CollegeBoard

The College Board

2009

International Student

HANDBOOK

2009

The College Board

International Student

HANDBOOK

CollegeBoard

Twenty-Second Edition

The College Board, New York

The College Board: Connecting Students to College Success

The College Board is a not-for-profit membership association whose mission is to connect students to college success and opportunity. Founded in 1900, the association is composed of more than 5,400 schools, colleges, universities, and other educational organizations. Each year, the College Board serves seven million students and their parents, 23,000 high schools, and 3,500 colleges through major programs and services in college admissions, guidance, assessment, financial aid, enrollment, and teaching and learning. Among its best-known programs are the SAT®, the PSAT/NMSQT®, and the Advanced Placement Program® (AP®). The College Board is committed to the principles of excellence and equity, and that commitment is embodied in all of its programs, services, activities, and concerns.

For further information, visit www.collegeboard.com.

Editorial inquiries concerning this book should be directed to College Planning Services, The College Board, 45 Columbus Avenue, New York, NY 10023-6992; or telephone 212 713-8000.

Copies of this book are available from your local bookseller or may be ordered from College Board Publications, P.O. Box 869010, Plano, TX 75074-0998. The book may also be ordered online through the College Board Store at www.collegeboard.com. The price is $29.95.

Library of Congress Catalog Number: 97-76451

ISBN 13: 978-0-87447-828-0
ISBN-10: 0-87447-828-6

Printed in the United States of America

Distributed by Macmillan

Contents

Dear Friends,

The College Board is dedicated to connecting students to college success and opportunity. We believe in the principles of excellence and equity in education and try to promote them in all that we do. With the College Board's Handbook series, we hope to put an authoritative source of college information at your fingertips as you seek to further your education in the United States.

World events make it ever more evident that a broad knowledge of other cultures is essential for everyone. Through intercultural programs, we hope young people will come to a better understanding of one another and that these programs will foster greater cooperation among the people of the world.

College is a dream worth working hard to achieve. I've been a businessman, a governor, and now the president of the College Board, but nothing makes me prouder than to say that I am a college graduate. With perseverance, anyone who desires a college education can attain one. College Board publications can help you get there.

My best wishes on your journey to success.

Gaston Caperton
President
The College Board

Preface

The doors of U.S. educational institutions are open to all qualified students from around the world. The United States is proud of an educational system that attracts students and scholars from across the globe. In the words of President George W. Bush, "We... encourage international students to take part in our educational system....The relationships that are formed between individuals from different countries, as part of international education programs and exchanges...foster goodwill that develops into vibrant, mutually beneficial partnerships among nations."

—Bureau of Educational and Cultural Affairs,
U.S. Department of State

The importance of international educational exchange in promoting understanding across national, cultural, religious, and racial borders cannot be underestimated. Hundreds of thousands of students who study overseas each year create a global citizenry that is culturally aware and respectful of people of different backgrounds. These benefits translate into a more understanding and peaceful world society. Individually, students are enriched and draw lifetime benefits from the opportunity to learn a discipline in a different cultural context, acquire or perfect a foreign language, be immersed in and learn from another culture, and teach one's culture to others.

The United States has an unparalleled system of higher education in terms of the number of institutions and the variety and quality of their programs of study. There are more than 3,800 universities offering bachelor's and associate degrees in more than 600 subject areas. The sheer size and diversity of the U.S. higher education system can make the task of finding the institution that is right for you seem daunting. The process of researching, selecting, and applying to colleges and universities in the United States is difficult and time-consuming, but it is well worth the investment.

It is important for students to find the institution that will best meet their educational, professional, and personal needs. With this in mind, the objective of the *College Board International Student Handbook* is to provide international students with up-to-date, objective, and thorough information to help them make informed decisions about their education. The undergraduate institutions described in this book are fully accredited by agencies recognized by the U.S. Department of Education and encourage international student enrollment.

The book is designed to be used in conjunction with the *College Board College Handbook* and the *College Board Book of Majors*, as well as the wide array of resources available on the Internet, in order to find the college or university that best fits a student's needs. Nearly all colleges and universities have Web sites, which are listed in this publication. The College Board also has a Web site (www.collegeboard.com) where students can conduct a college search, register for the SAT®, and learn about materials to prepare for the exam.

We would like to acknowledge those who worked on the *International Student Handbook 2009*, especially the following nine admissions professionals who provided their expertise.

Peter Briggs, Director, Office for International Students and Scholars, Michigan State University, East Lansing, Michigan

Ken Bus, Director, International Education Program, Glendale Community College, Arizona

Joseph DeCrosta, Director of International Programs, Duquesne University, Pittsburgh, Pennsylvania

David Dillman, Director of Transfer and International Student Admission, Austin College, Sherman, Texas

Michael Gargano, Vice Chancellor of Student Affairs, University of Massachusetts, Amherst, Massachusetts

Ann Gogerty, Senior Admissions Counselor, Iowa State University, Ames, Iowa

Dr. Tatia Granger, Vice President for Enrollment Services, Bennett College, Greensboro, North Carolina

Judith Jurek, Senior Associate Director, Office of Admission, University of Southern California, Los Angeles, California

Mark G. Reid, Director of International Admission, University of Miami, Florida

This publication is a culmination of cooperation between the College Board's Office of International Education and College Planning Services department, government agencies involved with international educational exchange, EducationUSA advisers, and international admissions officers at U.S. colleges and universities. The data in this publication were provided to the College Board by the institutions themselves through the Annual Survey of Colleges 2008, conducted in the spring of 2008. The information was verified by a staff of data editors under the direction of Andy Costello, Roger Harris, Doris Chow, and Stan Bernstein, with the assistance of Cathy Serico. Tom Vanderberg and Mike Polizzi were responsible for the overall editorial direction of this book.

All these professionals share a common belief that the proper placement of and service to international students at U.S. campuses are critical to the development of mutual understanding through the exchange process.

Office of International Education
The College Board

Part I:
Applying to college in the United States

Planning calendar for U.S. study

Two years before admission...

For admission in August or September, begin two years in advance.

September

- If you have access to the Internet, visit the College Board's Web site at www.collegeboard.com. It has rich databases of information on colleges, careers, and scholarships.

- Find out about sources of U.S. college information in your country—libraries, advising centers, U.S. educational organizations or commissions, and the Internet. The U.S. Department of State sponsors a network of EducationUSA advising centers in more than 150 countries to provide students with free, up-to-date information and help to apply for degree programs at American colleges and universities. A listing of these centers is located in Part III of this book.

- Review the sections in this book on choosing and comparing colleges. Use the College Search on collegeboard.com, where you can find colleges that match the features you want. Once you have a manageable list, use this book to get essential international student information about each of those colleges. College Search also allows you to link directly to any college's Web site, where you can gather more information.

- If English is not your first language, learn about the English proficiency examination required. Two examples of this type of test are the Test of English as a Foreign Language (TOEFL) and the International English Language Testing System (IELTS). Get the information bulletin and registration materials. See also *Test information* on page 31.

- Be sure you are taking courses that prepare you for college or graduate study at U.S. educational institutions.

- Register for the SAT Reasoning Test™ or SAT Subject Tests™ if you plan to take the tests in November. You may also still be able to register to take the tests in October. Information on the SAT® is available on the College Board Web site, www.collegeboard.com, and on page 31.

October

- Take the SAT Reasoning Test or SAT Subject Tests if you registered for the October test date.

- Register for the SAT Reasoning Test or SAT Subject Tests if you plan to take the tests in December.

- Discuss your plans with an adviser. Ask your adviser or counselor whether U.S. college representatives will be visiting your country. Note the dates and places, and try to attend at least one meeting.

November

- Take the SAT Reasoning Test or SAT Subject Tests if you registered for the November test date.

- Register for the SAT Reasoning Test or SAT Subject Tests if you plan to take the tests in January. You may also still be able to register to take the tests in December.

- Discuss your plans with your teachers, family, people who work in your field of study and, if possible, people who have studied in the United States.

- Contact colleges by airmail or e-mail to request catalogs.

December

- Take the SAT Reasoning Test or the SAT Subject Tests if you registered for the December test date.

- Register for the SAT Reasoning Test or SAT Subject Tests if you plan to take the tests in January.

January

- Take the SAT Reasoning Test or SAT Subject Tests if you registered for the January date.

- Review college information you have collected from guidebooks, college catalogs, and online sources. Choose three to six colleges to research more fully.

February

- Develop your financial plan. Consider how you will pay for your education, living expenses, and transportation for each year of study in the United States.

- Find out about scholarships and other types of financial aid available in your country. Request the application materials.

March

- Register for the SAT Reasoning Test or SAT Subject Tests if you plan to take the tests in May.

- Schedule an appointment to take the TOEFL, or another English proficiency test.

April

- Register for the SAT Reasoning Test or SAT Subject Tests if you plan to take the tests in June.

- Write to the colleges you have selected to request a current catalog and application form, or go to their Web sites to get that material. Be sure to request financial aid and scholarship application forms if you intend to apply for aid.

May

- Take the SAT Reasoning Test or SAT Subject Tests if you registered for the May test date.

- Identify the teachers, counselors, and other adults you will ask for letters of recommendation.

June

- Take the SAT Reasoning Test or SAT Subject Tests if you registered for the June test date.

- If there is a break in your school schedule, use the time to improve your English skills by reading, writing, and speaking in English whenever you can.

July

- Read college application instructions carefully to find out what information is required and when it must reach each college to which you are applying.

One year before admission…

August

- Request information on intensive English language programs in the event you do not meet English proficiency requirements.

- If an essay is required for your applications, begin your first draft.

- If you have not yet taken admissions tests, or if you and your adviser think you can improve your scores, register for a test date, preferably no later than November.

September

- Find out the procedures at your school (and any other secondary school or college you have attended) for sending your academic records (transcripts) to the colleges to which you are applying.

- If colleges have provided forms for recommendations, give them to the teachers and other adults you have contacted.

- Register for the SAT Reasoning Test or SAT Subject Tests if you plan to take the tests in November.

October

- Take the SAT Reasoning Test or SAT Subject Tests if you registered for the October test date.

- Register for the SAT Reasoning Test or SAT Subject Tests if you plan to take the tests in December.

- Complete the essay for your applications.

- Complete the financial aid application forms.

- Apply early to colleges.

November

- Take the SAT Reasoning Test or SAT Subject Tests if you registered for the November test date.

- You may still be able to register for the SAT Reasoning Test or SAT Subject Tests if you plan to take the tests in December.

- Be sure you request that your scores on all required tests be sent to all the colleges on your list.

- Check to see that the people from whom you requested recommendations have sent them.

- Be sure that your school or college has sent your academic records to all the colleges on your list.

December

- Take the SAT Reasoning Test or SAT Subject Tests if you registered for the December test date.

- Reply promptly and completely to any requests for additional information you may receive from colleges to which you have applied.

January

- Be sure to keep up the quality of your studies. Your complete academic record can be important in admissions decisions.

- If you have not already completed all financial aid application forms, be sure to do so now and mail them as soon as possible.

February

- Review your financial plan for your education. If you think you may need additional help, investigate any sources of financial aid in your country that you may have overlooked.

March

- Some colleges with a rolling admissions policy require a response and a deposit soon. Note any reply dates that apply to you.

April

- You will probably hear from colleges this month or next. Review the section in this book on what to do if you are accepted at more than one college.

- Be sure to send your reply and deposit by the acceptance deadline.

- Apply for a passport.

May

- Write to colleges from which you have not heard.

- Review predeparture procedures.

- Confirm housing reservations at the college of your choice.

- Apply for a visa. Check with the U.S. embassy or consulate to be sure you meet all requirements for entry into the United States.

June

- Investigate predeparture orientation programs in your country. Ask the adviser at the EducationUSA advising center in your country (see Part III).

- Make travel arrangements.

July

- Use this opportunity to continue upgrading your English proficiency.

- If possible, earn money toward your expenses.

August

- Make sure all your predeparture activities are complete.

- Have a wonderful trip!

Why study in the United States?

Although travel of any kind is both exciting and informative, studying outside your home country offers unique possibilities. It allows you to completely immerse yourself in a new environment: in the classroom you gain exposure to new learning techniques and perspectives; outside the classroom you have the opportunity to meet people from different cultures. This can be a life-changing experience, giving you a new understanding of international political, social, and economic issues. In addition, study abroad develops self-confidence, cross-cultural awareness, and open-mindedness to new ideas and values. Employers worldwide consider these important assets.

Of all the possible places international students choose to study, the largest proportion choose the United States. In fact, today about 22 percent of all international students in the world are studying in the United States. There are a number of features that make U.S. education so popular.

Quality. The U.S. higher education system has an international reputation for quality. There are distinguished programs available at both the undergraduate and graduate levels in almost every field of study. Many universities attract world-renowned faculty and stand at the forefront of research and technological development. State-of-the-art facilities include libraries, laboratories, computers, and other resources.

Diversity of institutions and programs available. The range of educational opportunities in the United States is enormous. No matter what college experience you are seeking, you will find it at one or more of the 3,800 higher education institutions throughout the country. Here are just a few of the features you can choose among.

- **Size:** Institutions range from fewer than 1,000 to more than 50,000 students.

- **Student body:** Most colleges are coeducational, but there are 66 for men only and 53 for women only.

- **Selectivity:** College admissions policies range from highly selective to open admissions.

- **Setting:** Campuses are located in small and large cities, suburban areas, and rural communities, and in a variety of climates.

- **Field of study:** With more than 600 major fields of study to select from, you are likely to find a program that suits your interests.

- **Type of institution:** Choices range from liberal arts colleges that emphasize broad preparation in academic disciplines to technical schools that provide focused, career-related training. Some offer vocational programs, and a growing number of colleges offer options in distance learning.

Flexibility. One of the hallmarks of U.S. education is flexibility. At the undergraduate level, universities emphasize a broad, well-rounded education. You will be offered a wide range of classes—mathematics, science, the arts, social science, and languages—before finally having to choose a specialization. Even at the graduate level, related courses might be offered outside the department and in interdisciplinary fields. Students are actively involved in designing their course schedules because so many options are available. It is even possible to combine academic classes with work experience that will be recognized as part of the degree program. Most institutions have qualified staff on hand to help you make the best decisions to attain your academic goals. In the classroom, you are encouraged to be an active participant in the learning process. Faculty welcome, and generally expect, student input and encourage you to develop your own ideas and questions, and to express them.

Campus life. A successful college experience involves more than academic work. You will find a wide range of social, cultural, and sports activities outside the classroom that will match your interests, such as internships and clubs. These give you a chance to make friends and at the same time develop team and leadership skills that will be useful in your future career.

It is important to understand the differences between the U.S. system of education and your own country's system. Please review the next section on U.S. higher education before continuing.

U.S. higher education

Organization of the U.S. education system

How education systems are organized varies from country to country. Higher education in the United States may be very different from education in your country.

Preuniversity studies in the United States consist of one or more years of preschool, kindergarten, and 12 years of elementary and secondary school (also called "high school"). The chart in this section shows that the structure of preuniversity studies varies in how it is organized, but the body of knowledge to be covered is similar across the 50 states, regardless of how the school system is organized. The United States does not have a mandated course for secondary schools or a national examination. However, educators apply a common set of standards for assessing the basic competencies expected of secondary school graduates. The typical student receives a secondary school diploma at age 17 or 18.

The first level of higher (postsecondary) education is called "undergraduate" study and includes two-year and four-year programs. Two-year programs generally lead to an associate degree. An associate degree may be earned at a two-year community or junior college, or at a four-year college or university. There are two types of associate degree programs. Transfer programs provide the first two years of general education for transfer to a four-year program. Terminal programs (sometimes called vocational or technical) prepare students for a career in a specific trade.

Four-year colleges and universities offer programs that lead to a bachelor's degree (sometimes called the baccalaureate). The first two years usually are spent in courses that give you a broad foundation for future specialization. They may include English composition, world history, natural sciences, mathematics, languages, and social sciences, plus some courses determined by your chosen field of study. The second two years are devoted to your major

academic subject. Five years of undergraduate study may be required for some fields. A few specialized institutions offer only the last two years of undergraduate study; these are called upper-division institutions.

"Graduate study" follows the completion of undergraduate education at the bachelor's degree level. It leads to the master's and doctoral degrees in academic disciplines or first-professional degrees such as law (J.D.), medicine (M.D.), and dentistry (D.D.S.). A master's degree generally requires one or two years of full-time study, but three-year master's degree programs exist. Doctoral and first-professional degrees require at least three years of full-time study and, with some research projects, will take even longer. Admission to graduate programs can be very competitive, and some first-professional degree programs limit admission to applicants who earned their bachelor's degrees at a U.S. college.

Types of institutions

Degree programs are offered at many different types of institutions in the United States. Some institutions are public and some private. Although nearly all institutions receive some financial support from federal and state governments, public institutions rely heavily on public funds, while private institutions depend more on tuition, fees, and contributions from foundations and private citizens. There are also some postsecondary schools called "proprietary" schools, which are operated on a for-profit basis by their owners.

Admissions Advice

"One advantage of community colleges is pricing. Students can earn two years of credit at a much lower cost to them and their families than at a public or private university. Community colleges also have smaller classes, and there's a lot of support available to international students for improving their English."

—Ken Bus, Glendale Community College, Glendale, Arizona

"One of the draws of an all-women institution is that families of international students are more comfortable sending their daughters to the U.S. knowing that they're going to an institution that is women-focused and women-centered."

—Tatia Granger, Bennett College, Greensboro, North Carolina

Education in the United States

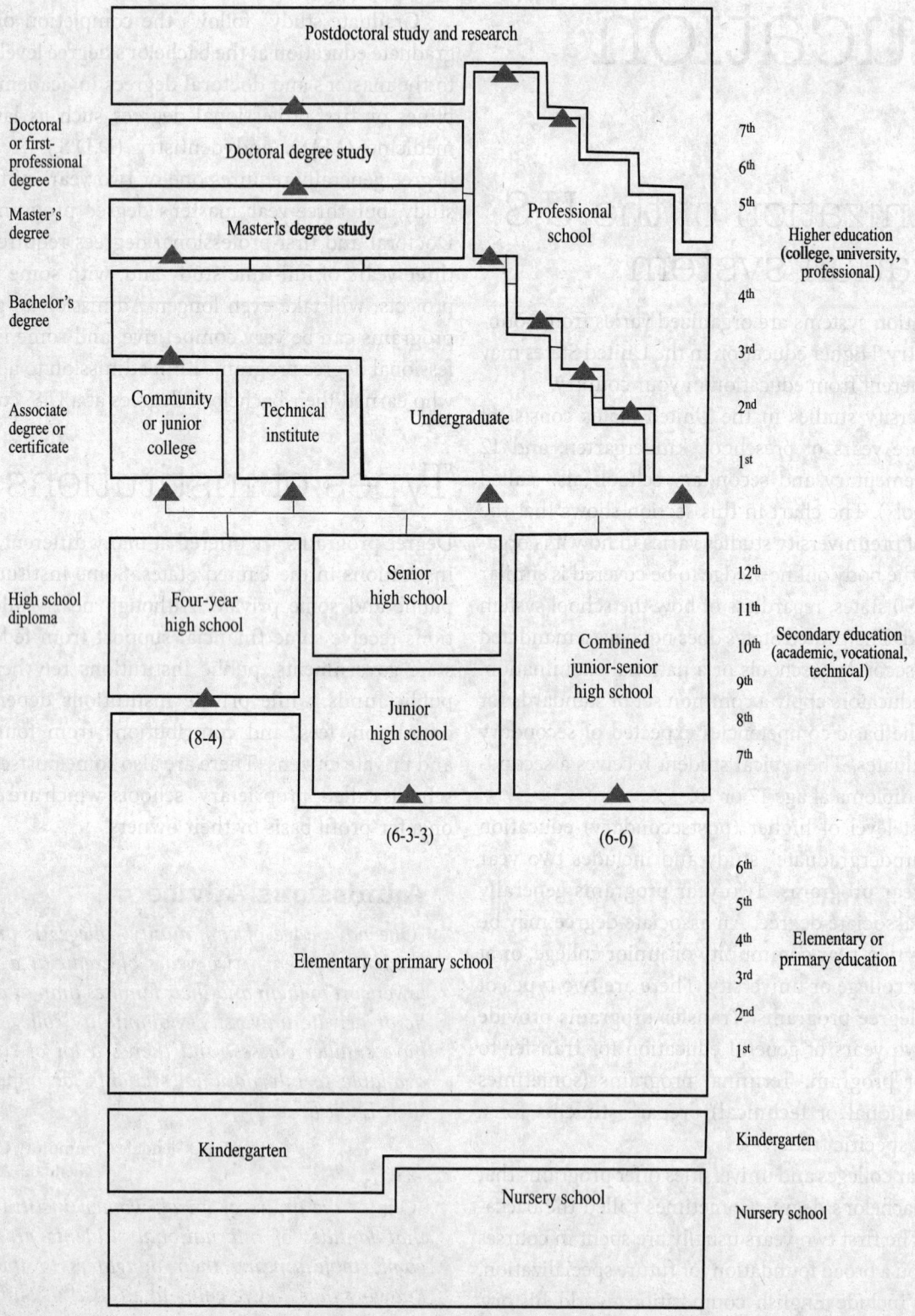

Postdoctoral study and research

Doctoral or first-professional degree — Doctoral degree study

Master's degree — Master's degree study

Professional school

7th
6th
5th

Higher education (college, university, professional)

Bachelor's degree

4th

Associate degree or certificate — Community or junior college — Technical institute — Undergraduate

3rd
2nd
1st

High school diploma — Four-year high school — Senior high school — Junior high school — Combined junior-senior high school

12th
11th
10th
9th
8th
7th

Secondary education (academic, vocational, technical)

(8-4)

(6-3-3)   (6-6)

6th
5th
4th
3rd
2nd
1st

Elementary or primary education

Elementary or primary school

Kindergarten

Kindergarten

Nursery school

Nursery school

Degrees offered

Undergraduate degrees

Associate degree programs are offered at two-year colleges, most of which are public *community colleges*, though some are private institutions called *junior colleges*. Associate degrees are also offered at some four-year colleges and universities. If you plan to earn an associate degree and then go on to a four-year bachelor's degree program, after you have enrolled be sure to consult with a transfer adviser to develop a program of study comparable to the first two years of a bachelor's program.

Bachelor's degrees are earned at four-year public or private *colleges* and *universities*. The terms *college* and *university* are used interchangeably in the United States and imply an institution that offers a bachelor's degree. Some *institutes*, such as the California Institute of Technology (Cal Tech) or the Massachusetts Institute of Technology (MIT), also offer bachelor's degrees. Some colleges and institutes, and all universities, also offer graduate degrees. Whether your bachelor's degree is earned at a college, university, or institute, it will have the same value as a credential for applying to graduate school, provided that the institution is accredited. (See the accreditation information later in this section.)

Graduate degrees

Graduate degree programs also are offered at several types of higher education institutions. Master's degrees can be earned at some four-year colleges as well as at universities and institutions that offer graduate study only. Master's degree programs generally take one or two years of full-time study to complete, but there are some that require three years of study. Doctoral and first-professional degree programs are offered at universities and graduate-only institutions. Doctoral degrees usually require a minimum of three years beyond the bachelor's degree.

It is possible to take a professional degree program without first earning a bachelor's degree, but those programs are highly selective and often require a very heavy course load. First-professional degrees require a total of at least six years of study, including appropriate undergraduate preparation. An example of this type of program is the six-year medical program.

Academic calendar

The academic year can be divided in a variety of ways. The most common is the semester system, in which the academic year is divided into two 16-week terms in fall and spring, with a long summer vacation and a shorter winter break. In the quarter system, the 12-month academic year is divided into four equal parts; most students take classes for three quarters of the year and take a break in the remaining quarter. There is also a trimester system, which divides the year into three 15-week terms. Under that system, students can attend school year-round and earn the same number of credits in the summer as they do in the fall or spring semesters. Some schools use a modified semester system called 4-1-4; they have a one-month intersession (or "winter term") between the two semesters, during which students take short courses, travel for a short study abroad experience, or do an internship. Regardless of how the calendar is arranged, you will cover approximately the same amount of material in a year of study. If you transfer from a college using the semester system to a university using a quarter system, the university will know how to convert your semester credits to quarter credits, and you will not lose any time.

Accreditation

Accreditation in the United States is managed entirely by the institutions themselves, in cooperation with regional accrediting bodies. Reviews are conducted by committees of educators and other private citizens rather than by the government. Although institutions are not required to seek accreditation, most do because accreditation indicates that an institution meets standards of quality in its faculty and academic programs.

There are six regional accrediting associations that cover the entire country. A college or university that is regionally accredited has the highest type of institutional accreditation granted in the United States. Some institutions are accredited by national agencies that accredit specific types of schools, such as religious or technical schools.

Accreditation by a recognized agency is important for several reasons:

- Credits are more easily transferred from one accredited institution to another.

- Most scholarship, fellowship, and grant programs are available only for study in accredited institutions.

- Degrees and diplomas are more generally recognized among accredited institutions within the United States as well as by governments and universities in other countries.

Specific academic or professional programs at a university, such as the engineering department, may also be accredited. Professional associations, concerned about standards of education, offer accreditation reviews to assure that the course offerings, facilities, and program administration (such as faculty qualifications and teaching load) meet agreed-upon standards. Two examples of such professional accrediting agencies are the Association to Advance Collegiate Schools of Business (AACSB) and the Accreditation Board for Engineering and Technology (ABET), but there are many others. Each institution you consider will be able to tell you the standing of their academic programs with accrediting bodies.

Accreditation alone is not a guarantee of high standards, but the lack of accreditation may be a warning that the degree or credit earned may not be accepted by other institutions or your country's government. All the colleges and universities listed in Part II of this book are accredited by either regional associations or national agencies recognized by the U.S. Department of Education and the Council for Higher Education Accreditation. (A list of these agencies appears on page 14.)

Information on accreditation can be found in the current edition of *Accredited Institutions of Postsecondary Education*, which is available in many libraries and advising centers, or at the Council for Higher Education Accreditation's Web site (www.chea.org). If a college is not accredited by a regional accrediting association or other nationally recognized agency, you should consult an adviser to find out more about the college before you send any application forms or money.

Credits, grading, and evaluation

The "credit" system in the United States is sometimes confusing. Each course is assigned a value, called a credit or unit. The number of credits usually reflects the number of hours the class will meet with the professor during one week. In a three-credit course, the class typically will meet Monday, Wednesday, and Friday for one hour of lecture each day. A four-credit course might meet Tuesday and Thursday for two hours of lecture each day, or meet three days a week for lecture and have one hour of discussion or lab. Each professor will make reading or writing assignments, usually weekly, and students should plan to work two to three hours outside of class for every hour inside class. In other words, a three-credit course may produce nine hours of homework a week.

Classroom examinations are given frequently throughout the years of undergraduate education in the United States. While small weekly written tests are common, testing may be limited to two or three large written examinations each semester, often called midterms. Almost all classes conclude with a final examination or large project. Testing gives the instructor or professor a basis for awarding grades and gives students an indication of their academic progress compared with other students in the class. At the graduate level, grades are more likely to be based on research papers in combination with some written or oral examinations.

Grades are determined by a series of evaluations and may include the cumulative assessment of all of the following: weekly quizzes, midterms, final exams, and papers, as well as class attendance and class participation. Each assignment or examination is usually graded, but your permanent record reflects only the final grade earned by the end of the course. If you do not do well on a midterm examination, there are other opportunities during the balance of the term to show the professor that you have improved. Although there is great variation in grading practices, particularly at the graduate level, most colleges in the United States use some version of the following grading system.

Grade	Represents
A or 4	Consistently high performance
B or 3	Above average
C or 2	Average
D or 1	Minimally passing
E, F, or 0	Failure

Grades are recorded in your permanent record at the end of each term by the registrar. Using the points noted above and the credits assigned to each course, a grade point average (GPA) is determined for each semester and accumulated for the entire time you are in the degree program. Each university has its own grading policies, and that information is usually explained in the university catalog or can be obtained from the office of the registrar.

Regional Accrediting Associations

Middle States Commission on Higher Education
3624 Market Street
Philadelphia, Pennsylvania 19104-2680
www.msche.org
Delaware, District of Columbia, Maryland, New Jersey, New York, Pennsylvania, Puerto Rico, Virgin Islands

New England Association of Schools and Colleges
209 Burlington Road
Bedford, Massachusetts 01730-1433
www.neasc.org
Connecticut, Maine, Massachusetts, New Hampshire, Rhode Island, Vermont

North Central Association of Colleges and Schools
30 North LaSalle Street, Suite 2400
Chicago, Illinois 60602-2504
www.ncacihe.org
Arizona, Arkansas, Colorado, Illinois, Indiana, Iowa, Kansas, Michigan, Minnesota, Missouri, Nebraska, New Mexico, North Dakota, Ohio, Oklahoma, South Dakota, West Virginia, Wisconsin, Wyoming

Northwest Association of Colleges and Schools
1510 Robert Street, Suite 103
Boise, Idaho 83705-5194
www.northwestaccreditation.org
Alaska, Idaho, Montana, Nevada, Oregon, Utah, Washington

Southern Association of Colleges and Schools
1866 Southern Lane
Decatur, Georgia 30033-4097
www.sacs.org
Alabama, Florida, Georgia, Kentucky, Louisiana, Mississippi, North Carolina, South Carolina, Tennessee, Texas, Virginia

Western Association of Schools and Colleges
www.wascweb.org
American Samoa, California, Guam, Hawaii, Trust Territory of the Pacific

Accrediting Commission for Senior Colleges and Universities
1985 Atlantic Avenue, Suite 100
Alameda, California 94501
www.wascsenior.org/wasc

Accrediting Commission for Community and Junior Colleges
10 Commercial Boulevard, Suite 204
Novato, California 94949
www.accjc.org

National Accrediting Associations

ACICS — **Accrediting Council for Independent Colleges and Schools**
750 First Street NE, Suite 980
Washington, D.C. 20002-4241
www.acics.org

ACCSCT — **Accrediting Commission of Career Schools and Colleges of Technology**
2101 Wilson Boulevard, Suite 302
Arlington, Virginia 22201
www.accsct.org

ABHE — **The Association for Biblical Higher Education**
5575 S. Semoran Boulevard, Suite 26
Orlando, Florida 32822-1781
www.abhe.org

AARTS — **Association of Advanced Rabbinical and Talmudic Schools**
11 Broadway, Suite 405
New York, New York 10004

ATS — **Association of Theological Schools in the United States and Canada**
10 Summit Park Drive
Pittsburgh, Pennsylvania 15275-1110
www.ats.edu

DETC — **Distance Education and Training Council**
1601 18th Street NW
Washington, D.C. 20009
www.detc.org

New York Board of Regents
Office of College and University Evaluation
New York State Education Department
Room 110EB
Albany, New York 12234
www.regents.nysed.gov

For specialized program accreditation, see *Accredited Institutions of Postsecondary Education* (Washington, D.C.: American Council on Education), available from:

Greenwood Publishing Group
88 Post Road West
Westport, Connecticut 06881
www.greenwood.com

Community Colleges in the United States

Judy Irwin
Director, International Programs & Services
American Association of Community Colleges

U.S. community colleges, sometimes called junior or technical colleges, are the "gateway to higher education" for international students. They provide the first two years of a four-year university degree program, at affordable costs, leading to an associate degree. Students with associate degrees can transfer their course credits they earn toward a bachelor's degree at a four-year college or university. Most community colleges have special arrangements with four-year institutions, called articulation agreements, to ensure a seamless transfer process. This process is often called "2+2" in reference to the two years students spend at a community college and the two years at a university.

All U.S. higher education institutions (community colleges, four-year colleges and major universities) are accredited by the same accrediting agencies. Community college programs must meet the same stringent criteria as four-year colleges and universities to attain accreditation status. That's why universities will accept course credits obtained at community colleges.

There are nearly 1,200 two-year, associate-degree granting institutions in the United States, serving more than 11 million students. Forty-six percent (46%) of all U.S. undergraduates begin their higher education studies at a community college.

U.S. community colleges are attracting approximately 15 percent of the international students who study in the United States because of their numerous benefits and opportunities: significantly (approximately 50 percent) lower costs; transfer options to universities; intensive English programs to advance language ability and skills; small class sizes with a focus on indi-vidual student success; a wide range of student support services; cutting-edge technologies; hundreds of programs from which to choose; strong ties with the community leading to hands-on access to U.S. culture; and the ability to take one year of optional practice training (OPT) related to one's degree, upon completion of an associate degree. (Another year of OPT can be undertaken upon completion of a bachelor's degree.)

Community colleges differ widely. Some are large, multicampus institutions located in big cities, while others are much smaller schools located in rural settings and serving smaller student populations. Housing opportunities at community colleges range from living in campus dormitories or nearby apartments, to renting rooms or arranging homestays with host families.

Alumni from community colleges include U.S. government officials, Nobel and Pulitzer Prize recipients, and award-winning producers, actors, and musicians. Some well-known alumni include Arnold Schwarzenegger, governor of California; Eileen Collins, NASA space shuttle commander; George Lucas, producer/director of the "Star Wars" movie series; Tom Hanks and Clint Eastwood, film actors; Walt Disney, founder of Disney studios and Disney World; Calvin Klein, designer; and Craig Ventnor, genome scientist.

Community colleges are a key component of higher education in the United States. They provide academically qualified and motivated international students with an opportunity to obtain high-quality and affordable education in a supportive learning environment as they begin their higher education experience in the United States.

Planning for study in the United States

Applying to college in the United States from another country can be exciting and challenging. The process may be different from the one in your country, but it need not be difficult if you get accurate information and follow the required procedures carefully.

There are over a half million students from other countries enrolled in degree programs at nearly 2,000 two-year and four-year colleges and universities in the United States. This represents 4 percent of the U.S. higher education enrollment each year. Many of these institutions have more applicants than they can accept in any year. As a result, college admissions can be very competitive, especially for applicants from outside the United States.

The key to successful admission lies in careful planning and timely completion of the required steps. Keep in mind the following advice during your college planning.

Consider your own characteristics

- What kind of person are you?
- What makes you happy?
- What are your interests?
- Are you sure you know what you want to study?
- Why do you think studying in another country will be good for you?
- What about studying in another country makes you feel anxious?

- Have you been away from your family for long periods of time before?

Planning Guide

- Begin planning about 24 months before the date you wish to start studying in the United States. Contact universities that interest you at least one year in advance.

- Identify the things that are most important to you when looking for a college in the United States. Make a list of those characteristics to help you compare the colleges that interest you.

- Review and use this book. If you have access to a computer with an Internet browser, link to the College Search on collegeboard.com, where you can find out quickly which colleges have the features you want. College Search also allows you to link directly to college Web sites, which are a rich source of information about degrees and courses offered, costs, student services, and financial aid. Some even provide a virtual campus tour.

- Consult an EducationUSA advising center or the EducationUSA Web site (http://educationusa.state.gov). Locate the center nearest you in the list at the back of this book. You can also e-mail questions in your native language to the Virtual Consulting Office of EducationUSA (www.vco-edusa.net).

- Talk with students in your country who have studied in the United States.

- Start planning your college budget. Be realistic about how you will pay for your education.

- If you plan to apply for scholarships, do so before leaving home. Little financial help is available once the school year starts.

- Be sure that your information is current and correct. Don't rely on hearsay or someone else's experience. Contact universities directly to get information and instructions about admissions.

- Complete all the steps in the admissions and financial aid process as early as possible. If you do not understand why a college asks for particular information or requires a particular process, ask them for more information about it.

The picture you have of yourself—your academic ability, interests, attitudes, and personality—is very useful in choosing colleges and in completing the application forms you will be asked to submit. Colleges will ask you about yourself because they are interested in you and believe that personal factors play an important role in academic success.

Consider your English language skills

One of the main challenges many international students face is their English language proficiency. If your first language is not English and if your previous education was not in English, it is important to take all English language proficiency tests as soon as possible.

You will be expected to read, write, understand, and speak English properly and fluently to carry out your studies. Conversational English will not be sufficient.

Colleges and universities require proof of English language proficiency when you apply and measure your skills by asking you to take a standardized test of English, such as the TOEFL. Even with excellent academic qualifications, you may not be admitted if your English language proficiency is too low.

International students often underestimate the stress caused by suddenly changing cultures, education and economic systems, friends, methods of teaching and learning, and living environments. Moving suddenly from speaking and thinking in the language of your country to thinking, listening, and speaking in English is very stressful. Get an accurate estimate of your ability in English so that you can enroll in a language school if needed to improve your ability before starting studies in the United States. Be sure to ask the admissions office if the institution offers an intensive course in English as a second language.

Answer the questions below to help you assess your English.

Circle one

1. **I can read textbooks written in English…**
    - A.   easily with the help of a dictionary to check new or difficult words.
    - B.   with difficulty and the frequent use of a dictionary.
    - C.   with great difficulty, constant use of a dictionary, and help from others.
    - D.   I have never tried reading a textbook in English.

2. **I can write an essay in English…**
    - A.   easily, using a dictionary to check the spelling and meaning of some words.
    - B.   with difficulty and the frequent use of a dictionary and grammar book.
    - C.   with great difficulty, translating what I have written in my language into English, with constant use of a dictionary and help from others.
    - D.   I have never tried writing an essay in English.

3. **I can understand spoken English about a current news topic…**
    - A.   easily except for special words.
    - B.   with some difficulty, and only if the information is repeated at least once.
    - C.   with difficulty and the use of a dictionary.
    - D.   I have not listened to someone speak in English about a current news topic.

4. **I can speak in English…**
    - A.   about any topic, with the occasional use of a dictionary.
    - B.   about certain topics with which I am most familiar.
        - ▪ if I am asked simple questions.
        - ▪ I have not had the opportunity to speak in English.

College cost and paying for your education

College cost

The profiles in Part II of this book give academic-year costs broken down by tuition and fees and living expenses. Remember that college costs are rising and are likely to be higher by the time you enter a program of study. Confirm current costs with the school when you apply.

Just as the types of educational institutions in the United States vary widely, so does the cost of education. Cost may be a major factor in deciding which college to attend. In academic year 2007-08, the average cost for U.S. residents living on campus at four-year undergraduate colleges varied from about $13,600 to $33,000 for nine months. The cost for international students was higher. You must consider living expenses during holidays and the summer and round-trip transportation from your home country. Actual tuition, fees, and estimated living expenses for international students are listed in Part II of this book. The estimates do not include expenses for an automobile, unless specified. The cost of going to college in the United States is something you and your family should think about early in your college planning. Cost differs from one institution to another, so you should estimate a budget for the college you are considering. Your total budget should include the following expenses for each year of study.

Tuition and fees

Tuition and fees are generally charged on the basis of a nine-month (September–May) academic year. Some colleges also offer course work in the summer period (June–August); if you plan to take courses in the summer, increase your budget to allow for expenses for a 12-month period. Some universities charge a flat rate for tuition and some calculate tuition by the credit hour. Each course is assigned a number of credits, usually reflecting the number of "contact hours" with the professor per week for one term. A typical course in a U.S. institution is worth three credit hours. Thus, to calculate the additional cost of a summer program, multiply the number of courses you intend to take by three to obtain the total number of credit hours, then multiply that by the tuition per credit hour charge.

Tuition and fees for international students listed in this book are for the 2008-09 academic year unless otherwise stated; the cost has increased by about 9 to 10 percent per year in recent years. Be sure to confirm current costs with the college when you apply. To estimate future costs, add this increase for each year.

The items included in fees vary from institution to institution. To compare accurately, ask what is included in the fees. Some typical fees are health insurance, student activity fees, scholarship funds, building funds, lab fees, and computer usage fees.

Room and board

Room and board means basic living expenses for food and housing. No matter where you go to college, you will have to consider these expenses. Many colleges have on-campus housing. Some require students to live in a college dormitory, at least for the first year. Others do not, and students commute from housing near the college. Commuting students in general pay somewhat less for housing than students living in college dormitories, but their cost of transportation is higher. Most colleges have housing offices that can help you find local housing in an apartment or a home that you can share with other students.

The room and board cost for colleges with on-campus housing assumes that you will share a room with one student, and have regular meals in the college cafeteria. Find out if the room charges include bedding (sheets, pillows, and blankets) and regular linen service.

If you will be attending college during the summer, add an estimate of the cost for housing and meals for three additional months to your budget.

Books and supplies

Colleges estimate the cost for books and supplies for the academic year. If you are planning to study in a field that requires special supplies, such as engineering, art, or film, your expenses are likely to be greater than the average. If you attend summer school, add a sum to your budget for books for the summer classes.

Computers

Computers are a common requirement on college campuses today. Most universities have computer labs for student use, but some require students to have their own computers. Ask whether the university you are applying to requires you to have a personal computer. If so, calculate that into your expenses.

Transportation

The living cost figures in this book do not cover trips between the United States and your home country. Be sure to add expenses to your yearly budget for round-trip travel between your home country and college.

If you plan to live off campus and commute to college, you will incur local travel expenses. Commuter colleges have included an estimate of these expenses.

Personal expenses

These expenses include the cost of basic goods such as clothing, services such as laundry, and activities such as movies and sports events. Health insurance is required. If you have dependents or if you have special medical needs, substantial additional funds will be needed to meet your living expenses. Most institutions have an estimate of the basic cost.

Sources of funding

Although there are government-sponsored and institutional financial aid programs, most of those funds are for U.S. citizens or permanent residents. For international students, the cost of higher education in the United States is primarily the student's responsibility. Although many colleges have some financial aid available for students from outside the United States, there is not enough aid to meet the need of all students.

There is more financial aid available for graduate students than for undergraduate students. In 2006-07, 62 percent of international undergraduate students paid for their education with personal or family funds. After personal and family funds, U.S. colleges and universities are the most significant source of funding for international students. In 2006-07, U.S. colleges and universities provided funding for 26 percent of students from abroad. In Part II of this book, which lists detailed information about undergraduate institutions, the far right-hand column indicates whether an institution offers financial aid to international students, the number of awards, and the average amount of the awards. These lists will give you a realistic idea of your chances of receiving financial assistance from a specific institution.

You are responsible for planning how you will pay for your educational, living, and travel expenses. Answer the questions below to begin your financial plan.

- Have you consulted your family, a prospective sponsor, or others about your plans for financing your stay in the United States?

- Have they agreed to support you?

- If you are applying for a scholarship, have you submitted all the required documents?

- When will you be notified of the results?

Financial aid

Financial aid to students in the United States includes (1) scholarships or grants, (2) loans, which have to be repaid, and (3) jobs, which provide money to help pay college costs. Financial aid may cover all college costs or only a very small fraction. Jobs require a commitment of a specified number of hours per week; teaching and research assistantships for graduate students require up to 20 hours per week.

U.S. sources of financial aid include federal and state governments, private foundations, companies, and universities. Financial aid programs usually have specific requirements, such as financial need, citizenship, or a particular field and level of study. International students may apply for privately sponsored scholarships where the criteria allow, but should be aware that these scholarships have a very early deadline for applications. If you have Internet access, be sure to use the Scholarship Search on the College Board's Web site (www.collegeboard.com) to find potential sources of funding.

It is a good idea to investigate sources of financial aid in your own country as well as those in the United States. Keep in mind that the application process for scholarships and other financial aid programs may begin as early as 18 months before your planned date of enrollment. Contact an EducationUSA advising center, the U.S. embassy or consulate in your country, or other organizations about financial aid as soon as possible.

Part-time work outside of the college or university is sometimes a possible source of additional income once a student is in the United States. Keep in mind, however, that people traveling in the United States on a student visa are not allowed to work off campus until one year of academic study has been completed successfully. Then you have to get permission from the college and the Bureau of Citizenship and Immigration Services before you can work off campus part-time. International students can usually work on campus. In either case, your earnings from part-time work will not cover much more than personal expenses. You should not count on employment to pay the major cost of your education.

> "International students can typically find scholarship information in the college's publications or Web site. Many schools will offer merit scholarship consideration, and that information is pretty easy to find on the Web site, usually in the financial aid or scholarship section."
>
> —Judith Jurek, University of Southern California, Los Angeles, California

Understanding your U.S. federal income tax obligations

Many students from other countries studying in the United States are not aware that they may incur U.S. federal income tax obligations. According to the U.S. Internal Revenue Service (IRS), the international students most likely to incur U.S. tax obligations are those who receive grants or stipends or who earn income as graduate assistants.

According to IRS officials, a large number of international students actually overpay their taxes because they mistakenly believe that the government will automatically withhold the correct amount of taxes and that they therefore do not have to file a return. Seek advice in the personnel office on your campus about your tax withholding, and familiarize yourself with the U.S. tax regulations. Watch for tax seminars on your campus, or ask your international student adviser for advice.

Advice for undergraduate applicants

Choosing a college

Attending college in another country can be a very exciting and rewarding experience. It is important that you select an institution that best matches your interests and needs and offers the academic program you want to study. To find a college that offers what you need, decide what college characteristics are important to you. When you compare your own needs and interests with the characteristics of the college, you will find a good match.

Choosing a college

Make a list of what is important to you when choosing a college. Consider this list and then add other characteristics you seek.

- Does the college offer the degree you are seeking in your desired field of study?

- What type of college is it (for example, two-year community college, four-year university, private or public, urban or rural, religious affiliation)?

- How many students are enrolled? How many of them specialize in the field you're interested in? How many of them are from outside the United States?

- Can you describe the campus environment from what you have read about it?

- Is housing available on campus?

- What is the total cost of tuition, fees, room, and board (meals)? Are scholarships or other forms of financial aid available for international students?

- Is there an orientation program specifically for international students? Are there student services to help you outside the classroom, including an international student advising office? If you need help with your English skills, does the college offer an intensive language learning program?

Admissions Advice

"It's all about finding the right fit, or the best fit, for that student. What you need to do is ask questions about yourself first. What kind of environment do I want to be in? What do I want to study? Do I want a preprofessional education or a liberal arts education? Do I want a big city or a small city? Do I want a religiously affiliated institution? Once you ask those questions, you can start plugging your desires and priorities into the schools that fit best."

—Joseph DeCrosta, Duquesne University, Pittsburgh, Pennsylvania

"It's important to decide whether you need an active international student community and how much support you think you will need. If there's an international student organization that you can become a part of, how active is it? If you can, determine whether international students are mainstreamed into the college community or whether they're more of a segregated population. That said, any international student should be sure that the college has an international student adviser."

—David Dillman, Austin College, Sherman, Texas

Finding out more about colleges

Learning as much as you can about the colleges you are considering increases your chances of making a good decision on where to apply. One of the best sources today is the Internet. Most U.S. colleges have Web sites that provide you with complete information about academic programs and course offerings, admissions requirements, and procedures for applying. Their sites may include photos of the campus and its environment or a virtual campus tour. The College Board's Web site (www.collegeboard.com) provides detailed resources to plan for, apply to, and pay for college. In addition, there are many other sources of information and advising that may be available in your country. The U.S. government, foreign governments, and nonprofit organizations support these activities. There is usually no cost to you, although a minimal charge may be requested to cover the expense of printing booklets or the postage if you request information by mail. The U.S. Department of State promotes American higher education through its EducationUSA advising network, located in the following types of centers:

- U.S. embassies, consulates, American centers, American corners, and libraries

- Fulbright commissions and foundations

- Binational centers

- Nonprofit exchange organizations, such as the Institute of International Education or AMIDEAST

- University information centers and libraries

- Public libraries

You may also check listings in local telephone books or call or write the U.S. embassy or the ministry of education in your country, stating that (1) you are seeking information and advice about academic study in the United States and (2) you would like to know where to visit or write.

A list of advising centers is provided in Part III of this book. Advice from knowledgeable and experienced advisers can help you make realistic plans and complete the admissions process successfully.

Another helpful source of information in your country is people who have studied in the United States. Talk to them, but remember that their experiences will be influenced by how recently they were there and by the location and type of institution they attended. The environment they chose may be different from the one you seek. However, they should be able to give you some ideas about adjusting to college life in the United States. An advising center may offer discussions or workshops with returnees and U.S. college alumni.

Admissions Advice

"It's very important for prospective international students to communicate with current students, especially from their home country, even perhaps from their own high school, who may be attending an institution. That way, culturally at least, they can ask the types of questions that are most relevant to them. A student from small-town Iowa and a student calling from Thailand—they might not quite relate on the same level. Speaking with someone from your own culture is probably most helpful. Speaking to parents of current students from your home country is also very helpful."

—Mark G. Reid, Director of International Admission, University of Miami, Florida

The following sources can provide important facts about U.S. colleges:

The Internet. Most colleges have Web sites, and their addresses are listed in the alphabetical list of colleges in Part III. When you contact an organization, ask for its Web site address.

You can also use the Internet to search for colleges with the features you want, using a free service such as the College Board's College Search (www.collegeboard.com/collegesearch).

Other college guidebooks and software. The book you're reading provides current information on international student enrollment, tests required, application deadlines, application fees, tuition and fees, room and board, financial aid, and the availability of international student advisers, orientation, and intensive English language programs at U.S. colleges. The *College Board College Handbook* provides in-depth, current information on size, location, degrees and majors offered, admissions requirements, cost, student profile, activities, athletics, and special programs and services. The *College Board Book of Majors* provides lists of major fields of study at the undergraduate and graduate degree levels and the colleges that offer each major. It also provides descriptions of the most popular majors.

College catalogs. Colleges produce catalogs and bulletins that give up-to-date information on their admissions requirements, major fields of study, faculty, college costs, and other important factors. Most catalogs are available on the Internet as well as in paper form.

College representatives. Some institutions send representatives to other countries to talk about their colleges and to meet students who may be interested in applying. Contact the U.S. embassy, an advising center, or the ministry of education to find out whether representatives from colleges will be visiting your country or participating in an online college fair.

Once you have investigated the colleges that you are considering and determined where you wish to study, you are ready to send an application. Since the procedures for applying to college in the United States are likely to be different from those in your own country, here are guidelines to help make this a smooth process.

When to apply

You should begin the application process as soon as you have decided which colleges best meet your needs. This usually should be no later than 12 months before the date you expect to begin study in the United States. Review the planning calendar at the beginning of this book.

Colleges may give a deadline for applications. Usually the deadline is the final date by which they must receive the application. Some colleges will continue to accept applications after the deadline, but they will only process the application if they do not fill their class with applications from students who applied by the deadline. For late applicants, there may be no housing and no financial assistance.

Make a checklist of the admissions requirements and deadlines from your college comparison worksheet. Set your own completion dates well ahead of the colleges' stated deadlines, and check off each step as you complete it. Remember to send all required documents and forms as soon as possible. U.S. colleges usually review applications only when *all* the required documents have been received.

Applying to college in the United States

Requesting and filing the application

Most colleges will respond to e-mail requests for information. Whether writing by airmail or using electronic mail, in your first contact with a college in the United States supply enough information so that you will receive correct information in return: include your intended field of study, your educational background, the term in which you wish to start, and information about your source of funds for paying for your education.

The use of computers in the application process and in completing other college procedures is very common. If at all possible, use the electronic application provided by the college. This will accelerate the application process for you and make it easier for the college to process your application.

After you have received an application packet from the colleges of your choice, you should:

- Review the programs offered and the academic preparation required for them.

- Note the important dates, such as deadlines.

- Note which parts of the application will require a contribution by another person—does the college ask for teacher recommendations, for example?

- Pay special attention to the information about tuition, fees, and living costs to be sure you understand the financial commitment involved.

You are now ready to file your application for admission. Plan to apply to more than one college in order to increase your opportunities for admission.

Admissions Advice

"Some international students will have limited English skills, especially when they are looking at our intensive English program, and may be shy about asking questions because of this. I encourage students to e-mail us anyway."

—Ann Gogerty, Iowa State University, Ames, Iowa

"Before e-mailing a college, look at its Web site to see if your question can be answered with information that's there. Keep the questions short, clear, and succinct. The other thing is to be patient. It may take a few days for someone to get to your e-mail."

—Judith Jurek, University of Southern California, Los Angeles

"Don't write chat-room English to college administrators!"

—Ken Bus, Glendale Community College, Glendale, Arizona

Completing the application form

Many colleges use a preliminary application for an initial review of your background. This preliminary decision may save both you and the university some time and money. Whether you complete a preliminary application or the official application, be sure to read all instructions carefully and answer every question. Many colleges offer an electronic application on the Internet. Be sure to look for it and use it if you have access to appropriate technology.

Application fee

Most colleges charge a nonrefundable application fee. Some colleges waive the fee if you use their electronic application. The fee must be sent in U.S. dollars; follow the instructions provided with the application form.

Writing the essay

As part of the application for admission, most colleges require one or more essays in which you respond to questions provided by the college, write a biographical statement, or describe your academic goals, your previous accomplishments, and reasons why you wish to attend college. Instructions for specific information requested as part of the essays will be included in the application packet. Give each essay a lot of thought because it is given careful consideration by the admissions staff when making a decision about your application. Type the essay or write very clearly.

Admissions Advice

"We ask for an essay and give students flexibility on what they write about. It's important for us to see that they can communicate well in English, grammatically and logically."

—David Dillman, Austin College, Sherman, Texas

"I want the essay to come alive. I want to know that person as well as I can on paper. And that's a hard thing, because we want somebody to self-disclose, and that's not necessarily the model in a lot of non-Western cultures."

—Peter Briggs, Michigan State University, East Lansing, Michigan

Important things to remember when completing your application

- Use the same translation of your name on all documents, preferably the one on your passport. If the name is different on some records, enclose an explanation.

- Note the proper dates for filing the application.

- Read and follow the essay instructions carefully.

- Enclose proper financial documentation.

- Include all fees requested.

- If you have an e-mail address and/or fax number, be sure to include it.

- Type the application form and essay, or write clearly.

- Send complete official academic records or certified copies of your academic records along with your application. Have official translations prepared, where necessary, and attach them to the original/official documents.

- Take all required tests in time for your scores to be considered with your application.

Your academic records

The colleges to which you apply will require a complete set of records of your academic performance at previous schools attended. Many colleges will accept unofficial copies for their preliminary evaluation but will require original or official documents to confirm their review. If your original records are not in English, submit an official translation with your academic records. Some EducationUSA advising centers can provide "apostille," or internationally certified, copies or translations of your academic records.

Placement and assessment tests

Almost all institutions will require you to take one or more tests as part of the application process. Most colleges and universities require assessment tests, such as the SAT Reasoning Test and SAT Subject Tests. The tests can be used for admissions decisions or for placement— that is, deciding whether you need additional study in some areas or whether you are equal to or ahead of other students being accepted to the college. Tests that are computer-based may be taken any time that is convenient for you. You are advised to register in advance, particularly if you intend to take a test from November through January. Where tests are given on a fixed date, you must register well in advance for a space to take the test. See the test registration schedule on page 31.

Each college will list the required tests in its application instructions. Be sure to take all required tests as early as possible because they will be considered when the college makes a decision about your admission to the university. Check the college application for required tests. See the test information section on page 31 for a description of the various tests.

Undergraduates may also be required to take placement tests in specific subject areas such as English, mathematics, or the sciences to assess knowledge in a particular subject. Placement tests are usually taken after arrival on campus and the information is used in course selection so that students neither repeat things they already know nor are placed in a course for which they do not have the sufficient background.

Letters of recommendation

Some colleges require letters of recommendation from one or more adults who know you well. Letters of recommendation by themselves will not ensure admission, and letters that do not appear to assess the candidate honestly may hinder an applicant's chance. The following guidelines may be useful when requesting letters of recommendation:

- Letters of recommendation should be honest and balanced. A letter that is unrealistically favorable is less useful than one that explains possible areas where you need improvement.

- You should request letters from two or three different people who are familiar with your academic or professional achievement—among them teachers, professors, school counselors, and employers. A family member or personal friend is usually not acceptable.

- Letters should focus on your academic abilities more than on your character, but may include information about your community service, volunteer work, employment, service to others, and leadership qualities.

- Admissions officers reading letters of recommendation find the following information useful:

    Academic record: discussion of your stronger and weaker academic areas; explanation of any gaps in your schooling, such as time off, school closings, and so forth.

    Achievements: special accomplishments in school, work, or family should be mentioned. Awards you have received should be described so that the admissions officer will understand their significance.

Unusual talents: special skills with languages or in the arts, athletic ability, and so on, should be mentioned.

- Give the person writing the letter clear instructions for sending the letter airmail to the address the college provides. Ask them to type or print clearly.

Auditions and portfolios

Schools of architecture, film, and the arts usually require additional information about you in order to assess your qualifications for admission to their programs. This may include portfolios of your work for art, architecture, and design programs, and auditions for music and theater programs. They will often accept audiotaped or videotaped representations of auditions from applicants who are unable to perform in person.

Interviews

Some colleges require interviews for admission to some or all of their programs. Interviews may be conducted in your home country by alumni, by visiting staff from the colleges, at recruitment fairs, or by individuals designated by the college. During the interview, be clear about your education goals and the reasons you want to attend this particular college, and be prepared to ask questions.

Your English skills

Strong English language skills will be very important to your success while studying in the United States. The level of proficiency expected by each college should be identified in the application for admission. Some colleges offer English as a second language (ESL) programs on the campus or nearby to help you improve your English language skills. Be sure to take the English language test required by your chosen college so the college can assess your readiness to study in English. Please refer to the test information on page 33 to find out more about the Test of English as a Foreign Language (TOEFL).

Other Requirements

Health forms and health insurance

Once you are admitted, you may be required to complete forms about your health. If a form is not provided, have a health examination and obtain a certificate written in English.

Most colleges and universities require health insurance while you are enrolled. Refer to the section on health on page 41 for more detailed information.

Financial documentation

A document certifying the amount and source of income available to you for study in the United States will be required. Most U.S. institutions will send you instructions and a special form to complete. The form should be submitted with your application for admission. The documentation must show that you have resources to pay for the first year of your college program and a reasonable financial plan for paying for the balance of your education. Once an admissions decision is made, the college will send you the appropriate U.S. government form so you can apply for a student or exchange visitor visa. Refer to the visa information on page 35 for more information regarding financial documentation and procedures for coming to the United States.

Financial aid forms

Many colleges and universities that offer financial aid to international students require applicants to complete a detailed financial aid application form, which is separate from the college application form. Typically, these forms ask the following kinds of questions:

- What is your parents' total annual income?

- What is your annual income?

- What are your annual living expenses?

- What is the value of any assets you and your parents have, such as a house, a car, savings, and investments?

- How many family members are in college?

- What plans do you have for locating financial aid from sources other than the college or university?

Ask each college to send you the financial aid application form it wants you to fill out. Some institutions use their own form. Others use the International Student Financial Aid Application or the CSS/Financial Aid PROFILE®, which are sponsored by the College Board, and which you may be able to submit to several institutions.

Request a financial aid application when you request an application for admission and submit the financial aid application when you apply for admission. Be sure to answer the questions as completely as possible. Most colleges will ask for documentation of the information you provide on the financial aid application; gather and save those documents as you complete the forms.

Be sure to send the financial aid form by airmail or courier to the correct address, which may be different from the address you use for the college application.

What happens next

Notice of receipt. Most colleges will send you a notice confirming that they have received your application. If you have not received such a notice within a month to six weeks from the time you submit your application (either by mail or e-mail), you should inquire to be sure it was received and is complete.

Evaluating your application. The evaluation of all the admissions applications a college receives can take several months. Some colleges send notifications to all students at one time; others respond as soon as an individual admissions decision is made. You can eliminate delays in your evaluation by following application instructions carefully and responding to requests for additional information immediately.

Offers of admission. Accompanying your offer of admission will be a packet of information about the college and its programs—things you need to know to get ready to enter the college. It will usually include information about campus housing and orientation programs, and may have forms for you to complete and return. You may be asked to submit a fee to hold a place at the college once you have been offered admission. (See *After colleges decide* on page 35.)

Orientation. Most colleges have orientation programs for new students; some offer special orientation programs for international students. You should try to attend these programs to acquaint yourself with the college environment as well as to obtain program advice.

Other things you should know

Transferring from one U.S. college to another. It is quite common in the United States for students to transfer from one college to another. They may attend a community college for one or two years and then transfer to a four-year college or university; sometimes they transfer from one four-year college to another. If you begin your studies in a community college and want to go on to a four-year college for a bachelor's degree, be sure to plan your studies with an adviser. Without careful course selection, you may extend the time it takes to earn your degree because the college you transfer to may require basic courses other than the ones you have taken.

Transferring academic credits. In the United States, colleges allow the transfer of university-level academic credits from one institution to another and will apply those credits toward your degree at the new institution. This is particularly important when transferring from a two-year to a four-year college. Transferring credits is also possible at the graduate level, though usually only a limited number are allowed. The previous course work must be comparable in content to an equivalent course offered at your new university and must be applicable to the degree you are pursuing. Although there is no guarantee that all previous course work will be accepted, universities make every effort to

apply courses either as general education credit or as fulfillment of a major subject requirement. Your new university will provide you with an evaluation of your credentials as well as documentation of your progress toward your degree. This information will enable you to determine the length of time it may take you to complete your degree.

Comparing colleges and universities

The more information you can gather on colleges and universities, the better your chance of making a good decision about applying to appropriate institutions. Look at the college listings in Part II of this book. If you are interested in undergraduate study, also use the College Search on www.collegeboard.com to identify colleges that have the features you want, read the descriptions in the College Board *College Handbook*, and consult other sources of information that are available to you.

There is no ideal number of colleges and universities to select for application, but advisers often recommend that students identify at least three to six institutions.

The worksheets on the following pages can help you compare institutions on the basis of the characteristics important in choosing and applying to colleges. For each characteristic, write how each college matches (or does not match) your preference. Some of the characteristics you may be comparing are:

- **Degree level.** For which degree do you plan to study at this college or university?

- **Location.** In what city or town, state, and region of the country is the college or university located?

- **Type of institution.** Is this a public or private institution? Is it a two-year community college, four-year liberal arts college, university, or graduate institution? Does the college admit men only, women only, or is it coeducational?

- **Major/field of study.** What field or fields of study that interest you does the institution offer?

- **Religious affiliation.** Was the college or university founded by or is it administered by a religious organization? Does this affect student lifestyle?

- **Enrollment size.** How many students are enrolled in the undergraduate colleges or graduate divisions in which you would be enrolled?

- **International student enrollment.** Does the college enroll many or few students from outside the United States?

- **Campus environment.** Is the institution's campus urban, suburban, or rural?

- **Housing.** Is on-campus housing available?

- **Academic background of students.** Do most students successfully complete their first year at the college? Do they return as sophomores?

- **Student activities.** Are there groups or organizations on campus to support the cultural, political, social, or other activities that interest you?

- **Athletics.** If athletic competition is important to you, does the college offer the sports programs you want?

- **Test requirements.** Is TOEFL required? What is the minimum acceptable score? Is the SAT or ACT required?

- **Cost.** What is the estimated international student cost for tuition, fees, room, and board for nine months? For 12 months? (Remember, your miscellaneous personal expenses, health insurance, and travel expenses will also be part of your total budget.)

- **Financial aid.** Is financial aid available to international students? How many international students receive aid? What is the average amount available for each student who receives aid?

- **English as a second language program.** Is an intensive ESL program available on campus? Is there a writing center for additional help?

- **Conditional admission based on English proficiency.** Will the institution provisionally accept students for academic study who do not meet English proficiency requirements?

- **Deadlines.** When must applications for admission and financial aid be completed and received by the institution?

College comparison worksheet (sample)

Characteristics important to you	College 1	College 2	College 3
	Yoder College	State University	Harrison University
Degree level	Bachelor's	Bachelor's	Bachelor's
Location	Baltimore, MD (Mid-Atlantic)	Minneapolis, MN (Midwest)	Boston, MA (New England)
Type of institution	Private college	Public university	Private university
Major	Engineering	Engineering	Engineering
Enrollment size	2,100	10,500 (very large)	6,800
International student enr.	18	113	182
Housing	yes	yes	yes
Academic background	Top half of class, 90% continue after first year	Top half	Most in top third, 45% continue to graduate studies
Test requirements	TOEFL SAT	TOEFL 550 mins. ACT	TOEFL 550 mins. SAT
Cost	$8,030 (9 months) $11,100 (12 months)	$13,400 (9 months) $17,850 (12 months)	$11,950 (9 months) $15,180 (12 months)
Financial aid	yes 12 applied for financial aid, 50% received aid	no	yes 109 applied for aid, 30% received aid
Application deadline	15 February	30 January	1 March
Financial aid deadline	15 March		30 December

College comparison worksheet

Characteristics important to you	College 1	College 2	College 3

Test information

The information tables in this book tell you which tests may be required of international students. Verify which tests are required by the colleges that interest you. Also, familiarize yourself with the format of the test you will be taking. When you register to take a test, ask for the information bulletin and work through the sample questions or sample test in the bulletin.

If you have access to the Internet, go to the Web sites of the various testing organizations to review the test formats, or take a sample test.

It is important to get up-to-date information about tests that are required by colleges to which you may apply. Although these standardized tests are offered at test centers throughout the world, they are not offered in every country on each test date or in each test format. For example, TOEFL, the test used by most colleges to evaluate English language proficiency, is now most widely offered in an Internet-based format, but is also offered as a paper-based test at designated testing centers. Write or call for information well ahead of time; registration dates often fill up to two months before the test date, particularly between October and February.

College Board tests commonly required or recommended by U.S. institutions are described below.

The SAT®

Type of test: Undergraduate admissions and placement.

Purpose: To help college admissions officers determine whether a student is likely to succeed in the first year of college. The SAT measures skills learned in school that are needed for academic success in college. SAT scores are intended to supplement the secondary school record.

Generally required of: Students seeking admission to the first year of undergraduate study.

Format: The SAT includes critical reading, mathematics, and writing sections. Each section of the SAT is scored on a scale of 200–800, and the writing section contains two subscores—one for multiple-choice questions and the other for a 25-minute written essay. The SAT is typically taken by high school juniors and seniors. It is administered six times a year outside the United States (a calendar of testing dates appears on page 32). The SAT is 3 hours and 45 minutes.

For more information: Consult the College Board Web site (www.collegeboard.com), where you can register online. You can also refer to the international edition of the *SAT Registration Booklet* or the *SAT Preparation Booklet*™, both of which you can obtain at no charge from your local EducationUSA advising center.

SAT Subject Tests™

Type of test: Undergraduate admissions and placement.

Purpose: To measure knowledge and the ability to apply knowledge in specific subject areas. Students take the SAT Subject Tests to demonstrate to colleges their mastery of specific subjects like English, history and social studies, mathematics, science, and language.

Generally required of: Undergraduates applying for admission as first-year students to selective institutions. One or more Subject Tests may be required. See the list of colleges that require or recommend the Subject Tests in Part III of this book.

Format: One-hour multiple-choice tests in the following subjects: English Literature, U.S. History, World History, Mathematics Level 1 and Level 2 (a calculator is required for some of the questions in the math tests), Biology Ecological/Molecular, Chemistry, Physics, Chinese with Listening, French, French with Listening, German, German with Listening, Modern Hebrew, Italian, Japanese with Listening, Korean with Listening, Latin, Spanish, and Spanish with Listening.

For more information: Consult the College Board Web site (www.collegeboard.com), where you can register online and review practice questions. You can also refer to the International Edition of the *SAT Registration Booklet* or the *SAT Subject Tests Preparation Booklet*, both of which you can get at no charge from your local EducationUSA advising center.

2008–2009 SAT Program Test Calendar

Test Dates	Oct. 4*	Nov. 1	Dec. 6	Jan. 24*	May 2*	June 6
Registration Deadlines						
*Early**	Aug. 26	Sept. 10	Oct. 15	Dec. 3	Mar. 11	Apr. 15
Regular	Sept. 9	Sept. 26	Nov. 5	Dec. 26	Mar. 31	May 5
SAT	■	■	■	■	■	■
SAT Subject Tests						
Literature	■	■	■	■	■	■
United States (U.S.) History	■	■	■	■	■	■
World History			■			■
Math Level 1	■	■	■	■	■	■
Math Level 2	■	■	■	■	■	■
Biology E/M (Ecological/Molecular)	■	■	■	■	■	■
Chemistry	■	■	■	■	■	■
Physics	■	■	■	■	■	■
Languages: *Reading Only*						
French	■		■		■	■
German						■
Modern Hebrew						■
Italian			■			
Latin			■			■
Spanish	■		■		■	■
Languages: *Reading and Listening*						
Chinese		■				
French		■				
German		■				
Japanese		■				
Korean		■				
Spanish		■				

* Question-and-Answer Service available.
** Applies to closer-to-home testing and registration through SAT International Representatives.
Note: Sunday test dates follow each Saturday test date for students who cannot test on Saturday because of religious observance.

Advanced Placement Program® (AP®) Exams

Type of test: Undergraduate credit, advanced placement, or both are awarded by almost every university in the United States and Canada, as well as by select institutions in Mexico and the United Kingdom. In addition, universities in more than 45 countries worldwide recognize AP when making admissions decisions.

Purpose: To measure students' mastery of content within university-level courses taught in secondary schools throughout the world. Universities grant advanced placement, credit, or both for successful AP Exam grades. Thirty-seven exams are administered during a two-week period in May.

Format: Most AP Exams are approximately three hours in length; some are shorter. Except for the three Studio Art exams, which consist of a portfolio assessment, AP Exams include a multiple-choice section and a free-response section. World language exams include a speaking section with recorded student responses.

For more information: Visit the College Board Web site (www.collegeboard.com/apstudents) or contact:

AP Services
P.O. Box 6671
Princeton, NJ 08541-6671
USA
+011 609 771-7300
877 274-6474 (toll free in the United States and Canada)
e-mail: apexams@info.collegeboard.org

2009 AP Exam Schedule

Week 1	Morning Session 8 a.m.	Afternoon Session 12 Noon
Monday, May 4	Government and Politics: United States	French Language* Government and Politics: Comparative
Tuesday, May 5	Computer Science A* Computer Science AB* Spanish Language*	Statistics
Wednesday, May 6	Calculus AB Calculus BC	Chinese Language and Culture
Thursday, May 7	English Literature * German Language*	French Literature* Japanese Language and Culture
Friday, May 8	United States History	European History Studio Art (portfolios due)

Week 2	Morning Session 8 a.m.	Afternoon Session 12 Noon
Monday, May 11	Biology* Music Theory*	Physics B* Physics C*†
Tuesday, May 12	Chemistry* Environmental Science*	Psychology
Wednesday, May 13	English Language* Italian Language and Culture*	Art History
Thursday, May 14	Macroeconomics* World History*	Microeconomics
Friday, May 15	Human Geography* Spanish Literature*	Latin Literature* Latin: Vergil*

*Coordinators should contact AP Services if a student would like to take exams that are scheduled for the same slot.

†Physics C: Mechanics will be given at 12 noon; Physics C: Electricity & Magnetism will be given at 2 p.m.

Up-to-date information on AP credit policies of U.S. universities may be found at www.collegeboard.com/ap/creditpolicy.

Policies of universities outside the United States may be found at www.collegeboard.com/apintl.

CLEP® (College-Level Examination Program®)

Type of test: Undergraduate credit-by-examination program.

Purpose: To measure knowledge of material normally taught in introductory college courses and give students the opportunity to earn undergraduate credit. Knowledge may have been acquired in the classroom or through independent study, academic interests, or on-the-job training. The individual colleges and universities determine whether they grant credit for CLEP® and for which exams, what score is required for credit, and how much credit is granted. There are 34 CLEP exams available in various subject areas, including mathematics, science, social sciences and history, literature, foreign languages, and business.

Who takes CLEP: Adults returning to college, students currently enrolled in college, recent high school graduates, and international students who wish to obtain credit from a U.S. university for knowledge acquired at an institution in another country.

Format: The exam is administered on computer at 1,400 colleges and universities in the United States and at some international locations.

For more information: Consult the CLEP Web site (www.collegeboard.com/clep), call +011 609 771-7865, or write to:
CLEP
P.O. Box 6600
Princeton, NJ 08541-6600
USA
e-mail: clep@info.collegeboard.org

Other Tests

ACT

The ACT is another admission test that measures English, Math, Science, and Reading skills. Consult the ACT Web site for more information.

TOEFL (Test of English as a Foreign Language)

Type of test: English proficiency.

Purpose: To measure the ability of nonnative speakers of English to use and understand English as it is spoken, written, and heard in college and university settings.

Required of: Undergraduates seeking a first degree and graduate students seeking an advanced degree.

Format: There are two versions of the TOEFL test: Internet-based (TOEFL iBT) and paper-based (TOEFL PBT). Results for all versions are valid for two years from the test administration date. It is important to understand where each version will be administered and the differences between them.

Internet-based test (TOEFL iBT): Test-takers have up to four hours to complete the TOEFL iBT, which has four sections: Reading, Listening, Speaking, and Writing. For more information consult the TOEFL Web site.

After colleges decide

You should receive a reply about two or three months after the college receives all your application documents. If not, write to the admissions office and ask about its decision.

If you are accepted. You will be asked to let the college know by a specific date whether you will enroll. Many colleges require a deposit to confirm enrollment, usually $50 to $100, which may not be refundable. This is credited to your tuition when you register. In your admissions packet, you will receive a document for use in applying for a visa (SEVIS Form I-20A-B or Form DS-2019 for study in the United States). Be sure to confirm housing reservations with the college and submit the required housing deposits, which average about $190.

If you are accepted by more than one college. If you already know which college you prefer, notify the other colleges that you will not attend, so that admission can be offered to another student. If you are not sure which college you prefer, review your college comparison worksheet to help you decide.

Admissions Advice

"International students, given that they can seldom visit campuses, are strongly influenced by family members and others who have been to the institution. Ask around and try to get a feel for each institution. If you're from Malaysia, try to contact a Malaysian student association at the college and ask everything from 'What's it really like there?' to 'Will you pick me up at the airport?'"

—Peter Briggs, Michigan State University, East Lansing, Michigan

---

If you are not offered the financial aid you need. Some colleges may not be able to offer financial aid, or you may have to choose between one that offers aid and another that offers none or a lesser amount. If you can't meet the college expense budget without additional help, find out if there are any resources in your country from which you can get financial help. Contact an EducationUSA advising center or the ministry of education to see if there are organizations that have helped other students in your country in recent years. However, keep in mind that deadlines for scholarships and financial aid are often earlier than the college application deadlines. Start your financial planning as soon as possible. Your admitting institution may ask you to submit a special form documenting your financial status or to complete the College Board International Student Certification of Finances and/or International Student Financial Aid Application.

Looking ahead

Once you have made your decision, there are many responsibilities to take care of.

Obtaining a passport and visa. You must have a valid passport to apply for a student visa. Your U.S. college or university will send you the documentation necessary to obtain a nonimmigrant student visa from the U.S. embassy or consulate in the country where you are located. The U.S. Department of State maintains consular offices at U.S. embassies and in many major cities around the world. Information on their location and details about the visa application process can be found at www.unitedstatesvisas.gov. Apply for a visa early to avoid any possible delays.

An F-1 student visa is granted to most students who have been accepted for admission to an academic institution in the United States. To obtain an F-1 visa, you must have a SEVIS Form I-20A-B, Certificate of Eligibility for Nonimmigrant (F-1) Student Status, from your U.S. college or university, as well as financial documentation proving that you have the funds to complete an academic program at that college. The documentation may consist of a notarized affidavit from a relative or other person who is supporting you financially, a bank statement showing that you have funds to meet at least your first-year expenses at college, and/or a letter from a government or private agency that is providing funds to support you.

Students entering on an international exchange program or with funding other than their personal funds may have to get a J-1 nonimmigrant Exchange Visitor visa rather than an F-1 visa. This includes students who are being supported by funds from the U.S. government, the government of the student's country, international organizations, or a U.S. college or university. If your U.S. college requires a J-1 visa, the college will send you a Form DS-2019, Certificate of Eligibility for Exchange Visitor (J-1) Status. You must take the Form DS-2019, with required financial documentation, to the U.S. embassy or consulate in your country to apply for a J-1 visa.

Students applying for either an F-1 or J-1 visa may have to provide additional documentation. For complete information about U.S. visa issuance requirements, contact the U.S. embassy or consulate. Be sure to read the rules governing the visa status on the form you receive from the university, as it provides different privileges for employment, dependents, practical training, and length of stay in the United States. With either visa, you are eligible to enroll as a full-time student and pursue the educational objective for which you entered the United States. You are advised not to enter the United States as a tourist (B-2) or without a visa, because you will not be eligible to enroll in college and pursue full-time studies in the United States.

If you wish to bring a spouse and/or children under age 21 with you, you must prove that you have the funds to support them. The college or university you will be attending will determine the amount of money necessary to support dependents.

Be sure to contact your local EducationUSA advising center for information about the visa application process and tips on preparing for your consular interview.

Upon arrival in the United States. As a guest in the United States, from the time you enter the United States until the time you complete studies and return home, you will be subject to U.S. laws and regulations. These affect your ability to enter the United States, study, work, and travel. Although you don't need to know every detail about U.S. immigration law, you should become familiar with the most important regulations that affect your status as a student.

While in the United States, you alone will be responsible for maintaining your status as a student in the United States. The best place to find accurate information about immigration regulations is the international student office on your campus. Although your friends might be willing to share their own experiences and advice with you, every student's situation is different, and the information given by your friends might not be the right information for you.

When you arrive at the U.S. port of entry, usually an airport, you will encounter various representatives of the U.S. government. One will request the Arrival-Departure Record (Form I-94), which you will have received on the airplane, and your passport. The inspector may ask you some questions about your plans and your source of support while in the United States. Such questions are routine, and if you have the proper documents you will be admitted without delay. The I-94 will be stapled into your passport. This card indicates the period of time you have permission to remain in the United States to study. For nonimmigrant students, the notation is "D/S," or "Duration of Status," to signify that you may remain in the United States for the time necessary to complete your program of study.

The inspector will take either your SEVIS Form I-20A-B or DS-2019. After making appropriate notations on the form, part of it will be returned to you—page 3 of Form I-20A-B if you are an F-1 student or a copy of the Form DS-2019 if you are a J-1 Exchange Visitor. It is very important that you check the immigration notations on your documents immediately for possible errors and retain this copy with your passport; it is a record of your stay in the United States, which includes date of entry, employment authorization, and expected school graduation date. Keep these documents in a safe place at all times. Also make copies and file them separately.

Upon arrival on your campus. Meet the international student adviser on your campus as soon as possible. Most colleges and universities hold orientation programs for new students, and some have special sessions for new international students. Many of your questions will be answered during these programs, and you will meet other new students before classes begin.

In addition to providing an orientation to your new surroundings and important details about your new community and college, the international adviser can help you with any required modifications to your immigration status, such as getting stay extensions once you are in the United States. Note that your passport must be valid for six months into the future at all times. The international adviser can also give you information on work eligibility and practical training. Students with F-1 or J-1 immigrant status may get permission to work in the United States subject to certain restrictions and the availability of jobs. Be sure not to work without permission, or you will jeopardize your student status.

Important regulations for F-1 and J-1 students

There are some important regulations that apply to international students while studying in the United States. You are responsible for being aware of, and following, these guidelines.

Full course of study

International students are expected to register for a full course of study during each semester or term. For undergraduate students, this means a minimum of 12 credit hours or its equivalent each semester. You are not required to carry a full course of study during your annual vacation or during your final semester of study. The full course of study requirements may vary at colleges that are on the quarter or trimester system. Consult your international student adviser about the requirements for you. Failure to carry a full course of study could result in your losing eligibility for employment and other important benefits.

Processing changes in your I-20A-B or DS-2019

If you change your major field of study or your degree objective, transfer from one college to another, or need an extension of the expected completion date of the academic program indicated on your I-20A-B or DS-2019, you must request a new I-20A-B or DS-2019 form and process the change officially. Consult your international student adviser or J-1 sponsor.

Departing and reentering the United States

You must have your I-20A-B or DS-2019 form endorsed each time you leave and reenter the United States. For an endorsement, F-1 students should consult the international student adviser; J-1 students should contact the sponsor.

Employment in the United States

Many international students are anxious to work in the United States. Employment can be a means of learning about American culture, developing professional skills, and earning additional income. However, employment of nonimmigrants in the United States is strictly regulated, and failure to follow U.S. employment law can result in loss of your student or exchange visitor status. Therefore, it is important to understand and follow the rules that govern your prospective employment. Refer to the overview provided below for general information, and consult your international student adviser for details.

You are eligible to apply for and accept employment only if you are in good standing with the immigration authorities. This means that you must carry a full course of study and process all the appropriate forms for change of major, degree objective, and school transfer for approval. If you do not maintain your approved status, you may face serious consequences.

Most student employment falls into one of these three categories:

- **Part-time employment on campus:** F-1 students are eligible to accept on-campus employment up to 20 hours per week while school is in session, and full-time (more than 20 hours per week) during holidays, school breaks, and vacation periods. Provided that a student is properly maintaining F-1 status, no written authorization is required. J-1 students are also eligible for part-time on-campus employment, but J-1 employment must be authorized in writing on the DS-2019 or in a separate letter from the sponsor.

- **Employment for economic necessity:** Some students experience unexpected financial crises after beginning study in the United States. Examples of such crises could include sudden devaluation of home-country currency, loss of scholarship, or the illness or death of a private sponsor. In such cases, if a student is able to show that off-campus part-time employment could provide a solution to the emergency, he or she may request employment authorization. Check with the international student office for the most current regulations and procedures. Off-campus employment must always be authorized in writing before a student begins work.

- **F-1 Practical Training/J-1 Academic Training:** Employment that applies the concepts learned in the student's academic program is considered practical or curricular training, and may be requested regardless of a student's economic need. Such employment is generally authorized only after the student has had a chance to participate in classroom activities and gain some theoretical background, which she or he would then apply in a practical setting. F-1 students are required to maintain their full-time student status for a minimum of one academic year or nine consecutive months before they become eligible to request practical training. J-1 students, similarly, may not request academic training for a period longer than their length of study in the United States. Both academic training and practical training may be undertaken prior to or following a student's completion of his or her program of studies. The length of authorization for academic or practical training, the type of job, and the employer are all generally regulated for both F-1 and J-1 students. In every case, employment for practical or academic training must be authorized in writing before a student begins work.

Predeparture checklist

❑ Get or renew your passport.

❑ Obtain a student or exchange visitor visa.

❑ Make airline reservations. Find out about baggage charges or shipping rates. Plan to arrive in time for the orientation program. Try to arrive at the college during regular office hours (8 a.m. to 5 p.m., Monday through Friday).

❑ Make hotel reservations if you will be stopping en route. If you have not received a housing assignment or need to find temporary living accommodations, be sure to have sufficient traveler's checks to cover these living expenses.

❑ Get inoculations and have your doctor complete a World Health Organization yellow immunization card. Have a physical examination and send the report to your college if it is requested. If you wear glasses, get and carry with you a prescription from your doctor. If you take special medication, get a reasonable supply and a new prescription, written in English, from your doctor to take with you.

❑ Request information on health insurance and services from your college. Obtain health insurance.

❑ If you want on-campus housing, send in your housing reservation form and deposit.

❑ Write to the international student adviser to notify him or her of the date and approximate time of your arrival. Ask about airport arrival services.

❑ If you would like help on arrival, check with your local EducationUSA adviser, or inquire about the help offered by the YMCA Arrivals Program, c/o International YMCA, 71 West 23rd Street, Suite 1904, New York, NY 10010 USA. Visit its Web site at www.ymcanyc.org.

❑ Be sure you understand U.S. currency (bills and coins) and the exchange rate between your country and the United States.

❑ Arrange to set up and transfer money to an account at a bank in the United States.

❑ Buy traveler's checks (in U.S. currency) to cover expenses while traveling to college and for your first month in the United States. A credit card in your name, such as a Visa or MasterCard, will also be extremely helpful.

❑ If possible, take about $150 in U.S. currency in small denominations ($1, $5, $10, $20) for use on arrival. Do not keep all the cash in one place.

❑ Ask the college or check on its Web site about the best transportation from the airport to the college. If arriving in a large city, ask how much it should cost to get from the airport to the college. If you take a taxi, be sure to confirm the price of the trip with the driver before leaving the airport. Some colleges offer airport pickup services, particularly if arranged in advance.

❑ Arrange in advance to ship belongings that will be over the baggage limit on airlines, unless you are willing to pay the excess baggage charges.

❑ Prepare items to be carried on your person or in a carry-on bag (not checked). Be sure to set aside your passport, visa documents, U.S. currency, medication and prescriptions, and the college deposit receipt or registration form to carry with you. Your carry-on bag should contain any items you will need in case your regular baggage is temporarily delayed.

❑ Label all of your luggage on the inside and outside with your name and the name and address of the college to which you are going.

Accompanying dependents

Students in F-1 and J-1 status may bring eligible dependents (spouse and children), who enter the United States with F-2 or J-2 visas. Additional funds are required for the support of dependents, and these funds must be documented before the dependents can enter the United States. F-2 dependents are not permitted to work under any circumstances. J-2 dependents may request employment authorization but can earn money only to support themselves and other J-2 dependents. If you wish to bring dependents with you when you first come to the United States, notify your university or your J-1 program sponsor so the required dependent information can be included on your I-20A-B or DS-2019 form. If you want your dependents to follow separately after you are settled, consult your international student adviser or sponsor for advice several months before your dependents plan to travel.

SEVIS (Student and Exchange Visitor Information System)

Students planning to study in the United States must be aware of the automated tracking system called "SEVIS." This system is designed to track international students through an electronic network among colleges and universities, U.S. immigration services, and U.S. consular posts overseas. While you are a student in the United States, it will be important to maintain contact with the international student adviser at your institution to report any changes to your status. You can learn more about visa procedures and your responsibilities under the SEVIS program by logging on to the Web site www.unitedstatesvisas.gov.

Keeping yourself in good standing with the U.S. government

- Learn the immigration regulations that apply to your student or exchange visitor status in the United States.

- Consult your international student adviser or J-1 program sponsor for current information and answers to your questions. Do not rely on the advice of friends.

- Process all changes of your status (school transfers, change of major or degree objective, extension of stay) promptly, following the advice of your international student adviser or program sponsor.

- Know your responsibilities under SEVIS.

- Answer all questions truthfully when applying for a U.S. visa abroad and when requesting entry into the United States.

- Enroll for a full course of study every academic term during your program of study. Discuss any need to reduce your academic course load with your international student adviser or J-1 program sponsor.

- Learn the rules for various kinds of employment. Work only if you have permission and if you are in good standing with the immigration authorities.

- Remember, all off-campus employment requires written authorization before you begin work.

Consider your health

Your good health is essential for your success as a student. If you have been relatively healthy for most of your life, you may take your good health for granted. But before you leave for the United States, you should take steps to prepare for the big changes ahead.

If you have any unresolved health concerns, take care of them before you leave home. Do you need a new pair of glasses? Have you had a recent dental examination? Have you experienced some unexplained symptoms that need to be checked? Be sure to have these and any similar problems solved before you depart for the United States.

Your U.S. university may request health records from your physician at home, but you should bring copies of your records for yourself. These include your medical history, immunization records, eyeglass prescription, drug prescriptions, and a written record of any remedy that you use on a regular basis. These records should be written in English or you should bring translations with you.

Learn as much as you can about health resources on your chosen campus ahead of time so you are prepared when you arrive. These may include a small infirmary or a large hospital, depending on the size of your college. After arriving on campus, find out where you can go for emergency health care if the health center is closed. Do not wait for an emergency to find out where such a facility is located.

Expect changes in your health as you adjust to your new surroundings. Many factors, including your eating habits, sleeping patterns, local climate, and level of stress, contribute to your physical health and emotional well-being. When you arrive in a new place and are surrounded by a different culture, these factors change and your health may be affected. Give yourself time to adjust, and if you become uncomfortable or unhappy, consult the international student adviser, student health service, or counselors available at your college or university.

Student health insurance

There is no socialized medicine in the United States. Be sure that you have health insurance. If your sponsor provides health coverage, be sure that it covers treatment in the United States and that it covers catastrophic illnesses. Otherwise, purchase medical insurance for yourself and your dependents through your campus health insurance plan or through a U.S. health insurance agent. Medical insurance is absolutely essential to meet health care costs in the United States. Many U.S. universities require medical insurance for international students who enroll, and all J-1 exchange visitor students are required by law to carry medical insurance. But whether your school requires insurance or not, you should buy it as soon as you arrive. Policies differ in the expenses they will pay; find a policy with a reasonable deductible, affordable copayments, and limited exclusions. To learn more about how to shop for a health insurance policy, consult with the student health service or international student adviser on your campus.

Be prepared for the cost of health care in the United States. Services available on your campus may be provided at a low cost, but most university health centers only take care of routine problems. If you have a major health problem or a serious accident, you will probably be sent to an off-campus hospital. You will be expected to pay the charges yourself.

Glossary

Accelerated program. A college program of study completed in less time than is usually required, most often by attending classes in summer or by taking extra courses during the regular academic terms. Completion of a bachelor's degree program in three years is an example of acceleration.

Accreditation. Recognition by an accrediting organization or agency that a college meets certain acceptable standards in its educational programs, services, and facilities. Regional accreditation applies to a college as a whole and not to any particular programs or courses of study. Specialized accreditation of specific types of schools, such as Bible colleges or trade and technical schools, may also be determined by a national organization. Information about the accreditation of specialized programs within a college by organizations, such as the American Chemical Society, American Dietetic Association, etc., is given in *Accredited Institutions of Postsecondary Education*, published for the Commission on Recognition of Postsecondary Accreditation by the American Council on Education.

ACT. A college entrance examination given at specific locations in the United States and other countries on specified dates throughout the year. It includes tests in English, mathematics, reading, and science.

Advanced placement. Admission or assignment of a freshman to an advanced course in a certain subject on the basis of evidence that the student has already completed the equivalent of the college's freshman course in that subject.

Advanced Placement Program® (AP®). A program of the College Board that provides high schools with course descriptions of college subjects and examinations in those subjects. The AP Program offers 38 exams in 22 subject areas. Most colleges and universities in the United States accept qualifying AP Exam grades for credit, advanced placement, or both.

Associate degree. A degree granted by a college or university after the satisfactory completion of a two-year full-time program of study or its part-time equivalent. In general, the associate of arts (A.A.) or associate of science (A.S.) degree is granted after students complete a program of study similar to the first two years of a four-year college curriculum. The associate in applied science (A.A.S.) is awarded by many colleges upon completion of technological or vocational programs of study.

Bachelor's, or baccalaureate, degree. A degree received after the satisfactory completion of a four- or five-year full-time program of study (or its part-time equivalent) at a college or university. The bachelor of arts (B.A.) and bachelor of science (B.S.) are the most common baccalaureates. There is no absolute difference between the degrees, and policies concerning their award vary from college to college.

Calendar. The system by which an institution divides its year into shorter periods for instruction and awarding credit. The most common calendars are those based on the semester, trimester, quarter, and 4-1-4.

Certificate. An award for completing a particular program or course of study, sometimes given by two-year colleges or vocational or technical schools.

College-Level Examination Program® (CLEP®). Examinations in undergraduate college subjects that provide students of any age the opportunity to demonstrate college-level achievement, thereby reducing costs and time to degree completion. The examinations, which are sponsored by the College Board, are administered at colleges year-round via computer, providing test-takers with instant score results. International students are encouraged to take CLEP exams once they arrive at a U.S. institution to begin their studies.

College-preparatory subjects. A term used to describe subjects required for admission to, or recommended as preparation for, college. It is usually understood to mean subjects from the fields of English, history and social studies, foreign languages, mathematics, science, and the arts.

Combined bachelor's/graduate degree. A program in which students complete a bachelor's degree and a master's degree or first-professional degree in less than the usual amount of time. In most programs, students apply to undergraduate study, and begin the graduate program in their fourth year of college. Successful completion results in the awarding of both bachelor's and graduate degrees. At some colleges, this option is called a joint-degree program.

Common Application. The standard application form distributed by the National Association of Secondary School Principals to private colleges that are subscribers to the Common Application Group.

Community/junior college. A college offering a two-year program rather than a four-year program. A junior college usually offers vocational programs as well as the first two years of a four-year program. The student in the vocational program usually goes directly into a vocation after graduation, while the student in the academic program transfers to a four-year institution.

Comprehensive fee. If the college combines tuition, fees, room, and board expenses, that single figure is called a comprehensive fee.

Consortium. When there are several colleges and universities within close geographical proximity, they often join together in a consortium. The advantages of attending a college that is a member of a consortium are that students have the resources of many libraries instead of just one; they have the opportunity to take courses not available at their own college by doing so at a member institution; and they can take advantage of many of the combined cultural and educational opportunities offered when the members of the consortium unite and present panel discussions, special lectures, and unusual courses.

Consumer Price Index (CPI). A measure of inflation or deflation at the consumer level, updated monthly by the U.S. Bureau of Labor Statistics.

Cooperative education (co-op). A program that provides for alternative class attendance and employment in business, industry, or government. Students are typically paid for their work. Under a cooperative plan, five years are normally required to complete a bachelor's degree, but graduates have the advantage of about a year's practical work experience in addition to their studies.

Credit by examination. Academic credit granted by a college to entering students who have demonstrated proficiency in college-level studies through examinations, such as those sponsored by the College Board's AP and CLEP programs. This is a means of cutting college costs by reducing the number of courses needed to earn a degree.

Credit hour. A unit of measure representing an hour of instruction over a 15-week period in a semester or trimester system, or a 10-week period in a quarter system. It is applied toward the total number of hours needed for completing the requirements of a degree, diploma, certificate, or other formal award.

Credit/no credit grading system. *See* Pass/fail grading system.

Cross-registration. The practice, through agreements between colleges, of permitting students enrolled at one college or university to enroll in courses at another institution without formally applying for admission to the second institution.

Deferred admission. The practice of permitting students to postpone enrollment, usually for one year, after acceptance to college.

Distance learning. An option for earning course credit off campus via cable television, the Internet, satellite classes, videotapes, correspondence courses, or other means.

Double major. Any program in which a student completes the requirements of two majors concurrently.

Exchange student program. Any arrangement that permits a student to study for a semester or more at another college in the United States without extending the amount of time required for a degree.

First-professional degree. A degree granted upon completion of academic requirements to become licensed in a recognized profession, such as medicine or the law. The programs of study require at least two years of previous college work for entrance, and at least six years of college work for completion.

4-1-4. A variation of the semester calendar system, the 4-1-4 calendar consists of two terms of about 16 weeks each, separated by a one-month intersession used for intensive short courses, independent study, off-campus work, or other types of instruction.

Gift aid. Scholarships and grants that do not have to be repaid.

Grade point average or ratio (GPA). A system used by many schools for evaluating the overall scholastic performance of students. Grade points are determined by first multiplying the number of hours given for a course by the numerical value of the grade and then dividing the sum of all grade points by the total number of hours carried. The most common system of numerical values for grades is: A = 4, B = 3, C = 2, D = 1, and E or F = 0. Also called a quality point average ratio.

Graduate study. A program leading to a master's degree or doctoral degree; advanced study generally following a bachelor's degree.

High school. The final three to four years of preuniversity education in the United States. Students usually receive their high school diplomas when they are 17 or 18. Also called "secondary school."

Honors program. A plan designed to encourage superior students to engage in more challenging programs in their areas of concentration than are required. Students who succeed in meeting the stringent requirements of an honors program are usually granted "honor" degrees.

IB. *See* International Baccalaureate.

Independent study. Academic work chosen or designed by the student with the approval of the department concerned, under an instructor's supervision. This work is usually undertaken outside of the regular classroom structure.

Interdisciplinary. Refers to programs or courses that use the knowledge from a number of academic disciplines, such as a combination of environmental science and government policy, or of engineering and business.

International Baccalaureate (IB). A comprehensive and rigorous two-year curriculum (usually taken in the final two years of high school) that is similar to the final year of secondary school in Europe. Some colleges award credit or advanced placement to students who have completed an IB program.

Internships. Short-term supervised work experiences, usually related to a student's major field, for which the student earns academic credit. The work can be full- or part-time, on or off campus, paid or unpaid. Student teaching and apprenticeships are examples.

Liberal arts. The study of the humanities (literature, the arts, and philosophy), history, foreign languages, social sciences, mathematics, and natural sciences. Study of the liberal arts and humanities prepares students to develop general knowledge and reasoning ability rather than specific skills.

Major. Short for "major field of concentration," a student's academic field of specialization. In general, most courses in the major are taken at the degree-granting institution during the junior and senior years.

Master's degree. A degree awarded after one or more years of graduate work following the bachelor's degree.

Matriculation. The process whereby a student is accepted, pays fees, and enrolls in classes, officially becoming a student at the college. This term is only applied to freshmen or to a transfer student's first enrollment.

Open admissions. The college admissions policy of admitting high school graduates and other adults generally without regard to conventional academic qualifications, such as high school subjects, high school grades, and admissions test scores. Virtually all applicants with high school diplomas or their equivalent are accepted.

Optional Practical Training (OPT). This program, sponsored by the U.S. Citizenship and Immigration Services, gives students on F-1 visas the opportunity to work for up to a year in a field related to their program of study.

Pass/fail grading system. Some colleges permit students to take courses where their performance is simply rated as either passing or failing, rather than graded to indicate various levels of passing work. The college's entire grading system may follow this pattern, or it may be an option for individual students in specific courses. It may also be referred to as a credit/no credit grading option.

Prerequisite. A requirement that must be met before a certain course can be taken.

Private institution. An institution of higher education not supported by public taxes. It may be independent or related to a church.

Public college/university. An institution of higher education supported by public taxes.

Quarter system. An academic calendar period of about 12 weeks. Four quarters make up an academic year, but at colleges using the quarter system, students make normal academic progress by attending three quarters each year. In some colleges, students can accelerate their progress by attending all four quarters in one or more years.

Residency requirements. Most colleges and universities require that a student spend a minimum number of terms taking courses on campus (as opposed to independent study, transfer credits from other colleges, or credit by examination) to be eligible for graduation. Also, residency requirements can refer to the minimum amount of time a student is required to have lived in a state to be eligible for in-state tuition at a public (state-controlled) college or university.

Rolling admissions. An admissions procedure by which the college considers each student's application as soon as all the required credentials, such as school records and test scores, have been received. The college usually notifies an applicant of its decision without delay. At many colleges, rolling admissions allows for early notification and works much like nonbinding Early Action programs.

SAT Question-and-Answer Service. A service of the College Board that provides students with a copy of their SAT Reasoning Test, their answers and the correct answers, scoring instructions, and information about the questions. The service is only available for certain test dates.

SAT®. The College Board's test of critical reading, writing, and mathematical reasoning abilities, given on specific dates throughout the year at test centers in the United States and other countries. The SAT is required by many colleges and sponsors of financial aid programs, and many colleges use scores on the SAT as criteria for the awarding of merit scholarships.

SAT Subject Tests™. College Board tests in specific subjects, given at test centers in the United States and other countries on specified dates throughout the year. Used by colleges not only to help with decisions about admission but also in course placement and exemption of enrolled freshmen.

Secondary school. *See* High school.

Semester. A period of about 16 weeks. Colleges on a semester system offer two semesters of instruction a year; there may also be an additional summer session.

Student and Exchange Visitor Information System (SEVIS). An automated system created by the U.S. government to track international students.

Terminal program. A program of study in which the student completes his or her studies in a preselected period of time. This type of program is usually directed toward vocational preparation. The amount of time taken to complete the program will vary, but is not usually longer than two years.

Test of English as a Foreign Language (TOEFL). This test helps international students demonstrate their English language proficiency at the advanced level required for study at colleges and universities in the United States. Many colleges require that their applicants from non-English-speaking countries take the test as part of the admissions requirements.

Test of Spoken English (TSE). A 20-minute tape-recorded test given to evaluate the spoken English proficiency of nonnative speakers. The TSE may be required for international students who apply for teaching and research assistantships and who cannot take the TOEFL iBT.

TOEFL. *See* Test of English as a Foreign Language.

Transcript. A copy of a student's official academic record listing all courses taken and grades required.

Transfer program. An educational program in a two-year college (or four-year college that offers associate degrees) primarily for students who plan to continue their studies in a four-year college or university.

Transfer student. A student who has attended another college for any period, which may be defined by various colleges as any time from a single term up to three years. A transfer student may receive credit for all or some of the courses successfully completed before the transfer.

Trimester. An academic calendar period of about 15 weeks. Three trimesters make up one year. Students normally progress by attending two of the trimesters each year and in some colleges can accelerate their progress by attending all three trimesters in one or more years.

Undergraduate study. A program leading to an associate or a bachelor's degree; generally follows high school.

Upper-division college. A college offering bachelor's degree programs that begin with the junior year. Entering students must have completed the freshman and sophomore years at other colleges.

Virtual university. A degree-granting, accredited institution wherein all courses are delivered by distance learning, with no physical campus.

Part II:
Information tables on U.S. colleges and universities

Part II:

How to use the information tables

The information tables provide detailed information on more than 2,800 undergraduate institutions in the United States. The data were collected directly from the institutions by written questionnaires and telephone follow-up from January through April 2008.

Undergraduate information

The names of the colleges are listed alphabetically by state. Institutions are listed by their full names, which are not always the ones in popular use. For example, UCLA is listed as University of California: Los Angeles. The mailing address, telephone number, Web site address, and fax number (when available) of each college are given in the *College addresses* starting on page 236. The columns in this section include the following information.

Control/degrees. This column shows whether the institution is private (Pr) or public (Pu), and whether the college offers associate degrees (A), bachelor's degrees (B), or both (AB).

Undergraduate enrollment. The first figure is the total number of undergraduate students enrolled in the fall of 2007. The second figure is the number of undergraduate international students enrolled.

Tests required. If the college requires one or more of the following standardized admissions tests, they are indicated in this column: SAT Reasoning Test, SAT Subject Test,

ACT, or TOEFL. A slash (/) between two tests means that either test is required; for example, SAT/TOEFL means that applicants must take either the SAT Reasoning Test or the TOEFL. A plus (+) between tests means that both are required; for example, SAT + TOEFL means that applicants must take both the SAT Reasoning Test and the TOEFL.

TOEFL minimum and average. The minimum score listed is generally acceptable to the college as an indicator of English language proficiency. The average may be significantly higher at some colleges. The scores indicated, which range from 310 to 667, are for the paper-based test. For iBT (Internet-based) scores, which range from 0 to 300, see the concordance table on the TOEFL Web site.

Applications. The deadline is generally the last date by which the college will accept application forms, test scores, transcripts, and other documents required for the admissions process. Remember that many colleges fill their classes well in advance of this date, so complete your applications as soon as possible before the deadline. The application fee is required at the time you send your application form; the figure here is in U.S. dollars.

Student services. These columns indicate whether the college offers the following services for international students: student adviser, student orientation program, or English as a second language (ESL) program on campus.

Housing. These two columns indicate whether the college has housing during the academic year (September–May) and/or summer months (June, July, and August) for international students.

Academic year cost. The figure for tuition/fees represents the tuition and general fees the college charges most first-year, full-time international students for the nine-month academic year. For colleges with on-campus housing, the nine-month living cost includes room and board, books and supplies, and personal expenses, such as clothing, laundry, and health insurance. For colleges that do not offer on-campus housing, the living cost figure includes an estimated expense for room and board. The cost per credit is indicated along with the maximum number of credits the institution allows a student to take during the summer. The cost does not include travel to and from your home country. Cost is for 2008-09, unless otherwise indicated.

Financial aid. The first column indicates whether the institution offers financial aid for undergraduates from other countries. The number of international students who received aid is shown next, followed by the average award (in U.S. dollars). The last column shows the deadline for applying for financial aid. Remember that there is not enough financial aid to meet the needs of all applicants, so complete any financial aid application requirements as soon as possible.

Lists and indexes

International undergraduate student enrollment. Colleges are listed in descending order by enrollment size. If a college did not provide international enrollment information this year, it is not included on the list.

Total financial aid for international undergraduate students. Colleges are listed in descending order by the total dollar amount of financial aid awarded to international students.

Conditional admission based on English language proficiency. Colleges that will admit applicants whose English skills will not permit them to pursue academic course work during their first term are listed here. These colleges require that the student spend time in the first term increasing their English language skills to the required level. English language proficiency is defined differently by different institutions. If you have questions about your English language skills, be sure to check with the colleges of interest to you.

SAT Subject Tests required or recommended. Some colleges require one or more SAT Subject Tests of undergraduate international applicants, and some recommend these tests.

Credit/placement for International Baccalaureate (IB). These colleges offer credit or advanced standing for the IB diploma and/or certificates from individual IB exams. They do not necessarily offer credit for every IB exam, and qualifying scores will vary. Check with the colleges to learn more about their policies.

Credit/placement for Advanced Placement (AP). These colleges offer credit or advanced placement to students with qualifying grades on certain AP Exams. They do not necessarily offer credit for every AP Exam, and qualifying grades will vary. Check with the colleges, or use the AP Credit Policy Info tool at www.collegeboard.com/ap/creditpolicy, to learn more about the colleges' policies.

ESL programs on campus. Colleges that offer English as a second language programs on campus are listed in alphabetical order by state.

Special housing for international students. Colleges that offer a special on-campus dormitory for international students are listed in alphabetical order by state.

Housing guaranteed for all freshmen. These colleges guarantee that incoming freshmen will be offered on-campus accommodations.

College size (undergraduate enrollment). Colleges are grouped into categories from very small (fewer than 750 undergraduates) to very large (15,000 or more undergraduates).

College type. Colleges are grouped into types that describe the type of courses you'll find at the college, such as liberal arts colleges, business colleges, engineering colleges, and military academies. Separate lists show colleges that are affiliated with a religious denomination and colleges that cater to a specific type of student, for example colleges for women.

Directory of colleges

This listing gives the full name and mailing address for each institution listed in the undergraduate and graduate tables in this section. It includes the school's telephone number and, when available, the Web site address, fax number, and e-mail address. The office to contact for further information about the institution and for application procedures and forms is also given.

Colleges and universities

Institution	Control/ degrees	Undergraduates		Tests required (Fall 2009)	TOEFL		Application	
		Total	Internat'l		minimum	average	Deadline	Fee
Alabama								
Alabama Agricultural and Mechanical University	Pu/B	4,716	112	TOEFL	500	650	5/15	20
Alabama State University	Pu/B	4,589	16	TOEFL	500		3/1	25
Andrew Jackson University	Pr/AB	200		TOEFL	550		None	75
Athens State University	Pu/B	2,858		TOEFL	500		7/11	30
Auburn University	Pu/B	19,794	111	TOEFL, SAT/ACT	550	580		50
Auburn University at Montgomery	Pu/B	4,134		TOEFL, SAT/ACT	500		8/1	25
Birmingham-Southern College	Pr/B	1,339	3	TOEFL	500		3/1	40
Bishop State Community College	Pu/A	2,812		TOEFL	500		7/1	
Calhoun Community College	Pu/A	9,228		TOEFL	500	525		
Chattahoochee Valley Community College	Pu/A	1,929		TOEFL	500		None	
Columbia Southern University	Pr/AB			TOEFL	500			50
Concordia College	Pr/AB	554		TOEFL	580		None	25
Faulkner State Community College	Pu/A	3,612		TOEFL	500		7/15	
Faulkner University	Pr/AB	2,534		TOEFL	450	500	None	10
Gadsden State Community College	Pu/A	5,516	162	TOEFL	500	515	None	
George C. Wallace Community College at Dothan	Pu/A	3,708		TOEFL	500			10
Heritage Christian University	Pr/AB	129					3/30	25
Huntingdon College	Pr/B	943		TOEFL, SAT/ACT	500		5/1	20
J. F. Drake State Technical College	Pu/A	675		TOEFL	500		None	
Jacksonville State University	Pu/B	7,391	157	TOEFL	500		None	20
Jefferson State Community College	Pu/A	6,070	101	TOEFL	500		8/15	
Judson College	Pr/B	311	4	TOEFL	500	517	None	32
Lawson State Community College	Pu/A	3,173		TOEFL	500	540	6/1	10
Marion Military Institute	Pu/A	389		TOEFL	500	570	8/15	40
Miles College	Pr/B	1,812		TOEFL	450	550	None	
Oakwood University	Pr/AB	1,778	121	TOEFL	500		6/30	30
Remington College: Mobile	Pr/AB	400					7/4	50
Samford University	Pr/AB	2,841		TOEFL	550		5/1	35
Shelton State Community College	Pu/A			TOEFL	500		None	
Southeastern Bible College	Pr/AB	213	1	TOEFL, SAT/ACT	500		7/1	30
Southern Union State Community College	Pu/A	4,960		TOEFL			None	
Spring Hill College	Pr/AB	1,268	8	TOEFL	550		7/1	35
Stillman College	Pr/B	915		TOEFL, SAT/ACT	500		4/1	25
Troy University	Pu/AB	21,046	390	TOEFL	500		3/30	30
Tuskegee University	Pr/B	2,514		TOEFL	500		6/15	35
United States Sports Academy	Pr/B	259						50
University of Alabama	Pu/B	20,910	168	TOEFL	500		5/1	35
University of Alabama at Birmingham	Pu/B	10,228	222	TOEFL, SAT/ACT	500		3/1	30
University of Alabama in Huntsville	Pu/B	5,562	182	TOEFL, SAT/ACT	500	575	5/21	30
University of Mobile	Pr/AB	1,346	32	TOEFL, SAT/ACT	500	541	7/1	30
University of Montevallo	Pu/B	2,473	50	TOEFL	525	560	6/1	25
University of North Alabama	Pu/B	5,299	485	TOEFL	500		6/27	25
University of South Alabama	Pu/B	10,459	509	TOEFL	500	580	7/1	35
University of West Alabama	Pu/AB	2,004		TOEFL	500	530	None	50
Virginia College at Huntsville	Pr/AB	862						100
Alaska								
Alaska Pacific University	Pr/AB	452	2	TOEFL	550		7/1	25
Ilisagvik College	Pu/A							
Prince William Sound Community College	Pu/A			TOEFL	450	550	7/31	10
University of Alaska Anchorage	Pu/AB	10,471	157	TOEFL, SAT/ACT	450			40
University of Alaska Fairbanks	Pu/AB	4,744	114	TOEFL, SAT/ACT	550		3/1	40
University of Alaska Southeast	Pu/AB	1,108		TOEFL	550		7/1	40

| Student services | | | Housing | | Academic year costs | | Maximum credits/ summer | Credit hour charge | International financial aid | | | |
Adviser	Orien-tation	ESL	Academic year	Summer	Tuition/ fees	Living costs			Avail-able	Number receiving aid	Average award	Deadline
Yes	Yes		Yes	Yes	9,220†	3,592	10	286	Yes			
Yes	Yes		Yes	Yes	8,516†	7,460	9	334	Yes			None
			No		5,550†	1,000		185				
Yes			Yes		7,350†	3,800	19	220	Yes			None
Yes	Yes	Yes	Yes		16,334†	11,100		651				
Yes	Yes	Yes	Yes	Yes	14,490†	7,580	18	474				
Yes	Yes		Yes	Yes	25,586	11,995	12	1033	Yes			
Yes	Yes		No		4,830†	5,493	15	142				
Yes			No		4,980†	3,700	19	142	Yes			None
Yes			No		4,830†	8,000	23	142				
					4,800			185				
Yes			Yes		6,826†	3,600		142				
Yes			Yes		4,920†	5,850		142				
Yes			Yes	Yes	12,770	10,650	12	445				
Yes	Yes	Yes	Yes	Yes	4,830†	4,904	14	142				
Yes			No		4,830†	3,400	21	143				
Yes	Yes		Yes	Yes	9,810†	3,000	15	307				
		Yes	Yes	Yes	20,020‡	9,495	12	800	Yes	7	$12,104	None
Yes			No		4,830†	550	15	142				
Yes			Yes	Yes	10,140†	10,555	18	338	Yes	10		None
Yes	Yes		No		5,190†	5,168	19	142				
Yes			Yes		11,120†	10,320	10	360				
Yes					5,130†	5,610	21	142				
Yes			Yes		12,796†	3,450			Yes			None
Yes			Yes		7,051†	6,766		275				
Yes	Yes		Yes		13,174	7,458						
			No				16					
Yes			Yes	Yes	17,920†	10,955			Yes	13	$15,120	None
Yes			No		4,830†	1,750	20		Yes			None
			Yes		10,035†	2,300		330	Yes			8/15
Yes			Yes		4,830†	4,500		142				
Yes			Yes	Yes	24,240	13,060	12	850	Yes	8	$22,190	None
			Yes		12,186†	5,572	12	456	Yes			None
Yes	Yes	Yes	Yes	Yes	8,428†	9,814	21	348				
Yes			Yes		15,450	10,056	9	420				
					8,200†		12	250				
Yes	Yes	Yes	Yes	Yes	16,518†	9,820						
Yes	Yes		Yes	Yes	11,546†	11,937	18	353				
Yes	Yes	Yes	Yes	Yes	11,024†	9,696	18	413	Yes	24	$2,446	7/31
Yes			Yes	Yes	13,970	11,420	18	480				
Yes		Yes	Yes	Yes	11,930†	8,164	14	390		37	$11,359	
Yes	Yes	Yes	Yes	Yes	9,203†	5,290	12	274	Yes			None
Yes	Yes	Yes	Yes		8,842†	5,698		268				
Yes			Yes	Yes	8,713†	6,624 4,562	18	348				
Yes	Yes		Yes		22,610	12,984	15	940	Yes			None
Yes		Yes	Yes	Yes	3,660†	1,800	15		Yes			None
Yes	Yes	Yes	Yes		13,370†	13,788	15	427	Yes			8/1
Yes	Yes		Yes	Yes	13,466†	10,514	18	427	Yes	56	$11,320	7/1
Yes	Yes		Yes	Yes	13,338†	10,708	12	427	Yes			None

† Tuition and fees are for 2007-08. ‡ Tuition and fees are projected for 2008-09. * Comprehensive Fee

Institution	Control/ degrees	Undergraduates		Tests required (Fall 2009)	TOEFL		Application	
		Total	Internat'l		minimum	average	Deadline	Fee
Arizona								
Arizona Automotive Institute	Pr/A	540					None	100
Arizona State University	Pu/B	38,597	970	TOEFL	500		6/1	50
Arizona State University West	Pu/B	5,860	40	TOEFL	500		6/1	50
Arizona Western College	Pu/A	6,056	762	TOEFL	500		None	25
Art Center Design College	Pr/AB	325		TOEFL, SAT/ACT	500		None	25
Art Institute of Phoenix	Pr/AB	1,109		TOEFL	500		10/13	50
Brown Mackie College: Tucson	Pr/AB	283						
Central Arizona College	Pu/A	4,951		TOEFL	500		8/1	22
Chandler-Gilbert Community College: Pecos	Pu/A	1,471			500		7/15	
Cochise College	Pu/A	3,113	5				8/1	50
DeVry University: Phoenix	Pr/AB	1,017	8	TOEFL	500		None	50
Dine College	Pu/A	1,681		TOEFL	500	520	None	20
Eastern Arizona College	Pu/A	3,058	29	TOEFL	500	540	8/1	25
Embry-Riddle Aeronautical University: Prescott Campus	Pr/B	1,667	60	TOEFL	500	630	6/1	50
Estrella Mountain Community College	Pu/A	5,973		TOEFL	500		6/1	5
Everest College: Phoenix	Pr/AB	2,766		TOEFL	450		None	
Gateway Community College	Pu/A			TOEFL	500		2/9	
Glendale Community College	Pu/A	4,446	45	TOEFL	500		7/1	
Golf Academy of Arizona	Pr/A	238						
Grand Canyon University	Pr/B	4,803	35	TOEFL	500		None	100
International Import-Export Institute	Pr/B	50		TOEFL				50
International Institute of the Americas: Mesa	Pr/AB	133						200
Long Technical College	Pr/A	322						25
Mesa Community College	Pu/A			TOEFL	500		7/7	
Midwestern University: Glendale	Pr/B	26						50
Mohave Community College	Pu/A	5,469		TOEFL	500			
Northcentral University	Pr/B	248		TOEFL	550		None	50
Northern Arizona University	Pu/B	15,362	365	TOEFL	525	553	5/1	50
Paradise Valley Community College	Pu/A	8,574		TOEFL	500		7/1	
Paralegal Institute	Pr/A	500						
Penn Foster College	Pr/A	25,000					None	200
Phoenix College	Pu/A	11,097		TOEFL	500		None	
Pima Community College	Pu/A	32,982		TOEFL	450		None	25
Prescott College	Pr/B	689	6	TOEFL	550		8/15	25
Rio Salado College	Pu/A	18,331		TOEFL	500		None	
Scottsdale Community College	Pu/A	10,371		TOEFL	500		None	
South Mountain Community College	Pu/A						7/1	
Tohono O'odham Community College	Pu/A	96						
Universal Technical Institute	Pr/A	1,761					None	
University of Advancing Technology	Pr/AB	1,195	12	TOEFL	550		6/8	
University of Arizona	Pu/B	28,670	721	TOEFL	500	595	4/1	50
University of Phoenix	Pr/AB	247,566		TOEFL	550		None	45
Western International University	Pr/AB	2,083		TOEFL	500		None	100
Yavapai College	Pu/A	4,718		TOEFL	450		4/1	50
Arkansas								
Arkansas State University	Pu/AB	8,791	60	TOEFL, SAT/ACT	500	550	4/1	40
Arkansas State University: Mountain Home	Pu/A	1,055		TOEFL	500		5/1	
Arkansas State University: Newport	Pu/A	1,175		TOEFL, SAT/ACT	500		5/1	
Arkansas Tech University	Pu/AB	6,558	206	TOEFL, SAT/ACT	500		5/1	50
Black River Technical College	Pu/A	1,954						

Student services			Housing		Academic year costs		Maximum credits/ summer	Credit hour charge	International financial aid			
Adviser	Orien- tation	ESL	Academic year	Summer	Tuition/ fees	Living costs			Avail- able	Number receiving aid	Average award	Deadline
			Yes				15					
Yes	Yes	Yes	Yes	Yes	17,003 †	7,320	12	702	Yes	481	$8,720	None
	Yes		Yes	Yes	16,999 †	12,240	14	702	Yes	9	$8,567	3/1
Yes	Yes	Yes	Yes		5,940 †	10,856	8	52				
Yes			No		15,360 †	6,134		640				
Yes	Yes		Yes		12,240 †		15	403				
			No									
Yes		Yes	Yes		7,501	9,045	7	120	Yes			7/15
			Yes		8,415 †	15,572		280				
Yes	Yes	Yes	Yes	Yes	7,330	9,321	12		Yes	3	$7,809	4/15
Yes					13,220 †	16,375		490				
			Yes	Yes	850 †	8,664	12		Yes			None
Yes			Yes		6,540 †	7,990	18	110	Yes			
Yes	Yes		Yes	Yes	27,180	13,048	18	1100	Yes	44	$10,989	None
			No		8,595	6,180	12	286	Yes			
	Yes		No			975		272				
Yes	Yes		No		7,905 †		12	263	Yes			None
Yes	Yes	Yes	No		8,410 †	5,942	12	280				
					9,850 †	4,342						
Yes	Yes		Yes	Yes	16,030	9,744	15	645	Yes			None
			No		11,400 ‡	11,100						
			No									
Yes	Yes	Yes	Yes		8,430 †	500	9	280	Yes			None
					18,311 †							
		Yes	No		5,390		7	177				
			No			1,200		250				
Yes	Yes	Yes	Yes	Yes	14,498 †	14,864	12	594	Yes	61	$4,643	None
			No		8,430 †	700	6	280				
					7,500 ‡			125				
			No									
Yes	Yes		No		8,130 †	700	12	270				
Yes	Yes	Yes	No		7,235 †	7,120	12	80	Yes			None
			Yes		21,792	5,200	24	597				
Yes			No		8,610	9,184	18	286	Yes			None
Yes	Yes	Yes	No		8,460 †	5,042		280	Yes			None
		Yes	No		8,430 †	6,100	12	280				
					6,340	750		72				
Yes			No		15,630							
			Yes		17,400	12,590	18		Yes			None
Yes	Yes	Yes	Yes	Yes	16,271 †	12,346	12	669	Yes			None
Yes			No		10,290 †	525		343				
Yes	Yes		No						Yes			None
Yes	Yes		Yes	Yes	8,140 †	7,750	12	327	Yes			None
Yes	Yes		Yes	Yes	13,390 †	10,111	12	400				
Yes			No		3,900 †	4,900	6	122				
			No		3,930 †		14	126				
Yes	Yes	Yes	Yes	Yes	9,710 †	8,132	12	306	Yes	63	$4,609	None
					5,412 †			178				

Institution	Control/ degrees	Undergraduates		Tests required (Fall 2009)	TOEFL		Application	
		Total	Internat'l		minimum	average	Deadline	Fee
Crowley's Ridge College	Pr/A	168		TOEFL, ACT	500	573		
East Arkansas Community College	Pu/A	1,121		TOEFL, ACT	500		2/28	25
Ecclesia College	Pr/AB			TOEFL	500		6/1	50
Harding University	Pr/B	4,063	201	TOEFL	550		None	100
Henderson State University	Pu/AB	3,092	76	TOEFL, SAT/ACT	500		None	30
Hendrix College	Pr/B	1,189	16	TOEFL	550	620	5/1	100
John Brown University	Pr/AB	1,666		TOEFL, SAT/ACT, SAT Subject Test(s)	550		None	100
Lyon College	Pr/B	483	12	TOEFL, SAT/ACT	550		5/1	50
National Park Community College	Pu/A	2,503		TOEFL	500	540	6/30	
Ouachita Baptist University	Pr/AB	1,448	38	TOEFL	550		7/31	50
Ouachita Technical College	Pu/A	1,558		TOEFL	500		None	100
Philander Smith College	Pr/B	561		TOEFL, SAT/ACT	500		4/5	75
Phillips Community College of the University of Arkansas	Pu/A	2,336		TOEFL	500		None	
Pulaski Technical College	Pu/A	7,606	10	TOEFL, ACT	550		6/1	50
South Arkansas Community College	Pu/A	1,319		TOEFL				
Southeast Arkansas College	Pu/A	1,710					None	
Southern Arkansas University	Pu/AB	2,660	146	TOEFL	500	560	7/1	25
Southern Arkansas University Tech	Pu/A	787	4	TOEFL	500		5/15	
University of Arkansas	Pu/B	14,442	331	TOEFL	550	577	5/31	50
University of Arkansas at Fort Smith	Pu/AB	5,833	7	TOEFL	500		6/15	
University of Arkansas at Little Rock	Pu/AB	8,908	127	TOEFL	525		6/1	30
University of Arkansas at Monticello	Pu/AB	2,604	7	TOEFL, SAT/ACT	500			30
University of Arkansas at Pine Bluff	Pu/AB	3,048	15	TOEFL	500	520	8/1	
University of Central Arkansas	Pu/AB	9,921	425	TOEFL	500		7/15	50
University of the Ozarks	Pr/B	612	118	TOEFL	500	540	8/1	30
Williams Baptist College	Pr/AB	502	3	TOEFL	500		None	20
California								
Academy of Art University	Pr/AB	8,210	1,147				None	100
Allan Hancock College	Pu/A	15,456		TOEFL	475	500	6/1	
Alliant International University	Pr/B	179	42	TOEFL, SAT, SAT Subject Test(s), or ACT	550		None	45
American Academy of Dramatic Arts: West	Pr/A	250		TOEFL	500		8/1	50
American Jewish University	Pr/B	107	6	TOEFL	550	585	6/30	35
American River College	Pu/A	34,338		TOEFL	510	530	7/1	50
Antelope Valley College	Pu/A	14,035		TOEFL	450		5/1	
Antioch University Los Angeles	Pr/B	150		TOEFL	600	610	8/1	60
Antioch University Santa Barbara	Pr/B			TOEFL	550		None	60
Art Institute of California: Los Angeles	Pr/AB	2,149		TOEFL	480		None	50
Art Institute of California: Orange County	Pr/AB	1,761		TOEFL	500		None	50
Art Institute of California: San Diego	Pr/AB			TOEFL			None	50
Art Institute of California: San Francisco	Pr/AB	1,568		TOEFL	500		None	150
Azusa Pacific University	Pr/B	4,615		TOEFL	500	525	6/1	65
Bakersfield College	Pu/A	17,580		TOEFL	500		3/15	50
Barstow Community College	Pu/A	4,060		TOEFL	450		None	
Berkeley City College	Pu/A	5,420		TOEFL				50
Bethany University	Pr/AB	456		TOEFL	500		None	35
Bethesda Christian University	Pr/B	254		TOEFL	500		None	160
Biola University	Pr/B	3,550		TOEFL	500	589	3/1	45
Brooks College	Pr/A	266		TOEFL	450	510	None	250
Brooks Institute	Pr/AB			TOEFL	500		None	100
Bryan College: Sacramento	Pr/A							35
Butte College	Pu/A	13,875		TOEFL	450	475		100

| Student services | | | Housing | | Academic year costs | | Maximum credits/ summer | Credit hour charge | International financial aid | | | |
Adviser	Orientation	ESL	Academic year	Summer	Tuition/ fees	Living costs			Available	Number receiving aid	Average award	Deadline
			Yes		8,410‡	5,850	12	245	Yes			None
			No		2,370†	5,700		71	Yes			7/1
Yes			Yes	Yes	15,090‡	8,732	12	475	Yes			None
Yes		Yes	Yes	Yes	13,130	8,500	16	423	Yes	109	$7,459	None
Yes	Yes	Yes	Yes	Yes	10,944	9,590	14		Yes			None
Yes	Yes		Yes		26,080	11,328			Yes	13	$19,010	None
Yes	Yes	Yes	Yes		18,066	11,630	6	720	Yes	37		None
Yes			Yes		19,034	9,990	10	695	Yes	11	$15,778	None
Yes			No		5,880†	10,071	12	194	Yes			None
Yes	Yes	Yes	Yes	Yes	18,400	12,330	15	515	Yes	32	$15,527	6/1
			No		5,420	12,414	12	165	Yes			6/30
Yes	Yes		Yes	Yes	8,490†	8,381	12		Yes			None
			No		3,320†	11,145	8	99	Yes			6/30
Yes			No		8,000	5,357	6	256	Yes			None
			No		3,880†	5,070	14	123	Yes			None
			No		3,220†	8,400		100	Yes			None
Yes	Yes		Yes	Yes	7,534†	8,300	12	227	Yes			None
Yes	Yes		Yes	Yes	3,049†	17,850	14	84				
Yes	Yes	Yes	Yes	Yes	14,492†	11,119	12	441	Yes	105	$7,472	None
Yes			Yes	Yes	8,950†	9,530	14	267				
Yes	Yes	Yes	Yes		13,199†	5,700	12	404				
			Yes	Yes	8,230†	8,090	12	239	Yes			None
Yes	Yes		Yes	Yes	8,909†	8,272	12	257				
Yes	Yes	Yes	Yes	Yes	10,892†	10,611	12	322	Yes			7/1
Yes	Yes		Yes		17,330	10,342	7	700	Yes	117	$19,507	None
			Yes	Yes	10,950	9,030		425	Yes	11	$8,456	None
Yes	Yes	Yes	Yes	Yes	20,380‡	18,036	9	670				
		Yes	No		5,832†	15,008	8	193				
Yes	Yes	Yes	Yes	Yes	15,210‡	12,744	18	550	Yes			None
Yes			No		20,000	5,010			Yes			None
			Yes	Yes	22,352	17,152			Yes			
Yes	Yes		No		6,362†	13,134	8	211				
		Yes	No		5,792†	14,292	9	193				
Yes			No		15,252†	1,500	15	501				
Yes	Yes		No		14,718†	1,750	15	490				
Yes	Yes		Yes	Yes	22,322†	3,233		464	Yes			None
Yes			Yes	Yes		14,248	18		Yes			None
Yes	Yes		Yes		22,272			464				
Yes	Yes		Yes		29,184‡	11,805	15	456				
Yes	Yes	Yes	Yes	Yes	26,640	11,742	16	1075	Yes	64	$6,615	7/1
Yes	Yes	Yes	No		7,628†	9,370	7	253				
Yes		Yes	No		5,790†	4,770		193				
Yes		Yes	No		5,970†	15,168	6	199				
Yes			Yes	Yes	17,360†	12,393	6	685	Yes			None
Yes		Yes	No		6,420†	1,500	18	210	Yes			3/14
Yes	Yes	Yes	Yes	Yes	26,424	11,586	12	1101	Yes			
Yes		Yes	Yes	Yes		1,500	18					
			No		17,840		12					
					17,507†							
Yes		Yes	No		6,326†	12,918		205				

† Tuition and fees are for 2007-08.   ‡ Tuition and fees are projected for 2008-09.   * Comprehensive Fee

Institution	Control/ degrees	Undergraduates		Tests required (Fall 2009)	TOEFL		Application	
		Total	Internat'l		minimum	average	Deadline	Fee
Cabrillo College	Pu/A	15,131		TOEFL	450	480	5/30	
California Baptist University	Pr/B	2,952		TOEFL	525		7/15	45
California Coast University	Pr/AB							75
California College of the Arts	Pr/B	1,285	89	TOEFL	550		None	50
California College San Diego	Pr/AB	550						
California Culinary Academy	Pr/A	200		TOEFL	500		None	65
California Design College	Pr/AB	882		TOEFL	500		None	50
California Institute of the Arts	Pr/B	820	67	TOEFL	550	570	1/4	85
California Institute of Integral Studies	Pr/B	56						65
California Institute of Technology	Pr/B	913	86				1/1	60
California Lutheran University	Pr/B	2,126	74	TOEFL	530		6/1	45
California Maritime Academy	Pu/B	865		TOEFL, SAT/ACT	500		5/1	55
California National University for Advanced Studies	Pr/B	350						100
California Polytechnic State University: San Luis Obispo	Pu/B	18,728	138	TOEFL	550	555	11/30	55
California School of Culinary Arts	Pr/A	1,586		TOEFL	500		None	100
California State Polytechnic University: Pomona	Pu/B	19,615	1,095	TOEFL, SAT, SAT Subject Test(s), or ACT	525	544	None	55
California State University: Bakersfield	Pu/B	5,594		TOEFL	500	530	8/1	55
California State University: Channel Islands	Pu/B	3,289		TOEFL	500			55
California State University: Chico	Pu/B	15,645	349	TOEFL	500		5/1	55
California State University: Dominguez Hills	Pu/B	8,409	174	TOEFL, SAT/ACT	550		5/1	55
California State University: East Bay	Pu/B	10,391	621	TOEFL	530	558	3/31	55
California State University: Fresno	Pu/B	19,191		TOEFL	500		2/1	55
California State University: Fullerton	Pu/B	29,788	1,091	TOEFL, SAT/ACT	500	563	4/15	55
California State University: Long Beach	Pu/B	30,605	1,431	TOEFL, SAT/ACT	500	547	11/30	55
California State University: Los Angeles	Pu/B	15,727		TOEFL	550			55
California State University: Monterey Bay	Pu/B	3,604	38	TOEFL	525		5/1	55
California State University: Sacramento	Pu/B	23,724	276	TOEFL, SAT/ACT	510			55
California State University: San Bernardino	Pu/B	13,311	346	TOEFL	500	570	None	55
California State University: San Marcos	Pu/B	7,997		TOEFL	550		5/1	55
California State University: Stanislaus	Pu/B	7,088		TOEFL	500		7/1	55
California University of Management and Sciences	Pr/AB	95		TOEFL	450	500	None	100
Canada College	Pu/A	6,691		TOEFL	480	500	4/15	
Cerritos College	Pu/A	23,857		TOEFL	450		5/1	40
Cerro Coso Community College	Pu/A	4,797		TOEFL	500		None	
Chabot College	Pu/A	14,069		TOEFL	500	525	5/15	100
Chaffey College	Pu/A	19,715		TOEFL	450	460	None	35
Chapman University	Pr/B	4,169	96	TOEFL	550	605	3/1	55
Charles R. Drew University of Medicine and Science	Pr/AB	294		TOEFL			1/15	35
Citrus College	Pu/A	13,095		TOEFL	450		6/1	40
City College of San Francisco	Pu/A	22,332	1,209	TOEFL	475	500	5/15	50
Claremont McKenna College	Pr/B	1,135	56	TOEFL, SAT/ACT	600	639	1/2	60
Coastline Community College	Pu/A	12,129		TOEFL	500		9/7	30
Cogswell Polytechnical College	Pr/B	230		TOEFL	525		3/1	55
Coleman College	Pr/AB	481		TOEFL	500	520	None	100
Coleman College: San Marcos	Pr/A	132						
College of Alameda	Pu/A	6,501		TOEFL	500		1/1	
College of the Canyons	Pu/A	18,459	97	TOEFL	450		6/1	
College of the Desert	Pu/A	10,926	178	TOEFL	400	420	7/15	25
College of Marin: Kentfield	Pu/A	6,572		TOEFL	500	535	7/31	50
College of the Redwoods	Pu/A	4,516		TOEFL	500		None	162

Student services			Housing		Academic year costs		Maximum credits/summer	Credit hour charge	International financial aid			
Adviser	Orien-tation	ESL	Academic year	Summer	Tuition/fees	Living costs			Avail-able	Number receiving aid	Average award	Deadline
Yes	Yes	Yes	No		5,948 †	13,735	8	197				
Yes	Yes	Yes	Yes	Yes	22,620	11,190	6	805	Yes			None
Yes	Yes	Yes	Yes		31,382	11,550	6	1293	Yes	2		None
Yes			Yes		28,000	600						
Yes	Yes			Yes	20,980 ‡	13,995	15	464				
Yes	Yes		Yes		33,436	13,373			Yes			3/2
			No		13,720			585				
Yes	Yes			Yes	34,437	11,340			Yes	31	$37,191	1/15
Yes	Yes		Yes		27,850	14,215	12		Yes	62	$9,531	None
Yes			Yes	Yes	13,898 †	13,508			Yes			None
Yes		Yes	Yes		14,859 †	13,236			Yes			
Yes						10,621						
Yes	Yes	Yes	Yes	Yes	13,448 †	12,441						
Yes		Yes	Yes		13,878 †	11,406			Yes			4/1
Yes			Yes		13,502 †	15,330						
Yes	Yes	Yes	Yes	Yes	13,860 †	13,692	12					
Yes	Yes	Yes	Yes	Yes	13,547 †	13,082	12					
Yes	Yes	Yes	Yes	Yes	13,434 †	11,268	22					
Yes	Yes	Yes	Yes	Yes	13,469 †	10,777	16					
Yes	Yes	Yes	Yes		13,512 †	9,803	18	339				
Yes	Yes	Yes	Yes	Yes	13,286 †	12,002	12	339				
Yes	Yes	Yes	Yes	Yes	13,502 †	8,898	12					
Yes	Yes		Yes		13,426 †	14,210						
Yes	Yes		Yes		13,728 †	14,592	12					
Yes	Yes	Yes	Yes	Yes	13,610 †	13,593	20		Yes			None
Yes	Yes	Yes	Yes		13,544 †	14,166	12					
Yes	Yes		Yes	Yes	13,477 †	12,942	9		Yes	9		None
Yes		Yes			5,790 †							
Yes	Yes		No		6,408 †	16,416	19	212				
Yes		Yes	No		6,628 †	10,764		220				
Yes		Yes			7,590 †	9,470	7	253				
Yes	Yes		No		5,876 †	14,148	18	195				
Yes	Yes	Yes	No		6,420 †	13,824	14	213				
Yes	Yes		Yes		34,700	14,315		1050	Yes	15	$9,680	None
Yes	Yes					11,279						
Yes	Yes	Yes	No		6,631 †	14,476	6	220				
Yes	Yes	Yes	No		5,732 †	14,582	7	190				
Yes	Yes		Yes		37,060	13,830			Yes	5	$30,000	2/1
Yes		Yes	No		5,848 †	5,256	9	193	Yes			None
			Yes	Yes	16,548 †		16	682				
Yes			No			8,741	12	255				
								255				
Yes			No		5,974 †	14,468	10	199				
Yes	Yes	Yes	No	Yes	5,168 †	4,770	12	171	Yes			3/2
Yes	Yes	Yes	No	Yes	5,640 †	14,752	9	187	Yes			None
Yes		Yes	No		6,270 †	10,251	7	208				
Yes			Yes		7,104 †	9,534	12	236				

† Tuition and fees are for 2007-08.   ‡ Tuition and fees are projected for 2008-09.   * Comprehensive Fee

Institution	Control/ degrees	Undergraduates		Tests required (Fall 2009)	TOEFL		Application	
		Total	Internat'l		minimum	average	Deadline	Fee
College of San Mateo	Pu/A	10,960		TOEFL	480	520	4/15	
College of the Sequoias	Pu/A	11,855		TOEFL	500		4/1	100
College of the Siskiyous	Pu/A	1,336		TOEFL	470	485	6/30	35
Columbia College	Pu/A	3,368		TOEFL	480	520	5/1	
Columbia College: Hollywood	Pr/AB	314		TOEFL	550		6/30	50
Concorde Career College: Garden Grove	Pr/A							
Concorde Career College: North Hollywood	Pr/A	525						
Concorde Career College: San Bernardino	Pr/A							
Concorde Career College: San Diego	Pr/A							
Concordia University	Pr/B	1,203	27	TOEFL	550		None	125
Contra Costa College	Pu/A	8,574					5/1	
Copper Mountain College	Pu/A	1,866						
Cosumnes River College	Pu/A	13,203		TOEFL	510	520		50
Crafton Hills College	Pu/A	5,120		TOEFL	500	510	5/1	100
Cuesta College	Pu/A	12,157		TOEFL	500		6/1	
Cuyamaca College	Pu/A	11,467		TOEFL	450		6/1	
Cypress College	Pu/A	13,634		TOEFL	500		7/1	40
De Anza College	Pu/A	24,965		TOEFL	500	517	6/1	
Deep Springs College	Pr/A	25					11/15	
Design Institute of San Diego	Pr/B	510						25
DeVry University: Fremont	Pr/AB	1,411	7					50
DeVry University: Long Beach	Pr/AB	826	2	TOEFL	500		None	50
DeVry University: Pomona	Pr/AB	1,543	7	TOEFL	500		None	50
DeVry University: Sherman Oaks	Pr/AB	462	3	TOEFL	500		None	50
Diablo Valley College	Pu/A	20,876		TOEFL	500		None	25
Dominican School of Philosophy and Theology	Pr/B	2		TOEFL	550	570	None	40
Dominican University of California	Pr/B	1,469	24	TOEFL	550		6/1	40
East Los Angeles College	Pu/A	22,287		TOEFL	450		7/15	35
El Camino College	Pu/A	24,968		TOEFL	450		6/30	25
El Camino College: Compton Center	Pu/A	3,637		TOEFL	400	450	8/25	
Empire College	Pr/A	87		TOEFL	450	475	None	100
Evergreen Valley College	Pu/A	9,365		TOEFL	500		4/15	100
Ex'pression College for Digital Arts	Pr/B							
Fashion Careers College	Pr/A	85						25
Fashion Institute of Design and Merchandising: Los Angeles	Pr/AB	4,457	304	TOEFL	483		None	300
Fashion Institute of Design and Merchandising: San Diego	Pr/A	260	7	TOEFL	483		None	300
Fashion Institute of Design and Merchandising: San Francisco	Pr/A	959	27	TOEFL	483		None	300
Feather River College	Pu/A	1,241		TOEFL	550		8/14	
Folsom Lake College	Pu/A	8,446		TOEFL	450			
Foothill College	Pu/A	19,566		TOEFL	500		6/20	50
Fremont College	Pr/A			TOEFL	500		None	85
Fresno City College	Pu/A	21,163		TOEFL	500	515	5/1	
Fresno Pacific University	Pr/AB	1,515		TOEFL	500		7/30	40
Fullerton College	Pu/A	20,136		TOEFL	500	510	4/15	25
Glendale Community College	Pu/A	21,227	1,758	TOEFL	430	450		50
Golden Gate University	Pr/B	492		TOEFL	525		7/1	90
Golden West College	Pu/A	13,536		TOEFL	500	515	6/15	30
Grossmont College	Pu/A	17,664		TOEFL	450	478	6/1	
Hartnell College	Pu/A	9,869		TOEFL	500	570	None	
Harvey Mudd College	Pr/B	737	29	TOEFL, SAT/ACT, SAT Subject Test(s)			1/15	60

Student services			Housing		Academic year costs		Maximum credits/ summer	Credit hour charge	International financial aid			
Adviser	Orien- tation	ESL	Academic year	Summer	Tuition/ fees	Living costs			Avail- able	Number receiving aid	Average award	Deadline
Yes	Yes	Yes	No		6,388 †		8	212				
Yes		Yes	No		6,672 †	14,292	8	221				
Yes	Yes	Yes	Yes		6,174 †	31,174	12	205				
Yes		Yes	Yes	Yes	5,832 †	8,964	8	193	Yes			
Yes	Yes		Yes	Yes	13,983 †		16	367				
Yes	Yes	Yes	Yes	Yes	23,930	12,330	11	665	Yes			4/1
Yes			No		5,910 †			197				
			No		5,792 †	14,292		193				
Yes		Yes	No		6,362 †	13,134	9	211				
Yes		Yes	No		6,342 †	5,274	6	210				
Yes	Yes	Yes	No		5,850 †	13,761	6	193				
Yes	Yes	Yes	No		5,528 †	12,400		183				
Yes	Yes	Yes	No		6,088 †	11,484		202				
Yes	Yes		No		5,346 †		17	118				
			Yes	Yes		1,500			Yes			None
					15,600	3,266						
Yes					14,640 †	8,528		525				
Yes					14,010 †	8,528		500				
Yes					14,020 †	15,410		500				
Yes					14,020 †	8,528		500				
Yes	Yes		No		5,920 †	14,238	9	197	Yes			5/1
			Yes		13,300	2,971		550	Yes			None
		Yes	Yes		30,570 †	16,320	18	1270				
Yes	Yes		No		6,112 †		7	203				
Yes	Yes	Yes	No	Yes	6,389 †	8,508	10	212				
Yes	Yes		No		5,819 †	650	8	193				
			No		8,625 ‡	2,918						
Yes			No		6,118 †	700	6	203				
			No		17,400 †							
Yes	Yes	Yes	No	Yes	19,700	2,060	15					
Yes	Yes	Yes	No		19,700	2,060	15					
Yes	Yes		No		19,700	2,060	15					
Yes			Yes		6,054 †	7,094	6	200	Yes			None
Yes		Yes	No		6,362 †	13,134		211				
Yes	Yes	Yes	No		5,350 †	13,882	12	118				
			No			12,688						
Yes	Yes	Yes	No		6,480 †	10,130	11	215				
Yes	Yes	Yes	Yes	Yes	23,202	11,816	18	820	Yes	56	$17,653	
Yes	Yes	Yes	No		6,088 †	2,844		202				
Yes	Yes	Yes	No		5,583 †	13,158	7	185				
Yes	Yes	Yes	No		16,200		17	510	Yes	20		None
Yes	Yes		No		5,848 †	5,652	9	193				
Yes	Yes		No		5,520 †	10,150	8	183				
Yes	Yes	Yes	No	Yes	5,888 †	2,924		196				
Yes	Yes		Yes		36,635 ‡	13,671			Yes	15	$35,623	2/1

Institution	Control/ degrees	Undergraduates		Tests required	TOEFL		Application	
		Total	Internat'l	(Fall 2009)	minimum	average	Deadline	Fee
Heald College: Concord	Pr/A			TOEFL	550		None	250
Heald College: Fresno	Pr/A						11/1	250
Heald College: Hayward	Pr/A			TOEFL	500			250
Heald College: Rancho Cordova	Pr/A			TOEFL				250
Heald College: Roseville	Pr/A							250
Heald College: Salinas	Pr/A			TOEFL	480		None	250
Heald College: San Francisco	Pr/A			TOEFL				250
Heald College: San Jose	Pr/A			TOEFL	480	520	None	250
Heald College: Stockton	Pr/A							250
Holy Names University	Pr/B	656	26	TOEFL	490		7/1	50
Hope International University	Pr/AB	674		TOEFL, SAT/ACT	500	601	6/1	50
Humphreys College	Pr/AB	666	3	TOEFL	450	490	3/8	200
Irvine Valley College	Pu/A	9,869			470			39
John F. Kennedy University	Pr/B	236		TOEFL	550		7/1	55
The King's College and Seminary	Pr/AB			TOEFL	500		7/1	45
LA College International	Pr/AB							35
La Sierra University	Pr/B	1,422	161	TOEFL	550		None	30
Laguna College of Art and Design	Pr/B			TOEFL	500		6/15	35
Lake Tahoe Community College	Pu/A	3,264		TOEFL	580		5/1	
Laney College	Pu/A	12,754		TOEFL	500		None	50
Las Positas College	Pu/A	8,407		TOEFL	500		None	100
Lassen College	Pu/A	1,923		TOEFL	450	460	8/1	
Life Pacific College	Pr/AB	399	1	TOEFL	550	553	5/1	35
Lincoln University	Pr/AB	114	13	TOEFL	500	525	None	75
Loma Linda University	Pr/AB	1,126		TOEFL	550		6/30	60
Long Beach City College	Pu/A	27,885		TOEFL	500	535	7/1	25
Los Angeles City College	Pu/A	2,833					6/15	
Los Angeles County College of Nursing and Allied Health	Pu/A							5
Los Angeles Harbor College	Pu/A	8,086		TOEFL	450	460	6/20	
Los Angeles Mission College	Pu/A	8,457		TOEFL	500	515	8/23	
Los Angeles Pierce College	Pu/A	19,782		TOEFL	450		6/15	35
Los Angeles Southwest College	Pu/A	6,034						
Los Angeles Trade and Technical College	Pu/A	12,973		TOEFL			6/1	
Los Angeles Valley College	Pu/A	16,111		TOEFL	450		6/30	35
Los Medanos College	Pu/A	9,000		TOEFL			7/1	50
Loyola Marymount University	Pr/B	5,585	92	TOEFL, SAT/ACT	550		1/15	50
Maric College: Palm Springs	Pr/A							
Maric College: Panorama City	Pr/A			TOEFL	477		None	100
Maric College: Salida	Pr/A	882						20
Maric College: Vista	Pr/A							20
Marymount College	Pr/A	674	70				None	35
The Master's College	Pr/B	1,112		TOEFL	525		None	40
Menlo College	Pr/B	680	70	TOEFL	500	530	8/1	40
Merritt College	Pu/A	7,409		TOEFL	500		4/1	50
Mills College	Pr/B	930	14	TOEFL, SAT/ACT	550	567	3/1	50
MiraCosta College	Pu/A	13,999		TOEFL	450		None	
Mission College	Pu/A	9,759		TOEFL	500	525	5/1	
Modesto Junior College	Pu/A	19,236		TOEFL	450	490	5/1	
Monterey Peninsula College	Pu/A	13,089		TOEFL	460	490	None	
Moorpark College	Pu/A	14,926		TOEFL	450		7/1	50
Mount San Antonio College	Pu/A	21,160	295	TOEFL	450			30
Mount San Jacinto College	Pu/A	16,540		TOEFL	450		6/1	100
Mt. Sierra College	Pr/B				500		None	20
MTI College	Pr/A							50
Napa Valley College	Pu/A	7,052		TOEFL	480	491	5/1	25

| Student services | | | Housing | | Academic year costs | | Maximum credits/ summer | Credit hour charge | International financial aid | | | |
Adviser	Orien- tation	ESL	Academic year	Summer	Tuition/ fees	Living costs			Avail- able	Number receiving aid	Average award	Deadline
Yes			No		10,800‡	1,500	20					
			No		10,800‡	1,500						
					10,800‡	1,500			Yes			None
					10,800‡	1,500			Yes			None
					10,800‡	1,500						
					10,800‡	3,900	12		Yes			None
					10,800‡	1,500						
			No		10,800‡	1,500						
			No		10,800‡	1,500						
Yes	Yes	Yes	Yes		26,300	17,776		870	Yes			6/30
Yes	Yes	Yes	Yes	Yes	21,885	12,928		799	Yes			3/2
Yes	Yes		Yes	Yes	12,240‡	4,662	16	255	Yes			6/30
Yes	Yes	Yes	No		6,572†	4,968	16	218				
Yes			No		15,468†	14,112		340				
			No		7,935†	900	15	170	Yes			None
					12,375†	210		375				
Yes	Yes	Yes	Yes	Yes	23,354‡	11,181		620	Yes	152	$7,598	None
Yes	Yes		No		20,600‡	4,939	4					
			No		6,222†	14,706	9	138				
Yes	Yes				5,974†	6,408	12	199				
Yes	Yes	Yes	No		5,876†	14,049		195				
Yes	Yes	Yes	Yes		6,105†	4,100	12	203				
Yes			Yes	Yes	11,450	10,290		375	Yes			7/1
Yes	Yes	Yes	No		10,150‡	6,899	9					
Yes			Yes		24,879	7,740	16	520				
Yes	Yes	Yes	No		6,148†	13,275	7	204	Yes			None
Yes		Yes	No		6,112†	840	7	203				
					2,400†							
Yes	Yes	Yes	No		6,112†	13,752	6	203				
Yes		Yes	No		6,112†		6	203				
Yes	Yes	Yes	No		6,566†	13,860	5	218	Yes			None
Yes	Yes	Yes	No		6,112†		7	203				
Yes		Yes	No		6,112†		6	203				
Yes	Yes	Yes	No		6,114†		7	203				
		Yes	No		5,920†		6	197				
Yes			Yes		33,902	16,388	12	1386				
			No		11,845†	4,318						
Yes	Yes	Yes	Yes	Yes	23,548	15,065	6		Yes			None
Yes	Yes		Yes	Yes	23,120	12,796		965	Yes	35	$15,430	None
Yes	Yes		Yes	Yes	30,900	15,110	18		Yes	39	$13,882	8/1
Yes		Yes	No		5,974†	14,302	18	199	Yes			6/30
Yes	Yes	Yes	Yes	Yes	35,190	13,850			Yes	11	$19,000	2/15
Yes	Yes	Yes	No		5,708†	15,588	8	189				
Yes		Yes	No		5,994†	15,726	6	198				
Yes	Yes	Yes	No		5,830†	14,292	12	193				
Yes	Yes	Yes	No		5,850†	5,616		193				
Yes			No		6,314†	14,292	7	209				
Yes		Yes	No		5,260†	13,720	14	197				
Yes	Yes		No		5,790†	11,944	12	193				
			No		14,237†	2,000		308				
			No		11,025	1,778						
Yes	Yes		No		5,636†	3,042	6	187				

† Tuition and fees are for 2007-08.   ‡ Tuition and fees are projected for 2008-09.   * Comprehensive Fee

Institution	Control/ degrees	Undergraduates		Tests required (Fall 2009)	TOEFL		Application	
		Total	Internat'l		minimum	average	Deadline	Fee
National Hispanic University	Pr/AB	399		TOEFL	450		None	50
National Polytechnic College of Science	Pr/A	500		TOEFL	475		None	200
National University	Pr/AB	6,675	69	TOEFL	525		None	60
NewSchool of Architecture & Design	Pr/B	304		TOEFL	550	580	None	75
Northwestern Polytechnic University	Pr/B	176		TOEFL, SAT	550		8/25	60
Notre Dame de Namur University	Pr/B	747	21	TOEFL	500		8/1	50
Occidental College	Pr/B	1,855	40	TOEFL, SAT/ACT	600		1/10	50
Ohlone College	Pu/A	11,595		TOEFL	510		4/10	100
Orange Coast College	Pu/A	24,555	369	TOEFL	500	535	6/30	30
Otis College of Art and Design	Pr/B	1,117		TOEFL, SAT/ACT	550	571	6/1	50
Oxnard College	Pu/A	6,763		TOEFL	505		7/1	
Pacific Oaks College	Pr/B	237		TOEFL	550		6/1	55
Pacific States University	Pr/B	34		TOEFL	450	500	None	100
Pacific Union College	Pr/AB	1,358	99	TOEFL	525		None	30
Palo Verde College	Pu/A	4,024		TOEFL	450	475	None	
Palomar College	Pu/A	32,260		TOEFL	470	472	5/1	25
Pasadena City College	Pu/A	29,424		TOEFL	450	470	6/15	25
Patten University	Pr/AB			TOEFL, SAT/ACT	550	565	7/31	30
Pepperdine University	Pr/B	3,381	218	TOEFL	550	590	1/15	65
Pitzer College	Pr/B	999	32	TOEFL	520		1/1	50
Platt College: Huntington Beach	Pr/AB			TOEFL	400	425	None	75
Platt College: Los Angeles	Pr/AB			TOEFL	400	425	None	75
Platt College: Ontario	Pr/AB	250		TOEFL	400	425	None	75
Platt College: San Diego	Pr/AB	281	7				None	
Point Loma Nazarene University	Pr/B	2,337	11	TOEFL	550		3/1	50
Pomona College	Pr/B	1,521	44	TOEFL, SAT, SAT Subject Test(s), or ACT	600		12/15	65
Porterville College	Pu/A	3,844		TOEFL	450	500	None	
Professional Golfers Career College	Pr/A	150		TOEFL	473			75
Reedley College	Pu/A	12,646		TOEFL	500	511	None	
Rio Hondo College	Pu/A	20,859		TOEFL	450		None	
Riverside Community College	Pu/A	33,027		TOEFL	450		6/1	50
Sacramento City College	Pu/A	24,966		TOEFL	450	487	7/10	50
Saddleback College	Pu/A	23,492		TOEFL	470		7/15	50
Sage College	Pr/A							100
St. Mary's College of California	Pr/B	2,504	49	TOEFL	525	550	5/1	55
Samuel Merritt College	Pr/B	368		TOEFL	550		3/1	35
San Bernardino Valley College	Pu/A	12,550		TOEFL	450		5/1	25
San Diego Christian College	Pr/B	469	6	TOEFL	500	510	8/1	100
San Diego City College	Pu/A	15,698		TOEFL	500		6/1	100
San Diego Mesa College	Pu/A	20,444		TOEFL	500		6/1	100
San Diego Miramar College	Pu/A	9,020		TOEFL	500	563	6/1	100
San Diego State University	Pu/B	30,460	773	TOEFL	550	570	11/30	55
San Francisco Art Institute	Pr/B	391		TOEFL	550		8/1	75
San Francisco Conservatory of Music	Pr/B	240		TOEFL	500	527	12/1	100
San Francisco State University	Pu/B	24,376	1,371	TOEFL	500		6/15	55
San Joaquin Delta College	Pu/A	18,802		TOEFL	500		None	50
San Joaquin Valley College	Pr/A	1,040						
San Jose City College	Pu/A	10,802		TOEFL	500	505	4/15	35
San Jose State University	Pu/B	24,390	954	TOEFL				55
Santa Ana College	Pu/A	29,260		TOEFL	450	500	7/1	50
Santa Barbara Business College	Pr/A							25
Santa Barbara Business College: Bakersfield	Pr/A	400						25
Santa Barbara Business College: Santa Maria	Pr/A							25
Santa Barbara City College	Pu/A	7,771	701				7/1	50
Santa Clara University	Pr/B	4,799	148	TOEFL, SAT/ACT	550	604	1/7	55

Student services			Housing		Academic year costs		Maximum credits/ summer	Credit hour charge	International financial aid			
Adviser	Orien- tation	ESL	Academic year	Summer	Tuition/ fees	Living costs			Avail- able	Number receiving aid	Average award	Deadline
	Yes		No		6,080	5,706		235				
Yes	Yes		No									
Yes	Yes	Yes	No		9,720†	4,162	18		Yes			None
Yes		Yes		Yes	18,945‡	3,700	18	600	Yes			None
Yes	Yes	Yes	Yes	Yes	9,140‡	2,550	16	300				
Yes	Yes	Yes	Yes	Yes	25,570‡	16,006		545	Yes			None
Yes	Yes		Yes		37,071	13,338	12		Yes	20	$34,424	2/1
Yes		Yes	No		6,142†	12,534	6	203				
Yes	Yes		No		5,848†	14,926	12	193				
Yes	Yes	Yes	Yes		30,464	13,500	18	993	Yes	16	$7,912	None
		Yes	No		6,314†	14,292	10	209				
Yes			No		23,910†	20,244	6	795				
Yes	Yes	Yes	Yes	Yes	13,400‡	1,200	20	210	Yes			None
Yes	Yes		Yes	Yes	22,695	11,295		656				
Yes		Yes	No		5,790†	11,146	6	193	Yes			None
Yes	Yes	Yes	No		5,730†	8,647		190				
Yes	Yes	Yes	No		6,058†	13,400	14	201				
Yes	Yes	Yes	Yes	Yes	11,880†	8,340	12	495	Yes			None
Yes	Yes		Yes	Yes	36,770	12,780	18	1135				
Yes	Yes	Yes	Yes	Yes	37,870	13,380						
			No									
			No									
			No									
Yes	Yes		No									
Yes	Yes		Yes	Yes	25,120	12,706			Yes	9	$18,475	3/2
Yes	Yes		Yes	Yes	35,625	14,670			Yes	23	$40,000	2/1
Yes		Yes	No		7,024†		6	233				
Yes			Yes	Yes		200						
Yes			Yes		6,478†	7,690	18	215	Yes			None
Yes			No		5,816†	14,726	7	193				
Yes	Yes	Yes			6,408†	14,104		212				
Yes	Yes	Yes	No		6,362†	13,134	7	211				
Yes	Yes	Yes	No		6,568†	5,382	9	218				
					7,675†							
Yes	Yes	Yes	Yes		33,250	15,784			Yes			None
Yes		Yes	Yes	Yes	33,572	25,813		1370				
Yes			No		5,884†	12,057		195				
Yes	Yes	Yes	Yes	Yes	20,980	11,860	12	832	Yes			7/15
Yes	Yes		No		5,516†	14,706	12	180				
Yes	Yes		No		5,516†	12,753	12	183				
Yes	Yes		No		5,516†	6,003	12	183				
Yes	Yes	Yes	Yes	Yes	13,598†	16,166			Yes	55	$11,163	None
Yes	Yes	Yes	Yes		30,196	14,508	15	1378	Yes			5/31
Yes	Yes		Yes		32,154	10,700		1500	Yes			None
Yes	Yes	Yes	Yes		13,626†	16,860	12					
Yes	Yes	Yes	No		5,790†	14,292	9	193				
			No									
Yes		Yes	No		6,118†	1,535	7	203	Yes			None
Yes	Yes	Yes	Yes		13,802†	14,563			Yes	52		6/22
Yes	Yes	Yes	No	Yes	6,118†	13,298	6	203				
Yes	Yes	Yes			6,040†	5,394	3	199				
Yes	Yes		Yes		34,950	15,606		1165				

† Tuition and fees are for 2007-08.   ‡ Tuition and fees are projected for 2008-09.   * Comprehensive Fee

Institution	Control/degrees	Undergraduates		Tests required (Fall 2009)	TOEFL		Application	
		Total	Internat'l		minimum	average	Deadline	Fee
Santa Monica College	Pu/A	32,082		TOEFL	450	500	6/10	50
Santa Rosa Junior College	Pu/A	32,943		TOEFL	475		6/15	25
Santiago Canyon College	Pu/A	14,200		TOEFL	500		7/1	50
School of Urban Missions: Oakland	Pr/AB	62		TOEFL	550			20
Scripps College	Pr/B	889	5	TOEFL, SAT/ACT	600	616	1/1	50
Shasta College	Pu/A	10,141		TOEFL	450		None	
Sierra College	Pu/A	20,030		TOEFL	450	470	7/1	100
Simpson University	Pr/AB	891	6	TOEFL	500		None	40
Skyline College	Pu/A	8,720		TOEFL	480	495	4/15	
Soka University of America	Pr/B	362	173				1/15	45
Solano Community College	Pu/A	11,153		TOEFL	500	520	6/1	
Sonoma State University	Pu/B	7,603		TOEFL	500	525	5/31	55
Southern California Institute of Architecture	Pr/B	256	35	TOEFL	550		2/1	60
Southern California Institute of Technology	Pr/AB			TOEFL	400		None	100
Southwestern College	Pu/A	19,839		TOEFL	460	470	5/1	
Stanford University	Pr/B	6,520		TOEFL, SAT/ACT			1/1	75
Taft College	Pu/A	10,003		TOEFL	450	513	6/1	150
University of California: Berkeley	Pu/B	24,636	786	TOEFL, SAT, SAT Subject Test(s), or ACT	550		11/30	70
University of California: Davis	Pu/B	23,373	445	TOEFL, SAT/ACT, SAT Subject Test(s)	550		11/30	70
University of California: Irvine	Pu/B	21,696	563	TOEFL, SAT, SAT Subject Test(s), or ACT	550		11/30	70
University of California: Los Angeles	Pu/B	25,928	1,075	TOEFL, SAT/ACT, SAT Subject Test(s)	550		11/30	70
University of California: Merced	Pu/B	1,750	17	TOEFL, SAT/ACT, SAT Subject Test(s)	550		11/30	70
University of California: Riverside	Pu/B	14,973	273	TOEFL, SAT/ACT, SAT Subject Test(s)	550	561	11/30	70
University of California: San Diego	Pu/B	22,048		TOEFL, SAT/ACT, SAT Subject Test(s)	550		11/30	70
University of California: Santa Barbara	Pu/B	18,412	218	TOEFL, SAT Subject Test(s)	550		11/30	70
University of California: Santa Cruz	Pu/B	14,381	99	TOEFL, SAT/ACT, SAT Subject Test(s)	550		11/30	70
University of La Verne	Pr/AB	1,671	24	TOEFL	500		4/1	50
University of the Pacific	Pr/B	3,456	108	TOEFL	475	543	None	60
University of Redlands	Pr/B	2,353	23	TOEFL	550		2/1	45
University of San Diego	Pr/B	4,906	117	TOEFL, SAT/ACT	550	590	1/15	55
University of San Francisco	Pr/B	4,872	363	TOEFL	550		1/15	55
University of Southern California	Pr/B	16,091	1,399		600		1/10	65
University of the West	Pr/B				500		6/1	100
Vanguard University of Southern California	Pr/B	1,872	22	TOEFL	550		8/6	45
Ventura College	Pu/A	12,066		TOEFL			None	50
Victor Valley College	Pu/A	11,447		TOEFL	500		5/15	
West Coast University	Pr/AB							
West Hills College: Coalinga	Pu/A	1,371					7/15	100
West Hills College: Lemoore	Pu/A	3,619					7/15	100
West Los Angeles College	Pu/A	9,261		TOEFL	450	460	6/15	35
West Valley College	Pu/A	14,615		TOEFL	500	520	6/1	
Western Career College: Antioch	Pr/A							100
Western Career College: Stockton	Pr/A	300						100
Westmont College	Pr/B	1,333	9	TOEFL, SAT/ACT	560	630	None	50
Westwood College: Anaheim	Pr/AB							25

Student services			Housing		Academic year costs		Maximum credits/ summer	Credit hour charge	International financial aid			
Adviser	Orien-tation	ESL	Academic year	Summer	Tuition/ fees	Living costs			Avail-able	Number receiving aid	Average award	Deadline
Yes	Yes	Yes	No		6,182†		8	205				
Yes	Yes				6,688†	15,588		222				
Yes	Yes	Yes	No	Yes	6,148†		6	204				
			Yes		7,180‡	9,177		235	Yes			None
Yes	Yes		Yes		37,950	13,300	8	1179	Yes	3		None
Yes		Yes	Yes		5,653†	6,660		186				
Yes	Yes	Yes	Yes	Yes	5,980†	10,654	18	198				
Yes			Yes	Yes	19,500	11,482		825	Yes	6	$17,850	None
Yes	Yes		No		6,388†	17,926	9	212				
Yes	Yes	Yes	Yes		23,434	12,000			Yes			3/1
		Yes	No		5,827†	10,485		193				
Yes	Yes	Yes	Yes	Yes	14,116†	14,788						
Yes			No		21,544	1,400			Yes			None
		Yes	No		11,185†	13,500		178				
Yes	Yes	Yes	No		5,514†	2,160		183				
Yes	Yes		Yes		36,030	15,157			Yes	210	$30,994	None
Yes		Yes	Yes		5,790†	5,836		193				
Yes	Yes		Yes		26,784†	13,848	10					
Yes	Yes	Yes	Yes	Yes	27,729†	14,999				66	$13,495	
Yes	Yes	Yes	Yes	Yes	27,175†	14,704						
Yes	Yes	Yes	Yes	Yes	26,658†	16,938	18		Yes	156	$10,715	None
			Yes		26,768†	14,745						
Yes	Yes	Yes	Yes	Yes	26,975†	15,400	10					
Yes	Yes	Yes	Yes		27,019†	14,203			Yes			
Yes	Yes	Yes	Yes		27,516†	11,946						
Yes	Yes	Yes	Yes		27,229†	16,148	20					
Yes	Yes	Yes	Yes	Yes	26,910‡	15,161		760	Yes	10	$4,500	None
Yes	Yes	Yes	Yes	Yes	30,730	14,721	18	1044				
Yes	Yes		Yes		32,294	14,454		1000	Yes			None
Yes	Yes	ESL	Yes		34,264	16,184	13					
Yes	Yes	Yes	Yes	Yes	33,500	15,440	18	1180				
Yes	Yes	Yes	Yes	Yes	37,890	14,228		1249	Yes	261	$26,670	
Yes	Yes	Yes	Yes	Yes	9,750	11,408	6	315				
			Yes	Yes	22,986	11,708	9	936				
Yes		Yes	No		6,312†	14,292	8	209				
Yes		Yes	No		6,220†	13,842	8	207	Yes			None
Yes	Yes	Yes	Yes	Yes	6,030†	9,413		201				
Yes	Yes	Yes		Yes								
Yes	Yes	Yes	No		6,114†	13,752	18	203				
Yes	Yes	Yes	No		5,994†	14,976	6	198				
Yes	Yes		Yes	Yes	33,170	14,616	9		Yes	6	$5,909	

Institution	Control/ degrees	Undergraduates		Tests required (Fall 2009)	TOEFL		Application	
		Total	Internat'l		minimum	average	Deadline	Fee
Westwood College: Los Angeles	Pr/AB							100
Westwood College: South Bay	Pr/AB	600						100
Whittier College	Pr/B	1,257	31	TOEFL, SAT/ACT	550	590	None	50
William Jessup University	Pr/AB	504	3	TOEFL	500		4/1	35
Woodbury University	Pr/B	1,277	75	TOEFL	500	527	None	50
World Mission University	Pr/B	76					None	50
WyoTech: Fremont	Pr/A							
WyoTech: Long Beach	Pr/A							
Yuba Community College District	Pu/A	10,444		TOEFL	480	490	5/15	25
Colorado								
Adams State College	Pu/AB	2,104		TOEFL	550	594	6/1	20
Aims Community College	Pu/A	4,590		TOEFL	520		8/19	
American Sentinel University	Pr/AB	750		TOEFL	550		None	40
Arapahoe Community College	Pu/A	5,318	9	TOEFL			None	
Art Institute of Colorado	Pr/AB	2,245		TOEFL	500		None	150
Aspen University	Pr/B	625		TOEFL	500		None	75
Cambridge College	Pr/A	585					None	50
CollegeAmerica: Fort Collins	Pr/AB	135						
Colorado Christian University	Pr/AB	920		TOEFL, SAT/ACT	550		8/1	50
Colorado College	Pr/B	2,034	50	TOEFL, SAT/ACT	550	620	1/15	50
Colorado Mountain College	Pu/A	14,900		TOEFL	500		5/1	
Colorado Northwestern Community College	Pu/A	3,768		TOEFL	500		5/15	
Colorado School of Mines	Pu/B	3,300	204	TOEFL	550	575	5/1	45
Colorado School of Trades	Pr/A	135					None	25
Colorado State University	Pu/B	20,765	343	TOEFL	525	579	5/9	50
Colorado State University: Pueblo	Pu/B	3,947	91	TOEFL	500	540	None	30
Colorado Technical University	Pr/AB	1,500		TOEFL	550		10/1	100
Community College of Aurora	Pu/A	5,031		TOEFL	500		None	
Community College of Denver	Pu/A	5,566	333	TOEFL	480		8/1	
DeVry University: Westminster	Pr/AB	596	1	TOEFL	500		None	50
Everest College: Aurora	Pr/A	61					None	25
Everest College: Colorado Springs	Pr/A	400		TOEFL	450		None	50
Fort Lewis College	Pu/B	3,788	30	TOEFL	500		6/1	30
Front Range Community College	Pu/A	12,537	33	TOEFL	475	480	None	
Institute of Business & Medical Careers	Pr/A	365						75
IntelliTec College	Pr/A	500					None	
IntelliTec College: Grand Junction	Pr/A							
Johnson & Wales University: Denver	Pr/AB	1,465	28	TOEFL	550		None	
Jones International University	Pr/B	320		TOEFL	550		None	100
Kaplan College: Denver	Pr/A	210						20
Lamar Community College	Pu/A	1,000					6/1	
Mesa State College	Pu/AB	5,585	14	TOEFL, SAT/ACT	525	550	5/1	30
Metropolitan State College of Denver	Pu/B	21,425		TOEFL	500	542	7/19	40
Morgan Community College	Pu/A	1,748		TOEFL	490		None	
Naropa University	Pr/B	456	9	TOEFL	550		None	50
National American University: Denver	Pr/AB	165		TOEFL	500		None	45
Northeastern Junior College	Pu/A	1,082		TOEFL	475		7/15	
Otero Junior College	Pu/A	1,500		TOEFL	450		8/1	
Pikes Peak Community College	Pu/A	10,797		TOEFL	450		None	
Pueblo Community College	Pu/A	5,050		TOEFL	450	480	4/1	
Red Rocks Community College	Pu/A	5,065	16				7/15	

Adviser	Orientation	ESL	Academic year	Summer	Tuition/ fees	Living costs	Maximum credits/ summer	Credit hour charge	Available	Number receiving aid	Average award	Deadline
					13,518‡	1,020		314				
Yes	Yes		Yes		32,270	15,086	13	1340	Yes			6/30
			Yes		20,480	12,006		868	Yes			8/15
Yes	Yes	Yes	Yes	Yes	25,198†	12,980	18	811				
Yes		Yes			4,600‡							
			No									
Yes	Yes				6,462†	1,260	9	215	Yes			3/1
Yes			Yes		10,808†	11,694	15					
Yes			No		10,685†	600		336				
Yes	Yes	Yes	No		10,889†	850		357				
Yes	Yes		Yes		21,985‡	11,968		436	Yes			None
					7,500†			250				
			No									
Yes	Yes		Yes	Yes	20,130	14,557	12	850	Yes			None
Yes	Yes		Yes		35,844	14,156	12	1120	Yes	31	$36,820	2/15
Yes	Yes		Yes		7,130†	10,136		231				
Yes			Yes		5,218†	10,650	12	166				
Yes	Yes	Yes	Yes	Yes	23,244†	10,450	10	806				
Yes	Yes	Yes	Yes	Yes	18,859†	12,704		874				
Yes	Yes	Yes	Yes	Yes	14,757‡	12,212	18		Yes	56	$4,668	None
			No		13,025	11,317	17	285				
Yes		Yes	Yes	Yes	10,832†	400	15	357				
Yes		Yes	No		11,357†	11,378		345	Yes			None
Yes					14,020†	8,528		500				
			No			4,374			Yes			None
			No			2,045	12		Yes			None
Yes	Yes	Yes	Yes	Yes	14,994†	11,276	18	692	Yes			None
Yes	Yes	Yes	No		11,002†	1,198		357				
					12,375†	1,400		275				
			No			1,200						
			No		17,000†	1,500						
Yes	Yes		Yes	Yes	21,717†	10,794		379	Yes			None
			No									
Yes			Yes		5,309†	6,340	18	166				
Yes	Yes		Yes	Yes	12,245†	14,191	12	441	Yes			None
Yes	Yes	Yes	No		11,134†		12	439				
Yes			No		10,882†	1,825		357				
Yes	Yes		Yes		22,074	11,960	12	712	Yes	7	$9,852	None
Yes		Yes	No		12,500†	1,200	20	275				
Yes	Yes		Yes	Yes	5,579†	11,226	12	166				
Yes	Yes		Yes		5,179†	8,942	10	166				
Yes		Yes			10,981†	4,277		357	Yes			None
Yes			No		10,981†	11,563		357				
Yes		Yes	No		10,990†	13,857	8	357				

Institution	Control/ degrees	Undergraduates		Tests required (Fall 2009)	TOEFL		Application	
		Total	Internat'l		minimum	average	Deadline	Fee
Redstone College	Pr/A	535		TOEFL	470		None	100
Regis University	Pr/B	1,623	20	TOEFL	550		8/1	40
Remington College: Colorado Springs	Pr/AB	175		TOEFL				50
Rocky Mountain College of Art & Design	Pr/B	496	7	TOEFL, SAT/ACT	500		None	50
Teikyo Loretto Heights University	Pr/AB	372					None	50
Trinidad State Junior College	Pu/A			TOEFL	450		None	10
University of Colorado at Boulder	Pu/B	25,521	381	TOEFL, SAT/ACT	500		1/15	70
University of Colorado at Colorado Springs	Pu/B	6,181	26	TOEFL, SAT/ACT	550		6/1	100
University of Colorado at Denver	Pu/B	8,327	98	TOEFL	525		7/22	75
University of Denver	Pr/B	5,260	235	TOEFL	525		None	50
University of Northern Colorado	Pu/B	10,038	98	TOEFL, SAT/ACT	520	523	5/27	60
Western State College of Colorado	Pu/B	2,400		TOEFL, SAT/ACT	550		6/1	40
Westwood College: Denver South	Pr/AB	325		TOEFL	475		None	25
Connecticut								
Albertus Magnus College	Pr/AB	1,682	4	TOEFL	550	575	7/1	35
Briarwood College	Pr/AB	663	2	TOEFL	540		None	25
Capital Community College	Pu/A	3,177		TOEFL	500		5/31	20
Central Connecticut State University	Pu/B	9,161	112	TOEFL	500		4/1	50
Charter Oak State College	Pu/AB	1,557						75
Clemens College	Pr/A	62		TOEFL	520	550	None	40
Connecticut College	Pr/B	1,746	77	TOEFL	600		1/1	60
Eastern Connecticut State University	Pu/AB	4,704	39	TOEFL	550		None	50
Fairfield University	Pr/AB	3,893		TOEFL	550	562	1/15	55
Gateway Community College	Pu/A	4,787	73	TOEFL	500	530	7/1	20
Goodwin College	Pr/A	1,419						50
Holy Apostles College and Seminary	Pr/AB	32	4	TOEFL	510		8/15	50
Housatonic Community College	Pu/A	4,514		TOEFL	530		6/1	20
Manchester Community College	Pu/A	5,420	35	TOEFL	500		3/1	20
Middlesex Community College	Pu/A	1,849	4	TOEFL	500		7/1	20
Mitchell College	Pr/AB	868		TOEFL	500	520	7/1	30
Naugatuck Valley Community College	Pu/A	4,964	31	TOEFL	500	575	5/1	20
Norwalk Community College	Pu/A	6,231					None	20
Paier College of Art	Pr/AB	207		TOEFL	500		8/15	25
Post University	Pr/AB	1,271		TOEFL	500	525	None	40
Quinnipiac University	Pr/AB	5,650	72	TOEFL	550	570	2/1	45
Sacred Heart University	Pr/AB	4,188	54	TOEFL, SAT/ACT	550		None	100
St. Joseph College	Pr/B	945	4	TOEFL				50
Southern Connecticut State University	Pu/B	8,515	63	TOEFL	525		6/15	50
Trinity College	Pr/B	2,243	87	TOEFL, SAT/ACT		623	1/1	60
Tunxis Community College	Pu/A	2,951		TOEFL	500		7/1	20
University of Bridgeport	Pr/AB	1,791	250	TOEFL, SAT/ACT	500	540	None	25
University of Connecticut	Pu/AB	16,036	161	TOEFL, SAT/ACT	550	596	2/1	70
University of New Haven	Pr/AB	2,963		TOEFL	520		None	50
Wesleyan University	Pr/B	2,787	173	TOEFL, SAT, SAT Subject Test(s), or ACT	600	628	1/1	55
Yale University	Pr/B	5,291	444	TOEFL, SAT, SAT Subject Test(s), or ACT	600		12/31	75
Delaware								
Delaware State University	Pu/B	3,374	2	TOEFL, SAT/ACT			6/1	25
Goldey-Beacom College	Pr/AB	874		TOEFL	475	505	6/1	30
University of Delaware	Pu/AB	15,318	153	TOEFL	550		1/15	60
Wesley College	Pr/AB	2,056		TOEFL	550		7/1	25

	Student services			Housing		Academic year costs		Maximum credits/ summer	Credit hour charge		International financial aid		
Adviser	Orien-tation	ESL	Academic year	Summer	Tuition/ fees	Living costs			Avail-able	Number receiving aid	Average award	Deadline
			Yes									
			Yes		28,700	12,516	12	888	Yes	17	$24,746	None
			No				12					
Yes				Yes	19,752 †	8,440	18	823	Yes			None
Yes	Yes	Yes	Yes	Yes	14,970 †	7,300		499	Yes			None
Yes	Yes	Yes	Yes		5,292 †	8,613	12	166				
Yes	Yes	Yes	Yes	Yes	24,797 †	14,998	15		Yes	86	$6,847	None
Yes			Yes	Yes	16,381 †	6,898	12		Yes	2	$550	None
Yes	Yes	Yes	Yes		17,771 †	12,230	12	709	Yes			4/1
Yes	Yes	Yes	Yes	Yes	33,810	9,093	18	916	Yes	124	$22,124	None
Yes	Yes	Yes	Yes	Yes	12,893 †	12,627	15		Yes			None
Yes			Yes		12,405 †	12,917	8	480				
			No		22,275 †	1,250	19					
Yes			Yes		22,724	11,602		907				
Yes		Yes	Yes	Yes	17,135 †	7,975	18	540	Yes			None
Yes			No		8,444 †	9,905		312				
Yes	Yes	Yes	Yes	Yes	15,454 †	11,604	12					
			No					244				
Yes	Yes	Yes	Yes	Yes	19,770 †	6,690	18					
Yes	Yes		Yes	Yes	49,385 *	1,000	8		Yes	77	$43,519	2/1
Yes	Yes		Yes	Yes	14,446 †	13,419			Yes	6	$916	None
Yes	Yes		Yes	Yes	36,075	16,815	18	475	Yes			2/15
Yes		Yes	No		8,444 †	9,790	12	312				
					13,820 †			425				
		Yes	No		7,800 ‡	630	9	325				
Yes		Yes	No		8,444 †	2,200	12	312				
Yes		Yes	No		8,444 †	9,128	12	312				
Yes		Yes	No		8,444 †	2,400	6	316				
Yes		Yes	Yes		23,093 †	13,356	11	275				
Yes	Yes	Yes	No		8,444 †	4,489	6	312				
Yes		Yes	No		8,444 †	4,870		448				
Yes					12,365	4,500	8	380	Yes			None
Yes			Yes	Yes	22,550 †	10,950	9	725	Yes			None
Yes	Yes		Yes		30,900	14,800	12	710	Yes	65	$30,736	None
Yes	Yes	Yes	Yes	Yes	27,150 †	12,916	15	425	Yes	18	$27,895	None
			Yes		25,940	12,980		540	Yes			None
Yes	Yes		Yes	Yes	14,110 †	10,352	12					
Yes	Yes		Yes	Yes	38,733	11,928			Yes	61	$42,673	3/1
Yes		Yes	No		8,444 †	2,220	15	312				
Yes	Yes	Yes	Yes	Yes	24,470	16,847	12	750	Yes			None
Yes	Yes	Yes	Yes	Yes	24,050	12,840	14	913				
Yes	Yes		Yes		28,190	13,666		900	Yes	15	$5,960	3/1
Yes	Yes		Yes	Yes	38,934	12,946			Yes	48	$43,141	2/15
Yes	Yes	Yes	Yes		35,300	13,700			Yes	261		3/1
Yes	Yes	Yes	Yes	Yes	13,100 †	14,082	9	513				
Yes	Yes		Yes	Yes	16,980	7,669	7	556	Yes			None
Yes	Yes	Yes	Yes	Yes	19,400 †	11,023	14					
Yes			Yes	Yes	18,530	10,750	12	740	Yes			None

† Tuition and fees are for 2007-08. ‡ Tuition and fees are projected for 2008-09. * Comprehensive Fee

Institution	Control/ degrees	Undergraduates		Tests required (Fall 2009)	TOEFL		Application	
		Total	Internat'l		minimum	average	Deadline	Fee
District of Columbia								
American University	Pr/AB	5,824	354	TOEFL	550	610	1/15	45
Catholic University of America	Pr/B	3,245	76	TOEFL, SAT/ACT	560		2/15	55
Corcoran College of Art and Design	Pr/AB	337		TOEFL	550		7/31	45
Gallaudet University	Pr/B			TOEFL	550		1/15	50
George Washington University	Pr/AB	10,370	466	TOEFL, SAT/ACT	550		1/10	60
Georgetown University	Pr/B	6,623	363	TOEFL, SAT/ACT			1/10	65
Howard University	Pr/B	6,973	357	TOEFL, SAT/ACT, SAT Subject Test(s)	550		2/15	45
Potomac College	Pr/AB	600		TOEFL	550		None	15
Southeastern University	Pr/AB	562		TOEFL	500		6/15	45
Trinity Washington University	Pr/B	1,047		TOEFL	550		8/1	40
University of the District of Columbia	Pu/AB	5,137		TOEFL	550	560	None	50
Florida								
Angley College	Pr/AB	86		TOEFL	450	500	None	450
Art Institute of Fort Lauderdale	Pr/AB	2,821		TOEFL	480	500	None	50
Ave Maria University	Pr/B			TOEFL			5/1	
Baptist College of Florida	Pr/AB	539	1	TOEFL, SAT/ACT	500		8/1	20
Barry University	Pr/B	5,053	221	TOEFL	550		None	30
Bethune-Cookman University	Pr/B	3,312	58	TOEFL, SAT/ACT	550	600	5/30	25
Brevard Community College	Pu/A	13,024	137	TOEFL	500		8/15	60
Broward Community College	Pu/A	26,028	1,969		500	510	5/24	75
Brown Mackie College: Miami	Pr/A	517						
Carlos Albizu University	Pr/B	425					None	25
Central Florida College	Pr/A	450						50
Central Florida Community College	Pu/A	5,615		TOEFL	420			50
Chipola Junior College	Pu/AB	2,100		TOEFL	525		8/1	100
City College: Casselberry	Pr/A	110						25
City College: Fort Lauderdale	Pr/AB	439						25
City College: Gainesville	Pr/AB	228						
City College: Miami	Pr/AB	271						25
College of Business and Technology: Flagler	Pr/A	153					None	25
College of Business and Technology: Kendall	Pr/A	93						
Daytona Beach Community College	Pu/AB			TOEFL, SAT/ACT	500	550	8/5	50
DeVry University: Miramar	Pr/AB	886	46	TOEFL	500			50
DeVry University: Orlando	Pr/AB	1,249	24	TOEFL	500		None	50
Eckerd College	Pr/B	1,826	54	TOEFL, SAT/ACT	550	590	4/15	35
Edward Waters College	Pr/B	811	7	TOEFL			6/30	75
Embry-Riddle Aeronautical University	Pr/AB	4,531	410	TOEFL	500	572	6/1	50
Everest University: Brandon	Pr/AB	875		TOEFL	450			25
Everest University: Lakeland	Pr/AB							25
Everest University: Pompano Beach	Pr/AB			TOEFL	450	490	None	25
Everest University: South Orlando	Pr/AB							
Everest University: Tampa	Pr/AB	1,300		TOEFL	450	500	None	50
Flagler College	Pr/B	2,537	29	TOEFL, SAT/ACT	550	569	3/1	40
Florida Agricultural and Mechanical University	Pu/AB	9,566	84	TOEFL, SAT/ACT	500	530	5/13	20
Florida Atlantic University	Pu/AB	20,525	583	TOEFL, SAT/ACT	550		4/1	30
Florida Career College: Hialeah	Pr/AB						None	
Florida Career College: Miami	Pr/AB							
Florida Career College: Pembroke Pines	Pr/AB							
Florida Career College: West Palm Beach	Pr/AB							
Florida Christian College	Pr/AB	226		TOEFL, SAT/ACT			7/15	35
Florida College of Natural Health: Bradenton	Pr/A	168						
Florida Community College at Jacksonville	Pu/AB	19,016		TOEFL	460	470	5/31	80
Florida Gulf Coast University	Pu/AB	7,996	93	TOEFL, SAT/ACT	550		6/2	30

| Student services | | | Housing | | Academic year costs | | Maximum credits/summer | Credit hour charge | International financial aid | | | |
Adviser	Orientation	ESL	Academic year	Summer	Tuition/fees	Living costs			Available	Number receiving aid	Average award	Deadline
Yes	Yes		Yes	Yes	33,283	14,318	12	1093	Yes	129	$16,538	2/15
Yes	Yes	Yes	Yes	Yes	30,670	11,320		1125				
Yes	Yes		Yes		27,380	14,738			Yes			None
Yes	Yes	Yes	Yes	Yes	21,436 †	13,930	8	527	Yes			None
Yes	Yes	Yes	Yes	Yes	40,437	12,970	12	1123	Yes			2/1
Yes	Yes	Yes	Yes	Yes	37,947	15,933	12	1564	Yes	34	$30,662	2/1
Yes	Yes		Yes	Yes	15,010	13,336	12	592	Yes			8/15
Yes			No		13,480 †	630		445				
Yes	Yes	Yes	No		12,525 †	19,667	12	255				
Yes	Yes	Yes	Yes	Yes	18,960	13,950	9	650				
Yes	Yes	Yes	No		7,070	4,500	9	215	Yes			None
Yes	Yes	Yes	No		15,075	9,127	15	315				
Yes	Yes	Yes	Yes	Yes	18,945 †	10,867	18	421				
Yes	Yes	Yes	Yes	Yes	16,255 †	7,140	8					
Yes			Yes		8,150	5,186	10	260	Yes			4/15
Yes	Yes	Yes	Yes	Yes	25,500	12,915	12	765	Yes	67	$14,634	None
Yes	Yes		Yes	Yes	12,966	12,302	9	516	Yes			None
Yes			No		6,990 †	11,224	18	220				
Yes	Yes	Yes	No		7,172 †	4,995	18		Yes			7/1
					11,472 †							
Yes	Yes	Yes	No		12,468 †	9,615	18					
Yes	Yes	Yes			7,382 †	4,616	15					
Yes					6,001 †	10,536	12		Yes			None
					9,675			215				
Yes	Yes		No		9,975 †	5,352		195				
					10,075 †	5,508		195				
					9,900 †			195				
Yes	Yes		No		11,772 †	1,350	12	322	Yes			None
					11,772 †			322				
Yes	Yes	Yes	No		8,225 †	800	12					
Yes					14,020 †	3,076		500				
Yes					14,020 †	3,662		500				
Yes	Yes	Yes	Yes	Yes	30,590	12,904	14	1043	Yes	62		None
Yes			Yes		10,618 ‡	8,224		382	Yes			4/15
Yes	Yes	Yes	Yes	Yes	27,540	14,782	18	1100	Yes	241	$5,937	None
			No		13,695 †	4,657		299				
					13,695 †			299				
Yes	Yes	Yes	Yes	Yes	13,695 †	3,192	12	299				
					13,695 †	800		299				
Yes	Yes	Yes	No		13,695 †	2,619	16	299				
			Yes		13,600	11,700	9	455	Yes	15	$6,059	None
Yes	Yes		Yes	Yes	15,186 †	9,924	9		Yes	24	$17,008	6/30
Yes	Yes	Yes	Yes	Yes	16,409 †	12,222	12	488	Yes	255	$6,802	None
Yes						1,000		370				
								370				
								370				
								370				
			Yes		10,200 †	18,365		325	Yes			7/15
			No									
Yes	Yes	Yes	No		7,452 †	10,340	12		Yes			None
Yes	Yes		Yes	Yes	16,174 †	10,650	12		Yes	20	$26,321	6/30

† Tuition and fees are for 2007-08.   ‡ Tuition and fees are projected for 2008-09.   * Comprehensive Fee

Institution	Control/ degrees	Undergraduates		Tests required (Fall 2009)	TOEFL		Application	
		Total	Internat'l		minimum	average	Deadline	Fee
Florida Institute of Technology	Pr/B	2,508	492	TOEFL	550		7/1	50
Florida International University	Pu/AB	29,584	1,054	TOEFL, SAT/ACT	500	550	3/1	30
Florida Keys Community College	Pu/A	1,405		TOEFL	560	570	7/1	50
Florida Memorial University	Pr/B	1,669		TOEFL, SAT/ACT	500		5/7	15
Florida National College	Pr/A	2,058						150
Florida Southern College	Pr/B	1,687	62	TOEFL	550		3/1	30
Florida State University	Pu/AB	31,231	141	TOEFL, SAT/ACT	550	614	2/14	30
Florida Technical College: Deland	Pr/A	340		TOEFL	500			25
Florida Technical College: Orlando	Pr/A	411		TOEFL	500		None	25
Full Sail University	Pr/AB	5,697		TOEFL	550		None	150
Gulf Coast Community College	Pu/A	7,251		TOEFL	550		6/9	
Heritage Institute: Jacksonville	Pr/A							
Hillsborough Community College	Pu/A	17,487		TOEFL	500		5/23	50
Hodges University	Pr/AB	1,475	1	TOEFL	500		None	20
Indian River Community College	Pu/AB	14,953			500	550	8/8	
International Academy of Design and Technology: Orlando	Pr/AB						None	50
International Academy of Design and Technology: Tampa	Pr/AB			TOEFL	550		None	50
Jacksonville University	Pr/B	2,893	58	TOEFL, SAT/ACT	540		6/1	30
Johnson & Wales University: North Miami	Pr/AB	1,955		TOEFL	550		None	
Jones College	Pr/AB	650		TOEFL	450	500	None	
Jones College: Miami	Pr/AB	108		TOEFL	450	500	None	
Keiser University	Pr/AB	1,527					None	50
Key College	Pr/A	181		TOEFL	400	420	None	95
Lake City Community College	Pu/A	2,723	13	TOEFL	500	510	None	50
Lake-Sumter Community College	Pu/A	3,337	27	TOEFL	550		None	70
Lynn University	Pr/B	2,144	273	TOEFL, SAT/ACT	500	550	8/1	35
Manatee Community College	Pu/A	8,814	140	TOEFL, SAT/ACT	500		7/24	75
Miami Dade College	Pu/AB	46,674	1,470		550		5/26	20
Miami International University of Art and Design	Pr/AB	1,275		TOEFL			None	50
New College of Florida	Pu/B	767	5	TOEFL, SAT/ACT	560		4/15	30
North Florida Community College	Pu/A	1,779		TOEFL	500		None	20
North Florida Institute: Orange Park	Pr/A	348						
Northwood University: Florida	Pr/AB	673	216	TOEFL	500	550	None	25
Nova Southeastern University	Pr/AB	5,403	284	TOEFL			8/1	50
Okaloosa-Walton College	Pu/AB	14,898		TOEFL	525		None	
Palm Beach Atlantic University	Pr/AB	2,471	60	TOEFL	550	600	None	30
Palm Beach Community College	Pu/A	14,588		TOEFL	450		8/1	30
Pasco-Hernando Community College	Pu/A			TOEFL	550	571	6/1	20
Pensacola Junior College	Pu/A	7,268		TOEFL, SAT/ACT	500		None	30
Polk Community College	Pu/A	6,063	58	TOEFL	525	537	5/15	20
Professional Golfers Career College: Orlando	Pr/A	200		TOEFL	473			75
Remington College: Largo	Pr/AB	158			•		None	50
Remington College: Tampa	Pr/AB	261					None	50
Ringling College of Art and Design	Pr/B	1,199	54	TOEFL	500		None	50
Rollins College	Pr/B	1,778	64	TOEFL	550	619	3/15	40
St. Leo University	Pr/AB	1,587	160	TOEFL	550	619	6/1	35
St. Petersburg College	Pu/AB	19,827	241	TOEFL		450	6/1	135
Saint Thomas University	Pr/B	1,150	98	TOEFL	525		8/1	40
Sanford-Brown Institute: Jacksonville	Pr/A	460						25
Santa Fe Community College	Pu/A	16,588		TOEFL	400		None	75

| Student services | | | Housing | | Academic year costs | | Maximum credits/ summer | Credit hour charge | International financial aid | | | |
Adviser	Orien- tation	ESL	Academic year	Summer	Tuition/ fees	Living costs			Avail- able	Number receiving aid	Average award	Deadline
Yes	Yes	Yes	Yes	Yes	30,190	13,450	12	898	Yes	233	$11,245	None
Yes	Yes	Yes	Yes		15,865 †	17,128	18					
Yes	Yes	Yes	No		8,069 †	15,130	15		Yes			None
Yes			Yes	Yes	12,254	10,040	12	438	Yes			None
					12,594	1,278	15	400				
Yes			Yes	Yes	22,145	10,650	18	650	Yes	62	$13,625	7/1
Yes	Yes	Yes	Yes	Yes	17,403 †	8,000	15					
			No						Yes			None
			No									
Yes	Yes		No									
Yes			No		7,109 †	9,150	12					
Yes			No		7,468 †	7,425	12	249				
		Yes	No		13,130 †	13,586	16	425				
Yes		Yes	Yes	Yes	7,295 †	6,806	12					
			No		18,780 †	12,859		385	Yes			None
Yes	Yes		Yes	Yes	23,900	10,760	18	795	Yes	64		3/15
Yes	Yes	Yes	Yes	Yes	21,717 †	11,844		379	Yes			None
Yes			No		8,340	5,772	15	275				
Yes			No		8,340 ‡	750		275				
			No			7,900						
Yes	Yes				9,210	1,050	16					
			Yes		7,638 †	7,545	12					
Yes			No		7,581 †	16,229	18		Yes			None
Yes	Yes	Yes	Yes		29,300	14,100	18		Yes	117	$18,798	None
Yes			No		7,908 †	16,525	12		Yes			7/28
Yes	Yes	Yes	No		6,863 †		12		Yes	918	$1,341	None
Yes	Yes		Yes	Yes	19,445 †	4,550		421				
Yes			Yes		16,682 †	11,436			Yes			None
Yes			No		6,826 †	2,975	12					
Yes	Yes		Yes	Yes	17,544	10,879	24	346	Yes	153	$9,562	None
Yes	Yes	ESL	Yes	Yes	20,350	14,363	18	660	Yes			None
Yes			No		6,730 †	974						
Yes	Yes		Yes	Yes	21,550	12,308	9		Yes	50	$5,100	None
Yes		Yes			7,110 †	8,428	17		Yes			None
		Yes	No		7,371 †	7,250	18					
Yes			No		7,123 †	12,058	6					
Yes		Yes	No		7,393 †	6,200	18		Yes			None
Yes			Yes		10,780 †	6,000						
			No			6,700	15					
Yes	Yes		Yes		27,110	16,340		1230				
Yes	Yes		Yes		34,520	14,440	8		Yes	36	$28,089	3/1
Yes	Yes		Yes	Yes	17,150	16,060	12		Yes	154	$8,904	None
Yes	Yes	Yes	No		7,558 †	9,640	12					
Yes	Yes	Yes	Yes	Yes	19,680 †	11,366	18	656	Yes			None
Yes		Yes	No		7,577 †	7,932	18					

† Tuition and fees are for 2007-08.   ‡ Tuition and fees are projected for 2008-09.   * Comprehensive Fee

Institution	Control/ degrees	Undergraduates		Tests required (Fall 2009)	TOEFL		Application	
		Total	Internat'l		minimum	average	Deadline	Fee
Schiller International University	Pr/AB			TOEFL	500		None	50
Seminole Community College	Pu/A	10,634					None	50
South Florida Community College	Pu/A	1,822	22	TOEFL	500		7/15	
South University: West Palm Beach Campus	Pr/AB			TOEFL	550		9/1	25
Southeastern University	Pr/AB	2,646	3	TOEFL, SAT/ACT	500		5/1	40
Southwest Florida College	Pr/AB	1,489		TOEFL	500		None	25
Stetson University	Pr/B	2,219	68	TOEFL	550		3/15	50
Tallahassee Community College	Pu/A	13,890		TOEFL	500	550	6/16	
Trinity College of Florida	Pr/AB	174	1	TOEFL, SAT/ACT	500		None	25
Universidad FLET	Pr/AB	303						20
University of Central Florida	Pu/AB	41,051	574	TOEFL, SAT/ACT	550		3/1	30
University of Florida	Pu/B	34,534	326	TOEFL, SAT/ACT	550	612	11/1	30
University of Miami	Pr/B	9,997	613	TOEFL	550		1/15	65
University of North Florida	Pu/AB	14,250	172	TOEFL, SAT/ACT	500	559	5/1	30
University of South Florida	Pu/B	33,998	491	TOEFL, SAT/ACT	550		6/1	30
University of Tampa	Pr/AB	4,887	386	TOEFL	550	583	None	40
University of West Florida	Pu/AB	8,334	112	TOEFL	525		5/15	30
Valencia Community College	Pu/A	26,707	717	TOEFL	450		5/9	25
Virginia College at Pensacola	Pr/A	293						100
Warner Southern College	Pr/AB	1,025	18	TOEFL, SAT/ACT	500	603	5/15	20
Webber International University	Pr/AB	535	79	TOEFL	500	570	8/1	75

Georgia

Abraham Baldwin Agricultural College	Pu/A			TOEFL	500		9/1	20
Agnes Scott College	Pr/B	827		TOEFL, SAT/ACT	577		1/1	35
Albany State University	Pu/B	3,614		TOEFL, SAT	523		7/1	20
Albany Technical College	Pu/A	2,346		TOEFL, SAT/ACT			8/31	15
American InterContinental University	Pr/AB	946		TOEFL	500		None	50
Andrew College	Pr/A			TOEFL	500	520	None	20
Armstrong Atlantic State University	Pu/AB	5,997	246	TOEFL	523		6/30	25
Art Institute of Atlanta	Pr/AB	3,187		TOEFL	480		None	50
Ashworth University	Pr/AB	3,200						
Atlanta Metropolitan College	Pu/A	1,814		TOEFL	523	525	None	20
Atlanta Technical College	Pu/A	2,937						15
Augusta State University	Pu/AB	5,479	60	TOEFL, SAT/ACT	500		7/15	20
Augusta Technical College	Pu/A	4,045	4	TOEFL	500			15
Bauder College	Pr/AB	834		TOEFL	460		None	100
Berry College	Pr/B	1,719	37	TOEFL, SAT/ACT	550	552	2/1	50
Beulah Heights University	Pr/AB	611						35
Brenau University	Pr/B	851	53	TOEFL	550		None	35
Brewton-Parker College	Pr/AB	1,030	13					25
Brown Mackie College: Atlanta	Pr/A							
Carver Bible College	Pr/AB	153						15
Central Georgia Technical College	Pu/A	4,999	2					15
Chattahoochee Technical College	Pu/A	4,300	104	TOEFL, ACT	550		9/1	15
Clark Atlanta University	Pr/B	3,533	34	TOEFL, SAT/ACT	500		5/1	55
Clayton State University	Pu/AB	6,061		TOEFL	550	564	7/1	40
Coastal Georgia Community College	Pu/A	2,943	16	TOEFL	523		7/15	20
Columbus State University	Pu/AB	6,462	75	TOEFL	550		5/1	25
Columbus Technical College	Pu/A	3,467	4	TOEFL	500			15
Covenant College	Pr/AB	989	14	TOEFL, SAT/ACT	540	630	8/1	45
Darton College	Pu/A	4,760	50	TOEFL	520		None	20

Student services			Housing		Academic year costs		Maximum credits/summer	Credit hour charge	International financial aid			
Adviser	Orientation	ESL	Academic year	Summer	Tuition/fees	Living costs			Available	Number receiving aid	Average award	Deadline
Yes	Yes	Yes	Yes	Yes	17,465†	12,700	10	490	Yes			4/1
Yes	Yes	Yes	No		7,571†	9,210	17		Yes			None
Yes	Yes		Yes	Yes	7,672†	14,743	7					
			No		12,570†	8,370	16					
Yes			Yes	Yes	14,470	9,900	12	540				
			No		9,710	4,676		255	Yes			None
Yes	Yes	Yes	Yes		30,216	11,056	9	870	Yes	61	$19,011	None
Yes	Yes		No		6,705†	10,600	18		Yes			None
Yes			Yes		10,550	10,405		405	Yes			8/2
Yes	Yes	Yes	Yes	Yes	17,763†	12,890	15		Yes			6/30
Yes	Yes	Yes	Yes		17,150†	11,700	15	537				
Yes	Yes	Yes	Yes	Yes	34,834	10,254	12	1424	Yes	208	$20,237	None
Yes	Yes	Yes	Yes	Yes	15,134†	10,601	18		Yes	63		
Yes	Yes	Yes	Yes	Yes	16,155†	8,390			Yes			None
Yes	Yes		Yes	Yes	21,692	10,910	16		Yes	142	$4,954	None
Yes	Yes		Yes	Yes	16,233†	11,105	15					
Yes	Yes	Yes	No		7,858†	12,600	19					
					11,625†			230				
			Yes		13,860†	10,083	12		Yes	24		
Yes	Yes	Yes	Yes	Yes	17,000	14,610	12	235	Yes	76	$10,034	8/1
Yes		Yes	Yes		7,990†	8,755	18	312				
Yes	Yes		Yes	Yes	29,060	13,800	12	1175	Yes	31	$19,455	5/1
Yes	Yes		Yes		12,074†	8,364						
					4,707†	7,848		124				
Yes	Yes		Yes		16,386†	7,820	18	430				
Yes		Yes	Yes		10,976	9,394	12		Yes			8/1
Yes	Yes		Yes	Yes	12,028†	6,000		478	Yes	14	$153	None
Yes	Yes		Yes	Yes	19,575	11,226	16	435	Yes			None
Yes			No		7,280†	10,954	12	292				
	Yes		No		2,478†	13,200	21	62				
Yes		Yes	Yes		12,008†	9,080	18	478	Yes	36	$5,138	6/1
Yes			No		4,719†	450		124				
Yes			Yes			2,000			Yes			None
Yes	Yes		Yes	Yes	22,370	10,828	12	739	Yes			
Yes	Yes	Yes	Yes	Yes	6,530†	2,250		210				
Yes	Yes		Yes	Yes	17,700†	12,350	12	583	Yes	30	$21,179	None
Yes	Yes		Yes	Yes	14,730	10,140	12	420	Yes	17	$11,296	None
					9,303†							
					6,000†			190				
			No		4,707†	6,182		124				
Yes		Yes	No		4,728†	1,020	22	124				
Yes	Yes		Yes	Yes	17,038	12,272	9	680				
Yes	Yes		Yes		12,186†	11,100	12	478	Yes			None
Yes			No		7,202†	3,700	18	292	Yes			
Yes	Yes		Yes	Yes	12,118†	9,877	13	478	Yes	40	$3,856	None
			No		4,695†	4,600		124				
Yes			Yes	Yes	24,320	9,200	3	985	Yes	14	$12,385	None
Yes	Yes	Yes	No		7,350†	5,400	15	292	Yes			None

† Tuition and fees are for 2007-08.　　‡ Tuition and fees are projected for 2008-09.　　* Comprehensive Fee

Institution	Control/ degrees	Undergraduates		Tests required (Fall 2009)	TOEFL		Application	
		Total	Internat'l		minimum	average	Deadline	Fee
DeKalb Technical College	Pu/A	3,691						15
DeVry University: Alpharetta	Pr/AB	672	10	TOEFL	500		None	50
DeVry University: Decatur	Pr/AB	2,087	16	TOEFL	500		None	50
East Georgia College	Pu/A			TOEFL	500	525	None	20
Emory University	Pr/AB	5,094	339	TOEFL, SAT/ACT		600	1/15	50
Everest Institute	Pr/A	407						
Fort Valley State University	Pu/AB			TOEFL, SAT/ACT	500		7/15	20
Gainesville State College	Pu/AB	7,476		TOEFL	480	560	5/1	25
Georgia College and State University	Pu/B	5,292	86	TOEFL	500		None	40
Georgia Highlands College	Pu/A	4,346		TOEFL, SAT/ACT	550		7/1	20
Georgia Institute of Technology	Pu/B	12,316	565	TOEFL, SAT	600		1/15	50
Georgia Military College	Pu/A	3,186		TOEFL		460	6/1	40
Georgia Perimeter College	Pu/A	19,847	899	TOEFL	460	495	7/1	20
Georgia Southern University	Pu/B	14,157	122	TOEFL	500		5/1	30
Georgia Southwestern State University	Pu/B	2,209	51	TOEFL	523		7/1	25
Georgia State University	Pu/B	19,282	518	TOEFL, SAT/ACT	550	593	3/1	50
Gordon College	Pu/AB	3,629		TOEFL	525		None	20
Griffin Technical College	Pu/A	3,635	1					15
Gupton Jones College of Funeral Service	Pr/A	175						50
Gwinnett College	Pr/A							
Herzing College	Pr/AB	441		TOEFL	500		None	
Kennesaw State University	Pu/B	18,213	552	TOEFL, SAT/ACT	527		6/29	40
LaGrange College	Pr/AB	989	17	TOEFL	500			30
Le Cordon Bleu College of Culinary Arts	Pr/A	1,035						50
Life University	Pr/AB	536		TOEFL	500		8/15	50
Mercer University	Pr/B	2,245	36	TOEFL	550		6/1	50
Middle Georgia College	Pu/AB	3,445		TOEFL	527	530	8/1	20
Middle Georgia Technical College	Pu/A	2,498		TOEFL	500			15
Morehouse College	Pr/B	2,810	74	TOEFL	500	550	2/15	45
North Georgia College & State University	Pu/AB	4,498	66	TOEFL, SAT/ACT	550		7/1	25
North Metro Technical College	Pu/A	2,062						15
Oglethorpe University	Pr/B	943	45	TOEFL	550	556	8/1	30
Paine College	Pr/B	908	3	TOEFL, SAT/ACT	500		8/1	45
Piedmont College	Pr/B	1,056	2	TOEFL, SAT/ACT	550		7/1	
Reinhardt College	Pr/AB	971	5	TOEFL	500	540	None	25
Savannah College of Art and Design	Pr/B	7,423	547	TOEFL	450	554	None	50
Savannah River College	Pr/A	268						50
Savannah State University	Pu/B	2,991		TOEFL, SAT/ACT	500		7/15	20
Savannah Technical College	Pu/A	3,748	57				None	15
Shorter College	Pr/B	1,019	59	TOEFL, SAT/ACT	500		8/1	25
South Georgia College	Pu/A	1,756		TOEFL	500		None	20
South University	Pr/AB			TOEFL	550		None	25
Southeastern Technical College	Pu/A							15
Southern Polytechnic State University	Pu/AB	3,827	210	TOEFL, SAT/ACT	550	560	8/1	20
Southwest Georgia Technical College	Pu/A	1,154						20
Spelman College	Pr/B	2,337	58	TOEFL, SAT/ACT	500		2/1	35
Thomas University	Pr/AB	456		TOEFL	550		7/1	125
Toccoa Falls College	Pr/AB	969	9	TOEFL	550		8/1	20
Truett-McConnell College	Pr/AB	472		TOEFL, SAT/ACT	500		8/1	25
University of Georgia	Pu/B	24,971	185	TOEFL, SAT/ACT	550		1/15	50
University of West Georgia	Pu/B	8,842		TOEFL, SAT/ACT	523		None	30
Valdosta State University	Pu/AB	9,696	124	TOEFL	523		4/1	40
Waycross College	Pu/A			TOEFL, SAT/ACT	523		5/1	20
Wesleyan College	Pr/B	547		TOEFL, SAT/ACT	550	597	5/15	30
West Central Technical College	Pu/A	3,216						25
Young Harris College	Pr/A	639		TOEFL, SAT/ACT	550		6/1	30

Student services			Housing		Academic year costs		Maximum credits/ summer	Credit hour charge	International financial aid			
Adviser	Orien- tation	ESL	Academic year	Summer	Tuition/ fees	Living costs			Avail- able	Number receiving aid	Average award	Deadline
Yes			No		2,523 †	9,200		62				
Yes					13,220 †	8,528		490				
Yes					13,220 †	15,194		490				
Yes			No		7,162 †	3,600		292	Yes			None
Yes	Yes		Yes	Yes	36,336	13,772	16		Yes			4/1
Yes	Yes		Yes	Yes	12,162 †	9,075	18	478				
Yes	Yes	Yes	No		7,728 †	5,630	15	312				
Yes	Yes		Yes	Yes	17,688 †	11,418		638	Yes			None
Yes					7,188 †	10,400	17	292				
Yes	Yes	Yes	Yes		23,366 †	7,924	16	926				
			Yes		12,050 †	7,365	15					
Yes	Yes	Yes	No		7,474 †	4,200		292	Yes			6/1
Yes	Yes	Yes	Yes	Yes	12,954 †	13,160	12	493	Yes	19	$6,397	4/20
Yes	Yes	Yes	Yes	Yes	12,130 †	6,274	18	478				
Yes	Yes	Yes	Yes	Yes	18,972 †	9,944	18	750	Yes			11/1
			Yes		7,768 †	6,724	18	312				
					4,707 †	737		124				
			No		8,400 †	8,000						
					8,350							
Yes			No		11,100 †		16	370	Yes			None
Yes	Yes	Yes	Yes		12,678 †	8,444	15	493				
Yes	Yes		Yes	Yes	19,900	11,143	17	820				
Yes	Yes	Yes	Yes	Yes	7,605 †	760	20	158	Yes			6/15
Yes	Yes		Yes	Yes	26,960 †	10,616	12	892	Yes			None
Yes			Yes	Yes	7,862 †	6,500	20	312	Yes	5		None
					2,475 †			62				
Yes			Yes		20,358	15,724	9	771	Yes			4/1
Yes	Yes	Yes	Yes	Yes	12,414 †	7,962	20	478	Yes			None
					2,475 †							
Yes	Yes		Yes	Yes	25,580	12,000	15		Yes			None
Yes			Yes		10,694 †	9,036	12	412	Yes			None
Yes			Yes	Yes	16,500 †	12,650	18	688	Yes			None
Yes			Yes	Yes	14,970 †	7,784	21	495	Yes			None
Yes	Yes	Yes	Yes	Yes	25,965	16,953	25	577	Yes	448	$1,948	None
					10,495	12,915			Yes			None
Yes	Yes		Yes	Yes	12,090 †	7,598	9	478	Yes			4/1
Yes	Yes	Yes	No		2,475 †	12,600	21	62	Yes	2		None
Yes	Yes		Yes		15,770	14,100	19	420	Yes			None
			Yes	Yes	7,316 †	9,205		292				
Yes			Yes			750	18					
					2,556 †			62				
Yes	Yes	Yes	Yes	Yes	13,590 †	11,180	15	540				
			No		4,707 †	5,390		124				
Yes	Yes		Yes		18,615 †	13,494			Yes			None
Yes			Yes	Yes	11,040 †	5,836	15	415				
Yes			Yes		14,625	10,860	12	604	Yes	8		8/1
Yes			Yes		14,000	8,170	12	450	Yes			None
Yes	Yes		Yes		20,726 †	8,092	9	817				
Yes		Yes	Yes	Yes	12,790 †	6,406	18	493				
Yes	Yes	Yes	Yes	Yes	12,910 †	12,190	21	493				
			No		7,144 †	2,000		292				
Yes	Yes		Yes	Yes	17,000	10,300	12	405	Yes	69		6/3
					4,707 †	6,519		124				
Yes			Yes		16,630	8,428	12	500	Yes			None

† Tuition and fees are for 2007-08.   ‡ Tuition and fees are projected for 2008-09.   * Comprehensive Fee

Institution	Control/ degrees	Undergraduates		Tests required (Fall 2009)	TOEFL		Application	
		Total	Internat'l		minimum	average	Deadline	Fee
Hawaii								
Brigham Young University-Hawaii	Pr/B	2,312	1,009	TOEFL	475	523	2/15	30
Chaminade University of Honolulu	Pr/AB			TOEFL, SAT/ACT	550			50
Hawaii Pacific University	Pr/AB	6,128		TOEFL	550	569	None	50
Hawaii Tokai International College	Pr/A	51	47	TOEFL	400	450	5/29	50
Heald College: Honolulu	Pr/A			TOEFL	500		None	250
Remington College: Honolulu	Pr/AB	455		TOEFL	400		None	50
TransPacific Hawaii College	Pr/A	176	176				8/31	50
University of Hawaii at Hilo	Pu/B	3,229			500		6/1	25
University of Hawaii at Manoa	Pu/B	13,386		TOEFL, SAT/ACT	500	565	2/1	50
University of Hawaii: Hawaii Community College	Pu/A			TOEFL	475		8/1	25
University of Hawaii: Honolulu Community College	Pu/A	4,027		TOEFL	500	530	6/15	25
University of Hawaii: Kapiolani Community College	Pu/A	7,300		TOEFL	500	600	7/17	50
University of Hawaii: Kauai Community College	Pu/A	201		TOEFL	450		7/1	25
University of Hawaii: Maui Community College	Pu/A	2,303		TOEFL	480		7/1	25
University of Hawaii: West Oahu	Pu/B	911	2	TOEFL	550		6/15	50
University of Hawaii: Windward Community College	Pu/A	1,854		TOEFL	500		6/1	25
Idaho								
Boise State University	Pu/AB	16,571	226	TOEFL	500	583	6/1	40
Brigham Young University-Idaho	Pr/AB	13,155		TOEFL	500	541	2/15	25
College of Idaho	Pr/B	813	26	TOEFL	550	600	6/1	
College of Southern Idaho	Pu/A	7,204		TOEFL	450		None	
Idaho State University	Pu/AB	9,347	174	TOEFL, ACT	500		6/1	40
Lewis-Clark State College	Pu/AB	2,944	112	TOEFL	500	533	6/1	45
North Idaho College	Pu/A	3,789		TOEFL	500	550	7/7	15
Northwest Nazarene University	Pr/B	1,189	7	TOEFL, SAT/ACT	500	550	None	25
Stevens-Henager College: Boise	Pr/AB	318		TOEFL			None	
University of Idaho	Pu/B	8,471	157	TOEFL	525	580	5/1	60
Illinois								
Augustana College	Pr/B	2,518	26	TOEFL, SAT/ACT	550		4/1	35
Aurora University	Pr/B	2,065	2	TOEFL	550		3/8	25
Benedictine University	Pr/AB	2,883		TOEFL	525	550	7/1	40
Black Hawk College	Pu/A	4,801					None	
Black Hawk College: East Campus	Pu/A	892		TOEFL	480			
Blackburn College	Pr/B	613	2	TOEFL	515	530	6/1	
Blessing-Rieman College of Nursing	Pr/B	211		TOEFL, SAT/ACT	500		None	
Bradley University	Pr/B	5,205	39	TOEFL	530		6/1	35
Carl Sandburg College	Pu/A	2,693		TOEFL	600		None	
Chicago State University	Pu/B	5,217		TOEFL	500	525	5/1	30
City Colleges of Chicago: Harold Washington College	Pu/A			TOEFL	450	500	8/15	25
City Colleges of Chicago: Kennedy-King College	Pu/A			TOEFL	450	500	7/1	100
City Colleges of Chicago: Malcolm X College	Pu/A			TOEFL	450		7/15	100
City Colleges of Chicago: Olive-Harvey College	Pu/A						6/30	100

| Student services | | | Housing | | Academic year costs | | Maximum credits/ summer | Credit hour charge | International financial aid | | | |
Adviser	Orientation	ESL	Academic year	Summer	Tuition/ fees	Living costs			Available	Number receiving aid	Average award	Deadline
Yes	Yes	Yes	Yes	Yes	3,600	7,968	9		Yes			3/15
Yes			Yes	Yes	16,140	13,738	12	533	Yes	19		None
Yes	Yes	Yes	Yes	Yes	13,080‡	13,660	21	542	Yes	119	$6,611	None
Yes	Yes	Yes	Yes	Yes	9,450	8,375	14					
	Yes		No		10,800	1,500			Yes			None
			No			2,601						
Yes	Yes	Yes	No		16,300†	12,524	12					
Yes	Yes	Yes	Yes	Yes	11,212†	9,218	10	461				
Yes	Yes	Yes	Yes	Yes	14,654†	11,073	16	600	Yes	560	$5,467	None
	Yes		Yes		7,814†	10,232	10	256				
			No		7,710†	9,611	6	256				
Yes	Yes		Yes		7,740†	9,551	6	256				
Yes	Yes		No		7,720†		6	256				
Yes	Yes	Yes	Yes	Yes	9,650†		6	320	Yes			None
Yes			No		10,186†	11,465	18	424				
			No		7,720†	10,407		256	Yes			None
Yes	Yes	Yes	Yes	Yes	12,578†	9,531	7					
Yes	Yes		Yes	Yes	3,360†	9,920	20		Yes			None
Yes	Yes	Yes	Yes		18,990	8,781		760	Yes	26	$11,162	None
Yes	Yes	Yes	Yes		5,900†	9,120	12	295	Yes			None
Yes	Yes	Yes	Yes	Yes	13,084†	9,930		341	Yes	82	$4,328	None
Yes	Yes	Yes	Yes	Yes	11,382†	13,500	15		Yes	180	$2,563	
Yes	Yes	Yes	Yes		7,478†	9,170	6	426				
Yes			Yes		21,170	8,320	6	905	Yes			None
			No		16,350†							
Yes	Yes	Yes	Yes	Yes	14,490†	12,180	18	360	Yes	49	$5,231	None
Yes	Yes		Yes	Yes	30,150	9,925	9	1300	Yes			None
Yes			Yes	Yes	17,500	10,572	6	530	Yes			None
Yes	Yes		Yes	Yes	21,310	11,205	12	695				
Yes	Yes	Yes	No		8,220†	11,965	12	267	Yes	13	$3,455	None
			No		8,220†	600	6	267				
Yes			Yes		13,610†	6,113	6	450				
			Yes	Yes	17,775†	10,900		465	Yes			None
Yes	Yes		Yes	Yes	22,814	8,850	15					
Yes		Yes	No		5,010†	6,530	6					
Yes	Yes		Yes		13,850†	10,952	6	410	Yes			None
Yes	Yes	Yes	No		9,543†	950	6	310				
Yes		Yes	No		9,543†	7,510	6	310				
Yes		Yes	No		9,543†	5,800	6	310				
Yes	Yes	Yes	No		9,543†	670	6	310				

† Tuition and fees are for 2007-08.   ‡ Tuition and fees are projected for 2008-09.   * Comprehensive Fee

Institution	Control/ degrees	Undergraduates		Tests required (Fall 2009)	TOEFL		Application	
		Total	Internat'l		minimum	average	Deadline	Fee
City Colleges of Chicago: Richard J. Daley College	Pu/A			TOEFL	450		5/30	100
City Colleges of Chicago: Wright College	Pu/A			TOEFL	450		7/1	
College of DuPage	Pu/A	21,988		TOEFL	550		6/7	10
College of Lake County	Pu/A	12,192			525		7/7	
College of Office Technology	Pr/A	368						50
Columbia College Chicago	Pr/B	11,256	114	TOEFL	533		5/1	65
Concordia University	Pr/B	1,026		TOEFL, SAT/ACT	525		5/5	
Cooking & Hospitality Institute of Chicago	Pr/A	1,002		TOEFL	500		None	100
Danville Area Community College	Pu/A	4,345		TOEFL	500		7/15	
DePaul University	Pr/B	14,661	201	TOEFL	550		7/1	40
DeVry University: Addison	Pr/AB	1,312	61	TOEFL	500		None	50
DeVry University: Chicago	Pr/AB	1,791	98	TOEFL	500		None	50
DeVry University: Online	Pr/AB	8,596	1					50
DeVry University: Tinley Park	Pr/AB	1,059	2	TOEFL	500		None	50
Dominican University	Pr/B	1,531	32	TOEFL	550	560	6/1	100
East-West University	Pr/AB	1,150		TOEFL			None	200
Eastern Illinois University	Pu/B	10,152	50	TOEFL	500		5/15	30
Elgin Community College	Pu/A	6,589	22	TOEFL				50
Elmhurst College	Pr/B	2,808		TOEFL, SAT/ACT	550	600	5/1	
Eureka College	Pr/B			TOEFL	550		6/15	
Governors State University	Pu/B	2,370	7	TOEFL	500	520	None	50
Greenville College	Pr/B	1,353	17	TOEFL	500		7/1	25
Harper College	Pu/A	13,343	147	TOEFL	550		None	25
Heartland Community College	Pu/A	4,758		TOEFL	550		6/15	
Highland Community College	Pu/A	1,844		TOEFL	500		7/18	
Illinois Central College	Pu/A	8,719	13	TOEFL	500	520	None	
Illinois College	Pr/B	990	17	TOEFL, SAT/ACT	550	580	6/1	
Illinois Eastern Community Colleges: Frontier Community College	Pu/A	2,102		TOEFL	500		None	35
Illinois Eastern Community Colleges: Lincoln Trail College	Pu/A	902		TOEFL	500		None	35
Illinois Eastern Community Colleges: Olney Central College	Pu/A	890		TOEFL	500		None	35
Illinois Eastern Community Colleges: Wabash Valley College	Pu/A	841		TOEFL	500		None	35
Illinois Institute of Art: Chicago	Pr/AB	3,000		TOEFL	480		None	50
Illinois Institute of Art: Schaumburg	Pr/AB	1,238		TOEFL				50
Illinois Institute of Technology	Pr/B	2,479	399	TOEFL	550		4/15	
Illinois State University	Pu/B	17,637	101	TOEFL, SAT/ACT	550	612	5/15	40
Illinois Wesleyan University	Pr/B	2,088	52	TOEFL, SAT/ACT	550		3/1	
International Academy of Design and Technology: Chicago	Pr/AB			TOEFL	500		None	50
International Academy of Design and Technology: Schaumburg	Pr/AB							
John A. Logan College	Pu/A	2,306	3	TOEFL	520		None	
John Wood Community College	Pu/A	1,873	7	TOEFL	470		None	
Joliet Junior College	Pu/A	13,194		TOEFL	500		None	
Judson University	Pr/B	1,250		TOEFL	550	580	8/1	35
Kankakee Community College	Pu/A	2,551	4	TOEFL	520		7/1	250
Kaskaskia College	Pu/A	2,795	13	TOEFL	550		6/1	
Kishwaukee College	Pu/A	4,617		TOEFL	485	495	6/1	15
Knox College	Pr/B	1,353	81	TOEFL	550		2/1	40
Lake Forest College	Pr/B	1,408	112	TOEFL, SAT/ACT	550	603	2/15	40
Lake Land College	Pu/A	7,182		TOEFL	500	525	None	
Lewis University	Pr/AB	3,822	100	TOEFL	500	515	None	40

Adviser	Orien-tation	ESL	Academic year	Summer	Tuition/fees	Living costs	Maximum credits/summer	Credit hour charge	Available	Number receiving aid	Average award	Deadline
		Yes	No		9,543†	1,760	6	310				
Yes	Yes	Yes	No		9,543†	730	8	310				
Yes		Yes	No		10,770	12,251	18	339				
Yes	Yes	Yes	No		8,580‡	12,738	12	272	Yes			None
					9,925‡	15,104						None
Yes	Yes	Yes	Yes	Yes	17,564†	15,124	12	592	Yes			
Yes			Yes	Yes	22,390	9,000	16	685	Yes	1	$5,000	8/15
Yes			No			7,294						
Yes			No		4,800†	11,511	12	150				
Yes	Yes	Yes	Yes	Yes	24,110†	12,526	16	422	Yes			5/1
Yes					13,220†	16,375		490				
Yes		Yes			13,220†	8,193		490				
						8,528						
Yes					13,220†	15,194		490				
Yes	Yes	Yes	Yes	Yes	23,950	10,800	12	790	Yes	7	$11,835	None
Yes			No		12,825†	3,500	16	405				
Yes	Yes		Yes	Yes	19,654†	9,304		583				
Yes	Yes	Yes	No		13,127†	14,350		437				
Yes	Yes		Yes	Yes	24,760†	10,679	8	700	Yes			None
Yes	Yes		Yes	Yes	15,270†	8,430		395	Yes			None
Yes	Yes		No		16,706†	5,800	16	537	Yes			10/1
			Yes	Yes	19,428	11,364	12	406	Yes			None
Yes	Yes	Yes	No		12,504	4,917	9	399				
Yes		Yes	No		6,630‡	7,802	9	216				
Yes		Yes	No		3,870†	10,222	9	123	Yes			None
Yes		Yes	No	Yes	5,400	2,825	10	180				
Yes	Yes		Yes	Yes	20,300	9,400	6		Yes			None
Yes	Yes	Yes	No	Yes	6,905†	6,587	9	227	Yes			None
Yes	Yes	Yes	No	Yes	6,905†	6,587	9	227	Yes			None
Yes	Yes	Yes	No	Yes	6,905†	6,587	9	227	Yes			None
Yes	Yes	Yes	No	Yes	6,905†	6,587	9	227	Yes			None
Yes			No		20,784†	7,570	9	433	Yes			None
			Yes		20,784†	9,345		433				
Yes	Yes	Yes	Yes	Yes	27,513	9,226	9	832	Yes	314	$9,101	None
Yes	Yes	Yes	Yes	Yes	16,339†	10,809	12	477				
Yes	Yes		Yes	Yes	32,434	8,780		1008	Yes	42	$23,877	3/1
Yes					17,250†	12,078	16		Yes			None
					15,000†	1,200						
			No		6,984	7,755		233				
		Yes	No		6,120†	2,736	10	196				
		Yes	No		9,784†	8,150	9	312	Yes			6/30
Yes	Yes		Yes	Yes	20,420†	9,700		675	Yes	30		8/1
Yes			No		9,275†	8,582	9	309				
Yes			No		8,416†		9	274	Yes			None
Yes	Yes	Yes	No		8,706†	10,120	9	281				
Yes	Yes		Yes	Yes	30,507	9,390	3		Yes	80	$17,865	None
Yes	Yes		Yes	Yes	32,520	10,260		1004	Yes	116		None
Yes	Yes		No		8,769†	318	10	277				
Yes	Yes	Yes	Yes	Yes	21,990	10,955	8	705				

† Tuition and fees are for 2007-08.   ‡ Tuition and fees are projected for 2008-09.   * Comprehensive Fee

Institution	Control/ degrees	Undergraduates Total	Internat'l	Tests required (Fall 2009)	TOEFL minimum	TOEFL average	Application Deadline	Fee
Lexington College	Pr/AB	57	3	TOEFL	547		None	75
Lincoln Christian College and Seminary	Pr/AB	708		TOEFL	550		3/1	25
Lincoln College	Pr/AB	800		TOEFL	480	490	8/1	25
Lincoln Land Community College	Pu/A	5,196	6	TOEFL	500		None	
Loyola University Chicago	Pr/B	9,365	111	TOEFL, SAT/ACT	550	602		25
MacCormac College	Pr/A	171		TOEFL	480		None	20
MacMurray College	Pr/AB			TOEFL	550	580	None	
McHenry County College	Pu/A			TOEFL	550		None	15
McKendree University	Pr/AB	2,363	56	TOEFL, SAT/ACT	520		None	40
Millikin University	Pr/B	2,295		TOEFL	550		5/1	25
Monmouth College	Pr/B	1,331	17	TOEFL	550	585	5/1	
Moody Bible Institute	Pr/AB			TOEFL	550		3/1	35
Moraine Valley Community College	Pu/A	10,758	146					
Morrison Institute of Technology	Pr/A	144		TOEFL	425		8/1	100
Morton College	Pu/A	2,183	60	TOEFL	500			10
National-Louis University	Pr/B			TOEFL	550		None	25
North Central College	Pr/B	2,142	23	TOEFL	520		4/15	25
North Park University	Pr/B	2,160	77	TOEFL	550		6/1	40
Northern Illinois University	Pu/B	18,915	133	TOEFL	550		5/1	
Northwestern Business College	Pr/A	1,987		TOEFL	500		None	100
Northwestern University	Pr/B	8,176	407	TOEFL, SAT/ACT	600	637	1/1	65
Oakton Community College	Pu/A			TOEFL	520		6/1	25
Olivet Nazarene University	Pr/AB	3,190	18	TOEFL	500		5/1	25
Parkland College	Pu/A	9,210	334	TOEFL	470		8/1	40
Prairie State College	Pu/A	5,507		TOEFL	570		None	10
Quincy University	Pr/AB	982	6	TOEFL	550	570	8/1	25
Richland Community College	Pu/A	2,502	2	TOEFL	500	550	None	
Robert Morris College: Chicago	Pr/AB	4,535	32	TOEFL	500		None	100
Rock Valley College	Pu/A			TOEFL	550		6/15	
Rockford College	Pr/B	862	4	TOEFL	550		8/1	50
Roosevelt University	Pr/B	3,861	109	TOEFL	525	570	7/1	35
Rosalind Franklin University of Medicine and Science	Pr/B	4		TOEFL	600		4/1	20
St. John's College	Pr/B	69						
St. Xavier University	Pr/B	3,251	18	TOEFL	550		7/30	25
Sauk Valley Community College	Pu/A	1,933		TOEFL	500	530	8/1	
School of the Art Institute of Chicago	Pr/B	2,330	422	TOEFL	550		6/1	85
Shimer College	Pr/B	76	2	TOEFL				25
Southeastern Illinois College	Pu/A	2,606		TOEFL	500		7/15	
Southern Illinois University Carbondale	Pu/AB	16,125	240	TOEFL	520		None	30
Southern Illinois University Edwardsville	Pu/B	10,843	75	TOEFL, SAT/ACT	550	555	6/1	30
Spoon River College	Pu/A	2,139		TOEFL	500		None	
Springfield College in Illinois	Pr/A	608	3	TOEFL	515		7/15	50
Trinity Christian College	Pr/B	1,217	21	TOEFL	550		None	20
Trinity College of Nursing and Health Sciences	Pr/AB							50
Trinity International University	Pr/B	1,048	17	TOEFL	580		5/1	25
Triton College	Pu/A	10,603	21	TOEFL	500	520	7/1	
University of Chicago	Pr/B	4,898	387	TOEFL, SAT/ACT	600	615	1/2	60
University of Illinois at Chicago	Pu/B	15,565	227	TOEFL, SAT/ACT	520		1/15	50
University of Illinois at Urbana-Champaign	Pu/B	30,395	1,485	TOEFL, SAT/ACT	550		1/2	50
University of Illinois: Springfield	Pu/B	2,696	27	TOEFL, SAT/ACT	500		None	50
University of St. Francis	Pr/B	1,282	8	TOEFL	550		8/1	30
VanderCook College of Music	Pr/B	116	1	TOEFL	500		None	50
Vatterott College: Quincy	Pr/A							
West Suburban College of Nursing	Pr/B	212						30
Western Illinois University	Pu/B	11,145	155	TOEFL	550	570	3/1	30

	Student services			Housing		Academic year costs		Maximum credits/ summer	Credit hour charge		International financial aid			
Adviser	Orien- tation	ESL	Academic year	Summer		Tuition/ fees	Living costs			Avail- able	Number receiving aid	Average award	Deadline
Yes			Yes			22,800	11,600		727	Yes			None
			Yes			11,790	8,155	3	393				
Yes			Yes			18,000 †	7,440	9	600	Yes			7/1
		Yes	No			6,915	12,671	10	221				
Yes	Yes	Yes	Yes			29,486	13,740	12	580				
Yes		Yes	No			10,060	1,000	16	415				
Yes	Yes		Yes	Yes		17,450	12,695	9	565	Yes			None
			No			9,674 †	12,914	9	313				
Yes	Yes		Yes	Yes		21,270	15,520	12	690	Yes			None
Yes	Yes	Yes	Yes	Yes		25,295	10,935	9	820	Yes	5	$9,359	None
Yes	Yes		Yes			24,000	8,900		800	Yes			None
Yes	Yes		Yes	Yes			2,100	9		Yes	24		None
Yes	Yes	Yes	No	Yes		7,712 ‡	5,730	9	252				
			Yes	Yes		13,360	4,650		545				
Yes		Yes	No			8,212 †		19	256				
Yes		Yes	Yes			18,075	4,205	21	399				
Yes		Yes	Yes	Yes		25,938	10,719	9	645	Yes	22	$12,865	None
Yes	Yes	Yes	Yes	Yes		18,600	12,830	12	650	Yes			8/1
Yes	Yes		Yes			14,039 †	10,934	12	454				
Yes			No			18,997 ‡	16,965	20	370				
Yes	Yes		Yes			37,125	14,995			Yes	30	$33,150	2/15
Yes	Yes		No			9,016 †	9,590		297	Yes	3		
Yes			Yes	Yes		21,590	9,500	12	865	Yes			None
Yes		Yes	No			10,230 †	4,200	8	338				
Yes			No			9,980 †	10,050	9	332				
Yes	Yes		Yes	Yes		20,790	11,640	12	480	Yes			None
Yes		Yes	No			11,625 †	1,000	6	388				
Yes			Yes	Yes		18,000 ‡	8,300	16	442				
Yes			No			12,284 †	900	9	401	Yes			None
		Yes	Yes	Yes		23,500	12,950	9	625	Yes	8	$14,656	None
Yes	Yes	Yes	Yes	Yes		16,930 †	14,442	12	600				
Yes			Yes			14,803 †	300						
						12,068 ‡	12,372		486				
Yes	Yes		Yes	Yes		22,926	10,315	6	753	Yes			None
Yes		Yes	Yes	Yes		8,340 †	4,631	9	276	Yes			None
Yes	Yes	Yes	Yes			31,040 †	14,610	9	1025	Yes	99		None
Yes			Yes	Yes		26,110	26,355		850	Yes	2	$33,678	None
Yes			No			3,270 †	8,919		107	Yes			None
Yes	Yes	Yes	Yes	Yes		18,421 †	10,002	6	529	Yes	91	$8,404	None
Yes	Yes		Yes	Yes		14,874 †	11,135	15					
Yes		Yes	No			7,110	600	9	227				
Yes			Yes			7,744 †	5,260		312	Yes	4		None
Yes			Yes	Yes		20,256	11,204		664	Yes			4/15
			No			11,105			366				
Yes			Yes	Yes		21,930	9,480	6	900	Yes	3	$5,666	None
Yes		Yes	No			7,150	6,550	12	230				
Yes			Yes			37,632	14,666			Yes	57	$41,061	2/1
Yes	Yes	Yes	Yes			22,134 †	11,878	12		Yes	46	$2,255	
Yes	Yes	Yes	Yes	Yes		25,216 †	12,490	8		Yes			None
Yes	Yes	Yes	Yes	Yes		16,976 †	8,446		517	Yes	7	$3,876	11/15
Yes			Yes	Yes		21,860	10,044	6	715	Yes			None
			Yes	Yes		18,800 †	12,420	4	760	Yes			4/30
						20,270 †	400		670	Yes			None
Yes	Yes	Yes	Yes	Yes		12,056	11,245	6	323	Yes			None

† Tuition and fees are for 2007-08. ‡ Tuition and fees are projected for 2008-09. * Comprehensive Fee

Institution	Control/ degrees	Undergraduates		Tests required (Fall 2009)	TOEFL		Application	
		Total	Internat'l		minimum	average	Deadline	Fee
Westwood College: Chicago Loop	Pr/AB	830						25
Westwood College: DuPage	Pr/AB	634		TOEFL				100
Westwood College: O'Hare Airport	Pr/AB	519		TOEFL	475		8/6	25
Westwood College: River Oaks	Pr/AB	625						
Wheaton College	Pr/B	2,357	30	TOEFL	550		1/10	50
Indiana								
Ancilla College	Pr/A	511		TOEFL	550		None	
Ball State University	Pu/AB	16,422	6	TOEFL	550	575	5/15	40
Bethel College	Pr/AB	2,099	41	TOEFL	540		6/1	25
Brown Mackie College: Fort Wayne	Pr/A	1,200						20
Butler University	Pr/AB	3,593	104	TOEFL	550	595	7/1	35
Calumet College of St. Joseph	Pr/AB	1,025		TOEFL	515		None	
College of Court Reporting	Pr/A	230						50
DePauw University	Pr/B	2,350	57		560		2/1	40
DeVry University: Indianapolis	Pr/AB	185	1					50
Earlham College	Pr/B	1,156	116	TOEFL	550	600	2/1	30
Franklin College	Pr/B	1,130	2	TOEFL	550	570	None	30
Goshen College	Pr/B	955	55	TOEFL	550	595	7/1	25
Hanover College	Pr/B	916	31	TOEFL, SAT/ACT	550	590	3/1	35
Holy Cross College	Pr/AB	481		TOEFL, SAT/ACT	500		8/15	50
Huntington University	Pr/AB	866	31	TOEFL	527	600	5/1	20
Indiana Business College: Indianapolis Northwest	Pr/A	218						50
Indiana Institute of Technology	Pr/AB	3,026	15	TOEFL	477		6/20	50
Indiana State University	Pu/AB	8,303	110	TOEFL	500	536	6/15	25
Indiana University Bloomington	Pu/AB	29,734	1,366					60
Indiana University East	Pu/AB	1,974	5				3/13	35
Indiana University Kokomo	Pu/AB	2,387	8	TOEFL, SAT/ACT	550		8/3	50
Indiana University Northwest	Pu/AB	3,965	8	TOEFL, SAT/ACT	500		2/1	25
Indiana University South Bend	Pu/AB	5,718	110	TOEFL	530		None	59
Indiana University Southeast	Pu/AB	5,167	15	TOEFL, SAT/ACT	530			30
Indiana University-Purdue University Fort Wayne	Pu/AB	10,659	143	TOEFL, SAT/ACT	550	560	8/1	30
Indiana University-Purdue University Indianapolis	Pu/AB	20,136	447	TOEFL, SAT/ACT	500		3/1	60
Indiana Wesleyan University	Pr/AB	2,881	11	TOEFL, SAT/ACT	550		5/1	25
International Business College	Pr/AB	785						50
Ivy Tech Community College: Bloomington	Pu/A	4,435	44	TOEFL	550		4/15	
Ivy Tech Community College: Central Indiana	Pu/A	12,639	278	TOEFL	550		4/15	
Ivy Tech Community College: Columbus	Pu/A	2,407	15	TOEFL	550		4/15	
Ivy Tech Community College: East Central	Pu/A	5,610	8	TOEFL	550		4/15	
Ivy Tech Community College: Kokomo	Pu/A	3,194	5	TOEFL	550		4/15	
Ivy Tech Community College: Lafayette	Pu/A	4,573	85	TOEFL	550		4/15	
Ivy Tech Community College: North Central	Pu/A	4,625	89	TOEFL	550		4/15	
Ivy Tech Community College: Northeast	Pu/A	5,704	99	TOEFL	550		4/15	
Ivy Tech Community College: Northwest	Pu/A	4,540	16	TOEFL	550		4/15	
Ivy Tech Community College: Richmond	Pu/A	1,976	5	TOEFL	550		4/15	
Ivy Tech Community College: South Central	Pu/A	3,181	6	TOEFL	550		4/15	
Ivy Tech Community College: Southeast	Pu/A	1,792	2	TOEFL	550		4/15	
Ivy Tech Community College: Southwest	Pu/A	4,393	32	TOEFL	550		4/15	
Ivy Tech Community College: Wabash Valley	Pu/A	4,647	24	TOEFL	550		4/15	
Kaplan College: Hammond	Pr/A	408						20
Kaplan College: Merrillville	Pr/A	347		TOEFL	477		None	100
Manchester College	Pr/AB	1,011	44	TOEFL	550	575	5/1	20

Student services			Housing		Academic year costs		Maximum credits/ summer	Credit hour charge	International financial aid			
Adviser	Orientation	ESL	Academic year	Summer	Tuition/ fees	Living costs			Available	Number receiving aid	Average award	Deadline
						500						
Yes					13,902†	900	15	484				
Yes	Yes		Yes	Yes	25,500	13,322	8	1063	Yes	12	$14,925	None
Yes			No		12,080	12,280	9	395	Yes			3/1
Yes	Yes	Yes	Yes	Yes	19,304	11,104	12					
Yes			Yes	Yes	19,996	7,820			Yes	35	$35,630	None
						1,100						
Yes		Yes	Yes	Yes	28,266	12,260	12	1150	Yes			
Yes					12,610	8,950	18	385	Yes			None
					6,600†			275				
Yes	Yes		Yes		31,825	10,400			Yes	55	$25,545	
					13,020†	16,375		490				
Yes	Yes	Yes	Yes	Yes	34,030	11,164		1109	Yes	64	$23,049	3/1
Yes	Yes		Yes	Yes	22,445	6,390			Yes	2	$16,710	3/1
Yes	Yes		Yes	Yes	22,300	10,650	8	890	Yes	57	$13,530	None
Yes	Yes		Yes	Yes	25,220	10,700		686	Yes	31	$22,048	
Yes		Yes	Yes		15,660†	8,750		520	Yes			None
Yes		Yes	Yes		20,300	10,750	8	570	Yes	24	$12,684	None
Yes			Yes		20,280	10,650	9	666	Yes			3/10
Yes	Yes	Yes	Yes	Yes	15,402‡	11,848	15					
Yes	Yes	Yes	Yes	Yes	22,316†	10,458		671	Yes	607	$4,284	None
			No		12,831†	4,624	18	416	Yes			None
Yes			No		12,861†	4,252		415	Yes	2	$200	3/1
			No		12,906†	6,630	18	416	Yes	2	$1,558	None
Yes	Yes	Yes	Yes	Yes	13,918†	4,512	12	450	Yes	34	$6,004	3/1
Yes	Yes		No		12,913†	5,130	12	416	Yes	4	$1,862	
Yes	Yes	Yes	Yes	Yes	14,666†	9,722	12	463	Yes	52	$7,284	
Yes	Yes	Yes	Yes	Yes	18,905†	11,892	12	609	Yes	138	$4,461	None
Yes	Yes		Yes	Yes	19,376	9,254	12	692	Yes			3/1
			Yes			900						
Yes			No		5,653†	8,992	18	186	Yes			None
Yes			No		5,653†	8,992	18	186	Yes			None
Yes			No		5,653†	8,992	18	186	Yes			None
Yes			No		5,653†	8,992	18	186	Yes			None
Yes			No		5,653†	8,992	18	186	Yes			None
Yes			No		5,653†	8,992	18	186	Yes			None
Yes			No		5,653†	8,992	18	186	Yes			None
Yes			No		5,653†	8,992	18	186	Yes			None
Yes			No		5,653†	8,992	18	186	Yes			None
Yes			No		5,653†	8,992	18	186	Yes			None
Yes			No		5,653†	8,992	18	186	Yes			None
Yes			No		5,653†	8,992	18	186	Yes			None
Yes			No		5,653†	8,992	18	186	Yes			None
Yes			No		5,653†	8,992	18	186	Yes			None
Yes			No		5,653†	8,992	18	186	Yes			None
					10,200	1,545						
			No		9,813†							
Yes	Yes		Yes	Yes	22,700	13,550	12	670	Yes			None

† Tuition and fees are for 2007-08.   ‡ Tuition and fees are projected for 2008-09.   * Comprehensive Fee

Institution	Control/ degrees	Undergraduates		Tests required (Fall 2009)	TOEFL		Application	
		Total	Internat'l		minimum	average	Deadline	Fee
Marian College	Pr/AB	1,906		TOEFL	530		7/1	20
National College: Indianapolis	Pr/AB							30
Oakland City University	Pr/AB	1,492	33	TOEFL, SAT/ACT	500	510	None	50
Purdue University	Pu/AB	30,952	2,024	TOEFL	550		3/1	30
Purdue University Calumet	Pu/AB	8,097	223	TOEFL	550	577	5/1	
Purdue University North Central	Pu/AB	3,512		TOEFL	550		5/1	
Rose-Hulman Institute of Technology	Pr/B	1,821	28	TOEFL, SAT/ACT	550	595	3/1	40
St. Mary-of-the-Woods College	Pr/AB	1,279	3	TOEFL	500	534	None	50
Saint Mary's College	Pr/B	1,591	7	TOEFL	500	550	None	30
Taylor University	Pr/AB	1,858	31	TOEFL, SAT/ACT	550		None	25
Taylor University Fort Wayne	Pr/AB	363		TOEFL	550		None	20
Tri-State University	Pr/AB	1,265		TOEFL	550		6/1	
University of Evansville	Pr/AB	2,539	157	TOEFL	500		7/15	50
University of Indianapolis	Pr/AB	3,474	158	TOEFL, SAT/ACT	500	555	None	25
University of Notre Dame	Pr/B	8,369	243	TOEFL, SAT/ACT	600		12/31	65
University of Southern Indiana	Pu/AB	9,008	130	TOEFL	525		5/1	25
University of St. Francis	Pr/AB	1,789		TOEFL	500		None	20
Valparaiso University	Pr/AB	2,834	75	TOEFL, SAT/ACT	550		5/1	50
Vincennes University	Pu/AB	8,203	80	TOEFL	528		None	20
Wabash College	Pr/B	910	43	TOEFL, SAT/ACT	550	635	2/1	30

Iowa

Institution	Control/ degrees	Total	Internat'l	Tests required	minimum	average	Deadline	Fee
AIB College of Business	Pr/AB	956		TOEFL	550		5/1	25
Ashford University	Pr/AB	9,805	26	TOEFL	420		8/15	20
Briar Cliff University	Pr/AB	1,074	5	TOEFL, SAT	500		7/1	20
Buena Vista University	Pr/B	1,022	10	TOEFL	550		8/1	
Central College	Pr/B	1,452		TOEFL	530	560	None	25
Clarke College	Pr/AB	1,008		TOEFL, SAT/ACT	527		7/1	25
Clinton Community College	Pu/A	996	4	TOEFL	500	530	8/25	
Coe College	Pr/B	1,298		TOEFL, SAT/ACT	500	550	3/1	30
Cornell College	Pr/B	1,075	33	TOEFL	550	618	5/1	30
Des Moines Area Community College	Pu/A	18,320	144	TOEFL	500		6/8	100
Divine Word College	Pr/AB			TOEFL	550		7/15	25
Drake University	Pr/B	3,362	246	TOEFL, SAT/ACT	530	545	None	25
Ellsworth Community College	Pu/A			TOEFL	500		7/30	
Faith Baptist Bible College and Theological Seminary	Pr/AB	320	1	TOEFL	500		1/1	25
Graceland University	Pr/B	1,698	157	TOEFL	450	504	None	50
Grand View College	Pr/AB	1,680	13	TOEFL, SAT/ACT	550		6/15	35
Grinnell College	Pr/B	1,623	183	TOEFL, SAT/ACT	550		1/20	30
Hamilton Technical College	Pr/AB							25
Hawkeye Community College	Pu/A	4,434	15	TOEFL	500		None	
Indian Hills Community College	Pu/A	3,019	17				None	
Iowa Central Community College	Pu/A	5,731		TOEFL	450		None	
Iowa Lakes Community College	Pu/A	1,982		TOEFL	500		7/1	
Iowa State University	Pu/B	20,613	656	TOEFL	500	530	7/1	50
Iowa Wesleyan College	Pr/B	833		TOEFL, SAT/ACT	500		8/15	
Iowa Western Community College	Pu/A	5,300		TOEFL	525		None	
Kaplan University: Cedar Falls	Pr/AB			TOEFL	477			100
Kaplan University: Cedar Rapids	Pr/AB	542		TOEFL	525		None	25
Kaplan University: Davenport	Pr/AB			TOEFL	477		None	25
Kaplan University: Des Moines	Pr/AB	728		TOEFL	477		None	100
Kaplan University: Mason City	Pr/AB	296		TOEFL	525			20

Student services			Housing		Academic year costs		Maximum credits/ summer	Credit hour charge	International financial aid			
Adviser	Orien- tation	ESL	Academic year	Summer	Tuition/ fees	Living costs			Avail- able	Number receiving aid	Average award	Deadline
Yes			Yes	Yes	20,800 † 9,585	9,360	9	870 212	Yes	9	$8,005	3/10
Yes	Yes		Yes	Yes	14,820 †	10,400	15	482	Yes			3/1
Yes	Yes		Yes	Yes	22,224 †	10,982	9	723	Yes	139	$2,108	
Yes	Yes	Yes	Yes	Yes	12,797 †	1,050	9	409				
			No		13,593 †	5,468	9	434		2	$3,609	
Yes	Yes		Yes	Yes	32,826	11,868	16	939	Yes	26	$3,636	None
Yes	Yes		Yes	Yes	21,550	13,240	12	396	Yes	24	$17,544	None
Yes	Yes		Yes	Yes	28,212	12,338	6	1091	Yes	5	$34,472	None
Yes	Yes		Yes		24,546	7,252	12	691	Yes	30	$12,922	3/10
Yes	Yes		Yes	Yes	21,164	8,210	12		Yes	4	$8,535	None
Yes	Yes	Yes	Yes	Yes	23,450	11,400	18	730	Yes	8	$8,164	3/10
Yes	Yes	Yes	Yes	Yes	25,845	10,970	9	690	Yes	104	$15,112	None
Yes	Yes	Yes	Yes	Yes	20,470	12,000		847	Yes	48		
Yes	Yes		Yes	Yes	36,847	12,078		1514	Yes	93	$26,297	2/15
Yes		Yes	Yes	Yes	12,154 ‡	10,998	12	378				
Yes			Yes	Yes	20,720	9,350	12	625				
Yes	Yes	Yes	Yes	Yes	26,950	12,460	14	620	Yes	23	$15,044	None
Yes	Yes	Yes	Yes	Yes	9,932 ‡	10,636	12	327	Yes			5/1
Yes	Yes		Yes	Yes	27,950	10,300			Yes			3/1
			Yes		12,120	5,676	12	220	Yes			None
Yes		Yes	Yes	Yes	15,890 †	7,400	6	447	Yes	5	$14,311	
Yes	Yes		Yes	Yes	21,510	10,646	10	696	Yes	2	$12,500	None
Yes	Yes	Yes	Yes	Yes	24,796	9,514	12	833	Yes			None
Yes	Yes		Yes	Yes	23,944	11,006	17	818	Yes	22	$7,582	None
Yes	Yes	Yes	Yes	Yes	22,378	10,174	9	550	Yes			None
Yes		Yes	No		4,590 †	11,846	12	153				
Yes	Yes	Yes	Yes	Yes	27,720	11,290	2		Yes			None
Yes	Yes		Yes		27,860	9,596		865	Yes	31	$20,214	3/1
Yes	Yes	Yes	No		6,120 †	9,332		204				
		Yes	Yes		10,500	4,100		347	Yes			None
Yes	Yes	Yes	Yes	Yes	24,872	14,120	16	450	Yes	218	$12,348	None
Yes			Yes	Yes	4,905 †	7,330	15	140				None
Yes			Yes	Yes	12,706	5,010	8	450	Yes			None
Yes	Yes	Yes	Yes	Yes	17,900 †	10,925	6	560	Yes			None
Yes	Yes		Yes	Yes	18,554	9,814		475	Yes	13	$11,664	None
Yes	Yes		Yes		35,428	11,222		1092	Yes	166	$25,203	2/1
			No						Yes			None
Yes	Yes		No		6,810 †	18,853	9	216				
Yes		Yes	Yes	Yes	5,310	7,961	15	177				
Yes			Yes	Yes	5,235	8,500	10	164				
Yes			Yes	Yes	3,942 †	6,300	12	117	Yes			None
Yes	Yes	Yes	Yes	Yes	16,919 †	11,024	12	672	Yes	156	$3,346	None
Yes			Yes	Yes	20,000	7,040	14	495	Yes			None
Yes	Yes	Yes	Yes	Yes	5,280 †	10,540	12	159	Yes			None
			No		11,250 †			375	Yes			None
			No		13,532 †	4,509		375	Yes			None
Yes			No		13,680 †	9,180	16	380				
			No		13,482 †	4,100	16	300				
			No									

† Tuition and fees are for 2007-08.   ‡ Tuition and fees are projected for 2008-09.   * Comprehensive Fee

Institution	Control/ degrees	Undergraduates		Tests required (Fall 2009)	TOEFL		Application	
		Total	Internat'l		minimum	average	Deadline	Fee
Kirkwood Community College . . . . .Pu/A	Pu/A	15,091		TOEFL	500	515	None	
Loras College . . . . .Pr/AB	Pr/AB	1,500	44	TOEFL	550		None	25
Luther College . . . . .Pr/B	Pr/B	2,405	90	TOEFL	550	566	6/1	25
Maharishi University of Management . . . . .Pr/B	Pr/B	199	34				8/1	30
Marshalltown Community College . . . . .Pu/A	Pu/A			TOEFL	400	500	8/20	100
Morningside College .Pr/B	Pr/B	1,181	16	TOEFL	450		8/15	25
Mount Mercy College .Pr/B	Pr/B	1,480		TOEFL, SAT/ACT	550		6/1	20
Muscatine Community College . . . . .Pu/A	Pu/A	1,355	5	TOEFL	500	530	8/1	
North Iowa Area Community College . . . . .Pu/A	Pu/A	3,100	28	TOEFL	500		None	50
Northeast Iowa Community College . . . . .Pu/A	Pu/A	3,028	9	TOEFL	500		None	
Northwestern College .Pr/B	Pr/B	1,269	32	TOEFL	475	520	None	25
St. Ambrose University . . . . .Pr/B	Pr/B	2,779	23	TOEFL	500	552	6/1	25
St. Luke's College . . . . .Pr/A	Pr/A	148		TOEFL	500		None	100
Scott Community College . . . . .Pu/A	Pu/A	3,954	24	TOEFL	500	530	8/25	
Simpson College . . . . .Pr/B	Pr/B	1,910	15	TOEFL	550		None	
Southeastern Community College: North Campus . . . . .Pu/A	Pu/A	2,404		TOEFL	525		None	
Southwestern Community College . . . . .Pu/A	Pu/A	1,464		TOEFL	500		None	75
University of Dubuque . . . . .Pr/AB	Pr/AB	1,250		TOEFL	500	525	None	25
University of Iowa . . . . .Pu/B	Pu/B	20,207		TOEFL	530		4/1	60
University of Northern Iowa . . . . .Pu/B	Pu/B	10,756	177	TOEFL	550		None	50
Upper Iowa University .Pr/AB	Pr/AB	749		TOEFL	500			15
Waldorf College . . . . .Pr/AB	Pr/AB	630		TOEFL	500	520	7/15	
Wartburg College . . . . .Pr/B	Pr/B	1,764	99	TOEFL	480		None	
Western Iowa Tech Community College . . . . .Pu/A	Pu/A	2,444		TOEFL	550		None	10
William Penn University . . . . .Pr/AB	Pr/AB	1,833		TOEFL	500		7/1	50
Kansas								
Allen County Community College . . . . .Pu/A	Pu/A	2,800		TOEFL	520		None	25
Baker University . . . . .Pr/B	Pr/B	911	12	TOEFL	525		7/1	
Barclay College . . . . .Pr/AB	Pr/AB	114		TOEFL			None	10
Barton County Community College . . . . .Pu/A	Pu/A	3,057		TOEFL	500		5/1	150
Benedictine College . . . . .Pr/AB	Pr/AB	1,306	38	TOEFL, SAT/ACT	535		None	25
Bethany College . . . . .Pr/B	Pr/B	520	18	TOEFL, SAT, SAT Subject Test(s), or ACT	525		4/15	20
Bethel College . . . . .Pr/B	Pr/B	541	57	TOEFL	540	620	None	20
Butler County Community College . . . . .Pu/A	Pu/A	5,290	178	TOEFL	500	514	6/15	
Central Christian College of Kansas . . . . .Pr/AB	Pr/AB	307	10	TOEFL, SAT/ACT	500	525	4/1	25
Cloud County Community College . . . . .Pu/A	Pu/A	2,858		TOEFL	550		None	
Coffeyville Community College . . . . .Pu/A	Pu/A	1,375		TOEFL		450	None	100
Colby Community College . . . . .Pu/A	Pu/A	594	19	TOEFL	500		7/1	100
Cowley County Community College . . . . .Pu/A	Pu/A	4,280	39	TOEFL	500		None	
Dodge City Community College . . . . .Pu/A	Pu/A			TOEFL	500		7/31	50
Donnelly College . . . . .Pr/AB	Pr/AB		52	TOEFL	500		None	250
Emporia State University . . . . .Pu/B	Pu/B	4,240	221	TOEFL	450	550	6/1	50
Fort Hays State University . . . . .Pu/AB	Pu/AB	7,926	2,382	TOEFL	500		7/1	35
Friends University . . . . .Pr/AB	Pr/AB	2,228		TOEFL	470		7/31	40
Garden City Community College . . . . .Pu/A	Pu/A			TOEFL	500		7/1	150
Haskell Indian Nations University . . . . .Pu/AB	Pu/AB							10
Hesston College . . . . .Pr/A	Pr/A	420	35	TOEFL	500	510	None	15
Hutchinson Community College . . . . .Pu/A	Pu/A	3,447	16	TOEFL	500	530	7/1	
Independence Community College . . . . .Pu/A	Pu/A	1,143		TOEFL	400	490	None	50
Kansas City Kansas Community College . . . . .Pu/A	Pu/A	4,339	102	TOEFL	520		6/1	85
Kansas State University . . . . .Pu/AB	Pu/AB	18,235	366	TOEFL	550		6/1	55

90

Student services			Housing		Academic year costs		Maximum credits/ summer	Credit hour charge	International financial aid			
Adviser	Orientation	ESL	Academic year	Summer	Tuition/ fees	Living costs			Available	Number receiving aid	Average award	Deadline
Yes	Yes	Yes	No		6,420	2,580	8	214	Yes			None
Yes	Yes	Yes	Yes	Yes	24,438	8,677	9	465	Yes	41	$12,383	None
Yes	Yes		Yes	Yes	31,707	8,480	8	1104	Yes	82	$22,143	None
Yes	Yes		Yes	Yes	24,430	10,280		550	Yes	30	$12,752	7/30
Yes	Yes	Yes	Yes		4,890 †	4,935	12	140				
Yes	Yes	Yes	Yes	Yes	20,010 †	9,266			Yes	16	$9,139	None
Yes			Yes		20,070	10,454	16	585	Yes	4	$9,800	None
Yes		Yes	Yes		4,590 †	4,290	12	153				
	Yes		Yes	Yes	4,861 †	7,077		149	Yes			None
		Yes	No		4,050 ‡	10,495	9					
Yes	Yes	Yes	Yes	Yes	22,950	11,906	8		Yes			6/30
Yes	Yes		Yes	Yes	21,610	9,950	18	672	Yes	11	$13,521	None
			No		13,725	11,274	9	375	Yes			None
Yes	Yes	Yes	No		4,590 †	11,846	12	153				
Yes	Yes		Yes	Yes	24,771	10,523	12	275	Yes	15	$20,432	None
Yes		Yes	Yes		3,570 †		6	119				
Yes			Yes	Yes	4,934 †	7,248	12	155	Yes			None
Yes	Yes	Yes	Yes	Yes	19,180 †	10,770	12	425	Yes			None
Yes	Yes	Yes	Yes	Yes	19,465 †	11,985	12	816	Yes	147	$8,816	None
Yes	Yes	Yes	Yes	Yes	14,282 †	10,285	12	561	Yes	50	$5,359	None
Yes	Yes		Yes	Yes	19,625 †	9,675	6		Yes			None
Yes	Yes	Yes	Yes	Yes	19,504	10,271	17	442	Yes			None
Yes	Yes		Yes	Yes	26,160	8,155	4	910	Yes	76	$12,032	None
Yes		Yes	Yes	Yes	4,455 ‡	9,350	12	133				
Yes	Yes		Yes	Yes	18,034	11,162	12		Yes			
Yes			Yes		4,350 †	7,270	9	129				
Yes	Yes		Yes	Yes	19,965	12,480	14	600	Yes			None
Yes			Yes		12,300 †	9,000	6	350	Yes			7/15
Yes		Yes	Yes	Yes	4,350 †	9,226	12	127				
Yes	Yes	Yes	Yes	Yes	18,800	13,600			Yes			None
Yes	Yes		Yes	Yes	18,124	9,650	12	300	Yes	17	$9,512	None
Yes	Yes		Yes		18,900	10,300	15	680	Yes	7	$12,606	None
Yes	Yes	Yes	Yes		5,843 †	8,150	9	180	Yes			None
Yes	Yes		Yes		16,000	9,000		450	Yes	10	$3,865	None
		Yes	Yes		2,970 †	6,790	9	99				
Yes		Yes	Yes	Yes	2,925 †	6,075	9	65				
Yes			Yes	Yes	3,924 †	7,188	14	102				
Yes		Yes	Yes		5,170 †	5,850	12	151				
Yes		Yes	Yes		4,350 †	6,810	12	100	Yes			None
Yes	Yes	Yes	No	Yes	4,900 †	12,290	6	175	Yes			
Yes	Yes	Yes	Yes	Yes	11,976 †	10,178	12	373	Yes			None
Yes	Yes	Yes	Yes	Yes	10,543 †	9,814		351	Yes			None
Yes	Yes		Yes	Yes	18,320 ‡	10,066	12	607	Yes			None
Yes			Yes	Yes	2,580 †	8,180	12	65	Yes			None
			Yes			220						
Yes	Yes	Yes	Yes		17,416 †	10,080	9		Yes			None
Yes			Yes	Yes	3,353 †	8,040	9	97				
Yes		Yes	Yes		4,125 †	4,700	9	110	Yes			None
Yes		Yes	No		4,710 †	15,675		147				
Yes	Yes	Yes	Yes	Yes	15,970 †	10,785	6	512				

† Tuition and fees are for 2007-08.   ‡ Tuition and fees are projected for 2008-09.   * Comprehensive Fee

Institution	Control/ degrees	Undergraduates		Tests required (Fall 2009)	TOEFL		Application	
		Total	Internat'l		minimum	average	Deadline	Fee
Kansas Wesleyan University	Pr/AB			TOEFL	500		None	30
Labette Community College	Pu/A	934	13	TOEFL	520		None	40
Manhattan Area Technical College	Pu/A			TOEFL	490		None	40
McPherson College	Pr/B	531	2	TOEFL	550		6/1	50
MidAmerica Nazarene University	Pr/AB	1,283	23	TOEFL, SAT/ACT	550		5/15	25
Neosho County Community College	Pu/A	1,994		TOEFL			6/1	50
Newman University	Pr/AB	1,116	66	TOEFL	600		7/15	40
North Central Kansas Technical College	Pu/A						None	50
Ottawa University	Pr/B			TOEFL	530	540	None	15
Pittsburg State University	Pu/AB	5,824	314	TOEFL	520	575	6/1	50
Pratt Community College	Pu/A	778	24	TOEFL	500	515	7/1	
Southwestern College	Pr/B	1,415	18	TOEFL	550	576	8/1	20
Sterling College	Pr/B	569	4	TOEFL	520		6/1	25
Tabor College	Pr/AB	561		TOEFL	525	530	8/1	30
University of Kansas	Pu/B	19,943	598				4/1	75
University of Kansas Medical Center	Pu/B	512	7	TOEFL				60
University of St. Mary	Pr/AB	475	2	TOEFL, SAT/ACT	500		6/9	25
Washburn University	Pu/AB	5,675		TOEFL	520		6/15	60
Wichita State University	Pu/AB	10,261	563	TOEFL	530	567	7/1	50

Kentucky

Institution	Control/ degrees	Undergraduates		Tests required (Fall 2009)	TOEFL		Application	
		Total	Internat'l		minimum	average	Deadline	Fee
Alice Lloyd College	Pr/B	607	1	TOEFL	550	575	3/1	
Ashland Community and Technical College	Pu/A			TOEFL, ACT	500		8/20	
Bellarmine University	Pr/B	2,032	48	TOEFL	550		5/1	25
Berea College	Pr/B	1,528	106	TOEFL	500		3/1	
Bluegrass Community and Technical College	Pu/A	11,617		TOEFL	500			
Brescia University	Pr/AB	553		TOEFL	550		None	75
Brown Mackie College: North Kentucky	Pr/A	474						
Campbellsville University	Pr/AB	1,549	82	TOEFL, SAT/ACT	500	600	7/15	20
Centre College	Pr/B	1,184	23	TOEFL, SAT/ACT	580	621	3/1	40
Daymar College: Louisville	Pr/A	344						
Eastern Kentucky University	Pu/AB	12,996		TOEFL, SAT/ACT	500	525	7/15	30
Georgetown College	Pr/B	1,335	15	TOEFL	520		6/1	30
Hazard Community College	Pu/A			TOEFL, SAT/ACT	500		None	
Henderson Community College	Pu/A	2,053		TOEFL, ACT	500		None	
Jefferson Community and Technical College	Pu/A	11,205		TOEFL, ACT	500		None	
Kentucky Christian University	Pr/B	570	19	TOEFL	550		None	30
Kentucky Mountain Bible College	Pr/AB	59		TOEFL	500		6/1	25
Kentucky State University	Pu/AB	2,201	28	TOEFL, SAT/ACT	525		None	100
Lindsey Wilson College	Pr/AB	1,562	76	TOEFL	500		9/1	
Louisville Technical Institute	Pr/AB	583		TOEFL	500	560	None	100
Maysville Community and Technical College	Pu/A			TOEFL, ACT	500		8/1	5
Mid-Continent University	Pr/AB	1,541	52	TOEFL	500		7/1	35
Midway College	Pr/AB	1,395	1	TOEFL	530		None	25
Morehead State University	Pu/AB	6,863	29	TOEFL, SAT/ACT	500	535	None	55
Murray State University	Pu/AB	7,749	114	TOEFL	500		8/1	30
National College: Danville	Pr/A						None	125
National College: Florence	Pr/A							125
National College: Lexington	Pr/A						None	125
Northern Kentucky University	Pu/AB	12,058	152	TOEFL	500	540	6/1	25
Owensboro Community and Technical College	Pu/A	2,802	1	TOEFL, ACT	500		None	
St. Catharine College	Pr/AB	671		TOEFL	425	430		15
Somerset Community College	Pu/A			TOEFL, ACT	500		None	

| Student services | | | Housing | | Academic year costs | | Maximum credits/summer | Credit hour charge | International financial aid | | | |
Adviser	Orientation	ESL	Academic year	Summer	Tuition/ fees	Living costs			Available	Number receiving aid	Average award	Deadline
Yes		Yes	Yes		17,400 †	7,700	6					
Yes					2,880 †	6,240	12	67				
					2,250 †				Yes			None
Yes	Yes		Yes		17,200	12,110	12		Yes	2	$10,450	None
Yes	Yes		Yes	Yes	18,216	10,048	15	576	Yes	20	$10,587	None
Yes	Yes	Yes	Yes	Yes	5,070 †	7,920	12	113				
Yes	Yes		Yes	Yes	17,988 †	10,841	12	589	Yes			None
			Yes		3,171 †	5,525			Yes			None
Yes	Yes		Yes	Yes	17,350 †	9,730	12	565	Yes			None
Yes	Yes	Yes	Yes	Yes	11,866 †	9,188	12	368				
Yes	Yes		Yes	Yes	3,480 †	12,821	8	87	Yes			8/1
Yes	Yes		Yes	Yes	18,700	11,736		775	Yes	17	$10,217	8/15
			Yes		16,700	7,530			Yes	4	$2,068	None
Yes			Yes		17,650 †	12,550		720	Yes	6	$13,010	8/30
Yes	Yes	Yes	Yes	Yes	17,556 †	10,714		560	Yes	69	$1,869	None
Yes	Yes		No		15,701 †	20,421		512				
Yes	Yes		Yes	Yes	18,120 ‡	10,076	12	580	Yes	2	$5,000	None
Yes	Yes	Yes	Yes	Yes	12,686 †	12,311	6	420	Yes			None
Yes	Yes	Yes	Yes	Yes	12,151 †	13,860		375	Yes	36	$857	None
Yes			Yes		8,250 †	16,732		212	Yes	1	$1,648	None
			No		10,350 †	450	14	345	Yes			None
Yes	Yes		Yes	Yes	28,030	8,406		640	Yes	44	$18,330	None
Yes	Yes	Yes	Yes	Yes		5,294	6		Yes	106	$30,881	None
Yes	Yes	Yes	Yes	Yes	10,350 †	8,854		345	Yes			None
Yes	Yes	Yes	Yes	Yes	15,440	10,550	9	475	Yes			8/23
					8,805 †	1,380		189				
Yes	Yes	Yes	Yes	Yes	17,260 †	9,860	12	703	Yes	63	$10,525	None
Yes	Yes		Yes	Yes	37,000 *	3,500		1070	Yes	22	$25,936	3/1
						950						
Yes	Yes	Yes	Yes	Yes	15,382 †	7,829	12	641	Yes	73		
Yes			Yes	Yes	24,150	10,230	14	1000	Yes			8/1
			No		10,350 †	8,480	6	345				
			No		10,350 †	500	9	345				
Yes	Yes	ESL	No		10,350 †	6,640	6	345				
Yes			Yes		12,120	5,298		399	Yes	19	$12,117	None
Yes			Yes	Yes	5,940	8,250		180	Yes	5	$2,210	6/30
Yes	Yes	Yes	Yes	Yes	12,490 †	6,340	6	450	Yes			6/30
Yes	Yes		Yes		16,670	10,050	12	685	Yes			None
			Yes	Yes		13,769	20		Yes			None
			No		10,350 †	6,300	9	345	Yes			None
Yes			Yes	Yes	13,100	11,325	12	395	Yes			5/30
Yes			Yes	Yes	15,750 †	10,900	12	525	Yes			8/1
Yes	Yes		Yes	Yes	13,340 †	7,070	12	560	Yes	4		None
Yes	Yes	Yes	Yes	Yes	14,718 †	7,658		613	Yes	114	$10,939	None
			No		9,090 †	1,200		202				
			No		9,090 †	1,200		202				
			No		9,090 †	1,200		202				
			Yes	Yes	10,776 †	9,549	15	449				
			No		10,350 †	7,415	10	345	Yes			None
Yes	Yes		Yes		12,008 †	8,580	9	450				
			No		10,350 †	3,240	10	345	Yes			

† Tuition and fees are for 2007-08.   ‡ Tuition and fees are projected for 2008-09.   * Comprehensive Fee

Institution	Control/ degrees	Undergraduates		Tests required (Fall 2009)	TOEFL		Application	
		Total	Internat'l		minimum	average	Deadline	Fee
Southeast Kentucky Community and Technical College	Pu/A	2,061		TOEFL, ACT	500		None	
Southwestern College: Florence	Pr/A	342						20
Spencerian College: Lexington	Pr/A	646					None	90
Sullivan University	Pr/AB	4,201		TOEFL, SAT/ACT	500		9/1	100
Thomas More College	Pr/AB	1,293	6	TOEFL	515		8/15	25
Transylvania University	Pr/B	1,153		TOEFL	550	570	2/1	30
Union College	Pr/B	694	35	TOEFL, SAT/ACT	550		6/1	20
University of the Cumberlands	Pr/B	1,463	54	TOEFL, SAT/ACT	550		6/1	100
University of Kentucky	Pu/B	18,770		TOEFL	527	579	2/15	40
University of Louisville	Pu/AB	14,101	173	TOEFL, SAT/ACT	550		7/1	40
Western Kentucky University	Pu/AB	15,502	220	TOEFL, SAT/ACT	525		4/1	35
Louisiana								
Baton Rouge Community College	Pu/A	5,889		TOEFL	500			7
Bossier Parish Community College	Pu/A	4,227	5	TOEFL	450		7/6	25
Centenary College of Louisiana	Pr/B	854		TOEFL	550		6/1	30
Delgado Community College	Pu/A	13,217	68		500		7/1	25
Delta School of Business & Technology	Pr/A							
Dillard University	Pr/B	956		TOEFL, SAT/ACT	550		6/1	50
Grambling State University	Pu/AB	4,747	326	TOEFL, SAT/ACT	450		7/15	30
ITI Technical College	Pr/A	323					None	
Louisiana College	Pr/AB	1,056		TOEFL, ACT	550	600	None	25
Louisiana State University and Agricultural and Mechanical College	Pu/B	23,063	359	TOEFL, SAT/ACT	550	603	4/15	40
Louisiana State University at Eunice	Pu/A	2,864		TOEFL, ACT	500	550	5/15	20
Louisiana State University Health Sciences Center	Pu/AB	573						50
Louisiana State University in Shreveport	Pu/B	3,556		TOEFL, ACT	500		5/15	20
Louisiana Tech University	Pu/AB	8,375		TOEFL	500		6/1	30
Loyola University New Orleans	Pr/B	2,591	68	TOEFL, SAT/ACT	550		5/1	20
McNeese State University	Pu/AB	7,041	206	TOEFL, SAT/ACT	500		5/15	30
Nicholls State University	Pu/AB	6,118	78	TOEFL, SAT/ACT	500		7/17	30
Northwestern State University	Pu/AB	7,677	42	TOEFL, SAT/ACT	500		7/6	30
Nunez Community College	Pu/A	847					12/1	20
Remington College: Baton Rouge	Pr/A	410						50
Remington College: Lafayette	Pr/A	363					None	50
St. Joseph Seminary College	Pr/B	77		TOEFL, ACT	520		None	
School of Urban Missions: New Orleans	Pr/AB	20		TOEFL	550		7/31	20
South Louisiana Community College	Pu/A	2,944						5
Southeastern Louisiana University	Pu/AB	13,253	114	TOEFL, SAT/ACT	500		6/1	30
Southern University and Agricultural and Mechanical College	Pu/AB	6,830	112	TOEFL	500		5/1	30
Southern University at New Orleans	Pu/AB	2,139	33	TOEFL, SAT/ACT	500		7/1	15
Southern University at Shreveport	Pu/A	2,403					6/30	15
Southwest University	Pr/AB							50
Tulane University		6,408		TOEFL, SAT/ACT	550		1/15	
University of Louisiana at Lafayette	Pu/B	14,449	226	TOEFL	525	533	6/1	30
University of Louisiana at Monroe	Pu/AB	7,262	91	TOEFL, SAT/ACT	500		3/1	30
University of New Orleans	Pu/B	8,653	267	TOEFL	525		6/1	40
Xavier University of Louisiana	Pr/B	2,316	60	TOEFL, SAT/ACT	550		3/1	25
Maine								
Andover College	Pr/A	1,062		TOEFL	477		None	100
Bates College	Pr/B	1,660	88	TOEFL			1/1	60
Bowdoin College	Pr/B	1,710	51	TOEFL	600		1/1	60
Central Maine Community College	Pu/A	1,881		TOEFL	500		None	20

Student services			Housing		Academic year costs		Maximum credits/ summer	Credit hour charge	International financial aid			
Adviser	Orientation	ESL	Academic year	Summer	Tuition/ fees	Living costs			Available	Number receiving aid	Average award	Deadline
Yes			No		10,350 †	4,414	10	345	Yes			None
			No		10,900 †							
			Yes	Yes		11,804	20					
			Yes			7,639	20		Yes			None
Yes	Yes		Yes	Yes	22,220	12,070	12	515	Yes	7	$9,246	None
Yes			Yes		23,810	9,950	2		Yes	1	$5,500	None
			Yes	Yes	16,820	5,750	15	280	Yes	33	$12,913	None
	Yes	Yes	Yes	Yes	14,658	10,426	7	460	Yes	54	$10,278	None
Yes	Yes	Yes	Yes	Yes	14,896 †	8,117	15	607	Yes			None
Yes	Yes	Yes	Yes	Yes	17,734 †	5,722	17	739				
Yes	Yes	Yes	Yes	Yes	15,470 †	8,964	15	645	Yes	53	$9,760	None
Yes					4,614 †	4,361						
Yes			No		3,900 †	12,238			Yes			7/1
Yes			Yes		21,630	11,030	12	700	Yes	17		None
Yes	Yes	Yes	No		4,908 †	12,022	9					
			No			800						
Yes	Yes		Yes		12,240 †	11,316	9	490	Yes			5/1
Yes			Yes	Yes	8,972 †	9,761	14		Yes			6/1
			No									
Yes	Yes		Yes	Yes	11,490 †	6,241	14	340	Yes			None
Yes	Yes	Yes	Yes	Yes	12,843 †	11,020	12		Yes	324	$9,266	None
Yes			No		5,192 †	12,095	10		Yes			None
Yes	Yes	Yes	Yes	Yes	7,110 †	2,210						
			Yes	Yes	7,847 †	12,670	10					
Yes		Yes	Yes		10,893 †	7,170	12		Yes			None
Yes	Yes		Yes	Yes	28,044	11,818	12	775	Yes	43	$9,653	6/1
Yes		Yes	Yes	Yes	9,299 †	10,030	12		Yes			None
Yes	Yes		Yes	Yes	9,043 †	8,423	12		Yes	15	$6,007	None
Yes			Yes		9,606 †	5,850	12		Yes	18	$6,453	None
		Yes	No		4,290 †	10,204	10					
			No									
			No									
		Yes	Yes		12,769	13,971			Yes			None
			Yes	Yes	7,105 ‡	9,177	6	220	Yes			None
					2,229 †							
Yes	Yes	Yes	Yes	Yes	9,561 †	6,110	10	342	Yes	103	$6,550	None
Yes	Yes		Yes	Yes	9,458 †	10,925	10					
Yes	Yes		No		6,742 †	9,400	10					
			No		3,382 †	2,300	10					
			No		5,500			175				
Yes	Yes	Yes	Yes	Yes	36,610 †	10,479	18	1488	Yes	48	$15,950	2/1
Yes	Yes	Yes	Yes	Yes	9,612 †	7,355	10					
Yes	Yes	Yes	Yes	Yes	9,559 †	6,000	6		Yes			None
Yes	Yes	Yes	Yes	Yes	11,028 †	10,082	12	345	Yes	184	$8,116	None
Yes			Yes	Yes	14,700 †	10,467	12	600				
					8,100 †		18	230	Yes			None
Yes	Yes		Yes	Yes	46,800 *	2,050			Yes	75	$41,848	2/1
Yes			Yes	Yes	36,370 †	11,890			Yes	31	$35,354	2/15
		Yes	Yes		5,490 †	9,626		161				

† Tuition and fees are for 2007-08.   ‡ Tuition and fees are projected for 2008-09.   * Comprehensive Fee

Institution	Control/ degrees	Undergraduates		Tests required (Fall 2009)	TOEFL		Application	
		Total	Internat'l		minimum	average	Deadline	Fee
Colby College	Pr/B	1,867	118	TOEFL, SAT/ACT	600	632	1/1	65
College of the Atlantic	Pr/B	327	44	TOEFL	550		2/15	45
Eastern Maine Community College	Pu/A	1,577		TOEFL	500		8/15	20
Husson College	Pr/AB	1,855	15	TOEFL	500		None	25
Kennebec Valley Community College	Pu/A	2,064						20
Maine College of Art	Pr/B	343	1	TOEFL	500		None	40
Maine Maritime Academy	Pu/AB	883		TOEFL	550		7/1	15
New England School of Communications	Pr/AB	393		TOEFL	500		None	15
Northern Maine Community College	Pu/A	901		TOEFL	550			20
St. Joseph's College	Pr/B	1,071		TOEFL	500		4/15	50
Southern Maine Community College	Pu/A	4,947		TOEFL	500			20
Thomas College	Pr/AB	739	1	TOEFL, SAT/ACT	530	600	None	50
Unity College	Pr/AB	552	2	TOEFL	500	530	4/2	50
University of Maine	Pu/B	8,777	139	TOEFL, SAT/ACT	530	572	3/1	40
University of Maine at Augusta	Pu/AB	4,207	2	TOEFL	530		5/1	40
University of Maine at Farmington	Pu/B	2,137	10	TOEFL	550		None	40
University of Maine at Fort Kent	Pu/AB	917	274	TOEFL	500	525	None	40
University of Maine at Machias	Pu/B	554	22	TOEFL	500		None	40
University of New England	Pr/AB	1,985	4	TOEFL	550		5/1	40
University of Southern Maine	Pu/AB	6,603	10	TOEFL	550	564	5/1	40
Washington County Community College	Pu/A	370		TOEFL	500		None	20
York County Community College	Pu/A	889		TOEFL				20
Maryland								
Allegany College of Maryland	Pu/A	2,887		TOEFL	550	570	8/15	
Anne Arundel Community College	Pu/A	14,834		TOEFL	550		7/31	
Baltimore City Community College	Pu/A	6,814					8/1	10
Baltimore Hebrew University	Pr/B			TOEFL			None	50
Baltimore International College	Pr/AB	478		TOEFL			6/15	40
Bowie State University	Pu/B	4,179	31	TOEFL			4/1	40
Capitol College	Pr/AB	360		TOEFL	450	525	8/15	200
Carroll Community College	Pu/A	3,413	4	TOEFL	550		6/15	
Chesapeake College	Pu/A	2,620		TOEFL	500		None	
College of Notre Dame of Maryland	Pr/B	3,402		TOEFL	500		2/15	25
College of Southern Maryland	Pu/A	5,912	28	TOEFL	500		6/15	
Columbia Union College	Pr/AB	876		TOEFL			6/1	25
Community College of Baltimore County	Pu/A	16,097		TOEFL	450		6/1	15
Coppin State University	Pu/B	3,151	127	TOEFL	500		5/1	35
DeVry University: Bethesda	Pr/B	45	1					50
Frostburg State University	Pu/B	4,268	13	TOEFL, SAT	550		6/1	30
Garrett College	Pu/A	777		TOEFL	550		6/1	
Goucher College	Pr/B	1,462	7	TOEFL	550		2/1	40
Griggs University	Pr/AB			TOEFL	250			50
Harford Community College	Pu/A	5,883	45	TOEFL	500		6/1	
Hood College	Pr/B	1,380	27	TOEFL, SAT/ACT	550		2/15	35
Howard Community College	Pu/A	6,702	418	TOEFL	537		6/1	50
Johns Hopkins University	Pr/B	4,578	239	TOEFL, SAT/ACT	600	624	1/1	70
Johns Hopkins University: Peabody Conservatory of Music	Pr/B	318		TOEFL	550		4/1	100
Kaplan College: Hagerstown	Pr/AB	611						20
Loyola College in Maryland	Pr/B	3,542	29	TOEFL, SAT	550		1/15	30
Maryland Institute College of Art	Pr/B	1,668	72	TOEFL	550		2/15	50
McDaniel College	Pr/B	1,687	1	TOEFL	550	667	2/1	50

Student services			Housing		Academic year costs		Maximum credits/ summer	Credit hour charge	International financial aid			
Adviser	Orientation	ESL	Academic year	Summer	Tuition/ fees	Living costs			Available	Number receiving aid	Average award	Deadline
Yes	Yes	Yes	Yes		48,520*	2,100			Yes	128	$41,645	2/1
Yes	Yes		Yes		31,470	10,620		1033	Yes	44	$37,970	2/15
			Yes	Yes	5,745†	9,410	12	161				
Yes			Yes	Yes	12,750	9,210	12	415	Yes	8	$4,693	None
			No		5,370†	737	9	161	Yes			None
			Yes		26,090†	12,990		1059	Yes			None
Yes			Yes	Yes	15,305†	10,000	12		Yes			None
Yes		Yes	Yes	Yes	10,690	10,290	15	320	Yes			
			Yes		5,420†	8,140		161				
			Yes		23,300†	15,300		750	Yes			None
Yes	Yes		Yes	Yes	5,765†	12,008	12	161				
Yes			Yes		19,750	10,970		801	Yes	1	$18,750	None
Yes			Yes		19,620†	8,960		700	Yes			None
Yes	Yes	Yes	Yes	Yes	20,540†	11,062	9	625	Yes	5	$14,372	
Yes			No		13,395†	910	12	421	Yes	2	$15,451	None
Yes	Yes		Yes	Yes	14,837†	10,427	16	444	Yes	7		
Yes		Yes	Yes	Yes	13,440†	10,285	9	426	Yes			None
Yes			Yes		14,800†	9,570		471	Yes			None
			Yes		25,290†	13,130		880	Yes			None
Yes	Yes	Yes	Yes	Yes	17,140†	11,624		547	Yes			None
			Yes		5,420†	5,151		161				
			No		5,480†	6,200		161	Yes			None
Yes		Yes	Yes	Yes	6,490†	7,281	8	208	Yes			None
Yes	Yes	Yes	No		9,040†	10,800	7	292				
Yes		Yes	No		5,422‡	900	12		Yes			None
Yes			No		11,250‡	7,600	6	467				
			Yes	Yes		12,230	18					
Yes	Yes		Yes	Yes	15,629†	10,451	12	589	Yes	1	$1,500	3/1
Yes		Yes	Yes	Yes	19,404†	8,458	12	602	Yes			None
		Yes	No		6,788†	6,200						
		Yes	No		7,494†	12,620	9	234				
Yes	Yes	Yes	Yes	Yes	25,750	10,900	9	390	Yes			None
Yes	Yes		No		7,524†	7,950	6	209	Yes			None
Yes		Yes	Yes	Yes	19,350	8,159	6		Yes			3/31
Yes	Yes	Yes	No		7,396†	1,000	12	236	Yes			3/1
Yes	Yes		Yes		12,753†	10,884	9	388				
					14,440†	8,528		525				
Yes	Yes		Yes	Yes	16,162†	8,396	12	411				
Yes	Yes		Yes		7,590	10,900	6	232	Yes			3/1
Yes	Yes		Yes		32,636	12,234		1075	Yes	3	$17,166	2/15
					8,540†			280				
Yes	Yes		No		7,347‡	10,300	6	237	Yes	23	$1,382	None
Yes	Yes		Yes	Yes	26,580	11,980		755	Yes	27	$19,983	None
Yes	Yes	Yes	No		8,193‡	14,054	12		Yes			
Yes	Yes		Yes	Yes	38,200	14,378		1260	Yes	26	$26,959	3/1
Yes	Yes		Yes		34,060	12,625		940	Yes			2/1
			Yes			7,325						
Yes	Yes		Yes	Yes	36,240	10,120	12	580				
Yes	Yes		Yes	Yes	32,680	13,050	9	1318	Yes			3/1
Yes	Yes		Yes		30,780	7,850	12	962	Yes			None

† Tuition and fees are for 2007-08.   ‡ Tuition and fees are projected for 2008-09.   * Comprehensive Fee

Institution	Control/ degrees	Undergraduates		Tests required (Fall 2009)	TOEFL		Application	
		Total	Internat'l		minimum	average	Deadline	Fee
Morgan State University	Pu/B			TOEFL, SAT/ACT	550	560	4/1	20
Mount St. Mary's University	Pr/B	1,681	13	TOEFL, SAT/ACT	550		6/1	35
National Labor College	Pr/B							50
Prince George's Community College	Pu/A	10,512	540	TOEFL	450		5/1	25
St. John's College	Pr/B	481	2	TOEFL, SAT/ACT	550		None	
St. Mary's College of Maryland	Pu/B	1,922	32	TOEFL, SAT/ACT	550		1/15	40
Salisbury University	Pu/B	6,726	40	TOEFL	550	617	3/1	45
Sojourner-Douglass College	Pr/B	1,246		TOEFL	500		None	25
TESST College of Technology: Baltimore	Pr/A	900						20
TESST College of Technology: Beltsville	Pr/A							
TESST College of Technology: Towson	Pr/A						None	20
Towson University	Pu/B	15,488	434	TOEFL	500	533	6/1	30
University of Baltimore	Pu/B	2,412		TOEFL, SAT/ACT	550		2/15	45
University of Maryland: Baltimore	Pu/B	803	39	TOEFL	550		4/1	50
University of Maryland: Baltimore County	Pu/B	9,304	342	TOEFL	550		11/1	50
University of Maryland: College Park	Pu/B	25,251	515	TOEFL	575	589	12/1	55
University of Maryland: Eastern Shore	Pu/B	3,539	109	TOEFL	500	550	7/15	25
University of Maryland: University College	Pu/AB	19,893	365	TOEFL	550		None	50
Villa Julie College	Pr/B	3,047	25	TOEFL	550		8/1	25
Washington Bible College	Pr/AB	254		TOEFL	550		None	35
Washington College	Pr/B	1,162		TOEFL	500	550	2/15	45
Yeshiva College of the Nations Capital	Pr/B							
Massachusetts								
American International College	Pr/AB	1,510	47	TOEFL	500	520	8/1	25
Amherst College	Pr/B	1,683	120	TOEFL, SAT, SAT Subject Test(s), or ACT	600	670	1/1	55
Anna Maria College	Pr/AB	882	4	TOEFL	470		None	40
Assumption College	Pr/B	2,172	8	TOEFL			2/15	50
Atlantic Union College	Pr/AB	469		TOEFL, SAT/ACT	525	550	7/1	25
Babson College	Pr/B	1,799	321	TOEFL, SAT/ACT	600		1/15	65
Bard College at Simon's Rock	Pr/AB	408		TOEFL			5/31	50
Bay Path College	Pr/AB	1,322	13	TOEFL, SAT/ACT	500		7/1	25
Bay State College	Pr/AB	810		TOEFL	550		8/15	25
Becker College	Pr/AB	1,694		TOEFL	500		None	30
Benjamin Franklin Institute of Technology	Pr/AB	513		TOEFL	500	520	7/15	50
Bentley College	Pr/AB	4,148	311	TOEFL, SAT/ACT	550	604	1/15	75
Berklee College of Music	Pr/B	4,090		TOEFL	500		2/1	150
Berkshire Community College	Pu/A	1,776	38	TOEFL	500		None	35
Boston Architectural College	Pr/B	584		TOEFL				50
Boston College	Pr/B	9,081	192	TOEFL, SAT, SAT Subject Test(s), or ACT	600	630	1/1	70
Boston Conservatory	Pr/B	459		TOEFL	550		2/1	105
Boston University	Pr/B	16,673	1,059	TOEFL, SAT, SAT Subject Test(s), or ACT	550		1/1	75
Brandeis University	Pr/B	3,203	239	TOEFL	600		1/15	55
Bridgewater State College	Pu/B	7,931	82	TOEFL	500	520	2/15	25
Bristol Community College	Pu/A	7,388	13				8/1	35
Bunker Hill Community College	Pu/A	8,806		TOEFL	423		7/2	35
Cambridge College	Pr/B	1,199		TOEFL				30
Cape Cod Community College	Pu/A	4,434		TOEFL	550		5/1	35
Caritas Laboure College	Pr/A	548		TOEFL	550		None	25
Clark University	Pr/B	2,217	181	TOEFL, SAT/ACT	550	605	1/15	55
College of the Holy Cross	Pr/B	2,817	29	TOEFL	550		1/15	50
Curry College	Pr/B	2,641	13	TOEFL, SAT/ACT	500	550	4/1	40

| Student services | | | Housing | | Academic year costs | | Maximum credits/ summer | Credit hour charge | International financial aid | | | |
Adviser	Orientation	ESL	Academic year	Summer	Tuition/ fees	Living costs			Available	Number receiving aid	Average award	Deadline
Yes			Yes		14,438†	11,101	6	481				
Yes			Yes	Yes	27,560	11,420	12	900	Yes	9	$18,662	3/1
Yes		Yes	No		7,670†	700	12	263				
Yes	Yes		Yes		39,154	11,244			Yes	3	$25,203	None
Yes	Yes		Yes		23,454	13,025			Yes			3/1
Yes	Yes		Yes		14,500†	12,454	6	537	Yes			12/31
Yes			No		7,478†	4,000						
Yes	Yes	Yes	Yes	Yes	17,174†	12,761	15	566	Yes	136	$9,085	None
Yes	Yes		No		19,716†	730	6	754	Yes			None
Yes	Yes		Yes		20,261†	6,995		503	Yes			None
Yes	Yes	Yes	Yes	Yes	17,449†	8,658	12	633				
Yes	Yes	Yes	Yes	Yes	22,208†	12,903	16	867				
Yes	Yes		Yes	Yes	12,555†	11,905	6	386	Yes			4/1
Yes			No		11,334†	5,836	18	466				
Yes			Yes		19,200	14,036		455				
Yes			Yes		11,810†	8,750	9	380	Yes	4		3/1
Yes	Yes		Yes		34,005	7,180		1391	Yes			None
			Yes		9,000†	7,000		266				
Yes	Yes	Yes	Yes	Yes	24,100	13,350	12	497	Yes			None
Yes	Yes		Yes		36,232†	12,970			Yes	82	$45,152	
	Yes		Yes		25,850	12,350	18	783	Yes	1	$3,000	None
Yes			Yes	Yes	28,851	12,026	12	956	Yes	7	$17,516	2/1
Yes		Yes	Yes	Yes	16,570	9,100	12		Yes	34	$4,244	None
Yes	Yes		Yes		36,096	13,020	8		Yes			2/15
Yes			Yes		36,550†	12,955	10	1430	Yes			
Yes	Yes	Yes	Yes		23,840	12,050	6	450	Yes			None
Yes	Yes	Yes	Yes	Yes	16,850†	12,450		550				
Yes	Yes		Yes	Yes	24,780	12,530	12	1000				
Yes		ESL	No		12,750†	2,150	17	531				
Yes	Yes		Yes	Yes	34,488	13,620	15		Yes	21	$11,005	2/1
Yes	Yes	Yes	Yes		31,298‡	18,110	16	917	Yes			None
Yes		Yes	No		10,846†	20,260		260				
			No		9,940‡	15,962		826	Yes			None
Yes	Yes		Yes		37,950	15,210	12					
Yes	Yes	Yes	Yes		30,110†	20,950	6	1170	Yes			2/1
Yes	Yes	Yes	Yes	Yes	37,050	15,667	16	1142	Yes	128	$28,306	2/15
Yes	Yes	Yes	Yes	Yes	37,294	12,054	12		Yes	118	$29,441	None
Yes	Yes	Yes	Yes	Yes	12,174†	11,670	6	294				
		Yes	No		9,930†	10,090	15	230				
Yes	Yes		No		9,360†	10,600	12	230	Yes			None
Yes					10,350†			345				
			No		10,126†	8,372	6	230				
Yes			No			800		495	Yes			None
Yes	Yes	Yes	Yes	Yes	32,865†	8,050	8	1019	Yes	134	$21,442	2/1
Yes	Yes		Yes		37,242	12,160						
Yes	Yes		Yes		27,540	13,780	12					

† Tuition and fees are for 2007-08. ‡ Tuition and fees are projected for 2008-09. * Comprehensive Fee

Institution	Control/ degrees	Undergraduates		Tests required (Fall 2009)	TOEFL		Application	
		Total	Internat'l		minimum	average	Deadline	Fee
Dean College	Pr/AB	1,093		TOEFL	500	528	7/31	35
Eastern Nazarene College	Pr/AB	678		TOEFL, SAT/ACT	500		5/1	25
Elms College	Pr/AB	996		TOEFL	450	520	6/15	30
Emerson College	Pr/B	3,293	80	TOEFL	550	611	1/5	65
Emmanuel College	Pr/B	2,139	30	TOEFL, SAT/ACT	550		3/1	40
Endicott College	Pr/AB	2,128		TOEFL	550	597	2/15	40
Fisher College	Pr/AB	589		TOEFL	500	510	None	50
Fitchburg State College	Pu/B	3,605	21	TOEFL, SAT/ACT	550		3/1	40
Framingham State College	Pu/B	3,503	26	TOEFL, SAT/ACT	550	560	2/15	40
Gordon College	Pr/B	1,521	37	TOEFL	550	583	4/1	50
Greenfield Community College	Pu/A	1,854		TOEFL	550		None	35
Hampshire College	Pr/B	1,412	43	TOEFL	577	634	1/15	55
Harvard College	Pr/B	6,648	645				1/1	65
Hellenic College/Holy Cross	Pr/B	72		TOEFL	500		None	50
Lasell College	Pr/B	1,304	30	TOEFL	500		8/15	40
Lesley University	Pr/AB	1,225	30	TOEFL, SAT/ACT	550	578	3/1	40
Marian Court College	Pr/A	257		TOEFL	500		None	25
Massachusetts Bay Community College	Pu/A	4,473	121	TOEFL	500		None	20
Massachusetts College of Art	Pu/B	1,687	47	TOEFL	550		3/1	65
Massachusetts College of Liberal Arts	Pu/B	1,491		TOEFL, SAT/ACT	550		4/1	25
Massachusetts College of Pharmacy and Health Sciences	Pr/B	2,411	46	TOEFL, SAT/ACT	550		2/1	70
Massachusetts Institute of Technology	Pr/B	4,163	343		577	642	1/1	65
Massachusetts Maritime Academy	Pu/B	1,100		TOEFL	500		5/1	50
Merrimack College	Pr/AB	2,062		TOEFL	550	590	6/1	60
Middlesex Community College	Pu/A	8,124		TOEFL	500		None	
Mount Holyoke College	Pr/B	2,185	353	TOEFL	600	640	1/15	60
Mount Ida College	Pr/AB			TOEFL	425		None	35
Mount Wachusett Community College	Pu/A	3,604	47	TOEFL	550		5/15	10
New England College of Finance	Pr/A	672						50
New England Conservatory of Music	Pr/B	384	83	TOEFL	500	525	12/1	100
New England Institute of Art	Pr/AB	1,684		TOEFL			None	150
Newbury College	Pr/AB			TOEFL	500		None	50
Nichols College	Pr/AB	1,271		TOEFL	550		None	25
North Shore Community College	Pu/A	6,331		TOEFL	500		8/3	
Northeastern University	Pr/B	15,339	742	TOEFL, SAT/ACT	550		1/15	75
Northern Essex Community College	Pu/A	5,618		TOEFL	500		8/1	25
Pine Manor College	Pr/AB	491	30	TOEFL	500	528	None	25
Quincy College	Pu/A	3,800		TOEFL	500		8/1	20
Quinsigamond Community College	Pu/A	5,262		TOEFL	500		6/30	50
Regis College	Pr/AB	934	11	TOEFL	550	590	6/15	50
Rhodec International	Pr/AB	160						
Roxbury Community College	Pu/A	2,167	47				None	135
Salem State College	Pu/B	7,014	276	TOEFL, SAT/ACT	527	545	3/1	40
School of the Museum of Fine Arts	Pr/B	640	43	TOEFL	550		2/1	80
Simmons College	Pr/B	2,064	49	TOEFL, SAT/ACT	560		2/1	35
Smith College	Pr/B	2,569	176	TOEFL	600		1/15	60
Springfield College	Pr/B	2,188		TOEFL, SAT	525		4/1	50
Springfield Technical Community College	Pu/A	5,145	39	TOEFL	525		6/1	35
Stonehill College	Pr/B	2,413	9	TOEFL, SAT/ACT	550		1/15	60
Suffolk University	Pr/AB	5,289	453	TOEFL, SAT/ACT	550		7/1	50
Tufts University	Pr/B	5,015	286	TOEFL, SAT, SAT Subject Test(s), or ACT	600		1/1	70
University of Massachusetts Amherst	Pu/AB	19,621	179	TOEFL, SAT/ACT	550		1/15	60
University of Massachusetts Boston	Pu/B	8,999	275	TOEFL		575	7/1	60
University of Massachusetts Dartmouth	Pu/B	7,600	23	TOEFL, SAT/ACT	520		6/15	60
University of Massachusetts Lowell	Pu/AB	7,663	71	TOEFL, SAT/ACT	500		7/1	60

Student services			Housing		Academic year costs		Maximum credits/ summer	Credit hour charge	International financial aid			
Adviser	Orien- tation	ESL	Academic year	Summer	Tuition/ fees	Living costs			Avail- able	Number receiving aid	Average award	Deadline
Yes	Yes	Yes	Yes	Yes	25,420†	12,460						
			Yes		22,014	12,513			Yes			None
Yes	Yes	Yes	Yes		23,755†	10,945		460				
Yes	Yes		Yes	Yes	28,969‡	13,802	16	886	Yes	8	$11,877	None
Yes	Yes		Yes		28,350	15,035	4	881	Yes	11	$13,904	None
Yes	Yes		Yes	Yes	24,530	14,380		740	Yes	29	$12,916	None
Yes	Yes	Yes	Yes	Yes	23,225	15,400	12		Yes			None
Yes			Yes	Yes	12,072†	9,082						
Yes		Yes	Yes		11,879†	9,717	16	294				
Yes	Yes		Yes	Yes	27,294	11,624			Yes			3/1
Yes	Yes	Yes	No		12,138†	8,700	18	281				
Yes	Yes		Yes		38,649	11,080			Yes	29	$37,086	
Yes	Yes		Yes	Yes	36,173	11,042			Yes	474	$43,311	2/1
Yes			Yes	Yes	17,325†	14,390	6		Yes			4/1
Yes			Yes		21,850†	13,050		700				
Yes	Yes		Yes	Yes	27,510	15,125	9	1135	Yes	10	$7,745	None
			No		13,956†	600						
Yes	Yes	Yes	No		9,830†	11,927	19	230				
Yes	Yes		Yes	Yes	21,900†	14,310						
			Yes	Yes	17,474†	10,809						
Yes		Yes	Yes	Yes	22,700†	14,740	12	810				
Yes	Yes		Yes	Yes	36,390	13,710		565	Yes	250	$37,732	2/15
Yes			Yes		15,114†	10,195			Yes	4		None
Yes	Yes	Yes	Yes		29,810	17,240	15	1085	Yes	5	$11,400	2/1
Yes	Yes		No		13,010†	9,630						
Yes	Yes		Yes	Yes	37,646	12,920		1175	Yes	347	$39,432	3/1
Yes	Yes	Yes	Yes	Yes	22,500	14,100			Yes			None
Yes	Yes	Yes	No		10,570†	9,900	12	230				
			No				6					
Yes	Yes	Yes	Yes		30,975†	14,702	8	1000	Yes	69	$18,469	12/1
Yes	Yes		Yes		20,900†	11,300	15	675	Yes			None
Yes	Yes		Yes		20,000†	13,750	18		Yes			5/1
Yes			Yes		26,970	11,850		795	Yes	3	$11,000	6/1
Yes			No		10,590†	11,700	12	257				
Yes	Yes	Yes	Yes	Yes	31,899†	14,120			Yes	95	$24,092	2/15
Yes		Yes	No		10,650†	7,025	12	266				
Yes	Yes	Yes	Yes	Yes	17,750†	13,170	8		Yes			None
Yes	Yes	Yes	No		4,470†	400	5					
Yes			No		10,050†	9,972	12	230				
Yes	Yes		Yes	Yes	27,800	14,770	12		Yes	9	$18,423	None
Yes	Yes	Yes	No		10,290†	10,070	9	247	Yes			None
Yes	Yes	Yes	Yes		12,264†	8,561	18					
Yes	Yes		Yes	Yes	27,970†	15,700		1130	Yes	12	$14,017	
Yes	Yes		Yes	Yes	28,302†	13,188		857	Yes	16	$22,774	3/1
Yes	Yes		Yes	Yes	34,186†	16,100	12	1060	Yes	113	$38,730	2/15
Yes	Yes	Yes	Yes	Yes	24,075†	12,030		719				
Yes		Yes	No		10,086†	13,700	12	242				
Yes	Yes		Yes	Yes	28,440†	11,430	18					
Yes	Yes	Yes	Yes	Yes	24,250†	16,983	16		Yes	134	$7,179	3/1
Yes	Yes		Yes		36,700†	12,160			Yes	53	$39,020	2/15
Yes	Yes	Yes	Yes	Yes	20,499†	11,352	12					
Yes	Yes	Yes	No		20,658†		12					
Yes	Yes		Yes	Yes	18,178†	11,593						
Yes			Yes	Yes	20,386†	8,858		357				

† Tuition and fees are for 2007-08.   ‡ Tuition and fees are projected for 2008-09.   * Comprehensive Fee

Institution	Control/ degrees	Undergraduates		Tests required	TOEFL		Application	
		Total	Internat'l	(Fall 2009)	minimum	average	Deadline	Fee
Wellesley College	Pr/B	2,247	180	TOEFL		636	1/15	50
Wentworth Institute of Technology	Pr/AB	3,688	107	TOEFL	525		None	30
Western New England College	Pr/AB	2,749	6	TOEFL	500		None	50
Wheaton College	Pr/B	1,551	39	TOEFL	580	595	1/15	55
Wheelock College	Pr/B	787	8	TOEFL, SAT/ACT	500	550	3/1	45
Williams College	Pr/B	1,962	132	TOEFL, SAT/ACT, SAT Subject Test(s)			1/1	60
Worcester Polytechnic Institute	Pr/B	3,009	226	TOEFL	550	598	2/1	60
Worcester State College	Pu/B	4,020	63	TOEFL, SAT/ACT	550		4/1	20
Michigan								
Adrian College	Pr/AB	1,269	52	TOEFL	500		3/15	
Albion College	Pr/B	1,922	15	TOEFL	550		4/1	20
Alma College	Pr/B	1,304	5	TOEFL	525		7/1	25
Andrews University	Pr/AB	1,622	213	TOEFL	550		None	30
Aquinas College	Pr/AB	1,779	4	TOEFL, SAT/ACT	550	600	5/1	
Baker College of Allen Park	Pr/AB							20
Baker College of Auburn Hills	Pr/AB			TOEFL	500			20
Baker College of Cadillac	Pr/AB			TOEFL	550		9/20	20
Baker College of Jackson	Pr/AB			TOEFL	550		None	20
Baker College of Muskegon	Pr/AB			TOEFL	500		9/22	20
Baker College of Owosso	Pr/AB			TOEFL	500		None	20
Baker College of Port Huron	Pr/AB			TOEFL	550		None	20
Bay de Noc Community College	Pu/A	1,993		TOEFL	550	575	5/1	25
Calvin College	Pr/B	4,078	278	TOEFL, SAT/ACT	550	570	4/1	35
Central Michigan University	Pu/B	19,632	238	TOEFL, ACT	550	555	6/1	35
Cleary University	Pr/AB	644	3	TOEFL	550		None	25
College for Creative Studies	Pr/B	1,307	57	TOEFL	527		7/1	35
Concordia University	Pr/AB	493	7	TOEFL, SAT/ACT	520		8/1	100
Cornerstone University	Pr/AB	1,798	18	TOEFL	500		6/1	25
Davenport University	Pr/AB	10,579	23	TOEFL	500		None	100
Delta College	Pu/A	10,422		TOEFL	500	550	5/20	20
Eastern Michigan University	Pu/B	17,609	224	TOEFL	500		3/1	30
Ferris State University	Pu/AB	11,421	98	TOEFL	500		None	30
Finlandia University	Pr/AB	543		TOEFL	500		None	30
Glen Oaks Community College	Pu/A	925		TOEFL	500			
Gogebic Community College	Pu/A	847	3	TOEFL	500		6/1	100
Grand Rapids Community College	Pu/A	13,998		TOEFL	525	608	6/1	40
Grand Valley State University	Pu/B	19,643	156	TOEFL	550		6/1	30
Hillsdale College	Pr/B	1,326	22	TOEFL	560	570	2/15	35
Hope College	Pr/B	3,135	33	TOEFL, SAT/ACT	550		2/1	35
International Academy of Design and Technology: Detroit	Pr/AB							50
Kalamazoo College	Pr/B	1,340	15	TOEFL, SAT/ACT	550	600	2/15	45
Kalamazoo Valley Community College	Pu/A	11,113		TOEFL	500			
Kellogg Community College	Pu/A	4,368	23	TOEFL	500	550	6/1	
Kendall College of Art and Design of Ferris State University	Pu/B	1,043		TOEFL	500	615	7/1	30
Kettering University	Pr/B	2,178	33	TOEFL	550	660	None	35
Kirtland Community College	Pu/A	1,488		TOEFL	550		None	
Kuyper College	Pr/AB	291	26	TOEFL	550	560	None	25
Lake Michigan College	Pu/A	2,916	9	TOEFL	500		7/13	
Lake Superior State University	Pu/AB	2,455	245	TOEFL	550		8/15	35
Lansing Community College	Pu/A	13,453	131	TOEFL	500	540	6/15	
Lawrence Technological University	Pr/AB	2,361	201		550		6/15	30

Student services			Housing		Academic year costs		Maximum credits/ summer	Credit hour charge	International financial aid			
Adviser	Orien- tation	ESL	Academic year	Summer	Tuition/ fees	Living costs			Avail- able	Number receiving aid	Average award	Deadline
Yes	Yes		Yes	Yes	36,640	14,336			Yes	115	$42,403	1/22
Yes	Yes		Yes	Yes	20,150†	12,650	20	630		22	$4,159	
Yes	Yes		Yes		25,942†	12,718		481	Yes			None
Yes	Yes		Yes		36,690†	10,640			Yes	27	$29,217	2/1
			Yes		26,080†	12,580		794	Yes			
Yes			Yes		37,640	12,390			Yes	127	$43,483	2/1
Yes	Yes	Yes	Yes	Yes	34,830†	13,262	15		Yes	162	$20,417	2/1
Yes	Yes	Yes	Yes	Yes	11,944†	12,642		294				
	Yes	Yes	Yes		21,620†	9,125	12	650	Yes			3/1
Yes	Yes		Yes	Yes	28,880	9,540		1206	Yes	15	$17,333	None
Yes			Yes		24,850	13,292		955	Yes			None
Yes	Yes	Yes	Yes	Yes	19,940	9,030		805	Yes			None
Yes	Yes		Yes	Yes	21,150	8,910	12	662	Yes	3	$4,583	None
					8,550‡			190				
Yes			No		8,550‡	1,000	16	190				
Yes			No		8,550‡	9,300	16	190				
Yes					8,550‡	975	16	190				
			Yes	Yes	8,550‡	6,290	16	190				
Yes			Yes		8,550‡	3,700	16	190				
Yes			No		8,550‡	11,100	16	190				
Yes			Yes	Yes	4,785†	4,645	8	153				
Yes	Yes		Yes	Yes	23,165	10,745	13	550	Yes	300	$11,000	None
Yes	Yes	Yes	Yes	Yes	21,210†	10,901	12	707	Yes	151	$4,933	None
Yes			No		14,880‡	2,742	12	310				
Yes	Yes		Yes	Yes	28,275‡	8,500	6	903	Yes	56	$4,181	None
			Yes		19,770†	9,500		650	Yes	7	$6,642	3/1
Yes			Yes		19,530	11,742	8	735	Yes	15	$9,560	None
Yes	Yes	Yes	Yes	Yes	12,445†	4,589		409	Yes			None
Yes			No		5,310†	2,530		165				
Yes	Yes	Yes	Yes	Yes	19,925†	9,792		628	Yes	118	$14,777	None
Yes			Yes	Yes	16,062†	11,034	15	530				
Yes	Yes	Yes	Yes		17,514†	8,000	12	540	Yes			8/1
Yes			No		2,610†	1,280	18		Yes			None
Yes			Yes	Yes	4,231†	5,970	12	125				
Yes	Yes		No		7,280‡	7,157	12	240				
Yes	Yes	Yes	Yes	Yes	12,510†	9,948	16	532	Yes	86	$9,405	None
Yes			Yes		19,920	10,470	8	760	Yes	14	$12,000	3/15
Yes	Yes		Yes	Yes	24,920	7,650	12		Yes	29	$18,991	None
					16,620†							
Yes	Yes		Yes		30,823	10,121			Yes			
Yes		Yes	No		4,230†	3,514		141				
Yes	Yes		No		4,980†	8,882	12					
Yes	Yes		Yes		19,640†	5,682			Yes			2/15
Yes	Yes		Yes	Yes	26,936	13,755	20	828				
			Yes	Yes	6,279†	6,575	9	191	Yes			None
Yes	Yes		Yes	Yes	13,869	8,272			Yes	11	$14,480	None
Yes			No		5,190†	3,410	18	142	Yes			None
Yes			Yes	Yes	14,562†	9,469		598	Yes	81	$4,137	None
Yes	Yes	Yes	No		5,450†	7,320		180				
Yes	Yes	Yes	Yes	Yes	21,979	12,918	30	722	Yes			

† Tuition and fees are for 2007-08. ‡ Tuition and fees are projected for 2008-09. * Comprehensive Fee

Institution	Control/ degrees	Undergraduates		Tests required (Fall 2009)	TOEFL		Application	
		Total	Internat'l		minimum	average	Deadline	Fee
Macomb Community College	Pu/A	12,902	601	TOEFL	550		7/21	
Madonna University	Pr/AB	2,779	112	TOEFL	540		7/1	200
Marygrove College	Pr/AB	780		TOEFL	520		3/15	25
Michigan Jewish Institute	Pr/AB	115		TOEFL	550		None	50
Michigan State University	Pu/B	35,772	1,456	TOEFL, SAT/ACT	550			50
Michigan Technological University	Pu/AB	5,722	276	TOEFL	500	549	None	
Michigan Theological Seminary	Pr/B	20						
Montcalm Community College	Pu/A	2,356		TOEFL	500		5/1	
Mott Community College	Pu/A	7,255	19	TOEFL	500		None	
Muskegon Community College	Pu/A	4,707		TOEFL	500	600	None	
North Central Michigan College	Pu/A	2,770		TOEFL	550		6/1	
Northern Michigan University	Pu/AB	8,287	44	TOEFL	500		6/1	30
Northwestern Michigan College	Pu/A	4,600		TOEFL	550	570	7/30	15
Northwood University: Michigan	Pr/AB	1,979	166	TOEFL	500	550	None	25
Oakland Community College	Pu/A	13,598	933	TOEFL	350		6/1	
Oakland University	Pu/B	13,605	130	TOEFL	550	570	7/1	40
Olivet College	Pr/B	920	17	TOEFL	500	520	7/15	25
Rochester College	Pr/AB	957	15	TOEFL, ACT	500		None	25
Saginaw Chippewa Tribal College	Pu/A	135						
Saginaw Valley State University	Pu/B	7,785	195	TOEFL	525		None	25
St. Clair County Community College	Pu/A	4,000		TOEFL	500	550	7/1	10
Siena Heights University	Pr/AB	1,915		TOEFL	525	540	8/1	50
Southwestern Michigan College	Pu/A	2,032	65	TOEFL	550		6/1	
Spring Arbor University	Pr/AB	2,611		TOEFL	525		4/1	30
University of Detroit Mercy	Pr/AB	2,989	124				4/1	50
University of Michigan	Pu/B	25,916	1,211	TOEFL, SAT/ACT	570	600	2/1	55
University of Michigan: Dearborn	Pu/B	6,212		TOEFL, SAT/ACT	550	560	8/15	75
University of Michigan: Flint	Pu/B	5,655	69	TOEFL	550		None	30
Walsh College of Accountancy and Business Administration	Pr/B	1,047		TOEFL	550		None	25
Washtenaw Community College	Pu/A	13,000		TOEFL	500		8/1	15
Wayne County Community College	Pu/A	17,877	69	TOEFL	500	550	8/7	10
Wayne State University	Pu/B	19,964	859	TOEFL	550	571	5/1	50
Western Michigan University	Pu/B	19,572	362	TOEFL	550		5/1	35
Minnesota								
Academy College	Pr/AB	150	1					30
Alexandria Technical College	Pu/A	2,141		TOEFL	500		6/1	20
Anoka Technical College	Pu/A	1,590		TOEFL	500	526		20
Art Institutes International Minnesota	Pr/AB	1,722		TOEFL	480		None	50
Augsburg College	Pr/B	2,829	27	TOEFL	550		7/15	25
Bemidji State University	Pu/AB	4,274		TOEFL	550	565	None	20
Bethany Lutheran College	Pr/B	617	3	TOEFL	500	530	7/1	140
Bethel University	Pr/AB	3,250	11	TOEFL	525		None	25
Brown College	Pr/AB	1,437		TOEFL	500	550	None	150
Carleton College	Pr/B	1,986	114	TOEFL, SAT/ACT	600		1/15	30
Central Lakes College	Pu/A	3,228		TOEFL	500		8/1	20
Century Community and Technical College	Pu/A	7,631	76	TOEFL	500		5/1	20
College of St. Benedict	Pr/B	2,049	98	TOEFL	550		5/1	
College of St. Catherine	Pr/AB	3,731	56	TOEFL	500	540	5/15	20
College of St. Scholastica	Pr/B	1,986	88	TOEFL	550	581	6/1	50
College of Visual Arts	Pr/B	170	1	TOEFL	500		None	40
Concordia College: Moorhead	Pr/B	2,720	96	TOEFL	533	620	None	20

Student services			Housing		Academic year costs		Maximum credits/summer	Credit hour charge	International financial aid			
Adviser	Orientation	ESL	Academic year	Summer	Tuition/fees	Living costs			Available	Number receiving aid	Average award	Deadline
Yes		Yes	No		4,210†	4,882	12	139				
Yes	Yes	Yes	Yes	Yes	14,575†	8,800		483	Yes			None
Yes			Yes		14,690†	10,160	7	512				
Yes		Yes	No		10,800†	2,275		336				
Yes	Yes	Yes	Yes	Yes	23,500†	9,018	6	742	Yes	95	$5,507	None
Yes	Yes	Yes	Yes	Yes	21,589†	10,875	18	698	Yes	196	$7,503	None
					11,660			380				
Yes			No		4,425†	14,489	8	149				
Yes			No		5,172†	9,687	8	164				
Yes			No		4,610†	6,700	12	145				
Yes			Yes		4,444†	4,625	6	140	Yes			4/1
Yes	Yes	Yes	Yes	Yes	10,645†	9,782	16	420	Yes	29	$1,941	None
Yes			Yes	Yes	5,621†	8,952	18	164	Yes			None
Yes	Yes	Yes	Yes	Yes	17,544	10,863	24	346	Yes			None
Yes	Yes	Yes	No		4,236†	9,660	16	139	Yes	8	$500	None
Yes	Yes	Yes	Yes	Yes	17,625†	14,359	16		Yes			None
Yes	Yes	Yes	Yes	Yes	19,302†	9,022		580	Yes			None
Yes			Yes	Yes	14,860†	8,920		435				
					1,786†							
Yes	Yes	Yes	Yes	Yes	14,283†	8,471	12	461	Yes	106	$6,316	None
Yes			No		6,237†	2,414		199	Yes			None
Yes			Yes	Yes	18,494†	7,990	6		Yes			8/15
Yes		Yes	No		4,785†	4,294	12	139				
Yes	Yes	Yes	Yes	Yes	19,240	8,912	8	470	Yes	26	$9,041	None
Yes	Yes	Yes	Yes	Yes	27,319	13,440		655	Yes			
Yes	Yes	Yes	Yes	Yes	31,301†	11,210		1268				
Yes	Yes		No		17,499†	7,682				20	$7,666	
Yes	Yes	Yes	No		13,998†	11,160	9	552	Yes	9	$550	None
Yes			No		8,280†	2,516		268	Yes			None
Yes		Yes	No		4,860†	4,100	12	155				
Yes	Yes	Yes	No		3,053†	1,330	9	93				
Yes	Yes	Yes	Yes	Yes	16,400†	11,351		518				
Yes	Yes	Yes	Yes	Yes	16,806†	11,039		537	Yes	100	$85,000	None
Yes			No			2,900						
Yes			No		4,329†	4,800		132	Yes			None
			No		4,586†			139				
Yes			Yes		19,872†	5,279	16	414				
Yes	Yes	Yes	Yes	Yes	26,103	9,831	3		Yes			8/1
Yes	Yes	Yes	Yes	Yes	6,740†	8,724	16	208				
Yes	Yes		Yes	Yes	18,710	9,800		780	Yes	9	$16,099	None
Yes	Yes		Yes	Yes	25,860	11,080	8	1035	Yes	3	$21,104	None
			Yes		16,340†	4,309	20					
Yes	Yes		Yes	Yes	38,046	11,954			Yes	73	$30,672	2/15
Yes			No		4,419†	9,008	16		Yes			None
Yes	Yes	Yes	No		4,409†	17,467	18	132	Yes			None
Yes	Yes	Yes	Yes	Yes	28,668	9,459		1171	Yes	92	$17,213	None
Yes	Yes	Yes	Yes	Yes	25,803	11,545		848	Yes			None
Yes	Yes		Yes	Yes	26,489	11,690		819	Yes			None
Yes			No		22,426	9,249	6		Yes			
Yes	Yes		Yes	Yes	24,120	9,900	8	940	Yes	110	$14,628	None

† Tuition and fees are for 2007-08. ‡ Tuition and fees are projected for 2008-09. * Comprehensive Fee

Institution	Control/ degrees	Undergraduates Total	Undergraduates Internat'l	Tests required (Fall 2009)	TOEFL minimum	TOEFL average	Application Deadline	Application Fee
Concordia University: St. Paul	Pr/AB	1,418	8	TOEFL	500		8/1	30
Dakota County Technical College	Pu/A	2,760		TOEFL	500		6/1	20
DeVry University: Edina	Pr/AB	161						50
Dunwoody College of Technology	Pr/AB	1,476	2	TOEFL	475	500	None	50
Globe University	Pr/AB						None	50
Gustavus Adolphus College	Pr/B	2,577		TOEFL	550	587	3/1	
Hamline University	Pr/B	1,986	66	TOEFL	550	565	None	
Hennepin Technical College	Pu/A	12,855			500		None	20
Hibbing Community College	Pu/A	1,415		TOEFL	500		3/31	20
Inver Hills Community College	Pu/A	4,574	20	TOEFL	500		6/1	20
Itasca Community College	Pu/A	984	1	TOEFL	500		8/1	20
Lake Superior College	Pu/A	4,317		TOEFL	513		7/16	20
Lakeland Academy Division of Herzing College	Pr/AB			TOEFL				
Le Cordon Bleu College of Culinary Arts	Pr/A	675						50
Macalester College	Pr/B	1,912	237	TOEFL, SAT/ACT	573	636	1/15	40
Mesabi Range Community and Technical College	Pu/A	1,351		TOEFL	500		None	20
Minneapolis Business College	Pr/A	360					None	50
Minneapolis College of Art and Design	Pr/B	731		TOEFL, SAT/ACT		550	5/1	50
Minneapolis Community and Technical College	Pu/A		213	TOEFL	310		None	20
Minneapolis Drafting School Division of Herzing College	Pr/AB	254		TOEFL	500			
Minnesota School of Business: Plymouth	Pr/AB	531						
Minnesota School of Business: Rochester	Pr/AB	626						50
Minnesota School of Business: Shakopee	Pr/AB	445	2					50
Minnesota State College - Southeast Technical	Pu/A	1,863	61	TOEFL	500		None	20
Minnesota State Community and Technical College: Fergus Falls	Pu/A	6,054		TOEFL	550		6/8	20
Minnesota State University: Mankato	Pu/AB	12,813		TOEFL	500	530	4/1	20
Minnesota State University: Moorhead	Pu/AB			TOEFL	500		6/1	20
Minnesota West Community and Technical College	Pu/A			TOEFL	500		6/8	20
Normandale Community College	Pu/A	9,239		TOEFL	500	520	7/15	20
North Central University	Pr/AB	1,181		TOEFL, SAT/ACT	500		5/1	25
North Hennepin Community College	Pu/A	6,255	81	TOEFL	500		6/1	20
Northland Community & Technical College	Pu/A	1,957		TOEFL	500		None	20
Northwest Technical College	Pu/A	891		TOEFL	500		None	20
Northwest Technical Institute	Pr/A	126		TOEFL			None	25
Northwestern College	Pr/AB	1,845	6	TOEFL, SAT/ACT	530	551	6/1	30
Northwestern Health Sciences University	Pr/B	82						50
Pillsbury Baptist Bible College	Pr/AB	153		TOEFL	500			25
Pine Technical College	Pu/A	779		TOEFL	500		None	20
Rainy River Community College	Pu/A			TOEFL	550		None	20
Rasmussen College: Eagan	Pr/AB	505		TOEFL	500		None	60
Rasmussen College: Eden Prairie	Pr/A	808		TOEFL	500		None	60
Rasmussen College: Mankato	Pr/A	610					None	60
Riverland Community College	Pu/A	3,477		TOEFL	500	520	6/1	20
Rochester Community and Technical College	Pu/A	5,896		TOEFL	450		7/1	20
Saint Cloud State University	Pu/AB	13,381	685	TOEFL	500		4/1	20
St. Cloud Technical College	Pu/A	3,333	7	TOEFL	500		7/1	20
St. John's University	Pr/B	1,917		TOEFL	550		5/1	
St. Mary's University of Minnesota	Pr/B	1,979	28	TOEFL	520	550	5/1	25
St. Olaf College	Pr/B	2,988	23	TOEFL, SAT/ACT	550	601	None	
St. Paul College	Pu/A	4,596						20

Student services			Housing		Academic year costs		Maximum credits/ summer	Credit hour charge	International financial aid			
Adviser	Orien-tation	ESL	Academic year	Summer	Tuition/ fees	Living costs			Avail-able	Number receiving aid	Average award	Deadline
Yes			Yes	Yes	24,900	9,400		520	Yes	1	$10,000	None
Yes	Yes	Yes	No		8,994†	15,831		283				
					13,020†	16,375		490				
Yes			No		12,633†	11,238		174				
			No		21,150†	12,600	12	470				
Yes	Yes		Yes	Yes	28,535†	8,605		863	Yes	33	$13,329	4/15
Yes	Yes	Yes	Yes	Yes	28,143	10,184	8	863	Yes	60	$17,584	None
Yes	Yes	Yes	No		4,187†	800	12	131				
Yes			Yes		5,312†	2,600	12	161				
Yes	Yes	Yes	No		4,534†		9	137				
Yes			Yes	Yes	5,305†	10,838	6	161				
Yes		Yes	No		7,745†	10,275	19	239				
Yes			No									
Yes	Yes		Yes	Yes	36,504	10,902	8	1135	Yes	220	$22,821	3/1
Yes			Yes	Yes	5,312†	3,676	9	161				
			Yes		13,160†	6,600						
Yes	Yes	Yes	Yes	Yes	29,300	7,860	12	940	Yes	7	$1,392	
Yes	Yes	Yes	No		4,442†				Yes			None
					11,605†			386				
					22,610†			370				
					22,610†			370				
					23,570‡			390				
Yes			Yes		8,645†	13,776		276				
Yes		Yes	Yes	Yes	4,737†	2,450	18	138				
Yes	Yes	Yes	Yes	Yes	12,854†	8,774	12	484	Yes	74	$5,624	
Yes	Yes		Yes	Yes	5,948†	9,196	12		Yes			None
Yes			No		4,692†	600	20					
		Yes	No		4,512†	14,000	13	134	Yes			None
Yes			Yes	Yes	14,586	6,170	15	456	Yes			None
Yes	Yes	Yes	No		4,420†	7,766	10	137	Yes			None
Yes			No		4,764†	3,450						
Yes		Yes	Yes	Yes	4,704†	1,200		147				
			No		14,845	14,154		463				
Yes	Yes		Yes		22,250	9,870	12	950	Yes	11	$15,924	6/1
					15,436†							
			Yes		10,228	5,796		285				
	Yes		No		7,986†	8,500	9	252				
Yes			Yes	Yes	5,348†	4,950		161	Yes			None
			No									
			No			450			Yes			None
Yes	Yes	Yes	Yes	Yes	4,590†	12,150	6		Yes			None
Yes			No		4,656†	7,293		136				
Yes	Yes	Yes	Yes	Yes	12,097†	5,592	9	380				
Yes	Yes	Yes	No		4,424†	6,403						
Yes	Yes	Yes	Yes	Yes	28,668	8,748		1171	Yes	94	$20,183	None
Yes	Yes	Yes	Yes	Yes	24,150	8,850		790	Yes	27	$14,448	None
Yes	Yes		Yes		34,300	9,700	4	1075	Yes	20	$14,705	4/15
			No		8,304†	3,240		266	Yes			None

† Tuition and fees are for 2007-08.   ‡ Tuition and fees are projected for 2008-09.   * Comprehensive Fee

Institution	Control/degrees	Total	Internat'l	Tests required (Fall 2009)	TOEFL minimum	TOEFL average	Application Deadline	Fee
South Central College	Pu/A	2,838		TOEFL	500		3/1	20
Southwest Minnesota State University	Pu/AB	2,600		TOEFL, SAT, SAT Subject Test(s), or ACT	500		6/15	20
University of Minnesota: Crookston	Pu/AB	1,142	79	TOEFL	520	540	5/1	30
University of Minnesota: Duluth	Pu/B	9,184	123	TOEFL	550	560	8/1	50
University of Minnesota: Morris	Pu/B	1,686		TOEFL, SAT/ACT	550		3/15	75
University of Minnesota: Twin Cities	Pu/B	28,703	556	TOEFL	475		None	45
University of St. Thomas	Pr/B	5,939	50	TOEFL	550		None	30
Walden University	Pr/B	1,369	497	TOEFL	550	609	None	50
White Earth Tribal and Community College	Pr/A	130						
Winona State University	Pu/AB	7,443	206	TOEFL	550		3/4	20

Mississippi

Institution	Control/degrees	Total	Internat'l	Tests required (Fall 2009)	TOEFL minimum	TOEFL average	Application Deadline	Fee
Alcorn State University	Pu/AB	3,004	46	TOEFL, SAT/ACT	525		None	
Antonelli College: Hattiesburg	Pr/A	293						75
Antonelli College: Jackson	Pr/A	287						75
Belhaven College	Pr/AB	2,071	30	TOEFL	500		None	25
Blue Cliff College: Gulfport	Pr/A	113						100
Blue Mountain College	Pr/B	406	1	TOEFL, SAT/ACT	500			10
Coahoma Community College	Pu/A	2,216		TOEFL, SAT/ACT		500		
Delta State University	Pu/B	3,356		TOEFL, SAT/ACT	525	530	8/1	25
East Central Community College	Pu/A	2,273		TOEFL, ACT	500		6/15	
Hinds Community College	Pu/A	10,235		TOEFL	500		8/17	
Jackson State University	Pu/B	6,823	19	TOEFL	525	560	8/15	
Meridian Community College	Pu/A	3,506			500	535	None	
Millsaps College	Pr/B	1,029	12	TOEFL	550		7/1	
Mississippi College	Pr/B	2,911	107	TOEFL		500	8/15	
Mississippi Gulf Coast Community College: Jefferson Davis Campus	Pu/A	8,724		TOEFL	525	540	7/1	
Mississippi State University	Pu/B	13,049		TOEFL, SAT/ACT	525	598		35
Mississippi University for Women	Pu/AB	2,379		TOEFL	525		7/15	25
Mississippi Valley State University	Pu/B	2,574		TOEFL, SAT/ACT	525	560	6/15	
Northeast Mississippi Community College	Pu/A	3,429		TOEFL	525		None	
Northwest Mississippi Community College	Pu/A	6,825		TOEFL	500		7/15	
Rust College	Pr/AB	979		TOEFL	540	570	7/15	10
Tougaloo College	Pr/AB	856		TOEFL	500		4/30	25
University of Mississippi	Pu/B	12,597	130	TOEFL, SAT/ACT	550	565		40
University of Southern Mississippi	Pu/B	11,924	100	TOEFL	525	540	7/1	25
William Carey University	Pr/B	1,679	47	TOEFL, SAT/ACT	523		7/15	30

Missouri

Institution	Control/degrees	Total	Internat'l	Tests required (Fall 2009)	TOEFL minimum	TOEFL average	Application Deadline	Fee
Avila University	Pr/B	1,065	31	TOEFL	500	573	None	25
Baptist Bible College	Pr/AB	544	9	TOEFL, ACT	550		1/1	40
Bolivar Technical College	Pr/A	98						45
Calvary Bible College and Theological Seminary	Pr/AB	254	2	TOEFL	525		7/15	30
Central Methodist University	Pr/AB	914	11	TOEFL	500		6/1	20
College of the Ozarks	Pr/B	1,336	18	TOEFL	550	556	2/15	
Columbia College	Pr/AB	1,034	85	TOEFL, SAT/ACT	500	523	7/1	50
Cottey College	Pr/A	327		TOEFL	500	547	None	20
Crowder College	Pu/A	2,604		TOEFL	500		None	25
Culver-Stockton College	Pr/B	807		TOEFL	500		None	
DeVry University: Kansas City	Pr/AB	950	2	TOEFL	500		None	50
Drury University	Pr/AB	1,605		TOEFL	550	610	None	25
East Central College	Pu/A	2,305		TOEFL	550		7/15	
Evangel University	Pr/AB	1,534		TOEFL	490	604	6/1	25
Fontbonne University	Pr/B	1,993	15	TOEFL	525		8/1	25

Student services			Housing		Academic year costs		Maximum credits/ summer	Credit hour charge	International financial aid			
Adviser	Orien- tation	ESL	Academic year	Summer	Tuition/ fees	Living costs			Avail- able	Number receiving aid	Average award	Deadline
Yes	Yes		No		4,436†	3,650			Yes			None
Yes	Yes		Yes	Yes	6,517†	9,322	20		Yes	22	$2,766	None
Yes	Yes	Yes	Yes	Yes	8,821†	13,022			Yes	6	$2,645	None
Yes	Yes		Yes	Yes	19,227†	9,310	12	666	Yes	73		None
Yes	Yes	Yes	Yes	Yes	9,331†	8,670	20		Yes			
Yes	Yes	Yes	Yes	Yes	21,515†	7,062		753	Yes			None
Yes	Yes	Yes	Yes	Yes	27,822	7,612	16		Yes	20	$16,162	None
					11,520‡			250				
					3,050	13,700		90				
Yes	Yes	Yes	Yes	Yes	10,798†	7,510	12	335	Yes			None
Yes			Yes	Yes	9,816†	10,739	12	409	Yes			None
					11,370†	900						
			No		11,370†	1,200						
Yes	Yes	Yes	Yes		16,460	8,420	15	350	Yes	30	$3,800	None
					11,350†			200				
			Yes		8,020†	5,952	14	245	Yes			8/1
			Yes		4,700†	5,414	12					
Yes	Yes		Yes		10,258†	6,096	12	427				
			Yes		3,610†	5,090	12	162				
Yes			Yes	Yes	3,946†	4,950	12	170				
Yes	Yes		Yes	Yes	9,976†	9,634	12	416				
Yes	Yes		Yes	Yes	2,950†	6,976	12	137	Yes			None
Yes	Yes		Yes	Yes	24,754	11,300	16	720	Yes	6	$15,338	None
Yes	Yes	Yes	Yes		12,800	9,221	12	382	Yes			None
Yes			Yes		3,548†	7,760		152				
Yes	Yes	Yes	Yes	Yes	11,469†	11,059						
Yes	Yes		Yes	Yes	10,723†	8,211		447	Yes			None
Yes			Yes	Yes	10,198†	4,542	12	340				
Yes		Yes	Yes		3,950	5,813	12	223				
			Yes		3,700	3,675	12	125				
Yes			Yes		6,600†	6,050	6	283	Yes			5/1
			Yes			5,000	12					
Yes	Yes	Yes	Yes	Yes	11,436†	5,398	12		Yes	101	$9,185	None
Yes	Yes	Yes	Yes	Yes	11,952†	9,352	19	488	Yes	103	$7,198	None
Yes	Yes		Yes	Yes	9,750	10,647	12	310	Yes			9/1
Yes	Yes	Yes	Yes	Yes	20,150	9,400	12	495	Yes			4/1
Yes			Yes		13,610	6,240	15	206				
					11,620†	1,000		325				
Yes			Yes	Yes	8,500†	6,500		260	Yes			4/1
			Yes	Yes	17,980	9,950	9	170	Yes	1	$5,000	None
Yes		Yes	Yes	Yes		7,890			Yes			None
Yes	Yes	Yes	Yes	Yes	13,034†	8,372	8	279	Yes			None
Yes	Yes		Yes		13,510†	8,400			Yes			None
Yes		Yes	Yes	Yes	3,900†	6,720	9	118	Yes			None
Yes			Yes		16,850†	11,600	9	450	Yes	3	$10,666	6/1
Yes					13,220†	8,528		490				
Yes	Yes	Yes	Yes	Yes	18,409	10,384	13	600	Yes	28	$2,737	3/15
Yes			No		4,530	10,686	9	141	Yes			None
Yes			Yes		14,340†	9,620	12	528	Yes			6/1
Yes	Yes	Yes	Yes	Yes	19,320	9,100	15	508	Yes	8	$4,375	

† Tuition and fees are for 2007-08.   ‡ Tuition and fees are projected for 2008-09.   * Comprehensive Fee

Institution	Control/ degrees	Undergraduates		Tests required (Fall 2009)	TOEFL		Application	
		Total	Internat'l		minimum	average	Deadline	Fee
Global University	Pr/AB	4,858					None	40
Grantham University	Pr/AB	8,500		TOEFL	500		None	
Hannibal-LaGrange College	Pr/AB	1,150	42	TOEFL, SAT/ACT	520		None	150
Harris-Stowe State University	Pu/B	1,800		TOEFL	500		None	15
Jefferson College	Pu/A	4,418		TOEFL	475	558	6/1	20
Kansas City Art Institute	Pr/B	671	6	TOEFL	550	558	3/15	35
Lincoln University	Pu/AB	2,483	92	TOEFL, SAT/ACT	500		12/1	20
Lindenwood University	Pr/B	5,872	557	TOEFL	500		None	100
Linn State Technical College	Pu/A	861						
Maryville University of Saint Louis	Pr/B	2,674	11	TOEFL	500	619	7/15	50
Metro Business College	Pr/A							
Metropolitan Community College: Blue River	Pu/A	2,030	1	TOEFL	550		7/1	50
Metropolitan Community College: Longview	Pu/A	3,906	1	TOEFL	550		7/1	50
Metropolitan Community College: Maple Woods	Pu/A	3,100	1	TOEFL	550		7/1	50
Metropolitan Community College: Penn Valley	Pu/A	3,509	1	TOEFL	500		7/1	50
Missouri Baptist University	Pr/AB	1,414	62	TOEFL	500		None	30
Missouri Southern State University	Pu/AB	5,593		TOEFL, SAT/ACT	535	545	4/1	25
Missouri State University	Pu/B	14,491	277	TOEFL	500	520	4/15	50
Missouri University of Science and Technology	Pu/B	4,705	121	TOEFL	550	604	6/1	35
Missouri Valley College	Pr/AB	1,430		TOEFL	500		5/1	75
Moberly Area Community College	Pu/A	2,984		TOEFL	450	487	None	
Northwest Missouri State University	Pu/AB	5,607		TOEFL	500	515	7/1	50
Ozarks Technical Community College	Pu/A	8,934	3	TOEFL	550		None	
Park University	Pr/AB	11,824		TOEFL, SAT/ACT	500	510	7/1	25
Patricia Stevens College	Pr/AB	175					None	15
Pinnacle Career Institute: Kansas City	Pr/A							50
Research College of Nursing	Pr/B	280		TOEFL, SAT/ACT	550		5/1	50
Rockhurst University	Pr/B	1,598	13	TOEFL, SAT/ACT	550		7/1	50
St. Louis Community College at Florissant Valley	Pu/A	6,240		TOEFL	500		4/20	
Saint Louis University	Pr/B	7,365	193	TOEFL	525		3/1	25
Sanford-Brown College: Hazelwood	Pr/A							25
Sanford-Brown College: St. Peters	Pr/A							
Southeast Missouri Hospital College of Nursing and Health Sciences	Pr/A							40
Southeast Missouri State University	Pu/AB	8,485	120	TOEFL	500		6/1	100
Southwest Baptist University	Pr/AB	2,443	23	TOEFL, SAT/ACT	550		4/1	100
State Fair Community College	Pu/A	2,941		TOEFL	450	475	7/1	25
Stephens College	Pr/AB	861	3	TOEFL	550		5/30	25
Three Rivers Community College	Pu/A	2,641	1	TOEFL	550		None	20
Truman State University	Pu/B	5,496	212	TOEFL	550		6/1	
University of Central Missouri	Pu/AB	8,333	216	TOEFL, SAT/ACT	500	527	5/1	50
University of Missouri: Columbia	Pu/B	21,385	267	TOEFL	500		5/1	60
University of Missouri: Kansas City	Pu/B	6,953	175	TOEFL	500	599	8/1	50
University of Missouri: St. Louis	Pu/B	8,947	176	TOEFL	500	537	5/7	40
Vatterott College	Pr/AB							
Washington University in St. Louis	Pr/B	6,467	260	TOEFL, SAT/ACT	550		1/15	55
Webster University	Pr/B	3,523	97	TOEFL, SAT/ACT	550	560	3/1	35
Wentworth Military Junior College	Pr/A	565					None	100
Westminster College	Pr/B	953	132	TOEFL	550	603	5/1	25
William Jewell College	Pr/B	1,329	6	TOEFL	550		7/15	25
William Woods University	Pr/AB	963	27	TOEFL	525	550	None	25

Student services			Housing		Academic year costs		Maximum credits/ summer	Credit hour charge	International financial aid			
Adviser	Orien- tation	ESL	Academic year	Summer	Tuition/ fees	Living costs			Avail- able	Number receiving aid	Average award	Deadline
			No			600	6					
			No		7,950			265	Yes			None
Yes	Yes	Yes	Yes	Yes	14,506	8,531	17	466	Yes			7/1
Yes			Yes		9,680 †	12,000	9	311	Yes			None
Yes	Yes	Yes	Yes	Yes	5,100	7,599	9	170	Yes	11	$7,432	None
Yes			Yes		27,220	13,294	6	1134	Yes	4	$13,725	None
Yes	Yes		Yes	Yes	10,885	8,827	9	346	Yes			None
Yes	Yes		Yes	Yes	13,000	22,260	12	360				
					9,390 †	6,530		280				
Yes	Yes		Yes	Yes	20,275	13,900	16	590	Yes	2	$11,200	None
Yes		Yes	No		5,700 †	9,100		185				
Yes		Yes	No		5,700 †	9,100		185				
					5,700 †	9,100		185				
Yes	Yes	Yes	No		5,700 †	9,100		185				
Yes	Yes		Yes	Yes	15,850 †	16,540	21	505	Yes			None
Yes	Yes	Yes	Yes	Yes	8,326 †	7,420	8	270	Yes			None
Yes	Yes	Yes	Yes	Yes	11,088 †	12,412	10	349	Yes	275	$5,376	None
Yes	Yes	Yes	Yes	Yes	18,828 †	9,816	9	591	Yes			None
Yes	Yes	Yes	Yes		15,950	11,950	12		Yes			None
Yes	Yes		Yes		4,380 †	5,480	12	135	Yes	3	$1,066	None
Yes	Yes	Yes	Yes	Yes	10,896 †	9,176	18	356	Yes			None
		Yes			4,725 †	5,955	6	140				
Yes	Yes	Yes	Yes	Yes	7,800 †	10,135	6	260	Yes			8/1
	Yes				10,050 †	500	18	195				
						965						
Yes	Yes		Yes	Yes	24,480	9,260	12	790				
			Yes	Yes	24,700	11,758	18	792	Yes	13	$21,434	6/30
					4,740 †	6,760	9	158				
Yes	Yes	Yes	Yes	Yes	30,728	15,413		1060	Yes	167	$11,679	None
						909						
					10,764	500						
Yes	Yes	Yes	Yes	Yes	10,320 †	9,429	15	323	Yes	26	$8,667	None
	Yes		Yes	Yes	15,704	8,166	12		Yes			None
Yes			Yes	Yes	5,820	9,200	9	180	Yes			None
Yes	Yes		Yes	Yes	23,000	12,910	12	265				
			Yes		4,245 †	3,572	12	128				
Yes	Yes		Yes	Yes	11,042 †	10,615	12	450	Yes	201	$4,923	None
Yes	Yes	Yes	Yes	Yes	11,845 †	8,646		375	Yes	2		None
Yes	Yes	Yes	Yes	Yes	18,755 †	10,842	12	591	Yes			None
	Yes	Yes	Yes		18,642 †	13,276		591				
Yes	Yes	Yes	Yes	Yes	18,920 †	15,602	9	591	Yes	104	$6,847	None
Yes	Yes	Yes	Yes	Yes	37,248	15,966	14		Yes			2/15
Yes	Yes	Yes	Yes	Yes	20,440	12,800	9	525	Yes			None
Yes	Yes	Yes	Yes	Yes	16,430	9,360			Yes			6/30
Yes	Yes		Yes	Yes	17,250	10,755	3	750	Yes	123	$14,195	None
Yes	Yes		Yes	Yes	23,000	10,330	8	725	Yes	2	$8,350	None
		Yes	Yes		16,690	14,450	18	540	Yes	17	$11,823	None

† Tuition and fees are for 2007-08.   ‡ Tuition and fees are projected for 2008-09.   * Comprehensive Fee

Institution	Control/ degrees	Undergraduates		Tests required (Fall 2009)	TOEFL		Application	
		Total	Internat'l		minimum	average	Deadline	Fee
Montana								
Carroll College	Pr/AB	1,272	11	TOEFL	550	585	None	35
Dawson Community College	Pu/A	322		TOEFL	500		5/1	30
Flathead Valley Community College	Pu/A	1,291		TOEFL	500	510	None	15
Fort Peck Community College	Pu/A							15
Helena College of Technology of the University of Montana	Pu/A			TOEFL	500		None	30
Montana State University: Billings	Pu/AB	4,283	22	TOEFL	500		None	30
Montana State University: Bozeman	Pu/B	10,461	199	TOEFL	525	583	5/15	30
Montana State University: Northern	Pu/AB	1,388		TOEFL	500		8/1	30
Montana Tech of the University of Montana	Pu/AB	2,173		TOEFL	525		None	30
Rocky Mountain College	Pr/AB	834		TOEFL	525	647	None	40
University of Great Falls	Pr/AB	612		TOEFL	500		6/1	35
University of Montana: Missoula	Pu/AB	11,799		TOEFL	500	525	7/1	30
University of Montana: Western	Pu/AB	1,148		TOEFL	500	550	5/1	30
Nebraska								
Bellevue University	Pr/B	5,515		TOEFL	500		None	75
Chadron State College	Pu/B	2,287		TOEFL	550		6/1	15
College of Saint Mary	Pr/AB	793	8	TOEFL	550		None	30
Concordia University	Pr/B	1,066	11	TOEFL, SAT/ACT	500	525	6/15	
Creighton University	Pr/AB	4,104	44	TOEFL	550		5/1	40
Dana College	Pr/B	613	2	TOEFL	500	544	5/1	
Doane College	Pr/B	921	7	TOEFL	525		8/15	15
Grace University	Pr/AB	358		TOEFL, ACT	550		None	35
Hastings College	Pr/B	1,067	10	TOEFL, SAT/ACT	600	650	6/15	50
Kaplan University: Lincoln	Pr/AB	522		TOEFL	560		None	25
Metropolitan Community College	Pu/A	6,627	120	TOEFL	480		6/7	
Mid-Plains Community College Area	Pu/A			TOEFL	500		2/15	
Midland Lutheran College	Pr/AB	827		TOEFL	500		4/1	30
Nebraska College of Technical Agriculture	Pu/A	327		TOEFL, ACT	575		8/1	25
Nebraska Indian Community College	Pu/A						None	10
Nebraska Methodist College of Nursing and Allied Health	Pr/AB	504		TOEFL	550		4/1	25
Nebraska Wesleyan University	Pr/B	1,854	3	TOEFL	525		5/1	30
Northeast Community College	Pu/A	2,573	6	TOEFL	500			
Peru State College	Pu/B			TOEFL	550	570	8/1	10
Union College	Pr/AB	867		TOEFL, ACT	550		None	
University of Nebraska - Kearney	Pu/B	5,090	383	TOEFL	500	541	5/1	45
University of Nebraska - Lincoln	Pu/AB	18,053	499	TOEFL	525		5/1	25
University of Nebraska - Omaha	Pu/B	11,080	259	TOEFL	500		7/1	45
Vatterott College: Spring Valley	Pr/A	500						
Wayne State College	Pu/B	2,802	23	TOEFL	550		6/1	50
Western Nebraska Community College	Pu/A	1,541	43	TOEFL	500	515	8/1	
York College	Pr/AB	385	5	TOEFL, SAT/ACT	500		7/1	100
Nevada								
Art Institute of Las Vegas	Pr/AB	1,198		TOEFL	500		None	50
Career College of Northern Nevada	Pr/A	241		TOEFL	500		None	25
College of Southern Nevada	Pu/AB	38,990		TOEFL	450		None	50
DeVry University: Henderson	Pr/AB	127	1					50
International Academy of Design and Technology: Henderson	Pr/AB	418		TOEFL	550			50

Student services			Housing		Academic year costs		Maximum credits/summer	Credit hour charge	International financial aid			
Adviser	Orientation	ESL	Academic year	Summer	Tuition/fees	Living costs			Available	Number receiving aid	Average award	Deadline
Yes	Yes	Yes	Yes	Yes	19,620†	11,758	13		Yes			None
Yes			Yes		8,499†	7,647	12	244				
Yes		Yes	No		9,240†	7,400	12	330				
			No		1,840†	500						
			No		7,922†	6,100	12					
Yes	Yes	Yes	Yes	Yes	13,707†	8,252	18		Yes	48	$6,960	None
Yes	Yes	Yes	Yes	Yes	16,338†	10,726				45	$4,131	
Yes			Yes		14,493†	7,624	14		Yes			None
Yes	Yes		Yes	Yes	15,067†	9,860	12		Yes			None
Yes	Yes	Yes	Yes	Yes	17,679†	9,250	12		Yes			None
Yes	Yes		Yes	Yes	16,400	8,240	12	495	Yes			None
Yes	Yes	Yes	Yes	Yes	15,504†	10,074	18	588	Yes			None
			Yes		12,428†	9,445	16		Yes			None
Yes	Yes	Yes	Yes		6,165	15,360	12	220	Yes			None
Yes			Yes		7,512†	6,691	18	220	Yes			None
Yes			Yes	Yes	21,260	11,496	11	685	Yes			None
Yes			Yes		20,700	8,380	12	640	Yes	6		None
Yes	Yes	Yes	Yes	Yes	28,542	11,716	15	853	Yes	12	$6,042	None
Yes	Yes	Yes	Yes	Yes	20,120	10,250	9	550	Yes			None
Yes	Yes	Yes	Yes	Yes	20,150	8,150	12	660	Yes			None
Yes			Yes	Yes	14,490	6,390	6	390	Yes			None
Yes	Yes		Yes	Yes	19,604†	8,442	9	779	Yes			None
			No		23,420‡			390	Yes			None
Yes	Yes	Yes	Yes	Yes	2,993†	9,684		62				
Yes			Yes		2,970	7,450	9	85	Yes			None
Yes			Yes	Yes	20,925†	8,580	12		Yes			None
			Yes		5,949†	7,034	6	184				
			No		3,200†	1,950			Yes			None
			Yes	Yes	13,440	12,650	9	428	Yes			None
Yes	Yes		Yes	Yes	21,274	8,710	12	788	Yes			None
Yes		Yes	Yes	Yes	2,910†	6,997		86				
Yes			Yes	Yes	7,366†	7,216	6	220	Yes			None
Yes	Yes	Yes	Yes	Yes	16,110†	7,818		660	Yes			None
Yes	Yes	Yes	Yes	Yes	9,341†	10,394	15		Yes	124		None
Yes	Yes	Yes	Yes	Yes	16,236†	10,851	15	504	Yes			None
Yes	Yes	Yes	Yes	Yes	14,522†	8,830	12		Yes			None
Yes	Yes		Yes	Yes	7,622†	7,798		220	Yes			None
Yes		Yes	Yes		2,580†	8,124	12	73	Yes	29	$3,899	None
Yes			Yes		14,000†	9,200	9	390	Yes			None
Yes			Yes	Yes			16		Yes			None
			No			10,532			Yes			5/30
Yes	Yes	Yes	No		7,148†	7,752	12					
					13,020†	8,528		490				
					16,560							

† Tuition and fees are for 2007-08. ‡ Tuition and fees are projected for 2008-09. * Comprehensive Fee

Institution	Control/ degrees	Undergraduates		Tests required (Fall 2009)	TOEFL		Application	
		Total	Internat'l		minimum	average	Deadline	Fee
Le Cordon Bleu College of Culinary Arts	Pr/A	705						50
Nevada State College	Pu/B	1,545						30
Sierra Nevada College	Pr/B	315		TOEFL	500		7/15	
Truckee Meadows Community College	Pu/A	12,774		TOEFL	500	520	None	10
University of Nevada: Las Vegas	Pu/B	20,971	852	TOEFL	500		2/1	95
University of Nevada: Reno	Pu/B	12,659	260	TOEFL	500	567	3/1	100
University of Southern Nevada	Pr/B	139		TOEFL	550		6/15	100
Western Nevada College	Pu/AB	3,218		TOEFL	500		5/1	15
New Hampshire								
Chester College of New England	Pr/B	222		TOEFL	550		7/31	35
Colby-Sawyer College	Pr/AB	942	14	TOEFL	500		7/1	45
Daniel Webster College	Pr/AB	711		TOEFL	520	525	7/8	35
Dartmouth College	Pr/B	4,085	262	TOEFL, SAT/ACT, SAT Subject Test(s)			1/1	70
Franklin Pierce University	Pr/B	1,721		TOEFL	500		None	
Granite State College	Pu/AB	1,065		TOEFL	550		None	45
Great Bay Community College	Pu/A	2,308		TOEFL	300		None	10
Hesser College	Pr/AB	3,800		TOEFL	450	475	None	10
Lakes Region Community College	Pu/A	1,050						10
Magdalen College	Pr/AB	69	2				5/1	35
Manchester Community College	Pu/A	3,122		TOEFL	500		None	10
Nashua Community College	Pu/A	1,537		TOEFL	500		None	10
New England College	Pr/AB	1,052	73	TOEFL		420	None	30
Plymouth State University	Pu/B	4,221		TOEFL	520	560	4/1	35
River Valley Community College	Pu/A	879		TOEFL	500		8/1	10
Rivier College	Pr/AB	1,432		TOEFL	500		7/1	25
St. Anselm College	Pr/B	1,936	8	TOEFL, SAT/ACT	550	600	2/1	55
Southern New Hampshire University	Pr/AB	1,953	74	TOEFL	530		None	40
Thomas More College of Liberal Arts	Pr/B	100					8/20	
University of New Hampshire	Pu/AB	11,622	89	TOEFL, SAT/ACT	550		2/1	60
University of New Hampshire at Manchester	Pu/AB	773		TOEFL	550		4/1	60
White Mountains Community College	Pu/A	1,014		TOEFL			None	10
New Jersey								
Atlantic Cape Community College	Pu/A	6,922		TOEFL			5/1	100
Berkeley College	Pr/AB	3,041	51	TOEFL	500		None	50
Bloomfield College	Pr/B	2,033	33	TOEFL	550	613	4/30	40
Brookdale Community College	Pu/A	14,026		TOEFL	430		7/1	25
Burlington County College	Pu/A	7,147	28	TOEFL	450	518	None	100
Caldwell College	Pr/B	1,604	98				6/30	40
Centenary College	Pr/AB	2,238	59	TOEFL	450	550	7/1	50
The College of New Jersey	Pu/B	6,164	9	TOEFL, SAT/ACT	550	600	2/15	60
College of St. Elizabeth	Pr/B	1,112	51	TOEFL	500	527	8/15	35
County College of Morris	Pu/A	8,330					7/1	25
Cumberland County College	Pu/A	3,527		TOEFL			None	25
DeVry University: North Brunswick	Pr/AB	1,370	26	TOEFL	500		None	50
Drew University	Pr/B	1,620	33	TOEFL	550	618	2/15	50
Essex County College	Pu/A	10,094	848				7/8	25
Fairleigh Dickinson University: College at Florham	Pr/B	2,470	26	TOEFL	550		7/1	40
Fairleigh Dickinson University: Metropolitan Campus	Pr/AB	3,458	257	TOEFL	550		7/1	40
Felician College	Pr/AB	1,615		TOEFL	500	550	None	30
Georgian Court University	Pr/B	1,718	10	TOEFL	550		3/1	40
Gloucester County College	Pu/A	6,169		TOEFL	500		9/1	20
Hudson County Community College	Pu/A	7,018					7/1	15

| Student services | | | Housing | | Academic year costs | | Maximum credits/ summer | Credit hour charge | International financial aid | | | |
Adviser	Orientation	ESL	Academic year	Summer	Tuition/ fees	Living costs			Available	Number receiving aid	Average award	Deadline
			Yes									
					10,790†							
Yes			Yes		22,305†	11,695	15	986	Yes			None
Yes	Yes		No		7,148†	12,836	9					
Yes	Yes	Yes	Yes	Yes	14,842†	12,938	18		Yes	41	$1,823	None
Yes	Yes	Yes	Yes	Yes	14,839†	9,879	15		Yes	76	$11,011	None
			No									
Yes			No		7,148†	20,600	12					
Yes			Yes		15,930†	10,450	12	640	Yes			None
Yes	Yes	Yes	Yes		29,620	12,090		990	Yes	9	$17,040	3/1
Yes			Yes	Yes	27,032	13,069	12	1038	Yes			None
Yes	Yes		Yes	Yes	37,250	14,429	4		Yes	181	$34,719	2/1
Yes	Yes	Yes	Yes		28,300	14,424	16	810	Yes	11	$10,000	3/1
Yes			No		7,460†	3,375		240				
Yes	Yes	Yes	No		12,150†	6,755	18	400				
Yes	Yes		Yes	Yes		3,145	15					
					12,120†			400				
			Yes		11,470†	7,050			Yes			6/30
Yes		Yes	No		12,180†	550		400				
			No		12,480†	2,700		400				
Yes	Yes	Yes	Yes		26,472	12,078	18	821	Yes	15	$15,433	None
Yes	Yes		Yes	Yes	15,494†	10,676	9	572	Yes	12	$1,917	None
			No		12,090†	2,350	18	400				
Yes	Yes	Yes	Yes	Yes	23,750	11,823	12	760				
Yes	Yes		Yes	Yes	29,170	11,560	9		Yes	8	$40,207	3/15
Yes	Yes	Yes	Yes		24,954	12,800	12		Yes			None
			Yes		12,250†	10,500		500	Yes			None
Yes	Yes	Yes	Yes	Yes	24,030†	12,573		907	Yes	63	$24,338	None
		Yes	No		21,145†	18,110	8	870	Yes			3/1
			No		12,120†	7,300		400				
Yes		Yes	No		10,500†	11,360		332	Yes			None
Yes	Yes		Yes	Yes	19,050	10,300	18	435	Yes			None
Yes	Yes		Yes	Yes	20,080	12,215			Yes	22	$9,574	6/1
			No		7,428†	13,064		225				
Yes		Yes	No		5,205†	4,638		157	Yes			None
Yes	Yes	Yes	Yes	Yes	23,600	12,600	12	640	Yes			None
Yes	Yes	Yes	Yes	Yes	24,930	11,400	18	445	Yes			None
Yes	Yes		Yes		18,530†	12,442	12	542				
Yes	Yes		Yes		22,547†	15,416	9	623	Yes			None
Yes			No		8,505†	5,470	11	269	Yes			None
	Yes		No		10,890†	5,953	12	336				
Yes			No		13,220†	3,662		490				
Yes	Yes		Yes	Yes	36,470	17,260	20	1496	Yes			2/15
Yes	Yes	Yes	No		6,615	4,461		190				
Yes	Yes	Yes	Yes	Yes	28,228†	9,582	9	799	Yes			None
Yes	Yes	Yes	Yes	Yes	26,232†	10,422	9	797	Yes	5		None
Yes	Yes	Yes	Yes	Yes	21,900†	13,917	9	675	Yes	13	$17,499	None
Yes		Yes	Yes	Yes	23,360	14,262	9		Yes	7	$23,110	None
Yes			No		5,370†	1,500	16	160	Yes			None
	Yes	Yes	No		6,123†	3,300	6	258				

† Tuition and fees are for 2007-08. ‡ Tuition and fees are projected for 2008-09. * Comprehensive Fee

Institution	Control/ degrees	Undergraduates		Tests required (Fall 2009)	TOEFL		Application	
		Total	Internat'l		minimum	average	Deadline	Fee
Kean University	Pu/B	10,137	204				3/1	150
Mercer County Community College	Pu/A	7,817	450	TOEFL	400	500	None	50
Monmouth University	Pr/AB	4,694	20	TOEFL	550	577	6/1	50
Montclair State University	Pu/B	12,559	295	TOEFL, SAT	539		4/1	40
New Jersey City University	Pu/B	6,242	71	TOEFL, SAT	500	520	4/1	35
New Jersey Institute of Technology	Pu/B	4,967		TOEFL	550		None	35
Ocean County College	Pu/A	7,908		TOEFL	500		7/7	
Passaic County Community College	Pu/A						None	
Princeton University	Pr/B	4,833	451				1/2	65
Ramapo College of New Jersey	Pu/B	5,116	140	TOEFL	550		3/1	75
Raritan Valley Community College	Pu/A	5,462	144	TOEFL	500		6/1	225
Richard Stockton College of New Jersey	Pu/B	6,600	25	TOEFL	525		3/15	50
Rider University	Pr/AB	4,534	123	TOEFL, SAT/ACT	550	577	3/15	50
Rowan University	Pu/B	8,499		TOEFL	500	525	3/1	50
Rutgers, The State University of New Jersey: Camden Regional Campus	Pu/B	3,657	10	TOEFL, SAT/ACT	550		4/15	50
Rutgers, The State University of New Jersey: New Brunswick/Piscataway Campus	Pu/B	26,479	438	TOEFL, SAT/ACT	550		4/15	60
Rutgers, The State University of New Jersey: Newark Regional Campus	Pu/B	6,115	115	TOEFL, SAT/ACT	550		4/15	50
Saint Peter's College	Pr/AB	2,259	82	TOEFL, SAT/ACT	520		4/1	40
Salem Community College	Pu/A	1,303		TOEFL	520		7/1	25
Seton Hall University	Pr/B	4,896	86	TOEFL	550	563	3/1	55
Stevens Institute of Technology	Pr/B	2,040	114	TOEFL, SAT/ACT	550	581	7/1	55
Sussex County Community College	Pu/A	3,732					None	15
Thomas Edison State College	Pu/AB	15,963	240	TOEFL	500		None	75
Union County College	Pu/A	9,776	283				7/1	35
University of Medicine and Dentistry of New Jersey: School of Health Related Professions	Pu/AB			TOEFL	550		3/7	50
William Paterson University of New Jersey	Pu/B	8,760	69	TOEFL, SAT/ACT	550		5/1	50

New Mexico

Institution	Control/ degrees	Total	Internat'l	Tests required	minimum	average	Deadline	Fee
Art Center Design College	Pr/AB	294		TOEFL				25
Clovis Community College	Pu/A	1,724						
College of Santa Fe	Pr/B	657	3	TOEFL	550		None	35
College of the Southwest	Pr/B	386		TOEFL, SAT/ACT	550		None	25
Dona Ana Branch Community College of New Mexico State University	Pu/A	7,801		TOEFL	500		None	15
Eastern New Mexico University	Pu/AB	2,966	79	TOEFL, SAT/ACT	500	525	6/15	
Eastern New Mexico University: Roswell Campus	Pu/A	3,918		TOEFL	500		None	
Institute of American Indian Arts	Pu/AB	221		TOEFL	500		4/1	5
International Institute of the Americas: Albuquerque	Pr/AB	200						200
Mesalands Community College	Pu/A	313		TOEFL	540			
National American University: Rio Rancho	Pr/AB	535		TOEFL	490		None	25
Navajo Technical College	Pu/A	447						
New Mexico Highlands University	Pu/AB	1,882		TOEFL	500	540	4/1	15
New Mexico Institute of Mining and Technology	Pu/AB	1,138	23	TOEFL	540	556	6/1	50
New Mexico Junior College	Pu/A			TOEFL	500	550	7/1	
New Mexico Military Institute	Pu/A	466		TOEFL, SAT/ACT	500		7/30	85
New Mexico State University	Pu/AB	13,056	521	TOEFL	500		3/1	50
New Mexico State University at Alamogordo	Pu/A			TOEFL	500		None	50
Northern New Mexico College	Pu/AB	2,237		TOEFL			5/1	

Student services			Housing		Academic year costs		Maximum credits/ summer	Credit hour charge	International financial aid			
Adviser	Orien-tation	ESL	Academic year	Summer	Tuition/ fees	Living costs			Avail-able	Number receiving aid	Average award	Deadline
Yes	Yes	Yes	Yes	Yes	12,645†	9,190	12	323	Yes	18	$1,640	
Yes	Yes	Yes	No		6,270†	9,510	18	209	Yes			None
Yes	Yes		Yes	Yes	24,098	18,056	12	680	Yes	19	$18,839	None
Yes	Yes	Yes	Yes	Yes	16,164†	14,491	8	455	Yes	66	$4,508	None
Yes	Yes	Yes	Yes	Yes	14,759†	12,548	12	418				
Yes	Yes	Yes	Yes		20,082‡	12,208		788	Yes	149		5/15
		Yes	No		6,900†	1,000	22	203	Yes			None
Yes		Yes	No		5,601†	12,689	12	165				
Yes	Yes		Yes	Yes	34,290	15,540			Yes	323	$36,622	None
Yes	Yes		Yes		15,536†	14,260	12	390	Yes	67	$1,925	None
Yes	Yes	Yes	No		3,890†	7,000	12		Yes			None
Yes			Yes	Yes	13,685†	14,466	24	352				
Yes	Yes		Yes	Yes	27,730	14,530	14	870	Yes	3	$8,900	None
Yes	Yes		Yes	Yes	17,376†	12,042	12	564				
Yes			Yes		19,700†	11,754	12	574	Yes	2		None
Yes	Yes	Yes	Yes	Yes	19,854†	12,492	12	574	Yes	1		None
Yes	Yes	Yes	Yes		19,435†	12,764	12	574	Yes	4		None
Yes	Yes	Yes	Yes	Yes	24,026†	11,550	12	784	Yes			None
Yes			No		3,695†	5,100	12	93				
Yes	Yes	Yes	Yes	Yes	29,630	15,860	12	844	Yes	96	$15,627	None
Yes	Yes		Yes	Yes	36,800	12,750	18	1164	Yes			None
		Yes	No		5,490†	8,044		164				
Yes			No		6,150†			165				
Yes	Yes	Yes	No		6,210	5,560		180				
Yes			No		11,926†	13,000	12	380				
Yes	Yes	Yes	Yes	Yes	16,242†	25,980	12	399	Yes	8	$7,932	
					23,040†	1,200						
		Yes	No		1,552†	6,900		51				
			Yes	Yes	28,558	11,714			Yes			None
Yes			Yes	Yes	11,700†	11,955	12	390	Yes			6/1
Yes	Yes	Yes	Yes	Yes	3,600	9,726	14	150				
	Yes		Yes	Yes	8,700†	11,813	9		Yes			None
Yes			Yes		4,540†	9,141	12	184				
Yes			Yes		4,950†	10,036		200	Yes			None
			No		11,400‡	11,100						
			No		2,387†			69				
			No		11,930†	2,859	16	260				
			Yes		840	4,856						
Yes	Yes		Yes	Yes	4,868†	8,676	9		Yes			5/1
Yes	Yes		Yes	Yes	11,761†	10,037	6	467	Yes	11		None
Yes			Yes	Yes	1,674†	7,745	14	51	Yes			None
Yes			Yes		8,421	6,030	2		Yes			None
Yes	Yes	Yes	Yes	Yes	14,180†	10,262	12	591				
Yes	Yes	Yes	No		4,008†	9,026	12	165				
Yes			Yes		2,206†	7,220	9	85				

† Tuition and fees are for 2007-08.   ‡ Tuition and fees are projected for 2008-09.   * Comprehensive Fee

Institution	Control/ degrees	Undergraduates		Tests required (Fall 2009)	TOEFL		Application	
		Total	Internat'l		minimum	average	Deadline	Fee
St. John's College	Pr/B	436	8	TOEFL, SAT/ACT	550		3/1	
San Juan College	Pu/A	4,773	3	TOEFL	550	580	5/29	
Santa Fe Community College	Pu/A	5,670		TOEFL	517		7/1	
University of New Mexico	Pu/AB			TOEFL	520		3/1	50
Western New Mexico University	Pu/AB	1,747	25		550		6/1	
New York								
Adelphi University	Pr/AB	4,973	195	TOEFL	550		None	50
Adirondack Community College	Pu/A	3,408		TOEFL	500		7/1	40
Albany College of Pharmacy	Pr/B	1,015	85	TOEFL, SAT/ACT	600		3/1	75
Alfred University	Pr/B	2,030		TOEFL, SAT/ACT		550	2/1	40
American Academy of Dramatic Arts	Pr/A			TOEFL, SAT/ACT	500		8/1	50
Art Institute of New York City	Pr/A	1,590	1		500			50
ASA Institute of Business and Computer Technology	Pr/A	2,958	135				9/1	25
Bard College	Pr/AB	1,737	160	TOEFL	600	620	1/15	50
Barnard College	Pr/B	2,346	86	TOEFL, SAT, SAT Subject Test(s), or ACT	600	620	1/1	45
Berkeley College	Pr/AB	704	48	TOEFL	500		None	50
Berkeley College of New York City	Pr/AB	2,595	459	TOEFL	500		None	50
Briarcliffe College	Pr/AB	1,996		TOEFL	500		None	35
Broome Community College	Pu/A	5,336	137	TOEFL	527		None	
Bryant & Stratton College: Albany	Pr/A	617		TOEFL	500			
Bryant & Stratton College: Buffalo	Pr/A	614						25
Bryant & Stratton College: Henrietta	Pr/A	715						
Bryant & Stratton College: Rochester	Pr/A	720					None	25
Bryant & Stratton College: Southtowns	Pr/A	315						25
Bryant & Stratton College: Syracuse North	Pr/A	498						
Business Informatics Center	Pr/A						None	50
Canisius College	Pr/AB	3,301	99	TOEFL	500		7/15	40
Cayuga County Community College	Pu/A	2,704	8	TOEFL	500		None	
Cazenovia College	Pr/AB	1,024	3	TOEFL	550		None	30
City University of New York: Baruch College	Pu/B	12,626	1,613	TOEFL	620	650	2/1	65
City University of New York: Borough of Manhattan Community College	Pu/A	19,259		TOEFL	450	550		50
City University of New York: Bronx Community College	Pu/A	8,767		TOEFL	500		8/15	60
City University of New York: Brooklyn College	Pu/B	11,923	725	TOEFL	500		None	65
City University of New York: City College	Pu/B	10,683		TOEFL	500	562	3/15	65
City University of New York: College of Staten Island	Pu/AB	11,197	390	TOEFL	450		3/1	65
City University of New York: CUNY Online	Pu/B	498			580		6/1	70
City University of New York: Hostos Community College	Pu/A	4,416	505				7/15	50
City University of New York: Hunter College	Pu/B	14,573	1,456	TOEFL	500		11/15	65
City University of New York: John Jay College of Criminal Justice	Pu/AB	12,634	445	TOEFL, SAT/ACT	500		1/16	65
City University of New York: Kingsborough Community College	Pu/A	10,943	656	TOEFL	475		9/1	65
City University of New York: LaGuardia Community College	Pu/A	12,678	1,425	TOEFL	450		11/15	65
City University of New York: Lehman College	Pu/B	8,236	381	TOEFL	500		5/1	65
City University of New York: Medgar Evers College	Pu/AB	5,245	133	TOEFL	475	480	None	65
City University of New York: Queens College	Pu/B	13,901	910	TOEFL	500		10/15	65
City University of New York: Queensborough Community College	Pu/A	13,353		TOEFL	475		None	65
City University of New York: York College	Pu/B	5,868		TOEFL			3/1	65

| Student services | | | Housing | | Academic year costs | | Maximum credits/summer | Credit hour charge | International financial aid | | | |
Adviser	Orientation	ESL	Academic year	Summer	Tuition/fees	Living costs			Available	Number receiving aid	Average award	Deadline
Yes			Yes	Yes	39,154	11,059			Yes	7	$34,143	None
Yes			No		6,000†	3,400	12	250				
Yes		Yes	No		2,439†	13,196	7	78	Yes			None
Yes	Yes	Yes	Yes	Yes	14,942†	7,020	9	623	Yes			None
		Yes	Yes	Yes	11,887†	8,015	12					
Yes	Yes	Yes	Yes	Yes	25,240	13,100	24	750	Yes	185	$11,653	None
Yes			No		6,487†	9,190	12	262				
Yes			Yes		24,450	9,300		735	Yes	7	$10,467	3/1
Yes	Yes	Yes	Yes	Yes	24,278	14,596	16	760	Yes	48	$8,126	3/15
Yes	Yes		No		20,000	9,690			Yes			None
Yes	Yes		No		24,485†	650		470				
Yes		Yes	No		11,499	6,531	18	470	Yes	139	$4,166	None
Yes		Yes	Yes	Yes	38,374	12,866		1176	Yes	143	$33,234	2/15
Yes			Yes	Yes	37,538	14,438		1200	Yes	7	$26,406	2/1
Yes	Yes		Yes	Yes	19,050	10,300	18	435	Yes			None
Yes	Yes		No		19,050	1,300	18	435	Yes			None
			Yes		15,979†		12	638				
Yes	Yes	Yes	No		6,421†	7,186		256				
			No		13,740		20					
			No		13,740	3,270	21	458				
					13,080†			436				
			No		13,080†	1,000		436				
					13,080†	1,200						
					12,450†							
			No		10,950†		15					
Yes	Yes	Yes	Yes	Yes	26,427†	9,770	9	724	Yes	99	$20,467	None
Yes			No		6,970†	8,739	15	240				
			Yes		22,894	11,602	12		Yes	2	$10,320	None
Yes	Yes	Yes	No		11,120†	15,743	12	360	Yes	34	$3,777	4/30
Yes	Yes	Yes	No		5,968†	9,712	6	190				
Yes			No		6,004†	2,561		190				
Yes	Yes	Yes	No		11,177†	8,850	6	360	Yes	51		None
Yes	Yes	Yes	Yes		11,079†	8,074	6	360	Yes			None
Yes	Yes	Yes	No		11,128†	18,318	8	360	Yes			None
					4,330†	1,016	12					
Yes	Yes	Yes	No		6,005†	11,193	6	190				
Yes		Yes	Yes		11,149†	9,912	7	360	Yes			None
Yes			No		11,079†	875	6	360	Yes			
Yes			No		6,000†	15,743	8	190				
Yes	Yes	Yes	No		5,992†	13,440		190	Yes			
Yes	Yes	Yes	No		11,090†	15,743	8	360	Yes			None
Yes			No		11,052†	8,154	9	360				
Yes	Yes	Yes	No		11,177†	13,732	11	360				
Yes	Yes		No		5,986†	8,817		190				
Yes	Yes	Yes	No		11,062†	3,382	12	360	Yes	5	$775	None

† Tuition and fees are for 2007-08. ‡ Tuition and fees are projected for 2008-09. * Comprehensive Fee

Institution	Control/ degrees	Undergraduates		Tests required (Fall 2009)	TOEFL		Application	
		Total	Internat'l		minimum	average	Deadline	Fee
Clarkson University	Pr/B	2,521	61	TOEFL, SAT/ACT	550		3/1	50
Clinton Community College	Pu/A	2,120		TOEFL	425		7/1	
Colgate University	Pr/B	2,800	133	TOEFL, SAT/ACT			1/15	55
College of Mount St. Vincent	Pr/AB	1,417	7	TOEFL, SAT/ACT	550	600	7/1	35
College of New Rochelle	Pr/B	933	5	TOEFL	550	605	None	20
College of Saint Rose	Pr/B	3,116		TOEFL	500		5/1	35
Columbia University	Pr/B	5,602	498	TOEFL, SAT, SAT Subject Test(s), or ACT	600	630	1/2	70
Columbia University: School of General Studies	Pr/B	1,190		TOEFL	600		4/1	65
Columbia-Greene Community College	Pu/A	1,438	3	TOEFL	575		None	30
Concordia College	Pr/AB	673	68	TOEFL	550	553	7/1	100
Cooper Union for the Advancement of Science and Art	Pr/B	889	125	TOEFL, SAT/ACT	600	650	1/1	65
Cornell University	Pr/B	13,455	1,028	TOEFL, SAT/ACT	600		1/1	65
Corning Community College	Pu/A	5,072		TOEFL	550		5/1	25
Culinary Institute of America	Pr/AB	2,738		TOEFL		534	None	50
Daemen College	Pr/B	1,571	11	TOEFL	500	570	None	25
Davis College	Pr/AB	225		TOEFL				25
DeVry Institute of Technology: New York	Pr/AB	880	13	TOEFL	500		None	50
Dominican College of Blauvelt	Pr/AB	1,698	14	TOEFL	550		None	35
Dowling College	Pr/B	2,914	181	TOEFL	500		None	25
Dutchess Community College	Pu/A	8,248		TOEFL	500	520	6/15	
D'Youville College	Pr/B	1,532	172	TOEFL	500	515	5/1	25
Eastman School of Music of the University of Rochester	Pr/B	506		TOEFL			12/1	100
Elmira College	Pr/AB	1,415		TOEFL	500	585	3/1	50
Erie Community College: City Campus	Pu/A	2,656	2	TOEFL	460	470	5/31	25
Erie Community College: North Campus	Pu/A	5,204	59	TOEFL	460	470	5/31	25
Erie Community College: South Campus	Pu/A	3,216	9	TOEFL	460	470	5/31	25
Eugene Lang College The New School for Liberal Arts	Pr/B	1,281	44	TOEFL, SAT/ACT			2/1	50
Excelsior College	Pr/AB	33,422	246				None	75
Fashion Institute of Technology	Pu/AB	7,535	861	TOEFL	550	558	1/1	40
Five Towns College	Pr/AB	1,093		TOEFL	520		None	35
Fordham University	Pr/B	7,541	141	TOEFL	550	575	2/1	50
Fulton-Montgomery Community College	Pu/A	1,722	91	TOEFL	500		8/1	
Genesee Community College	Pu/A	3,753	113	TOEFL	460	500		
Globe Institute of Technology	Pr/AB	2,305					None	200
Hamilton College	Pr/B	1,810	94	TOEFL	600	640	1/1	50
Hartwick College	Pr/B	1,513	44	TOEFL	550	600	2/15	35
Herkimer County Community College	Pu/A	3,328		TOEFL	500	525	None	
Hobart and William Smith Colleges	Pr/B	1,998	37	TOEFL	550	600	2/1	45
Hofstra University	Pr/B	8,298	122	TOEFL	550		6/1	75
Houghton College	Pr/AB	1,324	43	TOEFL	550		3/15	40
Hudson Valley Community College	Pu/A	12,346		TOEFL	450		None	30
Institute of Design and Construction	Pr/A	175					None	30
Iona College	Pr/B	3,480	47	TOEFL, SAT/ACT	550	561	2/15	50
Island Drafting and Technical Institute	Pr/A	123		TOEFL				25
Ithaca College	Pr/B	6,185	121	TOEFL, SAT/ACT	550		2/1	60
Jamestown Community College	Pu/A	2,983		TOEFL	500		6/1	40
Juilliard School	Pr/B	491	82	TOEFL			12/1	100
Keuka College	Pr/B	1,441		TOEFL	500		None	30
King's College	Pr/B	215	13	TOEFL, SAT/ACT	580		2/1	30
Laboratory Institute of Merchandising	Pr/AB	1,107	15	TOEFL	550		None	40

Student services			Housing		Academic year costs		Maximum credits/summer	Credit hour charge	International financial aid			
Adviser	Orientation	ESL	Academic year	Summer	Tuition/fees	Living costs			Available	Number receiving aid	Average award	Deadline
Yes	Yes	Yes	Yes	Yes	31,010	13,790	12	1011	Yes	30	$12,433	None
Yes			Yes		8,296†	4,870	12	335				
Yes	Yes		Yes		39,545	11,505			Yes	94	$42,010	1/15
	Yes		Yes		24,600	11,320	9	700	Yes			None
Yes		Yes	Yes	Yes	23,700†	11,300	6	781	Yes	9		None
Yes	Yes		Yes	Yes	21,972	12,086	12		Yes			None
Yes	Yes	Yes	Yes	Yes	37,223†	11,997			Yes	186	$34,981	3/1
Yes	Yes	Yes	Yes		36,013†	18,890	15	1146	Yes	94	$8,364	6/1
Yes			No		6,394†	1,870	15	256				
Yes	Yes	Yes	Yes	Yes	21,950†	13,520			Yes			None
Yes			Yes		34,600	15,725	6		Yes	100	$30,000	6/1
Yes	Yes	Yes	Yes	Yes	36,504	15,210	13		Yes	217	$21,896	2/11
			No		7,076†	5,100	12	280				
Yes			Yes		22,370†	7,865			Yes	62		None
Yes	Yes	Yes	Yes		18,750†	11,410	9	610				
					12,250	6,000		375				
Yes					14,640†	8,528		525				
			Yes		20,300	11,130		640	Yes	10	$17,321	None
Yes	Yes	Yes	Yes	Yes	19,270†	12,418	15	606	Yes	82	$13,390	None
Yes			No		6,017†	9,750	12	230	Yes			None
Yes	Yes		Yes	Yes	19,000	12,900	9		Yes			None
Yes	Yes	Yes	Yes	Yes	32,626†	13,277	6	990	Yes			2/28
Yes	Yes	Yes	Yes	Yes	33,200	14,600	9		Yes	97	$21,966	6/30
Yes	Yes	Yes	No		6,326†	8,050		250				
Yes	Yes	Yes	No		6,326†	8,050		250				
Yes	Yes	Yes	No		6,326†	8,050		250				
Yes			Yes	Yes	33,060	16,674		1100	Yes	32	$6,025	None
Yes			No						Yes			None
Yes		Yes	Yes	Yes	10,316†	13,795		412				
Yes			Yes		17,800	18,150	12	725				
Yes	Yes	Yes	Yes	Yes	35,257‡	16,150	12	739	Yes	40	$21,999	2/1
Yes	Yes	Yes	No	Yes	6,562†	500	12	256				
Yes	Yes			Yes	4,190†	9,405	12	154				
Yes	Yes	Yes	Yes	Yes	11,040	5,800	19	450	Yes			None
Yes	Yes	Yes	Yes	Yes	38,600	9,810			Yes	89	$33,941	2/8
Yes	Yes		Yes		31,900	10,610		952	Yes	49		None
Yes	Yes	Yes	Yes	Yes	5,430†	4,070	15	208				
Yes	Yes	Yes	Yes	Yes	38,860	11,496			Yes	32	$18,862	2/15
Yes	Yes		Yes	Yes	26,730†	13,940	15	785	Yes	58	$21,537	None
Yes	Yes		Yes	Yes	22,990	9,080		960	Yes	40	$12,811	None
Yes			No		9,104†	2,250	12	348				
Yes			No		7,800	800		260				
Yes	Yes		Yes		26,206	15,250	12	810	Yes	41	$18,305	4/15
					12,800†	6,831		415				
Yes	Yes		Yes	Yes	30,606	13,726	15	1020	Yes	127		None
Yes			Yes	Yes	7,150†	8,480	12	253				
Yes	Yes	Yes	Yes	Yes	28,640	16,340			Yes	82	$23,974	3/1
Yes			Yes		21,760	11,800	15	705	Yes	4	$10,371	None
Yes			Yes	Yes	22,850	11,050		950	Yes	13	$13,276	None
Yes			Yes		19,825	23,000	9	600	Yes			None

† Tuition and fees are for 2007-08.   ‡ Tuition and fees are projected for 2008-09.   * Comprehensive Fee

Institution	Control/ degrees	Undergraduates		Tests required (Fall 2009)	TOEFL		Application	
		Total	Internat'l		minimum	average	Deadline	Fee
Le Moyne College	Pr/B	2,490	20	TOEFL	550		2/1	35
Long Island Business Institute	Pr/A	610	17				None	50
Long Island University: Brooklyn Campus	Pr/AB	5,047	38	TOEFL	500	510		30
Long Island University: C. W. Post Campus	Pr/B	5,139	117	TOEFL	527	560	None	30
Manhattan College	Pr/B	2,986		TOEFL	550		5/1	40
Manhattan School of Music	Pr/B	415	94	TOEFL	550		12/1	100
Manhattanville College	Pr/B	1,752		TOEFL	550	595	None	60
Mannes College The New School for Music	Pr/B	189	63	TOEFL	550		12/1	100
Marist College	Pr/B	4,769	12	TOEFL, SAT/ACT	550	580	2/15	50
Marymount Manhattan College	Pr/AB	1,813	50	TOEFL	550	600	None	60
Medaille College	Pr/AB	1,640		TOEFL, SAT/ACT	550	553	None	25
Mercy College	Pr/AB	4,905	66	TOEFL	500		8/1	37
Metropolitan College of New York	Pr/AB	651		TOEFL	550		7/1	30
Mildred Elley	Pr/A	409					None	25
Mohawk Valley Community College	Pu/A	4,635	67				None	
Molloy College	Pr/AB	2,848		TOEFL	500		None	30
Monroe College	Pr/AB	6,232	368	TOEFL	450		4/25	35
Monroe Community College	Pu/A	17,482		TOEFL	500		6/1	20
Nassau Community College	Pu/A	19,872					8/1	40
Nazareth College of Rochester	Pr/B	2,120	19	TOEFL	550	630	2/15	40
New York Career Institute	Pr/A	563					None	50
New York Institute of Technology	Pr/AB	6,267	352	TOEFL, SAT/ACT	550	560	7/15	50
New York School of Interior Design	Pr/AB	685		TOEFL	550		None	75
New York University	Pr/AB	20,899	1,154	TOEFL, SAT/ACT	600		1/15	75
Niagara County Community College	Pu/A	4,175	23	TOEFL	500		8/1	
Niagara University	Pr/AB	3,219	381	TOEFL	500		4/15	30
North Country Community College	Pu/A	1,054	22	TOEFL	500	520	None	
Nyack College	Pr/AB			TOEFL	550		None	25
Onondaga Community College	Pu/A	7,138	40	TOEFL	500		6/15	40
Pace University	Pr/AB	7,178		TOEFL	570		7/15	45
Parsons The New School for Design	Pr/AB	3,537	1,159	TOEFL	580			50
Paul Smith's College	Pr/AB	930		TOEFL	500		None	30
Phillips Beth Israel School of Nursing	Pr/A	225	9	TOEFL	550	580	5/1	50
Polytechnic University	Pr/B	1,467	192	TOEFL, SAT	550		None	50
Pratt Institute	Pr/AB	3,040	302	TOEFL	530	543	2/1	90
Rensselaer Polytechnic Institute	Pr/B	5,119	112	TOEFL, SAT/ACT	570	610	1/15	70
Roberts Wesleyan College	Pr/AB	1,312	24	TOEFL	550		2/1	35
Rochester Institute of Technology	Pr/AB	12,779		TOEFL	550	600	6/1	50
Rockland Community College	Pu/A	6,653					7/15	30
Russell Sage College	Pr/B	655		TOEFL	550		7/1	30
Sage College of Albany	Pr/AB	883	2	TOEFL	550			30
Saint Bonaventure University	Pr/B	1,947		TOEFL	550	619	4/1	30
St. Elizabeth College of Nursing	Pr/A	184		TOEFL	500		None	30
St. Francis College	Pr/AB	2,224	154	TOEFL	500	515	None	35
St. John Fisher College	Pr/B	2,796	9	TOEFL, SAT/ACT	550		2/15	30
St. John's University	Pr/AB	12,178	481	TOEFL	500	555	5/1	30
St. Joseph's College	Pr/B	1,059	8	TOEFL, SAT	550	580	3/1	25
St. Joseph's College: Suffolk Campus	Pr/B	3,400		TOEFL	550		4/1	25
St. Lawrence University	Pr/B	2,160	117	TOEFL	600		2/1	60
St. Thomas Aquinas College	Pr/AB	1,437	15	TOEFL	500	520	3/1	30
Sarah Lawrence College	Pr/B	1,314	32	TOEFL	600		1/1	60
Schenectady County Community College	Pu/A	3,644		TOEFL	550		3/1	
School of Visual Arts	Pr/B	3,323	434	TOEFL		567	None	80
Siena College	Pr/B	3,151	15	TOEFL, SAT/ACT	550		3/1	50
Skidmore College	Pr/B	2,771	77	TOEFL, SAT/ACT	590	611	1/15	60

| Student services | | | Housing | | Academic year costs | | Maximum credits/ summer | Credit hour charge | International financial aid | | | Deadline |
Adviser	Orien- tation	ESL	Academic year	Summer	Tuition/ fees	Living costs			Avail- able	Number receiving aid	Average award	
Yes	Yes		Yes	Yes	25,000	11,800	12	509	Yes	19	$21,964	None
Yes		Yes	No		10,200	4,850	21	325	Yes			None
Yes		Yes	Yes		25,922 †	9,410		771	Yes			None
Yes	Yes		Yes	Yes	25,950 †	9,600		771				
Yes	Yes	Yes	Yes	Yes	23,240 ‡	11,550	12					
Yes	Yes	Yes	Yes		30,475	17,775		1300	Yes	40	$20,525	3/1
Yes	Yes	Yes	Yes	Yes	31,620	15,390	12	700	Yes			3/1
Yes	Yes	ESL	Yes		32,150	16,674		1030	Yes			None
Yes	Yes		Yes	Yes	24,040 †	15,020	9	550	Yes	8	$20,572	5/1
Yes	Yes	Yes	Yes	Yes	21,792	15,760	6	663	Yes	11	$4,890	None
			Yes		18,230	13,046	6	645	Yes	5	$10,000	None
Yes	Yes	Yes	Yes	Yes	15,470	9,820	18	630	Yes			None
Yes		Yes	No		16,750	13,336	16		Yes			None
			No		9,900 †			338	Yes			None
Yes	Yes	Yes	Yes		6,704 †	12,714	12	240	Yes			None
Yes		Yes	No		18,570 †	11,480		585	Yes			5/1
Yes			Yes		11,212	13,772	15	438	Yes			3/31
Yes			Yes		5,990 †	5,835	12	234				
Yes	Yes	Yes	No		6,864 †	18,828	15	276	Yes			None
Yes	Yes		Yes		24,226	11,916	12	549				
			No			5,400						
Yes	Yes		Yes	Yes	22,750	14,260		747	Yes			None
Yes	Yes		No		19,790	18,100	6	650				
Yes	Yes	Yes	Yes	Yes	35,290 †	13,900	16	980				
Yes			No		5,102 †	11,410	12	199				
Yes	Yes	Yes	Yes	Yes	23,575	12,100	12	750				
Yes			Yes		9,250 †	10,550	12	390				
Yes		Yes	Yes		18,300	11,850			Yes			None
Yes	Yes	Yes	Yes		6,921 †	11,964	18	258				
Yes	Yes	Yes	Yes	Yes	31,357	13,828	12	879	Yes	159	$7,708	None
Yes	Yes	Yes	Yes	Yes	34,460	16,674	18	1150	Yes	710	$6,540	None
Yes			Yes		19,250	13,100			Yes			None
Yes			No		16,310	2,210	7	340	Yes			6/1
Yes			Yes		32,644	12,222	12	994	Yes	135	$16,123	None
Yes	Yes	Yes	Yes	Yes	32,990	13,566		1026	Yes	6		2/1
Yes	Yes	Yes	Yes	Yes	37,990	12,545	16	1155	Yes	50	$28,778	2/15
Yes		Yes	Yes	Yes	22,600	11,477	12		Yes	26	$13,586	None
Yes	Yes	Yes	Yes	Yes	28,035	11,731	18	597	Yes	150	$6,000	None
Yes	Yes	Yes	No	Yes	6,665 †	2,400	15	266				
Yes			Yes		26,740	12,260		860	Yes			None
Yes			Yes		19,490	12,410		610	Yes			None
Yes	Yes		Yes	Yes	23,605 †	12,240	12	680	Yes			None
					12,350 †	12,150		300	Yes			None
Yes	Yes		No		14,970 †	13,642	12		Yes	97		None
Yes			Yes	Yes	23,690	11,840	14	625	Yes			None
Yes	Yes	Yes	Yes		28,790	17,970	12	937	Yes	308	$19,521	None
Yes					14,532	7,210	9	460	Yes			None
Yes			No		14,532 †	2,800	9	460	Yes			None
Yes	Yes		Yes		37,915	11,145	12		Yes	117	$42,610	2/1
Yes	Yes	Yes	Yes	Yes	20,000	13,730	12	630	Yes			None
Yes			Yes		40,350	15,116			Yes	13	$37,545	2/1
Yes			No		5,994 †	4,650	6	234				
Yes	Yes	Yes	Yes	Yes	25,500	17,050	18	850	Yes	92	$6,221	None
Yes	Yes	Yes	Yes	Yes	23,950	11,820		450	Yes			2/15
Yes	Yes		Yes	Yes	38,888	12,612		1270	Yes	37	$35,000	1/15

† Tuition and fees are for 2007-08.   ‡ Tuition and fees are projected for 2008-09.   * Comprehensive Fee

Institution	Control/ degrees	Undergraduates		Tests required (Fall 2009)	TOEFL		Application	
		Total	Internat'l		minimum	average	Deadline	Fee
State University of New York at Albany . . . . .Pu/B		12,449	240	TOEFL	550		3/1	40
State University of New York at Binghamton . . . . .Pu/B		11,435	971	TOEFL	550		3/15	40
State University of New York at Buffalo . . . . .Pu/B		18,470	1,815	TOEFL	550	584	None	40
State University of New York at Farmingdale . . . . . . .Pu/AB		5,569	48	TOEFL	500		6/1	40
State University of New York at New Paltz . . . . .Pu/B		5,803	118	TOEFL	550		4/1	40
State University of New York at Oswego . . . . .Pu/B		6,962	87	TOEFL	550	570	4/15	40
State University of New York at Purchase . . . . .Pu/B		3,764	90	TOEFL, SAT/ACT	550		1/1	40
State University of New York at Stony Brook . . . . . . .Pu/B		15,222	884	TOEFL	550		4/1	40
State University of New York College at Brockport . . . . .Pu/B		6,841	52	TOEFL	530	620	7/1	40
State University of New York College at Buffalo . . . . .Pu/B		8,935	65	TOEFL, SAT, SAT Subject Test(s), or ACT	500			40
State University of New York College at Cortland . . . . .Pu/B		5,904	15	TOEFL, SAT/ACT	550		6/1	30
State University of New York College at Fredonia . . . . .Pu/B		5,067	2	TOEFL	500	510	None	40
State University of New York College at Geneseo . . . . .Pu/B		5,376	119	TOEFL	525	586	6/1	40
State University of New York College at Old Westbury . . . . .Pu/B		3,405	44	TOEFL	513		None	40
State University of New York College at Oneonta . . . . .Pu/B		5,620	119	TOEFL	500	525	None	40
State University of New York College at Plattsburgh . . . . .Pu/B		5,516	390	TOEFL	540	558	4/1	40
State University of New York College at Potsdam . . . . .Pu/B		3,571	136	TOEFL	550	608	None	40
State University of New York College of Agriculture and Technology at Cobleskill . . . . . . .Pu/AB		2,559	74	TOEFL	500		None	40
State University of New York College of Agriculture and Technology at Morrisville . . . . . . .Pu/AB		3,388		TOEFL	500	550		40
State University of New York College of Environmental Science and Forestry . . . . .Pu/AB		1,455	11	TOEFL	550		None	40
State University of New York College of Technology at Alfred . . . . .Pu/AB		3,027		TOEFL	500	530	5/1	40
State University of New York College of Technology at Canton . . . . .Pu/AB		2,384	18	TOEFL	550		5/1	40
State University of New York College of Technology at Delhi . . . . .Pu/AB		2,778		TOEFL	450		None	40
State University of New York Empire State College . . . . .Pu/AB		10,731		TOEFL	550		None	
State University of New York Institute of Technology at Utica/Rome . . . . .Pu/B		1,913	11		550		8/15	40
State University of New York Maritime College . . . . .Pu/AB		1,327	108	TOEFL	500		None	40
State University of New York Upstate Medical University . . . . .Pu/B		247	2	TOEFL	550	575	None	40
Suffolk County Community College . . . . .Pu/A		22,664		TOEFL	500		7/15	35
Sullivan County Community College . . . . .Pu/A		1,611		TOEFL	550		5/1	25
Swedish Institute . . . . .Pr/A		511		TOEFL				45
Syracuse University . . . . .Pr/AB		11,796	447	TOEFL, SAT/ACT	550	603	1/1	70
Technical Career Institutes . . . . .Pr/A		3,193					None	75
Tompkins-Cortland Community College . . . . .Pu/A		2,842	70	TOEFL	450	480	7/15	15
Touro College . . . . .Pr/AB				TOEFL	500	525	4/15	30
Trocaire College . . . . .Pr/A		1,025		TOEFL	550		None	25
Ulster County Community College . . . . .Pu/A		2,137	9	TOEFL	500	550	8/1	25
Union College . . . . .Pr/B		2,134	48	TOEFL	600		1/15	50
United States Merchant Marine Academy . . . . .Pu/B		995		TOEFL, SAT/ACT	533	614	2/1	
University of Rochester . . . . .Pr/B		4,964	280	TOEFL	600	610	1/15	50
Utica College . . . . .Pr/B		2,336	40	TOEFL	525		None	40

Student services			Housing		Academic year costs		Maximum credits/summer	Credit hour charge	International financial aid			
Adviser	Orientation	ESL	Academic year	Summer	Tuition/fees	Living costs			Available	Number receiving aid	Average award	Deadline
Yes	Yes	Yes	Yes	Yes	12,278†	11,782		442				
Yes	Yes	Yes	Yes	Yes	12,272†	12,688	16	442	Yes	35	$17,668	None
Yes	Yes	Yes	Yes	Yes	12,478†	9,480	12	442	Yes	108		None
Yes			Yes	Yes	11,600†	17,264	12	442	Yes			None
Yes	Yes	Yes	Yes	Yes	11,650†	13,820	12	442				
Yes	Yes	Yes	Yes	Yes	11,694†	13,920	12	442	Yes	9	$5,146	None
Yes	Yes	Yes	Yes	Yes	12,031†	12,144	8	442	Yes			None
Yes	Yes	Yes	Yes	Yes	12,020†	11,426	16	442	Yes	110	$8,296	None
Yes	Yes		Yes		11,666†	13,413	16	442	Yes	29	$11,411	None
Yes	Yes	Yes	Yes	Yes	11,635†	12,814	16	442				
Yes	Yes		Yes		11,699†	11,860	12	442				
Yes	Yes		Yes	Yes	11,802†	11,278	12	442	Yes	26	$1,961	5/15
Yes	Yes	Yes	Yes	Yes	11,876†	10,850		442	Yes			2/15
Yes	Yes		Yes	Yes	11,437†	12,020	16	442				
Yes	Yes	Yes	Yes	Yes	11,730†	12,006	12	442				
Yes	Yes	Yes	Yes	Yes	11,667†	13,757	12	442	Yes	366	$5,773	None
Yes	Yes		Yes	Yes	11,666†	11,520	18	442	Yes	118	$8,248	None
Yes	Yes	Yes	Yes	Yes	11,709†	11,942	6	442	Yes	1	$500	2/15
Yes	Yes	Yes	Yes		11,605†	11,218	12	442				
Yes	Yes	Yes	Yes	Yes	11,360†	13,570		442				
Yes	Yes	Yes	Yes		8,266†	10,178		300	Yes			None
Yes			Yes	Yes	8,358†	11,260	6	300	Yes			
Yes	Yes	Yes	Yes		8,508†	11,760						
Yes			No		10,835†	11,430		442				
Yes	Yes		Yes	Yes	11,665†	10,770	8	442	Yes			None
Yes	Yes		Yes	Yes	12,624†	12,324	9	442	Yes	2	$3,250	7/15
Yes			Yes	Yes	11,136†	9,140		442				
Yes	Yes	Yes	No		6,830†	1,875	12		Yes			6/1
Yes			No		7,096†	1,300	10	168	Yes			None
					8,420†	13,708		275				
Yes	Yes	Yes	Yes	Yes	32,339‡	16,779		1401	Yes			2/1
Yes	Yes	Yes	No		10,165†	6,986		400				
Yes	Yes	Yes	Yes	Yes	7,538†	1,000	12	266				
Yes			Yes		12,800†	9,084	6		Yes			6/1
			No		11,054†	5,300	12	431				
			No		7,131†	3,000	24	240	Yes			None
Yes	Yes		Yes	Yes	48,552*	3,008			Yes	36	$33,207	2/1
Yes			Yes			692						
Yes	Yes	Yes	Yes	Yes	37,250	13,300	16	1138	Yes	33		2/1
Yes	Yes		Yes	Yes	26,058	12,966	12	818	Yes	19	$11,481	None

† Tuition and fees are for 2007-08.   ‡ Tuition and fees are projected for 2008-09.   * Comprehensive Fee

Institution	Control/ degrees	Undergraduates		Tests required (Fall 2009)	TOEFL		Application	
		Total	Internat'l		minimum	average	Deadline	Fee
Utica School of Commerce	Pr/A	386					None	20
Vassar College	Pr/B	2,409	134	TOEFL, SAT, SAT Subject Test(s), or ACT	600	640	1/1	60
Vaughn College of Aeronautics and Technology	Pr/AB	1,063	32	TOEFL	600	640	None	40
Villa Maria College of Buffalo	Pr/AB	436		TOEFL	450		None	
Wagner College	Pr/B	1,926	16	TOEFL	550		2/15	75
Webb Institute	Pr/B	91						25
Wells College	Pr/B	544	9	TOEFL	550		3/1	40
Westchester Community College	Pu/A	10,476		TOEFL	500		None	25
Yeshiva Mikdash Melech	Pr/B	105	1				None	
North Carolina								
Appalachian State University	Pu/B	13,763	53	TOEFL, SAT/ACT	500		None	50
Art Institute of Charlotte	Pr/AB	880		TOEFL	500		None	150
Asheville-Buncombe Technical Community College	Pu/A	6,341	3	TOEFL	550		7/15	
Barton College	Pr/B	1,103	17	TOEFL	525		None	50
Belmont Abbey College	Pr/B	1,300	39	TOEFL	550	590	7/15	35
Bennett College	Pr/B	662	7	TOEFL	500		None	30
Bladen Community College	Pu/A	1,450						
Brevard College	Pr/B	647	16	TOEFL	550		5/1	30
Brunswick Community College	Pu/A							
Cabarrus College of Health Sciences	Pr/AB	353						35
Campbell University	Pr/AB	2,806		TOEFL	500		None	35
Carolina Christian College	Pr/AB							50
Carteret Community College	Pu/A	1,175		TOEFL	550		None	
Catawba College	Pr/B	1,291	17	TOEFL	525		None	30
Central Piedmont Community College	Pu/A	15,569		TOEFL	500		6/1	35
Chowan University	Pr/AB	893		TOEFL, SAT/ACT	475	500	8/1	20
College of the Albemarle	Pu/A	1,653		TOEFL	500		None	
Davidson College	Pr/B	1,667	58	TOEFL, SAT/ACT	600		1/2	50
DeVry University: Charlotte	Pr/B	107						50
Duke University	Pr/B	6,260	360	TOEFL, SAT, SAT Subject Test(s), or ACT			1/2	75
Durham Technical Community College	Pu/A							
East Carolina University	Pu/B	19,651	94	TOEFL, SAT/ACT	550		4/15	60
Elizabeth City State University	Pu/B	2,658		TOEFL, SAT/ACT	450		None	30
Elon University	Pr/B	4,939	106	TOEFL, SAT/ACT	550		6/1	50
Fayetteville State University	Pu/B	5,678		TOEFL, SAT/ACT	550		7/1	25
Fayetteville Technical Community College	Pu/A	8,471		TOEFL	550	575	3/1	
Gardner-Webb University	Pr/AB	2,638		TOEFL, SAT/ACT	500	515	None	40
Greensboro College	Pr/B	901		TOEFL, SAT/ACT	550		7/15	35
Guilford College	Pr/B	2,688	26	TOEFL	550	604	2/15	25
Guilford Technical Community College	Pu/A	10,608		TOEFL	486		6/8	
Halifax Community College	Pu/A						None	
High Point University	Pr/B	2,736		TOEFL	500	530	6/2	40
John Wesley College	Pr/AB	107		TOEFL	500		5/6	35
Johnson & Wales University: Charlotte	Pr/AB	2,569	22	TOEFL	550			
Johnson C. Smith University	Pr/B	1,463	2	TOEFL, SAT/ACT	550		None	25
Johnston Community College	Pu/A	4,174	4	TOEFL	550			
Lees-McRae College	Pr/B	871		TOEFL	500		None	
Lenoir-Rhyne College	Pr/B	1,366	12	TOEFL	550		7/1	35
Livingstone College	Pr/B	960		TOEFL			7/1	25
Louisburg College	Pr/A	730		TOEFL	500	590	None	25
Mars Hill College	Pr/B			TOEFL, SAT/ACT	500		None	25

Student services			Housing		Academic year costs		Maximum credits/ summer	Credit hour charge	International financial aid			
Adviser	Orientation	ESL	Academic year	Summer	Tuition/ fees	Living costs			Available	Number receiving aid	Average award	Deadline
			No		11,200 †	1,185	15	450				
Yes			Yes		40,210	11,585		1335	Yes	133	$42,127	2/1
Yes	Yes		Yes		15,100 ‡	14,950	12	500	Yes			None
Yes			No		13,990	2,500	12	455	Yes			None
Yes	Yes		Yes	Yes	31,000	11,960	4		Yes	3	$6,766	None
			Yes			16,450						
Yes	Yes		Yes		19,080	11,200		740	Yes	7	$7,142	None
Yes	Yes	Yes	No		8,979 †	2,150		360				
			Yes	Yes	6,500	3,800			Yes			None
Yes	Yes	Yes	Yes		13,983 †	8,890						
Yes			Yes	Yes	18,090 †		16	402				
		Yes	No		7,043 †	550	18	233				
Yes			Yes		19,938	6,782	12	785	Yes			None
Yes	Yes		Yes		21,039	16,866	6	637	Yes			None
Yes			Yes		14,648 †	12,678	7	531	Yes			4/15
			No		7,065 †	800		233				
			Yes		20,050	11,240			Yes	16	$11,668	None
			No		7,072 †	6,200		233				
			No		8,750 †	1,300		275				
Yes	Yes		Yes	Yes	20,350	12,170	12	325				
					2,430 †			125				
Yes		Yes	No		7,050 †	13,990		233	Yes			None
			Yes		22,290	10,900	6	590	Yes	16	$19,274	None
Yes	Yes	Yes	No		7,179 †	2,896	15	233	Yes			6/1
Yes			Yes	Yes	16,920 †	10,034	9	315	Yes			None
Yes		Yes	No		7,535 †	1,000	12	233	Yes			None
Yes	Yes		Yes	Yes	33,479	12,246			Yes	41	$31,379	2/15
					13,020 †	8,528		490				
Yes	Yes	Yes	Yes	Yes	37,925	13,625	16	1127	Yes			3/1
Yes		Yes	No		7,069 †	5,880		233	Yes			
Yes	Yes		Yes	Yes	14,732 †	12,140	14					
Yes			Yes		11,779 †	7,717			Yes			8/15
Yes	Yes	Yes	Yes	Yes	24,076	11,270	8	746				
Yes			Yes		13,202 †	6,160	18					
			No		7,059 †	7,600		233	Yes			7/15
Yes	Yes		Yes	Yes	20,465	7,500		328	Yes			None
Yes			Yes	Yes	20,810 †	9,930	16	565	Yes			None
Yes	Yes	Yes	Yes	Yes	26,030	10,040	16	795	Yes	12	$11,800	None
Yes	Yes	Yes	No		7,131 †	8,578	12	233				
			No		7,095 †	2,000		233	Yes			None
Yes	Yes	Yes	Yes	Yes	31,000 *	7,800	12	588				
			Yes	Yes	10,914 †	6,344	12	465	Yes			None
Yes	Yes		Yes	Yes	21,717 †	10,794		379	Yes			None
Yes	Yes		Yes		15,754	11,482	9	361	Yes			None
			No		7,069 †	15,009	9	233				
Yes	Yes	Yes	Yes		20,500	11,845	12	569	Yes			None
Yes			Yes	Yes	23,070	11,750	12	960	Yes	12	$12,299	8/1
Yes			Yes		12,474 †	10,441		507	Yes			6/30
Yes			Yes		13,185	9,894	15		Yes			None
Yes	Yes	Yes	Yes	Yes	19,894	10,791	18	660	Yes			None

† Tuition and fees are for 2007-08.   ‡ Tuition and fees are projected for 2008-09.   * Comprehensive Fee

Institution	Control/ degrees	Undergraduates		Tests required (Fall 2009)	TOEFL		Application	
		Total	Internat'l		minimum	average	Deadline	Fee
Martin Community College	Pu/A	797						
Mayland Community College	Pu/A	1,800		TOEFL	500		6/8	
McDowell Technical Community College	Pu/A	1,205		TOEFL	450			
Meredith College	Pr/B	1,937	17	TOEFL	500	564	2/15	40
Methodist University	Pr/AB	1,940		TOEFL	500	575	None	25
Miller-Motte Technical College: Cary	Pr/A	459						35
Montreat College	Pr/AB	984	15	TOEFL	500		5/1	30
Mount Olive College	Pr/AB	3,116		TOEFL	500		8/15	20
Nash Community College	Pu/A			TOEFL	550		6/1	
North Carolina Central University	Pu/B	6,326		TOEFL, SAT/ACT	500		5/1	30
North Carolina School of the Arts	Pu/B	743		TOEFL	550		3/1	100
North Carolina State University	Pu/AB	22,070	228	TOEFL	550		2/1	70
North Carolina Wesleyan College	Pr/B	1,510		TOEFL, SAT/ACT	500	550	5/1	25
Pamlico Community College	Pu/A	450						
Peace College	Pr/B	658		TOEFL, SAT/ACT	550	560	12/15	25
Pfeiffer University	Pr/B	1,069	41	TOEFL, SAT/ACT	500		8/1	25
Piedmont Baptist College	Pr/AB	258		TOEFL, ACT	500		None	50
Piedmont Community College	Pu/A	5,315		TOEFL	550			
Queens University of Charlotte	Pr/AB	1,688	93	TOEFL	550		7/1	40
Roanoke Bible College	Pr/AB	141		TOEFL	500		5/23	50
Roanoke-Chowan Community College	Pu/A			TOEFL	500		None	
Robeson Community College	Pu/A			TOEFL	500			
Rockingham Community College	Pu/A	1,777	2	TOEFL	550	560	None	
St. Andrews Presbyterian College	Pr/B	726		TOEFL	500	550	5/1	30
St. Augustine's College	Pr/B	1,284		TOEFL	500		7/1	25
Salem College	Pr/B	741	94	TOEFL, SAT/ACT	550		5/1	30
Sandhills Community College	Pu/A	3,580		TOEFL	550		3/1	
Shaw University	Pr/AB	2,606	34	TOEFL, SAT/ACT			7/30	40
Southeastern Community College	Pu/A	1,949		TOEFL			None	
Southwestern Community College	Pu/A	2,167		TOEFL	500		None	
University of North Carolina at Asheville	Pu/B	3,251	27	TOEFL	550	667	4/1	50
University of North Carolina at Chapel Hill	Pu/B	17,138	231	TOEFL, SAT/ACT	600	620	1/15	70
University of North Carolina at Charlotte	Pu/B	17,481		TOEFL	507		5/1	50
University of North Carolina at Greensboro	Pu/B	13,245	129	TOEFL	550			45
University of North Carolina at Pembroke	Pu/B	5,002	49	TOEFL	500		7/15	40
University of North Carolina at Wilmington	Pu/B	10,481	39	TOEFL, SAT/ACT	550	580	2/1	45
Vance-Granville Community College	Pu/A	4,167		TOEFL			6/1	
Wake Forest University	Pr/B	4,405	47	TOEFL, SAT/ACT	600		1/15	50
Wake Technical Community College	Pu/A	13,112			540		5/1	30
Warren Wilson College	Pr/B	869		TOEFL	550	560	3/15	15
Western Carolina University	Pu/B	7,006	89	TOEFL, SAT/ACT	550		6/1	40
Wilson Community College	Pu/A	1,820		TOEFL	550			
Wingate University	Pr/B	1,462	38	TOEFL	550	575	6/1	30
Winston-Salem State University	Pu/B	5,423	30	TOEFL	550		None	40

North Dakota

Institution	Control/ degrees	Undergraduates		Tests required (Fall 2009)	TOEFL		Application	
		Total	Internat'l		minimum	average	Deadline	Fee
Bismarck State College	Pu/A	3,591		TOEFL	525		6/15	35
Dickinson State University	Pu/AB	2,669	328	TOEFL	525	540	None	35
Fort Berthold Community College	Pu/A	201						
Jamestown College	Pr/B	981	49	TOEFL	525		6/1	20
Lake Region State College	Pu/A	1,520		TOEFL	525		None	35
Mayville State University	Pu/AB	769	32	TOEFL	525	550	None	35

Student services			Housing		Academic year costs		Maximum credits/summer	Credit hour charge	International financial aid			
Adviser	Orientation	ESL	Academic year	Summer	Tuition/fees	Living costs			Available	Number receiving aid	Average award	Deadline
			No		7,037 †	7,834		233				
Yes		Yes	No		7,071 †	1,730		233	Yes			None
Yes			No		7,055 †	11,344	18	233	Yes			None
Yes	Yes		Yes	Yes	23,550	9,240	12	615	Yes			None
Yes	Yes	Yes	Yes	Yes	21,944	10,746	18	675	Yes	66	$14,145	7/1
					10,440			232				
Yes			Yes		18,700	13,289		480	Yes			None
Yes			Yes		13,126	7,520	12	250	Yes	19	$8,400	None
		Yes	No		7,089 †	6,600		233				
Yes		Yes	Yes		13,411 †	8,901			Yes			None
Yes			Yes		16,491 †	9,185			Yes	4		None
Yes	Yes	Yes	Yes	Yes	17,315 †	10,080	15		Yes	49	$17,506	None
Yes			Yes		18,900 ‡	10,300	14	285	Yes			None
			No		7,034 †	3,560	20	233				
Yes			Yes		22,993	12,170	15	600	Yes			None
Yes	Yes		Yes	Yes	18,570	9,410	14	425	Yes			None
			Yes	Yes	10,800	7,310	18	435	Yes			None
			No		7,029 †	5,986	12	233				
Yes	Yes		Yes	Yes	22,068	10,482	12	335	Yes	44	$16,427	None
			Yes		9,150	12,790		295	Yes			
			No		7,133 †	3,735		233	Yes			None
			No		7,059 †	2,400		233	Yes			None
Yes			No		7,534 †	8,800		233				
Yes	Yes		Yes		18,192 †	12,492	6	420	Yes	10	$9,033	None
Yes	Yes		Yes	Yes	13,206 †	10,830	12	440	Yes			3/15
	Yes		Yes		19,190 †	14,300	16	965	Yes			None
Yes		Yes	No		7,069 †	11,225		233				
Yes	Yes		Yes	Yes	11,696	9,400	9	389	Yes			None
Yes			No		7,068 †	10,776		233				
			No		7,060 †	5,769		233	Yes			None
Yes	Yes		Yes	Yes	15,154 †	9,980						
Yes	Yes		Yes	Yes	20,988 †	10,720	12					
Yes	Yes	Yes	Yes	Yes	14,565 †	10,004	6					
Yes	Yes		Yes	Yes	15,297 †	9,041	6		Yes	15	$10,435	None
Yes	Yes	Yes	Yes	Yes	12,767 †	11,488	14		Yes			3/15
Yes	Yes	ESL	Yes	Yes	14,361 †	10,364	12		Yes			None
			No		7,037 †	10,330		233				
Yes	Yes		Yes	Yes	36,975	12,845	12	1517	Yes	4	$36,894	3/1
Yes	Yes	Yes	No		7,059 †	6,150	14	233	Yes			None
Yes	Yes		Yes	Yes	21,384 †	9,120			Yes			None
Yes	Yes		Yes	Yes	13,861 †	8,117	12					
		Yes	No		7,040 †	7,496	20	233	Yes			None
Yes			Yes		19,350	10,600	12	610				
Yes			Yes		11,940 †	8,321	12		Yes			3/15
			Yes		9,124 †	7,504	10	285	Yes			None
Yes		Yes	Yes	Yes	11,143 †	6,901	7		Yes			None
			No		3,340 †	4,200	18					
			Yes	Yes	15,035	8,650	12		Yes	49	$5,052	None
Yes	Yes	Yes	Yes	Yes	8,141 †	4,537	12	122	Yes			None
Yes			Yes		11,775 †	8,537	10	422	Yes	22	$3,392	None

† Tuition and fees are for 2007-08. ‡ Tuition and fees are projected for 2008-09. * Comprehensive Fee

Institution	Control/ degrees	Undergraduates		Tests required (Fall 2009)	TOEFL		Application	
		Total	Internat'l		minimum	average	Deadline	Fee
Minot State University	Pu/AB	3,140	234	TOEFL, ACT	525	553	None	35
Minot State University: Bottineau Campus	Pu/A	637	23	TOEFL, SAT/ACT			None	35
North Dakota State College of Science	Pu/A	3,190			400		8/1	35
North Dakota State University	Pu/B	10,403		TOEFL	525	550	5/1	35
Rasmussen College: Bismarck	Pr/AB	380						
Turtle Mountain Community College	Pu/AB	956						
United Tribes Technical College	Pr/A	602		TOEFL	500			
University of Mary	Pr/AB	2,010	31	TOEFL	550		8/1	25
University of North Dakota	Pu/B	10,085	253	TOEFL	525	560	4/1	35
Valley City State University	Pu/B	901	41	TOEFL	525		5/1	35
Williston State College	Pu/A	731		TOEFL	525		None	35
Ohio								
Allegheny Wesleyan College	Pr/B							35
Art Academy of Cincinnati	Pr/AB	137		TOEFL, SAT/ACT	550		6/30	
Art Institute of Cincinnati	Pr/A	75					None	100
Art Institute of Ohio: Cincinnati	Pr/A	569		TOEFL	500		None	50
Ashland University	Pr/AB	2,712	53	TOEFL, SAT/ACT	500		7/1	50
Aultman College of Nursing and Health Sciences	Pr/A							30
Baldwin-Wallace College	Pr/B	3,491	45	TOEFL	523	567	7/1	25
Bluffton University	Pr/B	921	21	TOEFL	500	600	6/1	20
Bowling Green State University	Pu/B	15,391		TOEFL	500		5/1	40
Bowling Green State University: Firelands College	Pu/AB	2,019		TOEFL				35
Brown Mackie College: Cincinnati	Pr/A	1,496		TOEFL	500		None	20
Bryant & Stratton College: Parma	Pr/AB	696		TOEFL	500	525	9/10	25
Bryant & Stratton College: Willoughby Hills	Pr/AB	520		TOEFL	500	575	9/12	25
Capital University	Pr/B	2,634	31	TOEFL	500	570	None	25
Case Western Reserve University	Pr/B	4,120	133	TOEFL	550		1/15	
Cedarville University	Pr/B	2,951	15	TOEFL	550		None	30
Central Ohio Technical College	Pu/A	3,105		TOEFL	550		6/1	20
Central State University	Pu/B	1,955	6	TOEFL, SAT/ACT	500	520	None	20
Cincinnati Christian University	Pr/AB	775		TOEFL	550		2/15	40
Cincinnati College of Mortuary Science	Pr/AB	125						25
Cincinnati State Technical and Community College	Pu/A	7,487	117	TOEFL	500	525	None	
Clark State Community College	Pu/A	3,385	3	TOEFL	500		None	15
Cleveland Institute of Art	Pr/B	478		TOEFL	550		5/1	30
Cleveland Institute of Electronics	Pr/A	2,002					None	
Cleveland Institute of Music	Pr/B	230		TOEFL	550		12/1	100
Cleveland State University	Pu/B	9,221	186	TOEFL, SAT/ACT	525	530	5/15	30
College of Mount St. Joseph	Pr/AB	1,916	3	TOEFL	510		None	25
College of Wooster	Pr/B	1,754	95	TOEFL	550	600	2/15	40
Columbus College of Art and Design	Pr/B	1,375	75	TOEFL	500	550	None	25
Columbus State Community College	Pu/A	23,057		TOEFL	480		6/15	
Cuyahoga Community College: Metropolitan Campus	Pu/A	11,073	216				None	
David N. Myers University	Pr/AB			TOEFL, SAT/ACT	520		8/15	25
Defiance College	Pr/AB	869	3	TOEFL, SAT/ACT	550		7/1	25
Denison University	Pr/B	2,212	92	TOEFL	550		1/15	40
DeVry University: Columbus	Pr/AB	2,379	2	TOEFL	500		None	50
Edison State Community College	Pu/A	3,025	5	TOEFL	500		None	20
ETI Technical College of Niles	Pr/A	296						50
Franciscan University of Steubenville	Pr/AB	1,976	22	TOEFL	550	653	5/1	20
Gallipolis Career College	Pr/A	138						50

| Student services | | | Housing | | Academic year costs | | Maximum credits/summer | Credit hour charge | International financial aid | | | |
Adviser	Orientation	ESL	Academic year	Summer	Tuition/fees	Living costs			Available	Number receiving aid	Average award	Deadline
Yes	Yes		Yes	Yes	11,415†	3,914	18	443	Yes	93	$3,618	None
			Yes		5,120†	7,680		310	Yes			None
Yes			Yes	Yes	9,051†	7,708	12	285	Yes			None
Yes	Yes	Yes	Yes	Yes	14,346†	11,378	15	558	Yes			3/15
					11,700†							
Yes			Yes	Yes	2,000†	4,064	7					
						600						
Yes	Yes		Yes		12,164	7,620	12	375	Yes			None
Yes	Yes	Yes	Yes	Yes	14,523†	12,911	12	559	Yes	100	$10,913	None
Yes			Yes	Yes	12,165†	8,433	9	351	Yes	38	$6,049	None
			Yes	Yes	4,466†	6,194		144	Yes			None
			Yes		5,550	5,442						
			Yes		21,300	8,000	18	875				
			No		13,147†	1,515						
				Yes		7,106	20					
Yes	Yes	Yes	Yes	Yes	22,898†	11,135	12	682	Yes			None
					11,925†							
Yes	Yes	Yes	Yes	Yes	23,524	10,828	20	748	Yes	24	$8,414	9/1
Yes	Yes		Yes	Yes	22,920	10,826	17	936	Yes	20	$18,084	10/1
Yes	Yes		Yes	Yes	16,368†	6,878	18	729	Yes			None
Yes	Yes		No		11,536†	6,140			Yes			None
			No			675	12		Yes			None
			No		13,080‡	8,425	15	436				
					14,540†	7,206	21		Yes			None
Yes	Yes	Yes	Yes	Yes	27,680	10,420	18	925	Yes	14		None
Yes	Yes	Yes	Yes	Yes	35,572	12,850	9	1436				
Yes	Yes		Yes		20,992	7,244	12	656				
Yes			Yes		6,300†	10,908	19	175				
Yes		Yes	Yes	Yes	11,462†	10,702	18		Yes	6	$15,064	None
Yes	Yes		Yes	Yes	12,143	9,780	9	368	Yes			None
Yes			No		14,250†	3,850	18		Yes			None
Yes		Yes	No		7,476†	4,460	18	160				
Yes					6,828†	3,550	17	143				
Yes	Yes		Yes		31,010	14,398		1215	Yes	8	$7,957	None
			No		3,540‡	675						
Yes		Yes	Yes		34,482‡	13,720		1329	Yes	25		None
Yes	Yes	Yes	Yes	Yes	10,664†	14,074	18	444	Yes	47	$14,245	None
Yes			Yes	Yes	22,000	8,700	9	465	Yes	3	$22,739	None
Yes			Yes	Yes	33,770	10,650	8		Yes	89	$25,042	None
Yes	Yes		Yes		23,564	11,836	18	955	Yes			6/4
Yes	Yes	Yes	No		9,450†	10,590	18	210	Yes			None
Yes	Yes	Yes			6,541†	3,620	16	218	Yes	39	$4,312	None
Yes					13,500†	7,183	9	450	Yes			None
Yes	Yes		Yes	Yes	21,830	10,500	12	345	Yes			None
Yes	Yes		Yes		33,010†	8,570		1000	Yes	89	$24,989	None
Yes					13,220†	8,528		490				
Yes			No		6,420†	9,828	6	198				
					7,317‡	10,040		227				
Yes	Yes		Yes	Yes	18,180†	10,400	15	595	Yes			None
			No		9,170†	18,600		190				

† Tuition and fees are for 2007-08.   ‡ Tuition and fees are projected for 2008-09.   * Comprehensive Fee

Institution	Control/ degrees	Undergraduates		Tests required (Fall 2009)	TOEFL		Application	
		Total	Internat'l		minimum	average	Deadline	Fee
Heidelberg College	Pr/B	1,255	27	TOEFL	550		6/1	25
Hiram College	Pr/B	1,271		TOEFL, SAT/ACT	550	598	3/15	35
Hocking College	Pu/A	3,792					None	50
Hondros College	Pr/A	45						100
International College of Broadcasting	Pr/A							100
James A. Rhodes State College	Pu/A	3,386		TOEFL	550		None	25
John Carroll University	Pr/B	3,022		TOEFL	550		2/1	25
Kent State University	Pu/B	17,674	172	TOEFL	525	550	None	30
Kenyon College	Pr/B	1,653	55	TOEFL, SAT/ACT	570		1/15	50
Kettering College of Medical Arts	Pr/AB	738	3	TOEFL	550		1/31	25
Lake Erie College	Pr/B	795		TOEFL	550		None	50
Lakeland Community College	Pu/A	8,780		TOEFL	500		8/1	15
Laura and Alvin Siegal College of Judaic Studies	Pr/B	13		TOEFL			None	50
Lorain County Community College	Pu/A	10,894		TOEFL	500		None	
Lourdes College	Pr/AB	1,700	2	TOEFL	500		8/1	25
Malone College	Pr/B	1,964	22	TOEFL	550		7/1	20
Marietta College	Pr/AB	1,466	89	TOEFL	550		5/1	50
MedCentral College of Nursing	Pr/B	365		TOEFL	600			50
Miami University: Hamilton Campus	Pu/AB	3,247		TOEFL	530		None	35
Miami University: Middletown Campus	Pu/AB	1,784						35
Miami University: Oxford Campus	Pu/AB	14,479	139	TOEFL, SAT/ACT	533	580	3/1	45
Mount Union College	Pr/B	2,128	45	TOEFL	550		None	
Mount Vernon Nazarene University	Pr/AB	2,033	10	TOEFL, SAT/ACT	500	550	5/1	25
Muskingum College	Pr/B	1,648	27	TOEFL	550	583	6/1	
National College: Cincinnati	Pr/A							30
National College: Dayton	Pr/A							30
National College: Stow	Pr/A							30
National College: Youngstown	Pr/A							30
North Central State College	Pu/A	3,147		TOEFL	500		None	
Notre Dame College	Pr/AB			TOEFL	550	600	7/1	30
Oberlin College	Pr/B	2,762	166	TOEFL, SAT/ACT	600	630	1/15	35
Ohio Business College	Pr/A	231					None	25
Ohio College of Massotherapy	Pr/A	264						25
Ohio Dominican University	Pr/AB	2,250	12	TOEFL	550		6/1	25
Ohio Institute of Health Careers: Columbus	Pr/A	240						40
Ohio Institute of Health Careers: Elyria	Pr/A							35
Ohio Institute of Photography and Technology	Pr/A	566		TOEFL	477		None	
Ohio Northern University	Pr/B	2,534	39	TOEFL	550		7/15	30
Ohio State University Agricultural Technical Institute	Pu/A	723	3	TOEFL, SAT/ACT	527	598		40
Ohio State University: Columbus Campus	Pu/AB	37,848	904	TOEFL, SAT/ACT	527		2/1	50
Ohio State University: Lima Campus	Pu/AB	1,194		TOEFL, SAT/ACT	527		3/1	50
Ohio State University: Mansfield Campus	Pu/AB	1,180	1	TOEFL, SAT/ACT	527		3/1	50
Ohio State University: Marion Campus	Pu/AB	1,437	2	TOEFL, SAT/ACT	527		3/1	50
Ohio State University: Newark Campus	Pu/AB	2,325		TOEFL, SAT/ACT	527		3/1	50
Ohio University	Pu/AB	16,920	286	TOEFL, SAT/ACT	550		2/1	45
Ohio University: Zanesville Campus	Pu/AB	1,799						20
Ohio Wesleyan University	Pr/B	1,960	169	TOEFL, SAT/ACT	550	608	3/1	35
Otterbein College	Pr/B	2,715	6	TOEFL	523	530	7/1	30
Owens Community College: Toledo	Pu/A	9,191	372	TOEFL	500		None	
Remington College: Cleveland	Pr/A						None	50
Remington College: Cleveland West	Pr/A	580						
Shawnee State University	Pu/AB	2,798	19	TOEFL	500	525	6/30	55
Sinclair Community College	Pu/A	19,103		TOEFL	520		7/7	20
Southwestern College: Vine Street Campus	Pr/A	416						20
Stark State College of Technology	Pu/A			TOEFL	500	505	6/1	65

Adviser	Orientation	ESL	Academic year	Summer	Tuition/fees	Living costs	Maximum credits/summer	Credit hour charge	Available	Number receiving aid	Average award	Deadline
							Student services — Housing — Academic year costs — Maximum / Credit — International financial aid					
Yes	Yes		Yes	Yes	19,922	11,138	16		Yes	27	$8,284	None
Yes	Yes	Yes	Yes	Yes	24,895†	10,975	12	808	Yes			None
Yes	Yes	Yes	Yes	Yes	7,092†	3,185	18	197	Yes			None
			No		6,850†			150				
					8,715†	5,526						
Yes					8,382†	13,430	21	185				
Yes	Yes		Yes	Yes	26,434†	10,790	21	791	Yes	8		None
Yes	Yes	Yes	Yes	Yes	15,862†	9,312	12	722	Yes	95	$11,502	None
Yes	Yes		Yes	Yes	40,240‡	9,020			Yes	55	$42,242	2/15
Yes			Yes	Yes	9,690	8,272	13	315	Yes			None
Yes	Yes		Yes		25,220	13,388	6	560	Yes			None
Yes	Yes				7,067†	10,204	12	225	Yes			None
			No		15,775†	500	6	525	Yes			None
Yes		Yes	No		5,838†	2,667	18	220	Yes			None
Yes			No		14,730	12,138		431	Yes			None
Yes			Yes	Yes	20,020	10,260	18	340	Yes	21	$13,671	7/31
Yes	Yes	Yes	Yes	Yes	26,080	9,704	11		Yes	64	$4,562	4/15
			Yes		10,545†	13,490		325	Yes			9/15
Yes		Yes			16,452†	7,648	12	708				
			No		17,210†	3,140		716	Yes			None
Yes	Yes		Yes	Yes	24,377†	13,884	12	875	Yes			None
Yes	Yes	Yes	Yes	Yes	23,120	9,150	12	965	Yes	23	$11,946	None
Yes			Yes	Yes	19,330	9,545	8	670	Yes	9	$14,547	None
Yes	Yes	Yes	Yes		19,125	10,240	12	385	Yes	27	$11,407	8/1
					9,585			212				
					9,090†			202				
					9,585			212				
					9,585			212				
			No		5,804†	2,235	18	162	Yes			None
Yes			Yes		21,090†	10,870	12	425	Yes			5/1
Yes	Yes		Yes		36,500†	11,088		1500	Yes			1/15
			No		9,705	1,080		205				
Yes	Yes		Yes	Yes	21,794†	10,150	16	425	Yes			None
			No		19,833†	13,590	12	333				
Yes	Yes		Yes	Yes	31,020‡	11,310	16		Yes			6/1
			Yes	Yes	18,468†	6,075			Yes			None
Yes	Yes	Yes	Yes	Yes	21,285†	12,792			Yes	117	$5,409	None
		Yes			17,559†	6,075			Yes			None
Yes	Yes	Yes	Yes		18,273†	10,350			Yes			None
Yes	Yes	Yes			18,273†	6,075			Yes			None
Yes	Yes	Yes	Yes		18,273†	6,075			Yes			None
Yes	Yes	Yes	Yes	Yes	17,871†	12,906		578	Yes			4/1
			No		8,904†	7,276	20	270				
Yes	Yes		Yes	Yes	31,930†	13,140	2		Yes	167	$20,373	5/1
Yes	Yes		Yes	Yes	25,065†	9,397	15		Yes			None
Yes	Yes		No		5,932†	750		231	Yes			
			No									
					13,910†							
Yes	Yes	Yes	Yes	Yes	9,972†	12,620	20	389	Yes			None
Yes		Yes		Yes	6,525†	6,087	19	145	Yes			8/1
Yes					5,610†	900		163				

† Tuition and fees are for 2007-08. ‡ Tuition and fees are projected for 2008-09. * Comprehensive Fee

Institution	Control/ degrees	Undergraduates		Tests required (Fall 2009)	TOEFL		Application	
		Total	Internat'l		minimum	average	Deadline	Fee
Technology Education College	Pr/A	406						20
Tiffin University	Pr/AB	1,565		TOEFL	500	510	None	20
University of Akron	Pu/AB	17,988	170	TOEFL	500		5/1	50
University of Akron: Wayne College	Pu/A	1,856						30
University of Cincinnati	Pu/AB	19,796	246	TOEFL	515		4/1	40
University of Cincinnati: Clermont College	Pu/A	2,506	11	TOEFL	515		None	35
University of Dayton	Pr/B	7,154	62	TOEFL	523		5/1	50
University of Findlay	Pr/AB	3,187	227	TOEFL	500		None	
University of Northwestern Ohio	Pr/AB	3,247		TOEFL	500	550	None	50
University of Rio Grande	Pr/AB	1,861		TOEFL	400	600	None	25
University of Toledo	Pu/AB	16,527		TOEFL	500		7/1	40
Ursuline College	Pr/B	1,158	5	TOEFL	500		6/1	25
Virginia Marti College of Art and Design	Pr/A			TOEFL	450		None	200
Walsh University	Pr/AB	2,146		TOEFL	500		None	25
Wilberforce University	Pr/B			TOEFL	500		6/1	20
Wilmington College	Pr/B	1,428		TOEFL	500		6/1	25
Wittenberg University	Pr/B	1,897		TOEFL	550	580	4/15	40
Wright State University	Pu/AB	11,912	160	TOEFL, SAT/ACT	500	530	5/10	30
Wright State University: Lake Campus	Pu/AB	588	2	TOEFL	500	530	5/10	30
Xavier University	Pr/AB	3,814	54	TOEFL	530	557	2/1	35
Youngstown State University	Pu/AB	11,912	60	TOEFL	500		3/1	30
Zane State College	Pu/A	1,751		TOEFL	450			20
Oklahoma								
Bacone College	Pr/AB	880		TOEFL, SAT/ACT	500	550	None	25
Cameron University	Pu/AB	4,686		TOEFL	500	537	6/15	35
Carl Albert State College	Pu/A			TOEFL, ACT	500		None	
DeVry University: Oklahoma City Center	Pr/AB	44						50
East Central University	Pu/B	3,657	93	TOEFL	500		7/15	50
Family of Faith College	Pr/B							25
Langston University	Pu/AB	2,461	60	TOEFL	500		7/1	25
Northeastern Oklahoma Agricultural and Mechanical College	Pu/A	1,767	20	TOEFL	500		6/20	
Northeastern State University	Pu/B	8,181	260	TOEFL	500	540	8/1	25
Northwestern Oklahoma State University	Pu/B	1,698	29	TOEFL	500		6/8	15
Oklahoma Baptist University	Pr/AB	1,583		TOEFL	500	525	4/15	25
Oklahoma Christian University	Pr/B	1,998		TOEFL	500	510	8/1	25
Oklahoma City Community College	Pu/A	10,151	463	TOEFL	500	515	7/20	25
Oklahoma City University	Pr/B	2,129	369	TOEFL	500		None	70
Oklahoma Panhandle State University	Pu/AB	1,078	39	TOEFL, SAT, SAT Subject Test(s), or ACT	500	571	None	
Oklahoma State University	Pu/B	18,205	554	TOEFL, SAT/ACT	500	538	5/15	75
Oklahoma State University: Oklahoma City	Pu/AB	5,824		TOEFL	500	510	None	15
Oklahoma State University: Okmulgee	Pu/AB	2,855		TOEFL	500		None	15
Oklahoma Wesleyan University	Pr/AB	1,001		TOEFL, SAT/ACT	500	550	None	25
Oral Roberts University	Pr/B	2,714		TOEFL, SAT/ACT	500	521	7/1	35
Platt College: Oklahoma City Central	Pr/A	325						100
Platt College: Tulsa	Pr/A	160						100
Redlands Community College	Pu/A		4	TOEFL	500		None	25
Rose State College	Pu/A	7,107	3	TOEFL	500		None	
St. Gregory's University	Pr/AB	750	45	TOEFL	500	540	None	40
Southeastern Oklahoma State University	Pu/B	3,585		TOEFL	500	538	6/15	55
Southern Nazarene University	Pr/AB	1,665		TOEFL	500	510	7/1	25
Southwestern Christian University	Pr/AB	178		TOEFL	500		None	200
Southwestern Oklahoma State University	Pu/AB	4,146	129	TOEFL, SAT/ACT	500	515	8/8	15

Student services			Housing		Academic year costs		Maximum credits/summer	Credit hour charge	International financial aid			
Adviser	Orien-tation	ESL	Academic year	Summer	Tuition/fees	Living costs			Avail-able	Number receiving aid	Average award	Deadline
			Yes			700						
Yes	Yes		Yes	Yes	16,800 †	12,930	9		Yes	50	$8,083	None
Yes	Yes	Yes	Yes	Yes	17,632 †	11,407			Yes	28	$2,519	None
					12,854 †	8,227	9		Yes			3/15
Yes	Yes		Yes	Yes	23,922 †	13,608	19	665	Yes			None
Yes			No		11,394 †			317	Yes			None
Yes	Yes	Yes	Yes	Yes	27,330	10,880	18	873	Yes	20	$8,450	None
Yes	Yes	Yes	Yes	Yes	24,670	10,606	9	528	Yes	150	$1,800	9/1
Yes			Yes	Yes	8,820 †	7,491	19	190	Yes			None
Yes	Yes		Yes	Yes	16,600 †	10,041	15		Yes			None
Yes	Yes	Yes	Yes	Yes	16,738 †	11,828	21	651	Yes	29		None
			Yes		22,060	9,550	12	728	Yes			None
		Yes	No		15,075 †	4,080	18	325	Yes			None
Yes	Yes	Yes	Yes	Yes	20,050	10,534	12	640	Yes			None
Yes			Yes		11,560 †	12,250		438	Yes			6/1
Yes			Yes	Yes	22,078 †	8,700	18	395	Yes			6/1
Yes	Yes	Yes	Yes	Yes	31,400 †	11,780	15	1037	Yes	37	$18,515	None
Yes	Yes	Yes	Yes	Yes	14,004 †	7,180		425				
Yes	Yes		No		11,619 †		18	354				
Yes	Yes	Yes	Yes	Yes	26,860	11,570	14	483	Yes	29	$14,157	None
Yes	Yes	Yes	Yes	Yes	12,394 †	9,667		516	Yes			None
Yes			No		7,650 †	6,400	20	170				
	Yes		Yes	Yes	10,056 †	8,050	9		Yes			None
Yes	Yes		Yes	Yes	9,105 †	5,826	9	264				
Yes			Yes		5,115 †	6,943	9	147				
						8,528						
Yes	Yes		Yes	Yes	9,314 †	4,760	10	271	Yes			3/1
					5,110 †	1,600		165				
Yes			Yes		8,711 †	8,577		251				
Yes	Yes		Yes	Yes	5,761 †	6,651	9	169	Yes			None
Yes		Yes	Yes	Yes	9,318 †	9,116	12	281	Yes	92	$6,597	None
Yes			Yes	Yes	9,300 †	6,740		289	Yes	50	$1,674	None
Yes	Yes	Yes	Yes	Yes	16,790	10,285	12		Yes			None
Yes	Yes	Yes	Yes	Yes	16,566	9,910	12	612	Yes	43	$5,884	8/31
Yes	Yes	Yes	No		6,240 †	3,812	12	185				
Yes	Yes	Yes	Yes	Yes	20,800 †	10,650	12	670	Yes			6/30
Yes		Yes	Yes	Yes	8,139 †	3,540	9	246	Yes			None
Yes	Yes	Yes	Yes	Yes	14,916 †	11,397		434	Yes	7	$4,357	None
Yes			No		7,175 †	9,369	9	220	Yes			None
Yes			Yes	Yes	8,370 †	6,702	21	248				
Yes			Yes		16,585	8,950	12	650	Yes			None
Yes	Yes	Yes	Yes	Yes	18,386	12,210	16	742	Yes			None
			No									
			No									
Yes			Yes		4,890 †	6,460	6	163				
Yes			No		6,798 †	8,122	9	209				
Yes	Yes	Yes	Yes	Yes	14,710 †	11,150	12	460	Yes	41	$1,284	None
Yes			Yes		9,720 †	7,871	12	301	Yes	26	$5,363	None
Yes			Yes		15,924 †	7,820	9	510	Yes			None
Yes			Yes		9,020 †	6,900	6	299				
Yes			Yes	Yes	8,550 †	8,250	10	260				

† Tuition and fees are for 2007-08.   ‡ Tuition and fees are projected for 2008-09.   * Comprehensive Fee

Institution	Control/ degrees	Undergraduates		Tests required (Fall 2009)	TOEFL		Application	
		Total	Internat'l		minimum	average	Deadline	Fee
Spartan College of Aeronautics and Technology	Pr/AB	953		TOEFL	500	515	None	100
Tulsa Community College	Pu/A	11,512		TOEFL	500	520	None	15
Tulsa Welding School	Pr/A	736					None	
University of Central Oklahoma	Pu/B	14,181	919	TOEFL, SAT/ACT	500		6/1	25
University of Oklahoma	Pu/B	20,400	366	TOEFL	550		4/1	90
University of Science and Arts of Oklahoma	Pu/B	1,096	39	TOEFL	500	557	8/1	15
University of Tulsa	Pr/B	2,920	318	TOEFL	500	566	7/15	35
Vatterott College	Pr/AB							
Western Oklahoma State College	Pu/A	1,524		TOEFL	500		None	15
Oregon								
Art Institute of Portland	Pr/AB	1,722	17	TOEFL	500		None	50
Blue Mountain Community College	Pu/A	2,190		TOEFL	550		None	
Cascade College	Pr/B	262	5	TOEFL	500		None	50
Chemeketa Community College	Pu/A	6,350		TOEFL				
Clackamas Community College	Pu/A	6,500					8/24	50
Clatsop Community College	Pu/A	1,141		TOEFL	520		8/1	150
Concordia University	Pr/AB	1,036	18	TOEFL	530		7/1	50
Corban College	Pr/AB	861		TOEFL, SAT, SAT Subject Test(s), or ACT	500		6/1	35
DeVry University: Portland	Pr/B	66						50
Eastern Oregon University	Pu/AB	2,793	51	TOEFL	520		8/15	50
George Fox University	Pr/B	1,907	44	TOEFL	550		7/1	40
Heald College: Portland	Pr/A							
Lane Community College	Pu/A	8,750		TOEFL	480	490	8/1	
Lewis & Clark College	Pr/B	1,926	87	TOEFL	550		8/1	50
Linfield College	Pr/B	1,646	41	TOEFL	550		None	40
Linn-Benton Community College	Pu/A	4,986		TOEFL	500		8/5	100
Marylhurst University	Pr/B	837		TOEFL	550		None	50
Mount Angel Seminary	Pr/B	90		TOEFL	475		6/15	27
Mt. Hood Community College	Pu/A	6,964	4	TOEFL	500		8/1	15
Northwest Christian College	Pr/AB	395		TOEFL	500		None	
Oregon Health & Science University	Pu/B	591	7	TOEFL	560		1/15	120
Oregon Institute of Technology	Pu/AB	3,134	27	TOEFL, SAT/ACT	520		None	50
Oregon State University	Pu/B	15,515	243	TOEFL, SAT/ACT	550		6/15	50
Pacific Northwest College of Art	Pr/B	417	4	TOEFL	550		7/1	35
Pacific University	Pr/B	1,427	4	TOEFL	550	570	7/15	40
Pioneer Pacific College	Pr/AB	333		TOEFL	500		None	50
Pioneer Pacific College: Springfield	Pr/A	166		TOEFL	500		None	50
Portland Community College	Pu/A	24,363		TOEFL	470	500	7/1	50
Portland State University	Pu/B	16,524	737	TOEFL	525	550	3/1	50
Reed College	Pr/B	1,426		TOEFL, SAT Subject Test(s)	600		1/15	50
Rogue Community College	Pu/A	2,731	5	TOEFL	490		8/20	
Southern Oregon University	Pu/B	4,058		TOEFL	520	553	None	50
Southwestern Oregon Community College	Pu/A	2,120		TOEFL	450	480	None	30
Treasure Valley Community College	Pu/A	1,820	3	TOEFL	500		7/30	
Umpqua Community College	Pu/A	994	1	TOEFL	500	505	None	50
University of Oregon	Pu/B	16,422	790	TOEFL	500		3/15	50
University of Portland	Pr/B	2,967	54	TOEFL	525	603	3/1	50
Warner Pacific College	Pr/AB	722	6	TOEFL	525			25
Western Oregon University	Pu/AB	4,390		TOEFL	500	520	None	50
Willamette University	Pr/B	1,821	14	TOEFL	560	590	2/1	50

| Student services | | | Housing | | Academic year costs | | Maximum credits/ summer | Credit hour charge | International financial aid | | | |
Adviser	Orien- tation	ESL	Academic year	Summer	Tuition/ fees	Living costs			Avail- able	Number receiving aid	Average award	Deadline
Yes			Yes			9,478						
Yes	Yes	Yes	No		6,880 †	2,280	9	201	Yes			None
									Yes			None
Yes			Yes		9,729 †	10,995	12	306				
Yes	Yes	Yes	Yes	Yes	15,621 †	12,549	9	413	Yes	108	$1,955	
Yes	Yes		Yes	Yes	9,630 †	4,690	20	282	Yes	36	$9,714	None
Yes	Yes	Yes	Yes	Yes	23,940	12,918	12	856	Yes	80	$15,779	None
			Yes	Yes	5,771 †	8,350	12	162	Yes			None
Yes	Yes		Yes		19,395 †	15,807	18	431	Yes			None
Yes		Yes	No		8,704 †	18,775		191	Yes			None
			Yes		14,250	6,700		550				
Yes	Yes	Yes	No		9,135 †	10,014		199				
Yes	Yes	Yes	No		9,360	12,650	18	203	Yes			None
			No		10,170 †	10,248		220				
Yes	Yes	Yes	Yes	Yes	22,100 ‡	9,400	12	680				
Yes			Yes	Yes	22,320	9,768		918	Yes	4		None
					13,020 †	15,194		490				
Yes	Yes		Yes	Yes	6,072 †	12,169			Yes	6	$2,118	None
Yes	Yes	Yes	Yes		25,190	10,980		750	Yes	36	$8,927	
					11,000 †	1,500						
Yes	Yes	Yes	No		11,625 †	10,347		251	Yes			None
Yes	Yes	Yes	Yes	Yes	31,840 †	12,050	20	1592	Yes	61	$18,727	None
Yes	Yes	Yes	Yes	Yes	27,414	9,810		845	Yes	36	$15,342	None
Yes	Yes	Yes	No		8,467 †	11,664	20	184				
Yes	Yes	Yes	No	Yes	16,200	9,900	15	349				
		Yes	Yes		13,681 †	11,734						
Yes			No		10,890 †	3,627	16	236	Yes			None
Yes			Yes	Yes	21,481 †	8,495	9	716	Yes			None
Yes	Yes		No		20,176 †	11,521		444	Yes	2	$13,250	None
Yes	Yes		Yes	Yes	16,179 †	9,785	18		Yes	29	$4,441	None
Yes	Yes	Yes	Yes	Yes	18,187 †	11,172	19	465	Yes	64		5/1
			Yes	Yes	19,359 †	9,475	6		Yes			8/1
Yes	Yes	ESL	Yes		26,470 †	8,884	9	1076	Yes			None
Yes			No		10,677 ‡	4,357		411				
Yes			No		10,677 ‡	4,357		411				
Yes	Yes	Yes	No		9,045 †	9,555	9	195	Yes			None
Yes	Yes	Yes	Yes	Yes	17,831 †	13,548	21		Yes	98	$5,615	None
Yes	Yes		Yes	Yes	38,190	14,470		1625	Yes			1/15
Yes		Yes	No		10,545	4,650	15	227				
Yes	Yes	Yes	Yes	Yes	17,580 †	12,012	18		Yes			None
Yes	Yes	Yes	Yes	Yes	9,240	8,500	18		Yes			6/30
Yes	Yes	Yes	Yes		5,850 ‡	10,215		120				
Yes			No		8,775 †	10,800		186				
Yes	Yes	Yes	Yes	Yes	19,332 †	14,208			Yes			6/30
Yes	Yes	Yes	Yes	Yes	30,450	11,556	9	925	Yes			None
Yes	Yes		Yes	Yes	21,500 †	9,482		900	Yes			8/30
Yes	Yes	Yes	Yes	Yes	16,332 †	11,355	12	355	Yes			None
Yes	Yes		Yes		33,960	8,850			Yes	13	$20,158	2/1

† Tuition and fees are for 2007-08.   ‡ Tuition and fees are projected for 2008-09.   * Comprehensive Fee

Institution	Control/ degrees	Undergraduates		Tests required (Fall 2009)	TOEFL		Application	
		Total	Internat'l		minimum	average	Deadline	Fee
Pennsylvania								
Albright College	Pr/B	2,153	90	TOEFL	530	548	7/15	25
Allegheny College	Pr/B	2,163	25	TOEFL, SAT/ACT	550		2/15	35
Alvernia College	Pr/AB	1,922	10	TOEFL, SAT/ACT			None	25
Antonelli Institute of Art and Photography	Pr/A	235		TOEFL	480	540	None	25
Arcadia University	Pr/B	2,075		TOEFL	530	576	3/1	30
Art Institute of Philadelphia	Pr/AB	3,742		TOEFL	480		None	50
Art Institute of Pittsburgh	Pr/AB	16,586		TOEFL	490		None	50
Art Institute Online	Pr/AB	9,000						50
Baptist Bible College of Pennsylvania	Pr/AB	668	15	TOEFL, SAT/ACT	500		2/28	30
Berean Institute	Pr/A	240		TOEFL				25
Bloomsburg University of Pennsylvania	Pu/B	7,667	49	TOEFL	500	550	3/1	30
Bradford School: Pittsburgh	Pr/A	425						50
Bryn Mawr College	Pr/B	1,275	88	TOEFL, SAT, SAT Subject Test(s), or ACT	600	616	1/15	50
Bucknell University	Pr/B	3,495	96	TOEFL, SAT/ACT	550	621	1/1	60
Bucks County Community College	Pu/A	9,649	609	TOEFL	550		5/1	30
Business Institute of Pennsylvania	Pr/A	140					None	50
Butler County Community College	Pu/A	3,656		TOEFL	500		None	25
Cabrini College	Pr/B	1,820	17	TOEFL	550		None	35
California University of Pennsylvania	Pu/AB	6,606	63	TOEFL	450	510	6/1	35
Cambria-Rowe Business College: Indiana	Pr/A	195						15
Career Training Academy	Pr/A	85						30
Career Training Academy: Monroeville	Pr/A	45						30
Career Training Academy: Pittsburgh	Pr/A	45						
Carlow University	Pr/B	1,555	6	TOEFL	500	543	None	20
Carnegie Mellon University	Pr/B	5,758	821	TOEFL, SAT/ACT	600		1/1	65
Cedar Crest College	Pr/B	1,709	1	TOEFL	500		None	30
Central Pennsylvania College	Pr/AB	1,102		TOEFL	550		None	20
Chatham University	Pr/B	651	41	TOEFL	580		None	35
Chestnut Hill College	Pr/AB	1,248	10	TOEFL	500	520	7/15	35
Cheyney University of Pennsylvania	Pu/B	1,319		TOEFL, SAT	500		6/15	20
CHI Institute: Franklin Mills	Pr/A	700						
Clarion University of Pennsylvania	Pu/AB	5,691	45	TOEFL	500		7/15	30
Commonwealth Technical Institute	Pr/A	94						
Community College of Allegheny County	Pu/A	16,907	74				6/1	
Community College of Beaver County	Pu/A	1,865		TOEFL	450		6/15	
Community College of Philadelphia	Pu/A	17,339						20
Curtis Institute of Music	Pr/B	137	56	TOEFL	550		12/15	135
Delaware Valley College	Pr/AB	1,851	1	TOEFL, SAT/ACT	500	550	5/1	35
DeSales University	Pr/B	2,207		TOEFL	550	600	5/1	30
DeVry University: Fort Washington	Pr/AB	812	6	TOEFL	500			50
Dickinson College	Pr/B	2,349	132	TOEFL	600	623	2/1	65
Drexel University	Pr/AB	12,722	835		550		None	75
DuBois Business College	Pr/A	265		TOEFL	500		None	25
DuBois Business College: Huntingdon	Pr/A	70						25
DuBois Business College: Oil City	Pr/A	85						25
Duquesne University	Pr/B	5,562	115		575		None	50
East Stroudsburg University of Pennsylvania	Pu/AB	5,841	19	TOEFL	560		3/1	50
Eastern University	Pr/AB	2,528		TOEFL	500		None	25
Edinboro University of Pennsylvania	Pu/AB	6,127	58	TOEFL	500		7/1	30
Elizabethtown College	Pr/AB	2,233		TOEFL	525	565	5/1	30

| | *Student services* | | | *Housing* | | *Academic year costs* | | *Maximum* | *Credit* | | *International financial aid* | | |
Adviser	*Orien- tation*	*ESL*	*Academic year*	*Summer*	*Tuition/ fees*	*Living costs*	*credits/ summer*	*hour charge*	*Avail- able*	*Number receiving aid*	*Average award*	*Deadline*
Yes	Yes	Yes	Yes	Yes	30,570	10,670	8		Yes	22	$9,285	None
Yes	Yes		Yes	Yes	32,000	10,500		1320	Yes	23	$14,673	None
			Yes		23,200	12,562	12	630				
Yes			Yes	Yes	19,325	19,778		640				
Yes	Yes		Yes		29,700‡	12,680	16	490	Yes			None
Yes	Yes		Yes	Yes			18					
Yes	Yes		Yes	Yes	20,556‡	7,423	15	436	Yes			None
					13,024†							
			Yes		15,060†	7,344	6	490	Yes			5/1
Yes			No			1,900	6					
Yes		Yes	Yes	Yes	14,390†	10,028	12	539	Yes	35	$9,938	None
			Yes									
Yes	Yes		Yes	Yes	36,540	13,520	8		Yes	62	$39,515	3/1
Yes	Yes		Yes	Yes	39,652	11,533	8		Yes	11	$41,111	1/1
Yes	Yes	Yes	No		9,614†	6,450	12	279				
			No		9,240†	1,500	15	240				
			No		7,170†	12,185		219				
Yes	Yes		Yes	Yes	30,010	13,321	12		Yes	2	$16,060	4/1
Yes	Yes		Yes	Yes	14,706†	11,680	12	345	Yes			None
					9,440‡			250				
			No									
			No			11,891						
Yes	Yes	Yes	Yes	Yes	19,514†	9,884	18	612	Yes	6	$10,493	None
Yes	Yes		Yes	Yes	39,564	12,396		544				
Yes	Yes	Yes	Yes	Yes	26,542‡	13,808	12		Yes	1	$5,500	None
			Yes	Yes	12,648†	9,560		333	Yes			None
Yes	Yes	Yes	Yes	Yes	25,816†	11,614	12		Yes			None
Yes	Yes	Yes	Yes	Yes	26,000‡	11,650	12	550	Yes			4/15
Yes			Yes		14,179†	10,556		539	Yes			None
			No			1,065						
Yes	Yes		Yes	Yes	14,634†	9,493	19	539	Yes	41	$1,837	4/15
			Yes		11,224†	9,516						
Yes	Yes	ESL	No		7,469†	7,187		240	Yes			None
			No		8,880†	4,000	15	255				
Yes	Yes	Yes	No		11,910†	7,354	12	345				
Yes		Yes	No						Yes	46	$11,600	3/1
			Yes		27,078	12,052	16	681	Yes	1	$6,500	None
Yes			Yes		25,800	13,530	15		Yes			5/1
Yes					14,640†	8,528		525				
Yes	Yes	Yes	Yes		38,259	12,100	8	1185	Yes	118	$36,289	2/1
Yes	Yes	Yes	Yes	Yes	30,440	17,685		785	Yes			3/1
Yes	Yes		Yes		9,000†	8,640	18	190				
					9,000†			190				
					9,000†	2,500		190				
Yes	Yes	Yes	Yes	Yes	25,475	10,638	12	765	Yes	70	$16,766	5/1
Yes	Yes		Yes	Yes	14,575†	9,184	15	539	Yes	21	$6,578	3/1
Yes	Yes		Yes	Yes	22,715	14,910	12	480	Yes			None
Yes	Yes		Yes	Yes	9,356†	8,976	12	324	Yes	82	$4,032	5/1
Yes	Yes	Yes	Yes	Yes	30,650	9,968	9	740	Yes			None

† Tuition and fees are for 2007-08.   ‡ Tuition and fees are projected for 2008-09.   * Comprehensive Fee

Institution	Control/ degrees	Undergraduates		Tests required (Fall 2009)	TOEFL		Application	
		Total	Internat'l		minimum	average	Deadline	Fee
Erie Business Center	Pr/A	350						25
Erie Business Center South	Pr/A	67						25
Erie Institute of Technology	Pr/A	190						25
Franklin & Marshall College	Pr/B	2,063	159	TOEFL	600		2/1	50
Gannon University	Pr/AB	2,460	25	TOEFL, SAT/ACT	500		6/1	25
Geneva College	Pr/AB	1,639	24	TOEFL	480	550	None	40
Gettysburg College	Pr/B	2,485		TOEFL, SAT/ACT	570		2/1	55
Gratz College	Pr/B	10		TOEFL	450	500	None	50
Grove City College	Pr/B	2,490	18	TOEFL, SAT/ACT	550	600	2/1	50
Gwynedd-Mercy College	Pr/AB	1,933	15	TOEFL, SAT/ACT	530		7/9	50
Harcum College	Pr/A	832		TOEFL	500		8/1	25
Harrisburg Area Community College	Pu/A	11,180	134				6/15	35
Harrisburg University of Science and Technology	Pr/B							30
Haverford College	Pr/B	1,169	41	TOEFL, SAT/ACT, SAT Subject Test(s)	600		1/15	60
Holy Family University	Pr/AB	2,122		TOEFL, SAT	550	582	7/1	25
Immaculata University	Pr/AB	2,647	21	TOEFL, SAT/ACT	550		8/15	35
Indiana University of Pennsylvania	Pu/AB	11,338	133	TOEFL	500		6/15	35
JNA Institute of Culinary Arts	Pr/A	75					None	
Johnson College	Pr/A	376		TOEFL	500	525	8/1	30
Juniata College	Pr/B	1,410		TOEFL	550	557	3/1	30
Keystone College	Pr/AB	1,757	10	TOEFL	550		6/1	25
Keystone Technical Institute	Pr/A						None	20
King's College	Pr/AB	2,031	6	TOEFL	530	550	6/1	30
Kutztown University of Pennsylvania	Pu/B	8,768	65	TOEFL	500	550	4/1	35
La Roche College	Pr/AB	1,306	152	TOEFL	550		None	50
La Salle University	Pr/AB	4,024	23	TOEFL	500	550	4/15	35
Lackawanna College	Pr/A	1,274		TOEFL	450		6/30	30
Lafayette College	Pr/B	2,366	147	TOEFL	550	625	1/1	60
Lansdale School of Business	Pr/A	417						30
Laurel Business Institute	Pr/A	310					None	55
Lebanon Valley College	Pr/AB	1,705	8	TOEFL	550		3/15	30
Lehigh University	Pr/B	4,732	117	TOEFL, SAT/ACT	570	626	1/1	65
Lincoln Technical Institute: Allentown	Pr/A	455						25
Lincoln Technical Institute: Northeast Philadelphia	Pr/A	204						
Lincoln Technical Institute: Philadelphia	Pr/A	540						25
Lincoln University	Pu/B	1,898	63	TOEFL, SAT/ACT	550		6/1	20
Lock Haven University of Pennsylvania	Pu/AB	4,779	67	TOEFL	550		3/1	100
Lycoming College	Pr/B	1,402		TOEFL, SAT/ACT	500	570	4/1	35
Manor College	Pr/A	768	6	TOEFL	480	530	8/1	25
Mansfield University of Pennsylvania	Pu/AB	2,849	21	TOEFL	550		6/15	25
Marywood University	Pr/B	1,950	20	TOEFL, SAT/ACT	500	584	None	30
Mercyhurst College	Pr/AB	3,921		TOEFL, SAT/ACT	550	560	7/1	30
Messiah College	Pr/B	2,798	53	TOEFL, SAT/ACT	550		None	30
Millersville University of Pennsylvania	Pu/AB	7,164	18	TOEFL	500	579	None	50
Misericordia University	Pr/B	2,003	2	TOEFL	500	550	None	25
Montgomery County Community College	Pu/A	11,592	169				7/1	25
Moore College of Art and Design	Pr/B	557		TOEFL, SAT/ACT	527		None	110
Moravian College	Pr/B	1,661	18	TOEFL, SAT/ACT	550	553	3/1	40
Mount Aloysius College	Pr/AB	1,483	11	TOEFL, SAT/ACT	500		None	30
Muhlenberg College	Pr/AB	2,324	5	TOEFL	550	580	2/15	45
Neumann College	Pr/AB	2,499	43	TOEFL	550		None	35
Northampton Community College	Pu/A	9,319	103				7/1	25
Oakbridge Academy of Arts	Pr/A	55						50

	Student services		Housing		Academic year costs		Maximum credits/ summer	Credit hour charge	International financial aid			
Adviser	Orientation	ESL	Academic year	Summer	Tuition/ fees	Living costs			Available	Number receiving aid	Average award	Deadline
			No		10,800†	800		328				
						2,567						
					9,920†							
Yes	Yes		Yes	Yes	38,630	11,470	16		Yes	139	$33,028	3/1
Yes	Yes	Yes	Yes		22,662	12,272	12	685	Yes	24	$15,902	None
Yes	Yes	Yes	Yes	Yes	20,400	9,540		680	Yes	11	$6,100	None
Yes	Yes		Yes	Yes	37,950	9,600			Yes	36	$37,876	2/15
Yes			No		11,340†	9,375	12					
Yes	Yes		Yes		12,074	8,190			Yes	11	$7,682	4/15
Yes	Yes	Yes	Yes	Yes	22,790‡	11,990	12	495				
Yes	Yes	Yes	Yes	Yes	16,200†	12,072	12	533	Yes			None
Yes		Yes	No		8,205	13,474	12	257				
Yes	Yes		Yes	Yes	37,525	14,281			Yes	13	$40,906	1/31
Yes			Yes		21,590	11,704	12	455	Yes			None
Yes	Yes	Yes	Yes	Yes	24,575	11,650	12	400	Yes	4	$14,270	4/15
Yes	Yes	Yes	Yes	Yes	14,461†	9,375	12	539	Yes			None
			No									
Yes			Yes		13,858†	10,000		350				
Yes	Yes	Yes	Yes	Yes	30,280	10,270	8	1230	Yes			3/1
Yes	Yes		Yes	Yes	17,265†	13,840	12	375	Yes	8	$2,843	None
			No		13,006†	1,430						
Yes		Yes	Yes	Yes	24,680	12,290	12	480	Yes	5	$13,690	None
Yes	Yes		Yes		14,640†	10,660		539	Yes	52	$10,971	None
Yes	Yes	Yes	Yes	Yes	20,330	11,088	15		Yes	114	$9,883	5/1
Yes	Yes		Yes	Yes	31,320	12,309	12		Yes			None
Yes		Yes	Yes	Yes	10,150†	10,040	6	335	Yes			None
Yes	Yes		Yes	Yes	36,090	15,273	16	403	Yes	127	$36,711	2/15
			No				10					
			No			750	18					
Yes	Yes		Yes	Yes	29,350	10,160	11	480	Yes	7	$9,948	None
Yes	Yes	Yes	Yes	Yes	37,550	11,990	16	1555	Yes	37	$41,619	2/1
			No									
Yes	Yes		Yes		12,190†	7,278	12	388	Yes	37	$9,619	5/1
Yes		Yes	Yes	Yes	14,445†	8,478		539	Yes	44	$10,225	3/15
Yes	Yes		Yes	Yes	28,764	11,872	12	882	Yes	9	$16,000	None
Yes	Yes		Yes	Yes	11,754†	9,988	18	245				
Yes		Yes	Yes	Yes	14,746†	9,036	12	539	Yes	19	$7,814	None
Yes	Yes	Yes	Yes	Yes	25,390	13,408	12		Yes	18	$16,225	None
Yes	Yes		Yes	Yes	23,286	12,796	6	723	Yes			None
Yes	Yes		Yes	Yes	25,670	10,400	8	1040	Yes	53	$15,540	None
Yes	Yes		Yes	Yes	14,391†	10,190	15	539	Yes	15	$6,995	3/15
Yes			Yes	Yes	23,150	11,500	12	450	Yes	2	$10,975	5/1
Yes	Yes	Yes	No	Yes	8,970‡	7,672	12	264				5/1
Yes	Yes		Yes	Yes	27,724‡	15,200	18		Yes			
Yes	Yes		Yes	Yes	30,062	12,836		821	Yes			3/15
Yes			Yes	Yes	15,990†	11,850	12	450	Yes	5	$5,265	None
Yes			Yes		35,375	8,060	8			2	$42,500	
Yes			Yes	Yes	19,486†	12,038	6	431	Yes			None
Yes	Yes	Yes	Yes	Yes	7,590	10,413	12	225				
			No		9,750‡	5,040						

† Tuition and fees are for 2007-08.   ‡ Tuition and fees are projected for 2008-09.   * Comprehensive Fee

Institution	Control/ degrees	Undergraduates		Tests required (Fall 2009)	TOEFL		Application	
		Total	Internat'l		minimum	average	Deadline	Fee
Orleans Technical Institute - Center City Campus	Pr/A	500						125
Pace Institute	Pr/A	210						10
Peirce College	Pr/AB	2,172	43				None	50
Penn Commercial Business and Technical School	Pr/A	375						25
Penn State Abington	Pu/AB	2,902	16	TOEFL	550		2/1	50
Penn State Altoona	Pu/AB	3,854	25	TOEFL	550		2/1	50
Penn State Beaver	Pu/AB	697	3	TOEFL	550		2/1	50
Penn State Berks	Pu/AB	2,557	15	TOEFL	550		2/1	50
Penn State Brandywine	Pu/AB	1,455	4	TOEFL	550		2/1	50
Penn State Dubois	Pu/AB	724		TOEFL	550		2/1	50
Penn State Erie, The Behrend College	Pu/AB	3,843	44	TOEFL	550		2/1	50
Penn State Fayette, The Eberly Campus	Pu/AB	942		TOEFL	550		2/1	50
Penn State Greater Allegheny	Pu/AB	681	7	TOEFL	550		2/1	50
Penn State Harrisburg	Pu/AB	2,294	36	TOEFL	550		2/1	50
Penn State Hazleton	Pu/AB	1,192		TOEFL	550		2/1	50
Penn State Lehigh Valley	Pu/AB	685	4	TOEFL	550		2/1	50
Penn State Mont Alto	Pu/AB	1,025	2	TOEFL	550		2/1	50
Penn State New Kensington	Pu/AB	734		TOEFL	550		2/1	50
Penn State Schuylkill	Pu/AB	827	2	TOEFL	550		2/1	50
Penn State Shenango	Pu/AB	677		TOEFL	550		2/1	50
Penn State University Park	Pu/AB	35,876	878	TOEFL	550		2/1	50
Penn State Wilkes-Barre	Pu/AB	563	1	TOEFL	550		2/1	50
Penn State Worthington Scranton	Pu/AB	1,185	3	TOEFL	550		2/1	50
Penn State York	Pu/AB	1,070	4	TOEFL	550		2/1	50
Pennco Tech	Pr/A	550						100
Pennsylvania College of Technology	Pu/AB	6,565	20	TOEFL	500		6/1	50
Pennsylvania Culinary Institute	Pr/A	1,100		TOEFL, SAT/ACT	550		None	100
Pennsylvania Highlands Community College	Pu/A	1,064						20
Pennsylvania Institute of Technology	Pr/A	668		TOEFL	500		8/7	25
Philadelphia Biblical University	Pr/B	1,060	17	TOEFL	520		5/31	25
Philadelphia University	Pr/AB	2,796	58	TOEFL, SAT/ACT	500		None	35
Pittsburgh Institute of Aeronautics	Pr/A	400		TOEFL	500	520	None	150
Pittsburgh Institute of Mortuary Science	Pr/A	165		TOEFL			None	40
Pittsburgh Technical Institute	Pr/A	2,065		TOEFL	500		None	
Point Park University	Pr/AB	3,089	37	TOEFL	500	520	6/1	40
Reading Area Community College	Pu/A	3,917		TOEFL	450		8/15	
Robert Morris University	Pr/B	3,878	77	TOEFL, SAT/ACT	500		7/1	30
Rosemont College	Pr/B	551	8	TOEFL	500	550	None	35
St. Charles Borromeo Seminary - Overbrook	Pr/B	54	2	TOEFL	400		7/15	
St. Francis University	Pr/AB	1,513		TOEFL	550		7/30	30
Saint Joseph's University	Pr/AB	4,825	77	TOEFL	550		3/1	60
St. Vincent College	Pr/B	1,617	20	TOEFL, SAT/ACT	525	530	2/15	25
Seton Hill University	Pr/B	1,535		TOEFL	550		8/1	35
Shippensburg University of Pennsylvania	Pu/B	6,560	16	TOEFL, SAT/ACT	550		None	30
Slippery Rock University of Pennsylvania	Pu/B	7,521	84	TOEFL	500	600	5/1	25
Susquehanna University	Pr/AB	1,976	15	TOEFL	550		3/1	35
Swarthmore College	Pr/B	1,480	98		600	646	1/2	60
Temple University	Pu/AB	24,861	680	TOEFL	550		3/1	50
Thiel College	Pr/AB	1,179	44	TOEFL	450	485	None	35
Thomas Jefferson University: College of Health Professions	Pr/AB	827	6	TOEFL			4/1	50
Tri-State Business Institute	Pr/A	435						50
Triangle Tech: Bethlehem	Pr/A	114					None	

Student services			Housing		Academic year costs		Maximum credits/ summer	Credit hour charge	International financial aid			
Adviser	Orien- tation	ESL	Academic year	Summer	Tuition/ fees	Living costs			Avail- able	Number receiving aid	Average award	Deadline
			No			2,000						
Yes	Yes		No		13,750 †	9,500		425	Yes			
						3,383						
Yes		Yes	No	Yes	16,506 †	15,712		665				
Yes	Yes	Yes	Yes		17,246 †	12,374		696				
			Yes		16,506 †	12,374		665				
Yes	Yes		Yes	Yes	17,246 †	13,044		696				
			No		16,506 †	15,712		665				
			No		16,496 †	15,712		665				
Yes	Yes		Yes	Yes	17,246 †	12,374		696				
			No		16,496 †	15,712		665				
Yes		Yes	Yes	Yes	16,506 †	12,374		665				
Yes	Yes		Yes	Yes	17,236 †	13,234		696				
			Yes		16,506 †	12,374		665				
			No		16,506 †	15,712		665				
			Yes	Yes	16,506 †	12,374		665				
Yes			No		16,506 †	15,712		665				
			Yes		16,496 †	15,712		665				
			No		16,506 †	15,712		665				
Yes	Yes	Yes	Yes	Yes	23,712 †	12,374		965				
			No		16,506 †	15,712		665				
Yes	Yes		No		16,486 †	15,712		665				
		Yes	No		16,486 †	15,712		665				
			Yes			850			Yes			None
Yes	Yes		Yes	Yes	14,130 †	11,220		415				
			Yes			10,196						
					8,450	900		258				
Yes	Yes		No		10,350	900	18					
Yes	Yes		Yes	Yes	17,785 ‡	10,450	6	526	Yes			None
Yes	Yes	Yes	Yes	Yes	26,700	12,831	12	472	Yes	37	$4,876	4/15
Yes			No		11,352 †	2,100						
			No		14,587 †	700	20					
Yes			Yes	Yes								
Yes	Yes	Yes	Yes	Yes	20,570	12,240	12	552	Yes			None
Yes	Yes	Yes	No		8,430 †	2,500	15	207				
Yes	Yes		Yes	Yes	19,740	13,880	15	640	Yes	61	$17,414	None
Yes			Yes	Yes	22,835 †	11,200	12	830	Yes	7	$16,615	None
		Yes	Yes	Yes	12,321 †	9,569	6					
Yes			Yes		23,494 †	12,034	16	701	Yes	10	$18,086	None
Yes	Yes	Yes	Yes		32,860	11,230	12		Yes			5/1
Yes			Yes	Yes	24,106 †	11,740	12	734	Yes	14	$16,595	5/1
Yes	Yes	Yes	Yes	Yes	25,006 †	12,740	12	660	Yes	22	$20,965	None
Yes	Yes		Yes		14,615 †	9,739	15	539	Yes	14	$11,109	None
Yes	Yes		Yes	Yes	9,260 †	10,829	18	539	Yes	83	$4,195	
Yes	Yes		Yes		31,080	12,695	8	975	Yes	15	$24,950	5/1
Yes	Yes		Yes	Yes	36,490	13,446			Yes	50	$39,265	2/15
Yes	Yes	Yes	Yes	Yes	19,320 †	13,418	12	668	Yes	696	$5,493	3/1
Yes	Yes	Yes	Yes	Yes	20,214 †	11,740	16		Yes			None
Yes			Yes		23,685 †	11,130		770				
					12,919 †			349	Yes			None

† Tuition and fees are for 2007-08.   ‡ Tuition and fees are projected for 2008-09.   * Comprehensive Fee

Institution	Control/ degrees	Undergraduates		Tests required (Fall 2009)	TOEFL		Application	
		Total	Internat'l		minimum	average	Deadline	Fee
Triangle Tech: Greensburg	Pr/A	266					None	
University of the Arts	Pr/B	2,181		TOEFL	500	560	None	75
University of Pennsylvania	Pr/AB	9,687	988	TOEFL, SAT, SAT Subject Test(s), or ACT	600		1/1	75
University of Pittsburgh	Pu/B	16,798	132	TOEFL	550		2/1	45
University of Pittsburgh at Bradford	Pu/AB	1,354	3	TOEFL	550		4/15	45
University of Pittsburgh at Greensburg	Pu/B	1,771	3	TOEFL	550		5/1	45
University of Pittsburgh at Johnstown	Pu/AB	3,116	1	TOEFL	550		2/1	45
University of Pittsburgh at Titusville	Pu/A	557		TOEFL	550		2/1	45
University of the Sciences in Philadelphia	Pr/B	2,116	29	TOEFL, SAT/ACT	550	590	5/1	45
University of Scranton	Pr/AB	3,994	16	TOEFL	550		3/15	40
Ursinus College	Pr/B	1,563	20	TOEFL	500	580	2/15	50
Valley Forge Christian College	Pr/AB	946	1	TOEFL	500		3/1	25
Valley Forge Military College	Pr/A	216		TOEFL	550	570	8/1	25
Villanova University	Pr/AB	6,949	161	TOEFL, SAT/ACT	550	631	1/7	70
Washington & Jefferson College	Pr/AB	1,514	2	TOEFL, SAT/ACT	500	592	3/1	25
Waynesburg University	Pr/AB	1,614	3	TOEFL	550		7/1	20
West Chester University of Pennsylvania	Pu/B	10,716	26	TOEFL	550		4/1	35
West Virginia Career Institute	Pr/A	175						25
Westminster College	Pr/B	1,364		TOEFL	550		4/1	35
Widener University	Pr/AB	3,213	50	TOEFL	500	550	7/7	35
Wilson College	Pr/AB	521	39	TOEFL	500	560	5/1	35
Yeshivath Beth Moshe	Pr/B							
York College of Pennsylvania	Pr/AB	5,219		TOEFL, SAT/ACT	530	600	5/31	30
YTI Career Institute: Lancaster	Pr/A							100
Puerto Rico								
American University of Puerto Rico	Pr/AB	2,923					None	15
Atlantic College	Pr/AB	996						30
Bayamon Central University	Pr/AB						None	15
Caribbean University	Pr/AB	3,798						25
Carlos Albizu University: San Juan	Pr/B	192						75
Colegio Pentecostal Mizpa	Pr/AB	250					None	40
Columbia Centro Universitario: Yauco	Pr/AB	440						50
Conservatory of Music of Puerto Rico	Pu/B	361					2/28	35
Huertas Junior College	Pr/A	1,665						25
Humacao Community College	Pr/A	750					None	17
ICPR Junior College	Pr/A	1,426					7/1	25
Inter American University of Puerto Rico: Aguadilla Campus	Pr/AB	3,953						
Inter American University of Puerto Rico: Arecibo Campus	Pr/AB						5/1	
Inter American University of Puerto Rico: Barranquitas Campus	Pr/AB	2,068					None	
Inter American University of Puerto Rico: Bayamon Campus	Pr/AB	4,983					5/15	
Inter American University of Puerto Rico: Fajardo Campus	Pr/AB	2,256						
Inter American University of Puerto Rico: Guayama Campus	Pr/AB	2,151					None	
Inter American University of Puerto Rico: Metropolitan Campus	Pr/AB	6,780					5/15	
Inter American University of Puerto Rico: Ponce Campus	Pr/AB	5,163						
Inter American University of Puerto Rico: San German Campus	Pr/AB	4,645					5/15	
National College of Business and Technology: Arecibo	Pr/AB						None	25

Student services			Housing		Academic year costs		Maximum credits/summer	Credit hour charge	International financial aid			
Adviser	Orien-tation	ESL	Academic year	Summer	Tuition/fees	Living costs			Avail-able	Number receiving aid	Average award	Deadline
			No		12,850†	14,214		349				
Yes	Yes	Yes	Yes		30,600	12,712		1230	Yes			None
Yes	Yes	Yes	Yes	Yes	37,526	13,731	12		Yes	258	$35,026	None
Yes	Yes	Yes	Yes	Yes	22,386†	10,900		900				
			Yes	Yes	20,880†	10,610	18	840	Yes	2	$3,250	None
			Yes	Yes	20,900†	10,760	15	840	Yes			
			Yes		20,912†	10,160		840				
			Yes		18,692†	10,244	15	748				
Yes		Yes	Yes		26,930†	14,944	12	1067	Yes	6	$7,000	3/15
Yes	Yes		Yes		31,576	13,840	12	807	Yes	13	$28,924	None
Yes	Yes	Yes	Yes	Yes	36,910	12,600		1148	Yes			2/15
	Yes		Yes		12,990‡	10,670			Yes	1	$1,165	None
Yes	Yes	Yes	Yes		26,441	9,985			Yes			5/1
Yes	Yes	Yes	Yes	Yes	34,620†	12,310	12		Yes	55	$33,256	2/7
Yes			Yes		31,496	10,188	12	780	Yes	1	$37,562	None
Yes	Yes		Yes		17,080	8,630	12	700	Yes	3	$6,000	None
Yes		Yes	Yes		14,443†	11,140	12	539	Yes	4	$12,296	None
Yes			Yes		28,100	9,685	7	820	Yes			5/1
Yes	Yes	Yes	Yes	Yes	30,450	13,585	12	1000	Yes	9	$7,177	None
Yes	Yes	Yes	Yes	Yes	25,900	10,830	4		Yes			
					9,200†	4,050						
Yes	Yes		Yes		13,680	9,900	15	385	Yes			None
			No		4,630†	1,633						
						1,052						
Yes	Yes	Yes	No		4,850†	6,385	12	145				
Yes	Yes		No			1,840	9		Yes			None
						19,396						
Yes			Yes		2,550†	6,950		80				
					3,850†			145				
Yes	Yes		No		2,292†	9,450			Yes			None
			No		4,960†	3,660			Yes			None
			No			937						
			No			9,968						
			No		4,874†			147				
		Yes	No		4,886†	5,636	12	147	Yes			
			No		4,874†	11,613	6	147	Yes			4/30
					4,912†	1,490	18	147	Yes			
	Yes		No		4,939†	2,186	6	147				
Yes	Yes		No		4,874†	5,475	18	147				
			No		4,926†	14,822	18	147	Yes			4/30
					4,886†	11,734		147				
Yes		Yes	Yes	Yes	4,939†	6,770	6	147				
					6,295†			135				

† Tuition and fees are for 2007-08.   ‡ Tuition and fees are projected for 2008-09.   * Comprehensive Fee

Institution	Control/ degrees	Undergraduates		Tests required (Fall 2009)	TOEFL		Application	
		Total	Internat'l		minimum	average	Deadline	Fee
National College of Business and Technology: Bayamon	Pr/AB						None	25
National College of Business and Technology: Rio Grande	Pr/AB						None	25
Ponce Paramedical College	Pr/A	2,693						25
Pontifical Catholic University of Puerto Rico	Pr/AB	5,321					7/15	15
Ramirez College of Business and Technology	Pr/A	512					None	25
Turabo University	Pr/AB	12,677					None	15
Universal Technology College of Puerto Rico	Pr/A	1,206						20
Universidad Adventista de las Antillas	Pr/AB	581					None	20
Universidad del Este	Pr/AB	10,471					None	15
Universidad Metropolitana	Pr/AB	9,314						15
Universidad Politecnica de Puerto Rico	Pr/B	4,469					7/28	100
University College of San Juan	Pu/AB	1,004					8/15	15
University of Puerto Rico: Aguadilla	Pu/AB	2,969					12/15	20
University of Puerto Rico: Arecibo	Pu/AB	3,868					11/30	20
University of Puerto Rico: Bayamon University College	Pu/AB	4,916		TOEFL, SAT, SAT Subject Test(s), or ACT			12/10	15
University of Puerto Rico: Carolina Regional College	Pu/AB	4,236					1/31	20
University of Puerto Rico: Cayey University College	Pu/AB	3,562					12/1	20
University of Puerto Rico: Humacao	Pu/AB	4,336					11/15	20
University of Puerto Rico: Mayaguez	Pu/B	11,534	101					20
University of Puerto Rico: Medical Sciences	Pu/AB	414						20
University of Puerto Rico: Ponce	Pu/AB	2,911					12/1	20
University of Puerto Rico: Rio Piedras	Pu/B	15,094					2/15	20
University of Puerto Rico: Utuado	Pu/AB	1,527					5/31	20
Rhode Island								
Brown University	Pr/B	5,813	409	TOEFL, SAT, SAT Subject Test(s), or ACT	600		1/1	70
Bryant University	Pr/B	3,328	105	TOEFL, SAT/ACT	550		2/1	50
Community College of Rhode Island	Pu/A	15,081	17	TOEFL				20
Johnson & Wales University: Providence	Pr/AB	9,053	432	TOEFL	550		None	
New England Institute of Technology	Pr/AB	2,993		TOEFL			None	25
Providence College	Pr/AB	3,959	35	TOEFL	550	600	1/15	55
Rhode Island College	Pu/B	7,197	33	TOEFL	550		5/1	50
Rhode Island School of Design	Pr/B	1,927	308	TOEFL, SAT/ACT	580		2/15	60
Roger Williams University	Pr/AB	4,353	78		500		None	50
Salve Regina University	Pr/AB	2,109	32	TOEFL	500	520	None	40
University of Rhode Island	Pu/B	12,268	42	TOEFL, SAT/ACT	550		2/1	50
Zion Bible College	Pr/B	251	7	TOEFL	500		8/1	75
South Carolina								
Aiken Technical College	Pu/A	2,529		TOEFL		500	None	
Allen University	Pr/B	651			450		None	
Anderson University	Pr/B	1,597	32	TOEFL	550	575	7/1	25
Benedict College	Pr/B	2,641		TOEFL	500		None	60
Central Carolina Technical College	Pu/A	3,283		TOEFL	500		None	25
Charleston Southern University	Pr/B	2,831	43	TOEFL, SAT/ACT	550		7/11	40
The Citadel	Pu/B	2,209	38	TOEFL, SAT/ACT	550		6/1	40
Claflin University	Pr/B	1,627	57	TOEFL, SAT	550		5/1	20
Clemson University	Pu/B	14,173		TOEFL, SAT/ACT	550		5/1	50
Coastal Carolina University	Pu/B	6,851	77	TOEFL	500	569	6/1	45

	Student services			Housing		Academic year costs		Maximum credits/ summer	Credit hour charge		International financial aid		
Adviser	Orien- tation	ESL	Academic year	Summer	Tuition/ fees	Living costs				Avail- able	Number receiving aid	Average award	Deadline
					6,295 †			135					
					6,295 †			135					
Yes			Yes	Yes	5,018 †	2,599	12	150		Yes			None
						4,666							
			No		4,340 †	6,493				Yes			None
			No			3,050				Yes			6/30
Yes			Yes	Yes	10,945 ‡	3,700	12	140		Yes			None
			No		4,340 †	6,493							
					4,340 †	6,493	12						
					6,033 †	7,082	12			Yes			6/30
			No		2,715 †	7,150	9						
Yes			No		3,938 †	10,580	6			Yes			5/6
			No		3,938 †	10,525							
		Yes	No		3,938 †	2,960	6						
					4,109 †	10,770							
			No		3,938 †	9,820	7			Yes			6/30
					3,938 †	13,259	7						
Yes		Yes	No	Yes	3,938 †	10,780	6						
			No		3,938 †	9,646							
			No		3,938 †	6,840	6						
	Yes		Yes		3,938 †	11,070	7			Yes			
					3,938 †	10,780	9						
Yes	Yes		Yes		37,718	12,842				Yes			2/1
Yes	Yes		Yes	Yes	30,871	11,251	12	345		Yes	31		2/15
Yes			No		7,766 †	3,716	12	356					
Yes	Yes	Yes	Yes	Yes	21,717 †	10,794	18	379		Yes			None
Yes		Yes	No		17,165 ‡	3,039		390					
Yes			Yes		31,379	13,110	6	1027		Yes	30	$35,882	2/1
Yes			Yes		13,664 †	10,110	14	532					
Yes	Yes		Yes		34,925 ‡	12,260		1150					
	Yes	Yes	Yes	Yes	25,942 †	13,215	12	1013		Yes	55	$10,751	2/1
Yes	Yes	Yes	Yes		31,500	14,400	12	965		Yes	9	$12,838	None
Yes	Yes		Yes	Yes	23,038 †	8,732		887					
Yes			Yes		7,640	5,700		235					
Yes			No		8,982 †	2,950	15			Yes			6/30
Yes			Yes		9,884	9,040				Yes			7/20
		Yes	Yes		17,850 †	12,850		500		Yes			6/30
Yes			Yes		14,570	9,902		436					
Yes			No		5,181 †	900	12						
Yes			Yes		18,678	8,228	12	360		Yes			None
Yes		Yes	Yes		19,291 †	5,390	12			Yes	11	$26,287	None
Yes			Yes		12,358 †	11,240	10			Yes			None
Yes	Yes		Yes	Yes	21,800 †	11,926	14						
Yes			Yes		16,590 †	6,680	15	691		Yes	59	$16,712	None

† Tuition and fees are for 2007-08.   ‡ Tuition and fees are projected for 2008-09.   * Comprehensive Fee

Institution	Control/ degrees	Undergraduates		Tests required (Fall 2009)	TOEFL		Application	
		Total	Internat'l		minimum	average	Deadline	Fee
Coker College	Pr/B			TOEFL	500	525	None	15
College of Charleston	Pu/B	9,499	93	TOEFL	550		4/1	45
Columbia College	Pr/B	1,224	16	TOEFL, SAT/ACT	550	562	6/1	25
Columbia International University	Pr/AB	462		TOEFL	525		5/30	45
Converse College	Pr/B	730	20	TOEFL	550		3/15	
Denmark Technical College	Pu/A	1,348					None	10
Erskine College	Pr/B	567	5	TOEFL, SAT	550		6/30	25
Florence-Darlington Technical College	Pu/A	3,956		TOEFL	500		5/15	15
Forrest Junior College	Pr/A	106					None	250
Francis Marion University	Pu/B	3,231	27	TOEFL, SAT/ACT	500		7/1	30
Furman University	Pr/B	2,737	53	TOEFL	570		1/15	
Greenville Technical College	Pu/A	12,899	2		500		5/1	35
Horry-Georgetown Technical College	Pu/A	5,249	102	TOEFL	500		None	25
Lander University	Pu/B	2,325		TOEFL, SAT/ACT	550		None	35
Limestone College	Pr/AB	780	46	TOEFL, SAT/ACT	500	588	9/1	25
Midlands Technical College	Pu/A	10,406		TOEFL	500	510	6/10	
Miller-Motte Technical College	Pr/A	650						35
Morris College	Pr/B	868		TOEFL	500		5/31	20
Newberry College	Pr/B	911	35	TOEFL, SAT/ACT			7/15	30
North Greenville University	Pr/AB	1,868		TOEFL, SAT/ACT	500		4/30	35
Northeastern Technical College	Pu/A	924						25
Orangeburg-Calhoun Technical College	Pu/A	2,188		TOEFL	500			50
Piedmont Technical College	Pu/A	4,852		TOEFL, SAT	500		None	
South Carolina State University	Pu/B	4,289		TOEFL, SAT/ACT	500		5/30	25
South University	Pr/AB	593		TOEFL	550		None	25
Southern Wesleyan University	Pr/AB	1,730	18	TOEFL, SAT/ACT	500		6/1	25
Spartanburg Community College	Pu/A	4,459		TOEFL	450		None	
Spartanburg Methodist College	Pr/A	770		TOEFL, SAT/ACT	525	570	6/30	20
Tri-County Technical College	Pu/A	5,201		TOEFL	500	525	None	20
Trident Technical College	Pu/A	10,700		TOEFL				25
University of South Carolina	Pu/AB	18,497	174	TOEFL	550		12/1	50
University of South Carolina at Aiken	Pu/B	2,867	46	TOEFL, SAT/ACT	550		6/1	45
University of South Carolina at Beaufort	Pu/AB	1,192	16	TOEFL, SAT/ACT	550		None	40
University of South Carolina at Lancaster	Pu/A	1,047		TOEFL, SAT/ACT		500	None	40
University of South Carolina at Sumter	Pu/A	1,174		TOEFL	550		None	40
University of South Carolina at Union	Pu/A	400		TOEFL	550		None	40
University of South Carolina Upstate	Pu/B	4,752	76	TOEFL, SAT/ACT	500	530	7/15	40
Voorhees College	Pr/B	603		TOEFL, SAT, SAT Subject Test(s)	500	550	5/1	25
Winthrop University	Pu/B	4,757	88	TOEFL, SAT/ACT	520		None	40
Wofford College	Pr/B	1,316	11	TOEFL	550		2/1	50
South Dakota								
Augustana College	Pr/B	1,718	20	TOEFL	550	590	8/1	
Black Hills State University	Pu/AB	4,004		TOEFL	520	535	7/1	108
Dakota State University	Pu/AB	1,403	12	TOEFL	550		3/1	114
Dakota Wesleyan University	Pr/AB	756	11	TOEFL	500	550	5/30	25
Kilian Community College	Pr/A	391						25
Lake Area Technical Institute	Pu/A			TOEFL	500			20
Mitchell Technical Institute	Pu/A	568		TOEFL	500			35
Mount Marty College	Pr/AB	829		TOEFL	500	550	8/1	35
National American University: Rapid City	Pr/AB	480		TOEFL	500		None	45
Northern State University	Pu/AB	1,725		TOEFL	500		6/15	20

Student services			Housing		Academic year costs		Maximum credits/summer	Credit hour charge	International financial aid			
Adviser	Orientation	ESL	Academic year	Summer	Tuition/fees	Living costs			Available	Number receiving aid	Average award	Deadline
Yes		Yes	Yes	Yes	18,552†	8,420	10		Yes			6/1
Yes	Yes		Yes	Yes	18,732†	12,433	15	781				
Yes	Yes		Yes		21,650†	12,032	16	570	Yes	16	$14,026	None
Yes	Yes		Yes		15,665‡	8,950		640				
		Yes	Yes		24,500	10,400	15	775	Yes			3/1
			Yes		4,466†	7,410	9		Yes			None
Yes			Yes		23,165	11,211	14	800	Yes			None
Yes			No		7,382†	8,043	25		Yes			None
			No		7,160†	1,054	18	148	Yes			None
Yes			Yes	Yes	13,841†	11,760	15	680	Yes			None
Yes	Yes		Yes	Yes	34,568	14,942	12	1064	Yes	47	$30,437	1/15
Yes				Yes	6,698†	12,049	12					
Yes			No		4,914†	9,556						
	Yes		Yes		14,776†	12,767	17	609	Yes			None
Yes	Yes		Yes	Yes	17,300	11,380	14	720	Yes	50	$14,328	None
Yes	Yes	Yes	No		9,532†	10,040	18					
					9,225†			205				
Yes			Yes		9,621	8,258	14	389				
Yes			Yes		21,560	12,000	12	500	Yes			
Yes		Yes	Yes	Yes	11,680	11,830	12	200	Yes			6/30
			No		5,454†	12,200						
Yes			No		4,464†	1,400	18					
Yes			No		4,734†	1,500						
Yes			Yes		14,322†	6,918		597	Yes			5/1
			No		12,390†		16	270	Yes			None
Yes			Yes		17,150†	9,900		695	Yes	14	$8,907	6/30
Yes			No		6,088†	900	18		Yes			5/1
Yes	Yes	Yes	Yes		11,731	8,441	14	312	Yes			8/22
Yes			No		6,594†	650	18		Yes			None
		Yes	No		6,200†	3,878						
Yes	Yes	Yes	Yes	Yes	21,632†	11,825	12	970				
Yes		Yes	Yes	Yes	13,952†	9,660	6	590	Yes			None
			Yes		13,992†	5,583	6	567	Yes			None
			No		11,500†	2,200	12	480	Yes			None
			No		11,800†	10,561	12	480				
			No		11,800†	3,661	6	480				
Yes			Yes		15,912†	7,550	12	665	Yes	21	$526	7/15
Yes			Yes		8,984†	11,807	10	273	Yes			None
Yes	Yes		Yes	Yes	19,034†	9,022		796	Yes	93	$12,756	None
Yes			Yes		29,465	11,640	12	1085	Yes	11		None
Yes	Yes		Yes	Yes	22,452	7,720	8	336	Yes			None
Yes		Yes	Yes		6,679†	7,928	12	124				
Yes	Yes	Yes	Yes	Yes	7,283†	7,911	12	124	Yes			None
Yes	Yes		Yes	Yes	17,500†	9,580	12	375	Yes			None
			No		6,675†	10,920		215				
Yes		Yes	No		4,000†	4,200						
			No		4,370	10,750	12					
Yes			Yes	Yes	17,468†	8,474	18	596	Yes			None
Yes	Yes	Yes	Yes	Yes	11,835†	4,843			Yes			None
Yes		Yes	Yes	Yes	7,032	8,236	14	132	Yes	12		None

† Tuition and fees are for 2007-08. ‡ Tuition and fees are projected for 2008-09. * Comprehensive Fee

Institution	Control/ degrees	Undergraduates		Tests required (Fall 2009)	TOEFL		Application	
		Total	Internat'l		minimum	average	Deadline	Fee
Oglala Lakota College	Pu/AB	1,362					None	
Presentation College	Pr/AB	773		TOEFL, ACT	500		5/1	25
Sisseton Wahpeton College	Pu/A	240		TOEFL				
South Dakota School of Mines and Technology	Pu/AB	1,578	20	TOEFL	530	570	None	20
South Dakota State University	Pu/AB	9,353	53	TOEFL	500		4/15	20
University of Sioux Falls	Pr/AB	1,490		TOEFL, SAT/ACT	500	610	None	25
University of South Dakota	Pu/AB	6,046	30	TOEFL	550		None	20
Tennessee								
American Baptist College of ABT Seminary	Pr/AB	108	5				7/1	35
Aquinas College	Pr/AB	846		TOEFL	525	545	None	25
Austin Peay State University	Pu/AB	8,282	145	TOEFL	500		7/27	15
Belmont University	Pr/B	3,979	39	TOEFL, SAT/ACT	500	540	None	50
Bethel College	Pr/B	1,996		TOEFL	513		None	30
Bryan College	Pr/AB	1,020		TOEFL, SAT/ACT	533		5/1	30
Carson-Newman College	Pr/B	1,815	35	TOEFL, SAT/ACT	550	570	5/1	50
Christian Brothers University	Pr/B	1,430		TOEFL	500	633	None	25
Cleveland State Community College	Pu/A	2,295		TOEFL, ACT	500		None	10
Crichton College	Pr/B	906	22	TOEFL, SAT/ACT	500		7/15	25
Cumberland University	Pr/AB	994	39	TOEFL, SAT/ACT	500	527	5/1	50
DeVry University: Memphis . . . . / . .	Pr/AB	38						50
Draughons Junior College: Clarksville	Pr/A	690						20
Draughons Junior College: Murfreesboro	Pr/A	540						
Draughons Junior College: Nashville	Pr/A	332	1	TOEFL	500		None	75
Dyersburg State Community College	Pu/A	2,078		TOEFL	450	475	7/1	10
East Tennessee State University	Pu/B	10,270	144	TOEFL, SAT/ACT	500	513	7/1	25
Free Will Baptist Bible College	Pr/AB	291	1	TOEFL, SAT/ACT	550		5/1	35
Freed-Hardeman University	Pr/AB	1,428	42	TOEFL	500		None	
Hiwassee College	Pr/A	341	21	TOEFL	500		None	
Huntington College of Health Sciences	Pr/A	185						
International Academy of Design and Technology: Nashville	Pr/AB							50
King College	Pr/B	1,192	37	TOEFL	523		None	50
Lambuth University	Pr/B	721	26	TOEFL, SAT/ACT	500		5/1	175
Lane College	Pr/B	1,766		TOEFL	325	339	6/15	
Lee University	Pr/B	3,586	205	TOEFL	450	520	8/1	25
LeMoyne-Owen College	Pr/B	569	8	TOEFL		475	3/15	25
Lincoln Memorial University	Pr/AB	1,481		TOEFL	500	520	5/1	25
Lipscomb University	Pr/B	2,319	31	TOEFL, SAT/ACT	550		6/1	25
Martin Methodist College	Pr/AB	286		TOEFL, SAT/ACT	450	480	8/1	25
Maryville College	Pr/B	1,176		TOEFL	525	550	None	25
Memphis College of Art	Pr/B	284	5	TOEFL	500	550	8/1	25
Middle Tennessee State University	Pu/AB	19,883		TOEFL, SAT/ACT	500		7/31	30
Miller-Motte Technical College: Clarksville	Pr/A			TOEFL	500		None	
Milligan College	Pr/B	761	20	TOEFL	550	578	6/1	30
Motlow State Community College	Pu/A	3,436		TOEFL, SAT/ACT	500	530	7/31	10
National College: Bartlett	Pr/A							30
National College: Knoxville	Pr/A							30
National College: Madison	Pr/A							30
National College: Memphis	Pr/A							30
Nossi College of Art	Pr/AB	400		TOEFL			None	100
O'More College of Design	Pr/B			TOEFL	500		None	50
Pellissippi State Technical Community College	Pu/A			TOEFL	450	520	8/1	10

Student services			Housing		Academic year costs		Maximum credits/ summer	Credit hour charge	International financial aid			
Adviser	Orien-tation	ESL	Academic year	Summer	Tuition/ fees	Living costs			Avail-able	Number receiving aid	Average award	Deadline
		Yes	Yes		2,900‡	1,205						
			Yes	Yes	13,150†	7,775	12	475	Yes			None
			No		3,790‡	440						
Yes	Yes		Yes	Yes	6,910†	9,200		124	Yes			None
Yes	Yes		Yes	Yes	7,128	13,525		132	Yes	7	$1,368	None
Yes	Yes		Yes	Yes	17,940†	8,840	12	280	Yes			None
Yes	Yes	Yes	Yes	Yes	7,148	9,402	12	132				
			Yes		5,820†	2,240	12	190				
					15,005†	16,500	12	486	Yes			None
Yes		Yes	Yes	Yes	15,514†	10,325	14	624				
Yes	Yes		Yes	Yes	21,110	11,000	12	770	Yes	18	$16,620	None
Yes	Yes		Yes	Yes	11,690†	10,722		341	Yes			6/30
Yes			Yes	Yes	17,020	8,595		725	Yes			None
Yes	Yes	Yes	Yes	Yes	16,980†	9,200	14	675	Yes	32	$629	None
Yes	Yes		Yes	Yes	22,600	7,250	14	690	Yes			None
Yes			No		9,703†	9,250		407				
	Yes		Yes	Yes	11,256†	18,996	12	445	Yes			None
Yes	Yes		Yes	Yes	16,720‡	10,640	18	660	Yes			None
						8,528						
						700						
					10,669†	2,250		215				
Yes		Yes	No				12					
Yes					9,711†	11,849	14	407	Yes			None
Yes	Yes		Yes	Yes	15,163†	12,764	17	624				
Yes			Yes		13,086	56,122	6	409	Yes			None
Yes			Yes		14,060	12,420	17	390	Yes	33	$12,185	None
Yes		Yes	Yes	Yes	11,130†	11,470	18	445	Yes			None
					5,150†	1,350		165				
					15,875†	1,800						
Yes	Yes	Yes	Yes		20,582	11,775	6	600	Yes	22	$14,405	None
Yes	Yes	Yes	Yes	Yes	17,400	12,970	12	710	Yes	25	$18,159	None
Yes			Yes		7,620†	9,675	8			5	$11,336	
Yes	Yes		Yes	Yes	11,094	9,276	18	451	Yes			None
			Yes	Yes	10,098†	8,152			Yes	5	$5,380	None
Yes			Yes	Yes	14,400†	5,380	12	600	Yes			None
Yes	Yes		Yes	Yes	18,580	11,900	12		Yes			None
Yes	Yes	Yes	Yes	Yes	16,554†	8,725	14	675	Yes			None
Yes	Yes	Yes	Yes	Yes	26,947	14,890	14	1095	Yes			None
Yes	Yes		Yes	Yes	21,560	13,040	6	915	Yes			None
Yes	Yes		Yes	Yes	15,554†	10,404		624				
					9,900†	3,150	12	220				
	Yes		Yes		19,510†	8,858	12	520	Yes	17		
					9,699†	11,800	12	407				
					9,585			212				
					9,540			212				
					9,585			212				
					9,585			212				
Yes	Yes		Yes			1,800	12					
					15,514†	750			Yes			7/30
Yes	Yes	Yes			9,733†	6,050	12	407				

† Tuition and fees are for 2007-08.   ‡ Tuition and fees are projected for 2008-09.   * Comprehensive Fee

Institution	Control/ degrees	Undergraduates		Tests required (Fall 2009)	TOEFL		Application	
		Total	Internat'l		minimum	average	Deadline	Fee
Remington College: Memphis	Pr/AB							50
Rhodes College	Pr/B	1,670	8	TOEFL, SAT/ACT	550	618	2/1	40
Roane State Community College	Pu/A	4,427	14	TOEFL	500			10
South College	Pr/AB			TOEFL	525		9/1	40
Southwest Tennessee Community College	Pu/A	10,617		TOEFL, SAT/ACT	500		None	30
Tennessee State University	Pu/AB	6,966	43	TOEFL, SAT/ACT	500	550	6/1	15
Tennessee Technological University	Pu/B	7,875	124	TOEFL, SAT/ACT	500		5/1	30
Tennessee Temple University	Pr/AB	503		TOEFL, ACT	500		7/1	30
Tennessee Wesleyan College	Pr/B	846		TOEFL	500		7/1	25
Trevecca Nazarene University	Pr/AB	1,200	22	TOEFL, SAT/ACT	500		None	25
Tusculum College	Pr/B	2,446	57	TOEFL, SAT/ACT	550	560	None	
Union University	Pr/AB	2,100	45	TOEFL, SAT/ACT	500	582	5/1	50
University of Memphis	Pu/B	15,228	320	TOEFL, SAT/ACT	500		5/1	50
University of the South	Pr/B	1,455	23	TOEFL	550	650	2/1	45
University of Tennessee Health Science Center	Pu/B	294						50
University of Tennessee: Chattanooga	Pu/B	7,987	52	TOEFL, SAT/ACT	500		6/15	30
University of Tennessee: Knoxville	Pu/B	21,001	210	TOEFL	523		12/1	30
University of Tennessee: Martin	Pu/B	5,827	121	TOEFL	500	520	8/1	80
Vanderbilt University	Pr/B	6,496	184	TOEFL, SAT/ACT	570		1/3	50
Vatterott College: Memphis	Pr/A	468						
Volunteer State Community College	Pu/A	5,446	35	TOEFL, ACT	500		6/1	10
Walters State Community College	Pu/A	4,607	9	TOEFL, SAT/ACT	550		6/15	10

Texas

Institution	Control/ degrees	Total	Internat'l	Tests required	minimum	average	Deadline	Fee
Abilene Christian University	Pr/AB	3,954	174	TOEFL	525	553	7/31	45
Angelo State University	Pu/AB	5,720	50	TOEFL, SAT/ACT	550		6/10	50
Arlington Baptist College	Pr/B	142	5	TOEFL	550		6/5	15
Art Institute of Dallas	Pr/AB	1,739		TOEFL				50
Art Institute of Houston	Pr/AB	1,793		TOEFL	500			50
Austin College	Pr/B	1,312	19	TOEFL, SAT/ACT	550	596	3/1	35
Austin Community College	Pu/A	33,508		TOEFL	530		6/1	100
Baptist University of the Americas	Pr/AB	204						25
Baylor University	Pr/B	11,851	191	TOEFL, SAT/ACT	540		2/1	50
Blinn College	Pu/A	14,710		TOEFL	500		7/15	200
Bradford School of Business	Pr/A							50
Brookhaven College	Pu/A	8,480	104	TOEFL	525		None	
Cedar Valley College	Pu/A	4,373		TOEFL	530		None	
Central Texas College	Pu/A	17,996	153	TOEFL	520		4/1	
Clarendon College	Pu/A	1,029	9	TOEFL	525		6/1	200
Coastal Bend College	Pu/A	3,142	11	TOEFL	500		5/1	10
College of Saint Thomas More	Pr/B	47					None	35
Collin County Community College District	Pu/A	19,754	321	TOEFL	525		None	
Commonwealth Institute of Funeral Service	Pr/A	115					None	50
Concordia University at Austin	Pr/AB	1,090	1	TOEFL	550	600	5/1	50
Court Reporting Institute of Houston	Pr/A	400						100
Criswell College	Pr/AB	475		TOEFL	550		6/30	30
Dallas Baptist University	Pr/AB	3,581	284	TOEFL	525		None	25
Del Mar College	Pu/A	11,168		TOEFL	550		None	
DeVry University: Houston	Pr/AB	926	5					50
DeVry University: Irving	Pr/AB	1,453	6	TOEFL	500		None	50
East Texas Baptist University	Pr/B	1,215	15	TOEFL	500	528	6/1	50
Eastfield College	Pu/A	5,427		TOEFL	530		7/15	

| Student services | | | Housing | | Academic year costs | | Maximum credits/ summer | Credit hour charge | International financial aid | | | |
Adviser	Orientation	ESL	Academic year	Summer	Tuition/ fees	Living costs			Available	Number receiving aid	Average award	Deadline
Yes	Yes		Yes	Yes	32,446	10,732	12		Yes			3/1
Yes					9,721 †	8,355	21	407	Yes			None
Yes			No		14,100 †	1,300	18					
Yes	Yes	Yes			9,725 †	7,860		407	Yes			None
Yes	Yes		Yes	Yes	15,132 †	9,497	12	624				
Yes	Yes	Yes	Yes	Yes	15,256 †	8,703	16	624				
Yes			Yes	Yes	9,520 †	10,360	12		Yes			None
Yes			Yes		17,050	9,830	18	455	Yes			None
			Yes		16,288	10,437			Yes	23	$13,778	None
Yes			Yes		17,385 †	10,465	12		Yes			2/15
Yes	Yes		Yes	Yes	19,610	14,200	14	625	Yes	5	$3,200	3/1
Yes	Yes	Yes	Yes	Yes	16,630 †	10,333	16	649	Yes	6	$10,525	6/30
Yes	Yes		Yes	Yes	30,660 †	10,680	9	1105	Yes	22	$39,623	None
			Yes		11,784 †	17,414			Yes	172	$12,876	None
Yes	Yes	Yes	Yes	Yes	15,024 †	10,732	16	709	Yes	48	$2,883	None
Yes	Yes	Yes	Yes	Yes	17,874 †	14,476	19	712	Yes	80	$8,374	None
Yes	Yes	Yes	Yes	Yes	15,045 †	8,866	12	592				
Yes	Yes	Yes	Yes	Yes	35,278 †	14,488			Yes	13	$23,351	None
		Yes	No		9,701 †		18	407				
Yes		Yes	No		10,043 †	4,330	21	407	Yes			None
Yes	Yes	Yes	Yes	Yes	18,855	11,570	14	596	Yes	168	$5,037	None
Yes	Yes		Yes	Yes	13,451 †	7,121	12	378	Yes			None
Yes			Yes	Yes	6,090 ‡	11,770	12	185				
						8,100			Yes			None
								437				
Yes			Yes		26,555	10,657		956	Yes			None
Yes	Yes	Yes	No		8,208 †	9,408	12	259	Yes			4/1
					4,490	1,740		170				
Yes	Yes		Yes		26,234	13,082	18	986				
Yes	Yes	Yes	Yes	Yes	5,040	7,823	14	140	Yes			None
					12,760 ‡							
Yes	Yes	ESL	No		3,450 †	4,920	6	115				
Yes			No		3,450 †	2,300	14	115				
Yes	Yes	Yes	Yes	Yes	4,290 †	6,277	12	130				
		Yes	Yes		3,420 †	8,225	12		Yes			9/1
Yes			Yes		3,950 †	4,084	14					
			Yes		12,150	6,500		400				
Yes	Yes	Yes	Yes		3,184	4,248	14	106				
			No		6,290	10,819	20	143				
Yes			Yes		18,910 †	10,190	15	620				
Yes			No		7,470 †	500	9	232	Yes			
Yes	Yes	Yes	Yes	Yes	16,440	9,504	17	548	Yes	204	$3,579	5/1
		Yes	No		6,024 †	9,694	18	172				
					13,220 †	8,528		490				
Yes					13,220 †	8,528		490				
Yes	Yes		Yes	Yes	16,140	7,991	21	560	Yes	15	$5,266	
Yes			No		3,450 †	1,500	14	115	Yes			None

† Tuition and fees are for 2007-08. ‡ Tuition and fees are projected for 2008-09. * Comprehensive Fee

Institution	Control/ degrees	Undergraduates		Tests required (Fall 2009)	TOEFL		Application	
		Total	Internat'l		minimum	average	Deadline	Fee
El Centro College	Pu/A	5,527	148	TOEFL	530	550	7/15	
Everest College: Arlington	Pr/A	500						25
Frank Phillips College	Pu/A	721	25	TOEFL	500		None	
Galveston College	Pu/A	2,044	32	TOEFL	500		7/7	
Grayson County College	Pu/A	3,786		TOEFL	450			
Hallmark College of Aeronautics	Pr/A	196		TOEFL	450		None	187
Hallmark College of Technology	Pr/A	484		TOEFL	450		None	187
Hardin-Simmons University	Pr/B	1,991	16	TOEFL	550		4/1	50
Hill College	Pu/A	3,556		TOEFL			None	50
Houston Baptist University	Pr/AB	1,992	120	TOEFL	550		7/1	100
Houston Community College System	Pu/A	43,518					7/1	75
Howard Payne University	Pr/AB	1,173		TOEFL	550		6/1	50
Huston-Tillotson University	Pr/B	724	16	TOEFL	500		7/1	75
Jacksonville College	Pr/A	310		TOEFL	450	500	None	100
Kilgore College	Pu/A	5,150					6/1	
Lamar Institute of Technology	Pu/A	2,590		TOEFL	500			
Lamar State College at Orange	Pu/A	1,756		TOEFL	500			
Lamar State College at Port Arthur	Pu/A	2,279		TOEFL	500		None	
Lamar University	Pu/AB	8,428	87	TOEFL, SAT/ACT	500	536	5/15	
Laredo Community College	Pu/A	6,914		TOEFL	450		None	
Lee College	Pu/A	5,754		TOEFL	500		None	25
LeTourneau University	Pr/AB	3,552	27	TOEFL, SAT/ACT	500		None	25
Lon Morris College	Pr/A	395		TOEFL	450		None	300
Lone Star College System	Pu/A	35,850	1,013				None	
Lubbock Christian University	Pr/AB	1,718	10	TOEFL, SAT/ACT	500	550	6/1	25
McLennan Community College	Pu/A	8,079		TOEFL	500		7/1	50
McMurry University	Pr/B	1,365	16	TOEFL, SAT/ACT	550		3/1	50
Midland College	Pu/AB	3,485		TOEFL	530	535	None	20
Midwestern State University	Pu/AB	5,348	274	TOEFL, SAT/ACT	550		4/1	50
Mountain View College	Pu/A	6,827		TOEFL	530	540	7/31	
Navarro College	Pu/A	7,560	159	TOEFL	450		None	60
North Central Texas College	Pu/A			TOEFL	550		8/1	
North Lake College	Pu/A	9,817		TOEFL	530	540	None	
Northeast Texas Community College	Pu/A	2,458		TOEFL	550		None	
Northwest Vista College	Pu/A	10,672		TOEFL	450		5/15	
Northwood University: Texas	Pr/AB	526	31	TOEFL	500	550	None	25
Odessa College	Pu/A	3,806	8	TOEFL	525		5/1	50
Our Lady of the Lake University of San Antonio	Pr/B	1,528	11	TOEFL	525		7/15	50
Palo Alto College	Pu/A	8,021		TOEFL	450			
Panola College	Pu/A	1,879	17	TOEFL	525		5/1	
Paris Junior College	Pu/A	4,342		TOEFL		475	8/15	
Prairie View A&M University	Pu/B	6,118		TOEFL, SAT/ACT	500		6/1	50
Ranger College	Pu/A			TOEFL	550		7/15	100
Remington College: Fort Worth	Pr/A	409					None	50
Remington College: Houston	Pr/A	461						50
Rice University	Pr/B	3,001	154	TOEFL, SAT, SAT Subject Test(s), or ACT	600		1/2	60
Richland College	Pu/A	14,505		TOEFL	530	535	7/1	
St. Edward's University	Pr/B	4,312	88	TOEFL	500		5/1	50
St. Mary's University	Pr/B	2,412	75	TOEFL	550	570		30
St. Philip's College	Pu/A	9,256	12	TOEFL	500		5/15	15
Sam Houston State University	Pu/B	14,149	111	TOEFL	550		8/1	40
San Antonio College	Pu/A	21,479					5/15	15
San Jacinto College	Pu/A	23,805		TOEFL	525		None	
Schreiner University	Pr/AB	926	5	TOEFL, SAT/ACT	550		7/15	25
South Plains College	Pu/A	9,197	59	TOEFL	550	560	7/31	20

Student services			Housing		Academic year costs		Maximum credits/ summer	Credit hour charge	International financial aid			
Adviser	Orien- tation	ESL	Academic year	Summer	Tuition/ fees	Living costs			Avail- able	Number receiving aid	Average award	Deadline
Yes	Yes	Yes	No		3,450†	600	14	115	Yes			None
					15,360†	680		268				
Yes			Yes		3,136†	6,120		120				
Yes			No		2,314	9,276	16	60				
Yes	Yes	Yes	Yes		1,344‡	6,240			Yes			None
Yes	Yes		No									
Yes	Yes		No									
Yes			Yes	Yes	18,380	9,562	15	580	Yes	12	$6,833	None
Yes			Yes		2,350†	7,680	12		Yes			None
Yes		Yes	Yes	Yes	18,820	8,959	14	700	Yes			4/15
Yes		Yes	No		3,856†							
Yes			Yes	Yes	17,400	8,301	14	510				
Yes			Yes		10,038†	8,598	9		Yes			4/1
Yes			Yes		6,146†	5,770	20	185				
Yes	Yes	Yes	Yes	Yes	3,660†	5,830	14	100	Yes			7/15
Yes		Yes	Yes		12,090			362				
			No		11,680†	7,318	18	360				
Yes		Yes			11,788†	8,780						
Yes	Yes	Yes	Yes	Yes	14,444	19,534	12	426	Yes			None
Yes		Yes	Yes		3,816†	9,071	14	105				
Yes			No		3,102†	7,869		85	Yes			None
Yes			Yes		19,140	11,000	16		Yes			None
Yes		Yes	Yes	Yes	10,950†	10,350	18		Yes	25		None
Yes	Yes	Yes	No		3,310	6,350	12	101				
Yes			Yes		14,700	9,840	12	429	Yes	8	$1,312	None
Yes	Yes		No		3,750†	8,861	14	116				
			Yes	Yes	18,135	10,657	14	535	Yes	16	$11,358	None
Yes		Yes	Yes		2,820†	6,759	14	94	Yes			6/1
Yes	Yes	Yes	Yes	Yes	14,348	9,464	18	331	Yes	208	$1,564	None
Yes		Yes	No		3,450†	2,864		115	Yes			
Yes		Yes	Yes		3,756‡	11,444	14					
Yes			Yes	Yes	3,210†	6,660	12	98				
Yes	Yes	Yes	No		3,450†	600	14	115				
			Yes		3,956†	7,009	7	96	Yes			None
Yes		Yes	No		5,750†		12		Yes			None
Yes	Yes		Yes	Yes	16,455†	10,611	24	330	Yes			None
Yes			Yes	Yes	2,790	8,999	16		Yes			None
Yes	Yes	Yes	Yes	Yes	19,116†	9,688	12	604	Yes			
Yes	Yes	Yes	No		5,384†	500	12					
Yes			Yes		3,330†	10,970	12		Yes			None
Yes	Yes		Yes	Yes	3,450	4,632						
Yes	Yes		Yes		14,728	18,092	14		Yes			3/1
Yes			Yes		2,294†	4,372	14	49	Yes			7/24
			No			9,297						
Yes	Yes	Yes	Yes		30,479	13,100	12	1249		57	$24,187	
Yes	Yes	Yes	No		3,450†	350	15	115	Yes			7/30
Yes	Yes		Yes	Yes	22,150	16,150	15	738				
Yes	Yes	Yes	Yes	Yes	21,156	10,169	12	640	Yes			None
Yes			No		5,762	10,660	14	183				
Yes		Yes	Yes		14,250	10,552		429	Yes	11	$6,717	5/31
Yes	Yes	Yes	No		5,356†	3,249	18	168	Yes			None
Yes		Yes	No		3,500		17	108	Yes			None
Yes			Yes	Yes	17,892	10,322	6	742	Yes	3	$9,333	
Yes		Yes	Yes	Yes	3,032	5,580	18					

† Tuition and fees are for 2007-08.   ‡ Tuition and fees are projected for 2008-09.   * Comprehensive Fee

Institution	Control/ degrees	Undergraduates		Tests required (Fall 2009)	TOEFL		Application	
		Total	Internat'l		minimum	average	Deadline	Fee
South Texas College	Pu/AB	19,973		TOEFL	500		None	
Southern Methodist University	Pr/B	6,081	296	TOEFL, SAT/ACT	550		None	60
Southwestern Adventist University	Pr/AB	820	78	TOEFL	520		7/1	
Southwestern Assemblies of God University	Pr/AB	1,543		TOEFL	450		7/1	30
Southwestern University	Pr/B	1,283	1	TOEFL, SAT/ACT	570		2/15	40
Stephen F. Austin State University	Pu/B	10,106	89	TOEFL, SAT/ACT	550		6/1	50
Sul Ross State University	Pu/AB	1,935		TOEFL, SAT/ACT	520		None	50
Tarleton State University	Pu/AB	7,781	63	TOEFL, SAT/ACT	520		None	125
Tarrant County College	Pu/A	37,951			550		7/15	
Texas A&M International University	Pu/B	4,065	144	TOEFL	550		6/1	
Texas A&M University	Pu/B	37,341	493	TOEFL	550	601	2/1	75
Texas A&M University-Commerce	Pu/B	5,166	47	TOEFL, SAT/ACT	500	530	8/1	50
Texas A&M University-Galveston	Pu/B	1,565		TOEFL, SAT/ACT	550		3/1	75
Texas A&M University-Kingsville	Pu/B	5,009						15
Texas A&M University-Texarkana	Pu/B	1,003	2	TOEFL	550			
Texas Christian University	Pr/B	7,264	332	TOEFL	550		3/1	50
Texas College	Pr/AB	741		TOEFL	500	537	4/1	20
Texas Culinary Academy	Pr/A	917						100
Texas Lutheran University	Pr/B	1,334	11	TOEFL	550	560	5/6	25
Texas Southern University	Pu/B	7,572	212	TOEFL, SAT/ACT	500		4/30	78
Texas Southmost College	Pu/A	10,539		TOEFL	500		7/1	
Texas State Technical College: Harlingen	Pu/A	4,957	27	TOEFL	450			
Texas State Technical College: Marshall	Pu/A	705						
Texas State Technical College: Sweetwater	Pu/A	1,498		TOEFL	550		None	
Texas State Technical College: Waco	Pu/A			TOEFL	550		7/30	
Texas State University: San Marcos	Pu/B	24,038	218	TOEFL, SAT/ACT	550		5/1	75
Texas Tech University	Pu/B	22,996	202	TOEFL	550	610	4/1	60
Texas Tech University Health Sciences Center	Pu/B	608	8					40
Texas Wesleyan University	Pr/B	1,422		TOEFL, SAT/ACT	520		None	50
Texas Woman's University	Pu/B	6,986	136	TOEFL, SAT/ACT	550	590	6/1	50
Trinity University	Pr/B	2,464	120	TOEFL, SAT/ACT	600		2/1	50
Trinity Valley Community College	Pu/A	5,615		TOEFL	450		None	80
University of Dallas	Pr/B	1,222	14	TOEFL, SAT/ACT	550		2/15	40
University of Houston	Pu/B	26,495	1,133	TOEFL, SAT/ACT	550		5/1	75
University of Houston: Clear Lake	Pu/B	4,282		TOEFL	550	555	6/1	75
University of Houston: Downtown	Pu/B	11,670	319	TOEFL	550		5/1	60
University of Houston: Victoria	Pu/B	1,386	6	TOEFL	550		6/1	
University of the Incarnate Word	Pr/AB	4,666		TOEFL	560		7/1	20
University of Mary Hardin-Baylor	Pr/B	2,481	29				7/15	135
University of North Texas	Pu/B	27,242	666	TOEFL	550		6/15	75
University of St. Thomas	Pr/B	1,609	69	TOEFL	550		7/15	25
University of Texas at Arlington	Pu/B	18,489		TOEFL, SAT	550		None	50
University of Texas at Austin	Pu/B	36,881	1,483	TOEFL, SAT/ACT	550		2/1	75
University of Texas at Brownsville	Pu/AB	9,724						
University of Texas at Dallas	Pu/B	9,096	364	TOEFL, SAT/ACT	550	606	5/1	100
University of Texas at El Paso	Pu/B	16,658	1,630	TOEFL	500		5/1	65
University of Texas at San Antonio	Pu/B	24,280	518	TOEFL, SAT/ACT	550		6/1	30
University of Texas at Tyler	Pu/B	4,938	32	TOEFL, SAT/ACT	550	579	5/30	50
University of Texas Health Science Center at San Antonio	Pu/B	690		TOEFL	550			
University of Texas Medical Branch at Galveston	Pu/B	562		TOEFL	550			30
University of Texas of the Permian Basin	Pu/B	2,634	11	TOEFL	550	560	7/15	

Student services			Housing		Academic year costs		Maximum credits/ summer	Credit hour charge	International financial aid			
Adviser	Orien- tation	ESL	Academic year	Summer	Tuition/ fees	Living costs			Avail- able	Number receiving aid	Average award	Deadline
			No		6,497 †	3,225						
Yes	Yes	Yes	Yes	Yes	33,170	14,275	12	1230	Yes			None
Yes		Yes	Yes	Yes	15,236	9,954	12	619	Yes			None
Yes			Yes	Yes	11,530 †	8,648	12	355	Yes	1	$1,010	6/1
Yes	Yes		Yes	Yes	27,940	10,600	12	1165	Yes	1	$25,740	3/1
Yes		Yes	Yes	Yes	14,502 †	11,502	12	425	Yes	62	$1,051	
			Yes	Yes	13,398	10,320	14	394	Yes			None
Yes	Yes		Yes	Yes	13,995	8,114	12	420				
Yes	Yes		No		4,950	11,056	14	165	Yes			
Yes	Yes	Yes	Yes	Yes	13,378 †	10,618	12	396	Yes	5		None
Yes	Yes	Yes	Yes	Yes	15,675 †	12,749	12	434	Yes	253	$14,352	None
Yes	Yes	Yes	Yes	Yes	13,440 †	11,126	14		Yes			
Yes	Yes	Yes	Yes	Yes	14,395 †	10,292		434				
Yes	Yes	Yes	Yes	Yes	13,218 †	8,852			Yes			None
			No		12,061 †	9,752						
Yes	Yes	Yes	Yes	Yes	26,948	12,400	15	1135	Yes	244	$19,295	5/1
Yes			Yes		8,746 †	8,550		330	Yes	5	$5,141	
					38,750	3,355						
Yes	Yes		Yes	Yes	20,970	11,440	14	700	Yes	7	$14,271	None
Yes	Yes	Yes	Yes	Yes	14,128 †	11,480	12	325	Yes			None
		Yes	No			7,422			Yes			6/1
Yes		Yes	Yes	Yes	6,200 †	6,925	12	182				
					6,220 †	2,390		182				
Yes			Yes	Yes	6,220 †	5,600		182				
			Yes	Yes	6,224 †	8,431	15	182				
Yes	Yes	Yes	Yes	Yes	15,424	10,472	12	451	Yes	67	$6,670	None
Yes	Yes	Yes	Yes	Yes	15,123 †	11,631	16	422	Yes			None
Yes	Yes	Yes	Yes	Yes	16,730	9,982	12	525	Yes	20	$5,000	None
Yes	Yes		Yes	Yes	14,880	10,138	16	421	Yes			None
Yes	Yes		Yes		27,699	10,822		1111	Yes	88	$17,667	4/1
Yes	Yes	Yes	Yes	Yes	2,400 †	5,710	12	65	Yes			None
Yes	Yes	Yes	Yes		24,770	12,485	12	975				
Yes	Yes	Yes	Yes	Yes	15,790 †	12,025	12	439	Yes			None
Yes	Yes		Yes		13,954 †	6,912	12		Yes			None
Yes	Yes	Yes	No		13,172 †	8,044	12	413	Yes	23	$2,788	
Yes			No		13,395 †			410	Yes	1	$1,000	None
Yes	Yes	Yes	Yes	Yes	20,260	10,850		640	Yes	54	$8,984	None
Yes	Yes	Yes	Yes	Yes	19,750	10,890	12	580	Yes			None
Yes	Yes	Yes	Yes	Yes	15,107	9,906		439				
Yes			Yes	Yes	20,550	11,836	12	673	Yes	25	$6,207	None
Yes	Yes	Yes	Yes	Yes	15,534 †	10,816	14	441	Yes	107	$3,648	None
Yes	Yes	Yes	Yes	Yes	24,544 †	12,616	14		Yes			None
Yes		Yes	Yes		13,005 †	12,985		394	Yes			8/15
Yes	Yes		Yes		17,854 †	11,945	12	595		136	$5,824	4/12
Yes	Yes	Yes	Yes	Yes	13,950 †	10,376	9	424	Yes	321	$6,502	3/15
Yes	Yes	Yes	Yes	Yes	15,530	11,903	24	441	Yes			None
Yes	Yes		Yes	Yes	14,172	10,288	15	331	Yes			None
			No		15,500 †	6,210	9	488	Yes			None
Yes			Yes	Yes	13,618 †			428				
Yes			Yes	Yes	13,189 †	1,555	12			2	$2,550	

† Tuition and fees are for 2007-08. ‡ Tuition and fees are projected for 2008-09. * Comprehensive Fee

Institution	Control/ degrees	Undergraduates		Tests required (Fall 2009)	TOEFL		Application	
		Total	Internat'l		minimum	average	Deadline	Fee
University of Texas Southwestern Medical Center at Dallas	Pu/B	118		TOEFL	550			10
University of Texas: Pan American	Pu/B	14,995	808	TOEFL, SAT/ACT	500		2/1	
Victoria College	Pu/A	3,988	19	TOEFL	500		None	
Wayland Baptist University	Pr/AB	934	22	TOEFL, SAT/ACT	500		8/1	35
Weatherford College	Pu/A	4,092	59	TOEFL	525	565	6/1	50
West Texas A&M University	Pu/B	5,849	105	TOEFL, SAT/ACT	525		5/1	75
Western Technical College	Pr/A	500						
Western Texas College	Pu/A	1,977		TOEFL	500		8/8	25
Westwood College: Houston South	Pr/A	390		TOEFL				25
Wiley College	Pr/AB	922		TOEFL	500		7/1	25
Utah								
Brigham Young University	Pr/B	30,873	1,273	TOEFL, SAT/ACT	550		2/15	30
Careers Unlimited	Pr/AB	104						
College of Eastern Utah	Pu/A	2,103		TOEFL	500		8/15	50
DeVry University: Sandy	Pr/AB	39						50
Dixie State College of Utah	Pu/AB	4,607		TOEFL	500		7/1	50
Neumont University	Pr/B			TOEFL	550		None	125
Salt Lake Community College	Pu/A	23,375	266	TOEFL	450	500	6/1	65
Snow College	Pu/A	3,745		TOEFL	500	550	None	50
Southern Utah University	Pu/AB	5,329	66	TOEFL	500		7/1	25
Stevens-Henager College: Murray	Pr/AB	401						
Stevens-Henager College: Ogden	Pr/AB	425					None	
University of Utah	Pu/B	20,560	522	TOEFL, SAT/ACT	500	543	4/1	55
Utah State University	Pu/AB	12,995	467	TOEFL	500		None	40
Utah Valley State College	Pu/AB	20,159	281	TOEFL	500		None	100
Weber State University	Pu/AB	17,617					7/1	45
Westminster College	Pr/B	2,020	32	TOEFL, SAT/ACT	550		None	40
Vermont								
Bennington College	Pr/B	583	18	TOEFL	577		1/3	60
Burlington College	Pr/AB	172	4	TOEFL	580		None	50
Castleton State College	Pu/AB	1,873	4	TOEFL	500		None	35
Champlain College	Pr/AB	2,493	8	TOEFL	500	580	None	50
College of St. Joseph in Vermont	Pr/AB	209		TOEFL	550		7/1	25
Community College of Vermont	Pu/A	6,000		TOEFL			None	
Green Mountain College	Pr/B	759	2	TOEFL	500	560	6/1	30
Johnson State College	Pu/AB	1,520		TOEFL	500		None	35
Landmark College	Pr/A	462	18	TOEFL	550		None	75
Lyndon State College	Pu/AB	1,371		TOEFL, SAT/ACT	500	510	None	36
Marlboro College	Pr/B	330		TOEFL, SAT/ACT	550	575	3/1	50
Middlebury College	Pr/B	2,475	243	TOEFL, ACT		641	1/1	65
New England Culinary Institute	Pr/AB	637		TOEFL	550		None	25
Norwich University	Pr/B			TOEFL, SAT/ACT	500		None	35
St. Michael's College	Pr/B	1,980	27	TOEFL	550		2/1	50
Southern Vermont College	Pr/AB	406	7	TOEFL	500	520	None	30
Sterling College	Pr/B	104		TOEFL	500		2/15	35
University of Vermont	Pu/B	9,454	47	TOEFL, SAT/ACT	550	600	1/15	45
Virginia								
Art Institute of Washington	Pr/AB	1,700		TOEFL	500		None	50
Averett University	Pr/AB	790	16	TOEFL	500	585	6/1	35
Aviation Institute of Maintenance: Virginia Beach	Pr/A	174						
Beta Tech: Richmond South	Pr/A	148						
Beta Tech: Richmond West	Pr/A	86						25

Student services			Housing		Academic year costs		Maximum credits/ summer	Credit hour charge	International financial aid			
Adviser	Orien- tation	ESL	Academic year	Summer	Tuition/ fees	Living costs			Avail- able	Number receiving aid	Average award	Deadline
Yes			No		12,380†	17,015						
Yes	Yes	Yes	Yes		13,555	7,700	12	419	Yes	610	$6,601	3/1
Yes			No		2,310†	1,400	14					
Yes			Yes	Yes	12,000	7,998	12	380	Yes	21	$10,433	None
Yes	Yes		Yes	Yes	3,750†	9,315	12	125				
Yes	Yes	Yes	Yes	Yes	13,260†	9,355	12	328	Yes			None
			No						Yes			None
Yes		Yes	Yes	Yes	2,340†	9,300	10	59				
						660						
Yes			Yes		9,150†	8,190	7	253	Yes			None
Yes	Yes	Yes	Yes	Yes	3,840†	11,518		197	Yes	659	$3,197	None
Yes	Yes	Yes	Yes	Yes	7,964†	7,425						
						8,528						
Yes		Yes	Yes	Yes	9,460†	3,098	12					
Yes			Yes	Yes	28,275†			495				
Yes	Yes	Yes	No		7,958†	11,750	18					
Yes	Yes	Yes	Yes	Yes	7,889†	4,730	18		Yes			7/15
Yes		Yes	Yes		11,327†	4,922			Yes			None
Yes			No		16,350†							
			Yes	Yes	19,933‡	17,800		1660				
Yes	Yes	Yes	Yes	Yes	15,662†	12,078			Yes	4	$2,154	3/15
Yes	Yes	Yes	Yes	Yes	12,224†	4,580	18					
Yes	Yes	Yes	No		11,028†	10,784			Yes			None
Yes	Yes	Yes	Yes	Yes	11,135†	12,246			Yes			None
Yes	Yes		Yes	Yes	23,790	9,897		975	Yes	19	$7,500	None
Yes	Yes		Yes		38,270	13,730		1165	Yes			None
Yes			Yes	Yes	19,640	10,770	15	650				
			Yes		16,948	9,209	18	673	Yes			None
Yes	Yes		Yes	Yes	22,550†	13,110	12	940	Yes			3/1
			Yes		15,760‡	9,800	15	250				
		Yes	No		10,900†	600		360				
Yes	Yes	ESL	Yes		24,565†	12,352		792	Yes			None
Yes		Yes	Yes	Yes	15,428†	8,970	18	635	Yes			None
Yes			Yes		43,575	10,250	12		Yes			None
Yes			Yes		15,428†	9,020	9	635				
Yes			Yes		30,680†	12,960		990	Yes			3/1
Yes	Yes		Yes	Yes	49,210*	1,950			Yes	182	$37,766	1/1
Yes			Yes	Yes	25,652†	7,492			Yes			None
Yes	Yes		Yes		26,064	10,832	20	725	Yes			None
Yes	Yes	Yes	Yes	Yes	31,940	9,920	12	1055	Yes	20	$16,894	
Yes			Yes	Yes	18,160	8,500	15	575	Yes			None
			Yes		21,655	9,242		650	Yes			None
Yes	Yes		Yes	Yes	27,938†	10,096		1096	Yes			None
Yes	Yes		Yes	Yes	20,880‡	8,370	16					
Yes			Yes	Yes	21,300	10,040	12		Yes	16	$11,732	None
					17,097							
					11,060†							
					11,060†							

† Tuition and fees are for 2007-08.   ‡ Tuition and fees are projected for 2008-09.   * Comprehensive Fee

Institution	Control/ degrees	Undergraduates		Tests required (Fall 2009)	TOEFL		Application	
		Total	Internat'l		minimum	average	Deadline	Fee
Bluefield College	Pr/B	761		TOEFL, SAT/ACT	500		None	30
Bridgewater College	Pr/B	1,527	7	TOEFL, SAT/ACT	500		6/1	30
Bryant & Stratton College: Richmond	Pr/AB	516						
Bryant & Stratton College: Virginia Beach	Pr/AB	477		TOEFL	500		None	25
Central Virginia Community College	Pu/A	4,914		TOEFL	500	525	None	
Christendom College	Pr/AB	397	10	TOEFL, SAT/ACT			3/1	25
Christopher Newport University	Pu/B	4,663	11	TOEFL, SAT/ACT	530	540	3/1	45
College of William and Mary	Pu/B	5,706	115	TOEFL, SAT/ACT			1/1	60
Danville Community College	Pu/A	4,016		TOEFL	560		4/30	
DeVry University: Arlington	Pr/AB	550	8	TOEFL	500			50
Eastern Mennonite University	Pr/AB	953	36	TOEFL	550		6/1	25
Emory & Henry College	Pr/B	977			550		6/1	30
Ferrum College	Pr/B	1,240		TOEFL	550		None	25
George Mason University	Pu/B	17,983	676	TOEFL, SAT/ACT	570		1/15	75
Germanna Community College	Pu/A	3,092					None	
Hampden-Sydney College	Pr/B	1,122	13	TOEFL, SAT/ACT	570	590	3/1	30
Hampton University	Pr/AB	4,874		TOEFL, SAT	550	575	3/1	35
Hollins University	Pr/B	772	22	TOEFL	550	608	2/15	35
J. Sargeant Reynolds Community College	Pu/A	12,557		TOEFL	550		None	
James Madison University	Pu/B	16,108	137	TOEFL	550		4/1	40
Jefferson College of Health Sciences	Pr/AB	927	4	TOEFL	550			250
Liberty University	Pr/AB	18,475	639	TOEFL	500	573	None	40
Longwood University	Pu/B	3,932	19	TOEFL, SAT/ACT	550		3/1	40
Lynchburg College	Pr/B	2,046	15	TOEFL	525	559	7/31	30
Mary Baldwin College	Pr/B	1,369	16	TOEFL	500	550	None	35
Marymount University	Pr/B	2,199	142	TOEFL, SAT/ACT	550	588	7/1	40
National College: Harrisonburg	Pr/A						None	125
National College: Roanoke Valley	Pr/AB						None	125
Norfolk State University	Pu/AB	5,259	45	TOEFL	500	525	None	25
Northern Virginia Community College	Pu/A	41,266		TOEFL	500		7/1	
Old Dominion University	Pu/B	15,655	281	TOEFL	550		4/15	40
Patrick Henry Community College	Pu/A			TOEFL	500		8/1	
Paul D. Camp Community College	Pu/A	1,539		TOEFL	450	500	None	
Piedmont Virginia Community College	Pu/A	2,953		TOEFL	500			
Potomac College	Pr/AB			TOEFL	550		None	15
Radford University	Pu/B	7,982	45	TOEFL	520	560	4/15	50
Randolph College	Pr/B	618	73	TOEFL	550		3/1	35
Randolph-Macon College	Pr/B	1,166	18	TOEFL	550	613	3/1	30
Rappahannock Community College	Pu/A	3,206		TOEFL	500		8/20	
Regent University	Pr/B	1,177		TOEFL	577		6/15	50
Richard Bland College	Pu/A	1,060		TOEFL	500		8/15	20
Roanoke College	Pr/B	1,945	14	TOEFL	520		3/1	30
St. Paul's College	Pr/B	687		TOEFL			None	20
Shenandoah University	Pr/AB	1,587	49	TOEFL	527		None	30
Southern Virginia University	Pr/B	698	11					35
Southwest Virginia Community College	Pu/A	2,481		TOEFL	500			
Sweet Briar College	Pr/B	636	5	TOEFL, SAT	550		2/1	40
Thomas Nelson Community College	Pu/A	9,368					None	
Tidewater Community College	Pu/A	25,857		TOEFL	500		None	
Tidewater Tech: Chesapeake	Pr/A	185						
Tidewater Tech: Newport News	Pr/A							25
Tidewater Tech: Norfolk	Pr/A							25
Tidewater Tech: Virginia Beach	Pr/A	187						25
University of Mary Washington	Pu/B	4,117	20	TOEFL, SAT/ACT	570	620	2/1	45
University of Northern Virginia	Pr/B	40		TOEFL	500		7/24	60

| Student services | | | Housing | | Academic year costs | | Maximum credits/summer | Credit hour charge | International financial aid | | | Deadline |
Adviser	Orientation	ESL	Academic year	Summer	Tuition/fees	Living costs			Available	Number receiving aid	Average award	
			Yes	Yes	15,640	10,360	21	490	Yes	4	$11,737	None
Yes			Yes	Yes	23,090	12,710	11	775	Yes	7	$16,638	None
					13,185†	6,009		415	Yes			None
			No		13,205‡	3,750	15	436	Yes			None
Yes			No		7,614†	7,550		249				
			Yes		18,806	7,888	18		Yes			6/1
Yes			Yes	Yes	14,150‡	12,212	18					
Yes	Yes		Yes		26,725†	9,155	9	790				
			No		7,601†	5,412		249				
Yes					14,640†	3,662		525				
Yes	Yes	Yes	Yes	Yes	21,960†	9,180	7		Yes	25		None
			Yes		23,860	10,780	12	985	Yes			8/1
Yes			Yes		22,545	9,830		450	Yes			None
Yes	Yes	Yes	Yes		19,728†	7,020		822				
			No		7,622†	5,995		249				
Yes			Yes		27,732†	10,912	6	854	Yes			None
Yes	Yes		Yes	Yes	15,610†	10,199	12	350	Yes			None
Yes	Yes		Yes		25,645†	14,090			Yes			None
Yes		Yes	No		7,761†	6,000	18	249				
Yes	Yes		Yes		18,458	12,024	15	497	Yes	61	$12,902	
Yes			Yes		15,500†	10,110	15	445	Yes			None
Yes	Yes	Yes	Yes		16,434	11,156	9	515	Yes	312		3/1
Yes	Yes		Yes		16,259†	13,740	20					
Yes	Yes		Yes	Yes	27,565	8,200	12	375	Yes			None
Yes	Yes	Yes	Yes	Yes	23,645	8,945		400	Yes	14	$2,528	None
Yes	Yes		Yes		21,528	11,360		690	Yes	40	$11,349	None
Yes	Yes		No		9,585	1,200		212				
Yes	Yes		Yes	Yes	9,585			212				
Yes	Yes		Yes		16,242†	10,896	9	599	Yes			None
Yes		Yes	No		7,959†	3,950		257				
Yes	Yes	Yes	Yes	Yes	18,588	10,975		613	Yes			3/15
			No		7,605†	7,130	18	249	Yes			None
Yes			No		7,569†	2,000		249				
Yes			No		7,634†	4,458	12	249	Yes			None
			No		13,480†			445				
Yes	Yes	Yes	Yes	Yes	15,550	10,193	14	550	Yes	9	$1,498	None
Yes	Yes		Yes		27,890	12,210		1120	Yes			None
Yes	Yes		Yes	Yes	28,355	12,110	8	1020	Yes	18	$17,384	3/1
			No		7,599†	2,440	18	249	Yes			None
			No	Yes	12,750	1,000		420	Yes	4	$5,560	None
			Yes		10,802†	3,726	15	451				
Yes	Yes	Yes	Yes	Yes	27,935	13,485	16		Yes	14	$23,246	None
Yes			Yes		12,020†	11,710	12	470	Yes			None
Yes	Yes	Yes	Yes	Yes	23,340	11,450	12	670	Yes			3/2
			Yes		16,500†	6,500		595	Yes			None
Yes			No		7,614†	8,300	15	249	Yes			None
Yes	Yes		Yes		26,995	12,310	18	890	Yes			
		Yes	No		7,610†	9,290		249				
Yes		Yes	No		7,730†	9,410	18	249				
					11,060†							
					15,075							
					11,060†							
					15,075							
Yes	Yes		Yes		18,600‡	11,600	12	725				
Yes	Yes	Yes		Yes	14,000	920		325				

† Tuition and fees are for 2007-08.   ‡ Tuition and fees are projected for 2008-09.   * Comprehensive Fee

Institution	Control/ degrees	Undergraduates		Tests required (Fall 2009)	TOEFL		Application	
		Total	Internat'l		minimum	average	Deadline	Fee
University of Richmond	Pr/AB	2,719	125	TOEFL, SAT/ACT			1/15	50
University of Virginia	Pu/B	13,726	631	TOEFL, SAT Subject Test(s)			1/2	60
University of Virginia's College at Wise	Pu/B	1,657	9	TOEFL, SAT/ACT	550	570	4/1	25
Virginia Commonwealth University	Pu/B	20,232	577	TOEFL	500		None	40
Virginia Intermont College	Pr/AB	627	13	TOEFL	500	550	None	25
Virginia Military Institute	Pu/B	1,378	22	TOEFL	500	572	3/1	35
Virginia Polytechnic Institute and State University	Pu/AB	22,940	418	TOEFL, SAT/ACT	550		2/1	70
Virginia State University	Pu/AB	4,195	1	TOEFL	500		5/1	25
Virginia Union University	Pr/B	1,194		TOEFL, SAT, SAT Subject Test(s)	500	520	6/15	25
Virginia Wesleyan College	Pr/B	1,379		TOEFL	550		6/1	40
Washington and Lee University	Pr/B	1,774	70	TOEFL, SAT/ACT, SAT Subject Test(s)	600		1/15	50
World College	Pr/B	445						

Washington

Institution	Control/ degrees	Total	Internat'l	Tests required	minimum	average	Deadline	Fee
Art Institute of Seattle	Pr/AB	2,261	146	TOEFL	480	500	None	50
Bastyr University	Pr/B	213		TOEFL	550		4/15	60
Bates Technical College	Pu/A	10,500		TOEFL			None	56
Bellevue Community College	Pu/A	13,700		TOEFL	500	550	None	50
Bellingham Technical College	Pu/A	2,575		TOEFL	470		None	35
Big Bend Community College	Pu/A	1,154		TOEFL	450		7/25	30
Cascadia Community College	Pu/A	2,397		TOEFL				
Central Washington University	Pu/B	9,463	146	TOEFL	525		4/1	50
Centralia College	Pu/A	4,043	54		400	490	8/1	35
City University of Seattle	Pr/AB	1,443		TOEFL	540		8/15	50
Clark College	Pu/A				520		7/15	35
Clover Park Technical College	Pu/A						8/30	50
Columbia Basin College	Pu/A		4	TOEFL	500		4/1	28
Cornish College of the Arts	Pr/B	800		TOEFL	530		None	35
DeVry University: Federal Way	Pr/AB	661	3	TOEFL	500			50
DigiPen Institute of Technology	Pr/B	818		TOEFL	550		None	75
Edmonds Community College	Pu/A	7,208			480	510	None	50
Everett Community College	Pu/A	3,435	20				7/1	40
Evergreen State College	Pu/B	4,135	16	TOEFL, SAT/ACT	550		3/1	50
Gonzaga University	Pr/B	4,318	82	TOEFL	550	596	8/1	45
Grays Harbor College	Pu/A	578		TOEFL	500		None	
Green River Community College	Pu/A	6,898		TOEFL	500		8/25	50
Heritage University	Pr/AB	788		TOEFL	500		None	125
Highline Community College	Pu/A			TOEFL	480		None	50
International Academy of Design and Technology: Seattle	Pr/AB							50
Lake Washington Technical College	Pu/A	5,261		TOEFL	500		None	50
Lower Columbia College	Pu/A	1,408		TOEFL	460	500	None	66
North Seattle Community College	Pu/A	2,056			520		7/31	35
Northwest College of Art	Pr/B	128		TOEFL	500		6/1	100
Northwest Indian College	Pu/AB	1,224						
Northwest University	Pr/AB	1,053	23	TOEFL	500	575	6/1	30
Olympic College	Pu/AB	6,765	4	TOEFL	480	550	None	35
Pacific Lutheran University	Pr/B	3,271	173	TOEFL	550		7/1	40
Peninsula College	Pu/AB	980	66	TOEFL	500	510	None	35
Renton Technical College	Pu/A	1,906		TOEFL	500		None	25
Saint Martin's University	Pr/B	1,245	51	TOEFL	525	535	7/1	35
Seattle Pacific University	Pr/B	3,015	20	TOEFL	550	653	9/1	35
Seattle University	Pr/B	4,234	322	TOEFL	520	592	6/1	45

Student services			Housing		Academic year costs		Maximum credits/ summer	Credit hour charge	International financial aid			
Adviser	Orientation	ESL	Academic year	Summer	Tuition/ fees	Living costs			Available	Number receiving aid	Average award	Deadline
Yes	Yes	Yes	Yes	Yes	38,850	8,200	9	1940	Yes	101	$39,407	2/15
Yes	Yes	Yes	Yes		29,798	10,794	12					
Yes			Yes	Yes	17,715†	9,024	14	618	Yes			None
Yes	Yes	Yes	Yes	Yes	18,572†	7,567		703	Yes	386	$1,132	None
Yes	Yes		Yes		19,366†	12,685	8	220	Yes	66	$15,655	6/1
Yes					25,892†	9,283	14					
Yes	Yes	Yes	Yes	Yes	19,605†	9,412	14					
Yes			Yes	Yes	13,185†	9,715	10	444	Yes			5/1
Yes			Yes		13,662	10,208	6					
Yes	Yes		Yes	Yes	26,438	11,600	12	1081	Yes			None
Yes	Yes		Yes		37,412	12,530			Yes	60	$41,041	2/1
					3,540‡							
Yes	Yes		Yes	Yes	20,565‡	14,989	18	435				
	Yes		Yes		17,040†	4,775		340	Yes			None
Yes		Yes										
Yes	Yes	Yes	No		8,304†	10,062	18	253	Yes			None
Yes			No		3,345†	13,228						
Yes	Yes		Yes		7,794†	6,480	15	246				
			No		8,004†							
Yes	Yes	Yes	Yes	Yes	14,894†	11,387	12		Yes			None
Yes	Yes	Yes	No	Yes	8,154†	10,122	12	88	Yes			9/1
Yes	Yes	Yes	No		14,580	860	15	324				
Yes	Yes	Yes	No		8,048†	9,954	18	252				
Yes	Yes	Yes	No	Yes	7,757†	10,395			Yes			8/25
Yes	Yes	Yes	No		8,106†	3,894	18					
Yes			No		24,100†	10,100	16	1000	Yes			None
Yes					14,640†	16,136		525				
Yes	Yes		No			3,963			Yes			None
Yes	Yes	Yes		Yes	8,375†	9,414						
Yes	Yes	Yes	No	Yes	7,989†	12,432	18	246				
Yes	Yes		Yes	Yes	15,489†	10,375	20			7	$8,062	
Yes	Yes	Yes	Yes	Yes	28,262	11,510	14	810	Yes	26	$24,336	6/30
Yes		Yes	No		8,321†	3,684	10		Yes			None
Yes	Yes	Yes	Yes	Yes	8,247†	10,929	20	246				
		Yes	No		14,905	6,195	9	495				
Yes	Yes	Yes	No		7,959†	5,986	18	88				
					15,300†			340				
Yes	Yes	Yes	No			12,870	15					
Yes	Yes	Yes	No		8,289†	5,010	18	96				
Yes	Yes	Yes	No	Yes	8,143†	4,227	18	246	Yes			8/31
Yes					15,300		15	665	Yes			6/1
			Yes		7,332†			200				
Yes	Yes	Yes	Yes	Yes	20,790	9,478	10	855	Yes			8/1
Yes		Yes	No		8,089†	12,594	18	117				
Yes	Yes	Yes	Yes	Yes	26,800	11,318	12	838	Yes	126	$8,167	None
Yes	Yes	Yes			7,971†	3,974		90	Yes			None
Yes		Yes	No		3,618†	690						
Yes	Yes	Yes	Yes	Yes	24,110	12,040	12	794				
Yes	Yes	Yes	Yes	Yes	26,817	11,946	20	736	Yes	5	$9,280	None
Yes	Yes	Yes	Yes	Yes	28,260	12,408	18	628	Yes	41	$8,713	None

† Tuition and fees are for 2007-08.   ‡ Tuition and fees are projected for 2008-09.   * Comprehensive Fee

Institution	Control/ degrees	Undergraduates		Tests required (Fall 2009)	TOEFL		Application	
		Total	Internat'l		minimum	average	Deadline	Fee
South Puget Sound Community College	Pu/A	2,749		TOEFL	450	500	3/1	40
South Seattle Community College	Pu/AB	8,242			580		None	50
Spokane Community College	Pu/A	6,027		TOEFL	500		None	40
Spokane Falls Community College	Pu/A	5,392		TOEFL	500		None	40
Tacoma Community College	Pu/A	5,142					8/15	
Trinity Lutheran College	Pr/AB	105		TOEFL	500		None	30
University of Puget Sound	Pr/B	2,527	8	TOEFL, SAT/ACT	550	604	5/1	40
University of Washington	Pu/B	26,509	1,052	TOEFL	540		1/15	50
Walla Walla Community College	Pu/A	2,183		TOEFL	500	510	None	
Walla Walla University	Pr/AB	1,586	18	TOEFL			None	30
Washington State University	Pu/B	19,822	470	TOEFL	520		1/31	50
Wenatchee Valley College	Pu/A	2,878		TOEFL	520			
Western Washington University	Pu/B	12,967	63	TOEFL	550		3/1	50
Whatcom Community College	Pu/A	4,127			480	500	8/18	35
Whitman College	Pr/B	1,455	47	TOEFL, SAT/ACT	560		1/15	45
Whitworth University	Pr/B	2,310	17	TOEFL, SAT/ACT	550		None	
Yakima Valley Community College	Pu/A	2,829	8	TOEFL	480		None	25

West Virginia

Alderson-Broaddus College	Pr/AB	616	7	TOEFL, ACT	500		8/1	25
Appalachian Bible College	Pr/AB	223		TOEFL	500		8/10	20
Bethany College	Pr/B	815		TOEFL	500	574	None	25
Bluefield State College	Pu/AB	1,693	17	TOEFL	500			
Concord University	Pu/AB	2,671		TOEFL, SAT/ACT	500		7/15	
Davis and Elkins College	Pr/AB	599	35	TOEFL	500		5/30	35
Fairmont State University	Pu/AB	6,227	52	TOEFL, SAT/ACT	500	550	7/15	
Glenville State College	Pu/AB	1,155		TOEFL, SAT/ACT	550		None	25
Marshall University	Pu/AB	8,904	93	TOEFL, SAT/ACT	500		7/15	30
Mountain State University	Pr/AB	4,053	121	TOEFL	500	520	7/15	50
New River Community and Technical College	Pu/A	2,156						
Ohio Valley University	Pr/AB	526	38	TOEFL, SAT/ACT	500		None	20
Potomac State College of West Virginia University	Pu/AB	1,608		TOEFL	550		None	
Salem International University	Pr/AB	342					None	25
Shepherd University	Pu/B	3,548	21	TOEFL, SAT/ACT	550	600	None	35
University of Charleston	Pr/AB	1,134	108	TOEFL	500		None	25
Valley College of Technology	Pr/A	43					None	
West Liberty State College	Pu/AB	2,236		TOEFL	500	510	7/1	
West Virginia Business College	Pr/A	60						75
West Virginia Junior College: Bridgeport	Pr/A	230						
West Virginia State Community and Technical College	Pu/A	1,639		TOEFL, SAT/ACT	500			
West Virginia University	Pu/B	21,145	353	TOEFL	500		4/1	50
West Virginia University at Parkersburg	Pu/AB	3,141		TOEFL			4/1	
West Virginia Wesleyan College	Pr/B	1,210	49	TOEFL, SAT/ACT	500		3/1	35
Wheeling Jesuit University	Pr/B	1,093	30	TOEFL, SAT/ACT	550		None	25

Wisconsin

Alverno College	Pr/AB	2,251	14	TOEFL	520		5/15	20
Bellin College of Nursing	Pr/B	259		TOEFL, ACT			5/1	30
Beloit College	Pr/B	1,286	61	TOEFL	525	650	1/15	35
Cardinal Stritch University	Pr/AB	3,180	69	TOEFL	550		4/1	25
Carroll College	Pr/B	2,925	49	TOEFL	550	578	None	
Carthage College	Pr/B	2,372		TOEFL	500		None	30
Chippewa Valley Technical College	Pu/A	5,529		TOEFL	500		None	30
Concordia University Wisconsin	Pr/AB	3,356	27	TOEFL	500	509	7/1	125

Student services			Housing		Academic year costs		Maximum credits/summer	Credit hour charge	International financial aid			
Adviser	Orientation	ESL	Academic year	Summer	Tuition/fees	Living costs			Available	Number receiving aid	Average award	Deadline
Yes	Yes	Yes		Yes	7,982†	9,756	18	245				
Yes	Yes	Yes	No	Yes	8,105†	10,917	20					
Yes	Yes	Yes	No		8,057†	10,377	15	246				
Yes	Yes	Yes	No		8,015†	11,249	15	246				
Yes	Yes	Yes	No		8,147†	6,876						
Yes	Yes		Yes	Yes	14,170†	10,002		490	Yes			None
Yes	Yes		Yes		33,975	15,710	12	1065	Yes	3	$11,000	None
Yes	Yes		Yes	Yes	22,131†	12,867						
Yes	Yes				8,124†	10,186	15	254				
Yes	Yes		Yes	Yes	21,945‡	12,015	12	569	Yes	54	$7,938	None
Yes	Yes	Yes	Yes	Yes	17,180†	11,770			Yes			None
Yes			No		7,980†	4,164	18	246				
Yes	Yes	Yes	Yes	Yes	16,375†	11,230	18		Yes	10	$3,911	None
Yes	Yes	Yes	No	Yes	7,953†	11,310	20	248				
Yes	Yes		Yes	Yes	35,192	10,220		1462	Yes			2/1
Yes	Yes	Yes	Yes	Yes	27,420	11,110	12	1130	Yes	13	$21,483	None
	Yes	Yes	Yes	Yes	7,974†	7,155	18	246				
Yes	Yes		Yes	Yes	21,020	9,918	6	694	Yes	9	$17,038	None
Yes			Yes		9,880	8,738		351	Yes			6/15
Yes	Yes		Yes		18,695	11,060	4		Yes			5/1
Yes	Yes		No		8,160†	13,280	12					
Yes	Yes	Yes	Yes		9,806†	11,599		409	Yes			None
Yes	Yes	Yes	Yes	Yes	20,060	7,500	12	630	Yes			None
Yes	Yes	Yes	Yes	Yes	9,960†	9,524	12	415	Yes			2/1
Yes	Yes	Yes	Yes	Yes	9,990†	10,532	9	416	Yes	3	$6,150	None
Yes	Yes	Yes	Yes	Yes	11,264†	11,358	24	457				
Yes	Yes	Yes	Yes	Yes	8,400	10,416	12					
					6,150†			256				
Yes			Yes	Yes	15,120†	9,140	12	435	Yes	38	$2,500	None
			Yes		8,360†	7,244	14	348				
Yes	Yes	Yes	Yes	Yes	13,950†	6,720	20	450	Yes			None
Yes	Yes		Yes		12,036†	10,314	12	497	Yes	6	$13,695	None
Yes	Yes	Yes	Yes	Yes	23,150	11,075	12	400	Available			8/30
			No		7,300	16,446		225	Yes			Deadline
Yes			Yes		10,192†	10,534	18	425	Yes			None
			No			475						
Yes					7,718†	4,150						
Yes	Yes	Yes	Yes	Yes	14,600†	10,388		608				
			No		6,460†	4,400	12	269	Yes			None
Yes	Yes	Yes	Yes	Yes	22,880	12,470	12		Yes			None
Yes	Yes	Yes	Yes	Yes	24,390	9,550	12		Yes	28	$15,578	
Yes	Yes	Yes	Yes	Yes	18,161	10,352	18	739	Yes	7	$6,548	None
			No		16,839†	7,375		772				
Yes	Yes		Yes	Yes	31,540	8,296		985	Yes	56	$18,900	3/1
Yes	Yes		Yes	Yes	19,074†	7,800		582	Yes			None
Yes	Yes		Yes		21,926	10,013	20	260	Yes	39	$11,929	None
Yes			Yes	Yes	26,500	11,200	16	380	Yes			None
Yes		Yes	No		17,291†	8,019	9	571				
Yes		Yes	Yes	Yes	19,990	10,810	10	830	Yes	9	$4,111	None

† Tuition and fees are for 2007-08.   ‡ Tuition and fees are projected for 2008-09.   * Comprehensive Fee

Institution	Control/ degrees	Undergraduates		Tests required (Fall 2009)	TOEFL		Application	
		Total	Internat'l		minimum	average	Deadline	Fee
DeVry University: Milwaukee	Pr/B	108						50
Edgewood College	Pr/AB	1,996		TOEFL	525	540	8/1	25
Fox Valley Technical College	Pu/A	5,694		TOEFL, ACT			None	30
Herzing College	Pr/AB			TOEFL	500		None	
Lakeland College	Pr/AB	2,918	117	TOEFL	500		None	20
Lakeshore Technical College	Pu/A	2,121		TOEFL	550		None	30
Lawrence University	Pr/B	1,400	98	TOEFL	577	617	2/15	40
Madison Area Technical College	Pu/A	14,647		TOEFL	550			30
Madison Media Institute	Pr/A							30
Maranatha Baptist Bible College	Pr/AB	829	4	TOEFL, ACT	450		12/31	50
Marian College of Fond du Lac	Pr/B	1,958	25	TOEFL	525		5/1	25
Marquette University	Pr/B	7,742	114		525	560	None	40
Mid-State Technical College	Pu/A	2,960		TOEFL, SAT/ACT	500		None	30
Milwaukee Area Technical College	Pu/A	14,482		TOEFL	500	510	8/19	30
Milwaukee Institute of Art & Design	Pr/B	636		TOEFL	550		None	25
Milwaukee School of Engineering	Pr/B	2,317	49	TOEFL	550	580	8/1	25
Moraine Park Technical College	Pu/A	4,000		TOEFL	500		None	30
Mount Mary College	Pr/B	1,203	15	TOEFL, SAT/ACT	500	550	None	75
Northcentral Technical College	Pu/A	2,634		TOEFL	490		None	30
Northeast Wisconsin Technical College	Pu/A	5,853		TOEFL	550		8/31	30
Northland College	Pr/B	656	12	TOEFL	525	600	6/1	50
St. Norbert College	Pr/B	2,045	58	TOEFL	550	555	None	50
Silver Lake College	Pr/AB	380	7	TOEFL, SAT/ACT	550		6/1	35
Southwest Wisconsin Technical College	Pu/A			TOEFL	450		None	25
University of Wisconsin-Baraboo/Sauk County	Pu/A	652		TOEFL	500		6/1	35
University of Wisconsin-Eau Claire	Pu/AB	9,947	104	TOEFL	525	530	7/1	35
University of Wisconsin-Fox Valley	Pu/A	1,735		TOEFL	500		7/15	35
University of Wisconsin-Green Bay	Pu/AB	5,546	41	TOEFL	550		None	35
University of Wisconsin-La Crosse	Pu/AB	8,358	137	TOEFL	550		5/1	35
University of Wisconsin-Madison	Pu/B	28,999	1,133	TOEFL, SAT/ACT	550		2/1	44
University of Wisconsin-Marathon County	Pu/A			TOEFL, SAT/ACT	500	540	7/1	35
University of Wisconsin-Marinette	Pu/A			TOEFL, SAT/ACT			6/1	35
University of Wisconsin-Milwaukee	Pu/B	22,937	165	TOEFL	500			65
University of Wisconsin-Oshkosh	Pu/B	9,844	66	TOEFL	550		5/15	44
University of Wisconsin-Parkside	Pu/B	4,624	50	TOEFL	525		6/1	60
University of Wisconsin-Platteville	Pu/AB	6,252	19	TOEFL	500	580	6/1	35
University of Wisconsin-Richland	Pu/A	452		TOEFL	500		5/31	35
University of Wisconsin-River Falls	Pu/B	6,007	64	TOEFL	500	550	2/1	35
University of Wisconsin-Rock County	Pu/A	913		TOEFL	500		6/1	35
University of Wisconsin-Sheboygan	Pu/A			TOEFL	500		None	35
University of Wisconsin-Stevens Point	Pu/AB	8,621	156	TOEFL	523		7/1	50
University of Wisconsin-Stout	Pu/B	7,429	72	TOEFL	500	550	None	35
University of Wisconsin-Superior	Pu/AB	2,450	92	TOEFL	500	535	8/1	35
University of Wisconsin-Washington County	Pu/A	917		TOEFL	500		6/1	35
University of Wisconsin-Waukesha	Pu/A	1,777		TOEFL	500		6/1	35
University of Wisconsin-Whitewater	Pu/AB	9,180	106	TOEFL	500		6/6	35
Viterbo University	Pr/AB	1,922	23	TOEFL	525		6/1	25
Western Technical College	Pu/A	4,798					None	30
Wisconsin Indianhead Technical College	Pu/A	3,106		TOEFL	500		None	30

Wyoming

Institution	Control/ degrees	Undergraduates		Tests required (Fall 2009)	TOEFL		Application	
		Total	Internat'l		minimum	average	Deadline	Fee
Casper College	Pu/AB	2,875	25	TOEFL	500		None	

| Student services | | | Housing | | Academic year costs | | Maximum credits/ summer | Credit hour charge | International financial aid | | | |
Adviser	Orien- tation	ESL	Academic year	Summer	Tuition/ fees	Living costs			Avail- able	Number receiving aid	Average award	Deadline
					13,020†	8,528		490				
Yes	Yes		Yes		20,040‡	9,674	6	630	Yes			None
Yes		Yes	No		17,540†	8,570	12	571				
Yes			No						Yes			None
Yes	Yes	Yes	Yes	Yes	18,435	8,710	12	615	Yes			7/1
		Yes	No		17,250†	3,775		571				
Yes	Yes		Yes	Yes	33,264	10,337			Yes	95	$20,504	None
		Yes	No		17,366†	7,820	6	571				
Yes			Yes		9,486†	9,510	6	268	Yes			None
Yes	Yes	Yes	Yes	Yes	18,665†	10,870	15	300	Yes	18	$9,684	None
Yes	Yes	Yes	Yes	Yes	28,128	12,030	16	810	Yes	54	$11,096	None
			No		17,411†	9,198	6	571				
Yes	Yes		No		17,399†	1,000	12	571	Yes			None
Yes			Yes		24,900†	12,073		805	Yes			None
Yes	Yes	Yes	Yes	Yes	27,300	13,465	19	475	Yes	12	$4,000	None
Yes		Yes	No		17,248†	900	9	571				
Yes	Yes		Yes	Yes	20,350	12,230		575	Yes	1	$4,500	None
Yes	Yes	Yes	Yes	Yes	17,267†		12	571				
Yes	Yes		No		17,407†	10,220	3	571				
Yes			Yes	Yes	23,101	10,640		410	Yes	12	$14,883	None
Yes	Yes	Yes	Yes	Yes	25,926	8,781	12	798	Yes	54	$13,383	None
Yes		Yes	Yes	Yes	19,194	11,240	18	595	Yes	1	$17,980	None
		Yes	Yes	Yes	17,227†	7,348	6	571	Yes			None
Yes			No		11,694†	8,830	12	469				
Yes	Yes	Yes	Yes	Yes	13,414†	8,110	11	523	Yes	60	$4,706	None
Yes			No		11,476†	1,770	6	469	Yes			None
Yes	Yes		Yes	Yes	13,532†	8,478		516	Yes	35	$8,449	None
Yes	Yes	Yes	Yes	Yes	13,423†	7,665	8	519	Yes			None
Yes	Yes	Yes	Yes	Yes	21,438†	7,390						
Yes			Yes	Yes	11,491†	6,265	6	469				
Yes		Yes	No		11,474†	600	12	469				
Yes	Yes	Yes	Yes	Yes	16,686†	9,038		663				
Yes	Yes		Yes	Yes	13,262†	9,478	9	521				
Yes	Yes		Yes	Yes	13,332†	10,034		516	Yes	53	$7,534	None
Yes	Yes		Yes	Yes	13,319†	7,300	9	516	Yes			None
Yes	Yes		Yes		11,674†	7,455	9	469				
Yes	Yes	Yes	Yes	Yes	13,458†	8,014	8	519	Yes			
					11,527†	3,330	9	468				
Yes			No		11,519†	5,260	9	469	Yes			None
Yes	Yes	Yes	Yes	Yes	13,407†	7,262	6	516	Yes	101	$5,210	6/15
Yes	Yes		Yes	Yes	15,018†	7,620	10	437	Yes	72	$5,532	None
Yes	Yes		Yes	Yes	13,480†	8,620		523	Yes	84	$7,122	None
Yes			No		11,512†	7,314	9	469				
Yes			No		11,491†	10,115	6	469	Yes			None
Yes	Yes		Yes	Yes	13,431†	7,244	12		Yes			None
Yes	Yes		Yes	Yes	19,490	11,530	12	560	Yes			None
		Yes	Yes	Yes	17,353†	6,191	12	571				
			No		17,392†	7,226		571				
Yes	Yes		Yes		4,644†	6,968		187				

† Tuition and fees are for 2007-08.   ‡ Tuition and fees are projected for 2008-09.   * Comprehensive Fee

Institution	Control/ degrees	Undergraduates		Tests required	TOEFL		Application	
		Total	Internat'l	(Fall 2009)	minimum	average	Deadline	Fee
Central Wyoming College	Pu/A	1,155	11	TOEFL	500		None	
Eastern Wyoming College	Pu/A	618	6	TOEFL	520		None	
Laramie County Community College	Pu/A	2,931	38	TOEFL	500		None	20
Northwest College	Pu/A	1,765		TOEFL	500	525	7/1	50
Sheridan College	Pu/A	1,518	19	TOEFL	500	525	5/9	
University of Wyoming	Pu/B	9,140	168	TOEFL	525		6/1	40
Western Wyoming Community College	Pu/A	2,139	79	TOEFL	500		6/15	100
WyoTech: Laramie	Pr/A						None	

	Student services			Housing		Academic year costs		Maximum credits/ summer	Credit hour charge		International financial aid			
Adviser	Orien- tation	ESL	Academic year	Summer	Tuition/ fees	Living costs				Avail- able	Number receiving aid	Average award	Deadline
Yes	Yes		Yes	Yes	4,968 †	6,500			186	Yes			None
Yes			Yes		4,944 †	7,384			186	Yes			None
Yes		Yes	Yes		5,064 †	6,322			186				
Yes	Yes	Yes	Yes	Yes	4,998 †	6,665	6		186				
Yes		Yes	Yes	Yes	4,992 †	7,620	8		186	Yes			None
Yes	Yes	Yes	Yes		10,394 †	7,274	6		322	Yes	86	$7,992	None
Yes	Yes	Yes	Yes	Yes	4,804 †	4,810	12		178	Yes	19	$1,250	None
			Yes										

Part III:
Lists and indexes

International undergraduate student enrollment

Fort Hays State
University (KS) 2,382
Purdue University (IN) 2,024
Broward Community
College (FL) 1,969
State University of New
York at Buffalo (NY)............... 1,815
Glendale Community
College (CA) 1,758
University of Texas at El
Paso (TX) 1,630
City University of New
York: Baruch
College (NY) 1,613
University of Illinois at
Urbana-Champaign (IL)........... 1,485
University of Texas at
Austin (TX) 1,483
Miami Dade College (FL)............. 1,470
City University of New
York: Hunter
College (NY) 1,456
Michigan State
University (MI)...................... 1,456
California State University:
Long Beach (CA) 1,431
City University of New
York: LaGuardia
Community
College (NY) 1,425
University of Southern
California (CA)...................... 1,399
San Francisco State
University (CA) 1,371
Indiana University
Bloomington (IN).................. 1,366
Brigham Young
University (UT) 1,273
University of
Michigan (MI) 1,211
City College of San
Francisco (CA) 1,209
Parsons The New School
for Design (NY)..................... 1,159
New York University (NY).......... 1,154
Academy of Art
University (CA)...................... 1,147
University of Houston (TX)......... 1,133
University of Wisconsin-
Madison (WI) 1,133
California State Polytechnic
University:
Pomona (CA)........................ 1,095
California State University:
Fullerton (CA) 1,091
University of California:
Los Angeles (CA)................... 1,075
Boston University (MA) 1,059
Florida International
University (FL)...................... 1,054
University of
Washington (WA) 1,052
Cornell University (NY) 1,028
Lone Star College
System (TX) 1,013

Brigham Young University-
Hawaii (HI)............................. 1,009
University of
Pennsylvania (PA) 988
State University of New
York at
Binghamton (NY)...................... 971
Arizona State
University (AZ) 970
San Jose State
University (CA)......................... 954
Oakland Community
College (MI).............................. 933
University of Central
Oklahoma (OK).......................... 919
City University of New
York: Queens
College (NY) 910
Ohio State University:
Columbus Campus (OH)............. 904
Georgia Perimeter
College (GA)............................. 899
State University of New
York at Stony
Brook (NY).............................. 884
Penn State University
Park (PA) 878
Fashion Institute of
Technology (NY)....................... 861
Wayne State
University (MI).......................... 859
University of Nevada: Las
Vegas (NV) 852
Essex County College (NJ)............. 848
Drexel University (PA) 835
Carnegie Mellon
University (PA)......................... 821
University of Texas: Pan
American (TX) 808
University of Oregon (OR)............. 790
University of California:
Berkeley (CA) 786
San Diego State
University (CA)......................... 773
Arizona Western
College (AZ)............................. 762
Northeastern
University (MA) 742
Portland State
University (OR)......................... 737
City University of New
York: Brooklyn
College (NY) 725
University of Arizona (AZ)............. 721
Valencia Community
College (FL) 717
Santa Barbara City
College (CA) 701
Saint Cloud State
University (MN) 685
Temple University (PA) 680
George Mason
University (VA) 676
University of North
Texas (TX)............................... 666

City University of New
York: Kingsborough
Community
College (NY) 656
Iowa State University (IA)............... 656
Harvard College (MA)..................... 645
Liberty University (VA)................... 639
University of Virginia (VA) 631
California State University:
East Bay (CA) 621
University of Miami (FL) 613
Bucks County Community
College (PA) 609
Macomb Community
College (MI) 601
University of Kansas (KS).............. 598
Florida Atlantic
University (FL)......................... 583
Virginia Commonwealth
University (VA) 577
University of Central
Florida (FL) 574
Georgia Institute of
Technology (GA)...................... 565
University of California:
Irvine (CA) 563
Wichita State
University (KS) 563
Lindenwood
University (MO) 557
University of Minnesota:
Twin Cities (MN) 556
Oklahoma State
University (OK) 554
Kennesaw State
University (GA)........................ 552
Savannah College of Art
and Design (GA) 547
Prince George's
Community
College (MD) 540
University of Utah (UT) 522
New Mexico State
University (NM) 521
Georgia State
University (GA)........................ 518
University of Texas at San
Antonio (TX) 518
University of Maryland:
College Park (MD) 515
University of South
Alabama (AL)........................... 509
City University of New
York: Hostos
Community
College (NY) 505
University of Nebraska -
Lincoln (NE)............................ 499
Columbia University (NY) 498
Walden University (MN) 497
Texas A&M
University (TX) 493
Florida Institute of
Technology (FL)....................... 492
University of South
Florida (FL) 491
University of North
Alabama (AL)........................... 485
St. John's University (NY).............. 481
Washington State
University (WA) 470
Utah State University (UT)............. 467
George Washington
University (DC) 466
Oklahoma City Community
College (OK) 463
Berkeley College of New
York City (NY) 459
Suffolk University (MA)................. 453
Princeton University (NJ) 451
Mercer County Community
College (NJ) 450
Indiana University-Purdue
University
Indianapolis (IN) 447

Syracuse University (NY)................ 447
City University of New
York: John Jay College
of Criminal Justice (NY)........... 445
University of California:
Davis (CA) 445
Yale University (CT)....................... 444
Rutgers, The State
University of New
Jersey: New Brunswick/
Piscataway Campus (NJ)............ 438
School of Visual Arts (NY)............. 434
Towson University (MD)................. 434
Johnson & Wales
University:
Providence (RI) 432
University of Central
Arkansas (AR)........................... 425
School of the Art Institute
of Chicago (IL)......................... 422
Howard Community
College (MD) 418
Virginia Polytechnic
Institute and State
University (VA) 418
Embry-Riddle Aeronautical
University (FL)......................... 410
Brown University (RI) 409
Northwestern
University (IL)......................... 407
Illinois Institute of
Technology (IL)........................ 399
City University of New
York: College of Staten
Island (NY)............................. 390
State University of New
York College at
Plattsburgh (NY) 390
Troy University (AL).................... 390
University of Chicago (IL) 387
University of Tampa (FL) 386
University of Nebraska -
Kearney (NE) 383
City University of New
York: Lehman
College (NY) 381
Niagara University (NY)................. 381
University of Colorado at
Boulder (CO)........................... 381
Owens Community
College: Toledo (OH) 372
Oklahoma City
University (OK)........................ 369
Orange Coast College (CA)............. 369
Monroe College (NY) 368
Kansas State
University (KS)......................... 366
University of
Oklahoma (OK)........................ 366
Northern Arizona
University (AZ) 365
University of Maryland:
University College (MD)............. 365
University of Texas at
Dallas (TX)............................. 364
Georgetown
University (DC)........................ 363
University of San
Francisco (CA) 363
Western Michigan
University (MI)........................ 362
Duke University (NC).................... 360
Louisiana State University
and Agricultural and
Mechanical
College (LA)............................ 359
Howard University (DC)................ 357
American University (DC).............. 354
Mount Holyoke
College (MA) 353
West Virginia
University (WV)....................... 353
New York Institute of
Technology (NY)....................... 352

Brevard Community College (FL) 137

Broome Community College (NY) 137

James Madison University (VA) 137

University of Wisconsin-La Crosse (WI) 137

State University of New York College at Potsdam (NY) 136

Texas Woman's University (TX) 136

ASA Institute of Business and Computer Technology (NY) 135

Harrisburg Area Community College (PA) 134

Vassar College (NY) 134

Case Western Reserve University (OH) 133

City University of New York: Medgar Evers College (NY) 133

Colgate University (NY) 133

Indiana University of Pennsylvania (PA) 133

Northern Illinois University (IL) 133

Dickinson College (PA) 132

University of Pittsburgh (PA) 132

Westminster College (MO) 132

Williams College (MA) 132

Lansing Community College (MI) 131

Oakland University (MI) 130

University of Mississippi (MS) 130

University of Southern Indiana (IN) 130

Southwestern Oklahoma State University (OK) 129

University of North Carolina at Greensboro (NC) 129

Coppin State University (MD) 127

University of Arkansas at Little Rock (AR) 127

Cooper Union for the Advancement of Science and Art (NY) 125

University of Richmond (VA) 125

Tennessee Technological University (TN) 124

University of Detroit Mercy (MI) 124

Valdosta State University (GA) 124

Rider University (NJ) 123

University of Minnesota: Duluth (MN) 123

Georgia Southern University (GA) 122

Hofstra University (NY) 122

Ithaca College (NY) 121

Massachusetts Bay Community College (MA) 121

Missouri University of Science and Technology (MO) 121

Mountain State University (WV) 121

Oakwood University (AL) 121

University of Tennessee: Martin (TN) 121

Amherst College (MA) 120

Houston Baptist University (TX) 120

Metropolitan Community College (NE) 120

Southeast Missouri State University (MO) 120

Trinity University (TX) 120

State University of New York College at Geneseo (NY) 119

State University of New York College at Oneonta (NY) 119

Colby College (ME) 118

State University of New York at New Paltz (NY) 118

University of the Ozarks (AR) 118

Cincinnati State Technical and Community College (OH) 117

Lakeland College (WI) 117

Lehigh University (PA) 117

Long Island University: C. W. Post Campus (NY) 117

St. Lawrence University (NY) 117

University of San Diego (CA) 117

Earlham College (IN) 116

College of William and Mary (VA) 115

Duquesne University (PA) 115

Rutgers, The State University of New Jersey: Newark Regional Campus (NJ) 115

Carleton College (MN) 114

Columbia College Chicago (IL) 114

Marquette University (WI) 114

Murray State University (KY) 114

Southeastern Louisiana University (LA) 114

Stevens Institute of Technology (NJ) 114

University of Alaska Fairbanks (AK) 114

Genesee Community College (NY) 113

Alabama Agricultural and Mechanical University (AL) 112

Central Connecticut State University (CT) 112

Lake Forest College (IL) 112

Lewis-Clark State College (ID) 112

Madonna University (MI) 112

Rensselaer Polytechnic Institute (NY) 112

Southern University and Agricultural and Mechanical College (LA) 112

University of West Florida (FL) 112

Auburn University (AL) 111

Loyola University Chicago (IL) 111

Sam Houston State University (TX) 111

Indiana State University (IN) 110

Indiana University South Bend (IN) 110

Roosevelt University (IL) 109

University of Maryland: Eastern Shore (MD) 109

State University of New York Maritime College (NY) 108

University of Charleston (WV) 108

University of the Pacific (CA) 108

Mississippi College (MS) 107

Wentworth Institute of Technology (MA) 107

Berea College (KY) 106

Elon University (NC) 106

University of Wisconsin-Whitewater (WI) 106

Bryant University (RI) 105

West Texas A&M University (TX) 105

Brookhaven College (TX) 104

Butler University (IN) 104

Chattahoochee Technical College (GA) 104

University of Wisconsin-Eau Claire (WI) 104

Northampton Community College (PA) 103

Horry-Georgetown Technical College (SC) 102

Kansas City Kansas Community College (KS) 102

Illinois State University (IL) 101

Jefferson State Community College (AL) 101

University of Puerto Rico: Mayaguez (PR) 101

Lewis University (IL) 100

University of Southern Mississippi (MS) 100

Canisius College (NY) 99

Ivy Tech Community College: Northeast (IN) 99

Pacific Union College (CA) 99

University of California: Santa Cruz (CA) 99

Wartburg College (IA) 99

Caldwell College (NJ) 98

College of St. Benedict (MN) 98

DeVry University: Chicago (IL) 98

Ferris State University (MI) 98

Lawrence University (WI) 98

Saint Thomas University (FL) 98

Swarthmore College (PA) 98

University of Colorado at Denver (CO) 98

University of Northern Colorado (CO) 98

College of the Canyons (CA) 97

Webster University (MO) 97

Bucknell University (PA) 96

Chapman University (CA) 96

Concordia College: Moorhead (MN) 96

College of Wooster (OH) 95

East Carolina University (NC) 94

Hamilton College (NY) 94

Manhattan School of Music (NY) 94

Salem College (NC) 94

College of Charleston (SC) 93

East Central University (OK) 93

Florida Gulf Coast University (FL) 93

Marshall University (WV) 93

Queens University of Charlotte (NC) 93

Denison University (OH) 92

Lincoln University (MO) 92

Loyola Marymount University (CA) 92

University of Wisconsin-Superior (WI) 92

Colorado State University: Pueblo (CO) 91

Fulton-Montgomery Community College (NY) 91

University of Louisiana at Monroe (LA) 91

Albright College (PA) 90

Luther College (IA) 90

State University of New York at Purchase (NY) 90

California College of the Arts (CA) 89

Ivy Tech Community College: North Central (IN) 89

Marietta College (OH) 89

Stephen F. Austin State University (TX) 89

University of New Hampshire (NH) 89

Western Carolina University (NC) 89

Bates College (ME) 88

Bryn Mawr College (PA) 88

College of St. Scholastica (MN) 88

St. Edward's University (TX) 88

Winthrop University (SC) 88

Lamar University (TX) 87

Lewis & Clark College (OR) 87

State University of New York at Oswego (NY) 87

Trinity College (CT) 87

Barnard College (NY) 86

California Institute of Technology (CA) 86

Georgia College and State University (GA) 86

Seton Hall University (NJ) 86

Albany College of Pharmacy (NY) 85

Columbia College (MO) 85

Ivy Tech Community College: Lafayette (IN) 85

Florida Agricultural and Mechanical University (FL) 84

Slippery Rock University of Pennsylvania (PA) 84

New England Conservatory of Music (MA) 83

Bridgewater State College (MA) 82

Campbellsville University (KY) 82

Gonzaga University (WA) 82

Juilliard School (NY) 82

Saint Peter's College (NJ) 82

Knox College (IL) 81

North Hennepin Community College (MN) 81

Emerson College (MA) 80

Vincennes University (IN) 80

Eastern New Mexico University (NM) 79

University of Minnesota: Crookston (MN) 79

Webber International University (FL) 79

Western Wyoming Community College (WY) 79

Nicholls State University (LA) 78

Roger Williams University (RI) 78

Southwestern Adventist University (TX) 78

Coastal Carolina University (SC) 77

Connecticut College (CT) 77

North Park University (IL) 77

Robert Morris University (PA) 77

Saint Joseph's University (PA) 77

Northwestern State University (LA) 42
University of Rhode Island (RI) 42
Bethel College (IN)............ 41
Chatham University (PA)............ 41
Haverford College (PA) 41
Linfield College (OR) 41
Pfeiffer University (NC) 41
University of Wisconsin-Green Bay (WI)............ 41
Valley City State University (ND)............ 41
Arizona State University West (AZ)............ 40
Occidental College (CA)............ 40
Onondaga Community College (NY)............ 40
Salisbury University (MD) 40
Utica College (NY)............ 40
Belmont Abbey College (NC)............ 39
Belmont University (TN)............ 39
Bradley University (IL)............ 39
Cowley County Community College (KS)............ 39
Cumberland University (TN) 39
Eastern Connecticut State University (CT) 39
Ohio Northern University (OH)............ 39
Oklahoma Panhandle State University (OK)............ 39
Springfield Technical Community College (MA) 39
University of Maryland: Baltimore (MD)............ 39
University of North Carolina at Wilmington (NC)............ 39
University of Science and Arts of Oklahoma (OK)............ 39
Wheaton College (MA)............ 39
Wilson College (PA) 39
Benedictine College (KS) 38
Berkshire Community College (MA) 38
California State University: Monterey Bay (CA)............ 38
The Citadel (SC) 38
Laramie County Community College (WY)............ 38
Long Island University: Brooklyn Campus (NY) 38
Ohio Valley University (WV)............ 38
Ouachita Baptist University (AR)............ 38
Wingate University (NC)............ 38
Berry College (GA)............ 37
Gordon College (MA)............ 37
Hobart and William Smith Colleges (NY)............ 37
King College (TN) 37
Point Park University (PA) 37
Eastern Mennonite University (VA) 36
Mercer University (GA)............ 36
Penn State Harrisburg (PA)............ 36
Carson-Newman College (TN)............ 35
Davis and Elkins College (WV)............ 35
Grand Canyon University (AZ)............ 35
Hesston College (KS)............ 35
Manchester Community College (CT)............ 35
Newberry College (SC)............ 35
Providence College (RI) 35

Southern California Institute of Architecture (CA)............ 35
Union College (KY)............ 35
Volunteer State Community College (TN)............ 35
Clark Atlanta University (GA)............ 34
Maharishi University of Management (IA) 34
Shaw University (NC)............ 34
Bloomfield College (NJ)............ 33
Cornell College (IA)............ 33
Drew University (NJ)............ 33
Front Range Community College (CO)............ 33
Hope College (MI)............ 33
Kettering University (MI)............ 33
Oakland City University (IN)............ 33
Rhode Island College (RI) 33
Southern University at New Orleans (LA)............ 33
Anderson University (SC)............ 32
Dominican University (IL) 32
Galveston College (TX)............ 32
Ivy Tech Community College: Southwest (IN)............ 32
Mayville State University (ND)............ 32
Northwestern College (IA) 32
Pitzer College (CA)............ 32
Robert Morris College: Chicago (IL)............ 32
St. Mary's College of Maryland (MD) 32
Salve Regina University (RI) 32
Sarah Lawrence College (NY) 32
University of Mobile (AL)............ 32
University of Texas at Tyler (TX)............ 32
Vaughn College of Aeronautics and Technology (NY)............ 32
Westminster College (UT) 32
Avila University (MO)............ 31
Bowie State University (MD) 31
Capital University (OH) 31
Hanover College (IN) 31
Huntington University (IN)............ 31
Lipscomb University (TN)............ 31
Naugatuck Valley Community College (CT)............ 31
Northwood University: Texas (TX)............ 31
Taylor University (IN) 31
University of Mary (ND)............ 31
Whittier College (CA)............ 31
Belhaven College (MS)............ 30
Emmanuel College (MA)............ 30
Fort Lewis College (CO) 30
Lasell College (MA) 30
Lesley University (MA) 30
Pine Manor College (MA) 30
University of South Dakota (SD) 30
Wheaton College (IL) 30
Wheeling Jesuit University (WV) 30
Winston-Salem State University (NC)............ 30
College of the Holy Cross (MA)............ 29
Eastern Arizona College (AZ)............ 29
Flagler College (FL) 29
Harvey Mudd College (CA) 29
Loyola College in Maryland (MD) 29
Morehead State University (KY)............ 29

Northwestern Oklahoma State University (OK)............ 29
University of Mary Hardin-Baylor (TX) 29
University of the Sciences in Philadelphia (PA) 29
Burlington County College (NJ) 28
College of Southern Maryland (MD) 28
Johnson & Wales University: Denver (CO) 28
Kentucky State University (KY) 28
North Iowa Area Community College (IA)............ 28
Rose-Hulman Institute of Technology (IN) 28
St. Mary's University of Minnesota (MN) 28
Augsburg College (MN) 27
Concordia University (CA)............ 27
Concordia University Wisconsin (WI)............ 27
Fashion Institute of Design and Merchandising: San Francisco (CA) 27
Francis Marion University (SC)............ 27
Heidelberg College (OH) 27
Hood College (MD) 27
Lake-Sumter Community College (FL) 27
LeTourneau University (TX) 27
Muskingum College (OH) 27
Oregon Institute of Technology (OR) 27
St. Michael's College (VT) 27
Texas State Technical College: Harlingen (TX) 27
University of Illinois: Springfield (IL)............ 27
University of North Carolina at Asheville (NC) 27
William Woods University (MO) 27
Ashford University (IA)............ 26
Augustana College (IL)............ 26
College of Idaho (ID) 26
DeVry University: North Brunswick (NJ)............ 26
Fairleigh Dickinson University: College at Florham (NJ) 26
Framingham State College (MA) 26
Guilford College (NC) 26
Holy Names University (CA) 26
Kuyper College (MI)............ 26
Lambuth University (TN) 26
University of Colorado at Colorado Springs (CO)............ 26
West Chester University of Pennsylvania (PA) 26
Allegheny College (PA)............ 25
Casper College (WY) 25
Frank Phillips College (TX) 25
Gannon University (PA)............ 25
Marian College of Fond du Lac (WI) 25
Penn State Altoona (PA) 25
Richard Stockton College of New Jersey (NJ)............ 25
Villa Julie College (MD)............ 25
Western New Mexico University (NM) 25
DeVry University: Orlando (FL)............ 24
Dominican University of California (CA)............ 24
Geneva College (PA) 24

Ivy Tech Community College: Wabash Valley (IN)............ 24
Pratt Community College (KS) 24
Roberts Wesleyan College (NY) 24
Scott Community College (IA)............ 24
University of La Verne (CA) 24
Centre College (KY) 23
Davenport University (MI) 23
Kellogg Community College (MI)............ 23
La Salle University (PA) 23
MidAmerica Nazarene University (KS) 23
Minot State University: Bottineau Campus (ND)............ 23
New Mexico Institute of Mining and Technology (NM)............ 23
Niagara County Community College (NY) 23
North Central College (IL) 23
Northwest University (WA) 23
St. Ambrose University (IA) 23
St. Olaf College (MN) 23
Southwest Baptist University (MO)............ 23
University of Massachusetts Dartmouth (MA) 23
University of Redlands (CA)............ 23
University of the South (TN)............ 23
Viterbo University (WI) 23
Wayne State College (NE) 23
Crichton College (TN) 22
Elgin Community College (IL) 22
Franciscan University of Steubenville (OH)............ 22
Hillsdale College (MI) 22
Hollins University (VA)............ 22
Johnson & Wales University: Charlotte (NC) 22
Malone College (OH) 22
Montana State University: Billings (MT) 22
North Country Community College (NY)............ 22
South Florida Community College (FL) 22
Trevecca Nazarene University (TN) 22
University of Maine at Machias (ME)............ 22
Vanguard University of Southern California (CA) 22
Virginia Military Institute (VA) 22
Wayland Baptist University (TX) 22
Bluffton University (OH) 21
Fitchburg State College (MA) 21
Hiwassee College (TN) 21
Immaculata University (PA) 21
Mansfield University of Pennsylvania (PA) 21
Notre Dame de Namur University (CA) 21
Shepherd University (WV) 21
Trinity Christian College (IL) 21
Triton College (IL) 21
Augustana College (SD) 20
Converse College (SC) 20
Everett Community College (WA)............ 20

LeMoyne-Owen
  College (TN).................. 8
Odessa College (TX)................ 8
Rhodes College (TN)................ 8
Rosemont College (PA)................ 8
St. Anselm College (NH).................. 8
St. John's College (NM)................ 8
St. Joseph's College (NY)................ 8
Spring Hill College (AL)................ 8
Texas Tech University
  Health Sciences
  Center (TX) 8
University of Puget
  Sound (WA)................. 8
University of St.
  Francis (IL)................. 8
Wheelock College (MA)............ 8
Yakima Valley Community
  College (WA)................. 8
Alderson-Broaddus
  College (WV)................. 7
Bennett College (NC)................ 7
Bridgewater College (VA)................ 7
College of Mount St.
  Vincent (NY)................ 7
Concordia University (MI)................ 7
DeVry University:
  Fremont (CA)................. 7
DeVry University:
  Pomona (CA)................. 7
Doane College (NE)................ 7
Edward Waters
  College (FL)................. 7
Fashion Institute of Design
  and Merchandising: San
  Diego (CA)................. 7
Goucher College (MD)................ 7
Governors State
  University (IL)................. 7
John Wood Community
  College (IL)................. 7
Northwest Nazarene
  University (ID)................. 7
Oregon Health & Science
  University (OR)................ 7
Penn State Greater
  Allegheny (PA)................ 7
Platt College: San
  Diego (CA)................. 7
Rocky Mountain College of
  Art & Design (CO)................ 7
St. Cloud Technical
  College (MN)................. 7
Saint Mary's College (IN)................ 7
Silver Lake College (WI)................ 7
Southern Vermont
  College (VT)................. 7
University of Arkansas at
  Fort Smith (AR)................. 7
University of Arkansas at
  Monticello (AR)................. 7
University of Kansas
  Medical Center (KS)................ 7
Zion Bible College (RI)................ 7
American Jewish
  University (CA)................. 6
Ball State University (IN)................ 6
Carlow University (PA)................ 6
Central State
  University (OH)................. 6
DeVry University: Fort
  Washington (PA)................. 6
DeVry University:
  Irving (TX)................. 6
Eastern Wyoming
  College (WY)................. 6
Ivy Tech Community
  College: South
  Central (IN) 6
Kansas City Art
  Institute (MO)................ 6
King's College (PA)................ 6
Lincoln Land Community
  College (IL)................. 6
Manor College (PA)................ 6

Northeast Community
  College (NE)................ 6
Northwestern College (MN)................ 6
Otterbein College (OH)................ 6
Prescott College (AZ)................ 6
Quincy University (IL)................ 6
San Diego Christian
  College (CA)................. 6
Simpson University (CA)................ 6
Thomas Jefferson
  University: College of
  Health Professions (PA)................ 6
Thomas More College (KY)................ 6
University of Houston:
  Victoria (TX)................. 6
Warner Pacific
  College (OR)................. 6
Western New England
  College (MA)................. 6
William Jewell
  College (MO)................. 6
Alma College (MI)................ 5
American Baptist College
  of ABT Seminary (TN)................ 5
Arlington Baptist
  College (TX)................. 5
Bossier Parish Community
  College (LA)................. 5
Briar Cliff University (IA)................ 5
Cascade College (OR)................ 5
Cochise College (AZ)................ 5
College of New
  Rochelle (NY)................. 5
DeVry University:
  Houston (TX)................. 5
Edison State Community
  College (OH)................. 5
Erskine College (SC)................ 5
Indiana University
  East (IN)................. 5
Ivy Tech Community
  College: Kokomo (IN)................ 5
Ivy Tech Community
  College: Richmond (IN)................ 5
Memphis College of
  Art (TN)................. 5
Muhlenberg College (PA)................ 5
Muscatine Community
  College (IA)................. 5
New College of
  Florida (FL)................. 5
Reinhardt College (GA)................ 5
Rogue Community
  College (OR)................. 5
Schreiner University (TX)................ 5
Scripps College (CA)................ 5
Sweet Briar College (VA)................ 5
Ursuline College (OH)................ 5
York College (NE)................ 5
Albertus Magnus
  College (CT)................. 4
Anna Maria College (MA)................ 4
Aquinas College (MI)................ 4
Augusta Technical
  College (GA)................. 4
Burlington College (VT)................ 4
Carroll Community
  College (MD)................. 4
Castleton State
  College (VT)................. 4
Clinton Community
  College (IA)................. 4
Columbia Basin
  College (WA)................. 4
Columbus Technical
  College (GA)................. 4
Holy Apostles College and
  Seminary (CT)................. 4
Jefferson College of Health
  Sciences (VA)................. 4
Johnston Community
  College (NC)................. 4
Judson College (AL)................ 4
Kankakee Community
  College (IL)................. 4

Maranatha Baptist Bible
  College (WI) 4
Middlesex Community
  College (CT)................. 4
Mt. Hood Community
  College (OR)................. 4
Olympic College (WA)................ 4
Pacific Northwest College
  of Art (OR)................. 4
Pacific University (OR)................ 4
Penn State
  Brandywine (PA)................ 4
Penn State Lehigh
  Valley (PA)................. 4
Penn State York (PA)................ 4
Redlands Community
  College (OK)................. 4
Rockford College (IL)................ 4
St. Joseph College (CT)................ 4
Southern Arkansas
  University Tech (AR)................ 4
Sterling College (KS)................ 4
University of New
  England (ME)................. 4
Asheville-Buncombe
  Technical Community
  College (NC)................. 3
Bethany Lutheran
  College (MN)................. 3
Birmingham-Southern
  College (AL)................. 3
Cazenovia College (NY)................ 3
Clark State Community
  College (OH)................. 3
Cleary University (MI)................ 3
College of Mount St.
  Joseph (OH)................. 3
College of Santa Fe (NM)................ 3
Columbia-Greene
  Community
  College (NY)................. 3
Defiance College (OH)................ 3
DeVry University: Federal
  Way (WA)................. 3
DeVry University: Sherman
  Oaks (CA)................. 3
Gogebic Community
  College (MI)................. 3
Humphreys College (CA)................ 3
John A. Logan College (IL)................ 3
Kettering College of
  Medical Arts (OH)................ 3
Lexington College (IL)................ 3
Nebraska Wesleyan
  University (NE)................. 3
Ohio State University
  Agricultural Technical
  Institute (OH)................. 3
Ozarks Technical
  Community
  College (MO)................. 3
Paine College (GA)................ 3
Penn State Beaver (PA)................ 3
Penn State Worthington
  Scranton (PA)................. 3
Rose State College (OK)................ 3
St. Mary-of-the-Woods
  College (IN)................. 3
San Juan College (NM)................ 3
Southeastern
  University (FL)................. 3
Springfield College in
  Illinois (IL)................. 3
Stephens College (MO)................ 3
Treasure Valley Community
  College (OR)................. 3
University of Pittsburgh at
  Bradford (PA)................. 3
University of Pittsburgh at
  Greensburg (PA)................. 3
Waynesburg
  University (PA)................. 3
William Jessup
  University (CA)................. 3

Williams Baptist
  College (AR) 3
Alaska Pacific
  University (AK)................. 2
Aurora University (IL)................ 2
Blackburn College (IL)................ 2
Briarwood College (CT)................ 2
Calvary Bible College and
  Theological
  Seminary (MO)................. 2
Central Georgia Technical
  College (GA)................. 2
Dana College (NE)................ 2
Delaware State
  University (DE)................. 2
DeVry University:
  Columbus (OH)................. 2
DeVry University: Kansas
  City (MO)................. 2
DeVry University: Long
  Beach (CA)................. 2
DeVry University: Tinley
  Park (IL)................. 2
Dunwoody College of
  Technology (MN)................. 2
Erie Community College:
  City Campus (NY)................ 2
Franklin College (IN)................ 2
Green Mountain
  College (VT)................. 2
Greenville Technical
  College (SC)................. 2
Ivy Tech Community
  College: Southeast (IN)................ 2
Johnson C. Smith
  University (NC)................. 2
Lourdes College (OH)................ 2
Magdalen College (NH)................ 2
McPherson College (KS)................ 2
Minnesota School of
  Business:
  Shakopee (MN)................. 2
Misericordia
  University (PA)................. 2
Ohio State University:
  Marion Campus (OH)................ 2
Penn State Mont Alto (PA)................ 2
Penn State Schuylkill (PA)................ 2
Piedmont College (GA)................ 2
Richland Community
  College (IL)................. 2
Rockingham Community
  College (NC)................. 2
Sage College of
  Albany (NY)................. 2
St. Charles Borromeo
  Seminary -
  Overbrook (PA)................. 2
St. John's College (MD)................ 2
Shimer College (IL)................ 2
State University of New
  York College at
  Fredonia (NY)................. 2
State University of New
  York Upstate Medical
  University (NY)................. 2
Texas A&M University-
  Texarkana (TX)................. 2
Unity College (ME)................ 2
University of Hawaii: West
  Oahu (HI)................. 2
University of Maine at
  Augusta (ME)................. 2
University of St. Mary (KS)................ 2
Washington & Jefferson
  College (PA)................. 2
Wright State University:
  Lake Campus (OH)................ 2
Academy College (MN)................ 1
Alice Lloyd College (KY)................ 1
Art Institute of New York
  City (NY)................. 1
Baptist College of
  Florida (FL)................. 1

Blue Mountain
    College (MS) 1
Cedar Crest College (PA) 1
College of Visual
    Arts (MN) 1
Concordia University at
    Austin (TX) 1
Delaware Valley
    College (PA) 1
DeVry University:
    Bethesda (MD) 1
DeVry University:
    Henderson (NV) 1
DeVry University:
    Indianapolis (IN) 1
DeVry University:
    Online (IL) 1
DeVry University:
    Westminster (CO) 1
Draughons Junior College:
    Nashville (TN) 1
Faith Baptist Bible College
    and Theological
    Seminary (IA) 1
Free Will Baptist Bible
    College (TN) 1
Griffin Technical
    College (GA) 1
Hodges University (FL) 1
Itasca Community
    College (MN) 1
Life Pacific College (CA) 1
Maine College of Art (ME) 1
McDaniel College (MD) 1
Metropolitan Community
    College: Blue
    River (MO) 1
Metropolitan Community
    College: Longview (MO) 1
Metropolitan Community
    College: Maple
    Woods (MO) 1
Metropolitan Community
    College: Penn
    Valley (MO) 1
Midway College (KY) 1
Ohio State University:
    Mansfield Campus (OH) 1
Owensboro Community and
    Technical College (KY) 1
Penn State Wilkes-
    Barre (PA) 1
Southeastern Bible
    College (AL) 1
Southwestern
    University (TX) 1
Thomas College (ME) 1
Three Rivers Community
    College (MO) 1
Trinity College of
    Florida (FL) 1
Umpqua Community
    College (OR) 1
University of Pittsburgh at
    Johnstown (PA) 1
Valley Forge Christian
    College (PA) 1
VanderCook College of
    Music (IL) 1
Virginia State
    University (VA) 1
Yeshiva Mikdash
    Melech (NY) 1

Total financial aid for international undergraduate students

Harvard College (MA)	20,529,578
Mount Holyoke College (MA)	13,683,064
Princeton University (NJ)	11,829,138
Massachusetts Institute of Technology (MA)	9,433,169
University of Pennsylvania (PA)	9,036,883
Western Michigan University (MI)	8,500,000
University of Southern California (CA)	6,960,996
Middlebury College (VT)	6,873,468
Stanford University (CA)	6,508,740
Columbia University (NY)	6,506,525
Dartmouth College (NH)	6,284,280
St. John's University (NY)	6,012,763
Howard University (DC)	6,001,200
Vassar College (NY)	5,602,891
Williams College (MA)	5,522,437
Colby College (ME)	5,330,659
Macalester College (MN)	5,020,620
St. Lawrence University (NY)	4,985,420
Wellesley College (MA)	4,876,452
Bard College (NY)	4,752,547
Cornell University (NY)	4,751,644
Texas Christian University (TX)	4,708,000
Lafayette College (PA)	4,662,410
Parsons The New School for Design (NY)	4,643,400
Franklin & Marshall College (PA)	4,590,959
Smith College (MA)	4,376,597
Dickinson College (PA)	4,282,188
University of Miami (FL)	4,209,469
Arizona State University (AZ)	4,194,767
Grinnell College (IA)	4,183,757
University of Texas: Pan American (TX)	4,026,966
University of Richmond (VA)	3,980,182
Colgate University (NY)	3,949,032
Temple University (PA)	3,823,128
Amherst College (MA)	3,702,488
Texas A&M University (TX)	3,631,231
Boston University (MA)	3,623,260
Brandeis University (MA)	3,474,143
Ohio Wesleyan University (OH)	3,402,325
Connecticut College (CT)	3,350,971
Worcester Polytechnic Institute (MA)	3,307,600
Calvin College (MI)	3,300,000
Berea College (KY)	3,273,477
Bates College (ME)	3,138,663
University of Hawaii at Manoa (HI)	3,061,807
Hamilton College (NY)	3,020,819
Louisiana State University and Agricultural and Mechanical College (LA)	3,002,497

Cooper Union for the Advancement of Science and Art (NY)	3,000,000
Clark University (MA)	2,873,300
Illinois Institute of Technology (IL)	2,857,929
University of Denver (CO)	2,743,482
Drake University (IA)	2,692,071
Florida Institute of Technology (FL)	2,620,126
Trinity College (CT)	2,603,091
Indiana University Bloomington (IN)	2,600,515
Washington University in St. Louis (MO)	2,548,530
Washington and Lee University (VA)	2,462,492
Bryn Mawr College (PA)	2,449,931
University of Notre Dame (IN)	2,445,698
University of Chicago (IL)	2,340,478
Kenyon College (OH)	2,323,320
Northeastern University (MA)	2,288,754
University of the Ozarks (AR)	2,282,404
Carleton College (MN)	2,239,097
College of Wooster (OH)	2,228,816
Denison University (OH)	2,224,086
University of Tennessee Health Science Center (TN)	2,214,673
Lynn University (FL)	2,199,421
Polytechnic University (NY)	2,176,696
Adelphi University (NY)	2,155,960
American University (DC)	2,133,522
Elmira College (NY)	2,130,795
State University of New York College at Plattsburgh (NY)	2,112,998
Brigham Young University (UT)	2,107,139
University of Texas at El Paso (TX)	2,087,232
Whitman College (WA)	2,073,031
Wesleyan University (CT)	2,070,770
Tufts University (MA)	2,068,112
Canisius College (NY)	2,026,233
Quinnipiac University (CT)	1,997,851
Juilliard School (NY)	1,965,937
Swarthmore College (PA)	1,963,252
Saint Louis University (MO)	1,950,502
Lawrence University (WI)	1,947,968
St. John's University (MN)	1,897,246
Villanova University (PA)	1,829,086
Luther College (IA)	1,815,758
Westminster College (MO)	1,746,046
Eastern Michigan University (MI)	1,743,789
Florida Atlantic University (FL)	1,734,671
College of St. Scholastica (MN)	1,725,176

University of California: Los Angeles (CA)	1,671,661
College of the Atlantic (ME)	1,670,685
Concordia College: Moorhead (MN)	1,609,150
College of St. Benedict (MN)	1,583,637
University of Evansville (IN)	1,571,711
Trinity University (TX)	1,554,717
Lehigh University (PA)	1,539,933
University of New Hampshire (NH)	1,533,312
Seton Hall University (NJ)	1,500,239
University of New Orleans (LA)	1,493,447
Missouri State University (MO)	1,478,641
Earlham College (IN)	1,475,164
Michigan Technological University (MI)	1,470,656
Northwood University: Florida (FL)	1,462,997
Rensselaer Polytechnic Institute (NY)	1,438,900
Embry-Riddle Aeronautical University (FL)	1,431,011
Furman University (SC)	1,430,573
Knox College (IL)	1,429,217
DePauw University (IN)	1,405,028
Rice University (TX)	1,378,694
St. Leo University (FL)	1,371,315
Gettysburg College (PA)	1,363,562
University of Iowa (IA)	1,296,012
Skidmore College (NY)	1,295,000
Davidson College (NC)	1,286,559
New England Conservatory of Music (MA)	1,274,410
University of Tulsa (OK)	1,262,392
Hofstra University (NY)	1,249,186
Murray State University (KY)	1,247,158
Bethel College (IN)	1,247,076
Towson University (MD)	1,235,686
Miami Dade College (FL)	1,231,250
Pace University (NY)	1,225,684
Union College (NY)	1,195,486
Winthrop University (SC)	1,186,330
Duquesne University (PA)	1,173,657
Stetson University (FL)	1,159,675
La Sierra University (CA)	1,154,994
California Institute of Technology (CA)	1,152,933
Lewis & Clark College (OR)	1,142,397
Colorado College (CO)	1,141,420
Wabash College (IN)	1,130,428
La Roche College (PA)	1,126,750
Dowling College (NY)	1,097,980
Bowdoin College (ME)	1,095,975
Kent State University (OH)	1,092,690
University of North Dakota (ND)	1,091,330
Providence College (RI)	1,076,483
Hampshire College (MA)	1,075,500
Robert Morris University (PA)	1,062,261
Beloit College (WI)	1,058,409
Hamline University (MN)	1,055,044
Georgetown University (DC)	1,042,516
Virginia Intermont College (VA)	1,033,273
Pacific Lutheran University (WA)	1,029,062
Rollins College (FL)	1,011,222
Illinois Wesleyan University (IL)	1,002,865
Northwestern University (IL)	994,509
Truman State University (MO)	989,686
Fresno Pacific University (CA)	988,619

Coastal Carolina University (SC)	986,044
Barry University (FL)	980,543
State University of New York College at Potsdam (NY)	973,376
Suffolk University (MA)	962,059
Methodist University (NC)	933,633
Columbus College of Art and Design (OH)	932,162
University of Mississippi (MS)	927,780
Pomona College (CA)	920,000
Wartburg College (IA)	914,462
State University of New York at Stony Brook (NY)	912,568
Rochester Institute of Technology (NY)	900,000
University of California: Davis (CA)	890,711
Fordham University (NY)	879,960
Savannah College of Art and Design (GA)	873,063
University of the South (TN)	871,715
North Carolina State University (NC)	857,817
Abilene Christian University (TX)	846,257
Florida Southern College (FL)	844,769
University of Nevada: Reno (NV)	836,903
Messiah College (PA)	823,632
Manhattan School of Music (NY)	821,015
Harding University (AR)	813,078
Grand Valley State University (MI)	808,890
Bellarmine University (KY)	806,520
University of Texas at Dallas (TX)	792,104
Wheaton College (MA)	788,873
James Madison University (VA)	787,037
Hawaii Pacific University (HI)	786,817
Columbia University: School of General Studies (NY)	786,300
University of Arkansas (AR)	784,587
Goshen College (IN)	771,216
Tulane University (LA)	765,616
Southern Illinois University Carbondale (IL)	764,852
Webber International University (FL)	762,607
Iona College (NY)	750,525
Central Michigan University (MI)	745,003
University of Southern Mississippi (MS)	741,413
Dallas Baptist University (TX)	730,142
Queens University of Charlotte (NC)	722,790
St. Norbert College (WI)	722,719
Limestone College (SC)	716,448
University of Missouri: St. Louis (MO)	712,106
University of Tampa (FL)	703,500
Johns Hopkins University (MD)	700,942
Occidental College (CA)	688,490
University of Wyoming (WY)	687,342
Wittenberg University (OH)	685,056
Hanover College (IN)	683,488
Southeastern Louisiana University (LA)	674,710
University of Tennessee: Knoxville (TN)	669,935

Cleveland State University (OH).................... 669,520
Saginaw Valley State University (MI).................... 669,499
Campbellsville University (KY).................... 663,092
Brenau University (GA)............. 635,389
University of Alaska Fairbanks (AK).................... 633,974
Ohio State University: Columbus Campus (OH)...... 632,859
Gonzaga University (WA)........ 632,757
Cornell College (IA) 626,640
State University of New York at Binghamton (NY)................. 618,405
Indiana University-Purdue University Indianapolis (IN) 615,656
San Diego State University (CA) 614,000
Northeastern State University (OK).................... 606,960
Hobart and William Smith Colleges (NY)..................... 603,594
Agnes Scott College (GA) 603,122
Marquette University (WI) 599,192
University of Wisconsin-Superior (WI) 598,309
Roger Williams University (RI) 591,327
California Lutheran University (CA).................... 590,983
University of Colorado at Boulder (CO) 588,913
ASA Institute of Business and Computer Technology (NY)........ 579,140
School of Visual Arts (NY)....... 572,355
Centre College (KY) 570,610
Kutztown University of Pennsylvania (PA) 570,541
University of the Cumberlands (KY) 555,052
Linfield College (OR) 552,317
Hope College (MI).................... 550,745
Portland State University (OR)................... 550,287
Menlo College (CA) 541,436
The Master's College (CA)....... 540,075
Hood College (MD) 539,549
Harvey Mudd College (CA) 534,346
Curtis Institute of Music (PA)..................... 533,600
Haverford College (PA) 531,787
Florida Gulf Coast University (FL)..................... 526,438
University of Wisconsin-Stevens Point (WI) 526,212
Michigan State University (MI)..................... 523,208
Iowa State University (IA)........ 522,070
Western Kentucky University (KY).................... 517,305
Houghton College (NY)............ 512,477
Loras College (IA) 507,705
Sacred Heart University (CT) 502,123
Ouachita Baptist University (AR)................... 496,883
Sarah Lawrence College (NY) 488,092
University of the Incarnate Word (TX) 485,168
Embry-Riddle Aeronautical University: Prescott Campus (AZ) 483,545
Carroll College (WI) 465,250
Lewis-Clark State College (ID)..................... 461,459
Seton Hill University (PA)........ 461,242
Lambuth University (TN) 453,985
Marymount University (VA)................... 453,977
Bucknell University (PA)........... 452,221

Lock Haven University of Pennsylvania (PA) 449,919
Texas State University: San Marcos (TX) 446,906
Gustavus Adolphus College (MN) 439,872
Virginia Commonwealth University (VA) 437,302
Wheeling Jesuit University (WV) 436,200
Walla Walla University (WA) 428,674
Union College (KY) 426,138
Azusa Pacific University (CA) 423,410
St. Mary-of-the-Woods College (IN) 421,060
Regis University (CO) 420,693
University of Montevallo (AL).................... 420,316
Le Moyne College (NY) 417,324
Minnesota State University: Mankato (MN)...................... 416,235
Loyola University New Orleans (LA).................... 415,117
Xavier University (OH) 410,569
Florida Agricultural and Mechanical University (FL)..................... 408,213
Tiffin University (OH)............... 404,186
Freed-Hardeman University (TN) 402,109
University of Wisconsin-Parkside (WI) 399,314
University of Wisconsin-Stout (WI)............................ 398,366
University of Texas at Arlington (TX) 390,403
St. Mary's University of Minnesota (MN) 390,112
Alfred University (NY)............ 390,094
Taylor University (IN) 387,685
Saint Thomas University (FL)..................... 387,100
Maharishi University of Management (IA) 382,588
Gannon University (PA)............ 381,656
Indiana University-Purdue University Fort Wayne (IN) 378,814
University of Scranton (PA)..... 376,019
Endicott College (MA) 374,573
Susquehanna University (PA).................... 374,260
Clarkson University (NY)........ 373,000
Christian Brothers University (TN) 371,505
Simmons College (MA) 364,393
Bluffton University (OH) 361,697
Monmouth University (NJ)....... 357,953
Seattle University (WA)............ 357,253
Lincoln University (PA)............ 355,922
Idaho State University (ID)....... 354,963
Roberts Wesleyan College (NY) 353,255
University of Science and Arts of Oklahoma (OK)........ 349,704
Slippery Rock University of Pennsylvania (PA) 348,251
Bloomsburg University of Pennsylvania (PA) 347,843
Valparaiso University (IN)........ 346,030
St. Michael's College (VT)....... 337,885
Allegheny College (PA) 337,500
Minot State University (ND)..................... 336,522
Lake Superior State University (MI).................... 335,154
Montana State University: Billings (MT)...................... 334,100
State University of New York College at Brockport (NY) 330,933
Edinboro University of Pennsylvania (PA) 330,687

Roanoke College (VA)............. 325,444
Midwestern State University (TX) 325,339
University of St. Thomas (MN).................... 323,254
St. Anselm College (NH) 321,660
George Fox University (OR) 321,390
King College (TN) 316,913
Trevecca Nazarene University (TN) 316,900
Randolph-Macon College (VA)...................... 312,927
Catawba College (NC)............. 308,388
Muskingum College (OH) 308,000
Simpson College (IA) 306,481
Huntington University (IN)....... 304,420
Vanderbilt University (TN) 303,573
Belmont University (TN).......... 299,175
Montclair State University (NJ) 297,528
University of Wisconsin-Green Bay (WI) 295,726
St. Olaf College (MN) 294,100
Purdue University (IN) 293,018
Marywood University (PA)....... 292,057
Marietta College (OH) 292,000
Arkansas Tech University (AR) 290,384
College of Idaho (ID)............... 290,216
The Citadel (SC) 289,158
Malone College (OH) 287,100
Northern Arizona University (AZ) 283,250
North Central College (IL) 283,050
University of Wisconsin-Eau Claire (WI) 282,392
Whitworth University (WA) 279,287
Rockhurst University (MO)....... 278,646
Mount Union College (OH)...... 274,775
University of Findlay (OH)....... 270,000
University of Northern Iowa (IA) 267,953
Willamette University (OR)...... 262,060
Colorado State University: Pueblo (CO)......................... 261,456
Albion College (MI) 260,000
University of Idaho (ID) 256,320
Palm Beach Atlantic University (FL) 255,001
Oklahoma Christian University (OK).................... 253,053
Walsh University (OH) 251,865
Jamestown College (ND)........... 247,568
Hendrix College (AR)............... 247,138
College of the Ozarks (MO) 246,400
St. John's College (NM) 239,003
Spring Arbor University (MI)..................... 235,069
College for Creative Studies (MI)...................... 234,156
St. Vincent College (PA)........... 232,340
New England College (NH)...... 231,500
Bentley College (MA)............... 231,114
Kentucky Christian University (KY) 230,225
Valley City State University (ND).................... 229,876
Felician College (NJ) 227,487
Southeast Missouri State University (MO).................... 225,359
Columbia College (SC)............. 224,416
Heidelberg College (OH).......... 223,690
College of Saint Mary (NE)....... 221,892
Wayland Baptist University (TX) 219,106
Utica College (NY).................. 218,152
MidAmerica Nazarene University (KS) 211,747
University of Oklahoma (OK).................... 211,152
Bloomfield College (NJ)........... 210,639
Mills College (CA) 209,000
Albright College (PA) 204,284

Indiana University South Bend (IN)............................. 204,165
Baldwin-Wallace College (OH) 201,951
William Woods University (MO) 201,000
Samford University (AL).......... 196,562
Eugene Lang College The New School for Liberal Arts (NY) 192,804
Brewton-Parker College (GA) 192,032
Alabama State University (AL) 188,962
Averett University (VA)............ 187,713
Brevard College (NC) 186,700
Montana State University: Bozeman (MT) 185,924
Augusta State University (GA) 184,994
Barnard College (NY)............... 184,848
Oakland University (MI)........... 184,744
McMurry University (TX) 181,740
St. Francis University (PA) 180,864
Philadelphia University (PA)..................... 180,444
Wheaton College (IL) 179,106
Northland College (WI) 178,599
Spring Hill College (AL) 177,524
Northwestern College (MN) 175,174
Marian College of Fond du Lac (WI) 174,316
Southwestern College (KS)....... 173,702
Lyon College (AR).................... 173,564
Covenant College (GA) 173,400
Dominican College of Blauvelt (NY) 173,210
King's College (NY) 172,600
Saint Mary's College (IN)......... 172,362
University of Dayton (OH) 169,000
School of the Museum of Fine Arts (MA) 168,213
Cuyahoga Community College: Metropolitan Campus (OH) 168,200
Hillsdale College (MI).............. 168,000
Mount St. Mary's University (MD) 167,959
Central College (IA) 166,825
Point Loma Nazarene University (CA).................... 166,277
Regis College (MA).................. 165,810
Marist College (NY) 164,579
Georgian Court University (NJ) 161,772
Bethany College (KS)............... 161,710
Mount Olive College (NC) 159,608
Kuyper College (MI)................. 159,284
Peace College (NC).................. 158,600
University of North Carolina at Greensboro (NC) 156,533
Shippensburg University of Pennsylvania (PA) 155,537
University of St. Thomas (TX) 155,193
Columbus State University (GA)..................... 154,255
Colby-Sawyer College (NH) 153,360
Alderson-Broaddus College (WV) 153,350
University of Michigan: Dearborn (MI)...................... 153,336
Emmanuel College (MA)........... 152,950
Grand View College (IA) 151,637
Claremont McKenna College (CA) 150,000
St. Ambrose University (IA) 148,735
Mansfield University of Pennsylvania (PA) 148,468
Lenoir-Rhyne College (NC) 147,590
Wake Forest University (NC) 147,576

Total financial aid for international undergraduate students

Morningside College (IA).......... 146,236
Chapman University (CA)........ 145,200
Bethany Lutheran
  College (MN) 144,891
Atlantic Union
  College (MA) 144,301
Lycoming College (PA) 144,000
Cornerstone
  University (MI).................... 143,400
Westminster College (UT) 142,500
Guilford College (NC) 141,600
Southeastern Oklahoma
  State University (OK).......... 139,459
Augustana College (SD) 138,600
University of Tennessee:
  Chattanooga (TN)................. 138,414
East Stroudsburg University
  of Pennsylvania (PA)........... 138,140
Mount Vernon Nazarene
  University (OH)................... 130,924
University of Kansas (KS)........ 129,000
Ramapo College of New
  Jersey (NJ) 128,986
Oregon Institute of
  Technology (OR)................. 128,809
City University of New
  York: Baruch
  College (NY) 128,450
Otis College of Art and
  Design (CA) 126,600
Southern Wesleyan
  University (SC)................... 124,704
Assumption College (MA)........ 122,612
Georgia Southern
  University (GA)................... 121,552
Rockford College (IL).............. 117,250
Bridgewater College (VA)........ 116,470
Rosemont College (PA)............ 116,307
Northwestern State
  University (LA).................... 116,162
Salve Regina
  University (RI).................... 115,550
Belhaven College (MS)............ 114,000
Western Nebraska
  Community
  College (NE)....................... 113,086
Alma College (MI)................... 110,456
Franklin Pierce
  University (NH)................... 110,000
Simpson University (CA) 107,100
Millersville University of
  Pennsylvania (PA)............... 104,928
University of Illinois at
  Chicago (IL) 103,759
Riverland Community
  College (MN) 100,000
Texas Wesleyan
  University (TX) 100,000
Texas Lutheran
  University (TX) 99,900
Emerson College (MA).............. 95,020
Ohio Valley
  University (WV).................... 95,000
Rose-Hulman Institute of
  Technology (IN) 94,550
Williams Baptist
  College (AR) 93,018
Millsaps College (MS).............. 92,030
Wentworth Institute of
  Technology (MA)................... 91,500
Flagler College (FL) 90,892
Central State
  University (OH)..................... 90,389
St. Andrews Presbyterian
  College (NC) 90,334
Nicholls State
  University (LA) 90,111
University of New
  Haven (CT)........................... 89,400
Bethel College (KS).................. 88,245
Muhlenberg College (PA) 85,000
Huntingdon College (AL)........... 84,729
Grove City College (PA)............ 84,506
Northwestern Oklahoma
  State University (OK)............. 83,733

Dominican University (IL) 82,850
Shepherd University (WV) 82,175
Hardin-Simmons
  University (TX)...................... 82,000
Jefferson College (MO).............. 81,755
East Texas Baptist
  University (TX) 79,000
Tabor College (KS)................... 78,060
Lesley University (MA).............. 77,450
Arizona State University
  West (AZ)............................. 77,103
Drury University (MO).............. 76,650
St. John's College (MD) 75,610
Clarion University of
  Pennsylvania (PA)................. 75,336
University of Nevada: Las
  Vegas (NV) 74,757
Mayville State
  University (ND)..................... 74,641
Sam Houston State
  University (TX) 73,889
Albany College of
  Pharmacy (NY)..................... 73,270
Creighton University (NE).......... 72,504
Marian College (IN).................. 72,050
University of Maine (ME) 71,862
Ashford University (IA)............. 71,559
University of Akron (OH)........... 70,545
Lebanon Valley
  College (PA) 69,637
Naropa University (CO)............. 68,967
King's College (PA) 68,450
College of Mount St.
  Joseph (OH)......................... 68,218
Shimer College (IL)................... 67,356
Geneva College (PA) 67,100
Tri-State University (IN)............. 65,313
Stephen F. Austin State
  University (TX) 65,200
Thomas More College (KY) 64,724
Widener University (PA)............ 64,600
University of Houston:
  Downtown (TX) 64,141
Cleveland Institute of
  Art (OH) 63,660
William Paterson
  University of New
  Jersey (NJ)........................... 63,461
Bethel University (MN) 63,312
University of
  Memphis (TN)....................... 63,155
Carlow University (PA) 62,958
Southwest Minnesota State
  University (MN)..................... 60,861
University of Alabama in
  Huntsville (AL) 58,704
Immaculata University (PA) 57,080
Merrimack College (MA) 57,000
Lane College (TN) 56,680
Evergreen State
  College (WA)........................ 56,438
Northern Michigan
  University (MI)...................... 56,300
Kansas City Art
  Institute (MO) 54,900
Marymount Manhattan
  College (NY) 53,790
St. Gregory's
  University (OK)..................... 52,644
Goucher College (MD) 51,500
State University of New
  York College at
  Fredonia (NY) 51,000
Medaille College (NY) 50,000
Wells College (NY)................... 50,000
West Chester University of
  Pennsylvania (PA) 49,186
Milwaukee School of
  Engineering (WI)................... 48,000
Bluefield College (VA) 46,949
Millikin University (IL).............. 46,795
Concordia University (MI) 46,500
Seattle Pacific
  University (WA)..................... 46,404

State University of New
  York at Oswego (NY)............. 46,314
Alverno College (WI) 45,840
University of La
  Verne (CA) 45,000
Black Hawk College (IL)............ 44,916
University of the Sciences
  in Philadelphia (PA) 42,000
Keuka College (NY) 41,486
Mount Mercy College (IA)......... 39,200
Western Washington
  University (WA) 39,114
Central Christian College of
  Kansas (KS).......................... 38,650
Washington & Jefferson
  College (PA).......................... 37,562
Husson College (ME) 37,550
Concordia University
  Wisconsin (WI)...................... 37,000
Champlain College (VT)............. 36,445
Westmont College (CA) 35,456
Mary Baldwin
  College (VA) 35,399
Fontbonne University (MO) 35,000
Taylor University Fort
  Wayne (IN) 34,142
Franklin College (IN)................. 33,421
Nichols College (MA)................ 33,000
University of Puget
  Sound (WA) 33,000
Cabrini College (PA).................. 32,120
Culver-Stockton
  College (MO) 32,000
Harford Community
  College (MD) 31,800
University of Maine at
  Augusta (ME) 30,903
Wichita State
  University (KS) 30,887
Oklahoma State
  University (OK)..................... 30,500
Kean University (NJ) 29,525
Schreiner University (TX) 28,000
University of Illinois:
  Springfield (IL)...................... 27,132
LeMoyne-Owen
  College (TN)......................... 26,903
Rider University (NJ)................. 26,700
Oregon Health & Science
  University (OR)..................... 26,500
Mount Aloysius
  College (PA) 26,325
Southwestern
  University (TX) 25,740
Texas College (TX) 25,706
Briar Cliff University (IA) 25,000
Western Wyoming
  Community
  College (WY) 23,750
Cochise College (AZ) 23,427
Plymouth State
  University (NH) 23,013
Keystone College (PA)............... 22,750
Maryville University of
  Saint Louis (MO)................... 22,400
Regent University (VA) 22,243
Misericordia
  University (PA) 21,950
McPherson College (KS) 20,900
Cazenovia College (NY)............ 20,640
Wagner College (NY) 20,300
Carson-Newman
  College (TN)......................... 20,138
Thomas College (ME)................ 18,750
Glenville State
  College (WV) 18,450
Waynesburg
  University (PA)...................... 18,000
Silver Lake College (WI)............ 17,980
Trinity International
  University (IL)....................... 17,000
William Jewell
  College (MO) 16,700
Union University (TN)................ 16,000

University of Minnesota:
  Crookston (MN) 15,872
Aquinas College (MI) 13,750
Radford University (VA)............. 13,485
Eastern Oregon
  University (OR) 12,708
Kentucky Mountain Bible
  College (KY) 11,050
University of South
  Carolina Upstate (SC) 11,050
Lubbock Christian
  University (TX) 10,500
Mitchell Technical
  Institute (SD) 10,500
Concordia University: St.
  Paul (MN) 10,000
University of St. Mary (KS) 10,000
Minneapolis College of Art
  and Design (MN) 9,750
South Dakota State
  University (SD) 9,576
University of Utah (UT) 8,618
Sterling College (KS)................... 8,275
Indiana University
  Southeast (IN)....................... 7,450
Purdue University North
  Central (IN) 7,219
Delaware Valley
  College (PA) 6,500
State University of New
  York Maritime
  College (NY) 6,500
University of Pittsburgh at
  Bradford (PA) 6,500
Cedar Crest College (PA)............ 5,500
Eastern Connecticut State
  University (CT) 5,500
Transylvania
  University (KY) 5,500
University of Texas of the
  Permian Basin (TX)................. 5,100
Central Methodist
  University (MO) 5,000
Concordia University (IL)............ 5,000
University of Michigan:
  Flint (MI).............................. 4,950
Mount Mary College (WI) 4,500
Oakland Community
  College (MI) 4,000
City University of New
  York: York College (NY) 3,875
Moberly Area Community
  College (MO) 3,200
Indiana University
  Northwest (IN)....................... 3,117
Anna Maria College (MA)........... 3,000
Southeastern Bible
  College (AL).......................... 3,000
Armstrong Atlantic State
  University (GA)...................... 2,143
Alice Lloyd College (KY) 1,648
Bowie State
  University (MD) 1,500
Valley Forge Christian
  College (PA) 1,165
University of Colorado at
  Colorado Springs (CO)............ 1,100
Southwestern Assemblies of
  God University (TX) 1,010
University of Houston:
  Victoria (TX) 1,000
State University of New
  York College of
  Agriculture and
  Technology at
  Cobleskill (NY) 500
Indiana University
  Kokomo (IN)............................ 400

Conditional admission based on English-language proficiency

Alabama

Alabama Agricultural and Mechanical
   University
Auburn University
Bishop State Community College
Chattahoochee Valley Community
   College
Faulkner State Community College
Gadsden State Community College
J. F. Drake State Technical College
Jacksonville State University
Marion Military Institute
Miles College
Spring Hill College
University of Alabama
University of Mobile
University of North Alabama
University of South Alabama

Alaska

Alaska Pacific University
Prince William Sound Community
   College
University of Alaska Fairbanks

Arizona

Arizona Western College
Cochise College
Dine College
Everest College: Phoenix
Glendale Community College
Grand Canyon University
International Import-Export Institute
Northern Arizona University
Pima Community College
Rio Salado College
Scottsdale Community College
University of Advancing Technology
University of Arizona
Western International University

Arkansas

Arkansas State University
Arkansas State University: Newport
Arkansas Tech University
Crowley's Ridge College
Ecclesia College
Harding University
John Brown University
National Park Community College
Ouachita Baptist University
Phillips Community College of the
   University of Arkansas
University of Arkansas
University of Arkansas at Little Rock
University of Central Arkansas

California

Academy of Art University
Allan Hancock College
Alliant International University
Art Institute of California: San Diego
Art Institute of California: San Francisco
Azusa Pacific University
Biola University
California Baptist University
California Institute of the Arts
California Lutheran University
California State University: Chico
California State University: Fresno
California State University: Long Beach
California State University: Los Angeles
California State University: Stanislaus
California University of Management and
   Sciences
Canada College
Chaffey College
Charles R. Drew University of Medicine
   and Science
Citrus College
City College of San Francisco
Coastline Community College
Coleman College
College of the Desert
College of the Sequoias
College of the Siskiyous
Columbia College: Hollywood
Concordia University
Contra Costa College
East Los Angeles College
El Camino College
El Camino College: Compton Center
Empire College
Fashion Institute of Design and
   Merchandising: Los Angeles
Fashion Institute of Design and
   Merchandising: San Diego
Fashion Institute of Design and
   Merchandising: San Francisco
Feather River College
Foothill College
Fremont College
Fresno Pacific University
Glendale Community College
Golden Gate University
Holy Names University
Hope International University
Humphreys College
La Sierra University
Laguna College of Art and Design
Las Positas College
Lincoln University
Long Beach City College
Los Angeles City College
Los Angeles Pierce College
Maric College: Panorama City
Marymount College
The Master's College
Menlo College
Merritt College
Mills College
MiraCosta College

Mission College
Monterey Peninsula College
Mt. Sierra College
Napa Valley College
National Polytechnic College of Science
National University
NewSchool of Architecture & Design
Northwestern Polytechnic University
Notre Dame de Namur University
Otis College of Art and Design
Oxnard College
Pacific States University
Pacific Union College
Palomar College
Pasadena City College
Patten University
Pepperdine University
Pitzer College
Platt College: San Diego
Point Loma Nazarene University
Sacramento City College
Saddleback College
St. Mary's College of California
San Diego Christian College
San Diego Mesa College
San Diego State University
San Francisco Art Institute
San Francisco Conservatory of Music
San Joaquin Delta College
San Jose City College
Santa Ana College
Santa Barbara City College
Santa Monica College
Santiago Canyon College
School of Urban Missions: Oakland
Scripps College
Sierra College
Soka University of America
Solano Community College
Southern California Institute of
   Architecture
Southern California Institute of
   Technology
Taft College
University of California: Santa Barbara
University of La Verne
University of Redlands
University of San Diego
University of San Francisco
University of Southern California
University of the West
Ventura College
West Hills College: Coalinga
West Los Angeles College
Whittier College
World Mission University
Yuba Community College District

Colorado

Arapahoe Community College
Art Institute of Colorado
Colorado Christian University
Colorado Mountain College
Colorado Northwestern Community
   College
Colorado State University
Colorado State University: Pueblo
Front Range Community College
IntelliTec College
Johnson & Wales University: Denver
Mesa State College
Northeastern Junior College
Pikes Peak Community College
Red Rocks Community College
Rocky Mountain College of Art &
   Design
Teikyo Loretto Heights University
Trinidad State Junior College
University of Denver
University of Northern Colorado

Connecticut

Briarwood College
Central Connecticut State University
Clemens College
Gateway Community College
Housatonic Community College
Mitchell College
Naugatuck Valley Community College
Quinnipiac University
Sacred Heart University
Tunxis Community College
University of Bridgeport
University of Connecticut
University of New Haven

Delaware

Goldey-Beacom College
University of Delaware
Wesley College

District of Columbia

American University
Catholic University of America
Gallaudet University
George Washington University
Georgetown University
Howard University
Southeastern University
Trinity Washington University
University of the District of Columbia

Florida

Angley College
Ave Maria University
Barry University
Broward Community College
Carlos Albizu University
Central Florida College
Central Florida Community College
City College: Fort Lauderdale
College of Business and Technology:
   Flagler
Daytona Beach Community College
Eckerd College
Embry-Riddle Aeronautical University
Florida Institute of Technology
Florida Memorial University
Florida National College
Full Sail University
Johnson & Wales University: North
   Miami
Key College
Lynn University
Miami Dade College
Northwood University: Florida
Palm Beach Community College
Pensacola Junior College
Polk Community College
Remington College: Tampa
Ringling College of Art and Design
St. Leo University
Saint Thomas University
Schiller International University
Seminole Community College
Southwest Florida College
University of Miami
University of South Florida
University of Tampa
Valencia Community College
Webber International University

Georgia

Abraham Baldwin Agricultural College
American InterContinental University
Andrew College

Armstrong Atlantic State University
Art Institute of Atlanta
Augusta Technical College
Bauder College
Chattahoochee Technical College
DeKalb Technical College
Fort Valley State University
Gainesville State College
Georgia Highlands College
Georgia Southern University
Georgia Southwestern State University
Georgia State University
Life University
Mercer University
Middle Georgia College
North Georgia College & State University
Piedmont College
Savannah College of Art and Design
Savannah Technical College
South Georgia College
Thomas University
University of Georgia
Young Harris College

Hawaii

Brigham Young University-Hawaii
Chaminade University of Honolulu
Hawaii Pacific University
Hawaii Tokai International College
Heald College: Honolulu
TransPacific Hawaii College
University of Hawaii: Honolulu Community College
University of Hawaii: Kapiolani Community College
University of Hawaii: Windward Community College

Idaho

Boise State University
Idaho State University
Lewis-Clark State College
North Idaho College
Stevens-Henager College: Boise
University of Idaho

Illinois

Benedictine University
Black Hawk College
Carl Sandburg College
City Colleges of Chicago: Harold Washington College
City Colleges of Chicago: Malcolm X College
City Colleges of Chicago: Olive-Harvey College
City Colleges of Chicago: Richard J. Daley College
City Colleges of Chicago: Wright College
College of DuPage
College of Lake County
Columbia College Chicago
Concordia University
Danville Area Community College
DePaul University
Dominican University
East-West University
Elgin Community College
Harper College
Highland Community College
Illinois Central College
Illinois Eastern Community Colleges: Frontier Community College
Illinois Eastern Community Colleges: Lincoln Trail College
Illinois Eastern Community Colleges: Olney Central College

Illinois Eastern Community Colleges: Wabash Valley College
Kishwaukee College
Lake Land College
Lewis University
Lexington College
Lincoln College
Loyola University Chicago
MacCormac College
McKendree University
Moraine Valley Community College
Morrison Institute of Technology
National-Louis University
North Central College
North Park University
Northwestern Business College
Parkland College
Richland Community College
Rockford College
Roosevelt University
Sauk Valley Community College
School of the Art Institute of Chicago
Southern Illinois University Carbondale
Southern Illinois University Edwardsville
Trinity Christian College
Triton College
West Suburban College of Nursing
Western Illinois University

Indiana

Ancilla College
Ball State University
Butler University
Earlham College
Franklin College
Goshen College
Huntington University
Indiana State University
Indiana University Bloomington
Indiana University East
Indiana University-Purdue University Fort Wayne
Indiana University-Purdue University Indianapolis
Ivy Tech Community College: Bloomington
Ivy Tech Community College: Central Indiana
Ivy Tech Community College: Columbus
Ivy Tech Community College: East Central
Ivy Tech Community College: Kokomo
Ivy Tech Community College: Lafayette
Ivy Tech Community College: North Central
Ivy Tech Community College: Northeast
Ivy Tech Community College: Northwest
Ivy Tech Community College: Richmond
Ivy Tech Community College: South Central
Ivy Tech Community College: Southeast
Ivy Tech Community College: Southwest
Ivy Tech Community College: Wabash Valley
Marian College
Oakland City University
Taylor University
Taylor University Fort Wayne
University of Evansville
University of Indianapolis
Vincennes University

Iowa

Ashford University
Buena Vista University
Central College
Clarke College
Coe College
Des Moines Area Community College
Drake University
Ellsworth Community College

Graceland University
Hawkeye Community College
Iowa State University
Iowa Wesleyan College
Iowa Western Community College
Kaplan University: Des Moines
Kirkwood Community College
Loras College
Maharishi University of Management
Marshalltown Community College
Morningside College
Northwestern College
Scott Community College
Simpson College
University of Dubuque
University of Iowa
University of Northern Iowa
Upper Iowa University
Waldorf College
Wartburg College
Western Iowa Tech Community College
William Penn University

Kansas

Barclay College
Barton County Community College
Benedictine College
Cloud County Community College
Colby Community College
Dodge City Community College
Donnelly College
Emporia State University
Fort Hays State University
Hesston College
Independence Community College
Kansas City Kansas Community College
Kansas State University
McPherson College
Neosho County Community College
Ottawa University
Pittsburg State University
Pratt Community College
Southwestern College
University of Kansas
University of Kansas Medical Center
University of St. Mary
Washburn University
Wichita State University

Kentucky

Brescia University
Campbellsville University
Henderson Community College
Jefferson Community and Technical College
Kentucky Mountain Bible College
Lindsey Wilson College
Louisville Technical Institute
Maysville Community and Technical College
Mid-Continent University
Murray State University
Owensboro Community and Technical College
Somerset Community College
Southeast Kentucky Community and Technical College
Thomas More College
Transylvania University
University of the Cumberlands
University of Kentucky
University of Louisville
Western Kentucky University

Louisiana

Bossier Parish Community College
Delgado Community College
Louisiana College

Louisiana State University and Agricultural and Mechanical College
Louisiana State University at Eunice
Louisiana Tech University
McNeese State University
Nunez Community College
St. Joseph Seminary College
Tulane University
University of Louisiana at Lafayette
University of Louisiana at Monroe
University of New Orleans

Maine

Central Maine Community College
Colby College
Husson College
Maine Maritime Academy
Southern Maine Community College
Unity College
University of Maine
University of Maine at Fort Kent
University of New England
University of Southern Maine
Washington County Community College

Maryland

Anne Arundel Community College
Baltimore City Community College
Baltimore Hebrew University
Baltimore International College
Capitol College
Carroll Community College
Chesapeake College
Columbia Union College
Community College of Baltimore County
Garrett College
Griggs University
Harford Community College
Hood College
Johns Hopkins University: Peabody Conservatory of Music
Maryland Institute College of Art
Prince George's Community College
Salisbury University
TESST College of Technology: Towson
Towson University
University of Maryland: Baltimore County
University of Maryland: College Park
University of Maryland: Eastern Shore
University of Maryland: University College
Villa Julie College

Massachusetts

American International College
Atlantic Union College
Bay Path College
Benjamin Franklin Institute of Technology
Berklee College of Music
Berkshire Community College
Boston Conservatory
Boston University
Bristol Community College
Bunker Hill Community College
Clark University
Dean College
Elms College
Fisher College
Gordon College
Hellenic College/Holy Cross
Massachusetts Bay Community College
Merrimack College
Middlesex Community College
Mount Ida College
Mount Wachusett Community College
New England Conservatory of Music
Newbury College

Nichols College
Northeastern University
Northern Essex Community College
Pine Manor College
Quincy College
School of the Museum of Fine Arts
Springfield College
Suffolk University
University of Massachusetts Boston
Wentworth Institute of Technology
Wheaton College
Worcester Polytechnic Institute

Michigan

Albion College
Alma College
Andrews University
Baker College of Auburn Hills
Baker College of Cadillac
Baker College of Jackson
Baker College of Muskegon
Baker College of Port Huron
Calvin College
Central Michigan University
Cornerstone University
Davenport University
Eastern Michigan University
Finlandia University
Kettering University
Kuyper College
Lawrence Technological University
Macomb Community College
Madonna University
Michigan Jewish Institute
Michigan State University
Michigan Technological University
Muskegon Community College
Northern Michigan University
Northwood University: Michigan
Oakland Community College
Oakland University
Olivet College
Rochester College
Saginaw Valley State University
Siena Heights University
Southwestern Michigan College
Spring Arbor University
University of Detroit Mercy
University of Michigan: Dearborn
Wayne State University
Western Michigan University

Minnesota

Art Institutes International Minnesota
Augsburg College
Bemidji State University
Bethany Lutheran College
College of St. Benedict
College of St. Catherine
College of St. Scholastica
Concordia University: St. Paul
Dakota County Technical College
Globe University
Hamline University
Hennepin Technical College
Hibbing Community College
Itasca Community College
Lake Superior College
Minnesota State Community and
  Technical College: Fergus Falls
Minnesota West Community and
  Technical College
North Central University
North Hennepin Community College
Northwest Technical College
Pine Technical College
Rainy River Community College
Rochester Community and Technical
  College
Saint Cloud State University
St. Cloud Technical College

St. John's University
St. Mary's University of Minnesota
University of Minnesota: Crookston
University of St. Thomas
Winona State University

Mississippi

Belhaven College
Hinds Community College
Meridian Community College
Mississippi College
Northeast Mississippi Community
  College
Northwest Mississippi Community
  College
University of Mississippi
University of Southern Mississippi
William Carey University

Missouri

Avila University
Columbia College
Crowder College
Drury University
Grantham University
Jefferson College
Kansas City Art Institute
Lincoln University
Metropolitan Community College: Penn
  Valley
Missouri Baptist University
Missouri Southern State University
Missouri State University
Missouri University of Science and
  Technology
Missouri Valley College
Northwest Missouri State University
Rockhurst University
Saint Louis University
Southeast Missouri State University
Southwest Baptist University
Stephens College
University of Central Missouri
University of Missouri: Columbia
University of Missouri: Kansas City
University of Missouri: St. Louis
Washington University in St. Louis
Webster University
Westminster College
William Woods University

Montana

Carroll College
Montana State University: Bozeman
Montana Tech of the University of
  Montana
University of Great Falls
University of Montana: Missoula

Nebraska

Bellevue University
Creighton University
Dana College
Doane College
Hastings College
Metropolitan Community College
Nebraska Wesleyan University
Northeast Community College
Union College
University of Nebraska - Kearney
University of Nebraska - Lincoln
University of Nebraska - Omaha
Western Nebraska Community College
York College

Nevada

Career College of Northern Nevada
College of Southern Nevada
Sierra Nevada College
University of Nevada: Las Vegas
University of Nevada: Reno
Western Nevada College

New Hampshire

Chester College of New England
Colby-Sawyer College
Daniel Webster College
Franklin Pierce University
Hesser College
Magdalen College
Manchester Community College
New England College
Rivier College
Southern New Hampshire University
University of New Hampshire at
  Manchester

New Jersey

Atlantic Cape Community College
Brookdale Community College
Burlington County College
Caldwell College
Centenary College
College of St. Elizabeth
County College of Morris
Cumberland County College
Fairleigh Dickinson University: College
  at Florham
Fairleigh Dickinson University:
  Metropolitan Campus
Felician College
Hudson County Community College
Mercer County Community College
Montclair State University
New Jersey City University
New Jersey Institute of Technology
Rowan University
Seton Hall University
Stevens Institute of Technology
Sussex County Community College

New Mexico

College of the Southwest
Eastern New Mexico University
Institute of American Indian Arts
National American University: Rio
  Rancho
New Mexico Institute of Mining and
  Technology
New Mexico Military Institute
New Mexico State University
New Mexico State University at
  Alamogordo
Santa Fe Community College
University of New Mexico

New York

Adelphi University
Briarcliffe College
Broome Community College
Bryant & Stratton College: Albany
Bryant & Stratton College: Rochester
Canisius College
City University of New York: Baruch
  College
City University of New York: Borough of
  Manhattan Community College
City University of New York: Bronx
  Community College

City University of New York: Brooklyn
  College
City University of New York: City
  College
City University of New York: College of
  Staten Island
City University of New York: LaGuardia
  Community College
City University of New York: Queens
  College
City University of New York: York
  College
Clinton Community College
College of Mount St. Vincent
Columbia University: School of General
  Studies
Columbia-Greene Community College
Concordia College
Daemen College
Dowling College
Dutchess Community College
Eastman School of Music of the
  University of Rochester
Elmira College
Eugene Lang College The New School
  for Liberal Arts
Five Towns College
Fordham University
Fulton-Montgomery Community College
Globe Institute of Technology
Herkimer County Community College
Hofstra University
Iona College
Long Island Business Institute
Long Island University: C. W. Post
  Campus
Manhattan School of Music
Manhattanville College
Mannes College The New School for
  Music
Medaille College
Mercy College
Mohawk Valley Community College
Molloy College
Nazareth College of Rochester
New York Institute of Technology
New York University
Niagara County Community College
North Country Community College
Nyack College
Onondaga Community College
Pace University
Parsons The New School for Design
Polytechnic University
Pratt Institute
Rensselaer Polytechnic Institute
Roberts Wesleyan College
Rochester Institute of Technology
Rockland Community College
Saint Bonaventure University
St. Francis College
St. John's University
St. Thomas Aquinas College
School of Visual Arts
State University of New York at Albany
State University of New York at Buffalo
State University of New York at New
  Paltz
State University of New York College at
  Plattsburgh
State University of New York College of
  Agriculture and Technology at
  Morrisville
State University of New York College of
  Environmental Science and Forestry
State University of New York College of
  Technology at Alfred
State University of New York College of
  Technology at Canton
Suffolk County Community College
Syracuse University
Technical Career Institutes
Tompkins-Cortland Community College
Touro College
Union College

Utica College
Vaughn College of Aeronautics and
    Technology
Wagner College
Yeshiva Mikdash Melech

North Carolina

Appalachian State University
Belmont Abbey College
Brevard College
Central Piedmont Community College
Chowan University
College of the Albemarle
Elizabeth City State University
Elon University
Guilford College
John Wesley College
Mayland Community College
McDowell Technical Community College
Methodist University
Mount Olive College
North Carolina School of the Arts
Peace College
Piedmont Baptist College
Piedmont Community College
Southeastern Community College
University of North Carolina at Charlotte
Vance-Granville Community College
Warren Wilson College
Wilson Community College
Wingate University

North Dakota

Bismarck State College
Dickinson State University
Lake Region State College
North Dakota State College of Science
North Dakota State University
United Tribes Technical College
University of Mary

Ohio

Art Institute of Ohio: Cincinnati
Ashland University
Baldwin-Wallace College
Capital University
Central Ohio Technical College
Central State University
Cincinnati State Technical and
    Community College
Columbus College of Art and Design
Columbus State Community College
Cuyahoga Community College:
    Metropolitan Campus
Defiance College
Heidelberg College
Hiram College
Hocking College
Kent State University
Lake Erie College
Laura and Alvin Siegal College of Judaic
    Studies
Lorain County Community College
Miami University: Middletown Campus
Miami University: Oxford Campus
Mount Union College
Muskingum College
Oberlin College
Ohio Northern University
Ohio State University: Marion Campus
Ohio University
Otterbein College
Shawnee State University
Tiffin University
University of Akron
University of Dayton
University of Findlay
University of Northwestern Ohio
University of Rio Grande

University of Toledo
Virginia Marti College of Art and Design
Walsh University
Wilmington College
Wittenberg University
Xavier University
Youngstown State University

Oklahoma

Bacone College
Northeastern Oklahoma Agricultural and
    Mechanical College
Oklahoma Baptist University
Oklahoma Christian University
Oklahoma City Community College
Oklahoma City University
Oklahoma State University
Oklahoma State University: Oklahoma
    City
Oklahoma Wesleyan University
Oral Roberts University
St. Gregory's University
Southern Nazarene University
Southwestern Christian University
Southwestern Oklahoma State University
University of Oklahoma
University of Tulsa

Oregon

Blue Mountain Community College
Chemeketa Community College
Concordia University
George Fox University
Lewis & Clark College
Linfield College
Mt. Hood Community College
Oregon Institute of Technology
Oregon State University
Pacific University
Portland Community College
Portland State University
Southwestern Oregon Community
    College
Treasure Valley Community College
University of Oregon
University of Portland
Western Oregon University

Pennsylvania

Albright College
Arcadia University
Art Institute of Pittsburgh
Baptist Bible College of Pennsylvania
Bloomsburg University of Pennsylvania
Business Institute of Pennsylvania
Cabrini College
Carlow University
Chatham University
Curtis Institute of Music
Drexel University
DuBois Business College
Duquesne University
Geneva College
Gratz College
Gwynedd-Mercy College
Harcum College
Harrisburg Area Community College
Immaculata University
Juniata College
Keystone College
Keystone Technical Institute
King's College
La Roche College
Lackawanna College
Laurel Business Institute
Lehigh University
Lock Haven University of Pennsylvania
Lycoming College
Manor College

Mansfield University of Pennsylvania
Marywood University
Mercyhurst College
Messiah College
Misericordia University
Moore College of Art and Design
Oakbridge Academy of Arts
Penn State Abington
Penn State Altoona
Penn State Beaver
Penn State Berks
Penn State Brandywine
Penn State Dubois
Penn State Erie, The Behrend College
Penn State Fayette, The Eberly Campus
Penn State Greater Allegheny
Penn State Harrisburg
Penn State Hazleton
Penn State Lehigh Valley
Penn State Mont Alto
Penn State New Kensington
Penn State Schuylkill
Penn State Shenango
Penn State University Park
Penn State Wilkes-Barre
Penn State Worthington Scranton
Penn State York
Pennsylvania Institute of Technology
Pittsburgh Institute of Aeronautics
Pittsburgh Institute of Mortuary Science
Pittsburgh Technical Institute
Point Park University
Robert Morris University
Rosemont College
St. Charles Borromeo Seminary -
    Overbrook
St. Francis University
Saint Joseph's University
St. Vincent College
Seton Hill University
Thiel College
University of the Arts
University of Scranton
Valley Forge Christian College
Valley Forge Military College
Widener University

Puerto Rico

ICPR Junior College
Inter American University of Puerto
    Rico: San German Campus
University of Puerto Rico: Mayaguez

Rhode Island

Johnson & Wales University: Providence
New England Institute of Technology
Roger Williams University

South Carolina

Anderson University
Charleston Southern University
The Citadel
Coker College
Forrest Junior College
Greenville Technical College
Horry-Georgetown Technical College
Morris College
Newberry College
North Greenville University
Southern Wesleyan University
Spartanburg Community College
Spartanburg Methodist College
Tri-County Technical College
University of South Carolina at Beaufort
University of South Carolina at Sumter
University of South Carolina Upstate

South Dakota

Augustana College
Dakota State University
Lake Area Technical Institute
National American University: Rapid
    City
Presentation College
South Dakota State University
University of South Dakota

Tennessee

Carson-Newman College
East Tennessee State University
Hiwassee College
King College
Lane College
Lincoln Memorial University
Lipscomb University
Martin Methodist College
Maryville College
Nossi College of Art
O'More College of Design
Pellissippi State Technical Community
    College
Tennessee Wesleyan College
University of Memphis
University of Tennessee: Chattanooga
University of Tennessee: Martin
Volunteer State Community College

Texas

Abilene Christian University
Arlington Baptist College
Blinn College
Cedar Valley College
Central Texas College
Concordia University at Austin
Dallas Baptist University
East Texas Baptist University
El Centro College
Frank Phillips College
Galveston College
Grayson County College
Hallmark College of Aeronautics
Hallmark College of Technology
Hill College
Houston Community College System
Howard Payne University
Huston-Tillotson University
Kilgore College
Lamar State College at Port Arthur
LeTourneau University
Lon Morris College
Midland College
Midwestern State University
Mountain View College
Northwest Vista College
Northwood University: Texas
Our Lady of the Lake University of San
    Antonio
Richland College
St. Mary's University
Schreiner University
South Plains College
Southwestern Adventist University
Texas A&M University
Texas A&M University-Galveston
Texas Christian University
Texas Southern University
Texas Southmost College
Texas State Technical College: Harlingen
Texas State University: San Marcos
Texas Tech University
Texas Wesleyan University
Texas Woman's University
Trinity Valley Community College
University of Dallas
University of Houston: Downtown
University of the Incarnate Word

University of Mary Hardin-Baylor
University of North Texas
University of Texas at Arlington
University of Texas at El Paso
University of Texas at San Antonio
Wayland Baptist University
Weatherford College
West Texas A&M University
Wiley College

Utah

Brigham Young University
College of Eastern Utah
Dixie State College of Utah
Salt Lake Community College
Snow College
Southern Utah University
Stevens-Henager College: Ogden
University of Utah
Utah State University
Weber State University
Westminster College

Vermont

Burlington College
Community College of Vermont
Green Mountain College
Johnson State College
St. Michael's College

Virginia

Bryant & Stratton College: Virginia
  Beach
Christendom College
Eastern Mennonite University
George Mason University
J. Sargeant Reynolds Community
  College
James Madison University
Jefferson College of Health Sciences
Liberty University
Old Dominion University
Patrick Henry Community College
Paul D. Camp Community College
St. Paul's College
Shenandoah University
Thomas Nelson Community College
Tidewater Community College
University of Northern Virginia
University of Richmond
University of Virginia's College at Wise
Virginia Commonwealth University
Virginia Union University
Virginia Wesleyan College

Washington

Art Institute of Seattle
Bates Technical College
Bellevue Community College
Central Washington University
Centralia College
City University of Seattle
Clark College
Clover Park Technical College
Edmonds Community College
Everett Community College
Gonzaga University
Grays Harbor College
Heritage University
Highline Community College
Lake Washington Technical College
Lower Columbia College
North Seattle Community College
Olympic College
Pacific Lutheran University
Peninsula College
Saint Martin's University

Seattle Pacific University
Seattle University
South Puget Sound Community College
South Seattle Community College
Spokane Community College
Spokane Falls Community College
Trinity Lutheran College
Walla Walla Community College
Walla Walla University
Washington State University
Wenatchee Valley College
Western Washington University
Whatcom Community College
Whitworth University
Yakima Valley Community College

West Virginia

Alderson-Broaddus College
Appalachian Bible College
Bluefield State College
Concord University
Davis and Elkins College
Glenville State College
Marshall University
Mountain State University
Ohio Valley University
Salem International University
University of Charleston
West Virginia University
West Virginia Wesleyan College
Wheeling Jesuit University

Wisconsin

Beloit College
Concordia University Wisconsin
Edgewood College
Fox Valley Technical College
Lakeland College
Lakeshore Technical College
Marquette University
Milwaukee School of Engineering
Northcentral Technical College
Northland College
St. Norbert College
Silver Lake College
Southwest Wisconsin Technical College
University of Wisconsin-Baraboo/Sauk
  County
University of Wisconsin-Eau Claire
University of Wisconsin-La Crosse
University of Wisconsin-Milwaukee
University of Wisconsin-Platteville
University of Wisconsin-Richland
University of Wisconsin-Rock County
University of Wisconsin-Sheboygan
University of Wisconsin-Stevens Point
University of Wisconsin-Stout
University of Wisconsin-Superior
Viterbo University
Western Technical College

Wyoming

Central Wyoming College
Northwest College
Western Wyoming Community College

SAT Subject Tests required or recommended

Arkansas

John Brown University

California

Deep Springs College*
Harvey Mudd College
Marymount College*
Mills College*
Occidental College*
Stanford University*
University of California: Berkeley
University of California: Davis
University of California: Los Angeles
University of California: Merced
University of California: Riverside
University of California: San Diego
University of California: Santa Barbara
University of California: Santa Cruz
University of the Pacific*
University of Southern California*

Connecticut

Yale University*

District of Columbia

Catholic University of America*
Georgetown University*
Howard University

Georgia

Emory University*

Illinois

Northwestern University*

Indiana

Taylor University Fort Wayne*

Louisiana

Loyola University New Orleans*

Maryland

Hood College*

Massachusetts

Babson College*
Gordon College*
Harvard College
Massachusetts Institute of Technology
Smith College*
Williams College

Michigan

Hillsdale College*

Minnesota

Carleton College*

Montana

University of Great Falls*

New Hampshire

Dartmouth College

New Jersey

Princeton University
Stevens Institute of Technology*

New York

New York University*
Polytechnic University*
Skidmore College*

North Carolina

North Carolina State University*
Wake Forest University*

Ohio

Columbus College of Art and Design*
Ohio Wesleyan University*

Oregon

Reed College

Pennsylvania

Haverford College
Immaculata University*
Susquehanna University*

Puerto Rico

Inter American University of Puerto
  Rico: Barranquitas Campus
University of Puerto Rico: Aguadilla
University of Puerto Rico: Carolina
  Regional College
University of Puerto Rico: Cayey
  University College
University of Puerto Rico: Humacao
University of Puerto Rico: Mayaguez
University of Puerto Rico: Ponce
University of Puerto Rico: Utuado

South Carolina

Voorhees College

Tennessee

Cumberland University*

Texas

Hill College*

Vermont

Bennington College*
Green Mountain College*
Middlebury College

Virginia

Hampden-Sydney College*
University of Mary Washington*
University of Richmond*
University of Virginia
Virginia Union University
Washington and Lee University

Colleges that recommend SAT Subject Tests are noted with an asterisk

Credit/placement for International Baccalaureate (IB)

Alabama

Auburn University at Montgomery
Birmingham-Southern College
Huntingdon College
Jefferson State Community College
Samford University
Shelton State Community College
Southeastern Bible College
Spring Hill College
University of Alabama
University of Alabama at Birmingham
University of Alabama in Huntsville
University of Mobile

Alaska

Alaska Pacific University
Prince William Sound Community
  College
University of Alaska Anchorage
University of Alaska Fairbanks

Arizona

Arizona State University
Arizona State University West
Arizona Western College
Art Institute of Phoenix
Chandler-Gilbert Community College:
  Pecos
Eastern Arizona College
Embry-Riddle Aeronautical University:
  Prescott Campus
Estrella Mountain Community College
Gateway Community College
Grand Canyon University
International Import-Export Institute
Mesa Community College
Mohave Community College
Northcentral University
Northern Arizona University
Prescott College
South Mountain Community College
University of Advancing Technology
University of Arizona
University of Phoenix
Western International University
Yavapai College

Arkansas

Harding University
Hendrix College
John Brown University
Lyon College
Ouachita Baptist University
South Arkansas Community College
University of Arkansas
University of Arkansas at Monticello
University of Arkansas at Pine Bluff
University of Central Arkansas
Williams Baptist College

California

Academy of Art University
Alliant International University
American Jewish University
American River College
Antioch University Santa Barbara
Art Institute of California: Orange
  County
Art Institute of California: San Francisco
Azusa Pacific University
Bethany University
Bethesda Christian University
Biola University
Brooks College
California Baptist University
California College of the Arts
California Institute of the Arts
California Lutheran University
California State University: Chico
California State University: Dominguez
  Hills
California State University: East Bay
California State University: Fresno
California State University: Fullerton
California State University: Long Beach
California State University: Monterey
  Bay
California State University: Sacramento
California State University: San
  Bernardino
California State University: San Marcos
California State University: Stanislaus
Canada College
Chapman University
Charles R. Drew University of Medicine
  and Science
Claremont McKenna College
Cogswell Polytechnical College
College of San Mateo
Concordia University
Dominican University of California
El Camino College
Fashion Institute of Design and
  Merchandising: Los Angeles
Fashion Institute of Design and
  Merchandising: San Diego
Fashion Institute of Design and
  Merchandising: San Francisco
Feather River College
Fresno Pacific University
Golden Gate University
Harvey Mudd College
Holy Names University
Hope International University
Humphreys College
The King's College and Seminary
La Sierra University
Long Beach City College
Los Angeles Valley College
Loyola Marymount University
Marymount College
The Master's College
Menlo College
Mills College
MiraCosta College

Mt. Sierra College
National Hispanic University
Notre Dame de Namur University
Occidental College
Ohlone College
Otis College of Art and Design
Pacific States University
Pacific Union College
Pepperdine University
Pitzer College
Point Loma Nazarene University
Pomona College
St. Mary's College of California
San Diego Christian College
San Diego State University
San Francisco Art Institute
San Francisco State University
San Joaquin Delta College
San Jose City College
Santa Barbara City College
Santa Clara University
Santa Rosa Junior College
Scripps College
Southwestern College
Stanford University
University of California: Irvine
University of California: Los Angeles
University of California: Merced
University of California: Riverside
University of California: San Diego
University of California: Santa Cruz
University of the Pacific
University of Redlands
University of San Diego
University of San Francisco
University of Southern California
Vanguard University of Southern
  California
Westmont College
Whittier College
William Jessup University
Woodbury University
World Mission University

Colorado

Adams State College
Art Institute of Colorado
Colorado Christian University
Colorado College
Colorado Mountain College
Colorado School of Mines
Colorado State University
Colorado State University: Pueblo
Community College of Aurora
Fort Lewis College
Jones International University
Mesa State College
Metropolitan State College of Denver
Naropa University
Pikes Peak Community College
Red Rocks Community College
Regis University
Teikyo Loretto Heights University
University of Colorado at Boulder
University of Colorado at Colorado
  Springs
University of Colorado at Denver
University of Denver
University of Northern Colorado
Western State College of Colorado

Connecticut

Central Connecticut State University
Connecticut College
Fairfield University
Norwalk Community College
Paier College of Art
Quinnipiac University
Sacred Heart University
Trinity College
University of Bridgeport

University of Connecticut
University of New Haven
Wesleyan University
Yale University

Delaware

Goldey-Beacom College
University of Delaware

District of Columbia

American University
Catholic University of America
Corcoran College of Art and Design
George Washington University
Georgetown University
Southeastern University
University of the District of Columbia

Florida

Art Institute of Fort Lauderdale
Baptist College of Florida
Barry University
Bethune-Cookman University
Brevard Community College
Broward Community College
Carlos Albizu University
Central Florida Community College
Chipola Junior College
City College: Fort Lauderdale
Daytona Beach Community College
Eckerd College
Embry-Riddle Aeronautical University
Flagler College
Florida Agricultural and Mechanical
  University
Florida Atlantic University
Florida Christian College
Florida Gulf Coast University
Florida Institute of Technology
Florida International University
Florida Keys Community College
Florida Southern College
Florida State University
Gulf Coast Community College
Hillsborough Community College
Hodges University
Indian River Community College
Jacksonville University
Jones College: Miami
Lake City Community College
Lynn University
Miami Dade College
North Florida Community College
Northwood University: Florida
Nova Southeastern University
Palm Beach Atlantic University
Palm Beach Community College
Pasco-Hernando Community College
Pensacola Junior College
Polk Community College
Ringling College of Art and Design
Rollins College
St. Leo University
St. Petersburg College
Schiller International University
Seminole Community College
South Florida Community College
Southeastern University
Stetson University
Tallahassee Community College
University of Central Florida
University of Florida
University of Miami
University of North Florida
University of South Florida
University of Tampa
University of West Florida
Valencia Community College
Warner Southern College

Webber International University

Georgia

Agnes Scott College
American InterContinental University
Armstrong Atlantic State University
Art Institute of Atlanta
Atlanta Technical College
Berry College
Brenau University
Clark Atlanta University
Clayton State University
Columbus State University
Covenant College
Darton College
Emory University
Georgia College and State University
Georgia Institute of Technology
Georgia Perimeter College
Georgia Southern University
Georgia State University
Herzing College
Kennesaw State University
LaGrange College
Mercer University
Savannah College of Art and Design
Shorter College
South Georgia College
South University
Southern Polytechnic State University
Spelman College
University of Georgia
University of West Georgia
Valdosta State University
Wesleyan College
Young Harris College

Hawaii

Brigham Young University-Hawaii
Chaminade University of Honolulu
Hawaii Pacific University
University of Hawaii at Hilo
University of Hawaii at Manoa
University of Hawaii: West Oahu

Idaho

Brigham Young University-Idaho
College of Idaho
Idaho State University
Lewis-Clark State College
Northwest Nazarene University
University of Idaho

Illinois

Augustana College
Blessing-Rieman College of Nursing
Bradley University
City Colleges of Chicago: Wright
    College
Columbia College Chicago
Concordia University
DePaul University
Dominican University
Elmhurst College
Greenville College
Illinois College
Illinois Institute of Technology
Illinois Wesleyan University
International Academy of Design and
    Technology: Chicago
Knox College
Lake Forest College
Loyola University Chicago
MacCormac College
MacMurray College
McKendree University
Millikin University

Monmouth College
Moody Bible Institute
Morrison Institute of Technology
Morton College
North Central College
North Park University
Northwestern Business College
Northwestern University
Olivet Nazarene University
Quincy University
School of the Art Institute of Chicago
Southern Illinois University Carbondale
Spoon River College
Trinity Christian College
Trinity International University
University of Chicago
University of Illinois at Chicago
University of Illinois at
    Urbana-Champaign
University of Illinois: Springfield
University of St. Francis
Western Illinois University
Wheaton College

Indiana

Ball State University
Bethel College
Butler University
DePauw University
Earlham College
Goshen College
Hanover College
Indiana Institute of Technology
Indiana University Bloomington
Indiana University South Bend
Indiana University Southeast
Indiana University-Purdue University
    Fort Wayne
Indiana University-Purdue University
    Indianapolis
Indiana Wesleyan University
Manchester College
Marian College
Oakland City University
Purdue University
Rose-Hulman Institute of Technology
St. Mary-of-the-Woods College
Saint Mary's College
Tri-State University
University of Evansville
University of Indianapolis
University of Notre Dame
Valparaiso University
Vincennes University

Iowa

Briar Cliff University
Buena Vista University
Central College
Clarke College
Coe College
Cornell College
Drake University
Graceland University
Grand View College
Grinnell College
Iowa State University
Iowa Wesleyan College
Kirkwood Community College
Loras College
Luther College
Maharishi University of Management
Morningside College
Northwestern College
St. Ambrose University
Simpson College
University of Dubuque
University of Iowa
University of Northern Iowa
Upper Iowa University
Waldorf College

William Penn University

Kansas

Baker University
Barclay College
Barton County Community College
Benedictine College
Bethany College
Bethel College
Central Christian College of Kansas
Emporia State University
Friends University
Garden City Community College
Hesston College
Kansas City Kansas Community College
Kansas State University
McPherson College
MidAmerica Nazarene University
Newman University
Ottawa University
Pittsburg State University
Pratt Community College
Tabor College
University of Kansas
University of St. Mary
Wichita State University

Kentucky

Alice Lloyd College
Bellarmine University
Brescia University
Centre College
Georgetown College
Jefferson Community and Technical
    College
Kentucky Christian University
Midway College
Owensboro Community and Technical
    College
Sullivan University
Thomas More College
Transylvania University
University of the Cumberlands
University of Kentucky
University of Louisville
Western Kentucky University

Louisiana

Centenary College of Louisiana
Dillard University
Louisiana State University and
    Agricultural and Mechanical College
Loyola University New Orleans
St. Joseph Seminary College
Tulane University
University of New Orleans

Maine

Bates College
Bowdoin College
Central Maine Community College
Colby College
College of the Atlantic
Husson College
Unity College
University of Maine
University of Maine at Farmington
University of Maine at Fort Kent
University of New England
University of Southern Maine
Washington County Community College

Maryland

Baltimore City Community College
Baltimore Hebrew University

College of Notre Dame of Maryland
Coppin State University
Frostburg State University
Goucher College
Griggs University
Harford Community College
Hood College
Howard Community College
Johns Hopkins University
Johns Hopkins University: Peabody
    Conservatory of Music
Loyola College in Maryland
Maryland Institute College of Art
McDaniel College
Mount St. Mary's University
St. Mary's College of Maryland
Salisbury University
Towson University
University of Baltimore
University of Maryland: Baltimore
    County
University of Maryland: College Park
University of Maryland: Eastern Shore
University of Maryland: University
    College
Villa Julie College
Washington College

Massachusetts

American International College
Amherst College
Assumption College
Atlantic Union College
Babson College
Bay Path College
Bay State College
Becker College
Benjamin Franklin Institute of
    Technology
Bentley College
Berkshire Community College
Boston College
Boston University
Brandeis University
Bridgewater State College
Clark University
College of the Holy Cross
Dean College
Eastern Nazarene College
Elms College
Emerson College
Emmanuel College
Endicott College
Fisher College
Framingham State College
Gordon College
Hampshire College
Harvard College
Hellenic College/Holy Cross
Lasell College
Lesley University
Massachusetts Bay Community College
Massachusetts College of Art
Massachusetts College of Liberal Arts
Massachusetts College of Pharmacy and
    Health Sciences
Massachusetts Institute of Technology
Massachusetts Maritime Academy
Merrimack College
Mount Holyoke College
Mount Wachusett Community College
New England Conservatory of Music
Newbury College
Northeastern University
Pine Manor College
Quinsigamond Community College
Regis College
Simmons College
Smith College
Springfield College
Stonehill College
Suffolk University
Tufts University

University of Massachusetts Amherst
University of Massachusetts Dartmouth
Wellesley College
Wentworth Institute of Technology
Western New England College
Wheaton College
Williams College
Worcester Polytechnic Institute

Michigan

Adrian College
Albion College
Alma College
Andrews University
Baker College of Auburn Hills
Baker College of Cadillac
Baker College of Jackson
Baker College of Muskegon
Baker College of Owosso
Baker College of Port Huron
Calvin College
Central Michigan University
College for Creative Studies
Concordia University
Cornerstone University
Davenport University
Delta College
Eastern Michigan University
Finlandia University
Grand Valley State University
Hillsdale College
Hope College
Kalamazoo College
Kellogg Community College
Kettering University
Lake Superior State University
Lansing Community College
Lawrence Technological University
Madonna University
Michigan Jewish Institute
Michigan State University
Michigan Technological University
North Central Michigan College
Northern Michigan University
Northwood University: Michigan
Oakland University
Rochester College
Saginaw Valley State University
Spring Arbor University
University of Michigan
Walsh College of Accountancy and
    Business Administration
Wayne State University
Western Michigan University

Minnesota

Augsburg College
Bethany Lutheran College
Bethel University
Carleton College
Central Lakes College
Century Community and Technical
    College
College of St. Benedict
College of St. Catherine
College of St. Scholastica
Concordia College: Moorhead
Concordia University: St. Paul
Dunwoody College of Technology
Gustavus Adolphus College
Hamline University
Hibbing Community College
Inver Hills Community College
Itasca Community College
Macalester College
Minneapolis College of Art and Design
Minneapolis Community and Technical
    College
Minnesota State College - Southeast
    Technical

Minnesota State Community and
    Technical College: Fergus Falls
Minnesota State University: Mankato
Normandale Community College
North Hennepin Community College
Northwest Technical College
Northwestern College
Rainy River Community College
Saint Cloud State University
St. John's University
St. Mary's University of Minnesota
St. Olaf College
St. Paul College
South Central College
University of Minnesota: Crookston
University of Minnesota: Duluth
University of Minnesota: Morris
University of Minnesota: Twin Cities
University of St. Thomas
Winona State University

Mississippi

Belhaven College
Millsaps College
Mississippi College
Mississippi State University
Tougaloo College
University of Mississippi
William Carey University

Missouri

Avila University
Calvary Bible College and Theological
    Seminary
Central Methodist University
College of the Ozarks
Columbia College
Cottey College
Culver-Stockton College
Drury University
Evangel University
Grantham University
Lindenwood University
Maryville University of Saint Louis
Missouri Southern State University
Missouri State University
Missouri University of Science and
    Technology
Moberly Area Community College
Northwest Missouri State University
Ozarks Technical Community College
Research College of Nursing
Rockhurst University
Saint Louis University
Southwest Baptist University
Stephens College
Truman State University
University of Central Missouri
University of Missouri: Columbia
University of Missouri: Kansas City
University of Missouri: St. Louis
Washington University in St. Louis
Webster University
Westminster College
William Jewell College
William Woods University

Montana

Carroll College
Flathead Valley Community College
Montana State University: Bozeman
Montana Tech of the University of
    Montana
Rocky Mountain College
University of Great Falls

Nebraska

Bellevue University
College of Saint Mary
Concordia University
Creighton University
Dana College
Doane College
Hastings College
Nebraska Wesleyan University
Peru State College
Union College
University of Nebraska - Lincoln
Western Nebraska Community College
York College

Nevada

Art Institute of Las Vegas
Sierra Nevada College
University of Nevada: Las Vegas
University of Nevada: Reno

New Hampshire

Colby-Sawyer College
Daniel Webster College
Dartmouth College
Franklin Pierce University
Hesser College
Lakes Region Community College
New England College
Rivier College
St. Anselm College
Southern New Hampshire University
University of New Hampshire
University of New Hampshire at
    Manchester

New Jersey

Caldwell College
Centenary College
The College of New Jersey
College of St. Elizabeth
Drew University
Felician College
Hudson County Community College
Kean University
Monmouth University
Montclair State University
New Jersey City University
Princeton University
Ramapo College of New Jersey
Richard Stockton College of New Jersey
Rowan University
Rutgers, The State University of New
    Jersey: Camden Regional Campus
Rutgers, The State University of New
    Jersey: New Brunswick/Piscataway
    Campus
Rutgers, The State University of New
    Jersey: Newark Regional Campus
Saint Peter's College
Seton Hall University
Stevens Institute of Technology
Sussex County Community College
University of Medicine and Dentistry of
    New Jersey: School of Health Related
    Professions

New Mexico

College of the Southwest
Eastern New Mexico University: Roswell
    Campus
Northern New Mexico College
University of New Mexico
Western New Mexico University

New York

Adelphi University
Adirondack Community College
Alfred University
Bard College
Barnard College
Canisius College
Cazenovia College
City University of New York: Baruch
    College
City University of New York: Bronx
    Community College
City University of New York: Brooklyn
    College
City University of New York: City
    College
City University of New York: College of
    Staten Island
City University of New York: CUNY
    Online
City University of New York: Hunter
    College
City University of New York: Lehman
    College
City University of New York: Medgar
    Evers College
City University of New York: York
    College
Clarkson University
Clinton Community College
Colgate University
College of Mount St. Vincent
College of Saint Rose
Columbia University
Concordia College
Cornell University
Daemen College
Dominican College of Blauvelt
Dowling College
D'Youville College
Elmira College
Eugene Lang College The New School
    for Liberal Arts
Fashion Institute of Technology
Fordham University
Genesee Community College
Hamilton College
Hartwick College
Hobart and William Smith Colleges
Hofstra University
Houghton College
Ithaca College
King's College
Le Moyne College
Long Island University: Brooklyn
    Campus
Long Island University: C. W. Post
    Campus
Manhattanville College
Marist College
Marymount Manhattan College
Medaille College
Metropolitan College of New York
Molloy College
Monroe College
Nassau Community College
Nazareth College of Rochester
New York Institute of Technology
New York School of Interior Design
New York University
Niagara County Community College
Pace University
Parsons The New School for Design
Paul Smith's College
Polytechnic University
Rensselaer Polytechnic Institute
Roberts Wesleyan College
Rochester Institute of Technology
Rockland Community College
Russell Sage College
Sage College of Albany
Saint Bonaventure University
St. Francis College

St. John Fisher College
St. John's University
St. Joseph's College: Suffolk Campus
St. Lawrence University
St. Thomas Aquinas College
Sarah Lawrence College
School of Visual Arts
Siena College
Skidmore College
State University of New York at Albany
State University of New York at Binghamton
State University of New York at Buffalo
State University of New York at New Paltz
State University of New York at Oswego
State University of New York at Stony Brook
State University of New York College at Brockport
State University of New York College at Buffalo
State University of New York College at Cortland
State University of New York College at Fredonia
State University of New York College at Geneseo
State University of New York College at Old Westbury
State University of New York College at Oneonta
State University of New York College at Plattsburgh
State University of New York College at Potsdam
State University of New York College of Environmental Science and Forestry
State University of New York College of Technology at Alfred
State University of New York College of Technology at Canton
State University of New York College of Technology at Delhi
State University of New York Empire State College
State University of New York Institute of Technology at Utica/Rome
State University of New York Maritime College
Suffolk County Community College
Syracuse University
Tompkins-Cortland Community College
Union College
University of Rochester
Utica College
Vassar College
Vaughn College of Aeronautics and Technology
Wagner College
Wells College
Westchester Community College

North Carolina

Appalachian State University
Barton College
Belmont Abbey College
Brevard College
Campbell University
Catawba College
Chowan University
Davidson College
Duke University
East Carolina University
Elizabeth City State University
Elon University
Gardner-Webb University
Greensboro College
Guilford College
Guilford Technical Community College
High Point University
John Wesley College
Lees-McRae College

Lenoir-Rhyne College
Louisburg College
Mars Hill College
Meredith College
Methodist University
Montreat College
Nash Community College
North Carolina State University
Peace College
Pfeiffer University
Queens University of Charlotte
St. Andrews Presbyterian College
St. Augustine's College
Salem College
University of North Carolina at Asheville
University of North Carolina at Chapel Hill
University of North Carolina at Charlotte
University of North Carolina at Wilmington
Wake Forest University
Wake Technical Community College
Western Carolina University
Wingate University
Winston-Salem State University

North Dakota

Jamestown College
North Dakota State University
University of Mary
University of North Dakota

Ohio

Ashland University
Baldwin-Wallace College
Bryant & Stratton College: Parma
Capital University
Case Western Reserve University
Cedarville University
Central Ohio Technical College
Cincinnati Christian University
Cincinnati State Technical and Community College
Cleveland Institute of Art
Cleveland Institute of Music
Cleveland State University
College of Mount St. Joseph
College of Wooster
Columbus State Community College
Defiance College
Denison University
Franciscan University of Steubenville
Heidelberg College
Hiram College
John Carroll University
Kent State University
Kenyon College
Lake Erie College
Laura and Alvin Siegal College of Judaic Studies
Malone College
Marietta College
Miami University: Hamilton Campus
Miami University: Middletown Campus
Miami University: Oxford Campus
Mount Union College
Mount Vernon Nazarene University
Muskingum College
Oberlin College
Ohio Dominican University
Ohio Northern University
Ohio State University: Columbus Campus
Ohio University
Ohio Wesleyan University
Otterbein College
Sinclair Community College
Tiffin University
University of Akron
University of Cincinnati: Clermont College

University of Dayton
Wilmington College
Wittenberg University
Wright State University: Lake Campus
Xavier University
Youngstown State University

Oklahoma

Cameron University
Northeastern State University
Oklahoma Baptist University
Oklahoma Christian University
Oklahoma City Community College
Oklahoma City University
Oklahoma State University
Rose State College
St. Gregory's University
Southeastern Oklahoma State University
Southern Nazarene University
Southwestern Oklahoma State University
University of Oklahoma
University of Tulsa

Oregon

Art Institute of Portland
Chemeketa Community College
Eastern Oregon University
George Fox University
Lewis & Clark College
Linfield College
Marylhurst University
Northwest Christian College
Oregon Health & Science University
Oregon State University
Pacific University
Reed College
Southern Oregon University
University of Oregon
University of Portland
Western Oregon University
Willamette University

Pennsylvania

Albright College
Allegheny College
Alvernia College
Arcadia University
Art Institute of Philadelphia
Baptist Bible College of Pennsylvania
Bryn Mawr College
Bucknell University
Cabrini College
California University of Pennsylvania
Career Training Academy
Carlow University
Carnegie Mellon University
Cedar Crest College
Central Pennsylvania College
Chatham University
Chestnut Hill College
Clarion University of Pennsylvania
Dickinson College
Drexel University
Duquesne University
Eastern University
Elizabethtown College
Franklin & Marshall College
Gannon University
Geneva College
Gettysburg College
Grove City College
Harrisburg Area Community College
Haverford College
Holy Family University
Immaculata University
Indiana University of Pennsylvania
Juniata College
Keystone College
King's College

Kutztown University of Pennsylvania
Lackawanna College
Lebanon Valley College
Lehigh University
Lincoln University
Lock Haven University of Pennsylvania
Lycoming College
Mansfield University of Pennsylvania
Marywood University
Mercyhurst College
Messiah College
Misericordia University
Moravian College
Muhlenberg College
Peirce College
Penn State Abington
Penn State Altoona
Penn State Beaver
Penn State Berks
Penn State Brandywine
Penn State Dubois
Penn State Erie, The Behrend College
Penn State Fayette, The Eberly Campus
Penn State Greater Allegheny
Penn State Harrisburg
Penn State Hazleton
Penn State Lehigh Valley
Penn State Mont Alto
Penn State New Kensington
Penn State Schuylkill
Penn State Shenango
Penn State University Park
Penn State Wilkes-Barre
Penn State Worthington Scranton
Penn State York
Philadelphia Biblical University
Point Park University
Rosemont College
St. Francis University
Saint Joseph's University
St. Vincent College
Seton Hill University
Shippensburg University of Pennsylvania
Slippery Rock University of Pennsylvania
Susquehanna University
Swarthmore College
Temple University
Thiel College
University of the Arts
University of Pennsylvania
University of Pittsburgh
University of Pittsburgh at Bradford
University of Pittsburgh at Johnstown
University of the Sciences in Philadelphia
University of Scranton
Ursinus College
Villanova University
Washington & Jefferson College
Waynesburg University
West Chester University of Pennsylvania
Widener University
Wilson College
York College of Pennsylvania

Puerto Rico

University of Puerto Rico: Arecibo

Rhode Island

Bryant University
Providence College
Rhode Island School of Design
Roger Williams University
Salve Regina University

South Carolina

Anderson University
Charleston Southern University

Clemson University
Coastal Carolina University
Coker College
College of Charleston
Columbia College
Columbia International University
Converse College
Erskine College
Florence-Darlington Technical College
Furman University
Greenville Technical College
Lander University
Newberry College
North Greenville University
Piedmont Technical College
Trident Technical College
University of South Carolina
University of South Carolina at Lancaster
University of South Carolina Upstate
Voorhees College
Winthrop University
Wofford College

South Dakota

Augustana College
Dakota Wesleyan University
Mount Marty College
National American University: Rapid City
Northern State University
South Dakota School of Mines and Technology
South Dakota State University

Tennessee

Belmont University
Bryan College
Christian Brothers University
Crichton College
East Tennessee State University
Free Will Baptist Bible College
Freed-Hardeman University
Lambuth University
Lee University
LeMoyne-Owen College
Lincoln Memorial University
Lipscomb University
Maryville College
Memphis College of Art
Middle Tennessee State University
Milligan College
Pellissippi State Technical Community College
Rhodes College
Tennessee Technological University
Tennessee Temple University
Tennessee Wesleyan College
Trevecca Nazarene University
Union University
University of Memphis
University of the South
University of Tennessee: Knoxville
Vanderbilt University

Texas

Abilene Christian University
Austin College
Baylor University
Blinn College
Brookhaven College
Central Texas College
Concordia University at Austin
Dallas Baptist University
Del Mar College
East Texas Baptist University
Eastfield College
El Centro College
Frank Phillips College
Houston Baptist University

Lamar Institute of Technology
LeTourneau University
Lon Morris College
Lone Star College System
Lubbock Christian University
McMurry University
Midland College
Midwestern State University
Mountain View College
Northwood University: Texas
Our Lady of the Lake University of San Antonio
Rice University
St. Edward's University
Sam Houston State University
San Antonio College
Schreiner University
Southern Methodist University
Southwestern Adventist University
Southwestern University
Stephen F. Austin State University
Texas A&M International University
Texas A&M University
Texas A&M University-Commerce
Texas A&M University-Galveston
Texas A&M University-Texarkana
Texas Christian University
Texas Lutheran University
Texas State Technical College: Waco
Texas State University: San Marcos
Texas Tech University
Trinity University
University of Dallas
University of Houston
University of Mary Hardin-Baylor
University of North Texas
University of St. Thomas
University of Texas at Arlington
University of Texas at Austin
University of Texas at Brownsville
University of Texas at Dallas
University of Texas at El Paso
University of Texas at Tyler
University of Texas Medical Branch at Galveston
University of Texas: Pan American
Victoria College
Wayland Baptist University
West Texas A&M University

Utah

Brigham Young University
Salt Lake Community College
University of Utah
Utah State University
Utah Valley State College
Weber State University
Westminster College

Vermont

Bennington College
Burlington College
Champlain College
College of St. Joseph in Vermont
Green Mountain College
Lyndon State College
Marlboro College
Middlebury College
New England Culinary Institute
St. Michael's College
University of Vermont

Virginia

Art Institute of Washington
Averett University
Bluefield College
Bridgewater College
Central Virginia Community College
Christopher Newport University

College of William and Mary
Eastern Mennonite University
Emory & Henry College
Ferrum College
George Mason University
Hampden-Sydney College
Hampton University
Hollins University
J. Sargeant Reynolds Community College
James Madison University
Jefferson College of Health Sciences
Liberty University
Longwood University
Lynchburg College
Mary Baldwin College
Marymount University
Northern Virginia Community College
Old Dominion University
Radford University
Randolph College
Randolph-Macon College
Regent University
Roanoke College
Shenandoah University
Southern Virginia University
Sweet Briar College
University of Mary Washington
University of Northern Virginia
University of Richmond
University of Virginia
University of Virginia's College at Wise
Virginia Commonwealth University
Virginia Intermont College
Virginia Military Institute
Virginia Polytechnic Institute and State University
Virginia Union University
Virginia Wesleyan College
Washington and Lee University

Washington

Art Institute of Seattle
Bates Technical College
Central Washington University
Centralia College
City University of Seattle
Clark College
Columbia Basin College
DigiPen Institute of Technology
Everett Community College
Evergreen State College
Gonzaga University
North Seattle Community College
Northwest University
Olympic College
Pacific Lutheran University
Saint Martin's University
Seattle Pacific University
Seattle University
South Puget Sound Community College
South Seattle Community College
Tacoma Community College
Trinity Lutheran College
University of Puget Sound
University of Washington
Walla Walla University
Washington State University
Western Washington University
Whitman College
Whitworth University
Yakima Valley Community College

West Virginia

Bethany College
Bluefield State College
Davis and Elkins College
Fairmont State University
Marshall University
Mountain State University
Ohio Valley University

Salem International University
Shepherd University
University of Charleston
West Virginia University
West Virginia Wesleyan College

Wisconsin

Alverno College
Beloit College
Cardinal Stritch University
Carroll College
Carthage College
Concordia University Wisconsin
Edgewood College
Lakeland College
Lawrence University
Marian College of Fond du Lac
Marquette University
Milwaukee School of Engineering
Mount Mary College
Northcentral Technical College
Northland College
St. Norbert College
Silver Lake College
University of Wisconsin-Baraboo/Sauk County
University of Wisconsin-Eau Claire
University of Wisconsin-Green Bay
University of Wisconsin-La Crosse
University of Wisconsin-Madison
University of Wisconsin-Marathon County
University of Wisconsin-Oshkosh
University of Wisconsin-Parkside
University of Wisconsin-Richland
University of Wisconsin-River Falls
University of Wisconsin-Sheboygan
University of Wisconsin-Stevens Point
University of Wisconsin-Stout
University of Wisconsin-Superior
University of Wisconsin-Washington County
University of Wisconsin-Whitewater
Viterbo University

Wyoming

Casper College
Eastern Wyoming College
Laramie County Community College
University of Wyoming
Western Wyoming Community College

Credit/placement for Advanced Placement (AP)

Alabama

Alabama Agricultural and Mechanical
  University
Alabama State University
Andrew Jackson University
Athens State University
Auburn University
Auburn University at Montgomery
Birmingham-Southern College
Calhoun Community College
Faulkner University
George C. Wallace Community College
  at Dothan
Heritage Christian University
Huntingdon College
Jacksonville State University
Jefferson State Community College
Judson College
Lawson State Community College
Marion Military Institute
Oakwood University
Samford University
Shelton State Community College
Southeastern Bible College
Spring Hill College
Stillman College
Troy University
Tuskegee University
University of Alabama
University of Alabama at Birmingham
University of Alabama in Huntsville
University of Mobile
University of Montevallo
University of North Alabama
University of South Alabama
University of West Alabama

Alaska

Alaska Pacific University
Prince William Sound Community
  College
University of Alaska Anchorage
University of Alaska Fairbanks
University of Alaska Southeast

Arizona

Arizona State University
Arizona State University West
Arizona Western College
Art Center Design College
Art Institute of Phoenix
Central Arizona College
Chandler-Gilbert Community College:
  Pecos
Cochise College
Eastern Arizona College
Embry-Riddle Aeronautical University:
  Prescott Campus
Everest College: Phoenix
Gateway Community College
Glendale Community College
Grand Canyon University
Northcentral University
Northern Arizona University
Paradise Valley Community College
Pima Community College
Prescott College

Rio Salado College
Scottsdale Community College
University of Advancing Technology
University of Arizona
University of Phoenix
Western International University
Yavapai College

Arkansas

Arkansas State University
Arkansas State University: Mountain
  Home
Arkansas State University: Newport
Arkansas Tech University
East Arkansas Community College
Harding University
Henderson State University
Hendrix College
John Brown University
Lyon College
National Park Community College
Ouachita Baptist University
Ouachita Technical College
Philander Smith College
Pulaski Technical College
South Arkansas Community College
Southeast Arkansas College
Southern Arkansas University
Southern Arkansas University Tech
University of Arkansas
University of Arkansas at Fort Smith
University of Arkansas at Little Rock
University of Arkansas at Monticello
University of Central Arkansas
University of the Ozarks
Williams Baptist College

California

Academy of Art University
Allan Hancock College
Alliant International University
American Academy of Dramatic Arts:
  West
American Jewish University
American River College
Antelope Valley College
Antioch University Los Angeles
Antioch University Santa Barbara
Art Institute of California: San Diego
Art Institute of California: San Francisco
Azusa Pacific University
Barstow Community College
Bethany University
Biola University
Cabrillo College
California Baptist University
California College of the Arts
California Design College
California Institute of the Arts
California Institute of Integral Studies
California Lutheran University
California Maritime Academy
California Polytechnic State University:
  San Luis Obispo
California School of Culinary Arts
California State Polytechnic University:
  Pomona
California State University: Channel
  Islands

California State University: Chico
California State University: Dominguez
  Hills
California State University: East Bay
California State University: Fresno
California State University: Fullerton
California State University: Long Beach
California State University: Los Angeles
California State University: Monterey
  Bay
California State University: Sacramento
California State University: San
  Bernardino
California State University: San Marcos
California State University: Stanislaus
California University of Management and
  Sciences
Canada College
Cerro Coso Community College
Chapman University
Charles R. Drew University of Medicine
  and Science
Citrus College
City College of San Francisco
Claremont McKenna College
Coastline Community College
Cogswell Polytechnical College
Coleman College
College of the Canyons
College of San Mateo
College of the Siskiyous
Columbia College
Columbia College: Hollywood
Concordia University
Copper Mountain College
Crafton Hills College
Cuyamaca College
Diablo Valley College
Dominican University of California
East Los Angeles College
Evergreen Valley College
Fashion Institute of Design and
  Merchandising: Los Angeles
Fashion Institute of Design and
  Merchandising: San Diego
Fashion Institute of Design and
  Merchandising: San Francisco
Feather River College
Foothill College
Fresno City College
Fresno Pacific University
Fullerton College
Glendale Community College
Golden Gate University
Golden West College
Grossmont College
Harvey Mudd College
Holy Names University
Hope International University
Humphreys College
John F. Kennedy University
The King's College and Seminary
La Sierra University
Lassen College
Life Pacific College
Loma Linda University
Long Beach City College
Los Angeles Harbor College
Los Angeles Valley College
Loyola Marymount University
Maric College: Panorama City
Marymount College
The Master's College
Menlo College
Mills College
MiraCosta College
Modesto Junior College
Moorpark College
Mount San Jacinto College
National University
NewSchool of Architecture & Design
Northwestern Polytechnic University
Notre Dame de Namur University
Occidental College
Orange Coast College

Otis College of Art and Design
Pacific Union College
Palo Verde College
Palomar College
Patten University
Pepperdine University
Pitzer College
Platt College: San Diego
Point Loma Nazarene University
Pomona College
Reedley College
Riverside Community College
Saddleback College
St. Mary's College of California
San Bernardino Valley College
San Diego Christian College
San Diego City College
San Diego State University
San Francisco Art Institute
San Francisco Conservatory of Music
San Francisco State University
San Joaquin Delta College
San Jose State University
Santa Ana College
Santa Barbara City College
Santa Clara University
Santa Monica College
Santa Rosa Junior College
School of Urban Missions: Oakland
Scripps College
Sierra College
Simpson University
Solano Community College
Sonoma State University
Southern California Institute of
  Architecture
Southwestern College
Stanford University
Taft College
University of California: Berkeley
University of California: Davis
University of California: Irvine
University of California: Los Angeles
University of California: Merced
University of California: Riverside
University of California: San Diego
University of California: Santa Barbara
University of California: Santa Cruz
University of La Verne
University of the Pacific
University of Redlands
University of San Diego
University of San Francisco
University of Southern California
Vanguard University of Southern
  California
Ventura College
West Hills College: Coalinga
West Hills College: Lemoore
Westmont College
Westwood College: Anaheim
Whittier College
William Jessup University
Woodbury University

Colorado

Adams State College
Aims Community College
American Sentinel University
Arapahoe Community College
Colorado Christian University
Colorado College
Colorado Mountain College
Colorado Northwestern Community
  College
Colorado School of Mines
Colorado State University
Colorado State University: Pueblo
Community College of Denver
Everest College: Aurora
Everest College: Colorado Springs
Fort Lewis College
Institute of Business & Medical Careers

IntelliTec College
Mesa State College
Metropolitan State College of Denver
Morgan Community College
Naropa University
National American University: Denver
Northeastern Junior College
Otero Junior College
Pueblo Community College
Red Rocks Community College
Regis University
Remington College: Colorado Springs
Trinidad State Junior College
University of Colorado at Boulder
University of Colorado at Colorado
  Springs
University of Colorado at Denver
University of Denver
University of Northern Colorado
Western State College of Colorado

Connecticut

Albertus Magnus College
Briarwood College
Capital Community College
Central Connecticut State University
Charter Oak State College
Clemens College
Connecticut College
Eastern Connecticut State University
Fairfield University
Gateway Community College
Goodwin College
Holy Apostles College and Seminary
Manchester Community College
Mitchell College
Naugatuck Valley Community College
Norwalk Community College
Paier College of Art
Post University
Quinnipiac University
Sacred Heart University
Southern Connecticut State University
Trinity College
University of Bridgeport
University of Connecticut
University of New Haven
Wesleyan University
Yale University

Delaware

Delaware State University
Goldey-Beacom College
University of Delaware
Wesley College

District of Columbia

American University
Catholic University of America
Corcoran College of Art and Design
Gallaudet University
George Washington University
Georgetown University
Howard University
Southeastern University
Trinity Washington University
University of the District of Columbia

Florida

Angley College
Art Institute of Fort Lauderdale
Ave Maria University
Baptist College of Florida
Barry University
Bethune-Cookman University
Brevard Community College
Broward Community College

Central Florida Community College
Chipola Junior College
Daytona Beach Community College
Eckerd College
Edward Waters College
Embry-Riddle Aeronautical University
Everest University: Brandon
Flagler College
Florida Agricultural and Mechanical
  University
Florida Atlantic University
Florida Christian College
Florida Community College at
  Jacksonville
Florida Gulf Coast University
Florida Institute of Technology
Florida International University
Florida Keys Community College
Florida Memorial University
Florida National College
Florida Southern College
Florida State University
Full Sail University
Gulf Coast Community College
Hillsborough Community College
Hodges University
Indian River Community College
International Academy of Design and
  Technology: Orlando
International Academy of Design and
  Technology: Tampa
Jacksonville University
Jones College
Jones College: Miami
Lake-Sumter Community College
Lynn University
Manatee Community College
Miami Dade College
Miami International University of Art
  and Design
New College of Florida
North Florida Community College
Northwood University: Florida
Nova Southeastern University
Okaloosa-Walton College
Palm Beach Atlantic University
Palm Beach Community College
Pasco-Hernando Community College
Pensacola Junior College
Polk Community College
Ringling College of Art and Design
Rollins College
St. Leo University
St. Petersburg College
Saint Thomas University
Santa Fe Community College
Schiller International University
Seminole Community College
South Florida Community College
Southeastern University
Southwest Florida College
Stetson University
Tallahassee Community College
Trinity College of Florida
University of Central Florida
University of Florida
University of Miami
University of North Florida
University of South Florida
University of Tampa
University of West Florida
Valencia Community College
Warner Southern College
Webber International University

Georgia

Abraham Baldwin Agricultural College
Agnes Scott College
Albany Technical College
Andrew College
Armstrong Atlantic State University
Atlanta Metropolitan College
Atlanta Technical College

Augusta State University
Bauder College
Berry College
Brenau University
Brewton-Parker College
Clark Atlanta University
Clayton State University
Coastal Georgia Community College
Columbus State University
Columbus Technical College
Covenant College
Darton College
DeKalb Technical College
Emory University
Gainesville State College
Georgia College and State University
Georgia Highlands College
Georgia Institute of Technology
Georgia Military College
Georgia Perimeter College
Georgia Southern University
Georgia Southwestern State University
Georgia State University
Gordon College
Kennesaw State University
LaGrange College
Le Cordon Bleu College of Culinary Arts
Life University
Mercer University
Middle Georgia College
Middle Georgia Technical College
Morehouse College
North Georgia College & State
  University
Oglethorpe University
Paine College
Piedmont College
Reinhardt College
Savannah College of Art and Design
Savannah State University
Savannah Technical College
Shorter College
South Georgia College
South University
Southern Polytechnic State University
Spelman College
Thomas University
Toccoa Falls College
Truett-McConnell College
University of Georgia
University of West Georgia
Valdosta State University
Wesleyan College
Young Harris College

Hawaii

Brigham Young University-Hawaii
Chaminade University of Honolulu
Hawaii Pacific University
University of Hawaii at Manoa
University of Hawaii: Honolulu
  Community College
University of Hawaii: Kauai Community
  College
University of Hawaii: West Oahu

Idaho

Boise State University
Brigham Young University-Idaho
College of Idaho
College of Southern Idaho
Idaho State University
Lewis-Clark State College
Northwest Nazarene University
University of Idaho

Illinois

Augustana College
Aurora University

Benedictine University
Black Hawk College
Blackburn College
Bradley University
Carl Sandburg College
Chicago State University
City Colleges of Chicago: Harold
  Washington College
City Colleges of Chicago: Kennedy-King
  College
City Colleges of Chicago: Malcolm X
  College
City Colleges of Chicago: Olive-Harvey
  College
City Colleges of Chicago: Richard J.
  Daley College
City Colleges of Chicago: Wright
  College
College of DuPage
College of Lake County
College of Office Technology
Columbia College Chicago
Concordia University
Cooking & Hospitality Institute of
  Chicago
DePaul University
Dominican University
Eastern Illinois University
Elgin Community College
Elmhurst College
Eureka College
Governors State University
Greenville College
Harper College
Heartland Community College
Highland Community College
Illinois Central College
Illinois College
Illinois Eastern Community Colleges:
  Frontier Community College
Illinois Eastern Community Colleges:
  Lincoln Trail College
Illinois Eastern Community Colleges:
  Olney Central College
Illinois Eastern Community Colleges:
  Wabash Valley College
Illinois Institute of Technology
Illinois State University
Illinois Wesleyan University
International Academy of Design and
  Technology: Chicago
John Wood Community College
Joliet Junior College
Judson University
Kankakee Community College
Kishwaukee College
Knox College
Lake Forest College
Lake Land College
Lewis University
Lexington College
Lincoln Christian College and Seminary
Lincoln Land Community College
Loyola University Chicago
MacMurray College
McHenry County College
McKendree University
Millikin University
Monmouth College
Moody Bible Institute
Moraine Valley Community College
Morrison Institute of Technology
Morton College
National-Louis University
North Central College
North Park University
Northern Illinois University
Northwestern Business College
Northwestern University
Oakton Community College
Olivet Nazarene University
Parkland College
Quincy University
Richland Community College
Robert Morris College: Chicago

195

Rock Valley College
Rockford College
Roosevelt University
Rosalind Franklin University of Medicine and Science
St. Xavier University
Sauk Valley Community College
School of the Art Institute of Chicago
Southeastern Illinois College
Southern Illinois University Carbondale
Southern Illinois University Edwardsville
Spoon River College
Springfield College in Illinois
Trinity Christian College
Trinity International University
Triton College
University of Chicago
University of Illinois at Chicago
University of Illinois at Urbana-Champaign
University of Illinois: Springfield
University of St. Francis
Western Illinois University
Westwood College: O'Hare Airport
Wheaton College

Indiana

Ball State University
Butler University
Calumet College of St. Joseph
DePauw University
Earlham College
Franklin College
Goshen College
Hanover College
Holy Cross College
Huntington University
Indiana Institute of Technology
Indiana State University
Indiana University Bloomington
Indiana University East
Indiana University Kokomo
Indiana University Northwest
Indiana University South Bend
Indiana University Southeast
Indiana University-Purdue University Fort Wayne
Indiana University-Purdue University Indianapolis
Indiana Wesleyan University
Ivy Tech Community College: Bloomington
Ivy Tech Community College: Central Indiana
Ivy Tech Community College: Columbus
Ivy Tech Community College: East Central
Ivy Tech Community College: Kokomo
Ivy Tech Community College: Lafayette
Ivy Tech Community College: North Central
Ivy Tech Community College: Northeast
Ivy Tech Community College: Northwest
Ivy Tech Community College: Richmond
Ivy Tech Community College: South Central
Ivy Tech Community College: Southeast
Ivy Tech Community College: Southwest
Ivy Tech Community College: Wabash Valley
Manchester College
Marian College
Oakland City University
Purdue University
Purdue University Calumet
Rose-Hulman Institute of Technology
St. Mary-of-the-Woods College
Saint Mary's College
Taylor University
Taylor University Fort Wayne
Tri-State University
University of Evansville
University of Indianapolis

University of Notre Dame
University of Southern Indiana
University of St. Francis
Valparaiso University
Vincennes University
Wabash College

Iowa

AIB College of Business
Ashford University
Briar Cliff University
Buena Vista University
Central College
Clarke College
Clinton Community College
Coe College
Cornell College
Des Moines Area Community College
Divine Word College
Drake University
Ellsworth Community College
Faith Baptist Bible College and Theological Seminary
Graceland University
Grand View College
Grinnell College
Hawkeye Community College
Indian Hills Community College
Iowa Central Community College
Iowa State University
Iowa Wesleyan College
Kaplan University: Cedar Falls
Kaplan University: Cedar Rapids
Kaplan University: Des Moines
Loras College
Luther College
Maharishi University of Management
Marshalltown Community College
Morningside College
Mount Mercy College
Muscatine Community College
North Iowa Area Community College
Northeast Iowa Community College
Northwestern College
St. Ambrose University
St. Luke's College
Scott Community College
Simpson College
Southeastern Community College: North Campus
Southwestern Community College
University of Dubuque
University of Iowa
University of Northern Iowa
Upper Iowa University
Waldorf College
Wartburg College
Western Iowa Tech Community College
William Penn University

Kansas

Allen County Community College
Baker University
Barclay College
Barton County Community College
Benedictine College
Bethany College
Bethel College
Butler County Community College
Central Christian College of Kansas
Cloud County Community College
Coffeyville Community College
Colby Community College
Cowley County Community College
Emporia State University
Fort Hays State University
Garden City Community College
Hesston College
Hutchinson Community College
Kansas City Kansas Community College
Kansas State University

Kansas Wesleyan University
Labette Community College
Manhattan Area Technical College
McPherson College
MidAmerica Nazarene University
Newman University
Ottawa University
Pittsburg State University
Pratt Community College
Southwestern College
Sterling College
Tabor College
University of Kansas
University of St. Mary
Washburn University
Wichita State University

Kentucky

Alice Lloyd College
Ashland Community and Technical College
Bellarmine University
Berea College
Bluegrass Community and Technical College
Brescia University
Campbellsville University
Centre College
Daymar College: Louisville
Eastern Kentucky University
Georgetown College
Henderson Community College
Jefferson Community and Technical College
Kentucky Christian University
Kentucky Mountain Bible College
Kentucky State University
Lindsey Wilson College
Louisville Technical Institute
Maysville Community and Technical College
Midway College
Morehead State University
Murray State University
Northern Kentucky University
Owensboro Community and Technical College
St. Catharine College
Somerset Community College
Southeast Kentucky Community and Technical College
Thomas More College
Transylvania University
Union College
University of the Cumberlands
University of Kentucky
University of Louisville
Western Kentucky University

Louisiana

Bossier Parish Community College
Centenary College of Louisiana
Delgado Community College
Dillard University
Grambling State University
Louisiana College
Louisiana State University and Agricultural and Mechanical College
Louisiana State University at Eunice
Louisiana State University in Shreveport
Louisiana Tech University
Loyola University New Orleans
McNeese State University
Nicholls State University
Northwestern State University
Nunez Community College
St. Joseph Seminary College
School of Urban Missions: New Orleans
Southeastern Louisiana University
Southern University and Agricultural and Mechanical College

Tulane University
University of Louisiana at Lafayette
University of Louisiana at Monroe
University of New Orleans
Xavier University of Louisiana

Maine

Andover College
Bates College
Bowdoin College
Central Maine Community College
Colby College
College of the Atlantic
Husson College
Kennebec Valley Community College
Maine College of Art
Maine Maritime Academy
New England School of Communications
St. Joseph's College
Southern Maine Community College
Thomas College
Unity College
University of Maine
University of Maine at Augusta
University of Maine at Farmington
University of Maine at Fort Kent
University of Maine at Machias
University of New England
University of Southern Maine

Maryland

Allegany College of Maryland
Anne Arundel Community College
Baltimore International College
Bowie State University
Capitol College
Carroll Community College
College of Notre Dame of Maryland
College of Southern Maryland
Columbia Union College
Community College of Baltimore County
Coppin State University
Frostburg State University
Garrett College
Goucher College
Griggs University
Harford Community College
Hood College
Howard Community College
Johns Hopkins University
Johns Hopkins University: Peabody Conservatory of Music
Kaplan College: Hagerstown
Loyola College in Maryland
Maryland Institute College of Art
McDaniel College
Morgan State University
Mount St. Mary's University
Prince George's Community College
St. Mary's College of Maryland
Salisbury University
TESST College of Technology: Baltimore
Towson University
University of Baltimore
University of Maryland: Baltimore County
University of Maryland: College Park
University of Maryland: Eastern Shore
University of Maryland: University College
Villa Julie College
Washington Bible College
Washington College

Massachusetts

American International College
Amherst College
Anna Maria College

Assumption College
Atlantic Union College
Babson College
Bard College at Simon's Rock
Bay Path College
Becker College
Bentley College
Berkshire Community College
Boston Architectural College
Boston College
Boston University
Brandeis University
Bridgewater State College
Bunker Hill Community College
Cape Cod Community College
Clark University
College of the Holy Cross
Curry College
Dean College
Eastern Nazarene College
Elms College
Emerson College
Emmanuel College
Endicott College
Fisher College
Fitchburg State College
Framingham State College
Gordon College
Greenfield Community College
Hampshire College
Harvard College
Hellenic College/Holy Cross
Lasell College
Lesley University
Massachusetts Bay Community College
Massachusetts College of Liberal Arts
Massachusetts College of Pharmacy and
   Health Sciences
Massachusetts Institute of Technology
Massachusetts Maritime Academy
Merrimack College
Middlesex Community College
Mount Holyoke College
Mount Wachusett Community College
New England Institute of Art
Nichols College
North Shore Community College
Northeastern University
Northern Essex Community College
Pine Manor College
Quinsigamond Community College
Regis College
Salem State College
School of the Museum of Fine Arts
Simmons College
Smith College
Springfield College
Springfield Technical Community
   College
Stonehill College
Suffolk University
Tufts University
University of Massachusetts Amherst
University of Massachusetts Boston
University of Massachusetts Dartmouth
University of Massachusetts Lowell
Wellesley College
Wentworth Institute of Technology
Western New England College
Wheaton College
Wheelock College
Williams College
Worcester Polytechnic Institute
Worcester State College

Michigan

Adrian College
Albion College
Alma College
Andrews University
Aquinas College
Baker College of Auburn Hills
Baker College of Cadillac

Baker College of Jackson
Baker College of Muskegon
Baker College of Owosso
Baker College of Port Huron
Bay de Noc Community College
Calvin College
Central Michigan University
Cleary University
College for Creative Studies
Concordia University
Cornerstone University
Davenport University
Delta College
Eastern Michigan University
Ferris State University
Finlandia University
Glen Oaks Community College
Gogebic Community College
Grand Rapids Community College
Grand Valley State University
Hillsdale College
Hope College
Kalamazoo College
Kellogg Community College
Kendall College of Art and Design of
   Ferris State University
Kettering University
Kirtland Community College
Kuyper College
Lake Michigan College
Lake Superior State University
Lansing Community College
Lawrence Technological University
Macomb Community College
Madonna University
Marygrove College
Michigan Jewish Institute
Michigan State University
Michigan Technological University
Montcalm Community College
Mott Community College
Muskegon Community College
North Central Michigan College
Northern Michigan University
Northwestern Michigan College
Northwood University: Michigan
Oakland Community College
Oakland University
Olivet College
Rochester College
Saginaw Valley State University
St. Clair County Community College
Siena Heights University
Southwestern Michigan College
Spring Arbor University
University of Detroit Mercy
University of Michigan
University of Michigan: Dearborn
University of Michigan: Flint
Washtenaw Community College
Wayne County Community College
Wayne State University
Western Michigan University

Minnesota

Academy College
Alexandria Technical College
Art Institutes International Minnesota
Augsburg College
Bemidji State University
Bethany Lutheran College
Bethel University
Brown College
Carleton College
Central Lakes College
Century Community and Technical
   College
College of St. Benedict
College of St. Catherine
College of St. Scholastica
College of Visual Arts
Concordia College: Moorhead
Concordia University: St. Paul

Dakota County Technical College
Globe University
Gustavus Adolphus College
Hamline University
Hennepin Technical College
Inver Hills Community College
Itasca Community College
Lake Superior College
Macalester College
Minneapolis College of Art and Design
Minneapolis Community and Technical
   College
Minnesota State College - Southeast
   Technical
Minnesota State Community and
   Technical College: Fergus Falls
Minnesota State University: Mankato
Minnesota State University: Moorhead
Minnesota West Community and
   Technical College
Normandale Community College
North Central University
North Hennepin Community College
Northland Community & Technical
   College
Northwest Technical College
Northwest Technical Institute
Northwestern College
Pillsbury Baptist Bible College
Pine Technical College
Rainy River Community College
Riverland Community College
Rochester Community and Technical
   College
Saint Cloud State University
St. Cloud Technical College
St. John's University
St. Mary's University of Minnesota
St. Olaf College
St. Paul College
South Central College
Southwest Minnesota State University
University of Minnesota: Crookston
University of Minnesota: Duluth
University of Minnesota: Morris
University of Minnesota: Twin Cities
University of St. Thomas
Winona State University

Mississippi

Alcorn State University
Belhaven College
Blue Mountain College
Delta State University
Jackson State University
Millsaps College
Mississippi College
Mississippi State University
Mississippi University for Women
Mississippi Valley State University
Northeast Mississippi Community
   College
University of Mississippi
University of Southern Mississippi
William Carey University

Missouri

Avila University
Baptist Bible College
Calvary Bible College and Theological
   Seminary
Central Methodist University
College of the Ozarks
Columbia College
Cottey College
Crowder College
Culver-Stockton College
Drury University
East Central College
Evangel University
Fontbonne University

Hannibal-LaGrange College
Jefferson College
Kansas City Art Institute
Lincoln University
Lindenwood University
Maryville University of Saint Louis
Metropolitan Community College: Blue
   River
Metropolitan Community College:
   Longview
Metropolitan Community College: Maple
   Woods
Metropolitan Community College: Penn
   Valley
Missouri Baptist University
Missouri Southern State University
Missouri State University
Missouri University of Science and
   Technology
Missouri Valley College
Moberly Area Community College
Northwest Missouri State University
Park University
Patricia Stevens College
Research College of Nursing
Rockhurst University
Saint Louis University
Southeast Missouri Hospital College of
   Nursing and Health Sciences
Southeast Missouri State University
Southwest Baptist University
State Fair Community College
Stephens College
Three Rivers Community College
Truman State University
University of Central Missouri
University of Missouri: Columbia
University of Missouri: Kansas City
University of Missouri: St. Louis
Washington University in St. Louis
Webster University
Westminster College
William Jewell College
William Woods University

Montana

Carroll College
Flathead Valley Community College
Helena College of Technology of the
   University of Montana
Montana State University: Billings
Montana State University: Bozeman
Montana State University: Northern
Montana Tech of the University of
   Montana
Rocky Mountain College
University of Great Falls
University of Montana: Missoula
University of Montana: Western

Nebraska

Bellevue University
Chadron State College
College of Saint Mary
Concordia University
Creighton University
Dana College
Doane College
Grace University
Hastings College
Metropolitan Community College
Midland Lutheran College
Nebraska College of Technical
   Agriculture
Nebraska Methodist College of Nursing
   and Allied Health
Nebraska Wesleyan University
Northeast Community College
Union College
University of Nebraska - Lincoln
University of Nebraska - Omaha

Wayne State College
Western Nebraska Community College
York College

Nevada

Art Institute of Las Vegas
International Academy of Design and
    Technology: Henderson
Nevada State College
Sierra Nevada College
University of Nevada: Las Vegas
University of Nevada: Reno
Western Nevada College

New Hampshire

Chester College of New England
Colby-Sawyer College
Daniel Webster College
Dartmouth College
Franklin Pierce University
Granite State College
Hesser College
Nashua Community College
New England College
Plymouth State University
Rivier College
St. Anselm College
Southern New Hampshire University
University of New Hampshire
University of New Hampshire at
    Manchester

New Jersey

Berkeley College
Bloomfield College
Brookdale Community College
Burlington County College
Caldwell College
Centenary College
The College of New Jersey
College of St. Elizabeth
County College of Morris
Drew University
Essex County College
Fairleigh Dickinson University: College
    at Florham
Fairleigh Dickinson University:
    Metropolitan Campus
Felician College
Georgian Court University
Kean University
Mercer County Community College
Monmouth University
Montclair State University
New Jersey City University
New Jersey Institute of Technology
Ocean County College
Passaic County Community College
Princeton University
Ramapo College of New Jersey
Raritan Valley Community College
Richard Stockton College of New Jersey
Rider University
Rowan University
Rutgers, The State University of New
    Jersey: Camden Regional Campus
Rutgers, The State University of New
    Jersey: New Brunswick/Piscataway
    Campus
Rutgers, The State University of New
    Jersey: Newark Regional Campus
Saint Peter's College
Salem Community College
Seton Hall University
Stevens Institute of Technology
Thomas Edison State College
Union County College
William Paterson University of New
    Jersey

New Mexico

Clovis Community College
College of Santa Fe
College of the Southwest
Eastern New Mexico University
Mesalands Community College
National American University: Rio
    Rancho
New Mexico Highlands University
New Mexico Institute of Mining and
    Technology
New Mexico Junior College
New Mexico State University
New Mexico State University at
    Alamogordo
Northern New Mexico College
Santa Fe Community College
University of New Mexico
Western New Mexico University

New York

Adelphi University
Adirondack Community College
Albany College of Pharmacy
Alfred University
Art Institute of New York City
ASA Institute of Business and Computer
    Technology
Bard College
Barnard College
Berkeley College
Berkeley College of New York City
Broome Community College
Bryant & Stratton College: Buffalo
Bryant & Stratton College: Syracuse
    North
Business Informatics Center
Canisius College
Cayuga County Community College
Cazenovia College
City University of New York: Baruch
    College
City University of New York: Bronx
    Community College
City University of New York: Brooklyn
    College
City University of New York: City
    College
City University of New York: College of
    Staten Island
City University of New York: CUNY
    Online
City University of New York: Hunter
    College
City University of New York: John Jay
    College of Criminal Justice
City University of New York:
    Kingsborough Community College
City University of New York: LaGuardia
    Community College
City University of New York: Lehman
    College
City University of New York: Medgar
    Evers College
City University of New York: Queens
    College
City University of New York:
    Queensborough Community College
City University of New York: York
    College
Clarkson University
Clinton Community College
Colgate University
College of Mount St. Vincent
College of New Rochelle
Columbia University
Columbia University: School of General
    Studies
Columbia-Greene Community College
Concordia College

Cooper Union for the Advancement of
    Science and Art
Cornell University
Corning Community College
Daemen College
Dominican College of Blauvelt
Dowling College
Dutchess Community College
D'Youville College
Eastman School of Music of the
    University of Rochester
Elmira College
Erie Community College: City Campus
Erie Community College: North Campus
Erie Community College: South Campus
Excelsior College
Five Towns College
Fordham University
Fulton-Montgomery Community College
Genesee Community College
Globe Institute of Technology
Hamilton College
Hartwick College
Herkimer County Community College
Hobart and William Smith Colleges
Hofstra University
Houghton College
Iona College
Ithaca College
Jamestown Community College
Juilliard School
Keuka College
King's College
Laboratory Institute of Merchandising
Le Moyne College
Long Island Business Institute
Long Island University: Brooklyn
    Campus
Long Island University: C. W. Post
    Campus
Manhattan College
Manhattanville College
Marist College
Marymount Manhattan College
Medaille College
Mercy College
Mohawk Valley Community College
Molloy College
Monroe College
Monroe Community College
Nassau Community College
Nazareth College of Rochester
New York Career Institute
New York Institute of Technology
New York School of Interior Design
New York University
Niagara County Community College
Niagara University
North Country Community College
Nyack College
Onondaga Community College
Pace University
Paul Smith's College
Phillips Beth Israel School of Nursing
Polytechnic University
Rensselaer Polytechnic Institute
Roberts Wesleyan College
Rochester Institute of Technology
Rockland Community College
Russell Sage College
Sage College of Albany
Saint Bonaventure University
St. Francis College
St. John Fisher College
St. John's University
St. Joseph's College
St. Joseph's College: Suffolk Campus
St. Lawrence University
St. Thomas Aquinas College
Sarah Lawrence College
Schenectady County Community College
School of Visual Arts
Siena College
Skidmore College
State University of New York at Albany

State University of New York at
    Binghamton
State University of New York at Buffalo
State University of New York at
    Farmingdale
State University of New York at New
    Paltz
State University of New York at Oswego
State University of New York at Purchase
State University of New York at Stony
    Brook
State University of New York College at
    Brockport
State University of New York College at
    Buffalo
State University of New York College at
    Cortland
State University of New York College at
    Fredonia
State University of New York College at
    Geneseo
State University of New York College at
    Old Westbury
State University of New York College at
    Oneonta
State University of New York College at
    Plattsburgh
State University of New York College at
    Potsdam
State University of New York College of
    Agriculture and Technology at
    Cobleskill
State University of New York College of
    Agriculture and Technology at
    Morrisville
State University of New York College of
    Environmental Science and Forestry
State University of New York College of
    Technology at Alfred
State University of New York College of
    Technology at Canton
State University of New York College of
    Technology at Delhi
State University of New York Empire
    State College
State University of New York Institute of
    Technology at Utica/Rome
State University of New York Maritime
    College
State University of New York Upstate
    Medical University
Suffolk County Community College
Sullivan County Community College
Syracuse University
Tompkins-Cortland Community College
Touro College
Ulster County Community College
Union College
University of Rochester
Utica College
Vassar College
Vaughn College of Aeronautics and
    Technology
Villa Maria College of Buffalo
Wagner College
Wells College
Westchester Community College

North Carolina

Appalachian State University
Barton College
Belmont Abbey College
Bennett College
Brevard College
Brunswick Community College
Cabarrus College of Health Sciences
Campbell University
Carteret Community College
Catawba College
Central Piedmont Community College
Chowan University
College of the Albemarle
Davidson College

Duke University
Durham Technical Community College
East Carolina University
Elizabeth City State University
Elon University
Fayetteville State University
Fayetteville Technical Community College
Gardner-Webb University
Greensboro College
Guilford College
Guilford Technical Community College
High Point University
John Wesley College
Johnson C. Smith University
Johnston Community College
Lees-McRae College
Lenoir-Rhyne College
Louisburg College
Mars Hill College
Martin Community College
Mayland Community College
Meredith College
Methodist University
Montreat College
Mount Olive College
North Carolina Central University
North Carolina School of the Arts
North Carolina State University
North Carolina Wesleyan College
Peace College
Pfeiffer University
Piedmont Baptist College
Queens University of Charlotte
Roanoke Bible College
Rockingham Community College
St. Andrews Presbyterian College
Salem College
Sandhills Community College
Southeastern Community College
University of North Carolina at Asheville
University of North Carolina at Chapel Hill
University of North Carolina at Charlotte
University of North Carolina at Greensboro
University of North Carolina at Pembroke
University of North Carolina at Wilmington
Wake Forest University
Wake Technical Community College
Warren Wilson College
Western Carolina University
Wilson Community College
Wingate University
Winston-Salem State University

North Dakota

Bismarck State College
Dickinson State University
Jamestown College
Lake Region State College
Mayville State University
Minot State University
North Dakota State University
University of Mary
University of North Dakota
Valley City State University
Williston State College

Ohio

Allegheny Wesleyan College
Art Academy of Cincinnati
Ashland University
Baldwin-Wallace College
Bluffton University
Bowling Green State University
Bowling Green State University: Firelands College
Bryant & Stratton College: Parma

Bryant & Stratton College: Willoughby Hills
Capital University
Case Western Reserve University
Cedarville University
Central State University
Cincinnati Christian University
Cincinnati College of Mortuary Science
Cincinnati State Technical and Community College
Clark State Community College
Cleveland Institute of Art
Cleveland Institute of Music
Cleveland State University
College of Mount St. Joseph
College of Wooster
Columbus College of Art and Design
Columbus State Community College
Cuyahoga Community College: Metropolitan Campus
Defiance College
Denison University
Edison State Community College
Franciscan University of Steubenville
Heidelberg College
Hiram College
Hocking College
James A. Rhodes State College
John Carroll University
Kent State University
Kenyon College
Kettering College of Medical Arts
Lake Erie College
Lakeland Community College
Laura and Alvin Siegal College of Judaic Studies
Lorain County Community College
Lourdes College
Malone College
Marietta College
MedCentral College of Nursing
Miami University: Hamilton Campus
Miami University: Middletown Campus
Miami University: Oxford Campus
Mount Union College
Mount Vernon Nazarene University
Muskingum College
Oberlin College
Ohio Dominican University
Ohio Institute of Photography and Technology
Ohio Northern University
Ohio State University Agricultural Technical Institute
Ohio State University: Columbus Campus
Ohio State University: Lima Campus
Ohio State University: Mansfield Campus
Ohio State University: Marion Campus
Ohio State University: Newark Campus
Ohio University
Ohio University: Zanesville Campus
Ohio Wesleyan University
Otterbein College
Owens Community College: Toledo
Shawnee State University
Sinclair Community College
Tiffin University
University of Akron
University of Akron: Wayne College
University of Cincinnati
University of Cincinnati: Clermont College
University of Dayton
University of Findlay
University of Northwestern Ohio
University of Rio Grande
University of Toledo
Ursuline College
Walsh University
Wilberforce University
Wilmington College
Wittenberg University
Wright State University
Xavier University

Youngstown State University
Zane State College

Oklahoma

Bacone College
Cameron University
Carl Albert State College
East Central University
Langston University
Northeastern Oklahoma Agricultural and Mechanical College
Northeastern State University
Northwestern Oklahoma State University
Oklahoma Baptist University
Oklahoma Christian University
Oklahoma City Community College
Oklahoma City University
Oklahoma Panhandle State University
Oklahoma State University
Oklahoma State University: Okmulgee
Oklahoma Wesleyan University
Oral Roberts University
Redlands Community College
Rose State College
St. Gregory's University
Southeastern Oklahoma State University
Southern Nazarene University
Southwestern Christian University
Southwestern Oklahoma State University
University of Central Oklahoma
University of Oklahoma
University of Science and Arts of Oklahoma
University of Tulsa
Western Oklahoma State College

Oregon

Art Institute of Portland
Blue Mountain Community College
Cascade College
Chemeketa Community College
Clackamas Community College
Corban College
Eastern Oregon University
George Fox University
Lewis & Clark College
Linfield College
Linn-Benton Community College
Marylhurst University
Northwest Christian College
Oregon Institute of Technology
Oregon State University
Pacific Northwest College of Art
Pacific University
Portland Community College
Portland State University
Reed College
Rogue Community College
Southern Oregon University
Southwestern Oregon Community College
Treasure Valley Community College
Umpqua Community College
University of Oregon
University of Portland
Warner Pacific College
Western Oregon University
Willamette University

Pennsylvania

Albright College
Allegheny College
Alvernia College
Arcadia University
Art Institute of Pittsburgh
Baptist Bible College of Pennsylvania
Bloomsburg University of Pennsylvania
Bryn Mawr College
Bucknell University

Bucks County Community College
Butler County Community College
Cabrini College
California University of Pennsylvania
Cambria-Rowe Business College: Indiana
Carlow University
Carnegie Mellon University
Cedar Crest College
Central Pennsylvania College
Chatham University
Chestnut Hill College
Cheyney University of Pennsylvania
Clarion University of Pennsylvania
Community College of Allegheny County
Community College of Beaver County
Community College of Philadelphia
Curtis Institute of Music
Delaware Valley College
DeSales University
Dickinson College
Drexel University
DuBois Business College
Duquesne University
East Stroudsburg University of Pennsylvania
Eastern University
Edinboro University of Pennsylvania
Elizabethtown College
Franklin & Marshall College
Gannon University
Geneva College
Gettysburg College
Grove City College
Gwynedd-Mercy College
Harcum College
Harrisburg Area Community College
Haverford College
Holy Family University
Immaculata University
Indiana University of Pennsylvania
JNA Institute of Culinary Arts
Johnson College
Juniata College
Keystone College
Keystone Technical Institute
King's College
Kutztown University of Pennsylvania
La Roche College
La Salle University
Lackawanna College
Lafayette College
Laurel Business Institute
Lebanon Valley College
Lehigh University
Lincoln Technical Institute: Allentown
Lincoln University
Lock Haven University of Pennsylvania
Lycoming College
Manor College
Mansfield University of Pennsylvania
Marywood University
Mercyhurst College
Messiah College
Millersville University of Pennsylvania
Misericordia University
Montgomery County Community College
Moore College of Art and Design
Moravian College
Mount Aloysius College
Muhlenberg College
Neumann College
Northampton Community College
Peirce College
Penn State Abington
Penn State Altoona
Penn State Beaver
Penn State Berks
Penn State Brandywine
Penn State Dubois
Penn State Erie, The Behrend College
Penn State Fayette, The Eberly Campus
Penn State Greater Allegheny

Penn State Harrisburg
Penn State Hazleton
Penn State Lehigh Valley
Penn State Mont Alto
Penn State New Kensington
Penn State Shenango
Penn State University Park
Penn State Wilkes-Barre
Penn State Worthington Scranton
Penn State York
Pennsylvania College of Technology
Pennsylvania Culinary Institute
Pennsylvania Institute of Technology
Philadelphia Biblical University
Philadelphia University
Point Park University
Reading Area Community College
Robert Morris University
Rosemont College
St. Charles Borromeo Seminary -
  Overbrook
St. Francis University
Saint Joseph's University
St. Vincent College
Seton Hill University
Shippensburg University of Pennsylvania
Slippery Rock University of
  Pennsylvania
Susquehanna University
Swarthmore College
Temple University
Thiel College
Thomas Jefferson University: College of
  Health Professions
Triangle Tech: Greensburg
University of the Arts
University of Pennsylvania
University of Pittsburgh
University of Pittsburgh at Bradford
University of Pittsburgh at Greensburg
University of Pittsburgh at Johnstown
University of Pittsburgh at Titusville
University of the Sciences in
  Philadelphia
University of Scranton
Ursinus College
Valley Forge Christian College
Valley Forge Military College
Villanova University
Washington & Jefferson College
Waynesburg University
West Chester University of Pennsylvania
Westminster College
Widener University
Wilson College
York College of Pennsylvania

Puerto Rico

Bayamon Central University
Conservatory of Music of Puerto Rico
Humacao Community College
Inter American University of Puerto
  Rico: Aguadilla Campus
Inter American University of Puerto
  Rico: Arecibo Campus
Inter American University of Puerto
  Rico: Bayamon Campus
Inter American University of Puerto
  Rico: Metropolitan Campus
Inter American University of Puerto
  Rico: San German Campus
National College of Business and
  Technology: Arecibo
National College of Business and
  Technology: Bayamon
Pontifical Catholic University of Puerto
  Rico
Universidad Politecnica de Puerto Rico
University College of San Juan
University of Puerto Rico: Arecibo
University of Puerto Rico: Bayamon
  University College

University of Puerto Rico: Carolina
  Regional College
University of Puerto Rico: Cayey
  University College
University of Puerto Rico: Humacao
University of Puerto Rico: Mayaguez
University of Puerto Rico: Rio Piedras
University of Puerto Rico: Utuado

Rhode Island

Brown University
Bryant University
Community College of Rhode Island
New England Institute of Technology
Providence College
Rhode Island College
Rhode Island School of Design
Roger Williams University
Salve Regina University
University of Rhode Island
Zion Bible College

South Carolina

Aiken Technical College
Anderson University
Benedict College
Central Carolina Technical College
Charleston Southern University
The Citadel
Claflin University
Clemson University
Coastal Carolina University
Coker College
College of Charleston
Columbia College
Columbia International University
Converse College
Denmark Technical College
Erskine College
Florence-Darlington Technical College
Forrest Junior College
Francis Marion University
Furman University
Greenville Technical College
Lander University
Limestone College
Midlands Technical College
Morris College
Newberry College
North Greenville University
Northeastern Technical College
South Carolina State University
South University
Southern Wesleyan University
Spartanburg Community College
Spartanburg Methodist College
Tri-County Technical College
Trident Technical College
University of South Carolina
University of South Carolina at Aiken
University of South Carolina at Beaufort
University of South Carolina at Lancaster
University of South Carolina at Sumter
University of South Carolina at Union
University of South Carolina Upstate
Voorhees College
Winthrop University
Wofford College

South Dakota

Augustana College
Black Hills State University
Dakota State University
Dakota Wesleyan University
Kilian Community College
Mitchell Technical Institute
Mount Marty College
National American University: Rapid
  City

Northern State University
South Dakota School of Mines and
  Technology
South Dakota State University
University of South Dakota

Tennessee

Aquinas College
Austin Peay State University
Belmont University
Bethel College
Bryan College
Carson-Newman College
Christian Brothers University
Cleveland State Community College
Crichton College
Cumberland University
Dyersburg State Community College
East Tennessee State University
Free Will Baptist Bible College
Freed-Hardeman University
Hiwassee College
King College
Lambuth University
Lane College
Lee University
LeMoyne-Owen College
Lincoln Memorial University
Lipscomb University
Maryville College
Memphis College of Art
Middle Tennessee State University
Milligan College
Motlow State Community College
O'More College of Design
Pellissippi State Technical Community
  College
Rhodes College
Roane State Community College
Southwest Tennessee Community
  College
Tennessee State University
Tennessee Technological University
Tennessee Temple University
Tennessee Wesleyan College
Trevecca Nazarene University
Tusculum College
University of Memphis
University of the South
University of Tennessee: Chattanooga
University of Tennessee: Knoxville
University of Tennessee: Martin
Vanderbilt University
Volunteer State Community College
Walters State Community College

Texas

Abilene Christian University
Angelo State University
Arlington Baptist College
Austin College
Austin Community College
Baylor University
Blinn College
Central Texas College
Clarendon College
Concordia University at Austin
Dallas Baptist University
Del Mar College
East Texas Baptist University
El Centro College
Frank Phillips College
Grayson County College
Hallmark College of Aeronautics
Hallmark College of Technology
Hardin-Simmons University
Hill College
Houston Baptist University
Houston Community College System
Howard Payne University
Huston-Tillotson University

Jacksonville College
Kilgore College
Lamar University
Laredo Community College
LeTourneau University
Lon Morris College
Lone Star College System
Lubbock Christian University
McMurry University
Midland College
Midwestern State University
Mountain View College
North Central Texas College
North Lake College
Northwood University: Texas
Odessa College
Our Lady of the Lake University of San
  Antonio
Panola College
Prairie View A&M University
Rice University
Richland College
St. Edward's University
St. Mary's University
St. Philip's College
Sam Houston State University
San Antonio College
San Jacinto College
Schreiner University
South Plains College
Southern Methodist University
Southwestern Adventist University
Southwestern University
Stephen F. Austin State University
Sul Ross State University
Tarleton State University
Tarrant County College
Texas A&M International University
Texas A&M University
Texas A&M University-Commerce
Texas A&M University-Galveston
Texas A&M University-Kingsville
Texas A&M University-Texarkana
Texas Christian University
Texas College
Texas Lutheran University
Texas Southmost College
Texas State Technical College: Harlingen
Texas State Technical College:
  Sweetwater
Texas State Technical College: Waco
Texas State University: San Marcos
Texas Tech University
Texas Wesleyan University
Texas Woman's University
Trinity University
University of Dallas
University of Houston
University of Houston: Clear Lake
University of Houston: Downtown
University of the Incarnate Word
University of Mary Hardin-Baylor
University of North Texas
University of St. Thomas
University of Texas at Arlington
University of Texas at Austin
University of Texas at Brownsville
University of Texas at Dallas
University of Texas at El Paso
University of Texas at San Antonio
University of Texas at Tyler
University of Texas: Pan American
Victoria College
Wayland Baptist University
Weatherford College
West Texas A&M University
Western Texas College
Westwood College: Houston South
Wiley College

Utah

Brigham Young University
College of Eastern Utah

Dixie State College of Utah
Neumont University
Salt Lake Community College
Snow College
Southern Utah University
Stevens-Henager College: Ogden
University of Utah
Utah State University
Utah Valley State College
Weber State University
Westminster College

Vermont

Bennington College
Burlington College
Castleton State College
Champlain College
College of St. Joseph in Vermont
Community College of Vermont
Green Mountain College
Johnson State College
Landmark College
Lyndon State College
Marlboro College
Middlebury College
New England Culinary Institute
Norwich University
St. Michael's College
Sterling College
University of Vermont

Virginia

Art Institute of Washington
Averett University
Bluefield College
Bridgewater College
Bryant & Stratton College: Virginia
  Beach
Central Virginia Community College
Christendom College
Christopher Newport University
College of William and Mary
Danville Community College
Eastern Mennonite University
Emory & Henry College
Ferrum College
George Mason University
Germanna Community College
Hampden-Sydney College
Hampton University
Hollins University
J. Sargeant Reynolds Community
  College
James Madison University
Jefferson College of Health Sciences
Liberty University
Longwood University
Lynchburg College
Mary Baldwin College
Marymount University
Norfolk State University
Northern Virginia Community College
Old Dominion University
Paul D. Camp Community College
Piedmont Virginia Community College
Radford University
Randolph College
Randolph-Macon College
Rappahannock Community College
Regent University
Richard Bland College
Roanoke College
St. Paul's College
Shenandoah University
Southern Virginia University
Southwest Virginia Community College
Sweet Briar College
Thomas Nelson Community College
Tidewater Community College
University of Mary Washington
University of Northern Virginia

University of Richmond
University of Virginia
University of Virginia's College at Wise
Virginia Commonwealth University
Virginia Intermont College
Virginia Military Institute
Virginia Polytechnic Institute and State
  University
Virginia State University
Virginia Union University
Virginia Wesleyan College
Washington and Lee University

Washington

Art Institute of Seattle
Bastyr University
Bellevue Community College
Big Bend Community College
Cascadia Community College
Central Washington University
Centralia College
Clark College
Cornish College of the Arts
DigiPen Institute of Technology
Everett Community College
Evergreen State College
Gonzaga University
Grays Harbor College
Green River Community College
Heritage University
Lower Columbia College
North Seattle Community College
Northwest College of Art
Northwest University
Olympic College
Pacific Lutheran University
Peninsula College
Saint Martin's University
Seattle Pacific University
Seattle University
South Puget Sound Community College
Spokane Community College
Spokane Falls Community College
Tacoma Community College
Trinity Lutheran College
University of Puget Sound
University of Washington
Walla Walla Community College
Walla Walla University
Washington State University
Wenatchee Valley College
Western Washington University
Whatcom Community College
Whitman College
Whitworth University
Yakima Valley Community College

West Virginia

Alderson-Broaddus College
Appalachian Bible College
Bethany College
Bluefield State College
Concord University
Davis and Elkins College
Fairmont State University
Glenville State College
Marshall University
Mountain State University
Ohio Valley University
Potomac State College of West Virginia
  University
Salem International University
Shepherd University
University of Charleston
West Liberty State College
West Virginia University
West Virginia University at Parkersburg
West Virginia Wesleyan College
Wheeling Jesuit University

Wisconsin

Alverno College
Bellin College of Nursing
Beloit College
Cardinal Stritch University
Carroll College
Carthage College
Concordia University Wisconsin
Edgewood College
Fox Valley Technical College
Herzing College
Lakeland College
Lakeshore Technical College
Lawrence University
Maranatha Baptist Bible College
Marian College of Fond du Lac
Marquette University
Mid-State Technical College
Milwaukee Area Technical College
Milwaukee Institute of Art & Design
Milwaukee School of Engineering
Mount Mary College
Northcentral Technical College
Northeast Wisconsin Technical College
Northland College
St. Norbert College
Silver Lake College
University of Wisconsin-Baraboo/Sauk
  County
University of Wisconsin-Eau Claire
University of Wisconsin-Fox Valley
University of Wisconsin-Green Bay
University of Wisconsin-La Crosse
University of Wisconsin-Madison
University of Wisconsin-Marathon
  County
University of Wisconsin-Marinette
University of Wisconsin-Milwaukee
University of Wisconsin-Oshkosh
University of Wisconsin-Parkside
University of Wisconsin-Platteville
University of Wisconsin-Richland
University of Wisconsin-River Falls
University of Wisconsin-Rock County
University of Wisconsin-Sheboygan
University of Wisconsin-Stevens Point
University of Wisconsin-Stout
University of Wisconsin-Superior
University of Wisconsin-Washington
  County
University of Wisconsin-Waukesha
University of Wisconsin-Whitewater
Viterbo University
Western Technical College
Wisconsin Indianhead Technical College

Wyoming

Casper College
Central Wyoming College
Eastern Wyoming College
Laramie County Community College
Sheridan College
University of Wyoming
Western Wyoming Community College

ESL programs on campus

Alabama

Auburn University
Auburn University at Montgomery
Gadsden State Community College
Troy University
University of Alabama
University of Alabama in Huntsville
University of Montevallo
University of North Alabama
University of South Alabama

Alaska

Prince William Sound Community
    College
University of Alaska Anchorage

Arizona

Arizona State University
Arizona Western College
Central Arizona College
Cochise College
Glendale Community College
Mesa Community College
Mohave Community College
Northern Arizona University
Pima Community College
Scottsdale Community College
South Mountain Community College
University of Arizona

Arkansas

Arkansas Tech University
Harding University
Henderson State University
John Brown University
Ouachita Baptist University
University of Arkansas
University of Arkansas at Little Rock
University of Central Arkansas

California

Academy of Art University
Allan Hancock College
Alliant International University
Antelope Valley College
Azusa Pacific University
Bakersfield College
Barstow Community College
Berkeley City College
Bethesda Christian University
Biola University
Brooks College
Butte College
Cabrillo College
California Baptist University
California College of the Arts

California Polytechnic State University:
    San Luis Obispo
California State Polytechnic University:
    Pomona
California State University: Bakersfield
California State University: Chico
California State University: Dominguez
    Hills
California State University: East Bay
California State University: Fresno
California State University: Fullerton
California State University: Long Beach
California State University: Los Angeles
California State University: Sacramento
California State University: San
    Bernardino
California State University: San Marcos
California University of Management and
    Sciences
Cerritos College
Cerro Coso Community College
Chaffey College
Citrus College
City College of San Francisco
Coastline Community College
College of the Canyons
College of the Desert
College of Marin: Kentfield
College of San Mateo
College of the Sequoias
College of the Siskiyous
Columbia College
Concordia University
Cosumnes River College
Crafton Hills College
Cuesta College
Cuyamaca College
Cypress College
Dominican University of California
El Camino College
Fashion Institute of Design and
    Merchandising: Los Angeles
Fashion Institute of Design and
    Merchandising: San Diego
Folsom Lake College
Foothill College
Fresno City College
Fresno Pacific University
Fullerton College
Glendale Community College
Golden Gate University
Hartnell College
Holy Names University
Hope International University
Irvine Valley College
La Sierra University
Las Positas College
Lassen College
Lincoln University
Long Beach City College
Los Angeles City College
Los Angeles Harbor College
Los Angeles Mission College
Los Angeles Pierce College
Los Angeles Southwest College
Los Angeles Trade and Technical College
Los Angeles Valley College
Los Medanos College
Marymount College
Merritt College
Mills College

MiraCosta College
Mission College
Modesto Junior College
Monterey Peninsula College
Mount San Antonio College
National University
NewSchool of Architecture & Design
Northwestern Polytechnic University
Notre Dame de Namur University
Ohlone College
Otis College of Art and Design
Oxnard College
Pacific States University
Palo Verde College
Palomar College
Pasadena City College
Patten University
Pitzer College
Porterville College
Riverside Community College
Sacramento City College
Saddleback College
St. Mary's College of California
Samuel Merritt College
San Diego Christian College
San Diego State University
San Francisco Art Institute
San Francisco State University
San Joaquin Delta College
San Jose City College
San Jose State University
Santa Ana College
Santa Barbara City College
Santa Monica College
Santiago Canyon College
Shasta College
Sierra College
Soka University of America
Solano Community College
Sonoma State University
Southern California Institute of
    Technology
Southwestern College
Taft College
University of California: Davis
University of California: Irvine
University of California: Los Angeles
University of California: Riverside
University of California: San Diego
University of California: Santa Barbara
University of California: Santa Cruz
University of La Verne
University of the Pacific
University of San Diego
University of San Francisco
University of Southern California
University of the West
Ventura College
Victor Valley College
West Hills College: Coalinga
West Hills College: Lemoore
West Los Angeles College
West Valley College
Woodbury University
World Mission University

Colorado

Arapahoe Community College
Colorado School of Mines
Colorado State University
Colorado State University: Pueblo
Community College of Aurora
Community College of Denver
Fort Lewis College
Front Range Community College
Metropolitan State College of Denver
National American University: Denver
Pikes Peak Community College
Red Rocks Community College
Teikyo Loretto Heights University
Trinidad State Junior College
University of Colorado at Boulder

University of Colorado at Denver
University of Denver
University of Northern Colorado

Connecticut

Briarwood College
Central Connecticut State University
Clemens College
Gateway Community College
Holy Apostles College and Seminary
Housatonic Community College
Manchester Community College
Middlesex Community College
Mitchell College
Naugatuck Valley Community College
Norwalk Community College
Sacred Heart University
Tunxis Community College
University of Bridgeport
University of Connecticut
Yale University

Delaware

Delaware State University
University of Delaware

District of Columbia

Catholic University of America
Gallaudet University
George Washington University
Georgetown University
Southeastern University
Trinity Washington University
University of the District of Columbia

Florida

Angley College
Art Institute of Fort Lauderdale
Ave Maria University
Barry University
Broward Community College
Carlos Albizu University
Central Florida Community College
College of Business and Technology:
    Flagler
Daytona Beach Community College
Eckerd College
Embry-Riddle Aeronautical University
Everest University: Pompano Beach
Everest University: Tampa
Florida Atlantic University
Florida Community College at
    Jacksonville
Florida Institute of Technology
Florida International University
Florida Keys Community College
Florida State University
Hodges University
Indian River Community College
Johnson & Wales University: North
    Miami
Lynn University
Miami Dade College
Nova Southeastern University
Palm Beach Community College
Pasco-Hernando Community College
Polk Community College
St. Petersburg College
Saint Thomas University
Santa Fe Community College
Schiller International University
Seminole Community College
Stetson University
University of Central Florida

University of Florida
University of Miami
University of North Florida
University of South Florida
University of West Florida
Valencia Community College
Webber International University

Georgia

Abraham Baldwin Agricultural College
Andrew College
Augusta State University
Beulah Heights University
Chattahoochee Technical College
Darton College
Gainesville State College
Georgia Institute of Technology
Georgia Perimeter College
Georgia Southern University
Georgia Southwestern State University
Georgia State University
Kennesaw State University
Life University
North Georgia College & State
    University
Savannah College of Art and Design
Savannah Technical College
Southern Polytechnic State University
University of West Georgia
Valdosta State University

Hawaii

Brigham Young University-Hawaii
Hawaii Pacific University
Hawaii Tokai International College
TransPacific Hawaii College
University of Hawaii at Hilo
University of Hawaii at Manoa
University of Hawaii: Hawaii
    Community College
University of Hawaii: Maui Community
    College

Idaho

Boise State University
College of Idaho
College of Southern Idaho
Idaho State University
Lewis-Clark State College
North Idaho College
University of Idaho

Illinois

Black Hawk College
Carl Sandburg College
City Colleges of Chicago: Harold
    Washington College
City Colleges of Chicago: Kennedy-King
    College
City Colleges of Chicago: Malcolm X
    College
City Colleges of Chicago: Olive-Harvey
    College
City Colleges of Chicago: Richard J.
    Daley College
City Colleges of Chicago: Wright
    College
College of DuPage
College of Lake County
Columbia College Chicago
DePaul University
DeVry University: Chicago
Dominican University
Elgin Community College

Harper College
Heartland Community College
Highland Community College
Illinois Central College
Illinois Eastern Community Colleges:
    Frontier Community College
Illinois Eastern Community Colleges:
    Lincoln Trail College
Illinois Eastern Community Colleges:
    Olney Central College
Illinois Eastern Community Colleges:
    Wabash Valley College
Illinois Institute of Technology
Illinois State University
John Wood Community College
Joliet Junior College
Kishwaukee College
Lake Land College
Lewis University
Lincoln Land Community College
Loyola University Chicago
MacCormac College
Millikin University
Moraine Valley Community College
Morton College
National-Louis University
North Central College
North Park University
Parkland College
Richland Community College
Rockford College
Roosevelt University
Sauk Valley Community College
School of the Art Institute of Chicago
Southern Illinois University Carbondale
Spoon River College
Triton College
University of Illinois at Chicago
University of Illinois at
    Urbana-Champaign
University of Illinois: Springfield
Western Illinois University

Indiana

Ball State University
Butler University
Earlham College
Holy Cross College
Huntington University
Indiana State University
Indiana University Bloomington
Indiana University South Bend
Indiana University-Purdue University
    Fort Wayne
Indiana University-Purdue University
    Indianapolis
Purdue University Calumet
Tri-State University
University of Evansville
University of Indianapolis
University of Southern Indiana
Valparaiso University
Vincennes University

Iowa

Ashford University
Buena Vista University
Clarke College
Clinton Community College
Coe College
Des Moines Area Community College
Divine Word College
Drake University
Graceland University
Indian Hills Community College
Iowa State University
Iowa Western Community College
Kirkwood Community College
Loras College

Marshalltown Community College
Morningside College
Muscatine Community College
Northeast Iowa Community College
Northwestern College
Scott Community College
Southeastern Community College: North
    Campus
University of Dubuque
University of Iowa
University of Northern Iowa
Waldorf College
Western Iowa Tech Community College

Kansas

Barton County Community College
Benedictine College
Butler County Community College
Cloud County Community College
Coffeyville Community College
Cowley County Community College
Dodge City Community College
Donnelly College
Emporia State University
Fort Hays State University
Hesston College
Independence Community College
Kansas City Kansas Community College
Kansas State University
Kansas Wesleyan University
Neosho County Community College
Pittsburg State University
University of Kansas
Washburn University
Wichita State University

Kentucky

Berea College
Bluegrass Community and Technical
    College
Brescia University
Campbellsville University
Eastern Kentucky University
Jefferson Community and Technical
    College
Kentucky State University
Murray State University
University of the Cumberlands
University of Kentucky
University of Louisville
Western Kentucky University

Louisiana

Delgado Community College
Louisiana State University and
    Agricultural and Mechanical College
Louisiana State University Health
    Sciences Center
Louisiana Tech University
McNeese State University
Nunez Community College
St. Joseph Seminary College
Southeastern Louisiana University
Tulane University
University of Louisiana at Lafayette
University of Louisiana at Monroe
University of New Orleans

Maine

Central Maine Community College
Colby College
New England School of Communications
University of Maine
University of Maine at Fort Kent

University of Southern Maine

Maryland

Allegany College of Maryland
Anne Arundel Community College
Baltimore City Community College
Capitol College
Carroll Community College
Chesapeake College
College of Notre Dame of Maryland
Columbia Union College
Community College of Baltimore County
Howard Community College
Prince George's Community College
Towson University
University of Maryland: Baltimore
    County
University of Maryland: College Park

Massachusetts

American International College
Atlantic Union College
Bay Path College
Bay State College
Benjamin Franklin Institute of
    Technology
Berklee College of Music
Berkshire Community College
Boston Conservatory
Boston University
Brandeis University
Bridgewater State College
Bristol Community College
Bunker Hill Community College
Clark University
Dean College
Elms College
Fisher College
Framingham State College
Greenfield Community College
Lasell College
Massachusetts Bay Community College
Massachusetts College of Pharmacy and
    Health Sciences
Merrimack College
Mount Ida College
Mount Wachusett Community College
New England Conservatory of Music
Northeastern University
Northern Essex Community College
Pine Manor College
Quincy College
Roxbury Community College
Salem State College
Springfield College
Springfield Technical Community
    College
Suffolk University
University of Massachusetts Amherst
University of Massachusetts Boston
Worcester Polytechnic Institute
Worcester State College

Michigan

Adrian College
Andrews University
Central Michigan University
Davenport University
Eastern Michigan University
Finlandia University
Grand Valley State University
Kalamazoo Valley Community College
Lansing Community College
Lawrence Technological University
Macomb Community College
Madonna University
Michigan Jewish Institute

Michigan State University
Michigan Technological University
Northern Michigan University
Northwood University: Michigan
Oakland Community College
Oakland University
Olivet College
Saginaw Valley State University
Southwestern Michigan College
Spring Arbor University
University of Detroit Mercy
University of Michigan
University of Michigan: Flint
Washtenaw Community College
Wayne County Community College
Wayne State University
Western Michigan University

Minnesota

Augsburg College
Bemidji State University
Century Community and Technical
  College
College of St. Benedict
College of St. Catherine
Dakota County Technical College
Hamline University
Hennepin Technical College
Inver Hills Community College
Lake Superior College
Minneapolis College of Art and Design
Minneapolis Community and Technical
  College
Minnesota State Community and
  Technical College: Fergus Falls
Minnesota State University: Mankato
Normandale Community College
North Hennepin Community College
Northwest Technical College
Riverland Community College
Saint Cloud State University
St. Cloud Technical College
St. John's University
St. Mary's University of Minnesota
University of Minnesota: Crookston
University of Minnesota: Morris
University of Minnesota: Twin Cities
University of St. Thomas
Winona State University

Mississippi

Belhaven College
Mississippi College
Mississippi State University
Northeast Mississippi Community
  College
University of Mississippi
University of Southern Mississippi

Missouri

Avila University
College of the Ozarks
Columbia College
Crowder College
Drury University
Fontbonne University
Hannibal-LaGrange College
Jefferson College
Metropolitan Community College: Blue
  River
Metropolitan Community College:
  Longview
Metropolitan Community College: Penn
  Valley
Missouri Southern State University
Missouri State University

Missouri University of Science and
  Technology
Missouri Valley College
Northwest Missouri State University
Ozarks Technical Community College
Park University
Saint Louis University
Southeast Missouri State University
University of Central Missouri
University of Missouri: Columbia
University of Missouri: Kansas City
University of Missouri: St. Louis
Washington University in St. Louis
Webster University
Wentworth Military Junior College
William Woods University

Montana

Carroll College
Flathead Valley Community College
Montana State University: Billings
Montana State University: Bozeman
Rocky Mountain College
University of Montana: Missoula

Nebraska

Bellevue University
Creighton University
Dana College
Doane College
Metropolitan Community College
Northeast Community College
Union College
University of Nebraska - Kearney
University of Nebraska - Lincoln
University of Nebraska - Omaha
Western Nebraska Community College

Nevada

College of Southern Nevada
University of Nevada: Las Vegas
University of Nevada: Reno

New Hampshire

Colby-Sawyer College
Franklin Pierce University
Great Bay Community College
Manchester Community College
New England College
Rivier College
Southern New Hampshire University
University of New Hampshire
University of New Hampshire at
  Manchester

New Jersey

Atlantic Cape Community College
Bloomfield College
Burlington County College
Caldwell College
Centenary College
College of St. Elizabeth
County College of Morris
Cumberland County College
Essex County College
Fairleigh Dickinson University: College
  at Florham
Fairleigh Dickinson University:
  Metropolitan Campus
Felician College
Georgian Court University

Hudson County Community College
Kean University
Mercer County Community College
Montclair State University
New Jersey City University
New Jersey Institute of Technology
Ocean County College
Passaic County Community College
Raritan Valley Community College
Rutgers, The State University of New
  Jersey: New Brunswick/Piscataway
  Campus
Rutgers, The State University of New
  Jersey: Newark Regional Campus
Seton Hall University
Sussex County Community College
Union County College
William Paterson University of New
  Jersey

New Mexico

Clovis Community College
Dona Ana Branch Community College of
  New Mexico State University
New Mexico State University
New Mexico State University at
  Alamogordo
Santa Fe Community College
University of New Mexico
Western New Mexico University

New York

Adelphi University
Alfred University
ASA Institute of Business and Computer
  Technology
Bard College
Broome Community College
Canisius College
City University of New York: Baruch
  College
City University of New York: Borough of
  Manhattan Community College
City University of New York: Brooklyn
  College
City University of New York: City
  College
City University of New York: College of
  Staten Island
City University of New York: Hostos
  Community College
City University of New York: Hunter
  College
City University of New York: John Jay
  College of Criminal Justice
City University of New York:
  Kingsborough Community College
City University of New York: LaGuardia
  Community College
City University of New York: Lehman
  College
City University of New York: Medgar
  Evers College
City University of New York: Queens
  College
City University of New York:
  Queensborough Community College
City University of New York: York
  College
Clarkson University
College of New Rochelle
Columbia University
Columbia University: School of General
  Studies
Concordia College
Cornell University
Daemen College
Dowling College

Eastman School of Music of the
  University of Rochester
Elmira College
Erie Community College: City Campus
Erie Community College: North Campus
Erie Community College: South Campus
Eugene Lang College The New School
  for Liberal Arts
Fashion Institute of Technology
Fordham University
Fulton-Montgomery Community College
Globe Institute of Technology
Hamilton College
Herkimer County Community College
Hobart and William Smith Colleges
Juilliard School
Long Island Business Institute
Long Island University: Brooklyn
  Campus
Long Island University: C. W. Post
  Campus
Manhattan College
Manhattan School of Music
Manhattanville College
Mannes College The New School for
  Music
Marymount Manhattan College
Mercy College
Metropolitan College of New York
Mohawk Valley Community College
Molloy College
Nassau Community College
New York Institute of Technology
New York University
Niagara University
Nyack College
Onondaga Community College
Pace University
Parsons The New School for Design
Pratt Institute
Rensselaer Polytechnic Institute
Roberts Wesleyan College
Rochester Institute of Technology
Rockland Community College
St. John's University
St. Thomas Aquinas College
School of Visual Arts
Siena College
State University of New York at Albany
State University of New York at
  Binghamton
State University of New York at Buffalo
State University of New York at New
  Paltz
State University of New York at Oswego
State University of New York at Purchase
State University of New York at Stony
  Brook
State University of New York College at
  Buffalo
State University of New York College at
  Geneseo
State University of New York College at
  Oneonta
State University of New York College at
  Plattsburgh
State University of New York College of
  Agriculture and Technology at
  Cobleskill
State University of New York College of
  Agriculture and Technology at
  Morrisville
State University of New York College of
  Environmental Science and Forestry
State University of New York College of
  Technology at Alfred
State University of New York College of
  Technology at Delhi
Suffolk County Community College
Syracuse University
Technical Career Institutes
Tompkins-Cortland Community College
University of Rochester
Westchester Community College

North Carolina

Appalachian State University
Asheville-Buncombe Technical
  Community College
Carteret Community College
Central Piedmont Community College
College of the Albemarle
Duke University
Durham Technical Community College
Elon University
Guilford College
Guilford Technical Community College
High Point University
Lees-McRae College
Mars Hill College
Mayland Community College
Methodist University
Nash Community College
North Carolina Central University
North Carolina State University
Sandhills Community College
University of North Carolina at Charlotte
University of North Carolina at
  Pembroke
University of North Carolina at
  Wilmington
Wake Technical Community College
Wilson Community College

North Dakota

Dickinson State University
Lake Region State College
North Dakota State University
University of North Dakota

Ohio

Ashland University
Baldwin-Wallace College
Capital University
Case Western Reserve University
Central State University
Cincinnati State Technical and
  Community College
Cleveland Institute of Music
Cleveland State University
Columbus State Community College
Cuyahoga Community College:
  Metropolitan Campus
Hiram College
Hocking College
Kent State University
Lorain County Community College
Marietta College
Miami University: Hamilton Campus
Mount Union College
Muskingum College
Ohio State University: Columbus
  Campus
Ohio State University: Lima Campus
Ohio State University: Mansfield Campus
Ohio State University: Marion Campus
Ohio State University: Newark Campus
Ohio University
Shawnee State University
Sinclair Community College
University of Akron
University of Dayton
University of Findlay
University of Toledo
Virginia Marti College of Art and Design
Walsh University
Wittenberg University
Wright State University
Xavier University
Youngstown State University

Oklahoma

Northeastern State University
Oklahoma Baptist University
Oklahoma Christian University
Oklahoma City Community College
Oklahoma City University
Oklahoma Panhandle State University
Oklahoma State University
Oral Roberts University
St. Gregory's University
Tulsa Community College
University of Oklahoma
University of Tulsa

Oregon

Blue Mountain Community College
Chemeketa Community College
Clackamas Community College
Concordia University
George Fox University
Lane Community College
Lewis & Clark College
Linfield College
Linn-Benton Community College
Marylhurst University
Mount Angel Seminary
Oregon State University
Pacific University
Portland Community College
Portland State University
Rogue Community College
Southern Oregon University
Southwestern Oregon Community
  College
Treasure Valley Community College
University of Oregon
University of Portland
Western Oregon University

Pennsylvania

Albright College
Bloomsburg University of Pennsylvania
Bucks County Community College
Carlow University
Cedar Crest College
Chatham University
Chestnut Hill College
Community College of Allegheny
  County
Community College of Philadelphia
Curtis Institute of Music
Dickinson College
Drexel University
Duquesne University
Elizabethtown College
Gannon University
Geneva College
Gwynedd-Mercy College
Harcum College
Harrisburg Area Community College
Immaculata University
Indiana University of Pennsylvania
Juniata College
King's College
La Roche College
La Salle University
Lackawanna College
Lehigh University
Lock Haven University of Pennsylvania
Manor College
Mansfield University of Pennsylvania
Marywood University
Montgomery County Community
  College
Northampton Community College
Penn State Abington
Penn State Altoona

Penn State Greater Allegheny
Penn State University Park
Penn State York
Philadelphia University
Point Park University
Reading Area Community College
St. Charles Borromeo Seminary -
  Overbrook
Saint Joseph's University
Seton Hill University
Temple University
Thiel College
University of the Arts
University of Pennsylvania
University of Pittsburgh
University of the Sciences in
  Philadelphia
Ursinus College
Valley Forge Christian College
Valley Forge Military College
Villanova University
West Chester University of Pennsylvania
Widener University
Wilson College

Puerto Rico

Bayamon Central University
Inter American University of Puerto
  Rico: Arecibo Campus
Inter American University of Puerto
  Rico: San German Campus
University of Puerto Rico: Bayamon
  University College
University of Puerto Rico: Mayaguez

Rhode Island

Johnson & Wales University: Providence
New England Institute of Technology
Roger Williams University
Salve Regina University

South Carolina

The Citadel
Coker College
Converse College
Midlands Technical College
North Greenville University
Spartanburg Methodist College
Trident Technical College
University of South Carolina
University of South Carolina at Aiken

South Dakota

Black Hills State University
Dakota State University
Lake Area Technical Institute
National American University: Rapid
  City
Northern State University
Oglala Lakota College
University of South Dakota

Tennessee

Austin Peay State University
Carson-Newman College
Draughons Junior College: Nashville
Hiwassee College
King College
Lambuth University
Lee University
Lincoln Memorial University

Martin Methodist College
Maryville College
Pellissippi State Technical Community
  College
Southwest Tennessee Community
  College
Tennessee Technological University
University of Memphis
University of Tennessee: Chattanooga
University of Tennessee: Knoxville
University of Tennessee: Martin
Vanderbilt University
Volunteer State Community College
Walters State Community College

Texas

Abilene Christian University
Austin Community College
Blinn College
Brookhaven College
Central Texas College
Clarendon College
Collin County Community College
  District
Dallas Baptist University
Del Mar College
El Centro College
Grayson County College
Houston Baptist University
Houston Community College System
Kilgore College
Lamar Institute of Technology
Lamar State College at Port Arthur
Lamar University
Laredo Community College
Lon Morris College
Lone Star College System
Midland College
Midwestern State University
Mountain View College
Navarro College
North Lake College
Northeast Texas Community College
Northwest Vista College
Our Lady of the Lake University of San
  Antonio
Palo Alto College
Rice University
Richland College
St. Mary's University
Sam Houston State University
San Antonio College
San Jacinto College
South Plains College
Southern Methodist University
Southwestern Adventist University
Stephen F. Austin State University
Texas A&M International University
Texas A&M University
Texas A&M University-Commerce
Texas A&M University-Galveston
Texas A&M University-Kingsville
Texas Christian University
Texas Southern University
Texas Southmost College
Texas State Technical College: Harlingen
Texas State University: San Marcos
Texas Tech University
Texas Wesleyan University
Trinity Valley Community College
University of Dallas
University of Houston
University of Houston: Downtown
University of the Incarnate Word
University of Mary Hardin-Baylor
University of North Texas
University of Texas at Arlington
University of Texas at Austin
University of Texas at Brownsville
University of Texas at El Paso
University of Texas at San Antonio
University of Texas: Pan American

West Texas A&M University
Western Texas College

Utah

Brigham Young University
College of Eastern Utah
Dixie State College of Utah
Salt Lake Community College
Snow College
Southern Utah University
University of Utah
Utah State University
Utah Valley State College
Weber State University

Vermont

Community College of Vermont
Green Mountain College
Johnson State College
St. Michael's College

Virginia

Eastern Mennonite University
George Mason University
J. Sargeant Reynolds Community
  College
Liberty University
Mary Baldwin College
Northern Virginia Community College
Old Dominion University
Radford University
Roanoke College
Shenandoah University
Thomas Nelson Community College
Tidewater Community College
University of Northern Virginia
University of Richmond
University of Virginia
Virginia Commonwealth University
Virginia Polytechnic Institute and State
  University

Washington

Bates Technical College
Bellevue Community College
Central Washington University
Centralia College
City University of Seattle
Clark College
Clover Park Technical College
Columbia Basin College
Edmonds Community College
Everett Community College
Gonzaga University
Grays Harbor College
Green River Community College
Heritage University
Highline Community College
Lake Washington Technical College
Lower Columbia College
North Seattle Community College
Northwest University
Olympic College
Pacific Lutheran University
Peninsula College
Renton Technical College
Saint Martin's University
Seattle Pacific University
Seattle University
South Puget Sound Community College
South Seattle Community College
Spokane Community College
Spokane Falls Community College
Tacoma Community College

University of Washington
Washington State University
Western Washington University
Whatcom Community College
Whitworth University
Yakima Valley Community College

West Virginia

Concord University
Davis and Elkins College
Fairmont State University
Glenville State College
Marshall University
Mountain State University
Ohio Valley University
Salem International University
University of Charleston
West Virginia University
West Virginia Wesleyan College
Wheeling Jesuit University

Wisconsin

Alverno College
Beloit College
Chippewa Valley Technical College
Concordia University Wisconsin
Fox Valley Technical College
Lakeland College
Lakeshore Technical College
Madison Area Technical College
Marian College of Fond du Lac
Marquette University
Milwaukee School of Engineering
Moraine Park Technical College
Northcentral Technical College
St. Norbert College
Silver Lake College
Southwest Wisconsin Technical College
University of Wisconsin-Eau Claire
University of Wisconsin-La Crosse
University of Wisconsin-Madison
University of Wisconsin-Marinette
University of Wisconsin-Milwaukee
University of Wisconsin-River Falls
University of Wisconsin-Stevens Point
Western Technical College

Wyoming

Laramie County Community College
Northwest College
Sheridan College
University of Wyoming
Western Wyoming Community College

Special housing for international students

Alabama

Alabama State University
Birmingham-Southern College
Jacksonville State University
Troy University
University of North Alabama

Alaska

University of Alaska Anchorage

Arizona

University of Arizona

Arkansas

Henderson State University
University of Central Arkansas

California

California College of the Arts
California State University: Chico
California State University: Long Beach
California State University: Los Angeles
California State University: Sacramento
California State University: San Marcos
Loyola Marymount University
The Master's College
San Diego State University
San Francisco State University
San Jose State University
Shasta College
Simpson University
Sonoma State University
University of California: Berkeley
University of California: Irvine
University of California: Riverside
University of California: San Diego
University of California: Santa Cruz
University of Southern California

Colorado

Colorado College
Teikyo Loretto Heights University

Connecticut

University of Connecticut

Delaware

Delaware State University

District of Columbia

American University

Florida

Lynn University
Nova Southeastern University
University of Florida
University of Miami
University of South Florida

Georgia

Brenau University
Emory University
Fort Valley State University
Georgia College and State University
Georgia Southern University
Georgia Southwestern State University
Georgia State University
Mercer University
Toccoa Falls College
University of Georgia
University of West Georgia
Valdosta State University

Idaho

Brigham Young University-Idaho
College of Idaho
University of Idaho

Illinois

Eastern Illinois University
Illinois State University
Illinois Wesleyan University
Quincy University
Trinity International University
University of Illinois at
    Urbana-Champaign
University of Illinois: Springfield
Western Illinois University

Indiana

Ball State University
DePauw University
Earlham College
Indiana State University
Indiana University Bloomington
Indiana University South Bend
Indiana University-Purdue University
    Indianapolis

Iowa

Central College
Iowa State University

Kansas

Emporia State University

Kentucky

Centre College

Eastern Kentucky University
Morehead State University
University of Kentucky
Western Kentucky University

Louisiana

Louisiana Tech University
McNeese State University
Nicholls State University
Tulane University

Maine

University of Maine
University of Maine at Farmington

Maryland

Frostburg State University
Maryland Institute College of Art
Towson University
University of Maryland: Baltimore
    County
University of Maryland: College Park
Washington College

Massachusetts

Bridgewater State College
Curry College
Endicott College
Hampshire College
Merrimack College
Northeastern University
University of Massachusetts Amherst
Wheaton College
Worcester Polytechnic Institute

Michigan

Albion College
Central Michigan University
Eastern Michigan University
Ferris State University
Kirtland Community College
Michigan State University
Michigan Technological University
Oakland University
Olivet College
Spring Arbor University
University of Michigan
Western Michigan University

Minnesota

College of St. Scholastica
Concordia College: Moorhead
Gustavus Adolphus College
Hamline University
Northwest Technical College
Saint Cloud State University
University of Minnesota: Twin Cities
University of St. Thomas

Mississippi

Mississippi State University
University of Southern Mississippi

Missouri

Fontbonne University
Missouri State University
Truman State University
University of Central Missouri
Webster University

William Woods University

Montana

University of Montana: Missoula

Nebraska

University of Nebraska - Lincoln

New Hampshire

Dartmouth College
University of New Hampshire

New Jersey

Fairleigh Dickinson University:
    Metropolitan Campus
Montclair State University
Ramapo College of New Jersey
Rowan University

New Mexico

Dona Ana Branch Community College of
    New Mexico State University

New York

Canisius College
Columbia University: School of General
    Studies
Cornell University
Globe Institute of Technology
Herkimer County Community College
Hobart and William Smith Colleges
Hofstra University
Houghton College
Ithaca College
Jamestown Community College
Mohawk Valley Community College
New York Institute of Technology
Rochester Institute of Technology
St. Lawrence University
Skidmore College
State University of New York at Albany
State University of New York at Buffalo
State University of New York at New
    Paltz
State University of New York at Purchase
State University of New York College at
    Brockport
State University of New York College at
    Buffalo
State University of New York College at
    Cortland
State University of New York College at
    Plattsburgh
State University of New York College at
    Potsdam
State University of New York College of
    Agriculture and Technology at
    Cobleskill
State University of New York College of
    Environmental Science and Forestry
Syracuse University
University of Rochester
Vassar College

North Carolina

Appalachian State University
Elon University
Guilford College
Livingstone College
North Carolina State University
Pfeiffer University

Special housing for international students

University of North Carolina at Chapel
  Hill
University of North Carolina at Charlotte
University of North Carolina at
  Greensboro
University of North Carolina at
  Wilmington
Western Carolina University

Ohio

Baldwin-Wallace College
Cincinnati Christian University
Kenyon College
Miami University: Oxford Campus
Mount Union College
Ohio University
Ohio Wesleyan University
Tiffin University
University of Akron
University of Dayton
University of Findlay
University of Toledo
Wittenberg University

Oklahoma

Northeastern Oklahoma Agricultural and
  Mechanical College
University of Oklahoma

Oregon

Oregon State University
Southern Oregon University

Pennsylvania

Albright College
Bucknell University
Chatham University
Drexel University
DuBois Business College
East Stroudsburg University of
  Pennsylvania
Edinboro University of Pennsylvania
Franklin & Marshall College
Indiana University of Pennsylvania
Juniata College
Lehigh University
Messiah College
Muhlenberg College
Penn State University Park
Philadelphia Biblical University
St. Francis University
Susquehanna University
Thiel College
Ursinus College
Washington & Jefferson College
Waynesburg University
West Chester University of Pennsylvania

South Carolina

College of Charleston
Furman University
University of South Carolina

South Dakota

Northern State University
South Dakota State University

Tennessee

Belmont University
Tennessee Technological University
University of Tennessee: Knoxville

Vanderbilt University

Texas

Baylor University
Kilgore College
Texas A&M University-Commerce
Texas Woman's University
University of Houston
Western Texas College

Utah

Utah State University

Vermont

Champlain College
St. Michael's College

Virginia

College of William and Mary
Hampden-Sydney College
Hampton University
Hollins University
Longwood University
Lynchburg College
Mary Baldwin College
Old Dominion University
Radford University
Randolph-Macon College
Shenandoah University
University of Mary Washington
University of Richmond
University of Virginia
Virginia Commonwealth University
Virginia Polytechnic Institute and State
  University
Virginia Wesleyan College
Washington and Lee University

Washington

Central Washington University
Evergreen State College
Gonzaga University
Green River Community College
Pacific Lutheran University
University of Washington
Washington State University
Whitman College

West Virginia

Concord University
West Virginia University

Wisconsin

Marquette University
University of Wisconsin-La Crosse
University of Wisconsin-Madison
University of Wisconsin-Oshkosh
University of Wisconsin-Parkside
University of Wisconsin-Whitewater

Housing guaranteed for all freshmen

Alabama

Heritage Christian University
Samford University
Stillman College
University of Alabama
University of Mobile
University of Montevallo

Alaska

Alaska Pacific University

Arizona

Embry-Riddle Aeronautical University:
    Prescott Campus
University of Advancing Technology

Arkansas

Arkansas Tech University
Harding University
Henderson State University
Hendrix College
John Brown University
University of Central Arkansas
University of the Ozarks

California

Academy of Art University
Bethany University
California Baptist University
California Lutheran University
Chapman University
College of the Siskiyous
Columbia College: Hollywood
Concordia University
Harvey Mudd College
Hope International University
Life Pacific College
Loyola Marymount University
Marymount College
Menlo College
Notre Dame de Namur University
Occidental College
Pacific Union College
Pepperdine University
Pitzer College
Point Loma Nazarene University
St. Mary's College of California
Santa Clara University
Scripps College
Sonoma State University
University of California: Berkeley
University of California: Irvine
University of California: Los Angeles
University of California: Riverside
University of California: San Diego
University of California: Santa Barbara
University of California: Santa Cruz
University of the Pacific
University of Redlands
University of San Francisco
University of Southern California
Whittier College

William Jessup University

Colorado

Adams State College
Colorado Christian University
Colorado Mountain College
Colorado Northwestern Community
    College
Colorado School of Mines
Colorado State University
Colorado State University: Pueblo
Community College of Aurora
Lamar Community College
Naropa University
Regis University
University of Colorado at Boulder
University of Denver
Western State College of Colorado

Connecticut

Clemens College
Quinnipiac University
Trinity College
Yale University

Delaware

Delaware State University

District of Columbia

American University
Catholic University of America
Corcoran College of Art and Design
Gallaudet University
George Washington University
Georgetown University
Howard University

Florida

Bethune-Cookman University
Edward Waters College
Embry-Riddle Aeronautical University
Flagler College
Florida Atlantic University
Florida Institute of Technology
Florida Memorial University
Jacksonville University
Johnson & Wales University: North
    Miami
New College of Florida
Northwood University: Florida
Nova Southeastern University
Palm Beach Atlantic University
Rollins College
Schiller International University
Southeastern University
Webber International University

Georgia

Art Institute of Atlanta

Berry College
Brewton-Parker College
Clark Atlanta University
Covenant College
Georgia College and State University
Georgia Institute of Technology
Georgia Southwestern State University
LaGrange College
Mercer University
Morehouse College
Oglethorpe University
Reinhardt College
Shorter College
Spelman College
Thomas University
Toccoa Falls College
University of Georgia
University of West Georgia

Hawaii

Brigham Young University-Hawaii
Chaminade University of Honolulu
University of Hawaii at Manoa

Idaho

College of Idaho

Illinois

Bradley University
Concordia University
Dominican University
Eastern Illinois University
Illinois State University
Illinois Wesleyan University
Lake Forest College
Lincoln College
Loyola University Chicago
Millikin University
North Park University
Northern Illinois University
Northwestern University
Shimer College
Southern Illinois University Carbondale
Trinity Christian College
Trinity International University
University of Illinois at
    Urbana-Champaign
University of Illinois: Springfield
University of St. Francis
Wheaton College

Indiana

Ball State University
Hanover College
Indiana Institute of Technology
Indiana State University
Indiana University Bloomington
Manchester College
Marian College
Rose-Hulman Institute of Technology
Taylor University
Taylor University Fort Wayne
Tri-State University
University of Evansville
University of Notre Dame
University of St. Francis
Vincennes University

Iowa

Briar Cliff University
Clarke College
Cornell College
Drake University
Ellsworth Community College

Faith Baptist Bible College and
    Theological Seminary
Loras College
Morningside College
Mount Mercy College
St. Ambrose University
University of Dubuque
University of Northern Iowa
Wartburg College
William Penn University

Kansas

Baker University
Barclay College
Barton County Community College
Benedictine College
Dodge City Community College
Emporia State University
Fort Hays State University
Kansas Wesleyan University
MidAmerica Nazarene University
Neosho County Community College
Newman University
Ottawa University
Pittsburg State University
Southwestern College
Tabor College
University of St. Mary
Wichita State University

Kentucky

Bellarmine University
Brescia University
Eastern Kentucky University
Kentucky State University
Murray State University
Transylvania University
Union College
Western Kentucky University

Louisiana

Dillard University
Louisiana Tech University
Loyola University New Orleans
Southern University and Agricultural and
    Mechanical College
Tulane University

Maine

Bowdoin College
College of the Atlantic
New England School of Communications
Thomas College
University of Maine
University of Maine at Farmington
University of New England

Maryland

Baltimore International College
Columbia Union College
Goucher College
Johns Hopkins University
Johns Hopkins University: Peabody
    Conservatory of Music
Loyola College in Maryland
Maryland Institute College of Art
McDaniel College
St. John's College
Towson University
University of Maryland: Baltimore
    County
University of Maryland: College Park
Washington Bible College
Washington College

Massachusetts

Anna Maria College
Bard College at Simon's Rock
Becker College
Boston College
Brandeis University
Clark University
Eastern Nazarene College
Endicott College
Gordon College
Hampshire College
Hellenic College/Holy Cross
Massachusetts College of Pharmacy and
   Health Sciences
Massachusetts Institute of Technology
Merrimack College
Mount Ida College
New England Conservatory of Music
Newbury College
Northeastern University
Pine Manor College
Tufts University
University of Massachusetts Amherst
Western New England College
Wheelock College
Worcester Polytechnic Institute

Michigan

Aquinas College
Baker College of Owosso
Calvin College
Central Michigan University
Gogebic Community College
Grand Valley State University
Kettering University
Kuyper College
Lake Superior State University
Michigan State University
Michigan Technological University
Northwestern Michigan College
Northwood University: Michigan
Oakland University
Rochester College
Spring Arbor University
University of Michigan
Western Michigan University

Minnesota

Augsburg College
College of St. Benedict
College of St. Catherine
College of St. Scholastica
Concordia College: Moorhead
Concordia University: St. Paul
Macalester College
Minnesota State University: Mankato
North Central University
Northwestern College
St. John's University
University of Minnesota: Twin Cities
Winona State University

Mississippi

East Central Community College
Millsaps College
Mississippi State University
University of Mississippi
William Carey University

Missouri

Avila University
Baptist Bible College
Columbia College
Drury University
Evangel University
Kansas City Art Institute
Lincoln University
Missouri Southern State University
Missouri State University
Missouri University of Science and
   Technology
Northwest Missouri State University
Park University
Research College of Nursing
Southwest Baptist University
University of Missouri: Columbia
Washington University in St. Louis
Webster University
Westminster College
William Jewell College

Montana

Carroll College
Montana State University: Bozeman
Montana Tech of the University of
   Montana
Rocky Mountain College
University of Great Falls
University of Montana: Missoula
University of Montana: Western

Nebraska

Chadron State College
College of Saint Mary
Doane College
Grace University
Midland Lutheran College
Nebraska College of Technical
   Agriculture
Nebraska Methodist College of Nursing
   and Allied Health
Peru State College
University of Nebraska - Kearney
University of Nebraska - Lincoln
Wayne State College

Nevada

University of Nevada: Las Vegas

New Hampshire

Dartmouth College
Hesser College
Plymouth State University
University of New Hampshire

New Jersey

The College of New Jersey
Fairleigh Dickinson University: College
   at Florham
Fairleigh Dickinson University:
   Metropolitan Campus
Felician College
Ramapo College of New Jersey
Richard Stockton College of New Jersey
Rowan University
Rutgers, The State University of New
   Jersey: New Brunswick/Piscataway
   Campus

New Mexico

College of Santa Fe
Eastern New Mexico University
Institute of American Indian Arts
New Mexico Highlands University
St. John's College

New York

Albany College of Pharmacy
Alfred University
Bard College
Clarkson University
Clinton Community College
College of Saint Rose
Cornell University
Culinary Institute of America
Daemen College
D'Youville College
Eastman School of Music of the
   University of Rochester
Eugene Lang College The New School
   for Liberal Arts
Hartwick College
Hofstra University
Houghton College
Juilliard School
King's College
Long Island University: C. W. Post
   Campus
Manhattan School of Music
Marist College
Polytechnic University
Pratt Institute
Rensselaer Polytechnic Institute
Roberts Wesleyan College
Rochester Institute of Technology
Sage College of Albany
St. John Fisher College
St. Thomas Aquinas College
Sarah Lawrence College
Siena College
State University of New York at Albany
State University of New York at
   Binghamton
State University of New York at New
   Paltz
State University of New York College at
   Brockport
State University of New York College at
   Geneseo
State University of New York College at
   Oneonta
State University of New York College of
   Agriculture and Technology at
   Cobleskill
State University of New York College of
   Technology at Canton
State University of New York College of
   Technology at Delhi
State University of New York Institute of
   Technology at Utica/Rome
Syracuse University
Union College
University of Rochester
Utica College
Yeshiva Mikdash Melech

North Carolina

Appalachian State University
Barton College
Davidson College
Duke University
East Carolina University
Elizabeth City State University
Elon University
Guilford College
High Point University
Johnson C. Smith University
Lees-McRae College
Meredith College
Mount Olive College
North Carolina School of the Arts
North Carolina State University
North Carolina Wesleyan College
Peace College
Piedmont Baptist College
Queens University of Charlotte
St. Augustine's College
Salem College
University of North Carolina at Asheville
Western Carolina University

North Dakota

North Dakota State College of Science
North Dakota State University
University of Mary
University of North Dakota

Ohio

Baldwin-Wallace College
Bowling Green State University
Capital University
Case Western Reserve University
Central State University
Cleveland Institute of Art
College of Mount St. Joseph
Columbus College of Art and Design
Defiance College
Franciscan University of Steubenville
Kent State University
Lake Erie College
Marietta College
MedCentral College of Nursing
Miami University: Oxford Campus
Mount Vernon Nazarene University
Ohio Northern University
Ohio State University: Columbus
   Campus
Ohio University
Otterbein College
Tiffin University
University of Cincinnati
University of Dayton
University of Findlay
Wilberforce University
Xavier University

Oklahoma

Northeastern State University
Oklahoma State University
St. Gregory's University
Southern Nazarene University
University of Oklahoma
University of Science and Arts of
   Oklahoma
University of Tulsa

Oregon

Corban College
Eastern Oregon University
Lewis & Clark College
Linfield College
Northwest Christian College
Pacific University
Reed College
Southern Oregon University
Southwestern Oregon Community
   College
University of Portland
Warner Pacific College
Western Oregon University
Willamette University

Pennsylvania

Bloomsburg University of Pennsylvania
Carnegie Mellon University
Central Pennsylvania College
Cheyney University of Pennsylvania
Delaware Valley College
Drexel University
East Stroudsburg University of
   Pennsylvania
Edinboro University of Pennsylvania

Franklin & Marshall College
Gannon University
Holy Family University
Indiana University of Pennsylvania
Kutztown University of Pennsylvania
Lafayette College
Lehigh University
Lincoln University
Lock Haven University of Pennsylvania
Marywood University
Millersville University of Pennsylvania
Moore College of Art and Design
Philadelphia Biblical University
Philadelphia University
St. Francis University
Saint Joseph's University
Shippensburg University of Pennsylvania
Slippery Rock University of
   Pennsylvania
Temple University
University of Pennsylvania
University of Pittsburgh
University of Pittsburgh at Bradford
University of the Sciences in
   Philadelphia
Villanova University
Westminster College
Widener University
York College of Pennsylvania

Puerto Rico

Universidad Adventista de las Antillas

Rhode Island

Bryant University
Johnson & Wales University: Providence
Providence College
Rhode Island School of Design
Salve Regina University
University of Rhode Island

South Carolina

Allen University
Anderson University
Benedict College
Charleston Southern University
Claflin University
Clemson University
Coker College
Columbia College
Furman University
Limestone College
Morris College
Newberry College
South Carolina State University
University of South Carolina
Winthrop University

South Dakota

Black Hills State University
Dakota State University
Dakota Wesleyan University
Mount Marty College
South Dakota School of Mines and
   Technology
South Dakota State University
University of South Dakota

Tennessee

Belmont University
Bethel College
Carson-Newman College
Christian Brothers University
Freed-Hardeman University
Lambuth University

Lee University
Rhodes College
Tennessee Technological University
Tennessee Wesleyan College
Tusculum College
University of the South
University of Tennessee: Knoxville
University of Tennessee: Martin
Vanderbilt University

Texas

Abilene Christian University
Arlington Baptist College
Baylor University
Concordia University at Austin
Hardin-Simmons University
Houston Baptist University
Howard Payne University
Lamar University
Lubbock Christian University
Midwestern State University
Northwood University: Texas
Our Lady of the Lake University of San
   Antonio
Prairie View A&M University
Rice University
St. Edward's University
St. Mary's University
Sam Houston State University
Southern Methodist University
Southwestern Assemblies of God
   University
Southwestern University
Stephen F. Austin State University
Sul Ross State University
Tarleton State University
Texas A&M University-Kingsville
Texas Christian University
Texas College
Texas Lutheran University
Texas Southern University
Texas State University: San Marcos
Texas Tech University
University of Dallas
University of the Incarnate Word
University of Mary Hardin-Baylor
University of North Texas
Wayland Baptist University

Utah

Westminster College

Vermont

Castleton State College
Champlain College
Lyndon State College
Marlboro College
Southern Vermont College
University of Vermont

Virginia

Bluefield College
Christopher Newport University
College of William and Mary
Eastern Mennonite University
George Mason University
Hampton University
James Madison University
Longwood University
Marymount University
Radford University
Roanoke College
Shenandoah University
Southern Virginia University
University of Mary Washington
University of Virginia
Virginia Commonwealth University

Virginia Intermont College
Virginia Polytechnic Institute and State
   University
Virginia State University
Virginia Wesleyan College
Washington and Lee University

Washington

Central Washington University
Evergreen State College
Gonzaga University
Saint Martin's University
Seattle University
University of Puget Sound
University of Washington
Washington State University
Whitman College
Whitworth University

West Virginia

Fairmont State University
Glenville State College
Marshall University
Mountain State University
University of Charleston
West Virginia University

Wisconsin

Carroll College
Carthage College
Lakeland College
Marquette University
Milwaukee School of Engineering
Mount Mary College
Northland College
University of Wisconsin-Eau Claire
University of Wisconsin-Oshkosh
University of Wisconsin-Platteville
University of Wisconsin-River Falls
University of Wisconsin-Stout
University of Wisconsin-Superior
University of Wisconsin-Whitewater
Viterbo University

211

College size (undergraduate enrollment)

Very small (fewer than 750)

Four-year

Alabama

Andrew Jackson University
Concordia College
Heritage Christian University
Judson College
Southeastern Bible College
United States Sports Academy

Alaska

Alaska Pacific University

Arizona

Arizona Institute of Business and
    Technology
    International Institute of the
        Americas: Mesa
Art Center Design College
Brown Mackie College: Tucson
International Import-Export Institute
Midwestern University: Glendale
Northcentral University
Prescott College

Arkansas

Lyon College
Philander Smith College
University of the Ozarks
Williams Baptist College

California

Alliant International University
American Jewish University
Antioch Southern California
    Antioch University Los Angeles
Bethany University
Bethesda Christian University
California College San Diego
California Institute of Integral Studies
California National University for
    Advanced Studies
California University of Management and
    Sciences
Charles R. Drew University of Medicine
    and Science
Cogswell Polytechnical College
Coleman College
Columbia College: Hollywood
Design Institute of San Diego
DeVry University
    Sherman Oaks
Dominican School of Philosophy and
    Theology
Golden Gate University
Harvey Mudd College
Holy Names University
Hope International University
Humphreys College
John F. Kennedy University
Life Pacific College
Lincoln University
Menlo College
National Hispanic University
NewSchool of Architecture & Design
Northwestern Polytechnic University

Notre Dame de Namur University
Pacific Oaks College
Pacific States University
Platt College
    Ontario
    San Diego
Samuel Merritt College
San Diego Christian College
San Francisco Art Institute
San Francisco Conservatory of Music
School of Urban Missions: Oakland
Soka University of America
Southern California Institute of
    Architecture
Westwood College: South Bay
William Jessup University
World Mission University

Colorado

Aspen University
CollegeAmerica
    Fort Collins
DeVry University
    Westminster
Jones International University
Naropa University
National American University
    Denver
Rocky Mountain College of Art &
    Design
Teikyo Loretto Heights University
Westwood College of Technology
    Westwood College: Denver South

Connecticut

Briarwood College
Holy Apostles College and Seminary
Paier College of Art

District of Columbia

Corcoran College of Art and Design
Potomac College
Southeastern University

Florida

Angley College
Baptist College of Florida
Carlos Albizu University
City College
    Miami
City College: Fort Lauderdale
Florida Christian College
Jones College
Jones College: Miami
Northwood University
    Florida
Remington College: Largo
Remington College: Tampa
Trinity College of Florida
Universidad FLET
Webber International University

Georgia

Beulah Heights University
Carver Bible College
DeVry University
    Alpharetta
Herzing College
Life University

Thomas University
Truett-McConnell College
Wesleyan College

Illinois

Blackburn College
Blessing-Rieman College of Nursing
Lexington College
Lincoln Christian College and Seminary
Rosalind Franklin University of Medicine
    and Science
St. John's College
Shimer College
VanderCook College of Music
West Suburban College of Nursing
Westwood College of Technology
    Westwood College: O'Hare Airport
    Westwood College: River Oaks
Westwood College: DuPage

Indiana

DeVry University: Indianapolis
Holy Cross College
Taylor University Fort Wayne

Iowa

Faith Baptist Bible College and
    Theological Seminary
Kaplan University
    Cedar Rapids
    Des Moines
    Mason City
Maharishi University of Management
Upper Iowa University
Waldorf College

Kansas

Barclay College
Bethany College
Bethel College
Central Christian College of Kansas
McPherson College
Sterling College
Tabor College
University of Kansas Medical Center
University of St. Mary

Kentucky

Alice Lloyd College
Brescia University
Kentucky Christian University
Kentucky Mountain Bible College
St. Catharine College
Union College

Louisiana

Louisiana State University Health
    Sciences Center
St. Joseph Seminary College
School of Urban Missions: New Orleans

Maine

College of the Atlantic
Maine College of Art
New England School of Communications
Thomas College
Unity College
University of Maine
    Machias

Maryland

Baltimore International College
Capitol College
DeVry University: Bethesda
Johns Hopkins University: Peabody
    Conservatory of Music
St. John's College
Washington Bible College

Massachusetts

Atlantic Union College
Bard College at Simon's Rock
Boston Architectural College
Boston Conservatory
Eastern Nazarene College
Hellenic College/Holy Cross
New England Conservatory of Music
Pine Manor College

Rhodec International
School of the Museum of Fine Arts

Michigan

Cleary University
Concordia University
Finlandia University
Kuyper College
Michigan Jewish Institute
Michigan Theological Seminary

Minnesota

Academy College
Bethany Lutheran College
College of Visual Arts
DeVry University
    Edina
Minneapolis College of Art and Design
Minnesota School of Business: Plymouth
Minnesota School of Business: Rochester
Minnesota School of Business: Shakopee
Northwestern Health Sciences University
Pillsbury Baptist Bible College
Rasmussen College
    Eagan

Mississippi

Blue Mountain College

Missouri

Baptist Bible College
Calvary Bible College and Theological
    Seminary
Kansas City Art Institute
Research College of Nursing

Montana

University of Great Falls

Nebraska

Dana College
Grace University
Nebraska Methodist College of Nursing
    and Allied Health
York College

Nevada

DeVry University: Henderson
International Academy of Design and
    Technology: Henderson
Sierra Nevada College
University of Southern Nevada

New Hampshire

Chester College of New England
Daniel Webster College
Magdalen College
Thomas More College of Liberal Arts

New Mexico

Art Center Design College
College of Santa Fe
College of the Southwest
Institute of American Indian Arts
International Institute of the Americas:
    Albuquerque
National American University: Rio
    Rancho
St. John's College

New York

Berkeley College
City University of New York: CUNY
    Online
Concordia College
Davis College
Eastman School of Music of the
    University of Rochester
Juilliard School
King's College
Manhattan School of Music
Mannes College The New School for
    Music
Metropolitan College of New York
New York School of Interior Design
Russell Sage College
State University of New York
    Upstate Medical University
Webb Institute

Wells College
Yeshiva Mikdash Melech

North Carolina
Bennett College
Brevard College
Cabarrus College of Health Sciences
DeVry University: Charlotte
John Wesley College
North Carolina School of the Arts
Peace College
Piedmont Baptist College
Roanoke Bible College
St. Andrews Presbyterian College
Salem College

Ohio
Art Academy of Cincinnati
Bryant & Stratton College
   Parma
   Willoughby Hills
Cincinnati College of Mortuary Science
Cleveland Institute of Art
Cleveland Institute of Music
Kettering College of Medical Arts
Laura and Alvin Siegal College of Judaic
   Studies
MedCentral College of Nursing

Oklahoma
DeVry University: Oklahoma City Center
Southwestern Christian University

Oregon
Cascade College
DeVry University: Portland
Mount Angel Seminary
Northwest Christian College
Oregon Health & Science University
Pacific Northwest College of Art
Pioneer Pacific College
Warner Pacific College

Pennsylvania
Baptist Bible College of Pennsylvania
Chatham University
Curtis Institute of Music
Gratz College
Moore College of Art and Design
Penn State
   Beaver
   Dubois
   Greater Allegheny
   Lehigh Valley
   New Kensington
   Shenango
   Wilkes-Barre
Rosemont College
St. Charles Borromeo Seminary -
   Overbrook
Wilson College

Puerto Rico
Carlos Albizu University: San Juan
Colegio Pentecostal Mizpa
Conservatory of Music of Puerto Rico
Universidad Adventista de las Antillas
University of Puerto Rico
   Medical Sciences

Rhode Island
Zion Bible College

South Carolina
Allen University
Columbia International University
Converse College
Erskine College
South University
Voorhees College

South Dakota
National American University
   Rapid City

Tennessee
American Baptist College of ABT
   Seminary
DeVry University: Memphis

Free Will Baptist Bible College
Lambuth University
LeMoyne-Owen College
Martin Methodist College
Memphis College of Art
Tennessee Temple University
University of Tennessee Health Science
   Center

Texas
Arlington Baptist College
Baptist University of the Americas
College of Saint Thomas More
Criswell College
Huston-Tillotson University
Northwood University: Texas
Texas College
Texas Tech University Health Sciences
   Center
University of Texas
   Health Science Center at San
      Antonio
   Medical Branch at Galveston
   Southwestern Medical Center at
      Dallas

Utah
DeVry University: Sandy
Stevens-Henager College
   Murray
Stevens-Henager College: Ogden

Vermont
Bennington College
Burlington College
College of St. Joseph in Vermont
Marlboro College
Southern Vermont College
Sterling College

Virginia
Christendom College
DeVry University
   Arlington
Randolph College
St. Paul's College
Southern Virginia University
Sweet Briar College
University of Northern Virginia
Virginia Intermont College
World College

Washington
Bastyr University
DeVry University
   Federal Way
Northwest College of Art
Trinity Lutheran College

West Virginia
Alderson-Broaddus College
Appalachian Bible College
Davis and Elkins College
Ohio Valley University
Salem International University

Wisconsin
Bellin College of Nursing
DeVry University: Milwaukee
Milwaukee Institute of Art & Design
Northland College
Silver Lake College

Two-year

Alabama
J. F. Drake State Technical College
Marion Military Institute
Remington College
   Mobile

Arizona
Arizona Automotive Institute
Golf Academy of Arizona
Long Technical College
Paralegal Institute
Tohono O'odham Community College

Arkansas
Crowley's Ridge College

California
American Academy of Dramatic Arts:
   West
Brooks College
California Culinary Academy
Coleman College
   San Marcos
Concorde Career College: North
   Hollywood
Deep Springs College
Empire College
Fashion Careers College
Fashion Institute of Design and
   Merchandising
   San Diego
Marymount College
National Polytechnic College of Science
Professional Golfers Career College
Santa Barbara Business College
   Bakersfield
Western Career College: Stockton

Colorado
Cambridge College
Colorado School of Trades
Everest College: Aurora
Everest College: Colorado Springs
Institute of Business & Medical Careers
IntelliTec College
Kaplan College: Denver
Redstone College
Remington College
   Colorado Springs

Connecticut
Clemens College

Florida
Brown Mackie College: Miami
Central Florida College
City College
   Gainesville
City College: Casselberry
College of Business and Technology:
   Flagler
College of Business and Technology:
   Kendall
Florida College of Natural Health
   Bradenton
Florida Technical College
   Deland
   Orlando
Key College
North Florida Institute: Orange Park
Professional Golfers Career College:
   Orlando
Ultrasound Diagnostic School
   Sanford-Brown Institute:
      Jacksonville
Virginia College at Pensacola

Georgia
Everest Institute
Gupton Jones College of Funeral Service
Savannah River College
Young Harris College

Hawaii
Hawaii Tokai International College
Remington College
   Honolulu
TransPacific Hawaii College
University of Hawaii
   Kauai Community College

Idaho
Stevens-Henager College: Boise

Illinois
College of Office Technology
MacCormac College
Morrison Institute of Technology
Springfield College in Illinois

Indiana
Ancilla College
College of Court Reporting
Indiana Business College: Indianapolis
   Northwest
Kaplan College: Hammond
Kaplan College: Merrillville

Iowa
St. Luke's College

Kansas
Colby Community College
Hesston College

Kentucky
Daymar College
   Louisville
Louisville Technical Institute
Southern Ohio College
   Brown Mackie College: North
      Kentucky
Southwestern College: Florence
Spencerian College: Lexington

Louisiana
ITI Technical College
Remington College
   Baton Rouge
   Lafayette

Maine
Washington County Community College

Maryland
Kaplan College: Hagerstown

Massachusetts
Benjamin Franklin Institute of
   Technology
Caritas Laboure College
Fisher College
Marian Court College
New England College of Finance

Michigan
Saginaw Chippewa Tribal College

Minnesota
Herzing College
   Minneapolis Drafting School
      Division of
Le Cordon Bleu College of Culinary Arts
Minneapolis Business College
Northwest Technical Institute
Rasmussen College
   Mankato
White Earth Tribal and Community
   College

Mississippi
Antonelli College
   Hattiesburg
   Jackson
Blue Cliff College: Gulfport

Missouri
Bolivar Technical College
Cottey College
Patricia Stevens College
Wentworth Military Junior College

Montana
Dawson Community College

Nebraska
Kaplan University
   Lincoln
Nebraska College of Technical
   Agriculture
Vatterott College: Spring Valley

Nevada
Career College of Northern Nevada
Le Cordon Bleu College of Culinary Arts

New Mexico
Mesalands Community College
Navajo Technical College
New Mexico Military Institute

213

New York

Bryant & Stratton Business Institute
    Bryant & Stratton College: Albany
    Bryant & Stratton College: Buffalo
    Bryant & Stratton College:
      Rochester
    Bryant & Stratton College:
      Southtowns
Bryant & Stratton College: Henrietta
Bryant & Stratton College: Syracuse
    North
Institute of Design and Construction
Island Drafting and Technical Institute
Long Island Business Institute
Mildred Elley
New York Career Institute
Phillips Beth Israel School of Nursing
St. Elizabeth College of Nursing
Swedish Institute
Utica School of Commerce
Villa Maria College of Buffalo

North Carolina

Louisburg College
Miller-Motte Technical College: Cary
Pamlico Community College

North Dakota

Fort Berthold Community College
Minot State University: Bottineau
    Campus
Rasmussen College: Bismarck
United Tribes Technical College
Williston State College

Ohio

Art Institute of Cincinnati
Art Institute of Ohio: Cincinnati
ETI Technical College of Niles
Gallipolis Career College
Hondros College
Ohio Business College
Ohio College of Massotherapy
Ohio Institute of Health Careers:
    Columbus
Ohio Institute of Photography and
    Technology
Ohio State University
    Agricultural Technical Institute
Remington College: Cleveland West
Southwestern College of Business
    Southwestern College: Vine Street
    Campus
Technology Education College
Wright State University: Lake Campus

Oklahoma

Platt College
    Tulsa
Platt College: Oklahoma City Central
Tulsa Welding School

Oregon

Pioneer Pacific College: Springfield

Pennsylvania

Antonelli Institute of Art and
    Photography
Berean Institute
Bradford School: Pittsburgh
Business Institute of Pennsylvania
Cambria-Rowe Business College:
    Indiana
Career Training Academy
Career Training Academy: Monroeville
Career Training Academy: Pittsburgh
CHI Institute: Franklin Mills
Commonwealth Technical Institute
DuBois Business College
DuBois Business College
    Huntingdon
    Oil City
Erie Business Center
Erie Business Center South
Erie Institute of Technology
JNA Institute of Culinary Arts
Johnson College

Lansdale School of Business
Laurel Business Institute
Lincoln Technical Institute: Allentown
Lincoln Technical Institute: Northeast
    Philadelphia
Lincoln Technical Institute: Philadelphia
Oakbridge Academy of Arts
Orleans Technical Institute - Center City
    Campus
Pace Institute
Penn Commercial Business and
    Technical School
Pennco Tech
Pennsylvania Institute of Technology
Pittsburgh Institute of Aeronautics
Pittsburgh Institute of Mortuary Science
Tri-State Business Institute
Triangle Tech
    Greensburg
Triangle Tech: Bethlehem
University of Pittsburgh
    Titusville
Valley Forge Military College
West Virginia Career Institute

Puerto Rico

Columbia College
    Columbia Centro Universitario:
      Yauco
Ramirez College of Business and
    Technology

South Carolina

Forrest Junior College
Miller-Motte Technical College
University of South Carolina
    Union

South Dakota

Kilian Community College
Mitchell Technical Institute
Sisseton Wahpeton College

Tennessee

Draughons Junior College: Clarksville
Draughons Junior College: Murfreesboro
Draughons Junior College: Nashville
Hiwassee College
Huntington College of Health Sciences
Nossi College of Art
Vatterott College: Memphis

Texas

Commonwealth Institute of Funeral
    Service
Court Reporting Institute of Houston
Everest College: Arlington
Frank Phillips College
Hallmark College of Aeronautics
Hallmark College of Technology
Jacksonville College
Lon Morris College
Remington College
    Fort Worth
    Houston
Texas State Technical College: Marshall
Western Technical College
Westwood College: Houston South

Utah

Careers Unlimited

Vermont

Landmark College
New England Culinary Institute

Virginia

Aviation Institute of Maintenance:
    Virginia Beach
Beta Tech: Richmond South
Beta Tech: Richmond West
Bryant & Stratton College
    Richmond
Bryant & Stratton College: Virginia
    Beach
Tidewater Tech
    Virginia Beach
Tidewater Tech: Chesapeake

Washington

Grays Harbor College

West Virginia

Valley College of Technology
West Virginia Business College
West Virginia Junior College: Bridgeport

Wisconsin

University of Wisconsin
    Baraboo/Sauk County
    Richland

Wyoming

Eastern Wyoming College

Small (750-1,999)

Four-year

Alabama

Birmingham-Southern College
Huntingdon College
Miles College
Oakwood University
Spring Hill College
Stillman College
University of Mobile
Virginia College at Huntsville

Alaska

University of Alaska
    Southeast

Arizona

Art Institute
    of Phoenix
DeVry University
    Phoenix
Embry-Riddle Aeronautical University:
    Prescott Campus
University of Advancing Technology

Arkansas

Hendrix College
John Brown University
Ouachita Baptist University

California

Art Institute
    of California: Orange County
Art Institute of California: San Francisco
California College of the Arts
California Design College
California Institute of Technology
California Institute of the Arts
California Maritime Academy
Claremont McKenna College
Concordia University
DeVry University
    Fremont
    Long Beach
    Pomona
Dominican University of California
Fresno Pacific University
La Sierra University
Loma Linda University
The Master's College
Mills College
Occidental College
Otis College of Art and Design
Pacific Union College
Pitzer College
Pomona College
Scripps College
Simpson University
University of California: Merced
University of La Verne
Vanguard University of Southern
    California
Westmont College
Whittier College
Woodbury University

Colorado

American Sentinel University
Colorado Christian University

Colorado Technical University
Johnson & Wales University: Denver
Regis University

Connecticut

Albertus Magnus College
Charter Oak State College
Connecticut College
Mitchell College
Post University
St. Joseph College
University of Bridgeport

Delaware

Goldey-Beacom College

District of Columbia

Trinity Washington University

Florida

DeVry University
    Miramar
    Orlando
Eckerd College
Edward Waters College
Everest University: Brandon
Everest University: Tampa
Florida Memorial University
Florida Southern College
Hodges University
Johnson & Wales University: North
    Miami
Keiser University
Miami International University of Art
    and Design
New College of Florida
Ringling College of Art and Design
Rollins College
St. Leo University
Saint Thomas University
Warner Southern College

Georgia

Agnes Scott College
American InterContinental University
Bauder College
Berry College
Brenau University
Brewton-Parker College
Covenant College
LaGrange College
Oglethorpe University
Paine College
Piedmont College
Reinhardt College
Shorter College
Toccoa Falls College

Hawaii

University of Hawaii
    West Oahu

Idaho

College of Idaho
Northwest Nazarene University

Illinois

Concordia University
DeVry University
    Addison
    Chicago
    Tinley Park
Dominican University
East-West University
Greenville College
Illinois College
Illinois Institute of Art: Schaumburg
Judson University
Knox College
Lake Forest College
Monmouth College
Quincy University
Rockford College
Trinity Christian College
Trinity International University
University of St. Francis
Westwood College: Chicago Loop

Indiana
Calumet College of St. Joseph
Earlham College
Franklin College
Goshen College
Hanover College
Huntington University
Indiana University
    East
International Business College
Manchester College
Marian College
Oakland City University
Rose-Hulman Institute of Technology
Saint Mary's College
St. Mary-of-the-Woods College
Taylor University
Tri-State University
University of St. Francis
Wabash College

Iowa
Briar Cliff University
Buena Vista University
Central College
Clarke College
Coe College
Cornell College
Graceland University
Grand View College
Grinnell College
Iowa Wesleyan College
Loras College
Morningside College
Mount Mercy College
Northwestern College
Simpson College
University of Dubuque
Wartburg College
William Penn University

Kansas
Baker University
Benedictine College
MidAmerica Nazarene University
Newman University
Southwestern College

Kentucky
Berea College
Campbellsville University
Centre College
Georgetown College
Lindsey Wilson College
Mid-Continent University
Midway College
Thomas More College
Transylvania University
University of the Cumberlands

Louisiana
Centenary College of Louisiana
Dillard University
Louisiana College

Maine
Bates College
Bowdoin College
Colby College
Husson College
Maine Maritime Academy
St. Joseph's College
University of Maine
    Fort Kent
University of New England

Maryland
Columbia Union College
Goucher College
Hood College
Maryland Institute College of Art
McDaniel College
Mount St. Mary's University
St. Mary's College of Maryland
Sojourner-Douglass College
University of Maryland
    Baltimore

Washington College

Massachusetts
American International College
Amherst College
Anna Maria College
Babson College
Bay Path College
Becker College
Cambridge College
Elms College
Gordon College
Hampshire College
Lasell College
Lesley University
Massachusetts College of Art
Massachusetts College of Liberal Arts
Massachusetts Maritime Academy
New England Institute of Art
Nichols College
Regis College
Wheaton College
Wheelock College
Williams College

Michigan
Adrian College
Albion College
Alma College
Andrews University
Aquinas College
College for Creative Studies
Cornerstone University
Hillsdale College
Kalamazoo College
Kendall College of Art and Design of
    Ferris State University
Marygrove College
Northwood University: Michigan
Olivet College
Rochester College
Siena Heights University
Walsh College of Accountancy and
    Business Administration

Minnesota
Art Institutes International
    Minnesota
Brown College
Carleton College
College of St. Scholastica
Concordia University: St. Paul
Hamline University
Macalester College
North Central University
Northwestern College
St. John's University
St. Mary's University of Minnesota
University of Minnesota
    Crookston
    Morris
Walden University

Mississippi
Millsaps College
Rust College
Tougaloo College
William Carey University

Missouri
Avila University
Central Methodist University
College of the Ozarks
Columbia College
Culver-Stockton College
DeVry University
    Kansas City
Drury University
Evangel University
Fontbonne University
Hannibal-LaGrange College
Harris-Stowe State University
Missouri Baptist University
Missouri Valley College
Rockhurst University
Stephens College
Westminster College

William Jewell College
William Woods University

Montana
Carroll College
Montana State University
    Northern
Rocky Mountain College
University of Montana: Western

Nebraska
College of Saint Mary
Concordia University
Doane College
Hastings College
Midland Lutheran College
Nebraska Wesleyan University
Union College

Nevada
Art Institute
    of Las Vegas
Nevada State College

New Hampshire
Colby-Sawyer College
Franklin Pierce University
Granite State College
New England College
Rivier College
St. Anselm College
Southern New Hampshire University
University of New Hampshire at
    Manchester

New Jersey
Caldwell College
College of St. Elizabeth
DeVry University: North Brunswick
Drew University
Felician College
Georgian Court University

New Mexico
New Mexico Highlands University
New Mexico Institute of Mining and
    Technology
Western New Mexico University

New York
Albany College of Pharmacy
Bard College
Briarcliffe College
Cazenovia College
College of Mount St. Vincent
College of New Rochelle
Columbia University
    School of General Studies
Cooper Union for the Advancement of
    Science and Art
D'Youville College
Daemen College
DeVry Institute of Technology
    New York
Dominican College of Blauvelt
Elmira College
Eugene Lang College The New School
    for Liberal Arts
Five Towns College
Hamilton College
Hartwick College
Hobart and William Smith Colleges
Houghton College
Keuka College
Laboratory Institute of Merchandising
Manhattanville College
Marymount Manhattan College
Medaille College
Paul Smith's College
Polytechnic University
Roberts Wesleyan College
Sage College of Albany
Saint Bonaventure University
St. Joseph's College
St. Thomas Aquinas College
Sarah Lawrence College

State University of New York
    College of Environmental Science
    and Forestry
    Institute of Technology at
    Utica/Rome
    Maritime College
United States Merchant Marine Academy
Vaughn College of Aeronautics and
    Technology
Wagner College

North Carolina
Art Institute
    of Charlotte
Barton College
Belmont Abbey College
Catawba College
Chowan University
Davidson College
Greensboro College
Johnson C. Smith University
Lees-McRae College
Lenoir-Rhyne College
Livingstone College
Meredith College
Methodist University
Montreat College
North Carolina Wesleyan College
Pfeiffer University
Queens University of Charlotte
St. Augustine's College
Warren Wilson College
Wingate University

North Dakota
Jamestown College
Mayville State University
Valley City State University

Ohio
Bluffton University
Central State University
Cincinnati Christian University
College of Mount St. Joseph
College of Wooster
Columbus College of Art and Design
Defiance College
Franciscan University of Steubenville
Heidelberg College
Hiram College
Kenyon College
Lake Erie College
Lourdes College
Malone College
Marietta College
Muskingum College
Ohio State University
    Lima Campus
    Mansfield Campus
    Marion Campus
Ohio University
    Zanesville Campus
Ohio Wesleyan University
Tiffin University
University of Rio Grande
Ursuline College
Wilmington College
Wittenberg University

Oklahoma
Bacone College
National Education Center
    Spartan College of Aeronautics and
    Technology
Northwestern Oklahoma State University
Oklahoma Baptist University
Oklahoma Christian University
Oklahoma Panhandle State University
Oklahoma Wesleyan University
St. Gregory's University
Southern Nazarene University
University of Science and Arts of
    Oklahoma

Oregon
Art Institute of Portland
Concordia University

Corban College
George Fox University
Lewis & Clark College
Linfield College
Marylhurst University
Pacific University
Reed College
Willamette University

Pennsylvania

Alvernia College
Bryn Mawr College
Cabrini College
Carlow University
Cedar Crest College
Central Pennsylvania College
Chestnut Hill College
Cheyney University of Pennsylvania
Delaware Valley College
DeVry University
    Fort Washington
Geneva College
Gwynedd-Mercy College
Haverford College
Juniata College
Keystone College
La Roche College
Lebanon Valley College
Lincoln University
Lycoming College
Marywood University
Moravian College
Mount Aloysius College
Penn State
    Brandywine
    Fayette, The Eberly Campus
    Hazleton
    Mont Alto
    Schuylkill
    Worthington Scranton
    York
Philadelphia Biblical University
St. Francis University
St. Vincent College
Seton Hill University
Susquehanna University
Swarthmore College
Thiel College
Thomas Jefferson University: College of
    Health Professions
University of Pittsburgh
    Bradford
    Greensburg
Ursinus College
Valley Forge Christian College
Washington & Jefferson College
Waynesburg University
Westminster College

Puerto Rico

Atlantic College
University College of San Juan
University of Puerto Rico
    Utuado

Rhode Island

Rhode Island School of Design

South Carolina

Anderson University
Claflin University
Columbia College
Limestone College
Morris College
Newberry College
North Greenville University
Southern Wesleyan University
University of South Carolina
    Beaufort
Wofford College

South Dakota

Augustana College
Dakota State University
Dakota Wesleyan University
Mount Marty College
Northern State University

Oglala Lakota College
Presentation College
South Dakota School of Mines and
    Technology
University of Sioux Falls

Tennessee

Aquinas College
Bethel College
Bryan College
Carson-Newman College
Christian Brothers University
Crichton College
Cumberland University
Freed-Hardeman University
King College
Lane College
Lincoln Memorial University
Maryville College
Milligan College
Rhodes College
Tennessee Wesleyan College
Trevecca Nazarene University
University of the South

Texas

Art Institute
    of Dallas
    of Houston
Austin College
Concordia University at Austin
DeVry University
    Irving
DeVry University: Houston
East Texas Baptist University
Hardin-Simmons University
Houston Baptist University
Howard Payne University
Lubbock Christian University
McMurry University
Our Lady of the Lake University of San
    Antonio
Schreiner University
Southwestern Adventist University
Southwestern Assemblies of God
    University
Southwestern University
Sul Ross State University
Texas A&M University
    Galveston
    Texarkana
Texas Lutheran University
Texas Wesleyan University
University of Dallas
University of Houston
    Victoria
University of St. Thomas
Wayland Baptist University
Wiley College

Vermont

Castleton State College
Green Mountain College
Johnson State College
Lyndon State College
St. Michael's College

Virginia

Art Institute
    of Washington
Averett University
Bluefield College
Bridgewater College
Eastern Mennonite University
Emory & Henry College
Ferrum College
Hampden-Sydney College
Hollins University
Jefferson College of Health Sciences
Mary Baldwin College
Randolph-Macon College
Regent University
Roanoke College
Shenandoah University
University of Virginia's College at Wise
Virginia Military Institute

Virginia Union University
Virginia Wesleyan College
Washington and Lee University

Washington

City University of Seattle
Cornish College of the Arts
DigiPen Institute of Technology
Heritage University
Northwest University
Saint Martin's University
Walla Walla University
Whitman College

West Virginia

Bethany College
Bluefield State College
Glenville State College
University of Charleston
West Virginia Wesleyan College
Wheeling Jesuit University

Wisconsin

Beloit College
Edgewood College
Lawrence University
Maranatha Baptist Bible College
Marian College of Fond du Lac
Mount Mary College
Viterbo University

Two-year

Alabama

Chattahoochee Valley Community
    College

Arizona

Chandler-Gilbert Community College
    Pecos
Dine College
Universal Technical Institute

Arkansas

Arkansas State University
    Mountain Home
Arkansas State University: Newport
Black River Technical College
East Arkansas Community College
Ouachita Technical College
South Arkansas Community College
Southeast Arkansas College
Southern Arkansas University Tech

California

California School of Culinary Arts
College of the Siskiyous
Copper Mountain College
Fashion Institute of Design and
    Merchandising
    San Francisco
Feather River College
Lassen College
Maric College: Salida
San Joaquin Valley College
West Hills College: Coalinga

Colorado

Lamar Community College
Morgan Community College
Northeastern Junior College
Otero Junior College

Connecticut

Goodwin College
Middlesex Community College

Florida

Florida Keys Community College
North Florida Community College
South Florida Community College
Southwest Florida College

Georgia

Atlanta Metropolitan College
Le Cordon Bleu College of Culinary Arts
South Georgia College
Southwest Georgia Technical College

Hawaii

University of Hawaii
    Windward Community College

Illinois

Black Hawk College: East Campus
Cooking & Hospitality Institute of
    Chicago
Highland Community College
Illinois Eastern Community Colleges
    Lincoln Trail College
    Olney Central College
    Wabash Valley College
John Wood Community College
Lincoln College
Northwestern Business College
Sauk Valley Community College

Indiana

Brown Mackie College: Fort Wayne
Ivy Tech Community College: Richmond
Ivy Tech State College
    Ivy Tech Community College:
        Southeast

Iowa

AIB College of Business
Clinton Community College
Iowa Lakes Community College
Muscatine Community College
Southwestern Community College

Kansas

Coffeyville Community College
Independence Community College
Labette Community College
Neosho County Community College
Pratt Community College

Louisiana

Nunez Community College

Maine

Andover College
Central Maine Community College
Eastern Maine Community College
Northern Maine Community College
York County Community College

Maryland

Garrett College
TESST College of Technology
    Baltimore

Massachusetts

Bay State College
Berkshire Community College
Dean College
Greenfield Community College

Michigan

Bay de Noc Community College
Glen Oaks Community College
Gogebic Community College
Kirtland Community College

Minnesota

Anoka Technical College
Dunwoody College of Technology
Hibbing Community College
Itasca Community College
Mesabi Range Community and Technical
    College
Minnesota State College - Southeast
    Technical
Northland Community & Technical
    College
Northwest Technical College
Pine Technical College
Rasmussen College
    Eden Prairie

Missouri

Linn State Technical College

Montana

Flathead Valley Community College

Nebraska

Western Nebraska Community College

New Hampshire
Lakes Region Community College
Nashua Community College
River Valley Community College
White Mountains Community College

New Jersey
Salem Community College

New Mexico
Clovis Community College

New York
Art Institute
　　of New York City
Columbia-Greene Community College
Fulton-Montgomery Community College
North Country Community College
Sullivan County Community College
Trocaire College

North Carolina
Bladen Community College
Carteret Community College
College of the Albemarle
Martin Community College
Mayland Community College
McDowell Technical Community College
Rockingham Community College
Southeastern Community College
Wilson Community College

North Dakota
Lake Region State College
Turtle Mountain Community College

Ohio
Brown Mackie College: Cincinnati
Miami University
　　Middletown Campus
University of Akron: Wayne College
Zane State College

Oklahoma
Northeastern Oklahoma Agricultural and
　　Mechanical College
Western Oklahoma State College

Oregon
Clatsop Community College
Treasure Valley Community College
Umpqua Community College

Pennsylvania
Community College of Beaver County
Harcum College
Lackawanna College
Manor College
Pennsylvania Culinary Institute
Pennsylvania Highlands Community
　　College

Puerto Rico
Huertas Junior College
Humacao Community College
ICPR Junior College
Universal Technology College of Puerto
　　Rico

South Carolina
Denmark Technical College
Northeastern Technical College
Spartanburg Methodist College
University of South Carolina
　　Lancaster
　　Sumter

Texas
Clarendon College
Lamar State College at Orange
Panola College
Texas Culinary Academy
Texas State Technical College
　　Sweetwater
Western Texas College

Virginia
Paul D. Camp Community College
Richard Bland College

Washington
Big Bend Community College
Lower Columbia College
Northwest Indian College
Peninsula College
Renton Technical College

West Virginia
Potomac State College of West Virginia
　　University
West Virginia State Community and
　　Technical College

Wisconsin
University of Wisconsin
　　Fox Valley
　　Rock County
　　Washington County
　　Waukesha

Wyoming
Central Wyoming College
Northwest College
Sheridan College

Medium to large (2,000-7,499)

Four-year

Alabama
Alabama Agricultural and Mechanical
　　University
Alabama State University
Athens State University
Auburn University at Montgomery
Faulkner University
Jacksonville State University
Samford University
Tuskegee University
University of Alabama
　　Huntsville
University of Montevallo
University of North Alabama
University of West Alabama

Alaska
University of Alaska
　　Fairbanks

Arizona
Arizona State University West
Grand Canyon University
Western International University

Arkansas
Arkansas Tech University
Harding University
Henderson State University
Southern Arkansas University
University of Arkansas
　　Fort Smith
　　Monticello
　　Pine Bluff

California
Azusa Pacific University
Biola University
California Baptist University
California Lutheran University
California State University
　　Bakersfield
　　Monterey Bay
　　Stanislaus
California State University: Channel
　　Islands
Chapman University
Loyola Marymount University
National University
Pepperdine University
Point Loma Nazarene University
St. Mary's College of California
Santa Clara University
Stanford University
University of Redlands
University of San Diego
University of San Francisco

University of the Pacific

Colorado
Adams State College
Art Institute
　　of Colorado
Colorado College
Colorado School of Mines
Colorado State University
　　Pueblo
Fort Lewis College
Mesa State College
University of Colorado
　　Colorado Springs
University of Denver
Western State College of Colorado

Connecticut
Eastern Connecticut State University
Fairfield University
Quinnipiac University
Sacred Heart University
Trinity College
University of New Haven
Wesleyan University
Yale University

Delaware
Delaware State University
Wesley College

District of Columbia
American University
Catholic University of America
Georgetown University
Howard University
University of the District of Columbia

Florida
Art Institute of Fort Lauderdale
Barry University
Bethune-Cookman University
Chipola Junior College
Embry-Riddle Aeronautical University
Flagler College
Florida Institute of Technology
Jacksonville University
Lynn University
Nova Southeastern University
Palm Beach Atlantic University
Southeastern University
Stetson University
University of Tampa

Georgia
Albany State University
Armstrong Atlantic State University
Art Institute
　　of Atlanta
Ashworth University
Augusta State University
Clark Atlanta University
Clayton State University
Columbus State University
DeVry University
　　Decatur
Emory University
Georgia College and State University
Georgia Southwestern State University
Mercer University
Morehouse College
North Georgia College & State
　　University
Savannah College of Art and Design
Savannah State University
Southern Polytechnic State University
Spelman College

Hawaii
Brigham Young University-Hawaii
Hawaii Pacific University
University of Hawaii
　　Hilo

Idaho
Lewis-Clark State College

Illinois
Augustana College
Aurora University
Benedictine University
Bradley University
Chicago State University
Elmhurst College
Governors State University
Illinois Institute of Art: Chicago
Illinois Institute of Technology
Illinois Wesleyan University
Lewis University
McKendree University
Millikin University
North Central College
North Park University
Olivet Nazarene University
Robert Morris College: Chicago
Roosevelt University
St. Xavier University
School of the Art Institute of Chicago
University of Chicago
University of Illinois
　　Springfield
Wheaton College

Indiana
Bethel College
Butler University
DePauw University
Indiana Institute of Technology
Indiana University
　　Kokomo
　　Northwest
　　South Bend
　　Southeast
Indiana Wesleyan University
Purdue University
　　North Central
University of Evansville
University of Indianapolis
Valparaiso University

Iowa
Drake University
Luther College
St. Ambrose University

Kansas
Emporia State University
Friends University
Pittsburg State University
Washburn University

Kentucky
Bellarmine University
Kentucky State University
Morehead State University
Sullivan University

Louisiana
Grambling State University
Louisiana State University
　　Shreveport
Loyola University New Orleans
McNeese State University
Nicholls State University
Southern University
　　New Orleans
Southern University and Agricultural and
　　Mechanical College
Tulane University
University of Louisiana at Monroe
Xavier University of Louisiana

Maine
University of Maine
　　Augusta
　　Farmington
University of Southern Maine

Maryland
Bowie State University
College of Notre Dame of Maryland
Coppin State University
Frostburg State University
Johns Hopkins University

217

Loyola College in Maryland
Salisbury University
University of Baltimore
University of Maryland
    Eastern Shore
Villa Julie College

Massachusetts

Assumption College
Bentley College
Berklee College of Music
Brandeis University
Clark University
College of the Holy Cross
Curry College
Emerson College
Emmanuel College
Endicott College
Fitchburg State College
Framingham State College
Harvard College
Massachusetts College of Pharmacy and
    Health Sciences
Massachusetts Institute of Technology
Merrimack College
Mount Holyoke College
Salem State College
Simmons College
Smith College
Springfield College
Stonehill College
Suffolk University
Tufts University
Wellesley College
Wentworth Institute of Technology
Western New England College
Worcester Polytechnic Institute
Worcester State College

Michigan

Calvin College
Hope College
Kettering University
Lake Superior State University
Lawrence Technological University
Madonna University
Michigan Technological University
Spring Arbor University
University of Detroit Mercy
University of Michigan
    Dearborn
    Flint

Minnesota

Augsburg College
Bemidji State University
Bethel University
College of St. Benedict
College of St. Catherine
Concordia College: Moorhead
Gustavus Adolphus College
St. Olaf College
Southwest Minnesota State University
University of St. Thomas
Winona State University

Mississippi

Alcorn State University
Belhaven College
Delta State University
Jackson State University
Mississippi College
Mississippi University for Women
Mississippi Valley State University

Missouri

Global University
Lincoln University
Lindenwood University
Maryville University of Saint Louis
Missouri Southern State University
Northwest Missouri State University
Saint Louis University
Southwest Baptist University
Truman State University

University of Missouri
    Kansas City
    Missouri University of Science and
        Technology
Washington University in St. Louis
Webster University

Montana

Montana State University
    Billings
Montana Tech of the University of
    Montana

Nebraska

Bellevue University
Chadron State College
Creighton University
University of Nebraska
    Kearney
Wayne State College

New Hampshire

Dartmouth College
Hesser College
Plymouth State University

New Jersey

Berkeley College
Bloomfield College
Centenary College
The College of New Jersey
Fairleigh Dickinson University
    College at Florham
    Metropolitan Campus
Monmouth University
New Jersey City University
New Jersey Institute of Technology
Princeton University
Ramapo College of New Jersey
Richard Stockton College of New Jersey
Rider University
Rutgers, The State University of New
    Jersey
        Camden Regional Campus
        Newark Regional Campus
Saint Peter's College
Seton Hall University
Stevens Institute of Technology

New Mexico

Eastern New Mexico University

New York

Adelphi University
Alfred University
Barnard College
Berkeley College of New York City
Canisius College
City University of New York
    Medgar Evers College
    York College
Clarkson University
Colgate University
College of Saint Rose
Columbia University
Culinary Institute of America
Dowling College
Globe Institute of Technology
Iona College
Ithaca College
Le Moyne College
Long Island University
    Brooklyn Campus
    C. W. Post Campus
Manhattan College
Marist College
Mercy College
Molloy College
Monroe College
Nazareth College of Rochester
New York Institute of Technology
Niagara University
Pace University
Parsons The New School for Design
Pratt Institute
Rensselaer Polytechnic Institute
St. Francis College

St. John Fisher College
St. Joseph's College: Suffolk Campus
St. Lawrence University
School of Visual Arts
Siena College
Skidmore College
State University of New York
    College at Brockport
    College at Cortland
    College at Fredonia
    College at Geneseo
    College at Old Westbury
    College at Oneonta
    College at Plattsburgh
    College at Potsdam
    College of Technology at Canton
    Farmingdale
    New Paltz
    Oswego
    Purchase
Union College
University of Rochester
Utica College
Vassar College

North Carolina

Campbell University
Duke University
Elizabeth City State University
Elon University
Fayetteville State University
Gardner-Webb University
Guilford College
High Point University
Johnson & Wales University: Charlotte
Mount Olive College
North Carolina Central University
Shaw University
University of North Carolina
    Asheville
    Pembroke
Wake Forest University
Western Carolina University
Winston-Salem State University

North Dakota

Dickinson State University
Minot State University
University of Mary

Ohio

Ashland University
Baldwin-Wallace College
Capital University
Case Western Reserve University
Cedarville University
Denison University
DeVry University
    Columbus
John Carroll University
Mount Union College
Mount Vernon Nazarene University
Oberlin College
Ohio Dominican University
Ohio Northern University
Ohio State University
    Newark Campus
Otterbein College
Shawnee State University
University of Dayton
University of Findlay
Walsh University
Xavier University

Oklahoma

Cameron University
East Central University
Langston University
Oklahoma City University
Oral Roberts University
Southeastern Oklahoma State University
Southwestern Oklahoma State University
University of Tulsa

Oregon

Eastern Oregon University
Oregon Institute of Technology

Southern Oregon University
University of Portland
Western Oregon University

Pennsylvania

Albright College
Allegheny College
Arcadia University
Art Institute
    of Philadelphia
Bucknell University
California University of Pennsylvania
Carnegie Mellon University
Clarion University of Pennsylvania
DeSales University
Dickinson College
Duquesne University
East Stroudsburg University of
    Pennsylvania
Eastern University
Edinboro University of Pennsylvania
Elizabethtown College
Franklin & Marshall College
Gannon University
Gettysburg College
Grove City College
Holy Family University
Immaculata University
King's College
La Salle University
Lafayette College
Lehigh University
Lock Haven University of Pennsylvania
Mansfield University of Pennsylvania
Mercyhurst College
Messiah College
Millersville University of Pennsylvania
Misericordia University
Muhlenberg College
Neumann College
Peirce College
Penn State
    Abington
    Altoona
    Berks
    Erie, The Behrend College
    Harrisburg
Pennsylvania College of Technology
Philadelphia University
Point Park University
Robert Morris University
Saint Joseph's University
Shippensburg University of Pennsylvania
University of Pittsburgh
    Johnstown
University of Scranton
University of the Arts
University of the Sciences in
    Philadelphia
Villanova University
Widener University
York College of Pennsylvania

Puerto Rico

American University of Puerto Rico
Caribbean University
Inter American University of Puerto Rico
    Aguadilla Campus
    Barranquitas Campus
    Bayamon Campus
    Fajardo Campus
    Guayama Campus
    Metropolitan Campus
    Ponce Campus
    San German Campus
Pontifical Catholic University of Puerto
    Rico
Universidad Politecnica de Puerto Rico
University of Puerto Rico
    Aguadilla
    Arecibo
    Bayamon University College
    Carolina Regional College
    Cayey University College
    Humacao
    Ponce

Rhode Island

Brown University
Bryant University
New England Institute of Technology
Providence College
Rhode Island College
Roger Williams University
Salve Regina University

South Carolina

Benedict College
Charleston Southern University
The Citadel
Coastal Carolina University
Francis Marion University
Furman University
Lander University
South Carolina State University
University of South Carolina
    Aiken
    Upstate
Winthrop University

South Dakota

Black Hills State University
University of South Dakota

Tennessee

Belmont University
Lee University
Lipscomb University
Tennessee State University
Tusculum College
Union University
University of Tennessee
    Martin
Vanderbilt University

Texas

Abilene Christian University
Angelo State University
Dallas Baptist University
LeTourneau University
Midwestern State University
Prairie View A&M University
Rice University
St. Edward's University
St. Mary's University
Southern Methodist University
Texas A&M International University
Texas A&M University
    Commerce
    Kingsville
Texas Christian University
Texas Woman's University
Trinity University
University of Houston
    Clear Lake
University of Mary Hardin-Baylor
University of Texas
    Tyler
    of the Permian Basin
University of the Incarnate Word
West Texas A&M University

Utah

Dixie State College of Utah
Southern Utah University
Westminster College

Vermont

Champlain College
Middlebury College

Virginia

Christopher Newport University
College of William and Mary
Hampton University
Longwood University
Lynchburg College
Marymount University
Norfolk State University
University of Mary Washington
University of Richmond
Virginia State University

Washington

Art Institute of Seattle

Evergreen State College
Gonzaga University
Pacific Lutheran University
Seattle Pacific University
Seattle University
University of Puget Sound
Whitworth University

West Virginia

Concord University
Fairmont State University
Mountain State University
Shepherd University
West Liberty State College
West Virginia University at Parkersburg

Wisconsin

Alverno College
Cardinal Stritch University
Carroll College
Carthage College
Concordia University Wisconsin
Lakeland College
Milwaukee School of Engineering
St. Norbert College
University of Wisconsin
    Green Bay
    Parkside
    Platteville
    River Falls
    Stout
    Superior

Two-year

Alabama

Bishop State Community College
Faulkner State Community College
Gadsden State Community College
George C. Wallace State Community
    College
        George C. Wallace Community
            College at Dothan
Jefferson State Community College
Lawson State Community College
Southern Union State Community
    College

Arizona

Arizona Western College
Central Arizona College
Cochise College
Eastern Arizona College
Estrella Mountain Community College
Everest College
    Phoenix
Glendale Community College
Mohave Community College
Yavapai College

Arkansas

National Park Community College
Phillips Community College of the
    University of Arkansas

California

Art Institute
    of California: Los Angeles
Barstow Community College
Berkeley City College
Canada College
Cerro Coso Community College
College of Alameda
College of Marin: Kentfield
College of the Redwoods
Columbia College
Crafton Hills College
El Camino College: Compton Center
Fashion Institute of Design and
    Merchandising
        Los Angeles
Lake Tahoe Community College
Los Angeles City College
Los Angeles Southwest College
Merritt College
Napa Valley College
Oxnard College

Palo Verde College
Porterville College
West Hills College: Lemoore

Colorado

Aims Community College
Arapahoe Community College
Colorado Northwestern Community
    College
Community College of Aurora
Community College of Denver
Pueblo Community College
Red Rocks Community College

Connecticut

Capital Community College
Gateway Community College
Housatonic Community College
Manchester Community College
Naugatuck Valley Community College
Norwalk Community College
Tunxis Community College

Florida

Central Florida Community College
Florida National College
Full Sail University
Gulf Coast Community College
Lake City Community College
Lake-Sumter Community College
Pensacola Junior College
Polk Community College

Georgia

Albany Technical College
Atlanta Technical College
Augusta Technical College
Central Georgia Technical College
Chattahoochee Technical College
Coastal Georgia Community College
Columbus Technical College
Darton College
DeKalb Technical College
Gainesville State College
Georgia Highlands College
Georgia Military College
Gordon College
Griffin Technical College
Middle Georgia College
Middle Georgia Technical College
North Metro Technical College
Savannah Technical College
West Central Technical College

Hawaii

University of Hawaii
    Honolulu Community College
    Kapiolani Community College
    Maui Community College

Idaho

College of Southern Idaho
North Idaho College

Illinois

Black Hawk College
Carl Sandburg College
Danville Area Community College
Elgin Community College
Heartland Community College
Illinois Eastern Community Colleges
    Frontier Community College
John A. Logan College
Kankakee Community College
Kaskaskia College
Kishwaukee College
Lake Land College
Lincoln Land Community College
Morton College
Prairie State College
Richland Community College
Southeastern Illinois College
Spoon River College

Indiana

Ivy Tech State College
    Ivy Tech Community College:
        Bloomington
    Ivy Tech Community College:
        Columbus
    Ivy Tech Community College: East
        Central
    Ivy Tech Community College:
        Kokomo
    Ivy Tech Community College:
        Lafayette
    Ivy Tech Community College:
        North Central
    Ivy Tech Community College:
        Northeast
    Ivy Tech Community College:
        Northwest
    Ivy Tech Community College:
        South Central
    Ivy Tech Community College:
        Southwest
    Ivy Tech Community College:
        Wabash Valley

Iowa

Hawkeye Community College
Indian Hills Community College
Iowa Central Community College
Iowa Western Community College
North Iowa Area Community College
Northeast Iowa Community College
Scott Community College
Southeastern Community College
    North Campus
Western Iowa Tech Community College

Kansas

Allen County Community College
Barton County Community College
Butler County Community College
Cloud County Community College
Cowley County Community College
Hutchinson Community College
Kansas City Kansas Community College

Kentucky

Henderson Community College
Owensboro Community and Technical
    College
Southeast Kentucky Community and
    Technical College

Louisiana

Baton Rouge Community College
Bossier Parish Community College
Louisiana State University
    Eunice
South Louisiana Community College
Southern University
    Shreveport

Maine

Kennebec Valley Community College
Southern Maine Community College

Maryland

Allegany College of Maryland
Baltimore City Community College
Carroll Community College
Chesapeake College
College of Southern Maryland
Harford Community College
Howard Community College

Massachusetts

Bristol Community College
Cape Cod Community College
Massachusetts Bay Community College
Mount Wachusett Community College
North Shore Community College
Northern Essex Community College
Quincy College
Quinsigamond Community College
Roxbury Community College
Springfield Technical Community
    College

Michigan

Kellogg Community College
Lake Michigan College
Montcalm Community College
Mott Community College
Muskegon Community College
North Central Michigan College
Northwestern Michigan College
St. Clair County Community College
Southwestern Michigan College

Minnesota

Alexandria Technical College
Central Lakes College
Dakota County Technical College
Inver Hills Community College
Lake Superior College
Minnesota State Community and
    Technical College: Fergus Falls
North Hennepin Community College
Riverland Community College
Rochester Community and Technical
    College
St. Cloud Technical College
St. Paul College
South Central College

Mississippi

Coahoma Community College
East Central Community College
Meridian Community College
Northeast Mississippi Community
    College
Northwest Mississippi Community
    College

Missouri

Crowder College
East Central College
Jefferson College
Metropolitan Community College: Blue
    River
Metropolitan Community College:
    Longview
Metropolitan Community College: Maple
    Woods
Metropolitan Community College: Penn
    Valley
Moberly Area Community College
St. Louis Community College
    Florissant Valley
State Fair Community College
Three Rivers Community College

Nebraska

Metropolitan Community College
Northeast Community College

Nevada

Western Nevada College

New Hampshire

Great Bay Community College
Manchester Community College

New Jersey

Atlantic Cape Community College
Burlington County College
Cumberland County College
Gloucester County College
Hudson County Community College
Raritan Valley Community College
Sussex County Community College

New Mexico

Eastern New Mexico University: Roswell
    Campus
Northern New Mexico College
San Juan College
Santa Fe Community College

New York

Adirondack Community College
ASA Institute of Business and Computer
    Technology
Broome Community College
Cayuga County Community College

City University of New York
    Hostos Community College
Clinton Community College
Corning Community College
Erie Community College
    City Campus
    North Campus
    South Campus
Genesee Community College
Herkimer County Community College
Jamestown Community College
Mohawk Valley Community College
Niagara County Community College
Onondaga Community College
Rockland Community College
Schenectady County Community College
State University of New York
    College of Agriculture and
        Technology at Cobleskill
    College of Agriculture and
        Technology at Morrisville
    College of Technology at Alfred
    College of Technology at Delhi
Technical Career Institutes
Tompkins-Cortland Community College
Ulster County Community College

North Carolina

Asheville-Buncombe Technical
    Community College
Johnston Community College
Piedmont Community College
Sandhills Community College
Southwestern Community College
Vance-Granville Community College

North Dakota

Bismarck State College
North Dakota State College of Science

Ohio

Bowling Green State University:
    Firelands College
Central Ohio Technical College
Cincinnati State Technical and
    Community College
Clark State Community College
Cleveland Institute of Electronics
Edison State Community College
Hocking College
James A. Rhodes State College
Miami University
    Hamilton Campus
North Central State College
University of Cincinnati
    Clermont College
University of Northwestern Ohio

Oklahoma

Oklahoma State University
    Oklahoma City
    Okmulgee
Rose State College

Oregon

Blue Mountain Community College
Chemeketa Community College
Clackamas Community College
Linn-Benton Community College
Mt. Hood Community College
Rogue Community College
Southwestern Oregon Community
    College

Pennsylvania

Butler County Community College
Pittsburgh Technical Institute
Reading Area Community College

Puerto Rico

Ponce Paramedical College

South Carolina

Aiken Technical College
Central Carolina Technical College
Florence-Darlington Technical College
Horry-Georgetown Technical College
Orangeburg-Calhoun Technical College

Piedmont Technical College
Spartanburg Community College
Tri-County Technical College

Tennessee

Cleveland State Community College
Dyersburg State Community College
Motlow State Community College
Roane State Community College
Volunteer State Community College
Walters State Community College

Texas

Cedar Valley College
Coastal Bend College
Eastfield College
El Centro College
Galveston College
Grayson County College
Hill College
Kilgore College
Lamar Institute of Technology
Lamar State College at Port Arthur
Laredo Community College
Lee College
Midland College
Mountain View College
Northeast Texas Community College
Odessa College
Paris Junior College
Texas State Technical College
    Harlingen
Trinity Valley Community College
Victoria College
Weatherford College

Utah

College of Eastern Utah
Snow College

Vermont

Community College of Vermont

Virginia

Central Virginia Community College
Danville Community College
Germanna Community College
Piedmont Virginia Community College
Rappahannock Community College
Southwest Virginia Community College

Washington

Bellingham Technical College
Cascadia Community College
Centralia College
Edmonds Community College
Everett Community College
Green River Community College
Lake Washington Technical College
North Seattle Community College
Olympic College
South Puget Sound Community College
Spokane Community College
Spokane Falls Community College
Tacoma Community College
Walla Walla Community College
Wenatchee Valley College
Whatcom Community College
Yakima Valley Community College

West Virginia

New River Community and Technical
    College

Wisconsin

Chippewa Valley Technical College
Fox Valley Technical College
Lakeshore Technical College
Mid-State Technical College
Moraine Park Technical College
Northcentral Technical College
Northeast Wisconsin Technical College
Western Technical College
Wisconsin Indianhead Technical College

Wyoming

Casper College
Laramie County Community College

Western Wyoming Community College

Large (7,500-14,499)

Four-year

Alabama

University of Alabama
    Birmingham
University of South Alabama

Alaska

University of Alaska
    Anchorage

Arkansas

Arkansas State University
University of Arkansas
University of Arkansas
    Little Rock
University of Central Arkansas

California

Academy of Art University
California State University
    Dominguez Hills
    East Bay
    San Bernardino
    San Marcos
Sonoma State University
University of California
    Riverside
    Santa Cruz

Colorado

University of Colorado
    Denver
University of Northern Colorado

Connecticut

Central Connecticut State University
Southern Connecticut State University

District of Columbia

George Washington University

Florida

Florida Agricultural and Mechanical
    University
Florida Gulf Coast University
Okaloosa-Walton College
University of Miami
University of North Florida
University of West Florida

Georgia

Georgia Institute of Technology
Georgia Southern University
University of West Georgia
Valdosta State University

Hawaii

University of Hawaii
    Manoa

Idaho

Brigham Young University-Idaho
Idaho State University
University of Idaho

Illinois

Columbia College Chicago
DePaul University
DeVry University: Online
Eastern Illinois University
Loyola University Chicago
Northwestern University
Southern Illinois University Edwardsville
Western Illinois University

Indiana

Indiana State University
Indiana University-Purdue University
    Fort Wayne
Purdue University
    Calumet
University of Notre Dame
University of Southern Indiana

Iowa

Ashford University
University of Northern Iowa

Kansas

Fort Hays State University
Wichita State University

Kentucky

Eastern Kentucky University
Murray State University
Northern Kentucky University
University of Louisville

Louisiana

Louisiana Tech University
Northwestern State University
Southeastern Louisiana University
University of Louisiana at Lafayette
University of New Orleans

Maine

University of Maine

Maryland

University of Maryland
    Baltimore County

Massachusetts

Boston College
Bridgewater State College
University of Massachusetts
    Boston
    Dartmouth
    Lowell

Michigan

Davenport University
Ferris State University
Northern Michigan University
Oakland University
Saginaw Valley State University

Minnesota

Minnesota State University
    Mankato
Saint Cloud State University
University of Minnesota
    Duluth

Mississippi

Mississippi State University
University of Mississippi
University of Southern Mississippi

Missouri

Grantham University
Missouri State University
Park University
Southeast Missouri State University
University of Central Missouri
University of Missouri
    St. Louis

Montana

Montana State University
    Bozeman
University of Montana: Missoula

Nebraska

University of Nebraska
    Omaha

Nevada

University of Nevada
    Reno

New Hampshire

University of New Hampshire

New Jersey

Kean University
Montclair State University
Rowan University
William Paterson University of New
    Jersey

New Mexico

New Mexico State University

New York

City University of New York
    Baruch College
    Brooklyn College
    City College
    College of Staten Island
    Hunter College
    John Jay College of Criminal
        Justice
    Lehman College
    Queens College
Cornell University
Fashion Institute of Technology
Fordham University
Hofstra University
Rochester Institute of Technology
St. John's University
State University of New York
    Albany
    Binghamton
    College at Buffalo
    Empire State College
Syracuse University

North Carolina

Appalachian State University
University of North Carolina
    Greensboro
    Wilmington

North Dakota

North Dakota State University
University of North Dakota

Ohio

Cleveland State University
Miami University
    Oxford Campus
Wright State University
Youngstown State University

Oklahoma

Northeastern State University
University of Central Oklahoma

Pennsylvania

Art Institute
    Online
Bloomsburg University of Pennsylvania
Drexel University
Indiana University of Pennsylvania
Kutztown University of Pennsylvania
Slippery Rock University of
    Pennsylvania
University of Pennsylvania
West Chester University of Pennsylvania

Puerto Rico

Turabo University
Universidad del Este
Universidad Metropolitana
University of Puerto Rico
    Mayaguez

Rhode Island

Johnson & Wales University: Providence
University of Rhode Island

South Carolina

Clemson University
College of Charleston

South Dakota

South Dakota State University

Tennessee

Austin Peay State University
East Tennessee State University
Tennessee Technological University
University of Tennessee
    Chattanooga

Texas

Baylor University
Lamar University
Sam Houston State University
Stephen F. Austin State University
Tarleton State University
Texas Southern University

University of Houston
    Downtown
University of Texas
    Brownsville
    Dallas
    Pan American

Utah

Utah State University

Vermont

University of Vermont

Virginia

Radford University
University of Virginia

Washington

Central Washington University
South Seattle Community College
Western Washington University

West Virginia

Marshall University

Wisconsin

Marquette University
University of Wisconsin
    Eau Claire
    La Crosse
    Oshkosh
    Stevens Point
    Whitewater

Wyoming

University of Wyoming

Two-year

Alabama

Calhoun Community College

Arizona

Paradise Valley Community College
Phoenix College
Scottsdale Community College

Arkansas

Pulaski Technical College

California

Antelope Valley College
Butte College
Chabot College
Citrus College
Coastline Community College
College of San Mateo
College of the Desert
College of the Sequoias
Contra Costa College
Cosumnes River College
Cuesta College
Cuyamaca College
Cypress College
Evergreen Valley College
Folsom Lake College
Golden West College
Hartnell College
Irvine Valley College
Laney College
Las Positas College
Los Angeles Harbor College
Los Angeles Mission College
Los Angeles Trade and Technical College
Los Medanos College
MiraCosta College
Mission College
Monterey Peninsula College
Moorpark College
Ohlone College
Reedley College
San Bernardino Valley College
San Diego Miramar College
San Jose City College
Santa Barbara City College
Santiago Canyon College
Shasta College
Skyline College
Solano Community College

Taft College
Ventura College
Victor Valley College
West Los Angeles College
West Valley College
Yuba Community College District

Colorado

Colorado Mountain College
Front Range Community College
Pikes Peak Community College

Florida

Brevard Community College
Indian River Community College
Manatee Community College
Palm Beach Community College
Seminole Community College
Tallahassee Community College

Illinois

College of Lake County
Harper College
Illinois Central College
Joliet Junior College
Moraine Valley Community College
Parkland College
Triton College

Indiana

Ivy Tech State College
    Ivy Tech Community College:
        Central Indiana
Vincennes University

Kentucky

Bluegrass Community and Technical
    College
Jefferson Community and Technical
    College

Louisiana

Delgado Community College

Maryland

Anne Arundel Community College
Prince George's Community College

Massachusetts

Bunker Hill Community College
Middlesex Community College

Michigan

Delta College
Grand Rapids Community College
Kalamazoo Valley Community College
Lansing Community College
Macomb Community College
Oakland Community College
Washtenaw Community College

Minnesota

Century Community and Technical
    College
Hennepin Technical College
Normandale Community College

Mississippi

Hinds Community College
Mississippi Gulf Coast Community
    College
    Jefferson Davis Campus

Missouri

Ozarks Technical Community College

Nevada

Truckee Meadows Community College

New Jersey

Brookdale Community College
County College of Morris
Essex County College
Mercer County Community College
Ocean County College
Union County College

New Mexico

Dona Ana Branch Community College of
    New Mexico State University

Large (7,500-14,499)

New York
City University of New York
  Bronx Community College
  Kingsborough Community College
  LaGuardia Community College
  Queensborough Community
    College
Dutchess Community College
Hudson Valley Community College
Westchester Community College

North Carolina
Fayetteville Technical Community
  College
Guilford Technical Community College
Wake Technical Community College

Ohio
Cuyahoga Community College
  Metropolitan Campus
Lakeland Community College
Lorain County Community College
Owens Community College
  Toledo

Oklahoma
Oklahoma City Community College
Tulsa Community College

Oregon
Lane Community College

Pennsylvania
Bucks County Community College
Harrisburg Area Community College
Montgomery County Community
  College
Northampton Community College

South Carolina
Greenville Technical College
Midlands Technical College
Trident Technical College

Tennessee
Southwest Tennessee Community
  College

Texas
Blinn College
Brookhaven College
Del Mar College
McLennan Community College
Navarro College
North Lake College
Northwest Vista College
Palo Alto College
Richland College
St. Philip's College
South Plains College
Texas Southmost College

Virginia
J. Sargeant Reynolds Community
  College
Thomas Nelson Community College

Washington
Bates Technical College
Bellevue Community College

Wisconsin
Madison Area Technical College
Milwaukee Area Technical College

Very large (15,000 or more)

Four-year

Alabama
Auburn University
Troy University
University of Alabama

Arizona
Arizona State University
Northern Arizona University
University of Arizona

University of Phoenix

California
California Polytechnic State University:
  San Luis Obispo
California State Polytechnic University:
  Pomona
California State University
  Chico
  Fresno
  Fullerton
  Long Beach
  Los Angeles
  Sacramento
San Diego State University
San Francisco State University
San Jose State University
University of California
  Berkeley
  Davis
  Irvine
  Los Angeles
  San Diego
  Santa Barbara
University of Southern California

Colorado
Colorado State University
Metropolitan State College of Denver
University of Colorado
  Boulder

Connecticut
University of Connecticut

Delaware
University of Delaware

Florida
Florida Atlantic University
Florida International University
Florida State University
St. Petersburg College
University of Central Florida
University of Florida
University of South Florida

Georgia
Georgia State University
Kennesaw State University
University of Georgia

Idaho
Boise State University

Illinois
Illinois State University
Northern Illinois University
Southern Illinois University Carbondale
University of Illinois
  Chicago
  Urbana-Champaign

Indiana
Ball State University
Indiana University
  Bloomington
Indiana University-Purdue University
  Indianapolis
Purdue University

Iowa
Iowa State University
University of Iowa

Kansas
Kansas State University
University of Kansas

Kentucky
University of Kentucky
Western Kentucky University

Louisiana
Louisiana State University and
  Agricultural and Mechanical College

Maryland
Towson University

University of Maryland
  College Park
  University College

Massachusetts
Boston University
Northeastern University
University of Massachusetts
  Amherst

Michigan
Central Michigan University
Eastern Michigan University
Grand Valley State University
Michigan State University
University of Michigan
Wayne State University
Western Michigan University

Minnesota
University of Minnesota
  Twin Cities

Missouri
University of Missouri
  Columbia

Nebraska
University of Nebraska
  Lincoln

Nevada
University of Nevada
  Las Vegas

New Jersey
Rutgers, The State University of New
  Jersey
    New Brunswick/Piscataway
    Campus
Thomas Edison State College

New York
Excelsior College
New York University
State University of New York
  Buffalo
  Stony Brook

North Carolina
East Carolina University
North Carolina State University
University of North Carolina
  Chapel Hill
  Charlotte

Ohio
Bowling Green State University
Kent State University
Ohio State University
  Columbus Campus
Ohio University
University of Akron
University of Cincinnati
University of Toledo

Oklahoma
Oklahoma State University
University of Oklahoma

Oregon
Oregon State University
Portland State University
University of Oregon

Pennsylvania
Art Institute
  of Pittsburgh
Penn State
  University Park
Temple University
University of Pittsburgh

Puerto Rico
University of Puerto Rico
  Rio Piedras

South Carolina
University of South Carolina

Tennessee
Middle Tennessee State University
University of Memphis
University of Tennessee
  Knoxville

Texas
Texas A&M University
Texas State University: San Marcos
Texas Tech University
University of Houston
University of North Texas
University of Texas
  Arlington
  Austin
  El Paso
  San Antonio

Utah
Brigham Young University
University of Utah
Utah Valley State College
Weber State University

Virginia
George Mason University
James Madison University
Liberty University
Old Dominion University
Virginia Commonwealth University
Virginia Polytechnic Institute and State
  University

Washington
University of Washington
Washington State University

West Virginia
West Virginia University

Wisconsin
University of Wisconsin
  Madison
  Milwaukee

Two-year

Arizona
Penn Foster College
Pima Community College
Rio Salado College

California
Allan Hancock College
American River College
Bakersfield College
Cabrillo College
Cerritos College
Chaffey College
City College of San Francisco
College of the Canyons
De Anza College
Diablo Valley College
East Los Angeles College
El Camino College
Foothill College
Fresno City College
Fullerton College
Glendale Community College
Grossmont College
Long Beach City College
Los Angeles Pierce College
Los Angeles Valley College
Modesto Junior College
Mount San Antonio College
Mount San Jacinto College
Orange Coast College
Palomar College
Pasadena City College
Rio Hondo College
Riverside Community College
Sacramento City College
Saddleback College
San Diego City College
San Diego Mesa College
San Joaquin Delta College
Santa Ana College
Santa Monica College

Santa Rosa Junior College
Sierra College
Southwestern College

Florida
Broward Community College
Florida Community College at
    Jacksonville
Hillsborough Community College
Miami Dade College
Santa Fe Community College
Valencia Community College

Georgia
Georgia Perimeter College

Illinois
College of DuPage

Iowa
Des Moines Area Community College
Kirkwood Community College

Maryland
Community College of Baltimore County

Michigan
Wayne County Community College

Nevada
College of Southern Nevada

New York
City University of New York
    Borough of Manhattan Community
        College
Monroe Community College
Nassau Community College
Suffolk County Community College

North Carolina
Central Piedmont Community College

Ohio
Columbus State Community College
Sinclair Community College

Oregon
Portland Community College

Pennsylvania
Community College of Allegheny
    County
Community College of Philadelphia

Rhode Island
Community College of Rhode Island

Texas
Austin Community College
Central Texas College
Collin County Community College
    District
Houston Community College System
Lone Star College System
San Antonio College
San Jacinto College
South Texas College
Tarrant County College

Utah
Salt Lake Community College

Virginia
Northern Virginia Community College
Tidewater Community College

College type

Four-year

Alabama

Andrew Jackson University
Birmingham-Southern College
Concordia College
Faulkner University
Huntingdon College
Judson College
Miles College
Oakwood University
Spring Hill College
Stillman College
Tuskegee University
University of Mobile
University of Montevallo

Alaska

Alaska Pacific University
University of Alaska
    Southeast

Arizona

Prescott College

Arkansas

Arkansas Tech University
Ecclesia College
Henderson State University
Hendrix College
John Brown University
Lyon College
Ouachita Baptist University
Philander Smith College
University of the Ozarks
Williams Baptist College

California

American Jewish University
Antioch Southern California
    Antioch University Los Angeles
    Antioch University Santa Barbara
Bethany University
California Baptist University
California Institute of Integral Studies
California Lutheran University
California State University
    Bakersfield
    Chico
    Monterey Bay
    San Bernardino
    Stanislaus
Chapman University
Claremont McKenna College
Concordia University
Dominican University of California
Fresno Pacific University
Harvey Mudd College
Hope International University
Humphreys College
John F. Kennedy University
The Master's College
Menlo College
Mills College
NewSchool of Architecture & Design
Notre Dame de Namur University
Occidental College
Pacific Union College
Patten University
Pepperdine University
Pitzer College
Point Loma Nazarene University
Pomona College
St. Mary's College of California
San Diego Christian College

San Jose State University
Scripps College
Simpson University
Soka University of America
Sonoma State University
University of La Verne
University of Redlands
University of the West
Vanguard University of Southern
    California
Westmont College
Whittier College
William Jessup University

Colorado

Adams State College
Colorado Christian University
Colorado College
Fort Lewis College
Mesa State College
Metropolitan State College of Denver
Naropa University
Regis University
Teikyo Loretto Heights University
Western State College of Colorado

Connecticut

Albertus Magnus College
Charter Oak State College
Connecticut College
Eastern Connecticut State University
Holy Apostles College and Seminary
Mitchell College
Sacred Heart University
St. Joseph College
Trinity College
Wesleyan University

Delaware

Wesley College

District of Columbia

Gallaudet University
Southeastern University
Trinity Washington University
University of the District of Columbia

Florida

Ave Maria University
Bethune-Cookman University
Eckerd College
Edward Waters College
Flagler College
Florida Memorial University
Florida Southern College
Jacksonville University
New College of Florida
Palm Beach Atlantic University
Rollins College
Southeastern University
University of Tampa
Warner Southern College

Georgia

Agnes Scott College
Albany State University
Augusta State University
Berry College
Brenau University
Brewton-Parker College
Clayton State University
Columbus State University
Covenant College
Fort Valley State University
Georgia College and State University
Georgia Southwestern State University
LaGrange College
Morehouse College

Oglethorpe University
Paine College
Piedmont College
Savannah State University
Shorter College
Spelman College
Thomas University
Toccoa Falls College
Truett-McConnell College
Wesleyan College

Hawaii

Brigham Young University-Hawaii
Hawaii Pacific University
University of Hawaii
    West Oahu

Idaho

College of Idaho
Lewis-Clark State College

Illinois

Augustana College
Benedictine University
Blackburn College
Columbia College Chicago
Dominican University
Elmhurst College
Eureka College
Greenville College
Illinois College
Illinois Wesleyan University
Judson University
Knox College
Lake Forest College
MacMurray College
McKendree University
Monmouth College
North Central College
North Park University
Olivet Nazarene University
Quincy University
Rockford College
Shimer College
Trinity Christian College
Trinity International University
University of Chicago
University of Illinois
    Springfield
University of St. Francis
Wheaton College

Indiana

Bethel College
Calumet College of St. Joseph
DePauw University
Earlham College
Franklin College
Goshen College
Hanover College
Holy Cross College
Huntington University
Indiana Wesleyan University
Manchester College
Marian College
Oakland City University
Saint Mary's College
St. Mary-of-the-Woods College
Taylor University
Taylor University Fort Wayne
University of Evansville
University of Indianapolis
University of St. Francis
University of Southern Indiana
Wabash College

Iowa

Briar Cliff University
Buena Vista University
Central College
Clarke College
Coe College
Cornell College
Divine Word College
Graceland University
Grand View College
Grinnell College

Iowa Wesleyan College
Loras College
Luther College
Maharishi University of Management
Morningside College
Mount Mercy College
Northwestern College
St. Ambrose University
Simpson College
Waldorf College
Wartburg College
William Penn University

Kansas

Baker University
Benedictine College
Bethany College
Bethel College
Central Christian College of Kansas
Friends University
Kansas Wesleyan University
McPherson College
MidAmerica Nazarene University
Newman University
Ottawa University
Southwestern College
Sterling College
Tabor College

Kentucky

Alice Lloyd College
Bellarmine University
Berea College
Brescia University
Centre College
Georgetown College
Kentucky Christian University
Kentucky State University
Lindsey Wilson College
Mid-Continent University
Midway College
St. Catharine College
Thomas More College
Transylvania University
Union College
University of the Cumberlands

Louisiana

Centenary College of Louisiana
Dillard University
Louisiana College
Loyola University New Orleans
St. Joseph Seminary College

Maine

Bates College
Bowdoin College
Colby College
College of the Atlantic
St. Joseph's College
Thomas College
Unity College
University of Maine
    Farmington
    Machias
University of Southern Maine

Maryland

College of Notre Dame of Maryland
Columbia Union College
Coppin State University
Goucher College
Hood College
Loyola College in Maryland
McDaniel College
Morgan State University
Mount St. Mary's University
National Labor College
St. John's College
St. Mary's College of Maryland
Salisbury University
Sojourner-Douglass College
University of Baltimore
Villa Julie College
Washington College

Massachusetts
American International College
Amherst College
Anna Maria College
Assumption College
Atlantic Union College
Bard College at Simon's Rock
Becker College
Bridgewater State College
Cambridge College
Clark University
College of the Holy Cross
Curry College
Eastern Nazarene College
Elms College
Emmanuel College
Endicott College
Fitchburg State College
Framingham State College
Gordon College
Hampshire College
Hellenic College/Holy Cross
Lasell College
Lesley University
Massachusetts College of Liberal Arts
Merrimack College
Mount Holyoke College
Mount Ida College
Newbury College
Nichols College
Pine Manor College
Regis College
Simmons College
Smith College
Springfield College
Stonehill College
Wellesley College
Wheaton College
Wheelock College
Williams College
Worcester State College

Michigan
Adrian College
Albion College
Alma College
Aquinas College
Calvin College
Concordia University
Cornerstone University
Finlandia University
Hillsdale College
Hope College
Kalamazoo College
Madonna University
Marygrove College
Michigan Jewish Institute
Olivet College
Rochester College
Spring Arbor University

Minnesota
Augsburg College
Bethany Lutheran College
Bethel University
Brown College
Carleton College
College of St. Benedict
College of St. Catherine
College of St. Scholastica
Concordia College: Moorhead
Gustavus Adolphus College
Hamline University
Macalester College
Northwestern College
St. John's University
St. Olaf College
Southwest Minnesota State University
University of Minnesota
    Morris
University of St. Thomas

Mississippi
Belhaven College
Blue Mountain College
Millsaps College

Mississippi University for Women
Mississippi Valley State University
Rust College
Tougaloo College
William Carey University

Missouri
Avila University
Central Methodist University
College of the Ozarks
Columbia College
Culver-Stockton College
Drury University
Evangel University
Fontbonne University
Hannibal-LaGrange College
Lincoln University
Lindenwood University
Missouri Baptist University
Missouri Southern State University
Missouri Valley College
Rockhurst University
Stephens College
Truman State University
Westminster College
William Jewell College
William Woods University

Montana
Carroll College
Montana State University
    Northern
Rocky Mountain College
University of Great Falls
University of Montana: Missoula
University of Montana: Western

Nebraska
Chadron State College
College of Saint Mary
Dana College
Doane College
Hastings College
Midland Lutheran College
Nebraska Wesleyan University
Peru State College
Union College
Wayne State College
York College

Nevada
Nevada State College
Sierra Nevada College

New Hampshire
Chester College of New England
Colby-Sawyer College
Dartmouth College
Franklin Pierce University
Granite State College
Magdalen College
New England College
Rivier College
St. Anselm College
Thomas More College of Liberal Arts
University of New Hampshire at
    Manchester

New Jersey
Bloomfield College
Caldwell College
Centenary College
The College of New Jersey
College of St. Elizabeth
Drew University
Felician College
Georgian Court University
Kean University
Ramapo College of New Jersey
Richard Stockton College of New Jersey
Rowan University
Saint Peter's College
Thomas Edison State College
William Paterson University of New
    Jersey

New Mexico
College of Santa Fe

College of the Southwest
New Mexico Institute of Mining and
    Technology
St. John's College

New York
Bard College
Barnard College
Canisius College
Cazenovia College
City University of New York
    Baruch College
    Brooklyn College
    College of Staten Island
    Hunter College
    Lehman College
    Medgar Evers College
    Queens College
    York College
Colgate University
College of Mount St. Vincent
College of New Rochelle
College of Saint Rose
Columbia University
    School of General Studies
Concordia College
D'Youville College
Daemen College
Dominican College of Blauvelt
Dowling College
Elmira College
Eugene Lang College The New School
    for Liberal Arts
Excelsior College
Five Towns College
Hamilton College
Hartwick College
Hobart and William Smith Colleges
Houghton College
Iona College
Ithaca College
Keuka College
King's College
Le Moyne College
Long Island University
    C. W. Post Campus
Manhattan College
Manhattanville College
Marist College
Marymount Manhattan College
Medaille College
Mercy College
Metropolitan College of New York
Molloy College
Nazareth College of Rochester
Nyack College
Paul Smith's College
Roberts Wesleyan College
Russell Sage College
Sage College of Albany
St. Francis College
St. John Fisher College
St. Joseph's College
St. Joseph's College: Suffolk Campus
St. Lawrence University
St. Thomas Aquinas College
Sarah Lawrence College
Siena College
Skidmore College
State University of New York
    College at Brockport
    College at Buffalo
    College at Cortland
    College at Fredonia
    College at Geneseo
    College at Old Westbury
    College at Oneonta
    College at Plattsburgh
    College at Potsdam
    College of Environmental Science
        and Forestry
    Empire State College
    New Paltz
    Purchase
Touro College

Union College
Vassar College
Wagner College
Wells College

North Carolina
Barton College
Belmont Abbey College
Bennett College
Brevard College
Campbell University
Catawba College
Chowan University
Davidson College
Elizabeth City State University
Elon University
Gardner-Webb University
Greensboro College
Guilford College
Johnson C. Smith University
Lees-McRae College
Lenoir-Rhyne College
Livingstone College
Mars Hill College
Meredith College
Methodist University
Montreat College
Mount Olive College
North Carolina Wesleyan College
Peace College
Pfeiffer University
St. Andrews Presbyterian College
St. Augustine's College
Salem College
Shaw University
University of North Carolina
    Asheville
    Pembroke
Warren Wilson College
Wingate University

North Dakota
Jamestown College
Minot State University
Valley City State University

Ohio
Ashland University
Baldwin-Wallace College
Bluffton University
Cedarville University
Central State University
College of Mount St. Joseph
College of Wooster
Defiance College
Denison University
Heidelberg College
Hiram College
John Carroll University
Kenyon College
Lake Erie College
Laura and Alvin Siegal College of Judaic
    Studies
Lourdes College
Malone College
Marietta College
Mount Union College
Muskingum College
Notre Dame College
Oberlin College
Ohio Dominican University
Ohio Wesleyan University
Otterbein College
University of Rio Grande
Ursuline College
Walsh University
Wilberforce University
Wilmington College
Wittenberg University

Oklahoma
Bacone College
Cameron University
Langston University
Oklahoma Baptist University
Oklahoma Christian University

Oklahoma City University
Oklahoma Panhandle State University
Oklahoma Wesleyan University
Oral Roberts University
St. Gregory's University
Southeastern Oklahoma State University
Southern Nazarene University
University of Science and Arts of
    Oklahoma

Oregon

Art Institute of Portland
Cascade College
Concordia University
Corban College
Eastern Oregon University
Lewis & Clark College
Linfield College
Marylhurst University
Northwest Christian College
Reed College
Southern Oregon University
Warner Pacific College
Western Oregon University
Willamette University

Pennsylvania

Albright College
Allegheny College
Alvernia College
Bloomsburg University of Pennsylvania
Bryn Mawr College
Cabrini College
Carlow University
Cedar Crest College
Chatham University
Chestnut Hill College
Delaware Valley College
Dickinson College
Edinboro University of Pennsylvania
Elizabethtown College
Franklin & Marshall College
Geneva College
Gettysburg College
Grove City College
Gwynedd-Mercy College
Haverford College
Holy Family University
Immaculata University
Juniata College
Keystone College
King's College
La Roche College
La Salle University
Lafayette College
Lebanon Valley College
Lincoln University
Lock Haven University of Pennsylvania
Lycoming College
Mansfield University of Pennsylvania
Mercyhurst College
Messiah College
Millersville University of Pennsylvania
Misericordia University
Moravian College
Mount Aloysius College
Muhlenberg College
Neumann College
Rosemont College
St. Francis University
St. Vincent College
Seton Hill University
Susquehanna University
Swarthmore College
Thiel College
University of Pittsburgh
    Greensburg
    Johnstown
University of Scranton
Ursinus College
Valley Forge Christian College
Washington & Jefferson College
Waynesburg University
Westminster College
Wilson College
York College of Pennsylvania

Puerto Rico

Atlantic College
Caribbean University
Inter American University of Puerto Rico
    Aguadilla Campus
    Arecibo Campus
Turabo University
Universidad Adventista de las Antillas
Universidad del Este
Universidad Metropolitana
University of Puerto Rico
    Aguadilla
    Cayey University College
    Humacao

Rhode Island

Brown University
Bryant University
Providence College
Rhode Island College
Roger Williams University
Salve Regina University

South Carolina

Allen University
Anderson University
Benedict College
Charleston Southern University
Claflin University
Coker College
College of Charleston
Columbia College
Converse College
Erskine College
Francis Marion University
Furman University
Lander University
Limestone College
Morris College
Newberry College
North Greenville University
Southern Wesleyan University
University of South Carolina
    Aiken
    Beaufort
Voorhees College
Wofford College

South Dakota

Augustana College
Black Hills State University
Dakota Wesleyan University
Mount Marty College
Northern State University
Oglala Lakota College
University of Sioux Falls

Tennessee

Aquinas College
Austin Peay State University
Bethel College
Bryan College
Carson-Newman College
Crichton College
Cumberland University
Freed-Hardeman University
King College
Lambuth University
Lane College
Lee University
LeMoyne-Owen College
Lincoln Memorial University
Lipscomb University
Martin Methodist College
Maryville College
Milligan College
Rhodes College
South College
Tennessee Wesleyan College
Trevecca Nazarene University
Tusculum College
Union University

Texas

Austin College
College of Saint Thomas More
Concordia University at Austin

East Texas Baptist University
Houston Baptist University
Howard Payne University
Huston-Tillotson University
Lubbock Christian University
McMurry University
Midwestern State University
St. Edward's University
Schreiner University
Southwestern Adventist University
Southwestern University
Texas College
Texas Lutheran University
Trinity University
University of Dallas
University of North Texas
University of St. Thomas
University of the Incarnate Word
Wayland Baptist University
Wiley College

Utah

Stevens-Henager College: Ogden
Westminster College

Vermont

Bennington College
Burlington College
Castleton State College
Champlain College
College of St. Joseph in Vermont
Green Mountain College
Johnson State College
Lyndon State College
Marlboro College
Middlebury College
St. Michael's College
Southern Vermont College
Sterling College

Virginia

Averett University
Bluefield College
Bridgewater College
Christendom College
Christopher Newport University
Eastern Mennonite University
Emory & Henry College
Ferrum College
Hampden-Sydney College
Hollins University
Lynchburg College
Mary Baldwin College
Randolph College
Randolph-Macon College
Roanoke College
St. Paul's College
Southern Virginia University
Sweet Briar College
University of Mary Washington
University of Richmond
University of Virginia's College at Wise
Virginia Intermont College
Virginia Military Institute
Virginia Union University
Virginia Wesleyan College
Washington and Lee University

Washington

Gonzaga University
Heritage University
Northwest University
Saint Martin's University
Trinity Lutheran College
University of Puget Sound
Walla Walla University
Whitman College
Whitworth University

West Virginia

Alderson-Broaddus College
Bethany College
Bluefield State College
Davis and Elkins College
Glenville State College
Ohio Valley University
Salem International University

University of Charleston
West Liberty State College
West Virginia Wesleyan College
Wheeling Jesuit University

Wisconsin

Alverno College
Beloit College
Carroll College
Carthage College
Concordia University Wisconsin
Edgewood College
Lakeland College
Lawrence University
Marian College of Fond du Lac
Mount Mary College
Northland College
St. Norbert College
Silver Lake College
University of Wisconsin
    Green Bay
    River Falls
    Superior
Viterbo University

Two-year

Arkansas

Arkansas State University: Newport
National Park Community College

California

Deep Springs College
Feather River College
Fresno City College
Marymount College

Colorado

Colorado Mountain College

Georgia

Andrew College
Georgia Highlands College
Georgia Perimeter College
Waycross College
Young Harris College

Hawaii

Hawaii Tokai International College
TransPacific Hawaii College

Illinois

Springfield College in Illinois

Indiana

Ancilla College

Kansas

Donnelly College

Massachusetts

Dean College
Fisher College

Michigan

Montcalm Community College
Wayne County Community College

Minnesota

Itasca Community College
White Earth Tribal and Community
    College

Missouri

Cottey College
Crowder College
Patricia Stevens College

New York

State University of New York
    College of Technology at Alfred
Villa Maria College of Buffalo

Pennsylvania

University of Pittsburgh
    Titusville

South Carolina

Spartanburg Methodist College

Tennessee
Hiwassee College

Texas
Eastfield College
Jacksonville College
Lamar State College at Orange
Lon Morris College
North Lake College
Tarrant County College

Vermont
Landmark College

Virginia
Richard Bland College

Washington
Olympic College

Wisconsin
University of Wisconsin
Baraboo/Sauk County
Fox Valley
Marinette
Richland
Rock County
Washington County

Upper-division colleges

Alabama
Athens State University
United States Sports Academy

Arizona
Midwestern University: Glendale

California
Alliant International University
Antioch Southern California
Antioch University Los Angeles
Antioch University Santa Barbara
California Institute of Integral Studies
Dominican School of Philosophy and
Theology
Pacific Oaks College
Samuel Merritt College

Illinois
Governors State University
Rosalind Franklin University of Medicine
and Science
St. John's College
West Suburban College of Nursing

Kansas
University of Kansas Medical Center

Louisiana
Louisiana State University Health
Sciences Center

Maryland
University of Maryland
Baltimore

Michigan
Walsh College of Accountancy and
Business Administration

Minnesota
Northwestern Health Sciences University
Walden University

Nevada
University of Southern Nevada

New Jersey
University of Medicine and Dentistry of
New Jersey
School of Health Related
Professions

New York
State University of New York
Upstate Medical University

Pennsylvania
Penn State
Shenango
Thomas Jefferson University: College of
Health Professions

Puerto Rico
Carlos Albizu University: San Juan

Tennessee
University of Tennessee Health Science
Center

Texas
Texas A&M University
Texarkana
Texas Tech University Health Sciences
Center
University of Houston
Clear Lake
Victoria
University of Texas
Health Science Center at San
Antonio
Medical Branch at Galveston
Southwestern Medical Center at
Dallas

Washington
Bastyr University
City University of Seattle

Agricultural and technical colleges

Four-year
Alabama Agricultural and Mechanical
University, AL
Alcorn State University, MS
Art Institute
of Colorado, CO
of Pittsburgh, PA
Art Institute of Fort Lauderdale, FL
Art Institute of Seattle, WA
Baker College
of Auburn Hills, MI
of Jackson, MI
of Muskegon, MI
of Owosso, MI
of Port Huron, MI
Bluefield State College, WV
Boise State University, ID
Briarcliffe College, NY
California Design College, CA
Central Pennsylvania College, PA
City College: Fort Lauderdale, FL
Clayton State University, GA
Coleman College, CA
CollegeAmerica
Fort Collins, CO
Colorado Technical University, CO
Delaware Valley College, PA
Design Institute of San Diego, CA
DeVry Institute of Technology
New York, NY
DeVry University: Memphis, TN
Dixie State College of Utah, UT
Ex'pression College for Digital Arts, CA
Fairmont State University, WV
Hamilton Technical College, IA
Herzing College, GA
Herzing College, WI
International Academy of Design and
Technology: Chicago, IL
International Academy of Design and
Technology: Detroit, MI
International Academy of Design and
Technology: Henderson, NV
International Academy of Design and
Technology: Schaumburg, IL
International Academy of Design and
Technology: Tampa, FL
Kansas State University, KS
LA College International, CA
Lewis-Clark State College, ID

Louisiana State University and
Agricultural and Mechanical College,
LA
Minnesota School of Business:
Plymouth, MN
Minnesota School of Business:
Shakopee, MN
Montana State University
Billings, MT
Montana Tech of the University of
Montana, MT
Mt. Sierra College, CA
National American University
Rapid City, SD
National Education Center
Spartan College of Aeronautics and
Technology, OK
Neumont University, UT
New England Institute of Art, MA
New England Institute of Technology, RI
Oklahoma Panhandle State University,
OK
Oregon Institute of Technology, OR
Peirce College, PA
Pennsylvania College of Technology, PA
Pioneer Pacific College, OR
Platt College
Ontario, CA
San Diego, CA
Remington College: Largo, FL
Remington College: Tampa, FL
Southern California Institute of
Architecture, CA
Southwest Minnesota State University,
MN
State University of New York
College of Technology at Canton,
NY
Farmingdale, NY
Sterling College, VT
University College of San Juan, PR
University of Arkansas
Monticello, AR
University of Puerto Rico
Aguadilla, PR
Bayamon University College, PR
Utuado, PR
Utah Valley State College, UT
Vaughn College of Aeronautics and
Technology, NY
Virginia College at Huntsville, AL
Wentworth Institute of Technology, MA
Westwood College of Technology
Westwood College: Denver South,
CO
Westwood College: O'Hare Airport,
IL
Westwood College: Chicago Loop, IL
Westwood College: Anaheim, CA
Westwood College: DuPage, IL
Westwood College: South Bay, CA
World College, VA

Two-year
Abraham Baldwin Agricultural College,
GA
Aiken Technical College, SC
Albany Technical College, GA
Alexandria Technical College, MN
Anoka Technical College, MN
Antonelli College
Hattiesburg, MS
Jackson, MS
Arizona Automotive Institute, AZ
Arkansas State University
Mountain Home, AR
Art Institute
of New York City, NY
Art Institute of Ohio: Cincinnati, OH
Asheville-Buncombe Technical
Community College, NC
Atlanta Technical College, GA
Augusta Technical College, GA
Aviation Institute of Maintenance:
Virginia Beach, VA

Bates Technical College, WA
Bellingham Technical College, WA
Benjamin Franklin Institute of
Technology, MA
Berean Institute, PA
Black River Technical College, AR
Blue Cliff College: Gulfport, MS
Bluegrass Community and Technical
College, KY
Bolivar Technical College, MO
Bradford School of Business, TX
Brooks College, CA
Brown Mackie College: Atlanta, GA
Bryan College: Sacramento, CA
Business Institute of Pennsylvania, PA
Cambria-Rowe Business College:
Indiana, PA
Cambridge College, CO
Capital Community College, CT
Career College of Northern Nevada, NV
Carteret Community College, NC
CEI College
Maric College: Panorama City, CA
Central Carolina Technical College, SC
Central Florida College, FL
Central Georgia Technical College, GA
Central Lakes College, MN
Central Maine Community College, ME
Central Ohio Technical College, OH
Central Texas College, TX
Century Community and Technical
College, MN
Chattahoochee Technical College, GA
CHI Institute: Franklin Mills, PA
Chippewa Valley Technical College, WI
Cincinnati State Technical and
Community College, OH
Cleveland Institute of Electronics, OH
Clover Park Technical College, WA
Coleman College
San Marcos, CA
College of Business and Technology:
Flagler, FL
College of Court Reporting, IN
College of the Sequoias, CA
Colorado School of Trades, CO
Columbus State Community College, OH
Columbus Technical College, GA
Commonwealth Technical Institute, PA
Concorde Career College
Garden Grove, CA
Concorde Career College: San
Bernardino, CA
Court Reporting Institute of Houston, TX
Cowley County Community College, KS
Dakota County Technical College, MN
Daytona Beach Community College, FL
DeKalb Technical College, GA
Delta School of Business & Technology,
LA
Denmark Technical College, SC
Dodge City Community College, KS
DuBois Business College, PA
Dunwoody College of Technology, MN
Durham Technical Community College,
NC
Eastern Maine Community College, ME
Erie Institute of Technology, PA
ETI Technical College of Niles, OH
Everest College
Phoenix, AZ
Everest College: Arlington, TX
Everest College: Aurora, CO
Fayetteville Technical Community
College, NC
Florence-Darlington Technical College,
SC
Florida Career College: Hialeah, FL
Florida Career College: Miami, FL
Florida Career College: Pembroke Pines,
FL
Florida Career College: West Palm
Beach, FL

Florida Technical College
  Deland, FL
  Orlando, FL
Fox Valley Technical College, WI
Full Sail University, FL
Fullerton College, CA
Gadsden State Community College, AL
Gallipolis Career College, OH
Gateway Community College, AZ
Grayson County College, TX
Great Bay Community College, NH
Greenville Technical College, SC
Griffin Technical College, GA
Gupton Jones College of Funeral Service, GA
Hallmark College of Aeronautics, TX
Hallmark College of Technology, TX
Hawkeye Community College, IA
Hazard Community College, KY
Heald College
  Fresno, CA
  Hayward, CA
  Honolulu, HI
  Rancho Cordova, CA
Heald College: Portland, OR
Helena College of Technology of the University of Montana, MT
Hennepin Technical College, MN
Herzing College
  Minneapolis Drafting School Division of , MN
Hibbing Community College, MN
Hocking College, OH
Hondros College, OH
Horry-Georgetown Technical College, SC
Huertas Junior College, PR
Institute of Business & Medical Careers, CO
Institute of Design and Construction, NY
IntelliTec College, CO
IntelliTec College: Grand Junction, CO
International College of Broadcasting, OH
Iowa Western Community College, IA
Island Drafting and Technical Institute, NY
ITI Technical College, LA
J. F. Drake State Technical College, AL
James A. Rhodes State College, OH
Jefferson College, MO
Jefferson Community and Technical College, KY
JNA Institute of Culinary Arts, PA
Johnson College, PA
Johnston Community College, NC
Kaplan College: Denver, CO
Kaplan College: Hammond, IN
Kaplan College: Merrillville, IN
Kennebec Valley Community College, ME
Key College, FL
Keystone Technical Institute, PA
Lake Area Technical Institute, SD
Lake Region State College, ND
Lake Superior College, MN
Lake Washington Technical College, WA
Lakes Region Community College, NH
Lakeshore Technical College, WI
Lamar Institute of Technology, TX
Lamar State College at Port Arthur, TX
Laurel Business Institute, PA
Le Cordon Bleu College of Culinary Arts, GA
Le Cordon Bleu College of Culinary Arts, MN
Lincoln Technical Institute: Allentown, PA
Lincoln Technical Institute: Northeast Philadelphia, PA
Lincoln Technical Institute: Philadelphia, PA
Linn State Technical College, MO
Long Technical College, AZ

Los Angeles Trade and Technical College, CA
Louisville Technical Institute, KY
Madison Area Technical College, WI
Manchester Community College, NH
Manhattan Area Technical College, KS
Maric College
  Vista, CA
Maric College: Palm Springs, CA
Maric College: Salida, CA
Martin Community College, NC
Maysville Community and Technical College, KY
McDowell Technical Community College, NC
Mesabi Range Community and Technical College, MN
Mesalands Community College, NM
Metropolitan Community College, NE
Mid-Plains Community College Area, NE
Mid-State Technical College, WI
Middle Georgia Technical College, GA
Midlands Technical College, SC
Miller-Motte Technical College, SC
Miller-Motte Technical College: Cary, NC
Milwaukee Area Technical College, WI
Minneapolis Business College, MN
Minneapolis Community and Technical College, MN
Minnesota State College - Southeast Technical, MN
Minnesota State Community and Technical College: Fergus Falls, MN
Minnesota West Community and Technical College, MN
Mitchell Technical Institute, SD
Moraine Park Technical College, WI
Morrison Institute of Technology, IL
MTI College, CA
Nashua Community College, NH
National College
  Dayton, OH
  Knoxville, TN
National College of Business and Technology: Arecibo, PR
National College of Business and Technology: Bayamon, PR
National College of Business and Technology: Rio Grande, PR
National Park Community College, AR
National Polytechnic College of Science, CA
Naugatuck Valley Community College, CT
Navajo Technical College, NM
Nebraska College of Technical Agriculture, NE
New Mexico Junior College, NM
New River Community and Technical College, WV
North Central Kansas Technical College, KS
North Central State College, OH
North Dakota State College of Science, ND
North Metro Technical College, GA
Northcentral Technical College, WI
Northeast Wisconsin Technical College, WI
Northeastern Technical College, SC
Northern Maine Community College, ME
Northland Community & Technical College, MN
Northwest Technical College, MN
Northwest Technical Institute, MN
Northwestern Business College, IL
Norwalk Community College, CT
Nossi College of Art, TN
Nunez Community College, LA
Ohio Institute of Photography and Technology, OH

Ohio State University
  Agricultural Technical Institute, OH
Oklahoma State University
  Oklahoma City, OK
  Okmulgee, OK
Orangeburg-Calhoun Technical College, SC
Orleans Technical Institute - Center City Campus, PA
Ouachita Technical College, AR
Owensboro Community and Technical College, KY
Ozarks Technical Community College, MO
Pellissippi State Technical Community College, TN
Penn Commercial Business and Technical School, PA
Pennco Tech, PA
Pennsylvania Culinary Institute, PA
Pennsylvania Institute of Technology, PA
Piedmont Technical College, SC
Pima Community College, AZ
Pine Technical College, MN
Pinnacle Career Institute: Kansas City, MO
Pioneer Pacific College: Springfield, OR
Pittsburgh Institute of Aeronautics, PA
Pittsburgh Institute of Mortuary Science, PA
Pittsburgh Technical Institute, PA
Platt College
  Huntington Beach, CA
  Los Angeles, CA
Pratt Community College, KS
Pulaski Technical College, AR
Rainy River Community College, MN
Ramirez College of Business and Technology, PR
Redstone College, CO
Remington College
  Baton Rouge, LA
  Cleveland, OH
  Colorado Springs, CO
  Fort Worth, TX
  Houston, TX
  Memphis, TN
  Mobile, AL
Remington College: Cleveland West, OH
Renton Technical College, WA
River Valley Community College, NH
Riverland Community College, MN
Robeson Community College, NC
Rochester Community and Technical College, MN
Sage College, CA
St. Cloud Technical College, MN
St. Paul College, MN
Salt Lake Community College, UT
San Jacinto College, TX
Sanford-Brown College
  Hazelwood, MO
Savannah River College, GA
Savannah Technical College, GA
Shelton State Community College, AL
Sisseton Wahpeton College, SD
Somerset Community College, KY
South Central College, MN
South Florida Community College, FL
South Texas College, TX
Southeast Arkansas College, AR
Southeast Kentucky Community and Technical College, KY
Southeastern Technical College, GA
Southern Arkansas University Tech, AR
Southern Maine Community College, ME
Southern Union State Community College, AL
Southwest Georgia Technical College, GA
Southwest Tennessee Community College, TN
Southwest Wisconsin Technical College, WI

Spartanburg Community College, SC
Spencerian College: Lexington, KY
Springfield Technical Community College, MA
Stark State College of Technology, OH
State University of New York
  College of Agriculture and Technology at Cobleskill, NY
  College of Agriculture and Technology at Morrisville, NY
  College of Technology at Alfred, NY
Stevens-Henager College: Boise, ID
Technical Career Institutes, NY
Technology Education College, OH
TESST College of Technology
  Baltimore, MD
  Beltsville, MD
TESST College of Technology: Towson, MD
Texas Culinary Academy, TX
Texas State Technical College
  Harlingen, TX
  Sweetwater, TX
  Waco, TX
Texas State Technical College: Marshall, TX
Tidewater Tech
  Virginia Beach, VA
Tidewater Tech: Newport News, VA
Tri-County Technical College, SC
Triangle Tech
  Greensburg, PA
Triangle Tech: Bethlehem, PA
Trident Technical College, SC
Truckee Meadows Community College, NV
Tulsa Welding School, OK
United Tribes Technical College, ND
Universal Technical Institute, AZ
University of Hawaii
  Honolulu Community College, HI
University of Northwestern Ohio, OH
Vatterott College, MO
Vatterott College: Memphis, TN
Vatterott College: Quincy, IL
Vatterott College: Spring Valley, NE
Vincennes University, IN
Wake Technical Community College, NC
Walla Walla Community College, WA
Washington County Community College, ME
West Central Technical College, GA
West Virginia Business College, WV
West Virginia State Community and Technical College, WV
Western Career College: Antioch, CA
Western Career College: Stockton, CA
Western Technical College, TX
Western Technical College, WI
Westwood College of Technology
  Westwood College: Los Angeles, CA
Westwood College: Houston South, TX
White Mountains Community College, NH
Wisconsin Indianhead Technical College, WI
WyoTech: Fremont, CA
WyoTech: Laramie, WY
WyoTech: Long Beach, CA
York County Community College, ME
YTI Career Institute: Lancaster, PA
Zane State College, OH

Arts/music colleges

Four-year

Academy of Art University, CA
Art Academy of Cincinnati, OH
Art Center Design College, NM
Art Center Design College, AZ

Art Institute
  of Atlanta, GA
  of California: Orange County, CA
  of California: San Diego, CA
  of Charlotte, NC
  of Colorado, CO
  of Dallas, TX
  of Houston, TX
  of Las Vegas, NV
  of Philadelphia, PA
  of Phoenix, AZ
  of Pittsburgh, PA
  of Washington, VA
Art Institute of California: San Francisco, CA
Art Institute of Fort Lauderdale, FL
Art Institute of Portland, OR
Art Institute of Seattle, WA
Art Institutes International
  Minnesota, MN
Atlantic College, PR
Berklee College of Music, MA
Boston Conservatory, MA
Brooks Institute, CA
California College of the Arts, CA
California Design College, CA
California Institute of the Arts, CA
Chester College of New England, NH
Cleveland Institute of Art, OH
Cleveland Institute of Music, OH
Cogswell Polytechnical College, CA
College for Creative Studies, MI
College of Visual Arts, MN
Columbia College Chicago, IL
Columbia College: Hollywood, CA
Columbus College of Art and Design, OH
Conservatory of Music of Puerto Rico, PR
Converse College, SC
Cooper Union for the Advancement of Science and Art, NY
Corcoran College of Art and Design, DC
Cornish College of the Arts, WA
Curtis Institute of Music, PA
DePauw University, IN
DigiPen Institute of Technology, WA
Eastman School of Music of the University of Rochester, NY
Ex'pression College for Digital Arts, CA
Fashion Institute of Technology, NY
Five Towns College, NY
Illinois Institute of Art: Chicago, IL
Illinois Institute of Art: Schaumburg, IL
Institute of American Indian Arts, NM
International Academy of Design and Technology: Chicago, IL
International Academy of Design and Technology: Detroit, MI
International Academy of Design and Technology: Henderson, NV
International Academy of Design and Technology: Nashville, TN
International Academy of Design and Technology: Schaumburg, IL
International Academy of Design and Technology: Tampa, FL
Johns Hopkins University: Peabody Conservatory of Music, MD
Juilliard School, NY
Kansas City Art Institute, MO
Kendall College of Art and Design of Ferris State University, MI
Laguna College of Art and Design, CA
Lawrence University, WI
Maine College of Art, ME
Manhattan School of Music, NY
Mannes College The New School for Music, NY
Maryland Institute College of Art, MD
Massachusetts College of Art, MA
Memphis College of Art, TN
Miami International University of Art and Design, FL
Milwaukee Institute of Art & Design, WI

Minneapolis College of Art and Design, MN
Moore College of Art and Design, PA
New England Conservatory of Music, MA
New England Institute of Art, MA
New York School of Interior Design, NY
NewSchool of Architecture & Design, CA
North Carolina School of the Arts, NC
Northwest College of Art, WA
O'More College of Design, TN
Oberlin College, OH
Otis College of Art and Design, CA
Pacific Northwest College of Art, OR
Paier College of Art, CT
Parsons The New School for Design, NY
Platt College
  San Diego, CA
Pratt Institute, NY
Rhode Island School of Design, RI
Rhodec International, MA
Ringling College of Art and Design, FL
Rocky Mountain College of Art & Design, CO
San Francisco Art Institute, CA
San Francisco Conservatory of Music, CA
Savannah College of Art and Design, GA
School of the Art Institute of Chicago, IL
School of the Museum of Fine Arts, MA
School of Visual Arts, NY
Southern California Institute of Architecture, CA
State University of New York Purchase, NY
University of the Arts, PA
VanderCook College of Music, IL

Two-year

American Academy of Dramatic Arts, NY
American Academy of Dramatic Arts: West, CA
Antonelli Institute of Art and Photography, PA
Art Institute
  of California: Los Angeles, CA
Art Institute of Cincinnati, OH
Art Institute of Ohio: Cincinnati, OH
Fashion Institute of Design and Merchandising
  Los Angeles, CA
  San Diego, CA
  San Francisco, CA
Full Sail University, FL
Madison Media Institute, WI
Nossi College of Art, TN
Oakbridge Academy of Arts, PA
Platt College
  Huntington Beach, CA
  Los Angeles, CA
Villa Maria College of Buffalo, NY
Virginia Marti College of Art and Design, OH

Bible colleges

Four-year

Allegheny Wesleyan College, OH
American Baptist College of ABT Seminary, TN
Appalachian Bible College, WV
Arlington Baptist College, TX
Baptist Bible College, MO
Baptist Bible College of Pennsylvania, PA
Baptist College of Florida, FL
Baptist University of the Americas, TX
Barclay College, KS
Bethany University, CA
Bethesda Christian University, CA
Beulah Heights University, GA
Biola University, CA

Calvary Bible College and Theological Seminary, MO
Carolina Christian College, NC
Carver Bible College, GA
Colegio Pentecostal Mizpa, PR
Columbia International University, SC
Criswell College, TX
Davis College, NY
Faith Baptist Bible College and Theological Seminary, IA
Family of Faith College, OK
Florida Christian College, FL
Free Will Baptist Bible College, TN
Global University, MO
Grace University, NE
Griggs University, MD
Heritage Christian University, AL
John Wesley College, NC
Kaplan University
  Cedar Rapids, IA
Kentucky Christian University, KY
Kentucky Mountain Bible College, KY
The King's College and Seminary, CA
Kuyper College, MI
Life Pacific College, CA
Lincoln Christian College and Seminary, IL
Lipscomb University, TN
Maranatha Baptist Bible College, WI
Mid-Continent University, KY
Moody Bible Institute, IL
North Central University, MN
Northwestern College, MN
Philadelphia Biblical University, PA
Piedmont Baptist College, NC
Pillsbury Baptist Bible College, MN
Roanoke Bible College, NC
School of Urban Missions: New Orleans, LA
School of Urban Missions: Oakland, CA
Southeastern Bible College, AL
Southwestern Assemblies of God University, TX
Southwestern Christian University, OK
Tennessee Temple University, TN
Toccoa Falls College, GA
Trinity College of Florida, FL
Trinity Lutheran College, WA
Universidad FLET, FL
Washington Bible College, MD
William Jessup University, CA
World Mission University, CA
Zion Bible College, RI

Business colleges

Four-year

American University of Puerto Rico, PR
Angley College, FL
Aspen University, CO
Athens State University, AL
Atlantic College, PR
Babson College, MA
Baker College
  of Auburn Hills, MI
  of Cadillac, MI
  of Jackson, MI
  of Muskegon, MI
  of Owosso, MI
  of Port Huron, MI
Baker College of Allen Park, MI
Baltimore International College, MD
Bay Path College, MA
Bellevue University, NE
Bentley College, MA
Berkeley College, NY
Berkeley College, NJ
Berkeley College of New York City, NY
Briarcliffe College, NY
Brown College, MN
Bryant & Stratton College
  Willoughby Hills, OH
Bryant University, RI
California College San Diego, CA

California National University for Advanced Studies, CA
California State University
  Stanislaus, CA
California University of Management and Sciences, CA
Capitol College, MD
Central Pennsylvania College, PA
Chadron State College, NE
Champlain College, VT
City College
  Miami, FL
City College: Fort Lauderdale, FL
City University of New York
  Baruch College, NY
  Medgar Evers College, NY
Clarion University of Pennsylvania, PA
Cleary University, MI
CollegeAmerica
  Fort Collins, CO
Columbia Southern University, AL
Davenport University, MI
DeVry Institute of Technology
  New York, NY
DeVry University: Memphis, TN
Everest University: Brandon, FL
Everest University: Pompano Beach, FL
Everest University: South Orlando, FL
Everest University: Tampa, FL
Fashion Institute of Technology, NY
Friends University, KS
Globe Institute of Technology, NY
Globe University, MN
Goldey-Beacom College, DE
Herzing College, GA
Herzing College, WI
Hesser College, NH
Hodges University, FL
Humphreys College, CA
Husson College, ME
Huston-Tillotson University, TX
Indiana Institute of Technology, IN
International Business College, IN
International Import-Export Institute, AZ
Iona College, NY
John F. Kennedy University, CA
Jones College, FL
Jones College: Miami, FL
Keiser University, FL
King's College, PA
LA College International, CA
Lasell College, MA
Linfield College, OR
Loyola College in Maryland, MD
Maine Maritime Academy, ME
Mayville State University, ND
Menlo College, CA
Merrimack College, MA
Metropolitan College of New York, NY
Michigan Jewish Institute, MI
Millsaps College, MS
Minnesota School of Business: Plymouth, MN
Minnesota School of Business: Shakopee, MN
Monroe College, NY
Mount Ida College, MA
National American University
  Rapid City, SD
National American University: Rio Rancho, NM
National College
  Roanoke Valley, VA
New England College, NH
Newbury College, MA
Nichols College, MA
Northwestern Polytechnic University, CA
Northwood University
  Florida, FL
Northwood University: Michigan, MI
Northwood University: Texas, TX
Okaloosa-Walton College, FL
Peirce College, PA
Post University, CT
Potomac College, VA

Potomac College, DC
Presentation College, SD
Rasmussen College
    Eagan, MN
Reinhardt College, GA
Rockhurst University, MO
Sage College of Albany, NY
Savannah State University, GA
Silver Lake College, WI
South University, GA
South University: West Palm Beach
    Campus, FL
Southeastern University, DC
Southern California Institute of
    Technology, CA
State University of New York
    College at Old Westbury, NY
    Institute of Technology at
        Utica/Rome, NY
    Purchase, NY
Stevens-Henager College
    Murray, UT
Stonehill College, MA
Teikyo Loretto Heights University, CO
Thomas College, ME
Tiffin University, OH
University of Baltimore, MD
University of Northern Virginia, VA
Virginia College at Huntsville, AL
Walsh College of Accountancy and
    Business Administration, MI
Webber International University, FL
Western International University, AZ

Two-year

AIB College of Business, IA
Andover College, ME
Berean Institute, PA
Beta Tech: Richmond South, VA
Beta Tech: Richmond West, VA
Brown Mackie College: Atlanta, GA
Brown Mackie College: Cincinnati, OH
Brown Mackie College: Fort Wayne, IN
Brown Mackie College: Miami, FL
Bryant & Stratton Business Institute
    Bryant & Stratton College: Albany,
      NY
    Bryant & Stratton College: Buffalo,
      NY
    Bryant & Stratton College:
      Rochester, NY
    Bryant & Stratton College:
      Southtowns, NY
Bryant & Stratton College: Henrietta, NY
Bryant & Stratton College: Syracuse
    North, NY
Bryant & Stratton College: Virginia
    Beach, VA
Business Informatics Center, NY
Business Institute of Pennsylvania, PA
Cambria-Rowe Business College:
    Indiana, PA
Career College of Northern Nevada, NV
City College
    Gainesville, FL
Clemens College, CT
College of Court Reporting, IN
College of Office Technology, IL
Columbia College
    Columbia Centro Universitario:
      Yauco, PR
Daymar College
    Louisville, KY
Delta School of Business & Technology,
    LA
Draughons Junior College: Clarksville,
    TN
Draughons Junior College: Nashville, TN
DuBois Business College, PA
DuBois Business College
    Huntingdon, PA
    Oil City, PA
Empire College, CA
Erie Business Center, PA
Erie Business Center South, PA

Everest College
    Phoenix, AZ
Everest College: Arlington, TX
Everest College: Colorado Springs, CO
Fashion Careers College, CA
Fashion Institute of Design and
    Merchandising
    Los Angeles, CA
    San Diego, CA
    San Francisco, CA
Florida Career College: Miami, FL
Florida Career College: Pembroke Pines,
    FL
Gallipolis Career College, OH
Hallmark College of Technology, TX
Heald College
    Concord, CA
    Fresno, CA
    Honolulu, HI
    Roseville, CA
    Salinas, CA
    San Francisco, CA
    San Jose, CA
    Stockton, CA
Heald College: Portland, OR
Hondros College, OH
Humacao Community College, PR
ICPR Junior College, PR
Indiana Business College: Indianapolis
    Northwest, IN
Kaplan College: Hagerstown, MD
Kaplan College: Hammond, IN
Key College, FL
Long Island Business Institute, NY
Metro Business College, MO
Mildred Elley, NY
Miller-Motte Technical College:
    Clarksville, TN
Minneapolis Business College, MN
MTI College, CA
National College
    Danville, KY
    Dayton, OH
    Florence, KY
    Harrisonburg, VA
    Knoxville, TN
    Lexington, KY
National College of Business and
    Technology: Arecibo, PR
National College of Business and
    Technology: Bayamon, PR
National College of Business and
    Technology: Rio Grande, PR
New England College of Finance, MA
North Florida Institute: Orange Park, FL
Ohio Business College, OH
Penn Commercial Business and
    Technical School, PA
Ramirez College of Business and
    Technology, PR
Rasmussen College
    Eden Prairie, MN
    Mankato, MN
Remington College
    Memphis, TN
Sanford-Brown College
    Hazelwood, MO
Santa Barbara Business College
    Bakersfield, CA
    Santa Maria, CA
Southern Ohio College
    Brown Mackie College: North
      Kentucky, KY
Southwestern College of Business
    Southwestern College: Vine Street
      Campus, OH
Technology Education College, OH
Tidewater Tech: Chesapeake, VA
Tidewater Tech: Newport News, VA
Tri-State Business Institute, PA
University of Northwestern Ohio, OH
Utica School of Commerce, NY
Valley College of Technology, WV
Virginia College at Pensacola, FL

Virginia Marti College of Art and Design,
    OH
West Central Technical College, GA
West Virginia Business College, WV
West Virginia Career Institute, PA
West Virginia Junior College: Bridgeport,
    WV
YTI Career Institute: Lancaster, PA

Culinary schools

Four-year

Art Institute
    of California: Orange County, CA
    of Houston, TX
    of Las Vegas, NV
    of Phoenix, AZ
    of Washington, VA
Art Institutes International
    Minnesota, MN
Baltimore International College, MD
Culinary Institute of America, NY

Two-year

Art Institute
    of New York City, NY
Art Institute of Ohio: Cincinnati, OH
Atlantic Cape Community College, NJ
California Culinary Academy, CA
California School of Culinary Arts, CA
Clemens College, CT
Cooking & Hospitality Institute of
    Chicago, IL
Le Cordon Bleu College of Culinary
    Arts, NV
Le Cordon Bleu College of Culinary
    Arts, MN
Mitchell Technical Institute, SD
New England Culinary Institute, VT
Pennsylvania Culinary Institute, PA
Southwestern Oregon Community
    College, OR
Walters State Community College, TN

Engineering colleges

Four-year

California National University for
    Advanced Studies, CA
Capitol College, MD
Cogswell Polytechnical College, CA
Colorado School of Mines, CO
Columbia University, NY
Cooper Union for the Advancement of
    Science and Art, NY
DigiPen Institute of Technology, WA
Harvey Mudd College, CA
Illinois Institute of Technology, IL
Indiana Institute of Technology, IN
Inter American University of Puerto Rico
    Bayamon Campus, PR
Kettering University, MI
Lafayette College, PA
Maine Maritime Academy, ME
Manhattan College, NY
Montana Tech of the University of
    Montana, MT
Neumont University, UT
New Mexico Institute of Mining and
    Technology, NM
Northwestern Polytechnic University, CA
Oregon Institute of Technology, OR
Rose-Hulman Institute of Technology, IN
South Dakota School of Mines and
    Technology, SD
Southern California Institute of
    Technology, CA
Southern Polytechnic State University,
    GA
Stevens Institute of Technology, NJ
Tri-State University, IN
Union College, NY

United States Merchant Marine
    Academy, NY
Universidad Politecnica de Puerto Rico,
    PR
University of Missouri
    Missouri University of Science and
      Technology, MO
University of Pittsburgh
    Johnstown, PA
Vaughn College of Aeronautics and
    Technology, NY
Webb Institute, NY
Wentworth Institute of Technology, MA

Maritime colleges

Four-year

California Maritime Academy, CA
Maine Maritime Academy, ME
Massachusetts Maritime Academy, MA
State University of New York
    Maritime College, NY
United States Merchant Marine
    Academy, NY
Webb Institute, NY

Two-year

National Polytechnic College of Science,
    CA
Northwestern Michigan College, MI

Military colleges

Four-year

The Citadel, SC
Massachusetts Maritime Academy, MA
North Georgia College & State
    University, GA
Norwich University, VT
United States Merchant Marine
    Academy, NY
Virginia Military Institute, VA

Two-year

Georgia Military College, GA
Marion Military Institute, AL
New Mexico Military Institute, NM
Valley Forge Military College, PA
Wentworth Military Junior College, MO

Nursing and health science colleges

Four-year

Albany College of Pharmacy, NY
Angley College, FL
Aquinas College, TN
Baker College
    of Cadillac, MI
Baker College of Allen Park, MI
Bastyr University, WA
Bellin College of Nursing, WI
Blessing-Rieman College of Nursing, IL
Bryant & Stratton College
    Parma, OH
Cabarrus College of Health Sciences, NC
California College San Diego, CA
California University of Management and
    Sciences, CA
Caribbean University, PR
Charles R. Drew University of Medicine
    and Science, CA
City College
    Miami, FL
College of New Rochelle, NY
College of St. Catherine, MN
College of Saint Mary, NE
CollegeAmerica
    Fort Collins, CO
Coppin State University, MD
Curry College, MA
D'Youville College, NY

Dominican College of Blauvelt, NY
Globe University, MN
Gwynedd-Mercy College, PA
Husson College, ME
Ithaca College, NY
Jefferson College of Health Sciences, VA
Keiser University, FL
Kettering College of Medical Arts, OH
King College, TN
Lincoln University, CA
Loma Linda University, CA
Louisiana State University Health
    Sciences Center, LA
Massachusetts College of Pharmacy and
    Health Sciences, MA
MedCentral College of Nursing, OH
Misericordia University, PA
Monroe College, NY
Mountain State University, WV
Nebraska Methodist College of Nursing
    and Allied Health, NE
Nevada State College, NV
New York Institute of Technology, NY
Northwestern Health Sciences University,
    MN
Oregon Health & Science University, OR
Oregon Institute of Technology, OR
Presentation College, SD
Regis College, MA
Research College of Nursing, MO
Rosalind Franklin University of Medicine
    and Science, IL
St. Anselm College, NH
St. Catharine College, KY
St. John's College, IL
Samuel Merritt College, CA
South University, GA
South University: West Palm Beach
    Campus, FL
Springfield College, MA
State University of New York
    Institute of Technology at
        Utica/Rome, NY
    Upstate Medical University, NY
Stevens-Henager College
    Murray, UT
Thomas Jefferson University: College of
    Health Professions, PA
Trinity College of Nursing and Health
    Sciences, IL
University of Findlay, OH
University of Kansas Medical Center, KS
University of Maryland
    Baltimore, MD
University of Medicine and Dentistry of
    New Jersey
    School of Health Related
        Professions, NJ
University of Tennessee Health Science
    Center, TN
University of Texas
    Health Science Center at San
        Antonio, TX
    Medical Branch at Galveston, TX
    Southwestern Medical Center at
        Dallas, TX
University of the Sciences in
    Philadelphia, PA
West Coast University, CA
West Suburban College of Nursing, IL
Winston-Salem State University, NC

Two-year

Aultman College of Nursing and Health
    Sciences, OH
Beta Tech: Richmond South, VA
Beta Tech: Richmond West, VA
Bolivar Technical College, MO
Brown Mackie College: Atlanta, GA
Brown Mackie College: Cincinnati, OH
Career College of Northern Nevada, NV
Careers Unlimited, UT
Caritas Laboure College, MA
City College
    Gainesville, FL

College of Business and Technology:
    Kendall, FL
Columbia College
    Columbia Centro Universitario:
        Yauco, PR
Concorde Career College
    Garden Grove, CA
Concorde Career College: North
    Hollywood, CA
Concorde Career College: San Diego, CA
Everest Institute, GA
Florida College of Natural Health
    Bradenton, FL
Fremont College, CA
Goodwin College, CT
Heritage Institute: Jacksonville, FL
Hondros College, OH
Huntington College of Health Sciences,
    TN
Indiana Business College: Indianapolis
    Northwest, IN
Keystone Technical Institute, PA
Lakeland Academy Division of Herzing
    College, MN
Los Angeles County College of Nursing
    and Allied Health, CA
Maric College: Palm Springs, CA
Maric College: Salida, CA
Miller-Motte Technical College:
    Clarksville, TN
Minnesota State College - Southeast
    Technical, MN
North Florida Institute: Orange Park, FL
Ohio College of Massotherapy, OH
Ohio Institute of Health Careers:
    Columbus, OH
Ohio Institute of Health Careers: Elyria,
    OH
Phillips Beth Israel School of Nursing,
    NY
Platt College
    Tulsa, OK
Platt College: Oklahoma City Central,
    OK
Ponce Paramedical College, PR
St. Elizabeth College of Nursing, NY
St. Luke's College, IA
Southeast Missouri Hospital College of
    Nursing and Health Sciences, MO
Southern Ohio College
    Brown Mackie College: North
        Kentucky, KY
Southwestern College of Business
    Southwestern College: Vine Street
        Campus, OH
Southwestern College: Florence, KY
Swedish Institute, NY
Technology Education College, OH
Tidewater Tech: Chesapeake, VA
Ultrasound Diagnostic School
    Sanford-Brown Institute:
        Jacksonville, FL
Universal Technology College of Puerto
    Rico, PR
Virginia College at Pensacola, FL
West Virginia Junior College: Bridgeport,
    WV
Western Career College: Stockton, CA
White Earth Tribal and Community
    College, MN
WyoTech: Long Beach, CA

Schools of mortuary science

Four-year

Cincinnati College of Mortuary Science,
    OH

Two-year

Commonwealth Institute of Funeral
    Service, TX

Seminary/rabbinical colleges

Four-year

Baptist Bible College, MO
Baptist Bible College of Pennsylvania,
    PA
Calvary Bible College and Theological
    Seminary, MO
Criswell College, TX
Divine Word College, IA
Dominican School of Philosophy and
    Theology, CA
Earlham College, IN
Erskine College, SC
Faith Baptist Bible College and
    Theological Seminary, IA
George Fox University, OR
Global University, MO
Hellenic College/Holy Cross, MA
Holy Apostles College and Seminary, CT
The King's College and Seminary, CA
Liberty University, VA
Lincoln Christian College and Seminary,
    IL
The Master's College, CA
Michigan Theological Seminary, MI
Mount Angel Seminary, OR
Piedmont Baptist College, NC
St. Charles Borromeo Seminary -
    Overbrook, PA
St. Joseph Seminary College, LA
University of Dubuque, IA
Washington Bible College, MD
World Mission University, CA
Yeshiva College of the Nations Capital,
    MD
Yeshiva Mikdash Melech, NY
Yeshivath Beth Moshe, PA

Teacher's colleges

Four-year

Anderson University, SC
Arlington Baptist College, TX
Athens State University, AL
Augusta State University, GA
Austin College, TX
Baker University, KS
Baltimore Hebrew University, MD
Baptist College of Florida, FL
Black Hills State University, SD
Bloomfield College, NJ
Bridgewater State College, MA
California State University
    Monterey Bay, CA
Cambridge College, MA
Canisius College, NY
Chadron State College, NE
City University of New York
    Queens College, NY
Clarion University of Pennsylvania, PA
College of St. Joseph in Vermont, VT
College of Saint Mary, NE
College of Saint Rose, NY
College of the Southwest, NM
Concordia University, IL
Concordia University, MI
Eastern Illinois University, IL
Edinboro University of Pennsylvania, PA
Emporia State University, KS
Fitchburg State College, MA
Florida Christian College, FL
Fort Valley State University, GA
Framingham State College, MA
Free Will Baptist Bible College, TN
Frostburg State University, MD
Glenville State College, WV
Heritage University, WA
Howard Payne University, TX
Jones College, FL
Lander University, SC

Laura and Alvin Siegal College of Judaic
    Studies, OH
Lesley University, MA
Lyndon State College, VT
Manhattanville College, NY
Mayville State University, ND
National-Louis University, IL
Nevada State College, NV
New England College, NH
Northwestern Oklahoma State University,
    OK
Oglala Lakota College, SD
Pacific Oaks College, CA
Peru State College, NE
Piedmont College, GA
Plymouth State University, NH
Reinhardt College, GA
Rivier College, NH
St. Joseph's College, NY
Southeastern Oklahoma State University,
    OK
Southeastern University, FL
State University of New York
    College at Buffalo, NY
    College at Cortland, NY
    College at Plattsburgh, NY
    College at Potsdam, NY
Tennessee Wesleyan College, TN
Union College, KY
University of Hawaii
    West Oahu, HI
University of Maine
    Farmington, ME
University of Montana: Western, MT
Valley City State University, ND
VanderCook College of Music, IL
Wayne State College, NE
Western Oregon University, OR
Wheelock College, MA
Worcester State College, MA
York College, NE

Two-year

Northern New Mexico College, NM
White Earth Tribal and Community
    College, MN

Colleges for men

Four-year

Divine Word College, IA
Hampden-Sydney College, VA
Morehouse College, GA
Mount Angel Seminary, OR
St. Charles Borromeo Seminary -
    Overbrook, PA
St. John's University, MN
St. Joseph Seminary College, LA
Wabash College, IN
Yeshiva College of the Nations Capital,
    MD
Yeshiva Mikdash Melech, NY
Yeshivath Beth Moshe, PA

Two-year

Deep Springs College, CA

Colleges for women

Four-year

Agnes Scott College, GA
Alverno College, WI
Barnard College, NY
Bay Path College, MA
Bennett College, NC
Brenau University, GA
Bryn Mawr College, PA
Carlow University, PA
Cedar Crest College, PA
Chatham University, PA
College of New Rochelle, NY
College of Notre Dame of Maryland, MD
College of St. Benedict, MN

College of St. Catherine, MN
College of St. Elizabeth, NJ
College of Saint Mary, NE
Columbia College, SC
Converse College, SC
Georgian Court University, NJ
Hollins University, VA
Judson College, AL
Lexington College, IL
Mary Baldwin College, VA
Meredith College, NC
Midway College, KY
Mills College, CA
Moore College of Art and Design, PA
Mount Holyoke College, MA
Mount Mary College, WI
Peace College, NC
Pine Manor College, MA
Rosemont College, PA
Russell Sage College, NY
St. Joseph College, CT
Saint Mary's College, IN
St. Mary-of-the-Woods College, IN
Salem College, NC
Scripps College, CA
Simmons College, MA
Smith College, MA
Spelman College, GA
Stephens College, MO
Sweet Briar College, VA
Trinity Washington University, DC
Ursuline College, OH
Wellesley College, MA
Wesleyan College, GA
Wilson College, PA

Two-year
Cottey College, MO

Affiliated with a religion

Four-year
Trinity Lutheran College, WA
Valparaiso University, IN

African Methodist Episcopal Church

Four-year
Allen University, SC
Edward Waters College, FL
Wilberforce University, OH

African Methodist Episcopal Zion Church

Four-year
Livingstone College, NC

American Baptist Churches in the USA

Four-year
Alderson-Broaddus College, WV
Bacone College, OK
Benedict College, SC
Eastern University, PA
Florida Memorial University, FL
Franklin College, IN
Judson University, IL
Keuka College, NY
Linfield College, OR
Ottawa University, KS
University of Sioux Falls, SD

Assemblies of God

Four-year
Bethany University, CA
Evangel University, MO
Global University, MO
North Central University, MN
Northwest University, WA
School of Urban Missions: Oakland, CA
Southeastern University, FL

Southwestern Assemblies of God
University, TX
Valley Forge Christian College, PA
Vanguard University of Southern
California, CA
Zion Bible College, RI

Baptist faith

Four-year
American Baptist College of ABT
Seminary, TN
Arlington Baptist College, TX
Baptist Bible College, MO
Baptist Bible College of Pennsylvania,
PA
Baylor University, TX
Bluefield College, VA
Campbellsville University, KY
Cedarville University, OH
Corban College, OR
Cornerstone University, MI
Dallas Baptist University, TX
East Texas Baptist University, TX
Hardin-Simmons University, TX
Houston Baptist University, TX
Howard Payne University, TX
Judson College, AL
Liberty University, VA
Maranatha Baptist Bible College, WI
Mars Hill College, NC
Mercer University, GA
Missouri Baptist University, MO
Morris College, SC
Piedmont Baptist College, NC
Pillsbury Baptist Bible College, MN
Shaw University, NC
Tennessee Temple University, TN
University of Mary Hardin-Baylor, TX
University of Mobile, AL
University of the Cumberlands, KY
Virginia Intermont College, VA
Virginia Union University, VA
William Carey University, MS
Wingate University, NC

Two-year
Jacksonville College, TX

Baptist General Conference

Four-year
Bethel University, MN
Oakland City University, IN

Brethren Church

Four-year
Ashland University, OH

Christian and Missionary Alliance

Four-year
Nyack College, NY
Simpson University, CA
Toccoa Falls College, GA

Christian Church

Four-year
Bethesda Christian University, CA
The Master's College, CA
Taylor University Fort Wayne, IN
William Jewell College, MO

Christian Church (Disciples of Christ)

Four-year
Barton College, NC
Bethany College, WV
Chapman University, CA
Columbia College, MO
Culver-Stockton College, MO
Eureka College, IL
Hiram College, OH

Lynchburg College, VA
Midway College, KY
Northwest Christian College, OR
Texas Christian University, TX
Transylvania University, KY
William Woods University, MO

Christian Methodist Episcopal Church

Four-year
Lane College, TN
Miles College, AL
Texas College, TX

Christian Reformed Church

Four-year
Calvin College, MI

Church of Christ

Four-year
Abilene Christian University, TX
Carolina Christian College, NC
Cascade College, OR
Faulkner University, AL
Freed-Hardeman University, TN
Harding University, AR
Heritage Christian University, AL
Lincoln Christian College and Seminary,
IL
Lipscomb University, TN
Lubbock Christian University, TX
Ohio Valley University, WV
Oklahoma Christian University, OK
Pepperdine University, CA
Roanoke Bible College, NC
Rochester College, MI
York College, NE

Two-year
Crowley's Ridge College, AR

Church of God

Four-year
Lee University, TN
University of Findlay, OH
Warner Pacific College, OR
Warner Southern College, FL

Church of Jesus Christ of Latter-day Saints

Four-year
Brigham Young University, UT
Brigham Young University-Hawaii, HI
Brigham Young University-Idaho, ID
Southern Virginia University, VA

Church of the Brethren

Four-year
Bridgewater College, VA
Elizabethtown College, PA
Manchester College, IN
McPherson College, KS

Church of the Nazarene

Four-year
Eastern Nazarene College, MA
MidAmerica Nazarene University, KS
Mount Vernon Nazarene University, OH
Northwest Nazarene University, ID
Olivet Nazarene University, IL
Point Loma Nazarene University, CA
Southern Nazarene University, OK
Trevecca Nazarene University, TN

Episcopal Church

Four-year
Bard College, NY
St. Augustine's College, NC
St. Paul's College, VA

University of the South, TN
Voorhees College, SC

Evangelical Free Church of America

Four-year
Trinity International University, IL

Evangelical Lutheran Church in America

Four-year
Augsburg College, MN
Augustana College, IL
Augustana College, SD
Bethany College, KS
California Lutheran University, CA
Capital University, OH
Carthage College, WI
Concordia College: Moorhead, MN
Dana College, NE
Finlandia University, MI
Grand View College, IA
Gustavus Adolphus College, MN
Lenoir-Rhyne College, NC
Luther College, IA
Midland Lutheran College, NE
Muhlenberg College, PA
Newberry College, SC
Pacific Lutheran University, WA
Roanoke College, VA
St. Olaf College, MN
Susquehanna University, PA
Texas Lutheran University, TX
Thiel College, PA
Waldorf College, IA
Wartburg College, IA
Wittenberg University, OH

Evangelical Lutheran Synod

Four-year
Bethany Lutheran College, MN

Free Methodist Church of North America

Four-year
Central Christian College of Kansas, KS
Greenville College, IL
Roberts Wesleyan College, NY
Seattle Pacific University, WA
Spring Arbor University, MI

Free Will Baptists

Four-year
Free Will Baptist Bible College, TN
Mount Olive College, NC

General Association of Regular Baptist Churches

Four-year
Faith Baptist Bible College and
Theological Seminary, IA

Interdenominational tradition

Four-year
Azusa Pacific University, CA
Biola University, CA
Bryan College, TN
Ecclesia College, AR
Grace University, NE
Heritage University, WA
John Brown University, AR
John Wesley College, NC
Messiah College, PA
Moody Bible Institute, IL
Patten University, CA
Regent University, VA
Taylor University, IN
Trinity College of Florida, FL

Jewish faith

Four-year

American Jewish University, CA
Gratz College, PA
Laura and Alvin Siegal College of Judaic Studies, OH
Michigan Jewish Institute, MI
Yeshiva College of the Nations Capital, MD
Yeshiva Mikdash Melech, NY
Yeshivath Beth Moshe, PA

Lutheran Church - Missouri Synod

Four-year

Concordia College, NY
Concordia College, AL
Concordia University, IL
Concordia University, CA
Concordia University, MI
Concordia University, NE
Concordia University, OR
Concordia University at Austin, TX
Concordia University Wisconsin, WI
Concordia University: St. Paul, MN

Lutheran Church in America

Four-year

Wagner College, NY

Mennonite Brethren Church

Four-year

Fresno Pacific University, CA
Tabor College, KS

Mennonite Church

Four-year

Bethel College, KS
Bluffton University, OH
Eastern Mennonite University, VA
Goshen College, IN

Two-year

Hesston College, KS

Missionary Church

Four-year

Bethel College, IN

Moravian Church in America

Four-year

Moravian College, PA
Salem College, NC

Nondenominational tradition

Four-year

Appalachian Bible College, WV
Calvary Bible College and Theological Seminary, MO
Colorado Christian University, CO
Crichton College, TN
Davis College, NY
Friends University, KS
Gordon College, MA
King's College, NY
The King's College and Seminary, CA
LeTourneau University, TX
Northwestern College, MN
Occidental College, CA
Oral Roberts University, OK
Palm Beach Atlantic University, FL
San Diego Christian College, CA
Southeastern Bible College, AL
Washington Bible College, MD
Westmont College, CA
Wheaton College, IL
William Jessup University, CA

Pentecostal Holiness Church

Four-year

Southwestern Christian University, OK

Presbyterian Church (USA)

Four-year

Agnes Scott College, GA
Alma College, MI
Arcadia University, PA
Austin College, TX
Belhaven College, MS
Bethel College, TN
Blackburn College, IL
Bloomfield College, NJ
Buena Vista University, IA
Carroll College, WI
Centre College, KY
Coe College, IA
College of the Ozarks, MO
Davidson College, NC
Davis and Elkins College, WV
Eckerd College, FL
Grove City College, PA
Hampden-Sydney College, VA
Hanover College, IN
Hastings College, NE
Jamestown College, ND
King College, TN
Lafayette College, PA
Lake Forest College, IL
Lees-McRae College, NC
Lindenwood University, MO
Lyon College, AR
Macalester College, MN
Mary Baldwin College, VA
Maryville College, TN
Millikin University, IL
Missouri Valley College, MO
Monmouth College, IL
Montreat College, NC
Muskingum College, OH
Peace College, NC
Queens University of Charlotte, NC
Rhodes College, TN
St. Andrews Presbyterian College, NC
Schreiner University, TX
Sterling College, KS
Stillman College, AL
Trinity University, TX
Tusculum College, TN
University of Dubuque, IA
University of the Ozarks, AR
University of Tulsa, OK
Warren Wilson College, NC
Waynesburg University, PA
Westminster College, MO
Westminster College, PA
Whitworth University, WA
Wilson College, PA

Reformed Church in America

Four-year

Central College, IA
Hope College, MI
Northwestern College, IA

Reformed Presbyterian Church of North America

Four-year

Geneva College, PA

Roman Catholic Church

Four-year

Albertus Magnus College, CT
Alvernia College, PA
Alverno College, WI
Anna Maria College, MA
Aquinas College, MI
Aquinas College, TN
Assumption College, MA
Ave Maria University, FL
Avila University, MO
Barry University, FL
Bayamon Central University, PR
Bellarmine University, KY
Belmont Abbey College, NC
Benedictine College, KS
Benedictine University, IL
Boston College, MA
Brescia University, KY
Briar Cliff University, IA
Cabrini College, PA
Caldwell College, NJ
Calumet College of St. Joseph, IN
Canisius College, NY
Cardinal Stritch University, WI
Carlow University, PA
Carroll College, MT
Catholic University of America, DC
Chaminade University of Honolulu, HI
Chestnut Hill College, PA
Christendom College, VA
Christian Brothers University, TN
Clarke College, IA
College of Mount St. Joseph, OH
College of Mount St. Vincent, NY
College of New Rochelle, NY
College of Notre Dame of Maryland, MD
College of St. Benedict, MN
College of St. Catherine, MN
College of St. Elizabeth, NJ
College of St. Joseph in Vermont, VT
College of Saint Mary, NE
College of Saint Rose, NY
College of St. Scholastica, MN
College of Saint Thomas More, TX
College of the Holy Cross, MA
Creighton University, NE
DePaul University, IL
DeSales University, PA
Divine Word College, IA
Dominican School of Philosophy and Theology, CA
Dominican University, IL
Duquesne University, PA
Edgewood College, WI
Elms College, MA
Emmanuel College, MA
Fairfield University, CT
Felician College, NJ
Fontbonne University, MO
Fordham University, NY
Franciscan University of Steubenville, OH
Gannon University, PA
Georgetown University, DC
Georgian Court University, NJ
Gonzaga University, WA
Gwynedd-Mercy College, PA
Holy Apostles College and Seminary, CT
Holy Cross College, IN
Holy Family University, PA
Holy Names University, CA
Immaculata University, PA
Iona College, NY
John Carroll University, OH
King's College, PA
La Roche College, PA
La Salle University, PA
Le Moyne College, NY
Lewis University, IL
Lexington College, IL
Loras College, IA
Lourdes College, OH
Loyola College in Maryland, MD
Loyola Marymount University, CA
Loyola University Chicago, IL
Loyola University New Orleans, LA
Madonna University, MI
Magdalen College, NH
Manhattan College, NY
Marian College, IN
Marian College of Fond du Lac, WI
Marquette University, WI
Marygrove College, MI
Marylhurst University, OR
Marymount University, VA
Marywood University, PA
Mercyhurst College, PA
Merrimack College, MA
Misericordia University, PA
Molloy College, NY
Mount Aloysius College, PA
Mount Angel Seminary, OR
Mount Marty College, SD
Mount Mary College, WI
Mount Mercy College, IA
Mount St. Mary's University, MD
Neumann College, PA
Newman University, KS
Niagara University, NY
Notre Dame College, OH
Notre Dame de Namur University, CA
Ohio Dominican University, OH
Our Lady of the Lake University of San Antonio, TX
Pontifical Catholic University of Puerto Rico, PR
Presentation College, SD
Providence College, RI
Quincy University, IL
Regis College, MA
Regis University, CO
Rivier College, NH
Rockhurst University, MO
Rosemont College, PA
Sacred Heart University, CT
St. Ambrose University, IA
St. Anselm College, NH
Saint Bonaventure University, NY
St. Catharine College, KY
St. Charles Borromeo Seminary - Overbrook, PA
St. Edward's University, TX
St. Francis College, NY
St. Francis University, PA
St. Gregory's University, OK
St. John Fisher College, NY
St. John's College, IL
St. John's University, NY
St. John's University, MN
St. Joseph College, CT
St. Joseph Seminary College, LA
St. Joseph's College, ME
Saint Joseph's University, PA
St. Leo University, FL
Saint Louis University, MO
Saint Martin's University, WA
Saint Mary's College, IN
St. Mary's College of California, CA
St. Mary's University, TX
St. Mary's University of Minnesota, MN
St. Mary-of-the-Woods College, IN
St. Michael's College, VT
St. Norbert College, WI
Saint Peter's College, NJ
Saint Thomas University, FL
St. Vincent College, PA
St. Xavier University, IL
Salve Regina University, RI
Santa Clara University, CA
Seattle University, WA
Seton Hall University, NJ
Seton Hill University, PA
Siena College, NY
Siena Heights University, MI
Silver Lake College, WI
Spring Hill College, AL
Stonehill College, MA
Thomas More College, KY
Thomas More College of Liberal Arts, NH
Trinity Washington University, DC
University of Dallas, TX
University of Dayton, OH
University of Detroit Mercy, MI
University of Great Falls, MT
University of Mary, ND
University of Notre Dame, IN
University of Portland, OR
University of St. Francis, IN

University of St. Francis, IL
University of St. Mary, KS
University of St. Thomas, TX
University of St. Thomas, MN
University of San Diego, CA
University of San Francisco, CA
University of Scranton, PA
University of the Incarnate Word, TX
Ursuline College, OH
Villanova University, PA
Viterbo University, WI
Walsh University, OH
West Suburban College of Nursing, IL
Wheeling Jesuit University, WV
Xavier University, OH
Xavier University of Louisiana, LA

Two-year

Ancilla College, IN
Caritas Laboure College, MA
Donnelly College, KS
Marian Court College, MA
Marymount College, CA
St. Elizabeth College of Nursing, NY
Springfield College in Illinois, IL
Trocaire College, NY
Villa Maria College of Buffalo, NY

Seventh-day Adventists

Four-year

Andrews University, MI
Atlantic Union College, MA
Columbia Union College, MD
Griggs University, MD
Kettering College of Medical Arts, OH
La Sierra University, CA
Loma Linda University, CA
Oakwood University, AL
Pacific Union College, CA
Southwestern Adventist University, TX
Union College, NE
Universidad Adventista de las Antillas, PR
Walla Walla University, WA

Society of Friends (Quaker)

Four-year

Earlham College, IN
George Fox University, OR
Guilford College, NC
William Penn University, IA
Wilmington College, OH

Southern Baptist Convention

Four-year

Anderson University, SC
Baptist College of Florida, FL
Blue Mountain College, MS
Brewton-Parker College, GA
California Baptist University, CA
Carson-Newman College, TN
Charleston Southern University, SC
Chowan University, NC
Criswell College, TX
Gardner-Webb University, NC
Georgetown College, KY
Hannibal-LaGrange College, MO
Louisiana College, LA
Mid-Continent University, KY
Mississippi College, MS
North Greenville University, SC
Oklahoma Baptist University, OK
Ouachita Baptist University, AR
Samford University, AL
Shorter College, GA
Southwest Baptist University, MO
Truett-McConnell College, GA
Union University, TN
Wayland Baptist University, TX
Williams Baptist College, AR

Ukrainian Catholic Church

Two-year

Manor College, PA

United Brethren in Christ

Four-year

Huntington University, IN

United Church of Christ

Four-year

Catawba College, NC
Defiance College, OH
Doane College, NE
Elmhurst College, IL
Elon University, NC
Heidelberg College, OH
Lakeland College, WI
Northland College, WI
Pacific University, OR
Williams College, MA

United Methodist Church

Four-year

Adrian College, MI
Albion College, MI
Albright College, PA
Allegheny College, PA
American University, DC
Baker University, KS
Baldwin-Wallace College, OH
Bennett College, NC
Bethune-Cookman University, FL
Birmingham-Southern College, AL
Brevard College, NC
Centenary College, NJ
Centenary College of Louisiana, LA
Central Methodist University, MO
Claflin University, SC
Clark Atlanta University, GA
Columbia College, SC
Cornell College, IA
Dakota Wesleyan University, SD
DePauw University, IN
Drew University, NJ
Duke University, NC
Emory & Henry College, VA
Emory University, GA
Ferrum College, VA
Florida Southern College, FL
Green Mountain College, VT
Greensboro College, NC
Hamline University, MN
Hendrix College, AR
High Point University, NC
Huntingdon College, AL
Iowa Wesleyan College, IA
Kansas Wesleyan University, KS
LaGrange College, GA
Lambuth University, TN
Lebanon Valley College, PA
Lindsey Wilson College, KY
Lycoming College, PA
MacMurray College, IL
Martin Methodist College, TN
McKendree University, IL
McMurry University, TX
Methodist University, NC
Millsaps College, MS
Morningside College, IA
Mount Union College, OH
Nebraska Methodist College of Nursing and Allied Health, NE
Nebraska Wesleyan University, NE
North Carolina Wesleyan College, NC
North Central College, IL
Ohio Northern University, OH
Ohio Wesleyan University, OH
Oklahoma City University, OK
Otterbein College, OH
Pfeiffer University, NC
Philander Smith College, AR
Randolph College, VA

Randolph-Macon College, VA
Reinhardt College, GA
Rust College, MS
Shenandoah University, VA
Simpson College, IA
Southern Methodist University, TX
Southwestern College, KS
Southwestern University, TX
Tennessee Wesleyan College, TN
Texas Wesleyan University, TX
Union College, KY
University of Denver, CO
University of Evansville, IN
University of Indianapolis, IN
Virginia Wesleyan College, VA
Wesley College, DE
Wesleyan College, GA
West Virginia Wesleyan College, WV
Wiley College, TX
Willamette University, OR
Wofford College, SC

Two-year

Andrew College, GA
Hiwassee College, TN
Lon Morris College, TX
Louisburg College, NC
Spartanburg Methodist College, SC
Young Harris College, GA

Wesleyan Church

Four-year

Houghton College, NY
Indiana Wesleyan University, IN
Oklahoma Wesleyan University, OK
Southern Wesleyan University, SC

Historically Black colleges

Four-year

Alabama Agricultural and Mechanical University, AL
Alabama State University, AL
Albany State University, GA
Alcorn State University, MS
Allen University, SC
Benedict College, SC
Bennett College, NC
Bluefield State College, WV
Bowie State University, MD
Central State University, OH
Cheyney University of Pennsylvania, PA
Claflin University, SC
Clark Atlanta University, GA
Concordia College, AL
Coppin State University, MD
Delaware State University, DE
Dillard University, LA
Edward Waters College, FL
Elizabeth City State University, NC
Florida Agricultural and Mechanical University, FL
Florida Memorial University, FL
Fort Valley State University, GA
Grambling State University, LA
Hampton University, VA
Harris-Stowe State University, MO
Howard University, DC
Huston-Tillotson University, TX
Jackson State University, MS
Johnson C. Smith University, NC
Kentucky State University, KY
Lane College, TN
Langston University, OK
LeMoyne-Owen College, TN
Lincoln University, PA
Lincoln University, MO
Livingstone College, NC
Miles College, AL
Mississippi Valley State University, MS
Morehouse College, GA
Morgan State University, MD
Morris College, SC

Norfolk State University, VA
North Carolina Central University, NC
Oakwood University, AL
Paine College, GA
Philander Smith College, AR
Prairie View A&M University, TX
Rust College, MS
St. Augustine's College, NC
St. Paul's College, VA
Savannah State University, GA
Shaw University, NC
South Carolina State University, SC
Southern University
    New Orleans, LA
Southern University and Agricultural and Mechanical College, LA
Spelman College, GA
Stillman College, AL
Tennessee State University, TN
Texas College, TX
Texas Southern University, TX
Tougaloo College, MS
Tuskegee University, AL
University of Arkansas
    Pine Bluff, AR
University of Maryland
    Eastern Shore, MD
University of the District of Columbia, DC
Virginia State University, VA
Voorhees College, SC
Wilberforce University, OH
Wiley College, TX
Winston-Salem State University, NC
Xavier University of Louisiana, LA

Two-year

Bishop State Community College, AL
Coahoma Community College, MS
Denmark Technical College, SC
Hinds Community College, MS
J. F. Drake State Technical College, AL
Lawson State Community College, AL
St. Philip's College, TX
Southern University
    Shreveport, LA

Hispanic serving colleges

Four-year

Adams State College, CO
American University of Puerto Rico, PR
Atlantic College, PR
Barry University, FL
Bayamon Central University, PR
California State University
    Bakersfield, CA
    Dominguez Hills, CA
    Fresno, CA
    Los Angeles, CA
    Monterey Bay, CA
    San Bernardino, CA
    Stanislaus, CA
Caribbean University, PR
Carlos Albizu University, FL
City University of New York
    City College, NY
    John Jay College of Criminal Justice, NY
    Lehman College, NY
College of Santa Fe, NM
Conservatory of Music of Puerto Rico, PR
Dominican School of Philosophy and Theology, CA
Florida International University, FL
Heritage University, WA

Inter American University of Puerto Rico
    Aguadilla Campus, PR
    Arecibo Campus, PR
    Barranquitas Campus, PR
    Bayamon Campus, PR
    Fajardo Campus, PR
    Guayama Campus, PR
    Metropolitan Campus, PR
    Ponce Campus, PR
    San German Campus, PR
Lexington College, IL
Mercy College, NY
Mount Angel Seminary, OR
New Jersey City University, NJ
New Mexico State University, NM
Occidental College, CA
Our Lady of the Lake University of San Antonio, TX
Pontifical Catholic University of Puerto Rico, PR
Robert Morris College: Chicago, IL
St. Edward's University, TX
St. Mary's University, TX
Saint Peter's College, NJ
Saint Thomas University, FL
San Diego State University, CA
Sul Ross State University, TX
Texas A&M International University, TX
Texas A&M University
    Kingsville, TX
Turabo University, PR
Universidad Adventista de las Antillas, PR
Universidad del Este, PR
Universidad Metropolitana, PR
Universidad Politecnica de Puerto Rico, PR
University College of San Juan, PR
University of Houston
    Downtown, TX
University of La Verne, CA
University of Miami, FL
University of New Mexico, NM
University of Puerto Rico
    Aguadilla, PR
    Arecibo, PR
    Bayamon University College, PR
    Carolina Regional College, PR
    Cayey University College, PR
    Humacao, PR
    Mayaguez, PR
    Medical Sciences, PR
    Ponce, PR
    Rio Piedras, PR
    Utuado, PR
University of Texas
    Brownsville, TX
    El Paso, TX
    Health Science Center at San Antonio, TX
    Pan American, TX
    San Antonio, TX
    of the Permian Basin, TX
University of the Incarnate Word, TX
Vaughn College of Aeronautics and Technology, NY
Western New Mexico University, NM
Whittier College, CA
Woodbury University, CA

Two-year

Allan Hancock College, CA
Arizona Western College, AZ
Bakersfield College, CA
Central Arizona College, AZ
Cerritos College, CA
Chaffey College, CA
Citrus College, CA
City Colleges of Chicago
    Malcolm X College, IL
    Richard J. Daley College, IL
    Wright College, IL

City University of New York
    Borough of Manhattan Community College, NY
    Bronx Community College, NY
    Hostos Community College, NY
    LaGuardia Community College, NY
Coastal Bend College, TX
Cochise College, AZ
College of the Desert, CA
College of the Sequoias, CA
Community College of Denver, CO
Del Mar College, TX
Dodge City Community College, KS
Dona Ana Branch Community College of New Mexico State University, NM
East Los Angeles College, CA
Eastern New Mexico University: Roswell Campus, NM
El Camino College, CA
El Camino College: Compton Center, CA
Evergreen Valley College, CA
Fresno City College, CA
Fullerton College, CA
Hartnell College, CA
Heald College
    Fresno, CA
    Salinas, CA
    San Jose, CA
    Stockton, CA
Hudson County Community College, NJ
Humacao Community College, PR
Laredo Community College, TX
Long Beach City College, CA
Los Angeles City College, CA
Los Angeles Harbor College, CA
Los Angeles Mission College, CA
Los Angeles Trade and Technical College, CA
Los Angeles Valley College, CA
MacCormac College, IL
Miami Dade College, FL
Morton College, IL
Mount San Antonio College, CA
Mountain View College, TX
New Mexico Junior College, NM
Northern New Mexico College, NM
Odessa College, TX
Otero Junior College, CO
Oxnard College, CA
Palo Alto College, TX
Palo Verde College, CA
Pasadena City College, CA
Passaic County Community College, NJ
Phoenix College, AZ
Pima Community College, AZ
Porterville College, CA
Pueblo Community College, CO
Reedley College, CA
Rio Hondo College, CA
Riverside Community College, CA
St. Philip's College, TX
San Antonio College, TX
San Bernardino Valley College, CA
San Jose City College, CA
Santa Ana College, CA
Santa Fe Community College, NM
South Mountain Community College, AZ
South Plains College, TX
Southwestern College, CA
Texas Southmost College, TX
Texas State Technical College
    Harlingen, TX
Trinidad State Junior College, CO
Ventura College, CA
Victoria College, TX
West Hills College: Coalinga, CA

College addresses

Abilene Christian University
www.acu.edu
Center for International & Intercultural
Education
ACU Box 29000
Abilene, TX 79699
Fax: (325) 674-2966
E-mail: kehlk@acu.edu
Phone: (325) 674-2710

Abraham Baldwin Agricultural College
www.abac.edu
ABAC 4, 2802 Moore Highway
Tifton, GA 31793-2601
Fax: (229) 386-7481
Phone: (229) 391-5001

Academy College
www.academycollege.edu
Admissions
1101 East 78th Street
Bloomington, MN 55420
Fax: (952) 851-0094
E-mail: admissions@academycollege.edu
Phone: (952) 851-0066

Academy of Art University
www.academyart.edu
International Admissions Office
79 New Montgomery Street
San Francisco, CA 94105-3410
Fax: (415) 618-6278
E-mail: intladmissions@academyart.edu
Phone: (415) 274-2208

Adams State College
www.adams.edu
Academic Advising & Tutoring Services
Coordinator
208 Edgemont Boulevard
Alamosa, CO 81102
Fax: (719) 587-7522
E-mail: diegotrujillo@adams.edu
Phone: (719) 587-8189

Adelphi University
www.adelphi.edu
Office of International Admissions
One South Avenue, Levermore 110
PO Box 701
Garden City, NY 11530-0701
Fax: (516) 877-3039
E-mail: intladmissions@adelphi.edu
Phone: (516) 877-3020

Adirondack Community College
www.sunyacc.edu
Enrollment Management
640 Bay Road
Queensbury, NY 12804
Fax: (518) 743-2317
E-mail: linehans@sunyacc.edu
Phone: (518) 743-2264

Adrian College
www.adrian.edu
Admissions
110 South Madison Street
Adrian, MI 49221-2575
Fax: (517) 264-3878
E-mail: admissions@adrian.edu
Phone: (517) 265-5161 ext. 4326

Agnes Scott College
www.agnesscott.edu
Office of Admission
Office of Admissions
141 East College Avenue
Decatur, GA 30030-3797
Fax: (404) 471-6285
E-mail: admission@agnesscott.edu
Phone: (800) 868-8602

AIB College of Business
www.aib.edu
Admissions
2500 Fleur Drive
Des Moines, IA 50321-1799
Fax: (515) 246-5358
E-mail: haubert@aib.edu
Phone: (515) 244-4221

Aiken Technical College
www.atc.edu
Director of Admissions and Records
PO Drawer 696
Aiken, SC 29802
Fax: (803) 593-6526
E-mail: buttsd@atc.edu
Phone: (803) 593-9231

Aims Community College
www.aims.edu
Admissions and Records
5401 West 20th Street
PO Box 69
Greeley, CO 80632
E-mail: admissions.records@aims.edu
Phone: (970) 330-8008 ext. 443

**Alabama Agricultural and Mechanical
University**
www.aamu.edu
Admissions Office
Box 908
Normal, AL 35762
Fax: (256) 851-9747
E-mail: Juan.Alexander@aamu.edu
Phone: (256) 851-5245

Alabama State University
www.alasu.edu
Minority/International Student Affairs
PO Box 271
Montgomery, AL 36101-0271
Fax: (334) 229-4984
E-mail: dcrump@alasu.edu
Phone: (334) 229-6588

Alaska Pacific University
www.alaskapacific.edu
Admissions
4101 University Drive
Anchorage, AK 99508
Fax: (907) 564-8317
E-mail: kat@alaskapacific.edu
Phone: (907) 562-4276

Albany College of Pharmacy
www.acp.edu
Admissions
106 New Scotland Avenue
Albany, NY 12208-3492
Fax: (518) 694-7322
E-mail: admissions@acp.edu
Phone: (518) 694-7221

Albany State University
www.asurams.edu
Office of Recruitment and Admissions
504 College Drive
Albany, GA 31705-2796
Fax: (229) 430-3936
E-mail: fred.suttles@asurams.edu
Phone: (229) 430-7862

Albany Technical College
www.albanytech.edu
Admissions Office
1704 South Slappy Boulevard
Albany, GA 31701-3514
Fax: (229) 430-6180
Phone: (229) 430-3520

Albertus Magnus College
www.albertus.edu
Office of Admission
700 Prospect Street
New Haven, CT 06511-1189
Fax: (203) 773-5248
E-mail: admissions@albertus.edu
Phone: (203) 773-8501

Albion College
www.albion.edu
Associate Vice President for Enrollment
611 East Porter Street
Albion, MI 49224-1831
Fax: (517) 629-0569
E-mail: dkellar@albion.edu
Phone: (517) 629-0321

Albright College
www.albright.edu
Admission Office
13th & Bern Streets
PO Box 15234
Reading, PA 19612-5234
Fax: (610) 921-7294
E-mail: admission@alb.edu
Phone: (610) 921-7512

Alcorn State University
www.alcorn.edu
Admissions
1000 ASU Drive #300
Alcorn State, MS 39096-7500
Fax: (601) 877-6347
E-mail: ebarnes@alcorn.edu
Phone: (601) 877-6146

Alderson-Broaddus College
www.ab.edu
Admissions
101 College Hill Drive
Box 2003
Philippi, WV 26416
Fax: (304) 457-6239
E-mail: dionnemi@mail.ab.edu
Phone: (304) 457-6326

Alexandria Technical College
www.alextech.edu
Admissions
1601 Jefferson Street
Alexandria, MN 56308-3799
Fax: (320) 762-4603
E-mail: international@alextech.edu
Phone: (320) 762-4588

Alfred University
www.alfred.edu
Admissions
Alumni Hall
One Saxon Drive
Alfred, NY 14802-1205
Fax: (607) 871-2198
E-mail: mishalaniee@alfred.edu
Phone: (607) 871-2115

Alice Lloyd College
www.alc.edu
Admissions
100 Purpose Road
Pippa Passes, KY 41844
Fax: (606) 368-6215
E-mail: admissions@alc.edu
Phone: (606) 368-6036

Allan Hancock College
www.hancockcollege.edu
Admissions and Records
800 South College Drive
Santa Maria, CA 93454-6399
Fax: (805) 922-3477
E-mail:
aesquivel-swinson@hancockcollege.edu
Phone: (805) 922-6966 ext. 3248

Allegany College of Maryland
www.allegany.edu
Admissions Office
12401 Willowbrook Road, SE
Cumberland, MD 21502
Fax: (301) 784-5027
E-mail: ckauffman@allegany.edu
Phone: (301) 784-5199

Allegheny College
www.allegheny.edu
Admissions
520 North Main Street
Meadville, PA 16335
Fax: (814) 337-0431
E-mail: admissions@allegheny.edu
Phone: (814) 332-4351

Allegheny Wesleyan College
www.awc.edu
2161 Woodside Road
Salem, OH 44460-9598
Fax: (330) 337-6255
E-mail: college@awc.edu
Phone: (330) 337-6403

Allen County Community College
www.allencc.edu
Foreign Student Adviser
1801 North Cottonwood
Iola, KS 66749
Fax: (785) 654-2336
E-mail: supple@allencc.edu
Phone: (785) 654-2416

Allen University
www.allenuniversity.edu
Admissions
1530 Harden Street
Columbia, SC 29204
Fax: (803) 376-5793
E-mail: dfoster@allenuniversity.edu
Phone: (803) 765-6023

Alliant International University
www.alliant.edu
Office of Admissions
10455 Pomerado Road
San Diego, CA 92131-1799
Fax: (858) 635-4739
E-mail: admissions3@alliant.edu
Phone: (858) 635-4772

Alma College
www.alma.edu
Admissions
614 West Superior Street
Alma, MI 48801-1599
Fax: (989) 463-7057
E-mail: admissions@alma.edu
Phone: (989) 463-7139

Alvernia College
www.alvernia.edu
Admissions
400 St. Bernardine Street
Reading, PA 19607-1799
Fax: (610) 796-8336
E-mail: stephanie.garcia@alvernia.edu
Phone: (610) 568-1473

Alverno College
www.alverno.edu
International and Intercultural Center
3400 South 43rd Street
PO Box 343922
Milwaukee, WI 53234-3922
Fax: (414) 382-6354
E-mail: maryellen.spicuzza@alverno.edu
Phone: (414) 382-6099

American Academy of Dramatic Arts
www.aada.org
120 Madison Avenue
New York, NY 10016
Fax: (212) 686-1284
E-mail: admissions-ny@aada.org
Phone: (212) 686-0620

American Academy of Dramatic Arts: West
www.aada.org
1336 N. La Brea Avenue
Los Angeles, CA 90028
Fax: (323) 464-1250
E-mail: djustin@ca.aada.org
Phone: (323) 464-2777 ext. 103

American Baptist College of ABT Seminary
www.abcnash.edu
1800 Baptist World Center Drive
Nashville, TN 37207
Fax: (615) 226-7855
E-mail: mlockhart@abcnash.edu
Phone: (615) 256-1463

American InterContinental University
www.aiubuckhead.com
Admission
3330 Peachtree Road, NE
Buckhead Campus
Atlanta, GA 30326-1016
Fax: (404) 955-5701
E-mail: info@aiuniv.edu
Phone: (404) 965-5700 ext. 5953

American International College
www.aic.edu
Admissions
1000 State Street
Springfield, MA 01109
Fax: (413) 205-3051
E-mail: pauline.mortenson@aic.edu
Phone: (800) 242-3142

American Jewish University
www.ajula.edu
Office of Admissions
15600 Mulholland Drive
Los Angeles, CA 90077
Fax: (310) 471-3657
E-mail: admissions@ajula.edu
Phone: (310) 476-9777 ext. 247

American River College
www.arc.losrios.edu
Enrollment Services
4700 College Oak Drive
Sacramento, CA 95841
Fax: (916) 484-8864
Phone: (916) 484-8172

American Sentinel University
www.americansentinel.edu
2101 Magnolia Avenue, Suite 200
Birmingham, AL 35205-2827
Fax: (205) 328-2229
E-mail: admiss@americansentinel.edu
Phone: (205) 323-6191

American University
www.american.edu
Office of Admissions
4400 Massachusetts Avenue NW
Washington, DC 20016-8001
Fax: (202) 885-1025
E-mail: admissions@american.edu
Phone: (202) 885-6000

American University of Puerto Rico
www.aupr.edu
Box 2037
Bayamon, PR 00960-2037
Fax: (787) 785-7377
E-mail: oficinaadmisiones@aupr.edu
Phone: (787) 620-2040

Amherst College
www.amherst.edu
Admission Office
PO Box 5000
Amherst, MA 01002-5000
Fax: (413) 542-2040
E-mail: admission@amherst.edu
Phone: (413) 542-2328

Ancilla College
www.ancilla.edu
Admissions
9001 Union Road
PO Box 1
Donaldson, IN 46513
Fax: (574) 935-1773
E-mail: tara.minix@ancilla.edu
Phone: (574) 936-8898 ext. 375

Anderson University
www.andersonuniversity.edu
Admissions
316 Boulevard
Anderson, SC 29621-4002
Fax: (864) 231-2033
E-mail: pbryant@andersonuniversity.edu
Phone: (800) 542-3594

Andover College
www.andovercollege.edu
Admissions
901 Washington Avenue
Portland, ME 04103
Fax: (207) 774-1715
E-mail: enroll@andovercollege.edu
Phone: (207) 774-6126 ext. 8701

Andrew College
www.andrewcollege.edu
Office of Admission
413 College Street
Cuthbert, GA 39840-1395
Fax: (229) 732-2176
E-mail: admissions@andrewcollege.edu
Phone: (229) 732-2171

Andrew Jackson University
www.aju.edu
Office of Admissions
2919 John Hawkins Parkway
Birmingham, AL 35244
Fax: (205) 871-9288
E-mail: admissions@aju.edu
Phone: (205) 871-9288 ext. 107

Andrews University
www.andrews.edu
100 US Highway 31
Berrien Springs, MI 49104
Fax: (269) 471-3228
E-mail: enroll@andrews.edu
Phone: (800) 253-2874

Angelo State University
www.angelo.edu
Admissions and Retention
ASU Station #11014
San Angelo, TX 76909-1014
Fax: (325) 942-2078
E-mail: meghan.pace@angelo.edu
Phone: (325) 942-2041

Angley College
www.angley.edu
International Student Office
230 North Woodland Boulevard, Suite 310
Deland, FL 32720-4289
Fax: (386) 740-2077
E-mail: shensley@angley.edu
Phone: (386) 740-1215 ext. 160

Anna Maria College
www.annamaria.edu
Admissions
50 Sunset Lane, Box O
Paxton, MA 01612-1198
Fax: (508) 849-3362
E-mail: admission@annamaria.edu
Phone: (508) 849-3360

Anne Arundel Community College
www.aacc.edu
Admissions and Enrollment Development
101 College Parkway
Arnold, MD 21012-1895
Fax: (410) 777-4246
E-mail: 4info@aacc.edu
Phone: (410) 777-2246

Anoka Technical College
www.anokatech.edu
1355 West Highway 10
Anoka, MN 55303
Fax: (763) 576-4756
E-mail: admissions@anokatech.edu
Phone: (763) 576-4850

Antelope Valley College
www.avc.edu
Admissions and Records
3041 West Avenue K
Lancaster, CA 93536-5426
Fax: (661) 722-6531
E-mail: hahlgreen@avc.edu
Phone: (661) 722-6332

Antioch University Los Angeles
www.antiochla.edu
Admissions Office
400 Corporate Pointe
Culver City, CA 90230-7615
Fax: (310) 822-4824
E-mail: admissions@antiochla.edu
Phone: (800) 726-8462

Antioch University Santa Barbara
www.antiochsb.edu
Director of International Programs
801 Garden Street, Suite 101
Santa Barbara, CA 93101-1581
Fax: (805) 962-4786
E-mail: emulnix@antiochsb.edu
Phone: (805) 962-8179 ext. 335

Antonelli College: Hattiesburg
www.antonellicollege.edu
1500 North 31st Avenue
Hattiesburg, MS 39401
Fax: (601) 583-0839
E-mail: karen.gautreau@antonellicollege.edu
Phone: (601) 583-4100

Antonelli College: Jackson
www.antonellicollege.edu
2323 Lakeland Drive
Jackson, MS 39232
Phone: (601) 362-9991

Antonelli Institute of Art and Photography
www.antonelli.edu
300 Montgomery Avenue
Erdenheim, PA 19038-8242
Fax: (215) 836-2794
E-mail: admissions@antonelli.edu
Phone: (215) 836-2222

Appalachian Bible College
www.abc.edu
Admissions
PO Box ABC
Bradley, WV 25818-1353
Fax: (304) 877-5082
E-mail: admissions@abc.edu
Phone: (304) 877-6428

Appalachian State University
www.appstate.edu
Admissions
ASU Box 32004
Boone, NC 28608
Fax: (828) 262-4037
E-mail: nealal@appstate.edu
Phone: (828) 262-2120

Aquinas College
www.aquinas.edu
Dean of Admissions
1607 Robinson Road Southeast
Grand Rapids, MI 49506-1799
Fax: (616) 732-4435
E-mail: meehapau@aquinas.edu
Phone: (616) 632-2852

Aquinas College
www.aquinas-tn.edu
Admissions
4210 Harding Road
Nashville, TN 37205-2086
Fax: (615) 279-3893
E-mail: lejeuned@aquinas-tn.edu
Phone: (615) 297-7545 ext. 428

Arapahoe Community College
www.arapahoe.edu
Advising
PO Box 9002
5900 South Santa Fe Drive
Littleton, CO 80160-9002
Fax: (303) 797-5970
E-mail: janet.ludwig@arapahoe.edu
Phone: (303) 797-5652

Arcadia University
www.arcadia.edu
Enrollment Management
450 South Easton Road
Glenside, PA 19038-3295
Fax: (215) 572-4049
E-mail: international@arcadia.edu
Phone: (215) 572-2910

Arizona Automotive Institute
www.aai.edu
6829 North 46th Avenue
Glendale, AZ 85301
Fax: (623) 930-4948
E-mail: info@azautoinst.com
Phone: (623) 934-7273

Arizona State University
www.asu.edu
Assistant Director of International
Undergraduate Admissions
Box 870112
Tempe, AZ 85287-0112
Fax: (480) 965-3610
E-mail: ugradinq@asu.edu
Phone: (480) 965-2688

Arizona State University West
www.west.asu.edu
International Admission
PO Box 37100 MC 0250
Phoenix, AZ 85069-7100
Fax: (480) 965-3610
E-mail: west-info@asu.edu
Phone: (480) 965-7788

Arizona Western College
www.azwestern.edu
International Students Office
PO Box 929
Yuma, AZ 85366-0929
Fax: (928) 344-7710
E-mail: ken.kuntzelman@azwestern.edu
Phone: (928) 344-7699

Arkansas State University
www.astate.edu
International Programs
PO Box 1630
State University, AR 72467-1630
Fax: (870) 972-3288
E-mail: smarlay@astate.edu
Phone: (870) 972-2329

Arkansas State University: Mountain Home
www.asumh.edu
Assistant Vice Chancellor for Enrollment
1600 South College Street
Attention: Admissions
Mountain Home, AR 72653
Fax: (870) 508-6287
E-mail: rblagg@asumh.edu
Phone: (870) 508-6104

Arkansas State University: Newport
www.asun.edu
Registrar
7648 Victory Boulevard
Newport, AR 72112
Fax: (870) 512-7825
E-mail: tbyrd@asun.edu
Phone: (870) 512-7804

Arkansas Tech University
www.atu.edu
International and Multicultural Student
Services - Tomlinson
Doc Bryan Student Services Building #141
Russellville, AR 72801-2222
Fax: (479) 880-2039
E-mail: apennington@atu.edu
Phone: (479) 964-0832

Arlington Baptist College
www.abconline.edu
Academic Dean
3001 West Division
Arlington, TX 76012
Fax: (817) 274-1138
E-mail: hsullivan@abconline.org
Phone: (817) 461-8741 ext. 103

Armstrong Atlantic State University
www.armstrong.edu
Admissions Office
11935 Abercorn Street
Savannah, GA 31419-1997
Fax: (912) 921-5462
E-mail: adm-info@mail.armstrong.edu
Phone: (912) 921-5421

Art Academy of Cincinnati
www.artacademy.edu
Admissions
1212 Jackson Street
Cincinnati, OH 45202
Fax: (513) 562-8778
E-mail: admissions@artacademy.edu
Phone: (513) 562-8740

Art Center Design College
www.theartcenter.edu
Admissions Office
2525 North Country Club Road
Tucson, AZ 85716
Fax: (520) 325-5535
E-mail: inquiries@theartcenter.edu
Phone: (520) 325-0123

Art Center Design College
www.theartcenter.edu
5000 Marble Avenue NE
Albuquerque, NM 87119
Fax: (505) 254-4754
E-mail: inquire@theartcenter.edu
Phone: (505) 254-7575

Art Institute of Atlanta
www.aia.artinstitutes.edu
Admissions
6600 Peachtree Dunwoody Road
100 Embassy Row
Atlanta, GA 30328
Fax: (770) 394-0008
E-mail: aiaadm@aii.edu
Phone: (770) 394-8300

Art Institute of California: Los Angeles
www.artinstitutes.edu/losangeles
Admissions
2900 31st Street
Santa Monica, CA 90405-3035
Fax: (310) 752-4708
E-mail: wilkinso@aii.edu
Phone: (310) 752-4700

Art Institute of California: Orange County
www.artinstitutes.edu/orangecounty
Director of Admissions
3601 West Sunflower Avenue
Santa Ana, CA 92704-9888
Fax: (714) 556-1923
E-mail: aicaocadm@aii.edu
Phone: (714) 830-0200

Art Institute of California: San Diego
www.artinstitutes.edu/sandiego
7650 Mission Valley Road
San Diego, CA 92108-4423
E-mail: gdionisio@aii.edu
Phone: (858) 598-1217

Art Institute of California: San Francisco
www.artinstitutes.edu/sanfrancisco
Admissions
1170 Market Street
San Francisco, CA 94102
Fax: (415) 863-6344
E-mail: sfranklin@aii.edu
Phone: (888) 495-3261

Art Institute of Charlotte
www.artinstitutes.edu/charlotte
Admissions
Three LakePointe Plaza
2110 Water Ridge Parkway
Charlotte, NC 28217-4536
Fax: (704) 357-1133
E-mail: aichadmin@aii.edu
Phone: (704) 357-8020 ext. 5872

Art Institute of Cincinnati
www.theartinstituteofcincinnati.com
Admissions/Marketing
1171 East Kemper Road
Cincinnati, OH 45246
Fax: (513) 751-1209
E-mail: aic@theartinstituteofcincinnati.com
Phone: (513) 751-1206

Art Institute of Colorado
www.aic.artinstitutes.edu
International Admissions
1200 Lincoln Street
Denver, CO 80203
Fax: (303) 860-8520
E-mail: broerem@aii.edu
Phone: (303) 837-0825

Art Institute of Dallas
www.aid.edu
Two North Park, 8080 Park Lane
Suite 100
Dallas, TX 75231
E-mail: cwilliams@aii.edu
Phone: (214) 692-8080

Art Institute of Fort Lauderdale
www.aifl.edu
Admissions
1799 Southeast 17th Street
Fort Lauderdale, FL 33316
Fax: (954) 728-8637
E-mail: birgerc@aii.edu
Phone: (800) 275-7603 ext. 2122

Art Institute of Houston
www.artinstitutes.edu/houston
1900 Yorktown
Houston, TX 77056-4115
Fax: (713) 966-2797
E-mail: aihadm@aii.edu
Phone: (713) 623-2040

Art Institute of Las Vegas
www.ailv.artinstitutes.edu
2350 Corporate Circle
Henderson, NV 89074-7737
Phone: (702) 369-9944

Art Institute of New York City
www.ainyc.artinstitutes.edu
Admissions
75 Varick Street, 16th Floor
New York, NY 10013-1917
Fax: (212) 625-6055
E-mail: ajarmillo@edmc.edu
Phone: (212) 226-5500 ext. 6749

Art Institute of Ohio: Cincinnati
www.artinstitutes.edu/cincinnati/
8845 Governor's Hill Drive, Suite 100
Cincinnati, OH 45249-3317
E-mail: dichardson@aii.edu

Art Institute of Philadelphia
www.artinstitutes.edu/Philadelphia
Admissions
1622 Chestnut Street
Philadelphia, PA 19103-5198
Fax: (215) 405-6399
E-mail: panua@aii.edu
Phone: (215) 405-6363

Art Institute of Phoenix
www.artinstitutes.edu/phoenix
International Admissions
2233 West Dunlap Avenue
Phoenix, AZ 85021-2859
Fax: (602) 331-5301
E-mail: mdomblisky@aii.edu
Phone: (602) 331-7500

Art Institute of Pittsburgh
www.artinstitutes.edu/pittsburgh
Assistant Director of Admissions
420 Boulevard of the Allies
Pittsburgh, PA 15219-1328
Fax: (412) 263-6667
E-mail: aipadm@aii.edu
Phone: (412) 263-6600

Art Institute of Portland
www.aipd.artinstitutes.edu
Admissions
1122 Northwest Davis Street
Portland, OR 97209-2911
Fax: (503) 227-1945
E-mail: bkline@aii.edu
Phone: (503) 228-6528

Art Institute of Seattle
www.ais.edu
Admissions
2323 Elliott Avenue
Seattle, WA 98121-1622
Fax: (206) 269-0275
E-mail: bcicero@aii.edu
Phone: (206) 448-6600

Art Institute of Washington
www.aiw.artinstitutes.edu
Office of Admissions
1820 North Fort Myer Drive
Arlington, VA 22209-1802
Fax: (703) 358-9759
E-mail: aiwadm@aii.edu
Phone: (703) 358-9550

Art Institute Online
www.aionline.edu
1400 Penn Avenue
Pittsburgh, PA 15222
Fax: (412) 995-4320
E-mail: aioadm@aii.edu
Phone: (877) 872-8869

Art Institutes International Minnesota
www.artinstitutes.edu/minneapolis
Dean of Student Affairs
15 South Ninth Street
Minneapolis, MN 55402
Fax: (612) 332-3934
E-mail: pboersig@aii.edu
Phone: (612) 332-3361 ext. 6865

ASA Institute of Business and Computer Technology
www.asa.edu
International Student Services
151 Lawrence Street
Brooklyn, NY 11201
Fax: (212) 672-0362
E-mail: kfahey@asa.edu
Phone: (212) 672-6475

Asheville-Buncombe Technical Community College
www.abtech.edu
Admissions
340 Victoria Road
Asheville, NC 28801-4897
Fax: (828) 251-6718
E-mail: dharmon@abtech.edu
Phone: (828) 254-1921 ext. 146

Ashford University
www.ashford.edu
400 North Bluff Boulevard
Box 2967
Clinton, IA 52733-2967
Fax: (563) 243-6102
E-mail: admissns@ashford.edu
Phone: (563) 242-4153

Ashland Community and Technical College
www.ashland.kctcs.edu
Student Affairs/Admissions
1400 College Drive
Ashland, KY 41101-3683
Fax: (606) 326-2912
E-mail: willie.mccullough@kctcs.net
Phone: (606) 326-2193

Ashland University
www.ashland.edu
International Student Services
401 College Avenue
Ashland, OH 44805-9981
Fax: (419) 289-5629
E-mail: srosa@ashland.edu
Phone: (419) 289-5068

Ashworth University
www.ashworthuniversity.edu
430 Technology Parkway
Norcross, GA 30092-3406
Fax: (770) 729-9389
E-mail: info@ashworthcollege.com
Phone: (770) 729-8400

Aspen University
www.aspen.edu
501 South Cherry Street, Suite 350
Denver, CO 80246
E-mail: admissions@aspen.edu
Phone: (303) 333-4224

Assumption College
www.assumption.edu
Office of Student Affairs
500 Salisbury Street
Worcester, MA 01609-1296
Fax: (508) 799-4412
E-mail: rravanel@assumption.edu
Phone: (508) 767-7325

Athens State University
www.athens.edu
300 North Beaty Street
Athens, AL 35611
Fax: (256) 233-8128
E-mail: athstate@athens.edu
Phone: (256) 233-8171

Atlanta Metropolitan College
www.atlm.edu
Admissions
1630 Metropolitan Parkway, SW
Atlanta, GA 30310-4498
Fax: (404) 756-4407
E-mail: areid@atlm.edu
Phone: (404) 756-4004

Atlanta Technical College
www.atlantatech.org
Student Affairs
1560 Metropolitan Parkway, SW
Atlanta, GA 30310-4446
Fax: (404) 225-4451
E-mail: sbryant@atlantatech.edu
Phone: (404) 225- ext. 4474

Atlantic Cape Community College
www.atlantic.edu
Admissions
5100 Black Horse Pike
Mays Landing, NJ 08330
Fax: (609) 343-4921
E-mail: rskinner@atlantic.edu
Phone: (609) 343-4916

Atlantic College
www.atlanticcollege-pr.com
Admissions Office
PO Box 3918
Guaynabo, PR 00970
Fax: (787) 720-1092
E-mail: atlancol@coqui.net
Phone: (787) 720-1022 ext. 1104

Atlantic Union College
www.auc.edu
Student Accounts Office
Main Street
Box 1000
South Lancaster, MA 01561
Fax: (978) 368-2567
E-mail: rosita.lashley@auc.edu
Phone: (978) 368-2275

Auburn University
www.auburn.edu
Office of International Student Life &
Admissions
Quad Center
Auburn, AL 36849-5111
Fax: (334) 844-6754
E-mail: orgenny@auburn.edu
Phone: (334) 844-2401

Auburn University at Montgomery
www.aum.edu
Enrollment Services
7400 East Drive, Room 139 Taylor Center
Box 244023
Montgomery, AL 36124-4023
Fax: (334) 244-3795
E-mail: rblaesin@aum.edu
Phone: (334) 244-3758

Augsburg College
www.augsburg.edu
2211 Riverside Avenue
Minneapolis, MN 55454
Fax: (612) 330-1590
E-mail: admissions@augsburg.edu
Phone: (612) 330-1001

Augusta State University
www.aug.edu
Admissions
2500 Walton Way
Augusta, GA 30904-2200
Fax: (706) 667-4355
E-mail: cgiardin@aug.edu
Phone: (706) 737-1632

Augusta Technical College
www.augustatech.edu
Admissions
3200 Augusta Tech Drive
Augusta, GA 30906
Fax: (706) 771-4034
E-mail: broberts@augustatech.edu
Phone: (706) 771-4150

Augustana College
www.augustana.edu
Admissions
639 38th Street
Rock Island, IL 61201-2296
Fax: (309) 794-7422
E-mail: aaodc@augustana.edu
Phone: (309) 794-7314

Augustana College
www.augie.edu
Office of Admission
2001 South Summit Avenue
Sioux Falls, SD 57197-9990
Fax: (605) 274-5518
E-mail: donn.grinager@augie.edu
Phone: (605) 274-5516

Aultman College of Nursing and Health Sciences
www.aultmancollege.org
2600 Sixth St. SW
Canton, OH 44710
E-mail: mspeedy@aultman.com
Phone: (330) 363-5075

Aurora University
www.aurora.edu
Office of Admission
347 South Gladstone Avenue
Aurora, IL 60506-4892
Fax: (630) 844-5535
E-mail: admission@aurora.edu
Phone: (630) 844-5533

Austin College
www.austincollege.edu
Office of Admission
900 North Grand Avenue, Suite 6N
Sherman, TX 75090-4400
Fax: (903) 813-3198
E-mail: admission@austincollege.edu
Phone: (903) 813-3000

Austin Community College
www.austincc.edu
International Student Office
5930 Middle Fiskville Road
Austin, TX 78752-4390
Fax: (512) 223-6239
E-mail: intadm@austincc.edu
Phone: (512) 223-6241

Austin Peay State University
www.apsu.edu
Office of International Education
PO Box 4548
Clarksville, TN 37044
Fax: (931) 221-6168
E-mail: admissions@apsu.edu
Phone: (931) 221-7661

Ave Maria University
www.avemaria.edu
Admissions
5050 Ave Maria Boulevard
Ave Maria, FL 34142-9505
Fax: (239) 280-2559
E-mail: Alexander.Frain@avemaria.edu
Phone: (239) 280-2554

Averett University
www.averett.edu
Admissions
420 West Main Street
Danville, VA 24541
Fax: (434) 797-2784
E-mail: stephanie.mullins@averett.edu
Phone: (434) 791-5666

Aviation Institute of Maintenance: Virginia Beach
www.aviationmaintenance.edu
2211 South Military Highway
Chesapeake, VA 23320
Phone: (757) 363-2121

Avila University
www.avila.edu
International Language & Cultural Program
11901 Wornall Road
Kansas City, MO 64145-1007
Fax: (816) 501-2461
E-mail: bruce.inwards@avila.edu
Phone: (816) 501-3772

Azusa Pacific University
www.apu.edu
International Admissions
901 East Alosta Avenue
Box 7000
Azusa, CA 91702-7000
Fax: (626) 815-3801
E-mail: mgrams@apu.edu
Phone: (626) 815-6000 ext. 3055

Babson College
www.babson.edu
Undergraduate Admission Office
231 Forest Street
Babson Park, MA 02457-0310
Fax: (781) 239-4006
E-mail: afowkes@babson.edu
Phone: (781) 239-5522

Bacone College
www.bacone.edu
Admissions
2299 Old Bacone Road
Muskogee, OK 74403
Fax: (918) 781-7416
E-mail: admissions@bacone.edu
Phone: (918) 683-4581 ext. 7342

Baker College of Allen Park
www.baker.edu
Admissions
4500 Enterprise Drive
Allen Park, MI 48101
Phone: (313) 425-3700

Baker College of Auburn Hills
www.baker.edu
Academic Office
1500 University Drive
Auburn Hills, MI 48326
Fax: (248) 340-0608
Phone: (248) 276-8229

Baker College of Cadillac
www.baker.edu
Admissions
9600 East 13th Street
Cadillac, MI 49601
Fax: (231) 775-8505
E-mail: mike.tisdal@baker.edu
Phone: (231) 876-3100

Baker College of Jackson
www.baker.edu
2800 Springport Road
Jackson, MI 49202
Fax: (517) 789-7331
E-mail: adm-jk@baker.edu
Phone: (517) 788-7800

Baker College of Muskegon
www.baker.edu
Admissions
1903 Marquette Avenue
Muskegon, MI 49442
Fax: (231) 777-5201
E-mail: kathy.jacobson@baker.edu
Phone: (231) 777-5200

Baker College of Owosso
www.baker.edu
Admissions
1020 South Washington Street
Owosso, MI 48867
Fax: (989) 729-3359
E-mail: michael.konopacke@baker.edu
Phone: (989) 729-3350

Baker College of Port Huron
www.baker.edu
Admissions Office
3403 Lapeer Road
Port Huron, MI 48060-2597
Fax: (810) 985-7066
E-mail: daniel.kenny@baker.edu
Phone: (810) 985-7000

Baker University
www.bakeru.edu
Office of Admissions
618 Eighth Street
PO Box 65
Baldwin City, KS 66006-0065
Fax: (785) 594-8372
E-mail: admissions@bakeru.edu
Phone: (800) 873-4282

Bakersfield College
www.bakersfieldcollege.edu
Admissions and Records Office
1801 Panorama Drive
Bakersfield, CA 93305
Fax: (661) 395-4500
E-mail: lallday@bakersfieldcollege.edu
Phone: (661) 395-4332

Baldwin-Wallace College
www.bw.edu
Office of Undergraduate Admission
275 Eastland Road
Berea, OH 44017-2088
Fax: (440) 826-3830
E-mail: admission@bw.edu
Phone: (440) 826-2222

Ball State University
www.bsu.edu
Rinker Center for International Programs
2000 University Avenue
Muncie, IN 47306-1022
Fax: (765) 285-3710
E-mail: mabennett@bsu.edu
Phone: (765) 285-5422

Baltimore City Community College
www.bccc.edu
International Student Services
2901 Liberty Heights Avenue
Baltimore, MD 21215-7893
Fax: (410) 462-8345
E-mail: dedangerfield@bccc.edu
Phone: (410) 462-8311

Baltimore Hebrew University
www.bhu.edu
Admissions
5800 Park Heights Avenue
Baltimore, MD 21215
Fax: (410) 578-6840
E-mail: ekeyser@bhu.edu
Phone: (410) 578-6967

Baltimore International College
www.bic.edu
Admissions
17 Commerce Street
Baltimore, MD 21202-3230
Fax: (410) 752-3730
E-mail: admissions@bic.edu
Phone: (410) 752-4710 ext. 120

Baptist Bible College
www.baptist.edu
628 East Kearney Street
Springfield, MO 65803
Fax: (417) 268-6694
Phone: (417) 268-6013

Baptist Bible College of Pennsylvania
www.bbc.edu
Admissions - Michelle Hammaker
538 Venard Road
Clarks Summit, PA 18411-1297
Fax: (570) 585-9299
E-mail: admissions@bbc.edu
Phone: (570) 585-9385

Baptist College of Florida
www.baptistcollege.edu
Admissions
5400 College Drive
Graceville, FL 32440-3306
Fax: (850) 263-9026
E-mail: admissions@baptistcollege.edu
Phone: (800) 328-2660 ext. 460

Baptist University of the Americas
8019 South Pan Am Expressway
San Antonio, TX 78224
E-mail: mranjel@bua.edu
Phone: (210) 924-4338

Barclay College
www.barclaycollege.edu
Acting Director of Admissions
607 North Kingman
Haviland, KS 67059
Fax: (620) 862-5403
E-mail: admissions@barclaycollege.edu
Phone: (620) 862-5252 ext. 43

Bard College
www.bard.edu
Admissions
30 Campus Road
Box 5000
Annandale-on-Hudson, NY 12504-5000
Fax: (845) 758-5208
E-mail: admission@bard.edu
Phone: (845) 758-7472

Bard College at Simon's Rock
www.simons-rock.edu
Office of Admission
84 Alford Road
Great Barrington, MA 01230-1990
Fax: (413) 528-7334
E-mail: admit@simons-rock.edu
Phone: (413) 528-7355

Barnard College
www.barnard.edu
Admissions
3009 Broadway
New York, NY 10027-6598
Fax: (212) 854-6220
E-mail: admissions@barnard.edu
Phone: (212) 854-2014

Barry University
www.barry.edu
Division of Enrollment Management
11300 Northeast Second Avenue
Miami Shores, FL 33161-6695
Fax: (305) 899-2971
E-mail: ascott@mail.barry.edu
Phone: (305) 899-3100

Barstow Community College
www.barstow.edu
International Student Adviser
2700 Barstow Road
Barstow, CA 92311-9984
Fax: (760) 252-1875
E-mail: admit@barstow.edu
Phone: (760) 252-2411

Barton College
www.barton.edu
International Student Adviser
Box 5000
Wilson, NC 27893-7000
Fax: (252) 399-6572
E-mail: cbcombs@barton.edu
Phone: (252) 399-6321

Barton County Community College
www.bartonccc.edu
Admissions
245 North East 30th Road
Great Bend, KS 67530-9283
Fax: (620) 786-1160
E-mail: MooreT@bartonccc.edu
Phone: (620) 792-9241

Bastyr University
www.bastyr.edu
Admissions
14500 Juanita Drive, NE
Kenmore, WA 98028
Fax: (425) 602-3090
E-mail: tolsen@bastyr.edu
Phone: (425) 602-3101

Bates College
www.bates.edu
Admissions Office
23 Campus Avenue, Lindholm House
Lewiston, ME 04240-9917
Fax: (207) 786-6025
E-mail: wmitchel@bates.edu
Phone: (207) 786-6000

Bates Technical College
www.bates.ctc.edu
1101 South Yakima Avenue
Tacoma, WA 98405
E-mail: btraufler@bates.ctc.edu
Phone: (253) 680-7238

Baton Rouge Community College
www.mybrcc.edu
International Veteran Adviser
5310 Florida Boulevard
Baton Rouge, LA 70806
E-mail: chatmand@mybrcc.edu
Phone: (225) 216-6902

Bauder College
www.bauder.edu
Admissions (International)
384 Northyards Boulevard NW, Ste 190
Atlanta, GA 30313
Fax: (404) 237-1619
E-mail: llanier@bauder.edu
Phone: (404) 237-7573 ext. 1795

Bay de Noc Community College
www.baycollege.edu
Vice President for Student Services
2001 North Lincoln Road
Escanaba, MI 49829-2511
Fax: (906) 786-8515
E-mail: lesinerm@baycollege.edu
Phone: (906) 786-5802 ext. 1182

Bay Path College
www.baypath.edu
Admissions
588 Longmeadow Street
Longmeadow, MA 01106
Fax: (413) 565-1105
E-mail: mhudgik@baypath.edu
Phone: (413) 565-1331

Bay State College
www.baystate.edu
Admissions
122 Commonwealth Avenue
Boston, MA 02116
Fax: (617) 536-1735
E-mail: admissions@baystate.edu
Phone: (617) 236-8011

Bayamon Central University
www.ucb.edu.pr
Admissions
PO Box 1725
Bayamon, PR 00960-1725
Fax: (787) 740-2200
E-mail: chernandez@ucb.edu.pr
Phone: (787) 786-3030 ext. 2100

Baylor University
www.baylor.edu
International Programs
One Bear Place #97056
Waco, TX 76798-7056
Fax: (254) 710-1468
E-mail: alexine_burke@baylor.edu
Phone: (254) 710-1461

Becker College
www.becker.edu
Office of Admissions
61 Sever Street
Worcester, MA 01609
Fax: (508) 890-1500
E-mail: admissions@beckercollege.edu
Phone: (774) 354-0460

Belhaven College
www.belhaven.edu
Institutional Advancement
1500 Peachtree Street
Box 153
Jackson, MS 39202
Fax: (601) 968-8946
E-mail: admission@belhaven.edu
Phone: (800) 960-5940

Bellarmine University
www.bellarmine.edu
Admission
2001 Newburg Road
Louisville, KY 40205
Fax: (502) 452-8002
E-mail: dmahan@bellarmine.edu
Phone: (502) 452-8131

Bellevue Community College
www.bcc.ctc.edu
International Student Programs
3000 Landerholm Circle SE
Bellevue, WA 98007-6484
Fax: (425) 641-0246
E-mail: csamia@bcc.ctc.edu
Phone: (425) 564-2973

Bellevue University
www.bellevue.edu
International Programs
1000 Galvin Road South
Bellevue, NE 68005-3098
Fax: (402) 557-5423
E-mail: curtis.freerking@bellevue.edu
Phone: (402) 557-7283

Bellin College of Nursing
www.bcon.edu
Admissions Office
PO Box 23400
725 South Webster Avenue
Green Bay, WI 54305-3400
Fax: (920) 433-7416
E-mail: carol.rafferty@bcon.edu
Phone: (920) 433-5805

Bellingham Technical College
www.btc.ctc.edu
Admissions Office
3028 Lindbergh Avenue
Bellingham, WA 98225
Fax: (360) 676-2798
E-mail: erunestr@btc.ctc.edu
Phone: (360) 752-8324

Belmont Abbey College
www.belmontabbeycollege.edu
Admissions Office
100 Belmont - Mt. Holly Road
Belmont, NC 28012-2795
Fax: (704) 825-6220
E-mail: rogerljones@bac.edu
Phone: (888) 222-0110

Belmont University
www.belmont.edu
International Education
1900 Belmont Boulevard
Nashville, TN 37212-3757
Fax: (615) 460-5539
E-mail: skinnerk@mail.belmont.edu
Phone: (615) 460-5500

Beloit College
www.beloit.edu
Office of Admissions
700 College Street
Beloit, WI 53511-5595
Fax: (608) 363-2075
E-mail: admiss@beloit.edu
Phone: (608) 363-2500

Bemidji State University
www.bemidjistate.edu
Lamae Ritchie/Director of International
Services
1500 Birchmont Drive NE, D-102
Bemidji, MN 56601
Fax: (218) 755-4096
E-mail: lritchie@bemidjistate.edu
Phone: (218) 755-4096

Benedict College
www.benedict.edu
Student Records
1600 Harden Street
Columbia, SC 29204
Fax: (803) 253-5085
E-mail: scottkinney@benedict.edu
Phone: (803) 705-4680

Benedictine College
www.benedictine.edu
International Programs
1020 North Second Street
Atchison, KS 66002-1499
Fax: (913) 360-7160
E-mail: ssnaiderbaur@benedictine.edu
Phone: (800) 367-5340

Benedictine University
www.ben.edu
Enrollment Center
5700 College Road
Lisle, IL 60532
Fax: (630) 829-6301
E-mail: admissions@ben.edu
Phone: (630) 829-6300

Benjamin Franklin Institute of Technology
www.bfit.edu
41 Berkeley Street
Boston, MA 02116
Fax: (617) 482-3706
E-mail: nkraft@bfit.edu
Phone: (617) 423-4630

Bennett College
www.bennett.edu
Admissions
900 East Washington Street
Greensboro, NC 27401-3239
Fax: (336) 517-2166
E-mail: admiss@bennett.edu
Phone: (336) 370-8624

Bennington College
www.bennington.edu
Office of Admissions
One College Drive
Bennington, VT 05201-6003
Fax: (802) 440-4320
E-mail: admissions@bennington.edu
Phone: (800) 833-6845

Bentley College
www.bentley.edu
Undergraduate Admissions
175 Forest Street
Waltham, MA 02452-4705
Fax: (781) 891-3414
E-mail: ugadmission@bentley.edu
Phone: (781) 891-2244

Berea College
www.berea.edu
Admissions
CPO 2220
Berea, KY 40404
Fax: (859) 985-3512
E-mail: admissions@berea.edu
Phone: (800) 326-5948

Berean Institute
www.bereaninstitute.org
1901 West Girard Avenue
Philadelphia, PA 19130
Fax: (215) 236-6011
Phone: (215) 763-4833

Berkeley City College
www.berkeleycitycollege.edu
2050 Center Street
Berkeley, CA 94704
Fax: (510) 465-3257
E-mail: jng@peralta.edu
Phone: (510) 466-7380

Berkeley College
www.berkeleycollege.edu
International Division
44 Rifle Camp Road
West Paterson, NJ 07424-0440
Fax: (212) 986-7827
E-mail: international@berkeleycollege.edu
Phone: (212) 687-3730

Berkeley College
www.berkeleycollege.edu
International Division
99 Church Street
White Plains, NY 10601
Fax: (212) 986-7827
E-mail: international@berkeleycollege.edu
Phone: (212) 687-3730

Berkeley College of New York City
www.berkeleycollege.edu
Berkeley College, International Division
3 East 43rd Street
New York, NY 10017
Fax: (212) 986-7827
E-mail: international@berkeleycollege.edu
Phone: (212) 687-3730

Berklee College of Music
www.berklee.edu
Office of Admissions
1140 Boylston Street
Boston, MA 02215
Fax: (617) 747-2047
E-mail: admissions@berklee.edu
Phone: (617) 747-2222

Berkshire Community College
www.berkshirecc.edu
Office of Student Affairs and Enrollment
Services
1350 West Street
Pittsfield, MA 01201-5786
Fax: (413) 499-4576
E-mail: mbullock@berkshirecc.edu
Phone: (413) 236-1601

Berry College
www.berry.edu
Admissions
PO Box 490159
2277 Martha Berry Highway NW
Mount Berry, GA 30149-0159
Fax: (706) 290-2178
E-mail: admissions@berry.edu
Phone: (706) 236-2215

Beta Tech: Richmond South
www.betatech.edu
7914 Midlothian Turnpike
Richmond, VA 23608
E-mail: admdirbtr@betatech.edu
Phone: (804) 330-0111

Beta Tech: Richmond West
www.betatech.edu
7001 West Broad Street
Richmond, VA 23294
E-mail: admdirbtw@betatech.edu
Phone: (804) 672-2300

Bethany College
www.bethanylb.edu
Admissions
335 East Swensson
Lindsborg, KS 67456-1897
Fax: (785) 227-8993
E-mail: admissions@bethanylb.edu
Phone: (800) 826-2281

Bethany College
www.bethanywv.edu
Office of Admission
Office of Admission
Bethany, WV 26032-0428
Fax: (304) 829-7142
E-mail: kwilson@bethanywv.edu
Phone: (304) 829-7514

Bethany Lutheran College
www.blc.edu
700 Luther Drive
Mankato, MN 56001-4490
Fax: (507) 344-7376
E-mail: ryanbuch@blc.edu
Phone: (507) 344-7576

Bethany University
www.bethany.edu
Admissions
800 Bethany Drive
Scotts Valley, CA 95066-2898
Fax: (831) 461-1621
E-mail: info@fc.bethany.edu
Phone: (831) 438-3800 ext. 3900

Bethel College
www.bethelcollege.edu
Admissions
1001 West McKinley Avenue
Mishawaka, IN 46545
Fax: (574) 277-3335
E-mail: helmuta@bethelcollege.edu
Phone: (574) 257-3339

Bethel College
www.bethelks.edu
Admissions
300 East 27th Street
North Newton, KS 67117-0531
Fax: (316) 284-5870
E-mail: admissions@bethelks.edu
Phone: (800) 522-1887 ext. 230

Bethel College
www.bethel-college.edu
Office of Admissions
325 Cherry Avenue
McKenzie, TN 38201
Fax: (731) 352-4069
E-mail: admissions@bethel-college.edu
Phone: (731) 352-4030

Bethel University
www.bethel.edu
Office of Admissions
3900 Bethel Drive
Saint Paul, MN 55112-6999
Fax: (651) 635-1490
E-mail: d-yoshitani@bethel.edu
Phone: (800) 255-8706 ext. 6242

Bethesda Christian University
www.bcu.edu
Admissions
730 North Euclid Street
Anaheim, CA 92801
Fax: (714) 517-1948
E-mail: admission@bcu.edu
Phone: (714) 517-1945

Bethune-Cookman University
www.cookman.edu
Admissions
Dr. Mary McLeod Bethune Boulevard
Daytona Beach, FL 32114-3099
Fax: (386) 481-2601
E-mail: admissions@cookman.edu
Phone: (386) 481-2600

Beulah Heights University
www.beulah.org
Admissions
892 Berne Street SE
PO Box 18145
Atlanta, GA 30316
Fax: (404) 627-0702
E-mail: john.dreher@beulah.org
Phone: (404) 627-2681 ext. 117

Big Bend Community College
www.bigbend.edu
Admissions/Registration
7662 Chanute Street
Moses Lake, WA 98837-3299
Fax: (509) 762-6243
E-mail: maryannea@bigbend.edu
Phone: (509) 793-2062

Biola University
www.biola.edu
Admissions
13800 Biola Avenue
La Mirada, CA 90639-0001
Fax: (562) 903-4709
E-mail: carrie.stockton@biola.edu
Phone: (562) 903-4752

Birmingham-Southern College
www.bsc.edu
Office of International Programs
900 Arkadelphia Road
Box 549008
Birmingham, AL 35254
Fax: (205) 226-4805
E-mail: aledvina@bsc.edu
Phone: (205) 226-7722

Bishop State Community College
www.bishop.edu
Student Development Services
351 North Broad Street
Mobile, AL 36603-5898
Fax: (251) 438-5403
E-mail: mvodom@bishop.edu
Phone: (251) 690-6447

Bismarck State College
www.bismarckstate.edu
Admissions
PO Box 5587
Bismarck, ND 58506-5587
Fax: (701) 224-5643
E-mail: karla.gabriel@bsc.nodak.edu
Phone: (701) 224-5426

Black Hawk College
www.bhc.edu
International Office/ESL
6600 34th Avenue
Moline, IL 61265-5899
Fax: (309) 796-5124
E-mail: bollatia@bhc.edu
Phone: (309) 796-5183

Black Hawk College: East Campus
www.bhc.edu
1501 State Highway 78
Kewanee, IL 61443-8630
Fax: (309) 856-6005
E-mail: recruiter@bhc.edu
Phone: (309) 852-5671 ext. 6220

Black Hills State University
www.bhsu.edu
Admissions
University Street Box 9502
Spearfish, SD 57799-9502
Fax: (605) 642-6022
E-mail: admissions@bhsu.edu
Phone: (605) 642-6225

Black River Technical College
www.blackrivertech.org
Admissions
Highway 304 East
PO Box 468
Pocahontas, AR 72455
E-mail: elisec@blackrivertech.org
Phone: (870) 248-4000

Blackburn College
www.blackburn.edu
Admissions Office
700 College Avenue
Carlinville, IL 62626
Fax: (217) 854-3713
E-mail: jmali@blackburn.edu
Phone: (217) 854-3231 ext. 4252

Bladen Community College
www.bladencc.edu
Box 266
Dublin, NC 28332-0266
Fax: (910) 879-5564
E-mail: ywilloughby@bladencc.edu
Phone: (910) 879-5593

Blessing-Rieman College of Nursing
www.brcn.edu
Admissions
PO Box 7005
Quincy, IL 62305-7005
Fax: (217) 228-4661
E-mail: admissions@brcn.edu
Phone: (217) 228-5520 ext. 6949

Blinn College
www.blinn.edu
Student Services
902 College Avenue
Brenham, TX 77833
Fax: (979) 830-4110
E-mail: jharris@blinn.edu
Phone: (979) 830-4140

Bloomfield College
www.bloomfield.edu
Office of Enrollment Management and
Admission
One Park Place
Bloomfield, NJ 07003
Fax: (973) 748-0916
E-mail: admission@bloomfield.edu
Phone: (800) 848-4555 ext. 127

Bloomsburg University of Pennsylvania
www.bloomu.edu
Office of Admissions and Records
104 Student Service Center
400 East Second Street
Bloomsburg, PA 17815
Fax: (570) 389-4741
E-mail: buadmiss@bloomu.edu
Phone: (570) 389-4316

Blue Cliff College: Gulfport
www.bluecliffcollege.com
12251 Bernard Parkway
Gulfport, MS 39503
Fax: (228) 896-8659
Phone: (288) 896-9727

Blue Mountain College
www.bmc.edu
Office of Admissions
PO Box 160
Blue Mountain, MS 38610-0160
Fax: (662) 685-4776
E-mail: admissions@bmc.edu
Phone: (662) 685-4161 ext. 176

Blue Mountain Community College
www.bluecc.edu
Service Center
2411 Northwest Carden Avenue
PO Box 100
Pendleton, OR 97801
Fax: (541) 278-5871
E-mail: getinfo@bluecc.edu
Phone: (541) 278-5759

Bluefield College
www.bluefield.edu
Office of Enrollment Management
3000 College Drive
Bluefield, VA 24605
Fax: (276) 326-4602
E-mail: admissions@bluefield.edu
Phone: (800) 872-0175

Bluefield State College
www.bluefieldstate.edu
Enrollment Management
219 Rock Street
Bluefield, WV 24701
Fax: (304) 325-7747
E-mail: bscadmit@bluefield.wvnet.edu
Phone: (304) 327-4567

Bluegrass Community and Technical College
www.bluegrass.kctcs.edu
Admissions
200 Oswald Building, Cooper Drive
Lexington, KY 40506-0235
Fax: (859) 246-4666
E-mail: michelle.mossey@kctcs.edu
Phone: (859) 246-6296

Bluffton University
www.bluffton.edu
Admissions
1 University Drive
Bluffton, OH 45817-2104
Fax: (419) 358-3081
E-mail: admissions@bluffton.edu
Phone: (419) 358-3257

Boise State University
www.boisestate.edu
Foreign Student Admissions Office
1910 University Drive
Boise, ID 83725
Fax: (208) 426-3765
E-mail: bross@boisestate.edu
Phone: (208) 426-1757

Bolivar Technical College
www.bolivarcollege.org
PO Box 592
Bolivar, MO 65613
Fax: (417) 777-8908
E-mail: info@bolivarcollege.org
Phone: (417) 777-5062

Bossier Parish Community College
www.bpcc.edu
Registrar's Office
6220 East Texas Street
Bossier City, LA 71111-6922
Fax: (318) 678-6390
E-mail: pstewart@bpcc.edu
Phone: (318) 678-6034

Boston Architectural College
www.the-bac.edu
320 Newbury Street
Boston, MA 02115-2795
Fax: (617) 585-0121
E-mail: admissions@the-bac.edu
Phone: (617) 585-0123

Boston College
www.bc.edu
Office of Undergraduate Admissions
140 Commonwealth Avenue, Devlin Hall 208
Chestnut Hill, MA 02467-3809
Fax: (617) 552-0798
Phone: (617) 552-3100

Boston Conservatory
www.bostonconservatory.edu
Admissions
8 The Fenway
Boston, MA 02215
Fax: (617) 536-3176
E-mail: admissions@bostonconservatory.edu
Phone: (617) 912-9115

Boston University
www.bu.edu
Office of International Admissions
121 Bay State Road
Boston, MA 02215
Fax: (617) 353-5334
E-mail: intadmis@bu.edu
Phone: (617) 353-4492

Bowdoin College
www.bowdoin.edu
Admissions Office
5000 College Station
Brunswick, ME 04011-8441
Fax: (207) 725-3101
E-mail: aspring2@bowdoin.edu
Phone: (207) 725-3192

Bowie State University
www.bowiestate.edu
Career Co-Op and International Services
14000 Jericho Park Road
Attn: Admissions Office
Bowie, MD 20715
Fax: (301) 860-3824
E-mail: rbatton@bowiestate.edu
Phone: (301) 860-3830

Bowling Green State University
www.bgsu.edu
Office of International Programs
110 McFall Center
Bowling Green, OH 43403-0085
Fax: (419) 372-2429
E-mail: phofman@bgnet.bgsu.edu
Phone: (419) 372-2247

Bowling Green State University: Firelands College
www.firelands.bgsu.edu
International Programs
One University Drive
Huron, OH 44839
Fax: (419) 372-2429
E-mail: fireadm@bgsu.edu
Phone: (419) 372-2247

Bradford School of Business
www.bradfordschoolhouston.edu
4669 Southwest Freeway
Houston, TX 77027
E-mail: mortiz@bradfordschoolhouston.edu
Phone: (713) 629-1500

Bradford School: Pittsburgh
www.bradfordpittsburgh.edu
125 West Station Square Drive
Pittsburgh, PA 15219
Fax: (412) 471-6714
Phone: (412) 391-6710

Bradley University
www.bradley.edu
Undergraduate Admissions
1501 West Bradley Avenue
Peoria, IL 61625
Fax: (309) 677-2799
E-mail: intlam@bradley.edu
Phone: (309) 677-1000

Brandeis University
www.brandeis.edu
Undergraduate Admissions
Box 549110
Waltham, MA 02454-9110
Fax: (781) 736-3536
E-mail: kwest@brandeis.edu
Phone: (781) 736-3521

Brenau University
www.brenau.edu
Women's College Admission Office
500 Washington Street SE
Gainesville, GA 30501
Fax: (770) 538-4306
E-mail: Wcadmissions@brenau.edu
Phone: (770) 534-6100

Brescia University
www.brescia.edu
717 Frederica Street
Owensboro, KY 42301-3023
Fax: (270) 686-4314
E-mail: admissions@brescia.edu
Phone: (270) 686-4241

Brevard College
www.brevard.edu
Director of Admissions
One Brevard College Drive
Brevard, NC 28712
Fax: (828) 884-3790
E-mail: siglerkm@brevard.edu
Phone: (828) 884-8313

Brevard Community College
www.brevardcc.edu
International Student Services
1519 Clearlake Road
Cocoa, FL 32922-9987
Fax: (321) 433-7357
E-mail: gopakumars@brevardcc.edu
Phone: (321) 433-7342

Brewton-Parker College
www.bpc.edu
Admissions Office
Brewton-Parker College # 2011
201 David-Eliza Fountain Circle
Mount Vernon, GA 30445
Fax: (912) 583-3598
E-mail: kwuerzberger@bpc.edu
Phone: (912) 583-2241 ext. 265

Briar Cliff University
www.briarcliff.edu
Admissions
3303 Rebecca Street
PO Box 2100
Sioux City, IA 51104-0100
Fax: (712) 279-1632
E-mail: admissions@briarcliff.edu
Phone: (712) 279-5200

Briarcliffe College
www.briarcliffe.edu
1055 Stewart Avenue
Bethpage, NY 11714
Fax: (516) 470-6020
E-mail: info@bcl.edu
Phone: (516) 918-3600

Briarwood College
www.briarwood.edu
Admissions
2279 Mount Vernon Road
Southington, CT 06489-1057
Fax: (860) 628-6444
E-mail: brennanv@briarwood.edu
Phone: (860) 628-4751 ext. 214

Bridgewater College
www.bridgewater.edu
Admissions Office
402 East College Street
Bridgewater, VA 22812-1599
Fax: (540) 828-5481
E-mail: admissions@bridgewater.edu
Phone: (540) 828-5375

Bridgewater State College
www.bridgew.edu
Admissions
Gates House
Bridgewater, MA 02325
Fax: (508) 531-1746
E-mail: gmeyer@bridgew.edu
Phone: (508) 531-1237

Brigham Young University
www.byu.edu
International Admissions
A-153 ASB, BYU
Provo, UT 84602
Fax: (801) 422-0973
E-mail: intladm@byu.edu
Phone: (801) 422-2500

Brigham Young University-Hawaii
www.byuh.edu
Admissions
55-220 Kulanui Street, #1973
Laie, HI 96762-1294
Fax: (808) 293-3741
E-mail: sudlowm@byuh.edu
Phone: (808) 293-3535

Brigham Young University-Idaho
www.byui.edu
Admissions and Scholarships
120 Kimball Building
Rexburg, ID 83460-1615
Fax: (208) 496-1185
E-mail: coleck@byui.edu
Phone: (208) 496-1026

Bristol Community College
www.bristolcc.edu
Office of Admissions
777 Elsbree Street
Fall River, MA 02720-7395
Fax: (508) 730-3265
E-mail: Admission@bristolcc.edu
Phone: (508) 678-2811 ext. 2947

Brookdale Community College
www.brookdalecc.edu
Registration
765 Newman Springs Road
Lincroft, NJ 07738
Fax: (732) 224-2271
E-mail: kheuserschuck@brookdalecc.edu
Phone: (732) 224-2375

Brookhaven College
www.brookhavencollege.edu
Multi-Cultural Center
3939 Valley View Lane
Farmers Branch, TX 75244-4997
Fax: (972) 860-4886
E-mail: bhcMulticulturalCenter@dcccd.edu
Phone: (972) 860-4936

Brooks College
www.brookscollege.edu
4825 East Pacific Coast Highway
Long Beach, CA 90804
Fax: (562) 597-6209
Phone: (562) 597-6611 ext. 161

Brooks Institute
www.brooks.edu
801 Alston Road
Santa Barbara, CA 93108
Fax: (805) 565-1386
E-mail: admissions@brooks.edu
Phone: (888) 304-3456

Broome Community College
www.sunybroome.edu
Admissions Office
Box 1017
Binghamton, NY 13902
Fax: (607) 778-5310
E-mail: carra_m@sunybroome.edu
Phone: (607) 778-5001

Broward Community College
www.broward.edu
College Registrar's Office
225 East Las Olas Boulevard
Fort Lauderdale, FL 33301
Fax: (954) 201-7466
E-mail: sgreive@broward.edu
Phone: (954) 201-7468

Brown College
www.browncollege.edu
Admissions
1440 Northland Drive
Mendota Heights, MN 55120
Fax: (651) 905-3540
E-mail: info@browncollege.edu
Phone: (651) 905-3400

Brown Mackie College: Atlanta
6600 Peachtree Dunwoody NE
600 Embassy Row
Atlanta, GA 30328
E-mail: jthee@brownmackie.edu
Phone: (770) 638-0121

Brown Mackie College: Cincinnati
www.brownmackie.edu
Admission
1011 Glendale-Milford Road
Cincinnati, OH 45215
Fax: (513) 771-3413
E-mail: cmcneel@amedcts.com
Phone: (513) 771-2424

Brown Mackie College: Fort Wayne
www.brownmackie.com
3000 Coliseum Boulevard, Suite 100
Fort Wayne, IN 46805
Fax: (260) 484-2678
E-mail: ktaboh@brownmackie.edu
Phone: (260) 484-4400

Brown Mackie College: Miami
www.cbcaec.com
Academic Affairs
1501 Biscayne Boulevard
Miami, FL 33132
Fax: (305) 373-8814
E-mail: jrosenzweig@brownmackie.edu
Phone: (305) 341-6609

Brown Mackie College: North Kentucky
www.brownmackie.edu
309 Buttermilk Pike
Fort Mitchell, KY 41017
Phone: (859) 341-5627

Brown Mackie College: Tucson
www.chap-col.edu
4585 East Speedway Boulevard, Suite 204
Tucson, AZ 85712
Phone: (520) 327-6866

Brown University
www.brown.edu
Admission Office
45 Prospect Street
PO Box 1876
Providence, RI 02912
Fax: (401) 863-9300
E-mail: admission_undergraduate@brown.edu
Phone: (401) 863-2378

Brunswick Community College
www.brunswickcc.edu
Box 30
Supply, NC 28462
Fax: (910) 754-9609
E-mail: olsenj@brunswickcc.edu
Phone: (910) 755-7324

Bryan College
www.bryan.edu
Admissions
PO Box 7000
Dayton, TN 37321-7000
Fax: (423) 775-7199
E-mail: admissions@bryan.edu
Phone: (423) 775-7204

Bryan College: Sacramento
www.bryancollege.com
2317 Gold Meadow Way
Gold River, CA 95670
Fax: (916) 641-8649
E-mail: admissions@bryancollege.com
Phone: (916) 649-2400

Bryant & Stratton College: Albany
www.bryantstratton.edu
Admissions
1259 Central Avenue
Albany, NY 12205
Fax: (518) 437-1049
Phone: (518) 437-1802

Bryant & Stratton College: Buffalo
www.bryantstratton.edu
465 Main Street, Suite 400
Buffalo, NY 14203
Fax: (716) 884-0091
E-mail: mbrobinson@bryantstratton.edu
Phone: (716) 884-9120

Bryant & Stratton College: Henrietta
www.bryantstratton.edu
1225 Jefferson Road
Rochester, NY 14623
Phone: (585) 292-5627

Bryant & Stratton College: Parma
www.bryantstratton.edu
Admissions Department
12955 Snow Road
Parma, OH 44130-1013
Fax: (216) 265-0325
E-mail: flnelly@bryantstratton.edu
Phone: (216) 265-3151 ext. 229

Bryant & Stratton College: Richmond
www.bryantstratton.edu
8141 Hull Street Road
Richmond, VA 23235
Fax: (804) 745-6884
Phone: (804) 745-2444

Bryant & Stratton College: Rochester
www.bryantstratton.edu
1225 Jefferson Road
Rochester, NY 14623
Phone: (585) 292-5627

Bryant & Stratton College: Southtowns
www.bryantstratton.edu
200 Redtail
Orchard Park, NY 14127
Fax: (716) 677-9599
E-mail: prkehr@bryantstratton.edu
Phone: (716) 677-9500

Bryant & Stratton College: Syracuse North
www.bryantstratton.edu
8687 Carling Road
Liverpool, NY 13090
Phone: (315) 652-6500

Bryant & Stratton College: Virginia Beach
www.bryantstratton.edu
Admissions
301 Centre Pointe Drive
Virginia Beach, VA 23462-4417
Fax: (757) 499-9977
E-mail: dmsoutherland@bryantstratton.edu
Phone: (757) 499-7900

Bryant & Stratton College: Willoughby Hills
www.bryantstratton.edu
Admissions
27557 Chardon Road
Willoughby Hills, OH 44092
Fax: (440) 944-9260
E-mail: stkampa@bryantstratton.edu
Phone: (440) 944-6800

Bryant University
www.bryant.edu
Office of Admission
1150 Douglas Pike
Smithfield, RI 02917
Fax: (401) 232-6741
E-mail: admission@bryant.edu
Phone: (401) 232-6107

Bryn Mawr College
www.brynmawr.edu
Office of Admissions
101 North Merion Avenue
Bryn Mawr, PA 19010-2899
Fax: (610) 526-7471
E-mail: admissions@brynmawr.edu
Phone: (610) 526-5152

Bucknell University
www.bucknell.edu
Admissions Office
Freas Hall
Bucknell University
Lewisburg, PA 17837-9988
Fax: (570) 577-3538
E-mail: admissions@bucknell.edu
Phone: (570) 577-1101

Bucks County Community College
www.bucks.edu
Adult and Multicultural Student Services
275 Swamp Road
Office of Admissions
Newtown, PA 18940
Fax: (215) 968-8110
E-mail: barlowm@bucks.edu
Phone: (215) 968-8137

Buena Vista University
www.bvu.edu
International Programs Coordinator
610 West Fourth Street
Storm Lake, IA 50588
Fax: (712) 749-2037
E-mail: admissions@bvu.edu
Phone: (712) 749-2073

Bunker Hill Community College
www.bhcc.mass.edu
International Center
250 New Rutherford Avenue
Boston, MA 02129-2925
Fax: (617) 228-2442
E-mail: international@bhcc.mass.edu
Phone: (617) 228-2460

Burlington College
www.burlington.edu
Admissions
95 North Avenue
Burlington, VT 05401
Fax: (802) 660-4331
E-mail: admissions@burlington.edu
Phone: (802) 862-9616 ext. 104

Burlington County College
www.bcc.edu
Office Student Services
601 Pemberton-Browns Mills Road
Pemberton, NJ 08068-1599
Fax: (609) 726-0401
E-mail: dbusse@bcc.edu
Phone: (609) 894-9311 ext. 1350

Business Informatics Center
www.thecollegeforbusiness.com
Admissions
134 South Central Avenue
Valley Stream, NY 11580-5431
Fax: (516) 561-0074
Phone: (516) 561-0050 ext. 101

Business Institute of Pennsylvania
www.biop.edu
Admissions Officer
335 Boyd Drive
Sharon, PA 16146
Fax: (724) 983-8355
E-mail: info@biop.edu
Phone: (724) 983-0700

Butler County Community College
www.butlercc.edu
Counseling, Advising
901 South Haverhill Road
El Dorado, KS 67042-3280
Fax: (316) 322-6852
E-mail: mdugger@butlercc.edu
Phone: (316) 322-3255

Butler County Community College
www.bc3.edu
Admissions
PO Box 1203
Butler, PA 16003-1203
Fax: (724) 287-3460
E-mail: pattie.bajuszik@bc3.edu
Phone: (724) 287-8711 ext. 8212

Butler University
www.butler.edu
International Admissions
4600 Sunset Avenue
Indianapolis, IN 46208
Fax: (317) 940-8150
E-mail: intadmission@butler.edu
Phone: (888) 940-8100

Butte College
www.butte.edu
3536 Butte Campus Drive
Oroville, CA 95965
Fax: (530) 895-2411
E-mail: admissions@butte.edu
Phone: (530) 895-2361

Cabarrus College of Health Sciences
www.cabarruscollege.edu
401 Medical Park Drive
Concord, NC 28025-2405
Fax: (704) 783-2077
E-mail: admissions@cabarruscollege.edu
Phone: (704) 783-1556

Cabrillo College
www.cabrillo.edu
International Student Office
6500 Soquel Drive
Aptos, CA 95003
Fax: (831) 479-5782
Phone: (831) 479-6200

Cabrini College
www.cabrini.edu
Admissions Office
610 King of Prussia Road
Radnor, PA 19087-3698
Fax: (610) 902-8508
E-mail: charles.spencer@cabrini.edu
Phone: (610) 902-8556

Caldwell College
www.caldwell.edu
International Student Advisor
9 Ryerson Avenue
Caldwell, NJ 07006-6195
Fax: (973) 618-3600
E-mail: heatondwyer@caldwell.edu
Phone: (973) 618-3519

Calhoun Community College
www.calhoun.edu
Admissions and Records
Box 2216
Decatur, AL 35609-2216
Fax: (256) 306-2941
E-mail: bjt@calhoun.edu
Phone: (256) 306-2599

California Baptist University
www.calbaptist.edu
Director, International Services
8432 Magnolia Avenue
Riverside, CA 92504-3297
Fax: (951) 343-4728
E-mail: jbello@calbaptist.edu
Phone: (951) 343-4721

California Coast University
www.calcoast.edu
700 North Main Street
Santa Ana, CA 92701
E-mail: admissions@calcoast.edu
Phone: (714) 547-9625

California College of the Arts
www.cca.edu
Enrollment Services
1111 Eighth Street
San Francisco, CA 94107-2247
Fax: (415) 703-9539
E-mail: lcratty@cca.edu
Phone: (415) 703-9523

California College San Diego
www.cc-sd.edu
2820 Camino del Rio South 300
San Diego, CA 92108
Fax: (619) 295-5762
Phone: (619) 295-5785

California Culinary Academy
www.caculinary.edu
Admissions Office
350 Rhode Island
San Francisco, CA 94103
Fax: (415) 771-2194
E-mail: admissions@baychef.com
Phone: (415) 771-3500

California Design College
www.artinstitutes.edu/cdc
Admissions Office
3440 Wilshire Boulevard, 10th Floor
Los Angeles, CA 90010
Fax: (213) 385-3545
E-mail: jchang@aii.edu
Phone: (213) 251-3636

California Institute of the Arts
www.calarts.edu
International Student Adviser
24700 McBean Parkway
Valencia, CA 91355
Fax: (661) 291-3049
E-mail: pweston@calarts.edu
Phone: (661) 253-7845

California Institute of Integral Studies
www.ciis.edu
1453 Mission Street
San Francisco, CA 94103
E-mail: admissions@ciis.edu
Phone: (415) 575-6150

California Institute of Technology
www.caltech.edu
Office of Admissions
1200 East California Boulevard, MC 1-94
Pasadena, CA 91125
Fax: (626) 683-3026
E-mail: ugadmissions@caltech.edu
Phone: (626) 395-6341

California Lutheran University
www.callutheran.edu
Admission
60 West Olsen Road #1350
Thousand Oaks, CA 91360-2787
Fax: (805) 493-3114
E-mail: admissions@callutheran.edu
Phone: (805) 493-3135

California Maritime Academy
www.csum.edu
200 Maritime Academy Drive
Vallejo, CA 94590
Fax: (707) 654-1336
E-mail: admission@csum.edu
Phone: (707) 654-1330

California National University for Advanced Studies
www.cnuas.edu
8550 Balboa Boulevard, Suite 210
Northridge, CA 91325
Fax: (818) 830-2418
E-mail: cnuadms@mail.cnuas.edu
Phone: (818) 830-2411

California Polytechnic State University: San Luis Obispo
www.calpoly.edu
Admissions
Admissions Office, Cal Poly
San Luis Obispo, CA 93407-0031
Fax: (805) 756-5400
E-mail: admissions@calpoly.edu
Phone: (805) 756-2311

California School of Culinary Arts
www.csca.edu
Global Admissions
530 East Colorado Boulevard
Pasadena, CA 91101
Fax: (626) 403-4835
E-mail: jwilder@csca.edu
Phone: (626) 229-1300

California State Polytechnic University: Pomona
www.csupomona.edu
Coordinator of International Admissions
3801 West Temple Avenue
Pomona, CA 91768-4019
Fax: (909) 869-4529
E-mail: kevinmartin@csupomona.edu
Phone: (909) 869-2107

California State University: Bakersfield
www.csub.edu
Admission Office
9001 Stockdale Highway
Bakersfield, CA 93311-1099
Fax: (661) 654-3389
E-mail: jmimms@csub.edu
Phone: (661) 654-3036

California State University: Channel Islands
www.csuci.edu
One University Drive
Camarillo, CA 93012
E-mail: international@csuci.edu
Phone: (805) 437-3107

California State University: Chico
www.csuchico.edu
Coordinator International Admissions
400 West First Street
Chico, CA 95929-0722
Fax: (530) 898-4359
E-mail: IUGA@csuchico.edu
Phone: (530) 898-4895

California State University: Dominguez Hills
www.csudh.edu
International Student Services
1000 East Victoria Street
Carson, CA 90747
Fax: (310) 516-4132
E-mail: djoseffini@csudh.edu
Phone: (310) 243-2215

California State University: East Bay
www.csueastbay.edu
Director, International Admissions
25800 Carlos Bee Boulevard
Hayward, CA 94542-3095
Fax: (510) 885-3816
E-mail: admissions@csueastbay.edu
Phone: (510) 885-4038

California State University: Fresno
www.csufresno.edu
International Admissions
5150 North Maple Avenue, M/S JA 57
Fresno, CA 93740-8026
Fax: (559) 278-4812
E-mail: intladm@listserv.csufresno.edu
Phone: (559) 278-2409

California State University: Fullerton
www.fullerton.edu
Admissions and Records
800 North State College Boulevard, Langsdorf Hall-114
Fullerton, CA 92831-6900
Fax: (714) 278-2356
E-mail: admissions@fullerton.edu
Phone: (714) 278-2370

California State University: Long Beach
www.csulb.edu
Center for International Education
1250 Bellflower Boulevard
Long Beach, CA 90840-0106
Fax: (562) 985-4973
E-mail: pmlewis@csulb.edu
Phone: (562) 985-4106

California State University: Los Angeles
www.calstatela.edu
International Programs and Services
5151 State University Drive SA101
Los Angeles, CA 90032
Fax: (323) 343-6478
E-mail: admission@calstatela.edu
Phone: (323) 343-3170

California State University: Monterey Bay
www.csumb.edu
Admissions and Records
100 Campus Center, Building 47
Seaside, CA 93955-8001
Fax: (831) 582-4502
E-mail: holly_white@csumb.edu
Phone: (831) 582-4735

California State University: Sacramento
www.csus.edu
Global Education
6000 J Street
Lassen Hall, Lobby
Sacramento, CA 95819-6048
Fax: (916) 278-7471
E-mail: intlinfo@csus.edu
Phone: (916) 278-7772

California State University: San Bernardino
www.csusb.edu
Admissions (Foreign Evaluations)
5500 University Parkway
San Bernardino, CA 92407-2397
Fax: (909) 537-7020
E-mail: elsa@csusb.edu
Phone: (909) 537-5193

California State University: San Marcos
www.csusm.edu
Office of Global Education
333 South Twin Oaks Valley Road
San Marcos, CA 92096-0001
Fax: (760) 750-3284
E-mail: apply@csusm.edu
Phone: (760) 750-4090

California State University: Stanislaus
www.csustan.edu
Office of Global Affairs, International Student Services
801 West Monte Vista Avenue
Turlock, CA 95382-0256
Fax: (209) 667-3788
E-mail: IntlStudent@csustan.edu
Phone: (209) 667-3329

California University of Management and Sciences
www.calums.edu
Admissions
721 North Euclid Streeet
Anaheim, CA 92801
Fax: (714) 533-7778
E-mail: helenk@calums.edu
Phone: (714) 533-3946

California University of Pennsylvania
www.cup.edu
250 University Avenue
California, PA 15419-1394
Fax: (724) 938-4564
E-mail: inquiry@cup.edu
Phone: (724) 938-4404

Calumet College of St. Joseph
www.ccsj.edu
Admissions
2400 New York Avenue
Whiting, IN 46394-2195
Fax: (219) 473-4259
E-mail: cwalz@ccsj.edu
Phone: (877) 700-9100 ext. 215

Calvary Bible College and Theological Seminary
www.calvary.edu
Admissions
15800 Calvary Road
Kansas City, MO 64147
Fax: (816) 331-4474
E-mail: admissions@calvary.edu
Phone: (816) 322-3960

Calvin College
www.calvin.edu
Admissions
3201 Burton Street Southeast
Grand Rapids, MI 49546
Fax: (616) 526-6777
E-mail: intladm@calvin.edu
Phone: (616) 526-6106

Cambria-Rowe Business College: Indiana
www.crbc.net
422 South 13th Street
Indiana, PA 15701
E-mail: rhavener@crbc.net
Phone: (724) 463-0222

Cambridge College
www.cambridgecollege.com
350 Blackhawk Street
Aurora, CO 80011
Fax: (303) 338-9701
Phone: (720) 859-7900

Cambridge College
www.cambridgecollege.edu
International Students Office
1000 Massachusetts Avenue
Cambridge, MA 02138-5304
E-mail: bruce.grigsby@cambridgecollege.edu
Phone: (617) 868-1000 ext. 1142

Cameron University
www.cameron.edu
Admissions
2800 West Gore Boulevard
Lawton, OK 73505-6377
Fax: (580) 581-5416
E-mail: international@cameron.edu
Phone: (888) 454-7600

Campbell University
www.campbell.edu
International Admissions and Advisement Office
PO Box 546
Buies Creek, NC 27506
Fax: (910) 893-1288
E-mail: intl@campbell.edu
Phone: (910) 893-1200 ext. 1417

Campbellsville University
www.campbellsville.edu
Admissions Office
1 University Drive
Campbellsville, KY 42718-2799
Fax: (270) 789-5071
E-mail: admissions@campbellsville.edu
Phone: (270) 789-5020

Canada College
www.canadacollege.edu
Admissions & Records Office
4200 Farm Hill Boulevard
Redwood City, CA 94061
Fax: (650) 306-3113
E-mail: sohrabi@smccd.net
Phone: (650) 306-3494

Canisius College
www.canisius.edu
Admissions Office
2001 Main Street
Buffalo, NY 14208-1098
Fax: (716) 888-3230
E-mail: moscovia@canisius.edu
Phone: (716) 888-2200

Cape Cod Community College
www.capecod.edu
Admissions
2240 Iyanough Road
West Barnstable, MA 02668-1599
Fax: (508) 375-4089
E-mail: sklinesy@capecod.edu
Phone: (508) 362-2131 ext. 4311

Capital Community College
www.ccc.commnet.edu
Admissions
950 Main Street
Hartford, CT 06103-1207
E-mail: mball-davis@ccc.commnet.edu
Phone: (860) 906-5127

Capital University
www.capital.edu
Office of International Education
One College and Main
Columbus, OH 43209-2394
Fax: (614) 236-6171
E-mail: internation-education@capital.edu
Phone: (614) 236-7102

Capitol College
www.capitol-college.edu
11301 Springfield Road
Laurel, MD 20708
Fax: (301) 953-1442
E-mail: agmiller@capitol-college.edu
Phone: (301) 369-2800

Cardinal Stritch University
www.stritch.edu
Office of Undergraduate Admissions
6801 North Yates Road, Box 516
Milwaukee, WI 53217-7516
Fax: (414) 410-4058
E-mail: admityou@stritch.edu
Phone: (414) 410-4040

Career College of Northern Nevada
www.ccnn.edu
1195 A Corporate Boulevard
Reno, NV 89502-2331
E-mail: lgoldhammer@ccnn4u.com
Phone: (775) 856-2266

Career Training Academy
www.careerta.com
Admissions
950 Fifth Avenue
New Kensington, PA 15068
Fax: (724) 335-7140
E-mail: jreddy@careerta.com
Phone: (724) 337-1000

Career Training Academy: Monroeville
www.careerta.edu
4314 Old William Penn Highway #103
Monroeville, PA 15146
E-mail: Admissions2@careerta.edu
Phone: (412) 372-3900

Career Training Academy: Pittsburgh
www.careerta.edu
1500 Shoppes at Northway
Pittsburgh, PA 15237
E-mail: admissions3@careerta.edu
Phone: (412) 367-4000

Careers Unlimited
www.ucdh.edu/
1176 South 1480 West
Orem, UT 84058
E-mail: admissions@ucdh.edu
Phone: (801) 226-1081

Caribbean University
www.caribbean.edu
Office of Admissions
PO Box 493
Bayamon, PR 00960-0493
Fax: (787) 785-0101
E-mail: rvazquez@caribbean.edu
Phone: (787) 780-0070 ext. 1110

Caritas Laboure College
www.laboure.edu
Admissions Office
2120 Dorchester Avenue
Boston, MA 02124-5698
Fax: (617) 296-7947
E-mail: admit@laboure.edu
Phone: (617) 296-8300 ext. 4016

Carl Albert State College
www.carlalbert.edu
Admissions
1507 South McKenna
Poteau, OK 74953-5208
Fax: (918) 647-1306
E-mail: kcole@carlalbert.edu
Phone: (918) 647-1301

Carl Sandburg College
www.sandburg.edu
2400 Tom L. Wilson Boulevard
Galesburg, IL 61401
Fax: (309) 344-3291
E-mail: ckreider@csc.cc.il.us
Phone: (309) 344-2518

Carleton College
www.carleton.edu
Admissions
100 South College Street
Northfield, MN 55057
Fax: (507) 646-4526
E-mail: admissionsglobal@carleton.edu
Phone: (507) 646-4190

Carlos Albizu University
www.albizu.edu
Recruitment Department
2173 NW 99th Avenue
Miami, FL 33172
Fax: (305) 593-1854
E-mail: calicea@albizu.edu
Phone: (305) 593-1223 ext. 137

Carlos Albizu University: San Juan
www.albizu.edu
151 Tanca Street
San Juan, PR 00902-3711
Fax: (787) 721-7187
Phone: (787) 725-6500 ext. 21

Carlow University
www.carlow.edu
International Student Center
3333 Fifth Avenue
Pittsburgh, PA 15213-3165
Fax: (412) 578-8722
E-mail: nesgodajl@carlow.edu
Phone: (412) 578-6010

Carnegie Mellon University
www.cmu.edu
Admissions Office
5000 Forbes Avenue
Pittsburgh, PA 15213-3890
Fax: (412) 268-7838
E-mail:
undergraduate-admissions@andrew.cmu.edu
Phone: (412) 268-2082

Carolina Christian College
www.wsbc.edu
Box 777
Winston-Salem, NC 27105
Phone: (336) 744-0900

Carroll College
www.carroll.edu
International Programs
1601 North Benton Avenue
Helena, MT 59625
Fax: (406) 447-5461
E-mail: kkelley@carroll.edu
Phone: (406) 447-5460

Carroll College
www.cc.edu
Office of International Student Admission
100 North East Avenue
Waukesha, WI 53186-9988
Fax: (262) 524-7139
E-mail: morris@cc.edu
Phone: (800) 227-7655

Carroll Community College
www.carrollcc.edu
Office of Admissions
1601 Washington Road
Westminster, MD 21157
Fax: (410) 386-8446
E-mail: cedwards@carrollcc.edu
Phone: (410) 386-8435

Carson-Newman College
www.cn.edu
Office of Admissions
1646 Russell Avenue
Jefferson City, TN 37760
Fax: (865) 471-3502
E-mail: thuebner@cn.edu
Phone: (865) 471-3223

Carteret Community College
www.carteret.edu
Student Enrollment Resources
3505 Arendell Street
Morehead City, NC 28557-2989
Fax: (252) 222-6265
E-mail: mhw@carteret.edu
Phone: (252) 222-6155

Carthage College
www.carthage.edu
Admissions
2001 Alford Park Drive
Kenosha, WI 53140-1994
Fax: (262) 551-5762
E-mail: admissions@carthage.edu
Phone: (262) 551-6000

Carver Bible College
www.carver.edu
3837 Cascade Road, SW
Atlanta, GA 30313
Fax: (404) 527-4524
Phone: (404) 527-4520

Cascade College
www.cascade.edu
9101 East Burnside Street
Portland, OR 97216
Fax: (503) 257-1222
E-mail: admissions@cascade.edu
Phone: (503) 257-1202

Cascadia Community College
www.cascadia.edu
International
18345 Campus Way, NE
Bothell, WA 98011
E-mail: international@cascadia.edu
Phone: (425) 352-8587

Case Western Reserve University
www.case.edu
Undergraduate Admission
Tomlinson Hall
Cleveland, OH 44106-7055
Fax: (216) 368-5111
E-mail: admission@case.edu
Phone: (216) 368-4450

Casper College
www.caspercollege.edu
Office of Admissions
125 College Drive
Casper, WY 82601
Fax: (307) 268-2611
E-mail: amcnulty@caspercollege.edu
Phone: (307) 268-3123

Castleton State College
www.castleton.edu
Admissions Office
Seminary Street
Castleton, VT 05735
Fax: (802) 468-1476
E-mail: info@castleton.edu
Phone: (802) 468-1213

Catawba College
www.catawba.edu
Admissions
2300 West Innes Street
Salisbury, NC 28144
Fax: (704) 637-4222
E-mail: admission@catawba.edu
Phone: (800) 228-2922

Catholic University of America
www.cua.edu
Office of Undergraduate Admissions
620 Michigan Avenue, NE
Washington, DC 20064
Fax: (202) 319-6533
E-mail: cua-admissions@cua.edu
Phone: (202) 319-5305

Cayuga County Community College
www.cayuga-cc.edu
Admissions Office
197 Franklin Street
Auburn, NY 13021-3099
Fax: (315) 255-2117
E-mail: blodgett@cayuga-cc.edu
Phone: (315) 255-1743

Cazenovia College
www.cazenovia.edu
Admissions and Financial Aid
3 Sullivan Street
Cazenovia, NY 13035
Fax: (315) 655-4860
E-mail: jaustin@cazenovia.edu
Phone: (315) 655-7208

Cedar Crest College
www.cedarcrest.edu
Office of Admissions
100 College Drive
Allentown, PA 18104-6196
Fax: (610) 606-4647
E-mail: cccadmis@cedarcrest.edu
Phone: (800) 360-1222

Cedar Valley College
www.cedarvalleycollege.edu
Admissions
3030 North Dallas Avenue
Lancaster, TX 75134
Fax: (972) 860-8207
E-mail: cdw3310@dccd.edu
Phone: (972) 860-8203

Cedarville University
www.cedarville.edu
Admissions Department
251 North Main Street
Cedarville, OH 45314
Fax: (937) 766-7575
E-mail: admissions@cedarville.edu
Phone: (937) 766-7700

Centenary College
www.centenarycollege.edu
International Liaison
400 Jefferson Street
Hackettstown, NJ 07840-9989
Fax: (908) 852-3454
E-mail: young@centenarycollege.edu
Phone: (908) 852-1400 ext. 2221

Centenary College of Louisiana
www.centenary.edu
Admissions Office
Box 41188
Shreveport, LA 71134-1188
Fax: (318) 869-5005
E-mail: scallawa@centenary.edu
Phone: (318) 869-5131

Central Arizona College
www.centralaz.edu
Admissions Office
8470 North Overfield Road
Coolidge, AZ 85228-9778
Fax: (520) 494-5083
E-mail: sandra.todd@centralaz.edu
Phone: (520) 494-5260

Central Carolina Technical College
www.cctech.edu
Admissions
506 North Guignard Drive
Sumter, SC 29150-2499
Fax: (803) 778-6696
E-mail: brackenlm@cctech.edu
Phone: (803) 778-6652

Central Christian College of Kansas
www.centralchristian.edu
Admissions
1200 South Main
Box 1403
McPherson, KS 67460-5740
Fax: (620) 241-6032
E-mail: admissions@centralchristian.edu
Phone: (620) 241-0723 ext. 337

Central College
www.central.edu
Admission Office, Central College
812 University Street
Pella, IA 50219-1999
Fax: (641) 628-7637
E-mail: purnelld@central.edu
Phone: (877) 462-3687

Central Connecticut State University
www.ccsu.edu
Recruitment and Admissions
1615 Stanley Street
New Britain, CT 06050
Fax: (860) 832-2295
E-mail: admissions@ccsu.edu
Phone: (860) 832-2278

Central Florida College
www.centralfloridacollege.edu
Admissions
1573 West Fairbanks Avenue
Winter Park, FL 32789
Fax: (407) 843-9828
E-mail: admissions@centralfloridacollege.edu
Phone: (407) 843-3984

Central Florida Community College
www.cf.edu
3001 SW College Road
Ocala, FL 34474-4415
Fax: (352) 873-5882
E-mail: trexlerj@cf.edu
Phone: (352) 237-2111 ext. 1386

Central Georgia Technical College
www.cgtcollege.edu
3300 Macon Tech Drive
Macon, GA 31206
Fax: (478) 757-3454
E-mail: info@cgtcollege.org
Phone: (478) 757-3403

Central Lakes College
www.clcmn.edu
Admissions
501 West College Drive
Brainerd, MN 56401
Fax: (218) 855-8230
E-mail: cdaniels@clcmn.edu
Phone: (218) 855-8000

Central Maine Community College
www.cmcc.edu
Admissions
1250 Turner Street
Auburn, ME 04210
Fax: (207) 755-5493
E-mail: enroll@cmcc.edu
Phone: (207) 755-5334

Central Methodist University
www.centralmethodist.edu
Admissions
411 Central Methodist Square
Fayette, MO 65248-1198
Fax: (660) 248-1872
E-mail: admissions@centralmethodist.edu
Phone: (660) 248-6626

Central Michigan University
www.cmich.edu
Office of International Education
Admissions Office
Warriner Hall
Mount Pleasant, MI 48859
Fax: (989) 774-3690
E-mail: intlapp@cmich.edu
Phone: (989) 774-4308

Central Ohio Technical College
www.cotc.edu
Minority/Disadvantaged Recruiter-Admissions
1179 University Drive
Newark, OH 43055
Fax: (740) 366-5047
E-mail: cleblanc@cotc.edu
Phone: (740) 366-9392

Central Pennsylvania College
www.centralpenn.edu
Admissions
College Hill & Valley Roads
Summerdale, PA 17093-0309
Fax: (717) 732-5254
E-mail: katieborrelli@centralpenn.edu
Phone: (800) 759-2727 ext. 2214

Central Piedmont Community College
www.cpcc.edu
International Student Adviser
Box 35009
Charlotte, NC 28235-5009
Fax: (704) 330-6130
E-mail: dotty.holley@cpcc.edu
Phone: (704) 330-6456

Central State University
www.centralstate.edu
Admissions
PO Box 1004
Wilberforce, OH 45384-1004
Fax: (937) 376-6530
E-mail: admissions@centralstate.edu
Phone: (937) 376-6348

Central Texas College
www.ctcd.edu
International Student Services
Box 1800
Killeen, TX 76540
Fax: (254) 526-1481
E-mail: ctc.international@ctcd.edu
Phone: (254) 526-1107

Central Virginia Community College
www.cv.cc.va.us
Counseling
3506 Wards Road
Lynchburg, VA 24502-2498
Fax: (434) 386-4681
Phone: (434) 832-7800

Central Washington University
www.cwu.edu
Office of Admissions
400 East University Way
Ellensburg, WA 98926-7463
Fax: (509) 963-3022
E-mail: cwuadmis@cwu.edu
Phone: (509) 963-1211

Central Wyoming College
www.cwc.edu
Admissions
2660 Peck Avenue
Riverton, WY 82501
Fax: (307) 855-2093
E-mail: jason@cwc.edu
Phone: (307) 855-2270

Centralia College
www.centralia.edu
International Programs
600 Centralia College Boulevard
Centralia, WA 98531
Fax: (360) 736-9391
E-mail: intl@centralia.edu
Phone: (360) 736-9391 ext. 492

Centre College
www.centre.edu
Admission
600 West Walnut Street
Danville, KY 40422-1394
Fax: (859) 238-5373
E-mail: ned.frazier@centre.edu
Phone: (859) 238-5350

Century Community and Technical College
www.century.edu
Office of Admissions
3300 Century Avenue North
White Bear Lake, MN 55110
Fax: (651) 779-1796
E-mail: debbie.palm@century.edu
Phone: (651) 793-1222

Cerritos College
www.cerritos.edu
11110 Alondra Boulevard
Norwalk, CA 90650
Fax: (562) 860-9680
Phone: (562) 860-2451 ext. 2211

Cerro Coso Community College
www.cerrocoso.edu
Vice President
3000 College Heights Boulevard
Ridgecrest, CA 93555-7777
Fax: (760) 384-6377
E-mail: jboard@cerrocoso.edu
Phone: (760) 384-6354

Chabot College
www.chabotcollege.edu
Office of Special Admissions, Room 168,
Chabot College
25555 Hesperian Boulevard
Hayward, CA 94545
Fax: (510) 723-7510
E-mail: intladms@clpccd.cc.ca.us
Phone: (510) 723-6740

Chadron State College
www.csc.edu
1000 Main Street
Chadron, NE 69337
Fax: (308) 432-6229
E-mail: ccousin@csc.edu
Phone: (308) 432-6496

Chaffey College
www.chaffey.edu
International Student Admissions
5885 Haven Avenue
Rancho Cucamonga, CA 91701-3002
Fax: (909) 652-6006
E-mail: donna.colondres@chaffey.edu
Phone: (909) 652-6226

Chaminade University of Honolulu
www.chaminade.edu
Admissions Office
3140 Waialae Avenue
Honolulu, HI 96816
Fax: (808) 739-4647
E-mail: admissions@chaminade.edu
Phone: (808) 735-4735

Champlain College
www.champlain.edu
Office of International Programs
163 South Willard Street
PO Box 670
Burlington, VT 05402-0670
Fax: (802) 860-2773
E-mail: admission@champlain.edu
Phone: (802) 860-2727

**Chandler-Gilbert Community College:
Pecos**
www.cgc.maricopa.edu
International Education Programs
2626 East Pecos Road
Chandler, AZ 85225
Fax: (480) 866-8242
E-mail: iss@cgcmail.maricopa.edu
Phone: (480) 732-7391

Chapman University
www.chapman.edu
Office of Admission
One University Drive
Orange, CA 92866
Fax: (714) 997-6713
E-mail: admit@chapman.edu
Phone: (714) 997-6711

**Charles R. Drew University of Medicine and
Science**
www.cdrewu.edu
Office of Admissions
1731 East 120th Street
Los Angeles, CA 90059
Fax: (323) 569-0597
E-mail: makaylahall@cdrewu.edu
Phone: (323) 563-5886

Charleston Southern University
www.csuniv.edu
Enrollment Services
9200 University Boulevard
Box 118087
Charleston, SC 29423-8087
Fax: (843) 863-7070
E-mail: jrhoton@csuniv.edu
Phone: (843) 863-7050

Charter Oak State College
www.charteroak.edu
Admission
55 Paul Manafort Drive
New Britain, CT 06053-2142
Fax: (860) 832-3999
E-mail: info@charteroak.edu
Phone: (860) 832-3858

Chatham University
www.chatham.edu
Office of Admissions
Woodland Road
Pittsburgh, PA 15232
Fax: (412) 365-1609
E-mail: admissions@chatham.edu
Phone: (412) 365-1825

Chattahoochee Technical College
www.chattcollege.com
International Student Assistance
980 South Cobb Drive
Marietta, GA 30060-3300
Fax: (770) 528-4587
E-mail: ssessun@chat-tec.com
Phone: (770) 528-4484

Chattahoochee Valley Community College
www.cv.edu
2602 College Drive
Phenix City, AL 36869
Fax: (334) 291-4994
Phone: (334) 291-4929

Chemeketa Community College
www.chemeketa.edu
International Student Admissions
Admissions Office
4000 Lancaster Drive NE
Salem, OR 97305-1453
Fax: (503) 399-3918
E-mail: international@chemeketa.edu
Phone: (503) 399-2527

Chesapeake College
www.chesapeake.edu
Registrar
Box 8
1000 College Circle
Wye Mills, MD 21679-0008
Fax: (410) 827-9466
E-mail: cjewell@chesapeake.edu
Phone: (410) 822-5400 ext. 420

Chester College of New England
www.chestercollege.edu
Admissions
40 Chester Street
Chester, NH 03036
Fax: (603) 887-1777
E-mail: lsalazar@chestercollege.edu
Phone: (603) 887-7401

Chestnut Hill College
www.chc.edu
International Student Advisor
9601 Germantown Avenue
Philadelphia, PA 19118-2693
Fax: (215) 248-7155
E-mail: albruno@chc.edu
Phone: (215) 248-7166

Cheyney University of Pennsylvania
www.cheyney.edu
Admissions Office
1837 University Circle
PO Box 200
Cheyney, PA 19319-0019
Fax: (610) 399-2099
E-mail: abrown@cheyney.edu
Phone: (610) 399-2275

CHI Institute: Franklin Mills
www.chitraining.com
125 Franklin Mills Boulevard
Philadelphia, PA 19154
Phone: (215) 357-5100

Chicago State University
www.csu.edu
Office of Admissions
9501 South King Drive
Chicago, IL 60628
Fax: (773) 995-3820
E-mail: ug-admissions@csu.edu
Phone: (773) 995-2513

Chipola Junior College
www.chipola.edu
Admissions and Records
3094 Indian Circle
Marianna, FL 32446
Fax: (850) 718-2287
E-mail: robertsj@chipola.edu
Phone: (850) 718-2209

Chippewa Valley Technical College
www.cvtc.edu
620 West Clairemont Avenue
Eau Claire, WI 54701-6162
Fax: (715) 833-6470
E-mail: bread@chippewa.tec.wi.us
Phone: (715) 833-6247

Chowan University
www.chowan.edu
Office of Admissions
One University Place
Murfreesboro, NC 27855-9901
Fax: (252) 398-1190
E-mail: holtc@chowan.edu
Phone: (252) 398-6298

Christendom College
www.christendom.edu
134 Christendom Drive
Front Royal, VA 22630
Fax: (540) 636-1655
E-mail: admissions@christendom.edu
Phone: (540) 636-2900

Christian Brothers University
www.cbu.edu
Admissions
650 East Parkway South
Memphis, TN 38104-5519
Fax: (901) 321-3202
E-mail: tdysart@cbu.edu
Phone: (901) 321-3205

Christopher Newport University
www.cnu.edu
Office of the Registrar
1 University Place
Newport News, VA 23606
Fax: (757) 594-7711
E-mail: btracey@cnu.edu
Phone: (757) 594-7155

Cincinnati Christian University
www.ccuniversity.edu
Registrar
2700 Glenway Avenue
Cincinnati, OH 45204-3200
Fax: (513) 244-8453
E-mail: registrar@ccuniversity.edu
Phone: (513) 244-8170

Cincinnati College of Mortuary Science
www.ccms.edu
645 West North Bend Road
Cincinnati, OH 45224-1428
Fax: (513) 761-3333
Phone: (513) 761-2020

Cincinnati State Technical and Community College
www.cincinnatistate.edu
Foreign Student Advisor/Admission Office
3520 Central Parkway
Cincinnati, OH 45223-2690
Fax: (513) 569-1562
E-mail: yolanda.lawrence@cincinnatistate.edu
Phone: (513) 569-1543

The Citadel
www.citadel.edu
Director of Admissions
171 Moultrie Street
Charleston, SC 29409
Fax: (843) 953-7036
E-mail: powellj@citadel.edu
Phone: (843) 953-5200

Citrus College
www.citruscollege.edu
International Student Office
1000 West Foothill Boulevard
Glendora, CA 91741-1899
Fax: (626) 963-4854
E-mail: internationalstudents@citruscollege.edu
Phone: (626) 914-8549

City College of San Francisco
www.ccsf.edu
Foreign Student Admissions Office
Office of Admissions and Records E-107
50 Phelan Avenue
San Francisco, CA 94112
Fax: (415) 239-3936
E-mail: rbrovell@ccsf.edu
Phone: (415) 239-3837

City College: Casselberry
853 State Road 436, Suite 200
Casselberry, FL 32707-5353
Fax: (407) 831-1147
Phone: (407) 831-8466

City College: Fort Lauderdale
www.citycollege.edu
Admissions
2000 West Commercial Boulevard
Fort Lauderdale, FL 33309
Fax: (954) 491-1965
E-mail: rlohrmann@citycollege.edu
Phone: (954) 492-5353

City College: Gainesville
www.citycollege.edu
2400 SW 13th Street
Gainesville, FL 32608
Fax: (352) 335-4303
E-mail: kcartier@citycollege.edu
Phone: (352) 335-4000

City College: Miami
www.citycollege.edu
9300 South Dadeland Boulevard
Miami, FL 33156
Fax: (305) 666-9243
E-mail: sespath@citycollege.edu
Phone: (305) 666-9242

City Colleges of Chicago: Harold Washington College
www.ccc.edu
Admissions Office
30 East Lake Street
Chicago, IL 60601
Fax: (312) 553-6084
E-mail: ytownsend@ccc.edu
Phone: (312) 553-6004

City Colleges of Chicago: Kennedy-King College
www.ccc.edu
6800 South Wentworth Avenue
Chicago, IL 60621
Fax: (773) 602-5247
E-mail: wmurphy@ccc.edu
Phone: (773) 602-5080

City Colleges of Chicago: Malcolm X College
www.malcolmx.ccc.edu
Admissions
1900 West Van Buren Street
Chicago, IL 60612
Fax: (312) 850-7092
E-mail: mryniec@ccc.edu
Phone: (312) 850-7135

City Colleges of Chicago: Olive-Harvey College
www.ccc.edu
10001 South Woodlawn Avenue
Chicago, IL 60628
Fax: (773) 291-6185
Phone: (773) 291-6384

City Colleges of Chicago: Richard J. Daley College
daley.ccc.edu
7500 South Pulaski Road
Chicago, IL 60652
Fax: (773) 838-7605
Phone: (773) 838-7606

City Colleges of Chicago: Wright College
www.ccc.edu
Admissions
4300 North Narragansett Avenue
Chicago, IL 60634-4276
Fax: (773) 481-8053
E-mail: aaiello@ccc.edu
Phone: (773) 481-8200

City University of New York: Baruch College
www.baruch.cuny.edu
Office of Undergraduate Admissions
One Bernard Baruch Way, Box H-0720
New York, NY 10010-5585
Fax: (646) 312-1363
E-mail: admissions@baruch.cuny.edu
Phone: (646) 312-1400

City University of New York: Borough of Manhattan Community College
www.bmcc.cuny.edu
Office of Admissions Services
199 Chambers Street
New York, NY 10007-1097
Fax: (212) 220-2366
E-mail: amiddleton@bmcc.cuny.edu
Phone: (212) 947-4800

City University of New York: Bronx Community College
www.bcc.cuny.edu
West 181st Street and University Avenue
Bronx, NY 10453
Fax: (718) 289-6352
E-mail: alba.cancetty@bcc.cuny.edu
Phone: (718) 289-5888

City University of New York: Brooklyn College
www.brooklyn.cuny.edu
CUNY Office of Admissions Services
2900 Bedford Avenue
Brooklyn, NY 11210
Fax: (718) 951-4506
E-mail: adminqry@brooklyn.cuny.edu
Phone: (212) 947-4800

City University of New York: City College
www.ccny.cuny.edu
Admissions
160 Convent Avenue
Administration Building Room 101
New York, NY 10031
Fax: (212) 650-6417
E-mail: tstahis@ccny.cuny.edu
Phone: (212) 650-6483

City University of New York: College of Staten Island
www.csi.cuny.edu
Recruitment & Admissions
2800 Victory Boulevard 2A-104
Staten Island, NY 10314
Fax: (718) 982-2500
E-mail: bounacore@mail.csi.cuny.edu
Phone: (718) 982-2010

City University of New York: CUNY Online
www.cuny.edu/online
Admissions
101 West 31st Street, 7th Floor
New York, NY 10001
Fax: (212) 652-2887
E-mail: otilia.abraham@mail.cuny.edu
Phone: (212) 652-2879

City University of New York: Hostos Community College
www.hostos.cuny.edu
Office of Admissions
500 Grand Concourse
Bronx, NY 10451
Fax: (718) 518-4256
E-mail: rvelez@hostos.cuny.edu
Phone: (718) 518-4406

City University of New York: Hunter College
www.hunter.cuny.edu
International Student Office
695 Park Avenue
New York, NY 10021
E-mail:
internationalstudent.ser@hunter.cuny.edu
Phone: (212) 772-4864

City University of New York: John Jay College of Criminal Justice
www.jjay.cuny.edu/
Admissions
445 West 59th Street
New York, NY 10019
Fax: (212) 484-1185
E-mail: svavasis@jjay.cuny.edu
Phone: (212) 237-8777

City University of New York: Kingsborough Community College
www.kbcc.cuny.edu
Office of International Student Affairs
2001 Oriental Boulevard
Brooklyn, NY 11235
Fax: (718) 368-4535
E-mail: isa@kbcc.cuny.edu
Phone: (718) 368-6800

City University of New York: LaGuardia Community College
www.lagcc.cuny.edu
Foreign Student Office
31-10 Thomson Avenue
Long Island City, NY 11101
Fax: (718) 609-2023
E-mail: pnicolov@lagcc.cuny.edu
Phone: (718) 482-5143

City University of New York: Lehman College
www.lehman.cuny.edu
Office for International Students
250 Bedford Park Boulevard West
Bronx, NY 10468
Fax: (718) 960-8712
E-mail: enroll@lehman.cuny.edu
Phone: (718) 960-7274

City University of New York: Medgar Evers College
www.mec.cuny.edu
Admissions
1665 Bedford Avenue
Brooklyn, NY 11225-2201
Fax: (718) 270-6411
E-mail: jaugustin@mec.cuny.edu
Phone: (718) 270-6021

City University of New York: Queens College
www.qc.cuny.edu
Admissions
6530 Kissena Boulevard, Jefferson 117
Flushing, NY 11367-1597
Fax: (718) 997-5617
E-mail: admissions@qc.cuny.edu
Phone: (718) 997-5600

City University of New York: Queensborough Community College
www.qcc.cuny.edu
Admissions Services CUNY, 101 West 31
Street, NY 1001-3503
Springfield Boulevard & 56th Avenue
Bayside, NY 11364-1497
Fax: (718) 281-5189
Phone: (718) 631-6611

City University of New York: York College
www.york.cuny.edu
Admission Services
94-20 Guy R. Brewer Boulevard
Jamaica, NY 11451-9989
Fax: (718) 262-2601
E-mail: admissions@york.cuny.edu
Phone: (718) 262-2165

City University of Seattle
www.cityu.edu
International Student Admissions
11900 NE First Street
Bellevue, WA 98005
Fax: (425) 709-5361
E-mail: intladmissions@cityu.edu
Phone: (425) 637-1010 ext. 5308

Clackamas Community College
www.clackamas.edu
Admissions Specialist
19600 Molalla Avenue
Oregon City, OR 97045
Fax: (503) 722-5864
E-mail: pattyw@clackamas.edu
Phone: (503) 657-6958 ext. 2263

Claflin University
www.claflin.edu
Admissions
400 Magnolia Street
Orangeburg, SC 29115
Fax: (803) 535-5387
E-mail: mzeigler@claflin.edu
Phone: (803) 535-5340

Claremont McKenna College
www.claremontmckenna.edu
Office of Admission
890 Columbia Avenue
Claremont, CA 91711-6425
Fax: (909) 621-8516
E-mail: admission@claremontmckenna.edu
Phone: (909) 621-8088

Clarendon College
www.clarendoncollege.edu
Office of Admissions
PO Box 968
Clarendon, TX 79226
Fax: (806) 874-5080
E-mail: sharon.hannon@clarendoncollege.edu
Phone: (806) 874-3571 ext. 107

Clarion University of Pennsylvania
www.clarion.edu
Office of International Programs
840 Wood Street
Clarion, PA 16214
Fax: (814) 393-2341
E-mail: lheineman@clarion.edu
Phone: (814) 393-2340

Clark Atlanta University
www.cau.edu
Admissions
223 James P. Brawley Drive, SW
101 Trevor Arnett Hall
Atlanta, GA 30314-4391
Fax: (404) 880-6174
E-mail: mdavis@cau.edu
Phone: (404) 880-6605

Clark College
www.clark.edu
International Education
1933 Fort Vancouver Way
Vancouver, WA 98663
Fax: (360) 992-2868
E-mail: international@clark.edu
Phone: (360) 992-2495

Clark State Community College
www.clarkstate.edu
Records/Registration Office
Box 570
Springfield, OH 45501-0570
Fax: (937) 328-3853
E-mail: mabryt@clarkstate.edu
Phone: (937) 328-6014

Clark University
www.clarku.edu
950 Main Street
Worcester, MA 01610-1477
Fax: (508) 793-8821
E-mail: intadmissions@clarku.edu
Phone: (508) 793-7431

Clarke College
www.clarke.edu
Senior Admissions Representative
1550 Clarke Drive
Dubuque, IA 52001-3198
Fax: (563) 588-6789
E-mail: chris.pabon@clarke.edu
Phone: (563) 588-8176

Clarkson University
www.clarkson.edu
Transfer and International Admission
Holcroft House
Potsdam, NY 13699-5605
Fax: (315) 268-7647
E-mail: tdobbs@clarkson.edu
Phone: (315) 268-2125

Clatsop Community College
www.clatsopcollege.com
Admissions Office
1653 Jerome Avenue
Astoria, OR 97103
Fax: (503) 325-5738
E-mail: jswenson@clatsop.cc.or.us
Phone: (503) 338-2325

Clayton State University
www.clayton.edu
Office of the Registrar
5900 North Lee Street
Morrow, GA 30260-0285
Fax: (770) 961-4321
E-mail: jeanmyers@mail.clayton.edu
Phone: (770) 960-5110

Cleary University
www.cleary.edu
Admissions
3750 Cleary Drive
Howell, MI 48843
Fax: (517) 552-7805
E-mail: rosemsmith@cleary.edu
Phone: (517) 548-3670 ext. 2249

Clemens College
www.clemenscollege.edu
Admissions
1760 Mapleton Avenue
Suffield, CT 06078
Fax: (860) 668-7369
E-mail: admissions@clemenscollege.edu
Phone: (860) 668-3515

Clemson University
www.clemson.edu
Office of Admissions
105 Sikes Hall
Box 345124
Clemson, SC 29634-5124
Fax: (864) 656-2464
E-mail: cuadmissions@clemson.edu
Phone: (864) 656-2287

Cleveland Institute of Art
www.cia.edu
Admissions
11141 East Boulevard
Cleveland, OH 44106-1710
Fax: (216) 754-3634
E-mail: admiss@cia.edu
Phone: (216) 421-7418

Cleveland Institute of Electronics
www.cie-wc.edu
1776 East 17th Street
Cleveland, OH 44114-3679
Fax: (216) 781-0331
E-mail: instruct@cie-wc.edu
Phone: (216) 781-9400

Cleveland Institute of Music
www.cim.edu
11021 East Boulevard
Cleveland, OH 44106
Fax: (216) 795-3161
E-mail: cimadmission@po.cwru.edu
Phone: (216) 795-3107

Cleveland State Community College
www.clevelandstatecc.edu
Office of Admissions
3535 Adkisson Drive
Box 3570
Cleveland, TN 37320-3570
Fax: (423) 478-6255
E-mail: mburnette@clevelandstatecc.edu
Phone: (423) 478-6212

Cleveland State University
www.csuohio.edu
International Student Admissions Office
1806 East 22nd Street
Rhodes Tower West, Room 204
Cleveland, OH 44115-2403
Fax: (216) 687-3965
E-mail: cispcsu@csuohio.edu
Phone: (216) 687-4579

Clinton Community College
www.eicc.edu
Admissions Officer
1000 Lincoln Boulevard
Clinton, IA 52732
Fax: (563) 244-7107
E-mail: scarmody@eicc.edu
Phone: (563) 244-7007

Clinton Community College
www.clinton.edu
Admissions Advisor
136 Clinton Point Drive
Plattsburgh, NY 12901-4297
Fax: (518) 562-4380
E-mail: admissions@clinton.edu
Phone: (518) 562-4232

Cloud County Community College
www.cloud.edu
Office of Admissions
2221 Campus Drive
Box 1002
Concordia, KS 66901-1002
Fax: (785) 243-1459
E-mail: champlin@cloud.edu
Phone: (785) 243-1435 ext. 213

Clover Park Technical College
www.cptc.edu
International Programs
4500 Steilacoom Boulevard, SW
Lakewood, WA 98499-4098
Fax: (253) 589-6054
E-mail: international@cptc.edu
Phone: (253) 589-6089

Clovis Community College
www.clovis.edu
Admissions and Records
417 Schepps Boulevard
Clovis, NM 88101-8381
Fax: (575) 769-4190
E-mail: admissions@clovis.edu
Phone: (575) 769-4025

Coahoma Community College
www.coahomacc.edu
3240 Friars Point Road
Clarksdale, MS 38614-9799
Fax: (800) 844-1222
E-mail: wholmes@coahomacc.edu
Phone: (662) 621-4205

Coastal Bend College
www.coastalbend.edu
3800 Charco Road
Beeville, TX 78102
Fax: (361) 354-2254
E-mail: register@coastalbend.edu
Phone: (361) 354-2245

Coastal Carolina University
www.coastal.edu
International Programs
PO Box 261954
Conway, SC 29528-6054
Fax: (843) 349-2252
E-mail: parsons@coastal.edu
Phone: (843) 349-2054

Coastal Georgia Community College
www.cgcc.edu
Admissions
3700 Altama Avenue
Brunswick, GA 31520
Fax: (912) 262-3072
E-mail: cltoler@cgcc.edu
Phone: (912) 264-7253

Coastline Community College
www.coastline.edu
11460 Warner Avenue
Fountain Valley, CA 92708
Fax: (714) 241-6288
E-mail: jmcdonald@cccd.edu
Phone: (714) 241-6165

Cochise College
www.cochise.edu
Admissions
901 North Colombo Avenue
Sierra Vista, AZ 85635
Fax: (520) 515-5452
E-mail: international@cochise.edu
Phone: (520) 417-4038

Coe College
www.coe.edu
Admission Office
1220 First Avenue NE
Cedar Rapids, IA 52402
Fax: (319) 399-8816
E-mail: pcook@coe.edu
Phone: (319) 399-8500

Coffeyville Community College
www.coffeyville.edu
International
400 West 11th Street
Coffeyville, KS 67337-5064
Fax: (620) 251-7098
E-mail: marlal@coffeyville.edu
Phone: (620) 251-7700 ext. 2086

Cogswell Polytechnical College
www.cogswell.edu
Admissions
1175 Bordeaux Drive
Sunnyvale, CA 94089-1299
Fax: (408) 747-0764
E-mail: bsouza@cogswell.edu
Phone: (408) 541-0100 ext. 155

Coker College
www.coker.edu
Center of International and Experiential
Education
300 East College Avenue
Hartsville, SC 29550
Fax: (843) 383-8048
E-mail: dsmall@pascal.coker.edu
Phone: (843) 383-8038

Colby College
www.colby.edu
Admissions
4800 Mayflower Hill
Waterville, ME 04901-8848
Fax: (207) 859-4828
E-mail: admissions@colby.edu
Phone: (207) 859-4818

Colby Community College
www.colbycc.edu
Admissions
1255 South Range Avenue
Colby, KS 67701
Fax: (785) 460-4691
E-mail: doug.johnson@colbycc.edu
Phone: (785) 460-5498

Colby-Sawyer College
www.colby-sawyer.edu
Office of Admissions
541 Main Street
New London, NH 03257-7835
Fax: (603) 526-3452
E-mail: admissions@colby-sawyer.edu
Phone: (603) 526-3700

Colegio Pentecostal Mizpa
www.colmizpa.edu
DSO Student Dean
PO Box 20966
San Juan, PR 00928-0966
Fax: (787) 720-2012
E-mail: decanatoestudiante@colmizpa.edu
Phone: (787) 720-4476 ext. 228

Coleman College
www.coleman.edu
Office of International Admissions
8888 Balboa Avenue
San Diego, CA 92123
Fax: (619) 463-0162
E-mail: ateeple@coleman.edu
Phone: (619) 465-3990

Coleman College: San Marcos
www.coleman.edu
1284 West San Marcos Boulevard, Suite 110
San Marcos, CA 92069
Phone: (760) 747-3990

Colgate University
www.colgate.edu
13 Oak Drive
Hamilton, NY 13346-1383
Fax: (315) 228-7544
E-mail: ksryan@mail.colgate.edu
Phone: (315) 228-7401

College for Creative Studies
www.collegeforcreativestudies.edu
International Student Services
201 East Kirby
Detroit, MI 48202-4034
Fax: (313) 872-2739
E-mail: jdickey@collegeforcreativestudies.edu
Phone: (800) 952-2787

College of Alameda
alameda.peralta.edu
International Education
555 Ralph Appezzato Memorial Parkway
Alameda, CA 94501
Fax: (510) 748-5227
E-mail: jng@peralta.cc.ca.us
Phone: (510) 466-7295

College of the Albemarle
www.albemarle.cc.nc.us
Admissions
1208 North Road Street
PO Box 2327
Elizabeth City, NC 27906-2327
Fax: (252) 335-2011
E-mail: kkrentz@albemarle.cc.nc.us
Phone: (252) 335-0821 ext. 2220

College of the Atlantic
www.coa.edu
Admission
105 Eden Street
Bar Harbor, ME 04609
Fax: (207) 288-4126
E-mail: sbaker@coa.edu
Phone: (207) 288-5015

College of Business and Technology: Flagler
www.cbt.edu
International Students
8230 West Flagler Street
Miami, FL 33144
Fax: (305) 485-4411
E-mail: luis@cbt.edu
Phone: (786) 245-0227

College of Business and Technology: Kendall
www.cbt.edu
8991 SW 107 Avenue
Suite 200
Miami, FL 33176
E-mail: admissions@cbt.edu
Phone: (305) 273-4499

College of the Canyons
www.canyons.edu
International Students Programs
26455 Rockwell Canyon Road
Santa Clarita, CA 91355
Fax: (661) 259-8302
E-mail: isp@canyons.edu
Phone: (661) 362-3580

College of Charleston
www.cofc.edu
Admissions
Office of Admissions and Adult Student Services
66 George Street
Charleston, SC 29424-0001
Fax: (843) 953-6322
E-mail: admissions@cofc.edu
Phone: (843) 953-5670

College of Court Reporting
www.ccr.edu
111 West 10th Street, Suite 111
Hobart, IN 46342
Fax: (219) 942-1631
E-mail: information@ccr.edu
Phone: (219) 942-1459

College of the Desert
www.collegeofthedesert.edu
International Education Program
43-500 Monterey Avenue
Palm Desert, CA 92260
Fax: (760) 862-1361
E-mail: cdelgado@collegeofthedesert.edu
Phone: (760) 776-7205

College of DuPage
www.cod.edu
Admissions
425 Fawell Boulevard
Glen Ellyn, IL 60137-6599
Fax: (630) 790-2686
E-mail: carrma@cod.edu
Phone: (630) 942-2979

College of Eastern Utah
www.ceu.edu
International Student Affairs
451 East 400 North
Price, UT 84501
Fax: (435) 637-5418
E-mail: jane.johnson@ceu.edu
Phone: (435) 613-5333

College of the Holy Cross
www.holycross.edu
Admissions
One College Street
Fenwick 105
Worcester, MA 01610-2395
Fax: (508) 793-3888
E-mail: admissions@holycross.edu
Phone: (508) 793-2443

College of Idaho
www.collegeofidaho.edu
Admissions
2112 Cleveland Boulevard
Caldwell, ID 83605
Fax: (208) 459-5757
E-mail: admission@collegeofidaho.edu
Phone: (800) 224-3246 ext. 5534

College of Lake County
www.clcillinois.edu
International Education
19351 West Washington Street
Grayslake, IL 60030-1198
Fax: (847) 543-3733
E-mail: ssmith2@clcillinois.edu
Phone: (847) 543-2733

College of Marin: Kentfield
www.marin.edu
835 College Avenue
Kentfield, CA 94904
Phone: (415) 457-8811 ext. 7719

College of Mount St. Joseph
www.msj.edu
International Programs
5701 Delhi Road
Cincinnati, OH 45233-1670
Fax: (513) 244-4211
E-mail: international@mail.msj.edu
Phone: (513) 244-4241

College of Mount St. Vincent
www.mountsaintvincent.edu
Office of Admission
6301 Riverdale Avenue
Riverdale, NY 10471-1093
Fax: (718) 549-7945
E-mail: tim.nash@mountsaintvincent.edu
Phone: (718) 405-3268

The College of New Jersey
www.tcnj.edu
Admissions
Box 7718
Ewing, NJ 08628
Fax: (609) 637-5174
E-mail: admiss@tcnj.edu
Phone: (609) 771-2131

College of New Rochelle
www.cnr.edu
Admissions
29 Castle Place
New Rochelle, NY 10805-2339
Fax: (914) 654-5464
E-mail: admission@cnr.edu
Phone: (914) 654-5262

College of Notre Dame of Maryland
www.ndm.edu
Admissions Office
4701 North Charles Street
Baltimore, MD 21210
Fax: (410) 532-6287
E-mail: admiss@ndm.edu
Phone: (800) 435-0200

College of Office Technology
www.cot.edu
1520 West Division Street
Chicago, IL 60622-3312
Fax: (773) 278-0143
E-mail: info@cotedu.com
Phone: (773) 278-0042

College of the Ozarks
www.cofo.edu
Admissions
PO Box 17
Point Lookout, MO 65726-0017
Fax: (417) 335-2618
E-mail: admiss4@cofo.edu
Phone: (417) 334-6411 ext. 4218

College of the Redwoods
www.redwoods.edu
Enrollment Services
7351 Tompkins Hill Road
Eureka, CA 95501-9300
Fax: (707) 476-4406
E-mail: admissions@redwoods.edu
Phone: (707) 476-4200

College of Saint Mary
www.csm.edu
Admissions
7000 Mercy Road
Omaha, NE 68106
Fax: (402) 399-2412
E-mail: enroll@csm.edu
Phone: (800) 926-5534

College of Saint Rose
www.strose.edu
Undergraduate Admissions Office
432 Western Avenue
Albany, NY 12203
Fax: (518) 454-2013
E-mail: admit@mail.strose.edu
Phone: (518) 454-5150

College of Saint Thomas More
www.cstm.edu
3020 Lubbock Avenue
Fort Worth, TX 76109
Fax: (817) 924-3206
E-mail: jpatrick@cstm.edu
Phone: (817) 923-8459

College of San Mateo
www.collegeofsanmateo.edu
International Student Center
1700 West Hillsdale Boulevard
San Mateo, CA 94402-3784
Fax: (650) 574-6506
E-mail: villarealh@smccd.net
Phone: (415) 574-6525

College of Santa Fe
www.csf.edu
Office of Admissions
1600 Saint Michael's Drive
Santa Fe, NM 87505-7634
Fax: (505) 473-6129
E-mail: admissions@csf.edu
Phone: (800) 456-2673

College of the Sequoias
www.cos.edu
915 South Mooney Boulevard
Visalia, CA 93277
Fax: (559) 730-4820
E-mail: donaldm@cos.edu
Phone: (559) 737-4844

College of the Siskiyous
www.siskiyous.edu
Student Services
800 College Avenue
Weed, CA 96094-2899
Fax: (530) 938-5367
E-mail: info@siskiyous.edu
Phone: (530) 938-5374

College of Southern Idaho
www.csi.edu
Box 1238
Twin Falls, ID 83303-1238
Fax: (208) 736-3014
E-mail: kprestwich@csi.edu
Phone: (208) 732-6293

College of Southern Maryland
www.csmd.edu
Admissions Department
College of Southern Maryland-AOD
8730 Mitchell Road, POB 910
La Plata, MD 20646-0910
Fax: (301) 934-7698
E-mail: info@csmd.edu
Phone: (301) 934-7520

College of Southern Nevada
www.csn.edu
International Student Center
6375 West Charleston Boulevard
Las Vegas, NV 89146-1164
Fax: (702) 651-5821
E-mail: anneli_adams@ccsn.edu
Phone: (702) 651-5820

College of the Southwest
www.csw.edu
Office of Admissions
6610 Lovington Highway #506
Hobbs, NM 88240
Fax: (505) 392-6006
E-mail: admissions@csw.edu
Phone: (505) 392-6563 ext. 1007

College of St. Benedict
www.csbsju.edu
Admissions
PO Box 7155
Collegeville, MN 56321-7155
Fax: (320) 363-3206
E-mail: ryoung@csbsju.edu
Phone: (320) 363-2190

College of St. Catherine
www.stkate.edu
Aimee Thostenson
2004 Randolph Avenue #4-02
St. Paul, MN 55105
Fax: (651) 690-8824
E-mail: aethostenson@stkate.edu
Phone: (651) 690-6029

College of St. Elizabeth
www.cse.edu
2 Convent Road
Morristown, NJ 07960-6989
Fax: (973) 290-4710
E-mail: apply@cse.edu
Phone: (973) 290-4700

College of St. Joseph in Vermont
www.csj.edu
Director of Admissions
71 Clement Road
Rutland, VT 05701-3899
Fax: (802) 776-5258
E-mail: admissions@csj.edu
Phone: (802) 773-5900 ext. 3286

College of St. Scholastica
www.css.edu
Office of Admissions
1200 Kenwood Avenue
Duluth, MN 55811-4199
Fax: (218) 723-6394
E-mail: omeyer@css.edu
Phone: (218) 723-6045

College of Visual Arts
www.cva.edu
Director for Student Life
344 Summit Avenue
Saint Paul, MN 55102-2199
Fax: (651) 224-8854
E-mail: pgaines@cva.edu
Phone: (651) 224-3416

College of William and Mary
www.wm.edu
Office of Admissions
PO Box 8795
Williamsburg, VA 23187-8795
Fax: (757) 221-1242
E-mail: admiss@wm.edu
Phone: (757) 221-4223

College of Wooster
www.wooster.edu
Office of International Student Affairs
847 College Avenue
Wooster, OH 44691-2363
Fax: (330) 263-2594
E-mail: agates@wooster.edu
Phone: (330) 263-2545

CollegeAmerica: Fort Collins
www.collegeamerica.edu
4601 South Mason
Fort Collins, CO 80525
Phone: (970) 223-6060

Collin County Community College District
www.ccccd.edu
Admissions & Records Office
2800 East Spring Creek Parkway
Plano, TX 75074
Fax: (972) 881-5175
E-mail: smeinhardt@ccccd.edu
Phone: (972) 881-5710

Colorado Christian University
www.ccu.edu
Undergraduate Admission Office
8787 West Alameda Avenue
Lakewood, CO 80226
Fax: (303) 963-3201
E-mail: admission@ccu.edu
Phone: (303) 963-3200

Colorado College
www.coloradocollege.edu
Admission Office
14 East Cache La Poudre
Colorado Springs, CO 80903-9854
Fax: (719) 389-6816
E-mail: admission@coloradocollege.edu
Phone: (719) 389-6344

Colorado Mountain College
www.coloradomtn.edu
Enrollment Services
831 Grand Avenue
Glenwood Springs, CO 81601
Fax: (970) 947-8324
E-mail: bsommers@coloradomtn.edu
Phone: (800) 621-8559 ext. 8328

Colorado Northwestern Community College
www.cncc.edu
500 Kennedy Drive
Rangely, CO 81648
Fax: (970) 675-3343
E-mail: tresa.england@cncc.edu
Phone: (970) 675-2261 ext. 285

Colorado School of Mines
www.mines.edu
Office for International Students
Undergraduate Admissions
CSM Student Center - 1600 Maple Street
Golden, CO 80401
Fax: (303) 273-3099
E-mail: admit@mines.edu
Phone: (303) 273-3210

Colorado School of Trades
www.schooloftrades.com
Admissions
1575 Hoyt Street
Lakewood, CO 80215
Fax: (303) 233-4723
Phone: (303) 233-4697 ext. 16

Colorado State University
www.colostate.edu
Office of Admissions/Colorado State
University
1062 Campus Delivery
Fort Collins, CO 80523-1062
Fax: (970) 491-7799
E-mail: admissions@colostate.edu
Phone: (970) 491-5457

Colorado State University: Pueblo
www.colostate-pueblo.edu
International Programs
2200 Bonforte Boulevard
Pueblo, CO 81001-4901
Fax: (719) 549-2221
E-mail: intprog@colostate-pueblo.edu
Phone: (719) 549-2329

Colorado Technical University
www.coloradotech.edu
Admissions
4435 North Chestnut Street
Colorado Springs, CO 80907
Fax: (719) 598-3740
E-mail: cosadmissions@coloradotech.edu
Phone: (719) 598-0200

Columbia Basin College
www.columbiabasin.edu
Admissions
2600 North 20th Avenue
Pasco, WA 99301
Fax: (509) 546-0401
E-mail: pmcgarry@columbiabasin.edu
Phone: (509) 542-5500

Columbia Centro Universitario: Yauco
www.columbiaco.edu
Box 3062
Yauco, PR 00698-3062
Fax: (787) 744-7031
E-mail: rpadilla@columbiaco.edu
Phone: (787) 743-4041

Columbia College
www.gocolumbia.org
Counseling Office
11600 Columbia College Drive
Sonora, CA 95370
Fax: (209) 588-5330
E-mail: ramsarnna@yosemite.cc.ca.us
Phone: (209) 588-5109

Columbia College
www.ccis.edu
Admissions
1001 Rogers Street
Columbia, MO 65216
Fax: (573) 875-7506
E-mail: jhwilkerson@ccis.edu
Phone: (573) 875-7343

Columbia College
www.columbiacollegesc.edu
Admission
1301 Columbia College Drive
Columbia, SC 29203
Fax: (803) 786-3674
E-mail: admissions@colacollege.edu
Phone: (803) 786-3871

Columbia College Chicago
www.colum.edu
International Student Admissions
600 South Michigan Avenue
Room 301
Chicago, IL 60605-1996
Fax: (312) 344-8024
E-mail: gposejpal@colum.edu
Phone: (312) 344-7458

Columbia College: Hollywood
www.columbiacollege.edu
Admissions Office
18618 Oxnard Street
Tarzana, CA 91356
Fax: (818) 345-9053
E-mail: djustin@columbiacollege.edu
Phone: (818) 345-8414

Columbia International University
www.ciu.edu
Admissions Office
PO Box 3122
Columbia, SC 29230-3122
Fax: (803) 786-4209
E-mail: yesciu@ciu.edu
Phone: (800) 777-2227 ext. 5050

Columbia Southern University
www.columbiasouthern.edu
25326 Canal Road
PO Box 3110
Orange Beach, AL 36561
Fax: (251) 981-3815
E-mail: admissions@columbiasouthern.edu
Phone: (251) 981-3771 ext. 521

Columbia Union College
www.cuc.edu
Admissions
7600 Flower Avenue
Takoma Park, MD 20912
Fax: (301) 891-4230
E-mail: ejohn@cuc.edu
Phone: (301) 891-4079

Columbia University
www.columbia.edu
Undergraduate Admissions
212 Hamilton Hall, MC 2807
1130 Amsterdam Avenue
New York, NY 10027
Fax: (212) 854-1209
Phone: (212) 854-2522

**Columbia University: School of General
Studies**
www.gs.columbia.edu
Admissions
408 Lewisohn Hall, Mail Code 4101
2970 Broadway
New York, NY 10027
Fax: (212) 854-6316
E-mail: gsdegree@columbia.edu
Phone: (212) 854-2772

Columbia-Greene Community College
www.sunycgcc.edu
Admissions
4400 Route 23
Hudson, NY 12534
Fax: (518) 822-2015
E-mail: pepitone@sunycgcc.edu
Phone: (518) 828-4181 ext. 5513

Columbus College of Art and Design
www.ccad.edu
International Student Advisor
107 North Ninth Street
Columbus, OH 43215-3875
Fax: (614) 232-8344
E-mail: jneeley@ccad.edu
Phone: (614) 224-9101 ext. 3265

Columbus State Community College
www.cscc.edu
International Enrollment Services
550 East Spring Street
Box 1609
Columbus, OH 43216-1609
Fax: (614) 287-6019
E-mail: istudent@cscc.edu
Phone: (614) 287-2074

Columbus State University
www.colstate.edu
Admissions Office
4225 University Avenue
Columbus, GA 31907-5645
Fax: (706) 568-5091
E-mail: brinson_sherry@colstate.edu
Phone: (706) 568-2035

Columbus Technical College
www.columbustech.org
Student Services
928 Manchester Expressway
Columbus, GA 31904
Fax: (404) 649-1885
Phone: (706) 649-1800

Commonwealth Institute of Funeral Service
www.commonwealthinst.org
415 Barren Springs Drive
Houston, TX 77090-5913
Fax: (281) 873-5232
Phone: (281) 873-0262

Commonwealth Technical Institute
www.hgac.org
727 Goucher Street
Johnstown, PA 15905-3902
Phone: (814) 255-8237

Community College of Allegheny County
www.ccac.edu
International Student Services Office
800 Allegheny Avenue
Pittsburgh, PA 15233
Phone: (412) 237-2629

Community College of Aurora
www.ccaurora.edu
Advising
16000 East CentreTech Parkway
Aurora, CO 80011-9036
Fax: (303) 361-7401
E-mail: dino.madariaga@cca.cccoes.edu
Phone: (303) 360-4797

Community College of Baltimore County
www.ccbcmd.edu
Office of Admissions
7201 Rossville Boulevard
Baltimore, MD 21237
Fax: (410) 719-6546
E-mail: ddrake@ccbcmd.edu
Phone: (410) 455-4394

Community College of Beaver County
www.ccbc.edu
Registrar
One Campus Drive
Monaca, PA 15061-2588
Fax: (724) 728-7599
E-mail: dan.slater@ccbc.edu
Phone: (724) 775-8561 ext. 254

Community College of Denver
www.ccd.edu
Associate Director, Enrollment Services
Campus Box 201, PO Box 173363
Denver, CO 80217-3363
Fax: (303) 556-2431
E-mail: paula.marinez@ccd.edu
Phone: (303) 556-2430

Community College of Philadelphia
www.ccp.edu
1700 Spring Garden Street
Philadelphia, PA 19130-3991
Fax: (215) 972-6324
E-mail: internationaladmissions@ccp.edu
Phone: (215) 751-8981

Community College of Rhode Island
www.ccri.edu
Assistant Dean of Enrollment Services
400 East Avenue
Warwick, RI 02886-1807
Fax: (401) 825-2394
E-mail: nfigueroa@ccri.edu
Phone: (401) 333-7121

Community College of Vermont
www.ccv.edu
PO BOX 120
Waterbury, VT 05676-0120
Fax: (802) 254-3473
Phone: (802) 241-1192

Concord University
www.concord.edu
Admissions Office
PO Box 1000
Athens, WV 24712-1000
Fax: (304) 384-9044
E-mail: admissions@concord.edu
Phone: (304) 384-5248

Concorde Career College: Garden Grove
www.concorde.edu
12951 Euclid Street, #101
Garden Grove, CA 92840
E-mail: agueco@concorde.edu
Phone: (714) 703-1900

Concorde Career College: North Hollywood
www.concordecareercolleges.com
12412 Victory Boulevard
North Hollywood, CA 91606
Fax: (818) 766-1587
Phone: (818) 766-8151

Concorde Career College: San Bernardino
www.concorde.edu
201 East Airport Dr.
San Bernardino, CA 92408

Concorde Career College: San Diego
www.concorde.edu
4393 Imperial Avenue
San Diego, CA 92113
E-mail: creese@concorde.edu

Concordia College
www.concordiaselma.edu
1804 Green Street
Selma, AL 36701
Fax: (314) 874-5755
Phone: (334) 874-7143

Concordia College
www.concordia-ny.edu
Admission
171 White Plains Road
Bronxville, NY 10708
Fax: (914) 395-4636
E-mail: jcj@concordia-ny.edu
Phone: (914) 337-9300 ext. 2152

Concordia College: Moorhead
www.concordiacollege.edu
Admissions Office
901 Eighth Street South
Moorhead, MN 56562-9981
Fax: (218) 299-4720
E-mail: admissions@cord.edu
Phone: (800) 699-9897

Concordia University
www.cui.edu
International Admissions and Retention
1530 Concordia West
Irvine, CA 92612-3299
Fax: (949) 854-6852
E-mail: lonnie.lee@cui.edu
Phone: (949) 854-8002 ext. 1837

Concordia University
www.cuchicago.edu
Undergraduate Admission
7400 Augusta Street
River Forest, IL 60305-1499
Fax: (708) 209-3473
E-mail: crfadmis@cuchicago.edu
Phone: (708) 209-3100

Concordia University
www.cuaa.edu
Office of Admissions
4090 Geddes Road
Ann Arbor, MI 48105
Fax: (734) 995-4610
E-mail: admissions@cuaa.edu
Phone: (800) 253-0680

Concordia University
www.cune.edu
Office of Admission
800 North Columbia Avenue
Seward, NE 68434-1556
Fax: (402) 643-4073
E-mail: admiss@cune.edu
Phone: (800) 535-5494 ext. 7233

Concordia University
www.cu-portland.edu
Admissions
2811 Northeast Holman Street
Portland, OR 97211-6099
Fax: (503) 280-8531
E-mail: admissions@cu-portland.edu
Phone: (503) 493-6582

Concordia University at Austin
www.concordia.edu
Office of Admissions
3400 Interstate 35 North
Austin, TX 78705-2799
Fax: (512) 459-8517
E-mail: admissions@concordia.edu
Phone: (512) 486-1106

Concordia University Wisconsin
www.cuw.edu
Admissions
12800 North Lake Shore Drive
Mequon, WI 53097
Fax: (262) 243-4545
E-mail: ken.gaschk@cuw.edu
Phone: (262) 243-4305

Concordia University: St. Paul
www.csp.edu
Director of Undergraduate Admission
275 Syndicate Street North
St. Paul, MN 55104-5494
Fax: (651) 603-6320
E-mail: admission@csp.edu
Phone: (651) 641-8230

Connecticut College
www.conncoll.edu
270 Mohegan Avenue
New London, CT 06320-4196
Fax: (860) 439-4301
E-mail: admit@conncoll.edu
Phone: (860) 439-2200

Conservatory of Music of Puerto Rico
www.cmpr.edu
Counselor
Rafael Lamar #350 Esq. Roosevelt
San Juan, PR 00918-2199
Fax: (787) 758-8268
E-mail: pruibal@cmpr.gobierno.pr
Phone: (787) 751-0160 ext. 251

Contra Costa College
www.contracosta.edu
2600 Mission Bell Drive
San Pablo, CA 94806
Fax: (510) 236-6768
Phone: (510) 235-7800 ext. 4210

Converse College
www.converse.edu
Admissions
580 East Main Street
Spartanburg, SC 29302-0006
Fax: (864) 596-9225
E-mail: aaron.meis@converse.edu
Phone: (864) 596-9746

Cooking & Hospitality Institute of Chicago
www.chic.edu
Admissions
361 West Chestnut
Chicago, IL 60610-3050
Fax: (312) 798-2923
E-mail: vwieting@chicnet.org
Phone: (312) 544-7648

Cooper Union for the Advancement of Science and Art
www.cooper.edu
Admissions and Records
30 Cooper Square, Suite 300
New York, NY 10003-7183
Fax: (212) 353-4342
E-mail: falls@cooper.edu
Phone: (212) 353-4120

Copper Mountain College
www.cmccd.edu
6162 Rotary Way
PO Box 1398
Joshua Tree, CA 92252
Fax: (760) 366-5257
Phone: (760) 366-3791 ext. 4232

Coppin State University
www.coppin.edu
Office of Admissions
2500 West North Avenue
Baltimore, MD 21216
Fax: (410) 523-7351
E-mail: mgross@coppin.edu
Phone: (410) 951-3600

Corban College
www.corban.edu
Admissions
5000 Deer Park Drive SE
Salem, OR 97317-9392
Fax: (503) 585-4316
E-mail: admissions@wbc.edu
Phone: (503) 375-7005

Corcoran College of Art and Design
www.corcoran.edu
Office of Admissions
500 17th Street, NW
Washington, DC 20006-4804
Fax: (202) 639-1830
E-mail: admissions@corcoran.org
Phone: (202) 639-1814

Cornell College
www.cornellcollege.edu
Admissions
600 First Street SW
Mount Vernon, IA 52314-1098
Fax: (319) 895-4451
E-mail: international@cornellcollege.edu
Phone: (319) 895-4159

Cornell University
www.cornell.edu
Undergraduate Admissions
410 Thurston Avenue
Ithaca, NY 14850-2488
Fax: (607) 255-0659
E-mail: admissions@cornell.edu
Phone: (607) 255-5241

Cornerstone University
www.cornerstone.edu
Dean of Enrollment Management
1001 East Beltline NE
Grand Rapids, MI 49525-5897
Fax: (616) 222-1418
E-mail: admissions@cornerstone.edu
Phone: (616) 222-1426

Corning Community College
www.corning-cc.edu
Admissions
One Academic Drive
Corning, NY 14830
Fax: (607) 962-9582
E-mail: kbrown7@corning-cc.edu
Phone: (607) 962-9151

Cornish College of the Arts
www.cornish.edu
Admissions
1000 Lenora Street
Seattle, WA 98121
Fax: (206) 720-1011
E-mail: admissions@cornish.edu
Phone: (206) 726-5016

Cosumnes River College
www.crc.losrios.edu
8401 Center Parkway
Sacramento, CA 95823
Fax: (916) 691-7467
E-mail: kimuraj@exi.crc.losrios.cc.ca.us
Phone: (916) 691-7469

Cottey College
www.cottey.edu
Office of Enrollment Management
1000 West Austin Boulevard
Nevada, MO 64772
Fax: (417) 667-1025
E-mail: enrollmgt@cottey.edu
Phone: (417) 667-8181

County College of Morris
www.ccm.edu
Admissions
214 Center Grove Road
Randolph, NJ 07869-2086
Fax: (973) 328-5199
E-mail: julmer@ccm.edu
Phone: (973) 328-5095

Court Reporting Institute of Houston
www.crid.com
13101 Northwest Freeway, Suite 100
Houston, TX 77040
Fax: (713) 996-8360
E-mail: ssanders@crid.com
Phone: (713) 996-8300

Covenant College
www.covenant.edu
Admissions
14049 Scenic Highway
Lookout Mountain, GA 30750
Fax: (706) 820-0893
E-mail: todd.willison@covenant.edu
Phone: (706) 419-1230

Cowley County Community College
www.cowley.edu
Director of Admissions
PO Box 1147
Arkansas City, KS 67005-1147
Fax: (620) 441-5350
E-mail: schears@cowley.edu
Phone: (620) 442-0430

Crafton Hills College
www.craftonhills.edu
Counseling
11711 Sand Canyon Road
Yucaipa, CA 92399-1799
Fax: (909) 794-3863
E-mail: gmolino@craftonhills.edu
Phone: (909) 389-3366

Creighton University
www.creighton.edu
International Programs
2500 California Plaza
Omaha, NE 68178-0001
Fax: (402) 280-2211
E-mail: mkrane@creighton.edu
Phone: (402) 280-2221

Crichton College
www.crichton.edu
Admissions
255 North Highland
Memphis, TN 38111-1375
Fax: (901) 320-9791
E-mail: mtaylor@crichton.edu
Phone: (800) 960-9777 ext. 9753

Criswell College
www.criswell.edu
4010 Gaston Avenue
Dallas, TX 75246-1537
Fax: (214) 818-1310
E-mail: tccsa@criswell.edu
Phone: (214) 818-1305

Crowder College
www.crowder.edu
Coordinator of International Studies
601 LaClede Avenue
Neosho, MO 64850
Fax: (417) 455-5731
E-mail: jkoch@crowder.edu
Phone: (417) 455-5550

Crowley's Ridge College
www.crowleysridgecollege.edu
Registrar
100 College Drive
Paragould, AR 72450
Fax: (870) 236-7748
E-mail: pmcfadden@crowleysridgecollege.edu
Phone: (870) 236-6901

Cuesta College
www.cuesta.org
Box 8106
San Luis Obispo, CA 93403
Fax: (805) 546-3975
E-mail: admit@bass.cuesta.cc.ca.us
Phone: (805) 546-3140

Culinary Institute of America
www.ciachef.edu
Foreign Student Adviser
1946 Campus Drive
Hyde Park, NY 12538-1499
Fax: (845) 451-1068
E-mail: admissions@culinary.edu
Phone: (845) 452-9430

Culver-Stockton College
www.culver.edu
Registrar
One College Hill
Canton, MO 63435-1299
Fax: (573) 288-6616
E-mail: mellison@culver.edu
Phone: (573) 288-6541

Cumberland County College
www.cccnj.edu
PO Box 1500
3322 College Drive
Vineland, NJ 08362-9912
Fax: (609) 691-6157
Phone: (856) 691-8600

Cumberland University
www.cumberland.edu
Admissions
One Cumberland Square
Lebanon, TN 37087
Fax: (615) 444-2569
E-mail: ppope@cumberland.edu
Phone: (615) 444-2562 ext. 1224

Curry College
www.curry.edu
Admission
1071 Blue Hill Avenue
Milton, MA 02186-9984
Fax: (617) 333-2114
E-mail: sellis@curry.edu
Phone: (617) 333-2210

Curtis Institute of Music
www.curtis.edu
1726 Locust Street
Philadelphia, PA 19103-6187
Fax: (215) 893-7900
E-mail: admissions@curtis.edu
Phone: (215) 893-5262

**Cuyahoga Community College:
Metropolitan Campus**
www.tri-c.edu
Admissions
2900 Community College Avenue
Cleveland, OH 44115-2878
Fax: (216) 696-2567
E-mail: george.koussa@tri-c.edu
Phone: (216) 987-4167

Cuyamaca College
www.cuyamaca.net
Admissions and Records
900 Rancho San Diego Parkway
El Cajon, CA 92019-4304
Fax: (619) 660-4575
E-mail: Vanessa.Saenz@gcccd.edu
Phone: (619) 660-4565

Cypress College
www.cypresscollege.edu
International Students
9200 Valley View Street
Cypress, CA 90630
Fax: (714) 484-7446
E-mail: yhan@CypressCollege.edu
Phone: (714) 484-7050

Daemen College
www.daemen.edu
Admissions
4380 Main Street
Amherst, NY 14226-3592
Fax: (716) 839-8229
E-mail: admissions@daemen.edu
Phone: (716) 839-8225

Dakota County Technical College
www.dctc.edu
Office of Admissions
1300 145th Street East
Rosemount, MN 55068
Fax: (651) 423-8775
E-mail: patrick.lair@dctc.edu
Phone: (651) 423-8399

Dakota State University
www.dsu.edu
Enrollment Services
820 North Washington Avenue
Admissions Office
Madison, SD 57042
Fax: (605) 256-5020
E-mail: dsuinfo@dsu.edu
Phone: (605) 256-5139

Dakota Wesleyan University
www.dwu.edu
Academic Affairs Office
1200 West University Avenue
Mitchell, SD 57301-4398
Fax: (605) 995-2645
E-mail: admissions@dwu.edu
Phone: (800) 333-8506 ext. 2645

Dallas Baptist University
www.dbu.edu
International Office
3000 Mountain Creek Parkway
Dallas, TX 75211-9299
Fax: (214) 333-5409
E-mail: globalinfo@dbu.edu
Phone: (214) 333-5426

Dana College
www.dana.edu
Office of Admissions
2848 College Drive
Blair, NE 68008-1099
Fax: (402) 426-7386
E-mail: jwindmul@dana.edu
Phone: (402) 426-7372

Daniel Webster College
www.dwc.edu
Admissions
20 University Drive
Nashua, NH 03063
Fax: (603) 577-6001
E-mail: admissions@dwc.edu
Phone: (603) 577-6600

Danville Area Community College
www.dacc.edu
2000 East Main Street
Danville, IL 61832
Fax: (217) 443-8560
Phone: (217) 443-8803

Danville Community College
www.dcc.vccs.edu
Admissions
1008 South Main Street
Danville, VA 24541
Fax: (434) 797-8451
E-mail: pcastiglione@dcc.vccs.edu
Phone: (434) 797-8420

Dartmouth College
www.dartmouth.edu
Admissions Office
6016 McNutt Hall
Hanover, NH 03755
Fax: (603) 646-1216
E-mail:
admissions.international@dartmouth.edu
Phone: (603) 646-2875

Darton College
www.darton.edu
Student Affairs
2400 Gillionville Road
Albany, GA 31707-3098
Fax: (229) 317-1100
E-mail: dacia.stone@darton.edu
Phone: (229) 317-6866

Davenport University
www.davenport.edu
Senior Advisor for Study Abroad and
International Students
6191 Kraft Avenue SE
Grand Rapids, MI 49512-5926
Fax: (616) 554-5239
E-mail: Alex.Akulli@davenport.edu
Phone: (616) 698-7111

David N. Myers University
www.myers.edu
3921 Chester Avenue
Cleveland, OH 44114
Fax: (216) 361-9274
E-mail: Admissions@myers.edu
Phone: (216) 432-8992

Davidson College
www.davidson.edu
Admissions Office
Box 7156
Davidson, NC 28035-7156
Fax: (704) 894-2016
E-mail: admission@davidson.edu
Phone: (704) 894-2230

Davis and Elkins College
www.davisandelkins.edu
Admissions
100 Campus Drive
Elkins, WV 26241
Fax: (304) 637-1800
E-mail: summers@davisandelkins.edu
Phone: (304) 637-1230

Davis College
www.davisny.edu
Enrollment Management
400 Riverside Drive
Johnson City, NY 13790
Fax: (607) 729-2962
E-mail: admissions@davisny.edu
Phone: (607) 729-1581 ext. 406

Dawson Community College
www.dawson.edu
300 College Drive
Box 421
Glendive, MT 59330
Fax: (406) 377-8132
E-mail: lholte@dawson.edu
Phone: (406) 377-3396 ext. 404

Daymar College: Louisville
www.daymarcollege.edu
4400 Breckinridge Lane, Suite 415
Louisville, KY 40218
Phone: (502) 495-1040

Daytona Beach Community College
www.dbc.edu
Admissions Office
DBCC Admissions Office
1200 International Speedway Boulevard
Daytona Beach, FL 32114-2811
Fax: (386) 506-4489
E-mail: admissions@dbcc.edu
Phone: (386) 506-3000 ext. 3059

De Anza College
www.deanza.edu
Foreign Student Adviser
21250 Stevens Creek Boulevard
Cupertino, CA 95014
Fax: (408) 864-5638
E-mail: webreg@fhda.edu
Phone: (408) 864-8813

Dean College
www.dean.edu
Admissions
99 Main Street
Franklin, MA 02038-1994
Fax: (508) 541-8726
E-mail: cwalker@dean.edu
Phone: (508) 541-1512

Deep Springs College
www.deepsprings.edu
Applications Committee
Applications Committee
HC 72 Box 45001
Dyer, NV 89010-9803
Fax: (760) 872-4466
E-mail: apcom@deepsprings.edu
Phone: (760) 872-2000

Defiance College
www.defiance.edu
Admissions
701 North Clinton Street
Defiance, OH 43512-1695
Fax: (419) 783-2468
E-mail: bharsha@defiance.edu
Phone: (419) 783-2365

DeKalb Technical College
www.dekalbtech.edu
Admissions, International Student Advisors
495 North Indian Creek Drive
Clarkston, GA 30021-2397
Fax: (404) 294-3424
E-mail: nguyeny@dekalbtech.edu
Phone: (404) 297-9522 ext. 1156

Del Mar College
www.delmar.edu
Admissions and Registrar's Office
101 Baldwin Boulevard
Corpus Christi, TX 78404-3897
Fax: (361) 698-1595
E-mail: bthomps@delmar.edu
Phone: (361) 698-1255

Delaware State University
www.desu.edu
1200 North DuPont Highway
Dover, DE 19901
Fax: (302) 857-6103
E-mail: gcheatha@desu.edu
Phone: (302) 857-6103

Delaware Valley College
www.delval.edu
Admissions Office
700 East Butler Avenue
Doylestown, PA 18901-2697
Fax: (215) 230-2968
E-mail: admitme@delval.edu
Phone: (215) 489-2211

Delgado Community College
www.dcc.edu
Office of Admissions and Enrollment Services
615 City Park Avenue
New Orleans, LA 70119
Fax: (504) 483-1895
E-mail: gboutt@dcc.edu
Phone: (504) 671-5099

Delta College
www.delta.edu
Admissions
1961 Delta Road
University Center, MI 48710
Fax: (989) 667-2202
E-mail: danielsegura@delta.edu
Phone: (989) 686-9320

Delta School of Business & Technology
www.deltatech.edu
517 Broad Street
Lake Charles, LA 70601
Fax: (337) 436-5151
E-mail: barbara@deltatech.edu
Phone: (337) 439-5765

Delta State University
www.deltastate.edu
International Students Office
Kent Wyatt Hall Rm 117
Cleveland, MS 38733
Fax: (662) 846-4016
E-mail: makelly@deltastate.edu
Phone: (662) 846-4867

Denison University
www.denison.edu
Coordinator of International Admissions
Box H
Granville, OH 43023
Fax: (740) 587-6306
E-mail: leavell@denison.edu
Phone: (740) 587-6789

Denmark Technical College
www.denmarktech.edu
Solomon Blatt Boulevard
PO Box 327
Denmark, SC 29042
Fax: (803) 793-5942
Phone: (803) 793-5176

DePaul University
www.depaul.edu
Associate Director, International Admission
1 East Jackson Boulevard
Chicago, IL 60604-2287
Fax: (312) 362-8521
E-mail: kchrist2@depaul.edu
Phone: (312) 362-8300

DePauw University
www.depauw.edu
Admission
101 East Seminary Street
Greencastle, IN 46135-1611
Fax: (765) 658-4007
E-mail: rkonowicz@depauw.edu
Phone: (765) 658-4006

Des Moines Area Community College
www.dmacc.edu
International Student Advisor
2006 South Ankeny Boulevard
Ankeny, IA 50023-3993
Fax: (515) 964-6391
E-mail: khuang@dmacc.edu
Phone: (515) 964-6471

DeSales University
www.desales.edu
Enrollment Services
2755 Station Avenue
Center Valley, PA 18034-9568
Fax: (610) 282-0131
E-mail: peter.rautzhan@desales.edu
Phone: (610) 282-4443

Design Institute of San Diego
www.disd.edu
8555 Commerce Avenue
San Diego, CA 92121
Fax: (858) 566-2711
Phone: (858) 566-1200

DeVry Institute of Technology: New York
www.devry.edu
3020 Thomson Avenue
Long Island City, NY 11101-3051
Fax: (630) 571-0317
Phone: (630) 571-7700 ext. 3150

DeVry University: Addison
www.devry.edu
1221 North Swift Road
Addison, IL 60101-6106
Fax: (630) 571-0317
Phone: (630) 571-7700 ext. 3150

DeVry University: Alpharetta
www.devry.edu
2555 Northwinds Parkway
Alpharetta, GA 30004
Fax: (630) 571-0317
E-mail: admissions@devry.edu
Phone: (630) 571-7700 ext. 3150

DeVry University: Arlington
www.devry.edu
2450 Crystal Drive
Arlington, VA 22202
Fax: (630) 571-0317
E-mail: admissions@crys.devry.edu
Phone: (630) 571-7700 ext. 4006

DeVry University: Bethesda
www.devry.edu
4550 Montgomery Avenue, Suite 100 N
Bethesda, MD 20814
Fax: (301) 652-8577
Phone: (301) 652-8477

DeVry University: Charlotte
www.devry.edu
4521 Sharon Road
Charlotte, NC 28211
Phone: (704) 362-2345

DeVry University: Chicago
www.devry.edu
International Student Coordinator
3300 North Campbell Avenue
Chicago, IL 60618-5994
Fax: (630) 571-0317
E-mail: admissions2@devry.edu
Phone: (630) 571-7700 ext. 3150

DeVry University: Columbus
www.devry.edu
International Student Coordinator
1350 Alum Creek Drive
Columbus, OH 43209-2705
Fax: (630) 571-0317
E-mail: admissions@devry.edu
Phone: (630) 571-7700 ext. 3150

DeVry University: Decatur
www.devry.edu
International Student Coordinator
250 North Arcadia Avenue
Decatur, GA 30030-2198
Fax: (630) 571-0317
E-mail: dsilva@admin.atl.devry.edu
Phone: (630) 571-7700 ext. 3150

DeVry University: Edina
www.devry.edu
7700 France Avenue South, Suite 575
Edina, MN 55435
Phone: (877) 733-3879

DeVry University: Federal Way
www.devry.edu
3600 South 344th Way
Federal Way, WA 98001-9558
Fax: (630) 571-0317
E-mail: admissions@sea.devry.edu
Phone: (630) 571-7700 ext. 4006

DeVry University: Fort Washington
www.devry.edu
International Student Coordinator
1140 Virginia Drive
Fort Washington, PA 19034-3204
Fax: (630) 571-0317
E-mail: admissions@phi.devry.edu
Phone: (630) 571-7700 ext. 3150

DeVry University: Fremont
www.devry.edu
6600 Dumbarton Circle
Fremont, CA 94555-3615
Fax: (630) 571-0317
Phone: (630) 571-7700 ext. 3150

DeVry University: Henderson
www.devry.edu
2490 Paseo Verde Parkway, Suite 150
Henderson, NV 89074
Phone: (702) 933-9700

DeVry University: Houston
www.devry.edu
11125 Equity Drive
Houston, TX 77041-8217
Fax: (713) 896-7650
Phone: (713) 973-3000

DeVry University: Indianapolis
www.devry.edu
9100 Keystone Crossing, Suite 350
Indianapolis, IN 46240
Phone: (866) 513-3879

DeVry University: Irving
www.devry.edu
International Student Coordinator
4800 Regent Boulevard
Dallas, TX 75063-2439
Fax: (630) 571-0317
E-mail: cwilliams@mail.dal.devry.edu
Phone: (630) 571-7700 ext. 3150

DeVry University: Kansas City
www.devry.edu
International Student Coordinator
11224 Holmes Street
Kansas City, MO 64131-3626
Fax: (630) 571-0317
E-mail: ssmeed@kc.devry.edu
Phone: (630) 571-7700 ext. 3150

DeVry University: Long Beach
www.devry.edu
3880 Kilroy Airport Way
Long Beach, CA 90806
Fax: (630) 571-0317
Phone: (630) 571-7700 ext. 3150

DeVry University: Memphis
www.devry.edu
6401 Poplar Avenue, Ste. 600
Memphis, TN 38119

DeVry University: Milwaukee
www.devry.edu
100 East Wisconsin Avenue, Suite 2550
Milwaukee, WI 53202
Phone: (414) 278-7677

DeVry University: Miramar
www.devry.edu
International Student Coordinator
2300 Southwest 145th Avenue
Miramar, FL 33027
Fax: (630) 571-0317
E-mail: openhouse@mir.devry.edu
Phone: (630) 571-7700 ext. 3150

DeVry University: North Brunswick
www.devry.edu
International Student Coordinator
630 US Highway One
North Brunswick, NJ 08902-3362
Fax: (630) 571-0317
E-mail: admissions@devry.edu
Phone: (630) 571-7700 ext. 3150

DeVry University: Oklahoma City Center
www.devry.edu
Lakepointe Towers, 4013 NW Expressway
Street
Oklahoma City, OK 73116

DeVry University: Online
www.devry.edu
One Tower Lane
Oakbrook Terrace, IL 60181

DeVry University: Orlando
www.devry.edu
4000 Millennia Boulevard
Orlando, FL 32839-2426
Fax: (630) 571-0317
E-mail: krochford@orl.devry.edu
Phone: (630) 571-7700 ext. 3150

DeVry University: Phoenix
www.devry.edu
International Student Coordinator
2149 West Dunlap Avenue
Phoenix, AZ 85021-2995
Fax: (630) 571-0317
E-mail: admissions@phx.devry.edu
Phone: (630) 571-7700 ext. 3150

DeVry University: Pomona
www.devry.edu
901 Corporate Center Drive
Pomona, CA 91768-2642
Fax: (630) 517-0317
Phone: (630) 571-7700 ext. 3150

DeVry University: Portland
www.devry.edu
Peterkort Center II
9755 Southwest Barnes Road, Suite 150
Portland, OR 97225
Phone: (866) 543-3879

DeVry University: Sandy
9350 South 150 East, Suite 420
Sandy, UT 84070

DeVry University: Sherman Oaks
www.devry.edu
15301 Ventura Boulevard, D-100
Sherman Oaks, CA 91403
Fax: (630) 571-0317
Phone: (630) 571-7700 ext. 4006

DeVry University: Tinley Park
www.devry.edu
18624 West Creek Drive
Tinley Park, IL 60477-6243
Fax: (630) 571-0317
Phone: (630) 571-7700 ext. 3150

DeVry University: Westminster
www.devry.edu
1870 West 122 Avenue
Westminster, CO 80234-2010
Fax: (630) 571-0317
E-mail: denver-admissions@den.devry.edu
Phone: (630) 571-7700 ext. 3150

Diablo Valley College
www.dvc.edu
International Student Admissions and Services
321 Golf Club Road
Pleasant Hill, CA 94523
Fax: (925) 691-9503
E-mail: gzarabozo@dvc.edu
Phone: (925) 685-1230 ext. 2075

Dickinson College
www.dickinson.edu
PO Box 1773
Carlisle, PA 17013-2896
Fax: (717) 245-1442
E-mail: flemingd@dickinson.edu
Phone: (717) 245-1375

Dickinson State University
www.dsu.nodak.edu
Center for Multicultural Affairs
291 Campus Drive
Campus Box 169
Dickinson, ND 58601-4896
Fax: (701) 483-2831
E-mail: thy.yang@dickinsonstate.edu
Phone: (701) 483-2598

DigiPen Institute of Technology
www.digipen.edu
Admissions Office
5001-150th Avenue Northeast
Redmond, WA 98052
Fax: (425) 558-0378
E-mail: admissions@digipen.edu
Phone: (425) 558-0299

Dillard University
www.dillard.edu
Admissions
2601 Gentilly Boulevard
New Orleans, LA 70122-3097
Fax: (504) 816-4895
E-mail: lnash@dillard.edu
Phone: (800) 216-6637

Dine College
www.dinecollege.edu
Registrar
Box 67
Tsaile, AZ 86556
Fax: (928) 724-3349
E-mail: louise@dinecollege.edu
Phone: (928) 724-6630

Divine Word College
www.dwci.edu
102 Jacoby Drive SW
PO Box 380
Epworth, IA 52045
E-mail: svdvocations@dwci.edu
Phone: (563) 876-3332

Dixie State College of Utah
www.dixie.edu
International Student Admissions
225 South 700 East
St. George, UT 84770-3876
Fax: (435) 656-4070
E-mail: callahan@dixie.edu
Phone: (435) 652-7689

Doane College
www.doane.edu
Midwest Institute
1014 Boswell Avenue
Crete, NE 68333
Fax: (402) 826-8592
E-mail: mfranklin@doane.edu
Phone: (402) 826-8215

Dodge City Community College
www.dccc.cc.ks.us
2501 North 14th Avenue
Dodge City, KS 67801-2399
Fax: (620) 227-9227
E-mail: wmcclure@dc3.edu
Phone: (620) 227-9207

Dominican College of Blauvelt
www.dc.edu
Admissions
470 Western Highway
Orangeburg, NY 10962-1210
Fax: (845) 365-3150
E-mail: joyce.elbe@dc.edu
Phone: (845) 848-7900

Dominican School of Philosophy and Theology
www.dspt.edu
Admissions Office
2301 Vine Street
Berkeley, CA 94708
Fax: (510) 849-1372
E-mail: admissions@dspt.edu
Phone: (510) 883-2073

Dominican University
www.dom.edu
Undergraduate Office of Admissions
7900 West Division Street
River Forest, IL 60305-1099
Fax: (708) 524-5990
E-mail: domadmis@dom.edu
Phone: (708) 524-6800

Dominican University of California
www.dominican.edu
Admissions Office
50 Acacia Avenue
San Rafael, CA 94901-2298
Fax: (415) 485-3214
E-mail: mdillon@dominican.edu
Phone: (415) 485-3206

Dona Ana Branch Community College of New Mexico State University
www.dacc.nmsu.edu
International Programs, New Mexico State University
MSC-3DA
PO Box 30001
Las Cruces, NM 88003-8001
Fax: (575) 646-1517
E-mail: ibaca@nmsu.edu
Phone: (575) 646-4528

Donnelly College
www.donnelly.edu
International Student Admissions
608 North 18th Street
Kansas City, KS 66102-4210
Fax: (913) 621-0354
E-mail: cshadfar@donnelly.edu
Phone: (913) 621-8720

Dowling College
www.dowling.edu
International Student Office
150 Idle Hour Boulevard
Oakdale, NY 11769-1999
Fax: (631) 244-1035
E-mail: wangy@dowling.edu
Phone: (631) 244-5097

Drake University
www.drake.edu
Office of Admission
2507 University Avenue
Des Moines, IA 50311-4505
Fax: (515) 271-2831
E-mail: international@drake.edu
Phone: (515) 271-3181 ext. 2086

Draughons Junior College: Clarksville
www.draughons.edu
1860 Wilma Rudolph Boulevard
Clarksville, TN 37040
E-mail: chays@draughons.edu
Phone: (931) 552-7600

Draughons Junior College: Murfreesboro
www.draughons.edu
415 Golden Bear Court
Murfreesboro, TN 37128
E-mail: bday@draughons.edu
Phone: (615) 217-9347

Draughons Junior College: Nashville
www.draughons.edu
Admissions
340 Plus Park at Pavilion Boulevard
Nashville, TN 37217
Fax: (615) 367-2736
E-mail: admissions@draughons.org
Phone: (615) 361-7555

Drew University
www.drew.edu
Office of Admissions
36 Madison Avenue
Madison, NJ 07940-1493
Fax: (973) 408-3068
E-mail: cadm@drew.edu
Phone: (973) 408-3739

Drexel University
www.drexel.edu
International Admissions
3141 Chestnut Street
Philadelphia, PA 19104-2875
Fax: (215) 895-5939
E-mail: enroll@drexel.edu
Phone: (215) 895-2400

Drury University
www.drury.edu
International and IEP Admission
900 North Benton Avenue
Springfield, MO 65802-3712
Fax: (417) 866-3873
E-mail: jhockens@drury.edu
Phone: (417) 873-7506

DuBois Business College
www.dbcollege.com
One Beaver Drive
DuBois, PA 15801
Fax: (814) 371-3974
E-mail: admissions@dbcollege.com
Phone: (814) 371-6920

DuBois Business College: Huntingdon
www.dbcollege.com
1001 Moore Street
Huntingdon, PA 16652
Phone: (814) 371-6920

DuBois Business College: Oil City
www.dbcollege.com
701 East Third Street
Oil City, PA 16301
Phone: (814) 677-1322

Duke University
www.duke.edu
2138 Campus Drive
Box 90586
Durham, NC 27708
Fax: (919) 684-8128
E-mail: anne.sjostrom@duke.edu
Phone: (919) 684-3214

Dunwoody College of Technology
www.dunwoody.edu
Student Records
818 Dunwoody Boulevard
Minneapolis, MN 55403-1192
Fax: (612) 374-4128
E-mail: ychristenson@dunwoody.edu
Phone: (612) 381-3341

Duquesne University
www.duq.edu
Office of International Programs
600 Forbes Avenue, Administration Building
Pittsburgh, PA 15282-0201
Fax: (412) 396-5178
E-mail: oip@duq.edu
Phone: (412) 396-6113

Durham Technical Community College
www.durhamtech.edu
International Student Adviser
1637 Lawson Street
Durham, NC 27703
Fax: (919) 686-3669
E-mail: newhousem@durhamtech.edu
Phone: (919) 686-3305

Dutchess Community College
www.sunydutchess.edu
Student Services
53 Pendell Road
Poughkeepsie, NY 12601-1595
Fax: (845) 431-8997
E-mail: holst@sunydutchess.edu
Phone: (845) 431-8974

Dyersburg State Community College
www.dscc.edu
Admissions and Records
1510 Lake Road
Dyersburg, TN 38024
Fax: (731) 286-3325
E-mail: enroll@dscc.edu
Phone: (731) 286-3330

D'Youville College
www.dyc.edu
Admissions
320 Porter Avenue
Buffalo, NY 14201-1084
Fax: (716) 829-7788
E-mail: admissions@dyc.edu
Phone: (716) 829-8119

Earlham College
www.earlham.edu
International Student Admissions
801 National Road West
Richmond, IN 47374-4095
Fax: (765) 983-1560
E-mail: admissions@earlham.edu
Phone: (765) 983-1600

East Arkansas Community College
www.eacc.edu
Admissions and Records
1700 Newcastle Road
Forrest City, AR 72335-9598
Fax: (870) 633-3840
E-mail: dadams@eacc.edu
Phone: (870) 633-4480 ext. 300

East Carolina University
www.ecu.edu
International Affairs
Office of Undergraduate Admissions
106 Whichard Building
Greenville, NC 27858-4353
Fax: (252) 328-4813
E-mail: intlprgm@ecu.edu
Phone: (252) 328-6769

East Central College
www.eastcentral.edu
Academic Advising & Counseling
1964 Prairie Dell Road
Union, MO 63084-0529
Fax: (636) 583-1011
E-mail: weinhota@eastcentral.edu
Phone: (636) 583-5195 ext. 2226

East Central Community College
www.eccc.edu
Box 129
Decatur, MS 39327
Fax: (601) 635-4060
Phone: (601) 635-2111 ext. 392

East Central University
www.ecok.edu
International Student/Programs Office
PMBJ8, 1100 East 14th Street
Ada, OK 74820
Fax: (580) 310-5432
E-mail: erhynes@mailclerk.ecok.edu
Phone: (580) 332-8000

East Georgia College
www.ega.edu
Admissions
131 College Circle
Swainsboro, GA 30401-2699
Fax: (478) 289-2140
E-mail: kjones@ega.edu
Phone: (478) 289-2219

East Los Angeles College
www.elac.edu
1301 Avenida Cesar Chavez
Monterey Park, CA 91754
Fax: (213) 260-8192
E-mail: elac_iso@elac.edu
Phone: (213) 265-8796

East Stroudsburg University of Pennsylvania
www4.esu.edu
Undergraduate Admissions
200 Prospect Street
East Stroudsburg, PA 18301-2999
Fax: (570) 422-3933
E-mail: undergrads@po-box.esu.edu
Phone: (570) 422-3149

East Tennessee State University
www.etsu.edu
Admissions Office
ETSU Box 70731
Johnson City, TN 37614
Fax: (423) 439-4630
E-mail: go2etsu@etsu.edu
Phone: (423) 439-4213

East Texas Baptist University
www.etbu.edu
Admissions
1209 North Grove
Marshall, TX 75670-1498
Fax: (903) 923-2001
E-mail: admissions@etbu.edu
Phone: (903) 923-2000

East-West University
www.eastwest.edu
Admission
816 South Michigan Avenue
Chicago, IL 60605
Fax: (312) 939-0111
E-mail: agniezka@eastwest.edu
Phone: (312) 939-0111 ext. 1825

Eastern Arizona College
www.eac.edu
Records and Registration
615 North Stadium Avenue
Thatcher, AZ 85552-0769
Fax: (928) 428-8462
E-mail: admissions@eac.edu
Phone: (928) 428-8354

Eastern Connecticut State University
www.easternct.edu
Admissions
83 Windham Street
Willimantic, CT 06226-2295
Fax: (860) 465-5544
E-mail: satsukd@easternct.edu
Phone: (860) 465-5286

Eastern Illinois University
www.eiu.edu
International Program Services
600 Lincoln Avenue
Charleston, IL 61920-3011
Fax: (217) 581-7207
E-mail: interntl@eiu.edu
Phone: (217) 581-2321

Eastern Kentucky University
www.eku.edu
International Education
SSB CPO 54, 521 Lancaster Avenue
Richmond, KY 40475-3102
Fax: (859) 622-1552
E-mail: neil.wright@eku.edu
Phone: (859) 622-1478

Eastern Maine Community College
www.emcc.edu
354 Hogan Road
Bangor, ME 04401
Fax: (207) 974-4608
E-mail: gswett@emcc.edu
Phone: (207) 974-4604

Eastern Mennonite University
www.emu.edu
Admissions Office
1200 Park Road
Harrisonburg, VA 22802-2462
Fax: (540) 432-4444
E-mail: kratzj@emu.edu
Phone: (540) 432-4118

Eastern Michigan University
www.emich.edu
Admissions
400 Pierce Hall
Ypsilanti, MI 48197
Fax: (734) 487-6559
E-mail: international.admissions@emich.edu
Phone: (734) 487-3060

Eastern Nazarene College
www.enc.edu
Director of Admissions
23 East Elm Avenue
Quincy, MA 02170-2999
Fax: (617) 745-3929
E-mail: admissions@enc.edu
Phone: (617) 745-3711

Eastern New Mexico University
www.enmu.edu
Station Seven
Portales, NM 88130
Fax: (575) 562-2566
E-mail: Phillip.Gill@enmu.edu
Phone: (575) 562-4698

Eastern New Mexico University: Roswell Campus
www.roswell.enmu.edu
Box 6000
Roswell, NM 88202-6000
Fax: (505) 624-7144
E-mail: ida.stover@roswell.enmu.edu
Phone: (575) 624-7149

Eastern Oregon University
www.eou.edu
Admissions
One University Boulevard
LaGrande, OR 97850
Fax: (541) 962-3418
E-mail: admissions@eou.edu
Phone: (541) 962-3141

Eastern University
www.eastern.edu
Admission Office
1300 Eagle Road
St. Davids, PA 19087-3696
Fax: (610) 341-1723
E-mail: ugadm@eastern.edu
Phone: (610) 341-5967

Eastern Wyoming College
ewc.wy.edu
Admissions
3200 West C Street
Torrington, WY 82240
Fax: (307) 532-8222
E-mail: marilyn.cotant@ewc.wy.edu
Phone: (800) 658-3195

Eastfield College
www.efc.dcccd.edu
Admissions Office
3737 Motley Drive
Mesquite, TX 75150
Fax: (972) 860-8306
E-mail: efc@dcccd.edu
Phone: (972) 860-7059

Eastman School of Music of the University of Rochester
www.esm.rochester.edu
Admissions
26 Gibbs Street
Rochester, NY 14604-2599
Fax: (585) 232-8601
E-mail: admissions@esm.rochester.edu
Phone: (585) 274-1060

Ecclesia College
www.ecollege.edu
International Student Office
9653 Nations Drive
Springdale, AR 72762
Fax: (479) 248-1455
E-mail: abriggs@ecollege.edu
Phone: (479) 248-7236 ext. 225

Eckerd College
www.eckerd.edu
Assistant Director of Admissions
4200 54th Avenue South
St. Petersburg, FL 33711-4700
Fax: (727) 866-2304
E-mail: cruzcl@eckerd.edu
Phone: (727) 864-8331

Edgewood College
www.edgewood.edu
Admissions Office
1000 Edgewood College Drive
Madison, WI 53711-1997
Fax: (608) 663-3291
E-mail: cbenedict@edgewood.edu
Phone: (608) 663-2294

Edinboro University of Pennsylvania
www.edinboro.edu
Admissions
200 East Normal Street
Academy Hall
Edinboro, PA 16444
Fax: (814) 732-2420
E-mail: eup_admissions@edinboro.edu
Phone: (814) 732-2761

Edison State Community College
www.edisonohio.edu
Admissions
1973 Edison Drive
Piqua, OH 45356-9253
Fax: (937) 778-1920
E-mail: bogart@edisonohio.edu
Phone: (937) 778-7854

Edmonds Community College
www.edcc.edu
International Student Services Office
20000 68th Avenue West
Lynnwood, WA 98036-5912
Fax: (425) 774-0455
E-mail: iss_desk@edcc.edu
Phone: (425) 640-1518

Edward Waters College
www.ewc.edu
Academic Affairs
1658 Kings Road
Jacksonville, FL 32209
Fax: (904) 470-8041
E-mail: Tlittle@ewc.edu
Phone: (904) 347-08204

El Camino College
www.elcamino.edu
International Student Program Office
16007 Crenshaw Boulevard
Torrance, CA 90506
Fax: (310) 660-3818
E-mail: mchun@elcamino.cc.ca.us
Phone: (310) 660-3431

El Camino College: Compton Center
www.compton.edu
1111 East Artesia Boulevard
Compton, CA 90221
Fax: (310) 900-1695
Phone: (310) 900-1600 ext. 2043

El Centro College
www.elcentrocollege.edu
International Office Director
801 Main Street
Dallas, TX 75202
Fax: (214) 860-2022
E-mail: rxp5300@dcccd.edu
Phone: (214) 860-2664

Elgin Community College
www.elgin.edu
Admissions and Recruitment
1700 Spartan Drive
Elgin, IL 60123-7193
Fax: (847) 214-7484
E-mail: international@elgin.edu
Phone: (847) 214-7478

Elizabeth City State University
www.ecsu.edu
Director of Admissions
1704 Weeksville Road, Campus Box 901
Elizabeth City, NC 27909
Fax: (252) 335-3537
E-mail: gdeese@mail.ecsu.edu
Phone: (252) 335-3305

Elizabethtown College
www.etown.edu
Admission
One Alpha Drive
Elizabethtown, PA 17022-2298
Fax: (717) 361-1365
E-mail: admissions@etown.edu
Phone: (717) 361-1400

Ellsworth Community College
www.iavalley.cc.ia.us/ecc
Counseling Office
1100 College Avenue
Iowa Falls, IA 50126
Fax: (641) 648-3128
E-mail: nwalters@iavalley.cc.ia.us
Phone: (641) 648-4611 ext. 424

Elmhurst College
www.elmhurst.edu
Admission
190 South Prospect Avenue
Elmhurst, IL 60126-3296
Fax: (630) 617-5501
E-mail: admit@elmhurst.edu
Phone: (630) 617-3400

Elmira College
www.elmira.edu
Admissions
One Park Place
Elmira, NY 14901
Fax: (607) 735-1718
E-mail: bmoore@elmira.edu
Phone: (607) 735-1724

Elms College
www.elms.edu
Office of Admission
291 Springfield Street
Chicopee, MA 01013
Fax: (413) 594-2781
E-mail: admissions@elms.edu
Phone: (413) 592-3189

Elon University
www.elon.edu
Office of International Admissions
2700 Campus Box
100 Campus Drive
Elon, NC 27244-2010
Fax: (336) 278-7699
E-mail: interadm@elon.edu
Phone: (336) 278-7600

Embry-Riddle Aeronautical University
www.embryriddle.edu
International Student Services
600 South Clyde Morris Boulevard
Daytona Beach, FL 32114-3900
Fax: (386) 226-7070
E-mail: assadj@erau.edu
Phone: (386) 226-6125

Embry-Riddle Aeronautical University:
Prescott Campus
www.embryriddle.edu
3700 North Willow Creek Road
Prescott, AZ 86301-3720
Fax: (928) 777-6606
E-mail: frahera@erau.edu
Phone: (928) 777-3774

Emerson College
www.emerson.edu
Office of Undergraduate Admission
120 Boylston Street
Boston, MA 02116-4624
Fax: (617) 824-8609
E-mail: admission@emerson.edu
Phone: (617) 824-8600

Emmanuel College
www.emmanuel.edu
International Student Coordinator
400 The Fenway
Boston, MA 02115
Fax: (617) 735-9801
E-mail: enroll@emmanuel.edu
Phone: (617) 735-9715

Emory & Henry College
www.ehc.edu
Admissions Office
Box 10
Emory, VA 24327
Fax: (276) 944-6935
E-mail: ehadmiss@ehc.edu
Phone: (276) 944-6133

Emory University
www.emory.edu
Office of Admissions
200 Boisfeuillet Jones Center
Atlanta, GA 30322
Fax: (404) 727-4303
E-mail: admiss@learnlink.emory.edu
Phone: (404) 727-6036

Empire College
www.empcol.edu
3035 Cleveland Avenue
Santa Rosa, CA 95403-2100
Fax: (707) 546-4058
E-mail: rhurd@empcol.edu
Phone: (707) 546-4000

Emporia State University
www.emporia.edu
Office of International Education
1200 Commercial, Campus Box 4034
Emporia, KS 66801-5087
Fax: (620) 341-5918
E-mail: jharter@emporia.edu
Phone: (620) 341-5374

Endicott College
www.endicott.edu
Admission
376 Hale Street
Beverly, MA 01915-9985
Fax: (978) 232-2520
E-mail: tredman@endicott.edu
Phone: (978) 921-1000

Erie Business Center
www.eriebc.edu
246 West Ninth Street
Erie, PA 16501
Fax: (814) 459-3701
E-mail: admissions@eriebc.edu
Phone: (814) 456-7504 ext. 102

Erie Business Center South
www.eriebc.edu/newcastle
170 Cascade Galleria
New Castle, PA 16101
Fax: (724) 658-3083
E-mail: hallr@eriebcs.com
Phone: (724) 658-9066

Erie Community College: City Campus
www.ecc.edu
Foreign Student Adviser
121 Ellicott Street
Buffalo, NY 14203-2698
Fax: (716) 851-1429
E-mail: danna@ecc.edu
Phone: (716) 851-1359

Erie Community College: North Campus
www.ecc.edu
Foreign Student Adviser
6205 Main Street
Williamsville, NY 14221-7095
Fax: (716) 851-1429
E-mail: danna@ecc.edu
Phone: (716) 851-1359

Erie Community College: South Campus
www.ecc.edu
Foreign Student Adviser
4041 Southwestern Boulevard
Orchard Park, NY 14127-2199
Fax: (716) 851-1429
E-mail: danna@ecc.edu
Phone: (716) 851-1359

Erie Institute of Technology
www.erieit.org
940 Millcreek Mall
Erie, PA 16565
Fax: (814) 868-9977
Phone: (814) 868-9900

Erskine College
www.erskine.edu
Admissions
PO Box 338
Due West, SC 29639-0176
Fax: (864) 379-2167
E-mail: walker@erskine.edu
Phone: (864) 379-8838

Essex County College
www.essex.edu
Admissions
303 University Avenue
Newark, NJ 07102
Fax: (973) 623-6449
E-mail: dizdarev@essex.edu
Phone: (973) 877-3154

Estrella Mountain Community College
www.estrellamountain.edu
3000 North Dysart Road
Avondale, AZ 85392
Fax: (623) 935-8870
E-mail: barbara.boros@emcmail.maricopa.edu
Phone: (623) 935-8000

ETI Technical College of Niles
www.eticollege.edu
2076 Youngstown Warren Road
Niles, OH 44446-4398
Fax: (330) 652-4399
E-mail: etiadmissionsdir@hotmail.com
Phone: (330) 652-9919

Eugene Lang College The New School for
Liberal Arts
www.lang.edu
International Students Services
65 West 11th Street (3rd floor)
New York, NY 10011-8693
Fax: (212) 229-8992
E-mail: lang@newschool.edu
Phone: (212) 229-5592 ext. 3625

Eureka College
www.eureka.edu
Admissions
300 East College Avenue
Box 280
Eureka, IL 61530-1500
Fax: (309) 467-6576
E-mail: admissions@eureka.edu
Phone: (309) 467-6530

Evangel University
www.evangel.edu
Admissions
1111 North Glenstone
Springfield, MO 65802
Fax: (417) 865-9599
E-mail: Taylora@evangel.edu
Phone: (417) 865-2811 ext. 7450

Everest College: Arlington
www.everest-college.com
2801 East Division Street, Suite 250
Arlington, TX 76011
Fax: (817) 649-6033
E-mail: tevans@cci.edu
Phone: (817) 652-7790

Everest College: Aurora
www.cci.edu
Director of Admissions
14280 East Jewell Suite 100
Aurora, CO 80012
Fax: (303) 745-6245
E-mail: jrosenthal@cci.edu
Phone: (303) 745-6244 ext. 101

Everest College: Colorado Springs
www.cci.edu
1815 Jet Wing Drive
Colorado Springs, CO 80916
Fax: (719) 574-4493
E-mail: afi@cci.edu
Phone: (719) 638-6580

Everest College: Phoenix
www.everest-college.com
Admissions
10400 North 25th Avenue Suite 190
Phoenix, AZ 85021
Fax: (602) 943-0960
E-mail: jaskins@cci.edu
Phone: (602) 942-4141 ext. 2704

Everest Institute
www.georgia-med.com
1706 Northeast Expressway
Atlanta, GA 30329
Phone: (404) 327-8787

Everest University: Brandon
www.everest.edu
3924 Coconut Palm Drive
Tampa, FL 33619
Fax: (813) 628-0919
E-mail: spointer@cci.edu
Phone: (813) 621-0041 ext. 106

Everest University: Lakeland
www.everest.edu
995 East Memorial Boulevard, Suite 110
Lakeland, FL 33801-1919
Phone: (863) 686-1444

Everest University: Pompano Beach
www.everest.edu
225 North Federal Highway
Pompano Beach, FL 33062
Phone: (954) 783-7339

Everest University: South Orlando
www.everest.edu
9200 Southpark Center Loop
Orlando, FL 32819
Phone: (407) 851-2525

Everest University: Tampa
www.everest.edu
3319 West Hillsborough Avenue
Tampa, FL 33614
Fax: (813) 871-2483
Phone: (813) 879-6000

Everett Community College
www.everettcc.edu
Admissions Office
2000 Tower Street
Everett, WA 98201-1352
Fax: (425) 388-9173
E-mail: jfitzpatrick@everettcc.edu
Phone: (425) 388-9220

Evergreen State College
www.evergreen.edu
Admissions
2700 Evergreen Parkway NW
Olympia, WA 98505
Fax: (360) 867-6576
E-mail: admissions@evergreen.edu
Phone: (360) 867-6170

Evergreen Valley College
www.evc.edu
International Student Coordinator
3095 Yerba Buena Road
San Jose, CA 95135
Fax: (408) 223-9351
E-mail: beverly.lynch@evc.edu
Phone: (408) 274-7900 ext. 6638

Excelsior College
www.excelsior.edu
Admissions
7 Columbia Circle
Albany, NY 12203-5159
Fax: (518) 464-8777
E-mail: admissions@excelsior.edu
Phone: (888) 647-2388

Ex'pression College for Digital Arts
www.expression.edu
6601 Shellmound Street
Emeryville, CA 94608
Phone: (510) 654-2934

Fairfield University
www.fairfield.edu
Undergraduate Admission
1073 North Benson Road
Fairfield, CT 06824-5195
Fax: (203) 254-4199
E-mail: admis@mail.fairfield.edu
Phone: (203) 254-4000 ext. 2169

Fairleigh Dickinson University: College at Florham
www.fdu.edu
Office of International and Graduate Student Admissions
285 Madison Avenue
Madison, NJ 07940
Fax: (201) 692-2560
E-mail: global@fdu.edu
Phone: (201) 692-2205

Fairleigh Dickinson University: Metropolitan Campus
www.fdu.edu
Office of International and Graduate Student Admissions
1000 River Road, H-DH3-10
Teaneck, NJ 07666-1996
Fax: (201) 692-2560
E-mail: global@fdu.edu
Phone: (201) 692-2205

Fairmont State University
www.fairmontstate.edu
International Student Adviser
1201 Locust Avenue
Office of Admissions
Fairmont, WV 26554-2470
Fax: (304) 367-4995
E-mail: ghines@fairmontstate.edu
Phone: (304) 367-4490

Faith Baptist Bible College and Theological Seminary
www.faith.edu
Admissions
1900 NW Fourth Street
Ankeny, IA 50023
Fax: (515) 964-1638
E-mail: admissions@faith.edu
Phone: (515) 964-0601 ext. 233

Family of Faith College
www.familyoffaithcollege.com
PO Box 1805
Shawnee, OK 74802-1805
E-mail: ffc@allegiance.tv
Phone: (405) 273-5331

Fashion Careers College
www.fashioncareerscollege.com
1923 Morena Boulevard
San Diego, CA 92110
Fax: (619) 275-0635
E-mail: info@fashioncareerscollege.com
Phone: (619) 275-4700

Fashion Institute of Design and Merchandising: Los Angeles
www.fidm.edu
Out-of-State Admissions
919 South Grand Avenue
Los Angeles, CA 90015
Fax: (213) 624-4799
E-mail: laronoff@fidm.edu
Phone: (800) 421-0127

Fashion Institute of Design and Merchandising: San Diego
www.fidm.edu
Admissions
1010 Second Avenue, Suite 2000
San Diego, CA 92101
Fax: (213) 624-4799
E-mail: saronson@fidm.edu
Phone: (213) 624-1200

Fashion Institute of Design and Merchandising: San Francisco
www.fidm.com
55 Stockton Street
San Francisco, CA 94108-5805
Fax: (415) 296-7299
E-mail: tsmiles@fidm.edu
Phone: (415) 675-5200

Fashion Institute of Technology
www.fitnyc.edu
Admissions
Seventh Avenue at 27th Street
New York, NY 10001-5992
E-mail: fitinfo@fitnyc.edu
Phone: (212) 217-3760

Faulkner State Community College
www.faulknerstate.edu
Admissions
1900 Highway 31 South
Bay Minette, AL 36507
Fax: (334) 580-2186
E-mail: pduck@faulknerstate.edu
Phone: (334) 580-2111

Faulkner University
www.faulkner.edu
Admissions
5345 Atlanta Highway
Montgomery, AL 36109-3398
Fax: (334) 386-7137
E-mail: kmock@faulkner.edu
Phone: (334) 386-7200

Fayetteville State University
www.uncfsu.edu
Admissions
1200 Murchison Road
Fayetteville, NC 28301-4298
Fax: (910) 672-1414
E-mail: chogan@uncfsu.edu
Phone: (910) 672-1371

Fayetteville Technical Community College
www.faytechcc.edu
Admissions
PO Box 35236
2201 Hull Road
Fayetteville, NC 28303-0236
Fax: (910) 678-8407
E-mail: kelleyj@faytechcc.edu
Phone: (910) 678-8274

Feather River College
www.frc.edu
Admissions
570 Golden Eagle Avenue
Quincy, CA 95971
Fax: (530) 283-3757
E-mail: khayden@frc.edu
Phone: (530) 283-0202 ext. 285

Felician College
www.felician.edu
Director of International Student Services
262 South Main Street
Lodi, NJ 07644-2198
Fax: (201) 559-6188
E-mail: sindingj@felician.edu
Phone: (201) 559-6131

Ferris State University
www.ferris.edu
Coordinator of International Student
Recruiting
1201 South State Street, CSS 201
Big Rapids, MI 49307-2714
Fax: (231) 591-3944
E-mail: tartaril@ferris.edu
Phone: (231) 591-5444

Ferrum College
www.ferrum.edu
Spilman-Daniel House
PO Box 1000, 215 Ferrum Mountain Road
Ferrum, VA 24088
Fax: (540) 365-4266
E-mail: admissions@ferrum.edu
Phone: (540) 365-4290

Finlandia University
www.finlandia.edu
International Enrollment Officer
601 Quincy Street
Hancock, MI 49930-1882
Fax: (906) 487-7383
E-mail: kitti.loukus@finlandia.edu
Phone: (906) 487-7208

Fisher College
www.fisher.edu
Vice President of Enrollment Management
118 Beacon Street
Boston, MA 02116
Fax: (617) 236-5473
E-mail: international-advisor@fisher.edu
Phone: (617) 236-8818

Fitchburg State College
www.fsc.edu
Admissions
160 Pearl Street
Fitchburg, MA 01420-2697
Fax: (978) 665-4540
E-mail: admissions@fsc.edu
Phone: (978) 665-3144

Five Towns College
www.fivetowns.edu
Registrar's Office
305 North Service Road
Dix Hills, NY 11746-6055
Fax: (631) 656-2172
E-mail: MMaltz@ftc.edu
Phone: (631) 424-7000 ext. 2131

Flagler College
www.flagler.edu
Admissions Office
74 King Street
St. Augustine, FL 32084
Fax: (904) 819-6466
E-mail: ccutter@flagler.edu
Phone: (904) 829-6481

Flathead Valley Community College
www.fvcc.edu
777 Grandview Drive
Kalispell, MT 59901
Fax: (406) 756-3965
E-mail: gshryock@fvcc.edu
Phone: (406) 756-3886

Florence-Darlington Technical College
www.fdtc.edu
PO Box 100548
Florence, SC 29501-0548
Fax: (843) 661-8041
E-mail: admissions@fdtc.edu
Phone: (843) 661-8324

Florida Agricultural and Mechanical University
www.famu.edu
Office of Admissions
FHAC, G-9
Tallahassee, FL 32307-3200
Fax: (850) 599-3069
E-mail: kimberlya.davis@famu.edu
Phone: (850) 599-3796

Florida Atlantic University
www.fau.edu
International Students and Scholars
777 Glades Road
Box 3091
Boca Raton, FL 33431
Fax: (561) 297-2446
E-mail: ijones@fau.edu
Phone: (561) 297-3049

Florida Career College: Hialeah
www.careercollege.edu
3750 West 18th Avenue
Hialeah, FL 33012
Fax: (305) 825-3436
E-mail: pbrum@careercollege.edu
Phone: (954) 547-6989

Florida Career College: Miami
www.careercollege.edu
1321 SW 107 Avenue, Suite 201B
Miami, FL 3317-521
Phone: (305) 553-6065

Florida Career College: Pembroke Pines
www.careercollege.edu
7891 Pines Boulevard
Pembroke Pines, FL 33024
Fax: (954) 983-2707
E-mail: info@careercollege.edu
Phone: (954) 965-7272

Florida Career College: West Palm Beach
6065 Okeechobee Boulevard West
West Palm Beach, FL 33417
Fax: (561) 689-0739
Phone: (561) 689-0550

Florida Christian College
www.fcc.edu
Registrar's Office
1011 Bill Beck Boulevard
Kissimmee, FL 34744-4402
Fax: (321) 206-2007
E-mail: brian.smith@fcc.edu
Phone: (407) 569-1336

Florida College of Natural Health: Bradenton
www.fcnh.com
Admissions
616 67th Street Circle East
Bradenton, FL 34208
Fax: (941) 744-1242
E-mail: sarasota@fcnh.com
Phone: (941) 744-1244

Florida Community College at Jacksonville
www.fccj.edu
Office of Admissions
501 West State Street
Jacksonville, FL 32202
Fax: (904) 632-5105
E-mail: rdexter@fccj.edu
Phone: (904) 632-3375

Florida Gulf Coast University
www.fgcu.edu
Admissions
10501 FGCU Boulevard South
Ft. Myers, FL 33965-6565
Fax: (239) 590-7894
E-mail: admissions@fgcu.edu
Phone: (239) 590-7891

Florida Institute of Technology
www.fit.edu
International Admissions
150 West University Boulevard
Melbourne, FL 32901-6975
Fax: (321) 674-8004
E-mail: admission@fit.edu
Phone: (321) 674-8030

Florida International University
www.fiu.edu
Undergraduate Admissions
University Park Campus, PC 140
Miami, FL 33199
Fax: (305) 348-3648
E-mail: admiss@fiu.edu
Phone: (305) 348-2363

Florida Keys Community College
www.fkcc.edu
Office of Admissions
5901 College Road
Key West, FL 33040
Fax: (305) 292-5155
E-mail: runnels_s@firn.edu
Phone: (305) 809-3278

Florida Memorial University
www.fmuniv.edu
15800 Northwest 42 Avenue
Miami Gardens, FL 33054
Fax: (305) 623-1462
E-mail: admit@fmuniv.edu
Phone: (305) 626-3750

Florida National College
www.fnc.edu
4425 West 20th Avenue
Hialeah, FL 33012
Fax: (305) 362-0595
E-mail: jsanchez@fnc.edu
Phone: (305) 821-333

Florida Southern College
www.flsouthern.edu
Admissions Office
111 Lake Hollingsworth Drive
Lakeland, FL 33801-5698
Fax: (863) 680-4120
E-mail: fscadm@flsouthern.edu
Phone: (863) 680-4131

Florida State University
www.fsu.edu
Admissions
PO Box 3062400
Tallahassee, FL 32306-2400
Fax: (850) 644-0197
E-mail: intladms@admin.fsu.edu
Phone: (850) 644-3420

Florida Technical College: Deland
www.flatech.edu
1199 South Woodland Boulevard
Deland, FL 32720
Fax: (386) 734-5150
Phone: (386) 734-3303

Florida Technical College: Orlando
www.flatech.edu
Admissions
12689 Challenger Parkway, #130
Attn: Gabe Garces, Director
Orlando, FL 32826-2707
Fax: (407) 447-7301
E-mail: ggarces@flatech.edu
Phone: (407) 447-7300

Folsom Lake College
www.flc.losrios.edu
Admissions and Records
10 College Parkway
Folsom, CA 95630
Fax: (916) 608-6569
E-mail: rettere@flc.losrios.edu
Phone: (916) 608-5000

Fontbonne University
www.fontbonne.edu
Office of International Students
6800 Wydown Boulevard
St. Louis, MO 63105
Fax: (314) 889-1451
E-mail: rbahan@fontbonne.edu
Phone: (314) 889-4778

Foothill College
www.foothill.edu
International Student Admissions
12345 El Monte Road
Los Altos Hills, CA 94022
Fax: (650) 949-7048
E-mail: beersgeorge@foothill.edu
Phone: (650) 949-7293

Fordham University
www.fordham.edu
Admissions
East 441 Fordham Road
Bronx, NY 10458
Fax: (718) 367-9404
E-mail: messer@fordham.edu
Phone: (718) 817-4000

Forrest Junior College
www.forrestcollege.edu
Admissions
601 East River Street
Anderson, SC 29624
Fax: (864) 261-7471
E-mail: janieturmon@forrestcollege.edu
Phone: (864) 225-7653 ext. 210

Fort Berthold Community College
www.fbcc.bia.edu
Box 490
New Town, ND 58763
Fax: (701) 627-4790
Phone: (701) 627-4738 ext. 286

Fort Hays State University
www.fhsu.edu
600 Park Street
Hays, KS 67601
Fax: (785) 628-4085
E-mail: jmaxwell@fhsu.edu
Phone: (785) 628-4222

Fort Lewis College
www.fortlewis.edu
Admissions
1000 Rim Drive
Durango, CO 81301-3999
Fax: (970) 247-7179
E-mail: martin_b@fortlewis.edu
Phone: (970) 247-7187

Fort Peck Community College
www.fpcc.edu
Box 398 605 Indian
Poplar, MT 59255-0398
Fax: (406) 768-5552
Phone: (406) 768-5553

Fort Valley State University
www.fvsu.edu
1005 State University Drive
Fort Valley, GA 31030-4313
Fax: (478) 825-6169
E-mail: admissap@fvsu.edu
Phone: (478) 825-6307

Fox Valley Technical College
www.fvtc.edu
International Studies
1825 North Bluemound Drive
PO Box 2277
Appleton, WI 54912-2277
Fax: (920) 735-2538
E-mail: martinm@fvtc.edu
Phone: (920) 735-5677

Framingham State College
www.framingham.edu
Office of Undergraduate Admissions
100 State Street
PO Box 9101
Framingham, MA 01701-9101
Fax: (508) 626-4017
E-mail: admiss@frc.mass.edu
Phone: (508) 626-4500

Francis Marion University
www.fmarion.edu
Admissions Office
PO Box 100547
Florence, SC 29501-0547
Fax: (843) 661-4635
E-mail: jschlimmer@fmarion.edu
Phone: (843) 661-1231

Franciscan University of Steubenville
www.franciscan.edu
Student Life Office
1235 University Boulevard
Steubenville, OH 43952-1763
Fax: (740) 284-7225
E-mail: korbon@franciscan.edu
Phone: (740) 283-6470

Frank Phillips College
www.fpctx.edu
Student Services
Box 5118
Borger, TX 79008-5118
Fax: (806) 457-4224
E-mail: bgreen@fpctx.edu
Phone: (806) 457-4200 ext. 720

Franklin & Marshall College
www.fandm.edu
Admissions
PO Box 3003
Lancaster, PA 17604-3003
Fax: (717) 291-4389
E-mail: admission@fandm.edu
Phone: (717) 291-3953

Franklin College
www.franklincollege.edu
Admissions
101 Branigin Boulevard
Franklin, IN 46131-2623
Fax: (317) 738-8274
E-mail: jacosta@franklincollege.edu
Phone: (317) 738-8062

Franklin Pierce University
www.franklinpierce.edu
Admissions
40 University Drive
Rindge, NH 03461-0060
Fax: (603) 899-4372
E-mail: oehlscs@fpc.edu
Phone: (603) 899-497

Free Will Baptist Bible College
www.fwbbc.edu
Registrar
3606 West End Avenue
Nashville, TN 37205-2403
Fax: (615) 269-6028
E-mail: lgladson@fwbbc.edu
Phone: (615) 844-5233 ext. 5233

Freed-Hardeman University
www.fhu.edu
Admissions
158 East Main Street
Henderson, TN 38340
Fax: (731) 989-6047
E-mail: wscott@fhu.edu
Phone: (731) 989-6790

Fremont College
www.fremont.edu
Admissions
18000 Studebaker Road, 900A
Cerritos, CA 90703-5342
Fax: (562) 809-7100
E-mail: leads@fremont.edu
Phone: (562) 809-5100

Fresno City College
www.fresnocitycollege.edu
International Students
1101 East University Avenue
Fresno, CA 93741
Fax: (559) 237-4232
E-mail: info@scccd.com
Phone: (559) 442-8224

Fresno Pacific University
www.fresno.edu
International Programs Director
1717 South Chestnut Avenue
Fresno, CA 93702-4709
Fax: (559) 453-5501
E-mail: ipso@fresno.edu
Phone: (559) 453-2069

Friends University
www.friends.edu
Enrollment Services
2100 University
Wichita, KS 67213
Fax: (316) 295-5101
E-mail: newlina@friends.edu
Phone: (316) 295-5706

Front Range Community College
www.frontrange.edu
3645 West 112th Avenue
Westminster, CO 80031
Fax: (303) 404-5150
Phone: (303) 404-5471

Frostburg State University
www.frostburg.edu
Center for International Education
101 Braddock Road
Frostburg, MD 21532-1099
Fax: (301) 687-1069
E-mail: fsuadmissions@frostburg.edu
Phone: (301) 687-4714

Full Sail University
www.fullsail.com
International Liaison
3300 University Boulevard
Winter Park, FL 32792-7429
Fax: (407) 552-2067
E-mail: admissions@fullsail.com
Phone: (407) 679-0100

Fullerton College
www.fullcoll.edu
321 East Chapman Avenue
Fullerton, CA 92832-2095
Fax: (714) 870-7751
E-mail: admissions@fullcoll.edu
Phone: (714) 992-7580

Fulton-Montgomery Community College
www.fmcc.suny.edu
Director, International Students and ESL
Programs
2805 State Highway 67
Johnstown, NY 12095
Fax: (518) 762-6518
E-mail: intl@fmcc.suny.edu
Phone: (518) 762-4651 ext. 4750

Furman University
www.furman.edu
Admissions
3300 Poinsett Highway
Greenville, SC 29613
Fax: (864) 294-2018
E-mail: admissions@furman.edu
Phone: (864) 294-2034

Gadsden State Community College
www.gadsdenstate.edu
International Student Office
1001 George Wallace Drive
PO Box 227
Gadsden, AL 35902-0227
Fax: (256) 549-8344
E-mail: pross@gadsdenstate.edu
Phone: (256) 549-8324

Gainesville State College
www.gsc.edu
Admissions Office
PO Box 1358
Gainesville, GA 30503
Fax: (678) 717-3643
E-mail: admissions@gsc.edu
Phone: (678) 717-3941

Gallaudet University
www.gallaudet.edu
Admissions Office
800 Florida Avenue, NE
Washington, DC 20002
Fax: (202) 651-5774
E-mail: charity.reedyhines@gallaudet.edu
Phone: (202) 651-5750

Gallipolis Career College
www.gallipoliscareercollege.com
1176 Jackson Pike, Suite 312
Gallipolis, OH 45631
Fax: (740) 446-4124
Phone: (740) 446-4367 ext. 12

Galveston College
www.gc.edu
Admissions Office
4015 Avenue Q
Galveston, TX 77550-7447
Fax: (409) 944-1501
E-mail: rroark@gc.edu
Phone: (409) 944-4242 ext. 227

Gannon University
www.gannon.edu
Admissions
109 University Square
Erie, PA 16541-0001
Fax: (814) 871-5803
E-mail: international@gannon.edu
Phone: (814) 871-7480

Garden City Community College
www.gcccks.edu
Office of Admissions
801 Campus Drive
Garden City, KS 67846-6333
Fax: (620) 276-9573
E-mail: nikki.geier@gcccks.edu
Phone: (620) 276-9608

Gardner-Webb University
www.gardner-webb.edu
Undergraduate Admissions
Box 817
Boiling Springs, NC 28017
Fax: (704) 406-4488
E-mail: cforbes@gardner-webb.edu
Phone: (704) 406-4495

Garrett College
www.garrettcollege.edu
Coordinator of Career Services & Global
Education
687 Mosser Road
McHenry, MD 21541
Fax: (301) 387-3038
E-mail: globaled@garrettcollege.edu
Phone: (301) 387-3046

Gateway Community College
www.gatewaycc.edu
Admissions and Records
108 North 40th Street
Phoenix, AZ 85034
Fax: (602) 286-8072
E-mail: raeann.nunez@gwmail.maricopa.edu
Phone: (602) 286-8063

Gateway Community College
www.gwcc.commnet.edu
Admissions
60 Sargent Drive
New Haven, CT 06511-5970
Fax: (203) 285-2018
E-mail: kshea@gwcc.commnet.edu
Phone: (203) 285-2013

Genesee Community College
www.genesee.edu
Admissions
One College Road
Batavia, NY 14020-9704
Fax: (585) 345-6810
E-mail: tmlanemartin@genesee.suny.edu
Phone: (585) 345-6800

Geneva College
www.geneva.edu
Admissions Office
3200 College Avenue
Beaver Falls, PA 15010
Fax: (724) 847-6776
E-mail: int-admissions@geneva.edu
Phone: (724) 847-6500

George C. Wallace Community College at Dothan
www.wallace.edu
Admissions
1141 Wallace Drive
Dothan, AL 36303-0943
Fax: (334) 983-6066
E-mail: sjacobs@wallace.edu
Phone: (334) 556-2472

George Fox University
www.georgefox.edu
Undergraduate Admissions
414 North Meridian Street
Newberg, OR 97132-2697
Fax: (503) 554-3110
E-mail: admissions@georgefox.edu
Phone: (503) 554-2240

George Mason University
www.gmu.edu
Office of Admissions
4400 University Drive, MSN 3A4
Fairfax, VA 22030-4444
Fax: (703) 993-4622
E-mail: admissions@gmu.edu
Phone: (703) 993-2400

George Washington University
www.gwu.edu
2121 I Street NW, Suite 201
Washington, DC 20052
Fax: (202) 994-7266
E-mail: siskmn@gwunix2.gwu.edu
Phone: (202) 994-4940

Georgetown College
www.georgetowncollege.edu
Admissions
400 East College Street
Georgetown, KY 40324
Fax: (502) 868-7733
E-mail: julie_sams@georgetowncollege.edu
Phone: (502) 863-8013

Georgetown University
www.georgetown.edu
Undergraduate Admissions
103 White-Gravenor
Box 571002
Washington, DC 20057-1002
Fax: (202) 687-5084
Phone: (202) 687-3600

Georgia College and State University
www.gcsu.edu
International Education
Campus Box 23
Milledgeville, GA 31061-0490
Fax: (478) 445-2623
E-mail: intladm@gcsu.edu
Phone: (478) 445-4789

Georgia Highlands College
www.highlands.edu
Admissions
3175 Cedartown Highway SE
Rome, GA 30161
Fax: (706) 295-6341
E-mail: cgraham@highlands.edu
Phone: (706) 295-6339

Georgia Institute of Technology
www.gatech.edu
Office of Undergraduate Admission
Georgia Institute of Technology
Office of Undergraduate Admission
Atlanta, GA 30332-0320
Fax: (404) 894-9511
E-mail: steven.mclaughlin@ece.gatech.edu
Phone: (404) 894-4154

Georgia Military College
www.gmc.cc.ga.us
Admissions Office
201 East Greene Street
Milledgeville, GA 31061
Fax: (478) 445-6520
E-mail: admission@gmc.cc.ga.us
Phone: (478) 445-2963

Georgia Perimeter College
www.gpc.edu
Entry Services for International Students
555 North Indian Creek Drive
Clarkston, GA 30021-2361
Fax: (404) 299-4574
E-mail: rbeaubie@gpc.edu
Phone: (678) 891-3235

Georgia Southern University
www.georgiasouthern.edu
Admissions
PO Box 8024
Statesboro, GA 30460
Fax: (912) 486-7240
E-mail: intladmissions@georgiasouthern.edu
Phone: (912) 681-5391

Georgia Southwestern State University
www.gsw.edu
Admissions Office
800 Georgia Southwestern State University
Drive
Americus, GA 31709-9957
Fax: (229) 931-9283
E-mail: gswapps@canes.gsw.edu
Phone: (229) 928-1273

Georgia State University
www.gsu.edu
Admissions
Box 4009
Atlanta, GA 30302-4009
Fax: (404) 413-2002
E-mail: admissions@gsu.edu
Phone: (404) 413-2500

Georgian Court University
www.georgian.edu
Admissions
900 Lakewood Avenue
Lakewood, NJ 08701-2697
Fax: (732) 987-2000
E-mail: admissions@georgian.edu
Phone: (732) 987-2760

Germanna Community College
www.germanna.edu
Admissions and Records
2130 Germanna Highway
Locust Grove, VA 22508-2102
Fax: (540) 423-9158
Phone: (540) 423-9131

Gettysburg College
www.gettysburg.edu
Admissions Office
300 North Washington Street
Gettysburg, PA 17325-1484
Fax: (717) 337-6145
E-mail: intladmiss@gettysburg.edu
Phone: (717) 337-6100

Glen Oaks Community College
www.glenoaks.edu
Counseling Office-International Student
Adviser
62249 Shimmel Road
Centreville, MI 49032-9719
Fax: (269) 467-9068
E-mail: chayden@glenoaks.edu
Phone: (269) 467-9945 ext. 242

Glendale Community College
www.gccaz.edu
International Student Center
6000 West Olive Avenue
Glendale, AZ 85302
Fax: (623) 845-3136
E-mail: Ken.Bus@gcmail.maricopa.edu
Phone: (623) 845-3136

Glendale Community College
www.glendale.edu
International Students Admission
1500 North Verdugo Road
Glendale, CA 91208-2809
Fax: (818) 549-9436
E-mail: pkamarak@glendale.edu
Phone: (818) 240-1000 ext. 5440

Glenville State College
www.glenville.edu
Admissions
200 High Street
Glenville, WV 26351-1292
Fax: (304) 462-8619
E-mail: John.Fox@glenville.edu
Phone: (304) 462-4128 ext. 7132

Global University
www.globaluniversity.edu
International Student Services
1211 South Glenstone Avenue
Springfield, MO 65804
Fax: (417) 862-0863
E-mail: info@globaluniversity.edu
Phone: (417) 862-9533

Globe Institute of Technology
www.globe.edu
Admissions
291 Broadway
New York, NY 10007
Fax: (212) 227-5920
E-mail: admissions@globe.edu
Phone: (212) 349-4330

Globe University
www.globeuniversity.edu
8089 Globe Drive
Woodbury, MN 55125
Fax: (651) 730-5151
E-mail: admissions@globecollege.com
Phone: (651) 730-5100

Gloucester County College
www.gccnj.edu
Admissions
1400 Tanyard Road
Sewell, NJ 08080
Fax: (856) 468-8498
E-mail: kmomballou@gccnj.edu
Phone: (856) 415-2260

Gogebic Community College
www.gogebic.edu
Admissions
E4946 Jackson Road
Ironwood, MI 49938
Fax: (906) 932-2339
E-mail: jeanneg@gogebic.edu
Phone: (906) 932-4231 ext. 306

Golden Gate University
www.ggu.edu
International Admissions Office
536 Mission Street
San Francisco, CA 94105-2968
Fax: (415) 442-7807
E-mail: iss@ggu.edu
Phone: (415) 442-7290

Golden West College
www.goldenwestcollege.edu
International Students Office
15744 Golden West Street, Box 2748
Huntington Beach, CA 92647-2748
Fax: (714) 895-8960
E-mail: jleighton@gwc.cccd.edu
Phone: (714) 895-8146

Goldey-Beacom College
www.gbc.edu
Admissions
4701 Limestone Road
Wilmington, DE 19808
Fax: (302) 996-5408
E-mail: admissions@gbc.edu
Phone: (302) 225-6383

Golf Academy of Arizona
www.sdga.edu/locations_arizona.php
7373 North Scottsdale Road, Suite B-100
Scottsdale, AZ 85253
Fax: (480) 905-8705
E-mail: sdga@sdgagolf.com
Phone: (480) 905-9288

Gonzaga University
www.gonzaga.edu
International Student Programs
502 East Boone Avenue
Spokane, WA 99258-0001
Fax: (509) 323-5814
E-mail: fadeley@gonzaga.edu
Phone: (509) 323-6562

Goodwin College
www.goodwin.edu
745 Burnside Avenue
East Hartford, CT 06108
Fax: (860) 291-9550
E-mail: dnoonan@goodwin.edu
Phone: (860) 528-4111

Gordon College
www.gdn.edu
Admissions
419 College Drive
Barnesville, GA 30204
Fax: (770) 358-5080
E-mail: lisas@gdn.edu
Phone: (770) 358-5023

Gordon College
www.gordon.edu
Admissions Office
255 Grapevine Road
Wenham, MA 01984
Fax: (978) 867-4682
E-mail: admissions@gordon.edu
Phone: (978) 867-4218

277

Goshen College
www.goshen.edu
International Admissions
1700 South Main Street
Goshen, IN 46526
Fax: (574) 535-7609
E-mail: admission@goshen.edu
Phone: (574) 535-7535

Goucher College
www.goucher.edu
Admissions
1021 Dulaney Valley Road
Baltimore, MD 21204-2753
Fax: (410) 337-6354
E-mail: admissions@goucher.edu
Phone: (410) 337-6100

Governors State University
www.govst.edu
Office of International Programs
One University Parkway
University Park, IL 60466
Fax: (708) 534-1640
E-mail: v-mendoza@govst.edu
Phone: (708) 534-3087

Grace University
www.graceuniversity.edu
1311 South Ninth Street
Omaha, NE 68108-3629
Fax: (402) 449-2999
E-mail: admissions@graceuniversity.edu
Phone: (402) 449-2831

Graceland University
www.graceland.edu
Admissions
One University Place
Lamoni, IA 50140
Fax: (641) 784-5480
E-mail: washburn@graceland.edu
Phone: (641) 784-5423

Grambling State University
http://www.gram.edu
Center for International Affairs & Programs
(CIAP)
403 Main Street, GSU Box 4200
100 Founder Street- Grambling Hall, Suite 51
Grambling, LA 71245
Fax: (318) 274-6000
E-mail: lamadaniem@gram.edu
Phone: (318) 274-7798

Grand Canyon University
www.gcu.edu/clgbrd
3300 West Camelback Road
Phoenix, AZ 85017
Fax: (602) 589-2017
E-mail: admissionsonline@gcu.edu
Phone: (888) 261-2393

Grand Rapids Community College
www.grcc.edu
Office of Admissions
143 Bostwick Avenue NE
Grand Rapids, MI 49503-3295
Fax: (616) 234-4107
E-mail: mnicolet@grcc.edu
Phone: (616) 234-3567

Grand Valley State University
www.gvsu.edu
Office of Admissions
One Campus Drive
Allendale, MI 49401-9403
Fax: (616) 331-2000
E-mail: go2gvsu@gvsu.edu
Phone: (800) 748-0246

Grand View College
www.gvc.edu
Admissions
1200 Grandview Avenue
Des Moines, IA 50316-1599
Fax: (515) 263-2974
E-mail: dheaton@gvc.edu
Phone: (515) 263-2810

Granite State College
www.granite.edu
8 Old Suncook Road
Concord, NH 03301-7317
Fax: (603) 228-3000
E-mail: chris.zerillo@granite.edu
Phone: (603) 513-1389

Grantham University
www.grantham.edu
Admissions
7200 Northwest 86th Street
Kansas City, MO 64153
Fax: (816) 595-5757
E-mail: admissions@grantham.edu
Phone: (800) 955-2527

Gratz College
www.gratz.edu
7605 Old York Road
Melrose Park, PA 19027
Fax: (215) 635-7320
E-mail: rsandberg@gratz.edu
Phone: (215) 635-7300 ext. 168

Grays Harbor College
www.ghc.ctc.edu
Coordinator for Student Programs
1620 Edward P Smith Drive
Aberdeen, WA 98520
Fax: (360) 538-4293
E-mail: csvoboda@ghc.edu
Phone: (360) 538-4078

Grayson County College
www.grayson.edu
6101 Grayson Drive
Denison, TX 75020
Fax: (903) 463-8758
E-mail: pearcek@grayson.edu
Phone: (903) 463-8746

Great Bay Community College
www.stratham.nhctc.edu
Admissions
277 Portsmouth Avenue
Stratham, NH 03885
Fax: (603) 772-1198
E-mail: lshennett@ccsnh.edu
Phone: (603) 775-2306

Green Mountain College
www.greenmtn.edu
Admissions
One College Circle
Poultney, VT 05764
Fax: (802) 287-8099
E-mail: admiss@greenmtn.edu
Phone: (802) 287-8000

Green River Community College
www.greenriver.edu
International Programs
12401 SE 320th Street
Auburn, WA 98092
Fax: (253) 931-6346
Phone: (253) 288-3300

Greenfield Community College
www.gcc.mass.edu
Student Affairs
One College Drive
Greenfield, MA 01301
Fax: (413) 773-5129
E-mail: hentz@gcc.mass.edu
Phone: (413) 775-1809

Greensboro College
www.gborocollege.edu
Admissions Office
815 West Market Street
Greensboro, NC 27401-1875
Fax: (336) 378-0154
E-mail: admissions@gborocollege.edu
Phone: (336) 272-7102 ext. 211

Greenville College
www.greenville.edu
Admissions
315 East College Avenue
Greenville, IL 62246-0159
Fax: (618) 664-9841
E-mail: admissions@greenville.edu
Phone: (618) 664-7102

Greenville Technical College
www.gvltec.edu
Admissions
PO Box 5616
Greenville, SC 29606-5616
Fax: (864) 250-8534
E-mail: greenvilletech@gvltec.edu
Phone: (864) 250-8109

Griffin Technical College
www.griffintech.edu
501 Varsity Road
Griffin, GA 30223
Fax: (770) 229-3227
Phone: (770) 228-7348

Griggs University
www.griggs.edu
Admissions
12501 Old Columbia Pike
Silver Spring, MD 20904-6600
Phone: (301) 680-6570

Grinnell College
www.grinnell.edu
Admission
1103 Park Street
Grinnell, IA 50112-1690
Fax: (641) 269-4800
E-mail: askgrin@grinnell.edu
Phone: (641) 269-3600

Grossmont College
www.grossmont.edu
Admissions Office
8800 Grossmont College Drive
El Cajon, CA 92020
Fax: (619) 644-7933
E-mail: mika.miller@gcccd.edu
Phone: (619) 644-7182

Grove City College
www.gcc.edu
100 Campus Drive
Grove City, PA 16127-2104
Fax: (724) 458-3395
E-mail: admissions@gcc.edu
Phone: (724) 458-2100

Guilford College
www.guilford.edu
Admissions/Enrollment
Admissions, New Garden Hall
5800 West Friendly Avenue
Greensboro, NC 27410-4108
Fax: (336) 316-2443
E-mail: madenyikatb@guilford.edu
Phone: (800) 992-7759

Guilford Technical Community College
www.gtcc.edu
Foreign Student Adviser/Counselor
PO Box 309
Jamestown, NC 27282
Fax: (336) 819-2022
E-mail: mncarmon@gtcc.edu
Phone: (336) 334-4822 ext. 2356

Gulf Coast Community College
www.gulfcoast.edu
International Student Admissions
5230 West Highway 98
Panama City, FL 32401-1041
Fax: (850) 913-3308
E-mail: lbrouse@gulfcoast.edu
Phone: (850) 769-1551 ext. 4894

Gupton Jones College of Funeral Service
www.gupton-jones.edu
5141 Snapfinger Woods Drive
Decatur, GA 30035
Fax: (770) 593-1891
E-mail: jahinz@yahoo.com
Phone: (770) 593-2257

Gustavus Adolphus College
www.gustavus.edu
Office of International Education
800 West College Avenue
St. Peter, MN 56082
Fax: (507) 933-7474
E-mail: jeffa@gustavus.edu
Phone: (507) 933-7493

Gwinnett College
www.gwinnettcollege.edu
Director of Admissions
4230 Highway 29
Suite 11
Lilburn, GA 30047
Fax: (770) 381-0454
E-mail: admissions@gwinnettcollege.com
Phone: (770) 381-7200

Gwynedd-Mercy College
www.gmc.edu
International Students Office
1325 Sumneytown Pike
PO Box 901
Gwynedd Valley, PA 19437-0901
Fax: (215) 641-5556
E-mail: radi.y@gmc.edu
Phone: (215) 641-5544

Halifax Community College
www.hcc.cc.nc.us
Drawer 809
Weldon, NC 27890
Fax: (252) 538-4311
E-mail: vassorc@halifax.hcc.cc.nc.us
Phone: (252) 536-7220

Hallmark College of Aeronautics
www.hallmarkcollege.edu
Director of Admissions
8901 Wetmore Road
San Antonio, TX 78230
Fax: (210) 826-3707
E-mail: slross@hallmarkcollege.com
Phone: (210) 826-1000

Hallmark College of Technology
www.hallmarkcollege.com
Admissions Office
10401 IH 10 West
San Antonio, TX 78230-1737
Fax: (210) 697-8225
E-mail: sross@hallmarkinstitute.com
Phone: (210) 690-9000 ext. 207

Hamilton College
www.hamilton.edu
Admission
198 College Hill Road
Office of Admissions
Clinton, NY 13323-1293
Fax: (315) 859-4457
E-mail: szieseni@hamilton.edu
Phone: (800) 843-2655

Hamilton Technical College
www.hamiltontechcollege.com
1011 East 53rd Street
Davenport, IA 52807
Fax: (563) 386-6756
E-mail: mchristy@hamiltontechcollege.com
Phone: (563) 386-3570

Hamline University
www.hamline.edu
Office of Admission
1536 Hewitt Avenue
MS-C1930
St. Paul, MN 55104-1284
Fax: (651) 523-2458
E-mail: cla_admission@hamline.edu
Phone: (651) 523-2207

Hampden-Sydney College
www.hsc.edu
Admissions
Box 667
Hampden-Sydney, VA 23943
Fax: (434) 223-6346
E-mail: hsapp@hsc.edu
Phone: (434) 223-6120

Hampshire College
www.hampshire.edu
893 West Street
Amherst, MA 01002-9988
Fax: (413) 559-5631
E-mail: admissions@hampshire.edu
Phone: (413) 559-5471

Hampton University
www.hamptonu.edu
Admissions
Office of Admissions
Hampton University
Hampton, VA 23668
Fax: (757) 727-5095
E-mail: admissions@hamptonu.edu
Phone: (757) 727-5328

Hannibal-LaGrange College
www.hlg.edu
Admissions
2800 Palmyra Road
Hannibal, MO 63401
Fax: (573) 221-6594
E-mail: admissio@hlg.edu
Phone: (573) 629-3269

Hanover College
www.hanover.edu
Admission
PO Box 108
Hanover, IN 47243-0108
Fax: (812) 866-7098
E-mail: baer@hanover.edu
Phone: (800) 213-2178

Harcum College
www.harcum.edu
Center for International Programs or
Admissions
750 Montgomery Avenue
Bryn Mawr, PA 19010-3476
Fax: (610) 526-6191
E-mail: elaharcum@harcum.edu
Phone: (610) 526-6116

Hardin-Simmons University
www.hsutx.edu
PO Box 16050
Abilene, TX 79698-0001
Fax: (325) 670-1564
E-mail: maim@hsutx.edu
Phone: (325) 670-1299

Harding University
www.harding.edu
International student advisor
915 East Market Avenue
HU 12255
Searcy, AR 72149-2255
Fax: (501) 279-4122
E-mail: nboyd@harding.edu
Phone: (501) 279-4023

Harford Community College
www.harford.edu
Admissions
401 Thomas Run Road
Bel Air, MD 21015
Fax: (410) 836-4169
E-mail: BPace@harford.edu
Phone: (410) 836-4423

Harper College
www.harpercollege.edu
International Students Office
1200 West Algonquin Road
Palatine, IL 60067-7398
Fax: (847) 925-6048
E-mail: jizumika@harpercollege.edu
Phone: (847) 925-6227

Harris-Stowe State University
www.hssu.edu
Admissions Office
3026 Laclede Avenue
St. Louis, MO 63103-2199
Fax: (314) 340-3555
E-mail: admissions@hssu.edu
Phone: (314) 340-3300

Harrisburg Area Community College
www.hacc.edu
International Admissions Coordinator
One HACC Drive, Cooper 206
Harrisburg, PA 17110-2999
Fax: (717) 231-7674
E-mail: admit@hacc.edu
Phone: (717) 780-2400

**Harrisburg University of Science and
Technology**
www.harrisburgu.net
304 Market Street
Harrisburg, PA 17101
E-mail: admissions@harrisburgu.net
Phone: (717) 901-5160

Hartnell College
www.hartnell.edu
International Student Services
156 Homestead Avenue
Salinas, CA 93901
Fax: (831) 755-6751
Phone: (831) 755-6829

Hartwick College
www.hartwick.edu
Admissions
Box 4022
Oneonta, NY 13820-4022
Fax: (607) 431-4102
E-mail: admissions@hartwick.edu
Phone: (607) 431-4150

Harvard College
www.college.harvard.edu
86 Brattle Street
Cambridge, MA 02138
Fax: (617) 495-8821
E-mail: college@fas.harvard.edu
Phone: (617) 495-1551

Harvey Mudd College
www.hmc.edu
Admission
Kingston Hall, 301 Platt Boulevard
Claremont, CA 91711-5901
Fax: (909) 607-7046
E-mail: admission@hmc.edu
Phone: (909) 621-8011

Haskell Indian Nations University
www.haskell.edu
155 Indian Avenue #5031
Lawrence, KS 66046-4800
Fax: (913) 749-8429
Phone: (785) 749-8454

Hastings College
www.hastings.edu
Admissions Office
710 North Turner Avenue
Hastings, NE 68901-7621
Fax: (402) 461-7490
E-mail: mmolliconi@hastings.edu
Phone: (402) 461-7320

Haverford College
www.haverford.edu
Admission
370 Lancaster Avenue
Haverford, PA 19041-1392
Fax: (610) 896-1338
E-mail: admission@haverford.edu
Phone: (610) 896-1350

Hawaii Pacific University
www.hpu.edu
Office of International Recruitment
1164 Bishop Street
Honolulu, HI 96813
Fax: (808) 543-8065
E-mail: international@hpu.edu
Phone: (808) 543-8088

Hawaii Tokai International College
www.hawaiitokai.edu
Student Services
2241 Kapiolani Boulevard
Honolulu, HI 96826
Fax: (808) 983-4173
E-mail: ksimizu@tokai.edu
Phone: (808) 983-4122

Hawkeye Community College
www.hawkeyecollege.edu
Student Development
Box 8015
Waterloo, IA 50704-8015
Fax: (319) 296-4400
E-mail: adoyle@hawkeyecollege.edu
Phone: (319) 296-4014 ext. 1590

Hazard Community College
www.hazard.kctcs.edu
Director of Admissions
One Community College Drive
Hazard, KY 41701
Fax: (606) 672-6805
E-mail: Hallie.Bowling@kctcs.edu
Phone: (800) 246-7521 ext. 73486

Heald College: Concord
www.heald.edu
5130 Commercial Circle
Concord, CA 94520
Fax: (925) 288-5896
E-mail: info@heald.edu
Phone: (925) 288-5800

Heald College: Fresno
www.heald.edu
Dean
255 West Bullard
Fresno, CA 93704-1706
Fax: (559) 438-6368
E-mail: info@heald.edu
Phone: (559) 438-4222

Heald College: Hayward
www.heald.edu
25500 Industrial Boulevard
Hayward, CA 94545
Fax: (510) 783-3287
Phone: (510) 783-2100

Heald College: Honolulu
www.heald.edu
1500 Kapiolani Boulevard
Honolulu, HI 96814-3715
Fax: (808) 955-6964
Phone: (808) 955-1500

Heald College: Portland
www.heald.edu
625 SW Broadway
Portland, OR 97205
Phone: (503) 229-0492

Heald College: Rancho Cordova
www.heald.edu
2910 Prospect Park Drive
Rancho Cordova, CA 95670
Fax: (916) 638-1580
E-mail: info@heald.edu
Phone: (916) 638-1616

Heald College: Roseville
www.heald.edu
7 Sierra Gate Plaza
Roseville, CA 95678
Fax: (916) 789-8616
E-mail: rosevilleinfo@heald.edu
Phone: (916) 789-8600

Heald College: Salinas
www.heald.edu
1450 North Main Street
Salinas, CA 93906
Fax: (831) 443-1050
Phone: (831) 443-1700

Heald College: San Francisco
www.heald.edu
350 Mission Street
San Francisco, CA 94103
Fax: (418) 808-3005
Phone: (415) 808-3000

Heald College: San Jose
www.heald.edu
341 Great Mall Parkway
Milpitas, CA 95035
Fax: (415) 934-7777
E-mail: sanjoseinfo@heald.edu
Phone: (408) 934-4900

Heald College: Stockton
www.heald.edu
1605 East March Lane
Stockton, CA 95210
Fax: (209) 477-2739
Phone: (209) 473-5200

Heartland Community College
www.heartland.edu
Student Services
1500 West Raab Road
Normal, IL 61761
Fax: (309) 268-7992
E-mail: chris.riley@heartland.edu
Phone: (309) 268-8033

Heidelberg College
www.heidelberg.edu
Office of Admission
310 East Market Street
Tiffin, OH 44883-2462
Fax: (419) 448-2334
E-mail: adminfo@heidelberg.edu
Phone: (419) 448-2330

Helena College of Technology of the University of Montana
www.umhelena.edu
Student Services
1115 North Roberts Street
Helena, MT 59601-3098
Fax: (406) 444-6892
E-mail: info@umh.umt.edu
Phone: (406) 444-6800

Hellenic College/Holy Cross
www.hchc.edu
Admissions
50 Goddard Avenue
Brookline, MA 02445
Fax: (617) 850-1460
E-mail: admissions@hchc.edu
Phone: (617) 850-1260

Henderson Community College
www.hencc.kctcs.edu
Student Services
2660 South Green Street
Henderson, KY 42420
Fax: (270) 826-8391
E-mail: pattymitchell@kctcs.net
Phone: (270) 827-1867

Henderson State University
www.getreddie.com
Director of International Student Program
1100 Henderson Street
Box 7560
Arkadelphia, AR 71999-0001
Fax: (870) 230-5419
E-mail: smithc@hsu.edu
Phone: (870) 230-5265

Hendrix College
www.hendrix.edu
Office of Admission
1600 Washington Avenue
Conway, AR 72032-3080
Fax: (501) 450-3843
E-mail: frost@hendrix.edu
Phone: (800) 277-9017

Hennepin Technical College
www.hennepintech.edu
9000 Brooklyn Boulevard
Brooklyn Park, MN 55455
Fax: (952) 952-1391
E-mail: info@hennepintech.edu
Phone: (952) 995-1440

Heritage Christian University
www.hcu.edu
Office of Admissions
3625 Helton Drive
PO Box HCU
Florence, AL 35630
Fax: (256) 766-9289
E-mail: nhunnicutt@hcu.edu
Phone: (256) 766-6610

Heritage Institute: Jacksonville
www.heritage-education.com
4130 Salisbury Road North, Suite 1100
Jacksonville, FL 32216
Phone: (904) 332-0910 ext. 121

Heritage University
www.heritage.edu
Student Services Office
3240 Fort Road
Toppenish, WA 98948-9599
Fax: (509) 865-8659
E-mail: puente_m@heritage.edu
Phone: (509) 865-8508

Herkimer County Community College
www.herkimer.edu
International Programs
100 Reservoir Road
Herkimer, NY 13350-1598
Fax: (315) 866-0062
E-mail: simt@hccc.suny.edu
Phone: (315) 866-0300 ext. 8318

Herzing College
www.herzing.edu
Admissions
3393 Peachtree Road NE, Suite 1003
Atlanta, GA 30326
Fax: (404) 816-5576
E-mail: rhinton@atl.herzing.edu
Phone: (404) 816-4533

Herzing College
www.herzing.edu/madison
Admissions Advisor
5218 East Terrace Drive
Madison, WI 53718
Fax: (608) 249-8593
E-mail: info@msn.herzing.edu
Phone: (608) 249-6611

Hesser College
www.hesser.edu
Director of Admissions
3 Sundial Avenue
Manchester, NH 03103
Fax: (603) 666-4722
E-mail: kwilkinson@hesser.edu
Phone: (603) 668-6660

Hesston College
www.hesston.edu
Director of International Admissions
Box 3000
Hesston, KS 67062-2093
Fax: (620) 327-8300
E-mail: admissions@hesston.edu
Phone: (620) 327-8133

Hibbing Community College
www.hibbing.edu
Student Services
1515 East 25th Street
Hibbing, MN 55746
Fax: (218) 262-6717
E-mail: donnagrotteum@hibbing.edu
Phone: (218) 262-6786

High Point University
www.highpoint.edu
Admissions
833 Montlieu Avenue
PO Box 3188
High Point, NC 27262-3598
Fax: (336) 888-6382
E-mail: jmcilrat@highpoint.edu
Phone: (336) 841-9148

Highland Community College
www.highland.edu
Dean of Enrollment Services
2998 West Pearl City Road
Freeport, IL 61032-9341
Fax: (815) 235-6130
E-mail: karl.richards@highland.edu
Phone: (815) 235-6121 ext. 3486

Highline Community College
www.highline.edu
International Student Programs
2400 South 240th Street
PO Box 98000
Des Moines, WA 98198-9800
Fax: (206) 870-3782
E-mail: lwesterg@highline.edu
Phone: (206) 878-3710 ext. 3725

Hill College
www.hillcollege.edu
Admissions
Box 619
Hillsboro, TX 76645
Fax: (254) 582-7591
E-mail: rballew@hillcollege.edu
Phone: (254) 582-2555 ext. 288

Hillsborough Community College
www.hccfl.edu
Admissions, Registration and Records Officer
Box 31127
Tampa, FL 33631-3127
Fax: (813) 253-7196
E-mail: kcecil@hccfl.edu
Phone: (813) 253-7004

Hillsdale College
www.hillsdale.edu
Admissions
33 East College Street
Hillsdale, MI 49242
Fax: (517) 607-2223
E-mail: admissions@hillsdale.edu
Phone: (517) 607-2327

Hinds Community College
www.hindscc.edu
Foreign Student Counseling Office
505 East Main Street
P.O. Box 1100
Raymond, MS 39154-1100
Fax: (601) 857-3539
E-mail: records@hindscc.edu
Phone: (601) 857-3219

Hiram College
www.hiram.edu
Center for International Studies
Teachout Price Hall
Box 96
Hiram, OH 44234
Fax: (330) 569-5944
E-mail: mcgillsk@hiram.edu
Phone: (330) 569-5159

Hiwassee College
www.hiwassee.edu
Office of Admissions
225 Hiwassee College Drive
Office of Admission
Madisonville, TN 37354-6099
Fax: (423) 442-8521
E-mail: enroll@hiwassee.edu
Phone: (423) 420-1212

Hobart and William Smith Colleges
www.hws.edu
Admissions
629 South Main Street
Geneva, NY 14456
Fax: (315) 781-3814
E-mail: gage@hws.edu
Phone: (315) 781-3622

Hocking College
www.hocking.edu
International Admissions
3301 Hocking Parkway
Nelsonville, OH 45764-9704
Fax: (740) 753-7065
E-mail: springer_r@hocking.edu
Phone: (740) 753-7080

Hodges University
www.hodges.edu
Admissions
2655 Northbrooke Drive
Naples, FL 34119
Fax: (239) 513-9071
E-mail: rlampus@internationalcollege.edu
Phone: (239) 513-1122

Hofstra University
www.hofstra.edu
Multicultural & International Student Office
Admissions Center, 100 Hofstra University
Hempstead, NY 11549
Fax: (516) 463-5328
E-mail: admitme@hofstra.edu
Phone: (516) 463-6795

Hollins University
www.hollins.edu
Admissions Office
PO Box 9707
8060 Quadrangle Lane
Roanoke, VA 24020-1707
Fax: (540) 362-6218
E-mail: huadm@hollins.edu
Phone: (800) 456-9595

Holy Apostles College and Seminary
www.holyapostles.edu
Admissions
33 Prospect Hill Road
Cromwell, CT 06416-2005
Fax: (860) 632-3030
E-mail: admissions@holyapostles.edu
Phone: (860) 632-3012

Holy Cross College
www.hcc-nd.edu
Admissions
54515 State Road 933N
PO Box 308
Notre Dame, IN 46556-0308
Fax: (574) 233-7427
E-mail: vduke@hcc-nd.edu
Phone: (574) 239-8407

Holy Family University
www.holyfamily.edu
Admissions
9801 Frankford Avenue
Philadelphia, PA 19114-2009
Fax: (215) 281-1022
E-mail: lcampbell@holyfamily.edu
Phone: (215) 637-3050

Holy Names University
www.hnu.edu
Assistant Director of Undergraduate
Admissions
3500 Mountain Boulevard
Oakland, CA 94619-1699
Fax: (510) 436-1325
E-mail: admission@hnu.edu
Phone: (800) 430-1321

Hondros College
www.hondros.edu
4140 Executive Parkway
Westerville, OH 43081-3855
Fax: (614) 508-6269
E-mail: degreeadmissions@hondros.edu
Phone: (614) 508-6252

Hood College
www.hood.edu
Admissions
401 Rosemont Avenue
Frederick, MD 21701-8575
Fax: (301) 696-3819
E-mail: international@hood.edu
Phone: (301) 696-3813

Hope College
www.hope.edu
Admissions
69 East 10th Street
Box 9000
Holland, MI 49422-9000
Fax: (616) 395-7130
E-mail: admissions@hope.edu
Phone: (616) 395-7850

Hope International University
www.hiu.edu
Admissions
2500 East Nutwood Avenue
Fullerton, CA 92831-3199
Fax: (714) 681-7423
E-mail: rfbarnes@hiu.edu
Phone: (714) 879-3901 ext. 2234

Horry-Georgetown Technical College
www.hgtc.edu
PO Box 261966
Conway, SC 29528
Fax: (843) 349-7501
E-mail: Admissions@hgtc.edu
Phone: (843) 349-5277

Houghton College
www.houghton.edu
Admission
1 Willard Avenue/Box 128
Houghton, NY 14744-0128
Fax: (585) 567-9522
E-mail: admission@houghton.edu
Phone: (585) 567-9353

Housatonic Community College
www.hcc.commnet.edu
Dean of Learning
900 Lafayette Boulevard
Bridgeport, CT 06604-4704
Fax: (203) 332-5123
Phone: (203) 332-5061

Houston Baptist University
www.hbu.edu
Vice President of Enrollment Management
7502 Fondren Road
Houston, TX 77074-3298
Fax: (281) 649-3217
E-mail: jsteen@hbu.edu
Phone: (281) 649-3000 ext. 3208

Houston Community College System
www.hccs.edu
Director of Certification
3100 Main
Box 667517
Houston, TX 77266-7517
Fax: (713) 718-2111
Phone: (713) 718-8520

Howard Community College
www.howardcc.edu
Admissions and Advising
10901 Little Patuxent Parkway
Columbia, MD 21044-3197
Fax: (410) 772-4589
E-mail: intlstudent@howardcc.edu
Phone: (410) 772-4856

Howard Payne University
www.hputx.edu
International Program Office
1000 Fisk Avenue
Brownwood, TX 76801
Fax: (325) 649-8901
E-mail: enroll@hputx.edu
Phone: (325) 649-8406

Howard University
www.howard.edu
International Admission Counselor
2400 Sixth Street NW
Washington, DC 20059
Fax: (202) 806-9194
E-mail: gansah-birikorang@howard.edu
Phone: (202) 806-7517

Hudson County Community College
www.hccc.edu
Enrollment Services
70 Sip Avenue, 1st Floor
Jersey City, NJ 07306
Fax: (201) 714-2136
E-mail: rmartin@hccc.edu
Phone: (201) 360-4111

Hudson Valley Community College
www.hvcc.edu
International Student Office
80 Vandenburgh Avenue
Troy, NY 12180
Fax: (518) 629-4576
E-mail: deitcjay@hvcc.edu
Phone: (518) 629-7567

Huertas Junior College
www.huertas.edu
P.O. Box 8429
Caguas, PR 00726
Fax: (787) 743-0203
E-mail: admisiones@huertas.edu
Phone: (787) 743-1242

Humacao Community College
PO Box 9139
Georgetti St. #69
Humacao, PR 00792-9139
Fax: (787) 850-1577
Phone: (787) 852-1430 ext. 31

Humphreys College
www.humphreys.edu
Enrollment Management
6650 Inglewood Avenue
Stockton, CA 95207-3896
Fax: (209) 478-8721
E-mail: salopez@humphreys.edu
Phone: (209) 478-0800 ext. 202

Huntingdon College
www.huntingdon.edu
Office of Admission
1500 East Fairview Avenue
Montgomery, AL 36106-2148
Fax: (334) 833-4347
E-mail: admiss@huntingdon.edu
Phone: (334) 833-4497

Huntington College of Health Sciences
www.hchs.edu
1204D Kenesaw
Knoxville, TN 37919-7736
Fax: (865) 524-8339
E-mail: studentservices@hchs.edu
Phone: (865) 524-8079

Huntington University
www.huntington.edu
Admissions
2303 College Avenue
Huntington, IN 46750-1237
Fax: (260) 358-3699
E-mail: admissions@huntington.edu
Phone: (260) 359-4016

Husson College
www.husson.edu
ICLS
One College Circle
Bangor, ME 04401
Fax: (207) 941-7935
E-mail: hussonp@husson.edu
Phone: (207) 941-7470

Huston-Tillotson University
www.htu.edu
Enrollment Management
900 Chicon Street
Austin, TX 78702-2795
Fax: (512) 505-3190
E-mail: slstinson@htu.edu
Phone: (512) 505-3027

Hutchinson Community College
www.hutchcc.edu
Guidance and Counseling
1300 North Plum
Hutchinson, KS 67501
Fax: (620) 728-8155
E-mail: wintersd@hutchcc.edu
Phone: (620) 728-8163

ICPR Junior College
www.icprjc.edu
PO Box 190304
San Juan, PR 00919-0304
Fax: (787) 763-7249
E-mail: mvelez@icprjc.edu
Phone: (787) 763-1010

Idaho State University
www.isu.edu
International Student Programs and Services
921 South 8th Stop 8270
Pocatello, ID 83209-8270
Fax: (208) 282-4511
E-mail: intl@isu.edu
Phone: (208) 282-2314

Ilisagvik College
www.ilisagvik.cc
100 Stevenson Road
PO Box 749
Barrow, AK 99723
Fax: (907) 852-1784
E-mail: patty.stith@ilisagvik.cc
Phone: (907) 852-1763

Illinois Central College
www.icc.edu
One College Drive
East Peoria, IL 61635-0001
Fax: (309) 694-8461
E-mail: enroll@icc.edu
Phone: (309) 694-5354

Illinois College
www.ic.edu
Admission
1101 West College Avenue
Jacksonville, IL 62650
Fax: (217) 245-3034
E-mail: rlbystry@ic.edu
Phone: (217) 245-3030

Illinois Eastern Community Colleges:
Frontier Community College
www.iecc.edu/fcc
Program Director of International Students
2 Frontier Drive
Fairfield, IL 62837-9801
Fax: (618) 392-3293
E-mail: swansonp@iecc.edu
Phone: (618) 395-7777

Illinois Eastern Community Colleges:
Lincoln Trail College
www.iecc.edu/ltc
Program Director of International Students
11220 State Highway 1
Robinson, IL 62454-5707
Fax: (618) 392-3293
E-mail: swansonp@iecc.edu
Phone: (618) 395-7777

Illinois Eastern Community Colleges: Olney
Central College
www.iecc.edu/occ
Program Director of International Students
305 North West Street
Olney, IL 62450
Fax: (618) 392-3293
E-mail: swansonp@iecc.edu
Phone: (618) 395-7777

Illinois Eastern Community Colleges:
Wabash Valley College
www.iecc.edu/wvc
Program Director of International Students
2200 College Drive
Mount Carmel, IL 62863-2657
Fax: (618) 392-3293
E-mail: swansonp@iecc.edu
Phone: (618) 395-7777

Illinois Institute of Art: Chicago
www.ilic.artinstitutes.edu
350 North Orleans Street
Chicago, IL 60654
E-mail: antonj@aii.edu
Phone: (312) 280-3500

Illinois Institute of Art: Schaumburg
www.ilis.aii.edu
1000 North Plaza Drive
Schaumburg, IL 60173
Fax: (847) 619-3064
Phone: (847) 619-3450

Illinois Institute of Technology
www.iit.edu
Office of Undergraduate Admission
10 West 33rd Street
Perlstein Hall 101
Chicago, IL 60616
Fax: (312) 567-6939
E-mail: schoen@iit.edu
Phone: (312) 567-6940

Illinois State University
www.ilstu.edu
Office of International Studies
Campus Box 2200
Normal, IL 61790-2200
Fax: (309) 438-3987
E-mail: oisp@ilstu.edu
Phone: (309) 438-5365

Illinois Wesleyan University
www.iwu.edu
Admissions Office
PO Box 2900
Bloomington, IL 61702-2900
Fax: (309) 556-3820
E-mail: pschley@iwu.edu
Phone: (309) 556-3031

Immaculata University
www.immaculata.edu
Admission
PO Box 642
Immaculata, PA 19345-0642
Fax: (610) 640-0836
E-mail: admiss@immaculata.edu
Phone: (610) 647-4400 ext. 3046

Independence Community College
www.indycc.edu
Student Services
1057 West College Avenue
Independence, KS 67301
Fax: (620) 331-0946
E-mail: admissions@indycc.edu
Phone: (620) 331-4100

Indian Hills Community College
www.indianhills.edu
Enrollment Services
623 Indian Hills Drive, Building 12
Ottumwa, IA 52501
Fax: (641) 683-5184
E-mail: enrollment_services@ihcc.cc
Phone: (641) 683-5161

Indian River Community College
www.ircc.edu
3209 Virginia Avenue
Fort Pierce, FL 34981-5596
Fax: (772) 462-4699
E-mail: tspivey@ircc.edu
Phone: (772) 462-4327

Indiana Business College: Indianapolis
Northwest
www.ibcschools.edu
6300 Technology Center Drive
Indianapolis, IN 46278
E-mail: northwest@ibcschools.edu
Phone: (317) 873-6500

Indiana Institute of Technology
www.indianatech.edu
Director of Admissions
1600 East Washington Boulevard
Fort Wayne, IN 46803-1297
Fax: (260) 422-7696
E-mail: mlladig@indianatech.edu
Phone: (260) 422-5561 ext. 2348

Indiana State University
www.indstate.edu
Interim Executive Director, International
Affairs Center
Office of Admissions, Erickson 114
218 North 6th Street
Terre Haute, IN 47809-9989
Fax: (812) 237-4316
E-mail: ascemail2@isugw.indstate.edu
Phone: (812) 237-4391

Indiana University Bloomington
www.iub.edu
300 North Jordan Avenue
Bloomington, IN 47405
Fax: (812) 856-5378
E-mail: intladm@indiana.edu
Phone: (812) 855-4306

Indiana University East
www.iue.edu
International Admissions
2325 Chester Boulevard
Box WZ116
Richmond, IN 47374-1289
Fax: (765) 973-8288
E-mail: eaadmit@indiana.edu
Phone: (812) 855-4306

Indiana University Kokomo
www.iuk.edu
International Admissions
Box 9003, KC 230A
Kokomo, IN 46904-9003
Fax: (765) 455-9537
E-mail: iuadmis@iuk.edu
Phone: (812) 855-4306

Indiana University Northwest
www.iun.edu
3400 Broadway
Hawthorn 100
Gary, IN 46408
Fax: (219) 981-4219
E-mail: admit@iun.edu
Phone: (219) 980-6764

Indiana University of Pennsylvania
www.iup.edu
Office of International Affairs
117 John Sutton Hall, 1011 South Drive
Indiana, PA 15705-1088
Fax: (724) 357-2514
E-mail: intl-affairs@iup.edu
Phone: (724) 357-2295

Indiana University South Bend
www.iusb.edu
Director, International Programs
1700 Mishawaka Avenue
Box 7111
South Bend, IN 46634-7111
Fax: (574) 520-4590
E-mail: grobinso@iusb.edu
Phone: (574) 520-4419

Indiana University Southeast
www.ius.edu
Admissions
4201 Grant Line Road
Box UC-100
New Albany, IN 47150-6405
Fax: (812) 941-2595
E-mail: admissions@ius.edu
Phone: (812) 941-2212

Indiana University-Purdue University Fort Wayne
www.ipfw.edu
International Student Affairs
2101 East Coliseum Boulevard
Fort Wayne, IN 46805-1499
Fax: (260) 481-6880
E-mail: foreign@ipfw.edu
Phone: (260) 481-6034

Indiana University-Purdue University Indianapolis
www.iupui.edu
Office of International Affairs
425 North University Boulevard, Cavanaugh Hall R129
Indianapolis, IN 46202-5143
Fax: (317) 278-2213
E-mail: intlaff@iupui.edu
Phone: (317) 274-7294

Indiana Wesleyan University
www.indwes.edu
Admissions CAS
4201 South Washington Street
Marion, IN 46953-4999
Fax: (765) 677-2140
E-mail: tony.stevens@indwes.edu
Phone: (765) 677-2254

Institute of American Indian Arts
www.iaia.edu
Registrar
83 Avan Nu Po Road
Santa Fe, NM 87508-1300
Fax: (505) 424-4500
E-mail: tsjoblom@iaia.edu
Phone: (505) 424-2331

Institute of Business & Medical Careers
www.ibmc.edu
1609 Oakridge Drive
Fort Collins, CO 80525
E-mail: info@ibmc.edu
Phone: (970) 223-2669

Institute of Design and Construction
www.idc.edu
141 Willoughby Street
Brooklyn, NY 11201-5380
Fax: (718) 852-5889
Phone: (718) 855-3661 ext. 16

IntelliTec College
www.intelliteccollege.com
Financial Aid
2315 East Pikes Peak Avenue
Colorado Springs, CO 80909
Fax: (719) 632-7451
E-mail: twright@intelliteccollege.com
Phone: (719) 632-7626

IntelliTec College: Grand Junction
www.intelliteccollege.edu
772 Horizon Drive
Grand Junction, CO 81506
Fax: (970) 243-8074
Phone: (970) 245-8101

Inter American University of Puerto Rico: Aguadilla Campus
www.aguadilla.inter.edu
Box 20000
Aguadilla, PR 00605
Fax: (787) 882-3020
Phone: (787) 891-0925 ext. 2101

Inter American University of Puerto Rico: Arecibo Campus
www.arecibo.inter.edu
Admission Office
PO Box 4050
Arecibo, PR 00614-4050
Fax: (787) 880-1624
E-mail: pmontalvo@arecibo.inter.edu
Phone: (787) 878-5475 ext. 2268

Inter American University of Puerto Rico: Barranquitas Campus
www.br.inter.edu
Admission Office
PO Box 517
Barranquitas, PR 00794
Fax: (787) 857-2244
E-mail: mdiaz@br.inter.edu
Phone: (787) 857-3600 ext. 2011

Inter American University of Puerto Rico: Bayamon Campus
bc.inter.edu
Admissions
500 Dr. John Will Harris Road
Bayamon, PR 00957
Fax: (787) 279-2205
E-mail: calicea@bc.inter.edu
Phone: (787) 279-1912 ext. 2017

Inter American University of Puerto Rico: Fajardo Campus
fajardo.inter.edu
Call Box 70003
Fajardo, PR 00738-7003
Fax: (787) 863-3470
E-mail: adcaraba@inter.edu
Phone: (787) 863-2390 ext. 2210

Inter American University of Puerto Rico: Guayama Campus
www.guayama.inter.edu
PO Box 10004
Guayama, PR 00785
Fax: (787) 864-8232
E-mail: lferrer@inter.edu
Phone: (787) 864-7059

Inter American University of Puerto Rico: Metropolitan Campus
metro.inter.edu
Admission Office
Box 191293
San Juan, PR 00919-1293
Fax: (787) 250-1025
E-mail: jolivieri@metro.inter.edu
Phone: (787) 250-1912 ext. 2188

Inter American University of Puerto Rico: Ponce Campus
ponce.inter.edu
104 Turpo Industrial Park Road #1
Mercedita, PR 00715-1602
Fax: (787) 841-0103
E-mail: fldiaz@poce.inter.edu
Phone: (787) 841-0110

Inter American University of Puerto Rico: San German Campus
www.sg.inter.edu
Dean of Students
Box 5100
San German, PR 00683-9801
Fax: (787) 892-6350
E-mail: eanglero@sg.inter.edu
Phone: (787) 264-1912 ext. 7200

International Academy of Design and Technology: Chicago
www.iadtchicago.edu
Registrar's Office
One North State Street, Suite 500
Chicago, IL 60602
Fax: (312) 980-4829
E-mail: ttimmons@iadtchicago.com
Phone: (312) 980-9200

International Academy of Design and Technology: Detroit
www.iadtdetroit.com/
1850 Research Drive
Troy, MI 48083
Phone: (248) 457-2700

International Academy of Design and Technology: Henderson
www.iadtvegas.com
2495 Village View Drive
Henderson, NV 89074
E-mail: vegas_web@iadtvegas.com
Phone: (702) 990-0150

International Academy of Design and Technology: Nashville
www.iadtnashville.com
1 Bridgestone Park
Nashville, TN 37214
E-mail: admissions@iadtnashville.com
Phone: (866) 302-4238

International Academy of Design and Technology: Orlando
www.iadt.edu
Admissions
5959 Lake Ellenor Drive
Orlando, FL 32809
E-mail: trobinson@iadt.edu
Phone: (407) 857-2300

International Academy of Design and Technology: Schaumburg
www.iadtschaumburg.com
915 National Parkway
Schaumburg, IL 60173
Fax: (847) 969-0599
Phone: (847) 969-2800

International Academy of Design and Technology: Seattle
www.iadtseattle.com
645 Andover Park West
Seattle, WA 98188
Phone: (888) 424-8111

International Academy of Design and Technology: Tampa
www.academy.edu
International Admissions
5104 Eisenhower Boulevard
Tampa, FL 33634
Fax: (813) 881-0008
E-mail: Lbell@academy.edu
Phone: (813) 881-0007

International Business College
5699 Coventry Lane
Fort Wayne, IN 46804
Fax: (260) 436-1896
Phone: (260) 459-4500

International College of Broadcasting
www.icbcollege.com
6 South Smithville Road
Dayton, OH 45431
Fax: (937) 258-8714
E-mail: zenaicb@aol.com
Phone: (937) 258-8251 ext. 202

International Import-Export Institute
www.iiei.edu
Registrar
11225 North 28th Drive Suite B201
Suite 1026
Phoenix, AZ 85029
Fax: (62) 648-5755
E-mail: tandrews@expandglobal.com
Phone: (602) 648-5750

International Institute of the Americas: Albuquerque
www.iia.edu
4201 Central Avenue NW, Suite J
Albuquerque, NM 87105
Fax: (505) 352-0199
E-mail: jpalumbo@iia.edu
Phone: (505) 880-2877

International Institute of the Americas: Mesa
www.iia.edu
925 South Gilbert Road, Suite 201
Mesa, AZ 85204
Fax: (480) 926-1371
E-mail: jpalumbo@iia.edu
Phone: (480) 545-8755 ext. 209

Inver Hills Community College
www.inverhills.edu
Director, Prospective Students
2500 80th Street East
Inver Grove Heights, MN 55076-3224
Fax: (651) 450-8677
E-mail: sauldi@inverhills.edu
Phone: (651) 450-8510

Iona College
www.iona.edu
Admissions
715 North Avenue
New Rochelle, NY 10801-1890
Fax: (914) 637-2778
E-mail: SNastlkova@iona.edu
Phone: (914) 633-2249

Iowa Central Community College
www.iowacentral.edu
330 Avenue M
Fort Dodge, IA 50501
Fax: (515) 576-7724
Phone: (515) 576-0099 ext. 1175

Iowa Lakes Community College
www.iowalakes.edu
Admissions
300 South 18th Street
Estherville, IA 51334-2725
Fax: (712) 362-8342
E-mail: rguge@iowalakes.edu
Phone: (800) 521-5054

Iowa State University
www.iastate.edu
Admissions
100 Alumni Hall
Ames, IA 50011-2011
Fax: (515) 294-2592
E-mail: admissions@iastate.edu
Phone: (515) 294-5836

Iowa Wesleyan College
www.iwc.edu
Admissions Office
601 North Main Street
Mount Pleasant, IA 52641-1398
Fax: (319) 385-6240
E-mail: admit@iwc.edu
Phone: (319) 385-6231

Iowa Western Community College
www.iwcc.edu
Director of International Programs
2700 College Road
Box 4-C
Council Bluffs, IA 51502-3004
Fax: (712) 388-6803
E-mail: bduis@iwcc.edu
Phone: (712) 325-3419

Irvine Valley College
www.ivc.edu
International Student Office
5500 Irvine Center Drive
Irvine, CA 92618-4399
Fax: (949) 451-5466
E-mail: gvendley@ivc.edu
Phone: (949) 451-5624

Island Drafting and Technical Institute
www.idti.edu
Admissions
128 Broadway
Amityville, NY 11701-2704
Fax: (631) 691-8738
E-mail: info@idti.edu
Phone: (631) 691-8733

Itasca Community College
www.itascacc.edu
Enrollment Management Office
1851 Highway 169 East
Grand Rapids, MN 55744
Fax: (218) 327-4350
E-mail: cperry@it.cc.mn.us
Phone: (218) 327-4464

Ithaca College
www.ithaca.edu
Admission
100 Job Hall
Ithaca, NY 14850-7020
Fax: (607) 274-1900
E-mail: admission@ithaca.edu
Phone: (800) 429-4274

ITI Technical College
www.iticollege.edu
13944 Airline Highway
Baton Rouge, LA 70817
Fax: (225) 756-0903
E-mail: croubique@iticollege.edu
Phone: (225) 752-4233 ext. 233

Ivy Tech Community College: Bloomington
www.ivytech.edu
Registrar
200 Daniels Way
Bloomington, IN 47404-1511
Fax: (812) 332-8147
E-mail: bpless@ivytech.edu
Phone: (812) 330-6049 ext. 6012

Ivy Tech Community College: Central Indiana
www.ivytech.edu
Assistant Director of International Student Relations
50 West Fall Creek Parkway North Drive
Indianapolis, IN 46208-5752
Fax: (317) 917-5919
E-mail: tywebb@ivytech.edu
Phone: (317) 921-4580

Ivy Tech Community College: Columbus
www.ivytech.edu
Director of Admissions/Assistant Dean
4475 Central Avenue
Columbus, IN 47203-1868
Fax: (812) 372-0311
E-mail: nbagadio@ivytech.edu
Phone: (812) 374-5129

Ivy Tech Community College: East Central
www.ivytech.edu
Dean of Student Affairs
4301 South Cowan Road
Box 3100
Muncie, IN 47302-9448
Fax: (765) 289-2292
E-mail: mlewelle@ivytech.edu
Phone: (765) 289-2291 ext. 1391

Ivy Tech Community College: Kokomo
www.ivytech.edu
Director of Admissions
1815 East Morgan Street
Kokomo, IN 46903-1373
Fax: (765) 454-5111
E-mail: sdillman@ivytech.edu
Phone: (765) 459-0561 ext. 318

Ivy Tech Community College: Lafayette
www.ivytech.edu
Director of Admissions
3101 South Creasy Lane
Lafayette, IN 47905-6299
Fax: (765) 722-9293
E-mail: ihernand@ivytech.edu
Phone: (765) 269-5253

Ivy Tech Community College: North Central
www.ivytech.edu
Assistant Director of Admissions
220 Dean Johnson Boulevard
South Bend, IN 46601-3415
Fax: (574) 236-7177
E-mail: tteat@ivytech.edu
Phone: (574) 289-7001

Ivy Tech Community College: Northeast
www.ivytech.edu
Assistant Director of Diversity Affairs
3800 North Anthony Boulevard
Fort Wayne, IN 46805-1489
Fax: (260) 480-2053
E-mail: djackson@ivytech.edu
Phone: (260) 480-4115

Ivy Tech Community College: Northwest
www.ivytech.edu
Associate Dean of Student Affairs
1440 East 35th Avenue
Gary, IN 46409-1499
Fax: (219) 981-4415
E-mail: tlewis@ivytech.edu
Phone: (219) 981-1111 ext. 2273

Ivy Tech Community College: Richmond
www.ivytech.edu
Assistant Director of Admissions
2357 Chester Boulevard
Richmond, IN 47374-1298
Fax: (765) 962-8174
E-mail: lprzybys@ivytech.edu
Phone: (765) 966-2656 ext. 1214

Ivy Tech Community College: South Central
www.ivytech.edu
Assistant Director of Enrollment Services
8204 Highway 311
Sellersburg, IN 47172-1897
Fax: (812) 246-9905
E-mail: afelten@ivytech.edu
Phone: (812) 246-3301 ext. 4132

Ivy Tech Community College: Southeast
www.ivytech.edu
Executive Dean
590 Ivy Tech Drive
Madison, IN 47250-1881
Fax: (812) 265-4028
E-mail: dheiderm@ivytech.edu
Phone: (812) 265-2580

Ivy Tech Community College: Southwest
www.ivytech.edu
Director of Admissions
3501 First Avenue
Evansville, IN 47710-3398
Fax: (812) 429-9878
E-mail: ajohnson@ivytech.edu
Phone: (812) 429-1430

Ivy Tech Community College: Wabash Valley
www.ivytech.edu
International Student Coordinator
8000 South Education Drive
Terre Haute, IN 47802-4898
Fax: (812) 299-5723
E-mail: jfrey@ivytech.edu
Phone: (800) 377-4882

J. F. Drake State Technical College
www.drakestate.edu
Director of Admissions
3421 Meridian Street North
Huntsville, AL 35811
Fax: (256) 551-3142
E-mail: sudeall@drakestate.edu
Phone: (256) 551-3109

J. Sargeant Reynolds Community College
www.reynolds.edu
Admissions and Records
Box 85622
Richmond, VA 23285-5622
Fax: (804) 371-3650
E-mail: lmunson@reynolds.edu
Phone: (804) 523-5029

Jackson State University
www.jsums.edu
Office of International Programs
1400 JR Lynch Street
Box 17330
Jackson, MS 39217
Fax: (601) 973-3388
E-mail: ksims@jsums.edu
Phone: (601) 979-3794

Jacksonville College
www.jacksonville-college.edu
International Student Adviser
105 B.J. Albritton Drive
Jacksonville, TX 75766-4759
Fax: (903) 586-0743
E-mail: acadean@jacksonville-college.edu
Phone: (903) 586-2518 ext. 7108

Jacksonville State University
www.jsu.edu
Registrar's Office
700 Pelham Road North
Jacksonville, AL 36265-1602
Fax: (256) 782-5291
E-mail: kosterbi@jsu.edu
Phone: (256) 782-5400

Jacksonville University
www.ju.edu
Admissions Office
2800 University Boulevard North
Jacksonville, FL 32211-3394
Fax: (904) 256-7012
E-mail: ymartel@ju.edu
Phone: (800) 225-2027 ext. 7006

James A. Rhodes State College
www.rhodesstate.edu
Student Affairs Division
4240 Campus Drive, PS 148
Lima, OH 45804-3597
Fax: (419) 995-8112
E-mail: johnson.c@rhodesstate.edu
Phone: (419) 995-8304

James Madison University
www.jmu.edu
Office of Admissions
Sonner Hall, MSC 0101
Harrisonburg, VA 22807
Fax: (540) 568-3332
E-mail: mooneyms@jmu.edu
Phone: (540) 568-3453

Jamestown College
www.jc.edu
Admissions
6081 College Lane
Jamestown, ND 58405
Fax: (701) 253-4318
E-mail: jerickso@jc.edu
Phone: (701) 252-3467 ext. 5548

Jamestown Community College
www.sunyjcc.edu
Admissions
525 Falconer Street
PO Box 20
Jamestown, NY 14702-0020
Fax: (716) 338-1450
E-mail: WendyPresent@mail.sunyjcc.edu
Phone: (716) 665-5220 ext. 1070

Jefferson College
www.jeffco.edu
Admissions
1000 Viking Drive
Hillsboro, MO 63050-2441
Fax: (636) 789-5103
E-mail: sdean1@jeffco.edu
Phone: (636) 797-3000 ext. 216

Jefferson College of Health Sciences
www.jchs.edu
Office of Admissions
Box 13186
Roanoke, VA 24031-3186
Fax: (540) 224-6703
E-mail: jmckeon@jchs.edu
Phone: (540) 985-8483

Jefferson Community and Technical College
www.jefferson.kctcs.edu
International Student Services
109 East Broadway
Louisville, KY 40202
E-mail: SusanJ.Panfil@kctcs.edu
Phone: (502) 213-2496

Jefferson State Community College
www.jeffstateonline.com
International Student Office
2601 Carson Road
Birmingham, AL 35215-3098
Fax: (205) 856-6070
E-mail: cdbanks@jeffstateonline.com
Phone: (205) 856-7920

JNA Institute of Culinary Arts
www.culinaryarts.com
1212 South Broad Street
Philadelphia, PA 19146
E-mail: admissions@culinaryarts.edu
Phone: (215) 468-8800

John A. Logan College
www.jalc.edu
Admissions
700 Logan College Road
Carterville, IL 62918
Fax: (618) 985-4433
E-mail: terry.crain@jal.cc.il.us
Phone: (618) 985-3741

John Brown University
www.jbu.edu
Admissions
2000 West University Street
Siloam Springs, AR 72761-2121
Fax: (479) 524-4196
E-mail: jbuinfo@jbu.edu
Phone: (877) 528-4636

John Carroll University
www.jcu.edu
Admission
20700 North Park Boulevard
University Heights, OH 44118-4581
Fax: (216) 397-3098
E-mail: admission@jcu.edu
Phone: (216) 397-4249

John F. Kennedy University
www.jfku.edu
International Student Advisor
100 Ellinwood Way
Pleasant Hill, CA 94523-4817
Fax: (925) 969-3331
E-mail: ssermeno@jfku.edu
Phone: (925) 969-3339

John Wesley College
www.johnwesley.edu
Admissions
2314 North Centennial
High Point, NC 27265-3197
Fax: (336) 889-2261
E-mail: aziemba@johnwesley.edu
Phone: (336) 889-2262 ext. 127

John Wood Community College
www.jwcc.edu
Admissions
1301 South 48th Street
Quincy, IL 62305-8736
Fax: (217) 224-4208
E-mail: admissions@jwcc.edu
Phone: (217) 641-4339

Johns Hopkins University
www.jhu.edu
Office of Undergraduate Admissions
3400 North Charles Street, Mason Hall
Baltimore, MD 21218
Fax: (410) 516-6025
E-mail: Cowan@jhu.edu
Phone: (410) 516-8124

Johns Hopkins University: Peabody Conservatory of Music
www.peabody.jhu.edu
One East Mount Vernon Place
Baltimore, MD 21202
Phone: (410) 659-8100 ext. 3075

Johnson & Wales University: Charlotte
www.jwu.edu
801 West Trade Street
Charlotte, NC 28202
Fax: (980) 598-1111
E-mail: admissions.clt@jwu.edu
Phone: (980) 598-1100

Johnson & Wales University: Denver
www.jwu.edu
Academic Services Associate
7150 Montview Boulevard
Denver, CO 80220
Fax: (303) 256-9389
E-mail: CAbrahamson@jwu.edu
Phone: (303) 256-9557

Johnson & Wales University: North Miami
www.jwu.edu
International Admissions
1701 Northeast 127th Street
North Miami, FL 33181
Fax: (305) 892-7020
E-mail: mia@admissions.jwu.edu
Phone: (305) 892-7005

Johnson & Wales University: Providence
www.jwu.edu
International Admissions
8 Abbott Park Place
Providence, RI 02903-3703
Fax: (401) 598-4773
E-mail: admissons.pvd@jwu.edu
Phone: (401) 598-1074

Johnson C. Smith University
www.jcsu.edu
Admissions Office
100 Beatties Ford Road
Charlotte, NC 28216-5398
Fax: (704) 378-1242
E-mail: admissions@jcsu.edu
Phone: (704) 378-1010

Johnson College
www.johnson.edu
Admissions
3427 North Main Avenue
Scranton, PA 18508
Fax: (570) 348-2181
E-mail: admit@epix.net
Phone: (570) 342-6404 ext. 125

Johnson State College
www.jsc.vsc.edu
Admissions
337 College Hill
Johnson, VT 05656
Fax: (802) 635-1230
E-mail: jscadmissions@jsc.vsc.edu
Phone: (802) 635-1219 ext. 1223

Johnston Community College
www.johnstoncc.edu
Admissions
Box 2350
Smithfield, NC 27577
Fax: (919) 989-7862
E-mail: mclendonj@johnstoncc.edu
Phone: (919) 209-2079

Joliet Junior College
www.jjc.edu
Dean of Adminssions and Recruitment
1215 Houbolt Road
Joliet, IL 60431-8938
Fax: (815) 744-5507
E-mail: jkloberd@jjc.edu
Phone: (815) 280-2414

Jones College
www.jones.edu
Administrative Assistant to the CEO
5353 Arlington Expressway
Jacksonville, FL 32211
Fax: (904) 743-4446
E-mail: mbarber@jones.edu
Phone: (904) 743-1122 ext. 242

Jones College: Miami
www.jones.edu
Administrative Support, International Students
11430 North Kendall Drive, Suite 200
Miami, FL 33176
Fax: (904) 743-4446
E-mail: mbarber@jones.edu
Phone: (904) 743-1122 ext. 242

Jones International University
www.jonesinternational.edu
Enrollment Center
9697 East Mineral Avenue
Centennial, CO 80112
Fax: (303) 799-0966
E-mail: info@jonesinternational.edu
Phone: (800) 811-5663

Judson College
www.judson.edu
Admissions Office
302 Bibb Street
Marion, AL 36756
Fax: (334) 683-5282
E-mail: admissions@judson.edu
Phone: (334) 683-5110

Judson University
www.judsonu.edu
Admissions
1151 North State Street
Elgin, IL 60123-1404
Fax: (847) 628-2526
E-mail: admissions@JudsonU.edu
Phone: (847) 628-1572

Juilliard School
www.juilliard.edu
Admissions Office
60 Lincoln Center Plaza
New York, NY 10023-6588
Fax: (212) 724-0263
E-mail: admissions@juilliard.edu
Phone: (212) 799-5000 ext. 223

Juniata College
www.juniata.edu
Enrollment Office
1800 Moore Street
Huntingdon, PA 16652-2196
Fax: (814) 641-3100
E-mail: basomb@juniata.edu
Phone: (814) 641-3427

Kalamazoo College
www.kzoo.edu
Kalamazoo College Office of Admission
1200 Academy Street
Kalamazoo, MI 49006-3295
Fax: (269) 337-7390
E-mail: admission@kzoo.edu
Phone: (269) 337-7166

Kalamazoo Valley Community College
www.kvcc.edu
6767 West O Avenue
PO Box 4070
Kalamazoo, MI 49003-4070
Fax: (269) 488-4161
E-mail: mmccall@kvcc.edu
Phone: (269) 488-4207

Kankakee Community College
www.kcc.edu
Admissions
100 College Drive
Kankakee, IL 60901-6505
Fax: (815) 802-8101
E-mail: mdriscoll@kcc.edu
Phone: (815) 802-8524

Kansas City Art Institute
www.kcai.edu
Admissions
4415 Warwick Boulevard
Kansas City, MO 64111-1820
Fax: (816) 802-3309
E-mail: admiss@kcai.edu
Phone: (816) 474-5224

Kansas City Kansas Community College
www.kckcc.edu
English as a Second Language Office
7250 State Avenue
Kansas City, KS 66112
Fax: (913) 288-7648
E-mail: sneff@kckcc.edu
Phone: (913) 288-7201

Kansas State University
www.ksu.edu
International Student Center
119 Anderson Hall
Manhattan, KS 66506
Fax: (785) 532-6607
E-mail: kstate@ksu.edu
Phone: (785) 532-6448

Kansas Wesleyan University
www.kwu.edu
Admissions
100 East Claflin Avenue
Salina, KS 67401-6196
Fax: (785) 827-0927
E-mail: tina@kwu.edu
Phone: (785) 827-5541

Kaplan College: Denver
www.kaplancollege.com
500 East 84th Avenue, Suite W-200
Thornton, CO 80229
Fax: (303) 295-0102
Phone: (303) 295-0550

Kaplan College: Hagerstown
www.KC-Hagerstown.com
18618 Crestwood Drive
Hagerstown, MD 21742
Fax: (301) 791-7661
E-mail: info@kc-hagerstown.edu
Phone: (301) 739-2670

Kaplan College: Hammond
www.kaplan.com
7833 Indianapolis Boulevard
Hammond, IN 46324
Fax: (219) 844-0105
Phone: (219) 844-0100

Kaplan College: Merrillville
www.sawyercollege.edu
3803 East Lincoln Highway
Merrillville, IN 46410
Fax: (219) 942-3762
E-mail: cartim@kaplan.edu
Phone: (219) 947-8400

Kaplan University: Cedar Falls
www.kucampus.edu
7009 Nordic Drive
Cedar Falls, IA 50613
Fax: (319) 243-2961
E-mail: admissions@hamiltoncf.com
Phone: (319) 277-0220

Kaplan University: Cedar Rapids
www.kucampus.edu
Admissions
3165 Edgewood Parkway, SW
Cedar Rapids, IA 52404
Fax: (319) 363-3812
E-mail: druddy@kaplan.edu
Phone: (319) 363-0481

Kaplan University: Davenport
www.kucampus.edu
Director of Admissions
1801 East Kimberly Road, Suite 1
Davenport, IA 52807-2095
Fax: (563) 355-1320
E-mail: rhoffmann@kucampus.edu
Phone: (563) 441-2496

Kaplan University: Des Moines
www.kucampus.edu
Admissions Office
4655 121st Street
Urbandale, IA 50323
Fax: (515) 727-2115
E-mail: erogan_dm@hamiltonia.edu
Phone: (515) 727-2100

Kaplan University: Lincoln
www.kucampus.edu
Admissions
1821 K Street
Lincoln, NE 68508
Fax: (402) 474-5302
E-mail: jmathers@kaplan.edu
Phone: (402) 474-5315

Kaplan University: Mason City
www.kucampus.edu
2570 Fourth Street, SW
Mason City, IA 50401
Fax: (641) 423-7512
E-mail: mpischel@kaplan.edu
Phone: (641) 423-2530

Kaskaskia College
www.kaskaskia.edu
Admissions and Records
27210 College Road
Centralia, IL 62801
Fax: (618) 532-1990
E-mail: jripperda@kaskaskia.edu
Phone: (618) 545-3041

Kean University
www.kean.edu
Admissions Office
1000 Morris Avenue
PO Box 411
Union, NJ 07083-0411
Fax: (908) 737-7105
E-mail: admitme@kean.edu
Phone: (908) 737-7106

Keiser University
www.keiseruniversity.edu
1500 Northwest 49th Street
Fort Lauderdale, FL 33309
Fax: (954) 771-4894
E-mail: admissions-ftl@keisercollege.edu
Phone: (954) 776-4456

Kellogg Community College
www.kellogg.edu
Admissions
450 North Avenue
Battle Creek, MI 49017-3397
Fax: (269) 966-4089
Phone: (269) 965-4153

Kendall College of Art and Design of Ferris State University
www.kcad.edu
Admissions Office
17 Fountain Street NW
Grand Rapids, MI 49503-3002
Fax: (616) 831-9689
E-mail: brittons@ferris.edu
Phone: (616) 451-2787

Kennebec Valley Community College
www.kvcc.me.edu
Director of Admissions
92 Western Avenue
Fairfield, ME 04937-1367
Fax: (207) 453-5011
E-mail: jbourgoin@kvcc.me.edu
Phone: (207) 453-5035

Kennesaw State University
www.kennesaw.edu
International Admissions
1000 Chastain Road
Campus Box 0115
Kennesaw, GA 30144-5591
Fax: (770) 499-3430
E-mail: jespana@kennesaw.edu
Phone: (770) 423-6336

Kent State University
www.kent.edu
International Admissions
PO Box 5190
Kent, OH 44242-0001
Fax: (330) 672-2499
E-mail: intladm@kent.edu
Phone: (330) 672-2444

Kentucky Christian University
www.kcu.edu
Registrar
100 Academic Parkway
Box 2021
Grayson, KY 41143-2205
Fax: (606) 474-3155
E-mail: gww@email.kcc.edu
Phone: (606) 474-3212

Kentucky Mountain Bible College
www.kmbc.edu
Office of Recruiting
Box 10
Vancleve, KY 41385-0010
Fax: (606) 693-4884
E-mail: kmbc@kmbc.edu
Phone: (606) 693-5000 ext. 138

Kentucky State University
www.kysu.edu
Admissions
400 East Main Street, ASB 312
Frankfort, KY 40601
Fax: (502) 597-5978
E-mail: james.burrell@kysu.edu
Phone: (502) 597-6813

Kenyon College
www.kenyon.edu
Admissions
Ransom Hall
106 College-Park Street
Gambier, OH 43022
Fax: (740) 427-5770
E-mail: admissions@kenyon.edu
Phone: (800) 848-2468

Kettering College of Medical Arts
www.kcma.edu
3737 Southern Boulevard
Kettering, OH 45429-1299
Fax: (937) 395-8338
E-mail: studentadmissions@kcma.edu
Phone: (800) 422-5262

Kettering University
www.kettering.edu
Admissions
1700 West Third Avenue
Flint, MI 48504-4898
Fax: (810) 762-9837
E-mail: admissions@kettering.edu
Phone: (810) 762-7865

Keuka College
www.keuka.edu
Admissions
141 Cental Avenue
Keuka Park, NY 14478-0098
Fax: (315) 279-5386
E-mail: admissions@mail.keuka.edu
Phone: (800) 335-3852

Key College
www.keycollege.edu
Financial Services
225 Dania Beach Boulevard
Dania Beach, FL 33004
Fax: (954) 923-9226
E-mail: acirealtime@aol.com
Phone: (954) 923-4440

Keystone College
www.keystone.edu
Office of Admissions
One College Green
La Plume, PA 18440-1099
Fax: (570) 945-7916
E-mail: admissions@keystone.edu
Phone: (570) 945-8112

Keystone Technical Institute
www.kti.edu
2301 Academy Drive
Harrisburg, PA 17112-1012
Fax: (717) 901-9090
E-mail: info@kti.edu
Phone: (717) 545-4747

Kilgore College
www.kilgore.edu
1100 Broadway
Kilgore, TX 75662-3299
Fax: (903) 983-8607
E-mail: thornb@ranger.kilgore.cc.tx.us
Phone: (903) 983-8204

Kilian Community College
www.kilian.edu
300 East 6th Street
Sioux Falls, SD 57103-7020
Fax: (605) 336-2606
E-mail: amodrell@kilian.edu
Phone: (605) 221-3100

King College
www.king.edu
Admission Office
1350 King College Road
Bristol, TN 37620-2699
Fax: (423) 652-4861
E-mail: eabrowne@king.edu
Phone: (423) 652-4769

King's College
www.tkc.edu
Office of Admissions
350 Fifth Avenue, Lower Lobby
New York, NY 10118
Fax: (212) 659-3611
E-mail: info@tkc.edu
Phone: (212) 659-7200 ext. 3610

King's College
www.kings.edu
Admissions
133 North River Street
Wilkes-Barre, PA 18711
Fax: (570) 208-5971
E-mail: admissions@kings.edu
Phone: (570) 208-5858

The King's College and Seminary
www.kingscollege.edu
Office of Admission
14800 Sherman Way
Los Angeles, CA 91405-2233
Fax: (818) 779-8429
E-mail: admissions@kingscollege.edu
Phone: (818) 779-8040

Kirkwood Community College
www.kirkwood.edu
International Student Adviser Office
6301 Kirkwood Boulevard SW
PO Box 2068
Cedar Rapids, IA 52406
Fax: (319) 398-1244
E-mail: gglick@kirkwood.edu
Phone: (319) 398-5411 ext. 5579

Kirtland Community College
www.kirtland.edu
Student Services
10775 North Saint Helen Road
Roscommon, MI 48653
Fax: (989) 275-6727
E-mail: kochk@kirtland.edu
Phone: (989) 275-5000 ext. 253

Kishwaukee College
www.kishwaukeecollege.edu
Vice President of Student Services
21193 Malta Road
Malta, IL 60150-9699
Fax: (815) 825-2306
E-mail: apperson@kishwaukeecollege.edu
Phone: (815) 825-2086 ext. 249

Knox College
www.knox.edu
Admission Office
Knox College - Campus Box 148
Galesburg, IL 61401-4999
Fax: (309) 341-7070
E-mail: admission@knox.edu
Phone: (309) 341-7100

Kutztown University of Pennsylvania
www.kutztown.edu
Admissions
Admissions Office
PO Box 730
Kutztown, PA 19530-0730
Fax: (610) 683-1375
E-mail: admisson@kutztown.edu
Phone: (610) 683-4056

Kuyper College
www.kuyper.edu
Academic Office
3333 East Beltline Avenue Northeast
Grand Rapids, MI 49525-9749
Fax: (616) 988-3608
E-mail: mvandermeer@kuyper.edu
Phone: (616) 222-3000

LA College International
www.lac.edu
3200 Wilshire Boulevard, Suite 400
Los Angeles, CA 90010-1308
Fax: (213) 383-9369
Phone: (213) 381-3333

La Roche College
www.laroche.edu
Admissions
9000 Babcock Boulevard
Pittsburgh, PA 15237
Fax: (412) 536-1048
E-mail: hassett1@laroche.edu
Phone: (412) 536-1275

La Salle University
www.lasalle.edu
Admission and Financial Aid
1900 West Olney Avenue
Philadelphia, PA 19141-1199
Fax: (215) 951-1656
E-mail: arcangel@lasalle.edu
Phone: (215) 951-1500

La Sierra University
www.lasierra.edu
4500 Riverwalk Parkway
Riverside, CA 92515-8247
Fax: (951) 785-2477
E-mail: admissions@lasierra.edu
Phone: (951) 785-2176

Labette Community College
www.labette.edu
Admissions
200 South 14th Street
Parsons, KS 67357
Fax: (620) 421-2309
E-mail: tammyf@labette.edu
Phone: (620) 421-6700 ext. 1228

Laboratory Institute of Merchandising
www.limcollege.edu
Admissions Office
12 East 53rd Street
New York, NY 10022
Fax: (212) 421-4341
E-mail: aurmey@limcollege.edu
Phone: (800) 677-1323

Lackawanna College
www.lackawanna.edu
Admissions Office
501 Vine Street
Scranton, PA 18509
Fax: (570) 961-7843
E-mail: costanzob@lackawanna.edu
Phone: (570) 961-7841

Lafayette College
www.lafayette.edu
Admissions
118 Markle Hall
Easton, PA 18042-1770
Fax: (610) 330-5355
E-mail: admissions@lafayette.edu
Phone: (610) 330-5100

LaGrange College
www.lagrange.edu
Office of Admission
601 Broad Street
LaGrange, GA 30240-2999
Fax: (706) 880-8010
E-mail: kpirrman@lagrange.edu
Phone: (706) 880-8005

Laguna College of Art and Design
www.lagunacollege.edu
2222 Laguna Canyon Road
Laguna Beach, CA 92651-1136
Fax: (949) 376-6009
E-mail: admissions@lagunacollege.edu
Phone: (949) 376-6000

Lake Area Technical Institute
www.lakeareatech.edu
Registrar
PO Box 730
Watertown, SD 57201
Fax: (605) 882-6299
Phone: (605) 882-5284

Lake City Community College
www.lakecitycc.edu
Admissions
149 SE College Place
Lake City, FL 32025-8703
Fax: (386) 754-4788
E-mail: ricev@lakecitycc.edu
Phone: (386) 754-4288

Lake Erie College
www.lec.edu
Admissions
391 West Washington Street
Painesville, OH 44077-3389
Fax: (440) 375-7005
E-mail: evalyko@lec.edu
Phone: (440) 375-7050

Lake Forest College
www.lakeforest.edu
Admission Office
555 North Sheridan Road
Lake Forest, IL 60045-2399
Fax: (847) 735-6271
E-mail: international@lakefoest.edu
Phone: (847) 735-5000

Lake Land College
www.lakelandcollege.edu
Admissions
5001 Lake Land Boulevard
Mattoon, IL 61938-9366
Fax: (217) 234-5390
E-mail: klotz@lakeland.cc.il.us
Phone: (217) 234-5382

Lake Michigan College
www.lakemichigancollege.edu
One Stop Area
2755 East Napier Avenue
Benton Harbor, MI 49022-1899
Fax: (269) 927-6656
E-mail: LEE@lakemichigancollege.edu
Phone: (269) 927-8100 ext. 5173

Lake Region State College
www.lrsc.nodak.edu
Student Services
1801 College Drive North
Devils Lake, ND 58301-1598
Fax: (701) 662-1581
E-mail: laurel.goulding@lrsc.nodak.edu
Phone: (701) 662-1513

Lake Superior College
www.lsc.edu
Admissions
2101 Trinity Road
Duluth, MN 55811
Fax: (218) 733-5945
E-mail: k.tanski@lsc.edu
Phone: (218) 733-7617

Lake Superior State University
www.lssu.edu
Admissions
650 West Easterday Avenue
Sault Ste. Marie, MI 49783-1699
Fax: (906) 635-6696
E-mail: admissions@lssu.edu
Phone: (906) 635-2231

Lake Tahoe Community College
www.ltcc.edu
Admissions & Records
One College Drive
South Lake Tahoe, CA 96150-4524
Fax: (530) 542-1781
E-mail: admissions@ltcc.edu
Phone: (530) 541-4660 ext. 211

Lake Washington Technical College
www.lwtc.ctc.edu
11605 132nd Avenue, NE
Kirkland, WA 98034
Fax: (425) 739-8110
E-mail: international.students@lwtc.ctc.edu
Phone: (425) 739-8100 ext. 502

Lake-Sumter Community College
www.lscc.edu
Assistant Registrar
9501 U.S. Highway 441
Leesburg, FL 34788-8751
Fax: (352) 365-3553
E-mail: colbornc@lscc.edu
Phone: (352) 365-3571

Lakeland Academy Division of Herzing College
www.herzing.edu
5700 West Broadway
Crystal, MN 55428
E-mail: info@mpls.herzing.edu
Phone: (763) 535-3000

Lakeland College
www.lakeland.edu
International Student Advisor
Box 359
Sheboygan, WI 53082-0359
Fax: (920) 565-1556
E-mail: International@lakeland.edu
Phone: (920) 565-1337

Lakeland Community College
www.lakelandcc.edu
Admissions
7700 Clocktower Drive
Kirtland, OH 44094
Fax: (440) 975-4330
E-mail: tcooper@lakelandcc.edu
Phone: (440) 953-7230

Lakes Region Community College
www.laconia.ccsnh.edu
Admission
379 Belmont Road
Laconia, NH 03246-9204
Fax: (603) 524-8084
E-mail: wfraser@nhctc.edu
Phone: (603) 524-3207

Lakeshore Technical College
www.gotoltc.edu
1290 North Avenue
Cleveland, WI 53015-9761
Fax: (920) 693-3561
E-mail: scott.lieburn@gotoltc.edu
Phone: (920) 693-1378

Lamar Community College
www.lamarcc.edu
Admissions
2401 South Main Street
Lamar, CO 81052-3999
E-mail: admissions@lamarcc.edu
Phone: (719) 336-2248

Lamar Institute of Technology
www.lit.edu
International Admissions Office
PO Box 10043
Beaumont, TX 77705
Fax: (409) 880-8414
Phone: (409) 880-8356

Lamar State College at Orange
www.lsco.edu
410 Front Street
Orange, TX 77630
Fax: (409) 882-3374
Phone: (409) 883-7750

Lamar State College at Port Arthur
www.lamarpa.edu
Vice President for Student Services
Box 310
Port Arthur, TX 77641-0310
Fax: (409) 984-6025
E-mail: Tom.Neal@lamarpa.edu
Phone: (409) 984-6156

Lamar University
www.lamar.edu
International Student Services
Box 10009
Beaumont, TX 77705
Fax: (409) 880-8414
E-mail: intladm@hal.lamar.edu
Phone: (409) 880-8356

Lambuth University
www.lambuth.edu
Interim Vice President for Enrollment
705 Lambuth Boulevard
Jackson, TN 38301-5296
Fax: (731) 425-3496
E-mail: admit@lambuth.edu
Phone: (731) 425-3240

Lander University
www.lander.edu
Office of Admissions
Stanley Avenue
Box 6007
Greenwood, SC 29649-2099
Fax: (864) 388-8125
E-mail: admissions@lander.edu
Phone: (864) 388-8307

Landmark College
www.landmark.edu
Admissions
River Road South
PO Box 820
Putney, VT 05346
Fax: (802) 387-6868
E-mail: admissions@landmark.edu
Phone: (802) 387-6718

Lane College
www.lanecollege.edu
Admissions
545 Lane Avenue
Jackson, TN 38301-4598
Fax: (901) 426-7559
E-mail: ebrown@lanecollege.edu
Phone: (901) 426-7532

Lane Community College
www.lanecc.edu
International/Multi-Cultural Services
4000 East 30th Avenue
Eugene, OR 97405
Fax: (541) 744-3995
E-mail: strahanc@lanecc.edu
Phone: (541) 747-4501 ext. 2683

Laney College
laney.peralta.edu
International Student Admissions
900 Fallon Street
Oakland, CA 94607
Fax: (510) 465-3257
E-mail: Globaled@peralta.edu
Phone: (510) 466-7380

Langston University
www.lunet.edu
Box 728
Langston, OK 73050
Fax: (405) 466-3391
E-mail: gtrobertson@lunet.edu
Phone: (405) 466-3428

Lansdale School of Business
www.lsb.edu
201 Church Road
North Wales, PA 19454
Fax: (215) 699-8770
E-mail: mjohnson@lsb.edu
Phone: (215) 699-5700

Lansing Community College
www.lansing.cc.mi.us
Admissions
422 North Washington Square
Lansing, MI 48901
Fax: (517) 483-9668
Phone: (517) 483-1200

Laramie County Community College
www.lccc.wy.edu
1400 East College Drive
Cheyenne, WY 82007-3299
Fax: (307) 778-1350
E-mail: hallison@lccc.wy.edu
Phone: (307) 778-1117

Laredo Community College
www.laredo.edu
International Student and Veteran Office
West End Washington Street
Laredo, TX 78040-4395
Fax: (956) 721-5493
E-mail: vghernandez@laredo.edu
Phone: (956) 764-5768

Las Positas College
www.laspositascollege.edu
Admissions and Records
3033 Collier Canyon Road
Livermore, CA 94551
Fax: (925) 606-6437
E-mail: sdupree@clpccd.cc.ca.us
Phone: (925) 373-5815

Lasell College
www.lasell.edu
Undergraduate Admission
1844 Commonwealth Avenue
Newton, MA 02466
Fax: (617) 243-2380
E-mail: info@lasell.edu
Phone: (617) 243-2225

Lassen College
www.lassencollege.edu
Box 3000
Susanville, CA 96130
Fax: (530) 257-8964
Phone: (530) 251-8808

Laura and Alvin Siegal College of Judaic Studies
www.siegalcollege.edu
Office of Student Services
26500 Shaker Boulevard
Cleveland, OH 44122
Fax: (216) 464-5827
E-mail: admissions@siegalcollege.edu
Phone: (216) 464-4050 ext. 101

Laurel Business Institute
www.laurel.edu
11 East Penn Street
PO Box 877
Uniontown, PA 15401
Fax: (724) 439-3607
E-mail: ddecker@laurel.edu
Phone: (724) 439-4900

Lawrence Technological University
www.ltu.edu
Director of Admissions
21000 West Ten Mile Road
Southfield, MI 48075-1058
Fax: (248) 204-2228
E-mail: international@ltu.edu
Phone: (248) 204-3160

Lawrence University
www.lawrence.edu
Admissions
Box 599
Appleton, WI 54912-0599
Fax: (920) 832-6782
E-mail: excelinternational@lawrence.edu
Phone: (920) 832-6500 ext. 7067

Lawson State Community College
www.lawsonstate.edu
Admissions and Records
3060 Wilson Road SW
Birmingham, AL 35221-1717
Fax: (205) 923-7106
E-mail: dallen@lawsonstate.edu
Phone: (205) 929-6361

Le Cordon Bleu College of Culinary Arts
www.atlantaculinary.com
1927 Lakeside Parkway
Tucker, GA 30084
Fax: (773) 938-4571
Phone: (770) 938-4711

Le Cordon Bleu College of Culinary Arts
www.twincitiesculinary.com
1315 Mendota Heights Road
Mendota Heights, MN 55120
Fax: (651) 452-5282
E-mail: info@twincitiesculinary.com
Phone: (651) 675-4700

Le Cordon Bleu College of Culinary Arts
www.VegasCulinary.com
1451 Center Crossing Road
Las Vegas, NV 89144
Fax: (702) 851-5299
E-mail: info@vegasculinary.com
Phone: (702) 365-7690

Le Moyne College
www.lemoyne.edu
Admission Office
1419 Salt Springs Road
Syracuse, NY 13214-1301
Fax: (315) 445-4711
E-mail: admission@lemoyne.edu
Phone: (315) 445-4300

Lebanon Valley College
www.lvc.edu
Admission Office
101 North College Avenue
Annville, PA 17003-1400
Fax: (717) 867-6026
E-mail: admission@lvc.edu
Phone: (717) 867-6181

Lee College
www.lee.edu
Registrar
Box 818
Baytown, TX 77522
Fax: (281) 425-6831
E-mail: bgriffith@lee.edu
Phone: (281) 467-5611

Lee University
www.leeuniversity.edu
Office of Admissions
1120 North Ocoee Street
PO Box 3450
Cleveland, TN 37320-3450
Fax: (423) 614-8533
E-mail: admissions@leeuniversity.edu
Phone: (423) 614-8500

Lees-McRae College
www.lmc.edu
Admissions
Box 128
Banner Elk, NC 28604
Fax: (828) 898-8707
E-mail: weedm@lmc.edu
Phone: (828) 898-3432

Lehigh University
www.lehigh.edu
Admissions
27 Memorial Drive West
Bethlehem, PA 18015-3094
Fax: (610) 758-4361
E-mail: admissions@lehigh.edu
Phone: (610) 758-3100

LeMoyne-Owen College
www.loc.edu
Admissions
807 Walker Avenue
Memphis, TN 38126
Fax: (901) 435-1524
E-mail: june_chinn-jointer@loc.edu
Phone: (901) 435-1500

Lenoir-Rhyne College
www.lrc.edu
Admissions
PO Box 7227
Hickory, NC 28603
Fax: (828) 328-7356
E-mail: admission@lrc.edu
Phone: (800) 277-5721

Lesley University
www.lesley.edu/lc
29 Everett Street
Cambridge, MA 02138-2790
Fax: (617) 349-8810
E-mail: lcadmissions@lesley.edu
Phone: (617) 349-8800

LeTourneau University
www.letu.edu
Admissions
PO Box 7001
Longview, TX 75607-7001
Fax: (903) 233-3411
E-mail: admissions@letu.edu
Phone: (800) 759-8811

Lewis & Clark College
www.lclark.edu
International Students Office
0615 SW Palatine Hill Road
Portland, OR 97219-7899
Fax: (503) 768-7301
E-mail: iso@lclark.edu
Phone: (503) 768-7305

Lewis University
www.lewisu.edu
Admission
One University Parkway
Box 297
Romeoville, IL 60446-2200
Fax: (815) 836-5002
E-mail: admissions@lewisu.edu
Phone: (815) 838-0500 ext. 5250

Lewis-Clark State College
www.lcsc.edu
International Admissions
500 Eighth Avenue
Lewiston, ID 83501-2698
Fax: (208) 792-2824
E-mail: ssdecker@lcsc.edu
Phone: (208) 792-2177

Lexington College
www.lexingtoncollege.edu
Director of Advising
310 South Peoria Street, Suite 512
Chicago, IL 60607-3534
Fax: (312) 226-6405
E-mail: ckustner@lexingtoncollege.edu
Phone: (312) 226-6294

Liberty University
www.liberty.edu
Office of International Admissions
1971 University Boulevard
Lynchburg, VA 24502
Fax: (434) 582-2424
E-mail: international@liberty.edu
Phone: (434) 592-4118

Life Pacific College
www.lifepacific.edu
Admissions
Attn: Admissions
1100 West Covina Boulevard
San Dimas, CA 91773-3203
Fax: (909) 599-6690
E-mail: admissions@lifepacific.edu
Phone: (909) 599-5433 ext. 314

Life University
www.life.edu
New Student Development - International
1269 Barclay Circle
Marietta, GA 30060
Fax: (770) 426-2895
E-mail: wononvah@life.edu
Phone: (770) 426-2847

Limestone College
www.limestone.edu
Admissions
1115 College Drive
Gaffney, SC 29340-3799
Fax: (864) 487-8706
E-mail: cphenicie@limestone.edu
Phone: (800) 795-7151 ext. 4554

Lincoln Christian College and Seminary
www.lccs.edu
Admissions Office Manager
100 Campus View Drive
Lincoln, IL 62656-2167
Fax: (217) 732-4199
E-mail: coladmis@lccs.edu
Phone: (217) 732-3168 ext. 2251

Lincoln College
www.lincolncollege.edu
Admissions
300 Keokuk Street
Lincoln, IL 62656
Fax: (217) 732-7715
E-mail: srachel@lincolncollege.com
Phone: (800) 569-0556

Lincoln Land Community College
www.llcc.edu
Special Admissions
5250 Shepherd Road
Box 19256
Springfield, IL 62794-9256
Fax: (217) 786-2492
E-mail: ron.gregoire@llcc.cc.il.us
Phone: (217) 786-2296

Lincoln Memorial University
www.lmunet.edu
Admissions
6965 Cumberland Gap Parkway
Harrogate, TN 37752-1901
Fax: (423) 869-6444
E-mail: admissions@lmunet.edu
Phone: (423) 869-6280

Lincoln Technical Institute: Allentown
www.lincolntech.com
5151 Tilghman Street
Allentown, PA 18104
Fax: (610) 395-2706
Phone: (610) 398-5300

Lincoln Technical Institute: Northeast Philadelphia
www.lincolntech.com
2180 Hornig Road
Philadelphia, PA 19116
Fax: (215) 969-3457
Phone: (215) 969-0869

Lincoln Technical Institute: Philadelphia
www.lincolntech.com
9191 Torresdale Avenue
Philadelphia, PA 19136
E-mail: dcunningham@lincolntech.com
Phone: (215) 335-0800

Lincoln University
www.lincolnuca.edu
Admissions
401 15th Street
Oakland, CA 94612
Fax: (510) 628-8012
E-mail: registrar@lincolnuca.edu
Phone: (510) 628-8010

Lincoln University
www.lincolnu.edu
Admissions
820 Chestnut Street/B-7 Young Hall
Jefferson City, MO 65102-0029
Fax: (573) 681-5889
E-mail: kosherm@lincolnu.edu
Phone: (573) 681-5599

Lincoln University
www.lincoln.edu
International Programs and Services
PO Box 179
Lincoln University, PA 19352-0999
Fax: (610) 932-1219
E-mail: lundy@lincoln.edu
Phone: (610) 932-8300 ext. 3785

Lindenwood University
www.lindenwood.edu
International Admissions
209 South Kingshighway
St. Charles, MO 63301-1695
Fax: (636) 949-4108
E-mail: international@lindenwood.edu
Phone: (636) 949-4982

Lindsey Wilson College
www.lindsey.edu
International Student Services
210 Lindsey Wilson Street
Columbia, KY 42728
Fax: (270) 384-8060
E-mail: mcalpins@lindsey.edu
Phone: (270) 384-8236

Linfield College
www.linfield.edu
Admission Office
900 SE Baker Street
McMinnville, OR 97218-6894
Fax: (503) 883-2472
E-mail: admission@linfield.edu
Phone: (503) 883-2213

Linn State Technical College
www.linnstate.edu
One Technology Drive
Linn, MO 65051
E-mail: admissions@linnstate.edu
Phone: (573) 897-5196

Linn-Benton Community College
www.linnbenton.edu
Admissions
6500 SW Pacific Boulevard
Albany, OR 97321-3779
Fax: (541) 917-4868
E-mail: admissions@linnbenton.edu
Phone: (541) 917-4811

Lipscomb University
www.lipscomb.edu
Office of Transfer and International Students
One University Park Drive
Nashville, TN 37204-3951
Fax: (615) 966-1804
E-mail: sylvia.braden@lipscomb.edu
Phone: (615) 966-6151

Livingstone College
www.livingstone.edu
Admissions
701 West Monroe Street
Salisbury, NC 28144-5213
Fax: (704) 216-6215
Phone: (704) 216-6001

Lock Haven University of Pennsylvania
www.lhup.edu
Admissions
Akeley Hall
Lock Haven, PA 17745
Fax: (570) 484-2201
E-mail: admissions@lhup.edu
Phone: (570) 484-2027

Loma Linda University
www.llu.edu
International Student and Scholar Services
Admissions Processing
Loma Linda University
Loma Linda, CA 92350
Fax: (909) 558-4879
E-mail: intlstdsrv@univ.llu.edu
Phone: (909) 558-4955

Lon Morris College
www.lonmorris.edu
Admission
800 College Avenue
Jacksonville, TX 75766
Fax: (903) 586-8562
E-mail: phorton@lonmorris.edu
Phone: (903) 589-4063

Lone Star College System
www.nhmccd.edu
Admissions Office
5000 Research Forest Drive
The Woodlands, TX 77381-4356
Phone: (832) 813-6500

Long Beach City College
www.lbcc.edu
International Student Program
4901 East Carson Street
Long Beach, CA 90808
Fax: (562) 938-4747
E-mail: dkinsella@lbcc.edu
Phone: (562) 938-4745

Long Island Business Institute
www.libi.edu
Admissions
6500 Jericho Turnpike
Commack, NY 11725
Fax: (631) 499-7114
E-mail: wchong@libi.edu
Phone: (718) 939-5100 ext. 112

Long Island University: Brooklyn Campus
www.liu.edu
Office of Admissions
1 University Plaza
Office of Admissions
Brooklyn, NY 11201
Fax: (718) 797-2399
E-mail: admissions@brooklyn.liu.edu
Phone: (718) 488-1011

Long Island University: C. W. Post Campus
www.liu.edu
Admissions
720 Northern Boulevard
Brookville, NY 11548-1300
Fax: (516) 299-2137
E-mail: ois@cwpost.liu.edu
Phone: (516) 299-2900

Long Technical College
www.kc-phoenix.com
13610 North Black Canyon Highway, Suite 104
Phoenix, AZ 85029
Fax: (602) 548-1956
E-mail: mcrance@kaplan.edu
Phone: (602) 548-1955 ext. 1366

Longwood University
www.longwood.edu
Admissions Office
201 High Street
Farmville, VA 23909-1898
Fax: (434) 395-2332
E-mail: admissions@longwood.edu
Phone: (434) 395-2060

Lorain County Community College
www.lorainccc.edu
International Recruitment and Support Services
1005 Abbe Road North
Elyria, OH 44035-1691
Fax: (440) 366-4167
E-mail: darredon@lorainccc.edu
Phone: (440) 366-4794

Loras College
www.loras.edu
Admissions Office
1450 Alta Vista Street
Dubuque, IA 52004-0178
Fax: (563) 588-7119
E-mail: barb.harrington@loras.edu
Phone: (563) 588-4915

Los Angeles City College
www.lacitycollege.edu
International Student Center
855 North Vermont Avenue
Los Angeles, CA 90029-3589
Fax: (323) 953-4013
Phone: (323) 953-4516

Los Angeles County College of Nursing and Allied Health
www.ladhs.org/lacusc/lacnah
1237 North Mission Road
Los Angeles, CA 90033-1084
Phone: (323) 226-4911

Los Angeles Harbor College
www.lahc.edu
International Student Office
1111 Figueroa Place
Wilmington, CA 90744-2397
Fax: (310) 233-4223
E-mail: gradyp@lahc.edu
Phone: (310) 233-4112

Los Angeles Mission College
www.lamission.edu
Counseling Office
13356 Eldridge Avenue
Sylmar, CA 91342-3245
Fax: (818) 365-3623
Phone: (818) 364-7600

Los Angeles Pierce College
www.piercecollege.edu
International Student Services
6201 Winnetka Avenue
Woodland Hills, CA 91371
Fax: (818) 710-2504
E-mail: intlstu@laccd.edu
Phone: (818) 719-6417

Los Angeles Southwest College
www.lasc.edu
1600 West Imperial Highway
Los Angeles, CA 90047-4899
Phone: (323) 241-5321

Los Angeles Trade and Technical College
www.lattc.edu
Foreign Student Center
400 West Washington Boulevard
Los Angeles, CA 90015-4181
E-mail: grunbad@lattc.edu
Phone: (213) 763-7000

Los Angeles Valley College
www.lavc.edu
International Students Coordinator
5800 Fulton Avenue
Valley Glen, CA 91401-4096
Fax: (818) 778-5519
E-mail: dunnae@lavc.edu
Phone: (818) 778-5518

Los Medanos College
www.losmedanos.edu
International Students Admissions
2700 East Leland Road
Pittsburg, CA 94565
Fax: (925) 427-6351
E-mail: mherste@losmedanos.edu
Phone: (925) 439-2181

Louisburg College
www.louisburg.edu
Admissions
501 North Main Street
Louisburg, NC 27549
Fax: (919) 496-1788
E-mail: sbuchanan@louisburg.edu
Phone: (919) 497-3244

Louisiana College
www.lacollege.edu
Admissions
LC Box 566
Pineville, LA 71359
Fax: (318) 487-7550
E-mail: admissions@lacollege.edu
Phone: (318) 487-7259

Louisiana State University and Agricultural and Mechanical College
www.lsu.edu
Undergraduate Admissions
1146 Pleasant Halll
Baton Rouge, LA 70803-2750
Fax: (225) 578-4433
E-mail: admissions@lsu.edu
Phone: (225) 578-1175

Louisiana State University at Eunice
www.lsue.edu
Registrar
Box 1129
Eunice, LA 70535
Fax: (337) 550-1306
E-mail: bwilliam@lsue.edu
Phone: (337) 550-1302

Louisiana State University Health Sciences Center
www.lsuhsc.edu
433 Bolivar Street
New Orleans, LA 70112-2223
Phone: (504) 568-4808

Louisiana State University in Shreveport
www.lsus.edu
Admissions and Records
One University Place
Shreveport, LA 71115-2399
Fax: (318) 797-5286
E-mail: mdiez@pilot.lsus.edu
Phone: (318) 797-5063

Louisiana Tech University
www.latech.edu
Office of Admissions
Box 3178
Ruston, LA 71272
Fax: (318) 257-2499
E-mail: usjba@vm.cc.latech.edu
Phone: (318) 257-3036

Louisville Technical Institute
www.louisvilletech.edu
Admissions
3901 Atkinson Square Drive
Louisville, KY 40218-4524
Fax: (502) 456-2341
E-mail: kwoods@louisvilletech.edu
Phone: (502) 456-6509

Lourdes College
www.lourdes.edu
Admissions
6832 Convent Boulevard
Sylvania, OH 43560-2898
Fax: (419) 882-3987
E-mail: lcadmits@lourdes.edu
Phone: (419) 824-3677

Lower Columbia College
www.lowercolumbia.edu
International Student Admissions Office
1600 Maple Street
Box 3010
Longview, WA 98632-0310
Fax: (360) 442-2379
E-mail: sstonge@lcc.ctc.edu
Phone: (360) 442-2300

Loyola College in Maryland
www.loyola.edu
International Programs
4501 North Charles Street
Baltimore, MD 21210-2699
Fax: (410) 617-2176
E-mail: admissions@loyola.edu
Phone: (410) 617-2910

Loyola Marymount University
www.lmu.edu
International Student Office
Admissions, 1 LMU Drive
Xavier Hall 100
Los Angeles, CA 90045-8350
Fax: (310) 338-5976
E-mail: dfolga@lmu.edu
Phone: (310) 338-2937

Loyola University Chicago
www.luc.edu
Office of International Affairs
820 North Michigan Avenue
Chicago, IL 60611-9810
Fax: (773) 508-7125
E-mail: mtheis@luc.edu
Phone: (773) 508-3899

Loyola University New Orleans
www.loyno.edu
Admissions Office (Campus Box 18)
6363 St. Charles Avenue
Campus Box 18
New Orleans, LA 70118-6195
Fax: (504) 865-3383
E-mail: admit@loyno.edu
Phone: (504) 865-3240

Lubbock Christian University
www.lcu.edu
Admissions Office
5601 19th Street
Lubbock, TX 79407
Fax: (806) 720-7162
E-mail: admissions@lcu.edu
Phone: (806) 720-7151

Luther College
www.luther.edu
Executive Director of International Admissions and College Marketing
700 College Drive
Decorah, IA 52101-1042
Fax: (563) 387-2159
E-mail: lundjon@luther.edu
Phone: (563) 387-1428

Lycoming College
www.lycoming.edu
Admissions Office
700 College Place
Williamsport, PA 17701
Fax: (570) 321-4317
E-mail: admissions@lycoming.edu
Phone: (570) 321-4026

Lynchburg College
www.lynchburg.edu
Admissions
1501 Lakeside Drive
Lynchburg, VA 24501-3199
Fax: (434) 544-8653
E-mail: admissions@lynchburg.edu
Phone: (800) 426-8101 ext. 8300

Lyndon State College
www.lyndonstate.edu
Admission
1001 College Road
PO Box 919
Lyndonville, VT 05851
Fax: (802) 626-6335
E-mail: bernard.hartshorn@lyndonstate.edu
Phone: (802) 626-6413

Lynn University
www.lynn.edu
Admissions
3601 North Military Trail
Boca Raton, FL 33431-5598
Fax: (561) 237-7100
E-mail: admission@lynn.edu
Phone: (561) 237-7900

Lyon College
www.lyon.edu
Enrollment Services
PO Box 2317
Batesville, AR 72503-2317
Fax: (870) 307-7542
E-mail: admissions@lyon.edu
Phone: (800) 423-2542

Macalester College
www.macalester.edu
Admissions
1600 Grand Avenue
St. Paul, MN 55105-1899
Fax: (651) 696-6724
E-mail: admissions@macalester.edu
Phone: (651) 696-6357

MacCormac College
www.maccormac.edu
Registrar's Office
29 East Madison Street
Chicago, IL 60602
Fax: (312) 922-3196
E-mail: msilva@maccormac.edu
Phone: (312) 922-1884 ext. 203

MacMurray College
www.mac.edu
Admissions
447 East College Avenue
Jacksonville, IL 62650-2590
Fax: (217) 291-0702
E-mail: admiss@mac.edu
Phone: (217) 479-7056

Macomb Community College
www.macomb.edu
South Campus - G301
14500 East Twelve Mile Road
Warren, MI 48088-3896
Fax: (586) 445-7140
E-mail: hughesr@macomb.cc.mi.us
Phone: (586) 445-7183

Madison Area Technical College
www.madison.tec.wi.us
3350 Anderson Street
Madison, WI 53704-2599
Fax: (608) 258-2329
Phone: (608) 246-6205

Madison Media Institute
www.madisonmedia.edu
2702 Agriculture Drive
Madison, WI 53718
E-mail: mmi@madisonmedia.com
Phone: (800) 236-4997

Madonna University
www.madonna.edu
International Students Office
36600 Schoolcraft Road
Livonia, MI 48150-1176
Fax: (734) 432-5393
E-mail: gphilson@madonna.edu
Phone: (734) 432-5791

Magdalen College
www.magdalen.edu
Admissions
511 Kearsarge Mountain Road
Warner, NH 03278
Fax: (603) 456-2660
E-mail: admissions@magdalen.edu
Phone: (603) 456-2656

Maharishi University of Management
www.mum.edu
Office for International Student Admissions
1000 North Fourth Street
Fairfield, IA 52557
Fax: (641) 472-1179
E-mail: intadmiss@mum.edu
Phone: (641) 472-1110

Maine College of Art
www.meca.edu
Admissions
522 Congress Street
Portland, ME 04101
Fax: (207) 772-5069
E-mail: Ktownsend@meca.edu
Phone: (207) 775-5157 ext. 254

Maine Maritime Academy
www.mainemaritime.edu
Admissions Office
66 Pleasant Street
Castine, ME 04420
Fax: (207) 326-2515
E-mail: admissions@mma.edu
Phone: (207) 326-2206

Malone College
www.malone.edu
Admissions
515 25th Street Northwest
Canton, OH 44709-3897
Fax: (330) 471-8149
E-mail: jcrussell@malone.edu
Phone: (330) 471-8100 ext. 8145

Manatee Community College
www.mccfl.edu
Foreign Student Coordinator
Box 1849
Bradenton, FL 34206-1849
Fax: (941) 727-6179
E-mail: hekkinw@mccfl.edu
Phone: (941) 752-5418

Manchester College
www.manchester.edu
Admissions Office
604 East College Avenue
North Manchester, IN 46962-0365
Fax: (260) 982-5239
E-mail: international@manchester.edu
Phone: (260) 982-5055

Manchester Community College
www.mcc.commnet.edu
Great Path PO Box 1046, MS 12
Manchester, CT 06040-1046
Fax: (860) 512-3221
E-mail: jmesquita@mcc.commnet.edu
Phone: (860) 512-3205

Manchester Community College
www.manchester.nhctc.edu
Admissions Department
1066 Front Street
Manchester, NH 03102-8518
Fax: (603) 668-5354
E-mail: lbaia@ccsnh.edu
Phone: (603) 668-6706 ext. 208

Manhattan Area Technical College
www.matc.net
Director of Admissions
3136 Dickens Avenue
Manhattan, KS 66503-2499
Fax: (785) 587-28l04
E-mail: rsmith@matc.net
Phone: (785) 587-2800 ext. 104

Manhattan College
www.manhattan.edu
International Student Advisor
4513 Manhattan College Parkway
Riverdale, NY 10471
Fax: (718) 862-8019
E-mail: admit@manhattan.edu
Phone: (718) 862-7200

Manhattan School of Music
www.msmnyc.edu
Admission and Financial Aid
120 Claremont Avenue
New York, NY 10027-4698
Fax: (212) 749-3025
E-mail: admission@msmnyc.edu
Phone: (212) 749-2802 ext. 4501

Manhattanville College
www.manhattanville.edu
Admissions
2900 Purchase Street
Purchase, NY 10577
Fax: (914) 694-1732
E-mail: admissions@mville.edu
Phone: (914) 323-5464

Mannes College The New School for Music
www.mannes.edu
Admissions
150 West 85th Street
New York, NY 10024
Fax: (212) 580-1738
E-mail: mannesadmissions@newschool.edu
Phone: (212) 580-0210 ext. 4807

Manor College
www.manor.edu
Full-Time Admissions
700 Fox Chase Road
Jenkintown, PA 19046-3319
Fax: (215) 576-6564
E-mail: ftadmiss@mail.manor.edu
Phone: (215) 884-2216 ext. 203

Mansfield University of Pennsylvania
www.mansfield.edu
Admissions Office
Alumni Hall
Mansfield, PA 16933
Fax: (570) 662-4121
E-mail: tsoderbe@mansfield.edu
Phone: (570) 662-4243

Maranatha Baptist Bible College
www.mbbc.edu
Admissions Office
745 West Main Street
Watertown, WI 53094
Fax: (920) 261-9109
E-mail: admissions@mbbc.edu
Phone: (920) 261-9300

Marian College
www.marian.edu
Office of Admission
3200 Cold Spring Road
Indianapolis, IN 46222-1997
Fax: (317) 955-6401
E-mail: cstoughton@marian.edu
Phone: (317) 955-6326

Marian College of Fond du Lac
www.mariancollege.edu
Admissions
45 South National Avenue
Fond du Lac, WI 54935-4699
Fax: (920) 923-8755
E-mail: jhartzell@mariancollege.edu
Phone: (920) 923-8117

Marian Court College
www.mariancourt.edu
Admissions
35 Little's Point Road
Swampscott, MA 01907-2896
Fax: (781) 595-3560
E-mail: info@mariancourt.edu
Phone: (781) 595-6768

Maric College: Palm Springs
www.mariccollege.edu
2475 East Tahquitz Canyon Way
Palm Springs, CA 92262
Phone: (760) 327-4562

Maric College: Panorama City
www.mariccollege.edu
Admissions
14355 Roscoe Boulevard
Panorama City, CA 91402
Fax: (818) 672-8919
E-mail: kschepps@mariccollege.edu
Phone: (818) 672-8907 ext. 105

Maric College: Salida
www.mariccollege.edu
5172 Kiernan Court
Salida, CA 95368
E-mail: wtriplett@mariccollege.edu
Phone: (209) 543-7000

Maric College: Vista
www.mariccollege.edu
2022 University Drive
Vista, CA 92083
Fax: (760) 630-1656
Phone: (760) 630-1555

Marietta College
www.marietta.edu
Office of Admission
215 Fifth Street
Marietta, OH 45750-4005
Fax: (740) 376-8888
E-mail: tara.hildt@marietta.edu
Phone: (800) 331-7896

Marion Military Institute
www.marionmilitary.edu
Admissions
1101 Washington Street
Marion, AL 36756-0420
Fax: (334) 683-2383
E-mail: sgm-hastings@marionmilitary.edu
Phone: (800) 664-1842

Marist College
www.marist.edu
Undergraduate Admission
3399 North Road
Poughkeepsie, NY 12601-1387
Fax: (845) 575-3215
E-mail: admission@marist.edu
Phone: (845) 575-3226

Marlboro College
www.marlboro.edu
Admissions
PO Box A
2582 South Road
Marlboro, VT 05344-0300
Fax: (802) 451-7555
E-mail: admissions@marlboro.edu
Phone: (800) 343-0049

Marquette University
www.marquette.edu
Campus International Programs
PO Box 1881
Milwaukee, WI 53201-1881
Fax: (414) 288-3701
E-mail: world@marquette.edu
Phone: (414) 288-7289

Mars Hill College
www.mhc.edu
Admissions
Blackwell Hall, Box 370
Mars Hill, NC 28754
Fax: (828) 689-1473
E-mail: cquatela@mhc.edu
Phone: (828) 689-1392

Marshall University
www.marshall.edu
Graduate/International Admissions
One John Marshall Drive
Huntington, WV 25755
Fax: (304) 696-3135
E-mail: admissions@marshall.edu
Phone: (304) 696-2243

Marshalltown Community College
www.marshalltowncommunitycollege.com
Carole Permar
3700 South Center Street
Marshalltown, IA 50158
Fax: (641) 752-8149
E-mail: dtrawny@iavalley.edu
Phone: (641) 752-7106

Martin Community College
www.martincc.edu
1161 Kehukee Park Road
Williamston, NC 27892-9988
Fax: (252) 792-0826
E-mail: jbussell@martincc.edu
Phone: (252) 792-1521 ext. 268

Martin Methodist College
www.martinmethodist.edu
Admissions
433 West Madison
Pulaski, TN 38478-2799
Fax: (931) 363-9803
E-mail: gude@martinmethodist.edu
Phone: (931) 363-9805

Mary Baldwin College
www.mbc.edu
Office of Admissions
Box 1500
Staunton, VA 24401
Fax: (540) 887-7279
E-mail: hward@mbc.edu
Phone: (540) 887-7113

Marygrove College
www.marygrove.edu
Office of Admissions
8425 West McNichols Road
Detroit, MI 48221
Fax: (313) 927-1399
E-mail: info@marygrove.edu
Phone: (313) 927-1240

Maryland Institute College of Art
www.mica.edu
International Admissions
1300 Mount Royal Avenue
Baltimore, MD 21217-4134
Fax: (410) 225-2337
E-mail: mlynn@mica.edu
Phone: (410) 225-2222

Marylhurst University
www.marylhurst.edu
Admissions and Enrollment Relations
PO Box 261
Marylhurst, OR 97036-0261
Fax: (503) 636-9526
E-mail: admissions@marylhurst.edu
Phone: (800) 634-9982 ext. 3321

Marymount College
www.marymountpv.edu
Office of Admission
30800 Palos Verdes Drive East
Rancho Palos Verdes, CA 90275-6299
Fax: (310) 265-0962
E-mail: admissions@marymountpv.edu
Phone: (310) 377-5501 ext. 211

Marymount Manhattan College
www.mmm.edu
Admissions Office
221 East 71st Street
New York, NY 10021-4597
Fax: (212) 517-0541
E-mail: kzaba@mmm.edu
Phone: (212) 517-0430

Marymount University
www.marymount.edu
Office of Admissions
2807 North Glebe Road
Arlington, VA 22207-4299
Fax: (703) 522-0349
E-mail:
international.admissions@marymount.edu
Phone: (703) 284-1500

Maryville College
www.maryvillecollege.edu
International Services
502 East Lamar Alexander Parkway
Maryville, TN 37804-5907
Fax: (865) 981-8010
E-mail: micki.pruitt@maryvillecollege.edu
Phone: (865) 981-8186

Maryville University of Saint Louis
www.maryville.edu
Office of Admissions
650 Maryville University Drive
St. Louis, MO 63141-7299
Fax: (314) 529-9927
E-mail: intl@maryville.edu
Phone: (314) 529-9350

Marywood University
www.marywood.edu
Office of Undergraduate Admissions
2300 Adams Avenue
Scranton, PA 18509-1598
Fax: (570) 961-4763
E-mail: yourfuture@marywood.edu
Phone: (800) 346-5014

Massachusetts Bay Community College
www.massbay.edu
Admissions
50 Oakland Street
Wellesley Hills, MA 02481
Fax: (781) 239-2525
E-mail: info@massbay.edu
Phone: (781) 239-2500

Massachusetts College of Art
www.massart.edu
Admissions
621 Huntington Avenue
Boston, MA 02115-5882
Fax: (617) 879-7250
E-mail: aicasiano@massart.edu
Phone: (617) 879-7229

Massachusetts College of Liberal Arts
www.mcla.edu
Admission
375 Church Street
North Adams, MA 01247
Fax: (413) 662-5179
E-mail: admissions@mcla.edu
Phone: (413) 662-5410

Massachusetts College of Pharmacy and Health Sciences
www.mcphs.edu
Admissions Office
179 Longwood Avenue
Boston, MA 02115-5896
Fax: (617) 732-2118
E-mail: admissions@mcphs.edu
Phone: (617) 732-2850

Massachusetts Institute of Technology
www.mit.edu
Undergraduate Admissions
77 Massachusetts Avenue, Rm 3-108
Cambridge, MA 02139-4307
Fax: (617) 258-8304
E-mail: mitintl@mit.edu
Phone: (617) 253-3400

Massachusetts Maritime Academy
www.maritime.edu
101 Academy Drive
Blinn Hall
Buzzards Bay, MA 02532-1803
Fax: (508) 830-5077
E-mail: admissions@maritime.edu
Phone: (800) 544-3400

The Master's College
www.masters.edu
International Student Office
21726 Placerita Canyon Road
Santa Clarita, CA 91321-1200
Fax: (661) 254-6232
E-mail: jmelcon@masters.edu
Phone: (661) 259-3540 ext. 3375

Mayland Community College
www.mayland.edu
Registrar's Office
Box 547
Spruce Pine, NC 28777
Fax: (828) 765-0728
Phone: (828) 765-7351

Maysville Community and Technical College
www.maysville.kctcs.edu
1755 US 68
Maysville, KY 41056
Fax: (606) 759-5818
E-mail: patee.massie@kctcs.edu
Phone: (606) 759-7141 ext. 66186

Mayville State University
www.mayvillestate.edu
Academic Records
330 Third Street, NE
Mayville, ND 58257-1299
Fax: (701) 788-4748
E-mail: mary_iverson@mayvillestate.edu
Phone: (701) 788-4773

McDaniel College
www.mcdaniel.edu
Office of Admissions
Two College Hill
Westminster, MD 21157-4390
Fax: (410) 857-2757
E-mail: admissions@mcdaniel.edu
Phone: (800) 638-5005

McDowell Technical Community College
www.mcdowelltech.edu
Admissions
54 College Drive
Marion, NC 28752
Fax: (828) 652-1014
E-mail: rickw@mcdowelltech.edu
Phone: (828) 652-0632

McHenry County College
www.mchenry.edu
Admissions
8900 U.S. Highway 14
Crystal Lake, IL 60012-2761
Fax: (815) 455-3766
E-mail: mweniger@mchenry.edu
Phone: (815) 479-7620

McKendree University
www.mckendree.edu
Admission
701 College Road
Lebanon, IL 62254
Fax: (618) 537-6496
E-mail: cethomas@mckendree.edu
Phone: (618) 537-6408

McLennan Community College
www.mclennan.edu
1400 College Drive
Waco, TX 76708
Fax: (254) 299-8694
Phone: (254) 299-8628

McMurry University
www.mcm.edu
Admissions
South 14th and Sayles Boulevard
McMurry Station, Box 278
Abilene, TX 79697-0001
Fax: (325) 793-4701
E-mail: admissions@mcm.edu
Phone: (325) 793-4700

McNeese State University
www.mcneese.edu
International Student Affairs
Box 91740 MSU
Lake Charles, LA 70609-1740
Fax: (337) 475-5151
E-mail: memerson@mcneese.edu
Phone: (337) 475-5243

McPherson College
www.mcpherson.edu
Student Enrollment Services
1600 East Euclid Street
Box 1402
McPherson, KS 67460-1402
Fax: (620) 241-8443
E-mail: admiss@mcpherson.edu
Phone: (620) 241-0731 ext. 1270

Medaille College
www.medaille.edu
Admissions
18 Agassiz Circle
Buffalo, NY 14214
Fax: (716) 632-1811
E-mail: jmatheny@medaille.edu
Phone: (716) 635-5033 ext. 2012

MedCentral College of Nursing
www.medcentral.edu
Enrollment and Student Affairs
335 Glessner Avenue
Mansfield, OH 44903-2265
Fax: (419) 520-2662
E-mail: admissions@medcentral.edu
Phone: (419) 520-2600

Memphis College of Art
www.mca.edu
Admissions
1930 Poplar Avenue
Overton Park
Memphis, TN 38104-2764
Fax: (901) 272-5158
E-mail: info@mca.edu
Phone: (901) 272-5151

Menlo College
www.menlo.edu
Admission Office
1000 El Camino Real
Atherton, CA 94027
Fax: (650) 543-4496
E-mail: bwilms@menlo.edu
Phone: (650) 543-3812

Mercer County Community College
www.mccc.edu
International Students Coordinator
Box B
Trenton, NJ 08690-1099
Fax: (609) 570-3861
E-mail: bambhrol@mccc.edu
Phone: (609) 570-3438

Mercer University
www.mercer.edu
Admissions
1400 Coleman Avenue
Macon, GA 31207-0001
Fax: (478) 301-2828
E-mail: tatum_cr@mercer.edu
Phone: (478) 301-2653

Mercy College
www.mercy.edu
International Student Office
555 Broadway
Dobbs Ferry, NY 10522
Fax: (914) 693-9455
E-mail: sguisuraga@mercy.edu
Phone: (914) 674-7284

Mercyhurst College
www.mercyhurst.edu
International House
501 East 38th Street
Erie, PA 16546-0001
Fax: (814) 824-2071
E-mail: eevans@mercyhurst.edu
Phone: (814) 824-2478

Meredith College
www.meredith.edu
Office of Admissions
3800 Hillsborough Street
Raleigh, NC 27607-5298
Fax: (919) 760-2348
E-mail: admissions@meredith.edu
Phone: (919) 760-8581

Meridian Community College
www.meridiancc.edu
Admissions
910 Highway 19 North
Meridian, MS 39307-5890
Fax: (601) 484-8838
E-mail: lconner@meridiancc.edu
Phone: (601) 484-8631

Merrimack College
www.merrimack.edu
Admissions
315 Turnpike Street
North Andover, MA 01845
Fax: (978) 837-5133
E-mail: admission@merrimack.edu
Phone: (978) 837-5100

Merritt College
www.merritt.edu
Foreign Student Adviser
12500 Campus Drive
Oakland, CA 94619
Fax: (510) 436-2512
E-mail: admissions@peralta.edu
Phone: (510) 436-2572

Mesa Community College
www.mc.maricopa.edu
Director of International Education
1833 West Southern Avenue
Mesa, AZ 85202
Fax: (480) 461-7805
E-mail: ida.mansourian@mcmail.maricopa.edu
Phone: (480) 461-7000

Mesa State College
www.mesastate.edu
Admissions
1100 North Avenue
Grand Junction, CO 81501
Fax: (970) 248-1973
E-mail: intladmissions@mesastate.edu
Phone: (970) 248-1613

Mesabi Range Community and Technical College
www.mr.mnscu.edu
Enrollment Services
1001 Chestnut Street West
Virginia, MN 55792-3448
Fax: (218) 749-0318
E-mail: s.twaddle@mr.mnscu.edu
Phone: (218) 749-0313

Mesalands Community College
www.mesalands.edu
911 South Tenth Street
Tucumcari, NM 88401
Phone: (575) 461-4413

Messiah College
www.messiah.edu
Admissions
PO Box 3005
One College Avenue
Grantham, PA 17027-0800
Fax: (717) 796-5374
E-mail: CBlount@messiah.edu
Phone: (717) 691-6000

Methodist University
www.methodist.edu
International Programs
5400 Ramsey Street
Fayetteville, NC 28311-1498
Fax: (910) 630-7682
E-mail: mbaggett@methodist.edu
Phone: (910) 630-7159

Metro Business College
www.metrobusinesscollege.edu
1732 North Kingshighway
Cape Girardeau, MO 36701
Fax: (573) 334-0617
E-mail: randy@metrobusinesscollege.edu
Phone: (573) 334-9181

Metropolitan College of New York
www.metropolitan.edu
75 Varick Street
New York, NY 10013-1919
Fax: (212) 343-8470
E-mail: slenhart@metropolitan.edu
Phone: (212) 343-1234 ext. 2700

Metropolitan Community College
www.mccneb.edu
Office of International/Intercultural Education
Box 3777
Omaha, NE 68103-0777
Fax: (402) 457-2238
E-mail: bvelazquez@mccneb.edu
Phone: (402) 457-2253

Metropolitan Community College: Blue River
www.mcckc.edu
Associate Dean of Students
3200 Broadway
Kansas City, MO 64111-2429
Fax: (816) 759-4478
E-mail: carroll.oneal@mcckc.edu
Phone: (816) 759-4101

Metropolitan Community College: Longview
www.mcckc.edu
Associate Dean of Students
500 Longview Road
Lee's Summit, MO 64081-2105
Fax: (816) 672-2040
E-mail: carroll.oneal@mcckc.edu
Phone: (816) 672-2249

Metropolitan Community College: Maple Woods
www.mcckc.edu
Associate Dean of Students
2601 NE Barry Road
Kansas City, MO 64156-1299
Fax: (816) 759-4103
E-mail: carroll.oneal@kcmetro.edu
Phone: (816) 759-4339

Metropolitan Community College: Penn Valley
www.mcckc.edu
Registrar
3201 Southwest Trafficway
Kansas City, MO 64111-2429
Fax: (816) 759-4478
E-mail: carlton.fowler@kcmetro.edu
Phone: (816) 759-4134

Metropolitan State College of Denver
www.mscd.edu
Admission
Campus Box 16
Box 173362
Denver, CO 80217
Fax: (303) 556-6345
E-mail: rossic@mscd.edu
Phone: (303) 556-3066

Miami Dade College
www.mdc.edu
International Student Services
11011 SW 104th Street
Miami, FL 33176-3393
Fax: (305) 237-2586
E-mail: fgiol@mdc.edu
Phone: (305) 237-2363

Miami International University of Art and Design
www.artinstitutes.edu/miami/
Director of Admissions
1501 Biscayne Boulevard, Suite 100
Miami, FL 33132-1418
Fax: (305) 374-5933
E-mail: kryan@aii.edu
Phone: (305) 428-5600

Miami University: Hamilton Campus
www.ham.muohio.edu
Office of Admission
1601 University Boulevard
Hamilton, OH 45011-3399
Fax: (513) 785-1807
E-mail: leeje1@muohio.edu
Phone: (513) 785-3111

Miami University: Middletown Campus
www.mid.muohio.edu
4200 East University Boulevard
Middletown, OH 45042
Fax: (513) 727-3223
E-mail: mlflynn@muohio.edu
Phone: (513) 727-3216

Miami University: Oxford Campus
www.muohio.edu
International Education Services
301 South Campus Avenue
Oxford, OH 45056-3434
Fax: (513) 529-7383
E-mail: admission@muohio.edu
Phone: (513) 529-2512

Michigan Jewish Institute
www.mji.edu
Student Affairs
25401 Coolidge Highway
Oak Park, MI 48237
Fax: (248) 414-6907
E-mail: plevine@mji.edu
Phone: (248) 414-6900 ext. 106

Michigan State University
www.msu.edu
International Students and Scholars
250 Administration Building
East Lansing, MI 48824
Fax: (517) 355-4657
E-mail: inhadms@msu.edu
Phone: (517) 353-1720

Michigan Technological University
www.mtu.edu
International Programs and Services
1400 Townsend Drive
Houghton, MI 49931-1295
Fax: (906) 487-1891
E-mail: ssuleman@mtu.edu
Phone: (906) 487-2160

Michigan Theological Seminary
www.mts.edu
41550 East Ann Arbor Trail
Plymouth, MI 48170-1622
Phone: (734) 207-9581

Mid-Continent University
www.midcontinent.edu
Admissions
99 Powell Road East
Mayfield, KY 42066-0357
Fax: (270) 247-3115
E-mail: admissions@midcontinent.edu
Phone: (270) 247-8521 ext. 312

Mid-Plains Community College Area
www.mpcc.edu
Student Advising
1101 Halligan Drive
North Platte, NE 69101
Fax: (308) 535-3710
E-mail: mihels@mpcc.edu
Phone: (800) 658-4308 ext. 3710

Mid-State Technical College
www.mstc.edu
Director of Admissions
500 32nd Street North
Wisconsin Rapids, WI 54494
Fax: (715) 422-5561
E-mail: james.barrett@mstc.edu
Phone: (715) 422-5446

MidAmerica Nazarene University
www.mnu.edu
International Student Office
2030 East College Way
Olathe, KS 66062-1899
Fax: (913) 791-3410
E-mail: rorton@mnu.edu
Phone: (913) 971-3765

Middle Georgia College
www.mgc.edu
Admissions
1100 Second Street SE
Cochran, GA 31014
Fax: (478) 934-3403
E-mail: ltravis@mgc.edu
Phone: (478) 934-3136

Middle Georgia Technical College
www.middlegatech.edu
Admissions
80 Cohen Walker Drive
Warner Robins, GA 31088
Fax: (478) 988-6947
E-mail: cjackson@middlegatech.edu
Phone: (478) 988-6850

Middle Tennessee State University
www.mtsu.edu
International Programs and Services Office
1301 East Main Street
Cope Administration Building 208
Murfreesboro, TN 37132
Fax: (615) 898-5178
E-mail: twubneh@mtsu.edu
Phone: (615) 898-2238

Middlebury College
www.middlebury.edu
The Emma Willard House
Middlebury, VT 05753-6002
Fax: (802) 443-2056
E-mail: admissions@middlebury.edu
Phone: (802) 443-3000

Middlesex Community College
www.mxcc.commnet.edu
Admissions
100 Training Hill Road
Middletown, CT 06457
Fax: (860) 344-7488
E-mail: mshabazz@mxcc.commnet.edu
Phone: (860) 343-5719

Middlesex Community College
www.middlesex.mass.edu
International Student Office
33 Kearney Square
Lowell, MA 01852-1987
Fax: (978) 656-3322
E-mail: admissions@middlesex.mass.edu
Phone: (978) 656-3258

Midland College
www.midland.edu
Director of Counseling
3600 North Garfield
Midland, TX 79705
Fax: (432) 685-4623
E-mail: sgrinnan@midland.edu
Phone: (432) 685-4505

Midland Lutheran College
www.mlc.edu
Admissions Office
900 North Clarkson
Fremont, NE 68025
Fax: (402) 941-6513
E-mail: watson@mlc.edu
Phone: (402) 941-6501

Midlands Technical College
www.midlandstech.edu
International Admissions
PO Box 2408
Columbia, SC 29202
Fax: (803) 790-7584
E-mail: vinsons@midlandstech.edu
Phone: (803) 738-7811

Midway College
www.midway.edu
Director of Admissions
512 East Stephens Street
Midway, KY 40347-1120
Fax: (859) 846-5787
E-mail: admissions@midway.edu
Phone: (859) 846-5347

Midwestern State University
www.mwsu.edu
International Student Service
3410 Taft Boulevard
Wichita Falls, TX 76308-2099
Fax: (940) 397-4087
E-mail: kerrie.cale@mwsu.edu
Phone: (940) 397-4344

Midwestern University: Glendale
www.midwestern.edu
19555 North 59th Avenue
Glendale, AZ 85308
E-mail: admissaz@midwestern.edu
Phone: (623) 572-3215

Mildred Elley
www.mildred-elley.edu
Admission
800 New Loudon Road, Suite 5120
Latham, NY 12110
Fax: (518) 786-0011
E-mail: mebsadms@nycap.rr.com
Phone: (518) 786-3171

Miles College
www.miles.edu
Office of the Dean of Students
5500 Myron-Massey Boulevard
Fairfield, AL 35064
Fax: (205) 923-9292
E-mail: carolyn@miles.edu
Phone: (205) 929-1655

Miller-Motte Technical College
www.miller-motte.net
8085 Rivers Avenue, Suite E
North Charleston, SC 29406
Fax: (843) 266-3424
Phone: (843) 574-0101

Miller-Motte Technical College: Cary
www.mmccary.net
2205 Walnut Street
Cary, NC 27518

Miller-Motte Technical College: Clarksville
www.miller-motte.com
Admissions
1820 Business Park Drive
Clarksville, TN 37040
Fax: (931) 552-2916
E-mail: rgmmb@usit.net
Phone: (931) 553-0071

Millersville University of Pennsylvania
www.millersville.edu
Admissions
PO Box 1002
Millersville, PA 17551-0302
Fax: (717) 871-2147
E-mail: susan.kastner@millersville.edu
Phone: (717) 872-3371

Milligan College
www.milligan.edu
Admissions
Box 210
Milligan College, TN 37682
Fax: (423) 461-8982
E-mail: tnbrinn@milligan.edu
Phone: (423) 461-8730

Millikin University
www.millikin.edu
Admission Office
1184 West Main Street
Decatur, IL 62522-2084
Fax: (217) 425-4669
E-mail: admis@millikin.edu
Phone: (217) 424-6210

Mills College
www.mills.edu
Admission Office
5000 MacArthur Boulevard
Oakland, CA 94613
Fax: (510) 430-3298
E-mail: admission@mills.edu
Phone: (510) 430-2135

Millsaps College
www.millsaps.edu
Admissions
1701 North State Street
Jackson, MS 39210-0001
Fax: (601) 974-1059
E-mail: admissions@millsaps.edu
Phone: (601) 974-1057

Milwaukee Area Technical College
www.matc.edu
Admissions
700 West State Street
Milwaukee, WI 53233-1443
Fax: (414) 297-7800
E-mail: robertsp@matc.edu
Phone: (414) 297-7087

Milwaukee Institute of Art & Design
www.miad.edu
Admissions
273 East Erie Street
Milwaukee, WI 53202
Fax: (414) 291-8077
E-mail: kmeinke@miad.edu
Phone: (414) 291-8070

Milwaukee School of Engineering
www.msoe.edu
Director of Admissions
1025 North Broadway
Milwaukee, WI 53202-3109
Fax: (414) 277-7475
E-mail: borens@msoe.edu
Phone: (414) 277-6765

Minneapolis Business College
www.mplsbusinesscollege.com
1711 West County Road B
Roseville, MN 55113
Fax: (651) 636-8185
Phone: (651) 636-7406

Minneapolis College of Art and Design
www.mcad.edu
Admissions
2501 Stevens Avenue
Minneapolis, MN 55404
Fax: (612) 874-3701
E-mail: admissions@mcad.edu
Phone: (612) 874-3760

Minneapolis Community and Technical College
www.minneapolis.edu
International Students Counselor
1501 Hennepin Avenue
Minneapolis, MN 55403-1779
Fax: (612) 659-6210
E-mail: kevin.kujawa@minneapolis.edu
Phone: (612) 659-6705

Minneapolis Drafting School Division of Herzing College
www.herzing.edu
5700 West Broadway
Minneapolis, MN 55428
E-mail: info@mpls.herzing.edu
Phone: (763) 535-3000

Minnesota School of Business: Plymouth
www.msbcollege.edu
1455 County Road 101 North
Plymouth, MN 55447
Phone: (866) 476-2121

Minnesota School of Business: Rochester
www.msbcollege.edu
2521 Pennington Drive NW
Rochester, MN 55901
Phone: (507) 536-9500

Minnesota School of Business: Shakopee
www.msbcollege.edu
1200 Shakopee Town Square
Shakopee, MN 55379
Phone: (866) 776-1200

Minnesota State College - Southeast Technical
www.southeastmn.edu
Student Services
1250 Homer Road
PO Box 409
Winona, MN 55987-0409
Fax: (507) 453-1450
E-mail: aducett@southeastmn.edu
Phone: (877) 853-8324

Minnesota State Community and Technical College: Fergus Falls
www.minnesota.edu
Student Services
1414 College Way
Fergus Falls, MN 56537-1000
Fax: (218) 736-1510
E-mail: lon.laager@minnesota.edu
Phone: (218) 736-1516

Minnesota State University: Mankato
www.mnsu.edu
Admissions Office
122 Taylor Center
Mankato, MN 56001
Fax: (507) 389-1511
E-mail: diane.berge@mnsu.edu
Phone: (507) 389-1822

Minnesota State University: Moorhead
www.mnstate.edu
Office of International Programs
Owens Hall
1104 Seventh Avenue South
Moorhead, MN 56563
Fax: (218) 299-5928
E-mail: intladms@mnstate.edu
Phone: (218) 477-2956

Minnesota West Community and Technical College
www.mnwest.edu
Student Services
1593 11th Avenue
Granite Falls, MN 56241
Fax: (501) 372-5801
E-mail: rebecca.hoey@mnwest.edu
Phone: (507) 372-3418

Minot State University
www.minotstateu.edu
MSU International Office
500 University Avenue West
Minot, ND 58707-5002
Fax: (701) 858-3386
E-mail: libby.claerbout@minotstateu.edu
Phone: (701) 858-3348

Minot State University: Bottineau Campus
www.misu-b.nodak.edu
Student Services
105 Simrall Boulevard
Bottineau, ND 58318-1198
Fax: (701) 228-5499
E-mail: paula.berg@misu.nodak.edu
Phone: (800) 542-6866

MiraCosta College
www.miracosta.edu
Institute for International Perspectives
One Barnard Drive
Oceanside, CA 92056-3899
Fax: (760) 757-8209
E-mail: iip@miracosta.edu
Phone: (760) 795-6897

Misericordia University
www.misericordia.edu
Admissions
301 Lake Street
Dallas, PA 18612-1098
Fax: (570) 675-2441
E-mail: jdessoye@misericordia.edu
Phone: (570) 674-6168

Mission College
www.missioncollege.org
International Students
3000 Mission College Boulevard
Santa Clara, CA 95054-1897
Fax: (408) 980-8980
E-mail: carol_qazi@wvm.edu
Phone: (408) 855-5110

Mississippi College
www.mc.edu
International Center
PO Box 4026
200 South Capitol Street
Clinton, MS 39058
Fax: (601) 925-7704
E-mail: brackenr@mc.edu
Phone: (601) 925-7635

Mississippi Gulf Coast Community College: Jefferson Davis Campus
www.mgccc.edu
Admissions
PO Box 548
Perkinston, MS 39573
Fax: (601) 928-6345
E-mail: ladd.taylor@mgccc.edu
Phone: (601) 928-6333

Mississippi State University
www.msstate.edu
Admissions & Scholarships
Box 6334
Mississippi State, MS 39762
Fax: (662) 325-1678
E-mail: admit@msstate.edu
Phone: (662) 325-2224

Mississippi University for Women
www.muw.edu
Admissions
Box W-1613
Columbus, MS 39701
Fax: (662) 241-7421
E-mail: ctaylor@muw.edu
Phone: (662) 329-7106

Mississippi Valley State University
www.mvsu.edu
Admissions and Recruitment
14000 Highway 82 West
Box 7222
Itta Bena, MS 38941-1400
Fax: (662) 254-3759
E-mail: nbtaylor@mvsu.edu
Phone: (662) 254-3347

Missouri Baptist University
www.mobap.edu
Admissions Office
One College Park Drive
St. Louis, MO 63141-8698
Fax: (314) 392-2232
E-mail: cruseye@mobap.edu
Phone: (314) 744-5301

Missouri Southern State University
www.mssu.edu
International Student Exchange Program
3950 East Newman Road
Joplin, MO 64801-1595
Fax: (417) 659-4445
E-mail: goad-s@mssu.edu
Phone: (417) 625-9372

Missouri State University
www.missouristate.edu
Office of International Student Services
901 South National Avenue
Springfield, MO 65897
Fax: (417) 836-7656
E-mail:
InternationalStudentServices@MissouriState.edu
Phone: (417) 836-6618

Missouri University of Science and Technology
www.mst.edu
Admissions
106 Parker Hall
1870 Miner Circle
Rolla, MO 65409
Fax: (573) 341-4082
E-mail: admissions@mst.edu
Phone: (573) 341-4165

Missouri Valley College
www.moval.edu
Admissions
500 East College Street
Marshall, MO 65340
Fax: (660) 831-4129
E-mail: simicm@moval.edu
Phone: (660) 831-4129

Mitchell College
www.mitchell.edu
Enrollment Management
437 Pequot Avenue
New London, CT 06320-4498
Fax: (860) 444-1209
E-mail: brown_c@mitchell.edu
Phone: (800) 443-2811

Mitchell Technical Institute
www.mitchelltech.com
821 North Capital Street
Mitchell, SD 57301
Fax: (605) 996-3299
E-mail: questions@mitchelltech.edu
Phone: (605) 995-3025

Moberly Area Community College
www.macc.edu
Student Services Office
101 College Avenue
Moberly, MO 65270-1304
Fax: (660) 263-2406
E-mail: jamesg@macc.edu
Phone: (660) 263-4110 ext. 235

Modesto Junior College
www.mjc.edu
Counseling Office
435 College Avenue
Modesto, CA 95350-5800
Fax: (209) 575-6805
E-mail: sturbanb@yosemite.cc.ca.us
Phone: (209) 575-6012

Mohave Community College
www.mohave.edu
Registrar
1971 Jagerson Avenue
Kingman, AZ 86409
Fax: (928) 757-0808
E-mail: johwil@mohave.edu
Phone: (928) 757-0809

Mohawk Valley Community College
www.mvcc.edu
International Student Services
1101 Sherman Drive
Utica, NY 13501-5394
Fax: (315) 792-5527
E-mail: international_admissions@mvcc.edu
Phone: (315) 792-5350

Molloy College
www.molloy.edu
Admissions
PO Box 5002
Rockville Centre, NY 11570
Fax: (516) 256-2247
E-mail: mlane@molloy.edu
Phone: (516) 678-5000 ext. 6230

Monmouth College
www.monm.edu
Admission
700 East Broadway
Monmouth, IL 61462-9989
Fax: (309) 457-2141
E-mail: cjohnsto@monm.edu
Phone: (309) 457-2131

Monmouth University
www.monmouth.edu
Undergraduate Admission
400 Cedar Avenue
West Long Branch, NJ 07764-1898
Fax: (732) 263-5166
E-mail: admission@monmouth.edu
Phone: (732) 571-3456

Monroe College
www.monroecollege.edu
International Admissions
Monroe College Way
Bronx, NY 10468
Fax: (718) 364-3552
E-mail: glopez@monroecollege.edu
Phone: (914) 632-5400

Monroe Community College
www.monroecc.edu
Admission Office
Office of Admissions-Monroe Community College
Box 92808
Rochester, NY 14692-8908
Fax: (585) 292-3860
Phone: (585) 292-2200

Montana State University: Billings
www.msubillings.edu
International Studies
1500 University Drive
Billings, MT 59101-0298
Fax: (406) 657-2254
E-mail: jsmothers@msubillings.edu
Phone: (406) 657-1705

Montana State University: Bozeman
www.montana.edu
International Programs
PO Box 172190
Bozeman, MT 59717-2190
Fax: (406) 994-1619
E-mail: ddebode@montana.edu
Phone: (406) 994-4031

Montana State University: Northern
www.msun.edu
Multi-Cultural/Recruiting
Box 7751
Havre, MT 59501
Fax: (406) 265-3792
E-mail: sgonsalez@msun.edu
Phone: (800) 662-6132

Montana Tech of the University of Montana
www.mtech.edu
Admissions
1300 West Park Street
Butte, MT 59701-8997
Fax: (406) 496-4710
E-mail: tcampeau@mtech.edu
Phone: (406) 496-4632

Montcalm Community College
www.montcalm.edu
Enrollment Services
2800 College Drive
Sidney, MI 48885
Fax: (989) 328-2950
E-mail: admissions@montcalm.edu
Phone: (989) 329-1245

Montclair State University
www.montclair.edu
Undergraduate Admissions Office
One Normal Avenue
Upper Montclair, NJ 07043-1624
Fax: (973) 655-7700
E-mail: langdonj@mail.montclair.edu
Phone: (973) 655-5116

Monterey Peninsula College
www.mpc.edu
International Student Programs
980 Fremont Street
Monterey, CA 93940-4799
Fax: (831) 645-1390
E-mail: international_center@mpc.cc.ca.us
Phone: (831) 645-1357

Montgomery County Community College
www.mc3.edu
Office of Admissions
340 DeKalb Pike
PO Box 400
Blue Bell, PA 19422
Fax: (215) 619-7188
E-mail: amarcrof@mc3.edu
Phone: (215) 641-6550

Montreat College
www.montreat.edu
Admissions
Box 1267
Montreat, NC 28757-1267
Fax: (828) 669-0120
E-mail: jhiggins@montreat.edu
Phone: (828) 669-8012 ext. 3798

Moody Bible Institute
www.moody.edu
Associate Dean of Enrollment Management
820 North La Salle Boulevard
Chicago, IL 60610
Fax: (312) 329-8987
E-mail: annette.moy@moody.edu
Phone: (312) 329-4267

Moore College of Art and Design
www.moore.edu
Admissions Office
The Parkway at 20th Street
Philadelphia, PA 19103-1179
Fax: (215) 568-3547
E-mail: admiss@moore.edu
Phone: (215) 965-4014

Moorpark College
www.moorparkcollege.edu
International Student
7075 Campus Road
Moorpark, CA 93021
Fax: (805) 378-1499
E-mail: international@vcccd.net
Phone: (805) 378-1414

Moraine Park Technical College
www.morainepark.edu
Student Services
235 North National Avenue
Box 1940
Fond du Lac, WI 54935-1940
Fax: (920) 924-3421
E-mail: ahruska@morainepark.edu
Phone: (920) 924-6378

Moraine Valley Community College
www.morainevalley.edu
Office of International Student Affairs
9000 West College Parkway
Palos Hills, IL 60465-0937
Fax: (708) 974-0561
E-mail: viverito@morainevalley.edu
Phone: (708) 974-5334

Moravian College
www.moravian.edu
Admissions Office
1200 Main Street
Bethlehem, PA 18018
Fax: (610) 625-7930
E-mail: admissions@moravian.edu
Phone: (610) 861-1320

Morehead State University
www.moreheadstate.edu
Office of International Education
100 Admissions Center
Morehead, KY 40351
Fax: (606) 783-9118
E-mail: p.jaisingh@moreheadstate.edu
Phone: (606) 783-2096

Morehouse College
www.morehouse.edu
International Studies
830 Westview Drive SW
Atlanta, GA 30314
Fax: (404) 524-5635
E-mail: gwade@morehouse.edu
Phone: (404) 681-2800 ext. 2690

Morgan Community College
www.morgancc.edu
Student Services
920 Barlow Road
Fort Morgan, CO 80701
Fax: (970) 867-6608
Phone: (970) 867-3081

Morgan State University
www.morgan.edu
Admission & Recruiting
1700 East Cold Spring Lane
Baltimore, MD 21251
Fax: (443) 885-8200
E-mail: admissions@morgan.edu
Phone: (443) 885-3000

Morningside College
www.morningside.edu
Admissions
1501 Morningside Avenue
Sioux City, IA 51106
Fax: (712) 274-5101
E-mail: curryte@morningside.edu
Phone: (712) 274-5511

Morris College
www.morris.edu
Admissions and Records
100 West College Street
Sumter, SC 29150-3599
Fax: (803) 773-8241
E-mail: dcalhoun@morris.edu
Phone: (803) 934-3225

Morrison Institute of Technology
www.morrison.tec.il.us
Admissions
701 Portland Avenue
Morrison, IL 61270-2959
Fax: (815) 772-7584
E-mail: admissions@morrison.tec.il.us
Phone: (815) 772-7218

Morton College
www.morton.edu
Associate Dean Student Development &
Records
3801 South Central Avenue
Cicero, IL 60804-4398
Fax: (708) 656-9592
E-mail: Lizette.Urbina@morton.edu
Phone: (708) 656-8000 ext. 151

Motlow State Community College
www.mscc.cc.tn.us
Admissions and Records
Box 8500
Lynchburg, TN 37352-8500
Fax: (931) 393-1971
E-mail: galsup@mscc.edu
Phone: (931) 393-1529 ext. 1529

Mott Community College
www.mcc.edu
Executive Dean, Student Services
1401 East Court Street
Flint, MI 48503-2089
Fax: (810) 232-9442
E-mail: Delores.Deen@mcc.edu
Phone: (810) 762-0243

Mount Aloysius College
www.mtaloy.edu
Admissions
7373 Admiral Peary Highway
Cresson, PA 16630
Fax: (814) 886-6441
E-mail: admissions@mtaloy.eu
Phone: (814) 886-6383

Mount Angel Seminary
www.mtangel.edu
One Abbey Drive
St. Benedict, OR 97373
Fax: (503) 845-3126
Phone: (503) 845-3951

Mount Holyoke College
www.mtholyoke.edu
Office of Admission
Newhall Center
50 College Street
South Hadley, MA 01075-1488
Fax: (413) 538-2409
E-mail: admission@mtholyoke.edu
Phone: (413) 538-2773

Mount Ida College
www.mountida.edu
Admissions Office
777 Dedham Street
Newton, MA 02459
Fax: (617) 928-4507
E-mail: admissions@mountida.edu
Phone: (617) 928-4535

Mount Marty College
www.mtmc.edu
Admission
1105 West Eighth Street
Yankton, SD 57078
Fax: (605) 668-1508
E-mail: mmcadmit@mtmc.edu
Phone: (800) 658-4552

Mount Mary College
www.mtmary.edu
Admission
2900 North Menomonee River Parkway
Milwaukee, WI 53222
Fax: (414) 256-0180
E-mail: admiss@mtmary.edu
Phone: (414) 256-1219

Mount Mercy College
www.mtmercy.edu
Admissions
1330 Elmhurst Drive NE
Cedar Rapids, IA 52402-4797
Fax: (319) 363-5270
E-mail: mruss@mtmercy.edu
Phone: (319) 368-6460

Mount Olive College
www.mountolivecollege.edu
Vice President Student Development
634 Henderson Street
Mount Olive, NC 28365
Fax: (919) 658-7180
E-mail: dfried@moc.edu
Phone: (919) 658-2502

Mount San Antonio College
www.mtsac.edu
1100 North Grand Avenue
Walnut, CA 91789
Fax: (909) 468-4068
Phone: (909) 594-5611 ext. 4415

Mount San Jacinto College
www.msjc.edu
Student Services
1499 North State Street
San Jacinto, CA 92583
Fax: (951) 654-6738
E-mail: jvelkoff@msjc.edu
Phone: (951) 487-6752 ext. 1417

Mount St. Mary's University
www.msmary.edu
Admissions Office
16300 Old Emmitsburg Road
Emmitsburg, MD 21727
Fax: (301) 447-5860
E-mail: admissions@msmary.edu
Phone: (301) 447-5214

Mount Union College
www.muc.edu
International Admissions
1972 Clark Avenue
Alliance, OH 44601-3993
Fax: (330) 823-5097
E-mail: slabausa@muc.edu
Phone: (330) 829-8207

Mount Vernon Nazarene University
www.mvnu.edu
Admissions
800 Martinsburg Road
Mount Vernon, OH 43050
Fax: (740) 393-0511
E-mail: admissions@mvnu.edu
Phone: (866) 462-6868 ext. 4510

Mount Wachusett Community College
www.mwcc.edu
Admissions
444 Green Street
Gardner, MA 01440-1000
Fax: (978) 630-9554
E-mail: jwwalsh@mwcc.mass.edu
Phone: (978) 630-9110

Mountain State University
www.mountainstate.edu
Coordinator for International Student Services
609 South Kanawha Street
PO Box 9003
Beckley, WV 25802-9003
Fax: (304) 252-2896
E-mail: dheaster@mountainstate.edu
Phone: (304) 929-1551

Mountain View College
www.mvc.dcccd.edu
Office of Enrollment Management
4849 West Illinois Avenue
Dallas, TX 75211-6599
Fax: (214) 860-8570
E-mail: sxs6310@dcccd.edu
Phone: (214) 860-8817

Mt. Hood Community College
www.mhcc.cc.or.us
Admissions
26000 Southeast Stark Street
Gresham, OR 97030
Fax: (503) 491-6006
Phone: (503) 491-7393

Mt. Sierra College
www.mtsierra.edu
101 East Huntington Drive
Monrovia, CA 91016
Fax: (626) 359-1378
E-mail: pazadian@mtsierra.edu
Phone: (626) 873-2144

MTI College
www.mticollege.edu
Admissions
5221 Madison Avenue
Sacramento, CA 95841
Fax: (916) 339-0305
E-mail: epatterson@mticollege.edu
Phone: (916) 339-1500

Muhlenberg College
www.muhlenberg.edu
Office of Admissions
2400 Chew Street
Allentown, PA 18104
Fax: (484) 664-3234
E-mail: admissions@muhlenberg.edu
Phone: (484) 664-3245

Murray State University
www.murraystate.edu
Admissions
113 Sparks Hall
Murray, KY 42071
Fax: (270) 809-3780
E-mail: Lori.Brisendine@murraystate.edu
Phone: (270) 809-3755

Muscatine Community College
www.eicc.edu
Admissions
152 Colorado Street
Muscatine, IA 52761-5396
Fax: (563) 288-6104
E-mail: kwatson@eicc.edu
Phone: (563) 288-6012

Muskegon Community College
www.muskegoncc.edu
Enrollment Services
221 South Quarterline Road
Muskegon, MI 49442
Fax: (231) 777-0209
E-mail: donella.cooper@muskegoncc.edu
Phone: (231) 777-0404

Muskingum College
www.muskingum.edu
Director of International Admission and
Immigration Services Operations
163 Stormont Street
New Concord, OH 43762-1199
Fax: (740) 826-8100
E-mail: memerson@muskingum.edu
Phone: (740) 826-8127

Napa Valley College
www.napavalley.edu
2277 Napa-Vallejo Highway
Napa, CA 94558
Fax: (707) 253-3064
E-mail: snelson@napavalley.edu
Phone: (707) 253-3000

Naropa University
www.naropa.edu
Admissions
2130 Arapahoe Avenue
Boulder, CO 80302-6697
Fax: (303) 546-3583
E-mail: admissions@naropa.edu
Phone: (303) 546-4657

Nash Community College
www.nash.cc.nc.us
Box 7488
Rocky Mount, NC 27804-0488
Fax: (252) 443-0828
Phone: (252) 443-4011 ext. 300

Nashua Community College
www.nashua.ccsnh.edu
Admissions
505 Amherst Street
Nashua, NH 03063-1026
Fax: (603) 882-6923
E-mail: jcurtis@ccsnh.edu
Phone: (603) 882-6923 ext. 1547

Nassau Community College
www.ncc.edu
Admissions
One Education Drive
Garden City, NY 11530
Fax: (516) 572-9743
E-mail: admoff@ncc.edu
Phone: (516) 572-7345

National American University: Denver
www.national.edu
Admissions
1325 South Colorado Boulevard, Suite 100
Denver, CO 80222-3308
Fax: (303) 758-6810
E-mail: tdefice@national.edu
Phone: (303) 758-6700

National American University: Rapid City
www.national.edu/rc
International Admissions
321 Kansas City Street
Rapid City, SD 57701
Fax: (605) 394-4871
E-mail: mmerriam@national.edu
Phone: (605) 394-4896

National American University: Rio Rancho
www.national.edu
4775 Indian School Road Northeast, Suite 200
Albuquerque, NM 87110
Fax: (505) 348-3755
Phone: (505) 348-3750

**National College of Business and
Technology: Arecibo**
www.nationalcollegepr.edu
Admissions Director
PO Box 4035, MSC 452
Arecibo, PR 00614
Fax: (787) 780-5134
E-mail: mepagan@nationalcollegepr.edu
Phone: (787) 780-5134 ext. 4114

**National College of Business and
Technology: Bayamon**
www.nationalcollegepr.edu
Admissions Office
PO Box 2036
Bayamón, PR 00960
Fax: (787) 779-4909
E-mail: mepagan@nationalcollegepr.edu
Phone: (787) 780-5134 ext. 4114

**National College of Business and
Technology: Rio Grande**
www.nationalcollegepr.edu
PO Box 3064
Rio Grande, PR 00745
Fax: (787) 888-8280
E-mail: lbalseiro@nationalcollegepr.edu
Phone: (787) 809-5100

National College: Bartlett
5760 Stage Road
Bartlett, TN 38134
Phone: (901) 213-1681

National College: Cincinnati
6871 Steger Drive
Cincinnati, OH 45237
Phone: (513) 761-1291

National College: Danville
www.ncbt.edu
PO Box 6400
Roanoke, VA 24017
Fax: (859) 236-1063
E-mail: market@educorp.edu
Phone: (859) 236-6991

National College: Dayton
1837 Woodman Center Drive
Kettering, OH 45420
Phone: (937) 299-9450

National College: Florence
www.ncbt.edu
PO Box 6400
Roanoke, VA 24017
Fax: (606) 525-8961
E-mail: market@educorp.edu
Phone: (606) 525-6510

National College: Harrisonburg
www.national-college.edu
PO Box 6400
Roanoke, VA 24017
Fax: (540) 432-1133
E-mail: market@national-college.edu
Phone: (800) 664-1886

National College: Indianapolis
6060 Castleway Drive West
Indianapolis, IN 46250
Phone: (317) 578-7353

National College: Knoxville
www.ncbt.edu
8415 Kingston Pike
Knoxville, TN 37919
Phone: (865) 539-2011

National College: Lexington
www.ncbt.edu
PO Box 6400
Roanoke, VA 24017
Fax: (859) 233-3054
E-mail: market@educorp.edu
Phone: (859) 253-0621

National College: Madison
900 Madison Square
Madison, TN 37115
Phone: (615) 612-3015

National College: Memphis
3545 Lamar Avenue, Suite 1
Memphis, TN 38118
Phone: (901) 363-9046

National College: Roanoke Valley
www.national-college.edu
PO Box 6400
Roanoke, VA 24017-0400
Fax: (540) 444-4198
Phone: (540) 986-1800

National College: Stow
3855 Fishercreek Road
Stow, OH 44224

National College: Youngstown
3487 Belmont Avenue
Youngstown, OH 44505

National Hispanic University
www.nhu.edu
Admissions/Registrar
14271 Story Road
San Jose, CA 95127-3823
Fax: (408) 254-1369
Phone: (408) 273-2772

National Labor College
www.georgemeany.org
10000 New Hampshire Avenue
Silver Spring, MD 20904
Fax: (301) 431-5411
Phone: (301) 431-6400

National Park Community College
www.npcc.edu
Vice President of Student Affairs
101 College Drive
Hot Springs, AR 71913
Fax: (501) 760-4100
E-mail: mpicking@gccc.edu
Phone: (501) 760-4222

National Polytechnic College of Science
www.natpoly.edu
272 South Fries Avenue
Wilmington, CA 90744
Fax: (310) 834-7132
Phone: (310) 834-2501

National University
www.nu.edu
International Programs Office
11255 North Torrey Pines Road
La Jolla, CA 92037-1011
Fax: (858) 541-7995
E-mail: ipo@nu.edu
Phone: (858) 541-7960

National-Louis University
www.nl.edu
Student Affairs
122 South Michigan Avenue
Chicago, IL 60603
Fax: (847) 256-1057
E-mail: brouzan@nl.edu
Phone: (312) 261-3461

Naugatuck Valley Community College
www.nvcc.commnet.edu
Admissions
750 Chase Parkway
Waterbury, CT 06708-3089
Fax: (203) 596-2189
E-mail: jdaniels@nvcc.commnet.edu
Phone: (203) 575-8034

Navajo Technical College
www.navajotech.edu
PO Box 849
Crownpoint, NM 87313
Fax: (505) 786-5644
E-mail: rdamon@navajotech.edu
Phone: (505) 786-4326

Navarro College
www.navarrocollege.edu
3200 West Seventh Avenue
Corsicana, TX 75110
Fax: (903) 875-7353
E-mail: amy.connolly@navarrocollege.edu
Phone: (903) 875-7370

Nazareth College of Rochester
www.naz.edu
Center for International Education
4245 East Avenue
Rochester, NY 14618-3790
Fax: (585) 389-2372
E-mail: geisen1@naz.edu
Phone: (585) 389-2370

Nebraska College of Technical Agriculture
www.ncta.unl.edu
404 East 7th Street
Curtis, NE 69025-0069
Fax: (308) 367-5203
E-mail: sshaner3@unl.edu
Phone: (308) 367-4124 ext. 257

Nebraska Indian Community College
www.thenicc.edu
2451 St. Mary's Avenue
Omaha, NE 68105
Fax: (402) 344-8358
E-mail: estevens@thenicc.edu
Phone: (402) 344-8428 ext. 14

Nebraska Methodist College of Nursing and Allied Health
www.methodistcollege.edu
Admissions Office
720 North 87th Street
Omaha, NE 68114
Fax: (402) 354-7020
E-mail: deann.sterner@methodistcollege.edu
Phone: (402) 354-7200

Nebraska Wesleyan University
www.nebrwesleyan.edu
Admissions Office
5000 St. Paul Avenue
Lincoln, NE 68504
Fax: (402) 465-2177
E-mail: admissions@nebrwesleyan.edu
Phone: (402) 465-2218

Neosho County Community College
www.neosho.edu
Coordinator for International Services
800 West 14th Street
Chanute, KS 66720
Fax: (316) 431-0082
E-mail: aneff@neosho.edu
Phone: (316) 431-2820 ext. 240

Neumann College
www.neumann.edu
Admissions
One Neumann Drive
Aston, PA 19014-1298
Fax: (610) 558-5652
E-mail: neumann@neumann.edu
Phone: (610) 558-5616

Neumont University
www.neumont.edu
10701 South River Front Parkway, Suite 300
South Jordan, UT 84095
Fax: (801) 302-2880
E-mail: info@neumont.edu
Phone: (801) 302-2800

Nevada State College
www.nsc.nevada.edu
1125 Nevada State Drive
Henderson, NV 89002
E-mail: admissions@nsc.nevada.edu
Phone: (702) 992-2130

New College of Florida
www.ncf.edu
Office of Admissions
5800 Bay Shore Road
Sarasota, FL 34243-2109
Fax: (941) 487-5010
E-mail: admissions@ncf.edu
Phone: (941) 487-5000

New England College
www.nec.edu
Admissions
102 Bridge Street
Henniker, NH 03242
Fax: (603) 428-7230
E-mail: admission@nec.edu
Phone: (603) 428-2223

New England College of Finance
www.finance.edu
10 High Street, Suite 204
Boston, MA 02110
Fax: (617) 951-2533
Phone: (617) 951-2350

New England Conservatory of Music
www.newenglandconservatory.edu
Admissions
290 Huntington Avenue
Boston, MA 02115
Fax: (617) 585-1115
E-mail:
admissions@newenglandconservatory.edu
Phone: (617) 585-1101

New England Culinary Institute
www.neci.edu
Admissions
56 College Street
Montpelier, VT 05602
Fax: (802) 225-3280
E-mail: admissions@neci.edu
Phone: (877) 223-6324

New England Institute of Art
www.artinstitutes.edu/boston
Admissions
10 Brookline Place West
Brookline, MA 02445-7295
Fax: (617) 582-4680
E-mail: asanford@aii.edu
Phone: (800) 903-4425

New England Institute of Technology
www.neit.edu
Admissions Office
2500 Post Road
Warwick, RI 02886-2286
Fax: (401) 738-5122
E-mail: mseltzer@neit.edu
Phone: (401) 467-7744 ext. 3489

New England School of Communications
www.nescom.edu
Admissions
One College Circle
Bangor, ME 04401
Fax: (207) 947-3987
E-mail: grantl@nescom.edu
Phone: (207) 941-7176

New Jersey City University
www.njcu.edu
2039 Kennedy Boulevard
Jersey City, NJ 07305-1597
E-mail: admissions@njcu.edu
Phone: (201) 200-3234

New Jersey Institute of Technology
www.njit.edu
Office of International Students and Faculty
University Heights
Newark, NJ 07102
Fax: (973) 596-3461
E-mail: grundy@njit.edu
Phone: (973) 596-2451

New Mexico Highlands University
www.nmhu.edu
International Education Center
Box 9000
Las Vegas, NM 87701
Fax: (505) 454-3511
E-mail: eclayton@nmhu.edu
Phone: (505) 454-3058

New Mexico Institute of Mining and Technology
www.nmt.edu
International & Exchange Programs
801 Leroy Place
Socorro, NM 87801
Fax: (575) 835-5959
E-mail: bsamter@admin.nmt.edu
Phone: (575) 835-5022

New Mexico Junior College
www.nmjc.edu
Office of Admission
5317 Lovington Highway
Hobbs, NM 88240
Fax: (575) 392-0322
E-mail: jmcdonald@nmjc.edu
Phone: (575) 392-5112

New Mexico Military Institute
www.nmmi.edu
Student Assistance Center
101 West College Boulevard
Roswell, NM 88201-5173
Fax: (505) 624-8058
E-mail: admissions@nmmi.edu
Phone: (505) 624-8360

New Mexico State University
www.nmsu.edu
International Programs, MSC 3567
Box 30001, MSC 3A
Las Cruces, NM 88003-8001
Fax: (575) 646-2558
E-mail: cip@nmsu.edu
Phone: (575) 646-3199

New Mexico State University at Alamogordo
alamo.nmsu.edu/
Office of Student Services
2400 North Scenic Drive
Alamogordo, NM 88310
Fax: (505) 439-3760
Phone: (505) 439-3716

New River Community and Technical College
www.newriver.edu
167 Dye Drive
Beckley, WV 25801
Fax: (304) 255-5889
Phone: (304) 255-5812

New York Career Institute
www.nyci.com
11 Park Place
New York, NY 10007
Fax: (212) 385-7574
E-mail: cmcmahon@nyci.edu
Phone: (212) 962-0002

New York Institute of Technology
www.nyit.edu
Admissions
Box 8000
Old Westbury, NY 11568
Fax: (212) 977-3460
E-mail: jhopkins@nyit.edu
Phone: (212) 261-1513

New York School of Interior Design
www.nysid.edu
International Student Adviser
170 East 70th Street
New York, NY 10021-5110
Fax: (212) 472-1867
E-mail: douglasd@nysid.edu
Phone: (212) 472-1500 ext. 203

New York University
www.nyu.edu
Undergraduate Admissions
22 Washington Square North
New York, NY 10011-9108
Fax: (212) 995-4902
E-mail: admissions@nyu.edu
Phone: (212) 998-4500

Newberry College
www.newberry.edu
Admissions
2100 College Street
Newberry, SC 29108
Fax: (803) 321-5138
E-mail: admissions@newberry.edu
Phone: (803) 321-5129

Newbury College
www.newbury.edu
Admission
129 Fisher Avenue
Brookline, MA 02445
Fax: (617) 731-9618
E-mail: info@newbury.edu
Phone: (617) 730-7007

Newman University
www.newmanu.edu
Admissions
3100 McCormick
Wichita, KS 67213-2097
Fax: (316) 942-4483
E-mail: larreaa@newmanu.edu
Phone: (316) 942-4291 ext. 2487

NewSchool of Architecture & Design
www.newschoolarch.edu
1249 F Street
San Diego, CA 92101
Fax: (619) 235-4651
E-mail: admissions@newschoolarch.edu
Phone: (619) 235-4100

Niagara County Community College
www.niagaracc.suny.edu
Admissions Office
3111 Saunders Settlement Road
Sanborn, NY 14132-9460
Fax: (716) 614-6820
E-mail: ritter@niagaracc.suny.edu
Phone: (716) 614-4001

Niagara University
www.niagara.edu
Student Life
Niagara University, NY 14109
Fax: (716) 286-8477
E-mail: deb@niagara.edu
Phone: (716) 286-8405

Nicholls State University
www.nicholls.edu
Office of Admissions
PO Box 2004-NSU
Thibodaux, LA 70310
Fax: (985) 448-4929
E-mail: marilyn.gonzales@nicholls.edu
Phone: (985) 449-7038

Nichols College
www.nichols.edu
Admissions
PO Box 5000
Dudley, MA 01571-5000
Fax: (508) 943-9885
E-mail: paul.brower@nichols.edu
Phone: (508) 213-2371

Norfolk State University
www.nsu.edu
Admissions
700 Park Avenue
Norfolk, VA 23504
Fax: (757) 823-2078
E-mail: internationaladmissions@nsu.edu
Phone: (757) 823-2870

Normandale Community College
www.normandale.edu
Admissions
9700 France Avenue South
Bloomington, MN 55431
Fax: (952) 487-8230
E-mail:
antoinette.bowling-harris@normandale.edu
Phone: (952) 487-8207

North Carolina Central University
www.nccu.edu
Student Affairs
PO Box 19717
Durham, NC 27707
Fax: (919) 530-7645
E-mail: emosby@nccu.edu
Phone: (919) 530-7492

North Carolina School of the Arts
www.ncarts.edu
Admissions
1533 South Main Street
Winston-Salem, NC 27127-2188
Fax: (336) 770-3370
E-mail: Admissions@ncarts.edu
Phone: (336) 770-1471

North Carolina State University
www.ncsu.edu
Undergraduate Admissions
203 Peele Hall, Box 7103
Raleigh, NC 27695-7103
Fax: (919) 515-5039
E-mail: undergrad_admissions@ncsu.edu
Phone: (919) 515-2434

North Carolina Wesleyan College
www.ncwc.edu
Office of Admissions
3400 North Wesleyan Boulevard
Rocky Mount, NC 27804
Fax: (252) 985-5319
E-mail: adm@ncwc.edu
Phone: (800) 488-6292

North Central College
www.northcentralcollege.edu
Office of Admissions
PO Box 3063
Naperville, IL 60566-7063
Fax: (630) 637-5819
E-mail: admissions@noctrl.edu
Phone: (630) 637-5800

North Central Kansas Technical College
www.ncktc.edu
P.O. Box 507
Beloit, KS 67420
Fax: (785) 738-2903
Phone: (800) 658-4655

North Central Michigan College
www.ncmich.edu
Student Services
1515 Howard Street
Petoskey, MI 49770
Fax: (231) 348-6672
E-mail: pwelm@ncmc.cc.mi.us
Phone: (888) 298-6605

North Central State College
www.ncstatecollege.edu
Office of Admissions
Box 698
Mansfield, OH 44901
Fax: (419) 775-4757
E-mail: mmonnes@ncstatecollege.edu
Phone: (419) 775-4824

North Central Texas College
www.nctc.edu
1525 West California Street
Gainesville, TX 76240
Fax: (940) 668-6049
E-mail: admissions@nctc.edu
Phone: (940) 668-4404

North Central University
www.northcentral.edu
Admissions
910 Elliot Avenue
Minneapolis, MN 55404
Fax: (612) 343-4146
E-mail: arstumph@northcentral.edu
Phone: (612) 343-4460

North Country Community College
www.nccc.edu
Enrollment Management
23 Santanoni Avenue
PO Box 89
Saranac Lake, NY 12983
Fax: (518) 891-0898
E-mail: admissions@nccc.edu
Phone: (888) 879-6222 ext. 233

North Dakota State College of Science
www.ndscs.nodak.edu
Admissions Office
800 North 6th Street
Wahpeton, ND 58076
Fax: (701) 671-2201
E-mail: admissions@kitten.nodak.edu
Phone: (800) 342-4325 ext. 32202

North Dakota State University
www.ndsu.edu
Office of International Programs
Ceres Hall 124
PO Box 5454
Fargo, ND 58105-5454
Fax: (701) 231-1014
E-mail: ndsu.international@ndsu.nedu
Phone: (701) 231-7895

North Florida Community College
www.nfcc.edu
Admissions
325 NW Turner Davis Drive
Madison, FL 32340
Fax: (850) 973-1697
E-mail: wallerd@nfcc.edu
Phone: (850) 973-1622

North Florida Institute: Orange Park
560 Wells Road
Orange Park, FL 32073
Phone: (904) 269-7086

North Georgia College & State University
www.ngcsu.edu
Admissions
82 College Circle
Dahlonega, GA 30597
Fax: (706) 864-1478
E-mail: kapruitt@ngcsu.edu
Phone: (706) 864-1883

North Greenville University
www.ngu.edu
Admissions
PO Box 1892
Tigerville, SC 29688-1892
Fax: (864) 977-7177
E-mail: ewall@ngc.edu
Phone: (864) 977-7001

North Hennepin Community College
www.nhcc.edu
Admissions
7411 85th Avenue North
Minneapolis, MN 55445
Fax: (763) 493-0563
E-mail: AGemmell@nhcc.edu
Phone: (763) 424-0722

North Idaho College
www.nic.edu
Office of Admissions
1000 West Garden Avenue
Coeur d'Alene, ID 83814-2199
Fax: (208) 769-3399
E-mail: cahanhi@nic.edu
Phone: (208) 769-3311

North Iowa Area Community College
www.niacc.edu
Student Services
500 College Drive
Mason City, IA 50401
Fax: (641) 422-4385
E-mail: pierskar@niacc.edu
Phone: (641) 422-4245

North Lake College
www.northlakecollege.edu
International Center
5001 North MacArthur Boulevard
Irving, TX 75038-3899
Fax: (972) 273-3138
E-mail: nlcintl@dcccd.edu
Phone: (972) 273-3155

North Metro Technical College
www.northmetrotech.edu
5198 Ross Road
Acworth, GA 30102
Fax: (770) 975-4142
E-mail: info@northmetrotech.edu
Phone: (770) 975-4000

North Park University
www.northpark.edu
3225 West Foster Avenue
Chicago, IL 60625-4895
Fax: (773) 244-5243
E-mail: internationals@northpark.edu
Phone: (773) 244-5510

North Seattle Community College
www.northseattle.edu
International Student Programs
9600 College Way North
Seattle, WA 98103
Fax: (206) 527-3794
E-mail: international@sccd.ctc.edu
Phone: (206) 527-3672

North Shore Community College
www.northshore.edu
Enrollment Services
One Ferncroft Road
Box 3340
Danvers, MA 01923-0840
Fax: (781) 477-2143
E-mail: lbarrett@northshore.edu
Phone: (978) 762-4000 ext. 6225

Northampton Community College
www.northampton.edu
Admissions
3835 Green Pond Road
Bethlehem, PA 18020
Fax: (610) 861-4560
E-mail: pboulous@northampton.edu
Phone: (610) 861-5500

Northcentral Technical College
www.ntc.edu
International Education
1000 West Campus Drive
Wausau, WI 54401
Fax: (715) 675-0629
E-mail: bissonet@ntc.edu
Phone: (715) 675-3331 ext. 4807

Northcentral University
www.ncu.edu
Executive Director of Enrollment
10000 East University
Prescott Valley, AZ 86314
Fax: (928) 541-7817
E-mail: bpassey@ncu.edu
Phone: (928) 541-7777 ext. 8085

Northeast Community College
www.northeastcollege.com
Admissions
801 East Benjamin Avenue
Box 469
Norfolk, NE 68702-0469
Fax: (402) 844-7400
E-mail: shelley@northeastcollege.com
Phone: (402) 844-7282

Northeast Iowa Community College
www.nicc.edu
Admissions
Box 400
Calmar, IA 52132
Fax: (563) 562-4369
E-mail: keunem@nicc.edu
Phone: (800) 728-2256 ext. 307

Northeast Mississippi Community College
www.nemcc.edu
Admissions
101 Cunningham Boulevard
Booneville, MS 38829
Fax: (662) 720-7405
E-mail: admitme@nemcc.edu
Phone: (662) 720-7239

Northeast Texas Community College
www.ntcc.edu
Director of Admissions and Recruitment
Box 1307
Mount Pleasant, TX 75456-1307
Fax: (903) 572-6712
E-mail: skeys@ntcc.cc.tx.us
Phone: (903) 434-8136

Northeast Wisconsin Technical College
www.nwtc.edu
2740 West Mason Street
Box 19042
Green Bay, WI 54307-9042
Fax: (920) 498-6882
E-mail: mark.franks@nwtc.edu
Phone: (920) 498-6269

Northeastern Junior College
www.njc.edu
Admissions
100 College Avenue
Sterling, CO 80751
Fax: (970) 521-6801
E-mail: tina.joyce@njc.edu
Phone: (970) 521-7000

Northeastern Oklahoma Agricultural and Mechanical College
www.neo.edu
International Student Office
200 I Street Northeast
Miami, OK 74354-6497
Fax: (918) 540-6406
E-mail: kksutton@neo.edu
Phone: (918) 540-6229

Northeastern State University
www.nsuok.edu
International Student Services
600 North Grand Avenue
Tahlequah, OK 74464-2399
Fax: (918) 458-2342
E-mail: ranallo@nsuok.edu
Phone: (918) 444-2011

Northeastern Technical College
www.netc.edu
Drawer 1007
Cheraw, SC 29520
Fax: (843) 921-1476
E-mail: mnewton@netc.edu
Phone: (843) 921-6900

Northeastern University
www.northeastern.edu
International Admissions
360 Huntington Avenue, 150 Richards Hall
Boston, MA 02115-9959
Fax: (617) 373-8780
E-mail: internationaladmissions@neu.edu
Phone: (617) 373-2200

Northern Arizona University
www.nau.edu
International Student Admissions
PO Box 4084
Flagstaff, AZ 86011-4084
Fax: (928) 523-9489
E-mail: cie@nau.edu
Phone: (928) 523-2409

Northern Essex Community College
www.necc.mass.edu
100 Elliott Street
Haverhill, MA 01830-2399
E-mail: admissions@necc.mass.edu
Phone: (978) 556-3600

Northern Illinois University
www.niu.edu
International Student Office
DeKalb, IL 60115-2854
Fax: (815) 753-1488
E-mail: admission-info@niu.edu
Phone: (815) 753-8276

Northern Kentucky University
www.nku.edu
International Student Affairs
Administrative Center 401, Northern Kentucky University
Nunn Drive
Highland Heights, KY 41099
Fax: (859) 572-6178
E-mail: kimballv@nku.edu
Phone: (859) 572-6517

Northern Maine Community College
www.nmcc.edu
33 Edgemont Drive
Presque Isle, ME 04769
Fax: (207) 768-2831
E-mail: nbcasava@nmcc.edu
Phone: (207) 768-2700

Northern Michigan University
www.nmu.edu
International Studies
1401 Presque Isle Avenue
Marquette, MI 49855
Fax: (906) 227-2204
E-mail: iao@nmu.edu
Phone: (906) 227-2510

Northern New Mexico College
www.nnmc.edu
Registrar
921 Paseo de Onate
Espanola, NM 87532
Fax: (505) 747-2191
E-mail: mikec@nnmc.edu
Phone: (505) 471-2193

Northern State University
www.northern.edu
1200 South Jay Street
Aberdeen, SD 57401-7198
Fax: (605) 626-2587
E-mail: admissions1@wolf.northern.edu
Phone: (800) 678-5330

Northern Virginia Community College
www.nvcc.edu
4001 Wakefield Chapel Road
Annandale, VA 22003-3796
Phone: (703) 323-3000

Northland College
www.northland.edu
Admission Office
1411 Ellis Avenue
Ashland, WI 54806
Fax: (715) 682-1258
E-mail: admit@northland.edu
Phone: (715) 682-1677

Northland Community & Technical College
www.northlandcollege.edu
Admissions
1101 Highway One East
Thief River Falls, MN 56701
Fax: (218) 681-0774
E-mail: eugene.klinke@northlandcollege.edu
Phone: (218) 681-0701

Northwest Christian College
www.nwcc.edu
Admissions
828 East 11th Avenue
Eugene, OR 97401-3745
Fax: (541) 684-7317
E-mail: admissions@nwcc.edu
Phone: (541) 684-7201

Northwest College
www.northwestcollege.edu
Office of Enrollment Services
231 West 6th Street
Powell, WY 82435
Fax: (307) 754-6249
E-mail: admission@nwc.cc.wy.us
Phone: (307) 754-6101

Northwest College of Art
www.nca.edu
Registrar
16301 Creative Drive NE
Poulsbo, WA 98370
Fax: (360) 779-9933
E-mail: kstolp@nca.edu
Phone: (360) 697-8133

Northwest Indian College
www.nwic.edu
2522 Kwina Road
Bellingham, WA 98226-9217
Fax: (360) 392-4333
Phone: (360) 676-2772 ext. 4269

Northwest Mississippi Community College
www.northwestms.edu
Registrar/Admissions
4975 Highway 51 North
Senatobia, MS 38668
Fax: (662) 562-3221
E-mail: glspears@northwestms.edu
Phone: (662) 562-3209

Northwest Missouri State University
www.nwmissouri.edu
Admissions
800 University Drive
Maryville, MO 64468-6001
Fax: (660) 562-1821
E-mail: admissions@nwmissouri.edu
Phone: (660) 562-1149

Northwest Nazarene University
www.nnu.edu
Student Development
623 Holly Street
Nampa, ID 83686-5897
Fax: (208) 467-8468
E-mail: plrogers@nnu.edu
Phone: (208) 467-8768

Northwest Technical College
www.ntcmn.edu
Counseling Center
905 Grant Avenue Southeast
Bemidji, MN 56601-4907
Fax: (218) 333-6697
E-mail: debbie.grovum@ntcmn.edu
Phone: (218) 333-6618

Northwest Technical Institute
www.nti.edu
950 Blue Gentian Road
Eagan, MN 55121
Fax: (952) 944-9274
E-mail: info@nti.edu
Phone: (952) 944-0080

Northwest University
www.northwestu.edu
Director of Traditional Admissions
5520 108th Avenue, NE
Box 579
Kirkland, WA 98083-0579
Fax: (425) 889-5224
E-mail: ben.thomas@northwestu.edu
Phone: (425) 889-5212

Northwest Vista College
www.accd.edu/nvc
Student Success
3535 North Ellison Drive
San Antonio, TX 78251-4217
Fax: (210) 348-2024
E-mail: tmolina@accd.edu
Phone: (210) 348-2043

Northwestern Business College
www.northwesternbc.edu
Office of the Registrar
4839 North Milwaukee Avenue
Chicago, IL 60630
Fax: (773) 725-2731
E-mail: gdomke@northwesternbc.edu
Phone: (773) 777-4220 ext. 240

Northwestern College
www.nwciowa.edu
Director of International and Multicultural Affairs
101 Seventh Street, SW
Orange City, IA 51041
Fax: (712) 707-7164
E-mail: kmcmahan@nwciowa.edu
Phone: (712) 707-7016

Northwestern College
www.nwc.edu
Admissions Office
3003 Snelling Avenue North
Saint Paul, MN 55113-1598
Fax: (651) 631-5680
E-mail: admissions@nwc.edu
Phone: (651) 631-5111

Northwestern Health Sciences University
www.nwhealth.edu
2501 West 84th Street
Bloomington, MN 55431
E-mail: admit@nwhealth.edu
Phone: (952) 888-4777 ext. 409

Northwestern Michigan College
www.nmc.edu
Admissions Office
1701 East Front Street
Traverse City, MI 49686
Fax: (231) 995-1339
E-mail: jbensley@nmc.edu
Phone: (231) 995-1034

Northwestern Oklahoma State University
www.nwosu.edu
International Student Advisor
709 Oklahoma Boulevard
Alva, OK 73717-2799
Fax: (580) 327-8413
E-mail: bjpope@nwosu.edu
Phone: (580) 327-8435

Northwestern Polytechnic University
www.npu.edu
Director of Admissions
47671 Westinghouse Drive
Fremont, CA 94539
Fax: (510) 657-8975
E-mail: catherine@npu.edu
Phone: (510) 657-5913

Northwestern State University
www.nsula.edu
Admissions Office
Roy Hall, Room 209
Northwestern State University
Natchitoches, LA 71497
Fax: (318) 357-4660
E-mail: admissions@nsula.edu
Phone: (318) 357-4078

Northwestern University
www.northwestern.edu
Office of Undergraduate Admission
1801 Hinman Avenue
PO Box 3060
Evanston, IL 60204-3060
Fax: (847) 467-2331
E-mail: nuinternational@northwestern.edu
Phone: (847) 491-7271

Northwood University: Florida
www.northwood.edu
Admissions
2600 North Military Trail
West Palm Beach, FL 33409-2911
Fax: (561) 640-3328
E-mail: fladmit@northwood.edu
Phone: (561) 478-5500

Northwood University: Michigan
www.northwood.edu
Admissions
4000 Whiting Drive
Midland, MI 48640
Fax: (989) 837-4490
E-mail: miadmit@northwood.edu
Phone: (989) 837-4273

Northwood University: Texas
www.northwood.edu
Admissions
1114 West FM 1382
Cedar Hill, TX 75104
Fax: (972) 291-3824
E-mail: txadmit@northwood.edu
Phone: (800) 927-9663

Norwalk Community College
www.ncc.commnet.edu
International Student Office
188 Richards Avenue
Norwalk, CT 06854-1655
Fax: (203) 857-6948
E-mail: DBogusky@ncc.commnet.edu
Phone: (203) 857-7289

Norwich University
www.norwich.edu
158 Harmon Drive
Northfield, VT 05663
Fax: (802) 485-2002
E-mail: nuadm@norwich.edu
Phone: (802) 485-2002

Nossi College of Art
www.nossi.com
Admissions
907 Rivergate Parkway, Building E-6
Goodlettsville, TN 37072
Fax: (615) 851-1087
E-mail: admissions@nossi.com
Phone: (615) 851-1088

Notre Dame College
www.notredamecollege.edu
Admissions
4545 College Road
Cleveland, OH 44121-4293
Fax: (216) 381-3802
E-mail: cnolan@ndc.edu
Phone: (216) 381-1680 ext. 5355

Notre Dame de Namur University
www.ndnu.edu
Admission Office
1500 Ralston Avenue
Belmont, CA 94002-1908
Fax: (650) 508-3426
E-mail: admiss@ndnu.edu
Phone: (650) 508-3600

Nova Southeastern University
www.nova.edu
Individual Program Offices
3301 College Avenue
Fort Lauderdale, FL 33314
Fax: (954) 262-3846
E-mail: intl@nsu.nova.edu
Phone: (954) 262-7240

Nunez Community College
www.nunez.edu
Admissions Office
3710 Paris Road
Chalmette, LA 70043
Fax: (504) 278-7487
E-mail: bmaillet@nunez.edu
Phone: (504) 278-7467

Nyack College
www.nyack.edu
Admissions
1 South Boulevard
Nyack, NY 10960-3698
Fax: (845) 358-3047
E-mail: admissions@nyack.edu
Phone: (845) 358-1710 ext. 350

Oakbridge Academy of Arts
www.oaa.edu
Admissions
1250 Greensburg Road
Lower Burrell, PA 15068
Fax: (724) 335-3367
E-mail: jrs32076@cs.com
Phone: (724) 335-5336

Oakland City University
www.oak.edu
138 North Lucretia Street
Oakland City, IN 47660
Fax: (812) 749-1433
E-mail: ocuadmit@oak.edu
Phone: (800) 737-5125

Oakland Community College
www.oaklandcc.edu
International Student Advisor
2480 Opdyke Road
Bloomfield Hills, MI 48304-2266
Fax: (248) 232-4441
E-mail: ddschack@oaklandcc.edu
Phone: (248) 232-4440

Oakland University
www.oakland.edu
Office of Admissions
101 North Foundation Hall
Oakland University
Rochester, MI 48309-4401
Fax: (248) 370-4462
E-mail: ouinfo@oakland.edu
Phone: (248) 370-3360

Oakton Community College
www.oakton.edu
Admission & Enrollment Management Office
1600 East Golf Road
Des Plaines, IL 60016
Fax: (847) 635-1890
E-mail: lynn@oakton.edu
Phone: (847) 635-1713

Oakwood University
www.oakwood.edu
Enrollment Management
7000 Adventist Boulevard, NW
Huntsville, AL 35896
Fax: (256) 726-7154
E-mail: jbartholomew@oakwood.edu
Phone: (256) 726-7423

Oberlin College
www.oberlin.edu
Admissions
Carnegie Building, 101 North Professor Street
Oberlin, OH 44074
Fax: (440) 775-6905
E-mail: mary.conger@oberlin.edu
Phone: (440) 775-8411

Occidental College
www.oxy.edu
Admission
1600 Campus Road
Los Angeles, CA 90041
Fax: (323) 341-4875
E-mail: admission@oxy.edu
Phone: (323) 259-2700

Ocean County College
www.ocean.edu
Admissions/Records
College Drive
Box 2001
Toms River, NJ 08754-2001
Fax: (732) 255-0444
E-mail: mmehlmann@ocean.edu
Phone: (732) 255-0400 ext. 2969

Odessa College
www.odessa.edu
Admissions
201 West University
Odessa, TX 79764-7127
Fax: (432) 335-6824
E-mail: ngarcia@odess.edu
Phone: (432) 335-6313

Oglala Lakota College
www.olc.edu
Registrar
Box 490
Kyle, SD 57752-0490
Fax: (605) 455-2787
Phone: (605) 455-6033

Oglethorpe University
www.oglethorpe.edu
International Admissions Office
4484 Peachtree Road NE
Atlanta, GA 30319-2797
Fax: (404) 364-8500
E-mail: admission@oglethorpe.edu
Phone: (404) 364-8307

Ohio Business College
www.ohiobusinesscollege.edu
1907 North Ridge Road
Lorain, OH 44055
Fax: (440) 277-7989
E-mail: lorain@ohiobusinesscollege.edu
Phone: (440) 277-0021

Ohio College of Massotherapy
www.ocm.edu
225 Heritage Woods Drive
Akron, OH 44321
Fax: (330) 665-5021
E-mail: admissions@ocm.edu
Phone: (330) 665-1084

Ohio Dominican University
www.ohiodominican.edu
International Office
1216 Sunbury Road
Columbus, OH 43219
Fax: (614) 251-4639
E-mail: international@ohiodominican.edu
Phone: (614) 251-4646

Ohio Institute of Health Careers: Columbus
www.ohioinstituteofhealthcareers.edu
1880 East Dublin-Granville Road, Suite 100
Columbus, OH 43229
Phone: (614) 891-5030

Ohio Institute of Health Careers: Elyria
www.ohioinstituteofhealthcareers.edu
5095 Waterford Drive
Sheffield Village, OH 44035-0701
Fax: (440) 934-3105
Phone: (866) 636-47347

Ohio Institute of Photography and Technology
www.oipt.com
Admissions Office
2029 Edgefield Road
Dayton, OH 45439
Fax: (937) 294-2259
E-mail: info@oipt.com
Phone: (937) 294-6155

Ohio Northern University
www.onu.edu
International Admissions Office
525 South Main Street
Ada, OH 45810
Fax: (419) 772-2484
E-mail: j-fox@onu.edu
Phone: (419) 772-2483

Ohio State University Agricultural Technical Institute
www.ati.osu.edu
Ohio State University, Columbus Campus
Admissions
1328 Dover Road
Wooster, OH 44691
Fax: (330) 287-1333
E-mail: int.undergrad@osu.edu
Phone: (614) 292-3980

Ohio State University: Columbus Campus
www.osu.edu
Undergraduate Admissions and First Year Experience
110 Enarson Hall
154 West 12th Avenue
Columbus, OH 43210
Fax: (614) 292-4818
E-mail: askabuckeye@osu.edu
Phone: (614) 292-3980

Ohio State University: Lima Campus
www.lima.ohio-state.edu
Ohio State University Columbus Campus
4240 Campus Drive
Lima, OH 45804-3596
Fax: (419) 995-8483
E-mail: int.undergrad@osu.edu
Phone: (614) 292-3980

Ohio State University: Mansfield Campus
www.mansfield.ohio-state.edu
Ohio State University at Columbus
1680 University Drive
Mansfield, OH 44906
Fax: (419) 755-4241
E-mail: int.undergrad@osu.edu
Phone: (614) 292-3980

Ohio State University: Marion Campus
www.marion.ohio-state.edu
Ohio State University at Columbus
1465 Mount Vernon Avenue
Marion, OH 43302
Fax: (740) 386-2439
E-mail: int.undergrad@osu.edu
Phone: (614) 292-3980

Ohio State University: Newark Campus
www.newark.osu.edu
Ohio State University Columbus Campus
1179 University Drive
Newark, OH 43055
Fax: (740) 364-9645
E-mail: int.undergrad@osu.edu
Phone: (614) 292-3980

Ohio University
www.ohio.edu
Office of International Student Admissions
120 Chubb Hall
Athens, OH 45701-2979
Fax: (740) 593-0560
E-mail: pae@ohio.edu
Phone: (740) 593-4119

Ohio University: Zanesville Campus
www.zanesville.ohiou.edu
1425 Newark Road
Zanesville, OH 43701
Fax: (740) 588-1444
E-mail: ouzservices@ohio.edu
Phone: (740) 588-1439

Ohio Valley University
www.ovu.edu
Admissions Office
One Campus View Drive
Vienna, WV 26105
Fax: (304) 865-6175
E-mail: larry.lyons@ovu.edu
Phone: (304) 865-6035

Ohio Wesleyan University
www.owu.edu
International Recruitment
75 South Sandusky Street
Delaware, OH 43015-2398
Fax: (740) 368-3314
E-mail: owuintl@owu.edu
Phone: (740) 368-3020

Ohlone College
www.ohlone.edu
Admissions and Records
43600 Mission Boulevard
Fremont, CA 94539-0390
Fax: (510) 659-7321
E-mail: rtravenick@ohlone.cc.ca.us
Phone: (510) 659-6100

Okaloosa-Walton College
www.owc.edu
Counseling
100 College Boulevard
Niceville, FL 32578-1295
Fax: (850) 729-5215
E-mail: registrar@owc.edu
Phone: (850) 729-5372

Oklahoma Baptist University
www.okbu.edu
Dean of Enrollment Management
500 West University
OBU Box 61174
Shawnee, OK 74804
Fax: (405) 878-2046
E-mail: admissions@mail.okbu.edu
Phone: (405) 878-2023

Oklahoma Christian University
www.oc.edu
Office of International Programs
Box 11000
Oklahoma City, OK 73136-1100
Fax: (405) 425-5477
E-mail: internationalprograms@oc.edu
Phone: (405) 425-5475

Oklahoma City Community College
www.occc.edu
Coordinator of International Student Services
7777 South May Avenue
Oklahoma City, OK 73159
Fax: (405) 682-7521
E-mail: sgarner@occc.edu
Phone: (405) 682-7884

Oklahoma City University
www.okcu.edu
International Services
2501 North Blackwelder Avenue
Oklahoma City, OK 73106
Fax: (405) 208-5946
E-mail: iso@okcu.edu
Phone: (405) 208-5358

Oklahoma Panhandle State University
www.opsu.edu
High School Relations
OPSU Admissions
Box 430
Goodwell, OK 73939-0430
Fax: (580) 349-2302
E-mail: international@opsu.edu
Phone: (580) 349-1310

Oklahoma State University
osu.okstate.edu
Office of Undergraduate Admissions
219 Student Union
Stillwater, OK 74078-7042
Fax: (405) 744-7092
E-mail: admissions@okstate.edu
Phone: (405) 744-5358

Oklahoma State University: Oklahoma City
www.osuokc.edu
International Student Adviser
900 North Portland
Oklahoma City, OK 73107-6195
Fax: (405) 945-3277
E-mail: drarche@osuokc.edu
Phone: (405) 945-3324

Oklahoma State University: Okmulgee
www.osu-okmulgee.edu
International and Multicultural Coordinator
1801 East Fourth Street
Okmulgee, OK 74447-3901
Fax: (918) 293-4633
E-mail: thomas.kiipkirgat@okstate.edu
Phone: (918) 293-5071

Oklahoma Wesleyan University
www.okwu.edu
Admissions Office
2201 Silver Lake Road
Bartlesville, OK 74006
Fax: (918) 335-6229
E-mail: admissions@okwu.edu
Phone: (918) 335-6219

Old Dominion University
www.odu.edu
Office of International Admissions
108 Rollins Hall, 5115 Hampton Boulevard
Norfolk, VA 23529
Fax: (757) 683-3651
E-mail: intladm@odu.edu
Phone: (757) 683-3701

Olivet College
www.olivetcollege.edu
Admissions
Admissions Office
320 South Main Street
Olivet, MI 49076
Fax: (269) 749-6617
E-mail: egibbons@olivetcollege.edu
Phone: (269) 749-7635

Olivet Nazarene University
www.olivet.edu
International Student Admissions Counselor
One University Avenue
Bourbonnais, IL 60914
Fax: (815) 935-4998
E-mail: jfish1@olivet.edu
Phone: (815) 939-5011

Olympic College
www.olympic.edu
Admissions
1600 Chester Avenue
Bremerton, WA 98337-1699
Fax: (360) 475-7202
E-mail: gstamm@oc.ctc.edu
Phone: (360) 475-7128

O'More College of Design
www.omorecollege.edu
Admissions Office
423 South Margin Street
Franklin, TN 37064-0908
Fax: (615) 790-1662
E-mail: clee@omorecollege.edu
Phone: (615) 794-4254 ext. 232

Onondaga Community College
www.sunyocc.edu
Student Central
4585 West Seneca Turnpike
Syracuse, NY 13215-4585
Fax: (315) 469-6775
E-mail: occinfo@sunyocc.edu
Phone: (315) 498-2000

Oral Roberts University
www.oru.edu
International Admissions
7777 South Lewis Avenue
Tulsa, OK 74171
Fax: (918) 495-6788
E-mail: thannon@oru.edu
Phone: (918) 495-6488

Orange Coast College
www.orangecoastcollege.edu
International Center
2701 Fairview Road
Box 5005
Costa Mesa, CA 92628-5005
Fax: (714) 432-5191
E-mail: mniroumand@occ.cccd.edu
Phone: (714) 432-5940

Orangeburg-Calhoun Technical College
www.octech.edu
Admissions
3250 St. Matthews Road
Orangeburg, SC 29118-8222
Fax: (803) 535-1388
E-mail: felderb@octech.edu
Phone: (803) 536-0311

Oregon Health & Science University
www.ohsu.edu
Admissions
3181 SW Sam Jackson Park Road
SN-ADM
Portland, OR 97239
Fax: (503) 494-3400
E-mail: andersje@ohsu.edu
Phone: (503) 494-7725

Oregon Institute of Technology
www.oit.edu
Admissions Director
3201 Campus Drive
Klamath Falls, OR 97601
Fax: (541) 885-1115
E-mail: oit@oit.edu
Phone: (541) 885-1150

Oregon State University
www.oregonstate.edu
International Programs
104 Kerr Administration Building
Corvallis, OR 97331-2130
Fax: (541) 737-2482
E-mail: intl.advisor@oregonstate.edu
Phone: (541) 737-3006

Orleans Technical Institute - Center City Campus
www.orleanstech.edu
2770 Red Lion Road
Philadelphia, PA 19114
Fax: (215) 745-1689
E-mail: bellod@jevs.org
Phone: (215) 728-4426

Otero Junior College
www.ojc.edu
1802 Colorado Avenue
La Junta, CO 81050
Fax: (719) 384-6933
E-mail: brad.smith@ojc.cccoes.edu
Phone: (719) 384-6869

Otis College of Art and Design
www.otis.edu
Office of Admissions
9045 Lincoln Boulevard
Los Angeles, CA 90045-9785
Fax: (310) 665-6821
E-mail: admissions@otis.edu
Phone: (310) 665-6820

Ottawa University
www.ottawa.edu
Foreign Student Advisor
1001 South Cedar Street, #17
Ottawa, KS 66067-3399
Fax: (785) 229-1007
E-mail: murle.mordy@ottawa.edu
Phone: (785) 229-1072

Otterbein College
www.otterbein.edu
Office of Admission
One Otterbein College
Westerville, OH 43081
Fax: (614) 823-1200
E-mail: kmessenheimer@otterbein.edu
Phone: (614) 823-1500

Ouachita Baptist University
www.obu.edu
Director, International Studies
OBU Box 3776
Arkadelphia, AR 71998-0001
Fax: (870) 245-5312
E-mail: coshi@obu.edu
Phone: (870) 245-5197

Ouachita Technical College
www.otcweb.edu
Enrollment Management/Registrar
One College Circle
Malvern, AR 72104
Fax: (501) 337-9382
E-mail: ljohnson@otcweb.edu
Phone: (501) 337-5000 ext. 1133

Our Lady of the Lake University of San Antonio
www.ollusa.edu
Dean of Admissions
411 Southwest 24th Street
San Antonio, TX 78207-4689
Fax: (210) 431-4036
E-mail: boatm@lake.ollusa.edu
Phone: (210) 431-4145

Owens Community College: Toledo
www.owens.edu
International Student Services
PO Box 10000
Toledo, OH 43699-1947
Fax: (567) 661-7734
E-mail: cesar_hernandez@owens.edu
Phone: (567) 661-7504

Owensboro Community and Technical College
www.octc.kctcs.edu
4800 New Hartford Road
Owensboro, KY 42303-1899
Fax: (270) 686-4648
E-mail: barbara.tipmore@kctcs.net
Phone: (270) 686-4530

Oxnard College
www.oxnardcollege.edu
4000 South Rose Avenue
Oxnard, CA 93033
Fax: (805) 986-5943
E-mail: ocadmissions@vcccd.edu
Phone: (805) 986-5852

Ozarks Technical Community College
www.otc.edu
1001 East Chestnut Expressway
Springfield, MO 65802
Fax: (417) 447-6906
Phone: (417) 447-6900

Pace Institute
www.paceinstitute.com
606 Court Street
Reading, PA 19601
E-mail: pace4u2@aol.com
Phone: (610) 375-1212

Pace University
www.pace.edu
International Programs & Services
1 Pace Plaza
New York, NY 10038
Fax: (212) 346-1948
E-mail: infoctr@pace.edu
Phone: (212) 346-1323

Pacific Lutheran University
www.plu.edu
Admissions
Office of Admissions
1010 South 122nd Street
Tacoma, WA 98447-0003
Fax: (235) 536-5136
E-mail: Cheryl.hansen@plu.edu
Phone: (800) 274-6758

Pacific Northwest College of Art
www.pnca.edu
Admissions
1241 NW Johnson Street
Portland, OR 97209
Fax: (503) 821-8978
E-mail: csweet@pnca.edu
Phone: (503) 821-8972

Pacific Oaks College
www.pacificoaks.edu
Admissions Office
5 Westmoreland Place
Pasadena, CA 91103
Fax: (626) 666-1220
E-mail: apickens@pacificoaks.edu
Phone: (626) 397-1349

Pacific States University
www.psuca.edu
1516 South Western Avenue
Los Angeles, CA 90006
Fax: (323) 731-7276
E-mail: admissions@psuca.edu
Phone: (323) 731-2383 ext. 17

Pacific Union College
www.puc.edu
Enrollment Services
One Angwin Avenue
Angwin, CA 94508
Fax: (707) 965-6432
E-mail: enroll@puc.edu
Phone: (707) 965-6336

Pacific University
www.pacificu.edu
Office of Admission
2043 College Way
Forest Grove, OR 97116-1797
Fax: (503) 352-2975
E-mail: admissions@pacificu.edu
Phone: (503) 352-2218

Paier College of Art
www.paiercollegeofart.edu
Registrar
20 Gorham Avenue
Hamden, CT 06514-3902
Fax: (203) 287-3021
E-mail: paier.admin@snet.net
Phone: (203) 287-3032

Paine College
www.paine.edu
Office of Admissions
1235 15th Street
Augusta, GA 30901-3182
Fax: (706) 821-8648
E-mail: tinsleyj@mail.paine.edu
Phone: (706) 821-8320

Palm Beach Atlantic University
www.pba.edu
Undergraduate Admissions
PO Box 24708
West Palm Beach, FL 33416-4708
Fax: (561) 803-2115
E-mail: rod_sullivan@pba.edu
Phone: (561) 803-2000

Palm Beach Community College
www.pbcc.edu
International Student Admissions Office
4200 Congress Avenue
Lake Worth, FL 33461
Fax: (561) 868-3605
E-mail: Labordef@pbcc.edu
Phone: (561) 868-3031

Palo Alto College
www.accd.edu
Counseling Center
1400 West Villaret Boulevard
San Antonio, TX 78224-2499
Fax: (210) 921-5357
E-mail: nesparza@accd.edu
Phone: (210) 921-5242

Palo Verde College
www.paloverde.edu
Student Services
One College Drive
Blythe, CA 92225
Fax: (760) 921-3608
E-mail: mgracia@paloverde.edu
Phone: (760) 922-5405

Palomar College
www.palomar.edu
International Edcuation Office
1140 West Mission Road
San Marcos, CA 92069-1487
Fax: (760) 761-3592
E-mail: intladm@palomar.edu
Phone: (760) 744-1150 ext. 2167

Pamlico Community College
www.pamlicocc.edu
PO Box 185
Grantsboro, NC 28529
Fax: (252) 249-2377
E-mail: jgibbs@pamlicocc.edu
Phone: (252) 249-1851

Panola College
www.panola.edu
Testing Coordinator/Advisor/International Student Coordinator
1109 West Panola Street
Carthage, TX 75633
Fax: (903) 693-2031
E-mail: jdorman@panola.edu
Phone: (903) 693-2046

Paradise Valley Community College
www.pvc.maricopa.edu
18401 North 32nd Street
Phoenix, AZ 85032
Fax: (602) 787-6625
Phone: (602) 787-7020

Paralegal Institute
www.theparalegalinstitute.edu
18275 North 59th Avenue, Suite 186 Building N
Glendale, AZ 85308
Fax: (602) 212-0502
E-mail: paralegalinst@mindspring.com
Phone: (800) 354-1254

Paris Junior College
www.parisjc.edu
International Student Adviser
2400 Clarksville Street
Paris, TX 75460
Fax: (903) 784-9370
E-mail: bthomas@parisjc.edu
Phone: (214) 784-9434

Park University
www.park.edu
International Student Office
8700 River Park Drive
Parkville, MO 64152
Fax: (816) 505-5443
E-mail: admissions@park.edu
Phone: (816) 584-6379

Parkland College
www.parkland.edu
International Education
2400 West Bradley Avenue
Champaign, IL 61821-1899
Fax: (217) 353-2640
E-mail: mbowser-kiener@parkland.edu
Phone: (217) 351-2547

Parsons The New School for Design
www.parsons.edu
Office of Admissions
65 Fifth Avenue
New York, NY 10011
Fax: (212) 229-8975
E-mail: parsadm@newschool.edu
Phone: (212) 229-8910

Pasadena City College
www.pasadena.edu
International Students Office
1570 East Colorado Boulevard
Pasadena, CA 91106
Fax: (626) 585-7912
Phone: (818) 585-7391

Pasco-Hernando Community College
www.phcc.edu
Admissions and Student Records
10230 Ridge Road
New Port Richey, FL 34654-5199
Fax: (727) 816-3389
E-mail: bullard@phcc.edu
Phone: (727) 816-3261

Passaic County Community College
www.pccc.edu
One College Boulevard
Paterson, NJ 07505-1179
Fax: (973) 684-6778
Phone: (973) 684-6868

Patricia Stevens College
www.patriciastevenscollege.edu
Admissions
330 North Fourth Street, Suite 306
St. Louis, MO 63102
Fax: (314) 421-0304
E-mail:
admissions@patriciastevenscollege.edu
Phone: (314) 421-0949 ext. 12

Patrick Henry Community College
www.ph.vccs.edu
Admissions Office
Box 5311
Martinsville, VA 24115-5311
Fax: (276) 656-0352
E-mail: gvalentine@ph.vccs.edu
Phone: (276) 656-0311

Patten University
www.patten.edu
Admissions
2433 Coolidge Avenue
Oakland, CA 94601-2699
Fax: (510) 534-4344
E-mail: bailey@patten.edu
Phone: (510) 261-8500 ext. 7764

Paul D. Camp Community College
www.pc.vccs.edu
Admissions and Records
100 North College Drive
PO Box 737
Franklin, VA 23851-0737
Fax: (757) 569-6795
E-mail: mwilliams@pc.cc.va.us
Phone: (757) 569-6700

Paul Smith's College
www.paulsmiths.edu
Admissions
PO Box 265, Routes 30 & 86
Paul Smiths, NY 12970-0265
Fax: (518) 327-6016
E-mail: ccasey@paulsmiths.edu
Phone: (518) 327-6227

Peace College
www.peace.edu
Admissions
15 East Peace Street
Raleigh, NC 27604-1194
Fax: (919) 508-2306
E-mail: mtgreen@peace.edu
Phone: (919) 508-2000

Peirce College
www.peirce.edu
Admissions
1420 Pine Street
Philadelphia, PA 19102-4699
Fax: (215) 670-9366
E-mail: info@peirce.edu
Phone: (888) 467-3472 ext. 9214

Pellissippi State Technical Community College
www.pstcc.edu
International Admissions and Records
Box 22990
Knoxville, TN 37933-0990
Fax: (865) 539-7217
E-mail: latouzeau@pstcc.edu
Phone: (865) 539-7013

Peninsula College
www.pc.ctc.edu
International Coordinator Students
1502 East Lauridsen Boulevard
Port Angeles, WA 98362
Fax: (360) 417-6482
E-mail: gyl@pcadmin.ctc.edu
Phone: (360) 417-6491

Penn Commercial Business and Technical School
www.penncommercial.edu
242 Oak Spring Road
Washington, PA 15301
Fax: (724) 225-3561
E-mail: pcadmissions@penncommercial.edu
Phone: (724) 222-5330 ext. 1

Penn Foster College
www.pennfostercollege.edu
Manager, DP Services
14300 North Northsight Boulevard, Suite 111
Scottsdale, AZ 85254
Phone: (570) 342-7701

Penn State Abington
www.abington.psu.edu
Admissions
201 Shields Building
University Park, PA 16802-1294
Fax: (814) 863-7590
E-mail: admissions@psu.edu
Phone: (814) 865-5471

Penn State Altoona
www.aa.psu.edu
Admissions
201 Shields Building
University Park, PA 16802-1294
Fax: (814) 863-7590
E-mail: admissions@psu.edu
Phone: (814) 865-5471

Penn State Beaver
www.br.psu.edu
Admissions
201 Shields Building
University Park, PA 16802-1294
Fax: (814) 863-7590
E-mail: admissions@psu.edu
Phone: (814) 865-5471

Penn State Berks
www.bk.psu.edu
Admissions
201 Shields Building
University Park, PA 16802-1294
Fax: (814) 863-7590
E-mail: admissions@psu.edu
Phone: (814) 865-5471

Penn State Brandywine
www.de.psu.edu
Admissions
201 Shields Building
University Park, PA 16802-1294
Fax: (814) 863-7590
E-mail: admissions@psu.edu
Phone: (814) 865-5471

Penn State Dubois
www.ds.psu.edu
Admissions
201 Shields Building
University Park, PA 16802-1294
Fax: (814) 863-7590
E-mail: admissions@psu.edu
Phone: (814) 865-5471

Penn State Erie, The Behrend College
www.pserie.psu.edu
Admissions
201 Shields Building
University Park, PA 16801-1294
Fax: (814) 863-7590
E-mail: admissions@psu.edu
Phone: (814) 865-5471

Penn State Fayette, The Eberly Campus
www.fe.psu.edu
Admissions
201 Shields Building
University Park, PA 16802-1294
Fax: (814) 863-7590
E-mail: admissions@psu.edu
Phone: (814) 865-5471

Penn State Greater Allegheny
www.mk.psu.edu
Admissions
201 Shields Building
University Park, PA 16802-1294
Fax: (814) 863-7590
E-mail: admissions@psu.edu
Phone: (814) 865-5471

Penn State Harrisburg
www.hbg.psu.edu
Admissions
201 Shields Building
University Park, PA 16802-1294
Fax: (814) 863-7590
E-mail: admissions@psu.edu
Phone: (814) 865-5471

Penn State Hazleton
www.hn.psu.edu
Admissions
201 Shields Building
University Park, PA 16802-1294
Fax: (814) 863-7590
E-mail: admissions@psu.edu
Phone: (814) 865-5471

Penn State Lehigh Valley
www.lv.psu.edu
Admissions
201 Shields Building
University Park, PA 16802-1294
Fax: (814) 863-7590
E-mail: admissions@psu.edu
Phone: (814) 865-5471

Penn State Mont Alto
www.ma.psu.edu
Admissions
201 Shields Building
University Park, PA 16802-1294
Fax: (814) 863-7590
E-mail: admissions@psu.edu
Phone: (814) 865-5471

Penn State New Kensington
www.nk.psu.edu
Admissions
201 Shields Building
University Park, PA 16802-1294
Fax: (814) 863-7590
E-mail: admissions@psu.edu
Phone: (814) 865-5471

Penn State Schuylkill
www.sl.psu.edu
Admissions
201 Shields Building
University Park, PA 16802-1294
Fax: (814) 863-7590
E-mail: admissions@psu.edu
Phone: (814) 865-5471

Penn State Shenango
www.shenango.psu.edu
Admissions
201 Shields Building
University Park, PA 16802-1294
Fax: (814) 863-7590
E-mail: admissions@psu.edu
Phone: (814) 865-5471

Penn State University Park
www.psu.edu
Admissions
201 Shields Building
University Park, PA 16802-1294
Fax: (814) 863-7590
E-mail: admissions@psu.edu
Phone: (814) 865-5471

Penn State Wilkes-Barre
www.wb.psu.edu
Admissions
201 Shields Building
University Park, PA 16802-1294
Fax: (814) 863-7590
E-mail: admissions@psu.edu
Phone: (814) 865-5471

Penn State Worthington Scranton
www.sn.psu.edu
Admissions
201 Shields Building
University Park, PA 16802-1294
Fax: (814) 863-7590
E-mail: admissions@psu.edu
Phone: (814) 865-5471

Penn State York
www.yk.psu.edu
Admissions
201 Shields Building
University Park, PA 16802-1294
Fax: (814) 863-7590
E-mail: admissions@psu.edu
Phone: (814) 865-5471

Pennco Tech
www.penncotech.com
3815 Otter Street
Bristol, PA 19007
E-mail: admissions@penncotech.com
Phone: (215) 824-3200

Pennsylvania College of Technology
www.pct.edu
Admissions
One College Avenue
Williamsport, PA 17701
Fax: (570) 321-5551
E-mail: cschuman@pct.edu
Phone: (570) 327-4761

Pennsylvania Culinary Institute
www.paculinary.com
717 Liberty Avenue
Pittsburgh, PA 15222
Fax: (412) 566-2434
E-mail: info@paculinary.com
Phone: (800) 432-2433

**Pennsylvania Highlands Community
College**
www.pennhighlands.edu
Director of Admissions
PO Box 68
Johnstown, PA 15907-0068
Fax: (814) 262-6420
E-mail: jmaul@pennhighlands.edu
Phone: (814) 262-6431

Pennsylvania Institute of Technology
www.pit.edu
International Student Admissions
800 Manchester Avenue
Media, PA 19063-4098
Fax: (610) 892-1510
E-mail: info@pit.edu
Phone: (610) 565-7900 ext. 1505

Pensacola Junior College
www.pjc.edu
Director Admissions and Registrar
1000 College Boulevard
Pensacola, FL 32504-8998
Fax: (850) 484-1829
E-mail: mcaughey@pjc.edu
Phone: (850) 484-1623

Pepperdine University
www.pepperdine.edu
International Student Services
24255 Pacific Coast Highway
Malibu, CA 90263-4392
Fax: (310) 506-7403
E-mail: oiss@pepperdine.edu
Phone: (310) 506-4246

Peru State College
www.peru.edu
Admissions
Box 10
Peru, NE 68421-0010
Fax: (402) 872-2296
E-mail: admissions@oakmail.peru.edu
Phone: (402) 872-2221

Pfeiffer University
www.pfeiffer.edu
Office of Admissions
Box 960
Misenheimer, NC 28109
Fax: (704) 463-1363
E-mail: steve.cumming@pfeiffer.edu
Phone: (704) 463-3057

Philadelphia Biblical University
www.pbu.edu
Admissions
200 Manor Avenue
Langhorne, PA 19047-2990
Fax: (215) 702-4248
E-mail: admissions@pbu.edu
Phone: (215) 702-4241

Philadelphia University
www.philau.edu
Admissions Office
School House Lane and Henry Avenue
Philadelphia, PA 19144-5497
Fax: (215) 951-2907
E-mail: duffeyc@philau.edu
Phone: (215) 951-2800

Philander Smith College
www.philander.edu
Admissions
One Trudie Kibbe Reed Drive
Little Rock, AR 72202-3718
Fax: (501) 370-5225
E-mail: bevrich@philander.edu
Phone: (501) 370-5221

Phillips Beth Israel School of Nursing
www.futurenursebi.org
Admissions
776 Sixth Avenue, Fourth Floor
New York, NY 10001
Fax: (212) 614-6109
E-mail: bstern@bethisraelny.org
Phone: (212) 614-6176

**Phillips Community College of the
University of Arkansas**
www.pccua.edu
Admissions and Records
1000 Campus Drive
PO Box 785
Helena, AR 72342
Fax: (870) 338-7542
E-mail: lboone@pccua.edu
Phone: (870) 338-6474 ext. 1235

Phoenix College
www.pc.maricopa.edu
International Student Office
1202 West Thomas Road
Phoenix, AZ 85013
Fax: (602) 285-7813
E-mail: annette.duran@pcmail.maricopa.edu
Phone: (602) 285-7424

Piedmont Baptist College
www.pbc.edu
Admissions
420 South Boad Street
Winston-Salem, NC 27101-5133
Fax: (336) 725-5522
E-mail: holritzk@pbc.edu
Phone: (336) 725-8344 ext. 7927

Piedmont College
www.piedmont.edu
Admissions
165 Central Avenue
PO Box 10
Demorest, GA 30535-0010
Fax: (706) 776-0103
E-mail: jkelly@piedmont.edu
Phone: (800) 277-7020

Piedmont Community College
www.piedmontcc.edu
1715 College Drive
Box 1197
Roxboro, NC 27573-1197
Fax: (336) 597-3817
Phone: (336) 599-1181

Piedmont Technical College
www.ptc.edu
Admissions
PO Box 1467
Greenwood, SC 29648
Fax: (864) 941-8555
E-mail: king.m@ptc.edu
Phone: (864) 941-8373

Piedmont Virginia Community College
www.pvcc.edu
Office of Admissions
501 College Drive
Charlottesville, VA 22902-7589
Fax: (434) 961-5425
E-mail: mwalsh@pvcc.edu
Phone: (434) 961-6540

Pikes Peak Community College
www.ppcc.edu
Admissions
5675 South Academy Boulevard
Colorado Springs, CO 80906-5498
E-mail: vicki.furaus@ppcc.edu
Phone: (719) 502-2035

Pillsbury Baptist Bible College
www.pillsbury.edu
315 South Grove Avenue
Owatonna, MN 55060
E-mail: admissions@pillsbury.edu
Phone: (507) 451-2710

Pima Community College
www.pima.edu
International Student Admissions Office
4905B East Broadway
Tucson, AZ 85709-1120
Fax: (520) 206-3265
E-mail: coadmit@pima.edu
Phone: (520) 206-6732

Pine Manor College
www.pmc.edu
Admissions Office
400 Heath Street
Chestnut Hill, MA 02467
Fax: (617) 731-7102
E-mail: admissions@pmc.edu
Phone: (617) 731-7104

Pine Technical College
www.pinetech.edu
Admissions Office
900 Fourth Street, SE
Pine City, MN 55063
Fax: (320) 629-5101
E-mail: machn@pinetech.edu
Phone: (320) 629-5100

Pinnacle Career Institute: Kansas City
www.pcitraining.edu
1001 East 101st Terrace, Suite 325
Kansas City, MO 64131-3367
Fax: (816) 331-2026
E-mail: bricks@pcitraining.edu
Phone: (816) 331-5700

Pioneer Pacific College
www.pioneerpacific.edu
Admissions Office
27501 Southwest Parkway Avenue
Wilsonville, OR 97070
Fax: (503) 659-6107
E-mail: inquiries@pioneerpacific.edu
Phone: (503) 654-8000

Pioneer Pacific College: Springfield
www.pioneerpacific.edu
3800 Sports Way
Springfield, OR 97477
Fax: (541) 684-0665
E-mail: vchurch@pioneerpacific.edu
Phone: (541) 684-4644

Pittsburg State University
www.pittstate.edu
International Programs and Services
1701 South Broadway
Pittsburg, KS 66762
Fax: (620) 235-4962
E-mail: colcese@pittstate.edu
Phone: (620) 235-4680

Pittsburgh Institute of Aeronautics
www.pia.edu
Admissions
Box 10897
Pittsburgh, PA 15236-0897
Fax: (412) 466-0513
E-mail: admissions@pia.edu
Phone: (412) 346-2100

Pittsburgh Institute of Mortuary Science
www.pims.edu
5808 Baum Boulevard
Pittsburgh, PA 15206-3706
Fax: (412) 362-1684
E-mail: pims5808@aol.com
Phone: (412) 362-8500

Pittsburgh Technical Institute
www.pti.edu
Admissions
1111 McKee Road
Oakdale, PA 15071-3205
Fax: (412) 809-5351
E-mail: goodlin.nancy@pti.edu
Phone: (412) 809-5354

Pitzer College
www.pitzer.edu
International Programs Office
1050 North Mills Avenue
Claremont, CA 91711-6101
Fax: (909) 621-0518
E-mail: todd_sasaki@pitzer.edu
Phone: (909) 621-8308

Platt College: Huntington Beach
www.plattcollege.edu
7755 Center Avenue, Suite 400
Huntington Beach, CA 92647
Fax: (949) 833-0269
E-mail: lrhodes@plattcollege.edu
Phone: (949) 833-2300

Platt College: Los Angeles
www.plattcollege.edu
Admissions
1000 South Fremont Avenue A9W
Alhambra, CA 91803
Fax: (626) 300-3978
E-mail: jboylan@plattcollege.edu
Phone: (626) 300-5444

Platt College: Oklahoma City Central
www.plattcollege.org
309 South Ann Arbor
Oklahoma City, OK 73128
Fax: (405) 943-2150
E-mail: reneej@plattcollege.org
Phone: (405) 946-7799

Platt College: Ontario
www.plattcollege.edu
Admissions
3700 Inland Empire Boulevard
Ontario, CA 91764
Fax: (909) 941-9660
E-mail: cconceicao@plattcollege.edu
Phone: (909) 941-9410

Platt College: San Diego
www.platt.edu
6250 El Cajon Boulevard
San Diego, CA 92115
Fax: (619) 308-0570
E-mail: info@platt.edu
Phone: (619) 265-0107 ext. 37

Platt College: Tulsa
www.plattcollege.org
3801 South Sheridan
Tulsa, OK 74145-1132
Fax: (918) 622-1240
E-mail: stephanieh@plattcollege.org
Phone: (918) 663-9000

Plymouth State University
www.plymouth.edu
Admission Office
17 High Street MSC 52
Plymouth, NH 03264-1595
Fax: (603) 535-2714
E-mail: plymouthadmit@plymouth.edu
Phone: (800) 842-6900

Point Loma Nazarene University
www.pointloma.edu
Admissions
3900 Lomaland Drive
San Diego, CA 92106-2899
Fax: (619) 849-2601
E-mail: admissions@pointloma.edu
Phone: (619) 849-2273

Point Park University
www.pointpark.edu
201 Wood Street
Pittsburgh, PA 15222-1984
Fax: (412) 392-3902
E-mail: anwar@pointpark.edu
Phone: (412) 392-3903

Polk Community College
www.polk.edu
Enrollment Management, Winter Haven
Campus
999 Avenue H NE
Winter Haven, FL 33881-4299
Fax: (863) 297-1060
E-mail: mwestgate@polk.edu
Phone: (863) 297-1010 ext. 5201

Polytechnic University
www.poly.edu
Polytechnic Admissions
6 Metrotech Center
Brooklyn, NY 11201-2999
Fax: (718) 260-3446
E-mail: mgendel@poly.edu
Phone: (800) 765-9832

Pomona College
www.pomona.edu
Admissions Office
333 North College Way
Claremont, CA 91711-6312
Fax: (909) 621-8952
E-mail: admissions@pomona.edu
Phone: (909) 621-8134

Ponce Paramedical College
www.popac.edu
Calle Acacia L-1213, Urb. Villa Flores
Ponce, PR 00731
E-mail: admisiones@popac-pr.com
Phone: (787) 848-1589 ext. 413

Pontifical Catholic University of Puerto Rico
www.pucpr.edu
Admissions
2250 Las Americas Avenue, Suite 284
Ponce, PR 00717-9777
Fax: (787) 651-2044
E-mail: admisiones@pucpr.edu
Phone: (787) 841-2000 ext. 1000

Porterville College
www.portervillecollege.edu
Admissions and Records Office
100 East College Avenue
Porterville, CA 93257
Fax: (209) 791-2349
Phone: (209) 791-2222

Portland Community College
www.pcc.edu
International Student Admissions
Box 19000
Portland, OR 97280-0990
Fax: (503) 614-7351
E-mail: rchulufa@pcc.edu
Phone: (503) 614-7150

Portland State University
www.pdx.edu
Office of Admissions
PO Box 751-ADM
Portland, OR 97207-0751
Fax: (503) 725-5525
E-mail: harrisp@pdx.edu
Phone: (503) 725-5503

Post University
www.post.edu
Director of Admissions
800 Country Club Road
PO Box 2540
Waterbury, CT 06723-2540
Fax: (203) 596-4579
E-mail: jmurray@post.edu
Phone: (203) 596-4630

Potomac College
www.potomac.edu
Admissions
4000 Chesapeake Street NW
Washington, DC 20016
Fax: (202) 686-0818
E-mail: admissions@potomac.edu
Phone: (202) 686-0876

Potomac College
www.potomac.edu
1029 Herndon Parkway
Herndon, VA 20170
Fax: (703) 709-8972
Phone: (703) 709-5875

Potomac State College of West Virginia University
www.potomacstatecollege.edu
Enrollment Services
One Grand Central Park, Suite 2090
Keyser, WV 26726
Fax: (304) 788-6939
E-mail: BELittle@mail.wvu.edu
Phone: (304) 788-6820

Prairie State College
www.prairiestate.edu
Career and Transfer Center
202 South Halsted Street
Chicago Heights, IL 60411
Fax: (708) 755-2587
E-mail: rkiefer@prairie.cc.il.us
Phone: (708) 709-3512

Prairie View A&M University
www.pvamu.edu
Office of Admissions
PO Box 519, MS 1009
Prairie View, TX 77446-0519
E-mail: ntwoods@pvamu.edu
Phone: (936) 261-1067

Pratt Community College
www.prattcc.edu
Admissions
348 Northeast State Road 61
Pratt, KS 67124-8317
Fax: (620) 672-5288
E-mail: lynnp@prattcc.edu
Phone: (620) 450-2222

Pratt Institute
www.pratt.edu
International Admissions Office
200 Willoughby Avenue
Brooklyn, NY 11205-3817
Fax: (718) 399-4242
E-mail: admissions@pratt.edu
Phone: (718) 636-3683

Prescott College
www.prescott.edu
Admissions
220 Grove Avenue
Prescott, AZ 86301
Fax: (928) 776-5242
E-mail: admissions@prescott.edu
Phone: (877) 350-1201

Presentation College
www.presentation.edu
1500 North Main Street
Aberdeen, SD 57401
Fax: (605) 229-8332
E-mail: metzingerm@presentation.edu
Phone: (605) 229-8424

Prince George's Community College
www.pgcc.edu
Admissions and Records
301 Largo Road
Largo, MD 20774
Fax: (301) 322-0119
E-mail: enrollmentservices@pgcc.edu
Phone: (301) 322-0863

Prince William Sound Community College
www.pwscc.edu
Student Services
Box 97
Valdez, AK 99686
Fax: (907) 834-1691
E-mail: bpainter@pwscc.edu
Phone: (907) 834-1631

Princeton University
www.princeton.edu
Box 430
Princeton, NJ 08544-0430
Fax: (609) 258-6743
E-mail: uaoffice@Princeton.edu
Phone: (609) 258-3060

Professional Golfers Career College
www.golfcollege.edu
PO Box 892319
Temecula, CA 92589-2319
Fax: (951) 719-1643
E-mail: patti.paulsen@golfcollege.edu
Phone: (800) 877-4380

Professional Golfers Career College: Orlando
www.golfcollege.edu
Temecula
PO Box 892319
Temecula, CA 92589-2319
Fax: (951) 719-1643
E-mail: patti.paulsen@golfcollege.edu
Phone: (800) 877-4380

Providence College
www.providence.edu
Admissions
Harkins Hall 222, 549 River Avenue
Providence, RI 02918-0001
Fax: (401) 865-2826
E-mail: rfonts@providence.edu
Phone: (401) 865-2754

Pueblo Community College
www.pueblocc.edu
Admissions and Records
900 West Orman Avenue
Pueblo, CO 81004-1499
Fax: (719) 549-3012
E-mail: Maija.Kurtz@pueblocc.edu
Phone: (719) 549-3085

Pulaski Technical College
www.pulaskitech.edu
Student Services
3000 West Scenic Drive
North Little Rock, AR 72118-3347
Fax: (501) 812-2316
E-mail: catkins@pulaskitech.edu
Phone: (501) 812-2734

Purdue University
www.purdue.edu
Office of International Students and Scholars
475 Stadium Mall Drive
West Lafayette, IN 47907-2050
Fax: (765) 494-6340
E-mail: iss@purdue.edu
Phone: (765) 494-5770

Purdue University Calumet
www.calumet.purdue.edu
International Student Mentoring Center
2200 169th Street
Hammond, IN 46323-2094
Fax: (219) 989-2581
E-mail: grad@calumet.purdue.edu
Phone: (219) 989-2559

Purdue University North Central
www.pnc.edu
1401 South US Highway 421
Westville, IN 46391-9528
Fax: (219) 785-5538
E-mail: swilson@pnc.edu
Phone: (219) 785-5236

Queens University of Charlotte
www.queens.edu
Office of Admissions
1900 Selwyn Ave
Harris Welcome Center
Charlotte, NC 28274
Fax: (704) 337-2403
E-mail: parkerg@queens.edu
Phone: (704) 337-2212

Quincy College
www.quincycollege.edu
24 Saville Avenue
Quincy, MA 02169
Fax: (617) 984-1669
E-mail: admissions@quincycollege.edu
Phone: (617) 984-1700

Quincy University
www.quincy.edu
Admissions Office
1800 College Avenue
Quincy, IL 62301-2699
Fax: (217) 228-5479
E-mail: admissions@quincy.edu
Phone: (217) 228-5215

Quinnipiac University
www.quinnipiac.edu
Undergraduate or Graduate Admissions
275 Mount Carmel Avenue
Hamden, CT 06518-1908
Fax: (582) 582-8906
E-mail: jim.kirby@quinnipiac.edu
Phone: (582) 582-8600

Quinsigamond Community College
www.qcc.edu
Admissions
670 West Boylston Street
Worcester, MA 01606
Fax: (508) 854-7525
E-mail: qccadm@qcc.mass.edu
Phone: (508) 854-4262

Radford University
www.radford.edu
Admissions Office
209 Martin Hall
PO Box 6903
Radford, VA 24142
Fax: (540) 831-5038
E-mail: ruadmiss@radford.edu
Phone: (540) 831-5371

Rainy River Community College
www.rrcc.mnscu.edu
Admissions
1501 Highway 71
International Falls, MN 56649
Fax: (218) 285-2239
E-mail: bhagen@rrcc.mnscu.edu
Phone: (218) 285-2207

Ramapo College of New Jersey
www.ramapo.edu
Admissions
505 Ramapo Valley Road
Admissions- McBride Building
Mahwah, NJ 07430-1680
Fax: (201) 684-7964
E-mail: bperkins@ramapo.edu
Phone: (201) 684-7303

Ramirez College of Business and Technology
www.ramirezcollege.com
PO Box 21360
San Juan, PR 00928-1360
Fax: (787) 728-7023
E-mail: ramirezcollege@prtc.net
Phone: (787) 763-3120

Randolph College
www.randolphcollege.edu
Admissions Office
2500 Rivermont Avenue
Lynchburg, VA 24503-1555
Fax: (434) 947-8996
E-mail: admissions@randolphcollege.edu
Phone: (434) 947-8100

Randolph-Macon College
www.rmc.edu
Admissions
PO Box 5005
Ashland, VA 23005-5505
Fax: (804) 752-4707
E-mail: admissions@rmc.edu
Phone: (804) 752-7305

Ranger College
www.rangercollege.edu
Registrar
1100 College Circle
Ranger, TX 76470
Fax: (254) 647-3739
E-mail: rstephens@rangercollege.edu
Phone: (254) 647-3234

Rappahannock Community College
www.rappahannock.edu
Student Personnel Services
12745 College Drive
Glenns, VA 23149-2616
Fax: (804) 758-3852
Phone: (804) 758-6742

Raritan Valley Community College
www.raritanval.edu
Advising and Counseling
PO Box 3300
Office of Admissions - College Center
Somerville, NJ 08876-1265
Fax: (908) 253-6691
E-mail: iss@raritanval.edu
Phone: (908) 526-1200 ext. 8452

Rasmussen College: Bismarck
www.rasmussen.edu
1701 E. century Avenue
Bismarck, ND 58503
Fax: (701) 530-9604
Phone: (701) 530-9600

Rasmussen College: Eagan
www.rasmussen.edu
3500 Federal Drive
Eagan, MN 55122
Fax: (651) 687-0507
E-mail: brian.arndt@rasmussen.edu
Phone: (651) 687-9000

Rasmussen College: Eden Prairie
www.rasmussen.edu
7905 Golden Triangle Drive, Suite 100
Eden Prairie, MN 55344
Phone: (952) 545-2000

Rasmussen College: Mankato
www.rasmussen.edu
501 Holly Lane
Mankato, MN 56001
Fax: (507) 625-6557
E-mail: rascoll@ic.mankato.mn.us
Phone: (507) 625-6556

Reading Area Community College
www.racc.edu
Admissions Office
10 South Second Street
PO Box 1706
Reading, PA 19603-1706
Fax: (610) 607-6238
E-mail: jmelones@racc.edu
Phone: (610) 607-6224

Red Rocks Community College
www.rrcc.edu
Office of English Language/Intercultural Services
13300 West Sixth Avenue
Box 5
Lakewood, CO 80228-1255
Fax: (303) 314-6716
E-mail: international@rrcc.edu
Phone: (303) 914-6416

Redlands Community College
www.redlandscc.edu
Student Services
1300 South Country Club Road
El Reno, OK 73036
Fax: (405) 422-1239
E-mail: duel@redlandscc.edu
Phone: (405) 262-2552 ext. 1427

Redstone College
www.redstonecollege.com
10851 West 120th Avenue
Broomfield, CO 80021-3401
Fax: (303) 469-3797
Phone: (303) 466-1714

Reed College
www.reed.edu
International Programs
3203 SE Woodstock Boulevard
Portland, OR 97202-8199
Fax: (503) 777-7566
E-mail: paul.deyoung@reed.edu
Phone: (503) 777-7290

Reedley College
www.reedleycollege.edu
Admissions and Records
995 North Reed Avenue
Reedley, CA 93654
Fax: (559) 638-5040
E-mail: leticia.alvarez@reedleycollege.edu
Phone: (559) 638-0323

Regent University
www.regent.edu
Undergrad Admissions
1000 Regent University Drive, SC 218
Virginia Beach, VA 23464-9800
Fax: (757) 226-4509
E-mail: pfinch@regent.edu
Phone: (757) 226-4892

Regis College
www.regiscollege.edu
Admission
235 Wellesley Street
Weston, MA 02493-1571
Fax: (781) 768-7071
E-mail: wanda.suriel@regiscollege.edu
Phone: (781) 768-7100

Regis University
www.regis.edu
Office of Admissions
3333 Regis Boulevard, Mail Code B20
Denver, CO 80221-1099
Fax: (303) 964-5534
E-mail: regisadm@regis.edu
Phone: (303) 458-4900

Reinhardt College
www.reinhardt.edu
Admissions
7300 Reinhardt College Circle
Waleska, GA 30183
Fax: (770) 728-5899
E-mail: jtc@reinhardt.edu
Phone: (770) 720-5526

Remington College: Baton Rouge
www.remingtoncollege.edu/batonrouge
10551 Coursey Boulevard
Baton Rouge, LA 70816
Fax: (225) 922-6569
Phone: (225) 922-3990

Remington College: Cleveland
www.remingtoncollege.edu
Director of Recruitment
14445 Broadway Avenue
Cleveland, OH 44125
Fax: (216) 475-6055
E-mail: jeri.prochaska@remingtoncollege.edu
Phone: (216) 475-7520

Remington College: Cleveland West
www.remingtoncollege.edu/clevelandwest/
26350 Brookpark Road
North Olmsted, OH 44070
Phone: (440) 777-2560

Remington College: Colorado Springs
www.remingtoncollege.com
Recruiting
6050 Erin Park Drive
Colorado Springs, CO 80918
Fax: (719) 264-1234
E-mail: larry.schafer@remingtoncollege.edu
Phone: (719) 532-1234

Remington College: Fort Worth
www.remingtoncollege.edu
300 East Loop 820
Fort Worth, TX 76112
Fax: (817) 496-1257
E-mail: marcia.kline@remingtoncollege.edu
Phone: (817) 451-0017

Remington College: Honolulu
www.remingtoncollege.edu
Recruitment Office
1111 Bishop Street, Suite 400
Honolulu, HI 96813-2811
Fax: (808) 533-3064
E-mail: kheinema@remingtoncollege.edu
Phone: (808) 942-1000

Remington College: Houston
www.remingtoncollege.edu
Admissions
3110 Hayes Road, Suite 380
Houston, TX 77082
Fax: (281) 597-8466
E-mail:
kevin.wilkinson@remingtoncollege.edu
Phone: (281) 899-1240

Remington College: Lafayette
www.remingtoncollege.edu
303 Rue Louis XIV
Lafayette, LA 70508
Fax: (337) 983-7130
Phone: (337) 981-4010

Remington College: Largo
www.remingtoncollege.edu
8550 Ulmerton Road, Unit 100
Largo, FL 33771
Fax: (727) 530-7710
Phone: (727) 532-1999

Remington College: Memphis
www.remingtoncollege.edu
2710 Nonconnah Boulevard
Memphis, TN 38132
Fax: (901) 396-8310
Phone: (901) 345-1000

Remington College: Mobile
www.educationamerica.com
828 Downtowner Loop West
Mobile, AL 36609-5404
Fax: (251) 343-0577
Phone: (251) 343-8200

Remington College: Tampa
www.remingtoncollege.edu
International Department
2410 East Busch Boulevard
Tampa, FL 33612
Fax: (813) 935-7415
E-mail: gary.schwartz@remingtoncollege.edu
Phone: (813) 935-5700

Rensselaer Polytechnic Institute
www.rpi.edu
Admissions Office
110 Eighth Street
Troy, NY 12180-3590
Fax: (518) 276-4072
E-mail: admissions@rpi.edu
Phone: (518) 276-6216

Renton Technical College
www.RTC.edu
3000 NE Fourth Street
Renton, WA 98056-4195
Fax: (425) 235-7832
E-mail: bbennedsen@rtc.edu
Phone: (425) 235-5840

Research College of Nursing
www.researchcollege.edu
Student Development
2525 East Meyer Boulevard
Kansas City, MO 64132-1199
Fax: (816) 995-2813
Phone: (816) 501-4000

Rhode Island College
www.ric.edu
Admissions Office
600 Mount Pleasant Avenue
Forman Center
Providence, RI 02908
Fax: (401) 456-8817
E-mail: admissions@ric.edu
Phone: (401) 456-8234

Rhode Island School of Design
www.risd.edu
Admissions
Two College Street
Providence, RI 02903-2791
Fax: (401) 454-6309
E-mail: admissions@risd.edu
Phone: (401) 454-6300

Rhodec International
www.rhodec.edu/us
59 Coddington Street, Suite 104
Quincy, MA 02169
E-mail: uscontact@rhodec.edu
Phone: (617) 472-4942

Rhodes College
www.rhodes.edu
Office of Admissions
2000 North Parkway
Memphis, TN 38112
Fax: (901) 843-3631
E-mail: adminfo@rhodes.edu
Phone: (901) 843-3700

Rice University
www.rice.edu
Admission Office
6100 Main Street
Office of Admission MS-17 PO Box 1892
Houston, TX 77251-1892
Fax: (713) 348-5323
E-mail: admission@rice.edu
Phone: (713) 348-7423

Richard Bland College
www.rbc.edu
Division of Student Affairs
11301 Johnson Road
Petersburg, VA 23805
Fax: (804) 862-6490
E-mail: admit@rbc.edu
Phone: (804) 862-6249

Richard Stockton College of New Jersey
www.stockton.edu
Admissions Office
Jim Leeds Road
PO Box 195
Pomona, NJ 08240-0195
Fax: (609) 748-5541
E-mail: admissions@stockton.edu
Phone: (609) 652-4261

Richland College
www.rlc.dcccd.edu
Multicultural Center
12800 Abrams Road
Dallas, TX 75243-2199
Fax: (972) 682-6165
E-mail: tadams@dcccd.edu
Phone: (972) 238-6903

Richland Community College
www.richland.edu
Admissions & Records
One College Park
Decatur, IL 62521
Fax: (217) 875-7783
E-mail: jwirey@richland.edu
Phone: (217) 875-7200 ext. 284

Rider University
www.rider.edu
International Admissions
2083 Lawrenceville Road
Box 3001
Lawrenceville, NJ 08648-3099
Fax: (609) 895-6645
E-mail: admissions@rider.edu
Phone: (609) 896-5000 ext. 5194

Ringling College of Art and Design
www.ringling.edu
Admissions
2700 North Tamiami Trail
Sarasota, FL 34234-5895
Fax: (941) 359-7517
E-mail: afischer@ringling.edu
Phone: (941) 351-5100

Rio Hondo College
www.riohondo.edu
3600 Workman Mill Road
Whittier, CA 90601-1699
Fax: (562) 692-8318
Phone: (562) 692-0921 ext. 3134

Rio Salado College
www.riosalado.edu
Registration and Records
2323 West 14th Street
Tempe, AZ 85281
Fax: (480) 517-8199
E-mail: admissions@email.rio.maricopa.edu
Phone: (480) 517-8152

River Valley Community College
www.rivervalley.edu
One College Drive
Claremont, NH 03743-9707
Fax: (603) 543-1844
Phone: (603) 542-7744

Riverland Community College
www.riverland.edu
1900 Eighth Avenue, NW
Austin, MN 55912-1407
Fax: (507) 433-0515
E-mail: mmorem@river.cc.mn.us
Phone: (507) 433-0600

Riverside Community College
www.rcc.edu
Center for International Students and Programs
4800 Magnolia Avenue
Riverside, CA 92506
Fax: (951) 222-8376
E-mail: internationalcenter@rcc.edu
Phone: (951) 222-8160

Rivier College
www.rivier.edu
Director of Admissions
420 Main Street
Nashua, NH 03060-5086
Fax: (603) 891-1799
E-mail: dboisvert@rivier.edu
Phone: (603) 897-8507

Roane State Community College
www.roanestate.edu
Admission Office
276 Patton Lane
Harriman, TN 37748
Fax: (865) 882-4562
E-mail: gonzales_mr@roanestate.edu
Phone: (865) 882-4523

Roanoke Bible College
www.roanokebible.edu
Registrar
715 North Poindexter Street
Elizabeth City, NC 27909
Fax: (252) 334-2071
E-mail: jus@roanokebible.edu
Phone: (252) 334-2012

Roanoke College
www.roanoke.edu
Admissions
221 College Lane
Salem, VA 24153-3794
Fax: (540) 375-2267
E-mail: admissions@roanoke.edu
Phone: (540) 375-2270

Roanoke-Chowan Community College
www.roanokechowan.edu
Student Services
109 Community College Road
Ahoskie, NC 27910-9522
Fax: (252) 862-1355
E-mail: sandrac@roanokehowan.edu
Phone: (252) 862-1305

Robert Morris College: Chicago
www.robertmorris.edu
Student Information
401 South State Street
Chicago, IL 60605
Fax: (312) 935-4177
E-mail: studentrecords@robertmorris.edu
Phone: (312) 935-4180

Robert Morris University
www.rmu.edu
Office of Enrollment Management
6001 University Boulevard
Moon Township, PA 15108-1189
Fax: (412) 397-2425
E-mail: admissions@rmu.edu
Phone: (412) 397-5200

Roberts Wesleyan College
www.roberts.edu
Vice President for Admissions and Marketing
2301 Westside Drive
Rochester, NY 14624-1997
Fax: (585) 594-6371
E-mail: admissions@roberts.edu
Phone: (585) 594-6400

Robeson Community College
www.robeson.edu
PO Box 1420
5160 Fayetteville Road
Lumberton, NC 28359
Fax: (910) 618-5686
E-mail: jrevels@robeson.cc.nc.us
Phone: (910) 272-3700 ext. 3347

Rochester College
www.rc.edu
Enrollment Services
800 West Avon Road
Rochester Hills, MI 48307
Fax: (248) 218-2035
E-mail: admissions@rc.edu
Phone: (248) 218-2031

Rochester Community and Technical College
www.roch.edu
Office of Admissions and Records
851 30th Avenue SE
Rochester, MN 55904-4999
Fax: (507) 285-7496
E-mail: glen.saponari@roch.edu
Phone: (507) 285-7268

Rochester Institute of Technology
www.rit.edu
Undergraduate Admissions Office
60 Lomb Memorial Drive
Rochester, NY 14623-5604
Fax: (585) 475-7424
E-mail: admissions@rit.edu
Phone: (585) 475-6631

Rock Valley College
www.rockvalleycollege.edu
3301 North Mulford Road
Rockford, IL 61114-5699
Fax: (815) 921-4269
E-mail: m.foreman@rvc.cc.il.us
Phone: (815) 921-4251

Rockford College
www.rockford.edu
Admission
5050 East State Street
Rockford, IL 61108-2393
Fax: (818) 226-2822
E-mail: rcadmissions@rockford.edu
Phone: (815) 226-4050

324

Rockhurst University
www.rockhurst.edu
Admission
1100 Rockhurst Road
Kansas City, MO 64110-2561
Fax: (816) 501-4142
E-mail: admission@rockhurst.edu
Phone: (816) 501-4100

Rockingham Community College
www.rockinghamcc.edu
Box 38
Wentworth, NC 27375-0038
Fax: (336) 342-1809
E-mail: dunnm@rockinghamcc.edu
Phone: (336) 342-4261 ext. 2114

Rockland Community College
www.sunyrockland.edu
International Student Services
145 College Road
Suffern, NY 10901
Fax: (845) 574-4433
E-mail: info@sunyrockland.edu
Phone: (914) 574-4263

Rocky Mountain College
www.rocky.edu
International Programs
1511 Poly Drive
Billings, MT 59102-1796
Fax: (406) 259-9751
E-mail: briggsk@rocky.edu
Phone: (406) 657-1107

Rocky Mountain College of Art & Design
www.rmcad.edu
Dean of Students
1600 Pierce Street
Denver, CO 80214
Fax: (303) 759-4970
E-mail: bpantel@rmcad.edu
Phone: (303) 225-8538

Roger Williams University
www.rwu.edu
Admission
One Old Ferry Road
Bristol, RI 02809
Fax: (401) 254-3557
E-mail: admit@rwu.edu
Phone: (401) 254-3500

Rogue Community College
www.roguecc.edu
Enrollment Services
3345 Redwood Highway
Grants Pass, OR 97527
E-mail: Csullivan@roguecc.edu
Phone: (541) 956-7176

Rollins College
www.rollins.edu
Admissions
1000 Holt Avenue
PO Box 2720
Winter Park, FL 32789
Fax: (407) 646-1502
E-mail: admission@rollins.edu
Phone: (407) 646-2161

Roosevelt University
www.roosevelt.edu
Office of International Admissions
430 South Michigan Avenue
Chicago, IL 60605-1394
Fax: (312) 341-6377
E-mail: cearley@roosevelt.edu
Phone: (312) 341-3531

Rosalind Franklin University of Medicine and Science
www.rosalindfranklin.edu
Graduate Admissions Office
3333 Green Bay Road
North Chicago, IL 60064-3095
E-mail: grad.admissions@rosalindfranklin.edu
Phone: (847) 578-3209

Rose State College
www.rose.edu
Admissions
6420 SE 15th Street
Midwest City, OK 73110
Fax: (405) 736-0309
E-mail: dsorrell@rose.edu
Phone: (405) 736-0203

Rose-Hulman Institute of Technology
www.rose-hulman.edu
Dean of Admissions and Financial Aid
Office of Admissions
5500 Wabash Avenue, CM 1
Terre Haute, IN 47803-3999
Fax: (812) 877-8941
E-mail: james.goecker@rose-hulman.edu
Phone: (800) 248-7448

Rosemont College
www.rosemont.edu
Undergraduate Women's College Admissions
1400 Montgomery Avenue
Rosemont, PA 19010-1699
Fax: (610) 520-4399
E-mail: randrews@rosemont.edu
Phone: (610) 527-0200 ext. 2952

Rowan University
www.rowan.edu
International Student Services
Savitz Hall, 201 Mullica Hill Road
Glassboro, NJ 08028
Fax: (856) 256-5238
E-mail: katz@rowan.edu
Phone: (856) 256-4238

Roxbury Community College
www.rcc.mass.edu
Admissions
1234 Columbus Avenue
Roxbury Crossing, MA 02120-3400
Fax: (617) 541-5316
E-mail: msamuels@rcc.mass.edu
Phone: (617) 541-5310

Russell Sage College
www.sage.edu/rsc
Admissions
45 Ferry Street
Troy, NY 12180-4115
Fax: (518) 244-6880
E-mail: ruschk@sage.edu
Phone: (518) 244-2217

Rust College
www.rustcollege.edu
150 Rust Avenue
Holly Springs, MS 38635-2328
Fax: (662) 252-2258
E-mail: csmith@rustcollege.edu
Phone: (662) 252-8000 ext. 4056

Rutgers, The State University of New Jersey: Camden Regional Campus
www.rutgers.edu
406 Penn Street
Camden, NJ 08102
Fax: (856) 225-6498
Phone: (856) 225-6104

Rutgers, The State University of New Jersey: New Brunswick/Piscataway Campus
www.rutgers.edu
65 Davidson Road, Room 202
Piscataway, NJ 08854-8097
Fax: (732) 445-0237
Phone: (732) 932-4636

Rutgers, The State University of New Jersey: Newark Regional Campus
www.rutgers.edu
249 University Avenue
Newark, NJ 07102-1896
Fax: (973) 353-1440
Phone: (973) 353-5205

Sacramento City College
www.scc.losrios.edu
International Student Office
3835 Freeport Boulevard
Sacramento, CA 95822
Fax: (916) 558-2490
E-mail: sccaeinfo@scc.losrios.edu
Phone: (916) 558-2486

Sacred Heart University
www.sacredheart.edu
Admissions Office
5151 Park Avenue
Fairfield, CT 06825
Fax: (203) 365-7607
E-mail: enroll@sacredheart.edu
Phone: (203) 371-7880

Saddleback College
www.saddleback.edu
International Education Office
28000 Marguerite Parkway
Mission Viejo, CA 92692
Fax: (949) 582-4800
E-mail: intnled@saddleback.cc.ca.us
Phone: (949) 582-4635

Sage College
www.sagecollege.edu
12125 Day Street, Building L
Moreno Valley, CA 92557-6720
E-mail: admissions@sagecollege.edu
Phone: (951) 781-2727

Sage College of Albany
www.sage.edu
Sage College of Albany
140 New Scotland Avenue
Albany, NY 12208
Fax: (518) 292-1912
E-mail: sullia4@sage.edu
Phone: (518) 292-1730

Saginaw Chippewa Tribal College
www.sagchip.org/tribalcollege
7070 East Broadway
Mount Pleasant, MI 48858
Phone: (989) 775-4123

Saginaw Valley State University
www.svsu.edu
International Programs
7400 Bay Road
University Center, MI 48710
Fax: (989) 964-6066
E-mail: oip@svsu.edu
Phone: (989) 964-4473

St. Ambrose University
www.sau.edu
International Admissions
518 West Locust Street
Davenport, IA 52803-2898
Fax: (563) 333-6243
E-mail: spillmansherril@sau.edu
Phone: (563) 333-6309

St. Andrews Presbyterian College
www.sapc.edu
International Student Admissions
1700 Dogwood Mile
Laurinburg, NC 28352
Fax: (910) 277-5087
E-mail: wombleemc@sapc.edu
Phone: (910) 277-5555 ext. 5453

St. Anselm College
www.anselm.edu
Admission
100 Saint Anselm Drive
Manchester, NH 03102-1310
Fax: (603) 641-7550
E-mail: khrasky@anselm.edu
Phone: (603) 641-6009

St. Augustine's College
www.st-aug.edu
Admissions
1315 Oakwood Avenue
Raleigh, NC 27610-2298
Fax: (919) 516-4415
E-mail: admissions@es.st-aug.edu
Phone: (919) 516-4012

Saint Bonaventure University
www.sbu.edu
Office of Foreign Studies
Route 417
Box D
St. Bonaventure, NY 14778-2284
Fax: (716) 375-7882
E-mail: asayegh@sbu.edu
Phone: (716) 375-4009

St. Catharine College
www.sccky.edu
Admissions
2735 Bardstown Road
St. Catharine, KY 40061
Fax: (859) 336-5031
E-mail: cmedley@sccky.edu
Phone: (859) 336-5082 ext. 1273

St. Charles Borromeo Seminary - Overbrook
www.scs.edu
Vice Rector
100 East Wynnewood Road
Wynnewood, PA 19096
Fax: (610) 617-9267
E-mail: frdd@adphila.org
Phone: (610) 785-6271

St. Clair County Community College
www.sc4.edu
Dean of Student Services
323 Erie Street
Box 5015
Port Huron, MI 48061-5015
Fax: (810) 984-4730
E-mail: jmorris@sc4.edu
Phone: (810) 989-5560

Saint Cloud State University
http://www.stcloudstate.edu
Center for International Studies
720 Fourth Avenue South
St. Cloud, MN 56301
Fax: (320) 308-4223
E-mail: international@stcloudstate.edu
Phone: (320) 308-4287

St. Cloud Technical College
www.sctc.edu
Admissions
1540 Northway Drive
St. Cloud, MN 56303
Fax: (320) 308-5087
E-mail: jelness@sctc.edu
Phone: (800) 222-1009

St. Edward's University
www.stedwards.edu
Undergraduate Admission
3001 South Congress Avenue
Austin, TX 78704-6425
Fax: (512) 464-8877
E-mail: seu.admit@stedwards.edu
Phone: (512) 448-8500

St. Elizabeth College of Nursing
www.secon.edu
Registrar's Office
2215 Genesee Street
Utica, NY 13501
Fax: (315) 798-8271
E-mail: bcavoly@stemc.org
Phone: (315) 798-8253

St. Francis College
www.stfranciscollege.edu
Admissions
180 Remsen Street
Brooklyn Heights, NY 11201-9902
Fax: (718) 802-0453
E-mail: admissions@stfranciscollege.edu
Phone: (718) 489-5200

St. Francis University
www.francis.edu
Admissions
Box 600
117 Evergreen Drive
Loretto, PA 15940
Fax: (814) 472-3335
E-mail: admissions@francis.edu
Phone: (800) 472-3100

St. Gregory's University
www.stgregorys.edu
International Office
1900 West MacArthur Drive
Shawnee, OK 74804
Fax: (405) 878-5198
E-mail: int-admissions@stgregorys.edu
Phone: (405) 878-5177

St. John Fisher College
www.sjfc.edu
Admissions
3690 East Avenue
Rochester, NY 14618-3597
Fax: (585) 385-8386
E-mail: admissions@sjfc.edu
Phone: (585) 385-8064

St. John's College
www.st-johns.org/education/schools/nursing
729 East Carpenter Street
Springfield, IL 62702
E-mail: college@st-johns.org
Phone: (217) 525-5628

St. John's College
www.stjohnscollege.edu
Admissions
PO Box 2800
Annapolis, MD 21404
Fax: (410) 269-7916
E-mail: admissions@sjca.edu
Phone: (410) 626-2522

St. John's College
www.stjohnscollege.edu
Admissions Office, Undergraduate
1160 Camino Cruz Blanca
Santa Fe, NM 87505-4599
Fax: (505) 984-6162
E-mail: admissions@sjcsf.edu
Phone: (505) 984-6060

St. John's University
www.csbsju.edu
Admissions
PO Box 7155
Saint John's University
Collegeville, MN 56321-7155
Fax: (320) 363-3206
E-mail: ryoung@csbsju.edu
Phone: (320) 363-2190

St. John's University
www.stjohns.edu
Office of Admission
8000 Utopia Parkway
Queens, NY 11439
Fax: (718) 990-2346
E-mail: intladm@stjohns.edu
Phone: (718) 990-1342

St. Joseph College
www.sjc.edu
1678 Asylum Avenue
West Hartford, CT 06117
E-mail: admissions@sjc.edu
Phone: (860) 231-5216

St. Joseph Seminary College
www.sjasc.edu
Registrar
75376 River Road
St. Benedict, LA 70457-9990
Fax: (985) 327-1085
E-mail: gbinderregistrar@jsasc.edu
Phone: (985) 867-2248

St. Joseph's College
www.sjcme.edu
Admissions Office
278 Whites Bridge Road
Standish, ME 04084-5263
Fax: (207) 893-7862
E-mail: admission@sjcme.edu
Phone: (207) 893-7746

St. Joseph's College
www.sjcny.edu
245 Clinton Avenue
Brooklyn, NY 11205-3688
Fax: (718) 636-8303
E-mail: fsolorzano@sjcny.edu
Phone: (718) 636-6868

St. Joseph's College: Suffolk Campus
www.sjcny.edu
Admissions Office
155 West Roe Boulevard
Patchogue, NY 11772-2603
Fax: (631) 447-3601
E-mail: glamens@sjcny.edu
Phone: (631) 447-3219

Saint Joseph's University
www.sju.edu
Office of Undergraduate Admission
5600 City Avenue
Philadelphia, PA 19131
Fax: (610) 660-1314
E-mail: admit@sju.edu
Phone: (610) 660-1300

St. Lawrence University
www.stlawu.edu
Admissions
Payson Hall
Canton, NY 13617
Fax: (315) 229-5818
E-mail: admissions@stlawu.edu
Phone: (315) 229-5261

St. Leo University
www.saintleo.edu
Office of Admission
Office of Admission
Box 6665 MC2008
Saint Leo, FL 33574-6665
Fax: (352) 588-8257
E-mail: admission@saintleo.edu
Phone: (352) 588-8283

St. Louis Community College at Florissant Valley
www.stlcc.edu
3400 Pershall Road
St. Louis, MO 63135
Fax: (314) 513-4724
Phone: (314) 513-4244

Saint Louis University
www.slu.edu
International Center
221 North Grand Boulevard
St. Louis, MO 63103-2097
Fax: (314) 977-3412
E-mail: ndame@slu.edu
Phone: (314) 977-2490

St. Luke's College
www.stlukescollege.edu
Student Services
2720 Stone Park Boulevard
Box 2000
Sioux City, IA 51104
Fax: (712) 233-8017
E-mail: johanndd@stlukes.org
Phone: (712) 279-3377

Saint Martin's University
www.stmartin.edu
Office of International Programs
5300 Pacific Avenue SE
Lacey, WA 98503-7500
Fax: (360) 459-4124
E-mail: jyung@stmartin.edu
Phone: (360) 438-4504

St. Mary-of-the-Woods College
www.smwc.edu
Office of Admission
Guerin Hall, SMWC
St. Mary of the Woods, IN 47876
Fax: (812) 535-5010
E-mail: smwcadms@smwc.edu
Phone: (812) 535-5106

Saint Mary's College
www.saintmarys.edu
Admission Office
Notre Dame, IN 46556-5001
Fax: (574) 284-4716
E-mail: admission@saintmarys.edu
Phone: (574) 284-4587

St. Mary's College of California
www.stmarys-ca.edu
Admissions Office
Box 4800
Moraga, CA 94575-4800
Fax: (925) 376-7193
E-mail: international@stmarys-ca.edu
Phone: (925) 631-4307

St. Mary's College of Maryland
www.smcm.edu
Office of Admissions
18952 East Fisher Road
St. Mary's City, MD 20686-3001
Fax: (240) 895-5001
E-mail: rjedgar@smcm.edu
Phone: (240) 895-5000

St. Mary's University
www.stmarytx.edu
Admissions
One Camino Santa Maria
San Antonio, TX 78228
Fax: (210) 431-6742
E-mail: uadm@stmarytx.edu
Phone: (210) 436-3126

St. Mary's University of Minnesota
www.smumn.edu
Admissions
700 Terrace Heights, #2
Winona, MN 55987-1399
Fax: (507) 457-1752
E-mail: admissions@smumn.edu
Phone: (507) 457-1483

St. Michael's College
www.smcvt.edu
Office of Admission
One Winooski Park
Box 7
Colchester, VT 05439
Fax: (802) 654-2906
E-mail: admission@smcvt.edu
Phone: (802) 654-3000

St. Norbert College
www.snc.edu
Admissions
100 Grant Street
De Pere, WI 54115-2099
Fax: (920) 403-4072
E-mail: admit@snc.edu
Phone: (920) 403-3005

St. Olaf College
www.stolaf.edu
Admissions
1520 St. Olaf Avenue
Northfield, MN 55057
Fax: (507) 646-3832
E-mail: admissions@stolaf.edu
Phone: (507) 646-3995

St. Paul College
www.saintpaul.edu
235 Marshall Avenue
Saint Paul, MN 55102-1800
Fax: (651) 846-1468
E-mail: admissions@saintpaul.edu
Phone: (651) 846-1555

St. Paul's College
www.saintpauls.edu
Office of Admissions
115 College Drive
Lawrenceville, VA 23868
Fax: (434) 848-1846
E-mail: rlewis@saintpauls.edu
Phone: (434) 848-1856

Saint Peter's College
www.spc.edu
Admissions
2641 Kennedy Boulevard
Jersey City, NJ 07306
Fax: (201) 761-7105
E-mail: jgiglio@spc.edu
Phone: (201) 761-7100

St. Petersburg College
www.spcollege.edu
International Center
Box 13489
St. Petersburg, FL 33733-3489
Fax: (727) 341-3510
E-mail: le@spjc.edu
Phone: (727) 341-4370

St. Philip's College
www.accd.edu/spc
Advising
1801 Martin Luther King Drive
San Antonio, TX 78203
Fax: (210) 531-4790
E-mail: bcrow@mail.accd.edu
Phone: (210) 531-3263

St. Thomas Aquinas College
www.stac.edu
Admissions Office
125 Route 340
Sparkill, NY 10976
Fax: (845) 398-4372
E-mail: frodrigu@stac.edu
Phone: (845) 398-4103

Saint Thomas University
www.stu.edu
16401 Northwest 37th Avenue
Miami Gardens, FL 33054-6459
Fax: (305) 628-6510
E-mail: signup@stu.edu
Phone: (305) 628-6546

St. Vincent College
www.stvincent.edu
Admission
300 Fraser Purchase Road
Latrobe, PA 15650-2690
Fax: (724) 537-5069
E-mail: admission@stvincent.edu
Phone: (724) 537-4540

St. Xavier University
www.sxu.edu
Admission
3700 West 103rd Street
Chicago, IL 60655
Fax: (773) 298-3076
E-mail: admission@sxu.edu
Phone: (773) 298-3050

Salem College
www.salem.edu
Admissions
PO Box 10548
Winston-Salem, NC 27108
Fax: (336) 917-5972
E-mail: admissions@salem.edu
Phone: (336) 721-2621

Salem Community College
www.salemcc.edu
Admissions
460 Hollywood Avenue
Carneys Point, NJ 08069-2799
Fax: (856) 299-9193
E-mail: congle@salemcc.edu
Phone: (856) 351-2698

Salem International University
www.salemu.edu
Admissions
223 West Main Street
Box 500
Salem, WV 26426
Fax: (304) 326-1592
E-mail: lningi@salemu.edu
Phone: (304) 326-1518

Salem State College
www.salemstate.edu
Assistant Dean of Student Development
352 Lafayette Street
Salem, MA 01970-5353
Fax: (978) 542-6893
E-mail: admissions@salemstate.edu
Phone: (978) 542-6200

Salisbury University
www.salisbury.edu
Center for International Education
1200 Camden Avenue
Salisbury, MD 21801-6862
Fax: (410) 219-2853
E-mail: axliszkowska@salisbury.edu
Phone: (410) 334-3495

Salt Lake Community College
www.slcc.edu
International Students Office
4600 South Redwood Road
Box 30808
Salt Lake City, UT 84130-0808
Fax: (801) 957-4432
E-mail: nancy.fillat@slcc.edu
Phone: (801) 957-4528

Salve Regina University
www.salve.edu
Admissions Office
100 Ochre Point Avenue
Newport, RI 02840-4192
Fax: (401) 848-2823
E-mail: sruadmis@salve.edu
Phone: (401) 341-2908

Sam Houston State University
www.shsu.edu
Office of International Programs
Box 2418
Huntsville, TX 77341-2418
Fax: (936) 294-4620
E-mail: oip@shsu.edu
Phone: (936) 294-3892

Samford University
www.samford.edu
Admission
800 Lakeshore Drive
Birmingham, AL 35229
Fax: (205) 726-2171
E-mail: ppkimrey@samford.edu
Phone: (205) 726-2871

Samuel Merritt College
www.samuelmerritt.edu
Office of Admission
370 Hawthorne Avenue
Oakland, CA 94609-9954
Fax: (510) 869-6610
E-mail: admission@samuelmerritt.edu
Phone: (510) 869-6610

San Antonio College
www.accd.edu/sac
International Students Office
1300 San Pedro Avenue
San Antonio, TX 78212-4299
Fax: (210) 733-2030
E-mail: scecconi@accd.edu
Phone: (210) 733-2306

San Bernardino Valley College
www.valleycollege.edu
Foreign Student Adviser Counseling Office
701 South Mount Vernon Avenue
San Bernardino, CA 92410
E-mail: admissions@valleycollege.edu
Phone: (909) 384-4401

San Diego Christian College
www.sdcc.edu
2100 Greenfield Drive
El Cajon, CA 92019-1157
Fax: (619) 590-1763
E-mail: jmatauic@sdcc.edu
Phone: (619) 590-1113

San Diego City College
www.sdccd.edu
International Student Admissions
1313 Park Boulevard
San Diego, CA 92101-4787
Fax: (619) 388-3505
E-mail: dmeza@sdccd.net
Phone: (619) 388-3476

San Diego Mesa College
www.sandiegomesacollege.edu
International Admissions
7250 Mesa College Drive
San Diego, CA 92111
Fax: (619) 388-2960
E-mail: csawyer@sdccd.edu
Phone: (619) 388-2717

San Diego Miramar College
www.miramarcollege.net
Foreign Student Adviser
10440 Black Mountain Road
San Diego, CA 92126-2999
Fax: (619) 693-1899
Phone: (619) 536-7840

San Diego State University
www.sdsu.edu
International Student Center
5500 Campanile Drive
San Diego, CA 92182-7455
Fax: (619) 594-1973
E-mail: isc.reception@sdsu.edu
Phone: (619) 594-1982

San Francisco Art Institute
www.sfai.edu
Office of Admissions
800 Chestnut Street
San Francisco, CA 94133-2299
Fax: (415) 749-4517
E-mail: admissions@sfai.edu
Phone: (415) 749-4500

San Francisco Conservatory of Music
www.sfcm.edu
Office of Admission
50 Oak Street
San Francisco, CA 94102
Fax: (415) 503-6299
E-mail: admit@sfcm.edu
Phone: (415) 503-6231

San Francisco State University
www.sfsu.edu
Office of International Programs
1600 Holloway Avenue
San Francisco, CA 94132
Fax: (415) 338-6234
E-mail: ugadmit@sfsu.edu
Phone: (415) 338-1293

San Jacinto College
www.sanjac.edu
Call Center
8060 Spencer Highway
Pasadena, TX 77505-5999
Fax: (281) 478-2720
E-mail: information@sjcd.edu
Phone: (281) 998-6150

San Joaquin Delta College
www.deltacollege.edu
International Student Office
5151 Pacific Avenue
Stockton, CA 95207-6370
Fax: (209) 954-5769
E-mail: jwhiting@deltacollege.edu
Phone: (209) 954-5641

San Joaquin Valley College
www.sjvc.edu
8400 West Mineral King Avenue
Visalia, CA 93291-9283
Fax: (559) 651-0574
Phone: (559) 651-2500

San Jose City College
www.sjcc.edu
International Admissions
2100 Moorpark Avenue
San Jose, CA 95128-2798
Fax: (408) 297-3924
Phone: (408) 288-3750

San Jose State University
www.sjsu.edu
International Programs & Services
One Washington Square
San Jose, CA 95192-0011
Fax: (408) 924-5976
E-mail: hstevens@sjsu.edu
Phone: (408) 924-5916

San Juan College
www.sanjuancollege.edu
Admissions
4601 College Boulevard
Farmington, NM 87402-4699
Fax: (505) 566-3500
E-mail: coufalk@sanjuancollege.edu
Phone: (505) 566-3426

Sandhills Community College
www.sandhills.edu
Admissions
3395 Airport Road
Pinehurst, NC 28374
Fax: (910) 695-3981
E-mail: mcallisterr@sandhills.edu
Phone: (910) 695-3729

Sanford-Brown College: Hazelwood
www.sanford-brown.edu
75 Village Square
Hazelwood, MO 63042
Phone: (314) 731-1101

Sanford-Brown College: St. Peters
www.sbcstpeters.com
100 Richmond Center Boulevard
St. Peters, MO 63376
Phone: (636) 696-2300

Sanford-Brown Institute: Jacksonville
www.sbjacksonville.com
Admissions
10255 Fortune Parkway, Suite 501
Jacksonville, FL 32256
E-mail: tahmed@sbjacksonville.com
Phone: (904) 363-6221

Santa Ana College
www.sac.edu
International Students Office
1530 West 17th Street
Santa Ana, CA 92706
Fax: (714) 667-0751
E-mail: tolley_donna@sac.edu
Phone: (714) 564-6047

Santa Barbara Business College
www.sbbcollege.edu
506 Chapala Street
Santa Barbara, CA 93101
Fax: (805) 967-4248
Phone: (805) 967-9677

Santa Barbara Business College: Bakersfield
www.sbbcollege.edu
211 South Real Road
Bakersfield, CA 93309
Phone: (866) 749-7222

Santa Barbara Business College: Santa Maria
www.sbbcollege.edu
303 East Plaza Drive
Santa Maria, CA 93454
Fax: (805) 346-1862
Phone: (866) 749-7222

Santa Barbara City College
www.sbcc.edu
International Student Office
721 Cliff Drive
Santa Barbara, CA 93109-2394
Fax: (805) 965-0781
E-mail: smithc@sbcc.edu
Phone: (805) 965-0581 ext. 2243

Santa Clara University
www.scu.edu
Undergraduate Admissions
500 El Camino Real
Santa Clara, CA 95053
Fax: (408) 554-5255
E-mail: mmrubio@scu.edu
Phone: (408) 554-4700

Santa Fe Community College
www.santafe.cc.fl.us
International Student Office
3000 NW 83rd Street
Gainesville, FL 32606
Fax: (352) 395-4481
E-mail: james.earles@sfcc.edu
Phone: (352) 395-5504

Santa Fe Community College
www.sfccnm.edu
Admissions
6401 Richards Avenue
Santa Fe, NM 87508-4887
Fax: (505) 428-1237
E-mail: atupler@ofcanm.edu
Phone: (505) 428-1273

Santa Monica College
www.smc.edu
International Student Center
1900 Pico Boulevard
Santa Monica, CA 90405-1628
Fax: (310) 434-3645
Phone: (310) 434-4217

Santa Rosa Junior College
www.santarosa.edu
International Admissions
1501 Mendocino Avenue
Santa Rosa, CA 95401
Fax: (707) 527-4791
E-mail: khunt@santarosa.edu
Phone: (707) 524-1751

Santiago Canyon College
www.sccollege.edu
International Students
8045 East Chapman Avenue
Orange, CA 92869
Fax: (714) 667-0751
E-mail: tolley_donna@sac.edu
Phone: (714) 564-6047

Sarah Lawrence College
www.sarahlawrence.edu
Undergraduate Admissions
One Mead Way
Bronxville, NY 10708-5999
Fax: (914) 395-2515
E-mail: slcadmit@slc.edu
Phone: (914) 395-2510

Sauk Valley Community College
www.svcc.edu
Counseling
173 Illinois Route 2
Dixon, IL 61021-9110
Fax: (815) 288-3190
E-mail: breedt@svcc.edu
Phone: (815) 288-5511 ext. 390

Savannah College of Art and Design
www.scad.edu
Office of Admission
PO Box 2072
Savannah, GA 31402-2072
Fax: (912) 525-5986
E-mail: admission@scad.edu
Phone: (912) 525-5100

Savannah River College
www.savannahrivercollege.edu
2528 Center West Parkway, Building A
Augusta, GA 30909
Fax: (706) 736-3599
E-mail: jrainier@savannahrivercollege.edu
Phone: (706) 738-5046

Savannah State University
www.savstate.edu
Admissions
State College Branch
Box 20209
Savannah, GA 31404
Fax: (912) 356-2256
E-mail: ssvadms@savstate.edu
Phone: (912) 356-2181

Savannah Technical College
www.savannahtech.edu
Admissions
5717 White Bluff Road
Savannah, GA 31405-5521
Fax: (912) 443-5705
E-mail: jtuttle@savannahtech.edu
Phone: (912) 443-5706

Schenectady County Community College
www.sunysccc.edu
Admissions Office
78 Washington Avenue
Schenectady, NY 12305
Fax: (518) 346-1477
E-mail: sampsodg@gw.sunysccc.edu
Phone: (518) 381-1366

Schiller International University
www.schiller.edu
Admissions Office
300 East Bay Drive
Largo, FL 33770-3716
Fax: (727) 734-0359
E-mail: admissions@schiller.edu
Phone: (800) 336-4133

School of the Art Institute of Chicago
www.saic.edu
Office of Student Affairs/International
36 South Wabash Avenue
Chicago, IL 60603
Fax: (312) 629-6831
E-mail: intaff@saic.edu
Phone: (312) 629-6830

School of the Museum of Fine Arts
www.smfa.edu
Admissions
230 The Fenway
Boston, MA 02115
Fax: (617) 369-4264
E-mail: admissions@smfa.edu
Phone: (617) 369-3626

School of Urban Missions: New Orleans
www.sum.edu
511 Westbank Expressway
Gretna, LA 70053-3677
Fax: (504) 362-4895
E-mail: rmiller@sum.edu
Phone: (504) 362-6364

School of Urban Missions: Oakland
www.sum.edu
Vice President of Academics
735 105th Avenue
Oakland, CA 94603
Fax: (510) 568-1024
E-mail: pwilliams@sum.edu
Phone: (510) 567-6174

School of Visual Arts
www.sva.edu
Admissions Office
209 East 23rd Street
New York, NY 10010-3994
Fax: (212) 592-2242
E-mail: admissions@sva.edu
Phone: (212) 592-2100

Schreiner University
www.schreiner.edu
Admissions
2100 Memorial Boulevard
Kerrville, TX 78028-5697
Fax: (830) 792-7226
E-mail: admissions@schreiner.edu
Phone: (830) 792-7217

Scott Community College
www.eicc.edu
Admissions
500 Belmont Road
Bettendorf, IA 52722-6804
Fax: (563) 441-4101
E-mail: qmoreno@eicc.edu
Phone: (563) 441-4007

Scottsdale Community College
www.scottsdalecc.edu
International Education Program
9000 East Chaparral Road
Scottsdale, AZ 85256-2626
Fax: (480) 423-6099
E-mail: therese.tendick@sccmail.maricopa.edu
Phone: (480) 423-6590

Scripps College
www.scrippscollege.edu
Admissions
1030 Columbia Avenue
Claremont, CA 91711
Fax: (909) 607-7508
E-mail: admission@scrippscollege.edu
Phone: (909) 621-8149

Seattle Pacific University
www.spu.edu
Admissions
3307 Third Avenue West
Seattle, WA 98119-1997
Fax: (206) 281-2544
E-mail: admissions@spu.edu
Phone: (800) 366-3344

Seattle University
www.seattleu.edu
901 12th Avenue
Seattle, WA 98122-4340
Fax: (206) 296-5656
E-mail: admissions@seattleu.edu
Phone: (206) 296-5814

Seminole Community College
www.scc-fl.edu
Office of Admissions
100 Weldon Boulevard
Sanford, FL 32773-6199
Fax: (407) 708-2395
E-mail: smitha@scc-fl.edu
Phone: (407) 708-2041

Seton Hall University
www.shu.edu
Enrollment Services
400 South Orange Avenue
South Orange, NJ 07079-2680
Fax: (973) 275-2040
E-mail: thehall@shu.edu
Phone: (973) 761-9332

Seton Hill University
www.setonhill.edu
Office of Admissions
1 Seton Hill Drive
Greensburg, PA 15601
Fax: (724) 830-1294
E-mail: admit@setonhill.edu
Phone: (724) 838-4255

Shasta College
www.shastacollege.edu
Admissions and Records
Box 496006
Redding, CA 96049-6006
Fax: (530) 225-4995
E-mail: cryan@shastacollege.edu
Phone: (530) 254-867

Shaw University
www.shawuniversity.edu
Office of Admissions
118 East South Street
Raleigh, NC 27601
Fax: (919) 546-8271
E-mail: sclifton@shaw.edu
Phone: (919) 546-8275

Shawnee State University
www.shawnee.edu
Admissions
940 Second Street
Portsmouth, OH 45662
Fax: (740) 351-3111
E-mail: rmerb@shawnee.edu
Phone: (740) 351-3576

Shelton State Community College
www.sheltonstate.edu
International Student Liaison
9500 Old Greensboro Road
Tuscaloosa, AL 35405-8522
Fax: (205) 391-3910
E-mail: tbranch@sheltonstate.edu
Phone: (205) 391-2342

Shenandoah University
www.su.edu
Admissions
1460 University Drive
Winchester, VA 22601-5195
Fax: (540) 665-4627
E-mail: admit@su.edu
Phone: (540) 665-4581

Shepherd University
www.shepherd.edu
Admissions
PO Box 3210
Shepherdstown, WV 25443-3210
Fax: (304) 876-5165
E-mail: kscranag@shepherd.edu
Phone: (304) 876-5212

Sheridan College
www.sheridan.edu
Admissions
PO Box 1500
Sheridan, WY 82801-1500
Fax: (307) 674-3373
E-mail: ewiley@sheridan.edu
Phone: (307) 674-6446 ext. 2002

Shimer College
www.shimer.edu
Office of Admissions
3424 South State Street
Chicago, IL 60616
Fax: (312) 235-3501
E-mail: admissions@shimer.edu
Phone: (847) 623-8400

Shippensburg University of Pennsylvania
www.ship.edu
Associate Dean, Graduate Admissions
1871 Old Main Drive
Shippensburg, PA 17257-2299
Fax: (717) 477-4016
E-mail: rmpayn@ship.edu
Phone: (717) 477-1213

Shorter College
www.shorter.edu
Admissions
315 Shorter Avenue
Rome, GA 30165
Fax: (706) 233-7224
E-mail: jhead@shorter.edu
Phone: (706) 233-7310

Siena College
www.siena.edu
Admissions Office
515 Loudon Road
Loudonville, NY 12211-1462
Fax: (518) 783-2436
E-mail: admit@siena.edu
Phone: (518) 783-2423

Siena Heights University
www.sienahts.edu
1247 East Siena Heights Drive
Adrian, MI 49221-1796
Fax: (517) 264-7745
E-mail: admissions@sienahts.edu
Phone: (517) 264-7183

Sierra College
www.sierracollege.edu
International Students Office
5000 Rocklin Road
Rocklin, CA 95677
Fax: (916) 781-6210
E-mail:
internationalstudents@sierracollege.edu
Phone: (916) 789-2903

Sierra Nevada College
www.sierranevada.edu
Admission
999 Tahoe Boulevard
Incline Village, NV 89451-4269
Fax: (775) 831-1347
E-mail: admissions@sierranevada.edu
Phone: (775) 831-1314

Silver Lake College
www.sl.edu
Admissions
2406 South Alverno Road
Manitowoc, WI 54220-9319
Fax: (920) 684-7082
E-mail: admslc@silver.sl.edu
Phone: (920) 686-6175

Simmons College
www.simmons.edu
Undergraduate Admissions
300 The Fenway
Boston, MA 02115-5898
Fax: (617) 521-3190
E-mail: alexandra.krol@simmons.edu
Phone: (617) 521-2504

Simpson College
www.simpson.edu
Admissions
701 North C Street
Indianola, IA 50125
Fax: (515) 961-1870
E-mail: admiss@simpson.edu
Phone: (515) 961-1624

Simpson University
www.simpsonuniversity.edu
Enrollment Services
2211 College View Drive
Redding, CA 96003-8606
Fax: (530) 226-4861
E-mail: admissions@simpsonuniversity.edu
Phone: (530) 226-4606

Sinclair Community College
www.sinclair.edu
Registration/Student Records
444 West Third Street
Dayton, OH 45402-1460
Fax: (937) 512-3456
E-mail: intladm@sinclair.edu
Phone: (837) 512-3024

Sisseton Wahpeton College
www.swc.tc
Admissions Office
BIA 700, Box 689
Agency Village, SD 57262-0689
Fax: (605) 698-3132
E-mail: DRedday@swc.tc
Phone: (605) 698-3966 ext. 1180

Skidmore College
www.skidmore.edu
Admissions
815 North Broadway
Saratoga Springs, NY 12866
Fax: (518) 580-5584
E-mail: admissions@skidmore.edu
Phone: (518) 580-5570

Skyline College
www.skylinecollege.edu
Admissions and Records
3300 College Drive
San Bruno, CA 94066
Fax: (650) 738-4200
E-mail: acevedo@smccd.net
Phone: (650) 738-4251

Slippery Rock University of Pennsylvania
www.sru.edu
Office of International Services
1 Morrow Way
Slippery Rock, PA 16057-1383
Fax: (724) 738-2289
E-mail: pamela.frigot@sru.edu
Phone: (724) 738-2057

Smith College
www.smith.edu
Admission
7 College Lane
Northampton, MA 01063
Fax: (413) 585-2527
E-mail: kkristof@smith.edu
Phone: (413) 585-2500

Snow College
www.snow.edu
International Students Admissions
150 East College Avenue
Ephraim, UT 84627
Fax: (435) 283-7438
E-mail: diane.ogden@snow.edu
Phone: (435) 283-7430

Sojourner-Douglass College
www.sdc.edu
500 North Caroline Street
Baltimore, MD 21205
Fax: (410) 675-1811
Phone: (410) 276-0306 ext. 248

Soka University of America
www.soka.edu
Admission and Financial Aid
1 University Drive
Aliso Viejo, CA 92656-8081
Fax: (949) 480-4151
E-mail: cbrown@soka.edu
Phone: (949) 480-4048

Solano Community College
www.solano.edu
4000 Suisun Valley Road
Fairfield, CA 94534-3197
Fax: (707) 864-7175
E-mail: admissions@solano.edu
Phone: (707) 864-7171

Somerset Community College
www.somerset.kctcs.edu
Admissions
808 Monticello Street
Somerset, KY 42501
Fax: (606) 679-4369
E-mail: tracy.casada@kctcs.edu
Phone: (606) 679-8501

Sonoma State University
www.sonoma.edu
Coordinator, International Services
1801 East Cotati Avenue
Rohnert Park, CA 94928
Fax: (707) 664-2060
E-mail: marisa.thigpen@sonoma.edu
Phone: (707) 664-2582

South Arkansas Community College
www.southark.edu
Enrollment Services
Box 7010
El Dorado, AR 71731-7010
Fax: (870) 864-7137
E-mail: dinman@SouthArk.edu
Phone: (870) 862-8131

South Carolina State University
www.scsu.edu
Admissions and Recruitment
300 College Street NE
PO Box 7127
Orangeburg, SC 29117
Fax: (803) 536-8990
E-mail: aboyle@scsu.edu
Phone: (803) 536-8407

South Central College
www.southcentral.edu
Admissions
1920 Lee Boulevard
PO Box 1920
North Mankato, MN 56003
Fax: (507) 388-9951
E-mail: admissions@southcentral.edu
Phone: (507) 389-7336

South College
www.southcollegetn.edu
Admissions
3904 Lonas Drive
Knoxville, TN 37909
Fax: (865) 470-8737
E-mail: admissions@southcollegetn.edu
Phone: (865) 251-1800

South Dakota School of Mines and Technology
www.sdsmt.edu
501 East St. Joseph Street
Rapid City, SD 57701
Fax: (605) 394-6883
E-mail: susan.aadland@sdsmt.edu
Phone: (605) 394-6884

South Dakota State University
www.sdstate.edu
International Student Affairs
Box 2201 SAD 200
Brookings, SD 57007-0649
Fax: (605) 688-6540
E-mail: sdsu.intlstud@sdstate.edu
Phone: (605) 688-4122

South Florida Community College
www.southflorida.edu
Admissions
600 West College Drive
Avon Park, FL 33825
Fax: (863) 453-2365
E-mail: Deborah.Fuschetti@southflorida.edu
Phone: (863) 453-6661 ext. 7405

South Georgia College
www.sgc.edu
Enrollment Services
100 West College Park Drive
Douglas, GA 31533-5098
Fax: (912) 389-4388
E-mail: admissions@sgc.edu
Phone: (912) 389-4263

South Louisiana Community College
www.slcc.cc.la.us
320 Devalcourt
Lafayette, LA 70506-4124
Fax: (337) 262-2101
E-mail: admissions@slcc.cc.la.us
Phone: (337) 521-8923

South Mountain Community College
www.smc.maricopa.edu
7050 South 24th Street
Phoenix, AZ 85042
Fax: (602) 243-8199
Phone: (602) 243-8123

South Plains College
www.southplainscollege.edu
Admissions
1401 South College Avenue
Levelland, TX 79336
Fax: (806) 897-3167
E-mail: arangel@southplainscollege.edu
Phone: (806) 894-9611 ext. 2371

South Puget Sound Community College
www.spscc.ctc.edu
International Student Programs Office
2011 Mottman Road, SW
Olympia, WA 98512-6218
Fax: (360) 664-0780
E-mail: mcavendish@spscc.ctc.edu
Phone: (360) 596-5396

South Seattle Community College
www.southseattle.edu
International Programs Office
6000 16th Avenue, SW
Seattle, WA 98106-1499
Fax: (206) 764-5836
E-mail: ip@ssccd.ctc.edu
Phone: (206) 764-5360

South Texas College
www.southtexascollege.edu
Admissions
3201 West Pecan Boulevard
McAllen, TX 78502
Fax: (956) 872-8321
E-mail: olegarci@southtexascollege.edu
Phone: (956) 872-2250

South University
www.southuniversity.edu
Admissions office
709 Mall Boulevard
Savannah, GA 31406
Fax: (912) 201-8070
E-mail: mmills@southuniversity.edu
Phone: (912) 201-8000

South University
www.southuniversity.edu
Academics
9 Science Court
Columbia, SC 29203
Fax: (803) 799-5009
Phone: (803) 799-9082

**South University: West Palm Beach
Campus**
www.southuniversity.edu
Admissions
1760 North Congress Avenue
West Palm Beach, FL 33409-5178
Fax: (561) 697-9944
E-mail: wpbfdesk@southcollege.edu
Phone: (561) 697-9200

Southeast Arkansas College
www.seark.edu
Student Services
1900 Hazel Street
Pine Bluff, AR 71603
Fax: (870) 543-5903
E-mail: hpost@seark.edu
Phone: (870) 543-5900

**Southeast Kentucky Community and
Technical College**
www.secc.kctcs.edu
Admissions
700 College Road
Cumberland, KY 40823
Fax: (606) 589-5423
E-mail: cookie.baker@kctcs.net
Phone: (606) 589-2145

**Southeast Missouri Hospital College of
Nursing and Health Sciences**
www.sehosp.org
2001 William Street, Second Floor
Cape Girardeau, MO 63703
Fax: (573) 339-7805
E-mail: dpugh@sehosp.org
Phone: (573) 334-6825 ext. 23

Southeast Missouri State University
www.semo.edu
Office of International Programs
One University Plaza
MS 3550
Cape Girardeau, MO 63701
Fax: (573) 986-6866
E-mail: gdordoni@semo.edu
Phone: (573) 986-6863

Southeastern Bible College
www.sebc.edu
Admissions
2545 Valleydale Road
Birmingham, AL 35244-2083
Fax: (205) 970-9207
E-mail: lynngm@sebc.edu
Phone: (800) 749-8878

Southeastern Community College
www.sccnc.edu
Admissions Office
4564 Chadbourn Highway
PO Box 151
Whiteville, NC 28472-0151
Fax: (910) 642-5658
E-mail: jfowler@sccnc.edu
Phone: (910) 642-7141 ext. 265

**Southeastern Community College: North
Campus**
www.scciowa.edu
Enrollment Services
1500 West Agency Road
PO Box 180
West Burlington, IA 52655-0605
Fax: (319) 758-6725
E-mail: kthorarinsdottir@scciowa.edu
Phone: (319) 752-2731 ext. 5026

Southeastern Illinois College
www.sic.edu
Director of Counseling
3575 College Road
Harrisburg, IL 62946
Fax: (618) 252-3062
E-mail: david.nudo@sic.edu
Phone: (618) 252-5400 ext. 2430

Southeastern Louisiana University
www.selu.edu
Office of International Services
SLU 10752
Hammond, LA 70402
Fax: (985) 549-5882
E-mail: jmercante@selu.edu
Phone: (985) 549-5610

Southeastern Oklahoma State University
www.sosu.edu
Office of Admissions and Enrollment Services
1405 North Fourth Avenue, PMB 4225
Durant, OK 74701-0607
Fax: (580) 745-7502
E-mail: kingram@sosu.edu
Phone: (580) 745-2054

Southeastern Technical College
www.southeasterntech.org/
3001 East First Street
Vidalia, GA 30474
E-mail: brhart@southeasterntech.edu
Phone: (912) 538-3121

Southeastern University
www.seu.edu
International Admission
501 I Street SW
Washington, DC 20024
Fax: (202) 488-3172
E-mail: dharris@seu.edu
Phone: (202) 478-8210 ext. 255

Southeastern University
www.seuniversity.edu
Admission
1000 Longfellow Boulevard
Lakeland, FL 33801-6034
Fax: (863) 667-5200
E-mail: admission@seuniversity.edu
Phone: (863) 667-5018

Southern Arkansas University
www.saumag.edu
International Student Admissions
Box 9382
Magnolia, AR 71754-9382
Fax: (870) 235-5096
E-mail: cjlyons@saumag.edu
Phone: (870) 235-4082

Southern Arkansas University Tech
www.sautech.edu
VIce Chancellor for Student Services
PO Box 3499
100 Carr Road
Camden, AR 71711-1599
Fax: (870) 574-4478
E-mail: rcooper@sautech.edu
Phone: (870) 574-4504

**Southern California Institute of
Architecture**
www.sciarc.edu
Admissions
960 East 3rd Street
Los Angeles, CA 90013
Fax: (213) 613-2260
E-mail: shelby_ikeda@sciarc.edu
Phone: (213) 613-2200 ext. 320

Southern California Institute of Technology
www.scit-scu.edu
Student Affairs
222 South Harbor Boulevard, Suite 200
Anaheim, CA 92805
Fax: (714) 300-0310
E-mail: ssaboury@scit-scu.edu
Phone: (714) 300-0300

Southern Connecticut State University
www.southernct.edu
Admissions
131 Farnham Avenue
New Haven, CT 06515-1202
Fax: (203) 392-5727
E-mail: belchert1@southernct.edu
Phone: (203) 392-5726

Southern Illinois University Carbondale
www.siuc.edu
International Students and Scholars
Mailcode 4701
Carbondale, IL 62901-4701
Fax: (618) 453-7660
E-mail: coppi@siu.edu
Phone: (618) 453-7661

Southern Illinois University Edwardsville
www.siue.edu
Asstistant Director of Admissions
Campus Box 1600, Rendleman Hall, Rm 2120
Edwardsville, IL 62026-1600
Fax: (618) 650-2081
E-mail: intladm@siue.edu
Phone: (618) 650-3770

Southern Maine Community College
www.smccme.edu
Global Opportunities
2 Fort Road
South Portland, ME 04106
Fax: (207) 741-5653
E-mail: dandrews@smccme.edu
Phone: (207) 741-5791

Southern Methodist University
www.smu.edu
International Center
PO Box 750181
Dallas, TX 75275-0181
Fax: (214) 768-1051
E-mail: mclarke@smu.edu
Phone: (214) 768-4475

Southern Nazarene University
www.snu.edu
International Student Services
6729 NW 39th Expressway
Bethany, OK 73008
Fax: (405) 717-6270
E-mail: lcarr@snu.edu
Phone: (405) 491-6624

Southern New Hampshire University
www.snhu.edu
International Student Admission
2500 North River Road
Manchester, NH 03106-1045
Fax: (603) 645-9603
E-mail: s.harvey@snhu.edu
Phone: (603) 645-9629

Southern Oregon University
www.sou.edu
Admissions
1250 Siskiyou Boulevard
Ashland, OR 97520-5032
Fax: (541) 552-6614
E-mail: chambers@sou.edu
Phone: (541) 552-6981

Southern Polytechnic State University
www.spsu.edu
Admissions
1100 South Marietta Parkway
Marietta, GA 30060-2896
Fax: (678) 915-7292
E-mail: admiss@spsu.edu
Phone: (678) 915-4188

Southern Union State Community College
www.suscc.edu
Admissions
750 Roberts Street
P.O. Box 1000
Wadley, AL 36276
Fax: (256) 395-2215
E-mail: cstringfellow@suscc.edu
Phone: (256) 395-2215

Southern University and Agricultural and Mechanical College
www.subr.edu
Admissions Office
T.H. Harris Hall
PO Box 9426
Baton Rouge, LA 70813
Fax: (225) 771-2500
E-mail: yvonne_roberson@cxs.subr.edu
Phone: (225) 771-2430

Southern University at New Orleans
www.suno.edu
Admissions
6801 Press Drive
New Orleans, LA 70126
Fax: (504) 284-5481
E-mail: rgpratt@suno.edu
Phone: (504) 286-5314

Southern University at Shreveport
www.susla.edu
3050 Martin Luther King, Jr. Drive
Shreveport, LA 71107
Fax: (318) 674-3489
Phone: (318) 674-3342

Southern Utah University
www.suu.edu
351 West Center Street
Cedar City, UT 84720
Fax: (435) 865-8223
E-mail: adminfo@suu.edu
Phone: (435) 586-7740

Southern Vermont College
www.svc.edu
Admissions
982 Mansion Drive
Bennington, VT 05201
Fax: (802) 447-4695
E-mail: admis@svc.edu
Phone: (802) 447-6304

Southern Virginia University
www.svu.edu
One University Hill Drive
Buena Vista, VA 24416
E-mail: admissions@svu.edu
Phone: (540) 261-2756

Southern Wesleyan University
www.swu.edu
Admissions
PO Box 1020
Central, SC 29630-1020
Fax: (864) 644-5972
E-mail: admissions@swu.edu
Phone: (864) 644-5550

Southwest Baptist University
www.sbuniv.edu
Admissions
1600 University Avenue
Bolivar, MO 65613-2597
Fax: (417) 328-1514
E-mail: cstandley@sbuniv.edu
Phone: (417) 328-1810

Southwest Florida College
www.swfc.edu
1685 Medical Lane
Ft. Myers, FL 33907-1108
Fax: (239) 936-4040
E-mail: bland@swfc.edu
Phone: (239) 939-4766

Southwest Georgia Technical College
www.southwestgatech.edu
15689 US Highway 19N
Thomasville, GA 31792
Fax: (229) 227-2666
E-mail: info@southwestgatech.edu
Phone: (229) 225-5060

Southwest Minnesota State University
www.southwestmsu.edu
1501 State Street
Marshall, MN 56258-1598
Fax: (507) 537-7154
E-mail: shearerr@southwestmsu.edu
Phone: (507) 537-6286

Southwest Tennessee Community College
www.southwest.tn.edu
PO Box 780
Memphis, TN 38101-0780
Fax: (901) 333-4458
E-mail: cmeziere@southwest.tn.edu
Phone: (901) 333-4195

Southwest University
www.southwest.edu
Office of Admissions
2200 Veterans Boulevard
Kenner, LA 70062
Fax: (504) 468-3213
E-mail: admissions@southwest.edu
Phone: (800) 433-5923

Southwest Virginia Community College
www.sw.edu
Admissions
PO Box SVCC
Richlands, VA 24641
Fax: (276) 964-7716
E-mail: jim.farris@sw.edu
Phone: (276) 964-7300

Southwest Wisconsin Technical College
www.swtc.edu
1800 Bronson Boulevard
Fennimore, WI 53809
Fax: (608) 822-6019
E-mail: studentservices@swtc.edu
Phone: (608) 822-3262 ext. 2354

Southwestern Adventist University
www.swau.edu
Enrollment
Box 567
Keene, TX 76059
Fax: (817) 556-4744
E-mail: ccoy@swau.edu
Phone: (817) 645-3921 ext. 6252

Southwestern Assemblies of God University
www.sagu.edu
Admissions
1200 Sycamore Street
Waxahachie, TX 75165
Fax: (972) 937-0006
E-mail: pthompson@sagu.edu
Phone: (972) 937-4010 ext. 1229

Southwestern Christian University
www.swcu.edu
Academic Affairs
Box 340
Bethany, OK 73008
Fax: (405) 495-0078
E-mail: chuck.chitwood@swcu.edu
Phone: (405) 789-7661 ext. 3426

Southwestern College
www.swccd.edu
Dean, Student Services
900 Otay Lakes Road
Chula Vista, CA 91910-7297
Fax: (619) 482-6489
E-mail: mkerns@swccd.edu
Phone: (619) 482-6550

Southwestern College
www.sckans.edu
100 College Street
Winfield, KS 67156
Fax: (620) 229-6210
E-mail: todd.moore@sckans.edu
Phone: (620) 229-6236

Southwestern College: Florence
www.swcollege.net
8095 Connector Drive
Florence, KY 41042
Fax: (859) 282-7940
E-mail: cbaird@swcollege.net
Phone: (859) 282-9999

Southwestern College: Vine Street Campus
www.swcollege.net
632 Vine Street
Cincinnati, OH 45202
Fax: (513) 421-8325
Phone: (513) 421-3212

Southwestern Community College
www.swcciowa.edu
Admissions Coordinator
1501 West Townline Street
Creston, IA 50801
Fax: (641) 782-3312
E-mail: carstens@swcciowa.edu
Phone: (641) 782-7081 ext. 453

Southwestern Community College
www.southwesterncc.edu
447 College Drive
Sylva, NC 28779
Fax: (828) 586-3129
Phone: (828) 586-4091 ext. 352

Southwestern Michigan College
www.swmich.edu
Academic Support
58900 Cherry Grove Road
Dowagiac, MI 49047-9793
Fax: (269) 782-1331
E-mail: szovich@swmich.edu
Phone: (269) 782-1348

Southwestern Oklahoma State University
www.swosu.edu
Registrar's Office
100 Campus Drive
Weatherford, OK 73096
Fax: (580) 774-3795
E-mail: klaassb@swosu.edu
Phone: (580) 774-3777

Southwestern Oregon Community College
www.socc.edu
International Student Services
1988 Newmark Avenue
Coos Bay, OR 97420-2956
Fax: (541) 888-7247
E-mail: kneilsen@socc.edu
Phone: (541) 888-7185

Southwestern University
www.southwestern.edu
Admission
1001 East University Avenue
Georgetown, TX 78626
Fax: (512) 863-9601
E-mail: admission@southwestern.edu
Phone: (512) 863-1200

Spartan College of Aeronautics and Technology
www.spartan.edu
Box 582833
Tulsa, OK 74158-2833
Fax: (918) 831-5234
E-mail: spartan@mail.spartan.edu
Phone: (918) 836-6886 ext. 626

Spartanburg Community College
www.sccsc.edu
Box 4386
Spartanburg, SC 29305-4386
Fax: (864) 592-4642
E-mail: rogersp@sccsc.edu
Phone: (864) 592-4816

Spartanburg Methodist College
www.smcsc.edu
Admissions
1000 Powell Mill Road
Spartanburg, SC 29301-5899
Fax: (864) 587-4355
E-mail: admiss@smcsc.edu
Phone: (864) 587-4213

Spelman College
www.spelman.edu
Office of International and Commuter Students
350 Spelman Lane SW, Campus Box 277
Atlanta, GA 30314
Fax: (404) 270-5201
E-mail: aguinyard@spelman.edu
Phone: (404) 270-5143

Spencerian College: Lexington
www.spencerian.edu
Admissions
1575 Winchester Road
Lexington, KY 40505
Fax: (859) 224-7744
E-mail: cdouglas@spencerian.edu
Phone: (859) 223-9608

Spokane Community College
www.scc.spokane.edu
International Manager of Marketing and Recuriting
1810 North Greene Street
Spokane, WA 99217-5399
Fax: (509) 533-8860
E-mail: robertr@spokanefalls.edu
Phone: (509) 533-8885

Spokane Falls Community College
www.spokanefalls.edu
International Manager of Marketing and
Recruiting
3410 West Fort George Wright Drive
Spokane, WA 99224
Fax: (509) 533-3237
E-mail: robertr@spokanefalls.edu
Phone: (509) 533-8885

Spoon River College
www.src.edu
Dean of Macomb Campus
23235 North County Road 22
Canton, IL 61520
Fax: (309) 833-6062
E-mail: pshroyer@spoonrivercollege.edu
Phone: (309) 833-6029

Spring Arbor University
www.arbor.edu
106 East Main Street
Spring Arbor, MI 49283-9799
Fax: (517) 750-6620
E-mail: sharonh@arbor.edu
Phone: (517) 750-6468

Spring Hill College
www.shc.edu
Admissions Office
4000 Dauphin Street
Mobile, AL 36608-1791
Fax: (251) 460-2186
E-mail: admit@shc.edu
Phone: (251) 380-3030

Springfield College
www.spfldcol.edu
International Center
263 Alden Street
Springfield, MA 01109
Fax: (413) 731-1681
E-mail: dalm@spldcol.edu
Phone: (413) 748-3215

Springfield College in Illinois
www.sci.edu
Enrollment Services
1500 North Fifth Street
Springfield, IL 62702-2694
Fax: (217) 525-1497
E-mail: dbryant@sci.edu
Phone: (217) 525-1420 ext. 210

Springfield Technical Community College
www.stcc.edu
Admissions
One Armory Square
PO Box 9000, Suite 1
Springfield, MA 01102-9000
Fax: (413) 746-0344
E-mail: admissions@stcc.edu
Phone: (413) 755-4202

Stanford University
www.stanford.edu
Undergraduate Admission
Montag Hall
355 Galvez Street
Stanford, CA 94305-6106
Fax: (650) 723-6050
E-mail: admissions@stanford.edu
Phone: (650) 723-2091

Stark State College of Technology
www.starkstate.edu
Admissions
6200 Frank Avenue NW
North Canton, OH 44720
Fax: (330) 497-6313
E-mail: info@starkstate.edu
Phone: (330) 494-6170

State Fair Community College
www.sfccmo.edu
Student Services
3201 West 16th Street
Sedalia, MO 65301-2199
Fax: (660) 596-7472
E-mail: mbates@sfccmo.edu
Phone: (660) 596-7296

State University of New York at Albany
www.albany.edu
Office of Undergraduate Admissions,
University Hall 112
1400 Washington Avenue
Albany, NY 12222
Fax: (518) 442-5383
E-mail: ugadmissions@uamail.albany.edu
Phone: (518) 956-8198

**State University of New York at
Binghamton**
www.binghamton.edu
Admissions
Box 6001
Binghamton, NY 13902-6001
Fax: (607) 777-4445
E-mail: admit@binghamton.edu
Phone: (607) 777-2171

State University of New York at Buffalo
www.buffalo.edu
International Admissions
12 Capen Hall
Buffalo, NY 14260-1660
Fax: (716) 645-6121
E-mail: intiem@buffalo.edu
Phone: (716) 645-2368

**State University of New York at
Farmingdale**
www.farmingdale.edu
Admissions
2350 Broadhollow Road
Farmingdale, NY 11735-1021
Fax: (631) 420-2633
E-mail: admissions@farmingdale.edu
Phone: (631) 420-2200

State University of New York at New Paltz
www.newpaltz.edu
Director of International Student Programs
100 Hawk Drive
New Paltz, NY 12561-2499
Fax: (845) 257-3608
E-mail: intadmissions@newpaltz.edu
Phone: (845) 257-3596

State University of New York at Oswego
www.oswego.edu
Office of Admissions
229 Sheldon Hall
Oswego, NY 13126-3599
Fax: (315) 312-3260
E-mail: oberst@oswego.edu
Phone: (315) 312-2250

State University of New York at Purchase
www.purchase.edu
Admissions Office
735 Anderson Hill Road
Purchase, NY 10577-1400
Fax: (914) 251-6314
E-mail: barbaraw@purchase.edu
Phone: (914) 251-6300

**State University of New York at Stony
Brook**
www.stonybrook.edu
International Admissions
118 Administration Building
Stony Brook, NY 11794-1901
Fax: (631) 632-9898
E-mail: enrollintl@stonybrook.edu
Phone: (631) 632-6868

**State University of New York College at
Brockport**
www.brockport.edu
Leadership and Community Development
350 New Campus Drive
Brockport, NY 14420-2915
Fax: (585) 395-5291
E-mail: kpodsiad@brockport.edu
Phone: (585) 395-5245

**State University of New York College at
Buffalo**
www.buffalostate.edu
International Student Affairs
1300 Elmwood Avenue, Moot Hall
Buffalo, NY 14222-1095
Fax: (716) 878-5600
E-mail: gounarjf@buffalostate.edu
Phone: (716) 878-5331

**State University of New York College at
Cortland**
www.cortland.edu
Admissions
PO Box 2000
Cortland, NY 13045-0900
Fax: (607) 753-5998
E-mail: admissions@cortland.edu
Phone: (607) 753-4711

State University of New York College at Fredonia
www.fredonia.edu
Office of Admissions
178 Central Avenue
Fredonia, NY 14063-1136
Fax: (716) 673-3249
E-mail: admissions.office@fredonia.edu
Phone: (716) 673-3251

State University of New York College at Geneseo
www.geneseo.edu
International Student Services
1 College Circle
Geneseo, NY 14454-1471
Fax: (585) 245-5405
E-mail: hope@geneseo.edu
Phone: (585) 245-5404

State University of New York College at Old Westbury
www.oldwestbury.edu
Enrollment Services
Box 307
Old Westbury, NY 11568-0307
Fax: (516) 876-3307
E-mail: enroll@oldwestbury.edu
Phone: (516) 876-3073

State University of New York College at Oneonta
www.oneonta.edu
Office of International Education
Admissions Office, 116 Alumni Hall
State University College
Oneonta, NY 13820-4016
Fax: (607) 436-2475
E-mail: diverv@oneonta.edu
Phone: (607) 436-3369

State University of New York College at Plattsburgh
www.plattsburgh.edu
International Student Services
Kehoe Administration Building
Plattsburgh, NY 12901
Fax: (518) 564-3284
E-mail: iss@plattsburgh.edu
Phone: (518) 564-3287

State University of New York College at Potsdam
www.potsdam.edu
Office of Admissions
44 Pierrepont Avenue
Potsdam, NY 13676
Fax: (315) 267-2163
E-mail: admissions@potsdam.edu
Phone: (315) 267-2180

State University of New York College of Agriculture and Technology at Cobleskill
www.cobleskill.edu
Admissions
Knapp Hall
Cobleskill, NY 12043
Fax: (518) 255-6769
E-mail: admissions@cobleskill.edu
Phone: (518) 255-5525

State University of New York College of Agriculture and Technology at Morrisville
www.morrisville.edu
Admissions Office
PO Box 901
Morrisville, NY 13408-0901
Fax: (315) 684-6427
E-mail: admissions@morrisville.edu
Phone: (315) 684-6046

State University of New York College of Environmental Science and Forestry
www.esf.edu
Undergraduate Admissions
106 Bray Hall
One Forestry Drive
Syracuse, NY 13210
Fax: (315) 470-6933
E-mail: esfinfo@esf.edu
Phone: (315) 470-6600

State University of New York College of Technology at Alfred
www.alfredstate.edu
Admissions
Huntington Administration Building
Alfred, NY 14802-1196
Fax: (607) 587-4299
E-mail: admissions@alfredstate.edu
Phone: (607) 587-4215

State University of New York College of Technology at Canton
www.canton.edu
Admissions
34 Cornell Drive
Canton, NY 13617-1098
Fax: (315) 386-7929
E-mail: kentj@canton.edu
Phone: (315) 386-7123

State University of New York College of Technology at Delhi
www.delhi.edu
Admissions
2 Main Street
Delhi, NY 13753-1190
Fax: (607) 746-4104
E-mail: enroll@delhi.edu
Phone: (607) 746-4550

State University of New York Empire State College
www.esc.edu
Admissions
111 West Avenue
Saratoga Springs, NY 12866-4391
Fax: (518) 587-9759
E-mail: Melanie.Kaiser@esc.edu
Phone: (518) 587-2100 ext. 2447

State University of New York Institute of Technology at Utica/Rome
www.sunyit.edu
Admissions Office
Box 3050
Utica, NY 13504-3050
Fax: (315) 792-7837
E-mail: admissions@sunyit.edu
Phone: (315) 792-7500

State University of New York Maritime College
www.sunymaritime.edu
6 Pennyfield Avenue
Throggs Neck, NY 10465-4198
Fax: (718) 409-7465
E-mail: tfay@sunymaritime.edu
Phone: (718) 409-7401

State University of New York Upstate Medical University
www.upstate.edu
International Student Advisor
766 Irving Avenue
Syracuse, NY 13210
Fax: (315) 464-8857
E-mail: AbbottJ@upstate.edu
Phone: (315) 464-8817

Stephen F. Austin State University
www.sfasu.edu
Admissions Counselor
Box 13051, SFA Station
Nacogdoches, TX 75962-3051
Fax: (936) 468-3849
E-mail: slgee@sfasu.edu
Phone: (936) 468-2504

Stephens College
www.stephens.edu
Admission
1200 East Broadway
Box 2121
Columbia, MO 65215
Fax: (573) 876-7207
E-mail: apply@stephens.edu
Phone: (800) 876-7207

Sterling College
www.sterling.edu
Admissions
125 West Cooper
Sterling, KS 67579
Fax: (620) 278-4416
E-mail: admissions@sterling.edu
Phone: (620) 278-4275

Sterling College
www.sterlingcollege.edu
Admissions
PO Box 72
Craftsbury Common, VT 05827-0072
Fax: (802) 586-2596
E-mail: admissions@sterlingcollege.edu
Phone: (802) 586-7711 ext. 100

Stetson University
www.stetson.edu
Admissions
Campus Box 8378
DeLand, FL 32723
Fax: (386) 822-7112
E-mail: admissions@stetson.edu
Phone: (386) 822-7100

Stevens Institute of Technology
www.stevens.edu
Undergraduate Admissions
One Castle Point on Hudson
Wesley J Howe Center, 8th Floor
Hoboken, NJ 07030
Fax: (201) 216-8348
E-mail: efleming@stevens.edu
Phone: (201) 216-5194

Stevens-Henager College: Boise
www.stevenshenager.edu/shc/campus/
boise.cfm
Campus Director
1444 S Entertainment Avenue
Boise, ID 83709
Fax: (208) 345-6999
E-mail: shane.reeder@stevenshenager.edu
Phone: (208) 345-0700

Stevens-Henager College: Murray
www.stevenshenager.edu
383 West Vine Street
Salt Lake City, UT 84123
Fax: (801) 262-7660
Phone: (800) 622-2640

Stevens-Henager College: Ogden
www.stevenshenager.edu
1890 South 1350 West
Ogden, UT 84401
Fax: (801) 621-0853
Phone: (801) 394-7791

Stillman College
www.stillman.edu
Admissions
3600 Stillman Boulevard
PO Box 1430
Tuscaloosa, AL 35403
Fax: (205) 247-8156
E-mail: mfinch@stillman.edu
Phone: (205) 366-8814

Stonehill College
www.stonehill.edu
Admissions Office
320 Washington Street
Easton, MA 02357-0100
Fax: (508) 565-1545
E-mail: ssmith@stonehill.edu
Phone: (508) 565-1373

Suffolk County Community College
www.sunysuffolk.edu
Central Admissions
533 College Road
Selden, NY 11784
Fax: (631) 451-4415
E-mail: spagnoe@sunysuffolk.edu
Phone: (631) 451-4000

Suffolk University
www.suffolk.edu
Undergraduate Admissions
8 Ashburton Place
Boston, MA 02108
Fax: (617) 557-1574
E-mail: admission@suffolk.edu
Phone: (617) 573-8460

Sul Ross State University
www.sulross.edu
Recruiting/Admissions
Box C-2
Alpine, TX 79832
Fax: (432) 837-8431
E-mail: admissions@sulross.edu
Phone: (432) 837-8050

Sullivan County Community College
www.sullivan.suny.edu
112 College Road
Loch Sheldrake, NY 12759-5151
Fax: (845) 434-0923
Phone: (845) 434-5750 ext. 4287

Sullivan University
www.sullivan.edu
front desk personnel
3101 Bardstown Road
Louisville, KY 40205
Fax: (502) 456-0040
E-mail: admissions@sullivan.edu
Phone: (502) 456-6505

Susquehanna University
www.susqu.edu
Office of Admissions
514 University Avenue
Selinsgrove, PA 17870-1164
Fax: (570) 372-2722
E-mail: moy@susqu.edu
Phone: (570) 372-4260

Sussex County Community College
www.sussex.edu
Vice President of Student Services
One College Hill Road
Newton, NJ 07860
Fax: (973) 579-5226
E-mail: hdamato@sussex.edu
Phone: (973) 300-2219

Swarthmore College
www.swarthmore.edu
Admissions
500 College Avenue
Swarthmore, PA 19081
Fax: (610) 328-8580
E-mail: international@swarthmore.edu
Phone: (610) 328-8300

Swedish Institute
www.swedishinstitute.com
226 West 26th Street, 5th Floor
New York, NY 10001-6700
Fax: (212) 924-7600
E-mail: admissions@swedishinstitute.edu
Phone: (212) 914-5900 ext. 122

Sweet Briar College
www.sbc.edu
Admissions
PO Box B
Sweet Briar, VA 24595
Fax: (434) 381-6152
E-mail: admissions@sbc.edu
Phone: (434) 381-6142

Syracuse University
www.syr.edu
Admissions
100 Crouse-Hinds Hall
900 South Crouse Avenue
Syracuse, NY 13244-2130
Fax: (315) 443-4226
E-mail: orange@syr.edu
Phone: (315) 443-3611

Tabor College
www.tabor.edu
Enrollment Management
400 South Jefferson
Hillsboro, KS 67063-1799
Fax: (620) 947-6276
E-mail: admissions@tabor.edu
Phone: (620) 947-3121 ext. 1721

Tacoma Community College
www.tacomacc.edu
International Student Office
6501 South 19th Street
Tacoma, WA 98466-9971
Fax: (253) 566-6027
Phone: (253) 460-3935

Taft College
www.taftcollege.edu
Admissions
29 Emmons Park Drive
Taft, CA 93268
Fax: (661) 763-7758
E-mail: groberts@taft.org
Phone: (661) 763-7763

Tallahassee Community College
www.tcc.fl.edu
International Student Services
444 Appleyard Drive
Tallahassee, FL 32304
Fax: (850) 201-8474
E-mail: jensenb@tcc.fl.edu
Phone: (850) 201-8235

Tarleton State University
www.tarleton.edu
International Academic Programs
Box T-0030
Stephenville, TX 76402
Fax: (254) 968-9618
E-mail: koestler@tarleton.edu
Phone: (254) 968-9632

Tarrant County College
www.tccd.edu
International Admissions/Services
1500 Houston Street
Fort Worth, TX 76102-6599
Fax: (817) 515-55021
E-mail: noemi.vela@tccd.edu
Phone: (817) 515-5232

Taylor University
www.taylor.edu
Admissions Office
236 West Reade Avenue
Upland, IN 46989-1001
Fax: (765) 998-4925
E-mail: srhayhurst@tayloru.edu
Phone: (765) 998-5564

Taylor University Fort Wayne
www.fw.taylor.edu
Office of Enrollment Services
1025 West Rudisill Boulevard
Fort Wayne, IN 46807
Fax: (260) 744-8850
E-mail: admissions@fw.taylor.edu
Phone: (260) 744-8689

Technical Career Institutes
www.tcicollege.edu
Office of International Students
320 West 31st Street
New York, NY 10001
Fax: (212) 629-3937
E-mail: admissions@tcicollege.edu
Phone: (212) 594-4000 ext. 216

Technology Education College
www.teccollege.com
Admissions
2745 Winchester Pike
Columbus, OH 43232
Fax: (614) 456-4640
E-mail: sbode@teceducation.com
Phone: (614) 456-4600

Teikyo Loretto Heights University
www.tlhu.edu
Office of Admissions
3001 South Federal Boulevard
Denver, CO 80236
Fax: (303) 937-4224
E-mail: admissions@tlhu.edu
Phone: (303) 937-4221

Temple University
www.temple.edu
Office of Undergrad Admissions
103 Conwell Hall
1801 North Broad Street
Philadelphia, PA 19122-6096
Fax: (215) 204-5694
E-mail: Janusz.Baran@temple.edu
Phone: (215) 204-7200

Tennessee State University
www.tnstate.edu
Foreign Student Adviser
3500 John A. Merritt Boulevard
Nashville, TN 37209-1561
Fax: (615) 963-5051
E-mail: swingfield@tnstate.edu
Phone: (615) 963-5639

Tennessee Technological University
www.tntech.edu
Office of Admissions
Box 5006
Cookeville, TN 38505-0001
Fax: (931) 372-6111
E-mail: cwilkerson@tntech.edu
Phone: (931) 372-3634

Tennessee Temple University
www.tntemple.edu
International Admissions
1815 Union Avenue
Chattanooga, TN 37404
Fax: (423) 493-4497
E-mail: holritj@mail.tntemple.edu
Phone: (423) 493-4371

Tennessee Wesleyan College
www.twcnet.edu
Vice President of Enrollemnt Services
204 East College Street
P O Box 40
Athens, TN 37371-0040
Fax: (423) 744-9968
E-mail: sharrison@twcnet.edu
Phone: (423) 745-7504 ext. 5310

TESST College of Technology: Baltimore
www.tesst.com/tesstPortal
1520 South Caton Avenue
Baltimore, MD 21227-1063
Fax: (410) 644-6481
Phone: (410) 644-6400

TESST College of Technology: Beltsville
www.tesst.com
4600 Powder Mill Road
Beltsville, MD 20705
E-mail: dedmonds@tesst.com
Phone: (301) 937-8448

TESST College of Technology: Towson
www.tesst.com
803 Glen Eagles Court
Towson, MD 21286
Fax: (410) 296-5356
Phone: (410) 296-5350

Texas A&M International University
www.tamiu.edu
Admissions Office
5201 University Boulevard
Laredo, TX 78041-1900
Fax: (956) 326-2199
E-mail: adms@tamiu.edu
Phone: (956) 326-2200

Texas A&M University
www.tamu.edu
International Admissions
PO Box 30014
College Station, TX 77842-3014
Fax: (979) 458-1808
E-mail: admissions@tamu.edu
Phone: (979) 845-1079

Texas A&M University-Commerce
www.tamu-commerce.edu
International Studies
Box 3011
Commerce, TX 75429-3011
Fax: (903) 468-3200
E-mail: noi_prapan@tamu-commerce.edu
Phone: (903) 468-8144

Texas A&M University-Galveston
www.tamug.edu
Office of International Admissions
PO Box 1675
Galveston, TX 77553-1675
Fax: (979) 845-6979
E-mail: iss@iss.tamu.edu
Phone: (979) 845-1071

Texas A&M University-Kingsville
www.tamuk.edu
International Student Adviser
MSC 105
Kingsville, TX 78363-8201
Fax: (361) 593-2195
E-mail: ksossrx@tamuk.edu
Phone: (361) 593-2315

Texas A&M University-Texarkana
www.tamut.edu
Student Services
2600 North Robinson Road
Box 5518
Texarkana, TX 75505-5518
Fax: (903) 223-3118
E-mail: carl.greig@tamut.edu
Phone: (903) 223-3062

Texas Christian University
www.tcu.edu
International Admissions
TCU Box 297013
Fort Worth, TX 76129
Fax: (817) 257-7268
E-mail: frogmail@tcu.edu
Phone: (817) 257-7490

Texas College
www.texascollege.edu
Enrollment Services
2404 North Grand Avenue
PO Box 4500
Tyler, TX 75712-4500
Fax: (903) 596-0001
E-mail: rbrazzle@texascollege.edu
Phone: (903) 593-8311 ext. 2277

Texas Culinary Academy
www.tca.edu
11400 Burnet Road, Suite 2100
Austin, TX 78758
E-mail: info@txca.com
Phone: (512) 837-2665

Texas Lutheran University
www.tlu.edu
Enrollment Services
1000 West Court Street
Seguin, TX 78155-5999
Fax: (830) 372-8096
E-mail: jkocian@tlu.edu
Phone: (830) 372-8050

Texas Southern University
www.tsu.edu
International Student Affairs
3100 Cleburne Street
Bell Building 225
Houston, TX 77004
Fax: (713) 313-1878
E-mail: luckettph@tsu.edu
Phone: (713) 313-7930

Texas Southmost College
www.utb.edu
80 Fort Brown
Brownsville, TX 78520
Fax: (956) 882-8832
Phone: (956) 882-8254

Texas State Technical College: Harlingen
www.harlingen.tstc.edu
Admissions and Records
1902 North Loop 499
Harlingen, TX 78550-3697
Fax: (956) 364-5117
E-mail: blanca.guerra@harlingen.tstc.edu
Phone: (956) 364-4301

Texas State Technical College: Marshall
www.marshall.tstc.edu
2400 East End Boulevard South
Marshall, TX 75672
Phone: (903) 935-1010

Texas State Technical College: Sweetwater
www.westtexas.tstc.edu
Admissions and Records Office
300 Homer K Taylor Drive
Sweetwater, TX 79556
Fax: (325) 235-7443
E-mail: oretha.pack@tstc.edu
Phone: (325) 235-7377

Texas State Technical College: Waco
www.waco.tstc.edu
Director of Admission and Records
3801 Campus Drive
Waco, TX 76705
Fax: (254) 867-2250
E-mail: dawn.khoury@tstc.edu
Phone: (254) 867-2366

Texas State University: San Marcos
www.txstate.edu
International Undergraduate Admissions
Center
429 North Guadalupe Street
San Marcos, TX 78666-5709
Fax: (512) 245-8044
E-mail: admissions@txstate.edu
Phone: (512) 245-2364

Texas Tech University
www.ttu.edu
Admissions
Box 45005
Lubbock, TX 79409-5005
Fax: (806) 742-0062
E-mail: admissions@ttu.edu
Phone: (806) 742-1480

Texas Tech University Health Sciences Center
www.ttuhsc.edu
3601 Fourth Street
Lubbock, TX 79430
Phone: (806) 743-2300

Texas Wesleyan University
www.txwes.edu
International Student Advisor
1201 Wesleyan Street
Fort Worth, TX 76105-1536
Fax: (817) 531-4288
E-mail: aaustin@txwes.edu
Phone: (817) 531-4934

Texas Woman's University
www.twu.edu
International Student Office
Box 425589
Denton, TX 76204-5589
Fax: (940) 898-3157
E-mail: intloffice@twu.edu
Phone: (940) 898-3338

Thiel College
www.thiel.edu
Director of Admissions
75 College Avenue
Greenville, PA 16125-2181
Fax: (724) 289-2013
E-mail: slapikas@thiel.edu
Phone: (724) 589-2172

Thomas College
www.thomas.edu
Admissions
180 West River Road
Waterville, ME 04901
Fax: (207) 806-8013
E-mail: admiss@thomas.edu
Phone: (207) 859-1101

Thomas Edison State College
www.tesc.edu
Admissions
101 West State Street
Trenton, NJ 08608-1176
Fax: (609) 984-8447
E-mail: admissions@tesc.edu
Phone: (888) 442-8372

Thomas Jefferson University: College of Health Professions
www.jefferson.edu/jchp
Office of Admissions
130 South Ninth Street, Edison Building, Suite 100
Philadelphia, PA 19107
Fax: (215) 503-7241
E-mail: karen.jacobs@jefferson.edu
Phone: (215) 503-8890

Thomas More College
www.thomasmore.edu
Admissions Office
333 Thomas More Parkway
Crestview Hills, KY 41017-3495
Fax: (859) 344-4444
E-mail: jennifer.mason@thomasmore.edu
Phone: (859) 344-3332

Thomas More College of Liberal Arts
www.thomasmorecollege.edu
Admissions
Six Manchester Street
Merrimack, NH 03054-4818
Fax: (603) 880-9280
E-mail: admissions@thomasmorecollege.edu
Phone: (800) 880-8308

Thomas Nelson Community College
www.tncc.edu
Admissions and Records
Box 9407
Hampton, VA 23670
Fax: (757) 825-2763
E-mail: Admissions@tncc.edu
Phone: (757) 825-2800

Thomas University
www.thomasu.edu
Executive Director of Enrollment Management and Student Affairs
1501 Millpond Road
Thomasville, GA 31792-7499
Fax: (229) 227-6919
E-mail: mwest@thomasu.edu
Phone: (229) 226-1621 ext. 181

Three Rivers Community College
www.trcc.edu
Admissions
2080 Three Rivers Boulevard
Poplar Bluff, MO 63901-1308
Fax: (573) 840-9058
E-mail: mfields@trcc.edu
Phone: (573) 840-9675 ext. 675

Tidewater Community College
www.tcc.vccs.edu
International Student Services
7000 College Drive/Portsmouth Campus
Portsmouth, VA 23703
Fax: (757) 822-7544
E-mail: iss@tcc.edu
Phone: (757) 822-7342

Tidewater Tech: Chesapeake
www.tidewatertech.edu
932 Ventures Way
Chesapeake, VA 23320-2882
Fax: (757) 548-1196
E-mail: admdirttc@tidewatertech.edu

Tidewater Tech: Newport News
www.tidewatertech.edu
616 Denbigh Boulevard
Newport News, VA 23608
Fax: (757) 874-3857
E-mail: admdirttp@tidewatertech.edu
Phone: (757) 874-2121

Tidewater Tech: Norfolk
www.tidewatertech.edu/
tidewater-tech-norfolk.asp
7020 North Military Highway
Norfolk, VA 23518-4202
Fax: (757) 852-9017
E-mail: admdirttn@tidetech.com
Phone: (757) 853-2121

Tidewater Tech: Virginia Beach
www.tidewatertech.edu
2697 Dean Drive, Suite 100
Virginia Beach, VA 23452
Fax: (757) 340-9704
E-mail: directorttv@tidetech.com
Phone: (757) 340-2121

Tiffin University
www.tiffin.edu
Admissions
155 Miami Street
Tiffin, OH 44883
Fax: (419) 443-5006
E-mail: admissions@tiffin.edu
Phone: (419) 448-3423

Toccoa Falls College
www.tfc.edu
Admissions
PO Box 800899
Toccoa Falls, GA 30598-0368
Fax: (706) 282-6012
E-mail: admissions@tfc.edu
Phone: (706) 886-6831 ext. 5380

Tohono O'odham Community College
www.tocc.cc.az.us
PO Box 3129
Sells, AZ 85634-3129
Fax: (520) 383-0029
E-mail: lluna@tocc.cc.az.us
Phone: (520) 383-8401 ext. 35

Tompkins-Cortland Community College
www.TC3.edu
Enrollment Services Center
170 North Street
Box 139
Dryden, NY 13053-0139
Fax: (607) 844-6541
E-mail: armstrc@TC3.edu
Phone: (607) 844-6580

Tougaloo College
www.tougaloo.edu
Office of Admissions
500 West County Line Road
Tougaloo, MS 39174
E-mail: jjacobs@tougaloo.edu
Phone: (601) 977-7768

Touro College
www.touro.edu
Registrar
1602 Avenue J
Brooklyn, NY 11230
Fax: (212) 627-9542
E-mail: eddies@touro.edu
Phone: (212) 463-0400 ext. 607

Towson University
www.towson.edu
International Admissions
8000 York Road
Towson, MD 21252-0001
Fax: (410) 704-6070
E-mail: intladm@towson.edu
Phone: (410) 704-6069

TransPacific Hawaii College
www.transpacific.org
Admissions
5257 Kalanianaole Highway
Honolulu, HI 96821
Fax: (808) 373-9735
E-mail: akikotyler@transpacific.edu
Phone: (808) 377-5402 ext. 309

Transylvania University
www.transy.edu
Admissions
300 North Broadway
Lexington, KY 40508-1797
Fax: (859) 233-8797
E-mail: bgoan@transy.edu
Phone: (859) 233-8242

Treasure Valley Community College
www.tvcc.cc
Admissions
650 College Boulevard
Ontario, OR 97914
Fax: (541) 881-2721
E-mail: dmbell@tvcc.cc
Phone: (541) 881-8822 ext. 244

Trevecca Nazarene University
www.trevecca.edu
Office of Admissions
333 Murfreesboro Road
Nashville, TN 37210
Fax: (615) 248-7406
E-mail: admissions_und@trevecca.edu
Phone: (615) 248-1320

Tri-County Technical College
www.tctc.edu
Admissions
Box 587
Pendleton, SC 29670
Fax: (864) 646-1890
E-mail: lhall4@tctc.edu
Phone: (864) 646-1862

Tri-State Business Institute
www.tsbi.edu
5757 West Twenty-Sixth Street
Erie, PA 16506
Fax: (814) 838-8642
E-mail: webadmissions@tsbi.edu
Phone: (814) 838-7673

Tri-State University
www.tristate.edu
Admissions
One University Avenue
Angola, IN 46703
Fax: (260) 665-4578
E-mail: admit@tristate.edu
Phone: (260) 665-4100

Triangle Tech: Bethlehem
www.triangle-tech.edu
31 South Commerce Way, LVIP IV
Bethlehem, PA 18017
Fax: (610) 691-7525
Phone: (610) 691-1300

Triangle Tech: Greensburg
www.triangle-tech.edu
222 East Pittsburgh Street, Suite A
Greensburg, PA 15601-3304
Fax: (724) 834-0325
Phone: (724) 832-1050

Trident Technical College
www.tridenttech.edu
Office of International Student Admissions
Box 118067, AM-M
Charleston, SC 29423-8067
Fax: (843) 574-6483
E-mail: demetria.griffin@tridenttech.edu
Phone: (843) 574-6325

Trinidad State Junior College
www.trinidadstate.edu
Alumni Office
600 Prospect Street
Trinidad, CO 81082
Fax: (719) 846-5667
E-mail: Toni.DeAngelis@trinidadstate.edu
Phone: (719) 846-5649

Trinity Christian College
www.trnty.edu
Dean of Students
6601 West College Drive
Palos Heights, IL 60463
Fax: (708) 239-3980
E-mail: ginny.carpenter@trnty.edu
Phone: (708) 239-4703

Trinity College
www.trincoll.edu
Admissions
300 Summit Street
Hartford, CT 06106
Fax: (860) 297-2287
E-mail: Mandi.Haines@trincoll.edu
Phone: (860) 297-2551

Trinity College of Florida
www.trinitycollege.edu
Office of Admissions
2430 Welbilt Boulevard
Trinity, FL 34655-4401
Fax: (727) 569-1410
E-mail: msawyer@trinitycollege.edu
Phone: (727) 569-1412

Trinity College of Nursing and Health Sciences
www.trinitycollegeqc.edu
2122 25th Avenue
Rock Island, IL 61201
Fax: (309) 779-7748
Phone: (309) 779-7710

Trinity International University
www.tiu.edu
Undergraduate Admissions
2065 Half Day Road
Deerfield, IL 60015
Fax: (847) 317-8097
E-mail: tcadmissions@tiu.edu
Phone: (847) 317-7000

Trinity Lutheran College
www.tlc.edu
Registrar's Office
4221 228th Avenue Southeast
Issaquah, WA 98029
Fax: (425) 392-0404
E-mail: registrar@tlc.edu
Phone: (425) 961-5513

Trinity University
www.trinity.edu
Admissions
One Trinity Place
San Antonio, TX 78212-7200
Fax: (210) 999-8164
E-mail: Eric.Maloof@trinity.edu
Phone: (210) 999-7207

Trinity Valley Community College
www.tvcc.edu
Student Affairs
100 Cardinal Drive
Athens, TX 75751
Fax: (903) 675-6316
Phone: (903) 675-6220

Trinity Washington University
www.trinitydc.edu
125 Michigan Avenue, NE
Washington, DC 20017
Fax: (202) 884-9403
E-mail: peppind@trinitydc.edu
Phone: (202) 884-9019

Triton College
www.triton.edu
Record Evaluator
2000 North Fifth Avenue
River Grove, IL 60171
Fax: (708) 583-3147
E-mail: vhoward@triton.edu
Phone: (708) 456-0300 ext. 3444

Trocaire College
www.trocaire.edu
Admissions
360 Choate Avenue
Buffalo, NY 14220
Fax: (716) 828-6107
E-mail: lesinskic@trocaire.edu
Phone: (716) 826-1200 ext. 1218

Troy University
www.troy.edu
Dean of International Students
University Avenue, Adams Administration 111
Troy, AL 36082
Fax: (334) 670-3735
E-mail: dstewart@troy.edu
Phone: (334) 670-3335

Truckee Meadows Community College
www.tmcc.edu
Admissions and Records
7000 Dandini Boulevard
MS RDMT 319
Reno, NV 89512
Fax: (775) 673-7028
E-mail: csteppat@tmcc.edu
Phone: (775) 674-7042

Truett-McConnell College
www.truett.edu
Dean for Enrollment Services
100 Alumni Drive
Cleveland, GA 30528
Fax: (706) 865-7615
E-mail: ploggins@truett.edu
Phone: (706) 865-2134 ext. 210

Truman State University
www.truman.edu
International Student Office
McClain Hall 205
100 East Normal Street
Kirksville, MO 63501-9980
Fax: (660) 785-5395
E-mail: internat@truman.edu
Phone: (660) 785-4215

Tufts University
www.tufts.edu
Undergraduate Admissions
Bendetson Hall
Medford, MA 02155
Fax: (617) 627-3860
E-mail: admissions.inquiry@ase.tufts.edu
Phone: (617) 627-3170

Tulane University
www.tulane.edu
Undergraduate Admisson
6823 St. Charles Avenue
New Orleans, LA 70118-5680
Fax: (504) 862-8715
E-mail: interns@tulan.edu
Phone: (504) 865-5731

Tulsa Community College
www.tulsacc.edu
Northeast Campus Counseling and Testing Center
6111 East Skelly Drive
Tulsa, OK 74135
Fax: (918) 595-7598
E-mail: dklingha@tulsa.cc.ok.us
Phone: (918) 595-7533

Tulsa Welding School
www.weldingschool.com
2545 East 11th Street
Tulsa, OK 74104-3909
Fax: (918) 587-8170
E-mail: tws@ionet.net
Phone: (918) 587-6789 ext. 240

Tunxis Community College
www.tunxis.commnet.edu
Admissions
271 Scott Swamp Road
Farmington, CT 06032-3187
Fax: (860) 255-3559
E-mail: pmccluskey@txcc.commnet.edu
Phone: (860) 255-3555

Turabo University
www.suagm.edu/ut
Admissions and Financial Aid
PO Box 3030
Gurabo, PR 00778
Fax: (787) 743-7940
E-mail: ut_vgonzalez@suagm.edu
Phone: (787) 743-7979 ext. 4453

Turtle Mountain Community College
www.tm.edu
PO Box 340
Belcourt, ND 58316
Fax: (701) 477-7892
E-mail: jlafontaine@tm.edu
Phone: (701) 477-7862

Tusculum College
www.tusculum.edu
International Student Admissions Counselor
60 Shiloh Road
Box 5097
Greeneville, TN 37743
Fax: (423) 638-7166
E-mail: tengland@tusculum.edu
Phone: (423) 636-7300 ext. 5374

Tuskegee University
www.tuskegee.edu
102 Old Administration Building
Tuskegee, AL 36088
Fax: (334) 724-4402
E-mail: adm@tuskegee.edu
Phone: (334) 727-8953

Ulster County Community College
www.sunyulster.edu
Cottekill Road
Stone Ridge, NY 12484
Fax: (845) 687-5090
E-mail: admissions@sunyulster.edu
Phone: (845) 687-5022

Umpqua Community College
www.umpqua.edu
Student Services
1140 College Road
PO Box 967
Roseburg, OR 97470-0226
Fax: (541) 677-3289
E-mail: joyce.kelly@umpqua.edu
Phone: (541) 440-4705

Union College
www.unionky.edu
Admission
310 College Street, Box 005
Barbourville, KY 40906
Fax: (606) 546-1667
E-mail: jgjackson@unionky.edu
Phone: (606) 546-1221

Union College
www.ucollege.edu
Enrollment Services
3800 South 48th Street
Lincoln, NE 68506-4300
Fax: (402) 486-2895
E-mail: ucenroll@ucollege.edu
Phone: (800) 228-4600

Union College
www.union.edu
Office of Admissions
Grant Hall
Schenectady, NY 12308-2311
Fax: (518) 388-6986
E-mail: admissions@union.edu
Phone: (518) 388-6112

Union County College
www.ucc.edu
Registrar
1033 Springfield Avenue
Cranford, NJ 07016-1599
Fax: (908) 709-7125
E-mail: davis@ucc.edu
Phone: (908) 709-7127

Union University
www.uu.edu
Nikki Castles - Enrollment Counselor
1050 Union University Drive
Jackson, TN 38305-3697
Fax: (731) 661-5017
E-mail: ncastles@uu.edu
Phone: (731) 661-5006

United States Merchant Marine Academy
www.usmma.edu
Admissions
300 Steamboat Road, Admissions Center
Kings Point, NY 11024-1699
Fax: (516) 773-5390
E-mail: admissions@usmma.edu
Phone: (516) 773-5391

United States Sports Academy
www.ussa.edu
One Academy Drive
Daphne, AL 36526
E-mail: admissions@ussa.edu
Phone: (251) 626-3303

United Tribes Technical College
www.uttc.edu
Admission Department
3315 University Drive
Bismarck, ND 58504
Fax: (701) 530-0640
E-mail: vgillette@uttc.edu
Phone: (701) 255-3285 ext. 1334

Unity College
www.unity.edu
P.O. 532
Unity, ME 04988-0532
Fax: (207) 948-6277
E-mail: kfiedler@unity.edu
Phone: (207) 948-3131 ext. 275

Universal Technical Institute
www.uticorp.com
Campus Admissions
10695 West Pierce Street
Avondale, AZ 85323
Fax: (602) 245-4601
E-mail: info@uticorp.com
Phone: (623) 245-4600

Universal Technology College of Puerto Rico
www.unitecpr.edu/
Apartado 1955, Victoria Station
Aguadilla, PR 00605
Fax: (787) 891-2370
E-mail: admisiones@unitecpr.net
Phone: (787) 882-2065 ext. 308

Universidad Adventista de las Antillas
www.uaa.edu
PO Box 118
Mayaguez, PR 00681-0118
Fax: (787) 834-9597
E-mail: ojimenez@uaa.edu
Phone: (787) 834-9595 ext. 2213

Universidad del Este
www.suagm.edu/une
PO Box 2010
Carolina, PR 00984-2010
Fax: (787) 257-8444
E-mail: ue_rfuentes@suagm.edu
Phone: (787) 257-7373 ext. 3300

Universidad FLET
www.flet.edu
14540 SW 136th Street, Suite 108
Miami, FL 33186
Fax: (305) 232-5832
E-mail: admisiones@flet.edu
Phone: (305) 378-8700

Universidad Metropolitana
www.suagm.edu/umet
Apartado 21150
Rio Piedras, PR 00928
Fax: (787) 759-7663
Phone: (787) 765-6262

Universidad Politecnica de Puerto Rico
www.pupr.edu
Admissions Office
PO Box 192017
San Juan, PR 00919-2017
Fax: (787) 764-8712
E-mail: tcardona@pupr.edu
Phone: (787) 622-8000 ext. 309

University College of San Juan
www.cunisanjuan.edu
Admissions Office
180 Jose R. Oliver Avenue
San Juan, PR 00918
Fax: (787) 250-7395
E-mail: sanrivera@sanjuancapital.com
Phone: (787) 250-7375

University of Advancing Technology
www.uat.edu
Admissions
2625 West Baseline Road
Tempe, AZ 85283-1056
Fax: (602) 383-8228
E-mail: admissions@uat.edu
Phone: (800) 658-5744

University of Akron
www.uakron.edu
International Programs
The University of Akron
Akron, OH 44325-2001
Fax: (330) 972-8604
E-mail: international@uakron.edu
Phone: (330) 972-6349

University of Akron: Wayne College
www.wayne.uakron.edu
1901 Smucker Road
Orrville, OH 44667-9758
Fax: (330) 684-8989
E-mail: wayneadmissions@uakron.edu
Phone: (330) 683-2010

University of Alabama
www.ua.edu
Undergraduate Admissions
Box 870132
Tuscaloosa, AL 35487-0132
Fax: (205) 348-5298
E-mail: international@ua.edu
Phone: (205) 348-5666

University of Alabama at Birmingham
www.uab.edu
HUC 260, 1530 Third Avenue South
Birmingham, AL 35294-1150
Fax: (205) 975-7114
E-mail: UndergradAdmit@uab.edu
Phone: (205) 934-8221

University of Alabama in Huntsville
www.uah.edu
Office of Undergraduate Admissions
UAH Office of Undergraduate Admissions
301 Sparkman Drive
Huntsville, AL 35899
Fax: (256) 824-6073
E-mail: admitme@uah.edu
Phone: (256) 824-2744

University of Alaska Anchorage
www.uaa.alaska.edu
Enrollment Services
PO Box 141629
3901 Old Seward Highway
Anchorage, AK 99514-1629
Fax: (907) 786-4888
E-mail: ayenroll@uaa.alaska.edu
Phone: (907) 786-1558

University of Alaska Fairbanks
www.uaf.edu
Office of International Programs
PO Box 757480
Fairbanks, AK 99775-7480
Fax: (907) 474-5979
E-mail: fyoip@uaf.edu
Phone: (907) 474-5327

University of Alaska Southeast
www.uas.alaska.edu
Student and Enrollment Management
11120 Glacier Highway
Juneau, AK 99801-8681
Fax: (907) 796-6365
E-mail: shontay.king@uas.alaska.edu
Phone: (907) 796-6359

University of Arizona
www.arizona.edu
International Admissions
Robert L. Nugent Building
Box 210040
Tucson, AZ 85721-0040
Fax: (520) 621-9799
E-mail: intluga@arizona.edu
Phone: (520) 621-3111

University of Arkansas
www.uark.edu
International Admissions
232 Silas Hunt Hall
Fayetteville, AR 72701
Fax: (479) 575-5055
E-mail: mosesso@uark.edu
Phone: (479) 575-5346

University of Arkansas at Fort Smith
www.uafortsmith.edu
Student Advisement Center
PO Box 3649
Fort Smith, AR 72913-3649
Fax: (479) 788-7016
E-mail: amccaleb@uafortsmith.edu
Phone: (479) 788-7400

University of Arkansas at Little Rock
www.ualr.edu
International Student Affairs
2801 South University Avenue
Administration South, Room 208
Little Rock, AR 72204
Fax: (501) 569-8956
Phone: (501) 683-7567

University of Arkansas at Monticello
www.uamont.edu
Admissions
Box 3600
Monticello, AR 71656
Fax: (870) 460-1926
E-mail: whitingm@uamont.edu
Phone: (870) 460-1026

University of Arkansas at Pine Bluff
www.uapb.edu
Foreign Student Adviser
1200 North University Drive, Mail Slot 4981
Pine Bluff, AR 71601-2799
Fax: (870) 543-8004
E-mail: balogu_d@uapb.edu
Phone: (870) 575-8196

University of the Arts
www.uarts.edu
Student services
320 South Broad Street
Philadelphia, PA 19102
Fax: (215) 717-6045
E-mail: admissions@uarts.edu
Phone: (215) 875-2262

University of Baltimore
www.ubalt.edu
International Services Office
1420 North Charles Street
Baltimore, MD 21201-5779
Fax: (410) 837-4793
E-mail: admissions@ubalt.edu
Phone: (410) 837-4756

University of Bridgeport
www.bridgeport.edu
International Admissions
126 Park Avenue
Bridgeport, CT 06604
Fax: (203) 576-4941
E-mail: admit@bridgeport.edu
Phone: (203) 576-4552

University of California: Berkeley
www.berkeley.edu
110 Sproul Hall, #5800
Berkeley, CA 94720-5800
Phone: (510) 642-3175

University of California: Davis
www.ucdavis.edu
Services for International Students and
Scholars
178 Mrak Hall
Davis, CA 95616
Fax: (530) 752-5822
E-mail: siss@ucdavis.edu
Phone: (530) 752-0864

University of California: Irvine
www.uci.edu
Office of Admissions and Relations with
Schools
204 Aldrich Hall
Irvine, CA 92697-1075
Fax: (949) 824-2951
E-mail: aelsadr@uci.edu
Phone: (949) 824-4545

University of California: Los Angeles
www.ucla.edu
UCLA Undergraduate Admissions
1147 Murphy Hall
Box 951436
Los Angeles, CA 90095-1436
Fax: (310) 206-1206
E-mail: ugadm@saonet.ucla.edu
Phone: (310) 825-3101

University of California: Merced
www.ucmerced.edu
Admissions
5200 North Lake Road
Merced, CA 95343-5603
Fax: (209) 724-4244
E-mail: admissions@ucmerced.edu
Phone: (209) 381-7880

University of California: Riverside
www.ucr.edu
Office of Undergraduate Admissions
Admissions Office
1120 Hinderaker Hall
Riverside, CA 92521
Fax: (951) 827-6344
E-mail: discover@ucr.edu
Phone: (951) 827-3411

University of California: San Diego
www.ucsd.edu
International Admissions, 0021
9500 Gilman Drive, 0021
La Jolla, CA 92093-0021
Fax: (858) 534-5723
E-mail: admissionsinfo@ucsd.edu
Phone: (858) 534-4831

University of California: Santa Barbara
www.ucsb.edu
Office of International Students and Scholars
1210 Cheadle Hall
Santa Barbara, CA 93106-2014
Fax: (805) 893-7132
E-mail: oiss@sa.ucsb.edu
Phone: (805) 893-3753

University of California: Santa Cruz
www.ucsc.edu
Admissions
Cook House, 1156 High Street
Santa Cruz, CA 95064
Fax: (831) 459-4163
E-mail: myapplication@ucsc.edu
Phone: (831) 459-2131

University of Central Arkansas
www.uca.edu
Office of International Programs
201 Donaghey Avenue
Bernard 101
Conway, AR 72035
Fax: (501) 450-5095
E-mail: afaulkner@uca.edu
Phone: (501) 450-3442

University of Central Florida
www.ucf.edu
International Student Services
Box 160111
Orlando, FL 32816-0111
Fax: (407) 823-2526
E-mail: admission@mail.ucf.edu
Phone: (407) 823-2337

University of Central Missouri
www.ucmo.edu
Office of International Programs
WDE 1400
Warrensburg, MO 64093
Fax: (660) 543-4201
E-mail: intladmit@ucmo.edu
Phone: (660) 543-8502

University of Central Oklahoma
www.ucok.edu
International Office
100 North University Drive
Edmond, OK 73034-0151
Fax: (405) 974-3842
E-mail: ddunham1@ucok.edu
Phone: (405) 974-2390

University of Charleston
www.ucwv.edu
Admissions
2300 MacCorkle Avenue, SE
Charleston, WV 25304
Fax: (304) 357-4781
E-mail: amandapritt@ucwv.edu
Phone: (304) 357-4750

University of Chicago
www.uchicago.edu
1101 East 58th Street
Rosenwald Hall, Suite 105
Chicago, IL 60637
Fax: (773) 702-4199
E-mail: isabel@uchicago.edu
Phone: (773) 702-8661

University of Cincinnati
www.uc.edu
Admissions Office
PO Box 210091
Cincinnati, OH 45221-0091
Fax: (513) 556-1105
E-mail: admissions@uc.edu
Phone: (513) 556-1100

University of Cincinnati: Clermont College
www.ucclermont.edu
Senior Enrollment Advisor
4200 Clermont College Drive
Batavia, OH 45103
Fax: (513) 732-5303
E-mail: blaine.kelley@uc.edu
Phone: (513) 732-5301

University of Colorado at Boulder
www.colorado.edu
Office of Admissions
552 UCB
Boulder, CO 80309-0552
Fax: (303) 735-2501
E-mail: jeannine.bell@colorado.edu
Phone: (303) 735-2437

University of Colorado at Colorado Springs
www.uccs.edu
Admissions and Records
PO Box 7150
Colorado Springs, CO 80933-7150
Fax: (719) 262-3116
E-mail: jtidwell@mail.uccs.edu
Phone: (719) 262-3383

University of Colorado at Denver
www.ucdhsc.edu
Admissions and Records
Box 173364, Campus Box 167
Denver, CO 80217-3364
Fax: (303) 556-4838
E-mail: constance.costa@cudenver.edu
Phone: (303) 556-2704

University of Connecticut
www.uconn.edu
Office of Undergraduate Admissions
2131 Hillside Road, Unit 3088
Storrs, CT 06269-3088
Fax: (860) 486-1476
E-mail: beahusky@uconn.edu
Phone: (860) 486-3137

University of the Cumberlands
www.ucumberlands.edu
Admissions Office
6178 College Station Drive
Williamsburg, KY 40769
Fax: (606) 549-4303
E-mail: rfleenor@ucumberlands.edu
Phone: (606) 539-4241

University of Dallas
www.udallas.edu
Admissions
1845 East Northgate Drive
Irving, TX 75062-4736
Fax: (972) 721-5017
E-mail: ugadmis@udallas.edu
Phone: (972) 721-5266

University of Dayton
www.udayton.edu
International Admission
300 College Park
Dayton, OH 45469-1300
Fax: (937) 229-4729
E-mail: intl_adm@udayton.edu
Phone: (937) 229-4411

University of Delaware
www.udel.edu
Admissions
116 Hullihen Hall
Newark, DE 19716
Fax: (302) 831-6905
E-mail: admissions@udel.edu
Phone: (302) 831-8123

University of Denver
www.du.edu
International Student Admissions
2197 South University Boulevard
Denver, CO 80208
Fax: (303) 871-3301
E-mail: msmith@du.edu
Phone: (303) 871-2790

University of Detroit Mercy
www.udmercy.edu
International Services Office
4001 West McNichols Road
Detroit, MI 48221-3038
Fax: (313) 993-1192
E-mail: isoffice@udmercy.edu
Phone: (313) 993-1205

University of the District of Columbia
www.udc.edu
Office of Admission
4200 Connecticut Avenue NW
Washington, DC 20008
Fax: (202) 274-6180
E-mail: tjones@udc.edu
Phone: (202) 274-6088

University of Dubuque
www.dbq.edu
Admissions
2000 University Avenue
Dubuque, IA 52001-5099
Fax: (563) 589-3690
E-mail: jjames@dbq.edu
Phone: (800) 722-5583

University of Evansville
www.evansville.edu
Office of International Admission
1800 Lincoln Avenue
Evansville, IN 47722
Fax: (812) 488-6389
E-mail: international@evansville.edu
Phone: (812) 488-1392

University of Findlay
www.findlay.edu
Office of International Admissions and
Services
1000 North Main Street
Findlay, OH 45840-3653
Fax: (419) 434-5507
E-mail: gerdeman@findlay.edu
Phone: (419) 434-4558

University of Florida
www.ufl.edu
201 Criser Hall-PO Box 114000
Gainesville, FL 32611-4000
Fax: (352) 392-2115
E-mail: zevans@ufl.edu
Phone: (352) 392-1365

University of Georgia
www.uga.edu
Office of Undergraduate Admissions
Terrell Hall
Athens, GA 30602-1633
Fax: (706) 542-1466
E-mail: undergrad@admissions.uga.edu
Phone: (706) 542-8776

University of Great Falls
www.ugf.edu
Assistant Director of Admissions
1301 20th Street South
Great Falls, MT 59405
Fax: (406) 791-5209
E-mail: aclutter01@ugf.edu
Phone: (406) 791-5200

University of Hawaii at Hilo
www.uhh.hawaii.edu
Admissions
200 West Kawili Street
Hilo, HI 96720-4091
Fax: (808) 974-7691
E-mail: pgrossma@hawaii.edu
Phone: (808) 974-7414

University of Hawaii at Manoa
www.manoa.hawaii.edu
Admissions and Records
2600 Campus Road, QLC Rm 001
Honolulu, HI 96822
Fax: (808) 956-4148
E-mail: ar-info@hawaii.edu
Phone: (808) 956-8975

University of Hawaii: Hawaii Community College
www.hawcc.hawaii.edu
200 West Kawili Street
Hilo, HI 96720-4091
Fax: (808) 974-7692
E-mail: loeding@hawaii.edu
Phone: (808) 974-7662

University of Hawaii: Honolulu Community College
honolulu.hawaii.edu
Admissions
874 Dillingham Boulevard
Honolulu, HI 96817
Fax: (808) 847-9872
E-mail: admissions@hcc.hawaii.edu
Phone: (808) 845-9129

University of Hawaii: Kapiolani Community College
www.kcc.hawaii.edu
4303 Diamond Head Road
Honolulu, HI 96816-4421
Fax: (808) 734-9896
E-mail: liantmei@hawaii.edu
Phone: (808) 734-9312

University of Hawaii: Kauai Community College
www.kauai.hawaii.edu
Student Services
3-1901 Kaumualii Highway
Lihue, HI 96766-9500
Fax: (808) 245-8297
E-mail: tanakawa@hawaii.edu
Phone: (808) 245-8225

University of Hawaii: Maui Community College
www.maui.hawaii.edu
Student Services
310 West Kaahumanu Avenue
Kahului, HI 96732-1617
Fax: (808) 242-9618
Phone: (808) 984-3517

University of Hawaii: West Oahu
www.westoahu.hawaii.edu
Student Services Office
96-129 Ala Ike
Pearl City, HI 96782
Fax: (808) 453-6075
E-mail: robyno@hawaii.edu
Phone: (808) 454-4700

University of Hawaii: Windward Community College
www.wcc.hawaii.edu
Admissions and Records
45-720 Kea'ahala Road
Kaneohe, HI 96744
Fax: (808) 235-9148
E-mail: wccinfo@hawaii.edu
Phone: (808) 235-7432

University of Houston
www.uh.edu
International Admissions
122 East Cullen Building
Houston, TX 77204-2023
Fax: (713) 743-9652
E-mail: admissions@uh.edu
Phone: (713) 743-9607

University of Houston: Clear Lake
www.uhcl.edu
Enrollment Services, International Admissions
2700 Bay Area Boulevard
Houston, TX 77058-1098
Fax: (281) 283-2530
E-mail: Kabasele@uhcl.edu
Phone: (281) 283-2506

University of Houston: Downtown
www.uhd.edu
International Admissions
One Main Street, Suite 350-S
Houston, TX 77002
Fax: (713) 221-2718
E-mail: uhadmit@uhd.edu
Phone: (713) 221-8677

University of Houston: Victoria
www.uhv.edu
Admissions/Enrollment Services
3007 North Ben Wilson
Victoria, TX 77901-4450
Fax: (361) 570-4114
E-mail: kraatze@uhv.edu
Phone: (361) 570-4112

University of Idaho
www.uidaho.edu
International Programs
PO Box 444264
Moscow, ID 83844-4264
Fax: (208) 885-2859
E-mail: ipo@idaho.edu
Phone: (208) 885-8984

University of Illinois at Chicago
www.uic.edu
Admissions and Records
PO Box 5220
Chicago, IL 60680-5220
Fax: (312) 413-7628
E-mail: uicadmit@uic.edu
Phone: (312) 996-4350

University of Illinois at Urbana-Champaign
www.illinois.edu
International Admissions
901 West Illinois
Urbana, IL 61801-3028
Fax: (217) 244-4614
E-mail: gperry@uiuc.edu
Phone: (217) 333-3036

University of Illinois: Springfield
www.uis.edu
Admissions
One University Plaza, MS UHB 1080
Springfield, IL 62703
Fax: (217) 206-6620
E-mail: admissions@uis.edu
Phone: (217) 206-4847

University of the Incarnate Word
www.uiw.edu
Admissions
4301 Broadway
CPO 285
San Antonio, TX 78209-6397
Fax: (210) 829-3921
E-mail: levy@uiwtx.edu
Phone: (210) 805-3554

University of Indianapolis
www.uindy.edu
International Student Admissions
1400 East Hanna Avenue
Indianapolis, IN 46227-3697
Fax: (317) 788-3300
E-mail: kgunyon@uindy.edu
Phone: (317) 788-3600

University of Iowa
www.uiowa.edu
Admissions
107 Calvin Hall
Iowa City, IA 52242-1396
Fax: (319) 335-1535
E-mail: admissions@uiowa.edu
Phone: (800) 553-4692

University of Kansas
www.ku.edu
International Student and Scholar Services
1502 Iowa Street
Lawrence, KS 66045-7576
Fax: (785) 864-5244
E-mail: isss@ku.edu
Phone: (785) 864-3617

University of Kansas Medical Center
www.kumc.edu
International Programs
3901 Rainbow Boulevard
Kansas City, KS 66160-7116
Fax: (913) 588-1462
E-mail: jshaw@kumc.edu
Phone: (913) 588-1485

University of Kentucky
www.uky.edu
100 W.D. Funkhouser Building
Lexington, KY 40506-0054
Fax: (859) 257-3823
E-mail: mlkrin0@uky.edu
Phone: (859) 257-4708

University of La Verne
www.ulv.edu
Undergraduate Admissions
1950 Third Street
La Verne, CA 91750
Fax: (909) 392-2714
E-mail: mckinney@ulv.edu
Phone: (909) 392-2800

University of Louisiana at Lafayette
www.louisiana.edu
Box 41210
Lafayette, LA 70504-1210
Fax: (337) 482-6195
E-mail: admissions@louisiana.edu
Phone: (337) 482-6467

University of Louisiana at Monroe
www.ulm.edu
International Student Office
700 University Avenue
Monroe, LA 71209-1160
Fax: (318) 342-6764
E-mail: loeb@ulm.edu
Phone: (318) 342-3678

University of Louisville
www.louisville.edu
Admissions
2211 South Brook Street
Louisville, KY 40292
Fax: (502) 852-6526
E-mail: admitme@louisville.edu
Phone: (502) 852-4953

University of Maine
www.umaine.edu
Office of International Programs
5713 Chadbourne Hall
Orono, ME 04469-5713
Fax: (207) 581-2920
E-mail: umintprg@maine.edu
Phone: (207) 581-2905

University of Maine at Augusta
www.uma.edu
Admissions
46 University Drive
Augusta, ME 04330
Fax: (207) 621-3333
E-mail: trask@maine.edu
Phone: (207) 621-3140

University of Maine at Farmington
www.farmington.edu
Associate Director Admissions
246 Main Street
Farmington, ME 04938
Fax: (207) 778-8182
E-mail: ellrich@maine.edu
Phone: (207) 778-7050 ext. 7054

University of Maine at Fort Kent
www.umfk.maine.edu
Admissions
23 University Drive
Fort Kent, ME 04743
Fax: (207) 834-7609
E-mail: jillb@maine.edu
Phone: (207) 834-7602

University of Maine at Machias
www.umm.maine.edu
Admissions Office
9 O'Brien Avenue
Machias, ME 04654
Fax: (207) 255-1363
E-mail: mahmoud.sowe@maine.edu
Phone: (207) 255-1332

University of Mary
www.umary.edu
Enrollment Services
7500 University Drive
Bismarck, ND 58504-9652
Fax: (701) 255-7687
E-mail: heringer@umary.edu
Phone: (701) 355-8190

University of Mary Hardin-Baylor
www.umhb.edu
Office of International Student Services
900 College Street
UMHB Box 8004
Belton, TX 76513
Fax: (254) 295-4535
E-mail: etanaka@umhb.edu
Phone: (254) 295-4949

University of Mary Washington
www.umw.edu
Admissions
1301 College Avenue
Fredericksburg, VA 22401-5358
Fax: (540) 654-1857
E-mail: admit@umw.edu
Phone: (540) 654-2000

University of Maryland: Baltimore
www.umaryland.edu
Office of Records and Registration
660 West Redwood Street, Room 021
Baltimore, MD 21201
Fax: (410) 706-4053
E-mail: tday@umaryland.edu
Phone: (410) 706-7480

University of Maryland: Baltimore County
www.umbc.edu
Office of Undergraduate Admissions
1000 Hilltop Circle
Baltimore, MD 21250
Fax: (410) 455-1094
E-mail: massey@umbc.edu
Phone: (410) 455-6705

University of Maryland: College Park
www.maryland.edu
International Education Student Services
Mitchell Building
College Park, MD 20742-5235
Fax: (301) 314-9347
E-mail: iesadv@deans.umd.edu
Phone: (301) 314-7740

University of Maryland: Eastern Shore
www.umes.edu
Bird Hall
One Backbone Road
Princess Anne, MD 21853
Fax: (410) 651-8386
E-mail: snacquah@mail.umes.edu
Phone: (410) 651-6079

University of Maryland: University College
www.umuc.edu
3501 University Boulevard East
Adelphi, MD 20783-8010
Fax: (301) 985-7364
E-mail: emteam@umuc.edu
Phone: (301) 985-7000

University of Massachusetts Amherst
www.umass.edu
Undergraduate Admissions Office
University Admissions Center
37 Mather Drive
Amherst, MA 01003-9291
Fax: (413) 545-4312
E-mail: mail@admissions.umass.edu
Phone: (413) 545-0222

University of Massachusetts Boston
www.umb.edu
Undergraduate Admissions
100 Morrissey Boulevard
Boston, MA 02125-3393
Fax: (617) 287-5999
E-mail: undergrad@umb.edu
Phone: (617) 287-6100

University of Massachusetts Dartmouth
www.umassd.edu
Undergraduate Admissions Office
285 Old Westport Road
North Dartmouth, MA 02747-2300
Fax: (508) 999-8755
E-mail: skesman@umassd.edu
Phone: (508) 999-9107

University of Massachusetts Lowell
www.uml.edu
Admissions Office
883 Broadway Street, Room 110
Lowell, MA 01854-5104
Fax: (978) 934-3086
E-mail: admissions@uml.edu
Phone: (978) 934-3931

University of Medicine and Dentistry of New Jersey: School of Health Related Professions
www.shrp.umdnj.edu
Office od International Services - Office of the
University Registrar
65 Bergen Street
Room 149
Newark, NJ 07101-1709
Fax: (973) 972-8260
E-mail: shrpadm@umdnj.edu
Phone: (973) 972-6138

University of Memphis
www.memphis.edu
Office of Admissions, Graduate and
International
101 Wilder Tower
Memphis, TN 38152
Fax: (901) 678-3053
E-mail: dwelch@memphis.edu
Phone: (901) 678-2111

University of Miami
www.miami.edu
Office of International Admissions
132 Ashe Building
Box 248025
Coral Gables, FL 33124-4616
Fax: (305) 284-6811
E-mail: intl.admission@miami.edu
Phone: (305) 284-2271

University of Michigan
www.umich.edu
Office of Undergraduate Admissions
1220 Student Activities Building
515 East Jefferson Street
Ann Arbor, MI 48109-1316
Fax: (734) 936-0747
E-mail: ugadmiss@umich.edu
Phone: (734) 764-7433

University of Michigan: Dearborn
www.umd.umich.edu
Admissions
4901 Evergreen Road, 1145 UC
Dearborn, MI 48128-1491
Fax: (313) 436-9167
E-mail: reybrown@umd.umich.edu
Phone: (313) 593-5391

University of Michigan: Flint
www.umflint.edu
Admissions
303 East Kearsley Street
Flint, MI 48502-1950
Fax: (810) 762-3272
E-mail: admissions@umflint.edu
Phone: (810) 762-3302

University of Minnesota: Crookston
www.UMCrookston.edu
International Programs Office
2900 University Avenue
170 Owen Hall
Crookston, MN 56716-5001
Fax: (218) 281-8588
E-mail: gillette@umn.edu
Phone: (218) 281-8442

University of Minnesota: Duluth
www.d.umn.edu
Office of Admissions
25 Solon Campus Center
1117 University Drive
Duluth, MN 55812-3000
Fax: (218) 726-6724
E-mail: krobbin1@d.umn.edu
Phone: (218) 726-8962

University of Minnesota: Morris
www.morris.umn.edu
Office of Admissions
600 East 4th Street
Morris, MN 56267
Fax: (320) 589-1673
E-mail: schmidtt@morris.umn.edu
Phone: (320) 589-6035

University of Minnesota: Twin Cities
www.umn.edu/tc
Admissions
240 Williamson Hall, 231 Pillsbury Drive SE
Minneapolis, MN 55455-0115
Fax: (612) 626-1693
Phone: (800) 752-1000

University of Mississippi
www.olemiss.edu
Office of International Programs
145 Martindale
PO BOX 1848
University, MS 38677-1848
Fax: (662) 915-7486
E-mail: ipadmiss@olemiss.edu
Phone: (662) 915-7404

University of Missouri: Columbia
www.missouri.edu
International Student Admissions
230 Jesse Hall
Columbia, MO 65211
Fax: (573) 882-7887
E-mail: inter@missouri.edu
Phone: (573) 882-0102

University of Missouri: Kansas City
www.umkc.edu
International Student Affairs Office
5100 Rockhill Road, AC120
Kansas City, MO 64110-2499
Fax: (816) 235-6502
E-mail: gaults@umkc.edu
Phone: (816) 235-6234

University of Missouri: St. Louis
www.umsl.edu
Office of International Student and Scholar
Services
One University Boulevard
351 Millennium Student Center
St. Louis, MO 63121-4400
Fax: (314) 516-5636
E-mail: trudo@umsl.edu
Phone: (314) 516-5229

University of Mobile
www.umobile.edu
Assistant Director of Admissions for
Recruitment
5735 College Parkway
Mobile, AL 36613-2842
Fax: (251) 442-2498
E-mail: HaliW@mail.umobile.edu
Phone: (251) 442-2221

University of Montana: Missoula
www.umt.edu
Admissions
Lommasson Center 103
Missoula, MT 59812
Fax: (406) 243-5711
E-mail: JAlcala@mso.umt.edu
Phone: (406) 243-2049

University of Montana: Western
www.umwestern.edu
Admissions
710 South Atlantic Street
Dillon, MT 59725
Fax: (406) 683-7493
E-mail: admissions@umwestern.edu
Phone: (406) 683-7331

University of Montevallo
www.montevallo.edu
Admissions
Station 6030
Montevallo, AL 35115-6030
Fax: (205) 665-6032
E-mail: admissions@montevallo.edu
Phone: (205) 665-6030

University of Nebraska - Kearney
www.unk.edu
International Education Admissions
905 West 25th
Kearney, NE 68849
Fax: (308) 865-8160
E-mail: intladmin@unk.edu
Phone: (308) 865-8157

University of Nebraska - Lincoln
www.unl.edu
International Affairs
1410 Q Street
Box 880417
Lincoln, NE 68588-0417
Fax: (402) 472-5383
E-mail: hturner@unlnotes.unl.edu
Phone: (402) 472-5358

University of Nebraska - Omaha
www.unomaha.edu
International Admissions
6001 Dodge Street
Omaha, NE 68182-0005
Fax: (402) 554-2949
E-mail: world@unomaha.edu
Phone: (402) 554-2293

University of Nevada: Las Vegas
www.unlv.edu
4505 Maryland Parkway Box 451021
Las Vegas, NV 89154-1021
Fax: (702) 895-0169
E-mail: issssc@unlv.edu
Phone: (702) 895-0143

University of Nevada: Reno
www.unr.edu
Office of International Students & Scholars
Mail Stop 120
Reno, NV 89557
Fax: (775) 327-5843
E-mail: iap@unr.nevada.edu
Phone: (775) 784-6874

University of New England
www.une.edu
Admissions
Hills Beach Road
Biddeford, ME 04005
Fax: (207) 602-5900
E-mail: admissions@une.edu
Phone: (207) 283-0170 ext. 2297

University of New Hampshire
www.unh.edu
Admissions Office
Grant House
4 Garrison Avenue
Durham, NH 03824
Fax: (603) 862-0077
E-mail: admissions@unh.edu
Phone: (603) 862-3431

University of New Hampshire at Manchester
www.unhm.unh.edu
Admissions
400 Commercial Street
Manchester, NH 03101-1113
Fax: (603) 641-4342
E-mail: unhm.admissions@unh.edu
Phone: (603) 641-4150

University of New Haven
www.newhaven.edu
Office of International Admissions
300 Boston Post Road
West Haven, CT 06516
Fax: (203) 931-6093
E-mail: jspellman@newhaven.edu
Phone: (203) 932-7134

University of New Mexico
www.unm.edu
Office of International Admissions
Office of Admissions
PO Box 4895
Albuquerque, NM 87196-4895
Fax: (505) 277-6686
E-mail: goglobal@unm.edu
Phone: (505) 277-5829

University of New Orleans
www.uno.edu
Admissions
Administration Building Room 103
New Orleans, LA 70148
Fax: (504) 280-6552
E-mail: admissions@uno.edu
Phone: (504) 280-6595

University of North Alabama
www.una.edu
International Student Services
One Harrison Plaza, UNA Box 5011
Florence, AL 35632-0001
Fax: (256) 765-4960
E-mail: cbagcioglu@una.edu
Phone: (256) 765-4626

University of North Carolina at Asheville
www.unca.edu
Admissions
CPO#1320, UNCA
One University Heights
Asheville, NC 28804-8510
Fax: (828) 251-6482
E-mail: lmcbride@unca.edu
Phone: (828) 251-6481

University of North Carolina at Chapel Hill
www.unc.edu
Undergraduate Admissions
Jackson Hall CB #2200
Chapel Hill, NC 27599-2200
Fax: (919) 962-3045
E-mail: afelder@admissions.unc.edu
Phone: (919) 843-6156

University of North Carolina at Charlotte
www.uncc.edu
Office of International Admissions
9201 University City Boulevard
Charlotte, NC 28223-0001
Fax: (704) 687-3727
E-mail: intnladm@uncc.edu
Phone: (704) 687-3366

University of North Carolina at Greensboro
www.uncg.edu
Undergraduate Admissions
1400 Spring Garden Street
PO Box 26170
Greensboro, NC 27402-6170
Fax: (336) 334-4180
E-mail: admissions@uncg.edu
Phone: (336) 334-5243

University of North Carolina at Pembroke
www.uncp.edu
Admissions
Box 1510
Pembroke, NC 28372
Fax: (910) 521-6497
E-mail: admissions@uncp.edu
Phone: (910) 521-6264

University of North Carolina at Wilmington
www.uncw.edu
Admissions
601 South College Road
Wilmington, NC 28403-5904
Fax: (910) 962-3038
E-mail: admissions@uncw.edu
Phone: (910) 962-3243

University of North Dakota
www.und.edu
Undergraduate Admissions Office
Twamley Hall Room 205 264 Centennial Drive
Stop 8357
Grand Forks, ND 58202-8357
Fax: (701) 777-2721
E-mail: heidikippenhan@mail.und.nodak.edu
Phone: (701) 777-3821

University of North Florida
www.unf.edu
International Center
1 UNF Drive
Jacksonville, FL 32224-7699
Fax: (904) 620-3925
E-mail: intlctr@unf.edu
Phone: (904) 620-2768

University of North Texas
www.unt.edu
Office of International Admissions
1401 West Prairie, Suite 309
Box 311277
Denton, TX 76203
Fax: (940) 565-4822
E-mail: international@unt.edu
Phone: (940) 565-2442

University of Northern Colorado
www.unco.edu
Graduate School
Campus Box 10
Greeley, CO 80639
Fax: (970) 351-2371
E-mail: gradsch@unco.edu
Phone: (970) 351-2831

University of Northern Iowa
www.uni.edu
Admissions
Towers 130
Cedar Falls, IA 50614-0018
Fax: (319) 273-6103
E-mail: kristi.marchesani@uni.edu
Phone: (319) 273-2281

University of Northern Virginia
www.unva.edu
Admissions
10021 Balls Ford Road
Manassas, VA 20109
Fax: (703) 392-0756
E-mail: ibehery.admin@unva.edu
Phone: (703) 392-0771

University of Northwestern Ohio
www.unoh.edu
1441 North Cable Road
Lima, OH 45805
Fax: (419) 229-6926
E-mail: info@unoh.edu
Phone: (419) 998-3120

University of Notre Dame
www.nd.edu
Admissions
220 Main Building
Notre Dame, IN 46556
Fax: (574) 631-8865
E-mail: admissions@nd.edu
Phone: (574) 631-7505

University of Oklahoma
www.ou.edu
Office of Admissions
1000 Asp Avenue
Norman, OK 73019-4076
Fax: (405) 325-7124
E-mail: admrec@ou.edu
Phone: (405) 325-2252

University of Oregon
www.uoregon.edu
International Programs
1217 University of Oregon
Eugene, OR 97403-1217
Fax: (541) 346-1232
E-mail: magid@uoregon.edu
Phone: (541) 346-3206

University of the Ozarks
www.ozarks.edu
415 College Avenue
Clarksville, AR 72830
Fax: (479) 979-1239
E-mail: rjcasey@ozarks.edu
Phone: (479) 979-1232

University of the Pacific
www.pacific.edu
Admissions
3601 Pacific Avenue
Stockton, CA 95211-0197
Fax: (209) 946-2413
E-mail: bbrissen@pacific.edu
Phone: (209) 346-2211

University of Pennsylvania
www.upenn.edu
International Admissions Office
1 College Hall
Philadelphia, PA 19104
Fax: (215) 898-9670
E-mail: intl@admissions.upenn.edu
Phone: (215) 898-7901

University of Phoenix
www.phoenix.edu
University of Phoenix - On-Line Campus
4615 East Elwood Street
Mail Stop AA-E101
Phoenix, AZ 85040-1958
Fax: (602) 735-9589
E-mail: pete.martinez@apollogrp.edu
Phone: (602) 387-6169

University of Pittsburgh
www.pitt.edu
Office of International Services
4227 Fifth Avenue, 1st Floor, Alumni Hall
Pittsburgh, PA 15260
Fax: (412) 624-7105
E-mail: intladm@pitt.edu
Phone: (412) 624-7129

University of Pittsburgh at Bradford
www.upb.pitt.edu
Office of Admissions
300 Campus Drive
Bradford, PA 16701
Fax: (814) 362-5150
E-mail: admissions@upb.pitt.edu
Phone: (814) 362-7555

University of Pittsburgh at Greensburg
www.upg.pitt.edu
International Services
150 Finoli Drive
Greensburg, PA 15601
Fax: (412) 624-7105
E-mail: gfk1@pitt.edu
Phone: (412) 624-7128

University of Pittsburgh at Johnstown
www.upj.pitt.edu
Office of Admissions
450 Schoolhouse Road, 157 Blackington Hall
Johnstown, PA 15904-1200
Fax: (814) 269-7044
E-mail: jskist@pitt.edu
Phone: (814) 269-7050

University of Pittsburgh at Titusville
www.upt.pitt.edu
Foreign Student Admissions
UPT Admissions Office
Box 287
Titusville, PA 16354-0287
Fax: (412) 624-7105
E-mail: uptadm@pitt.edu
Phone: (412) 624-7125

University of Portland
www.up.edu
Office of Admissions
5000 North Willamette Boulevard
Portland, OR 97203-5798
Fax: (503) 943-7315
E-mail: mcdonaja@up.edu
Phone: (503) 943-7147

University of Puerto Rico: Aguadilla
www.uprag.edu
Admissions Office
Box 250160
Aguadilla, PR 00604
Fax: (787) 890-4543
E-mail: melba_serrano@hotmail.com
Phone: (787) 890-2681 ext. 280

University of Puerto Rico: Arecibo
www.upra.edu
PO Box 4010
Arecibo, PR 00614-4010
Fax: (787) 880-4972
E-mail: mmendez@upra.edu
Phone: (787) 815-0000 ext. 4110

University of Puerto Rico: Bayamon
University College
www.uprb.edu
174 State Road #170 Parque Industrial
Minillas
Bayamon, PR 00959
Fax: (787) 993-8929
E-mail: cmontes@uprb.edu
Phone: (787) 993-8952

University of Puerto Rico: Carolina Regional College
www.uprc.edu
Admissions Office
PO Box 4800
Carolina, PR 00984-4800
Fax: (787) 750-7940
Phone: (787) 757-1485

University of Puerto Rico: Cayey University College
www.cayey.upr.edu
Admissions Office
Oficina de Admisiones UPR- Cayey
205 Antonio Barcelo Avenue
Cayey, PR 00736
Fax: (787) 738-5633
E-mail: wilopez@cayey.upr.edu
Phone: (787) 738-2161

University of Puerto Rico: Humacao
www.uprh.edu
Director of Admissions
100 Road 908 CUH Station
Humacao, PR 00791
Fax: (787) 850-9428
E-mail: m_alvarez@uprh.edu
Phone: (787) 850-9301 ext. 9814

University of Puerto Rico: Mayaguez
www.uprm.edu
International Students Office
Admissions Office
PO Box 9021
Mayaguez, PR 00681-9021
Fax: (787) 265-5432
E-mail: gildreth@uprm.edu
Phone: (787) 265-3896

University of Puerto Rico: Medical Sciences
www.rcm.upr.edu
P.O. Box 365067
San Juan, PR 00936-5067
Fax: (787) 282-7117
E-mail: marrivera@rcm.upr.edu
Phone: (787) 758-2525 ext. 5211

University of Puerto Rico: Ponce
www.uprp.edu
Director Admission Office
Box 7186
Ponce, PR 00732
Fax: (787) 840-8108
E-mail: avelazquez@uprp.edu
Phone: (787) 844-8181 ext. 2530

University of Puerto Rico: Rio Piedras
www.rrp.upr.edu
Box 23344
San Juan, PR 00931-3344
Fax: (787) 763-4265
Phone: (787) 764-0000 ext. 5655

University of Puerto Rico: Utuado
www.uprutuado.edu
PO Box 2500
Utuado, PR 00641
Fax: (787) 894-2891
Phone: (787) 894-2828 ext. 2240

University of Puget Sound
www.ups.edu
Admission
1500 North Warner Street
Tacoma, WA 98416-1062
Fax: (253) 879-3993
E-mail: admission@ups.edu
Phone: (253) 879-3211

University of Redlands
www.redlands.edu
International Student Adviser
1200 East Colton Avenue
PO Box 3080
Redlands, CA 92373-0999
Fax: (909) 335-4089
E-mail: admissions@redlands.edu
Phone: (909) 793-2121 ext. 4583

University of Rhode Island
www.uri.edu
International Students and Scholars
14 Upper College Road
Kingston, RI 02881-1322
Fax: (401) 874-5523
E-mail: nancys@uri.edu
Phone: (401) 874-7100

University of Richmond
www.richmond.edu
28 Westhampton Way
University of Richmond, VA 23173
Fax: (804) 287-6535
E-mail: intladm@richmond.edu
Phone: (804) 289-6531

University of Rio Grande
www.rio.edu
Student Services
218 North College Avenue
Box F-30
Rio Grande, OH 45674
Fax: (749) 245-7341
E-mail: ericm@rio.edu
Phone: (740) 245-7128

University of Rochester
www.rochester.edu
Admissions Office
300 Wilson Boulevard
Box 270251
Rochester, NY 14627-0251
Fax: (585) 461-4595
E-mail:
international@admissions.rochester.edu
Phone: (585) 275-3221

University of San Diego
www.sandiego.edu
Admissions Office
5998 Alcala Park
San Diego, CA 92110
Fax: (619) 260-6836
E-mail: admissions@sandiego.edu
Phone: (619) 260-4506

University of San Francisco
www.usfca.edu
Admissions: Assistant Director for
International Student Admissions
2130 Fulton Street
San Francisco, CA 94117-1046
Fax: (415) 422-2217
E-mail: admissions@usfca.edu
Phone: (415) 422-6563

University of Science and Arts of Oklahoma
http://www.usao.edu
Office of Admissions
1727 West Alabama
Chickasha, OK 73018-5322
Fax: (405) 574-1220
E-mail: usao-admissions@usao.edu
Phone: (405) 574-1357

University of the Sciences in Philadelphia
www.usp.edu
Student Affairs
600 South 43rd Street
Philadelphia, PA 19104-4495
Fax: (215) 895-1100
E-mail: w.perry@usip.edu
Phone: (215) 596-8890

University of Scranton
www.scranton.edu
Director of International Student Affairs
800 Linden Street
St. Thomas Hall Room 409
Scranton, PA 18510-4699
Fax: (570) 941-5928
E-mail: blazespl@scranton.edu
Phone: (570) 941-7575

University of Sioux Falls
www.usiouxfalls.edu
Admissions Office
1101 West 22nd Street
Sioux Falls, SD 57105-1699
Fax: (605) 331-6615
E-mail: admissions@usiouxfalls.edu
Phone: (800) 888-1047

University of the South
www.sewanee.edu
Admission
Office of Admission
735 University Avenue
Sewanee, TN 37383-1000
Fax: (931) 538-3248
E-mail: admiss@sewanee.edu
Phone: (800) 522-2234

University of South Alabama
www.southalabama.edu
Office of International Services
Meisler Hall, Suite 2500
307 University Boulevard North
Mobile, AL 36688-0002
Fax: (251) 414-8213
E-mail: intlserv@jaguar1.usouthal.edu
Phone: (251) 460-6050

University of South Carolina
www.sc.edu
Admissions Office
Office of Undergraduate Admissions
Columbia, SC 29208
Fax: (803) 777-0101
E-mail: admissions-ugrad@sc.edu
Phone: (803) 777-7700

University of South Carolina at Aiken
www.usca.edu
Admissions Office
471 University Parkway
Aiken, SC 29801
Fax: (803) 641-3727
E-mail: admit@usca.edu
Phone: (803) 641-3366

University of South Carolina at Beaufort
www.uscb.edu
Admissions Office
One University Boulevard
Bluffton, SC 29909
Fax: (843) 208-8290
E-mail: mrwilli5@gwm.sc.edu
Phone: (843) 208-8112

University of South Carolina at Lancaster
usclancaster.sc.edu
Admissions
Box 889
Lancaster, SC 29721
Fax: (803) 313-7116
Phone: (803) 313-7071

University of South Carolina at Sumter
www.uscsumter.edu
Admissions
200 Miller Road
Sumter, SC 29150-2498
Fax: (803) 938-3901
E-mail: kbritton@uscsumter.edu
Phone: (803) 938-3882

University of South Carolina at Union
uscunion.sc.edu
PO Drawer 729
Union, SC 29379
Fax: (864) 427-3682
Phone: (864) 429-8728

University of South Carolina Upstate
www.uscupstate.edu
Admissions
800 University Way
Spartanburg, SC 29303
Fax: (864) 503-5727
E-mail: dstewart@uscupstate.edu
Phone: (864) 503-5280

University of South Dakota
www.usd.edu
International Student Advising Office
414 East Clark Street
Vermillion, SD 57069-2390
Fax: (605) 677-5073
E-mail: isa@usd.edu
Phone: (605) 677-6061

University of South Florida
www.usf.edu
International Admissions
4202 East Fowler Avenue, SVC 1036
Tampa, FL 33620-9951
Fax: (813) 974-8271
E-mail: pekovsky@iac.usf.edu
Phone: (813) 974-5004

University of Southern California
www.usc.edu
Admissions
Office of Admission
File 51158
Los Angeles, CA 90089-1158
Fax: (213) 740-1556
E-mail: diradmit@usc.edu
Phone: (213) 740-1111

University of Southern Indiana
www.usi.edu
Admission
8600 University Boulevard
Evansville, IN 47712
Fax: (812) 465-7154
E-mail: eotto@usi.edu
Phone: (812) 464-1765

University of Southern Maine
www.usm.maine.edu
Rachel Morales, Associate Director
37 College Avenue
Gorham, ME 04038
Fax: (207) 780-5640
E-mail: rmorales@usm.maine.edu
Phone: (207) 780-5670

University of Southern Mississippi
www.usm.edu
Office of International Student Affairs
118 College Drive #5166
Hattiesburg, MS 39406-0001
Fax: (601) 266-5723
E-mail: isa@usm.edu
Phone: (601) 266-4841

University of Southern Nevada
www.usn.edu
Dean, College of Nursing
11 Sunset Way
Henderson, NV 89014
Fax: (702) 968-2097
E-mail: bsnadmissions@usn.edu
Phone: (702) 968-2075

University of St. Francis
www.stfrancis.edu
Director Undergraduate Admissions
500 Wilcox Street
Joliet, IL 60435
Fax: (815) 740-5032
E-mail: mconnolly1@srfrancis.edu
Phone: (800) 735-7500

University of St. Francis
www.sf.edu
Admissions
2701 Spring Street
Fort Wayne, IN 46808
Fax: (260) 434-7590
E-mail: adinh@sf.edu
Phone: (260) 434-3279

University of St. Mary
www.stmary.edu
Office of Admission
4100 South Fourth Street Trafficway
Leavenworth, KS 66048
Fax: (913) 758-6307
E-mail: admiss@stmary.edu
Phone: (800) 752-7043

University of St. Thomas
www.stthomas.edu
International Education Center
2115 Summit Avenue, 32F
St. Paul, MN 55105-1096
Fax: (651) 962-5199
E-mail: international@stthomas.edu
Phone: (651) 962-6450

University of St. Thomas
www.stthom.edu
International Student Advisor
3800 Montrose Boulevard
Houston, TX 77006-4626
Fax: (713) 525-6968
E-mail: admissions@stthom.edu
Phone: (713) 525-3503

University of Tampa
www.ut.edu
Office of Admissions
401 West Kennedy Boulevard
Tampa, FL 33606-1490
Fax: (813) 258-7398
E-mail: admissions@ut.edu
Phone: (813) 253-6211

University of Tennessee Health Science Center
www.utmem.edu
Enrollment Management
800 Madison Avenue
Memphis, TN 38163
Fax: (901) 448-7772
E-mail: etaylor@utmem.edu
Phone: (901) 528-5560

University of Tennessee: Chattanooga
www.utc.edu
Foreign Student Advisor
615 McCallie Avenue
Dept 5105
Chattanooga, TN 37403
Fax: (423) 425-2292
E-mail: nancy-amberson@utc.edu
Phone: (423) 425-4573

University of Tennessee: Knoxville
www.tennessee.edu
Graduate and International Admissions
320 Student Services Building
Knoxville, TN 37996-0230
Fax: (865) 974-6541
E-mail: mickowit@utk.edu
Phone: (865) 974-3251

University of Tennessee: Martin
www.utm.edu
International Programs Office
200 Hall Moody Administration Building
Martin, TN 38238
Fax: (731) 881-7322
E-mail: sbaker@utm.edu
Phone: (731) 881-7340

University of Texas at Arlington
www.uta.edu
Admissions
Box 19111
Arlington, TX 76019
Fax: (817) 272-3435
E-mail: admissions@uta.edu
Phone: (817) 272-6287

University of Texas at Austin
www.utexas.edu
Graduate and International Admission Center
PO Box 8058
Austin, TX 78713-8058
Fax: (512) 475-7395
E-mail: adint@utxdp.its.utexas.edu
Phone: (512) 475-7398

University of Texas at Brownsville
www.utb.edu
Admissions Office
80 Fort Brown
Brownsville, TX 78520
Fax: (956) 983-7810
E-mail: admissions@utb.edu
Phone: (956) 544-8295

University of Texas at Dallas
www.utdallas.edu
Enrollment Services
Office of Admissions
PO Box 830688, HH10
Richardson, TX 75083-0688
Fax: (972) 883-2599
E-mail: interest@utdallas.edu
Phone: (972) 883-2258

University of Texas at El Paso
www.utep.edu
Admissions
500 West University Avenue
El Paso, TX 79968-0510
Fax: (915) 747-8893
E-mail: taragoncampos@utep.edu
Phone: (915) 747-5890

University of Texas at San Antonio
www.utsa.edu
Office of Admissions and Registrar
One UTSA Circle
San Antonio, TX 78249-0617
Fax: (210) 458-7564
E-mail: bunderwood@utsa.edu
Phone: (210) 458-6065

University of Texas at Tyler
www.uttyler.edu
Admissions
3900 University Boulevard
Tyler, TX 75799
Fax: (903) 566-7068
E-mail: acrockett@mail.uttyl.edu
Phone: (903) 566-7230

University of Texas Health Science Center at San Antonio
www.uthscsa.edu
Registrar
7703 Floyd Curl Drive
San Antonio, TX 78229
Fax: (210) 567-2685
E-mail: goode@uthscsa.edu
Phone: (210) 567-2629

University of Texas Medical Branch at Galveston
www.utmb.edu
Registrar
301 University Boulevard
Galveston, TX 77555-1305
Fax: (409) 772-4466
E-mail: enrollment.services@utmb.edu
Phone: (409) 772-1215

University of Texas of the Permian Basin
www.utpb.edu
Admissions
4901 East University Boulevard
Odessa, TX 79762
Fax: (915) 552-3605
E-mail: admissions@utpb.edu
Phone: (915) 552-2605

University of Texas Southwestern Medical Center at Dallas
www.utsouthwestern.edu
International Affairs
5323 Harry Hines Boulevard
Dallas, TX 75390-9162
Fax: (214) 648-2102
E-mail: admissions@utsouthwestern.edu
Phone: (214) 648-2780

University of Texas: Pan American
www.utpa.edu
Office of Undergraduate Admissions
1201 West University Drive
Edinburg, TX 78541-2999
Fax: (956) 381-2281
E-mail: intladvise@utpa.edu
Phone: (956) 381-2922

University of Toledo
www.utoledo.edu
Office of Undergraduate Admissions for Adult,
Transfer and International Students
2801 West Bancroft Street
Toledo, OH 43606-3398
Fax: (419) 530-1202
E-mail: enroll@utnet.utoledo.edu
Phone: (419) 530-1201

University of Tulsa
www.utulsa.edu
International Student Services
800 South Tucker Drive
Tulsa, OK 74104-3189
Fax: (918) 631-3322
E-mail: pamela-smith@utulsa.edu
Phone: (918) 631-2329

University of Utah
www.utah.edu
Admissions Office
201 South 1460 East, Room 250 S
Salt Lake City, UT 84112-9057
Fax: (801) 585-7864
E-mail: IAO@sa.utah.edu
Phone: (801) 581-3091

University of Vermont
www.uvm.edu
Admissions
194 South Prospect Street
Burlington, VT 05401-3596
Fax: (802) 656-8611
E-mail: admissions@uvm.edu
Phone: (802) 656-4620

University of Virginia
www.virginia.edu
Office of Undergraduate Admission
Box 400160
Charlottesville, VA 22904-4160
Fax: (434) 924-3587
E-mail: undergradadmission@virginia.edu
Phone: (434) 982-3200

University of Virginia's College at Wise
www.uvawise.edu
Admissions
1 College Avenue
Wise, VA 24293-4412
Fax: (276) 328-0251
E-mail: jcm6h@uvawise.edu
Phone: (276) 328-0104

University of Washington
www.washington.edu
Admissions
1410 Northeast Campus Parkway, Box 355852
Seattle, WA 98195-5852
Fax: (206) 685-3655
E-mail: intladm@u.washington.edu
Phone: (206) 543-9686

University of the West
www.uwest.edu
Office of Admission
1409 North Walnut Grove Avenue
Rosemead, CA 91770
Fax: (626) 571-1413
E-mail: info@uwest.edu
Phone: (626) 571-8811 ext. 311

University of West Alabama
www.uwa.edu
Registrar's Office
Station 4
Livingston, AL 35470
Fax: (205) 652-3708
E-mail: cwe@uwa.edu
Phone: (205) 652-3587

University of West Florida
www.uwf.edu
Office of Admissions
11000 University Parkway
Pensacola, FL 32514-5750
Fax: (850) 474-3360
E-mail: admissions@uwf.edu
Phone: (850) 474-2230

University of West Georgia
www.westga.edu
Admissions
1601 Maple Street
Carrollton, GA 30118
Fax: (678) 839-4747
E-mail: rjohnson@westga.edu
Phone: (678) 839-4000

University of Wisconsin-Baraboo/Sauk County
www.baraboo.uwc.edu
Office of Student Services
1006 Connie Road
Baraboo, WI 53913-1098
Fax: (608) 356-0752
E-mail: tmartin@uwc.edu
Phone: (608) 356-8351 ext. 255

University of Wisconsin-Eau Claire
www.uwec.edu
Center for International Education
112 Schofield Hall
Eau Claire, WI 54701
Fax: (715) 836-4948
E-mail: markgraf@uwec.edu
Phone: (715) 836-4411

University of Wisconsin-Fox Valley
www.uwfoxvalley.uwc.edu
Student Services
1478 Midway Road
Menasha, WI 54952-2850
Fax: (920) 832-2850
E-mail: foxinfo@uwc.edu
Phone: (920) 832-2620

University of Wisconsin-Green Bay
www.uwgb.edu
Office of International Student Services
2420 Nicolet Drive
Green Bay, WI 54311-7001
Fax: (920) 465-2949
E-mail: oie@uwgb.edu
Phone: (920) 465-2889

University of Wisconsin-La Crosse
www.uwlax.edu
Office of International Education
1725 State Street, Room 115 Main Hall
La Crosse, WI 54601
Fax: (608) 785-8923
E-mail: uwlworld@uwlax.edu
Phone: (608) 785-8016

University of Wisconsin-Madison
www.wisc.edu
Undergraduate Admissions Office
Armory & Gymnasium
716 Langdon Street
Madison, WI 53706-1481
Fax: (608) 262-7706
E-mail: onwisconsin@admissions.wisc.edu
Phone: (608) 262-3961

University of Wisconsin-Marathon County
www.uwmc.uwc.edu
Admissions
518 South Seventh Avenue
Wausau, WI 54401-5396
Fax: (715) 261-6331
E-mail: mhoppe@uwc.edu
Phone: (715) 261-6100

University of Wisconsin-Marinette
www.marinette.uwc.edu
Student Services
750 West Bay Shore Street
Marinette, WI 54143
Fax: (715) 735-4304
E-mail: cynthia.bailey@uwc.edu
Phone: (715) 735-4301

University of Wisconsin-Milwaukee
www.uwm.edu
International Admissions
Box 749
Milwaukee, WI 53201
Fax: (414) 229-0521
E-mail: isss@uwm.edu
Phone: (414) 229-4846

University of Wisconsin-Oshkosh
www.uwosh.edu
Dean of Students
800 Algoma Boulevard
Oshkosh, WI 54901-8602
Fax: (920) 424-1098
E-mail: mylrea@uwosh.edu
Phone: (920) 424-3100

University of Wisconsin-Parkside
www.uwp.edu
Admissions
PO Box 2000
Kenosha, WI 53141-2000
Fax: (262) 595-2008
E-mail: admissions@uwp.edu
Phone: (262) 595-2355

University of Wisconsin-Platteville
www.uwplatt.edu
Admissions
One University Plaza
Platteville, WI 53818
Fax: (608) 342-1122
E-mail: admit@uwplatt.edu
Phone: (608) 342-1125

University of Wisconsin-Richland
www.richland.uwc.edu
Registrar, University of Wisconsin Colleges
1200 Highway 14 West
Richland Center, WI 53581
Fax: (608) 262-7872
E-mail: cherie.hatlem@uwc.edu
Phone: (608) 262-9652

University of Wisconsin-River Falls
www.uwrf.edu
International Programs
410 South 3rd Street
112 South Hall
River Falls, WI 54022-5001
Fax: (715) 425-0693
E-mail: brent.d.greene@uwrf.edu
Phone: (715) 425-4891

University of Wisconsin-Rock County
www.rock.uwc.edu
Registrar
2909 Kellogg Avenue
Janesville, WI 53546-5699
Fax: (608) 758-6579
E-mail: rckinfo@uwc.edu
Phone: (608) 262-9652

University of Wisconsin-Sheboygan
www.sheboygan.uwc.edu
Student Services
One University Drive
Sheboygan, WI 53081
Fax: (920) 459-6662
E-mail: rcampopi@uwc.edu
Phone: (920) 459-6633

University of Wisconsin-Stevens Point
www.uwsp.edu
Foreign Student Office
Student Services Center
Stevens Point, WI 54481
Fax: (715) 346-3819
E-mail: fso@uwsp.edu
Phone: (715) 346-3849

University of Wisconsin-Stout
www.uwstout.edu
Office of International Programs
1 Clocktower Plaza
Menomonie, WI 54751
Fax: (715) 232-2500
E-mail: kuesterv@uwstout.edu
Phone: (715) 232-1896

University of Wisconsin-Superior
www.uwsuper.edu
Office of International Programs
Belknap and Catlin, PO Box 2000
Superior, WI 54880
Fax: (715) 394-8363
E-mail: international@uwsuper.edu
Phone: (715) 394-8052

University of Wisconsin-Washington County
washington.uwc.edu
Registrar's Office
400 University Drive
West Bend, WI 53095
Fax: (262) 335-5274
Phone: (608) 263-9652

University of Wisconsin-Waukesha
www.waukesha.uwc.edu
Registrar
1500 University Drive
Waukesha, WI 53188
Fax: (608) 265-9473
E-mail: cherie.hatlem@uwc.edu
Phone: (608) 262-9652

University of Wisconsin-Whitewater
www.uww.edu
International Education and Programs
800 West Main Street
Whitewater, WI 53190-1790
Fax: (262) 472-1491
E-mail: smithh@uww.edu
Phone: (262) 472-5178

University of Wyoming
www.uwyo.edu
Admissions Office
1000 East University Avenue/Department 3435
Knight Hall 146
Laramie, WY 82071
Fax: (307) 766-4042
E-mail: grzy@uwyo.edu
Phone: (307) 766-5160

Upper Iowa University
www.uiu.edu
Admission Office
Parker Fox Hall
PO Box 1859
Fayette, IA 52142
Fax: (563) 425-5277
E-mail: thongm@uiu.edu
Phone: (563) 425-5709

Ursinus College
www.ursinus.edu
Admissions
PO Box 1000
601 Main Street
Collegeville, PA 19426-1000
Fax: (610) 409-3662
E-mail: admissions@ursinus.edu
Phone: (610) 409-3200

Ursuline College
www.ursuline.edu
Admission
2550 Lander Road
Pepper Pike, OH 44124-4398
Fax: (440) 684-6138
E-mail: cmauer@ursuline.edu
Phone: (440) 449-4203

Utah State University
www.usu.edu
International Students and Scholars
0160 Old Main Hill
Logan, UT 84322-0160
Fax: (435) 797-3522
E-mail: jeannie.pacheco@usu.edu
Phone: (435) 797-1124

Utah Valley State College
www.uvsc.edu
International Admissions and Immigration
Affairs
800 West University Parkway
Orem, UT 84058-5999
Fax: (801) 225-4677
E-mail: info@uvsc.edu
Phone: (801) 863-8466 ext. 8475

Utica College
www.utica.edu
Director of International Admissions
1600 Burrstone Road
Utica, NY 13502-4892
Fax: (315) 792-3003
E-mail: cominsky@utica.edu
Phone: (315) 792-5290

Utica School of Commerce
www.uscny.edu
201 Bleecker Street
Utica, NY 13501
Fax: (315) 733-9281
E-mail: admissions@uscny.edu
Phone: (315) 733-2307

Valdosta State University
www.valdosta.edu
International Programs
1500 North Patterson Street
Valdosta, GA 31698
Fax: (229) 245-3849
E-mail: ibmcclel@valdosta.edu
Phone: (229) 333-7410

Valencia Community College
www.valenciacc.edu
Admissions and Records
PO Box 3028
Orlando, FL 32802-3028
Fax: (407) 582-1403
E-mail: rsimpson@valenciacc.edu
Phone: (407) 582-1506

Valley City State University
www.vcsu.edu
101 College Street SW
Valley City, ND 58072-4098
Fax: (701) 845-7299
E-mail: dan.klein@vcsu.edu
Phone: (701) 845-7204

Valley College of Technology
www.vct.edu
Admissions
287 Aikens Center
Martinsburg, WV 25404
Fax: (304) 263-2413
E-mail: gkennedy@vct.edu
Phone: (304) 263-0979

Valley Forge Christian College
www.vfcc.edu
Admissions
1401 Charlestown Road
Phoenixville, PA 19460
Fax: (610) 917-2069
E-mail: admissions@vfcc.edu
Phone: (800) 432-8322

Valley Forge Military College
www.vfmac.edu
1001 Eagle Road
Wayne, PA 19087
Fax: (610) 688-1545
E-mail: jlambert@vfmac.edu
Phone: (610) 989-1561

Valparaiso University
www.valpo.edu
Office of Admission
Kretzmann Hall, 1700 Chapel Drive
Valparaiso, IN 46383-6493
Fax: (219) 464-6898
E-mail: jennifer.smolnicky@valpo.edu
Phone: (219) 464-5011

Vance-Granville Community College
www.vgcc.edu
Registrar
Box 917
Henderson, NC 27536
Fax: (252) 430-0460
Phone: (252) 492-2061

Vanderbilt University
www.vanderbilt.edu
Undergraduate Admissions
2305 West End Avenue
Nashville, TN 37203-1727
Fax: (615) 343-7765
E-mail: intladmit@vanderbilt.edu
Phone: (615) 322-1906

VanderCook College of Music
www.vandercook.edu
3140 South Federal Street
Chicago, IL 60616-3731
Fax: (312) 225-5211
E-mail: admissions@vandercook.edu
Phone: (312) 225-6288 ext. 230

Vanguard University of Southern California
www.vanguard.edu
Undergraduate Admissions
55 Fair Drive
Costa Mesa, CA 92626-9601
Fax: (714) 966-5471
E-mail: cambria.larson@vanguard.edu
Phone: (714) 556-3610

Vassar College
www.vassar.edu
Office of Admissions
Box 10, 124 Raymond Avenue
Poughkeepsie, NY 12604-0077
Fax: (845) 437-7063
E-mail: admissions@vassar.edu
Phone: (845) 437-7300

Vatterott College
www.vatterott-college.edu
8580 Evans Avenue
Berkeley, MO 63134
Fax: (314) 522-6174
E-mail: adm@vatterot-college.edu
Phone: (314) 264-1040

Vatterott College
www.vatterott-college.com
4621 NW 23rd Street
Oklahoma City, OK 73127
Fax: (405) 945-0788
Phone: (405) 945-0088

Vatterott College: Memphis
www.vatterott-college.edu
2655 Dividend Drive
Memphis, TN 38132
Fax: (901) 763-2897
E-mail: paulette.thomas@vatterott-college.edu
Phone: (901) 761-5730

Vatterott College: Quincy
3609 North Marx Drive
Quincy, IL 62305
Fax: (217) 223-6771
Phone: (217) 224-0600

Vatterott College: Spring Valley
www.vatterott-college.com
11818 I Street
Omaha, NE 68137
Fax: (402) 891-9413
Phone: (402) 891-9411

Vaughn College of Aeronautics and Technology
www.vaughn.edu
Director of Admissions
86-01 23rd Avenue
Flushing, NY 11369
Fax: (718) 779-2231
E-mail: vincent.papandrea@vaughn.edu
Phone: (718) 429-6600 ext. 167

Ventura College
www.venturacollege.edu
Admissions & Records
4667 Telegraph Road
Ventura, CA 93003
Fax: (805) 654-6357
Phone: (805) 654-6457

Victor Valley College
www.vvc.edu
Admissions and Records
18422 Bear Valley Road
Victorville, CA 92392-5849
Fax: (760) 843-7707
E-mail: millenb@vvc.edu
Phone: (760) 245-4271 ext. 2668

Victoria College
www.victoriacollege.edu
Admissions and Records Office
2200 East Red River
Victoria, TX 77901
Fax: (361) 582-2525
E-mail: registrar@victoriacollege.edu
Phone: (361) 572-6400

Villa Julie College
www.vjc.edu
Admissions Office
1525 Greenspring Valley Road
Stevenson, MD 21153-0641
Fax: (443) 352-4440
E-mail: admissions@mail.vjc.edu
Phone: (443) 352-4410

Villa Maria College of Buffalo
www.villa.edu
Admissions
240 Pine Ridge Road
Buffalo, NY 14225-3999
Fax: (716) 896-0705
E-mail: admissions@villa.edu
Phone: (716) 896-0700 ext. 1870

Villanova University
www.villanova.edu
Office of University Admission
800 Lancaster Avenue
Villanova, PA 19085-1672
Fax: (610) 519-6450
E-mail: gotovu@villanova.edu
Phone: (610) 519-4000

Vincennes University
www.vinu.edu
Admissions
1002 North First Street
Vincennes, IN 47591
Fax: (812) 888-5707
E-mail: acrabtree@vinu.edu
Phone: (812) 888-4313

Virginia College at Huntsville
www.vc.edu
2800 Bob Wallace Avenue
Huntsville, AL 35805
Phone: (256) 533-7387

Virginia College at Pensacola
www.vc.edu/pensacola
19 West Garden Street
Pensacola, FL 32502
Fax: (850) 436-4838
E-mail: hrobbins@vc.edu
Phone: (850) 436-8444

Virginia Commonwealth University
www.vcu.edu
Office of International Admissions
Box 842526
821 West Franklin Street
Richmond, VA 23284-2526
Fax: (804) 828-1829
E-mail: vcuia@vcu.edu
Phone: (804) 828-6016

Virginia Intermont College
www.vic.edu
Admissions Office
1013 Moore Street
Campus Box D-460
Bristol, VA 24201
Fax: (276) 466-7855
E-mail: viadmit@vic.edu
Phone: (276) 466-7856

Virginia Marti College of Art and Design
www.vmcad.edu
Admissions
11724 Detroit Avenue
Lakewood, OH 44107
Fax: (216) 221-2311
E-mail: dmarti@virginiamarticollege.com
Phone: (216) 221-8584

Virginia Military Institute
www.vmi.edu
Admissions
319 Letcher Avenue
Lexington, VA 24450-9967
Fax: (540) 464-7746
E-mail: admissions@vmi.edu
Phone: (540) 464-7211

Virginia Polytechnic Institute and State University
www.vt.edu
201 Burruss Hall
Blacksburg, VA 24061-0202
Fax: (540) 231-3242
E-mail: vtadmiss@vt.edu
Phone: (540) 231-6267

Virginia State University
www.vsu.edu
Orientation and Advisement
One Hayden Street
PO Box 9018
Petersburg, VA 23806
Fax: (804) 524-5466
E-mail: fmarshall@vsu.edu
Phone: (804) 524-5562

Virginia Union University
www.vuu.edu
Office of Admissions
1500 North Lombardy Street
Richmond, VA 23220
Fax: (804) 342-3511
E-mail: admissions@vuu.edu
Phone: (804) 342-3571

Virginia Wesleyan College
www.vwc.edu
Admissions Office
1584 Wesleyan Drive
Norfolk, VA 23502-5599
Fax: (757) 461-5238
E-mail: admissions@vwc.edu
Phone: (757) 455-5717

Viterbo University
www.viterbo.edu
Office of Global Education
900 Viterbo Drive
La Crosse, WI 54601-8804
Fax: (608) 796-3050
E-mail: globaled@viterbo.edu
Phone: (608) 796-3172

Volunteer State Community College
www.volstate.edu
Admissions
1480 Nashville Pike
Gallatin, TN 37066
Fax: (615) 230-4875
E-mail: tim.amyx@volstate.edu
Phone: (615) 452-8600 ext. 3614

Voorhees College
www.voorhees.edu
Office of Admissions
213 Wiggins Road
PO Box 678
Denmark, SC 29042
Fax: (803) 780-1444
E-mail: williej@voorhees.edu
Phone: (803) 780-1049

Wabash College
www.wabash.edu
Coordinator of International Admissions
PO Box 352
Crawfordsville, IN 47933
Fax: (765) 361-6437
E-mail: merkelr@wabash.edu
Phone: (765) 361-6405

Wagner College
www.wagner.edu
Admissions
One Campus Road
Staten Island, NY 10301-4495
Fax: (718) 390-3105
E-mail: adm@wagner.edu
Phone: (718) 390-3411

Wake Forest University
www.wfu.edu
Admissions
PO Box 7305
Winston-Salem, NC 27109-7305
Fax: (336) 758-4324
E-mail: admissions@wfu.edu
Phone: (336) 758-5201

Wake Technical Community College
www.waketech.edu
International Student Coordinator
9101 Fayetteville Road
Raleigh, NC 27603
Fax: (919) 662-3529
E-mail: smcaison@waketech.edu
Phone: (919) 866-5428

Walden University
www.waldenu.edu
Admissions
650 South Exeter Street 8th Floor
Baltimore, MD 21202
E-mail: admissions@laureate-inc.com
Phone: (800) 925-3368

Waldorf College
www.waldorf.edu
International Admissions
106 South Sixth Street
Forest City, IA 50436-1713
Fax: (641) 585-8125
E-mail: admissions@waldorf.edu
Phone: (641) 585-8124

Walla Walla Community College
www.wwcc.edu
Admissions
500 Tausick Way
Walla Walla, WA 99362-9972
Fax: (509) 527-3661
E-mail: sally.wagoner@wwcc.edu
Phone: (509) 527-4283

Walla Walla University
www.wallawalla.edu
Admissions
204 South College Avenue
College Place, WA 99324-3000
Fax: (509) 527-2397
E-mail: dallas.weis@wallawalla.edu
Phone: (800) 541-8900 ext. 2608

Walsh College of Accountancy and Business Administration
www.walshcollege.edu
Admissions and Academic Advising
PO Box 7006
Troy, MI 48007-7006
Fax: (248) 823-1611
E-mail: admissions@walshcollege.edu
Phone: (248) 823-1610

Walsh University
www.walsh.edu
Admissions
2020 East Maple Street
North Canton, OH 44720-3396
Fax: (330) 490-7165
E-mail: admissions@walsh.edu
Phone: (330) 490-7172

Walters State Community College
www.ws.edu
Enrollment Development
500 South Davy Crockett Parkway
Morristown, TN 37813-6899
Fax: (423) 585-6786
E-mail: sherry.watson@ws.edu
Phone: (423) 585-2691

Warner Pacific College
www.warnerpacific.edu
2219 SE 68th Avenue
Portland, OR 97215-4026
Fax: (503) 517-1352
E-mail: jpowell@warnerpacific.edu
Phone: (503) 517-1024

Warner Southern College
www.warner.edu
Admissions
13895 Highway 27
Lake Wales, FL 33859
Fax: (863) 638-7290
E-mail: roej@warner.edu
Phone: (863) 638-7213

Warren Wilson College
www.warren-wilson.edu
Office of Admission
Box 9000
Asheville, NC 28815-9000
Fax: (828) 298-1440
E-mail: admit@warren-wilson.edu
Phone: (828) 771-2073

Wartburg College
www.wartburg.edu
Office of Admissions
100 Wartburg Boulevard, PO Box 1003
Waverly, IA 50677-0903
Fax: (319) 352-8579
E-mail: global.admissions@wartburg.edu
Phone: (319) 352-8511

Washburn University
www.washburn.edu
International Student Services
1700 Southwest College, Morgan 114
Topeka, KS 66621
Fax: (785) 670-1067
E-mail: international@washburn.edu
Phone: (785) 670-1051

Washington & Jefferson College
www.washjeff.edu
Admission Office
60 South Lincoln Street
Washington, PA 15301
Fax: (724) 223-6534
E-mail: bkoerber@washjeff.edu
Phone: (724) 223-6025

Washington and Lee University
www.wlu.edu
Admissions
204 West Washington Street
Lexington, VA 24450-2116
Fax: (540) 458-8062
E-mail: admissions@wlu.edu
Phone: (540) 458-8710

Washington Bible College
www.bible.edu
Admissions
6511 Princess Garden Parkway
Lanham, MD 20706-3599
Fax: (301) 552-2775
E-mail: admissions@bible.edu
Phone: (301) 552-1400 ext. 1208

Washington College
www.washcoll.edu
300 Washington Avenue
Chestertown, MD 21620-1197
Fax: (410) 778-7287
E-mail: tlittlefield2@washcoll.edu
Phone: (410) 778-7700

Washington County Community College
www.wccc.me.edu
Admissions
One College Drive
Calais, ME 04619
Fax: (207) 454-1026
E-mail: admissions@wccc.me.edu
Phone: (207) 454-1048

Washington State University
www.wsu.edu
International Programs, Enrollment
370 Lighty Student Services Bldg
PO Box 641067
Pullman, WA 99164-1067
Fax: (509) 335-2373
E-mail: international@wsu.edu
Phone: (509) 335-4508

Washington University in St. Louis
www.wustl.edu
Office of Undergraduate Admissions
Campus Box 1089, One Brookings Drive
St. Louis, MO 63130-4899
Fax: (314) 935-4290
E-mail: admissions@wustl.edu
Phone: (314) 935-6000

Washtenaw Community College
www.wccnet.edu
Enrollment Services
4800 East Huron River Drive
Box D-1
Ann Arbor, MI 48106-1610
Fax: (734) 677-5414
E-mail: studrec@wccnet.org
Phone: (734) 973-3315

Waycross College
www.waycross.edu
Admissions
2001 South Georgia Parkway
Waycross, GA 31503
Fax: (912) 295-6158
E-mail: sdukes@waycross.edu
Phone: (912) 285-6133

Wayland Baptist University
www.wbu.edu
Admissions
1900 West Seventh Street, CMB #712
Plainview, TX 79072
Fax: (806) 291-1960
E-mail: admityou@wbu.edu
Phone: (806) 291-3500

Wayne County Community College
www.wcccd.edu
801 West Fort Street
Detroit, MI 48226
Fax: (313) 962-1643
E-mail: mfinley1@wcccd.edu
Phone: (313) 496-2725

Wayne State College
www.wsc.edu
Admissions Office
1111 Main Street
Wayne, NE 68787
Fax: (402) 375-7204
E-mail: admit1@wsc.edu
Phone: (402) 375-7234

Wayne State University
www.wayne.edu
Office of Admissions
42 West Warren
Detroit, MI 48202
Fax: (313) 577-7536
E-mail: admissions@wayne.edu
Phone: (313) 577-3577

Waynesburg University
www.waynesburg.edu
Admission Counselor
51 West College Street
Waynessburg, PA 15370-1222
Fax: (724) 627-8124
E-mail: kwhite@waynesburg.edu
Phone: (724) 852-3216

Weatherford College
www.wc.edu
225 College Park Drive
Weatherford, TX 76086
Fax: (817) 598-6205
E-mail: sstorm@wc.edu
Phone: (817) 598-6349

Webb Institute
www.webb-institute.edu
298 Crescent Beach Road
Glen Cove, NY 11542-1398
Fax: (516) 674-9838
E-mail: admissions@webb-institute.edu
Phone: (516) 671-2213

Webber International University
www.webber.edu
Admissions
1201 North Scenic Highway
PO Box 96
Babson Park, FL 33827-0096
Fax: (863) 638-1591
E-mail: admissions@webber.edu
Phone: (863) 638-2910

Weber State University
www.weber.edu
Director of Admissions
1137 University Circle
Ogden, UT 84408-1137
Fax: (801) 626-6747
E-mail: ccrivera@weber.edu
Phone: (801) 626-7670

Webster University
www.webster.edu
International Recruitment and International
Services
470 East Lockwood Avenue
St. Louis, MO 63119-3194
Fax: (314) 968-7122
E-mail: intlstudy@webster.edu
Phone: (314) 968-7433

Wellesley College
www.wellesley.edu
Admissions Office
106 Central Street
Wellesley, MA 02481-8203
Fax: (781) 283-3678
E-mail: admission@wellesley.edu
Phone: (781) 283-2270

Wells College
www.wells.edu
Admissions
170 Main Street
Aurora, NY 13026
Fax: (315) 364-3227
E-mail: admissions@wells.edu
Phone: (315) 364-3264

Wenatchee Valley College
www.wvc.edu
Student Development
1300 Fifth Street
Wenatchee, WA 98801-1799
Fax: (509) 682-6801
E-mail: jkuhlmann@wvc.edu
Phone: (509) 682-6846

Wentworth Institute of Technology
www.wit.edu
Admissions Office
550 Huntington Avenue
Boston, MA 02115
Fax: (617) 989-4010
E-mail: hincheyr@wit.edu
Phone: (617) 989-4030

Wentworth Military Junior College
wjc.wma.edu
1880 Washington Avenue
Lexington, MO 64067-1799
Fax: (660) 259-3395
E-mail: admissions@wma1880.org
Phone: (660) 259-2221 ext. 517

Wesley College
www.wesley.edu
120 North State Street
Dover, DE 19901-3875
Fax: (302) 736-2301
E-mail: jacobsar@wesley.edu
Phone: (302) 736-2428

Wesleyan College
www.wesleyancollege.edu
Admissions
4760 Forsyth Road
Macon, GA 31210-4462
Fax: (478) 757-4030
E-mail: admission@wesleyancollege.edu
Phone: (478) 757-5206

Wesleyan University
www.wesleyan.edu
Office of Admission
70 Wyllys Avenue
Middletown, CT 06459-0260
Fax: (860) 685-3001
E-mail: toverton@wesleyan.edu
Phone: (860) 685-3000

West Central Technical College
www.westcentraltech.edu
176 Murphy Campus Boulevard
Waco, GA 30182
Fax: (770) 537-7995
Phone: (770) 537-5740

West Chester University of Pennsylvania
www.wcupa.edu
Messikomer Hall
West Chester, PA 19383
Fax: (610) 436-2907
E-mail: lkeiser@wcupa.edu
Phone: (610) 436-2943

West Coast University
www.westcoastuniversity.com/
4021 Rosewood Avenue
Los Angeles, CA 90004
Phone: (877) 505-4928

West Hills College: Coalinga
www.westhillscollege.com
300 Cherry Lane
Coalinga, CA 93210
Fax: (559) 935-2788
E-mail: danieltamayo@westhillscollege.com
Phone: (559) 934-2000 ext. 2432

West Hills College: Lemoore
www.westhillscollege.com
Daniel Tamayo
555 College Avenue
Lemoore, CA 93245
Fax: (559) 925-3837
E-mail: danieltamayo@westhillscollege.com
Phone: (559) 934-2000 ext. 2432

West Liberty State College
www.westliberty.edu
Box 295
West Liberty, WV 26074-0295
Fax: (304) 336-8403
E-mail: wladmsn1@wlsc.edu
Phone: (304) 336-8076

West Los Angeles College
www.wlac.edu
International Student Office
9000 Overland Avenue
Culver City, CA 90230
Fax: (310) 837-4062
Phone: (310) 287-4362

West Suburban College of Nursing
www.wscn.edu
Three Erie Court
Oak Park, IL 60302
Fax: (708) 763-1531
E-mail: wsadmis@wscn.edu
Phone: (708) 763-6530

West Texas A&M University
www.wtamu.edu
International Student Office
2501 Fourth Avenue, WTAMU Box 60907
Canyon, TX 79016-0001
Fax: (806) 651-2071
E-mail: kcombs@mail.wtamu.edu
Phone: (806) 651-2073

West Valley College
www.westvalley.edu
Counseling Center - Foreign Student Adviser
14000 Fruitvale Avenue
Saratoga, CA 95070-5698
Fax: (408) 867-5033
Phone: (408) 741-2009

West Virginia Business College
www.wvbc.edu
1052 Main Street
Wheeling, WV 26003
Fax: (304) 232-0363
E-mail: info@wvbc.edu
Phone: (304) 624-7695

West Virginia Career Institute
www.wvci.edu
Route 119 North and Mount Braddock Road
Mount Braddock, PA 15465
Fax: (724) 437-6053
Phone: (724) 437-4600

West Virginia Junior College: Bridgeport
www.wvjcinfo.net
176 Thompson Drive
Bridgeport, WV 26330
Phone: (304) 842-4007

West Virginia State Community and Technical College
www.wvsctc.edu
Admissions
PO Box 1000
106 Ferrell Hall
Institute, WV 25112-1000
Fax: (304) 766-4104
E-mail: admission@wvstateu.edu
Phone: (304) 766-3221

West Virginia University
www.wvu.edu
International Admissions
Admissions and Records Office
PO Box 6009
Morgantown, WV 26506-6009
Fax: (304) 293-8832
E-mail:
internationaladmissions@mail.wvu.edu
Phone: (304) 293-2124

West Virginia University at Parkersburg
www.wvup.edu
Admissions and Records
300 Campus Drive
Parkersburg, WV 26104-8647
Fax: (304) 424-8332
E-mail: cecelia.malhotra@mail.wvu.edu
Phone: (304) 424-8220

West Virginia Wesleyan College
www.wvwc.edu
Admission
59 College Avenue
Buckhannon, WV 26201-2998
Fax: (304) 473-8108
E-mail: admission@wvwc.edu
Phone: (304) 473-8510

Westchester Community College
www.sunywcc.edu
Office of Admissions
75 Grasslands Road
Valhalla, NY 10595
Fax: (914) 606-6540
E-mail: admissions@sunywcc.edu
Phone: (914) 606-6735

Western Career College: Antioch
www.westerncollege.edu
2157 Country Hills Road
Antioch, CA 94531
Fax: (925) 280-0267
Phone: (925) 280-0235

Western Career College: Stockton
www.westerncollege.edu
1313 West Robinhood Drive Suite B
Stockton, CA 95207

Western Carolina University
www.wcu.edu
International Programs and Services
102 Camp Building
Cullowhee, NC 28723
Fax: (828) 227-7422
E-mail: lmwaniki@email.wcu.edu
Phone: (828) 227-7494

Western Illinois University
www.wiu.edu
International Programs
One University Circle
115 Sherman Hall
Macomb, IL 61455-1390
Fax: (309) 298-2245
E-mail: international-ed@wiu.edu
Phone: (309) 298-2426

Western International University
www.wintu.edu
University Services
9215 North Black Canyon Highway
Phoenix, AZ 85021
Fax: (602) 944-1831
E-mail: jo.arney@apollogrp.edu
Phone: (602) 943-2311 ext. 1012

Western Iowa Tech Community College
www.witcc.com
Enrollment Services
Box 5199
Sioux City, IA 51102-5199
Fax: (712) 274-6412
E-mail: bolanol@witcc.cc.ia.us
Phone: (712) 274-8733 ext. 1241

Western Kentucky University
www.wku.edu
International Programs
1906 College Heights Boulevard
Bowling Green, KY 42101
Fax: (270) 745-6144
E-mail: robin.borczon@wku.edu
Phone: (270) 745-4857

Western Michigan University
www.wmich.edu
International Services and Student Affairs
1903 West Michigan Avenue
Kalamazoo, MI 49008-5211
Fax: (269) 387-5899
E-mail: rebecca.solomon@wmich.edu
Phone: (269) 387-5876

Western Nebraska Community College
www.wn.edu
Registrar
1601 East 27th Street
Scottsbluff, NE 69361
Fax: (308) 635-6732
E-mail: rhovey@wncc.net
Phone: (308) 635-6013

Western Nevada College
www.wnc.edu
Admission and Records
2201 West College Parkway
Carson City, NV 89703-7399
Fax: (775) 887-3147
E-mail: dianne@wnc.nevada.edu
Phone: (775) 445-3288

Western New England College
www.wnec.edu
Admissions
1215 Wilbraham Road
Springfield, MA 01119-2684
Fax: (413) 782-1777
E-mail: ugradmis@wnec.edu
Phone: (413) 782-1321

Western New Mexico University
www.wnmu.edu
Admissions
Castorena 106
Box 680
Silver City, NM 88062
Fax: (505) 538-6127
E-mail: tresslerd@wnmu.edu
Phone: (505) 538-6000

Western Oklahoma State College
www.wosc.edu
2801 North Main Street
Altus, OK 73521
Fax: (580) 477-7723
E-mail: larry.paxton@wosc.edu
Phone: (580) 477-7720

Western Oregon University
www.wou.edu
International Students and Scholar Affairs
345 North Monmouth Avenue
Monmouth, OR 97361
Fax: (503) 838-8067
E-mail: yangn@wou.edu
Phone: (503) 838-8590

Western State College of Colorado
www.western.edu
International Student Programs
600 North Adams Street
Gunnison, CO 81231
Fax: (970) 943-2212
E-mail: bsamter@western.edu
Phone: (970) 943-2176

Western Technical College
www.wtc-ep.edu
Admissions
9624 Plaza Circle
El Paso, TX 79927
E-mail: jmartin@wtc-ep.edu
Phone: (915) 760-8123

Western Technical College
www.westerntc.edu
Counseling Center
PO Box 908
La Crosse, WI 54602-0908
Fax: (608) 785-9094
E-mail: wellsj@westerntc.edu
Phone: (608) 785-9575

Western Texas College
www.wtc.edu
International Studies
6200 College Avenue
Snyder, TX 79549
Fax: (325) 573-9321
E-mail: jsentell@wtc.edu
Phone: (325) 573-8511 ext. 207

Western Washington University
www.wwu.edu
Office of Admissions
516 High Street
Bellingham, WA 98225-9009
Fax: (360) 650-7369
E-mail: admit@wwu.edu
Phone: (360) 650-3440

Western Wyoming Community College
www.wwcc.wy.edu
Admissions
Box 428
Rock Springs, WY 82902-0428
Fax: (307) 382-1636
E-mail: admissions@wwcc.wy.edu
Phone: (307) 382-1647

Westminster College
www.westminster-mo.edu
Office of Off-Campus and International
Programs
501 Westminster Avenue
Fulton, MO 65251-1299
Fax: (573) 592-5217
E-mail: veltrot@westminster-mo.edu
Phone: (573) 592-5175

Westminster College
www.westminster.edu
Admissions, Westminster College
South Market Street
New Wilmington, PA 16172-0001
Fax: (724) 946-7171
E-mail: admis@westminster.edu
Phone: (724) 946-7100

Westminster College
www.westminstercollege.edu
Admissions Office
1840 South 1300 East
Salt Lake City, UT 84105
Fax: (801) 832-3101
E-mail: admission@westminstercollege.edu
Phone: (801) 832-2200

Westmont College
www.westmont.edu
International Student Coordinator, Sandy Lyon
955 La Paz Road
Santa Barbara, CA 93108-1089
Fax: (805) 565-6234
E-mail: slyon@westmont.edu
Phone: (800) 777-9011

Westwood College: Anaheim
www.westwood.edu
1551 South Douglass Road
Anaheim, CA 92806
Phone: (714) 938-6140 ext. 60100

Westwood College: Chicago Loop
www.westwood.edu
17 North State Street, Suite 300
Chicago, IL 60602
Fax: (312) 739-1004
Phone: (312) 739-0850

Westwood College: Denver South
www.westwood.edu
Admissions
3150 South Sheridan Boulevard
Denver, CO 80227-5507
Fax: (303) 934-2583
Phone: (303) 934-1122

Westwood College: DuPage
www.westwood.edu
7155 Janes Avenue
Woodridge, IL 60517
Fax: (630) 434-8255
Phone: (630) 434-8244

Westwood College: Houston South
www.westwood.edu/
7322 Southwest Freeway
Suite 110
Houston, TX 77074
Fax: (713) 219-2088
E-mail: tlevinthal@westwood.edu
Phone: (866) 340-3677

Westwood College: Los Angeles
www.westwood.edu
3250 Wilshire Boulevard, Suite 400
Los Angeles, CA 90010
Phone: (213) 739-9999

Westwood College: O'Hare Airport
www.westwood.edu
Executive Director
8501 West Higgins Road
Suite 100
Chicago, IL 60631
Fax: (773) 714-0828
E-mail: astutts@westwood.edu
Phone: (773) 380-6820

Westwood College: River Oaks
www.westwood.edu
80 River Oaks Center, Suite D-49
Calumet City, IL 60409
Phone: (708) 832-1988

Westwood College: South Bay
19700 South Vermont Avenue #100
Long Beach, CA 90502
Phone: (310) 965-0888

Whatcom Community College
www.whatcom.ctc.edu
International Programs Office
237 West Kellogg Road
Bellingham, WA 98226
Fax: (360) 752-6767
E-mail: ied@whatcom.ctc.edu
Phone: (360) 676-2170 ext. 3910

Wheaton College
www.wheaton.edu
International Student Services
501 College Avenue
Wheaton, IL 60187-5593
Fax: (630) 752-5735
E-mail: karen.l.martin@wheaton.edu
Phone: (630) 752-5191

Wheaton College
www.wheatoncollege.edu
Office of Admission
26 East Main Street
Norton, MA 02766
Fax: (508) 286-8271
E-mail: admission@wheatoncollege.edu
Phone: (508) 286-8251

Wheeling Jesuit University
www.wju.edu
International Student Advisor's Office
316 Washington Avenue
Wheeling, WV 26003-6295
Fax: (304) 243-2243
E-mail: eileenv@wju.edu
Phone: (800) 624-6992 ext. 2346

Wheelock College
www.wheelock.edu
Office of Admission
200 The Riverway
Boston, MA 02215-4176
Fax: (617) 879-2449
E-mail: undergrad@wheelock.edu
Phone: (617) 879-2206

White Earth Tribal and Community College
www.wetcc.org
202 South Main Street
PO Box 478
Mahnomen, MN 56557
E-mail: molson@wetcc.org
Phone: (218) 936-5731

White Mountains Community College
www.berlin.ccsnh.edu
Admissions
2020 Riverside Drive
Berlin, NH 03570
Fax: (603) 752-6335
E-mail: mlaflamme@nhctc.edu
Phone: (603) 752-1113 ext. 1004

Whitman College
www.whitman.edu
Admission
345 Boyer Avenue
Walla Walla, WA 99362-2046
Fax: (509) 527-4967
E-mail: cabascja@whitman.edu
Phone: (509) 527-5176

Whittier College
www.whittier.edu
Admissions
13406 East Philadelphia Street
Box 634
Whittier, CA 90608-0634
Fax: (562) 907-4870
E-mail: admission@whittier.edu
Phone: (562) 907-4238

Whitworth University
www.whitworth.edu
Undergraduate Admissions
300 West Hawthorne Road
Spokane, WA 99251-0002
Fax: (509) 466-3758
E-mail: hdonkor@whitworth.edu
Phone: (509) 777-4571

Wichita State University
www.wichita.edu
Office of International Admissions
1845 Fairmount Box 124
Wichita, KS 67260-0124
Fax: (316) 978-3777
E-mail: international@wichita.edu
Phone: (316) 978-3232

Widener University
www.widener.edu
Office of Admissions
One University Place
Chester, PA 19013
Fax: (610) 499-4676
E-mail: admissions.office@widener.edu
Phone: (610) 499-4595

Wilberforce University
www.wilberforce.edu
Academic Affairs
1055 North Bickett Road
PO Box 1001
Wilberforce, OH 45384-1001
Fax: (937) 376-4751
E-mail: admissions@wilberforce.edu
Phone: (937) 708-5705

Wiley College
www.wileyc.edu
711 Wiley Avenue
Marshall, TX 75670
Fax: (903) 927-3366
E-mail: smasenda@wileyc.edu
Phone: (903) 927-3242 ext. 3242

Willamette University
www.willamette.edu
Office of Admission
900 State Street
Salem, OR 97301-3922
Fax: (503) 375-5363
E-mail: libarts@willamette.edu
Phone: (503) 370-6303

William Carey University
www.wmcarey.edu
Admissions
498 Tuscan Avenue
WCC Box 13
Hattiesburg, MS 39401
Fax: (601) 318-6765
E-mail: admissions@wmcarey.edu
Phone: (601) 318-6103 ext. 564

William Jessup University
www.jessup.edu
Admission Office
333 Sunset Boulevard
Rocklin, CA 95765
Fax: (916) 577-2220
E-mail: admissions@jessup.edu
Phone: (916) 577-2222

William Jewell College
www.jewell.edu
Office of International Studies
500 College Hill
Liberty, MO 64068
Fax: (816) 415-6996
E-mail: grovesj@william.jewell.edu
Phone: (816) 415-5985

William Paterson University of New Jersey
www.wpunj.edu
Admissions
300 Pompton Road
Wayne, NJ 07470
Fax: (973) 720-2910
E-mail: admissions@wpunj.edu
Phone: (973) 720-3508

William Penn University
www.wmpenn.edu
Admissions Office
201 Trueblood Avenue
Oskaloosa, IA 52577
Fax: (641) 673-2113
E-mail: ottossonj@wmpenn.edu
Phone: (641) 673-1012

William Woods University
www.williamwoods.edu
Office of Enrollment Services
One University Avenue
Fulton, MO 65251-2388
Fax: (573) 592-1146
E-mail: admissions@williamwoods.edu
Phone: (573) 592-4221

Williams Baptist College
www.wbcoll.edu
Admissions
PO Box 3665
Walnut Ridge, AR 72476
Fax: (870) 886-3924
E-mail: admissions@wbcoll.edu
Phone: (870) 759-4120

Williams College
www.williams.edu
33 Stetson Court
Williamstown, MA 01267
Fax: (413) 597-4052
E-mail: admission@williams.edu
Phone: (413) 597-2211

Williston State College
www.wsc.nodak.edu
Admission & Records Office
1410 University Avenue
Box 1326
Williston, ND 58802-1326
Fax: (701) 774-4211
E-mail: keith.dawson@wsc.nodak.edu
Phone: (701) 774-4554

Wilmington College
www.wilmington.edu
Student Life
Box 1325 Pyle Center
Wilmington, OH 45177
Fax: (937) 382-7077
E-mail: mark_denniston@wilmington.edu
Phone: (937) 382-6661 ext. 264

Wilson College
www.wilson.edu
Admissions
1015 Philadelphia Avenue
Chambersburg, PA 17201-1285
Fax: (717) 262-2546
E-mail: admissions@wilson.edu
Phone: (717) 262-2002

Wilson Community College
www.wilsoncc.edu
Student Services
Box 4305
Wilson, NC 27893-0305
Fax: (252) 246-1384
E-mail: jebison@wilsontech.edu
Phone: (252) 246-1230

Wingate University
www.wingate.edu
Admissions
Campus Box 3059
Wingate, NC 28174-0157
Fax: (704) 233-8110
E-mail: admit@wingate.edu
Phone: (704) 233-8202

Winona State University
www.winona.edu
Director of International Students
Office of Admissions
PO Box 5838
Winona, MN 55987
Fax: (507) 457-5620
E-mail: tmarkos@winona.msus.edu
Phone: (507) 457-5303

Winston-Salem State University
www.wssu.edu
International Student Affairs
601 Martin Luther King Jr Drive
PO Box 19413
Winston-Salem, NC 27110
Fax: (336) 750-2079
E-mail: ayuninjamf@wssu.edu
Phone: (336) 750-2306

Winthrop University
www.winthrop.edu
701 Oakland Avenue
Rock Hill, SC 29733
Fax: (803) 323-2137
E-mail: barberd@winthrop.edu
Phone: (803) 323-4764

Wisconsin Indianhead Technical College
www.witc.edu
Financial Aid
505 Pine Ridge Drive
Shell Lake, WI 54871
Fax: (715) 468-2819
E-mail: sevenson@witc.edu
Phone: (715) 468-2815 ext. 2246

Wittenberg University
www.wittenberg.edu
Assistant Director
Ward Street and North Wittenberg
PO Box 720
Springfield, OH 45501-0720
Fax: (937) 327-7453
E-mail: swelker@wittenberg.edu
Phone: (800) 677-7558 ext. 6376

Wofford College
www.wofford.edu
Admission
429 North Church Street
Spartanburg, SC 29303-3663
Fax: (864) 597-4147
E-mail: admission@wofford.edu
Phone: (864) 597-4130

Woodbury University
www.woodbury.edu
Admissions
7500 Glenoaks Boulevard
Burbank, CA 91510-7846
Fax: (818) 767-7520
E-mail: admissions@woodbury.edu
Phone: (800) 784-9663

Worcester Polytechnic Institute
www.wpi.edu
Admissions
100 Institute Road
Worcester, MA 01609-2280
Fax: (508) 831-5875
E-mail: intl_admissions@wpi.edu
Phone: (508) 831-5286

Worcester State College
www.worcester.edu
International Student Programs
486 Chandler Street
Worcester, MA 01602-2597
Fax: (508) 929-8012
E-mail: schao@worcester.edu
Phone: (508) 929-8747

World College
www.cie-wc.edu
Lake Shore Plaza, 5193 Shore Drive, Suite 105
Virginia Beach, VA 23455-2500
E-mail: instruct@cie-wc.edu
Phone: (800) 696-7532

World Mission University
www.wmu.edu
Admissions Department
500 Shatto Place
Los Angeles, CA 90020
Fax: (213) 385-2332
E-mail: wmuoffice@gmail.com
Phone: (213) 385-2322

Wright State University
www.wright.edu
University Center for International Education
3640 Colonel Glenn Highway
Dayton, OH 45435
Fax: (937) 775-5776
E-mail: claudia.espinoza@wright.edu
Phone: (937) 775-5745

Wright State University: Lake Campus
www.wright.edu/lake
University Center for International Education
7600 State Route 703
Celina, OH 45822-2952
Fax: (937) 775-5776
E-mail: claudia.espinoza@wright.edu
Phone: (937) 775-5745

WyoTech: Fremont
www.wyotech.com
200 Whitney Place
Fremont, CA 94539
Fax: (510) 490-8599
Phone: (510) 490-6900

WyoTech: Laramie
www.wyotech.com
Admissions
4373 North Third Street
Laramie, WY 82072
Fax: (307) 742-4852
E-mail: admissions@wyotech.com
Phone: (307) 742-3776

WyoTech: Long Beach
www.nitschools.com
2161 Technology Place
Long Beach, CA 90810
Fax: (562) 437-8111
Phone: (562) 624-9530

Xavier University
www.xavier.edu
Undergraduate Admission for ESL and
Undergraduate Programs
3800 Victory Parkway
Cincinnati, OH 45207-5311
Fax: (513) 745-4319
E-mail: goodloe@xavier.edu
Phone: (513) 745-3163

Xavier University of Louisiana
www.xula.edu
Center for Intercultural and International
Programs
1 Drexel Drive
New Orleans, LA 70125-1098
Fax: (504) 520-7920
E-mail: crbaquet@xula.edu
Phone: (504) 520-5491

Yakima Valley Community College
www.yvcc.edu
Manager, Housing and International Students
PO Box 22520
Yakima, WA 98907-2520
Fax: (509) 574-4882
E-mail: bmugleston@yvcc.edu
Phone: (509) 574-4880

Yale University
www.yale.edu
Undergraduate Admissions
Box 208234
New Haven, CT 06520-8234
Fax: (203) 432-9392
E-mail: undergraduate.admissions@yale.edu
Phone: (203) 432-9300

Yavapai College
www.yc.edu
Registration
1100 East Sheldon Street
Prescott, AZ 86301
Fax: (928) 776-2151
E-mail: registration@yc.edu
Phone: (928) 776-2188

Yeshiva College of the Nations Capital
1216 Arcola Avenue
Silver Spring, MD 20902
Phone: (301) 593-2534

Yeshiva Mikdash Melech
1326 Ocean Parkway
Brooklyn, NY 11230
Fax: (718) 998-9321
E-mail: mikdashmelech@covad.net
Phone: (718) 339-1090

Yeshivath Beth Moshe
930 Hickory Street
Scranton, PA 18505
Fax: (717) 346-2251
Phone: (717) 346-1747

York College
www.york.edu
1125 East 8th Street
York, NE 68467
Fax: (402) 363-5623
E-mail: clones@york.edu
Phone: (402) 363-5620

York College of Pennsylvania
www.ycp.edu
Admissions
441 Country Club Road
York, PA 17403-3651
Fax: (717) 849-1607
E-mail: admissions@ycp.edu
Phone: (800) 455-8018

York County Community College
www.yccc.edu
112 College Drive
Wells, ME 04090
E-mail: admissions@yccc.edu
Phone: (207) 646-9282 ext. 304

Young Harris College
www.yhc.edu
Admissions
PO Box 116
Young Harris, GA 30582-0116
Fax: (706) 379-3108
E-mail: mmashburn@yhc.edu
Phone: (706) 379-3111 ext. 5172

Youngstown State University
www.ysu.edu
International Undergraduate Admissions
One University Plaza
Youngstown, OH 44555-0001
Fax: (330) 941-3674
E-mail: intadm@ysu.edu
Phone: (330) 941-2000

YTI Career Institute: Lancaster
www.yti.edu
3050 Hempland Road
Lancaster, PA 17601
Fax: (717) 295-1135
E-mail: amy.daveler@yti.edu
Phone: (717) 295-1100

Yuba Community College District
www.yccd.edu
Dean, Student Development
2088 North Beale Road
Marysville, CA 95901
Fax: (530) 634-7709
E-mail: dfarrell@yccd.edu
Phone: (530) 741-6706

Zane State College
www.zanestate.edu
Student Success Center
1555 Newark Road
Zanesville, OH 43701-2626
Fax: (740) 454-0035
E-mail: sclapper@matc.tec.oh.us
Phone: (740) 588-1321

Zion Bible College
www.zbc.edu
Admissions Office
27 Middle Highway
Barrington, RI 02806
Fax: (401) 246-0906
E-mail: admissions@zbc.edu
Phone: (401) 246-0900 ext. 2132

 # EducationUSA
Advising Centers

Albania

Tirana
EducationUSA Advising Center
Rruga Deshmoret e 4 shkurtit
P 1, a 5
Tirana, Albania
Tel: 355-4269 955; 0692411335
E-mail: acie_albania@yahoo.com
Web: http://tirana.usembassy.gov/
    education_exchange.html

Algeria

Algiers
Educational Advising Center
US Embassy Public Affairs Section
4, Chemin Cheikh Bachir Ibrahimi
Algiers 16035, Algeria
Tel: 213-21-69 12 55
E-mail: Algiers_Public_Diplomacy@state.gov
Web: http://algiers.usembassy.gov/edu_
    training.html

Angola

Luanda
Educational Advising Center
US Embassy Public Affairs Section
Rua H. Boumedienne, 32,
Miramar
Luanda, Angola
Tel: 244-222-641122; 445727
E-mail: Luandapas1@yahoo.com
Web: http://angola.usembassy.gov

Anguilla, British West Indies

The Valley
Anguilla Library Service
Schools Librarian
The Valley
Anguilla, British West Indies
Tel: 264-497-2441
E-mail: meadsbayqueen@yahoo.com

Argentina

Buenos Aires
Fulbright Commission
Educational Adviser
Viamonte 1653, 2 piso
Buenos Aires C1055ABE
Argentina
Tel: 54-11-4814-3561
E-mail: info@fulbright.com.ar
Web: www.fulbright.edu.ar

Instituto Cultural Argentino-
    Norteamericano (ICANA)
Centro de Asesoria Estudiantil
Maipu 672
Buenos Aires C1006ACH
Argentina
Tel: 54-11-5382-1526
E-mail: advising@icana.org.ar
Web: www.icana.org.ar

Cordoba
Instituto de Intercambio Cultural Argentino
    Norteamericano (IICANA)
IICANA Dept de Orientacion
Educacional
Dean Funes 454
Cordoba 5000, Argentina
Tel: 54-351-4236396
E-mail: iicanaeduusa@fibertel.com.ar
Web: www.iicanacordoba.com.ar

Mendoza
Asociación Mendocina de Intercambio
    Cultural Argentino Norteamericano
    (AMICANA)
Chile 987
Mendoza 5500, Argentina
Tel: 54-261-4236271
E-mail: aeducacional@amicana.com
Web: www.amicana.com

Rosario
Asociación Rosarina de Intercambio Cultural
Argentino Norteamericano (ARICANA)
Buenos Aires 934
Rosario S2000, Argentina
Tel: 54-341-4217664
E-mail: advising-aricana@arnet.com.ar;
    advising@aricanabnc.com.ar
Web: www.aricanabnc.com.ar

Salta
Instituto Salteno de Intercambio
    Cultural Argentino-Norteamericano
    (ISICANA)
Santiago del Estero 865
Salta 4400, Argentina
Tel: 54-387-431-4040
E-mail: info@isicana.org.ar
Web: www.isicana.org.ar

Tucuman
Asociación Tucumana de
    Intercambio CulturalArgentino-
    Norteamericano (ATICANA)
Avda. Salta no. 581
Tucuman 4000, Argentina
Tel: 54-381-303070
E-mail: aticana@arnet.com.ar
Web: www.aticana.com

Armenia

Gyumri
Educational Advising Center
177A Shirakatsi Street, apt. 2
Gyumri 377518, Armenia
Tel: 374-312-344-97
E-mail: gyumrieac@yahoo.com

Yerevan
ACIE Educational Advising Center
American Councils
Baghramyan Ave. 1/1
Yerevan 0019, Armenia
Tel: 374-10-54-40-12;54-40-15
E-mail: americancouncils@americancouncils.am
Web: http://freenet.am/~yereveac

Australia

Brisbane
University of Queensland
Student Support
Relaxation Block, Union Building 21D
Brisbane Q5072, Australia
Tel: 61-7-33651718
E-mail: p.macgroarty@yahoo.com.au
Web: http://brisbane.usvpp.gov/brisbane/
    student.html

Canberra/Barton
EducationUSA Advising Center,
    US Office of Public Affairs
National Press Club Building
16 National Circuit
Barton ACT 2606, Australia
Tel: 61-2-6214-5766
E-mail: freuds@bigpond.net.au
Web: http://usembassy-australia.state.gov/
    education

Melbourne
EducationUSA Advising Center
US Consulate General
553 St. Kilda Road
Melbourne VIC 3004
Australia
Tel: 61-3-9526-5966
E-mail: edusa@usconmelbourne.org
Web: http://melbourne.usconsulate.gov/
    melbourne/student.html

Perth
EducationUSA Advising Center
US Consulate General
16 St. Georges Terrace, 4th FL
Perth WA 6000, Australia
Tel: 61-8-9225-6839
E-mail: leehealy@bigpond.net.au;
ccrass@globaldial.com
Web: http://perth.usconsulate.gov/perth/
student.html

Sydney
EducationUSA Advising Center,
US Consulate General
Level 59, MLC Center
19-29 Martin Place
Sydney NSW 2000, Australia
Tel: 61-2-9373-9230
E-mail: edadvsyd@uunet.com.au
Web: http://sydney.usconsulate.gov/sydney/
student.html

Austria

Wien (Vienna)
Centre International Universitaire
Educational Adviser
Schottengasse 1
Vienna 1010, Austria
Tel: 43-1-533 65 33
E-mail: advising@ciu.at
Web: www.ciu.at

Fulbright Commission
quartier21/MQ
Museumsplatz 1
Vienna 1070, Austria
Tel: 43-1-236 7878 0
E-mail: Aenzi@fulbright.at
Web: www.fulbright.at

Azerbaijan

Baku
Baku Education Information Center
'US Azerbaijan Education
Center', 4th floor
Suleyman Rahimov str, 183
Baku AZ 1014, Azerbaijan
Tel: 994-12-48 28 45
E-mail: GMassimova@beic.az
Web: www.beic.az

Ganja
Ganja Education Information Center
Mirali Gashgay 10
Ganja AZE 2000, Azerbaijan
Tel: 994-22-563025
E-mail: hhuseynli@geic.osi-az.org
Web: www.gitc.aznet.org

Bahrain

Manama
US Embassy Public Affairs Section
Bldg 979, Road 3119, Block 331
Zinj District
Manama, Bahrain
Tel: 973-17-242767
E-mail: hasansaf@state.gov
Web: http://bahrain.usembassy.gov/
resources/education-advising.html

Bangladesh

Dhaka
The American Center
House # 110, Road # 27
Banani Model Town
Dhaka 1213, Bangladesh
Tel: 880-2-883-7150 ext.4
E-mail: dhakapa@state.gov
Web: http://dhaka.usembassy.gov

Barbados

St. Michael
Counseling & Placement Centre
Barbados Community College
"Eyrie" Howell's Cross Road
Two Mile Hill
St. Michael, Barbados
Tel: 246-426-2858 ext 5295
E-mail: clicorish@bcc.edu.bb
Web: www.bcc.edu.bb

Belarus

Gomel
American Center for Education
and Research
Gomel EIC
Prospekt Lenina, 3/508
Gomel 246050, Belarus
Tel: 375-232-74 71 83
E-mail: gomel@amcenter.by
Web: www.amcenter.by

Minsk
Minsk Educational Advising Center
pr. Nezavisimosti 169-512 (south wing)
Minsk 220114, Belarus
Tel: 375-172-18-12-65
E-mail: eic@amcenter.by; advising@amcenter.by
Web: www.amcenter.by; www.vco-edusa.net

Mogilev
American Center for Education
and Research
Mogilev EIC
Arkhiereiskiy Val Kanisskogo, 3/213
Mogilev 212030, Belarus
Tel: 375-222-25 69 63
E-mail: mogilev@amcenter.by
Web: www.amcenter.by

Belgium

Brussels
Commission for Educational
Exchange
Boulevard de l'Empereur, 4
Keizerslaan
Brussels B-1000, Belgium
Tel: 32-2-519.57.72
E-mail: adviser@fulbright.be
Web: www.fulbright.be

Belize

Belize City
St. John's Junior College
Counseling and Educational Advising
Center
Princess Margret Drive
Belize City, Belize
Tel: 501-223-3732 ext.146/120
E-mail: tinacuellar19@hotmail.com
Web: http://belize.usembassy.gov/
educational_advising.html

Benin

Cotonou
Centre Culturel Americain
Boulevard de France
Pres du Conseil de l'Entente
Cotonou, Benin
Tel: 229-21-30 03 12
E-mail: marcosKV@state.gov
Web: http://cotonou.usembassy.gov

Bolivia

Cochabamba
Centro Boliviano Americano,
Asesoramiento EducativoEducationUSA
Information & Advising Center
Calle 25 de Mayo N-0365
Cochabamba, Bolivia
Tel: 591-4-422-9934
E-mail: rribera@cbacoch.org; info@cbacoch.org
Web: www.cbacoch.org

La Paz
Centro Boliviano Americano
Centro de Informacion y Asesoria Educativa
Avenida Arce-Parque Zenon
Iturralde No.121
La Paz, Bolivia
Tel: 591-2-2430998
E-mail: lapazeduusa@cba.edu.bo;
rosmycba@yahoo.com
Web: www.cba.edu.bo

Santa Cruz de la Sierra
Centro Boliviano Americano
Asesoria Educativa
Calle Cochabamba No. 66
Santa Cruz de la Sierra, Bolivia
Tel: 591-3-3342299
E-mail: cbascz@cotas.com.bo
Web: www.cba.com.bo

Sucre
Centro Boliviano Americano
Calle Calvo #301
or Calle Potosi #201
Sucre, Chuquisaca, Bolivia
Tel: 591-4-64-41608
E-mail: cba@entelnet.bo
Web: http://lapaz.usembassy.gov/cbasucre/
cba.htm

Bosnia & Herzegovina

Sarajevo
SUS BiH-US Educational
Advising Center
Zmaja od Bosne bb
Kampus Univerziteta u Sarajevu
Sarajevo 71000
Bosnia & Herzegovina
Tel: 387-33-200 070
E-mail: useac.adviser@sus.ba; useac@sus.ba
Web: www.sus.ba/useac

Botswana

Gaborone
US Embassy—Public Affairs Section
Government Enclave
Embassy Drive
Gaborone, Botswana
Tel: 267-357326
E-mail: OkaileN@state.gov
Web: http://gaborone.usembassy.gov/
  botswana/edu_adv.html

Brazil

Belem
Centro Cultural Brasil-Estados Unidos
  (CCBEU)
Travessa Padre Eutiquio, 1309
Batista Campos
Belem PA 66023-710, Brazil
Tel: 55-91-3242-9455 ext.240-211
E-mail: cultural@ccbeu.com.br
Web: www.ccbeu.com.br

Belo Horizonte
Instituto Cultural Brasil-Estados Unidos
  ICBEU
Educational Advising
Rua da Bahia, 1723 - Lourdes
Belo Horizonte MG 30160-011
Brazil
Tel: 55-31-3271-7255 ext.223
E-mail:advising@icbeu.com.br;
icbeu012@terra.com.br
Web: www.icbeu.com.br

Brasilia
Casa Thomas Jefferson
Escritorio de Consultas
Educacionais
SGAN 606 - Conj. B
Brasilia DF 70840-060
Brazil
Tel: 55-61-3347-4040 ext.46
E-mail: eao@thomas.org.br
Web: www.thomas.org.br

Campinas
Centro Cultural Brasil-Estados
Unidos-Campinas
Consultas Educacionais
Av. Julio de Mesquita, 606
Campinas SP 13025-061
Brazil
Tel: 55-19-3794-9700
E-mail: consedu@ccbeuc.com.br
Web: www.ccbeuc.com.br

Curitiba
ECE UniFAE Centro Universitario -
Escritorio de Consultas
Educacionais
Avenida Silva Jardim, 1499 -
Reboucas
80.250-200 Curitiba, Parana
Brazil
Tel: 55-41-2105-4444
E-mail: AretaGallat@fae.edu
Web: www.fae.edu/ece/index.asp

Interamericano EBC
Educational & Business Center
Rua Maranhao, 2088, Portao
Curitiba PR 80610-001
Brazil
Tel: 55-41-3229-3064
E-mail: eac_curitiba@interamericano.com.br
Web: www.interamericano.com.br

Fortaleza
IBEU-Ceara
Orientacao Educacional
Rua Nogueira Acioly, 891
Fortaleza CE 60110-140
Brazil
Tel: 55-85-4006.9941
E-mail: educacional@ibeuce.com.br
Web: www.ibeuce.com.br

Franca
Centro Cultural Brasil-Estados Unidos-
  Franca
Centro de Consultas Educacionais
Av. Major Nicacio, 1.907 – Cidade Nova
14401-135 Franca SP, Brazil
Tel: 55-16-3724-4300
E-mail: ccbeu@ccbeufranca.com.br
Web: www.ccbeufranca.com.br

Goiania
Centro Cultural Brasil-Estados Unidos
  (CCBEU)
Rua 4, n. 408, Setor Oeste
Av. T-5, n. 441, Setor Bueno
Goiania, Goias 74110-140
Brazil
Tel: 55-62-3533-1415, -1416
E-mail: soeex@ccbeu.com
Web: www.ccbeu.com

Joinville
Centro Cultural Brasil-EstadosUnidos-
  Joinville
Consultas Educacionales
Rua Tijucas, 370 Centro
Joinville SC 89204-020
Brazil
Tel: 55-47-3433-4110
E-mail: adviser@ccbeuj.com.br
Web: www.ccbeuj.com.br

Londrina
Instituto Cultural Brasil-Estados Unidos
Escritorio de Consultas Educacionais
Rua Professor Joao Candido, 1114 -Centro
Londrina PR 86010-001, Brazil
Tel: 55-43-3324-5372
E-mail: agardin@culturalweb.com.br
Web: www.culturalweb.com.br

Manaus
Instituto Cultural Brasil-Estados Unidos
Servico de Orientacao
Av. Joaquim Nabuco, 1286
Manaus AM 69020-030, Brazil
Tel: 55-92-3232-5919
E-mail: coord.cult@icbeu.com
Web: www.icbeu.com

Porto Alegre
Instituto Cultural Brasileiro
Norte-Americano ICBNA
Rua Riachuelo, #1257 2nd floor
Porto Alegre RS 90010-271
Brazil
Tel: 55-51-4009-2321
E-mail: culturalgrad@icbna.com.br;
ninarosa@icbna.com.br
Web: www.cultural.org.br

Recife
Associacao Brasil-America (ABA)
Servicos de Orientacao
Av. Rosa e Silva,1510 - Aflitos
Recife, Pernambuco 52050-220
Brazil
Tel: 55-81-3427-0200
E-mail: martha@abaweb.org
Web: www.abaweb.org

Ribeirao Preto
Associacao de Cultura Brasil-
Estados Unidos
Dep. de Consultas Educacionais
Rua General Osorio, 768 -Centro
Ribeirao Preto SP 14010-000
Brazil
Tel: 55-16-3625-4449
E-mail: acbeu@acbeu.com.br
Web: www.acbeu.com.br

Rio de Janeiro
Fulbright Office of Educational Advising,
  PUC Rio
Av. Marques de Sao Vicente, 225
Ed. Pe. Leonel Franca, sala 55, Gavea
Rio de Janeiro RJ 22451-041
Brazil
Tel: 55-21-2294-1177
E-mail: fulbrightrio@fulbright.org.br
Web: www.fulbright.org.br

Instituto Brasil-Estados Unidos-IBEU/BNC
Av. Nossa Senhora de
Copacabana, 690 -Room 1004
Rio de Janeiro RJ 22050-001
Brazil
Tel: 55-21-3816-9445
E-mail: ibeu@alternex.com.br
Web: www.ibeu.org.br

Salvador
ACBEU-Salvador
Consultas Educacionais
Av. Prof. Magalhaes Netto,
1520 - Stiep
Salvador, Bahia 41820-140
Brazil
Tel: 55-71-3340-5400
E-mail: mgsantos@acbeubahia.org.br
Web: www.acbeubahia.org.br

Santos
Centro Cultural Brasil-Estados Unidos
Servico de Orientacao, studos nos EUA
Rua Jorge Tibirica, 5/7
Santos SP 11055-250, Brazil
Tel: 55-13-3281-3993
E-mail: advising@ccbeunet.br
Web: www.ccbeunet.br/educationusa/index.html

Saõ José dos Campos
ICBEU Sao Jose dos Campos
Av. Dr. Adhemar de Barros, 464
Vila Ady'Anna
Sao Jose dos Campos SP 12243-610
Brazil
Tel: 55-12-3941-4978;3924-1000
E-mail: advising@icbeusjc.com.br
Web: www.icbeusjc.com.br

Saõ Paulo
Associacao Alumni
Dep. de Consultas Educacionais
Alameda Jau 1.208– Cerqueira Cesar
Saõ Paulo SP 01420-001 Brazil
Tel: 55-11-3067-2916
E-mail: advising@alumni.org.br
Web: www.alumni.org.br

Uniao Cultural Brasil Estados Unidos
Rua Coronel Oscar Porto, 208 Paraiso
Saõ Paulo SP 04003-000 Brazil
Tel: 55-11- 2148-2912
E-mail: studentadvising@uniaocultural.com.br
Web: www.uniaocultural.com.br

Brunei

Bandar Seri Begawan
US Embassy Public Affairs Section
Jalan Sultan (Corner of Jalan McArthur)
3rd Floor, Teck Guan Plaza
Bandar Seri Begawan BS 8811 Brunei
Tel: 673-222-9670 ext.2101
E-mail: education_brunei@state.gov
Web: http://brunei.usembassy.gov/higher_
    education.html

Bulgaria

Sofia
Bulgarian-American Fulbright Commission
Educational Adviser
17, Alexander Stamboliiski Boulevard
Sofia 1000, Bulgaria
Tel: 359-2-981 6830
E-mail: steneva@fulbright.bg
Web: www.fulbright.bg

Burkina Faso

Ouagadougou
EducationUSA Center
Centre Culturel Americain
674, Avenue John F. Kennedy
Ouagadougou 01, Burkina Faso
Tel: 226-50-30 67 23
E-mail: kalmogob@state.gov
Web: http://ouagadougou.usembassy.gov

Burma (Myanmar)

Yangon(Rangoon)
American Center
14, Tawwin Road
Dagon Township
Yangon, Burma (Myanmar)
Tel: 95-1-223106; 223140
E-mail: EDURangoon@state.gov
Web: http://burma.usembassy.gov/
    advisingservice.html

Cambodia

Phnom Penh
Educational Advising Center, Royal
    University of Phnom Penh
Room 103, Faculty of Science Building
Blvd. Confederation of Russia
Khan Tuol kok, Phnom Penh
Cambodia
Tel: 855-23-884-320;216-163
E-mail: caradvchthon@online.com.kh
Web: www.eacc-edu-kh.com;
http://cambodia.usembassy.gov/
    educational_advising_center.html

Cameroon

Yaounde
American Embassy Yaounde
Public Affairs Section
Avenue Rosa Parks
Yaounde, Cameroon
Tel: 237-220-1500
E-mail: yaoundeEdu@state.gov
Web: http://yaounde.usembassy.gov/
    educational_advising.html

Cape Verde

Praia
EducationUSA-US Embassy
Public Affairs Section
 Rua Abilio Macedo 6
Praia, Cape Verde
Tel: 238- 260-8900
E-mail: britomt@state.gov
Web: http://praia.usembassy.gov

Cayman Islands BWI

George Town
Employment Services Center (MOE)
Paddington Place, Ste 309-310
Godfrey Nixon Way
George Town, Grand Cayman
Cayman Islands BWI
Tel: 345-945-3114
E-mail: Jennifer.Smith@gov.ky
Web: http://employmentservices@gov.ky

Chad

N'Djamena
US Embassy, Public Diplomacy Section
Information Resource Center
Avenue Felix Eboue
N'Djamena, Chad
Tel: 235-51 70 09
E-mail: roassre@yahoo.fr
Web: http://ndjamena.usembassy.gov/
    educational_advising.html

Chile

Antofagasta
Instituto Chileno Norteamericano de
    Antofagasta
Educational Adviser
Carrera 1445
Antofagasta, Chile
Tel: 56-55-263 520
E-mail: inchafta@chilesat.net
Web: www.norteamericano.cl

Concepcion
Instituto Chileno Norteamericano de
    Cultura
Asesora Academica
Caupolican 315
Concepcion, Chile
Tel: 56-40-225506
E-mail: mtvilla@norteamericanoconcepcion.cl
Web: www.norteamericanoconcepcion.cl

Curicó
Instituto Chileno
Norteamericano de Cultura
Asesora Academica
Estado 563
Curicó, Chile
Tel: 56-75-311129
E-mail: mtsani@terra.cl
Web: www.inchinor.cl

Santiago
Centro de Asesoria Academica
Internacional
Instituto Chileno
Norteamericano de Cultura
Moneda 1467
Santiago, Chile
Tel: 56-2-677-7157
E-mail: advising@norteamericano.cl
Web: www.norteamericano.cl

Valparaíso
Instituto Chileno Norteamericano de
    Cultura
Esmeralda 1069
Valparaíso, Chile
Tel: 56-32-2686191;2450400
E-mail: ccarmona@chilenonorteamericano.cl
Web: www.chilenonorteamericano.cl

Vina del Mar
Instituto Chileno Norteamericano de
    Cultura
2 Oriente 385
Vina del Mar, Chile
Tel: 56-32-2686191;2450400
E-mail: ccarmona@chilenonorteamericano.cl
Web: www.chilenonorteamericano.cl

China

Beijing
American Center for EducationalExchange
    (IIE Beijing)
Suite 2801 Jingguang Center
Hu Jia Lou, Chaoyang District
Beijing 100020, China
Tel: 86-10-6597-3242 ext208
E-mail: mokfw@state.gov
Web: www.iie-china.org;
www.usembassy-china.org.cn/acee/

Beijing National Library
39 Baishiqiao Road
Haidian District
Beijing 100081, China
Tel: 86-10-8854-5381
E-mail: interco@publicf.nlc.gov.cn

Chinese Service Center for Scholarly
   Exchange
No. 15, Xue Yuan Road
Haidian District
Beijing 100083, China
Tel: 86-10-82301006-219;82301019
E-mail: xjli@cscse.edu.cn
Web: www.cscse.edu.cn

Chivast Education Intl/Chinese
Service Ctr for Scholarly Exchange
907-911 North Office Bldg,
New World Center
3B Chongwenmenwai Street
Beijing 100062, China
Tel: 86-10-6708 1943
E-mail: tracydian@yahoo.com;
topuniv@chivast.cscse.org
Web: www.chivast.com;
www.cscse.org/chivast/main/index.php

Dongfang International Center for
   Education Exchange CSC
Room 801, Jinyu Mansion
No. 129A Xuanwumen Xidajie
Beijing 100031, China
Tel: 86-10-66411821;66417264
E-mail: us@cscdf.org; Marketing@csc.edu.cn
Web: www.cscdf.org; www.csc-studyabroad.net

Education Information Center (EIC)
   Beijing Office
Room 1203, Block A, Jianwai
SOHO
39 East 3rd-Ring Rd, Chaoyang Dist.
Beijing 100022, China
Tel: 86-10-5869-6611
E-mail: us.beijing@eic.org.cn;
pantu@eic.org.cn
Web: www.eic.org.cn

EduChina Group (Open Minds Center)
Suite 808 Building 4 SOHO NewTown
No. 88 Jianguo Road, Chaoyang District
Beijing 100022, China
Tel: 86-10-8589-7942
E-mail: huijin@edusa.cn
Web: www.openmindsedu.org

Peking University Library
Beijing 100871, China
Tel: 86-10-62751053 x215; 62751051
E-mail: office@lib.pku.edu.cn
Web: www.lib.pku.edu.cn

Changchun
Jilin Provincial Library Changchun
No. 116 Xinmin Dajie
Changchun, Jilin 130021, China
Tel: 86-431-5643802; 5644115
E-mail: wLdgbk@21cn.com
Web: www.jlplib.com.cn

Changsha
Hunan Provincial Library Changsha
No. 38 Shaoshan Lu
Changsha, Hunan 410011, China
Tel: 86-731-413-8123
E-mail: hunanlib@library.hn.cn

Chengdu
Intensive Language Training
Center EIC
Sichuan University-West Campus
No. 24, South Section, First Ring
Chengdu, Sichuan 610065 China
Tel: 86-28-85460856;85407417
E-mail: iltcsuu1979@yahoo.com.cn
Web: www.iltcscu.org; iltc.scu.edu.cn

Sichuan Provincial Library Chengdu
222 Dongfeng Road
Chengdu, Sichuan 610016 China
Tel: 86-28-8667-2492
E-mail: yling803@sohu.com;
   scplib@mail.sc.cninfo.net

Sichuan Service Center for Scholarly
   Exchange
No. 8 Xi Yu Jie
A-26-A, Xi Yu Building
Chengdu, Sichuan 610015 China
Tel: 86-28-8612-4388; 8613-9696
E-mail: sclxfw@yahoo.com.cn;
cdchenbing@hotmail.com
Web: www.sc-studyabroad.com/index.asp

US Information ResourceCenter, Public
   Affairs Section
US Consulate General Chengdu
4 Lingshiguan Lu, Renmin Nan Lu Section 4
Chengdu, Sichuan 610041 China
Tel: 86-28-8558-3992 ext 6783
E-mail:usiscd@mail.sc.cninfo.net
Web: http://chengdu.usconsulate.gov/
   resources.html

Chongqing
Chongqing Library
No.106 Fengtian Avenue
Shapingba district
Chongqing, Sichuan 400037 China
Tel: 86-23-65210032
E-mail: cqtsg1947@163.com
Web: www.cqlib.cn

Service Centre for Studying Abroad
Sichuan International Studies University
Lieshimu, Shapingba
Chongqing, Sichuan 400031 China
Tel: 86-23-6538-5434, 6538-5271
E-mail: zzyan98@yahoo.com;
sisupxb@yahoo.com.cn
Web: www.sisu.edu.cn

Fuzhou
Fujian Provincial Library - Fuzhou
Foreign Language Section, Overseas Study
   Advising Center
No 227 Hudong Road
Fuzhou, Fujian Province 350001, China
Tel: 86-591-8750-8548 ext2401
E-mail: ksn@fjlib.net; mtzdh@public.fz.fj.cn

Guangzhou
Education Information Center (EIC)
   Guangdong
Guangzhou Library - 2nd Fl
42, Zhongshan Si (4th) Road
Guangzhou, Guangdong 510055, China
Tel: 86-20-83839376; 8386-6665
E-mail: us@eic.org.cn; usmkt@eic.org.cn
Web: www.eic.org.cn

Guangzhou Service Center for Scholarly
   Exchange-GSCSE
6/F Bei Xiu Building
266 Xiao Bei Road
Guangzhou, Guangdong 510050, China
Tel: 86-20-8356 8066 ext 8617
E-mail: gscse@163.net; John28@21cn.net
Web: www.gzscse.com

US Consulate General Guangzhou–Resource
   Center/PAS
R/F, Garden Hotel
368 Huan Shi Dong Road
Guangzhou, Guangdong 510064, China
Tel: 86-20-8335-4269 ext 29
E-mail: ircgz@state.gov
Web: http://guangzhou.usembassy-china.
   org.cn/study.html

Haikou
Hainan Provincial Service Center
for Scholarly Exchange
Room 715-716 Yaxi Building
No 12 Haifu Road
Haikou, Hainan 570203, China
Tel: 86-898-535-7858;6535-7858

Harbin
Heilongjiang Provincial Library Harbin
No. 218 Changjiang Road
Nangang District
Harbin, Heilongjiang 150090 China
Tel: 86-451-53969010
E-mail: hljlib@hljlib.cn; HLJlib@163.com
Web: http://dx.hljlib.cn/; www.HLJlib.gov.cn

Hefei
Anhui Provincial Library Hefei
Foreign Publication Section
74 Wu Hu Lu
Hefei, Anhui 230001, China
Tel: 86-551-2886188 x328
E-mail: qk@mail.ahlib.com;
   zhanghaiz@sohu.com
Web: www.ahlib.com

Jinan
Shandong Provincial Library Jinan
No. 2912 East Road, Second Ring
Licheng District
Jinan, Shandong 250100, China
Tel: 86-531-8559-0748
E-mail: mokfw@state.gov
Web: mokfw@state.gov

Kunming
Yunnan Provincial Library Kunming
Collection Center
No. 141 Cuihu Nan Road (South)
Kunming, Yunnan 650091, China
Tel: 86-871-532-2035; 53200554

Nanjing
Nanjing University Library
Personnel Department
No. 22 Hankou Road
Nanjing, Jiangsu 210093, China
Tel: 86-25-8359-2943
E-mail: majinch@netra.nju.edu.cn;
    ndszbli@nju.edu.cn
Web: www.nju.edu.cn

Nanning
Guangxi Zhuang
Autonomous Regional Library
No. 61 Minzu Dadao
Nanning, Guangxi 530022, China
Tel: 86-771-562-3636; 5860297; 5864579

Ningbo
Ningbo University Zone Library
928 Qianhu Road (South)
University Zone, Yinzhou
Ningbo, Zhejiang 315100 China
Tel: 86-574-8812-6507; 8812-6502
E-mail: ywll@sina100.com
Web: www.nlic.net.cn

Shanghai
EduShanghai International Co., Ltd.
Room 205, Education Hotel
No. 3 Fen Yang Road
Shanghai 200031, China
Tel: 86-21-6466-4150, -3147
E-mail: usoffice@edush.com
Web: www.edush.com

Fudan University
Personnel Division
Handan Road 220
Shanghai 200433, China
Tel: 86-21-6564-2658; 5566-4154
Web: www.fudan.edu.cn

Shanghai CIIC Education International
    Co., Ltd.
11 Floor, Suite A, ShengAi Plaza
No.88, Cao Xi Bei (North) Road
Shanghai 200030, China
Tel: 86-21-6486-8282 x230
E-mail: zhusa@shciic.com
Web: www.shciic.com

Shanghai Jiaotong University Library
    (Jiao Da)
1954 Huashan Road Xu Jia Hui
Shanghai 200030, China
Tel: 86-21-6293-3195, -3225
E-mail: refdesk@lib.sjtu.edu.cn
Web: www.lib.sjtu.edu.cn

Shanghai Municipal Library
Foreign University Reference Room
1555 Huai Hai Zhong Road, Room 4309
Shanghai 200031, China
Tel: 86-21-6445-5555 x1316
E-mail: gpfan@libnet.sh.cn;
    DLLU@libnet.sh.cn
Web: www.library.sh.cn/tsgc/lxzn/

US Consulate General, Public Affairs
    Section IRC
Suite 532, East Tower, Shanghai Center
1376 Nanjing Road West
Shanghai 200040, China
Tel: 86-21-6279-7662 ext4678
E-mail: ircshanghai@yahoo.com
Web: http://shanghai.usembassy-
    china.org.cn/education_study_usa.html

Shenyang
American Studies Center, North
East University
Lane #3, #11, Wenhua Road
Heping District
Shenyang, Liaoning 110004, China
Tel: 86-24-8368-8502
Web: www.neu.edu.cn

Liaoning International Exchange Center
    (LIEC)
5/F 56 Beijing Ave.
Shenyang, Liaoning 110032, China
Tel: 86-24-86907808;86909855
E-mail: LIEC@liec.com.cn
Web: www.liec.com.cn

Liaoning Provincial Library Shenyang
111 Wan Liu Tang Lu
Dong Ling Qu
Shenyang, Liaoning 110015, China
Tel: 86-24-24822241;24822449
E-mail: mingmingxue@yahoo.com
Web: www.library.ln.cninfo.net

Resource Center, Public Affairs Section
US Consulate General Shenyang
No. 52, 14 Wei Road, Heping District
Shenyang, Liaoning 110003 China
Tel: 86-24-2322-2976
E-mail: xiaob@state.gov;xiaobgrace@gmail.com
Web: http://shenyang.usconsulate.gov/
    usainfo/education.html

Shenyang Normal University
No.253 Huanghe North Street
Huang'gu District
Shenyang, Liaoning 110034, China
Tel: 86-24-8659-2441
E-mail: quyanna2004@163.com;
    quyanna2004@sohu.com
Web: www.synu.edu.cn

Shenyang University
International Business College
21 Wanghua South Street,
Dadong District
Shenyang, Liaoning 110044, China
Tel: 86-24-6226-8631
E-mail: swang1557@yahoo.com.cn
Web: www.syu.edu.cn/bumen/hetian/index.
    asp

Suzhou
Suzhou City Library
Reading Dept.
858 Renming Road
Suzhou, Jiangsu 215002, China
Tel: 86-512-6522-8568; 6522-0802
E-mail: mokfw@state.gov
Web: www.szlib.com

Tianjin
Tianjin Municipal Library
No. 15 Fu Kang Road
Nankai District
Tianjin 300191, China
Tel: 86-22-23368226;23369194
E-mail: kfe2915@sina.com
Web: www.tjl.tj.cn

Wuhan
Wuhan University
Library Reading Room
Luojia Hill, Wuhan 430072, Hubei, China
Tel: 86-27-68754352; 87682745
E-mail: zhangming@lib.whu.edu.cn
Web: www.lib.whu.edu.cn

Xi'an
Xi'an International Studies University
Study Abroad Agency,
Classroom Building 1
No. 437, Chang'an South Rd
Xi'an, Shaanxi 710061, China
Tel: 86-29-8530-9798
E-mail: catherinefan@hotmail.com
Web: http://lxzj.xisu.edu.cn

Zhengzhou
Henan Provincial Library Zhengzhou
Foreign Department
No. 150 Songshan Nan Lu
Zhengzhou, Henan 450052, China
Tel: 86-371-6718-1473
Web: www.henanlib.gov.cn

Colombia

Armenia
BNC Colombo Americano-Armenia
Educational Advising Center
Avenida Bolivar 1-55
Armenia, Quindio, Colombia
Tel: 57-67-463-588
E-mail: asesoria@bncarmenia.com
Web: www.bncarmenia.com

Barranquilla
Centro Cultural Colombo
Americano de Barranquilla-Asesoria
Carrera 43 No. 51 - 95
Barranquilla, Colombia
Tel: 57-5-379 3951
E-mail: colombolibrary@caribemovil.com;
colombolibrary@metrotel.net.co
Web: www.colomboamericano.org

Bogotá
Centro Colombo Americano
Centro de Asesoria Educativa
Calle 19 No. 2-49
Bogotá 1101, Colombia
Tel: 57-1-334-7640 ext.231
E-mail: advising@colombobogota.edu.co
Web: www.colombobogota.edu.co

COLFUTURO
Consejeria Academica
Carrera 15 No. 37-15, Barrio Teusaquillo
Bogota, Colombia
Tel: 57-1-340-5394 PBX
E-mail: yosoyfuturo@colfuturo.com.co
Web: www.colfuturo.com.co

Fulbright Commission
Consejeria Academica
Calle 38 # 13-37 Piso 11
Bogota, Colombia
Tel: 57-1-287-1481
E-mail: consejeria@fulbright.edu.co
Web: www.fulbright.edu.co

Bucaramanga
Centro Colombo Americano de
   Bucaramanga
Biblioteca
Carrera 22 No. 37-74
Bucaramanga, Santander
Colombia
Tel: 57-7-6352908
E-mail: ccolombo@colombobucaramanga.
   edu.co
Web: www.colombobucaramanga.edu.co

Cali
Centro Cultural Colombo
Americano Cali
Asesoria Estudiantil
Calle 13 Norte, # 8-45
Cali, Colombia
Tel: 57-2-667-3539 ext.114
E-mail: asesoria@colomboamericano.edu.co
Web: www.colomboamericano.edu.co

Cartagena
Centro Colombo Americano de Cartagena
Biblioteca
Calle de la Factoria No. 36-27
Cartagena 28-31, Colombia
Tel: 57-5-6641-714 ext.102
E-mail: information@colombocartagena.com
Web: www.colombocartagena.com

Manizales
Centro Colombo Americano
Asesoria
Calle 62 No. 24B-50
Manizales, Caldas, Colombia
Tel: 57-6-881-1525
E-mail: studyusa@colombomanizales.com
Web: www.colombomanizales.com

Medellín
Centro Colombo Americano
Educational Advising Office
Carrera 45 # 53-24
Medellin, Colombia
Tel: 57-4-513-4444 ext.227
E-mail: studyusa@colomboworld.com
Web: www.colomboworld.com

Pereira
Centro Colombo Americano Asesoria
   Estudiantil
Carrera 6 # 22-26
Pereira, Colombia
Tel: 57-6-325-40-32
E-mail: educationaladvisor@
   colombopereira.com
Web: www.colombopereira.com

Congo, Democratic Republic of

Kinshasa
Congo American Language Institute
Complex Utexafrica
Avenue Colonel Mondjiba
Kinshasa
Congo, Democratic Republic
Tel: 243-81-880 6045
E-mail: edadvisor@micronet.cd
Web: http://kinshasa.usembassy.gov

Costa Rica

San José
Centro Cultural Costarricense-
Norteamericano
Asesoria Educacional
150 Metros Norte de Gasolinera los Yoses
San José, Costa Rica
Tel: 506-207-7564
E-mail: cchaves@cccncr.com
Web: www.cccncr.com

Côte d'Ivoire

Abidjan
Centre Culturel Americain
Boulevard de l'Université, Angle
Avenue de l'Entente
Cocody, Riviera Golf
Abidjan 01, Côte d'Ivoire
Tel: 225-22-49 41 27
E-mail: AbjStudentAdvisor@state.gov
Web: http://french.cotedivoire.usembassy.
   gov/premier_cycle.html

Croatia

Zagreb
Institute for the Development of
Education IRO
EducationUSA Adviser
Preradoviceva 33/I
Zagreb 10000, Croatia
Tel: 385-1-4817-195
E-mail: iro@iro.hr
Web: www.iro.hr

Cyprus

Nicosia
Cyprus Fulbright Commission -
Koskluciftlik branch
5A Server Somuncuoglu Street
Koskluciftlik
Nicosia, Cyprus
Tel: 90-392-2271800
E-mail:fulbright@superonline.com
Web: www.fulbright.org.cy

Cyprus Fulbright Commission
Educational Adviser
2 Egypt Ave.
Nicosia 1097, Cyprus
Tel: 357-2-22 669757
E-mail: cfc@fulbright.org.cy
Web: www.fulbright.org.cy

Czech Republic

Prague
J. W. Fulbright Commission
Educational Adviser
Taboritska 23
Prague 130 87, Czech Republic
Tel: 420-222718452
E-mail: advisor@fulbright.cz
Web: www.fulbright.cz

Denmark

Copenhagen
Denmark-America Foundation/Fulbright
   Commission
Educational Adviser
Fiolstraede 24, 3rd floor
Copenhagen K DK-1171
Denmark
Tel: 45-33-12 82 23
E-mail: advising@daf-fulb.dk
Web: www.wemakeithappen.dk

Dominica

Roseau
Educational Advising Unit
Public Library
Victoria Street
Roseau, Dominica
Tel: 767-448-2401 ext. 3341
E-mail: dominicaedadvise@gmail.com

Dominican Republic

Santiago
Centro Cultural Dominico-Americano
Avda. Salvador Estrella Sahdala
La Rinconada
Santiago de los Caballeros
Dominican Republic
Tel: 809-582-6627,-28; 582-1244
E-mail: CCDAlibrary@yahoo.com

Santo Domingo
Instituto Cultural Dominico-Americano
Educational Advising Office
Ave. Abraham Lincoln #21,
Sector Mata Hambre
Santo Domingo 10102
Dominican Republic
Tel: 809-535-0665 ext.263
E-mail: eco@icda.edu.do
Web: www.icda.edu.do

Ecuador

Guayaquil
Fulbright Commission
Asesoria Academica
Luis Urdaneta 112 y Cordova
Guayaquil, Ecuador
Tel: 593-4-2302392
E-mail: advisorg@fulbright.org.ec
Web: www.fulbright.org.ec

Quito
Comision Fulbright del Ecuador
Centro de Asesoria Academica
EducationUSA
Almagro N25-41 y Av. Colon
Quito, Ecuador
Tel: 593-2-222-2103
E-mail: advisorq@fulbright.org.ec
Web: www.fulbright.org.ec/asesoria.htm

Egypt

Alexandria
AMIDEAST
American Center Alexandria
3 Pharana Street, Azarita
Alexandria, Egypt
Tel: 20-3-486-9091
E-mail: alexandria@amideast.org
Web: www.amideast.org

Cairo (Giza)
AMIDEAST
23, Mossadak St.
Dokki
Giza, Egypt
Tel: 20-2-337-8265; 19-263
E-mail: Hal-Hawary@amideast.org;
    CS-egypt@amideast.org
Web: www.amideast.org

El Salvador

San Salvador
Centro Cultural Salvadoreno
Student Advising Office
Avenida los Sisimiles, Costado
norte de Metrocentro
San Salvador, El Salvador
Tel: 503-2260 9024
E-mail: stadvisor@hotmail.com
Web: www.centroculturalsalvadoreno.com

Eritrea

Asmara
American Center
Public Affairs Section
Ala Street, #179
Asmara, Eritrea
Tel: 291-1-12-06-37
E-mail: AregahegnS@state.gov
Web: http://asmara.usembassy.gov

Estonia

Tallinn
EducationUSA Advising Center
Tallinn Technical University
Ehitajate tee 5, III korpus, room 211a
Tallinn 19086, Estonia
Tel: 372-2-620 3543
E-mail: EducationUSA@ttu.ee
Web: www.eac.ttu.ee

Tartu
EducationUSA Advising Center
Tartu University Library
W. Struve 1-325
Tartu 50091, Estonia
Tel: 372-7-427 243
E-mail: educentre@lists.ut.ee
Web: www.ut.ee/ameerika

Ethiopia

Addis Ababa
US Embassy, Public Affairs Section
Entoto Street
Woreda 11, Kebele 10
Addis Ababa, Ethiopia
Tel: 251-1-584007, 5174000
E-mail: ShiferawY@state.gov
Web: http://ethiopia.usembassy.gov

Fiji

Suva
U.S. Embassy Suva
Commercial Assistant/EducationUSA
    Adviser
31 Loftus Street
Suva, Fiji
Tel: 679-3314466
E-mail: usembsuva@connect.com.fj
Web: http://suva.usembassy.gov/ed_
    exchange.html

Finland

Helsinki
Fulbright Center
Kaisaniemenkatu 3 B 5th floor
Helsinki 00100, Finland
Tel: 358-9-5494 7400
E-mail: office@fulbright.fi
Web: www.fulbright.fi

France

Lyon
Centre d'Information Internationale (CII)
Universite de Lyon
25, rue Jaboulay
69007 Lyon, France
Tel: 33-4-72 73 24 95
E-mail: cii.lyon@ac-lyon.fr
Web: www.euroguidance-france.org;
www.universite-lyon.fr/cii

Paris
Centre Education USA
Franco-American Commission
 for Educational Exchange
9, rue Chardin
Paris 75016, France
Tel: 08 92 68 07 47 (inside France)
E-mail: doc@fulbright-france.org
Web: www.fulbright-france.org/htm/centred.
    asp

Rennes
Institut Franco-Americain, Rennes
7 quai Chateaubriand
35000 Rennes, France
Tel: 33-2-99 79 20 57
E-mail: thomas.hull@ifa-rennes.org
Web: www.ifa-rennes.org

Gambia, The

Banjul
US Embassy, Public Affairs Section
Kairaba Avenue
Fajara
Banjul, The Gambia
Tel: 220-4392856 ext.2189
E-mail: NjieMM@state.gov
Web: www.usembassybanjul.gm

Georgia

Batumi
Center for International Education—Batumi
International Student Advising Center
23 Ninoshvili Street
Batumi 6010, Georgia
Tel: 995-222-75817
E-mail: natia_andguladze@osgf.ge
Web: www.cie-batumi.org;
http://batumi.osgf.ge

K'ut'aisi
International Student Advising
Center
University of Law and Economics
Tsereteli str., 13
384000 Kutaisi, Georgia
Tel: 995-331-4-11-40
E-mail: isac-kutaisi@mail.osgf.ge

Tbilisi
Center for International Education
Open Society Georgia Foundation
ul. Chovelidze,10
0108 Tbilisi, Georgia
Tel: 995-32-25-04-63
E-mail: natia@isac.osgf.ge; nino@isac.osgf.ge
Web: www.cie.ge; www.osgf.ge/isac

Educational Advising Center Kvali
3, Chavchavadze Avenue
Tbilisi State University
Tbilisi 0128, Georgia
Tel: 995-32-91 24 31
E-mail: eac@kvali.com
Web: www.kvali.org/center

Germany

All cities
EducationUSA Berlin
Telephone Hotline Service
Tel: 49-030-31 80 08 99
E-mail: austausch@state.gov
Web: www.usembassy.de/germany/exchanges

Freiburg
Carl-Schurz-Haus,
German-American Institute
Eisenbahnstrasse 62
Freiburg im Breisgau 79098
Germany
Tel: 49-761-55652716
E-mail: bibliothek@carl-schurz-haus.de
Web: www.carl-schurz-haus.de

Hamburg
Amerikazentrum Hamburg
Am Sandtorkai 5
Hamburg 20457, Germany
Tel: 49-40-70 38 36 88
E-mail: info@amerikazentrum.de
Web: www.amerikazentrum.de

Hannover
Fachhochschule Hannover
Studienberatung USA
Hanomagstrasse 8, Zi.122
Hannover-Linden 30449
Germany
Tel: 49-511-9296-2154
E-mail: usa@fh-hannover.de
Web: www.fh-hannover.de/usa/

Heidelberg
German American Institute
Deutsch-amerikanisches Institut
Sofienstrasse 12
Heidelberg 69115, Germany
Tel: 49-6221-607315
E-mail: biblio@dai-heidelberg.de
Web: www.dai-heidelberg.de

Kiel
Kennedy Infozentrum Kiel
Amerika-Gesellschaft
Schleswig-Holstein
Olshausenstrasse 10
Kiel 24118, Germany
Tel: 49-431-586 999 3
E-mail: info@amerika-gesellschaft.de
Web: www.amerika-gesellschaft.de

Leipzig
Generalkonsulat der USA Leipzig
Amerika Haus
Wilhelm-Seyfferth-Strasse 4
Leipzig 04107, Germany
Tel: 49-341-213 84 65
E-mail: ircleipzig@state.gov
Web: http://germany.usembassy.gov/
   germany/exchanges/

Munich
Bavarian American Center -
Amerika Haus Munich
Section Education & Exchange
Karolinenplatz 3
Munich 80333, Germany
Tel: 49-89-55 25 37 17
E-mail: infothek@amerikahaus.de
Web: www.amerikahaus.de

Nürnberg (Nuremberg)
Deutsch-Amerikanisches Institut
GAI Nuernberg
Gleissbuhlstrasse 13
90402 Nürnberg, Germany
Tel: 49-911-2306912
E-mail: mail@dai-nuernberg.de
Web: www.dai-nuernberg.de/
   DAIFrameStudy.htm

Stuttgart
Deutsch-Amerikanisches Zentrum
James-F.-Byrnes Institut e.V.
Charlottenplatz 17
Stuttgart 70173, Germany
Tel: 49-711-22 81 80
E-mail: info@daz.org
Web: www.daz.org

Tübingen
German American Institute
Karlstrasse 3
Tübingen 72072, Germany
Tel: 49-7071-795-2616
E-mail: bibliothek@dai-tuebingen.de
Web: www.dai-tuebingen.de

Ghana

Accra
Educational Advising Center,
US Embassy Public Affairs Section
No. 24, Fourth Circular Road
Cantonments-Accra
Accra, Ghana
Tel: 233-21-741-150 ext.1116
E-mail: fiebb2000@yahoo.com
Web: http://accra.usembassy.gov

Kumasi
EducationUSA Advisory Center
ACE CONSULT
3rd FL Top Martin's Complex,
Asokwa, Kumasi, Ghana
Tel: 233-51-0244-369027
E-mail: ace_consult2006@yahoo.com
Web: http://accra.usembassy.gov

Greece

Athens
The Fulbright Foundation in
Greece—Athens
EducationUSA adviser
6 Vassilissis Sophias Avenue
Athens 10674, Greece
Tel: 30-210-7241811
E-mail: advisor@fulbright.gr;
info@fulbright.gr
Web: www.fulbright.gr

Thessaloniki
The Fulbright Foundation—Thessaloniki
EducationUSA adviser
4 Venizelou Str., 3rd floor
Thessaloniki 54625, Greece
Tel: 30-2310-242-904
E-mail: edadthes@fulbright.gr
Web: www.fulbright.gr

Grenada

St. George's
TA Marryshow Community College
Office of Student Affairs
Tanteen, St. George's, Grenada
Tel: 473-440-1389
E-mail: tamcc@caribsurf.com;
Web: www.tamcc.edu.gd

Guatemala

Guatemala City
Instituto Guatemalteco Americano
Walt Whitman Library
Ruta 1, 4-05, Zona 4,
1st Floor, Of. 108
Guatemala City 01004, Guatemala
Tel: 502-2422-5590
E-mail: educationUSA@iga.edu
Web: www.iga.edu

Quetzaltenango
EducationUSA–IGA Xela
14 avenida
Quetzaltenango 09001
Guatemala
Tel: (502) 7765-8160
E-mail: wcalva@iga.edu
Web: www.iga.edu

Guinea

Conakry
Conakry Educational Advising Center
Centre d'Etudes de la Langue
Anglaise CELA
Universite GLC de Sonfonia,
Rte Donka
Conakry 4027, Guinea
Tel: 224- 60-26 19 67
E-mail: marudaka@yahoo.fr
Web: http://conakry.usembassy.gov/
   edadvise.html

Guyana

Georgetown
US Embassy, Public Affairs Section
99-100 Young and Duke Streets
Kingston
Georgetown, Guyana
Tel: 592-225-4900 ext.235
E-mail: duncanjr@state.gov
Web: http://georgetown.usembassy.gov

Haiti

Port-au-Prince
US Embassy Information Resource Center
Port-au-Prince, Haiti
Tel: 509-222-3715
E-mail: GardereNM@state.gov
Web: http://haiti.usembassy.gov

Honduras

San Pedro Sula
Centro Cultural Sampedrano
3 Calle, 3 y 4 Avenida No. 22
Barrio El Centro
San Pedro Sula 511, Honduras
Tel: 504-553-3768;553-3911
E-mail: biblioteca@ centrocultural-sps.com
Web: www.centrocultural-sps.com

Tegucigalpa
Instituto Hondureno de Cultura
Interamericana
Boulevard Suyapa
Plaza Florencia, Colonia
Florencia Norte
Tegucigalpa, Honduras
Tel: 504-239-4323; 239-3424
E-mail: educationusaihci@yahoo.com
Web: http://honduras.usembassy.gov/.
embajada/secciones/ihci.htm; www.ihci.hn

Hong Kong

Hong Kong
IIE EducationUSA Advising Center
Room 601, General Commercial Building
156-164 Des Voeux Road Central
Hong Kong, Hong Kong
Tel: 852-2603-5771
E-mail: info@iiehongkong.org
Web: www.iiehongkong.org

Hungary

Budapest
Fulbright EducationUSA
Advising Center - FEAC
Baross utka 62, #111
Budapest 1082, Hungary
Tel: 36-1-462-8050
E-mail: advising@fulbright.hu
Web: www.fulbright.hu/advising

Pécs
American Corner-EducationUSA Advising
Center
International House/Europa Haz
Maria u. 9
Pécs 7621, Hungary
Tel: 36-72-514817
E-mail: pecs@americancorner.hu
Web: www.americancorner.hu;
www.interhouse.hu

Szeged
American Higher Education
Information Center
University of Szeged, University
Library
Ady ter 10
Szeged 6722, Hungary
Tel: 36-62-546-625
E-mail: ficzko@bibl.u-szeged.hu
Web: www.bibl.u-szeged.hu/afik/

Veszprém
American Corner-EducationUSA Advising
Eotvos Karoly Megyei Konyvtar
Komakut ter 3.
Veszprém 8200, Hungary
Tel: 36-88-560-600
E-mail: baranyait@ekmk.hu;
veszprem@americancorner.hu
Web: www.fulbright.hu/advising

Iceland

Reykjavík
Iceland–US Educational
Commission
Laugavegur 59
Reykjavik 101, Iceland
Tel: 354-551-0860
E-mail: advisor@fulbright.is
Web: www.fulbright.is

India

Ahmedabad
Indo-American Education
Society, USEFI Satellite Center
No.4 Malhar House, bh.Raindrops
Nr. National Handloom, off
C.G. Road, Navrangpura
Ahmedabad 3800096, Gujarat
India
Tel: 91-79-2644-2129; 2644-2209
E-mail: eduadviser@gmail.com
Web: http://iaesgujarat.org

Bangalore
Yashna Trust-USEFI Satellite Centre
102 Park View
40 Haines Road, Frazer
Bangalore 560005, India
Tel: 91-80-4125-1922
E-mail: info@yashnatrust.org
Web: www.yashnatrust.org

Chennai(Madras)
US Educational Foundation in
India (USEFI—Southern Region)
American Consulate Building,
Anna Salai
220 Mount Road
Chennai 600006, India
Tel: 91-44-2811-2049
E-mail: usefichennai@dataone.in
Web: www.fulbright-india.org

Hyderabad
UNITI Foundation—USEFI
Satellite Center
702 Paigah Plaza
Basheerbagh
Hyderabad 500063, India
Tel: 91-40-6666-8435
E-mail: info@unitifoundation.org
Web: www.unitifoundation.org

Kolkata (Calcutta)
US Educational Foundation in
India (USEFI)
American Center
38A, Jawaharlal Nehru Road
Calcutta 700071, West Bengal, India
Tel: 91-33-3984-6310
E-mail: Usefikolkata@fulbright-india.org;
usefical@dataone.in
Web: www.fulbright-india.org

Mumbai (Bombay)
US Educational Foundation in
India (USEFI)
Regional Office, American
Center Building
4, New Marine Lines
Mumbai 400020, India
Tel: 91-22-2262-4603
E-mail: usefibom@bom3.vsnL.net.in
Web: www.fulbright-india.org

New Delhi
US Educational Foundation in
India (USEFI)
Fulbright House
12 Hailey Road - City
New Delhi 110001, India
Tel: 91-11-4209-0909
E-mail: adviser@fulbright-india.org
Web: www.fulbright-india.org

Indonesia

Jakarta
AMINEF-American Indonesian
Exchange Foundation
Gedung Balai Pustaka 6th Fl.
Jl. Gunung Sahari Raya No. 4
Jakarta 10720, Indonesia
Tel: 62-21-345 2016
E-mail: infoeas@aminef.or.id
Web: www.aminef.or.id

Malang
AMINEF Satellite Office Malang
Universitas Muhammadiyah
Gedung Perpustakaan, Jl. Raya
Tlogomas no. 246
Malang 65144, Indonesia
Tel: 62-341-463 345
E-mail: umiatijawas@umm.ac.id;
    aminef@umm.ac.id
Web: www.aminef.or.id

Medan
YPPIA Medan
Educational Advising Service
(EAS-Medan)
Jalan Dr. Mansur III No. 1A
Medan 20121, North Sumatra
Indonesia
Tel: 62-61-821 1074
E-mail: donna_pasaribu@yahoo.com;
    yppia@indosat.net.id
Web: www.aminef.or.id

Surabaya
AMINEF/EAS
International Village, 2nd Floor
Universitas Surabaya
Surabaya 60293, Indonesia
Tel: 62-31-8471809
E-mail: eas_sby@rad.net.id
Web: www.aminef.or.id

Iran

All cities
EducationUSA Student Advising
Services
Online only
E-mail: adviser@educationusairan.com
Web:www.educationusairan.com

Ireland

Dublin
US Embassy, Office of Public
Diplomacy
42 Elgin Road
Ballsbridge
Dublin 4, Ireland
Tel: 353-1-668-8777
E-mail: edudublin@state.gov
Web: http://dublin.usembassy.gov

Israel

Tel Aviv
U.S. Israel Educational
Foundation
Fulbright Educational Adviser
1 Ben Yehuda Street
Tel Aviv 61261, Israel
Tel: 972-3-517-2131
E-mail: adviser@fulbright.org.il
Web: www.fulbright.org.il

Italy

Milano
EAC Milan, Public Affairs Section
US Consulate General
Via Principe Amedeo 2/10
Milano 20120, Italy
Tel: 39-2-2903-5503
E-mail: fulbrightmilan@yahoo.com;
    fulbrightmilan@fulbright.it
Web: www.fulbright.it

Napoli (Naples)
US Consulate General Naples
Public Affairs Section
Piazza della Repubblica, 2
Naples 80122, Italy
Tel: 39-81-669-989
E-mail: fulbrightnaples@fulbright.it
Web: www.fulbright.it

Palermo
US Consulate General Palermo
Public Affairs Section
Via Vaccarini 1
Palermo 90143, Italy
Tel: 39-91-346036
E-mail: fulbrightpalermo@fulbright.it
Web: www.fulbright.it

Roma (Rome)
Commission for Educational and Cultural
    Exchange between Italy & the United
    States
Via Castelfidardo, 8
Rome 00185, Italy
Tel: 39-6-4888.211
E-mail: info@fulbright.it
Web: www.fulbright.it

Jamaica

Kingston
Office of Public Affairs,
EducationUSA Adviser
US Embassy
142 Old Hope Road
Kingston 6, Jamaica
Tel: 876-702-6172
E-mail: opakgn@state.gov
Web: http://kingston.usembassy.gov

Japan

Fukuoka
Fukuoka International Exchange Foundation
ACROS Fukuoka 3F
1-1-1, Tenjin, Chuo-ku
Fukuoka 810-0001, Japan
Tel: 81-92-725-9201
E-mail: info@kokusaihiroba.or.jp
Web: www.kokusaihiroba.or.jp

Kyoto
Kyoto City International
Foundation
2-1, Torii-cho, Awataguchi
Sakyo-ku
Kyoto 606-8536, Japan
Tel: 81-75-752-3511
E-mail: office@kcif.or.jp
Web: www.kcif.or.jp

Nagoya
The Nagoya International Center
Nagoya International Center Bldg. 3F
Nagono 1-47-1, Nakamura-ku
Nagoya 450-0100, Japan
Tel: 81-52-581-0100
E-mail: info@nic-nagoya.or.jp
Web: www.nic-nagoya.or.jp

Okinawa
Okinawa Int'l Exchange &
Human Resources Dvpt Fndn
Higashicho Kaikan 9F
1-1, Higashimachi
Naha, Okinawa 900-0034
Japan
Tel: 81-98-941-6771
E-mail: ryugaku@oihf.or.jp
Web: www.oihf.or.jp

Osaka
Osaka International House
Information Center
8-2-6 Uenohonmachi, Tennoji-ku
Osaka 543-0001, Japan
Tel: 81-66-772-5931
E-mail: center@ih-osaka.or.jp
Web: www.ih-osaka.or.jp

Sapporo
Sapporo International Communication
    Plaza Foundation
Sapporo MN Bldg. 3F, Kita 1, Nishi 3
Chuo-ku,
Sapporo City, Hokkaido 060-0001
Japan
Tel: 81-11-211-2105
E-mail: sicpfexc@plaza-sapporo.or.jp
Web: http://plaza-sapporo.or.jp

Sendai
Sendai International Center
Aobayama, Aoba-ku
Miyagi-ken
Sendai 980-0856, Japan
Tel: 81-22-265-2471
E-mail: info@sira.or.jp
Web: www.sira.or.jp

Tokyo
Japan-U.S. Educational Commission
Sanno Grand Bldg. #207,
2-14-2 Nagata-cho, Chiyoda-ku
Tokyo 100-0014, Japan
Tel: 81-3-3580-3231
E-mail: eas@fulbright.jp
Web: www.fulbright.jp

Jordan

Amman
AMIDEAST Jordan
Rodeo Plaza, 3rd Fl near Café la Noisette
Nuh Al-Rumi Street, Sweifiyeh
Amman 11118, Jordan
Tel: 962-6-581-0930 ext. 113
E-mail: jordan@amideast.org
Web: www.amideast.org/programs_services/
    advising/jordan/default.htm

Kazakhstan

Aktobe
Aktobe Educational Advising Center
  AKEAC
ul. 101 Strelkovoi Brigady 6-A
Aktobe 030000, Kazakhstan
Tel: 7-3132-514 331
E-mail: info@akeac.com
Web: www.akeac.com

Almaty
BILIM Educational Center
next to the "Namedni" restaurant
31, Tulebayev str., 2nd entrance, 1st Fl
Almaty 050004, Kazakhstan
Tel: 7-7272-597-620; 597622
E-mail: info@bilim.kz
Web: http://eac.bilim.kz

Astana
Astana ACIE Educational
Advising Center
American Councils for
International Education
Ul. Beibitshilik, 18, office 409
Astana 010000, Kazakhstan
Tel: 7-7172-91 00 68
E-mail: astana_eac@americancouncils-kz.
  com
Web: www.kz.vco-edusa.net

Karaganda
BILIM Educational Center
 Karaganda
KarGU building, 1st Fl.
38 Gogolya Str.
Karaganda 100008, Kazakhstan
Tel: 7-7212-513650
E-mail: soros_kar_rc@nursat.kz
Web: http://eac.bilim.kz

Shymkent
BILIM Educational Center Shymkent
25, Gani Ilyaev Street
Shymkent 160012, Kazakhstan
Tel: 7-7252-211981
E-mail: aturdaliyev@mail.ru
Web: http://eac.bilim.kz

Kenya

Mombasa
Educational Center of Mombasa (EdCoM)
3rd Floor, Sea View Plaza
Mama Ngina Drive
Mombasa 80100, Kenya
Tel: 254-41-2223917
E-mail: edcom@aboogroup.com
Web: http://nairobi.usembassy.gov/
  educational_advising.html

Nairobi
American Educational Advising Center
Maksons Plaza, 2nd floor
Parklands Road
Nairobi 00606, Kenya
Tel: 254-2-3740759
E-mail: aeac@accesskenya.co.ke
Web: http://nairobi.usembassy.gov/
  educational_advising.html

Korea, South (ROK)

Seoul
Korean-American Educational Commission
  (Fulbright)
U.S. Education Center
168-15 Yomni-dong Mapo-Gu
Seoul 121-874, Korea, South (ROK)
Tel: 82-2-3275-4000;3275-4011
E-mail: usec@fulbright.or.kr
Web: www.fulbright.or.kr;
  www.educationusa.or.kr

Kosovo

Priština
American Advising Center - Kosova
American School of Kosova
Rr. Luan Haradinaj n.n. (Pallati i Rinise-
  Sportit)
Priština, Kosovo 10000
Tel: 381-38 227277;228288 ext.107
E-mail: ereblirk@askosova.org
Web: http://pristina.usmission.gov/
  exchange_programs.html

Kuwait

Salmiya
AMIDEAST Kuwait
Building 15, 1st Floor
Corner of 4th ST & Yousef Al-Qenai Sts.
Salmiya, Kuwait City
Kuwait
Tel: 965-575-0670 ext.6815
E-mail: kuwait@amideast.org
Web: www.amideast.org/offices/kuwait/

Kyrgyzstan

Bishkek
Bishkek Resource Center
Soros Foundation Kyrgyzstan
55a Logvinenko Str.
Bishkek 720040, Kyrgyzstan
Tel: 996-312-66-34-75
E-mail: ajamasheva@soros.kg
Web: www.soros.kg;
www.eac.to.kg

Jalal-Abad
Jalalabad Soros Resource Center
Jalal-Abad Oblast Theater
Erkendik #1, named Barpy
Jalalabad 715600, Kyrgyzstan
Tel: 996-3722-25 330
E-mail: djrc@users.kyrnet.kg
Web: www.soros.kg

Karakol
Karakol Soros Resource Center, Issyk-Kul
  Region
T. Satylganov School
uL. Esenina, 1
Karakol 722360, Issyk-Kul
Kyrgyzstan
Tel: 996-339-225-43-13
E-mail: karakol@users.kyrnet.kg
Web: www.soros.kg

Naryn
Naryn Soros Resource Center
Soros Foundation, Kyrgyzstan
47 Sagynbay Orozbak uulu Str.
Naryn 722600, Kyrgyzstan
Tel: 996-3522-5-04-27
E-mail: narynrc@users.kyrnet.kg
Web: www.soros.kg

Osh
Osh Soros Resource Center
Soros Foundation Kyrgyzstan
Kurmanjan-Datka str. 271
Osh 714000, Kyrgyzstan
Tel: 996-322-25-66-62
E-mail: oshrc@users.kyrnet.kg
Web: www.soros.kg

Talas
Talas Soros Resource Center
28 Islam Sarygulov Str.
Talas 724200, Kyrgyzstan
Tel: 996-3422-53419
E-mail: talasrc@users.kyrnet.kg
Web: www.soros.kg;
http://kyrgyz.usembassy.gov/educational_
  advising.html

Laos

Vientiane
US Embassy Public Affairs Section
Rue Bartholonie
That Dam
Vientiane, Laos
Tel: 856-21-26 7055
E-mail: vimolDX@state.gov
Web: http://laos.usembassy.gov

Latvia

Riga
EducationUSA Advising Center at RTU Riga
  Business School
Skolas 11
Riga LV-1010, Latvia
Tel: 371-7217921
E-mail: educationusa@rbs.lv
Web: www.educationusa.lv

Lebanon

Beirut
AMIDEAST
Bazerkan Building, 1st fl, Riad el Solh ST
Nijmeh Square
Beirut 2011 5601, Lebanon
Tel: 961-1-989901 ext 160
E-mail: lebanon@amideast.org
Web: www.amideast.org/offices/lebanon/

Lesotho

Maseru
US Embassy Maseru
Public Affairs
254 Kingsway Ave.
Maseru 100, Lesotho
Tel: 266-22-312-666
E-mail: InfoMaseru@state.gov
Web: http://maseru.usembassy.gov

Liberia

Monrovia
US Information Resource Center
Office of Public Affairs, US Embassy
111 United Nations Drive
Mamba Point, Monrovia
Liberia
Tel: 231-7-705-4826
E-mail:ConsularMonrovia@state.gov
Web: http://monrovia.usembassy.gov/
informationandadvising.html

Libya

Tripoli
United States Embassy
Public Affairs Section
Corinthia Hotel, Room 1053
Tripoli, Libya
Tel: 218-21-335-1831
E-mail: educationusalibya@state.gov
Web: http://libya.usembassy.gov

Lithuania

Kaunas
Youth Career and Advising Center
Vytautas Magnus University
S.Daukanto 27-310
Kaunas LT-44249, Lithuania
Tel: 370-37-228151
E-mail: jkc@jkc.vdu.lt
Web: http://vilnius.usembassy.gov/study.
html

Vilnius
American Center Vilnius
Educational Advising Center
Akmenu gatve 7
Vilnius 10133, Lithuania
Tel: 370-5-266-5470
E-mail: webemailvilnius@state.gov
Web: www.usembassy.lt

Vilnius Educational Information Center
Sauletekio 9
VU Skaiciavimo Centras rm 107
Vilnius 10222, Lithuania
Tel: 370-5-2366274
E-mail: eac@cr.vu.lt
Web: http://eac.osf.lt

Luxembourg

Luxembourg
Centre de Documentation et d'Information
sur l'Enseignement Supérieur—CEDIES
211, route d'Esch
Luxembourg L-1471, Luxembourg
Tel: 352-478-8650
E-mail: cedies@mcesr.etat.lu
Web: www.cedies.public.lu/index.html

Macau

Macau
University of Macau—American
Corner
International Library, T404 Tai
Fung Building
Av. Padre Tomas Pereira S.J., Taipa Island
Macao, Macau
Tel: 86-853-397-8191
Web: www.umac.mo

Macedonia

Bitola
American Corner Bitola
House of Culture (Dom na Kulturata)
Marshal Tito bb
Bitola 7000, Macedonia
Tel: 389-47-203-326
E-mail: acmbitola@on.net.mk
Web: http://skopje.usembassy.gov/
american_corner_bitola.html

Skopje
American Educational Center
City Library "Braka Miladinovci"
blvd Partizanski Odredi 22
Skopje 1000, Macedonia
Tel: 389-2-3112 464
E-mail: aec.mof@gmail.com
Web: www.mof.org.mk/aec

Madagascar

Antananarivo
University Studies Advisory Center
Centre Culturel Americain
7, rue Rainizanabololona
Antananarivo 101, Madagascar
Tel: 261-20-22 314-21
E-mail: raharijaf@yahoo.com
Web: www.antananarivo.usembassy.gov

Malawi

Lilongwe
United States Educational
Advising Center
US Embassy Public Affairs Section
Old Mutual Building, City Center
Lilongwe, Malawi
Tel: 265-1-772222
E-mail: cameronws@state.gov;
martKanj@hotmail.com
Web: http://malawi.usembassy.gov/
advising_services.html

Malaysia

Kuala Lumpur
Malaysian-American Commission on
Educational Exchange MACEE
18th Fl, Menara Yayasan Tun Razak
200, Jalan Bukit Bintang
Kuala Lumpur 50200, Malaysia
Tel: 60-3-21668878
E-mail: mea@pc.jaring.my
Web: www.macee.org.my

Penang
MACEE Penang
Tingkat 1 (1st Fl), KDU College
32 Jalan Anson
Penang 10400, Malaysia
Tel: 60-4-226-4924
E-mail: maceepg@po.jaring.my
Web: www.macee.org.my

Mali

Bamako
American Cultural Center
Badalabougou-Est
Derriere la Patisserie Amandine
Bamako, Mali
Tel: 223-222-5470
E-mail: gastonm1@yahoo.com;
addabasy@yahoo.com
Web: www.usa.org.ml;
http://mali.usembassy.gov/cultural_
activities.html

Malta

Msida
Reference Department
University of Malta Library
Msida MSD 06, Malta
Tel: 356-2340-2050
E-mail: joanna.felice@um.edu.mt
Web: www.lib.um.edu.mt

Marshall Islands

Majuro
U.S. Embassy Majuro
EducationUSA Advising Center
Public Affairs/Cultural & Education
Majuro 96960, Marshall Islands
Tel: 692-247-4011 ext.222
E-mail:publicmajuro@state.gov
Web: http://majuro.usembassy.gov

Mauritania

Nouakchott
Student Advising Center,
American Corner
Faculty of Arts & Human Sciences
University of Nouakchott
Nouakchott, Mauritania
Tel: 222-525-2660
E-mail: syab@state.gov
Web: http://mauritania.usembassy.gov/
studentadvisingcenter.html

Mauritius

Port-Louis
Educational Advising Center, US Embassy
4th Floor, Rogers House
John Kennedy Avenue
Port-Louis, Mauritius
Tel: 230-202 4445
E-mail: usainfo@intnet.mu
Web: http://mauritius.usembassy.gov/
eduadv_center.html

Mexico

Chihuahua

Scholarships and Studies Abroad
Bogota No. 1905 Fraccionamiento Gloria
Venusiano Carranza Building of
Revolutionary Heroes
Chihuahua 31139, Mexico
Tel: 52-614-442-56-07
E-mail: infosilvia@ch.cablemas.com
Web: www.chihuahua.gob.mx

Guadalajara

Instituto Cultural Mexicano Norteamericano
Enrique Diaz de Leon Sur 300
Colonia Moderna
Guadalajara 44170, Mexico
Tel: 52-33-3825-4101; 3825-5838
E-mail: advisingguad@yahoo.com

Hermosillo

Secretaria de Educacion y
Cultura de Sonora
Direccion General de
Intercambios Educativos y
Asuntos Internacionales
Guerrero #39 y Luis Donaldo
Colosio; Edif.Antiguo Cuartel
Hermosillo, Sonora 83000
Mexico
Tel: 52-662-289-7600 x2381
E-mail: arline.araiza@gmail.com

Merida

Instituto Benjamin Franklin de
Yucatan, A.C.
Calle 57 No. 474-A (52 y 54) Centro
Merida, Yucatan 97000
Mexico
Tel: 52-999-928-6005;928-0097
E-mail: franklin@benjaminfranklin.com.mx
Web: www.benjaminfranklin.com.mx

Mexicali

Centro de Orientacion Educativa -EUA
CETYS Universidad, Programas
 Internacionales
Calzada CETYS s/n, Colonia Rivera
Mexicali B.C. 21259, Mexico
Tel: 52-686-567-3745
E-mail: coe@cetys.mx
Web: www.mxl.cetys.mx/coe-eua

Mexico D.F (Mexico City)

Institute of International Education-
 EducationUSA
U.S. Trade Center
Liverpool 31, P.B., Colonia Juarez
Mexico D.F. 06600, Mexico
Tel: 52-55-5703-0167
E-mail: info@iielatinamerica.org
Web: www.iielatinamerica.org

Monterrey

Biblioteca Benjamin Franklin de
Monterrey, ABP
Porfirio Diaz 949 Sur
Col. Centro
Monterrey CP 64000, Mexico
Tel: 52-81-8343-3907
E-mail: biblioteca@relacionesculturales.edu.mx
Web: www.relacionesculturales.com/bbf

Morelia

Universidad Vasco de Quiroga,
Centro de Idiomas
Camino a Jesus del Monte 555
Santa Maria de Guido
Morelia 58290, Mexico
Tel: 52-443-3235171 ext.2189
E-mail: dricedi@uvaq.edu.mx
Web: www.uvaq.edu.mx

Oaxaca

Universidad Autonoma Benito
Juarez de Oaxaca (UABJO) - Biblioteca PB
Oficina de Educacion
Internacional; Unidad de
Atencion a Estudiantes Indigenas
C.U. ex-Hacienda de Cinco Senores
Oaxaca, Oaxaca, Mexico
Tel: 52-951-502-0763
E-mail: ebautista@iielatinamerica.org
Web: www.iielatinamerica.org

US Consular Agency
Plaza Santo Domingo, planta alta
Alcala 407, int. 20
Oaxaca, Oaxaca 68000, Mexico
Tel: 52-951-514-3054
E-mail: mleyes49@hotmail.com

Saltillo

Instituto Mexicano Norteamericano
de Relaciones Culturales
Av. Presidente Cardenas 840
Zona Centro
Saltillo, Coahuila 25000
Mexico
Tel: 52-844-414 8422
E-mail: cenasi_imarc@hotmail.com

San Luis Potosi

Universidad Autonoma de San Luis Potosi
Centro de Idiomas
Zaragoza 410
San Luis Potosi 78000, Mexico
Tel: 52-444-812-4955
E-mail: salomonvalles@yahoo.com.mx
Web: http://cidiomas.uaslp.mx

Tijuana

Universidad Autonoma de Baja
California
Edificio del Dept de Informacion
 Academica, 3 piso
Calz. Tecnologico #14418,
Mesa de Otay
Tijuana, Baja California 22390
Mexico
Tel: 52-664-979-7510 x53403
E-mail: aquintanaeducationusa@gmail.com;
 aquintana@uabc.mx
Web: www.uabc.mx

Tuxtla Gutierrez

Universidad Autonoma de Chiapas
Dept.Intercambio Acad.,
edif.Recursos Humanos, 2p
Blvd. Belisario Dominguez km 1081
Tuxtla Gutierrez, Chiapas 29020
Mexico
Tel: 52-961-615-3533
E-mail: intercambio@unach.mx
Web: www.unach.mx

Xalapa

Centro de Asesoria, Escuela para
 Estudiantes Extranjeros
Universidad Veracruzana
Zamora #25 Centro
Xalapa, Veracruz 91000
Mexico
Tel: 52-228-817-7380; 817-8687
E-mail: movilidad_eee@uv.mx;
 movilidaduv@yahoo.com.mx
Web: www.uv.mx/eee/caeuv

Micronesia, Federated States of

Kolonia

U.S. Embassy Kolonia
Public Diplomacy/Economic Assistant
101 Upper PICS Road
Kolonia, Pohnpei
Micronesia FSM
Tel: 691-320-2187
E-mail: bloomGD@state.gov;
usembassy@mail.fm
Web: http://kolonia.usembassy.gov

Moldova

Chisinau

Educational Advising Center
148 Stefan cel Mare si Sfant
Blvd., of. 22
Chisinau MD 2012, Moldova
Tel: 373-22-22 11 67
E-mail: eac@eac.md
Web: www.eac.md

Mongolia

Darkhan City

Educational Advising Center
Darkhan Library
Darkhan City 213800, Mongolia
Tel: 976-1-372-27937
E-mail: darkhanadvising@yahoo.com
Web: www.earcmn.org;
 http://mongolia.usembassy.gov

Dornod

Educational Advising Center
Public Library of Dornod
Dornod
Choibalsan 212600, Mongolia
Tel: 976-1-582-23259
E-mail: dornodadvising@yahoo.com
Web: www.earcmn.org;
 http://mongolia.usembassy.gov

Erdenet
Educational Advising Center
Mongolian National University in
Erdenet
Erdenet Book Center
Erdenet, Orkhon province
Mongolia
Tel: 976-1-352-21064
E-mail: erdenetadvising@yahoo.com
Web: www.earcmn.org;
http://mongolia.usembassy.gov

Khovd
Educational Advising Center
Central Library
Children's Book Palace
Khovd, Mongolia
Tel: 976-1-432-2-23892
E-mail: khovdadvising@yahoo.com
Web: www.earcmn.org;
http://mongolia.usembassy.gov

Ulaanbaatar
Educational Advising Resource Center
MKM 24th Building, 1st Floor
8th khoroo Student's Street,
Sukhbaatar district
Ulaanbaatar 210648, Mongolia
Tel: 976-11-319016
E-mail: info@earcmn.org
Web: www.earcmn.org;
http://mongolia.usembassy.gov

Montserrat, West Indies

Brades
Montserrat Public Library
Advising Center
BBC Building
Brades
Montserrat, West Indies
Tel: 664-491-4706; 491-6727
E-mail: publiclibrary@gov.ms

Morocco

Casablanca
AMIDEAST Casablanca
Dar America
10, place Bel Air
Casablanca, Morocco
Tel: 212-22-49 08 53
E-mail: morocco@amideast.org
Web: www.amideast.org

Rabat
AMIDEAST
35, Zanqat Oukaimeden
Agdal
Rabat 1000, Morocco
Tel: 212-37-67 50 81
E-mail: morocco@amideast.org
Web: www.amideast.org

Mozambique

Maputo
US Embassy Public Affairs Section
Martin Luther King, Jr. Library
Av. Mao Tse Tung, 542
Maputo, Mozambique
Tel: 258-21-49 19 16
E-mail: maputoIRC@state.gov
Web: http://maputo.usembassy.gov/irc.html

Namibia

Windhoek
American Cultural Center
154 Independence Avenue
3rd Floor, Sanlam
Windhoek, Namibia
Tel: 264-61-229801
E-mail: nauyomaSN@state.gov
Web: http://windhoek.usembassy.gov/
american_cultural_center.html

Nepal

Kathmandu
US Educational Foundation in Nepal
(USEF-Nepal)
American Center
Gyaneshwor
Kathmandu, Nepal
Tel: 977-1-4414598
E-mail: adviserusef@fulbrightnepal.org.np
Web: www.fulbrightnepal.org.np

Netherlands

Amsterdam
Fulbright Center
EducationUSA Adviser
Herengracht 472
Amsterdam 1017 CA
Netherlands
Tel: 31-20-5315930
E-mail: info@fulbright.nl
Web: www.fulbright.nl

New Zealand

Auckland
US Consulate General-Public Affairs
Assistant
3rd Floor, Citibank Building
23 Customs St.
Auckland, New Zealand
Tel: 64-9-303 2724 ext.2843
E-mail: McKennaPA@state.gov
Web: http://wellington.usembassy.gov

Wellington
Fulbright New Zealand
Level 8, 120 Featherston Street
Wellington, New Zealand
Tel: 64-4-472 2065
E-mail: educate@fulbright.org.nz
Web: www.fulbright.org.nz

Nicaragua

Managua
Centro Cultural Nicaraguense
Norteamericano
Centro Comercial Nejapa,
detras del Banco Popular
Contiguo a los Juzgados
Managua, Nicaragua
Tel: 505-265-2535
E-mail: advise@ccnn.org.ni
Web: www.ccnn.org.ni

Niger

Niamey
Centre Culturel Americain
Rue de la Tapoa
Niamey, Niger
Tel: 227-733169
E-mail: adamamaigao@state.gov
Web: http://niamey.usembassy.gov

Nigeria

Abuja
Educational Advising Center
Plot 1075, Diplomatic Drive
Central Area District
Abuja, Garki, Nigeria
Tel: 234-9-4614000
E-mail: usabuja@state.gov
Web: http://abuja.usembassy.gov/wwwhescc.
html

Lagos
EAC Lagos
Public Affairs Section
2, Broad Street
Lagos, Nigeria
Tel: 234-1-263-0933
E-mail: eaclagos@yahoo.com;
esclagos@state.gov
Web: http://abuja.usembassy.gov/wwwhescc.
html

Norway

Oslo
US-Norway Fulbright Foundation
for Educational Exchange -
EducationUSA Adviser
Arbinsgate 2
Oslo 0253, Norway
Tel: 47-22 01 40 10
E-mail: fulbright@fulbright.no
Web: www.fulbright.no

Oman

Muscat
AMIDEAST Muscat
11 Fahood Street
Qurum, Sultanate of Oman
Muscat 115, Oman
Tel: 968-24-56-4457
E-mail: salbadi@amideast.org
Web: www.amideast.org/oman/

Pakistan

Islamabad
US Educational Foundation in
Pakistan
House No. 5 Street 17 F-6/2
Islamabad 44000, Pakistan
Tel: 92-51-2877075, -76
E-mail: advising@usefpakistan.org
Web: www.usefpakistan.org

Karachi
World Educational Services
Suite 505, Marine Pride
Block-7 Clifton
Karachi 75600, Pakistan
Tel: 92-21-5361322
E-mail: wes@cyber.net.pk
Web: www.wes.edu.pk

Lahore
US Consulate Lahore
Public Affairs Section
50 Empress Road
Lahore 54000, Pakistan
Tel: 92-42-6034256
E-mail: anwarl@state.gov
Web: www.useducation.com.pk/stpages/
    default.html

Palestinian Territories

Ramallah
AMIDEAST West Bank
Al-Watanieh Towers, 1st Floor
34 El-Bireh Municipality St.
El-Bireh, Ramallah District
Palestinian Territories
Tel: 972-2-240-8023 (or ext.103)
E-mail: sitayim@amideast.org;
    westbank-gaza@amideast.org
Web: www.amideast.org/offices/
    westbank/default.htm

Gaza
AMIDEAST Gaza
Shaheed Raja St.
Besiso Building, 8th floor
Gaza, Palestinian Territories
Tel: 972-8-2824635
E-mail: abaghdadi@amideast.org
Web: www.amideast.org

Panama

Panama City
EducationUSA Advising Center USMA
Edificio de Postgrado e
Investigacion (Planta baja)
entrada hacia Canal TV 5, El Dorado
Tumba Muerto
Panama zona 6, Panama
Tel: 507-230-8398;230-8373
E-mail: educationusa@usma.ac.pa
Web: www.usma.ac.pa

Papua New Guinea

Port Moresby
US Embassy Port Moresby
Office of Protocol & Public Diplomacy
Douglas Street
Port Moresby N.C.D.
Papua New Guinea
Tel: 675-321-1455 ext.128
E-mail: PR&M@upng.ac.pg
Web: http://portmoresby.usembassy.gov

Paraguay

Asunción
Centro Cultural Paraguayo Americano
Asesoria Estudiantil
Avda Espana 352
Asunción, Paraguay
Tel: 595-21-224-831
E-mail: asesoria@ccpa.edu.py
Web: www.ccpa.edu.py

Peru

Arequipa
Centro Cultural Peruano Norteamericano de
    Arequipa
Asesoria Educacional
Melgar 109, Cercado
Arequipa, Peru
Tel: 51-54-391022 ext.226
E-mail: smolina@cultural.edu.pe
Web: www.cultural.edu.pe

Chiclayo
Instituto Cultural Peruano
Norteamericano de Chiclayo
Asesoria Educativa
Manuel Maria Izaga 807
Chiclayo, Peru
Tel: 51-74-231241
E-mail: jmblanco@icpnachi.edu.pe
Web: www.icpnachi.edu.pe

Cusco
Instituto Cultural Peruano
Norteamericano de Cusco
Asesoria Educativa
Av. Tullumayo 125
Cusco, Peru
Tel: 51-84-239451
E-mail: asesoriaedu@icpnacusco.org
Web: www.icpnacusco.org

Ilo
Centro Cultural Peruano
Norteamericano Ilo
Asesoria Educacional
Jiron Junin 414 Oficina 101
Ilo, Peru
Tel: 51-53-48-3008
E-mail: yobando@cultural.edu.pe
Web: www.cultural.edu.pe

Lima
Educational Advising Center
Fulbright Commission
Juan Romero Hidalgo 444
San Borja
Lima 41, Peru
Tel: 51-1-476-0666
E-mail: info@fulbrightperu.info
Web: www.fulbrightperu.info

Instituto Cultural Peruano Norteamericano
Asesoria Educacional
Av. Angamos Oeste 160,
Miraflores, Lima 18, Peru
Tel: 51-1-7067001ext.9060
E-mail: Educational_advising@icpna.edu.pe
Web: www.icpna.edu.pe

Tacna
Centro Cultural Peruano
Norteamericano
Asesoria Educacional
Coronel Bustios 146
Tacna 054, Peru
Tel: 51-52-24 44 06
E-mail: cbartesaghi@cultural.edu.pe
Web: www.cultural.edu.pe

Trujillo
Centro Peruano Americano
Asesoria Educacional
Av. Venezuela 125 Urb. El Recreo
Trujillo, Peru
Tel: 51-44-261944
E-mail: aeusa@elcultural.com.pe
Web: www.elcultural.com.pe

Philippines

Bacolod City
EducationUSA Advising Center,
University of St. La Salle
American Studies Resource Center (ASRC)
La Salle Ave.
Bacolod City 6100, Philippines
Tel: 63-34-435-2594
E-mail: tvjdera@usls.edu
Web: www.usls.edu

Baguio City
EducationUSA Advising Center, ASRC
St. Louis University
Charles Vath Library Bldg, 3rd fl,
Bonifacio ST
Baguio City 2600, Philippines
Tel: 63-74-444-8246 loc.310
E-mail: asrcbaguio@slu.edu.ph
Web: www.slu.edu.ph

Batac
EducationUSA Advising Center,
Mariano Marcos State University
American Studies Resource Center (ASRC)
Main Library
Batac 2906, Ilocos Norte
Philippines
Tel: 63-77-792-2583
E-mail: mmsu_asrc@hotmail.com
Web: www.paef.org.ph

Davao City
EducationUSA Advising Center,
Ateneo de Davao University
American Studies Resource Center(ASRC)
E. Jacinto ST
Davao City 8016, Philippines
Tel: 63-82-221-2411 loc.8322,8602
E-mail: escobido@gmail.com;
mayeleanor@yahoo.com
Web: www.paef.org.ph; www.addu.edu.ph

Dumaguete City
SU-PAEF Educational Advising Center
1st Floor Main Library
Silliman University
Dumaguete City 6200,
Negros Oriental, Philippines
Tel: 63-35-422-6002 loc.516,355
E-mail: paef@su.edu.ph
Web: www.su.edu.ph

Ilo-ilo City
EducationUSA Advising Center, ASRC
Central Philippine University
Henry Luce III Library
Lopez Jaena ST, Jaro
Iloilo City 5000, Philippines
Tel: 63-33-329-1971/79 loc.1019
E-mail: jofer@cpu.edu.ph;
jigsaw5000@yahoo.com
Web: www.cpu.edu.ph

Manila
Philippine-American Educational
  Foundation (PAEF)
10/F Ayala Life FGU Center
6811 Ayala Avenue
Makati City 1226, Philippines
Tel: 63-2-812-0945
E-mail: fulbright@paef.org.ph
Web: www.paef.org.ph

Zamboanga City
EducationUSA Advising Center, ASRC
Ateneo de Zamboanga
University, Graduate School
La Purisima Street
Zamboanga City 7000
Philippines
Tel: 63-62-991-0871 loc.2000/01
E-mail: shalili@mailcity.com
Web: www.adzu.edu.ph

Poland

Kraków
US Consulate General Krakow
Public Affairs
ul. Stolarska 9
Krakow 31-043, Poland
Tel: 48-12-424 5140
E-mail: brzostekmr@state.gov
Web: http://krakow.usconsulate.gov/krakow/
  studyus.html

Warsaw
Polish-U.S. Fulbright Commission
Educational Advising Center
Nowy Swiat 4
Warsaw 00-497, Poland
Tel: 48-22-625-6970
E-mail: ola.augustyniak@fulbright.edu.pl
Web: www.fulbright.edu.pl

Portugal

Lisboa (Lisbon)
Fulbright Information Center
Edificio da Reitoria,
Universidade de Lisboa
Cidade Universitaria, Campo Grande
Lisboa 1649-0004, Portugal
Tel: 351-21-7611130
E-mail: studyusa@ccla.pt
Web: www.fulbrightcenter.org

Qatar

Doha
US Embassy
Public Affairs Section
22 February Road
Doha, Qatar
Tel: 974-496-6749
E-mail: PASDoha@state.gov
Web: http://qatar.usembassy.gov;
www.amideast.org/qatar

Romania

Bucharest
Fulbright Educational Advising Center
Fulbright Commission
Str. Ing. Costinescu nr 2, sector 1
Bucharest 011878, Romania
Tel: 40-21-231 9015
E-mail: feac@fulbright.ro
Web: www.fulbright.ro/educationUSA;
www.usembassy.ro/fulbright/eac.html

Russia

Cheboksary
Cheboksary Cooperative Institute
American Educational Center
pr. Gorkogo 24, room 319
Cheboksary 428025, Russia
Tel: 7-8352-66-30-05
E-mail: kazakov@coop.chuvashia.ru
Web: http://vco-edusa.net

Kazan
Kazan State University
International Office
ul. Kremlyovskaya 18, room 17
Kazan, Tatarstan 420008, Russia
Tel: 7-8432-92-76-00
E-mail: olya@ksu.ru; olga.vershinina@ksu.ru
Web: www.ksu.ru/umc/index.ru.html

Moscow
EducationUSA Advising Center
American Councils
Ulitsa Nikoloyamskaya, dom 1, 3rd floor,
  EAC
Moscow 109189, Russia
Tel: 7-495-777 65 33
E-mail: eic@useic.ru
Web: www.useic.ru

Nizhny Novgorod
Nizhny Novgorod Linguistics University
Room 206, ul. Minina 31a
Nizhny Novgorod 603155, Russia
Tel: 7-8312-36-22-21; 36-20-49
E-mail: eac@lunn.ru; max@lunn.ru
Web: http://vco-edusa.net

Novosibirsk
Educational Advising Center -
EducationUSA
American Councils for
International Education
pr. Lavrentiaeva 17, 2nd Building
Novosibirsk 630090, Russia
Tel: 7-383-330-92-94
E-mail: eac@ieie.nsc.ru
Web: http://actr.nsk.ru

Obninsk
French-Russian Institute of
Business Administration
ul. Guryanova 19, room 234
Kaluga Region
Obninsk 249020, Russia
Tel: 7-4843-97-33-51
E-mail: id@fridas.ru
Web: www.fridas.ru; http://vco-edusa.net

Omsk
Omsk State Pedagogical University
nab. Tukhachevskogo 14, room 337
Omsk 644099, Russia
Tel: 7-3812-24-37-95
E-mail: common@omsk.edu;
sshirob@omsk.edu
Web: www.vco-edusa.net/omsk;
http://dic.omgpu.omsk.edu

Rostov-on-Don
EducationUSA Advising Center
Don State Public Library
ul. Pushkinskaya, 175 A
Rostov-on-Don 344049, Russia
Tel: 7-863-264-52-75
E-mail: edusa-rostov@yandex.ru
Web: www.ac-rnd.dspl.ru/education.asp

Samara
Samara Educational Advising Center
Center of American Culture and Education
ul. Novo-Vikzalnaya 213, 2nd Fl
Samara 443084, Russia
Tel: 7-902-371-7608
E-mail: samara@amcorners.ru
Web: http://vco-edusa.net

St. Petersburg
American Councils for
International Education
Mayakovsky Library
nab. Fontanka 46, 4th Floor
St. Petersburg 191025, Russia
Tel: 7-812-571-45-93
E-mail: adviser@americancouncils.spb.ru
Web: www.americancouncils.spb.ru

Tomsk
Tomsk State University
American Educational Information Center
34a, Lenin Pr.
Tomsk 634050, Russia
Tel: 7-3822-534284
E-mail: kichiginalena@gmail.com
Web: http://vco-edusa.net; www.tsu.ru

Vladimir
Vladimir Educational Advising Center
Regional Scientific Library
ul. Dzerzhinskogo 3
Vladimir 600000, Russia
Tel: 7-922-32-32-02, 32-26-08
E-mail: vladlib@vtsnet.ru
Web: www.library.vladimir.ru/otdels/kons_1.
htm

Vladivostok
Vladivostok Educational
Advising Center
American Councils
Okeanskiy pr-t, 15A, 3 floor
Vladivostok 690091, Russia
Tel: 7-4232-408071
E-mail: useac@vlad.ru; actrvlad@vlad.ru
Web: http://vco-edusa.net/vladivostok

Volgograd
American Center in Volgograd
Volgograd Regional Scientific Library
Ulitsa Mira 15, office 4-02
Volgograd 400131, Russia
Tel: 7-8442-90-30-93
E-mail: VolgogradAC@yandex.ru;
VolgogradAC@mail.ru
Web: www.amcorners.ru; http://vac.t-k.ru

Voronezh
Voronezh Regional Educational
Advising Center
ul. Kukolkina 3, office 203
Voronezh 394000, Russia
Tel: 7-732-77-49-26
E-mail: koshelevaa@mail333.com
Web: www.vreac.org.ru

Yekaterinburg
Municipal Information Library
American Center
ul. Mamina-Sibiryaka, 193
Yekaterinburg 620055, Russia
Tel: 7-3432-62 67 04
E-mail: tbabkina@yandex.ru
Web: http://vco-edusa.net; //ac.iatp.ru

Yoshkar-Ola
Mari State University
Russian-American Center
pl. Lenina 1
Yoshkar-Ola 424001, Russia
Tel: 7-8362-72 07 05
E-mail: sergey@marsu.ru
Web: http://vco-edusa.net

Rwanda

Kigali
US Embassy Public Affairs Section
Educational Advising Center
Boulevard de la Revolution
Kigali, Rwanda
Tel: 250-505 601
E-mail: irckigali@state.gov
Web: http://rwanda.usembassy.gov/
educational_advising.html

St. Kitts and Nevis

Charlestown
Nevis Public Library
Prince William Street
Charlestown, St. Kitts and Nevis
Tel: 869-469-0421ext 2055/2105
E-mail: nepublib@sisterisles.kn

St. Lucia, West Indies

Castries
Students Services Centre
Sir Arthur Lewis Community College
Morne Fortune,   Castries
St. Lucia, West Indies
Tel: 758-452-5507
E-mail: hbynoe@salcc.edu.lc
Web: www.salcc.edu.lc

St. Vincent & the Grenadines

Kingstown
National Documentation Center
Ministry of Finance, 2nd fl,
Administrative Center
Bay Street, Kingstown
St. Vincent & the Grenadines
Tel: 784-456-1689
E-mail: document@caribsurf.com

Saudi Arabia

Dhahran
US Consulate General Dhahran
Public Affairs Section
next to KFUPM
Dhahran 31942, Saudi Arabia
Tel: 966-3-330-3200 ext 3044
E-mail: VargheseSM@state.gov
Web: http://dhahran.usconsulate.gov/
dhahran/resources.html

Jeddah
US Consulate General Jeddah
Public Affairs Section
Falasteen Street, Al Ruwais District
Jeddah, Saudi Arabia
Tel: 966-2-667-0080 ext 4151
E-mail: AlsaiedNF@state.gov
Web: http://jeddah.usconsulate.gov/jeddah/
advising.html

Riyadh
Education Advising Office
US Embassy-Riyadh
Diplomatic Quarter
Riyadh 11693, Saudi Arabia
Tel: 966-1-488 3800 ext 4505
E-mail: bauerkm@state.gov
Web: http://riyadh.usembassy.gov/
saudi-arabia/resources.html

Senegal

Dakar
US Embassy Public Affairs Section
Avenue Jean XXIII x rue Bugnicourt
Immeuble Kleber II
Dakar, Senegal
Tel: 221-338292340
E-mail: FallAX@state.gov
Web: http://dakar.usembassy.gov/
educational_exchange.html

Serbia

Belgrade
International Academic Center
Educational Adviser
Majke Jevrosime 18/II
Belgrade 11000, Serbia
Tel: 38-11-334 5227
E-mail: office@iacbg.org
Web: www.iacbg.org

Sierra Leone

Freetown
Educational Advising Center
US Embassy
Public Affairs Section
Southridge - Hill Station
Freetown, Sierra Leone
Tel: 232-22-232-76-515-363
E-mail: RoweAA@state.gov
Web: http://freetown.usembassy.gov

Singapore

Singapore
United States Education Information Center
12 Prince Edward Road
01-03 Bestway Bldg Podium A
Singapore 079212, Singapore
Tel: 65-6223 4566
E-mail: inquiry@useic.org
Web: www.useic.org

Slovakia

Bratislava
Fulbright Commission Advising Center
Levicka 3
Bratislava 821 08, Slovakia
Tel: 421-2-5542 5606
E-mail: office@fulbright.gov.sk
Web: www.fulbright.sk

Slovak Academic Information Agency-SAIA,
N.O.
Nam. Slobody 23
Bratislava 1, 812 20 Slovakia
Tel: 421-2-5441 1426
E-mail: monika.breckova@saia.sk
Web: www.saia.sk

Slovenia

Ljubljana
American Library
US Embassy
Public Affairs Section
Presernova 31
1000 Ljubljana, Slovenia
Tel: 386-1-200-55-83
E-mail: USEmbassyLjubljana@state.gov
Web: http://slovenia.usembassy.gov/
resources2.html

South Africa

Cape Town
US Consulate General
EducationUSA Advising Center
2 Reddam Ave., Westlake 7945
Cape Town, Western Cape
South Africa
Tel: 27-21-702-7362
E-mail: bridgmanm@state.gov
Web: http://pretoria.usembassy.gov/
wwwhstudy.html

Durban
US Consulate General
Educational Advising Center
30th Floor, 303 West Street
Durban 4001, South Africa
Tel: 27-31-305-7693
E-mail: knowlesSD@state.gov
Web: http://pretoria.usembassy.gov/
wwwhstudy.html

Johannesburg
American Culture and Information Center
35 Pritchard Street, Corner Harrison
1066 Building, 3rd Floor
Johannesburg, South Africa
Tel: 27-11-838 2231
E-mail: ducationusajhb@state.gov
Web: http://pretoria.usembassy.gov/
wwwhstudy.html

Pretoria
US Embassy
Public Affairs Section
877 Pretorius Street
Arcadia 0083
Pretoria, South Africa
Tel: 27-12-431 4000
E-mail: wilsoncs@state.gov
Web: http://pretoria.usembassy.gov/
wwwhstudy.html

Soweto
American Library, Ipelegeng
Community Center
1283 Phera & Dlamini Streets
White City, Jabavu
Soweto, Gauteng, South Africa
Tel: 27-11-982 5580
E-mail: wilsoncs@state.gov
Web: http://pretoria.usembassy.gov/
wwwhstudy.html

Spain

Barcelona
Institut Nord-America
Academic Advising Office/IEN Library
Via Augusta, 123
Barcelona 08006, Spain
Tel: 34-93-240.51.10
E-mail: advising@ien.es
Web: www.ien.es

Madrid
Comision Espana-EE.UU.
Fulbright Program - Educational Adviser
Po General Martinez Campos, 24 bis
Madrid 28002, Spain
Tel: 34-91-319 1126
E-mail: adviser@comision-fulbright.org
Web: www.fulbright.es

Sri Lanka

Colombo
US-Sri Lanka Fulbright Commission
Educational Advising Center
7, Flower Terrace
Colombo 7, Sri Lanka
Tel: 94-11-256 4176
E-mail: advising@isplanka.lk
Web: www.fulbrightsrilanka.com

Suriname

Paramaribo
US Embassy Business Education Resource
Center
Dr. Sophie Redmondstraat 129
Paramaribo, Suriname
Tel: 597-472900 ext.2267
E-mail: dijksjb@state.gov

Swaziland

Mbabane
American Center
Embassy House
Gwamile Street
Mbabane H100, Swaziland
Tel: 268-404-2059
E-mail: balarinMN@state.gov
Web: http://mbabane.usembassy.gov

Sweden

Malmö
Malmö Borgarskola
EducationUSA Advising Center
Attn: Magnus Andresson
Regementsgatan 36
Malmö SE-200 10, Sweden
Tel: 46-40-34 70 20
E-mail: mb.educationusa@pub.malmo.se
Web: http://ib.borgarskolan.se

Stockholm
Swedish Fulbright Commission
Vasagatan 15-17, 4th floor
Stockholm SE-111 20, Sweden
Tel: 46-8-534 818 80
E-mail: fulbright@fulbright.se
Web: www.usemb.se/Fulbright

Switzerland

Bern
US Embassy
Public Affairs Office
Bern CH-3001, Switzerland
Tel: 41-31-3577 376
E-mail: bernpa@state.gov
Web: http://bern.usembassy.gov/study_in_
the_u.s.html

Syria

Damascus
Education Advising & Testing Office
American Cultural Center
87 Ata Al-Ayoubi Street, Abou Rumaneh
Damascus, Syria
Tel: 963-11-3391-4444
E-mail: eatosy@gmail.com
Web: http://damascus.usembassy.gov/eato2.
html

Taiwan

Taipei
American International
Education Foundation
5F-1 No. 237 Fu-Hsing S.Road, Sec. 1
Taipei 106, Taiwan
Tel: 886-2-2705-8840
E-mail: service@aief.org.tw
Web: www.aief.org.tw; www.uscampus.com.tw

Foundation for Scholarly Exchange
U.S. Education Information Center
3F, 45 Yanping S. Road
Taipei 10043, Taiwan
Tel: 886-2-2388-7600
E-mail: ustudy@ustudy.org.tw;
fse@saec.edu.tw
Web: www.ustudy.org.tw

Tajikistan

Dushanbe
American Councils for International
Education: ACTR/ACCELS
EducationUSA Advising Center
86 Tolstoy Street
Dushanbe 734003, Tajikistan
Tel: 992-3772-211795
E-mail: americancouncils@americancouncils.tj
Web: http://dushanbe.usembassy.gov/
exchange_programs.html

Khujand
Khujand Education Advising Center
120 Firdawsi Street, room 119
Khujand 735700, Tajikistan
Tel: 992-3422-45377
E-mail: naimjon@gmail.com
Web: http://dushanbe.usembassy.gov/
exchange_programs.html

Tanzania

Dar es Salaam
US Embassy Office of Public Affairs
Educational Advising Center
686 Old Bagamoyo Road,
Msasani
Dar es Salaam, Tanzania
Tel: 255-22-2668001
E-mail: eadar@state.gov
Web: http://tanzania.usembassy.gov/
   educational_advising.html

Thailand

Bangkok
American University Alumni
(AUA) Language Center
Library, 2nd Fl -Educational
Counseling Unit
179 Rajdamri Road, Lumpini,
Pathumwan
Bangkok 10330, Thailand
Tel: 66-2-252-8170 ext4006
E-mail: counseling@auathailand.org
Web: www.auathailand.org

Bangkok Bank Public Co., Ltd.
Educational Advisory Service
333 Silom Road (2nd Floor)
Bangkok 10500, Thailand
Tel: 66-2-230-1329
E-mail: daranee.lim@bbl.co.th
Web: www.bangkokbank.com

Civil Service Commission Office
Education Counseling Center
Siam Square Soi 7, Rama I Road,
   Pathumwan
Bangkok 10330, Thailand
Tel: 66-2-2529737 hotline 1786
E-mail: vatchara01@gmail.com;
vatchara@ocsc.go.th
Web: www.ocsc.go.th

Institute of International
Education-Southeast Asia
6th Floor, Maneeya Center North
518/3 Ploenchit Road, Pathumwan
Bangkok 10330, Thailand
Tel: 66-2-652-0653 ext.122
E-mail: advising@bkk.iie.org;
iiethai@bkk.iie.org
Web: www.iiethai.org

Knowledge Plus
Silom Shanghai Bldg,2nd fl
(opp.Silom Village)
807 Silom 17, Silom Road
Bangkok 10500, Thailand
Tel: 66-2-238-3933
E-mail: info@knowledgeplus.ac.th
Web: www.knowledgeplus.ac.th

Media and Cultural Section
U.S. Embassy
95 Wireless Road
Bangkok 10330, Thailand
Tel: 66-2-205-4000
E-mail: Bangkokpd@state.gov
Web: http://bangkok.usembassy.gov/
   education.hrml

Chiang Mai
ACE! Academy for EducationUSA
Chiang Mai University,
International Center Bldg
239 Nimmanhaemin RD, A.Muang
Chiang Mai 50200, Thailand
Tel: 66-53-942896
E-mail: hub.ace@gmail.com; info@ace-i.org
Web: www.ace-i.org

Khon Kaen
AUA Language Center, Khon
Kaen University
Faculty of Humanities & Social
Sciences, Bldg HS-03
123 Mitrphab Highway, A.Muang
Khon Kaen 40002, Thailand
Tel: 66-43-203-745;203-746
E-mail: khonhaen@auathailand.org;
ron@kku.ac.th
Web: www.kku.ac.th; www.auathailand.org

Togo

Lomé
US Embassy
Public Affairs Section
Rue Kouenou & Beniglato
Rue no. 15
Lome, Togo
Tel: 228-221 2991
E-mail: AwuteKK@state.gov;
awkpeter@yahoo.fr
Web: http://lome.usembassy.gov

Trinidad & Tobago, WI

Port of Spain
US Embassy Public Affairs Section
Information Resource Center
7-9 Marli Street
Port of Spain
Trinidad & Tobago, WI
Tel: 868-622-5979
E-mail: ircpos@state.gov
Web: http://trinidad.usembassy.gov

Tunisia

Tunis
AMIDEAST Tunisia
22 Rue Al Amine Al Abassi
Cite les Jardins
Tunis, Belvedere 1002
Tunisia
Tel: 216-71-790.559
E-mail: tunis@amideast.org
Web: www.amideast.org

Turkey

Ankara
Fulbright Commission
Sehit Ersan Caddesi 28/4
Cankaya
Ankara 06680, Turkey
Tel: 90-312-4284824
E-mail: advising@tr.net
Web: www.fulbright.org.tr

Istanbul
Fulbright Istanbul Ofisi
Dumen Sokak, Gumussuyu
No: 3/11 Taksim
Istanbul 34437, Turkey
Tel: 90-212-244 1105
E-mail: fulb-ist@tr.net
Web: www.fulbright.org.tr

Turkish American University Association
Rumeli Cad. 60-62, Titiz Apt.K:1-2
Osmanbey
Istanbul 34363, Turkey
Tel: 90-212-247 5785
E-mail: turkamerican@superonline.com
Web: www.turkamerican.org

Kavaklidere
EducationUSA Center at the
Turkish American Association
Cinnah caddesi No: 20
Kavaklidere Ankara 06690
Turkey
Tel: 90-312- 426 37 27
E-mail: useducation@taa-ankara.org.tr
Web: www.taa-ankara.org.tr/educationusa.
   php

Turkmenistan

Ashgabat
EAC/American Councils for
International Education in Turkmenistan
Gerogly Street 48/A, 2nd floor
Ashgabat 744000, Turkmenistan
Tel: 993-12-33-10-15
E-mail: eacashgabat@inbox.ru
Web: http://americancouncilstm.org

Dashoguz
Dashoguz American Corner
Educational Adviser
Turkmenbashy str. 7/2
746300 Dashoguz, Turkmenistan
Tel: 993-322-5-03-81
E-mail: acdash@mail.ru
Web: http://americancornerstm.org

Mary
Mary American Corner
Educational Adviser, 2nd floor
42a Agziberlik Avenue
Mary 745400, Turkmenistan
Tel: 993-522-7-38-65
E-mail: macorner@rambler.ru
Web: http://americancornerstm.org

Turkmenabat
Turkmenabat American Corner
3rd floor, Shatlyk Building
33 Pushkina Avenue
Turkmenabat 746100
Turkmenistan
Tel: 993-422-6-37-71
E-mail: tabat@americancornerstm.org
Web: http://americancornerstm.org

Türkmenbaşy
Türkmenbaşy American Corner
Educational Adviser
13 Dostluk Street, Balkan Velayat
Türkmenbaşy City 745000
Turkmenistan
Tel: 993-243-7-45-83; 2-13-95
E-mail: tbashy@americancornerstm.org
Web: http://americancornerstm.org

Uganda

Kampala
US Embassy Public Affairs Section
Educational Advising Center
Plot 1577 Ggaba Road
Nsambya–Kampala, Uganda
Tel: 256-41-259-795
E-mail: MutazindwaCB@state.gov
Web: http://kampala.usembassy.gov/
    educational_exchange.html

Mbarara
Mbarara University of Science & Technology
    (MUST)
Main Library-Educational Adviser
Mbarara, Uganda
Tel: 256-485-20393
E-mail: agakibayo@yahoo.co.uk
Web: http://kampala.usembassy.gov/
    educational_exchange.html

Ukraine

Dnipropetrovsk
"Osvita" Educational Information and
    Advising Center
K. Marksa 60, office 74, 75
Dnipropetrovsk 49000, Ukraine
Tel: 380-56-744-62-42
E-mail: osvita@fregat.com
Web: www.center-osvita.dp.ua

Kharkiv
Kharkiv "Osvita" Educational Advising
    Center
National University Library
4 Svobody Sq, room VII-45
Kharkiv 61077, Ukraine
Tel: 380-57-7020165
E-mail: bulgakova@univer.kharkov.ua
Web: www.osvita.kharkiv.org

Kyiv
US Education Information Center
American Councils for
International Education
vul. Melnykova, 63
Kyiv 04050, Ukraine
Tel: 380-44-483-2532
E-mail: receptionieac@america
    ncouncilskyiv.org.ua
Web: www.americancouncilskyiv.org.ua/
    EIC

Lviv
Osvita Educational Advising Center
prospekt Chornolova, 4, room 1
Lviv, Ukraine
Tel: 380-32-2971206
E-mail: info@osvita.org
Web: www.osvita.org

Odessa
American EIC for International Education
South Ukrainian Pedagogical University
Staroportofrankivska, 26 room 61 (3rd fl.)
Odesa 65020, Ukraine
Tel: 380-48-7155693
E-mail: eic@advisingcenter.odessa.ua
Web: www.advisingcenter.odessa.ua

"Osvita" Educational Information Center
Educational Adviser
vul. Gogolya, 16, kim. 113, Bd.16
Odesa 65026, Ukraine
Tel: 380-48-716-5288
E-mail: grade@farlep.net
Web: www.centerosvita.org

United Arab Emirates

Abu Dhabi
US Embassy Public Affairs Section
Embassies District
Al Sudan Street
Abu Dhabi, United Arab Emirates
Tel: 971-2-4142658
E-mail: EducationUSAabudhabi@state.gov
Web: http://uae.usembassy.gov/educational_
    advising.html

Dubai
US Consulate General
Public Affairs Office
World Trade Center, 20 FL
Dubai, United Arab Emirates
Tel: 971-4-311 6172
E-mail: EducationUSAdubai@state.gov
Web: http://dubai.usconsulate.gov/dubai/
    General_Information.html

United Kingdom

London
US Educational Advisory Service
Fulbright House
62 Doughty Street
London, WC1N 2JZ England
United Kingdom
Tel: 44-20-7404 6994
E-mail: education@fulbright.co.uk
Web: www.fulbright.co.uk/eas

Uruguay

Montevideo
Fulbright Commission
Centro de Asesoramiento Educativo
Colonia 810, Suite 703
Montevideo 11100, Uruguay
Tel: 598-2-901 41 60
E-mail: fulbrigh@chasque.apc.org
Web: www.fulbright.org.uy

Uzbekistan

Tashkent
US Embassy Public Affairs Section
Educational Advising Center
3 Moyqorghon Street, 5th
Block, Yunusobod District
100093 Tashkent, Uzbekistan
Tel: 998-71-120-54-50
E-mail: tashkent-advising@state.gov
Web: http://uzbekistan.usembassy.gov/advising

Venezuela

Caracas
Asociacion Venezolano Americana de
    Amistad
Ave. Libertador, Multicentro
Empresarial del Este
Torre Libertador A, piso 10 Ofic.A-103.
Chacao, Caracas 1060
Venezuela
Tel: 58-212-2637601
E-mail: info@avaa.org
Web: www.avaa.org

Maracaibo
Centro Venezolano Americano del Zulia
Departamento de Estudios en
Estados Unidos
Calle 63, #3E-60, Sector Las Mercedes
Maracaibo 4001, Venezuela
Tel: 58-61-793-4517
E-mail: estudiosusa@cevaz.com
Web: www.cevaz.org

Merida
Centro Venezolano Americano de Merida
Urbanizacion El Encanto
Avenida 2 (Lora) Esq. Calle 43 No. 1-55
Merida 5101, Venezuela
Tel: 58-74-263-1362
E-mail: cevam@intercable.net.ve
Web: www.cevam.org.ve

Vietnam

Hanoi
U.S. Education Information Center - IIE
C9 Giang Vo, Ba Dinh District
Hanoi, Vietnam
Tel: 84-4-726-2524
E-mail: iievietnam@iievn.org;
advisor@iievn.org
Web: www.iievn.org

Ho Chi Minh City
Institute of International Education
69 Hoang Hoa Tham Street
Ward 6, Binh Thanh District
Ho Chi Minh City, Vietnam
Tel: 84-8-510-8844
E-mail: advisorhcmc@iievn.org
Web: www.iievn.org

EducationUSA Advising Centers

Yemen

Aden
AMIDEAST Aden
Miswat Street-Villa 162
Khormaksar
Aden, Yemen
Tel: 967-2-232-345
E-mail: aden@amideast.org
Web: www.amideast.org/yemen/

Sana'a
AMIDEAST Yemen
66, Algiers Street
(near the Sana'a Trade Center)
Sana'a, Yemen
Tel: 967-1-400279/80/81
E-mail: salamri@amideast.org
Web: www.amideast.org/yemen/

Zambia

Lusaka
American Center
COMESA Building, Zone F
Ben Bella Road
Lusaka 10101, Zambia
Tel: 260-1-227993
E-mail: paslusaka@state.gov;
andersonAG@state.gov
Web: http://zambia.usembassy.gov

Zimbabwe

Bulawayo
Bulawayo Educational Advising Center
Bulawayo Public Library
100 Fort Street & 8th Avenue
Bulawayo, Zimbabwe
Tel: 263-9-60965
E-mail: advisingzw@yahoo.com
Web: http://harare.usembassy.gov

Harare
US Educational Advising
Center, US Embassy-PAS
Eastgate Mall, 7th Fl, Goldbridge
2nd Street
Harare, Zimbabwe
Tel: 263-4-758800/1/5
E-mail: useaczim@gmail.com
Web: http://harare.usembassy.gov

Also Available
from the College Board

Book of Majors 2009

What's the major for you? Where can you study it? In this book, 190 college professors describe the majors they teach: what you'll study, careers the major can lead to, and how to prepare for the major in high school. Includes listings showing which colleges offer each of 900 majors, and at what degree level.

1,328 pages, paperbound
ISBN 978-0-87447-824-2
$25.95

College Handbook 2009

Get instant access to crucial information on every accredited college in the United States. Completely updated and verified for 2009, this handbook contains detailed descriptions of 3,800 colleges, universities, and technical schools.

2,172 pages, paperbound
ISBN 978-0-87447-823-5
$29.95

Scholarship Handbook 2009

This no-nonsense guide speeds you straight to scholarships targeted to who you are, where you live, and what you want to study. Includes detailed profiles of more than 2,100 scholarship, internship, and loan programs.

632 pages, paperbound
ISBN 978-0-87447-827-3
$27.95

Campus Visits & College Interviews, 2nd Edition
by Zola Dincin Schneider

Visiting campuses and talking to admissions deans is a great way to learn more about which colleges are right for you. Experienced school counselor Zola Dincin Schneider shows you how to make the most of your visits and make a good impression during interviews. Includes interview tips for the shy.

160 pages, paperbound
ISBN 978-0-87447-675-0
$12.95

CollegeBoard
connect to college success®

Available wherever books are sold.
Distributed by Macmillan

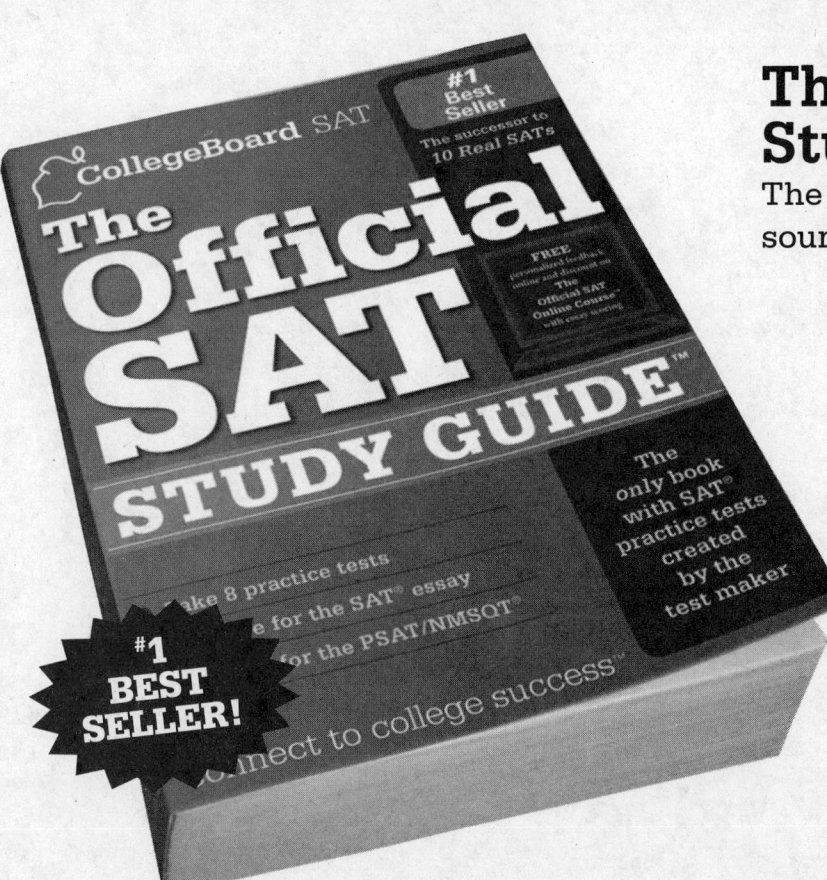